MOON HA   ...   S®

VIETNAM
CAMBODIA & LAOS

FOURTH EDITION

MICHAEL BUCKLEY

AVALON TRAVEL

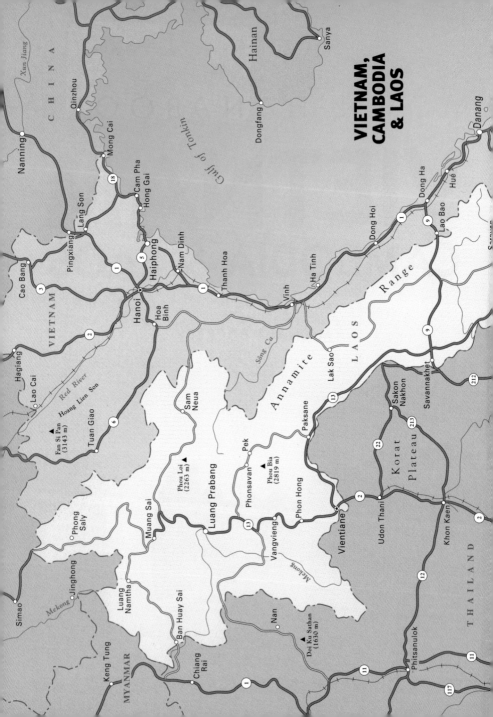

CONTENTS

Discover Vietnam, Cambodia & Laos

Explore Vietnam, Cambodia & Laos

Vietnam

Saigon 250

The South 302

Cambodia

Laos

Know Vietnam, Cambodia & Laos

MAPS

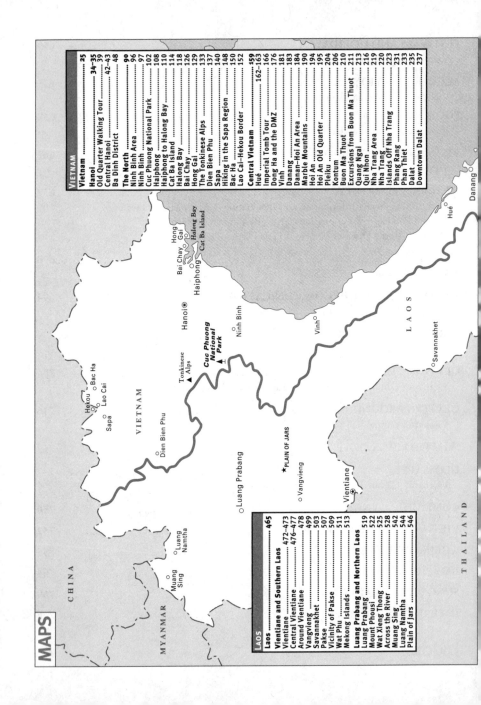

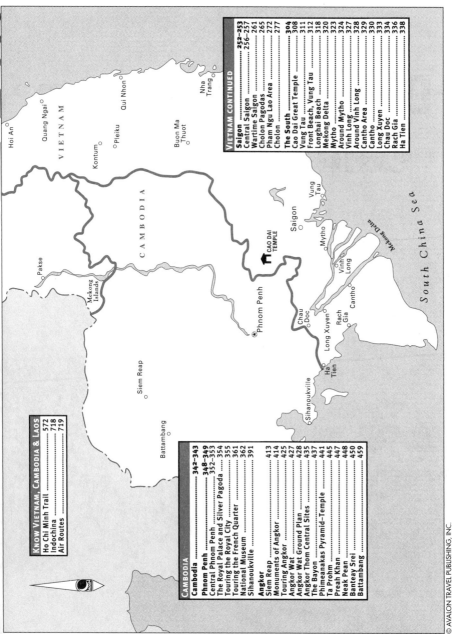

South China Sea

© AVALON TRAVEL PUBLISHING, INC.

Discover Vietnam, Cambodia & Laos

The 1990s marked a major turning point for travel to Vietnam, Cambodia, and Laos (collectively known as Indochina). With the normalization of relations between Laos, Thailand, Cambodia, Vietnam, and China, the region is more accessible than ever before. For the first time in more than three decades, it's possible to ride a bicycle around Angkor Wat, motorcycle through hilltribe areas of North Vietnam, or cruise on a cargo boat through the Mekong Delta. Throughout the region, authorities are busy turning battlefields into marketplaces. In Vietnam, they're turning battlefields into tourist attractions. The war has become a kind of theme park—christened "Cong World" by one Western reporter—where you can scramble through Vietcong tunnels or visit war museums.

Rounding the corner into the 21st century, travel in the nations of Vietnam, Cambodia, and Laos has never been easier: Complex permits in Vietnam and Laos have been rescinded, a number of new border crossings have opened to foreigners, and a host of new air links have made the region far more accessible.

In the early 1990s, individual travel in Vietnam was not

officially recognized, and travelers were hamstrung by complicated permit requirements. The system was scrapped in 1993, and areas such as the Central Highlands and the mountains north of Hanoi were opened for the first time. For cash-strapped Vietnam, tourism is seen as a quick way to earn vital foreign exchange. The normalization of relations between Vietnam and China in 1991 opened two new border crossings and promised reestablished rail links. With the 1994 lifting of the U.S. trade embargo, U.S. travel agents and banks began operating freely. With the visit of President Clinton in November 2000, relations between the United States and Vietnam entered a new phase.

Ironically, in the era of terrorism after 9/11, Vietnam has emerged as probably the safest travel destination in Asia. There are a number of reasons for this: strong police and army presence, small Muslim population, no known links with global terrorist groups.

Cambodia, previously a war zone off-limits to all but the foolish and/or well-heeled, is now freely accessible because of the U.N. peacekeeping operation in 1992. That year, all travel permit requirements in Cambodia were lifted; you can now go wherever you want (limitations being land mines and sporadic banditry). The Khmer Rouge menace evaporated in 1999, freeing previously inaccessible zones. Cambodia has since experienced a tourist boom, especially to the region of Angkor.

Laos at first adopted a tourism model that emphasized high-paying tour groups and lots of permit areas. Permits were needed for boat travel and to cross land borders. But those restrictions have all gone, and with borders open to foreigners into Thailand, Vietnam, and China, the landlocked country has become part of grander road links in Indochina. Sporadic banditry and insurgency, however, still bedevil Laos.

Visiting these three countries is a grand adventure. You're the center of attention in Vietnam; in Cambodia, the warmth and spontaneity of the people is infectious; in Laos, the approach is more reserved and dignified. More than anything else, it's the people you meet that make Indochina a real experience. Indochina is home to a great diversity of artists and intellectuals, farmers and duck herders, hardy hilltribe folk and French-educated city folk. At any given moment, you can find yourself being regaled with tales from a Vietnam War veteran, lines recited by an eccentric poet in Dalat, or sharing a bottle of lizard wine in the Central Highlands.

So go! I hope this book will inspire and inform. *Bon courage et bonne chance!*

How long should you spend in Indochina? Three weeks would be a minimum. Less time is possible if you cut a country out, or cover only one sector of a country (say northern Vietnam only, or northern Laos only). More reasonable would be six weeks for Indochina, allowing you to see a fair cross-section. Or you could go longer—until the visas run out, or even until the money runs out.

Should you fly directly into Indochina or go via a gateway? That is a decision you will have to consider carefully. There are direct flights into Vietnam from Australia and Europe and flights from Canada and the United States with stopovers. While there are direct international flights into Cambodia and Laos, the planes often transit through Bangkok. You might consider flying to a gateway city such as Bangkok or Hong Kong and arranging visas and onward travel from there (which could be overland travel as well as air connections). This stepping-stone strategy will be cheaper but will require time to garner visas and tickets. (For more about the logistics involved, see the *Getting There* section of the *Know Vietnam, Cambodia & Laos* chapter.)

Visa issue is something you have to keep in mind for all route planning. Usually you get a month's visa in each country—and that's about how long it would take to get to begin to get to know each. Cambodia and gateways such as Thailand and Hong Kong present no problem—you are stamped in on arrival for a month. Laos has a 15-day visa on arrival if by air (extensions could be tricky). You can generally get a one-month Lao visa ahead of time. Vietnam is the difficult one—you must always get the visa in advance. That can take 3–4 working days in a place such as Hong Kong or Bangkok. On a longer trip, you can solve the sticky Vietnamese visa problem by obtaining a three-month multiple-entry visa, which gives you lots of flexibility, since it is valid for entry or exit from all Vietnamese border points.

If you get the Vietnamese visa from your home base, you can skip Hong Kong or Bangkok gateway entry points. Be aware that obtaining a visa for Vietnam, Cambodia, or Laos from home may require several weeks or longer, depending on where the nearest relevant embassy or consulate is. Cost largely depends on nationality of the passport holder and the type of visa issued (the longer the visa, the more expensive). (Refer to the *Visas and Officialdom* section in the *Know Vietnam, Cambodia & Laos* chapter for information on the wonderful world of visas, red tape, and bureaucratic stonewalling—a legacy of the French in Indochina.)

WHEN TO GO

With different climate zones in the Indochina region, there is no optimum time to visit. November through to March would be the best overall timing to visit all three countries, but there are numerous variables at work. It will be chilly (even freezing) in the mountainous zones of northern Laos and northern Vietnam in January and February, but those same months are the best time to visit the far south of Cambodia and Vietnam—at Phu Quoc Island, for instance. In Vietnam, the best seasons to go would be the fall (October–December) and the spring (March–April); in Cambodia, the best season is December–February; while in Laos, the best time is November–February.

Vietnam, Cambodia, and Laos are characterized by a tropical monsoon climate, with wet and dry seasons. The monsoons fluctuate from north to south. You would do well to avoid monsoon rains, for a number of reasons: discomfort, mosquitoes, flooding, and decreased accessibility and enjoyment.

It is exciting to be in Indochina during festival periods, but these times can also be chaotic for transport and hotels can be overcrowded. This is especially true of Tet, or Vietnamese New Year, which falls in January or February (lunar calendar). Many overseas Vietnamese return home at this time, making it extremely difficult to secure flights, and making hotels in the larger cities tough to get into. Many businesses close down for more than a week at this time. A similar problem occurs at Lao New Year (April) in Luang Prabang.

WHAT TO TAKE

A notebook computer with negotiation software for Vietnam? A flak jacket for Cambodia? An armful of novels for those long languid trips down the Mekong in Laos? There's no end to the amount of stuff you could cram into your bags to cover all needs, but most of it would be dead weight. It's far more enjoyable to travel lightly and not worry about your stuff—and leave space for purchases en route. Travelers can become fixated with their belongings and spend hours agonizing needlessly over what to take. Get that part over quickly and shift your attention to more important matters, such as plotting your route, determining what to see, learning languages, and reading up on the areas you'll visit. Knowledge is the most important thing to carry with you.

Money: Take as much of this fine stuff as you can, in several different forms. The most useful form to have along is cash U.S. dollars in $50 bills. However, this is not insurable if lost or stolen, so you should place a personal ceiling on how much U.S. cash you are willing to risk carrying. You should carry a wad of traveler's checks for the trip: If you take U.S. dollar traveler's checks, these can be converted back into U.S. cash as needed for a 1–2 percent fee. You can depend on ATMs for drawing dong in larger cities in Vietnam, but these are not found in Cambodia or Laos. Credit cards have limited applications in all three countries, and in any case, will incur fees of 3–4 percent extra when used.

Clothing: For hot climates, cotton clothing or a cotton/polyester mix is best. Dress loosely, and choose clothing that is lightweight, washes quickly, and dries fast. Be prepared for adverse weather conditions: Carry a hat and sunglasses to counter the sun; take a pair of sturdy, lightweight walking shoes; and waterproof yourself with a light jacket and hood. If you're planning to visit highland areas, plan to layer T-shirt, shirt, pile sweater, and rain jacket to ward off the cold.

Medical Kit: This is one area where you should not skimp. Camping and outdoor stores sell prepackaged medical kits you can customize to your needs. Bring a large medical kit, perhaps shared between several people. Medicines are in short supply and of dubious quality in Indochina, so it's best to bring your own.

Communication Aids: One greatly overlooked consideration in travel gear is communication. Bring language phrasebooks. Take photos of family, friends, your neighborhood, city postcards, and so on. They're always great talking points and help answer the question you'll be asked everywhere you go: "Where are you from?" Gifts are good communicators: postcards, balloons, cosmetics, cigarettes, lighters, and pens. Presents need not be big or expensive—they're a way of saying thank you, not a redistribution of wealth.

(For much more about what to take and how to pack it, consult the *What to Pack* section in the *Know Vietnam, Cambodia & Laos* chapter.)

The Regions

VIETNAM

Hanoi

Hanoi is the hub of northern Vietnam—a launching pad for trips in the region but a fine sight in its own right. Hanoi is where they make the rules—cool and austere at times, but it's also the place where you will feel the pulse of 1,000 years of Vietnamese culture. Though it has a population of more than three million, Hanoi is still low-rise—a city of distinct neighborhoods, arrayed around lakes. It has the best-preserved French architecture in Indochina and a charming ambience with numerous restaurants, cafés, and art galleries. You can stroll around the lively Old Quarter or bicycle out to Ho Chi Minh's mausoleum.

At night you can see the fantastic art of water puppetry. Or take in a live performance at the magnificent Opera House—the pride of Hanoi.

The North

You could sum up the finest landscape of the north in one word: karst. Dramatic pockets of karst limestone punctuate the mountainous areas of the north—and the Gulf of Tonkin. At Halong Bay and Cat Ba National Park, you can commandeer a junk or kayak and cruise among hundreds of weird karst islets and outcrops. Karst limestone is porous, forming spectacular grottoes and caverns—many are found at Halong Bay, but more are found afield at Phong Nga, Ninh Binh, and elsewhere. Hardy hilltribe groups abound in the rugged and mountainous border regions of the north. The French called them montagnards—mountain people. They come together at weekend markets—they're seen at the charming town of Sapa, or the town of Bac Ha, where Flower Hmong women gather in gorgeous costume.

Central Vietnam

Vietnam boasts a 3,200-kilometer coastline, with about 125 large and small white-sand beaches and scores of fishing villages. The north-central coast is the poorest region of Vietnam; the south-central coast lags behind economically but is being boosted by the rise of beachfront resorts—especially around Phan Thiet and Danang. Central Vietnam's twin gateways of Hué and Danang are rather dull. The rising star of the center is Hoi An—a well-preserved maritime trading town and a World Heritage Site, and a firm favorite among travelers. It's one of the very few places in Vietnam where you can find traditional architecture—and gourmet food. For those who like getting off the track, the Central Highlands is the place to be. The mountainous highland region is sparsely populated and has a frontier feel to it, with forest cover, waterfalls, and diverse tribal groups.

Saigon

Saigon is the powerhouse of the south: noisy, raucous, rough and ready, brash. It is the industrial and economic leader of Vietnam. The city's population is hard to determine: probably in excess of five or six million. In any case, it is the most crowded metropolis in Vietnam, with the worst traffic. Downtown you can find faded colonial grandeur and the stark War Crimes Museum, while in Cholon there are bustling markets and pagodas filled with a fog of incense. Saigon boasts an excellent array of hotels, restaurants, and shopping facilities. Most travelers use Saigon as a base for exploring the south—particularly the Mekong Delta region.

The South

The south is blessed with the most consistently balmy weather in Vietnam, though some find it too humid. "Balmy" is a word that could equally be applied to the religious faiths of the south—such as the Cao Dai sect, with its synthesis of half a dozen creeds. The most striking feature of the south is the lush Mekong Delta—a tropical wonderland of deep-green rice fields, fruit orchards, floating markets, and more coconuts than you'd ever want to contemplate. The market towns of Vinh Long and Cantho are easily accessible from Saigon and make great bases for exploring surrounding channels and islands by small boat—the best way to see this fertile region.

CAMBODIA

Phnom Penh

This city of 1.5 million is back on its feet again after some very tough and tumultuous times. Phnom Penh has witnessed rapid—and disastrous—changes of fortune. Traces of the city's former splendor are visible at the lofty Royal Palace. The National Museum houses the world's finest collection of Khmer artifacts: Visiting is an uplifting experience—one that is offset by seeing the horrors of Tuol Sleng Holocaust Museum across town. By night, Phnom Penh can be dangerous, but it is fine if you keep to popular well-lit venues. A short ride from the capital is Sihanoukville, a relaxing place with abundant seafood and long stretches of sand. A handful of water corridors link Phnom Penh to distant border crossings. The most scenic is a trip of several days up the Mekong to Stung Treng, and then crossing into southern Laos.

Angkor

The awesome Angkor region casts its spell over all who visit. It is far and away the top archaeological site of Southeast Asia. The ruins of Angkor attest to the might of the Khmer Empire, which crumbled about 800 years ago. The romantic ruins are a wonder of the eastern world, with 70 sites sprawled over a forested zone of 200 square kilometers. Giant tree roots drape over sandstone Buddha faces, banyan trees sprout over cloister roofs, and lines of celestial nymphs appear on 100-meter friezes. Angkor Wat and Angkor Thom are the star sites. Siem Reap, the small gateway town to Angkor Wat, is a good place for rest and relaxation, with palatable food. Around town are quiet rural areas and forested zones, and within easy reach is Lake Tonle Sap—one of the richest fishing grounds in the world.

LAOS

Vientiane and Southern Laos

That's it? This is the capital? Vientiane is not an exciting metropolis—in fact, quite a dull one, with just a handful of temples to see. However, Vientiane is a great place to bicycle or walk around, with wide boulevards and little traffic. About 160 kilometers north of Vientiane lies a place with world-class scenery—the tiny town of Vangvieng. Set in an entrancing karst landscape, Vangvieng is a mecca for adventure sports such as kayaking and caving. Devoid of beaches or outstanding historical attractions, Laos's main draw is its laid-back lifestyle. Using Vientiane as the hub, you can easily get to the far south of Laos, where a main attraction is the beguiling region of Siphandon (4,000 Islands), also known as the Mekong Islands, close to the Cambodian border. Here the Mekong turns surly, with a frothing departure from Laos at Khong Papheng Falls—the widest in Asia. Travelers may spend a week or more at Siphandon, lounging in hammocks among coconut palms by the Mekong.

Luang Prabang and Northern Laos

The splendid former royal capital of Laos is steeped in history. Luang Prabang is considered one of the best-preserved traditional towns in Southeast Asia, with a number of 16th-century temples, as well as colonial and traditional timber houses. For these reasons the entire town and its surroundings were inscribed on the U.N. World Heritage List. Laos offers great natural beauty, with as-yet-unspoiled mountain, plateau, and river regions. Beyond Luang Prabang, you can follow Mekong tributaries such as the Nam Ou, snaking north through spectacular limestone gorges. In the mountain areas of northern Laos live numerous hilltribe groups—you can trek through villages from Luang Namtha.

You have three weeks and three countries to visit. And you want to see the best they have to offer, but you want to relax—you don't want to feel rushed. Tall order? No, actually. The World Heritage List Committee has already made the selection for you. Three weeks, three countries—and three wonders. The very best of Indochina can be found at these World Heritage sites: **Halong Bay (Vietnam)**, **Angkor (Cambodia)**, and **Luang Prabang (Laos)**. By visiting these three, you will experience a wonder-ful introduction to these lands and their special culture.

If you spend five days around each site, and build in five days spare for transiting points such as Bangkok and Hong Kong, or for delays, or simply for staying longer at one site, then you are looking at three weeks.

Glance at the map and you will find that the three sites form a rough triangle. There are a number of ways of linking up the dots, with a start or end point being Bangkok or Hong Kong. If your time is short, you need to fly between these sites. Here is one way to do it.

Luang Prabang

Fly from Bangkok directly to Luang Prabang. (It's also possible to get there via Vientiane.) A visa is issued on arrival if you're staying less than 15 days. You can completely slow down and lose track of time here, arguably the best-preserved traditional town in Asia, with the finest temples in Laos. Explore Luang Prabang and region for five days.

Angkor

Fly from Luang Prabang directly to Siem Reap (Angkor). This flight runs several times a week. If it's not available, you can fly to Pakse and connect from there directly to Siem Reap. Or fly back to Bangkok and transfer to a flight to Siem Reap. Cambodian visas are issued on arrival. You can sit back in a remork (breezy chariot) to visit the ruins of Angkor, the top archaeological site of Southeast Asia—with Angkor Wat as the crowning highlight. Explore the Angkor region for five days.

Halong Bay

Fly from Siem Reap directy to Hanoi (a Vietnamese visa is needed in advance). Make your way to Halong Bay, where a modified junk will take you on a relaxing cruise of several days through stunning karst scenery. Explore Halong Bay and the Cat Ba region for five days, with more time possible in Hanoi. Fly onward to Hong Kong or back to Bangkok.

Variations

Another way to explore this route is to start out by flying from Bangkok to Siem Reap (Angkor), then fly from Angkor to Hanoi (Halong Bay), and then fly from Hanoi to Vientiane, connecting to Luang Prabang. Or you could make Angkor the end point of the whole route, allowing more time there.

For longer trips, you can pick up more destinations along the way (as outlined in some other itineraries in this section). And if you have more time on your hands, and less money, consider overland travel for sections of the route—if not the whole route. Bangkok to Vientiane overland is not difficult with overnight VIP buses plying the route. From Vientiane, you can go overland to Luang Prabang. From Luang Prabang, there are overland routes via Phonsavan that cross into northern Vietnam and head for Hanoi, though these may take time.

Karst is eroded limestone that forms into bizarre caves, pinnacles, and outcrops. Karst means adventure—kayaking, caving, hilltribe trekking, and mountain biking through splendid scenery.

Numerous pockets of karst are scattered through northern Vietnam and northern Laos—some fall within national parks or biosphere reserves. The scenery is spectacular, but unfortunately there is very little wildlife to be seen. Numbers of many species have dwindled because of years of warfare, and in more recent times, because of poaching and illegal smuggling for the wildlife trade.

Halong Bay

You can cruise on a modified junk for days among the karst islets at Halong Bay and in **Cat Ba National Park**. A handful of karst caves at Halong Bay have been garishly lit up: You walk among bizarre formations of stalagmites and stalactites. To get in closer to karst islets, you can arrange a kayak—this is carried on the mothership. In a kayak you can pass under sea arches and reach tiny water-level caves, and even paddle through karst tunnels that lead to interior lagoons. You can also land at small beaches and go swimming.

Meovac Region

In the northeast, close to the Chinese border, road trips by Russian jeep or Japanese 4WD vehicle to the Meovac region reveal deep gorges and some of the most entrancing karst scenery in Vietnam. Numerous hilltribe groups live in the northern border areas of Vietnam and maintain their own customs, language, and dress. The French called them montagnards—people of the mountains. There are Hmong, Tai, Zao and Tay groups. **Hilltribe trekking tours** of a day, two days, or longer can be arranged in **Sapa** or **Bac Ha** to learn about the culture and tradition of these fascinating people.

Mai Chau

Another fine region for trekking and mountain biking amid karst and rice paddy terracing is at Mai Chau, a short distance from Hanoi. Close to Mai Chau is more karst: You can hike on a three-day limestone adventure trail from Mai Chau through Phu Long to reach **Cuc Phuong National Park**.

Red River Delta

Southwest of Hanoi lies **Perfume Pagoda**, a pilgrimage site set in splendid karst scenery. Directly south of Hanoi lies the region of **Ninh Binh**, famed for its rice paddies set among karst peaks. Villagers run boat rides through the area, but you can also bicycle out to the **Kenh Ga** region.

Northern Laos

The road between Vientiane and Luang Prabang affords views of dramatic karst scenery. You should break the journey at the town of **Vangvieng**, a magnet for adventure sports. **Cave-kayaking** is the big thing here—with several operators running tours. Other caves can be reached by trekking or biking out to them. Some karst cliffs have been scoped out for climbers.

From Luang Prabang, you can take a boat up the **Nam Ou** tributary, with karst cliffs and peaks looming. Farther north, the scenery grows more remote and more rugged—with more spectacular karst up around **Muang Khoua**, along with stands of giant bamboo and old-growth forest.

Laos's hard-to-reach northern provinces of Phong Saly, Udomxai, and Luang Namtha have the greatest diversity of hilltribes. Hilltribe trekking can be done here, and rafting is possible when water levels are high enough.

Central Laos

Stunning karst formations can be found at the Khammouan Plateau, where there are "stone forests" composed of karst pillars. This is karst at its best—along the Hinboun River are sheer-sided gorges with 400-meter-high cliffs on both sides. The labyrinth of cave networks in this region has yet to be explored. You can arrange a river trip to the interior of dazzling Khonglor Cave (strong headlamp required).

Colonial Architecture

Vietnam, Cambodia, and Laos are three nations whose histories have become entwined because of French colonization. You see the French legacy in the baguettes sold on the streets in the morning; you see it in the kilometer markers along major routes. But the most visible sign of French colonial presence remains in the architecture: The French threw up administrative offices, churches, schools, hospitals, prisons, and bridges—many still in use today. Colonial architecture also lives on in character hotels and restaurants and cafés.

Hanoi

The French pulse is strongest in Hanoi, the former capital of Indochina, where the French architectural styles change with the period—from plain brick edifices of the 1880s to stylish art deco structures from the 1930s.

You can dine at elegantly restored French villa restaurants and stay in historic hotels such as the Metropole. The Opera House, completed in 1911, today functions exactly the same way it used to—and if you buy a performance ticket, you can see the magnificent interior and experience the acoustics. Hanoi has some mixed-style architecture—combinations of French and Vietnamese—as at the History Museum. "Colonial architecture" does not always imply French. The Chinese were in Vietnam for 1,000 years—there's a lot of Chinese architectural influence in Hanoi too, especially seen in tiny temples such as Ngoc Son, a classic photo-op locale.

Phnom Penh

Phnom Penh would be next on the list for seeing well-preserved French colonial buildings. The Raffles hotel group has sunk millions into restoring the Hotel le Royal to its original colonial splendor. An interesting facet of French colonial architecture is that on occasion the French set out to construct edifices in local style, using local artisans. A spectacular example of this is Phnom Penh's National Museum. Designed by French archaeologist and painter George Groslier, it is based on Khmer temple structures and was completed by Cambodian craftsmen in 1918.

Saigon

In Saigon you can see the lofty Notre Dame Cathedral (best viewed from the inside), the nearby Post Office (the interior has a large glass dome), the Town Hall (not possible to see from the inside), **Municipal Theater,** and a slew of grand French administrative buildings.

Vietnamese wooden buildings from the 19th century.

Port Towns

French colonial buildings are more likely to be found along coastal or river sites because boats were the main form of access in early colonial days—before roads and railways were built. This would explain the lofty Municipal Theater found in the port of **Haiphong,** along with numerous other French buildings there.

The port town of **Hoi An** in central Vietnam has a smattering of French buildings, but it has more in the way of influence from other foreign naval visitors—Chinese-style and Japanese-style. And, a great rarity for Vietnam, Hoi An has intact

Luang Prabang

The French administration was not terribly active in Laos—not getting around to building until the 1920s, and even then halfheartedly. Luang Prabang, the former royal capital of Laos, has an eclectic mix of architecture—Lao, French, and Chinese. You can find old French villas here, as well as the **Palace Museum,** the former Royal Palace, which was commissioned by the French colonial administration and is a mix of Lao and French styles. The interior of the palace veers more to the French side, with French mirrors and crystal chandeliers, but it's filled with Lao lacquered furniture.

History and Culture

War and the preservation of culture are not a good mix—destruction of culture is the more likely result. In Indochina, you can't avoid seeing the aftermath of the ravages of war in the late 20th century. Turmoil and upheaval from this period have formed the context for the present era—let's hope one of peace. Traditional culture has survived—and is being revived—but it's a slow process. Indochina is not strong on historical and cultural attractions because, for one thing, many key sites were blown to bits by aerial bombing—such as the Royal Citadel of Hué (though this is under reconstruction today). And yet some towns have survived, today functioning as outdoor museums: the ancient towns of **Hoi An** (Vietnam) and **Luang Prabang** (Laos).

Hanoi

Miraculously, Hanoi, with a history stretching back a millennium, survived aerial bombing during the 1965é1975 war relatively intact. The city is the cultural nerve center of Vietnam, host to its best museums. The **Museum of Ethnology** showcases the customs and traditions of Vietnam's 53 ethnic groups, and the **Ho Chi Minh Museum** is the most elaborate of the many HCM museums in Vietnam. Hanoi is also the best place to see the performance art of **water puppetry.**

Angkor

Easily the most outstanding historical and cultural attraction of Indochina is Angkor. Somehow, the incredible stonework at Angkor has survived warfare through the centuries, and it stands as mute testament to the might of the ancient Khmer civilization. Put on your Indiana Jones hat—or Lara Croft tanktop—and head for the ruins. A bonus here is that classical and folk dance are performed nightly in nearby **Siem Reap**—including the sensuous *apsara dance.*

Cultural Museums

The brilliance of past cultures in Indochina is highlighted in a handful of museums in larger cities. In addition to the Hanoi museums, the best are the **National Museum** in Phnom Penh, which houses priceless Angkorian statuary, and the **Cham Museum** in Danang, which showcases the largely disappearing Cham culture.

War Museums

Museums are meant to be uplifting in some way—a celebration of the achievements and creative powers of a civilization. But in Phnom Penh is a museum that is a monument to the dark side of the human mind. **Tuol Sleng Genocide Museum** documents a prison of the Khmer Rouge, who tried to completely wipe out Khmer culture and history and return it to the Year Zero. Destruction, rather than creation, is a theme running through a string of war museums in Vietnam. The most notable are the **War Crimes Museum** in Saigon, documenting the 1965–1975 American assault on Vietnam; and the **Military Museum** at Dien Bien Phu, documenting the epic battle with French forces in 1954.

Religion

After years of civil war, the nations of Indochina came under the austere rule of communist governments, which attempted to stamp out traditional culture and religion. But these have proved resilient and are on the rebound. Buddhism has made a strong comeback—especially in Laos and Cambodia, where monks do the morning alms rounds (spectacular in **Luang Prabang**).

Festivals

One of the best places to see traditional culture and performing arts in action is at festivals. The Vietnamese are reinventing such festivals for the purpose of attracting tourism; the same thing is happening in Cambodia. Laos has preserved festivals that have long disappeared in other parts of Asia. (Check the *Festival and Holidays* section in the *Know Vietnam, Cambodia & Laos* chapter for ideas and timing.) The big festival event is New Year—**Tet** in Vietnam (usually around February), **Chaul Chhnam** in Cambodia (mid-April), and **Pimai** in Laos (also mid-April).

Do Nothing

Doing nothing is an art in Indochina. In some places, people have perfected the technique of sleeping on a motorcycle in the middle of a busy street, or of stringing up a hammock for a midday snooze. You might well follow suit. Some of the prime spots in Indochina are best for simply doing nothing—relax, put your feet up, read a book, catch some rays, contemplate your navel. Being on the road for a while can wear you down: Travelers may want to hone in on a place where they can stay still and take time out. A number of places in Vietnam, Cambodia, and Laos take the concept of Rest and Recreation to new heights. Here are some of them.

Northern Vietnam

The French, who were heavily into rest and recreation, set up cool hill resorts in Indochina to get away from insufferable humidity during the summer. Some of the hill resorts, which lay in ruins after the American War, have been revitalized—such as Tao Dao near Hanoi. But the prize is **Sapa**, today renowned for its weekend market, which draws ethnic minorities. Sapa is a pleasant place to take in some mountain air and drink in the views.

Central Vietnam

Vietnam boasts a 3,200-kilometer coastline with about 125 large and small beaches. It's not the Côte d'Azur—not yet, anyway—but upscale resorts are popping up along the Vietnamese coastline from Hué to Vung Tau. **Cua Dai Beach** (close to Hoi An) is very good. **China Beach**, near Danang, has waves—bodysurfing and boardsurfing are possible at certain times of year. In **Nha Trang**, you'll find lots of boating to offshore islands and sailboarding. **Mui Ne Beach** also has sailboarding and kite-surfing.

Southern Vietnam

Remote but not all that difficult to get to by air are **Phu Quoc Island** and **Con Dao Islands**. The former has blissful white sands; the latter has the best diving in Vietnam.

Cambodia

Low-key white-sand beaches stretch along the coast at **Sihanoukville**. You can hop on boats for day trips to outer islands for picnicking, swimming, snorkeling, and sun worship.

Laos

This is the ultimate place to chill out—time slows down here. A lot of sunset-watching and star-gazing are in order. At **Vangvieng**, you can hang out in a deck chair by the Song River with a Bia Lao—or float down the Song River in a tube with a Bia Lao. Laos is landlocked, but it does have coconut-lined riverbanks at the **Mekong Islands,** right down by the southern border with Cambodia. These islands will redefine your concept of "laid-back."

The sublime taste of mangosteen. The rank smell of durian. The pungent odor of fish sauce. The aroma of lemongrass. The crunchy texture of fried grasshopper. And the daunting prospect of eating sautéed tarantula or drinking lizard wine. Food is a real adventure in Indochina, with no shortage of gourmet treats. Markets and streetside foodstalls are the best places to rub shoulders with the locals and to observe local trading and bustle. And you will get the freshest food in town—look for small restaurants close to the markets.

Though there are markets in all the larger cities, these tend to be huge affairs with little character. Much better are the smaller open-air markets in towns or villages. Big cities have the best restaurants, however.

Most markets are bustling early in the morning. Across the region at this hour you can find fresh-baked baguettes, processed cheese, orange juice, and drip-filter coffee—for which you can thank the French, who instilled a strong café culture. This is what is so enticing about Indochina—it's a mix of the familiar (French legacy) and the strange (recipes handed down in the same family for generations). You can buy ice cream made with Italian machinery—but the flavors might be durian, soursop, or custard-apple. A salad in Vietnam might use the delicious banana flower as a base, while in Laos, it could be spicy pomelo or shredded green papaya.

If your time is limited, then the best places for combinations of markets and good restaurants would be these four culinary hotspots: **Sapa** (northern Vietnam—weekend market, mountain herbs and spices, minority groups), **Hoi An** (central Vietnam—fish markets, specialities cooked in local restaurants), **Cantho** (southern Vietnam—amazing floating markets with fruit from nearby orchards), and **Luang Prabang** (distinctive Laotian cuisine style, excellent restaurants).

Hanoi and the North

Hanoi restaurants cover a comprehensive range, with styles sometimes mixed (Vietnamese-French or Vietnamese-Chinese blends). There's excellent seafood on offer at **Halong Bay** (often cooked right on board your boat). **Sapa** in the northwest is famed for its wild mushrooms, honey, and unusual mountain herbs and spices—all of which find their way to the dinner table. Markets such as the weekend one at Sapa are a magnet for ethnic minority groups, who may use the opportunity to size up prospective spouses (a phenomenon sometimes referred to as a "love market"). Weekend markets at **Bac Ha** and **Can Cau** draw Flower Hmong women, with their intricately embroidered costumes. Along with food, cloth is sold here, and there are livestock sections where buyers haggle over pigs, water buffalo, and dogs (don't ask).

Central Vietnam

Fish markets are busy along the coast, and seafood is cooked with flair in places such as **Nha Trang**. **Hoi An** is a kind of gourmet's paradise, with its intimate bistros and its secret recipes handed down in families for generations. For the avid food tourist, cooking classes are also offered by restaurants in Hoi An: Your instructor will take you first to the markets to shop for fresh ingredients. **Dalat** hosts markets day and night.

Saigon and the South

Cosmopolitan Saigon offers a great variety of restaurants with innovative menus, while in **Cholon,** Chinese food reigns. The **Mekong Delta** has an amazing proliferation of fruit, with succulent varieties such as dragon fruit, spiny soursop, and miniature mangoes. At the crack of dawn, you can witness floating markets outside of **Cantho** at Cai Rang or a bit farther afield at **Phung Hiep.**

Cambodia

The food section of **Phnom Penh's Central Market** is extensive, and you will be lucky if you can identify more than half the varieties on display. Excellent seafood is served at beachside restaurants in **Sihanoukville.** Busy food markets are found in **Siem Reap.** Cambodian cuisine uses fish as a staple, with a great variety of species caught in Lake Tonle Sap.

Laos

Everything in Laos seems to come with a base of sticky rice, including dessert. Lao food combines the raw textures of Vietnamese food with the hot spicing of Thai cuisine. **Luang Prabang** is the best place to sample Lao dishes—and learn how to make them in cooking classes offered by some restaurants. As in Vietnam, markets in remote areas of the north draw in hardy hilltribe folk—a good one to get to is at **Muang Sing,** where Akha, Mien, Hmong, and Lolo groups converge.

Floating World

River life in Vietnam, Cambodia, and Laos is fascinating—with floating villages, extensive fish farming, and floating markets with stand-up rowers and leg-rowers. Naturally, the best way to see this is from the deck of a boat. And boat touring is an excellent way of viewing dramatic scenery in remote regions. This is the nuoc mam tour—you may smell of fish sauce by the time it's all done.

The original explorers of Indochina—both native and foreign—took to the rivers. The Mekong forms a natural link between the three countries, a river road of sorts. It is indeed possible to travel all the way from Saigon to Jinghong (China) on the Mekong, but lengthy sectors are no longer serviced by regular boats (superseded by faster and cheaper road transport). Another problem is that the river must be high enough for larger boats to be able to ride on it—in the dry season, the Mekong may not be navigable in parts because it is too low.

The following extensive itinerary—a sort of Great Indochina Loop—aims to explore the floating world of Indochina. The selection of vessels for these wild rides varies from red-sailed junks and leaky sampans to sleek "bullet boats" and even hydrofoils. In Laos, the rides are a bit too wild on occasion—a long-tailed speedboat driver will kindly supply you with a crash helmet. You would need at least six weeks to cover the overland loop described, but shorter trips are simply a matter of cutting out sectors, or flying over them.

Before you start out, obtain a three-month multiple-entry Vietnamese visa, valid for all border crossings, unless your endpoint is going to be Bangkok. Once in Hanoi, you can apply for a one-month Lao visa. And you will need a Cambodian visa, which you can pick up in either Hanoi or Vientiane.

ping at **Vangvieng** for kayaking and caving. Continue by road south via Vientiane all the way to **Pakse**. Boat from Pakse via Champassak to the **Mekong Islands,** landing at Muang Sene. Stay for a few days.

To Cambodia

Using a long-tailed speedboat, cross the water border at **Voeng Kham** to reach **Stung Treng** in Cambodia. Wild rides by bullet-boats all the way to **Kompong Cham**—this can be done in a single day, or take two. Go from Kompong Cham to **Phnom Penh** by road if no boat is running on this route.

Angkor

Take a bullet boat across **Tonle Sap** to Chong Kneas floating village (dock for **Siem Reap**). Visit **Angkor**. On the return trip, first head by boat from Siem Reap to Battambang: You can stop at **Preak Toal** floating village for the bird sanctuary boat trip, or just carry on through to **Battambang** (five hours). Continue overland from Battambang to Phnom Penh.

Hanoi Loop

Starting in Hanoi, mount your own trip to the Halong Bay area. Take a hydrofoil from **Haiphong** to Cat Ba, kayak at **Cat Ba National Park,** take a junk via Halong Bay to **Bai Chay,** and another hydrofoil to **Quan Lan Island.** This will all take five days or longer. Return to Hanoi.

Luang Prabang Loop

Once back in Hanoi, the next objective is Luang Prabang. There is a choice of several northern border crossings into Laos. The Nonghet border crossing goes via Phonsavan to reach Luang Prabang.

From Luang Prabang, take a loop of about four days. Proceed north of Luang Prabang up the **Nam Ou** river to Muang Khoua, cross by road to **Luang Namtha,** and arrange a kayak trip of several days down the **Namtha River** to Pak Tha. Take a regular boat from here back along the **Mekong** to Pakbeng and Luang Prabang.

To Southern Laos

Head south by road from Luang Prabang, stop-

From Phnom Penh

At this point you could exit Phnom Penh via **Sihanoukville** for a sea crossing into Thailand. Or you could head for Saigon by water. To cross into Vietnam, you need to use a multiple-entry visa, or obtain a new visa in Phnom Penh (while waiting, go and visit Sihanoukville).

To Saigon

If you take the Saigon route, there is regular speedboat service from Phnom Penh to **Chau Doc.** Chartering a boat along the Mekong from Chau Doc to **Cantho** is possible, but boats may be hard to find. Cantho has spectacular floating markets. Cantho to Saigon by chartered speedboat is possible, but it's very difficult and expensive to arrange. You would probably have to do this part by road.

The Vietnam Coast

From Saigon, take the hydrofoil to **Vung Tau.** Explore the beaches, resort towns, and fishing villages along the coast road. **Mui Ne, Nha Trang,** and **Cua Dai** (Hoi An) are among the best beaches. You can also make day trips by boat from these places. Close by are fishing villages: Marvel at the skill of Vietnamese fishermen in their basket boats.

Make it back to Hanoi. Home at last! After all that time on the water, catch up with a **water puppetry** performance and see more boats bobbing up and down, as well as marine dragons.

Explore Vietnam, Cambodia & Laos

Vietnam

Introduction

On April 30, 2005, Vietnam commemorated the 30th anniversary of the fall of Saigon. A sizeable percentage of the population cannot remember the war at all, because they were born after April 30, 1975. They are more preoccupied with what motorcycle to buy, what cellphone to wear, or what color to dye their hair. These youth are part of an economic boom in Vietnam—one of the fastest-growing economies in Asia.

The war is history now—relegated to museums. In 1994, the Clinton administration lifted the U.S. trade embargo against Vietnam, bringing the war to an official close and enabling Vietnam to get on with rebuilding its shattered economy. A year later, the U.S. flag was flying over the U.S. liaison office in Hanoi—the first American flag to fly over a U.S. government building in the north since 1955. In November 2000, Clinton and his entourage visited Hanoi: Clinton even managed to speak a few words of greeting in Vietnamese—the first U.S. president ever to do so.

Among the more unusual tourist attractions

CHINA

Simao
Mengzi
Ha Giang
Cao Bang
Nanning

Black River
Sapa
Lao Cai
BA BE LAKES ★ 3
Dong Dang
Lang Son
Mong Cai
Beihai
Zhanjiang

Jinghong
Lai Chau
Yen Bai
Red River
2
TAM DAO ★
1
18

Taichang
Dien Bien Phu
Son La
Viet Tri
Hanoi
CAT BA NATIONAL PARK ▲

Ban Boten
1
6
CUC PHUONG NATIONAL PARK ▲
1
Haiphong
Nam Dinh

Mekong River
Sam Neva
Song Ca
Nameo
Ninh Binh
Samson Beach
Than Hoa

Luang Prabang
7
Nong Het
Vinh
Ha Tinh

LAOS
13
Cau Treo
8
Lak Sao
Gulf of Tonkin
Hainan Island (China)
Haikou

Vientiane
Nong Khai
13
12
Dong Hoi
VIETNAM

2
22
Phong Nga Caves
1

Savannakhet
Lao Bao
Dong Ha
Thuan An Beach

Mukdahan
13
9
Hué
Danang
Hoi An

THAILAND
Paksé
BACH MA NATIONAL PARK ▲
Ai Nghia
MY SON RUINS ★

Chong Mek
18
Dak To
14
Quang Ngai
Sa Huynh Beach

Poipet
Voeng Kham
Central Highlands
Kontum
19
Binh Dinh
1

CAMBODIA
19
Pleiku
Qui Nhon

Lake Tônlé Sap
Stung Treng
Ban Don
Tuy Hoa

Mekong River
7
14
26
Buon Ma Thuot
Ninh Hoa
Nha Trang

Phnom Penh
5
Dalat
Cam Ranh Bay

Tonle Mekong
22
Moc Bai
20
Bao Loc
Phan Rang
Cana Beach

Chau Doc
Bavet
1
Saigon
Bien Hoa
51
Phan Thiet
Mui Ne Beach

Gulf of Thailand
Long Xuyen
Mytho
Vung Tau

Phu Quoc Island
Rach Gia
Cantho
Vinh Long
South China Sea

0   100 mi
0   100 km
U-MINH MANGROVE FOREST ★
Soc Trang
1
Mekong Delta

= BORDER CROSSING
Camau
Con Dao Islands

© AVALON TRAVEL PUBLISHING, INC.

in Vietnam today are the relics of war—captured weaponry at the War Crimes Museum in Saigon, preserved tactical tunnels at Cu Chi and Vinh Moc, and fragments of downed B-52s at the Army Museum in Hanoi. Mementos of the war bolster national unity and provide a sense of legitimacy to the rule of the Communist Party. For their part, the Vietnamese bear no animosity toward Americans or the French (the Vietnamese are eager to put the past behind them and forge ahead). In fact, Americans visiting the area say this is the friendliest place in Southeast Asia.

Though it's the Vietnam War that lingers with those who know Vietnam through film, television, and personal experience, it's the French presence that strikes those who actually visit. There are stately French-built mansions and tree-shaded boulevards in Hanoi, art galleries in Hanoi and Saigon selling works heavily influenced by French styles, cafés serving French bread and drip-filter coffee in Saigon, French villas dotting the hills of Dalat. The origin of some customs are French, but the interpretation is pure Vietnamese: One visitor spotted a black Citroën Traction, straight out of 1930s France except for the roof, which was covered in white geese. The Vietnamese still move at bicycle pace. On the streets, schoolgirls in graceful white *ao dais* cycle by, and women with conical hats sit on top of loads of produce, being wheeled around in bicycle-powered contraptions.

Equally important as the rapprochement with the United States is the reopening of the door to China, closed after bitter border warfare in 1979. Animosity between the Vietnamese and Chinese harks back several thousand years. However, in late 1991 Hanoi and Beijing agreed to put all that behind them, opening several trading frontiers. Renewed trade has boosted the economy in the north: Smuggled goods account for an even larger trade. Three border crossings to China are open to foreigners, including two international train crossings (Hanoi–Kunming and Hanoi–Beijing). The Vietnamese have opened five land crossings into Laos, making it possible to travel by land

from Thailand all the way to Hong Kong. Two borders have opened into Cambodia as well. After a long period of isolation, the tiny nation that defeated the French and the Americans—and gave the Chinese a bloody nose—is open for business.

Tourists are welcome in Vietnam—a sign of a return to normalcy after the years of insanity called "war." After being out in the cold for so long, the Vietnamese are keen to rejoin the international community. An international marathon in Saigon and international surfing competition in Danang are efforts in that direction. Ironically, Vietnam is today viewed as the safest place in Asia to travel—shielded from terrorist activity and from the ethnic conflicts that bedevil places like Thailand.

Now is the time to go to Vietnam. It's safe, it's inexpensive, it's new, it's exciting. The welcome mat is out, the doors are open, the people are friendly. So go and see for yourself!

THE LAND

Vietnam shares borders with Cambodia, Laos, and China and features 3,200 kilometers of coastline facing the South China Sea. With an area of 332,000 square kilometers, Vietnam's topography varies from coastal plains to mountain ranges.

Vietnam has a tropical monsoon climate, with dry and wet seasons. Conditions vary from north to south and with elevation changes.

THE PEOPLE

With a population of 83 million, Vietnam is the most densely populated country in Southeast Asia. There's a vigorous campaign to limit children to one or two per family.

A variety of ethnic groups inhabit the Central Highlands and northern mountain regions. Population distribution is roughly 80 percent rural and 20 percent urban. The largest cities in the north are Hanoi (Greater Hanoi district three million, urban Hanoi around 1.5 million) and Haiphong (Greater Haiphong district 1.7 million, urban area about 700,000);

in the center, Danang (1,100,000), Nha Trang (315,000), and Hué (350,000); in the south, Saigon (Ho Chi Minh City district five or six million, urban Saigon perhaps three million).

Language

Vietnamese is a tonal language that uses a Roman alphabet together with tone markers. Chinese, French, English, and Russian are also spoken. There are more than 55 minority languages. The literacy rate is 92 percent.

Religion

Officially there is none. Percentages on religious beliefs are impossible to come by since the government suppresses religion and does not permit proselytizing. It is believed an estimated 60 percent of the population adhere to some form of Buddhism, with strong Confucian and Taoist influences. Catholics account for perhaps 8 percent of the population; in the Mekong Delta, the Cao Dai and Hoa Hao faiths are strong.

Festivals

The most important festival is Tet, determined by the lunar calendar but usually falling in February. Before the onset of Tet, transportation is booked solid. Most businesses close for a five-day period.

GOVERNMENT AND ECONOMY

Vietnam is a socialist republic under the rule of the Communist Party, the only political party permitted. Its general secretary is the country's leader, and its Politburo the most powerful government body. The National Assembly rubberstamps party decisions.

The national flag is a bright yellow star centered on a blood-red background. The red is symbolic of lives lost in Vietnam's movement toward unification; the star represents a brighter future. The flag is based on the 1954 North Vietnam flag.

Economy

After switching to a market-based economy, Vietnam managed to overcome rampant infla-tion, the legacy of years of warfare. Vietnam's economy is mainly based on rice farming. Primary agricultural exports are rice, rubber, coffee, and tea. Major industries include chemical fertilizer, cement, textiles, steel, sawn logs, and paper. Vietnam also exports electricity, crude oil, and coal. Seaports are Saigon, Danang, and Haiphong. Per capita income is $300. The unit of currency is the dong (US$1=15,800 dong).

TOURISM IN VIETNAM

Vietnam opened to Western tourism in the 1980s. The early days of travel were harrowing, with snarls of frustrating red tape. For a long time, individual travelers were neither recognized nor allowed. Now they are, and travel permits are not required except in a handful of sensitive areas.

Vietnam's fledgling tourist industry appears to be taking off. From a paltry 60,000 visitors in 1989, arrivals rocketed to almost three million in 2004, according to the Vietnam National Tourism Administration. Although a complete breakdown of figures has not been released, a large contingent of arrivals were Vietnamese from overseas, half of them from the United States. Most certainly, Asian visitors from China, Taiwan, Japan, Singapore, and Hong Kong account for a large percentage of visitors. Up to a quarter of arrivals could be Chinese tourists, many on cross-border day trips.

HIGHLIGHTS

Vietnamese tourist authorities are fond of grafting pretty women in colorful *ao dai* dress onto the landscape to brighten up brochures. A photo of a row of soot-gray mandarin statues in Hué, for instance, may feature the addition of a young woman with a bright yellow *ao dai*. This may be because Hué's major attraction, the Royal Citadel, was leveled during the Vietnam War. A similar fate befell a number of key sites around the country, although the enterprising Vietnamese have created new attractions out of the debris of war, including tours to the DMZ and visits to tactical tunnels and

AN EARLY AMERICAN TOURIST

In December 1973, travel writer Paul Theroux entered Vietnam to ride what trains he could in South Vietnam. Theroux describes an encounter with the director of Vietnam Tourism in Saigon in his book *The Great Railway Bazaar*. The director tells Theroux that the train he is planning to take is the worst in the world and advises him instead to go to a beach such as Vung Tau. Or to the Central Highlands, so he can say he slept in a bunker at Pleiku. Or to Hué, described in the proffered *Lovely Hué* brochure as a "scenic beauty" (the booklet had not been updated; it failed to mention that Hué was obliterated five years previously). Posters were printed showing pretty Vietnamese girls in places such as Danang and Hué with the slogan,

"Follow Me!" The director was hoping to attract many tourists from Japan and America who had heard so much about the country. In his estimation, there were two main selling points: the beaches and the war.

An estimated 70,000 people had been killed since the cease-fire went into effect in 1972. When Theroux brought up the question of getting shot, the director told him there was nothing to worry about; tourists would visit only noncombat areas. While Theroux was riding the train from Saigon to Bien Hoa, the stationmaster mentioned to him at one point that this was usually where the Vietcong fired on the train. Theroux joked, "Perhaps we should close the windows then."

army museums. What remains in the way of architecture is mostly French: the grand public buildings in Hanoi and Saigon, the villas at the former hill station of Dalat.

The ethnic minorities of the northwest are fascinating—an array of groups unencumbered by the commercial hoopla found in Thailand. Among the natural wonders are the karst scenery of the mountainous north, Halong Bay's grottoes, Phong Nga Grotto, and the Mekong Delta waterways lined with lush tropical vegetation. Pristine beaches are a major draw and fishing villages dot the coastline, along with semideveloped resorts such as China Beach and Nha Trang.

Many visitors say the highlight of their trips to Vietnam is not the sights but the experiences. The Vietnamese are friendly and hospitable. After 30 years of warfare, the older folk have some tales to tell. More than half of Vietnam's current population were born after 1975, however, and have no experience of the wars that molded the older generation. The younger set are less concerned with patriotic fighting than with pleasure seeking, riding the right kind of motorcycle, wearing the right clothes, wearing the right cellphone, or being seen at the ritziest cafés.

Gourmet food is resurgent in Vietnam, with

superb Viet-French and Chinese cuisine available in Saigon and Hanoi. The food quality varies. Hoi An is excellent; Hué offers above-average fare. On the coast, there's seafood at Nha Trang and Halong Bay.

The weather in Vietnam can play havoc with travel plans—typhoons at beaches, thick fog at Halong Bay, flooding in the Mekong Delta. Because of the varied climate zones, no season can be described as "best all-around." If you want to cover the entire country, consider devoting half your time to the north, the other half to the center and south. You can travel the entire country via a series of stepping stones; Hanoi, Hué, Danang, Nha Trang, Dalat, and Saigon are the most common. It's also eminently possible to concentrate on one region alone—spend all your time in the north, south, or center—and return for the others some other time. Vietnam is the kind of place you'll want to return to.

Hanoi and the North

The north was the last area of Vietnam to open to tourism and holds the greatest potential. There's spectacular karst scenery with sugarloaf peaks at Halong Bay and Tam Coc Caves. The landscape is evocative of parts of Thailand, the Philippines, and the south of China. Hanoi is a common base for exploring the north. Options include touring from Hanoi to the Chinese border, or crossing over into China from either of the three open borders.

Hanoi offers most of the cultural and historical highlights in the north. It has the best-preserved French architecture in Indochina and a charming ambience with numerous cafés and art galleries. You can walk or bicycle around the lively Old Quarter or out to Ho Chi Minh Mausoleum and the Army Museum. At night you can visit a water puppet theater—a fantastic and unique art form. If you get a chance, go to a live performance at the magnificent Opera House, which is the pride of Hanoi.

The top day trips from Hanoi are the Perfume Pagoda trip or the Tam Coc Caves and Bich Dong tour. To the southwest, limited hiking is available at Cuc Phuong National Park, which, like other national parks in Vietnam, is a reserve in name only. Also in this area, Mai Chau offers fine scenery and markets and a look at various ethnic groups. Several Hanoi tour operators provide hiking trips to the southwest of 2–4 days, staying at minority villages en route. These are available for Cuc Phuong National Park, Hoa Binh, and Mai Chau.

In the Gulf of Tonkin, ugly, gray Haiphong is the gateway to the fascinating regions of Cat Ba Island and Halong Bay, where you can commandeer a converted fishing boat or a modified red-sailed junk for a leisurely cruise among hundreds of karst islands, cliffs, and outcrops. This area was once the domain of pirates, with hideaway caves and inlets. Allow 1–3 days for the entire trip from Hanoi, longer if returning via Cat Ba Island. Sunbathing, swimming, snorkeling, and caving are the order of the day. Limestone outcrops provide excellent caving. Halong Bay has deep grottoes to explore, and near Cat Ba National Park lie Trung Trang Caves.

Minority groups abound in the rugged and mountainous northwest near the Tonkinese Alps. There are lots of opportunities to get off the track and organize your own treks to villages, best arranged in a 4WD vehicle. Stopping points along the northwest route include Dien Bien Phu, Lai Chau, and the old French hill resort of Sapa, near the Chinese border. Ethnic groups are best seen at markets, where women dress in full costume and men occasionally do too. Because of poor roads, trips to the northwest are time-consuming: Allow a minimum of three days when traveling from Hanoi. You can carry on from Hanoi through the Lao Cai border into China. A rail spur leads all the way from Hanoi to Kunming.

The best place to experience Tet (Lunar New Year) is in the more traditional north. Villagers take time out from hard toil to get into the Tet spirit with special festivities. Firecracker competitions are held in several villages close to Hanoi.

Hué and Central Vietnam

Vietnam's central region is not universally popular. Some like it, some prefer to skip it. The center has beaches, but few historical sites. Most find it's on the way or in the way, so they check it out anyway. Gateway to the center is the Hué–Danang–Hoi An triangle, which holds the main historic and cultural interest. A land border crossing into Laos is possible about 150 kilometers due northwest of Hué at Lao Bao.

Hué, the former imperial capital, is the educational and cultural heart of central Vietnam. Dowdy tombs and the Royal Citadel (the main attractions) are somewhat overrated, if not destroyed. When it's not pouring rain, Hué is pleasant enough, offering quiet boating on the Perfume River and cycling along back roads.

The top day trip from Hué is the DMZ tour to Vinh Moc Tunnels and Khe Sanh base—all highly educational. Do not, however, believe any hype about trekking along the Ho Chi Minh Trail. Any section of the fabled trail not reclaimed by the jungle would be dangerous ground because of the massive amount of remaining unexploded ordnance lying around. Also, remember that the trail was chosen because it was inconspicuous; the scenery is on the boring side.

Danang is a nasty port city but host to the Cham Museum, which features a fine collection of artifacts from the fascinating Cham civilization. Within easy reach of Danang are China Beach (swimming) and the Marble Mountains.

Hoi An, a well-preserved maritime trading town and a World Heritage Site, is a favorite among travelers. It's one of the very few places in Vietnam where you can find traditional architecture. There's good food for a change, and it's an excellent place to stroll around. Nearby Cua Dai beach is home to several upscale resort hotels.

Central Vietnam has a long coastline with numerous white-sand beaches and fishing villages. Some remain pristine; others have been colonized by resort hotel consortiums. Duking it out at Cua Dai Beach (near Hoi An) are three upscale resort hotels. The same phenomenon occurs at Phan Thiet, with a golf course for the idle rich to boot. Other ritzy resort hotels are sprinkled around central Vietnam—at China Beach (Danang) and Nha Trang—and farther south at Longhai Beach.

Typhoons can lash the coast toward the latter part of the year. Nha Trang is an established beach resort, meaning it has a few umbrellas and seaside cafés and five kilometers of white sand and coconut palms. You have to put up with aggressive cyclos and mafia types around Nha Trang. But, it has some fine Cham towers and there are excellent day trips to offshore islands by fishing boat. There is limited diving and sailboarding equipment available. Apart from Nha Trang, hot spots for the foreign beach-potato include China Beach (near Danang, where occasional surf comes up), Cua Dai Beach near Hoi An, and Thuan An Beach near Hué. Pristine spots—still fishing villages—include Lang Co Lagoon north of Danang and Dai Lanh Beach north of Nha Trang.

If you want to get off the track, the Central Highlands is the place to go. Some prefer the solitude and open spaces here, compared to the more crowded coastal cities. The highlands have forest cover and deep waterfalls. Don't expect any wonders in the way of ethnic groups in the highlands; most have parted from their traditional ways and are increasingly becoming Vietnamized. Half-hearted—and expensive—elephant rides are available at Ban Don near Buon Ma Thuot.

Dalat is the former French hill resort set in pine woods, with many villas. The Vietnamese rave about this place, but it's quite ordinary. The pine woods around Dalat are great for motorcycling and hiking.

Saigon and the South

The south is blessed with the most consistently balmy weather in Vietnam, which gives you a chance to put your camera to good use (not to mention your beach towel; the humidity will make you sweat like a pig). What the south lacks in real attractions it more than compensates for in energy level and cultural exchange. Most travelers use Saigon as a base for exploring the south. It's possible to go by land from Saigon to Phnom Penh if your paperwork is in order.

Saigon is the powerhouse of the south: noisy, raucous, rough, and ready. It has the worst traffic in Vietnam, with bicycles now being replaced by motorcycles; it also has more than its share of beggars and prostitutes, con men, drug addicts, and hustlers. Downtown you can find faded colonial grandeur and the stark War Crimes Museum; over in Cholon stand peaceful pagodas. Saigon has great cuisine, with a selection of restaurants to suit anyone, and excellent shopping. It's also the only place in the country with anything resembling nightlife. Clubs vary from disco joints to karaoke bars; quieter alternatives include open-air cafés and boat cruises on the Saigon River.

A good day trip from Saigon is the Cao Dai Temple and Cu Chi Tunnels tour, which will delight seekers of the bizarre. Another option is a one-day trip to the Mekong Delta, particularly to the town of Mytho. Farther afield is Vung Tau, a mundane beach resort rife with prostitutes; a better bet is Long Hai Beach, with pristine coastline close by.

The Mekong Delta is a region of waterways, deep green rice fields, fruit orchards, floating markets, and more coconuts than you'd ever want to contemplate. A visit to this tropical wonderland is highly recommended. The towns of Mytho, Cantho, and Vinh Long are easily accessible from Saigon, and they make great bases for exploring surrounding areas by small boat. This is a fertile region; markets present exotic species of fruit. Getting right into the delta may require a week or longer; you can strike out for Ha Tien or Chau Doc at the extremities. Throw in some river trips if you can—that's the real way to see this region. Some travelers motorcycle around; you can often load motorcycles onto boats.

Hanoi

To visit Hanoi is to steep yourself in history, tradition, and legend in a capital that has been inhabited continuously for a millennium. Hanoi's present architecture is mainly from the 19th and 20th centuries, and the stately French-built section of town is largely intact. Hanoi is cleaner, leafier, and quieter than other big cities in Vietnam—in a word, it's "cooler." There's cooler weather, more drizzle, less traffic, less hype; the streets seem quieter, with few large billboards. There's a cooler mentality here, too—prouder,

more prudish. Hanoi is a magnet for intellectuals and artists, while Saigon seems to attract entrepreneurs and hustlers.

Hanoi street life is fascinating. In the morning, you can see tai chi practitioners, martial arts exponents, and joggers along Hoan Kiem Lake. Bicyclists wearing berets ride past with baguettes tucked into their baskets. Strolling through the old French sector, you can find a street occupied by outdoor barbers clipping their customers in front of mirrors hung off building walls. On

Must-Sees

HANOI

Museum of Ethnology

Old Quarter

Ba Dinh Square

Hoan Kiem Lake

Opera House

Water Puppetry

M Hoan Kiem Lake: The heart of Hanoi and abode of a mythical tortoise bearing a magic sword. Mix with Hanoians who gather to exercise at dawn, play badminton at dusk, or just stroll around the lake (page 38).

M Old Quarter: Stroll through the happily chaotic Quarter of the 36 Streets, formerly home to trade guilds. This is the oldest part of Hanoi, with some ancient temples (page 39).

M Opera House: Over-the-top French colonial masterpiece brings Paris to Hanoi. Experience the majestic architecture and the acoustics from the inside at performances (page 45).

M Ba Dinh Square: File past and see the revered Ho Chi Minh himself at this austere memorial. A well-designed museum about his life is part of the Ho Chi Minh mausoleum complex, along with Uncle Ho's humble House on Stilts (page 46).

M Museum of Ethnology: Well-thought-out displays about Vietnam's 53 ethnic minority groups. The museum has some innovative multimedia features as well as full-sized ethnic houses (page 54).

M Water Puppetry: Exuberant and magical art form that will thrill and delight. This fantastic art form is seen regularly only in Hanoi (page 69).

Trang Tien Street there's a beautician at work: a woman with a flashlight mounted on her head, cleaning a customer's ears. At street corners in the Old Quarter, men with green pith helmets chat over steaming bowls of noodles. Farther along the street, women sell fresh-cut flowers from the backs of bicycles.

The City Rises

Although the banks of the Red River have been inhabited for thousands of years, Hanoi traces its founding to 1010—the year Emperor Le Thai To moved his capital from Hoa Lu to this site. He named the town Thang Long, or Soaring Dragon, after an auspicious dream about a dragon arising from the city.

Originally, Hanoi was laid out in a pattern dictated by Chinese geomancy. At its center was a walled royal city with a cosmic mountain; ceremonial rites and recreational functions took place in this zone. The One Pillar Pagoda was constructed in 1049; the Temple of

Hanoi

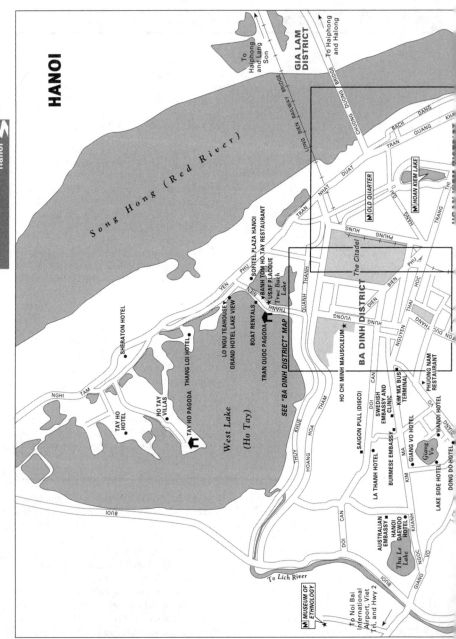

HANOI

Song Hong (Red River)

To Haiphong and Lang Son

GIA LAM DISTRICT

To Haiphong and Halong

LONG BIEN RAILWAY BRIDGE

CHUONG DUONG BRIDGE

BACH DANG

TRAN QUANG KHAI

DUAT

NHAT

TRAN

OLD QUARTER

HANG

HOAN KIEM LAKE

TRANG

THI

HUNG

PHUNG

TRAN PHU

SOFITEL PLAZA HANOI

BANH TOM HO TAY RESTAURANT

USAF PLAQUE

Truc Bach Lake

PHU

YEN

NHU

THANH

The Citadel

QUANH

BIEN

HOC

PHU

DIEN

NGUYEN

THAI

TON DUC THANG

VUONG

HUNG

BA DINH DISTRICT

SHERATON HOTEL

LO NGU TEAHOUSE

GRAND HOTEL LAKE VIEW

BOAT RENTALS

TRAN QUOC PAGODA

HO CHI MINH MAUSOLEUM

SEE "BA DINH DISTRICT" MAP

NGHI

TAM

TAY HO VILLAS

HO TAY HOTEL

TAY HO PAGODA   THANG LOI HOTEL

West Lake (Ho Tay)

THUY KHUE

HOA

THIAM

HOANG

CAN

DOI

MA

KIM

KHANH

VO

NGOC

GIANG

BUOI

CAN

DOI

PHUONG NAM RESTAURANT

KIM MA BUS TERMINAL

SWEDISH EMBASSY AND CLINIC

BURMESE EMBASSY

SAIGON PULL (DISCO)

LA THANH HOTEL

GIANG VO HOTEL

Giang Vo

HANOI HOTEL

LAKE SIDE HOTEL

DONG DO HOTEL

AUSTRALIAN EMBASSY

HANOI DAEWOO HOTEL

Thu Le Lake

To Lich River

MUSEUM OF ETHNOLOGY

To Noi Bai International Airport, Viet Tri, and Hwy 2

BUOI

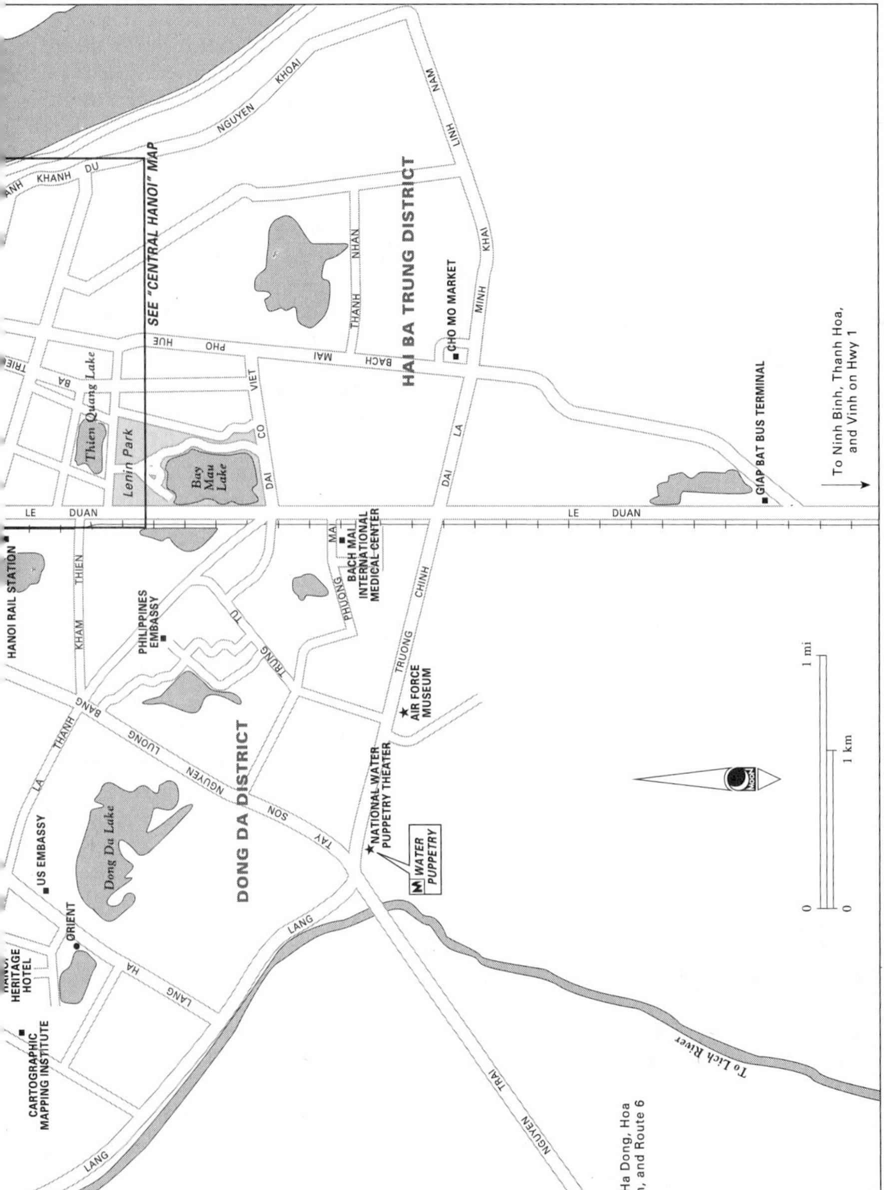

Hanoi

SEE "CENTRAL HANOI" MAP

KHANH DU

NGUYEN KHOAI

NAM

LINH

KHAI

MINH

HAI BA TRUNG DISTRICT

NHAN

THANH

BACH MAI

HUE

PHO

VIET

CO

DAI

KHANH

TRIE

BA

Thien Quang Lake

Lenin Park

Bay Mau Lake

■ CHO MO MARKET

LA

DAI

■ GIAP BAT BUS TERMINAL

To Ninh Binh, Thanh Hoa,
and Vinh on Hwy 1

LE   DUAN

LE   DUAN

MAI

PRUONG

TU

BACH MAI
INTERNATIONAL
MEDICAL CENTER

CHINH

HANOI RAIL STATION ■

THIEN

KHAM

PHILIPPINES
EMBASSY ■

TU

TRUNG

BANG

BAVAI

LA

LUONG

NGUYEN

SON

TAY

Dong Da Lake

DONG DA DISTRICT

TRUONG

★ AIR FORCE
MUSEUM

★ NATIONAL WATER
PUPPETRY THEATER

M WATER
PUPPETRY

US EMBASSY ■

● ORIENT

HANOI
HERITAGE
HOTEL ■

HA

LANG

LANG

CARTOGRAPHIC
MAPPING INSTITUTE ■

LANG

NGUYEN

TRAI

To Lich River

To Ha Dong, Hoa
Binh, and Route 6

0   1 mi

0   1 km

© AVALON TRAVEL PUBLISHING, INC.

Literature, to the south, was the first educational institution in Vietnam, established in 1070. East of the citadel and north of Hoan Kiem Lake was the artisan and commercial area, now the Old Quarter. On the other side of the lake, east and south, was the quarter for visiting residents; later this became the French zone. To the far south of the city lay a region of cemeteries, sickness, and death, where a leper colony and abattoir were relegated.

In the 12th century palaces built by Ly dynasty emperors sprouted along the Red River and around West Lake; the city was protected from Red River flooding by construction of a massive dike. Though flooding was contained, the Vietnamese could not keep out the Mongols. In the late 13th century the Mongols sacked the city, and for the next hundred-odd years the city's fortunes fluctuated. In 1428 Vietnamese leader Le Loi ousted the Chinese from the area and renamed the city Dong Kinh (Eastern Capital), later corrupted by the French to "Tonkin."

From the 16th century on, the city fell into a period of decline, culminating in the shifting of the imperial court to Hué. In 1805 Emperor Gia Long, ruling from Hué, ordered the ancient citadel of Thang Long destroyed, replacing it with a smaller citadel constructed in the style of French military architect Sébastien de Vauban. In 1831, Emperor Tu Duc renamed the city Hanoi, or City on the Bend of the River. This strategic bend attracted the French, who were investigating the Red River as an alternate trade route to the Mekong for shipping goods from China. In 1873 Francis Garnier was sent to reconnoiter the area. After negotiations with Emperor Tu Duc failed, Garnier attacked and destroyed Hanoi Citadel. Upon seeing what a small French force could accomplish, Tu Duc acceded to French demands. Many old structures in Hanoi were razed to make way for new French buildings. From 1882 on, Hanoi and Haiphong were the focal points of French exploitation of the north, and Hanoi was made capital of the new protectorate of Tonkin.

In 1902, after a merger of French protectorates and colonies, Hanoi was selected as the capital of the French Indochinese Union. It was a convenient base for exploring China routes, and its climate mild in comparison to Saigon's. French colonial rule came to an end in 1954; after the departure of the French, Ho Chi Minh set about expanding Hanoi's industrial base. The city's factories were targeted by U.S. bombers 1966–1972; oddly enough, central Hanoi survived the U.S. blitzkrieg. Parts of the city hit by B-52 bombing lay mainly to the south of Hanoi. The Old Quarter and Hoan Kiem District were not bombed, although Long Bien Bridge was a constant target. Between 1965 and 1973 up to three-quarters of the inner-city population was evacuated.

Cessation of hostilities led to rapid migration back to the capital. Today Hanoi is one of three independent municipalities in Vietnam, covering an area of 2,139 square kilometers. The inner city is distributed in four districts; Greater Hanoi comprises 11 peripheral districts. The present population is estimated at 3.1 million.

poster marking the 30th anniversary of the end of the Vietnam War

Hanoi at the Crossroads

Hanoi today is a city on the brink of transformation. With the opening of Vietnam to tourism and joint-venture projects, developers envision a Hanoi studded with high-rise buildings. Land prices in Hanoi are skyrocketing. Bids are in for 20- and 30-story office towers and apartment blocks in central Hanoi. The Hanoi People's Committee wish list includes 5,000 hotel rooms for businesspeople around West Lake, a region where present structures discharge waste straight into the water. Electronic goods, previously hard to come by, are now flooding in from China, arriving either legally or illegally. Unfortunately, motorcycles have taken over from bicycles as the primary mode of private transportation, while those with money have taken to buying large SUVs. Unleashing scores of new cars and hundreds of thousands of motorcycles has done more than create traffic and parking headaches—it has led to pollution. And it has made Hanoi very noisy because both motorcyclists and auto drivers are in the habit of hitting the horn all the time to announce their right of way.

Construction of high-rise office and apartment buildings and an increase in the number of hotel rooms will inevitably place more stress on road and sewage systems, power supply, and other facilities. Hanoi could become another nightmarish Asian metropolis of towering concrete monoliths and interminable traffic jams. Or, if managed properly, it could remain a low-rise city with high-density population, retaining its charming character.

An international foundation called Friends of Hanoi is raising several million dollars through sponsorship from foreign companies for a management initiative on Hanoi's architectural heritage. Friends of Hanoi has approved three projects: creation of a database containing information on buildings and infrastructure; development of internationally compatible planning and zoning laws; and a public awareness program. An example of what can be done to maintain harmony is the ANZ Bank initiative—the company renovated an old French villa along Hoan Kiem Lake for use as its place of business.

But careless decisions and thoughtless planning continue to plague Hanoi. In 1994 the authorities evicted tenants from 150 French villas in three major streets in central Hanoi with the intention of renovating the properties and renting them at inflated prices to those willing to pay, including foreigners. In 1995 a scandal surfaced involving illegal construction along a one-kilometer stretch of earth embankment that protects Hanoi from Red River flooding. Hundreds of villas, minihotels, and restaurants had appeared along the embankment, their combined weight resulting in dozens of cracks in the earth. If the embankment collapses, the flood could consume Hanoi. Trouble is, many of the new villas and buildings belong to senior party officials.

Meanwhile, the authorities have come up with a game-plan to save Hanoi from traffic jams and overcrowding: build another Hanoi. Building of a satellite town for Hanoi is going on, full of huge apartment blocks and shopping malls. The same strategy is being implemented in Saigon.

Neighborhoods

Hanoi, a city of distinct neighborhoods, is also a city of lakes. Once you sort out the lakes, it's easy to find your way around. The heart of Hanoi is the district around Hoan Kiem Lake. North of Hoan Kiem Lake is the Old Quarter, a fascinating jumble of alleys teeming with life, with some great guesthouses and cafés. Around the southern and eastern side of the lake is the former French zone, with cream-colored offices and green-shuttered apartment blocks and villas. Here you'll find the Opera House and former palatial residences. This is also the main commercial district, with large hotels, banks, department stores, art galleries, and shops.

In the northwest of Hanoi is Ba Dinh District, taking in the area of the former citadel. Little remains of the citadel, though the area is still used by the military and houses the Ministry of Defense, the Army Club, and other bodies. Speaking of bodies, Ho Chi Minh's mausoleum is out this way, along with the Ho Chi Minh Museum and high-priced villas used by Eastern European embassies. The area is leafy and green, with wide boulevards—ideal for bicycling. The Ba Dinh District also encompasses Giang Vo Lake, an area of nascent four-star hotels.

In the north end of Hanoi are Truc Bach Lake and West Lake (Ho Tay), two exclusive residential zones. West Lake offers low-key recreational facilities and is a relaxing place to go boating.

PLANNING YOUR TIME

At least two days are recommended to tour Hanoi and to take in the key sights, such as Ba Dinh Square (dedicated to Ho Chi Minh), the Old Quarter, the Ethnology Museum, colonial architecture (especially the Opera House), the Army Museum, and a water puppetry show at night. Museums are usually closed on Mondays. Ho Chi Minh's Mausoleum at Ba Dinh Square is open only early mornings, and closed Mondays and Fridays. Key parts of Hanoi such as Hoan Kiem Lake and the nearby Old Quarter are best covered on foot, including lingering at streetside cafés. Though there is a public bus system, few bother trying to figure it out. Bicycling rentals are available but cycling can be unnerving because of the large number of motorcycles in Hanoi. Use (inexpensive) taxis to cover longer stretches, or rent a car with driver or moto with driver by the day. Just for fun, take at least one cyclo ride in Hanoi—these are comfortable and you go slowly enough to be able to take photos along the way. Seeing the Old Quarter by cyclo is popular with group tours.

Sights

ⓜ HOAN KIEM LAKE

Hoan Kiem, or the Lake of the Restored Sword, is the center of Hanoi, both in spirit and in geographical location. You can bicycle or stroll around the lake, as thousands of Hanoians do on weekends. At the crack of dawn locals assemble on the thin parkland perimeter for an hour or so of tai chi, jogging, or badminton.

Associated with the lake is an Arthurian-type legend. In the early 15th century, so the story goes, a humble fisherman named Le Loi asked the heavens for help in resisting the Ming dynasty Chinese who occupied the north. A golden turtle from the lake then brought him a magic sword that flashed like lightning. After leading an insurrection against the Chinese, Le Loi returned to the lake, and the turtle reclaimed the sword.

At the northern end of Hoan Kiem is tiny **Ngoc Son Temple,** reached by the bright red Sunbeam Bridge, an arched Chinese–style wooden structure built in 1855. Before crossing the bridge you pass Penbrush and Inkslab towers, built in 1864 to commemorate the learned scholar Nguyen Van Sieu. Ngoc Son Temple is a mixture of temples and gift shops, and it is the desired place for Viet-namese to have their photos taken. Built in the early 19th century, it has undergone a few renovations, most recently in 1994. The temple honors several Vietnamese icons, including Van Xuong, the god of literature; Quan Vu, a martial arts exponent; physician La To; and 13th-century hero Tran Hung Dao. At the back of the shrine is the preserved body of a huge turtle found in the lake in 1968. It weighed 250 kilograms and was believed to be 400 years old—some say 500 years old, to make it old enough to serve as the turtle of legend. On an islet at the south end of the lake is a dilapidated three-tiered tower, built in honor of the valiant turtle. Turtles are occasionally still sighted in the lake. On the west bank, next to the ANZ Bank, is a small temple with a statue of Le Loi.

There are several other pagodas in the vicinity of the lake. Popular with locals is **Bada Pagoda,** or Heavenly Mistress of the Stone, to the west of Hoan Kiem on Nha Tho Street. The pagoda was built in the 15th century after the discovery of a stone statue of a woman. The statue, imbued with magic powers, disappeared and was replaced with a wooden replica. The pagoda bears bonsai trees, oriental vases, and an impressive array of Buddha statuary.

▶ OLD QUARTER

A stroll through Hanoi's happily chaotic Old Quarter will quickly lay to rest the conception that the city is gray, dull, reserved, and austere. In the anarchic jumble of the Old Quarter thrives a lively commerce in trade and handicrafts. The place is full of character—and characters. You might come across a woman trundling down a street with a shoulder pole of dual baskets bearing porcelain, or an old woman who reveals blackened teeth when she smiles, or a group of men crouched over bamboo bongs at tiny sidewalk stools. The quarter is a medieval maze of alleys lined with shops, homes, and cafés. It's best to tackle the area on foot, allowing time to stop and poke around. Unfortunately, the sidewalks are often blocked by parked motorcycles, the narrow roads filled with bicycles and motorbikes. Exercise care when walking.

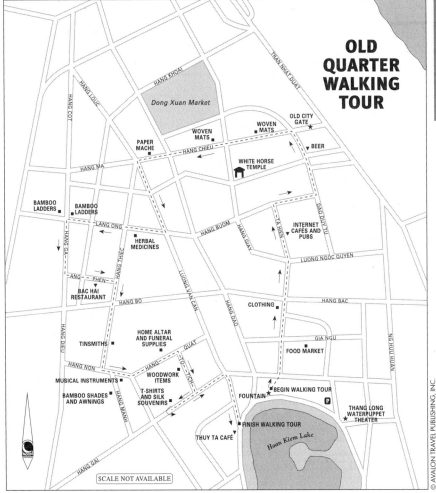

OLD
QUARTER
WALKING
TOUR

© AVALON TRAVEL PUBLISHING, INC.

OLD QUARTER WALKING TOUR

Although the following tour covers some of the more colorful streets in the Old Quarter, really you can dive in anywhere and wander at will. A good starting point is the fountain above Hoan Kiem Lake. From here you can proceed in a long counterclockwise arc through the area. Heading north up Dinh Liet Street you come across wool clothing—scarves from China, handmade sweaters, yarn products. There are more clothing and cosmetics outlets down the first side alley. To the left are Russian watch shops; to the right, running along Gia Ngu Street, is a busy food market well worth a detour.

Proceeding north you cross Hang Bac, one of the oldest streets in Hanoi. It was once known for its silversmiths, brought to the capital to cast silver bars and coins in a silver ingot factory. Some jewelers remain at this crossroads, though farther east along Hang Bac the main trade is in marble (for etching tombstones), wood (coffinmakers), and tourism (cybercafés, motorcycle rental outlets). Onward, upward, northward along Ta Hien Street, is "Chat Street," with a string of cybercafés and tiny pubs. And farther north lies Hang Buom Street, which could be dubbed "Smuggler's Alley"—luxury goods are smuggled in from China, Cambodia, or Thailand—the labels may be the real thing or fakes. Follow this street to Hang Buom.

White Horse Temple

A little way west on Hang Buom, at the corner of Hang Giay, is White Horse Temple (Bach Ma), one of the oldest in Hanoi and the most sacred in the Old Quarter. When Emperor Le Thai To set about building his capital, he went to a temple to consult the local land oracle. A white horse emerged from the temple and galloped west; the emperor decided to build his citadel walls along the hoof prints and declared the white horse the city guardian. The present White Horse Temple was reconstructed in the 18th and 19th centuries and used as a center of Taoist worship. The temple is an oasis from the traffic, with red-lacquered pillars and numerous small shrines; to the west side of the temple is a funeral palanquin shaded by twin umbrellas. Right at the back is a wooden white horse statue mounted on wheels: It has an elaborate phoenix saddle.

Go east along Hang Buom and turn north up Dao Duy Tu past some shops entirely stocked with beer (some smuggled in from China). Here you'll find an old brick city gate, Quan Chuong, built in the mid-18th century. This was one of the original 16 city gates, once closed at night with massive wooden doors. Noodle stalls now operate from inside the structure. Parts of a former city rampart and dike still stand along Tran Nhat Duat Street. On to the next street, Hang Chieu. *Chieu* means "mats"—you'll find all kinds of woven products.

Dong Xuan Market

Walking along Sugar Street (Hang Duong), just before you reach Sweet Potato Street (Hang Khoai), you'll run across Dong Xuan Market, Hanoi's oldest and newest and biggest. It's both 1,000 years old and brand-new. How so? Well, it burnt to the ground in 1994, with a fearful loss of merchandise. The market was completely rebuilt. Intriguing at Dong Xuan is the bird market to the east side. There's also a section for pets—hamsters, budgies, cats—and a rather grisly collection of lizards, pythons, macaques, and pangolins destined for restaurant tables or traditional medicines. The area outside the market to the east side features spice, rice, and dried-fish stalls.

Hanoi

Walk back to Hang Ma Street. "Ma" denotes paper offerings to the spirits of deceased relatives. Paper money, houses, cars, and fridges are burned to assist spirits in the afterlife. The street also offers other colorful paper products—gift wrapping, wedding decorations, lanterns, papier-mâché masks.

You can smell the next street before you see it—the odors of ginger, musk, powders, and potions. This is the street of herbal medicines, called Lan Ong, featuring a variety of roots, leaves, bark, and dried herbs. If you continue west you'll cross a street called Hang Dong. Originally this street specialized in copperware; now the trade is in collapsible metal door shutters used at night on Hanoi shop fronts.

Continuing west you'll reach Hang Vai, the street of the bamboo ladders. Bamboo is often used for construction scaffolding in Asia in place of metal—it's light, strong, and durable. Buildings in this section of the Old Quarter are obscured behind stacks of bamboo poles and ladders, the latter still made by hand.

Make your way down Hang Ga and turn left on Hang Phen. One of the Old Quarter's specialized restaurants lies along here—halfway along the street at number 7 on your right is a restaurant devoted solely to veal dishes. Uncle Hai's serves steak; cow brains, stomach, tongue, and liver; and fetal calves.

The next stop is Hang Thiec. *Thiec* means "tinsmiths." This area once produced metal products, candlesticks, oil lamps, opium boxes, and mirrors. Today sheet-metal workers on Hang Thiec bang away with a deafening din, producing metal storage boxes and plumbing supplies. Another side street in the area, Hang Manh, specializes in the manufacture of bamboo shades and awnings.

Red Banners and Ray-Bans

Hang Quat is the most colorful street in the whole quarter, with a riot of bright red banners and flags and eye-catching displays of objects for the home altar—most intended for religious use and funerals. For a funeral, relatives and friends in white headbands form a procession, bearing red banners and garlands of flowers.

Leading off Hang Quat at the east side is tiny To Tich, a wood-turner's street offering musical instruments and other wooden goods. Hang Gai features silk and cotton items, with embroidery and souvenir shops; the western end leads to Hang Bong. *Bong* means "cotton"—here you'll find knockoff Tintin-in-Halong T-shirts and other pirated logos. T-shirts can be custom-made.

On the street leading back to Hoan Kiem Lake, vendors sell eyeglasses, mostly sunglasses, so you might call it Ray-Ban Street. Ray-Bans here sell for $4, so Ray-Ban Copy Street might be more accurate. And to go with Ray-Bans, of course, are mafioso. You'll find them around the corner on a side street, sitting at cafés—all wearing fake Ray-Bans. Shiny new Honda Dream motorcycles are parked nearby.

The ideal place to finish your walking tour is at Thuy Ta Café by the side of Hoan Kiem Lake. The place has a derelict air, service is slow, and drinks are overpriced, but the views are great. You can get ice cream, fruit juice, or coffee at the ground-floor terrace overlooking the lake—an oasis of calm in the heart of Hanoi.

Hanoi

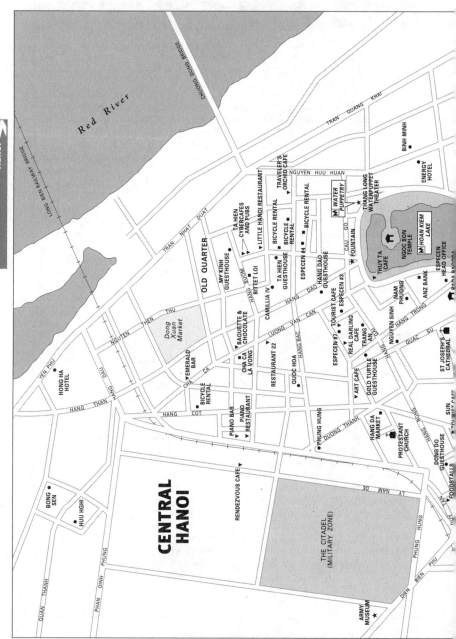

Hanoi

TRAN KHANH DU

HISTORY MUSEUM
REVOLUTIONARY MUSEUM
GMD/ARMY HOTEL
OPERA HOUSE

CAFE DE PARIS

TONG
DAN
ITALIAN EMBASSY
CLUB OPERA

LE THANH TONG

SMILING PUB
HANOI OPERA HILTON HOTEL
NAM PHUONG RESTAURANT
VIETCOMBANK/HSBC

250 yds
250 m

LE THACH
GOVERNMENT GUESTHOUSE
METROPOLE
LOTUS RESTAURANT
DAN CHU
MINIBUSES TO NORTHEAST
HANOI TOURISM

LE VAN HUU

FORMER TONKIN GOVERNOR'S OFFICES
IDD/TELECOM
BODEGA CAFE
TRANG TIEN HOTEL
BAC NAM
LE BISTROT

PHAN CHU TRINH
LO
DUC
NGO QUYEN

POST OFFICE
BODEGA I
VIETNAM TOURISM
HAO BINH
MOTORCYCLE SHOPS
HOA MA

HANG
SOPHIA GUESTHOUSE
CENTRAL BUILDING
IMMIGRATION POLICE
HANG BAI

PHU GIA
AIR FRANCE
ZEPHYR
FRENCH EMBASSY
TOURISTS' MEETING CAFE

RAINBOW CAFE-BAR
CHUNG
VIETNAM AIRLINES
HOAN KIEM DISTRICT
LOTUS GUESTHOUSE
TIEN
DINH
BA TRIEU

19 DECEMBER MARKET
MELIA HOTEL

CAMBODIAN EMBASSY
HOA SUA RESTAURANT
LAO VISA SECTION
BOSS HOTEL

CANADIAN EMBASSY

HANOI TOWERS
HOA LO MUSEUM
QUAN SU PAGODA
BOOKWORM
VIP CLUB

Thien Quang Lake

Lenin Park

HOAN KIEM GUESTHOUSE
ROSE HOTEL
GUOMAN HOTEL
TRAN HUNG DAO

ALPO
INDOCHINE
DONG LOI
SAIGON HOTEL
MANGO HOTEL
HANOI RAILWAY STATION
30-4 HOTEL
CAPITAL HOTEL

PHAN BOI CHAU
NGUYEN DU
LAOTIAN EMBASSY
CIRCUS ARENA

LE DUAN
BLUE

The Old Quarter is known as the Quarter of the 36 Streets. The derivation of the name is not clear. East of the former citadel was the artisan and merchant quarter; in the 15th century, workshop villages clustered around this area to satisfy the royal court's need for quality products. Houses and shops stood side by side in this royal city, in a cooperative system like that of imperial Beijing or medieval Florence. Guilds worked together to transport merchandise from outlying villages, often along the Red River. Guild names were applied to streets— Silk Street, Paper Street, Basket Street. Each guild maintained its own pagoda and patron deity; most of these "community centers" have since been turned over to other uses such as schools. Many street signs in this district begin with Pho Hang. "Pho" means "alley," "hang" means "shop" or "merchandise," and "bac" means "silversmiths," so Pho Hang Bac refers to the alley with the shops of silversmiths.

There may at one time have been 36 guild locations in the Old Quarter, but the number is more likely abstract or just plain lucky. In Asia, nine is an auspicious number; taken in the four compass directions, it multiplies to 36. In any case there are double that number of streets in the area now, and only a fraction of the activity revolves around handicrafts. Most streets are now concerned with trades—retail shops, tailors, repair shops. Trades have changed with the times—you'll find entire streets given over to the sale of Russian watches, smuggled cigarettes, bootleg whiskey, motorcycle parts, shoes, pillows, Korean-made luggage, and Chinese thermos flasks. Increasingly, parts of the Old Quarter are dedicated to minihotels and restaurants for tourists.

One thing that hasn't changed much in the Old Quarter is the size of its shophouses. Shops were taxed according to the width of their market frontage, so crafty old Hanoians built narrow shop fronts with long narrow homes behind them containing living space and storage. These red-tiled three- or four-story structures are called "tube houses," as they're only three meters wide at the front, but up to 60 meters deep. The local government is formulat-ing plans to preserve the Old Quarter from demolition or alteration, as developers have their beady eyes on this sector, dreaming of high-rise buildings. The Old Quarter is in surprisingly good condition, with few changes to the original layout; it has been recognized by UNESCO as an important heritage site.

FRENCHTOWN

Hanoi is home to the best-preserved colonial architecture in Indochina. From 1902 to 1953, Hanoi was the capital of the French Indochinese Union, and the grandiose public buildings and exquisite villas here attest to the fact.

When North Vietnam became a French protectorate in 1883, the French settled to the south and east of things Kiem Lake, razing Vietnamese housing except for some key pagodas and creating a *ville Française*, or Frenchtown, of several square kilometers. By 1884 the first avenues appeared, shaded with tamarind and banyan trees and lined with green-shuttered apartment blocks flung up by contract workers from France; in 1885 the first hotel appeared.

One of the oldest structures in Frenchtown is **St. Joseph's Cathedral,** built in 1886, on Nha Chung Street to the southwest of the lake. The somber Gothic exterior with its square towers is now grimy and gray; to see the interior illuminated by stained-glass windows, attend services in the early morning or late afternoon.

At the west side of Hoan Kiem Lake is the **ANZ Bank.** The bank moved into an early 1900s villa that had been converted into a warehouse. The bank eventually restored it to its former elegance, and the results are quite stunning.

From here stroll along Trang Thi Street, heading east to Trang Tien. This street, known in the French era as Rue Paul Bert, was one of the most elegant shopping thoroughfares in Hanoi.

At 15 Ngo Quyen is the **Hotel Metropole,** which opened under the same name in 1901. In its heyday the Metropole was the center of French social life, frequented by visiting celebrities and senior French officers and their wives or consorts. The building was showing its age when the French group Accor decided to pour $9 million into renovations in 1990. Architects were careful to preserve the character of the hotel, maintaining the original hardwood floors and shuttered windows in the rooms, as well as the vintage 1920s plumbing. Today the Metropole is once again the hub of foreign business and highbrow social life in the capital.

Opposite the Metropole and slightly to the north is the **Government Reception Hall,** formerly the offices of the governor-resident of Tonkin, built in 1918. This immaculately preserved specimen of belle epoque architecture has ornate and spacious rooms used for state functions, official receptions, and VIP guests, so you will have to content yourself with looking at the exterior through the wrought-iron railings at the front.

Opera House

Looming at the end of Trang Tien is the block-wide Opera House, a flamboyant structure built in 1911 in neoclassical style as an exact, though smaller, replica of the Paris Opera. The lavish 900-seat Hanoi Opera was the focal point for socializing during the French era, with patrons flocking to see productions of Victor Hugo or Molière. The interior is designed in such a way that everybody can see everybody else—no matter which little box or seat he or she is in. This was the whole point: to be seen. Aiming to be seen and heard, but more from the exterior, were the Vietminh, who in 1945 proclaimed the August Revolution from a balcony of the Opera House. The Opera House exterior, with its elaborate wrought ironwork and shutters, saw the addition of a large air-raid siren on the rooftop during the American War (that was removed during renovations).

In 1996–1997, a $15 million renovation added state-of-the-art sound and lighting equipment, as well as new seats and air-conditioning, in conjunction with the building of the Hilton Hanoi Opera Hotel on the same block. A team of Vietnamese and European preservationists and architects worked on this gem: The setting is a favorite backdrop for photography by Vietnamese visitors and locals alike (they seem to prefer the Hilton side). At night, the Opera House

may be floodlit, bringing out its elegance from a different light. The place is the pride of Hanoi and is often rented for special functions such as embassy-hosted performance soirees. Cocktail receptions for these events take place in the Mirror Room, lined with slim mirrors and chandeliers. If you are invited, check out several bullet holes to the mirrors, acquired in 1946. These have not been "renovated," apparently because of their historic value.

If you want to see the Opera House interior, attend an advertised evening cultural performance. Advertising banners appear at the Opera House to announce events. Performances are sporadic: usually twice or three times a month. (Opera House staff seem very rarely to be around except when an event is in progress, so phoning ahead to find out about events will not prove to be helpful.) Tickets are reasonable: You can check out the sweeping marble staircases, crystal chandeliers, the plush red seats—and the acoustics. Buy tickets from a small office tucked just inside the front of the building; you can also buy them through the nearby Metropole or Hilton Hanoi Opera hotels.

For special holidays, free concerts sometimes take place at night *outside* the Opera House, with a stage constructed at the front, and VIP seating in place. All traffic to the square facing the Opera House is blocked off—and thousands jam the square to see the concert.

Other Edifices

In the vicinity of the Opera House are several other buildings. The **Revolutionary Museum** was previously the neoclassical Museum of Indochinese Mines. The **History Museum** was built in 1926 and was formerly a museum and archaeological research institute under the auspices of the Ecole Française d'Extrême-Orient. It's an unusual structure with mixed Oriental and French features.

To the north of Hanoi is a curious piece of French and Vietnamese engineering. In 1902 Governor-general Paul Doumer cut the ribbon for a bridge named in his honor; the bridge, now called **Long Bien Railway Bridge,** spans 1.6 kilometers across the Red River. At the time

Hanoi

of the Vietnam War this was the only bridge across the river and was thus a prime target for U.S. bombers. As fast as American bombs knocked out the span, however, the Vietnamese repaired it; the bridge therefore became a hodgepodge of different styles. The best way to view the work up close, of course, is by traveling across it—it carries train and bicycle traffic, as well as handcart-pushers and pedestrians. **Chuong Dueng Bridge,** farther south, was built in 1985.

M BA DINH SQUARE

It was from Ba Dinh Square that Ho Chi Minh addressed half a million Vietnamese with his Declaration of Independence speech in 1945. Today the square is a shrine and pilgrimage site. Legions of schoolchildren and droves of visitors from all over Vietnam converge on Ho Chi Minh's mausoleum, museum, and house. A Ho Chi Minh Arch was completed to mark the 50th anniversary of the independence declaration. In the same area are the former Presidential Palace and the One Pillar Pagoda. If your timing is right, you can visit all the sites in one go—start early in the morning, visit the mausoleum and Ho's house, then see the One Pillar Pagoda and Ho Chi Minh Museum. Monday and Friday are bad days to visit—the mausoleum and museum are both closed.

UNCLE HO

Ho Chi Minh, roughly meaning "Bringer of Light," was the last of many pseudonyms adopted by the Vietnamese leader. He chose the name on his return to Vietnam in the early 1940s, and it remained unchanged until his death in 1969, though he preferred the appellation Boc Ho, or "Uncle Ho."

In the early part of his life, Uncle Ho was in the habit of altering his name to mark each new phase of his life—dozens of aliases have been recorded. Taking new names is acceptable in Asia when a change of circumstance warrants it, but Ho clearly carried this convention to a new extreme; like a character in a spy thriller, Ho changed names and disguises with abandon. Along the way, he mastered a number of languages—among them French, English, Russian, Mandarin, Cantonese, and Thai.

Born Nguyen Sinh Cung (or possibly Nguyen Van Thanh) in 1890 in a small village near Vinh, Ho attended Quoc Hoc college in Hué and worked for a while as a teacher in Phan Thiet. In 1911, at the age of 21, he left Vietnam as a galley boy on a French freighter bound for Europe, working under the name Nguyen Tat Thanh. In 1913 he boarded another French vessel, this time headed across the Atlantic. He spent almost a year in the United States, working as an itinerant laborer, before sailing for London. In Europe, Ho held a variety of jobs—pastry chef, waiter, photo retoucher. In 1917 he moved to Paris, where he lived for seven years, mixing with leftists and contributing to radical newspapers under the name Nguyen Ai Quoc, or Nguyen the Patriot. He joined the French Communist Party in 1920, and in 1924 he left Paris for Moscow for training by the Communist International, which he received under the name of Comrade Linh. He was sent to Canton in 1925, where, under the alias of Wang, he founded the Revolutionary Youth League of Vietnam and mobilized Vietnamese students.

It is difficult to track his movements during this period: In 1927 he secretly slipped back into Paris; in 1928 he was with Vietnamese dissidents in Thailand, bearing the shaven head and saffron robes of a Buddhist monk, traveling under the name Thau Chin. In 1929 he assembled rival factions in Hong Kong and in 1930 formed the Communist Party of Indochina. He was arrested and imprisoned in a hospital infirmary, but he managed to escape by persuading an employee to report him dead. He spent the 1930s drifting between China and the Soviet Union, waiting for the right moment to make a move in Vietnam. The Second World War provided it.

In 1940 Japan occupied Vietnam. Disguised

The Mausoleum

Getting into the mausoleum is not always easy. Plan to arrive early and be sure to bring your passport. Posted hours for the mausoleum are: Tuesday, Wednesday, Thursday, Saturday, and Sunday 0730–1030 in summer and 0800–1100 in winter. Ho Chi Minh's body is apparently taken away for upkeep September–October. Visitors entering the mausoleum area must be respectful. Posted rules require you to leave outside weapons, explosives, fire, radioactive materials, toxic products, and cameras. Inside, there's no talking, touching the walls, hands in pockets, smoking, sunglasses, or immodest clothing (including shorts, sleeveless tops, and hats).

When the mausoleum is open for visits, the surrounding boulevards are barricaded and guarded. There are car and bike parking areas to the west of Ho Chi Minh Museum off Ngoc Ha Street. Foreigners follow a different route through the Ho Chi Minh memorial complex than Vietnamese visitors, in effect jumping the queue. Just deposit bags (with camera) at 8 Hung Vuong Boulevard, and proceed to the corner of Chua Mot Cot Street east of the Ho Chi Minh Museum. Guards will check your passport, wait for a group to assemble, and then lead you through the mausoleum. From the mausoleum you can double back and get your bag and proceed to Ho Chi Minh's house.

Ho Chi Minh was embalmed using the same

as a Chinese journalist, Ho slipped back into Vietnam in 1941 for the first time in 30 years and founded the Vietminh Front. In late 1941 he entered China disguised as a blind man, intending to muster support for the Vietminh. However, he was arrested by the Nationalist Chinese on suspicion of being a Franco-Japanese spy. From August 1942 to September 1943 Ho was dragged from prison to prison in Guangxi province in China. He composed a series of poems in classical Chinese along the way—later reassembled under the title *Prison Diary*. Eventually, he was freed and given support in exchange for intelligence on the Japanese. In August 1945, as Japan was about to surrender, Ho led the August Revolution that took control of much of Vietnam. On September 2, 1945, Ho proclaimed the Democratic Republic of Vietnam, reading the Declaration of Independence near the present site of his mausoleum. In the south, the British ruthlessly suppressed the Vietminh, and with the return of the French to Vietnam, the Vietminh fled Hanoi and took up armed resistance—a struggle that would last for the next 30 years.

Ho never married, although evidence suggests he had several liaisons (which apparently resulted in several offspring). Supposedly he was wedded to the revolution—and he spent a good deal of time promoting a unified Vietnam as one happy family. Thus he cultivated the image of "Uncle Ho"—he preferred the informal name to the more formal "President." His personal charm, humility, simplicity, and sincerity enabled him to converse easily with farmers, monks, or politicians. In *A Vietcong Memoir,* Truong Nhu Trang describes a meeting with Uncle Ho:

I was immediately struck by Ho Chi Minh's appearance. Unlike the others, who were dressed in Western-style clothes, Ho wore a frayed, high-collared Chinese jacket. On his feet he had rubber sandals. In contrast to the tense-looking younger men around him, he gave off an air of fragility, almost sickliness. But these impressions only contributed to the imperturbable dignity that enveloped him as through it were something tangible.… He exuded a combination of inner strength and personal generosity that struck me with something like a physical blow. He looked directly at me, and at the others, with a magnetic expression of intensity and warmth.

Hanoi

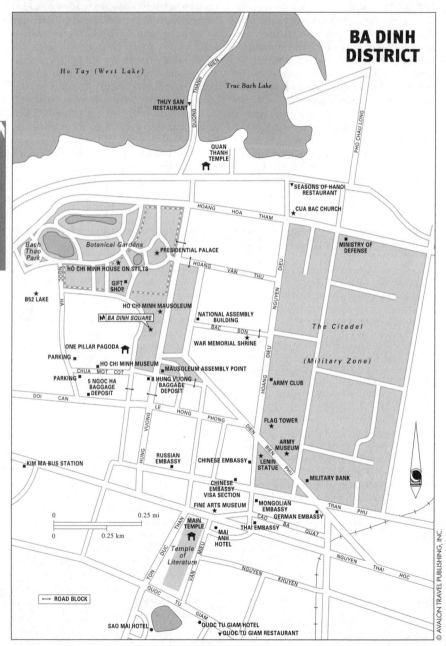

BA DINH DISTRICT

Ho Tay (West Lake)

Truc Bach Lake

PHO CHAU LONG

THUY SAN RESTAURANT

DUONG THANH NIEH

QUAN THANH TEMPLE

SEASONS OF HANOI RESTAURANT

HOANG HOA THAM

CUA BAC CHURCH

Bach Thao Park

Botanical Gardens

PRESIDENTIAL PALACE

MINISTRY OF DEFENSE

HO CHI MINH HOUSE ON STILTS

HOANG VAN THU

NGOC HA

GIFT SHOP

B52 LAKE

HO CHI MINH MAUSOLEUM

BA DINH SQUARE

NATIONAL ASSEMBLY BUILDING

NGUYEN

DIEU

The Citadel

BAC SON

WAR MEMORIAL SHRINE

ONE PILLAR PAGODA

PARKING

HO CHI MINH MUSEUM

CHUA MOT COT

(Military Zone)

DIEU

MAUSOLEUM ASSEMBLY POINT

PARKING

5 NGOC HA BAGGAGE DEPOSIT

8 HUNG VUONG BAGGAGE DEPOSIT

HOANG

ARMY CLUB

DOI CAN

LE HONG PHONG

HUNG VUONG

DIEN BIEN PHU

FLAG TOWER

KIM MA BUS STATION

RUSSIAN EMBASSY

CHINESE EMBASSY

ARMY MUSEUM

LENIN STATUE

CHINESE EMBASSY VISA SECTION

MILITARY BANK

FINE ARTS MUSEUM

MONGOLIAN EMBASSY

TRAN PHU

CAO BA QUAT

GERMAN EMBASSY

THAI EMBASSY

MAIN TEMPLE

MAI ANH HOTEL

0   0.25 mi

0   0.25 km

DUC

TON

QUOC

TU

THANH

VAN MIEU

GIAM

Temple of Literature

NGUYEN KHUYEN

NGUYEN THAI HOC

SAO MAI HOTEL

QUOC TU GIAM HOTEL

QUOC TU GIAM RESTAURANT

ROAD BLOCK

secret techniques applied to the body of Lenin. In his last years, Ho was quite frail, suffering from tuberculosis and recurrent malaria. As Ho lay dying, the chief Soviet embalmer, Dr. Sergei Debov, flew to Hanoi with two transport planes of air-conditioners and other equipment. Using special chemicals, the embalming team required a full year to complete their work, and the body is apparently sent back to Moscow for regular checkups. Dr. Debov is also responsible for pickling other communist luminaries: He is the director of the Scientific and Research Center for Biological Structures in Moscow, which cares for the body of Vladimir Lenin. Because of a falling out with the Russians, Mao Zedong was embalmed without Soviet help. The Chinese had to lean on the Vietnamese for information on the secret embalming process.

Ho Chi Minh's mausoleum is closely modeled on Lenin's in Moscow's Red Square. Lenin's mausoleum, built in 1930, was based on a cubist design—the cube was envisaged, like a pyramid, as a symbol of eternity. Mao Zedong occupies a similar squarish structure in Tiananmen Square, Beijing.

All this is quite odd when you consider communism emphasizes cremation as a way of conserving land, and none of the three leaders wanted to be on public display. Lenin asked to be buried next to his mother, and Ho Chi Minh and Mao Zedong both requested cremation.

Ba Dinh Square is sometimes used for large parades; to the north and south of the mausoleum are review stands. The mausoleum is guarded by an elite military regiment. At the front of the building, on the hour every hour there is a ceremonial changing of the guard, with a pair of goose-stepping Vietnamese soldiers relieving their cohorts. The white-gloved goose-stepping sentinels are modeled on those at Lenin's mausoleum in Red Square, where the ritual was suspended by Boris Yeltsin in 1993.

Ho's air-conditioned mausoleum consists of granite and marble quarried from the Marble Mountains near Danang. It was built 1973–1975. Inside, Ho's glass sarcophagus is guarded by four unblinking soldiers, one at each corner of the bier. Your escort propels you through the chilly vault, making sure you don't pause, talk, sneeze, or put your hands in your pockets. No time to dawdle here—just a few seconds to take in marble-faced Ho, with eerie lighting on his head and hands.

House on Stilts

After you exit the mausoleum, a guide will take you through to Ho Chi Minh's House on Stilts. If you want to come back at another time, you can visit the area from a gate just south of the large wrought-iron gates of the Presidential Palace. You may have to wait till a small group assembles before being allowed in, but there don't appear to be any restrictions on taking photos here. The house is open 0730–1100 and 1330–1630. Constructed in 1958, it was modeled on the house Ho lived in while fighting the French from a hideout near the Chinese border. The house sits next to a pond stocked with carp; Ho was fond of jogging in a leafy area nearby lined with mango trees.

The wooden house has been preserved as it was during Ho Chi Minh's working life. The house is raised on wooden pillars, with the lower section open. Upstairs are two rooms—a bedroom and a winter workroom with desk, telephone, and books. The portable typewriter here is said to be the one Ho used to type his Declaration of Independence. Ho used the open downstairs section for working in summer and for holding meetings. There are 10 chairs here for the 10 members of the politburo, and three telephones. A sobering thought—Ho Chi Minh ran the whole Vietnam War from here. Nearby is a concrete bunker under a hill, a bomb shelter 10 meters deep with room for 10 people. A hanging 105mm shell acted as a gong for an air-raid alarm. Behind the bomb shelter is the hut where Ho died in 1969.

If you entered the House on Stilts area from the mausoleum, you may be escorted back to the One Pillar Pagoda after a stop at a gift shop. You can then visit Ho Chi Minh Museum.

Presidential Palace

When the north achieved independence in 1954, Ho Chi Minh declined to move into the Presidential Palace, saying the building belonged to the people. Formerly the palace of the governor-general of Indochina, it was built between 1900 and 1908 in Edwardian style. The gardens surrounding the mansion once contained botanical specimens from around the world. There are frangipani, banyan, mango, and other trees in this area, and at the back of the palace is a French trellis draped with bougainvillea. Now air-conditioned, the palace is used for official functions and as a party guesthouse. The building itself and a large zone around it are off limits—the area is a working compound for high officials. Other mustard-colored colonial buildings in the area include the former servants' quarters and an electrical power station used during the time of the governor-general. Between 1954 and 1958, Ho Chi Minh lived in the gardener's quarters. One of the buildings is now a souvenir shop. A new white building near the palace was constructed in 1993 to house VIP guests.

Ho Chi Minh Museum

In contrast to the often dowdy exhibits in Ho Chi Minh museums in other parts of the country, the museum in Hanoi offers lavish and striking displays on the life and times of Uncle Ho. Most are captioned in Vietnamese and English. If you need further explanation, consult gung-Ho patriotic guides available (for a donation) at the ground-level reception area.

The museum is open 0800–1100 and 1330–1600 daily except Monday. Foreigners enter from the east side; Vietnamese enter from the north. No photography is allowed within the museum, and bags must be deposited on entry. Museum exhibits are on the top floor. The ground and first floors contain cloakrooms, meeting rooms, an auditorium, library and research facility, bookstore, several gift shops, and a small café.

The museum opened in 1990 to commemorate the centenary of Ho's birth. The concrete building was designed by a Soviet architect and has fluted sides to resemble a lotus, the Buddhist symbol of purity. In the front foyer is a larger-than-life-sized statue of Ho Chi Minh backed by another Buddhist sacred symbol, the banyan tree. Upstairs in the main display area, the lotus-petal motif is echoed in the design of several exhibits. Still, the museum manages to veer away from the propagandist tone that haunts others of its kind around Vietnam. The thought-provoking displays make you wonder what motivated Ho Chi Minh and other Vietnamese revolutionaries to take on what seemed at the time a hopeless cause.

The top-floor museum exhibits are arranged chronologically, from Ho's birth in 1890 to his death in 1969, with a small section on the victorious 1975 reunification of north and south. The arrangement can be quite confusing. There are several layers to the display: the personal life of Ho Chi Minh (photos, personal possessions); document display stands with newspaper clippings, letters, and so on, often in French or Russian; and displays depicting events in Vietnam and other parts of the world at specific dates. This all comes with a kind of revolutionary packaging of offbeat sculptural enhancement in metal, stone, and wood—no expense has been spared here.

As you proceed clockwise, exhibits are arrayed around four corner displays based on key events in Ho's life.

North Corner/1890: Birth of Ho Chi Minh. The display shows a model of Chua village, near Vinh, where Ho was born. Side exhibits portray world events and artistic and revolutionary movements 1890–1920, with pictures of Chaplin, Picasso, Toulouse-Lautrec, Rousseau, and Einstein. The impact of Marx and Lenin, and the October Revolution of 1917, are also depicted.

East Corner/1930: Founding of the Communist Party of Indochina by Ho Chi Minh in Hong Kong. Ho fled Hong Kong in 1933 with the help of a British lawyer—one section displays the Chinese gown and slippers that Ho used to disguise himself. A section devoted to world events 1930–1945 concerns the struggle against fascism, with paintings including Picasso's *Guernica* and works by Dali, Max Ernst, Matisse, Miro, and Chagall. Another side section here highlights the struggle between socialism and capitalism—between the United States (symbolized by a plaster cast of a Ford with Ohio plates coming out of a wall and a portrait of Dizzy Gillespie) and the USSR (with a picture of the Kremlin). Another wall shows pictures from the Nuremberg Trials.

South Corner/1945: Declaration of Independence by Ho Chi Minh and beginning of resistance to the French. The Vietnamese declaration was modeled on both the French and the American declarations. Side panels feature the world revolutionary movement in Africa, South America, and Asia in the 1950s. A video salon shows the struggle for independence and social progress in Vietnam.

West Corner/1969: Death of Ho Chi Minh, with his alarm clock stopped at 9:47 A.M., September 2. His rubber sandals, khaki suit, and pith helmet are displayed. Here are pictures of the funeral with gifts received at the time from provincial groups in Vietnam, and from Russia, China, Cuba, Chile, Mongolia, Laos, India, and other countries. The display is laid out in the shape of sacred lotus petals. Around it is a small section on the Ho Chi Minh Trail and the American War, with military hardware and part of a U.S. plane downed while attacking Hanoi. This section also contains a cigarette case, comb, and thermos made from recycled aluminum U.S. plane parts, and a watch donated by the U.S. Communist Party. The exhibit concludes with the 1975 reunification of Vietnam, the dream that Ho did not live to see realized. The last document case here emphasizes reestablishing diplomatic relations as a unified Vietnam—receiving foreign heads of state and the like.

After visiting the museum, check out the tacky Ho Chi Minh souvenir trinkets at the gift shops. Patrons can buy busts of Ho or framed pictures for the home altar, copies of Ho's poetry, Uncle Ho postcards, stamps, posters, Ho hats and badges, but no Uncle Ho T-shirts. Ho souvenirs are also sold by sidewalk vendors in front of the museum.

One Pillar Pagoda

The tiny One Pillar Pagoda (Chua Mot Cot)

was constructed in the 11th century after a vision by Emperor Ly Thai Tong. In a dream the emperor saw Bodhisattva Quan Am on a lotus, handing him a young boy. After seeking advice from court counselors, the emperor built a lotus-shaped temple at the center of a lily pond, and shortly after, his empress presented him a son. In Buddhism, the lotus represents purity and regeneration—the lotus is an object of great beauty arising from a muddy swamp. Made of wood, the frail pagoda had to be rebuilt several times; it was burned by the French before their 1954 withdrawal from Vietnam. In 1955 a replica was built using a concrete pillar instead of a wooden one. No monks are attached to the pagoda, so technically it's a shrine. The pagoda is highly revered, and childless couples make offerings to a statue of Quan Am on an interior altar. This place is also said to possess miraculous healing powers. A few meters from the One Pillar Pagoda is the entrance to small Dien Huu Pagoda, maintained by a monk who is an acupuncture expert. In the afternoon you'll see a queue of people waiting for free acupuncture treatment, said to cure many disorders.

MUSEUMS AND TEMPLES
Army Museum

The Army Museum, at 28 Dien Bien Phu St., is open Tuesday–Saturday 0800–1130 and 1330–1600, Sunday 0800–1500, closed Mondays. Those are generally the hours that all museums around Hanoi are open: forget Mondays. The Army Museum presents a Vietnamese point of view on the 1965–1975 war. You get an idea of what it must have been like living in Hanoi with B-52s flying overhead. In the central courtyard lies a mountain of metal, the twisted wreckage of a B-52 fuselage and part of an F-111.

The curators have run into some problems: In 1994, with the lifting of the U.S. trade embargo, the anti-American section was altered. A gallery of photos of captured pilots was removed, and a MiG-21, once positioned triumphantly over the wreckage of the B-52, was moved to the front courtyard. This MiG-21 shot down 14 aircraft

THE BOULEVARD BICYCLE TOUR

The Ba Dinh District, with its wide boulevards, leafy parks, and light traffic, is perfect for cycling. Before setting out on this tour, you might like to drop in and see Uncle Ho at the mausoleum in the morning, but perhaps come back another time for the Ho Chi Minh Museum, which is a real time-chewer. There are roadblocks around the mausoleum in the morning, but these disappear around 1100 or 1130, after which you can cycle past the front of the mausoleum. Only bicycles are allowed outside the mausoleum along Hung Vuong Boulevard—no cyclos or motorcycles.

Start the tour on the west side of Ho Chi Minh Museum, near the bicycle parking area. Ride north on Ngoc Ha Street toward **Bach Thao Park,** which used to be a botanical garden under the French and is now parkland. You can cycle through the park and exit at the north side.

A historical detour here if you're into it: you'll notice a location "B-52 Lake" south of the park. This is simply a lake where bits of a B-52 bomber landed, right in a residential zone. The B-52 was one of 23 shot down during the infamous Christmas Bombing of 1972—ordered by Nixon—which caused an estimated 1,300 deaths in Hanoi. The B-52 bits, poking out of a small lake, have been left *in situ* as a memorial to those who died, along with a plaque. To find this place, cycle along Phan Dinh Phung till you see a sign that reads May Bay B-52, and turn down an alley—the lake is about 100 meters in.

Back on track, at the north side of Bach Thao Park, carry on to **Quan Thanh Temple.** Inside this Taoist temple is a black bronze statue of General Tran Vo and a large bronze bell, both from the 17th century. The temple is known for its private school of *gong fu,* originating from a monastery in China. In the late afternoon, students dressed in black practice in the courtyard. There's an art gallery on the temple grounds.

Silk Lake and Shrimpcake

North of the temple a causeway cuts between two lakes. To your left is Ho Tay. To your right is **Ho Truc Bach,** or White Silk Lake. In the 18th century, a palace stood at this lakeside; concubines disloyal to the emperor were imprisoned here and forced to weave fine white silk.

A very different kind of prisoner landed here on October 26, 1967—U.S. Air Force Major John Sidney McCain. McCain's A-4 Skyhawk was shot down by antiaircraft gunners: There were gun emplacements around neighboring West Lake. McCain bailed out and parachuted into Truc Bach Lake—which probably saved his life as angry Vietnamese could not reach him. McCain survived his injuries and more than five years of prison life. He was elected to the U.S. Senate from Arizona and has returned to Hanoi on missions related to American MIAs. After the embargo was lifted in 1994, Senator McCain said, "I feel that we are finally putting the war behind us, as we have put every war behind us. A nation must do

in 1967–1968. There are few English captions for the exhibits, which makes you wonder what the Vietnamese references to Presidents Nichxon and Gion-xon are all about.

The front salon covers the period of Vietnam's battles with the Chinese (more than 1,000 years) and the French (for 100 years). The back salon is devoted to the American War. The display is dominated by a T54B tank mounted on a podium—similar to one that smashed down the palace gates at the fall of Saigon in 1975. To one side is a glass case displaying "things belonged to the Ameri-

cans" (captured American fliers' helmets and regiment insignia), while in an opposing case are "things belonged to the Saigon puppet government and army" (lots of medals). An adjacent wall display is devoted to North Vietnam's "things"—with a large display focusing on the Truong Son Trail (Ho Chi Minh Trail), showing medical instruments fashioned from downed U.S. aircraft, hammocks used on the trail, and pack-bicycles used for shuttling impossibly heavy loads of rice and other supplies. Behind the T54 tank and upstairs is a salon with a scratchy film of the

that, and I am grateful to have survived to see it when so many of my friends didn't." But later McCain backtracked and it seemed he could not put the war behind him. During a later visit to Vietnam, he criticized Vietnam's treatment of American POWs.

On a small promontory known as Goldfish Islet stands **Tran Quoc Temple,** one of the oldest temples in Hanoi. Originally reserved for high-ranking court monks, this temple contains some unique statuary. The temple was removed to this location in the 17th century after Red River floodwaters started to eat away its foundations.

The causeway between the two lakes is host to a number of restaurants. Good fare can be found at **Banh Tom Restaurant**—you can sit inside a circular building or outside under rooftop umbrellas and the branches of a huge tree. The specialty here is West Lake shrimpcake—crunchy unshelled shrimps cooked in batter (not always appealing to the Western palate). You can also order soup, fish, eel, snail, or rabbit. The snails come from West Lake. In this area you can hire a sculling boat; for longer forays across West Lake, try a speedboat or dragon boat. If you're feeling energetic, you could make a detour of a few hours out to Tay Ho Pagoda. In Truc Bach Lake you can hire pedal boats to cruise around. For an interesting lakeside perspective over Tay Ho, try to find **Co Ngu Teahouse,** at 8 Duong Thanh Nien—this funky place serves 27 different kinds of tea in a romantic atmosphere.

Ten-Ton Buddha

Chances of getting lost along the next stretch are quite good, but persevere and keep asking for directions—you'll get there. If you loop around the back of Truc Bach Lake, and turn west on Nu Xa Street, you'll come to **Ngu Xa Temple,** which holds the largest bronze Buddha statue in Vietnam—10 tons of it. The 3.5-meter-high Buddha is cast in a meditation pose. Ngu Xa is a bronze-working neighborhood where locals craft small Buddhas and other bronze objects.

Find your way out of the Nu Xa District and head down Pho Chau Long; cycling southward, turn down Nguyen Du Street, through an exclusive area of finely restored French villas, and past classic French-built Cua Bac Church. Turn right on Hoang Van Thu Street and head toward the Presidential Palace. At the palace gates, turn south on Hung Vuong Boulevard and you'll have the entire roadway to yourself—only bicycles are allowed south of the Presidential Palace. When visiting hours for the mausoleum are over—usually by 1130—roadblocks in this area come down and you can cycle past the front of the mausoleum. If you pass in front precisely on the hour, you can witness a Soviet-style goose-stepping changing of the guard. From this point, if you want to keep touring, you can visit Ho Chi Minh Museum and the One Pillar Pagoda, or head off through Eastern-bloc embassy-land to the Army Museum. The Temple of Literature and the Fine Arts Museum are also within easy reach.

heroic exploits of the North Vietnamese. Another salon displays some horrific pictures of damage wrought by U.S. bombing in southern Hanoi. Also on view are stacks of identity cards of fallen Vietnamese soldiers.

The Army Museum is positioned in what was once the area of Hanoi Citadel, still used today by the military. The citadel was largely destroyed by the French in 1882. All that remains today are rampart ruins on the east side and the Flag Tower (Cot Co) in the grounds of the Army Museum. The hexagonal Flag Tower was built in 1812 and is a symbol of Hanoi, featured on

maps and other items. In its day the tower was used for signaling outlying stations with lights. You can scramble to the top of the 60-meter-high turret for a fine view of the area.

Opposite the Army Museum is a park with the biggest *lien xo* in Vietnam—Vladimir Lenin. Although Lenin statues have toppled in Russia and many Eastern European countries, a few remain in far-flung places such as Mongolia and Vietnam. As elsewhere in the communist world, Hanoians joke about this particular pose of Lenin. They point out that Lenin has one hand over his coat pocket—a dig at the cheapskate reputation of Russians in Vietnam.

Special note: For those interested in aerial warfare, the **Air Force Museum,** on Truong Chinh Street, showcases a variety of Russian planes, helicopters, and antiaircraft guns. During the war Truong Chinh Street was known as Chien Thang B-52. The museum is on the southern outskirts of Hanoi.

Hoa Lo Prison Museum

This museum runs the length of a small street named after it: The former prison wall runs north-south between Ly Thuong Kiet and Hai Ba Trung Streets just west of December 19 Market. An easier landmark to navigate by is Hanoi Towers. Hoa Lo Prison once occupied the entire triangular block that today encompasses the three imposing Hanoi towers: Demolition has given way to swank Pierre Cardin and Shiseido boutiques on the ground floor of the main tower.

The prison—what's left of it—was called Maison Centrale under the French, and Hoa Lo by the Vietnamese. Hoa Lo roughly translates as "inferno" or "hot burner." Something like "burn in hell" might be the closest rendition. Though small, the prison makes a powerful statement about the fate of the Vietnamese under the French—which is why it has been preserved. There are two guillotines on display—one in an internal room, the other in the back courtyard. They were last used in the 1930s. Models of emaciated Vietnamese shackled in irons in dim cells occupy the north part of the displays. Around the midsection is a small room showing pictures of downed U.S. fliers, including John McCain and Pete Peterson (the first U.S. ambassador to Vietnam, postembargo).

Although the museum harps on the French prison operation 1898–1954, authorities gloss over the fact that it continued operations for another 20 years as a North Vietnamese prison. (See also the sidebar, *Tale of Two Hiltons.*)

Fine Arts Museum

At 38 Cao Ba Quat (address also given as 66 Nguyen Thai Hoc), the Fine Arts Museum is open 0800–1200 and 1300–1600 daily except Monday; entry is $1. It is across the street from the back wall of the Temple of Literature. The Fine Arts Museum is housed in a colonial building that served as the Ministry of Information under the French and contains three floors of sculpture, ceramics, and painting. On the top floor is an ethnology section with minority costumes, some Cham pieces, bronze drums (circa 1000 B.C.), stone lintels, and a fine 16th-century Quan Am statue with a forest of arms. On the second floor are paintings, ceramics, lacquerware, water puppets, folk art items, and an excellent display of 11th- to 18th-century Buddha statues.

The ground floor is devoted to painting. For almost 40 years Vietnamese painting was of the Social-Realism school, or "politically correct" art, featuring revolutionary fighters and happy peasants. Some examples can be found in the Fine Arts Museum, although such works are only a minor part of the collection. In modern Vietnam the style has been abandoned. At the Fine Arts Museum you'll find French-influenced work and modern and abstract themes. A shop sells sculpture and painting. Another wing of the Fine Arts Museum contains a sculpture salon, with antique wooden furniture on display upstairs.

Museum of Ethnology

On Nguyen Van Huyen Street, this museum will take a bit of effort to get to—it's about six kilometers due west of the Old Quarter, in the Cau Giay District. The easiest way to get there is to take a taxi. The museum is open daily 0830–1730 but closed Mondays, tel. 4/8360350. Plan to spend at least several hours—there's a lot to see. Housed in a striking modern edifice are some 10,000 artifacts and 15,000 photos related to Vietnam's 53 minority groups—and one Kinh majority group. The museum is well laid out for a change (design was assisted by liaison with the Musée de l'Homme in Paris), with displays and maps labelled in Vietnamese, French, and English. Displays vary from the making of conical hats to exhibits of weaving and fabric motifs, while dioramas portray village markets.

If you are heading north to minority regions such as Sapa, the museum will provide insights into the fast-disappearing customs and beliefs of the various ethnic groups. Exhibits highlight the intricate weaving and embroidery skills of groups such as the Lolo and the Hmong. Likewise, if you are headed for the Central Highlands, the museum has sections showcasing the basket-weaving skills of groups such as the Sedang.

Some innovative ideas come into play at the museum: Bringing things to life are sound recordings and videos of shamanist rites, for instance. Craft demonstrations by artisans and performances of traditional arts are sometimes organised at the museum. What the museum fails to tell you is about problems involving ethnic groups: Certain tribal groups have proved troublesome for the Vietnamese to subdue, particularly in the Central Highlands.

The museum occupies a vast area of land: Out back is an ambitious project to reconstruct a number of tribal houses, built by artisans from the original ethnic villages. You can see a huge Bahnar communal house, an Ede longhouse, a Hmong house, a Cham house, and others. A curious structure out this way is a Giarai tomb surrounded by sexually explicit fertility figures, apparently intended to accompany the dead into the afterlife.

Other Museums

In the vicinity of the Opera House is a glut of museums. The museums are usually open Tuesday–Sunday 0800–1130 and 1330–1600, closed Mondays. The **Revolutionary Museum** at 25 Tong Dan Street tells the story of Vietnam's 1,150-year struggle against the Chinese, French, Japanese, and Americans through gruesome displays of executions and torture devices. If you've seen the Ho Chi Minh Museum and the Army Museum, visiting this museum is overkill. The **History Museum,** down the street at 1 Pham Ngu Lao, covers Vietnam's Neolithic history, the arrival of Buddhism, and the unwelcome advent of the Chinese. The emphasis is on archaeology, with items culled from temples, citadels, and other sites throughout Vietnam, as well as other parts of Asia. The museum exhibits are difficult to decipher without a translator. The **Women's Museum,** at 36 Ly Thuong Kiet, gives a nod to female soldiers and their deeds, but it also offers a great deal of information on the costumes of Vietnam's far-flung minorities (the women being much more flamboyant in their dress than the men). There are four floors of exhibits, with ethnic material on the top floor.

Temple of Literature

Van Mieu, or the Temple of Literature, is Hanoi's best-preserved ancient site. The temple is long and narrow, and faces south, so you must go all the way to the southern entrance on Quoc Tu Giam Street. It's open daily from dawn to dusk.

Van Mieu is Vietnam's oldest institution of higher education, dating from the 11th century. A 10-year renovation project was completed in 2002: What you see at Van Mieu may be a fair bit of modern brick and concrete, but it is faithful to original designs. Dedicated to Confucius, the temple served as a national university for more than 700 years, educating mandarins (high court officials). Confucianism managed to break the Buddhist monopoly on education at the time. Students at Van Mieu used an ideographic writing called *cho nho* based on Chinese characters. In 1802 Emperor Gia Long transferred the seat of learning to Hué. The system of recruiting civil servants ended in the north in 1915, and in Hué in 1919.

The Temple of Literature is divided into five walled courtyards with adjoining doors and porticos. Entering at Van Mieu Gate in the south, the path leads through gardens to garden courtyards where wooden hostels for teachers and students once stood. From here, an ornate tower gate leads to a large central pool: To the east and west of this pool is a collection of 82 stone stele supported on massive tortoise pedestals. From the 15th to late 18th centuries, in the Le dynasty, triennial exams were held here—successful candidates had their names, birthdates, and deeds engraved on stone stele. Van Mieu thus became a kind of shrine to honor scholars.

Continuing north you cross a paved courtyard and come to the House of Ceremonies, the main temple where sacrifices were offered to Confucius on the second and 10th lunar months. Two dragons adorn the rooftop, with a lunar disc between them. The temple is built on wooden pillars and is lacquered in bright red, with Chinese and Vietnamese motifs and features. Around the interior altar are incense burners mounted on cranes—symbols of longevity—and tortoises, as well as bonsai plants in Chinese pots and gnarled frangipani trees. The temple is still used by the University of Hanoi for Vietnamese literature lectures. Otherwise, on a less intellectual note, building interiors cater to tourism, with vendors selling water puppets, artwork, books, postcards and other items. This section underwent major renovations in the 1920s, 1950s, and 1990s.

The northern part of the temple was destroyed by bombing in the late 1940s, but by 2002 it had been fully reconstructed, which is quite a feat, considering how much wood, brick, and tiling is involved in the structures. The northernmost structure is the most impressive: a double-story edifice with interior huge wooden columns and ornate lanterns. To either side of the structure are two towers sheltering large bronze bells. The area was originally the National Academy—an important seat of learning.

At Tet, Van Mieu is the site of traditional celebrations, including "live" games of Chinese chess. In a practice that dates to the 15th century, young people dressed in red or yellow outfits hold sticks indicating the piece they represent and are moved on instructions of the players. The games take place in an open courtyard at Van Mieu.

Quan Su Pagoda

Important as a Buddhist educational institution is Quan Su (Ambassador) Pagoda, at 73 Quan Su Street. The temple was founded in the 17th century as a haven for visiting Buddhist scholars from as far afield as Cambodia and Laos. The present pagoda was constructed 1936–1942 and is a major center for Buddhist instruction in Vietnam. Monks come from all over Vietnam

to study here. Quan Su is headquarters of the North Vietnam Buddhist Association.

West Lake and Tay Ho Pagoda

Named after a lake in Hangzhou, China, of similar shape, West Lake covers an area of five square kilometers and has a circumference of about 12 kilometers. The lake was once the site of palaces for emperors and lords, but all were destroyed during feudal wars. Today top party officials maintain luxurious villas on the quiet shores, and nouveau riche Vietnamese are moving in, too. Greedy joint-venture developers envisage an area bristling with hotels. Commercial uses of the lake vary from fishing to flower growing. Fish-breeding cages are laid in the lake, yielding up to 600 tons of fish in a good season. Egrets, cranes, and wading birds visit as well. On the east side of the lake are large flower villages where roses and peach trees are grown.

For visitors, West Lake is associated with quiet recreation. You can bicycle around the shores of the lake or take a cruise. A good place to aim for is Tay Ho Pagoda, which can also be reached by bike, or by boat from the southwest side of the lake.

Boat Rentals: For a relaxing paddle in a small area designated by red flags, you can rent a sculling boat, pedalboat, or rowboat for under $1.50 an hour. To go farther afield, you can rent a speedboat for $6–10 an hour—it takes about 15 minutes one-way from here to Tay Ho Pagoda. Mock-imperial dragon boats cost $20 an hour for up to 15 passengers, or $40 an hour for 16–40 passengers. For reservations, contact Olympic Café, tel. 4/8257105. There's an extra charge for onboard food service or if you want to dress like a mandarin (for some reason, French tourists love to dress as mandarins and sit on dragon boats).

Tay Ho Pagoda is considered a popular lucky site of the wish-fulfilling variety. There is a large wall mosaic here—the lower section depicts the realm of the sea, the middle band shows the earth, and the top band depicts the sky. Offerings placed at the various shrines include candied lotus seed, sticky rice in red conical packets, eggs, miniature bottles of apricot brandy or vodka, cake, fruit, and roses. Muttering, sometimes crying, supplicants burn paper money at lakeside urns. On the alley leading to the pagoda are eateries that serve aquatic snails from the lake, eaten with noodles and garnish. They also sell shrimpcakes—small shrimp fried in batter and sometimes mixed with sweet potato.

Accommodations

Hanoi offers a wide range of luxury hotels, business hotels, boutique hotels, minihotels, and guesthouses for foreign guests. The better hotels may be full, and some hotels in the moderate range seem to be permanently occupied by businesses. If you don't reserve ahead, try to time your arrival for midday checkout to increase your chances of securing a good room. It's best to find a place to drop your luggage, then head off to search for a hotel. Peak tourist season (June–August) is especially difficult: You're also competing with vacationing Vietnamese at this time.

Privately run minihotels offer much better service than government-run places. Minihotels are going up as Hanoi residents discover they can profit by converting an old building or part of their home into lodgings. Prices range $20–80 a room, depending on whether the place has air-conditioning, a minibar, and satellite TV. In the Old Quarter, narrow three- and four-story buildings sometimes have only two rooms to each floor—one at the front, one at the back. As part of a growing awareness of the city's architectural heritage, police have been instructed to ensure that housing development in this area is architecturally appropriate. This means new accommodations are supplied by renovating existing structures—which favors the rise of more minis.

Some important considerations for staying in Hanoi: quietness, hot water in winter, a/c in summer, secure luggage storage if going out of town, and advance reservation if returning from a trip out of town. Luxury hotels charge a 10 percent government tax and 5–10 percent for service; be wary of a 6 percent surcharge for use of a credit card. Room prices may include breakfast.

The largest hotel operator in Hanoi is Hanoi

Tourism, which owns seven hotels, including the Bong Sen and Hoa Binh, and has a share in the Sofitel Metropole.

OLD QUARTER

In this zone, north of Hoan Kiem Lake, minihotels and guesthouses have lots of character. These are two- or three-story structures; some may be five stories high. Smaller places can be like living in someone's house, with the gates locked between 2300 and 0500. Guesthouse owners sometimes run small restaurants and rent bicycles.

Under $20

Traveler cafés offer some rudimentary accommodations with shared bath facilities. **Real Darling Café,** at 33 Hang Quat, tel. 4/8269386, offers 10 rooms at around $10 each. Nearby **Lucky Tourist Café,** at 6 To Tich, has a few rooms with bath for $8–12.

Ta Hien Guesthouse, at 22 Ta Hien St., tel. 4/8255888, has 11 rooms for $10 (fan), $12 (phone), and $15 (a/c). At 24C Ta Hien St. is **Thuy Nga Hotel,** tel. 4/8266053, with six rooms for $12–18. **A Dong Hotel,** 46 Luong Ngoc Quyen, tel. 4/8256948, has nine rooms for $12–20 and its own small restaurant—clean and comfortable. This place operates its own travel agent. Opposite is **Nha Khach 55,** at 55 Luong Ngoc Quyen, tel. 4/8268539—half a dozen soulless and windowless rooms for $10–12. **My Kinh Hotel,** 72 Hang Buom, tel. 4/8255726, has 22 rooms for $10–30. At 10B Dinh Liet St. is **Nam Long Hotel,** tel. 4/8266054, with rooms for $6–12. So you won't forget the address, one guesthouse includes it in the name: **Guesthouse 73 Ma May Street,** tel. 4/8244425, has nine rooms for $10 each and operates a tour office on the ground floor. **Phuc Loc Hotel,** 23 Ma May St., tel. 4/8280396, offers eight rooms for $10–15. **Nam Phuong Hotel,** 64 Cau Go St., tel. 4/8258735, offers five rooms for $10–20. **North Hotel I,** at 15 Hang Ga St., tel. 4/8267242, has doubles $10–12 with hot shower. This guesthouse is recommended by two travelers who found the family here extremely helpful with laundry, sorting luggage, and so on. There is also a North Hotel II guesthouse.

At 7 Dong Thai St. is **Phong Lan Hotel,** tel. 4/8281645, a place run by a caring family with rooms $10–12. At the edge of the Old Quarter is **Dong Do Guesthouse,** 27 Tong Duy Tan St., tel. 4/8233275, with rooms for $15–50.

Phan Thai Hotel, 44 Hang Giay St.,.tel. 4/8243667, offers doubles at around $20 including breakfast. The hotel has large rooms with a/c and big bathrooms—good value, and well situated.

Especen, a private organization with French, Australian, and American partners, runs a number of minihotels—some around the lake, some tucked into the Old Quarter. The minis range from five to 16 rooms; prices range $10–15 with shared bathroom, and $20–40 with a/c and bath included, and are a good value. The front doors are closed around 2300—you have to ring the front bell after that. Especen's main office is at 22 Hang Be; attached to this is the Especen travel bureau and café.

$20–50

Phung Hung, 2 Duong Thanh St., tel. 4/8265556, is a minihotel run by the official Hanoi Tourism Service Company (TOSERCO) with rooms for $20–30. **Gold Turtle** (Kim Quy), 38 Hang Hom St., tel. 4/8243944, fax 4/8260082, has five rooms for $30 each. **Ngoc Minh Hotel,** 47 Luong Ngoc Quyen St., tel. 4/8268459, fax 4/8283184, is a clean family-run place with seven rooms going for $25–30 including breakfast. **Prince Hotel,** 51 Luong Ngoc Quyen, tel. 4/8280155, fax 4/8280156, offers 12 rooms for $20–25. **Vinh Quang,** 24 Hang Quat St., tel. 4/8266848, fax 4/8225420, has 11 rooms for $20–30. **Venus Hotel,** 10 Hang Can St., tel. 4/8261212, offers 11 rooms for $18–20.

Bat Dan minihotel, 10 Bat Dan St., tel. 4/8284528, fax 4/8267424, is a great hotel with a café and late-night bar on the ground floor emphasizing board games. Prices range $25 and up per room here. **Trang Anh Hotel,** 58 Hang Gai, tel. 4/8261135, fax 4/8258511, is a narrow five-story structure with 10 rooms with a/c and TV in the $45–75 range. On the edge of the Old Quarter near Hoan Kiem Lake is **Ho Guom Hotel,** at 76 Hang Trong St., tel. 4/8252225, fax 4/8243564, with 37 rooms for $30–50–80; this hotel is set back from the road and thus quieter. **Hang Trong Hotel,** 56 Hang Trong, tel. 4/8251346, fax 4/8285577, has seven rooms for $15–25; the better rooms are upstairs at the back. **Quoc Hoa Minihotel,** 10 Bat Dan, tel. 4/8284528, fax 4/8267424, claims to be the first privately owned hotel in Hanoi, operating since 1991. This 28-room hotel certainly leads the way with innovations in the Old Quarter—it has a business center, rooftop café, games room, and restaurant. Not bad for a minihotel. Prices range $30–60 for rooms, $70–120 for superior rooms and suites. **Kim Thanh Hotel,** 30 Hang Manh St., tel. 4/8259682, fax 4/8286933, has 15 rooms for $40–80 and a suite for $110.

HOAN KIEM DISTRICT
Under $20

Lotus GH, 42V Ly Thuong Kiet, has a few rooms for $6–12. A dorm setup costs $4 a bed. The small guesthouse is run by a doctor and his family. The entire block here is numbered 42—with 42A, 42B, 42C, and so on—which means 42V is toward the west end. **Trang Tien Hotel,** 35 Trang Tien, tel. 4/8256341, fax 4/8251416, offers 11 rooms for $8–10 with outside bath, and 22 rooms for $20–40 with bath and a/c, and 13 rooms for $40–60. Staff tend to be surly here, and so do the rats. **Bodega I,** 57 Trang Tien, tel. 4/8267784, fax 4/8267787, rents 15 rooms for $15–25. On the ground floor is a café; the next floor is a restaurant; the top floor is the hotel. Three blocks along 41 Hang Bai St. is **Bodega II,** with six rooms for $15–20.

Sophia GH, 6 Hang Bai St., tel. 4/8253069, has dilapidated rooms for $20—you might be able to reduce the price by bargaining.

Green Bamboo GH, 42 Nha Chung St., tel. 4/8268752, fax 4/8264949, offers nine rooms for $15–18, including bath. **Guesthouse 8,** at 8 Nha Chung, tel. 4/8268500, has rooms for $8 and up. **Guest House Culture** (Nha Khach Van Hoa), 22A Hai Ba Trung, tel. 4/8253044, features doubles for $10–15 and triples as low as $10. The guesthouse is one block south of Hoan Kiem Lake, set off the street through a passageway; bicycle rentals available. West of Hoan Kiem is **Especen 1,** at 76 Hang Trong, tel. 4/8266856, with rooms for $20–30.

$20–50

The following hotels lie to the west of the lake. **Phu Gia,** 136 Hang Trong St., tel. 4/8255493, fax 4/8259207, has 50 rooms for $20–42 in an older-style four-story hotel. Decor is a bit weird here; the front rooms include views over Hoan Kiem Lake. **Nam Phuong,** 16 Bao Khanh St., Hoan Kiem, tel. 4/8258030, fax 4/8258964, is a cheap and clean minihotel one block from Hoan Kiem Lake. Rooms are $20–35 d with a/c and hot water. **Thien Trang,** 24 Nha Chung St., tel. 4/8269823, is a reasonably priced minihotel; bicycle rentals available. To the south side of the lake lies **Bac Nam Hotel,** 20 Ngo Quyen, tel. 4/8267877, fax 4/8268998. This is a private hotel with 19 rooms for $25–40–50 and two suites for $70.

To the east side of Hoan Kiem are the following hotels. **Binh Minh Hotel,** 27 Le Thai To, tel. 4/8266441, fax 4/8266442, has good rooms for $30–40. **Energy Hotel** (Nan Luong), 30 Le Thai To, tel. 4/8253167, fax 4/8259226, is run by the Ministry of Energy. Rooms cost $30–55.

$50–100

The six-story **Huyen Trang Hotel,** 36 Hang Trong St., tel. 4/8247512, fax 4/8247449, has 20 rooms for $50–80 apiece, with satellite TV. **Dan Chu** (Souvenir Hotel), 29 Trang Tien, tel. 4/8254937, fax 4/8266786, is a renovated French hotel with 41 rooms for $65–

105 (standard to deluxe), $130 suite. The Dan Chu also operates a nearby villa-hotel called **Dan Chu Villa** at 2 Pham Su Manh St., tel. 4/8251865, with 12 rooms for $105–120. **Camellia Hotel,** 12 Hue St., tel. 4/8225140, fax 4/8225949, offers 33 a/c rooms for $70–100 and suites for $150. At 78 Tho Nhuom St. is **Eden Hotel,** tel. 4/8245273, fax 4/8245619, a well-managed minihotel with 30 rooms for $50–90 and suites for $115.

Facing Thien Quang Lake is the **Boss Hotel** at 60 Nguyen Du St., tel. 4/8265859, fax 4/8257634. This business hotel consists of 25 rooms but usually only half are available; rates $60–70 d. Businesses such as SOS International and Pacific Airlines operate from here; the place is run by Oscan Enterprises, a tour operator. The hotel is small, modern, and includes business center and VIP lounge. To the east of Thien Quang Lake is **Madison Hotel,** 16 Bui Thi Xuan, tel. 4/8228164, fax 4/8225533. This nine-story boutique hotel has 33 rooms for $64–95 and suites for $125–135. The in-house restaurant, Madison's, has a decent reputation.

Government Guesthouse, 2 Le Thach St., tel. 4/8255801, fax 4/8259227, has 48 rooms for $35–105, featuring French decor in spacious rooms. This building is in the back wing of what was once an office and residence complex of the governor of Tonkin. The front wing, on Ngo Quyen, opposite the Metropole Hotel, is reserved for VIPs and diplomats.

Popular with foreign businesspeople, the following two hotels, run by the Ministry of Defense, have a total of 89 rooms. The **MOD Palace** (Guesthouse of the Ministry of Defense), at 33A Pham Ngu Lao, tel. 4/8265540, fax 4/8265539, has 40 doubles for $63–105, a deluxe suite for $150, and two other suites for $420–450. Facilities include a business center. At the opposite end of the compound is the dreary **Army Hotel,** 33C Pham Ngu Lao, tel. 4/8252896, fax 4/8259276, with 77 rooms for $50–75 and suites for $70–200. Rooms feature a/c, satellite TV, and fridges, and there's a swimming pool. Between the two hotels is a VIP wing—an old colonial mansion reserved for state guests. This was constructed in 1874–

Hanoi

1877 and used to be the villa of the French army's chief of staff.

$100–200

To the southwest corner of the lake is **Zephyr Hotel,** 4 Ba Trieu, tel. 4/9341256, fax 4/9341262, with rooms for $100–160, and highly favorable reports from guests who have stayed there.

Hoa Binh Hotel (Peace), 27 Ly Thuong Kiet, tel. 4/8253315, fax 4/8269818, offers 120 a/c rooms. Although there are some rooms available for $20–40, most rooms at the Hoa Binh fall in the $96–165 category, with suites going for $160–185. This hotel has been in business since 1923 and features real French ambience—lobby with revolving doors, original mirrors and staircases, top-floor bar. On the ground floor is Le Splendide, a top-rated French restaurant. The Hoa Binh underwent major renovation in 1993 and is popular with French group tours. The hotel also operates a 16-room villa. Qi Spa, one of the best in the city, is to one side of the hotel.

De Syloia Hotel 17A Tran Hung Dao, tel. 4/8245346, fax 4/8241083, lies southeast of Hoan Kiem lake. This luxury hotel is small, compact, and superefficient—ideal for the visiting businessperson. There are 27 superior rooms for $135–155; four executive suites for $165–185; a deluxe suite for $195–215; and a VIP apartment for $250. The hotel has its own restaurant, bar, minigym and mini–business center.

Royal Hotel, 20 Hang Tre St., tel. 4/8244230, fax 4/8244234, offers 59 rooms for $145–175 and six suites for $235–365. The hotel lies to the northeast of Hoan Kiem Lake.

Over $200

The **Sofitel Metropole,** 15 Ngo Quyen St., tel. 4/8266919, fax 4/8266920, sofmet@

TALE OF TWO HILTONS

The "Hanoi Hilton," the downtown-Hanoi prison where downed American airmen were interned, interrogated, and tortured during the Vietnam War, had a long and infamous career. Known to the Vietnamese as Hoa Lo, the structure also was a prison under the French, who interned and tortured Vietnamese activists (including many North Vietnamese leaders) there. And, after the Vietnam War until 1994, the building served as a Vietnamese prison.

In the spring of 1973, *New York Times* reporter Malcolm Browne flew into Hanoi from Vientiane to visit the Hanoi Hilton. Foreign press correspondents had been invited in for a day to witness the release of the last group of American POWs. The correspondents strolled through the Hanoi Hilton, but they were not allowed to talk to the stony-faced prisoners, standing at attention in their purple-and-pink–striped prison garb. Browne records that "simply being in the enemy's capital and politely shaking their hands with smiling officials wearing olive-green pith helmets was the strangest experience of all."

At the end of 1994, workers began knocking down the walls of Hoa Lo to make way for a 22-story hotel and office complex, a Singapore joint-venture project called Hanoi Towers. Completed in 1997, the $60 million project encompasses three towers: Somerset Hotel Apartments tower (204 apartments), a minitower that houses a convention center, and a high-rise third tower with office space above and upscale shops at ground level. Building on the site was temporarily delayed because of a campaign to save the historic site: To level the prison would remove all trace of heroic Vietnamese struggle against imperialism. So a compromise was reached: One wing of the prison was saved to serve as an on-site museum to honor the memory of Vietnamese nationalists imprisoned at Hoa Lo.

Meanwhile, postembargo, representatives of the real Hilton Hotel group came to Hanoi to break ground on a megahotel next to the Opera House. They ran into a tricky naming problem—they eventually named it the Hilton Hanoi Opera, reversing the normal order of the moniker.

netnam.org.vn., boasts 244 rooms (109 rooms are in the old wing, and 135 in the new wing), including 22 suites. Rates range $230–270 for rooms, $280–460 for suites; add $30 for double occupancy. Depending on the season, the Metropole can be heavily booked—reservations at least one month in advance are advised. The Metropole is the grande dame of Hanoi hotels. It first opened in 1901. The long list of illustrious guests includes Charlie Chaplin (1936, on honeymoon with actress Paulette Godard, his costar from *Modern Times*), Graham Greene (1951, as a correspondent for *Paris Match*—he modeled a character in *The Quiet American* on a hard-nosed American reporter he met at the Met's bar), and Jane Fonda (who used the rundown Met as her base in 1972, when her controversial pro-Vietnam speech was broadcast on Radio Hanoi, directed against U.S. pilots bombing the north).

The Met underwent extensive renovations in the early 1990s as part of a joint venture with the French group Accor. In the mid-1990s, a 135-room wing in quasi-French style was added. Creature comforts include individually controlled air-conditioning, satellite TV, in-house video, and room safes. The Metropole is a Hanoi meeting point—visitors and travelers come for afternoon tea, to read international newspapers kept at the bar, use the pool, or sample the superb French cuisine. The Met Pub is a popular businessperson's rendezvous spot, especially at happy hour. Attached to the hotel is the International Center Building, devoted to office space, with Citibank and Singapore Airlines on-site.

Providing stiff competition as a business-class hotel is **Hilton Hanoi Opera,** 1 Le Thanh Tong St., tel. 4/9330500, fax 4/9330530, hanhitw@fpt.vn, www.hilton.com. The hotel has 269 rooms on deluxe and executive floors, a number of which offer a view of the Opera House. Rack rates start at $230 and range up to $930 a night for the Presidential Suite. This seven-story colossus was built to blend in with the French-designed Opera House next door. True to form, it has mock-French elements—but along the way, the Hilton has picked up some immense Grecian columns, which are

more suited to a bank or a museum. The hotel can cater for conventions of up to 550 participants. Facilities include health club, small swimming pool, and all the features you'd expect with the high-end price tag. The hotel's 24-hour business center offers secretarial and translation services as well. The Lobby Lounge is a good place for a quiet interlude—far from the madding crowd—and the adjoining Café Opera serves excellent cakes and coffee.

Renowned for its convention facilities is **Melia Hanoi,** 44B Ly Thuong Kiet, tel. 4/9343343, fax 4/9343344, www.meliahanoi.com, with rooms starting at $200. Efficient as it may be, the hotel will not garner any architecture or style awards.

RAILWAY STATION AREA
Under $20
Right near the station is **Mango Hotel** (Khach San Cay Xoai), at 118 Le Duan, tel. 4/8243704, with 24 rooms for $15–25–32. Opposite the station is **30-4 Hotel,** 115 Tran Hung Dao St., tel. 4/8260807, fax 4/8252611; the place has 24 rooms for $6–8 and five rooms for $30 each. **Nat Phuong,** 39 Le Duan, tel. 4/8253765, is a minihotel with five rooms for $15 s or $25–30 d. **Anh Duong GH,** at 33 Le Duan, tel. 4/8265220, is a six-room guesthouse with rooms for $15–20–50. **Hoan Kiem GH,** 76 Hai Ba Trung, tel. 4/8268944, has $20 doubles. Do not confuse this place with the pricier Hoan Kiem Hotel.

$20–50
Quoc Tu Giam Hotel, just west of the railway tracks at 27 Quoc Tu Giam, tel. 4/8257106, fax 4/8257691, has 16 a/c rooms for $30, and two suites for $45 each. Also in this area are **Mai Anh Hotel,** 109A Nguyen Thai Hoc, tel. 4/8232702, with rooms for $20–40; and **Sao Mai Hotel,** 17 Thong Phong Alley, tel. 4/8255827, with doubles for $20 and up. **Capital Hotel** (Thu Do), 109 Tran Hung Dao St., tel. 4/8261266, fax 4/8261121, offers 27 rooms for $40–70. The front desk rents bicycles. **Dong Loi,** at 94 Ly Thuong Kiet St.

on the corner of Le Duan, tel. 4/8255721, fax 4/8267999, has 30 rooms for $50 single or double, and two suites for $72 each. Built in the 1930s and operated by TOSERCO, this place has character—spiral staircase, molded ceilings, and art nouveau light fixtures. **Rose Hotel** (Hoa Hong), 20 Phan Boi Chau, tel. 4/8254438, fax 4/8254437, offers 21 elegant rooms in the $40–60 range.

$50–100

Just east of the railway tracks are several hotels. **Blue II Hotel,** 6 Dinh Ngang, tel. 4/8233541, fax 4/8236393, is a four-story minihotel with eight rooms for $40–80 with a/c, StarTV, fridge, and phone.

$100–200

Saigon Hotel, 80 Ly Thuong Kiet St., tel. 4/8268505, fax 4/8266631, has 44 rooms for $105; suites for $165. The hotel features a business center, rooftop terrace bar, and satellite TV. It's a joint venture between Saigon Tourist and the National Railway Company with a Hanoi Taxi rank out front.

GIANG VO LAKE

$20–50

More than three kilometers from town is a cluster of high-rise hotels around Giang Vo Lake. The cheap hotel of the area, patronized by Vietnamese, is **Giang Vo Hotel,** A1 Giang Vo, tel. 4/8256598, with several hundred rooms in five-story apartment blocks. Rooms range from $10 to $20 and up. **Trade Hotel,** 8 Ngoc Khanh St., tel. 4/8347164, fax 4/8343165, has 60 strangely decorated rooms for $40–75.

$50–100

Dong Do Hotel, Giang Vo Street, tel. 4/8351382, fax 4/8334228, has 24 rooms for $55–75, and a few suites for $120. **Orient** (Phuong Dong), 23 Lang Ha St., tel. 4/8345397, fax 4/8246396, farther out from Giang Vo Lake to the southwest, rents rooms for $50–90. **Hanoi Heritage Hotel,** 80 Giang Vo St., tel. 4/8344727, fax 4/8351458, has 41 rooms. Most

are $90 and up, while suites run $140; add $15 for double occupancy. This is a Singapore joint-venture hotel, favored by foreign businesspeople for its atmosphere. The hotel features a restaurant with Asian cuisine and the Club Bleu nightclub with karaoke booths.

$100–200

Lake Side Hotel, 6A Ngoc Khanh Rd., tel. 4/8350111, fax 4/8350121, has 78 rooms for $160–190 and suites for $210–380. **Hanoi Hotel,** D8 Giang Vo St., tel. 4/8452270, fax 4/8459209, comprises a 10-story wing with 76 rooms and an 18-floor wing with 148 rooms. Rates vary $148–178 standard, and $228–388 for a suite. This Hong Kong joint venture involved the renovation of a 10-year-old building at a cost of $6 million. Hanoi Hotel encompasses a business center, tennis court, nightclub, and a large Chinese restaurant.

Over $200

Hanoi Daewoo Hotel, 360 Kim Ma St., tel. 4/8315000, fax 4/8315010, is a Korean joint venture, one of Hanoi's five-star hotels. It even stages an afternoon tea buffet, just like the Metropole. Two enormous wings of the hotel enclose a landscaped area with palm-fringed pool and driveway. The main wing of the hotel is 18 floors—on the 18th is the art-deco Lakeview Sky Lounge, serving cocktails and panoramic views of Hanoi. The immense Palm Court lobby gives off an air of great opulence, with palm trees and neo-Roman columns. Reception staff dressed in smart *ao dais* must rank as Hanoi's most polite. There are 411 rooms at the Daewoo, including 34 luxurious suites; standard and deluxe rooms run $200–270; suites $320–360; special suites go for $900–1,200. The executive-floor Presidential Suite hits the jackpot at $1,500 a night. The hotel has extensive conference and meeting facilities, with the Grand Ballroom capable of accommodating 500 seated guests. The Daewoo is much more than a hotel—it aims to be the big business center of Hanoi. However, the complete collapse of the Daewoo Corporation in Korea does not set a good business model to emulate. On one side of the grounds is a 15-floor office tower, Daeha Business Center, with company offices and office rentals; at the back is a 15-story building with 193 high-end, fully furnished rental apartments, catering to embassy clientele who have gravitated to this area. The Daeha Business Center runs an 18-hole golf course and country club northwest of Hanoi.

Past Giang Vo Lake to the southwest is Dong Da Lake District. Here is the superluxury **Capital Garden Hotel,** at 48A Lang Ha St., tel. 4/8350373, fax 4/8350363, with 69 rooms for $180–215 and seven suites for $230–250. This European–style hotel is awkwardly sited but close to embassy-land, and there's enough room to swing a golf club out this way (the hotel offers golf workshops).

WEST LAKE, TRUC BACH LAKE

West Lake is an exclusive villa zone about five kilometers north of the city center. You need transport to commute. In the future this zone will see a lot of hotel building; some minihotels are also going up in the area, with much lower prices. Separated by a narrow causeway is Truc Bach Lake, also with prime real estate around its shores.

$20–50

Southeast of Truc Bach Lake and north of the Old Quarter is **Hong Ha Hotel** (Red River Hotel), at 78 Yen Phu, tel. 4/8254911, offering doubles for $20–35, as well as a few lower-priced rooms. **Bong Sen** (Lotus), 34 Hang Bun St., tel. 4/8254017, fax 4/8233232, has 26 rooms with a/c, TV, and fridge for $43–50–60. **Huu Nghi** (Friendship), 23 Quan Thanh, tel. 4/8253182, fax 4/8259272, features 38 a/c rooms for $35–60. **Ho Tay Villas,** tel. 4/8258241, has 68 rooms in the $40–55 range. It was once the Communist Party Guesthouse but is now open to those who can afford the rates.

$50–100

Tay Ho Hotel, Nghi Tam Street, tel. 4/8232380, fax 4/8232390, has 118 a/c rooms and 27 suites, with satellite TV and business center. Rooms cost $55 s, $70 d. **Hang Nga Hotel,** 65 Cua Bac St., tel. 4/8437777, fax 4/8437779, is a 12-story building with 40 rooms decorated in Chinese style; rooms range $75–95, with deluxe rooms costing over $100 each.

$100–200

Planet Hotel, 120 Quan Thanh St., tel. 4/8435888, fax 4/8435088, is a classy place with 53 rooms for $90–180; on the 10th floor is a restaurant serving French and Vietnamese food, with panoramic views. This hotel has business and health centers. **Grand Lake View Hotel,** at 28 Thanh Nien Rd., tel. 4/8292888, fax 4/8292999, is a Thai joint-venture luxury hotel that has 151 rooms, swimming pool, fitness center, and jetty bar. **Thang Loi Hotel,** Yen Phu Street, tel. 4/8268211, fax 4/8252800, has 175 rooms for $80–163. The main wing, built as a gift from Cuba in 1975, is an uninspiring concrete blockhouse; nearby are some traditional bamboo bungalows. The hotel occupies a landscaped site on a peninsula jutting into West Lake, with swimming pool and tennis courts. There's a nightly disco from 2000 to midnight; Sunday is the big night out.

Over $200

Looming over West Lake and Truc Bach Lake is the gigantic **Sofitel Plaza Hanoi,** 1 Thanh Nien St., tel. 4/8238888, fax 4/8298888, www.sofitel.com, which hosts 322 rooms and offers full amenities. The hotel is very popular with Asian guests. Prices range from a basic $190–250 for a superior room, and $300 up to $1,000 for suites. The Summit Lounge on the 20th floor, open from 1630–midnight, presents a terrific bird's-eye view of West Lake and Hanoi. A stunning all-weather swimming pool is near the fourth-floor gym and spa—the heated pool comes with a retractable glass roof.

To the northeast side of West Lake is the megasized **Sheraton Hanoi,** at 11 Xuan Dieu, tel. 4/7199000, fax 4/7199001, www.sheraton.com/hanoi, with rooms in the $200–450 range.

Food

RESTAURANTS

After a hiatus of several decades, the culinary arts have been kick-started in Hanoi, with excellent offerings of Vietnamese, Chinese, and European cuisine. Hanoi certainly has the most pleasant collection of cafés in all Vietnam—great atmosphere, and some in tranquil locations. Certain kinds of food are missing: Vegetarians visiting Hanoi often complain they get the same half dozen dishes over and over again (hence the special write-up, *Vegetarian Restaurants,* in this section). Poke around and you'll find good, cheap, tasty Vietnamese food at food stalls: The specialty of Hanoi is *pho* (chicken or beef soup). Arrive early for dinner, as many Hanoi restaurants get under way at 1800 and close by 2100. A few Western-oriented restaurants stay open to 2200 or 2300. A good test of a restaurant is to see how many cyclos are out front—if there are a lot waiting, it must be good.

An interesting feature of Hanoi restaurants is that they're often family-run and operate from converted two-story dwellings with the family living in the same quarters. This gives a place a real homey feel—true of a place such as Restaurant 22 (naming a restaurant after the street number is a Russian idea—to avoid being bourgeois).

Snakes and snails and puppy dog tails are sometimes featured on specialty restaurant menus—so avoid or seek out as befits your state of mind or palate. Hot dog means something quite different in Hanoi—dog meat is a delicacy, believed to enhance stamina in men. A string of shacks along the lower east side of West Lake specialize in dog, eaten at certain times of the month. Down by the railway tracks near Lenin Park in southern Hanoi, several restaurants feature large cat paintings outside—that's because cat is served inside. In the Old Quarter, at 7 Hang Phen, is Bac Hai, a restaurant solely devoted to the parts of the cow. Aquatic snails from West Lake are eaten particularly at Tay Ho Pagoda, along with West Lake shrimpcakes.

You may also find snakes from the village of Le Mat on offer. About 10 kilometers northeast of Hanoi, a zone contains more than a dozen cobra restaurants. You need to assemble a small group and arrange a Vietnamese speaker to experience an extraordinary multidish menu based entirely on cobras. Like the Chinese, the Vietnamese consider snake to be an aphrodisiac, and snake blood is meant to "strengthen" male impulses (it's not clear what it does for female impulses). Dishes vary from grilled snake, crunchy snake ribs, and snake liver to steamed snake skin. The courses are washed down with a variety of snake "liqueurs"—rice wine mixed with blood or greenish-brown snake bile, or a bottle of wine with the cobra coiled inside, imparting a reptilian aftertaste.

Old Quarter

In this area are lots of small eateries and pubs, intimate places in converted houses. **Cha Ca La Vong,** at 14 Cha Ca, has no menu. You don't need one: The chefs prepare only one dish—*cha ca,* or fried fish. The restaurant has been in the same family for five generations, so they've got that dish perfected. In keeping with the simplicity of the restaurant, the popular second-floor dining room is starkly furnished, with plastic chairs. At the table you'll get a charcoal brazier and a boneless river fish in a fry pan, usually enough for two people. You sprinkle herbs (cilantro), shallots, and peanuts on the fish, add the mix to cold noodles, spice it with chili sauce, and Bob's your uncle. Tasty! Costs about $6 a head. This place can be crowded. There are other restaurants tucked away in the Old Quarter that serve the same dish.

At 3B Cha Ca St. is **Baan Thai Restaurant,** tel. 4/8281120, serving palatable Thai food. Down the street, **Restaurant 22** at 22 Hang Can St. (2nd and 3rd floors), tel. 4/8267160, serves Viet-French food. Quality varies with the chef—from good to mediocre. A good

ESSENCE OF WATERBUG

If you ask for it, your server at **Cha Ca Restaurant**, at 14 Cha Ca St., will bring you a special flavoring. It's a liquid made from the scent gland of an insect known as *ca cuong*—a member of the Heteroptera (or bug) order. The highly prized secretion has a fruity aroma. At Cha Ca, it is dispensed with an eyedropper from a glass vial, and you're charged by the drop. This giant waterbug is found only in the summer in the north, and the gland from one waterbug produces only three or four drops. One hundred waterbugs must be harvested to produce a small vial of the liquid, which explains the 2,000-dong-a-drop price tag.

At number 17 Cha Ca Street is the restaurant **Tuyet Nhung**, which bases its business around waterbug liquid. Sometimes it's mixed with fish sauce or chili sauce—as a dip for fish, chicken, pork, or beef dishes, or as a condiment in bowls of noodles. The small restaurant keeps frozen specimens of the insect in jars and sells vials of the liquid. An artificial facsimile, called Maengdana, is produced in Thailand, but for gourmets there's a big difference between real and artificial—something akin to the difference between fresh and canned fruit.

place for Italian food, at reasonable prices, is **Datano,** at 10 Hang Hanh, tel. 4/8287936, with a real Italian chef at the helm.

A short way from the intersection of Ta Hien and Long Ngoc Quyen are twin branches of **Little Hanoi,** a tiny family-run restaurant with tasty fare and excellent atmosphere. Upper Ta Hien is bristling with cybercafés and tiny pubs. **Bittet Loi** (Loi's Beefsteak), 51 Hang Buom St., tel. 4/8251211, is open daily from 1600. It's a small place, packed at night. Serves beefsteak, prawn, pigeon, and crab. Good service—you can see dishes being prepared in Loi's kitchen. Excellent for steak and fries smothered in a scrumptious garlic sauce.

Vegetarian Restaurants

If all those dead animals don't interest you, or if your digestive system needs a break from red meat, try **Tamarind Restaurant** at 80 Ma May, tel. 4/9260580, in the Old Quarter, with a great selection of fresh fruit juices and tasty smoothies, though on the expensive side. For the Old Quarter, the interior of Tamarind is surprisingly deep—the atmosphere somewhere between Amsterdam and Kathmandu, with back section seating on low cushions. Very pleasant, even if only for drinks.

Tamarind Restaurant is a French-run operation. For Vietnamese vegetarian, you're more likely to find something close to a temple, catering to the monks or nuns. Next to Quoc Su Pagoda, at 65 Quan Su St., is **Au Lac**, a vegetarian restaurant with inexpensive prices. This is one of the very few in Hanoi that is exclusively vegetarian. Another vegetarian place is **Com Chay Nang Tam,** at 79a Tran Hung Dao, tel. 4/8266140. Inexplicably, Vietnamese vegetarians seem to like their food shaped to resemble meat, so the tofu and other vegetable matter is often warped to resemble pork chops or something similar.

Fresh Beer

Hanoians seem to enjoy passing time seated on plastic kindergarten stools at street corners. And with a glass of beer going for $.10, you begin to understand why. All around Hanoi are hundreds of no-name places bearing a BIA HOI banner, with the barrel sitting street side, and glasses siphoned off it. "Bia Hoi" means "fresh beer." Contrary to the belief that it is homebrewed on the premises, *bia hoi* is made by three major breweries in town: The barrel is delivered by motorcycle or other means, and outlets buy just enough to last the day. There are no additives or preservatives, so it's made to be consumed the day it leaves the factory. The beer is sweet, smooth, and light, with mild carbonation—and it has an alcohol content of between 4 percent and 4.5 percent. There are actually three varieties of fresh beer available around Hanoi: *bia hoi* (light, weak); *bia tuoi* (stronger brew, more alcoholic, pressurized beer); and *bia den* (it means "black beer," a darker stoutlike beer). Because beer goes through a fermenting

Hanoi

process, it is very safe to drink—and here's something to think about: It is actually cheaper than bottled water! It is estimated that about 500,000 liters of *bia hoi* are consumed in Hanoi and environs daily. Locals will tell you that it is best when served early in the day—before it gets too old. Beer for breakfast, anyone? Anyhow, parking yourself over a *bia hoi* will serve a number of useful purposes: Mainly, you get to mix with the locals, and you get ringside seats for watching what goes on along the street. Sorry, not seats. Little plastic kindergarten stools.

If you want to go up a few levels, try **Bia Minh,** a terrace restaurant just inside the Old Quarter at 7A Dinh Liet Street. Very popular with expats and travelers alike.

Street Treats

Many Hanoi streets feature impromptu food stalls. To the southwest fringe of the Old Quarter, near the railway tracks, is some unique street food, with both indoor seating and street-side seating at tiny wooden stools. The stalls are mostly clustered around Tong Duy Tan Street, which is about as close as you'll get to a "walking area" in Hanoi (meaning it is closed off to cars, but watch out—motorcycles still come zipping through). Cam Chi Street offers stir-fried food and noodles for about $.50 a dish. You can buy from any of the stalls and take the fare to another stall to sit down. Cam Chi means "Forbidden Way"—the street once led to a gate to Hanoi Citadel.

The western extension of Tong Duy Tan Street becomes Ga Tan, or Chicken Soup Alley. This avenue specializes in medicinal chicken or beef soup for around $.60 a serving. You get soup, bread, and chicken pieces. In the soup are lotus seeds, spinach, dates, ginger, and herbs—a booster for those cold winter days. On really cold days, patrons buy a shot glass of whiskey.

Farther south, nearer the railway station, is Nam Ngu Street, which is full of noodle stalls. You can get yellow noodles, white noodles, flat noodles, clear noodles, thin vermicelli, and soups. Indochine Restaurant is also on this street.

Known to Hanoians are tiny places that specialize in one or two tasty dishes. You have to work to find these spots, but language is not a problem with only one or two items on the menu, and the cost is right—it should be under $2 a head. **Dac Kim** restaurant, at 1 Hang Manh, in the Old Quarter, is famed for *bun cha,* or fresh rice noodles with barbecued pork; there are three floors of seating here, and the place is always packed at lunch. Serving *pho bo,* or rice noodles in beef-bone soup, is **Bat Dan** restaurant, at 49 Bat Dan, in the Old Quarter. Selling the chicken-bone version of *pho ga* are **Mai Anh** restaurant at 42 Le Van Huu St., and **Tiem Pho** restaurant at 2 Nguyen Du Street. Two other restaurants on Le Van Huu—at numbers 32 and 39—serve variations on rice noodles. At 67 Hang Dieu St. is **Bun Bo Nam Bo** restaurant, specializing in **bun bo**—cold fresh rice noodles with fried beef. At 17 Cha Ca is **Banh Cuo Nong** restaurant, specializing in *banh cuon,* which is meat and mushroom wrapped in a rice crepe.

Street Kid Restaurants

There are estimated to be several million kids on the street in Vietnam: Officially, there are more than 20,000 street kids in Hanoi alone—but the real figure could be much higher. You will no doubt be chased along the streets of Hanoi by more than a few of them, selling postcards and guidebooks or offering a shoe shine—even if you are wearing sandals. They are often not orphans but simply young people who have come from rural areas to escape the grind of poverty and seek a new life. Giving them a chance to realize that dream are two restaurants in Hanoi that are very popular with the expatriate community.

Hoa Sua, at 28 Ha Hoi St., tel. 4/9424448, www.hoasuaschool.com, is a restaurant in a restored colonial villa with a fine courtyard. It is tucked down a quiet alley toward the south end of Hanoi. The service can be slow and erratic, but the menu of Vietnamese and Western dishes is solid. Hoa Sua is part of a vocational training school that has been providing career-training opportunities for disadvantaged youth in Hanoi since 1995. All profits from the restaurant, brasserie, bakery, and catering service go to provide living expenses and training scholarships for students and to cover operational costs of the school. (See also the entry for Baguette & Chocolate under *Cafés and Bakeries*.)

Another training school for street kids is **Koto,** tel. 4/7470337, at 61 Van Mieu, near the entrance to the Temple of Literature. This is a training facility for up to 30 street kids, aged 16–22, drawn from the streets of Hanoi. Those lucky enough to be selected by Koto receive accommodation and a monthly wage and undergo a rigorous, intensive 18-month course—learning cooking and serving skills, English, and other facets. By the time they graduate, they are in demand from top Hanoi hotels. Koto is open for breakfast and lunch: In the evening, the teaching components take place. Instructors are largely Western volunteers.

Koto serves mostly Western fare—try the upstairs section. The concept is the brainchild of Jimmy Phan, a Vietnamese-Australian who set up a registered charity to help street kids. Jimmy plans to expand that concept to other parts of Vietnam. In November 2000, Koto got a surprise visit—from President Bill Clinton. The restaurant had three hours' notice to prepare lunch for Clinton and 30 of his entourage in the upstairs section—and 80 security and press people milling around downstairs.

Courtyard Restaurants

It's surprising what a bland street entrance can lead to: a tunnel that comes out into a great courtyard, such as **Hanoi Garden,** at 36 Hang Manh St., tel. 4/8243402. This airy place is centered around a garden area with outdoor tables. On three sides are interior rooms on several levels, and special rooms for up to 30 or 40 guests. Food is Vietnamese, Asian, and European. A quiet oasis in the heart of the Old Quarter.

Pho Bien Seafood, at 14 Trang Tien St., tel. 4/9285757, is another restaurant sited well off the road, and although it has no garden, it has a pleasant atmosphere. Fresh seafood here is sold by weight—which can get expensive. But to make calculations easier, the restaurant offers a range of set menus (minimum four people), with prices ranging $5–20 a head depending on choice.

With striking Chinese design elements showcased in the architecture and furniture is **Emperor,** at 18b Le Thanh Tong St., tel. 4/8268801, in the Hoan Kiem District, south of the Opera House. It houses two levels of tables, with a sumptuous bar facing the courtyard. Out toward the Temple of Literature is **Brother's Café,** at 26 Nguyen Thai Hoc St., tel. 4/7333866, which also features classic Chinese and Vietnamese design elements; its interior courtyard is shaded by banana trees. Great atmosphere, buffet-style offerings with faux market stalls cooking up noodles, and possible live music performance at night. Open lunch and dinner.

Villa Restaurants

For a touch of class—and food for the discerning palate—here are some exclusive restaurants housed in historic buildings or old French villas. As well as dinner, you might consider these places for brunch. Expect to pay $10 and up per person for food alone.

Indochine, 16 Nam Ngu, tel. 4/8246097, is in an alley near Saigon Hotel. The restaurant occupies a renovated historic building and serves Vietnamese cuisine. Staff dress in traditional costume; there may be traditional music performances. Alas, the restaurant has seen too many group tours and the quality of the food has dropped. Open for lunch from 1030, and dinner from 1700.

Nam Phuong, at 19 Phan Chu Trinh, tel. 4/8240926, is in a beautifully renovated villa. Elegantly presented Vietnamese dishes are accompanied by traditional live music. **Seasons of Hanoi,** at 95B Quan Thanh, tel. 4/8425444, serves French and Vietnamese food in the charm of a French villa. Tariff is high. **The Verandah,** downtown at 9 Nguyen Khac Can, tel. 4/8257220, serves French food in a French atmosphere—at French prices.

Hoan Kiem District

Restaurants in this zone are moderate to expensive. Western food comes with a Western price tag, and seafood is also pricey. Pizza can cost $4–8 depending on size; a dish of crab might run $7.

Overlooking the lake, above Thuy Ta Café, is **Thuy Ta Restaurant,** tel. 4/8286290, with pricey seafood. The banana flower salad with shrimp is good. Traditional live music is provided at night.

Nha Tho Street, running directly east of St. Joseph's Cathedral, is host to a number of upscale Western restaurants, including Salsa (Mexican) and La Brique (oven-fired pizza). Pick of the lot for atmosphere is **Moca Café,** at 14 Nha Tho, tel. 4/8256334, which offers an eclectic menu of Vietnamese, Western, and Indian food in a sumptuous colonial atmosphere of high ceilings, swirling fans, and marble-topped tables. There is an upstairs section, also with lofty ceiling. You can also come here for drinks alone—varying from cinnamon-flavored cappuccino to liqueurs. Almost opposite is **Mediterraneo,** at 23 Nha Tho St., tel. 4/8266288, an Italian restaurant serving real pasta and pizza; the chef makes his own rice-wine concoction—as a "digestif."

For pizza, Mexican food, and burgers, try **Al Fresco's,** at 23 Hai Ba Trung, tel. 4/8267782. For superior pizza, go to **La Primavera,** a restaurant inside the Camellia Hotel at 12 Pho Hue St., tel. 4/8263202.

Le Bistrot, 34 Tran Hung Dao, tel. 4/8266136, caters to the expatriate crowd, and dishes can get expensive. The restaurant features a French menu and French decor—the food is good, and the atmosphere pleasant. **Le Splendide** is a top-rated French restaurant in the Hoa Binh Hotel, tel. 4/8266087—decor includes chandeliers and stained-glass windows.

The **Pear Tree,** 78 Tho Nhuom St. (ground floor of Eden Hotel), tel. 4/8258167, is open for lunch and dinner. Unlike most Hanoi restaurants, it's open until 2300 during the week and midnight on Friday and Saturday. The restaurant serves pizza and pasta and features a cocktail bar.

Lotus Restaurant, 16 Ngo Quyen (on the 4th floor above the art galleries, opposite the Metropole), tel. 4/8267618, is a large salon with a garden terrace. It serves Vietnamese food, including Hanoi specialties. Prices are double those of other restaurants in the area, but the place is often booked. East of the Opera House is an upscale restaurant called **Au Palmier** on Dac Thai Than Street.

Le Beaulieu is the Metropole's top restaurant—for reservations call tel. 4/8266919, ext. 8028. This high-class restaurant serves French and Asian cuisine and features the best wine selection in Vietnam. The Metropole's **Spice Garden** specializes in Asian cuisine drawn from China, Indonesia, Thailand, and Vietnam.

Other Areas

Ba Dinh District: Quoc Tu Giam, close to the hotel of the same name, on the street of the same name, enjoys a good reputation. It serves crab, eel, snail, and other specialty dishes. **Phuong Nam,** on Giang Vo Street, is popular with Vietnam Tourism guides.

Giang Vo District: The restaurants at Hanoi Daewoo Hotel, tel. 4/8315000, are stylish—and priced accordingly. Here you'll find **Silk Road,** with Chinese cuisine; **Edo,** a Japanese restaurant and sushi bar; **La Paix,** for Italian continental dining; and **Café Promenade,** with European and Asian delicacies.

East of Lenin Park: Viet Phuong, at 4 Mai Hac De St., serves a delicious array of roast rabbit, eel soup, steamed crab, meat-stuffed tomatoes, and pork rolls. There are cheap food stalls on the southern end of Mai Hac De Street.

West Lake: There are a number of floating restaurants on the strip between West Lake and Truc Bach Lake, but the food is generally under par and overpriced. The best of the bunch is the nonfloating **Banh Tom Ho Tay,** a circular restaurant with a rooftop terrace. It's a pleasant place with good fare—eat outside under umbrellas, or inside if the weather is cold. The specialty of the house is West Lake shrimpcake.

CAFÉS AND BAKERIES

French habits linger in Hanoi, with cafés serving baguettes, drip-filter coffee, and even croissants and crème caramel. In the Old Quarter at 11 Cha Ca St. is **Baguette & Chocolate,** a branch of the Hoa Sua training school for disadvantaged youth. Fresh croissants, baguettes, and pastries are served here, as well as a variety of dishes. The upstairs section is an oasis from the rush of the Old Quarter. A number of traveler cafés in the Old Quarter serve backpacker fare—banana pancakes, yogurt, fruit salad, fruit shakes, and noodles—at low prices. There is a concentration of these places along Hang Bac Street. Hang Than Street, north on the perimeter of the Old Quarter, specializes in *banh com,* a kind of sticky rice filled with coconut and lotus seeds.

By the side of Hoan Kiem Lake is **Thuy Ta Café.** The food is on the boring side, but the views of the lake and quiet ambience make up for it—and if you sit here long enough you might even see the legendary giant turtle of Hoan Kiem surfacing. Close by a roundabout with a fountain up at the north end of the lake you will see a building with cafés stacked up: The one on the 5th floor, **City View Cafe,** has outdoor tables that provide a bird's-eye view of the lake.

One of the best places for sandwiches is **No Noodles,** at 20 Nha Chung St.—a tiny place that serves great eat-in or take-out food and fresh juices and yogurt. How about a chicken curry sandwich or a *croque monsieur?* No Noodles has those, in addition to the regular camembert and ham sandwiches.

South along Le Thai To Street are the best ice cream places in Hanoi. These are **Fanny** (Kem Phap), at number 48, and **Kem Carvel,** at number 32. Both places use imported equipment and assure customers that the ingredients are pristine, and hygiene standards are so high that you will not get sick from eating the ice cream. Right by Hoan Kiem Lake to the southwest is the open-air venue **Highlands,** serving cappuccino, Italian-style espresso, and café latte. This place also serves juices, ice cream, and snacks—it's a good place to mingle, though it attracts its share of street hawkers and postcard pushers. The **Bodega Café,** on the ground floor of 57 Trang Tien, mimics a dimly lit Halong Bay grotto. This place is a student hangout—the spring rolls are good, the ice cream is okay, but the rest is fairly bland.

And the last word on pastries and treats comes from the **⋈ Metropole Hotel's chocolate buffet,** which is a combination of high tea, chocolate, and the return of the French Empire. Some molten chocolate with your dragon fruit? That can be arranged—along with a mouthwatering array of pastries. The decadent chocolate buffet takes place 1500–1830 daily, and will set you back $10. French pastry addicts will be drawn to the Metropole Hotel's patisserie, operating from a shop at the back. The patisserie sells expensive goods that are delicious. The chefs make their own pastries, chocolate cake, pâté, and ice cream on the premises.

Nightlife

Cafés and bars are the nightlife in Hanoi. Hanoi dies after dark—the streets are deserted by 2300, when police regulations about closing down come into force. The city is so bereft of nightlife that various embassies organize their own beery get-togethers, alternating each week. You need inside knowledge or an invitation to crash an embassy function. In the basement of the German Embassy at 29 Tran Phu is a small restaurant serving schnitzel, open weekends only.

The French have gone to the trouble of throwing up a six-story French Cultural Center, called L'Espace, at 24 Trang Tien—a short distance from the Opera House. L'Espace stages events, exhibitions, and screenings of French movies.

⋈ WATER PUPPETRY

Without a doubt, one of the top attractions in Hanoi is water puppetry. This exuberant and magical art form is intended for children but will delight adults as well. Unique to Vietnam, it's seen regularly only in the north. The exact origins of water puppetry are uncertain, but it's known the Red River Delta area nurtured and preserved this traditional theater through many centuries. Water puppetry was a village festival art before it became a theatrical one. Temporary theaters were constructed in village ponds, and performances marked such auspicious occasions as the beginning or end of the agricultural cycle.

For performances, a dozen puppeteers stand waist-deep in water behind a pagoda set; invisible to the audience, they manipulate puppets with a series of bamboo poles, pulleys, and strings. The pagoda pool is roughly six meters long by four meters wide. The puppets are made of lacquered wood and appear remarkably lifelike when skipping across the water. What goes on under the water is a closely guarded secret—some puppeteers have to swim under other puppeteers. Water plays a key part in the show—the surface is seething during a naval battle, or romantically calm when a group of fairies drifts across. Underwater fireworks bring flashing dragons to life and furnish a haze of smoke for mythical settings. Puppeteers and percussionists provide explosive sound effects—rhythmic music and zany sound effects maintain the tempo.

Coated in lacquer to make them water-resistant, the wooden water puppets last only about three or four months, so new ones are constantly being produced by local artisans. The hand-carved puppets are a folk art in themselves, with larger pieces held in museum collections, and miniature copies sold as souvenirs at puppetry shows and in Hanoi shops.

Repertoire

The traditional water puppetry repertoire includes up to 100 short skits. A 75-minute performance usually presents 15–20 short pieces, derived from fables, local legends, historic events, or adapted from popular theater. Such mythical animals as the phoenix, lion-dog, unicorn, and dragon are often shown in aquatic dances. Satirical takes at rural life are common.

You may catch the story of the magic sword, a mixture of myth and history similar to the Arthurian legend of Excalibur.

Venues

There are several locations for viewing water puppetry shows in Hanoi. Show duration is usually around 60–75 minutes. In town is **Thang Long Water Puppetry Theater,** 57 Dinh Tien Hoang St., tel. 4/8249494, with performances every evening. Thang Long Theater is a 300-seat venue at the northeast side of Hoan Kiem Lake: The main clientele is foreign group tours who arrive in convoys. There are up to five shows daily, starting at 1600, with the last performance at 2100. Buy tickets in advance: Cost is $2 per seat, $4 for a front seat with a water puppetry audiocassette thrown in. There should be no charge for cameras. Hanoi's local Thang Long water puppetry troupe runs the show; the theater provides a live traditional music ensemble of five who sing, play instruments, and provide acoustic effects.

The National Water Puppetry Theater, at 32 Truong Chinh St., tel. 4/8534545, stages shows at 1930 on Tuesday, Thursday, Saturday, and Sunday, but performances are seasonal—there may only be Thursday and Sunday performances in winter, so phone ahead to check the schedule. The theater is at the southern edge of town; these performances are more for Vietnamese than tourists. Take a taxi out there. If you have a larger group, you can phone the theater and it will dispatch its bus to pick your group up. Entry is $3 for foreigners. The national troupe is Vietnam's best and has toured Japan, Australia, and Europe; it was set up in 1956 by Ho Chi Minh himself.

A third troupe called **Song Ngoc Troupe** occasionally performs in Hanoi. On the seventh day of the third lunar month, usually in April, there's a water puppetry festival at Thay Pagoda, 40 kilometers west of Hanoi.

CULTURAL SHOWS

The **Opera House**—also called the National Theater—stages performances of traditional theater and music and offers concerts by visiting artists. (Refer to the section on the *Opera House* under *Frenchtown* in the *Sights* section for ticketing information.) Fare could be a Cuban flamenco guitarist, Hungarian folk dance troupe, Shakespearean performance, Vietnamese modern ballet, Vietnamese folk dance, or Hanoi Philharmonic Orchestra. Yet to appear at this illustrious venue is the renowned soap opera *Miss Saigon*. Perhaps it is being held up by title problems—a change of name to Miss Ho Chi Minh City?

THE CIRCUS

Hanoi's Big Top is in a circular concrete building in the northwest corner of Lenin Park. Performers seem to derive their inspiration from Groucho Marx rather than Karl. Acts are amateurish and often hilarious, with out-of-control monkeys, an uncooperative elephant, and flawless performing dogs. See also a variety of jugglers, contortionists, gymnasts, and acrobats. Tickets are cheap. Inquire through your hotel for performance times—the troupe could be on tour in other parts of the country.

BARS AND PUBS

Nightspots in Hanoi are small; the venues are crosses between bars, cafés, bistros, and pubs. In the Old Quarter are several venues.

Running off the northwest edge of Hoan Kiem Lake, but still in the Old Quarter, are Hang Hanh and Bao Khanh streets, which have a number of small bars—popular here are the **Funky Monkey,** at 15 Hang Hanh, and **Polite Pub,** at 5 Bao Khanh. Also in this area is **Cyclo Bar,** at 38 Duong Thach: You sit in fancy padded cyclos when dining here. On the northeast side of the lake is **R&R Bar,** at 47 Lo Su St.—the owner is American. Music is mostly stuck in the '70s, and the menu is firmly stuck in Mexico—a great little bar.

The **Jazz Club** at 31 Luong Van Can is lively, with a singer sometimes showing up to front for a live jazz group; on Fridays is rock, with slightly warped lyrics but recognizable numbers. If you're looking for a place that's open after 2300 in the Old Quarter, go to **Bat Dan Café,** at 10 Bat Dan St.—this has great ice cream, draft beer, and a games room for chess and backgammon aficionados. **Art Café,** at 57 Hang Non, open 0900–2400, is a cocktail bar with a pleasant European atmosphere and tasteful music. The bar serves pizza, spaghetti, red wine, and beer; it's a family-run place—the owners have a couple of large dogs.

In the Hoan Kiem District, prices rise to $2 or $3 a drink and up, with food prices to match. The rooftop bar of the **Press Club,** at 59A Ly Thai To, is a great place for a drink—or food. Down the street is candlelit ambience at the upscale bar-café **Diva's,** at 57 Ly Thai To, with live music in the garden at night. At 59 Ly Thai To is the upscale **Club Opera,** in an old French mansion: a businessperson's venue with drinks and a Western menu (*croque* sandwich, spaghetti, steak).

Inside the Metropole Hotel is **Le Club,** where, 1500–1730, you can indulge in a fixed-price ($7) afternoon tea with pastries; furniture is luxurious; at night there's live music—traditional Vietnamese, classical, or jazz. The Metropole also features the poolside **Bamboo Bar** with exotic fruit cocktails and ice cream sundaes, and a barbecue in the evening. The **Met Pub,** on the north corner of the Metropole facing Ly Thai To Street, is a popular haunt for foreign businesspeople—prices drop at happy hour; this English-style pub is open late and serves tacos, fish and chips, and a large selection of beer and whisky.

To the southern side of Hanoi is **The Blue-beat Café,** a bar-restaurant at 78 Ba Trieu Street. Also south, at 5C Hoa Ma St., is **Apocalypse Now** bar, which has a large snooker table, MTV, dance floor, and no cover charge.

KARAOKE AND DISCO

Hanoi has little in the disco line, but lots of karaoke. Karaoke in Hanoi is largely synonymous with private cubicles stocked with women of dubious moral integrity; another variety is *bia om,* or "beer-cuddle" bars, which are small places with hostesses. Otherwise, legitimate karaoke and disco venues occupy larger hotels. The **Dong Loi** and **Hanoi Heritage** hotels feature karaoke lounges and dance floors. **Thang Loi Hotel** has regular *soirée dansante*—the big night is Sunday (2000–midnight), when a live band plays.

Two popular downtown discos are the **New Century,** at 10 Trang Thi St., mostly with a hip Vietnamese crowd (there is a cover charge), and **Apocalypse Now,** at 5C Hoa Ma St., mostly catering to Westerners (no cover charge). Both are open late, especially on weekends. Apocalypse Now is quiet early in the evening when the bar, pool table, and MTV screen dominate. But toward midnight, action shifts to the dance floor—continuing until early morning on weekends.

Shopping

The souvenir trade in Hanoi is concentrated around the Old Quarter and Hoan Kiem District. To the south side of Hoan Kiem Lake, along Hang Khay and Trang Tien streets, is a string of stores selling lacquerware, woodcarvings, silverware, antiques, and artwork; to the east side of Hoan Kiem are art galleries along Ngo Quyen Street; to the north side of Hoan Kiem are numerous small shops tucked into the Old Quarter.

Nha Tho Street, running west off Hoan Kiem Lake to St. Josephs Cathedral, is home to a number of fine shops that sell Vietnamese artifacts, clothing, and furniture. For finding out what's available, Nha Tho Street would make good reconnoitering grounds (the prices tend to be higher in the upscale shops here).

Handicrafts and Antiques

The **Tourist and Handicraft Shop** at the corner of Ly Thuong Kiet and Hang Bai streets is run by Hanoi Tourism and features a large range of handcrafted goods at reasonable prices. Items include sculpture, silk paintings, water puppetry figures, and chess games. You can buy mass-produced prints or silk paintings for $3–12. A few antique stores are strung along Le Duan, south of the station, opposite Lenin Park. However, it's advisable to shop in government-run stores for antiques, as you'll receive an official receipt, which may be demanded upon exiting the country.

Original Art

Hanoi is the top place for buying original art

in Vietnam, with more than 60 galleries and many well-known painters. Artists concentrate on Hanoi street scenes, portraits of women, and abstract and surrealist themes. There are numerous galleries in the Hang Khay and Trang Tien areas. A sampling of the art galleries: **Salon Natasha** at 30 Hang Bong is a tiny avant-garde place; **Red River Gallery** at 71A Nguyen Du St. caters to the international market, featuring up-and-coming artists. There are a number of small galleries tucked away in the Old Quarter, including **Thang Long Gallery,** 15 Hang Gai St.; **Trang An Gallery,** 15 Hang Buom St.; and **Art Gallery,** at 7 Hang Khay Street.

Clothing

Silk items—ready-made or custom-ordered—can be found on Hang Gai Street in the Old Quarter. Try **Khaisilk** at 96 Hang Gai, **Queen Silk** at 76 Hang Gai, or **Hoasilk** at number 86. You can buy silk kimonos with brocade designs here. Embroidery shops, such as the one at 109 Hang Gai, produce exquisite silk blouses and pajamas, as well as tablecloths and wall hangings. Designs feature majestic dragons, blue lotus flowers, or scenes of Vietnam. By leaving a picture behind, you can custom-order pieces; they may take time to produce. Around the corner from Hong Gai, along Luong Van Can Street, traditional *ao dai* dresses are made. Message T-shirts and hand-embroidered T-shirts are available on Ly Quoc Su Street. You can also have T-shirts custom-made. Custom-made silk lingerie is popular. Try the tailor **Le Minh Silk** at 79 and 111 Hang Gai Street.

Bia hoi (fresh beer) is available on many street corners in Hanoi. Here, men gather to drink beer on a street known for crafting headstones for graves.

Hanoi

Ho Chi Minh Souvenirs

The Vietnamese aren't above making a few bucks off old Ho—with Ho T-shirts, Ho buttons, badges, stamps, and posters. The gift shops and sidewalk stalls outside the Ho Chi Minh Museum carry a large selection. Be aware that Ho Chi Minh kitsch may not go down well with Western war veterans. Nor with the resident Vietnamese community in, say, California—to whom the Vietnamese flag and pictures of Ho are extremely offensive. The neighborhood of "Little Saigon" in the city of Westminster, California, is home to 200,000 ethnic Vietnamese, many of whom escaped pre-1975 and settled there. In 1999, video store owner Truong Van Tran hung a Vietnamese flag and a poster of Ho Chi Minh in his shop window display. After someone knocked down the Ho picture, Tran taunted Vietnamese anti-Communist activists, challenging them over the issue of freedom of speech. They responded with round-the-clock demonstrations and thousands of screaming protesters.

Pirateware

Probably not going down very well with Western customs officers are the bootleg CDs that are sold all over Hanoi—music CDs, game CDs, software CDs, movie DVDs. Hanoi has the widest (and cheapest) selection of bootleg music CDs in Vietnam—probably because of its proximity to the Chinese border. Little booths dispense these copies, going for a song, mostly in the Old Quarter. You come across all sorts of copycat stuff in Hanoi—bootleg computer-game CDs, pirated software (on a massive scale), Nike knockoffs. A lot of this pirateware comes from China, but the Vietnamese are pretty good at it too. Art-school students in Saigon fund their education by laboriously repainting Picassos or Gauguins—or, if you prefer, they'll copy an oil painting or watercolor of your choice. Any book that looks as if it will sell to foreigners is copied from an original—even books banned in Vietnam (how does that work?).

In the larger logo-stealing sweepstakes,

there's a fast-food place in the Old Quarter called "Mickey's," with the Disney character greeting you. Disney would come down like a ton of bricks on that business if it were elsewhere on the planet. A more brazen, larger-than-life Mickey stands outside a restaurant on Cao Ba Quat Street. And the Japanese are experiencing some logo-stealing trouble, too. There are Chinese clones of Honda motorcycles—with flashy model names such as Spacy or Future. The fakes sell for about a third of the price of a real Honda—which might explain why there are so many. Just a tad off a knockoff was one sly brand spotted: It bore the legend "Hongda," and the model name "Wise."

Old Quarter Specialty Shops

Some shops in the Old Quarter focus on one particular line of items. Hang Quat Street in the Old Quarter specializes in banners and flags, which are usually intended for service awards or funerals. For an unusual but attractive wall hanging, buy a scarlet banner with brightly embroidered gold or silver dragons and other symbols from one of the Hang Quat stores for $5–15. For a few dollars more, you can have your personal or business name and other information embroidered on the banner. At 11 Hang Non St. is a shop devoted to Vietnamese musical instruments—ingenious wooden items fashioned like frogs or fish. There is an innovative array of instruments here. At 44 Hang Ga St. is a shop, **The Culture of Vietnam Ethnic Groups,** which sells exclusively items made by minority peoples—baskets, pan pipes, clothing, textiles, and so on.

Markets

Dong Xuan Market, in the Old Quarter, is the largest market in Hanoi, stocking food, clothing, and other necessities. Smaller food markets are **Hang Da Market,** on the southwest side of the Old Quarter near the Protestant Church, and **19 December Market,** which runs between

REVOLUTIONARY TIMES

After she brought over the cup of tea and carefully placed it on the table, the waitress beamed and said, "Enjoy your meal!" I did a double-take, because in the early 1990s, customer service was not a strong suit in Hanoi. When you paid the bill, a gruff waitress dressed in baggy pants would actually throw the change onto your table with a look of disdain, and she would snarl if you tried to leave a tip—even lecture you about how insulting tips were. It was demeaning even to be serving a foreigner in the first place. This was all blunt and direct to the point of actually being funny. Restaurants were not named, they were numbered—Restaurant 22 or Restaurant 44—because luxurious dining was considered a decadent bourgeois habit. A vegetarian dish meant that you could pick the meat out of the stew if you were so inclined.

Yes, times have changed indeed! Restaurant staff in Hanoi do not lash out at the customers, and they don't mind tips at all. But traces of the Soviet hammer-and-sickle mentality remain. You still will find places called Restaurant 75 or Pho 24 in Hanoi. For those hankering after the nostalgic days of Soviet influence in all its tacky glory, Hanoi is one of the better places to go looking. Hanoi still has an intact Lenin statue, it has museums packed to the rafters with revolutionary kitsch, and it has more than its fair share of large Soviet blockhouse monstrosities—usually official buildings. The yellow hammer-and-sickle ensign, emblazoned on a blood-red background, appears on posters around the streets to mark special occasions, along with the Vietnamese flag with identical colours. On Hang Gai Street you can buy T-shirts bearing the same designs. Need some revolutionary home decor ideas? Nostalgia seekers can buy old revolutionary posters from **Propaganda Art,** at 8 Nha Chung Street.

Ly Thuong Kiet and Hai Ba Trung streets to the southwest of Hoan Kiem Lake. There are small street markets selling consumer goods in the Old Quarter. For army surplus, go to Le Duan Boulevard, south of the railway station. Here you can find green pith helmets, fake-furry Russian hats, army surplus jackets, gloves, and so on—useful for travel in the cold north.

HANOI HEADGEAR

Peculiar to northern Vietnam is the olive-green pith helmet worn during the Vietnam War. Originally copied from the French, the hat is called *mucoi* in Vietnamese because it is shaped like a mortar (as in mortar and pestle) when inverted. These helmets are often made from tree bark and covered with green canvas. The helmets are cheap—and useful in keeping off sun or rain or deflecting falling rocks when motorcycling along northern Vietnamese roads. Occasionally spotted are color variations on the standard green model: You can buy blue, black, or even pink pith helmets. Some tourist shops carry a wide range of colors.

It's odd that a helmet so closely associated with North Vietnam's Communist struggle should derive from the French. For nearly 100 years, the white cork helmet was the symbol of French imperialism, just as the khaki pith helmet symbolized the British Empire. Also derived from the French (although now mostly imported from Czech Republic) are the ubiquitous berets and French-style caps. Russian influence is evident in earflap headwarmers—the wearers look like delegates to a Snoopy convention, except for the fact they're crouched over bamboo bongs, taking hits of tobacco. You'll sometimes see Hanoi men smoking a B-52 bong. The bamboo stem of the pipe features an ailing B-52 heading earthward; attached to the smoking mouthpiece, the B-52 appears to be trailing smoke.

Hanoi

© MICHAEL BUCKLEY

fish market activity near the riverbanks

Services and Information

TRAVELER CAFÉS

There are traveler cafés all over Hanoi, with a high concentration in the Old Quarter. The cafés are prefabricated in Saigon and shipped north by train, complete with Sinh Café and Kim Café shingles. Well, something like that. Most traveler cafés arrange tours, handle paperwork, and book tickets; some rent motorcycles and bicycles. The larger ones will also store luggage if you head up-country—just make sure you attach a passport number to your baggage. In choosing a café, the best advice is to stick to older ones. The older cafés still exist because they have business licenses and, more important, have the right contacts to get permits needed for tours and transport. They have developed a long-term strategy instead of going for fast returns.

Because many smaller cafés manage to book only two or three travelers for a trip, they tend to pool resources. As a result, when you book a trip, you may end up being shuffled off to a totally different outfit—and you may end up with 50 other travelers on a big bus (yes, it has happened—and you might end up with 50 people on a boat at Halong Bay too). It is really tedious traveling in such unwieldy groups: at a rest stop, by the time everybody has wandered off to buy drinks or go to the toilet, half an hour has gone by—and then it takes another half an hour to round up the strays. And try taking discreet photos with 50 people walking around a small town.

So when inquiring about trips in cafés, the magic words are: small group. Groups of under 10 are viable; some prefer fewer than six on the trip. Be extra careful about gauging the number of people on your proposed trip—and make it very clear what you want, and hold the café owners to that agreement. The easiest way to do this is to specify a minibus—which will hold only 10–15 passengers. If it looks as if you're moving to a full-size bus, bail out immediately and ask for a refund. Likewise, if

you're promised an English-speaking guide, or a certain class of hotel or a certain type of transport, hold the operator to it. If you don't, you make it more difficult for the next traveler. Most traveler cafés are budget-conscious and tend to cut corners on accommodation, restaurants, and type of transport—that's why their tours are inexpensive.

Like a guidebook, a meeting café should get you going and point you in the right direction—and then you can find your own feet. Some travelers begin with a few day trips from traveler cafés, and then give up on the logistics of arranging trips themselves. They get lazy and rely totally on the cafés—they stay there, eat there, and take tours in minibuses. And then they use the Open Tour buses that ply the Hanoi-to-Saigon route. They spend all their time with other foreigners, a rather peculiar way of coming to grips with Vietnam.

Cafés are good for gathering information, but you should think twice about joining organized tours all the time—they're not always satisfying. Check café traveler books and tour itineraries for ideas. Café bulletin boards are great for seeking other riders for shared jeep rides or minibuses for custom trips or travel to the northwest. Finally, several of the cafés offer low-budget accommodations and they do also actually serve food, though it's generally bland. Traveler cafés are usually open all day, 0800–2230 or 2300.

Operators

The Old Quarter zone is bustling with traveler cafés and cybercafés. Good for budget adventure-touring in the north is **Handspan** at 80 Ma May, tel. 4/9260501, handspan@hn.vnn.vn, www.handspan. com. Handspan has a handful of locations in Hanoi—there's another at 116 Hang Bac. Handspan can arrange kayaking at Halong Bay, white-water kayaking on the Da River, motorcycling on a Minsk to Sapa, or camping-trek trips of a week or more in the

HANOI TOUR COMPANIES AND TRAVELER CAFÉ AGENTS

The reins of business have loosened in Hanoi, and small private entrepreneurs such as Queen Café and Old Darling Café are keen for a piece of the tourist trade. To get started, entrepreneurs need a government business license and must pay taxes on profits. Those with the right connections can organize tours for foreigners; this system of paperwork and kickbacks means some cafés are more powerful than others. Shoestring tours are provided by traveler cafés, including **Old Darling Café,** 4 Hang Quat, tel. 4/8243024; **Real Darling Café,** 33 Hang Quat, tel. 4/8269386; **Queen Café,** 65 Hang Bac, tel. 4/8260860; and **Green Bamboo Travel,** 42 Nha Chung, tel. 4/8264949. The Meeting Café and other small cafés also run day trips.

Ann Tourist, Dong Do Hotel, 27 Tong Duy Tan, tel. 4/8233275

Ecco, 50A Ba Trieu, tel. 4/8254615—this agency has a poor reputation and is prone to overcharging and botching arrangements

Especen Tourist Company, 79E Hang Trong St., tel. 4/8266856, fax 4/8269612—good agency for hotel bookings, car rentals

Hanoi Tourism Service Company (Hanoi TOSERCO), 8 To Hien Thanh St., tel. 4/8229076; also operating through Sinh Café, 18 Luong Van Can St., tel. 4/8287552

National Oil Services Company (OSC), 38 Yet Kieu, tel. 4/8264500, fax 4/8259260— good for tours and vehicle rentals

New Indochina Travel, 4 Dang Thai Than St., tel. 4/9330599, fax 4/9330499, new-indochina@fpt.vn, is efficient at organizing small group tours and tailor-made itineraries; this is the official STA rep for Vietnam

Oscan Enterprises, 60 Nguyen Du (Boss Hotel), tel. 4/8252690

Pacific Tours, 58B Tran Nhan Tong, tel. 4/8267942

Vidotour, 51 Phan Chu Trinh, tel. 4/8269875

Vietnam Veterans Tourism Service (VVTS), 192B Quan Thanh, tel. 4/8232966—liaises with touring veterans

Vinatour, at 54 Nguyen Du, near the Boss Hotel, tel. 4/8255963, fax 4/8252707— splinter group from Vietnam Tourism, can arrange Land Cruiser

Vung Tau Intourco, 136 Hang Trong, near Phu Gia Hotel, tel. 4/8252739

northeast. It runs the full range of local and other tours, too. At 80 Ma May the staff hand out a "menu" of their trips—you can scan it while eating in the attached vegetarian restaurant.

Love Planet, at 25 Hang Bac St., tel. 4/8284864, fax 4/8280913, loveplanet8@ hotmail.com, is run by Mr. Liem, who is very knowledgeable and helpful with touring around Hanoi and beyond. Love Planet has the largest selection of second-hand English books in Hanoi—there are lots on the ground floor, and more upstairs. The way this collection has been built up is through a two-for-one book exchange. If you have nothing to exchange, you can rent or buy a book.

Another reliable operator with good feedback from travelers is **Kangaroo Café,** at 18 Bao Khanh St., tel. 4/8289931, kangaroo@ hn.vnn.vn.

TOURIST INFORMATION

Vietnam Tourism is at 30A Ly Thuong Kiet near the Peace Hotel, tel. 4/8264319, fax 4/8257583—good for visa extensions, useless for anything else. **Hanoi Tourism,** 18 Ly Thuong Kiet, tel. 4/8254074, and **Hanoi Tourism Service Company** (TOSERCO), at 94 Ly Thuong Kiet, tel. 4/8255721, fax 4/8267999, also handle visa extensions and official paperwork. TOSERCO is the travel and touring arm, with overpriced vehicle rentals and guided tours to many parts of the north. The Hanoi branch of **Saigon Tourist** is at 55B Phan Chu Trinh, tel. 4/8250923.

Customized Small-Group Touring

If you have a group of, say, 10 people together with special interests and want to cue arrangements up, there are a number of agencies that would be delighted to help out. An example would be a student group coming to Hanoi to study Vietnamese and make weekend trips around Hanoi. **New Indochina Travel,** overlooking Truc Bach Lake at 60 Tran Vu St., tel. 4/7150343, fax 4/7150340, new-indochina@fpt.vn, www.stavietnam.com, is a reliable agency for arranging customized small-group touring; it also deals with STA air ticketing and International Student Cards.

Guides

Guides speaking English, French, German, and other languages are available from either official tourist organizations (expensive, $15–20 a day), private agencies (better deal), or by inquiring through traveler cafés (the least expensive option).

Miniguide to Hanoi

Because things tend to change (particularly with restaurants and clubs) you should supplement your information diet with two slim magazines: *Time Out,* which comes as a weekly addition to *Vietnam Investment Review,* and *The Guide,* a monthly addition to *Vietnam Economic Times.* Both of these give up-to-the-minute listings for both Hanoi and Saigon, but bear in mind that listings are a form of advertising. You should be able to buy these magazines separately from vendors.

Maps

The best scale map of Hanoi is a joint-venture Canadian map produced by International Travel Maps (ITM) and Hanoi's Cartographic Mapping Institute. Check the date on maps—older touring maps may be of limited use. Hanoi is such a sprawling place that it makes sense to have a booklet with section maps. This item exists: It's called *Hanoi Atlas*—you can track it down in one of the bookstores along Trang Tien. Could be out of date, however.

Street vendors around the GPO and in the area along Trang Tien Street sell all kinds of maps. If you require high detail, vendors have topo maps tucked away—you might have to preorder them. The **Cartographic Mapping**

Institute (CMI), the national mapmaking bureau of Vietnam, is out in the Dong Da District, at 73 Lang Trung Street. By the front gate is a small shop selling topo maps, atlases, giant wall maps of Vietnam, and thematic maps, all in a haphazard jumble of rolled sheafs.

Books

Because of stringent government restrictions on import of books, you may well be reduced to foraging for second-hand fiction titles or guidebooks left behind or sold by travelers. **Bookworm,** at 15 Ngo Van So St., tel. 4/9437226, stocks a good range of new and second-hand books—worth browsing. The foreign owner claims this is the only English bookshop in Hanoi. Around the Old Quarter, small places trade in second-hand books: The largest collection is held at **Love Planet,** at 25 Hang Bac.

Xunhasaba, the state corporation for import and export of books and periodicals, is at 32 Hai Ba Trung. Good for magazines on Vietnam, and it may even stock the *Tribbie (International Herald Tribune), Time,* and the *Asian Wall Street Journal.* The **Foreign Language Publishing House** is at 46 Tran Hung Dao St.; this place publishes propaganda in English, French, Russian, and other languages. The **Foreign Language Bookstore,** at 55 Trang Tien, and the **State Bookshop,** at 40 Trang Tien, both stock books effusive in their praise of things Vietnamese. Otherwise, bookstore offerings in Hanoi are spotty—because of government censorship. That may explain the book-pirating cottage industry—photocopied works include everything from French guides of the 1930s to erudite botany manuals. Major hotels such as the Metropole, Hilton Hanoi Opera, and Daewoo feature kiosks with magazines and books.

COMMUNICATIONS
Fax and Phone

The IDD/telecom center is next to the GPO on the southeast side of Hoan Kiem Lake; a branch at 66 Trang Tien also handles calls. Hotels can usually place IDD calls and send faxes. The country dial code for Vietnam is 84; the city code for Hanoi is 4, followed by the number. Help yourself to the information contained in the bilingual *Hanoi Telephone Directory and Yellow Pages,* issued annually. The information section at the front provides full charts of IDD rates, postal services, express mail, parcel costs, and other telecommunications details. Emergency numbers: police, 113; fire, 114; ambulance, 115.

Email and Internet

Cybercafés are found all over Hanoi, with the heaviest concentration in the Old Quarter. Connections come and go; connections can be very slow. Some places have laser printers and some can arrange scanning. Don't expect anything too high-tech—keep it simple because there are often problems with servers. Because the cybercafés are using different servers, if one connection is down, try another. In the Old Quarter, recommended are the places along Ta Hien Street, particularly at 18 Ta Hien and 9 Ta Hien. **Emotion CyberNet Café,** 52 Ly Thuong Kiet (upstairs), has a full Internet setup, charging less than $1 an hour.

Satellite TV

Luxury hotels—and an increasing number of smaller hotels—receive StarTV, BBC, CNN, and other cable programs. These include the Metropole, Hilton Hanoi Opera, Hanoi Daewoo, Royal, Hanoi Heritage, Hanoi Hotel, Saigon Hotel, MOD Hotel, and Tay Ho Hotel.

Post Office and Courier

The **GPO** is at 87 Dinh Tien Hoang St., on the southeast side of Hoan Kiem Lake. It handles *poste restante,* philatelic sales, and parcel mailing. Open daily 0700–2000. For postage and parcel rates, consult the Hanoi Directory. The GPO offers an express mail service (EMS), with a branch at 66 Trang Tien Street. Close to the GPO are the offices of **Federal Express,** tel. 4/8249054; **DHL,** tel. 4/8267020; and **TNT,** tel. 4/8257615. Around the post office cluster map vendors (semilegitimate), and money changers (illegitimate).

PHOTOGRAPHY AND FILM

Photo shops are scattered around the perimeter of Hoan Kiem Lake, particularly the northeast, northwest, and south sides. They sell imported slide and print film. Quality of print and slide film developing varies—shop around and try some test rolls. Recommended is **Minilab Nguyen Cau,** at 19 Ba Trieu, tel. 4/8261258—slide film is processed within a few hours and standard is good: You can choose to have slide film unmounted or mounted. Enlarged prints are good quality.

MONEY AND BUSINESS
Banks and ATMs

The **Vietcombank,** in the Sun Red River Building at 23 Phan Chu Trinh (between Ly Thuong Kiet and Tran Hung Dao streets), is the major exchange point, open weekdays 0800–1630, Saturday 0900–1500, closed Sundays. The bank offers commission-free conversions from American Express traveler's checks to dong, but it charges a commission for other brands (Isn't commerce wonderful? Ten years back these banks would not even touch an American Express check—you had to bring in Thomas Cook or other non-American kinds). You can also have American Express checks issued here. You can convert traveler's checks to U.S. cash for 1 percent commission, which is a good deal. In the lobby are some Vietcombank ATMs. In the same lobby are HSBC ATMs: The HSBC has a branch in the same building, on the same floor.

The **ANZ Bank,** at 14 Le Thai To, tel. 4/8258190, is open 0830–1530 and Saturday 0830–1200; it charges a $2 minimum commission to convert traveler's checks to dong and handles Visa and MasterCard cash advances with a 4 percent commission. Outside the building are two ATMs, which allow a maximum draw of two million dong each time (consecutive draws are possible). The ANZ has acquired a share of Sacombank, which will explain why you get ANZ-type statements from a Sacombank ATM. There are a number of Sacombank and Vietcombank ATMs around Hanoi.

Other foreign banks include **Bank of America,** on the ground floor of Hoa Binh Hotel; **Citibank,** in the International Center at 17 Ngo Quyen; **Commonwealth Bank of Australia,** in the Central Building, 31 Hai Ba Trung; **Banque National de Paris,** 8 Tran Hung Dao; **Credit Lyonnais,** 8 Trang Thi; **Hongkong Bank,** 51 Le Thai To; **Deutsche Bank,** 25 Tran Binh Trong; **Krung Thai Bank,** 34 Ba Trieu; and **Standard Chartered Bank,** Hanoi Towers, 49 Hai Ba Trung.

Street money changers lurk around the GPO—shortchangers would be a more accurate description of their profession. Changers often deliberately undercut on agreed amounts and actually offer less than bank rates. The only real advantage money changers offer is the ability to change dong back to dollars when you are leaving Vietnam. Avoid all street transactions.

Business Services

The Metropole Hotel, Hilton Hanoi Opera, and the Daewoo have the best business centers in town, with excellent secretarial and translation services. Other hotels with business centers include Boss Hotel, MOD Hotel, Saigon Hotel, Hanoi Hotel, Hanoi Heritage Hotel, and Tay Ho Hotel.

HEALTH CARE

Family Medical Practice, at Van Phuc Compound, 298D Kim Ma Rd., Ba Dinh District, tel. 4/8430748, is an efficient Western-run place with Western doctors, modern equipment, and a small on-site pharmacy. Down the road is **Family Dental Practice,** at 298D Kim Ma Rd., tel. 4/8230281, again with Western dentists and modern equipment. The website for both is www.vietnammedicalpractice.com.

Bach Mai International Medical Center, on Phuong Mai, tel. 4/8243728, has been upgraded with American equipment and drug supplies; this 56-bed facility deals with foreigners—the place is clean and uses disposable needles. The facility includes accident and emergency units, radiology and pathology sections, and a pharmacy.

Evacuation: International SOS, with an office in the Central Building, 31 Hai Ba Trung St., tel. 4/9340666, fax 4/9340556, arranges evacuation to Singapore. SOS also has 24-hour alarm numbers: tel. 4/9340555, fax 4/9340556. This large office has a dental practice and doctors for general consultation (nonemergency) but fees are high.

REST AND RECREATION

Major hotels include fitness centers and gym facilities. Several hotels have swimming pools and tennis courts. The Metropole charges nonguests $5 to use the pool—one of the few pools in Vietnam that won't turn your hair green. Check the notice boards at the Metropole for news of Hanoi Hash House Harrier runs (usually on Saturdays). Recreational boating opportunities can be found at the southeast corner of West Lake—sculling boats are for rent here.

Buses leave the Metropole Hotel on Sunday morning for **King's Island Golf and Country Club** at Dong Mo, 45 kilometers west of Hanoi. This is a $22 million resort with a luxury hotel and corporate villas; two 18-hole courses were under construction. In Hanoi, contact King's Valley Corporation, tel. 4/8260342. Also to the northwest is **Daeha Golf Course and Country Club,** connected with the Daeha Business Center at Hanoi Daewoo Hotel, tel. 4/8315000. This is an 18-hole course with country club and a full range of sports, leisure, and entertainment facilities, including tennis courts, swimming pool, and jogging track.

Getting There

BY AIR

There are a dozen carriers flying into Hanoi's Noi Bai Airport, whose new terminal has adequate facilities, though not exciting ones. Should you find yourself stuck out this way, try the Airport Hotel, Noi Bai Airport, tel. 4/8254745, with rooms for $40 double. An old French airfield at Gia Lam was being upgraded—some flights leave from there at present.

Entry Formalities

On arrival, you may have to fill in a document that looks like a visa application, sometimes with two photos required. Fill in the usual customs declaration form and entry-exit card—keep these with you, to be surrendered on departure. On the entry-exit card, look for the box specifying the place where you intend to stay: The best thing to write in here is "unknown." On the customs form, you must itemize cameras, video recorders, tape recorders, and other electronic equipment. You may have to declare currency above $3,000 but it's best to be vague about it. Avoid changing money at the airport—the rate is not good.

Transfers into Hanoi

Noi Bai Airport lies about 40 kilometers north of Hanoi. A taxi from the airport costs $10 for the 45-minute ride to downtown Hanoi. There is a booth at the airport where you can prepay that amount and get a ticket stub. Otherwise, you may fall victim to the taxi mafia, who will try and nail you for the highest price. Prices may vary with the number of passengers; be prepared to pay in dollars. Vietnam Airlines minibuses into Hanoi are considerably cheaper. In the reverse direction, from Hanoi to Noi Bai, you can get an Airport Taxi (a special line) for $7. The Vietnam Airlines yellow minibus is $2 a passenger; buy your ticket from the Vietnam Airlines international booking office near Hoan Kiem Lake, preferably the day before departure. Check bus times; buses leave from the

same place. There is a regular city bus that runs from Hanoi all the way to the airport.

Airline Offices

The Vietnam Airlines international booking office is at 1 Quang Trung St., tel. 4/8255229. This is the general agent for a few minor international carriers such as Lao Aviation. Vietnam Airlines operates direct flights from Hanoi to Bangkok, Vientiane, Phnom Penh, Guangzhou, Hong Kong, Seoul, Taipei, Beijing, Singapore, Dubai, Moscow, Paris, and Berlin. Other carriers also travel these routes.

If time is not a factor, consider indirect routes—they might work out cheaper and are certainly an adventure. Instead of flying direct to Bangkok for $160 on Vietnam Airlines (or $180 on Thai Airways), take a plane to Vientiane for $90 on Vietnam Airlines or Lao Aviation (twice-weekly service on Thursday and Sunday). Add $15 for a seven-day Lao transit visa, and $20 to cover the cost of a transfer into Nong Khai, and overnight sleeper to Bangkok, and your cost for a Lao layover is only $125.

Another spectacular route to consider is Hanoi to Kunming in stages by train, and a flight from Kunming to Bangkok. The Kunming–Bangkok flight is competitive in price with the Hanoi–Bangkok flight. Rail travel from Hanoi to Kunming is about $30 for sleepers; paperwork may cost another $50. Flying to Canton from Hanoi is much cheaper than direct flights into Hong Kong. If you add the Hanoi–Canton flight, Chinese visa, and Canton–Hong Kong boat, you can get to Hong Kong for around $190, which is below the $270 tariff for a direct flight from Hanoi to Hong Kong. China Southern Airlines operates one-way flights from Hanoi to Canton for $125, Nanning for $80, and Beijing for $260.

BY LAND

There are three border crossings from China in the north—at Lao Cai in the northwest, approached from Kunming; at Huu Nghi Quan (Friendship Gate) in the northeast near Lang Son, approached from Nanning; and at Mong Cai, on the northeast coast, also approached from Nanning via Dongxing. If entering this way, you need a valid Vietnamese visa. You can arrange visas in Hong Kong, or possibly Beijing. For exiting the north into China, you need a Chinese visa, which is easily obtained in Hanoi within a few days (or same day if you want to pay a premium).

Overland buses ply the route from Hanoi to Vientiane for around $15 a head. You probably won't get much sleep, but it's cheap. You may not be missing much in the way of scenery by overnight travel—much of the route is bland anyway.

Getting Around

Metered Taxis

Hanoi Taxi, tel. 4/8265252, runs a fleet of white Toyotas. These are radio controlled and can be called to a restaurant or other location for pickup. Some taxi ranks are found on the street, such as the one near the railway station. Hanoi Taxi is run by Hanoi People's Committee, which also operates Red Taxi, tel. 4/8353686, and PT Taxi, tel. 4/8533171. Another fleet, called V Taxi, tel. 4/8215668, is run by the Interior Ministry. Other outfits include Airport Taxi, Capital, CP, Five, Fujicab, T Taxi, and City Taxi. Metered taxis are about $.70 for the first kilometer and $.50 per kilometer after that. Hanoi Taxi and Red Taxi charge the highest rates. Older, nonmetered taxis are also found around Hanoi—negotiate the fare before boarding.

Motos and Cyclos

Hanoi moto drivers are not always easy to find (or recognize): Try intersections—look for someone with a battered baseball cap. Cyclos in Hanoi employ models with wooden seats. Prices depend on distance but should be $1 or less for a cross-town run. For stylish touring, the Metropole Hotel offers luxury white cyclos with padded seats. Cyclos are not permitted on certain streets in Hanoi, particularly the road encircling Hoan Kiem Lake and along Trang Tien, Hang Bong, and Trang Thi boulevards, and in certain parts of the Old Quarter. This may explain erratic maneuvering patterns by cyclos in this area. The traffic sign for "No Cyclos Allowed" is a red bordered circle with a painting of a cyclo or similar vehicle inside it (but no red slash across that).

Two-Wheel Rentals

For motorcycle rentals, inquire through traveler cafés. Rental agents require a deposit for Japanese motorcycle rental—either a large sum of cash, or your departure card, paper visa, credit card, passport, or plane ticket. Avoid leaving a credit card or a passport. For a Russian motorcycle, a photocopy of your passport might work. There's little in the way of insurance—

wired: overhead wires and bird cages in downtown Hanoi

HANOI VEHICLE RENTAL

A car with driver is around $25–35 a day within the city.

Especen's price list for vehicles is as follows: Volga car, three passengers, $25/100 kilometers; Toyota car $30/100 kilometers; nine-seat Japanese minibus, no a/c, $30/100 kilometers; same with a/c $35/100 kilometers; 12-seat minibus $40/100 kilometers; Land Cruiser, $45/100 kilometers for four passengers. Sun Tourist Café charges $25 a day for a car and driver; Vinatour charges $33/100 kilometers or for a one-day Hanoi tour.

inquire as to who's liable for the repair bill in case of an accident or mechanical breakdown, and who pays if the bike is stolen. Hondas are rented for about $8/day for a 70cc, and $15 for a 100cc. For a Russian motorcycle, the charges are $5/day for 125cc or 175cc. Czech motorcycles are cheaper than Japanese.

Bicycles are rented for $.30–.70 a day: You can negotiate keeping the bike overnight or for several days. If you do keep a bike overnight, park it in your hotel courtyard, off the street, or inside the hotel lobby. Rentals are fairly relaxed, with little required in the way of deposits. Go for the black Chinese bicycles with encased chains—these are less liable to fall apart. Always check brakes and adjust saddle height. In the Old Quarter is a string of rental places on Ta Hien Street, just north of Hang Bac Street.

Your Own Wheels

You can buy used Russian motorcycles in Hanoi; inquire through traveler cafés. You can buy a used Minsk 175cc for around $250; a new one sells for $500. No papers are involved—you use the bike, then resell to locals or other travelers.

Adventure Motorbike, at 40 Luong Ngoc Quyen St., tel. 4/8266586, minskwizard@ yahoo.com, specializes in buying, selling, and renting Minsks. You can buy motorcycle parts and helmets along Hué Boulevard, south of Nguyen Cong Tru Street east of Lenin Park, and also along Hang Bong Street in the Old Quarter.

Chinese-made black roadster bicycles are often smuggled in from the border. Vietnamese brands such as Doan The (Corporate) or Huu Nghi (Friendship) are turned out at a French-built factory in Hanoi. These cost only around $30 each. Chinese bikes run $55 and up.

Boat Rentals

At the southeast corner of West Lake, near Tran Quoc Pagoda, you can rent rowboats and sculling boats for exercise, or to go across the lake, speedboats or dragon boats. For dragon boat information and reservations at West Lake contact Olympic Café, 28 Thanh Nien, tel. 4/8257105.

Getting Away

BY AIR

The Vietnam Airlines office is at 1 Quang Trung St., tel. 4/8250888. There are flights from Hanoi to Dien Bien Phu (twice a week), Hué (five times a week), Danang (daily), Nha Trang (twice a week), and Ho Chi Minh City (daily).

Pacific Airlines has an office at 100 Le Duan, Dong Da District, tel. 4/8515350; this carrier mounts flights mainly from Hanoi to Saigon or Haiphong to Saigon.

Vietnam Air Service Company (VASCO) operates several Aerospatiale Squirrel AS-350 helicopters with French pilots, available for custom flights. Contact VASCO at the Metropole Hotel, tel. 4/8266919, ext. 8015. Scheduled routes: Noi Bai Airport to Gia Lam Airfield, $150 one-way per person for the five-minute trip; Gia Lam Airfield to Haiphong, $250 one-way for a 25-minute trip. VASCO will arrange a two-day overflight of Halong Bay for $2,000, for 1–4 passengers (there is a

HANOI AIRLINE OFFICES

Aeroflot, 4 Trang Thi, tel. 4/8256742—flies to Moscow twice weekly

Air France, 1 Ba Trieu, tel. 4/8253484—direct flights to Paris several times weekly via Bangkok

Cathay Pacific, in Hanoi Towers building, 49 Hai Ba Trung, tel. 4/8267298—flies to Hong Kong daily

China Airlines, 18 Tran Hung Dao, tel. 4/8242688, flies to Taipei five times a week

China Southern Airlines, Binh Minh Hotel, 27 Le Thai To, tel. 4/8269233, flies to Guangzhou, Nanning, and Beijing

Czechoslovakia Airlines, 404 A2 Van Phuc Quarter, tel. 4/8256512

Japan Airlines, 1 Ba Trieu, tel. 4/8266693

Lao Airlines, 41 Quang Trung St., tel. 4/8266538, flies to Vientiane twice weekly

Malaysia Airlines, in Metropole Hotel, 15 Ngo Quyen, tel. 4/8268821, flies to Kuala Lumpur twice weekly

Singapore Airlines, International Center, 17 Ngo Quyen (Metropole Hotel), tel. 4/8268888—flies to Singapore three times weekly

Thai Airways International, office in Melia Hanoi Hotel, Ly Thuong Kiet, tel. 4/8266893—frequent flights to Bangkok

United Airlines, office in Hilton Hanoi Opera, 1 Ly Thanh Tong, tel. 4/9333183—flights to San Francisco

regular one-day helitour of Halong for $195 per person on Saturdays).

BY RAIL

The foreign booking office at Hanoi railway station is open 0730–1130 and 1330–1530. You can also make reservations by phone. Reunification Express trains run from Hanoi to Saigon. Prices vary depending on speed. Hanoi to Danang is $31 soft seat, $46 hard sleeper, and $70 a/c soft sleeper, by the fastest train (S1). Hanoi to Saigon is 1,728 kilometers (46 hours) and costs $48 hard seat, $56 soft seat, $82–91–99 hard sleeper, and $108 soft sleeper. On the faster train, taking 36 hours, those prices might rise another $10–20; the a/c soft sleeper on an S1 train is $150 for Hanoi to Saigon, which is close to the cost of flying.

There are also rail spurs running from Hanoi to Haiphong (three hours by fastest train), Lao Cai (11–12 hours, one day train, one overnight train, leaves from small station just north of main Hanoi terminal, costs $10 soft seat or $16 hard sleeper), and Lang Son (eight hours, one day train, one overnight train). The through train from Hanoi to Kunming runs twice a week: It is a two-night journey taking more than 30 hours. Train LC5 leaves Hanoi at 2130 and arrives at Lao Cai at 0700 next morning; several hours are allowed for customs and immigration clearance at Lao Cai, and the train proceeds again at 0920, reaching Kunming the next day at 0600. In the opposite direction, train LC6 leaves Kunming at 1445 and arrives at Hanoi at 2020 the following day.

A twice-weekly Hanoi-to-Beijing direct train travels via Dong Dang, with about eight stops en route to Beijing, including Guilin and Changsha.

Be aware that not all trains leave from or arrive at Hanoi main station. All the southern departures are from the main station, but departures for northern destinations may leave from minor stations. Just north of the main station, near a busy crossroads, is a minor station at Tran Quy Cap Street, where trains leave for Lao Cai and points north; out toward Long Bien Bridge is Long Bien Station, the terminal for trains to Haiphong.

BY ROAD

Vehicle Rental
You can rent minibuses, Russian Army jeeps, Land Cruisers, and Toyota cars for up-country travel. For rough roads, you need a 4WD vehicle. Most tour agents can organize vehicle rental. Vinatour charges $44/100 kilometers for a minibus; $66/100 kilometers for a 25-seat bus; and $90/100 kilometers for a 50-seat bus. TOSERCO charges $35/100 kilometers for a 12-seat minibus and $40/100 kilometers for a 15-seat bus.

Traveler Buses and Minibuses
Though you can take an overnight train on the Hanoi–Hué leg, traveler minibuses also ply the route. You can get a ride from Hanoi to Hué for around $22–25, taking 17 hours straight through. Other travelers break the journey with a day or two stop-off in Ninh Binh. It might be worth negotiating a stop to tour the DMZ from Dong Ha en route also. Several tour companies handle Open Tour bus ticketing for Hanoi to Hué. A major operator is Sinh Café at 18 Luong Van Can St., tel. 4/8287552, in conjunction with partner Hanoi TOSERCO, 8 To Hien Thanh St., tel. 4/8229076.

Bus and Minibus Terminals
A shuttle bus runs between the various bus terminals and strategic points, including Hanoi main station and Long Bien Bridge, making transfers a little easier and considerably cheaper. It goes from Giap Bap to Bach Mai to Ga Hanoi (main station), and on to Kim Lien, Long Bien, and Gia Lam.

Northeast: Minibuses and buses to Halong Bay (Bai Chay) and Lang Son depart from Le Thanh Tong Street a short distance south of the Opera House, near the intersection of Dac Thai Than. Minibuses run to Lang Son between 2200 and 0100, taking five hours. On Dac Thai Than Street is a bus depot with departures to Hong Gai. On the east banks of the Red River is Gia Lam Ben Xe, with departures to Bai Chay 0630–1300, and buses to Haiphong and Lang Son.

Northwest: Kim Ma bus station, on the west side of Hanoi, handles departures to Hoa Binh, Moc Chau, Son La, and Tuan Giao daily, and Dien Bien Phu every two days. There are also departures to Tuyen Quang, Yen Bai, and Tuyen Quang.

South: Kim Lien bus station, at 100 Le Duan, and Giap Bat bus station, 15 kilometers south of central Hanoi, run departures in the direction of Thanh Hoa, Vinh, Hué, and points south.

VISA EXTENSIONS AND EXIT FORMALITIES
Although no one bothers checking the items on your customs form on exit, failure to produce the piece of paper can result in incredible hassles. Get rid of all dong before exiting—the dong isn't worth a damn outside the country. If you have a surplus of dong, you might have to change money on the streets in Hanoi to convert it back to U.S. dollars. International departure tax is $8. In case you're wondering why visa extensions and exit formalities are paired together here, it's because when you go to get a visa extension in Hanoi sometimes you're just presented with an exit stamp instead—which means, beat it—hit the road, Jack.

Regional Embassies
The **Laotian Embassy,** 22 Tran Binh Trong, tel. 4/8254576, maintains a visa-issuing office close by at 40 Quang Trung St., tel. 4/8252588. The **Embassy of Thailand,** 63 Hoang Dieu, tel. 4/8235092, is open daily except Saturday, with visa-issuing hours 0830–1200; a regular 30-day visa takes one day to issue and costs $15. The **Cambodian Embassy,** at 71A Tran Hung Dao, tel. 4/8253789, is open Mon.–Fri. 0830–1130. A visa costs $20 and takes several days to issue.

The **Chinese Embassy,** 46 Hoang Dieu, tel. 4/8253737, staffs a visa-issuing office south of

HANOI EMBASSIES

There are more than 40 embassies in Hanoi, grouped in several zones. Van Phuc Quarter is an enclave to the west side of Hanoi; Trung Tu Quarter lies to the southwest of Hanoi. At the time of writing, a number of embassies—including the Japanese and Korean embassies—were planning to move to the area just north of Hanoi Daewoo Hotel. Embassies in Hanoi include:

Australia, Van Phuc Quarter, tel. 4/8317755
Belgium, Room 105-108, D1 Van Phuc Quarter, tel. 4/8252263
Canada, 39 Nguyen Dinh Chieu, tel. 4/8265840
Finland, B3 Giang Vo Quarter, tel. 4/8256754
France, 49 Ba Trieu, tel. 4/8252719
Germany, 29 Tran Phu, tel. 4/8252836
India, 58 Tran Hung Dao, tel. 4/8253409
Indonesia, 50 Ngo Quyen, tel. 4/8253353
Italy, 9 Le Phung Hieu, tel. 4/8256246
Japan, 66 Truong Chinh St., tel. 4/8692600
Malaysia, A3 Van Phuc Quarter, tel. 4/8253371
Mongolia, 39 Tran Phu, tel. 4/8253009
Myanmar (Burma), A3 Van Phuc Quarter, tel. 4/8253369
New Zealand, 32 Hang Bai, tel. 4/8241481
Philippines, Room 305-308, E1 Trung Tu Quarter, tel. 4/8257948
Russian Federation, 58 Tran Phu, tel. 4/8254632
Sweden, 2-358 St., Van Phuc Quarter, tel. 4/8254824
Switzerland, 77B Kim Ma, tel. 4/8232019
Thailand, 63 Hoang Dieu, tel. 4/8235092
United Kingdom, Central Bldg., 31 Hai Ba Trung St., tel. 4/8252510
United States, 7 Lang Ha, tel. 4/8431500

the main embassy, around the corner at 40A Tran Phu. Application hours are Mon.–Fri. 0830–1100. A 30-day or 60-day visa is available. Fees depend on nationality, usually ranging $20–40 but going through the roof for Brazilians. The visa takes five working days to process, but you can get it faster—for a price. Hand over 50 bucks and you get the visa back the same afternoon; for 40 bucks you can pick it up the next day. All deals are in U.S. dollars—cash. Have exact bills ready to seal the deal.

Vietnamese Visa Modifications

Extending a visa in Hanoi is sometimes straightforward, other times complicated. The Hanoians like to play games. Sometimes they find irregularities in the issuance of the visa. On several occasions, travelers applying for extensions have instead been handed an exit visa, meaning they have 72 hours to leave the country. That may mean a rush visit to the Lao visa office, and a fast flight out. Allow at least three working days, and preferably five, to extend your visa in Hanoi.

Visa Extensions: The folks at the immigration office will not deal direct—they will refer you to an agency such as Vietnam Tourism. Agencies charge different fees—Vietnam Tourism, at 30A Ly Thuong Kiet, charges

$15 for a one-week extension, $20 for a two-week, and $25 for three- to four-week extensions; it requires three working days. Apply about five days before your visa expires; attach your entry/exit card and the name of the hotel where you are staying. Other outfits may be cheaper: Saigon Tourist, at 55B Phan Chu Trinh, processes a three-week extension in two days for $16.

Reentry Visa: It's possible to have your Vietnamese visa validated for reentry to Vietnam after a visit to, say, Kunming in China's Yunnan province. The reentry stamp turns your existing visa into a double-entry visa.

The North

Vietnam's greatest touring potential lies in the untapped north. The mountainous terrain, and the war, have isolated the area from travel since the 1940s. Now you can rediscover Sapa, a former French resort town up by the Chinese border, or Mai Chau, set in a beautiful valley near the Lao border. The north is intriguing because it is full of unknowns; it is less commercial than the south, and the people have an entirely different mentality. The north feels like a foreign place; central Vietnam seems nebulous; and in the south, everything looks a little too familiar.

The north has spectacular karst scenery—hills, deep gorges, and the kind of sugarloaf peaks found on islands in southern Thailand, in China's Yunnan province, and on Palawan in the Philippines. At Halong Bay, bizarre limestone formations sprinkle the coastline, creating a dreamlike landscape that inspires Vietnamese painters. Hundreds of grottoes are embedded in the karst islets. Karst formations also make for spectacular boat trips on rivers to the Perfume Pagoda and Tam Coc Caves to the southwest of Hanoi.

With scenery like this, trekking is only a step away, and a number of Hanoi tour operators offer hiking and camping itineraries. A jeep takes you to the trailhead, and then you march three or four days, staying in villages

Must-Sees

Look for M to find the sights and activities you can't miss and ⋈ for the best dining and lodging.

M Perfume Pagoda: A pilgrimage of sorts, to a cave-shrine southwest of Hanoi. The backdrop is splendid karst—you hike up a mountain trail to the shrine (page 94).

M Ninh Binh Area: A wondrous zone of beautiful karst formations and caves. There are organized boat trips for access to the area, or you can rent a mountain bike or moto and stop where you like. **Kenh Ga** island village has an especially entrancing setting (page 95).

M Mai Chau: Hiking and mountain biking are inspiring in this valley west of Hanoi. Highly photogenic is the rice terracing in this area, set among sugarloaf peaks (page 100).

M Kayaking in Cat Ba National Park: Kayaking is the best way to get in close to karst. You can explore sea-level tunnels and caves in this region—the best place to see them (page 116).

M Halong Bay: Hop aboard a modified junk and cruise past bizarre karst limestone islets and outcrops. You can view some formations from the inside at spectacular caves with stalagmites and stalactites (page 117).

M Military Museum, Dien Bien Phu: This marks the spot where an Asian guerrilla army took on mighty French forces—and won. A multimedia show recounts the fall of the French (page 137).

M Hiking in the Sapa Region: Vietnam's highest peak, Mt. Fansipan, looms in the distance on a clear day as you hike among ethnic villages. The hill resort of Sapa is positively charming, and the mountain air is bracing (page 147).

M Bac Ha Sunday Market: Lots of eye-popping color here because the market draws Flower Hmong women with their elaborately embroidered costumes (page 150).

The North

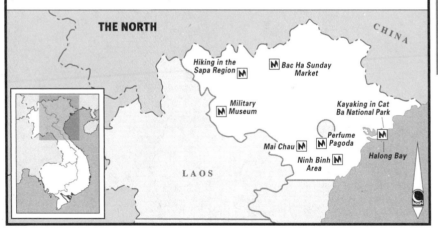

The North

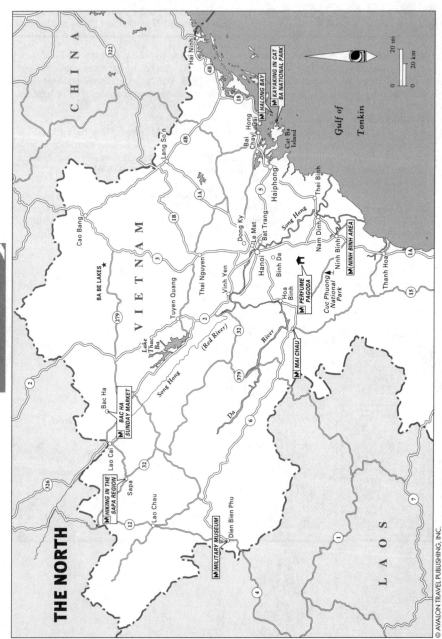

THE NORTH

© AVALON TRAVEL PUBLISHING, INC.

along the route. Porters can carry supplies if needed. Ideal points for hiking include Mai Chau in the southwest, and Dien Bien Phu, Lai Chau, Phong Tho, and Sapa in the northwest. Mediocre national parks in the north offer limited hiking facilities; the best is Cuc Phuong National Park. Old French hill stations undergoing redevelopment are potential bases for independent treks with your own guide. Two stations, Sapa and Tam Dao, are operational; others such as Bavi were soon to follow suit.

Many minority groups live in villages in the northwestern mountains, especially toward the Chinese and Lao borders on the Son La-to–Sapa route. The French word for minorities is *montagnard,* meaning mountain people. You'll often notice minorities at markets, which are more animated on weekends, especially Sunday. Here's where you have to think about the timing. A place such as Bac Ha is fairly dead until market day comes around. Then the place is hopping. Mornings from dawn to around 10 A.M. are best for market day. Market days are: Saturday and Sunday for Sapa; Saturday for Can Cau (Flower Hmong); Sunday for Bac Ha (Flower Hmong); Sunday for Muong Houm (many groups); Sunday for Muong Khuong; Tuesday for Coc Ly; Thursday and Saturday for Binh Lu; Sunday for Dongvan.

PLANNING YOUR TIME

In 1990, you couldn't beg, borrow, or rent a bicycle, much less a motorcycle, in Hanoi. Now you can rent—or buy—a Russian motorcycle and ride off into the hills all the way to the Chinese border. Travelers band together, rent a jeep or 4WD vehicle, and take off on wild 10-day journeys over dirt roads.

Because of a lack of bases in the north, trips tend to be round-trip loops radiating out of Hanoi. Favored day-trip destinations include Tam Coc Caves and Bich Dong, and the Perfume Pagoda. Top overnight trips from Hanoi are Halong Bay and Mai Chau. Traveler cafés and tour agencies in Hanoi organize tours to these and other areas. Prices and services vary considerably. Some tours offer transport only; others include food, accommodations, and entry fees. Agencies such as TOSERCO charge considerably more than the traveler cafés—they also use better hotels and transport and employ better guides.

For longer trips in the north, you should assemble a small group to split costs, and be prepared to negotiate. In Halong Bay you have to rent fishing boats; to get to Sapa via Dien Bien Phu, you must bargain for car, jeep, or Land Cruiser prices. Get as much finalized on paper as you can, as a kind of contract. If you paid half the cost of a jeep up front, for example, write the amount down and indicate the balance due at the end of the trip. Also sketch the route on paper to counter confusion and avoid possible misunderstandings. Make your trip flexible: Negotiate a fee in advance if you decide to add an extra day. Negotiate what happens if your vehicle breaks down.

An alternative to loops from Hanoi is a one-way trip from Hanoi to China. Along the 1,600-kilometer China-Vietnam border lie 25 major market points for cross-border trade. Two of them, Dong Dang, near Lang Son, and Lao Cai, are open to foreigners at present. Others may open in the future. The Kunming–Bangkok flight costs the same as the Hanoi–Bangkok flight, so you might consider traveling by rail north to Lao Cai and on to Kunming in China. Paperwork and fares might run you an extra $80, but what a ride! For an unusual loop in the north, travel up to Sapa, exit and carry on to Kunming, make your way back to Nanning, and reenter Vietnam at Lang Son. For this exercise, you need a Chinese visa and a reentry stamp on your Vietnamese visa.

Short Trips

Village Excursions: It's easy to get out of Hanoi into the surrounding countryside. There are villages within a 25-kilometer radius of Hanoi that have specialized for hundreds of years in a particular trade—silk production, wood carving, lacquerware. You don't need a bus to reach these—just hop on a bike.

Red River Delta: Excellent day trips from Hanoi, or good stops if you're coming north from Thanh Hoa, include the Perfume Pagoda and Tam Coc Caves near Ninh Binh. Both involve boat trips through majestic scenery. Traveler cafés offer day trips for $19 per person to Perfume Pagoda; $15–18 to Tam Coc and Bich Dong.

Southwest Loop: You'll need two days or longer for trips from Hanoi to this area. Good hikes here, with visits to ethnic villages in pretty Mai Chau Valley, and a glimpse of old-growth forest in Cuc Phuong National Park. You can travel round-trip to either Cuc Phuong or Mai Chau, or try the loop from Hanoi to Cuc Phuong to Mai Chau to Hoa Binh and back to Hanoi. For a longer trip, combine some destinations in the Red River Delta: Hanoi, Tam Coc Caves, Cuc Phuong, Mai Chau, Hoa Binh, Hanoi. Traveler cafés in Hanoi offer two-day trips to Mai Chau for around $25–28 a person and also organize area hikes. Especen charges $35 a head for a two-day trip to Cuc Phuong, based on three passengers.

North by Northeast: Here's a mixed bag, including Tam Dao Hill Resort, Ba Be Lakes Forest Reserve, and an exit to China via Lang Son. Minority groups live near the China border, in Cao Bang and Ha Giang. Hiking is possible at Ba Be Lakes. Old Darling Café at 4 Hang Quat offers a three-day trip to Ba Be, accommodations included, for $45–60 per person.

Gulf of Tonkin/Halong Bay: Visiting Halong Bay requires an overnight trip. Hire a fishing boat to tour the bay's wonders—waterscapes, grottoes, junks, marine activity. You'll find good accommodations and food at Bai Chay, the jumping-off point for Halong Bay. Traveler cafés in Hanoi offer two-day round-trips for $22–30 per person, based on 5–20 passengers. The price includes minibus and boat transport, as well as accommodations and food. If you have more time, consider spending 4–6 days or longer on this route, proceeding from Hanoi to Haiphong to Bai Chay to Halong Bay to Cat Ba Island and back to Haiphong and Hanoi.

Tonkinese Alps/Northwest: Key destinations in this direction are Dien Bien Phu and Sapa. You can travel to Sapa directly in one day, or take a long loop via Dien Bien Phu in five days. Along the way you'll find spectacular mountain scenery, rough roads, and numerous minority groups. There is excellent hiking in Dien Bien Phu, Lai Chau, and Sapa. At Lao Cai, you can cross into China and take a train to Kunming. A minimum four-day trip to Sapa's weekend market is recommended from Hanoi; on the longer route, you need at least six days, and preferably eight.

Traveler cafés in Hanoi offer direct car and minibus rides to Sapa, departing Hanoi on Friday and usually taking four days—two days of travel, two days in Sapa—for approximately $45–70 per person based on 4–14 passengers. Some traveler cafés in Hanoi and in Sapa arrange two-day hikes in Sapa and day hikes in Lai Chau and Phong Tho. You can organize your own jeep or Land Cruiser trips on the long route to Sapa via Dien Bien Phu. A jeep costs $300–400 for a six-day trip on the Hanoi–Son La–Dien Bien Phu–Lai Chau–Sapa–Lao Cai–Hanoi route; split expenses between four passengers. Especen offers a Hanoi–Dien Bien Phu round-trip in five days for $330 for a jeep, or $530 for a Land Cruiser, based on three passengers.

Accommodations

Tourism is new in the north, and there are few conventional hotels. Larger towns usually offer a UBND (People's Committee) guesthouse, where foreigners can secure a bed for $5 (local truckers pay $.50). These are basic places, but you usually get a warm quilt, mosquito net, and thermos of hot water—and that's the extent of the hot water. You can stay in a jungle lodge in Cuc Phuong National Park, on a fishing boat at Halong Bay, or in a village longhouse at Mai Chau. If worse comes to worst, seek out a noodlehouse or something similar and sleep on the floor. Food in the north is simple and monotonous, often a soup with beef, fried egg, rice, and cabbage, the national vegetable. At Halong Bay, however, you can get excellent seafood.

Gear

Some trips, such as those to Halong Bay, stay within range of civilization; other trips, especially to the northwest, verge on the expeditionary. If heading north to Sapa, or to Halong in winter, buy warm clothing in Hanoi. You can buy a silk or wool scarf, a padded cotton jacket, or a Chinese-made parka to counter the cold and wind in the north. You'll find sweaters and gloves in Hanoi's Old Quarter. Silk provides excellent insulation as long as it doesn't get wet; you can find silk items along Hang Gai Street. On Le Duan Boulevard south of the Hanoi railway station you can buy army surplus gear. A strong flashlight is necessary to compensate for lack of electricity and for stumbling through karst caves.

Village Excursions Outside Hanoi

There are a number of villages within a short distance of Hanoi where specialty trades—be it pottery and wood carving or fireworks—have been practiced for generations. The more "artistic" villages are particularly lively around Tet. After those torturous rides in buses, legs crammed into the back of a seat, it's good to know you can stretch your legs with longer bike rides around Hanoi. Though Hanoi is a large city, you can reach the countryside by simply cycling across Long Bien Railway Bridge. The bridge passes over areas of intensive vegetable farming in the Red River; the other side is immediately rural.

BAT TRANG

About 12 kilometers southeast of Hanoi, Bat Trang specializes in large-scale pottery and porcelain production using traditional methods. The village was founded in the 16th century by Thanh Hoa potters and features more than 800 family-operated and industrial kilns fired with wood and coal. Molding, firing, and painting are all done by hand, although clay-mixing is accomplished with machinery. Pottery is transported using industrial bicycles or lambros. There are small retail outlets in the town, and larger concerns have their own showrooms. You can reach Bat Trang under your own steam—if you're on a motorcycle, take the Chuong Duong toll bridge over the Red River and loop around to head south. If you're on a bicycle, use Long Bien Railway Bridge a bit farther north—on the other side, ride south back under Chuong Duong Bridge, turn inland, and keep asking for Bat Trang. It's a beautiful ride along an elevated road overlooking farmland, but watch for trucks. It takes about an hour to reach Bat Trang; the village is visible from the road on your right. A crossbar sentry at the entrance to the village charges big-noses $1 to enter.

BINH DA

Binh Da is a "firecracker village" 23 kilometers southwest of Hanoi. It's fallen on hard times because of Hanoi's mid-1990s decree banishing the use of fireworks at Tet. In 1994 the government imposed a Draconian tax on the sale of fireworks, equal to three times their cost. Fireworks are still used to keep demons at bay—at marriage engagements and wedding ceremonies, for official openings, and during house construction. Underwater fireworks, for use in water puppet shows, are also made in Binh Da. Since production of fireworks has been severely curtailed, the folk in this village have mostly turned to woodworking and other endeavors, but there are still some pyromaniacs lurking (in the woodwork).

DONG KY

Dong Ky, 18 kilometers northeast of Hanoi, specializes in antique Chinese–style wooden furniture, handmade and inlaid with mother-of-pearl or marble pieces. In the spring, a rocket festival features giant firecrackers eight meters long and two meters in diameter.

VAN HA AND VAN PHUC

Another village specializing in wood carving is **Van Ha,** to the south of Hanoi. Skillful carvers produce fine furniture, religious icons, and small souvenir items. Among the most commonly produced items are wooden statues of Buddha and bodhisattvas, including complex versions with multiple heads and arms. **Van Phuc Village,** 14 kilometers southwest of Hanoi, is of interest to those who seek silk by the meter. Watch families with motor looms spin and wash silk here.

LE MAT

Villagers from Le Mat, eight kilometers northeast of Hanoi, travel all over the north catching snakes. The serpents are kept in compounds around the house, in readiness for export to China or for use in snake wine or traditional medicine. In Hanoi's Old Quarter a shop sells medicines made from Le Mat snakes.

DONG HO

Dong Ho is a village along the Duong River in nearby Ha Bac province that produces traditional woodblock prints. There is great activity here in December in readiness for the Tet celebrations of February. A Dong Ho print for the house is considered essential for welcoming the new year.

Red River Delta

As the north's heartland and the cradle of northern Vietnamese culture, the Red River Delta has seen the rise and fall of emperors, dynasties, and a number of imperial capitals through the centuries. The Red River begins in China's Yunnan province. After coursing though northern Vietnam, the river merges with two tributaries near Hanoi and forms a fanlike delta that empties into the Gulf of Tonkin. What the Mekong Delta is to southern Vietnam, the Red River Delta is to the north. This area of rich alluvial plains is intensively farmed and densely populated. It is the north's main rice-producing zone, but it sometimes endures famines, when rice must be supplied from the south. Despite a system of canals and embankments, the Vietnamese have never been able to completely contain the Red River, particularly during monsoons.

The Red River Delta covers an area of 15,000 square kilometers and extends more than 200 kilometers inland from the coast. It is roughly delineated by a triangle formed by Viet Tri (northwest of Hanoi), Haiphong (east of Hanoi), and Ninh Binh (south of Hanoi). It covers the area bounded by Ha Tay, Hai Hung, Thai Binh, Nam Ha, and Ninh Binh provinces. You can make day trips or overnight sorties into the delta, if you are based in Hanoi. If traveling north from Vinh or Thanh Hoa, you can overnight in Ninh Binh. The top day trip from Hanoi is to either the Perfume Pagoda or Tam Coc Caves. Both offer similar karst scenery and boat rides, so you really should choose between them.

PAGODAS NEAR HANOI
Perfume Pagoda

Perfume Pagoda (Chua Huong) is a cave-shrine 60 kilometers southwest of Hanoi. The route features spectacular karst scenery, which really makes the trip worthwhile. Tens of thousands of visitors visit this site daily in peak pilgrimage season, usually March–April, during the spring festival. You can join an organized minibus tour from a traveler café in Hanoi or make your way out to the village of Ben Duc by hired car. At Ben Duc, two hours from Hanoi, hundreds of rowers clamor to transport you along the Swallow River to the Perfume Pagoda. The upstream boat trip takes one hour and is the only way to reach the pagoda. The open rowboats provide no shelter, so in summer take an umbrella and conical hat to avoid sunburn.

THE MARKET ECONOMY SHRINE

On peak days, the tiny shrine of **Den Ba Chua Kho** attracts up to 1,000 visitors. Nicknamed "the market economy shrine," it lies east of Hanoi in Ha Bac province. A government ban on superstitious practices has not prevented a flourishing trade at the shrine. Pilgrims once visited it only in the spring, but since the early 1990s the turnout has been year-round. Supplicants bring trays of offerings to a dozen different altars in the temple, filled with the smoke of joss sticks. Among the offerings are beer, cigarettes, fruit, flowers, paper gold ingots, and bundles of imitation American $100 bills.

The 11th-century shrine was built in honor of Ba Chua Kho, a queen involved in heroic battles against the Chinese during the Ly dynasty. It's believed the queen acknowledges the wishes of supplicants, wielding the power to multiply their symbolic offerings into affluence. Thus, wishes for material possessions such as real estate or a new motorcycle can be granted.

Unfortunately, the queen hails from the pre-French era and cannot read today's romanized Vietnamese script. So supplicants must rely on interpreters available on-site to translate their messages into Chinese characters, which the good queen can then read. Payment to cover the interpreter's service fee and a basic worship materials package makes this a very costly place to worship, but visitors don't seem to care; they're elated to reach the shrine in person. Another curious industry here is the hiring of porters to visit Den Ba Chua Kho by those physically unable to reach it—most likely because they're too busy making money elsewhere.

After the boat ride you face a one-hour hike on a rocky and sometimes slippery trail up the Mountain of Fragrant Traces, ending at a complex of Buddhist shrines thick with incense. The Perfume Pagoda itself is not impressive; it consists of a large cavern set into limestone cliffs. Inside, many of the stalactites and stalagmites are painted. Drops of water falling from stalactites are believed to possess healing powers. Legend has it that a Hindu bodhisattva transformed himself into Quan Am, Goddess of Compassion, in this cavern; an 18th-century statue of Quan Am carved from blue stone presides. Pilgrims burn paper offerings inside the pagoda to help their ancestors in the afterlife. They also consume lots of sodas—there's a big rubbish dump of empty cans inside the cavern.

The entry fee to the Perfume Pagoda, which includes a boat ride to get there, is a whopping $9 for foreigners, $1.40 for locals. If you join a tour from Hanoi, that entry price is usually included. Traveler cafés run tours for $18 a head.

Thay and Tay Phuong Pagodas

While spectacular boat rides enhance the trips to the Perfume Pagoda and the temples at Bich Dong, the itinerary taking in Thay and Tay Phuong pagodas wears a bit thin. Traveler cafés organizing day trips to this area throw in stops at Van Phuc, a silk-spinning village, and So, a noodle-making village. Thay Pagoda, 40 kilometers west of Hanoi in Sai Son, was built during the 11th century and includes a variety of enclosures with Buddhist figures. The pagoda is famed for a pavilion on stilts in a pond facing the pagoda. Water puppetry performances take place here at festival time, particularly in the third lunar month when pilgrims flock in. Eight kilometers away is Tay Phuong Pagoda, sited on a hilltop above the village of Thac Xa. Parts of the pagoda date to the 8th century, but most of the structure was built in the 18th century. Inside are 75 jackwood figures modeled on monks once associated with the pagoda.

NINH BINH AREA

Ninh Binh has become a major touring base in the north. Ninh Binh is a small town 95 kilometers south of Hanoi, reached by train (three hours), bus, or car (2.5 hours). Ninh Binh itself offers little to see but has enough hotels to make a base camp for visiting the spectacular karst landscapes nearby at Tam Coc

The North

NINH BINH AREA

To Cuc Phuong National Park

To Hanoi

Kenh Ga Village

1

To Nam Dinh and Haiphong

HOA LU TEMPLES

19

BAN LONG PAGODA

SEE "NINH BINH" MAP

THAIVI TEMPLE

To Phat Diem Church

Tam Coc Caves

1

BICH DONG TEMPLE

Van Lam

To Thanh Hoa

0   5 mi

0   5 km

© AVALON TRAVEL PUBLISHING, INC.

Caves, Bich Dong Temple, or Kenh Ga village. If you're coming from the south, Ninh Binh makes a great pit stop. If you're coming from the north, you can cover the area in a long day trip. A popular day-trip route is Hanoi to Ninh Binh to Hoa Lu Temples to Tam Coc Caves to Bich Dong Temple and back to Hanoi. A similar itinerary might run thus: 0730 depart Hanoi; 1000 reach Van Lam village to visit Tam Coc Caves; 1330 lunch; 1400 Bich Dong Temple; 1600 drive back to Hanoi; 1830 reach Hanoi. Another longer routing would be a two- or three-day trip from Hanoi by rented vehicle: Start in Hanoi, visit Tam Coc Caves and

Bich Dong Temple, stay overnight in Ninh Binh, carry on to Cuc Phuong National Park and/or Mai Chau, then drive back to Hanoi. You might also want to consider this triangle routing: Hanoi to Ninh Binh and back to Haiphong (the gateway to Cat Ba Island and Halong Bay). This makes an interesting double—karst scenery on land at Ninh Binh, and karst islets in the water at Halong Bay. Hanoi to Ninh Binh is about three hours' drive, while Ninh Binh to Haiphong is about five hours.

If you want to tackle the routes yourself and base out of Ninh Binh, you can rent a motor-cycle (or hire a moto driver) or a car. A car costs

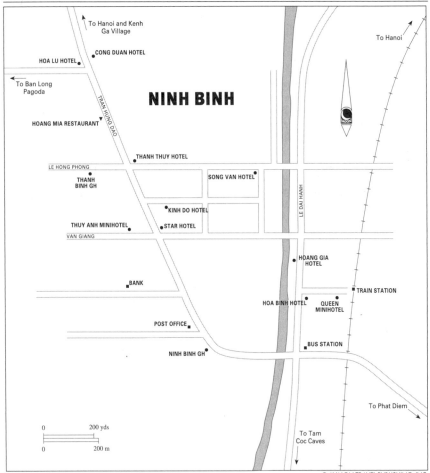

© AVALON TRAVEL PUBLISHING, INC.

$25–35 a day with driver, and a motorbike with driver is $7–10; a bicycle should be $1 a day. By bicycle it's only a five-kilometer ride to Tam Coc Caves from Ninh Binh, and the scenery is entrancing—something to savor at bicycle pace. You can rent bicycles from Star, Thanh Binh, or Thuy Anh hotels.

Accommodations and Food

There are at least a dozen hotels and guesthouses in Ninh Binh. On the railway station side of the river are **Hoang Gia, Queen mini** and **Hoa**

Binh hotels. Preferable to these are the guest-houses on the west side of the river. The **Star Hotel,** at 267 Tran Hung Dao, tel. 30/871522, fax 30/871200, has nine rooms for $8–15; the owner is very helpful with information, touring, and transport. The nearby **Thuy Anh mini,** at 55A Truong Han Sieu St., tel. 30/871602, fax 30/871200, offers seven rooms for $8/15/25 and hosts traveler services, including open-tour bus connections to Hanoi and Hué.

Thanh Binh GH, on Luong Van Tuy St., tel. 30/860072, is run by the superfriendly Nguyen family, who will provide meals; about 10 rooms here run $6–15 each. On the same street nearby are some hotels with taxi-girls; these include the **Sao Mai Hotel,** tel. 30/872190, with six rooms for $10–12. More pleasant is the family-run **Thanh Thuy GH,** 128 Le Hong Phong, tel. 30/871811, with six rooms for $5–9. Other places in Ninh Binh are either sterile, unwelcoming, or simply very strange. Among these are **Kinh Do Hotel,** 99 Phan Dinh Phung, tel. 30/873005, with 12 rooms for $20 each; **Ninh Binh Hotel,** 2 Tran Hung Dao, tel. 30/871337, with 10 rooms for $10 each; and the **Cong Doan Hotel,** at the north end of town. In the deluxe concrete nightmare category is the **Hoa Lu Hotel,** on Tran Hung Dao St., tel. 30/871217, fax 30/874126, with 115 rooms in several wings for $40–45 apiece. This hotel caters to group tours.

Most eating takes place in guesthouse or hotel restaurants, although there are some eateries strung out along Tran Hung Dao. You could try **Huong Mai Restaurant,** at 2 Tran Hung Dao St., serving Vietnamese and European fare.

Tam Coc Caves

Tam Coc is known as Halong Bay on land. In fact, in the French movie *Indochine,* the drifting junk that carries the star-crossed lovers through Halong Bay comes to rest at Tam Coc. The movie director splices footage from both locations and makes them appear as one; the lovers rest up in Bich Dong Temple. Tam Coc's karst sugarloaf mountains resemble the topography at Halong Bay—the big difference is that Tam Coc has rice paddies. The area supports duck farmers, stray goats on the karst hillsides, and electric fishermen (that is, they fish with pitchforks electrified by car batteries). You can take a similar dreamy boat ride through karst landscape near Ninh Binh. At the village of Van Lam you rent a tar-coated open rowboat for a two- to three-hour trip. Your rower will negotiate the boat through shallow rice paddies and under three splendid long caves. The rice paddies are surreally framed by giant karst outcrops and grottoes.

After gliding through the caves, you get off the boat and walk to a Chinese–style shrine called **Thien,** set in a high cave with views of the area. From here you continue to **Den Thai Vy,** a small 13th-century temple, and jump into the boat again to return to Van Lam.

To get to Tam Coc Caves, go south along Highway 1 from Ninh Binh for 3.5 kilometers. By the side of the road stands a sign for Ninh Binh Tourism—turn west there, cross a stone bridge, and drive along a dirt road for two kilometers to Van Lam village. There's a $3.50 entry fee for the village, which includes a boat ride—a three-hour circuit through the caves and rice paddies. There are no accommodations in Van Lam; food stalls provide a bit of nourishment. Traveler-café trips from Hanoi cost around $15 for the Tam Coc–Bich Dong trip, including entry fees and boat.

Be aware that Tam Coc has developed into a tourist trap, with vendors clamoring to sell you shirts and linen as soon as you set foot in the place. The rowers persistently try to squeeze you for "tips" (not a Vietnamese custom), coming up with lines such as "the rice harvest was poor" or "my baby is hungry" (if this approach fails, they might graduate to offering to exchange dollars to dong at an unfavorable rate). Establish a fixed price before you set out and stick by it to discourage this annoying and blatant coercion.

Bich Dong Temple

Three kilometers beyond Van Lam village lies Bich Dong, known for its small temple. There's a $2.50 entry fee to the area. Local children will act as guides, and they expect a donation. Bich Dong Temple is set into the base of a limestone peak. The upper temple, situated inside a cave, holds three blackened figures—a large stone Buddha in meditation posture, flanked by two protectors. From the upper temple you can climb to the top of a peak for splendid views over the entire area; watch out for the sharp limestone. There are two other small temples in the vicinity if you want to explore further: **Xuyen Thuy Dong,** reached by boat, and **Dong Tien Grotto,** a 500-meter walk from Bich Dong.

Hoa Lu

Site of an ancient royal capital, Hoa Lu is situated about 12 kilometers northwest of Ninh Binh. There are several ways of getting to Hoa Lu. If you're on a moto, you can connect via trails leading through rice paddies directly from Van Lam, via Thai Vy Temple, and the cave-temple of Ban Long Pagoda. Compared to Tam Coc or Bich Dong, there's not much to see at Hoa Lu. There are two-hour boat rides in the area, however, delving into the karst landscape for $2 a head. Guardians charge a $2.50 entry fee, which allows you to view a couple of temples restored in the mid-1990s. The main temple was dedicated to 10th-century Emperor Dinh Tien Hoang and rebuilt in the 17th century. Hoa Lu served as capital for 12 years under Hoang's reign and a further 29 years under the Le dynasty. There are half a dozen minor temples in the area. You can climb up Lang Ma Mountain to visit the tomb of the Dinh emperors, and the peak provides a panoramic view. You can see similar vistas from Bich Dong.

Kenh Ga Village

Entrancing karst scenery is the setting for an island village called Kenh Ga, about 20 kilometers to the northwest of Ninh Binh, off the route leading to Cuc Phuong National Park. You need a moto or car to reach the Kenh Ga area. Well worth the trip. Kenh Ga village is quite large; as well as fishing, activities in the area include quarrying sand and limestone. You can rent fishing boats in the area to make a circuit of the island, which could take 2–5 hours. If heading for Cuc Phuong, this might make a good detour on the route.

Nam Dinh

A slew of (yawn) royal temples and pagodas pack the area around Nam Dinh, a filthy industrial town 28 kilometers northeast of Ninh Binh. The temples and pagodas date from the 12th–14th centuries, with later additions and renovations.

Phat Diem Cathedral

About 28 kilometers southeast of Ninh Binh stands Phat Diem Cathedral, the center of Catholicism in north Vietnam. The stone structure is built in unique Sino-Vietnamese style with a pagoda-like belfry. The vaulted ceiling is supported by a series of massive wood columns; lining the nave are wooden carvings, and at the front is an altar sculpted from a single block of granite. The cathedral was founded in 1891 by a Vietnamese priest. Nearby is Thuan Dao Church, built in 1926 in an odd neo-Roman design, and a small seminary in Phuc Nac.

In the Southwest

Southwest of Hanoi you'll find several areas ideal for short hikes or longer treks—in the minority areas around Hoa Binh and Mai Chau, or the national park at Cuc Phuong. Visiting these places requires expeditionary planning—you need your own transportation, preferably a 4WD vehicle, and a guide. Although you can reach these places on day trips from Hanoi, a trip two days or longer is preferable. Longer itineraries might include Hanoi to Hoa Binh to Mai Chau to Cuc Phuong to Hanoi, or Hanoi to Ninh Binh to Tam Coc Caves to Bich Dong to Cuc Phuong to Mai Chau to Hoa Binh and back to Hanoi. If you plan to travel to the Tonkinese Alps, you can arrange to spend extra time in Mai Chau en route.

Hoa Binh

Site of a huge Russian-built dam on the Black River (Song Da), Hoa Binh, 75 kilometers southwest of Hanoi, is the largest hydroelectric plant in the country, with a capacity of 1,900 megawatts. Constructing the dam and reservoir involved flooding the valley and displacing an estimated 58,000 people, so the area has lost much of its attraction. However, Hoa Binh serves some tour companies as a base for jungle treks and visits to nearby Muong and Tai villages. The four-story **Khach San Song Da** hotel in Hoa Binh was built for Russian engineers. **Khach San Hoa Binh** displays more imagination, with Tai–style bungalows for $20.

M Mai Chau

Mai Chau lies in a pretty valley with a patchwork quilt of rice paddies, farms, and longhouses. It's 60 kilometers southwest of Hoa Binh, or about 135 kilometers from Hanoi. In the spring, Mai Chau displays a riot of color with blooming flowers and peach blossoms. Using Mai Chau as a base, you can traipse through rice paddies to reach Tai and Hmong villages. The Tais live in raised wooden longhouses in the shape of tortoise shells, with sloping roofs made from palm or sugarcane leaves. Inside are polished bamboo-slat floors with woven mats, a fireplace for cooking, and a handloom; buffalo, chickens, and pigs live under the house. There are usually fishponds in the area.

Hmong villages are harder to find. They're much poorer and composed of simple huts with earthen floors. The women wear elaborately patterned tops and skirts; the full outfit can take three years to embroider. The men smoke opium.

Opposite the bus station in Mai Chau is the central covered market, visited by minority groups in the area. The big day is Sunday. Moto drivers with Russian Minsks hang around outside the market and can take you to outlying villages. About 1.5 kilometers south of the market, the two-story **Mai Chau Guesthouse** offers nine comfortable rooms for $13 double with bath. A kilometer or so southwest of this guesthouse is a Tai village where longhouses are adapted for use by visitors. There are a dozen longhouses here accepting foreign guests on a regular basis, at a fixed charge of $3 a head per night. A minibus can park right next to the longhouse; you are supplied with a simple fold-up mattress and mosquito net. The longhouse family arranges for food to be served, local style, on the floor. Staying in a longhouse gives you an opportunity to see how the locals live, but these places are rather commercialized, with a tourist circus selling weavings down "longhouse row."

For an extra charge, Tai women will stage a dance soiree; the repertoire includes the delicate butterfly dance (performed with fans) and the striking bamboo dance (daintily dodging bamboo sticks that are smashed together); the performance is followed by a large pot of Tai homebrew rice wine, complete with superlong bamboo straws.

Using the village as a base camp, you can trek out through rice paddy trails to outlying villages in the area. On these walks you can attune yourself to the rhythms of rural life—watching locals harvesting rice, carrying baskets of goods around, or thatching a new house. One or two days should suffice, but longer treks of up to four days are possible. A guide may be needed.

To reach Mai Chau, take a bus from Hanoi's Kim Ma bus station to Hoa Binh, then change for Mai Chau. A jeep or minibus takes four or five hours to get to Mai Chau from Hanoi. If coming by hired vehicle, you can stop at Man Duc, a town close to Mai Chau with great karst scenery. Traveler cafés in Hanoi typically charge $15–30 per person for a two-day minibus trip to Mai Chau with an overnight stay in a village. Especen organizes a two-day Hanoi–Mai Chau–Hoa Binh–Hanoi loop in a Russian car for $97, or $145 in a Land Cruiser.

Cuc Phuong National Park

Cuc Phuong is the best of a rum bunch of "national parks" in the north. The park, roughly 11 kilometers wide and 25 kilometers long, was created in 1962—the first area in Vietnam set aside as a national park. It covers an area of 25,000 hectares, but for the moment it is a national park in name only. There are six Muong villages in the park: Villagers farm and raise cattle on park lands and hunt. Deforestation in the surrounding area steadily encroaches on parkland, and large amounts of brushwood disappear from the park daily. Rangers, poorly paid, turn a blind eye to poaching, or to weekend visitors carrying off orchids. Cuc Phuong is low-key: Those expecting spectacular scenery with animals everywhere will be sorely disappointed.

However, Cuc Phuong contains plenty of attractions for botanists. The park supports a wide variety of flora species and patches of primeval forest, including 50-meter-tall *Cinamomum, Parashorea,* and *Sandicorum* trees. You can find ancient trees with thick clusters of roots, and parasitic plants and ligneous creepers. Some tree species have been introduced from Myanmar (Burma), India, and Borneo. Clusters of orchids grow near cave entrances, where the moisture conditions and light are ideal. Varieties include coral, vanilla, snow-white, and butterfly orchids.

Larger mammals inhabit the park, including panthers and bears, but hunting has severely depleted their numbers. The park supports many varieties of monkeys and gibbons. The world's last Delacour's langurs live here—an estimated 20 are left in the park, and 100 in northern Vietnam. Other unusual mammals include a striped fox and a squirrel that glides between trees. A rare species of fish called *niec hang* lives in cave streams. There are more than 120 species of birds: Birding on the road at the park entrance is good, particularly around the botanical garden. There are many varieties of beetles; in April and May arrive swarms of butterflies. At night, millions of cicadas create a deafening din, and millions of fireflies flicker on and off, making the place look like something out of *The Hobbit.*

Lying in a limestone area, Cuc Phuong includes numerous caves. At Nguoi Xua (Cave of Early Man), two ancient tombs have been discovered, along with Neolithic remains and evidence of stone implements. There have been similar finds at Trang Khuyet (Crescent Moon), Thanh Minh, and Con Moong Caves. Hang Dan Cave is known for its bat population.

Endangered Primate Rescue Center

Vietnam is home to some quite rare primates, including Delacour's langur and the black-shanked Douc langur. These are very difficult to see in the wild—although you might be able to see Delacour's langur on the limestone cliffs of nearby Van Long Nature Reserve (reed boats operated by locals will take you there for possible sightings, usually around sunset). The same langur is found in Phu Luong Nature Reserve, which lies to the northwest of Cuc Phuong. Because Delacour's langur is found only in this region of northern Vietnam, it is a target for the wildlife trade. Close to Cuc Phuong Park headquarters is the Endangered Primate Rescue Center, which allows visitors to see at close range a number of rare species rescued from poachers. An interpretation center nearby provides information about the park.

Hiking

The best hike in the park is a six-kilometer trail starting at B-Block in the Park Center and looping back round to A-block. It's a cleared trail with steps in rough spots, slippery after rain. You hike through old-growth forest with long vines wrapped around strangled trees. Quite bizarre is *Eutada tonkinensis ganep,* a thick vine that shoots all over the place. You pass a *Parashorea assimica* tree, and halfway round the trail a large, double *Terminalia miriocarpa* tree stands 45 meters tall. Along the trail you also pass a small waterfall and a cave. Other notable plants include huge fern trees and the

CUC PHUONG NATIONAL PARK

To Mai Chau

DOUBLE TREE
(TERMINALIA MIRIOCARPA)

PARK CENTER

VIEWPOINT

TRANG KHUYET CAVE

To Gia Vien and
Ninh Binh

NGUOI XUA CAVE

CON MOONG CAVE

XUI XUAN CAVE

PARK ENTRY GATE
LODGES AND RESTAURANT
RESEARCH CENTER

0   5 mi

0   5 km

© AVALON TRAVEL PUBLISHING, INC.

san, or tent tree, anchored in shallow soil with trunks that resemble flying buttresses.

A longer hike proceeds 15 kilometers northwest from the Park Center to a Muong village, where you stay overnight. The next day you can hike four kilometers out to the roadway at the northwest side of the park, where an arranged van takes you on to Mai Chau, back to Cuc Phuong's lodges, or to Ninh Binh.

Accommodations and Food

Upon entering the park you pass two gates. At the second gate you pay the $5 entry fee. Near the second gate is a complex of bungalows, restaurant, research center, and meeting hall; 100 workers live in this area. Tourist accommodations include a concrete double room with bath for $35; a self-contained jungle lodge for $40; and an old temple structure with rooms for $10–20, no bath. There's a new wing with 17 rooms at the gate. Electricity comes from generators. The restaurant charges $2 per person for meals. At the Park Center, 20 kilometers into the park, is a large conference hall and two accommodation blocks, mainly intended for Vietnamese. Foreigners may stay if they can negotiate a deal. A-Block has 14 beds in seven rooms, for $10 a person, no bathrooms, one shared toilet. B-Block is for Vietnamese students and has 60 beds at $3 each plus camping on front lawn; a tent for five people costs foreigners $20. Vietnamese students arrive in buses to camp and cook out. Though no restaurant operates in the vicinity, you can arrange meals with sufficient notice.

Getting There

The park lies 140 kilometers from Hanoi, or 45 kilometers from Ninh Binh. It sits astride the junction of Hoa Binh, Ninh Binh, and Thanh Hoa provinces. The only way to get to Cuc Phuong at present is by rented vehicle. The drive in from Ninh Binh via Gia Vien is along a rough dirt road and takes about two hours. You can base yourself in Ninh Binh for a day trip to the park or stay overnight at Cuc Phuong. Especen in Hanoi charges $95 for a car and driver to Cuc Phuong and back, the cost split between three passengers for the two-day trip. Queen Café charges $20–35 for a two-day tour, transportation only, based on 2–10 passengers. Park entry fee is $5 for each foreigner; the price includes a guide. Try to time your visit for the October–January dry winter season, when there are no mosquitoes or leeches. The weather can be chilly at this time, as Cuc Phuong lies at 300 meters; it's generally a few degrees cooler than Hanoi. May–September is the rainy season, and June–August is very hot and humid, with leeches and mosquitoes.

North by Northeast

Historically, the border zone to the far north and northeast has been contested by the Vietnamese and Chinese. The dense and hilly area is pierced by several alluvial plains—Cao Bang and Lang Son being two of them. In the 1940s the Vietminh ousted the French from Cao Bang and used the area as their base; Ho Chi Minh took refuge in a grotto here. Major battles were fought with the French in the early 1950s around Lang Son and Cao Bang. In 1979 the Chinese launched a 17-day war with the Vietnamese, destroying buildings in many border towns in the area. Since the normalization of relations in 1991, trade between China and Vietnam once more thrives, as does smuggling.

Close to the Chinese border live minority groups, originally descended from China. A million Nung and Tay people live in the northeast, scattered in mountain valleys. Other groups include the Zao and the Hmong. Ethnic groups are found in larger concentrations around Cao Bang and Ha Giang.

The zone north by northeast of Hanoi hasn't sparked a lot of tourist interest yet, nor has it produced much in the way of hotels. It just doesn't seem to have the right kind of attractions or creature comforts to attract tourists.

TAM DAO HILL RESORT

Tam Dao is a scruffy resort 75 kilometers north of Hanoi. Set up in 1907 by the French as an escape from the heat of the Red River Delta, the resort lies at a 900-meter elevation and is 10 degrees cooler than the delta in the summer and actually cold in the winter. The forest has reclaimed the ruins of summer homes the French torched in 1954 rather than hand them over to the advancing Vietminh.

Some Hanoi traveler cafés organize day trips to the area, or you could get there via rented motorcycle. Local transportation falls short; there's a bus from Hanoi's Kim Ma bus station to Vinh Yen that takes 2.5 hours. Once you reach Vinh Yen, it's another 20 kilometers to Tam Dao, so you have to hitch on whatever comes past, usually a motorcycle. At the bottom of the hill at a guard post a man will ask you for $3—that's $1 for entry and $2 for "insurance." Other motorcyclists have been charged a "motorcycle fee," so at least the rip-off is customized. You may wish to negotiate.

There's not much left of the old French hill station. Most of the old buildings have been replaced with concrete-block structures, such as the Trade Union Hotel (which has double rooms for $10). There are some fancier places to stay: Mela Hotel and Cay Thong Hotel. Very strange things appear on the menus in these hotels—such as bamboo rat, porcupine, and bear. What to do in Tam Dao? Well, apart from eating endangered species, you can swim in a refreshing outdoor pool with mountain views. Or you can take a short walk to Silver Falls; nice if you can ignore the trash everywhere. Or you can hike around the forest. Close by is Tam Dao Forest Preserve, with an array of camellias, orchids, birds, and butterflies.

DONGVAN AND MEOVAC

In a rented vehicle you can reach the town of Hagiang, 300 km north of Hanoi, the same day, as the road is sealed. Hagiang is the gateway to the incredible Dongvan Plateau, an area studded with weird karst limestone formations and some of the best roadside scenery in all Vietnam. But there is a hitch. You must get permission to enter this area. You have to get that permission from police in Hagiang. It costs $10 per person, and route details and timing must be specified. Officials in Hagiang are

liable to play games, insisting that you take a guide along for an exorbitant fee (and the guide doesn't speak English!). Resist these blatant extortion methods. It's not clear why this area requires a permit—officials mumble something about its proximity to the Chinese border, but there are no such restrictions in place in other parts of the north.

If you can get through all that, then you should be able to drive to Dongvan to the east of Hagiang in a day. Take your time along here: There are stunning mountain views, overlooking karst peaks and rice terracing. Dongvan is a small town of wooden and concrete structures—crowded on Sundays when the weekly market is held. The Sunday market attracts minority groups from the area, including Green Hmong.

The best is yet to come: Along the 22-kilometer stretch between Dongvan and Meovac, the road winds along a cliff-face overlooking a canyon. The views are divine. This would be an excellent road for biking—and since it is paved, you could even use a road bike. Meovac has several hotels that accept foreigners. Beyond Meovac is the town of Khau Vai—but you may have a lot of trouble reaching this destination, as permission is not routinely granted to go there. Roads are few around here—you basically have to loop back to Hagiang to exit the area, though there are alternate roads (some quite rough—they would require a 4WD vehicle).

BA BE LAKES

Ba Be Lakes (Ho Ba Be), 230 kilometers north of Hanoi, was created as a forest reserve and tourist center in 1978. The name means "Three Seas," a reference to the three lakes within its confines. Two are minor lakes. The main lake, seven kilometers long, and between 200 meters and one kilometer wide, is surrounded by vertical rock walls to which many kinds of creepers cling, and a wild forest where many species of birds abound. Travelers find the lakes a bit boring. From Ba Be Town you can continue by land or boat along the Nang River for about

© MICHAEL BUCKLEY

rice fields among karst peaks in the Dongvan area

three kilometers to **Puong Cave,** Ba Be's major attraction. The cave opens into large chambers adorned with oddly shaped stalactites and stalagmites. You can reach **Dau Dang Falls** by foot or boat. When visiting the lakes, foreigners pay a $6 National Park entrance fee, and about $3 an hour when touring in a private boat that seats 10 people.

By hired car, it takes about eight hours to drive to Ba Be Lakes from Hanoi along Route 3 via Thai Nguyen and Bac Can. By bus you can go to Bac Can, transfer for another ride to Cho Ra, and then take a rough 16-kilometer moto ride into Ba Be Lakes. Construction of a guesthouse and restaurants was in progress on the shores of the lake. Several kilometers from the lake is an inexpensive guesthouse. You can stay in Cho Ra Town, which is 16 kilometers from the lakes, at Ba Be Guesthouse, across from the Sunday market area—rooms here are $12.

Traveler cafés in Hanoi offer the Ba Be Lakes trip on an irregular basis. A three-day trip costs $45–60 based on 6–12 people and includes admission fee, guide, accommodations, and food.

CAO BANG AREA

Farther northeast of Ba Be Lakes is a little-traveled zone of hilltribe villages toward the Chinese border. A 4WD vehicle is recommended to visit this area. The base for visits is the town of Cao Bang. Cao Bang's markets are busy and colorful, with lots of Chinese goods. At the main market, some minority people sell goods near the bridge. In the town of Cao Bang, a recommended minihotel is **Duc Chung GH,** on Be Van Road—very clean, rooms from $18. **Giao Te GH,** tel. 26/852803, and **Bang Giang GH,** tel. 26/853431, are both larger establishments with basic rooms—not as comfortable as Duc Chung GH but cheaper.

There are some fascinating 4WD trips you can make up to Chinese border zones from Cao Bang. About 10 kilometers west of Cao Bang, you can turn north on a road to Nuoc Hai and Ha Quang to visit **Uncle Ho's Cave,** which is sited almost right on the Chinese border. The

road condition is reasonable, but still suitable only for a 4WD vehicle. The scenery on this route is beautiful, with small villages backed by limestone peaks jutting from rice paddies and cornfields.

Another trip from Cao Bang heads northeast: You can try to reach **Ban Gioc Falls** on the Chinese border. However, this is a sensitive military zone and you may be turned back. If you succeed in reaching the falls, as a foreigner you must pay an entrance fee of a few dollars. The route goes through Ma Phuc, Quang Uyen, and Trung Khanh. Road conditions are very poor, and the route is best attempted in a 4WD vehicle. Close to Ma Phuc are Nung minority villages—the Nung are curious and welcoming to visitors. There is a large market in Trung Khanh, mostly visited by Tay people. This is another beautiful area of karst limestone scenery.

If making a round-trip from Hanoi to Ba Be Lakes and Cao Bang, you can return by a different route—drive from Cao Bang to Lang Son. However, this road is in poor condition and there's nothing of note in the way of scenery.

LANG SON AND THE CHINESE BORDER

Lang Son, 155 kilometers northeast of Hanoi, is the closest town to the Chinese border crossing at Huu Nghi Quan (Friendship Gate). The town is uninspiring, much of it newly built after Chinese attacks in early 1979 inflicted considerable damage. At that time 85,000 Chinese troops streamed across 26 points along the border with Vietnam. Within 10 days, they'd taken every provincial capital except for Lang Son, which became the scene of intense house-to-house fighting. Chinese troops captured the town six days later, and several hours after announcing their success, withdrew to China.

For the next 10 years, nothing happened at the border apart from a few skirmishes. The residents of Lang Son lived in the ruins of their city under strips of canvas and plastic, without running water or other facilities. With the normalization of relations in 1991, the town faced a new invasion—an avalanche of cheap Chinese goods. An estimated 70 percent of the trade in Chinese goods involves smuggling.

Lang Son to Hong Kong

To cross the Chinese border at Lang Son you must have a Chinese visa. Arrange to get that in Hanoi: Allow several days for processing (anything faster will cost more). To reach Lang Son, take a minibus near Hanoi Opera House, or a bus from Hanoi's Gia Lam bus station (six hours). A day trip is preferable so you can view the scenery. Several trains depart daily in the direction of Lang Son, taking 6–8 hours for the journey.

From Lang Son, hire a jeep or moto for the 20-kilometer ride to the border at Dong Dang, the terminus of Highway 1. Dong Dang features a bustling market with a sea of Chinese goods—cosmetics, toys, electric fans, Chinese beer. A black market in money also flourishes, with exchanges transacted in dong, dollars, and Chinese renminbi. About 600 meters of no-man's-land lies between border checkpoints. You cross on foot through the marble Huu Nghi Quan, or Friendship Gate (Youyi Guan in Chinese), to the Chinese side, where Vietnamese exports of coal, rubber, and coconut oil are stacked. For $5 you can take a share-taxi to Pingxiang, the first major town on the Chinese side, where you can catch a train or bus to Nanning (five hours). You'll find places to stay in both Pingxiang and Nanning. The journey from Nanning to Canton takes 24 hours by bus; from Canton, you can board an overnight boat to Hong Kong for about $25. The entire cost overland by rail, bus, and boat from Hanoi to Hong Kong should be under $50.

Hong Kong to Lang Son

Coming in the other direction, exiting China, you must have a valid Vietnamese visa. In Beijing you can obtain a Vietnamese visa in one week, though most travelers pick up a Vietnamese visa in Hong Kong. From Hong Kong you can travel overland via Nanning to the border crossing.

Gulf of Tonkin

The Gulf of Tonkin was once the haunt of Vietnamese and Chinese pirates. At Halong Bay the romance of old Vietnam still lingers, with bizarre karst islets randomly scattered and the odd red-sailed junk clipping across the waters. This timeless waterscape seems a long way off in the dreary port of Haiphong, the key access point to the area by boat, but Halong Bay is only a short hop away. Halong Bay is accessible principally from the seaside resort town of Bai Chay, which you can reach by land from Hanoi via Haiphong, or by ferry from Haiphong. The Haiphong ferry lands at Hong Gai, a mining town and fishing port five kilometers east of Bai Chay. Travelers consider Halong Bay one of the highlights of their trip in the north—seafaring in these waters is definitely an experience. You can laze about on deck, and opportunities abound for swimming, caving, and diving, not to mention enjoying fresh seafood.

HAIPHONG

Haiphong has the distinction of being the first place French warships landed in the Gulf of Tonkin in 1872, and the last place they left in May of 1955. In the late 1880s, after the harbor was widened, the port was developed by the French as the major conduit for extracting wealth from Tonkin, and Haiphong soon mushroomed into the second-largest city in the north. Visiting in 1918, Reverend James Walsh wrote in his *Observations in the Orient* that Haiphong had

> *the appearance of a neat, prosperous, French city with wide streets, attractive public buildings, comfortable-looking houses, well-equipped hotels, a large theater, and about every conceivable convenience for its French residents, of whom, in normal times there are 5,000.*

TOURING HALONG BAY

Plan a minimum two-day trip to Halong Bay. It's 105 kilometers from Hanoi to Haiphong, another 60 kilometers to Bai Chay, and a final five to Hong Gai. By sea, Cat Ba Island is 30 kilometers east of Haiphong. Allow five days to cover the Haiphong–Bai Chay–Halong Bay–Cat Ba Island route. A week's itinerary might run: Hanoi–Bai Chay on the first day; spend two days in Bai Chay exploring Halong Bay; transfer by boat to Cat Ba; spend 1–2 days in Cat Ba; leave for Haiphong and transfer to Hanoi. Build in extra time for delays that are due to poor transport connections. You could cut a day by sightseeing across Halong Bay en route to Cat Ba Island. Or make it a two-day jaunt: Sightsee in Halong, overnight on a boat in Halong, and continue to Cat Ba the next day. Mid-November–mid-March Halong Bay is colder and foggier, with increased rain and drizzle. Fog and rain can obscure visibility and defeat the purpose of the visit. At this time of year you need raingear, and blankets if sleeping overnight on boats.

Tour Options

Tour agencies and traveler cafés in Hanoi all offer one- to three-day tours of Halong Bay—typically $18–30 a person for a two-day trip, based on 5–20 people. This includes minibus and boat transport, one night's accommodations, and food. Queen Café organizes a two-day tour with an overnight on the boat and occasionally arranges a Halong–Cat Ba combination tour. It's easy to band together with other travelers in Bai Chay to rent fishing boats. You could also put together your own small group and set off in a car or minibus. A Hanoi agency might charge $120 for a three-day package, not including a boat, which breaks down to $25–30 per 100 kilometers of road travel, plus $15 for the driver, and $20 for a guide. TOSERCO charges $80–110 per person for a two-day trip to Halong, based on 3–9 people. The agency books more expensive hotels, and you hope the boats are superior for that price.

For those with money to burn, Vietnam Air Service Company (VASCO) offers a two-day overflight of Halong Bay in a Squirrel helicopter with a French pilot. The flight begins from Hanoi's Gia Lam Airport, continues to Haiphong and Cat Ba, then wings over Halong Bay to Hong Gai. After a night in Hong Gai, return the next day to Gia Lam Airport. Cost is $2,000 for 1–4 passengers. Contact VASCO at the Metropole Hotel, Hanoi, tel. 4/8266919, ext. 8015.

The North

From Haiphong, rice, rubber, coal, and mineral resources were shipped back to France. The Japanese, arriving in 1940, used the same infrastructure to divert the flow of goods to Japan.

In 1946, in a dispute about who should collect customs duties, the French clashed with the Vietminh and bombarded Haiphong, leading to an outbreak of warfare that continued for the next eight years. Between 1966 and 1972, Haiphong was repeatedly attacked by U.S. air and naval forces. In 1972 Haiphong harbor was mined in an attempt to reduce the flow of Russian military supplies, though the mines were cleared the following year as part of the Paris Accords. After 1975 Haiphong developed as an industrial town, with the establishment of brick, glass, cement, and textile plants, lime kilns, and shipyards.

Like Saigon and Hanoi, Haiphong functions as an independent municipality. The population of greater Haiphong, covering an area of 1,515 square kilometers, is estimated at 1.7 million; the city proper consists of three districts and supports a population of perhaps 700,000.

Haiphong remains an industrial port town. Adjectives that spring to mind are dreary, gray, run-down, ugly, sleepy, and sluggish. Still, you don't have to fight over hotel rooms. Not many foreigners bother to look around Haiphong, so they receive better treatment here than in Hanoi.

Sights

Colonial Haiphong: Traces of Haiphong's colonial splendor remain along Dien Bien

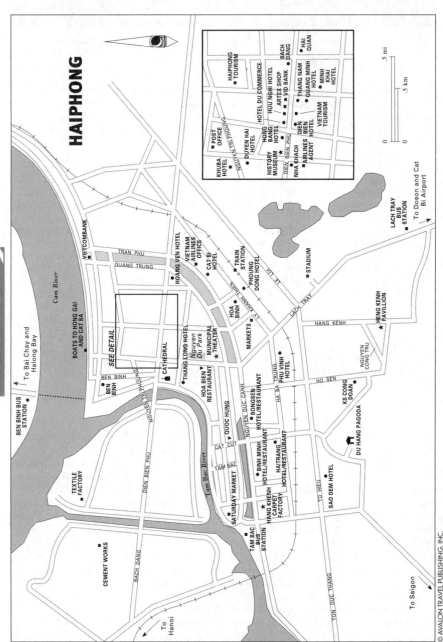

HAIPHONG

Cam River

To Bai Chay and Halong Bay

BEN BINH BUS STATION

BOATS TO HONG GAI AND CAT BA

SEE DETAIL

BEN BINH

BEN BINH

WE'COMBANK

TRAN PHU

QUANG TRUNG

HOANG VEN HOTEL

VIETNAM AIRLINES OFFICE

CAT BI HOTEL

TRAIN STATION

PHUONG DONG HOTEL

STADIUM

HOA BINH

LY KANH THIEN

LE LOI

THANG LONG HOTEL

Nguyen Du Park

MUNICIPAL THEATER

MARKETS

CATHEDRAL

HOA BIEN RESTAURANT

QUOC HUNG

NGUYEN DUC CANH

BONGSEN HOTEL/RESTAURANT

PHU VINH HOTEL

HA BA TRUNG

HANG KENH

HENG KENH PAVILLION

NGUYEN CONG TRU

HO SEN

KS CONG DOAN

DU HANG PAGODA

LACH TRAY

LACH TRAY BUS STATION

To Doson and Cat Bi Airport

NGUYEN TRI PHUONG

DIEN BIEN PHU

Tam Bac River

CAT CUT

TAM BAC

BINH MINH HOTEL/RESTAURANT

HAITRANG HOTEL/RESTAURANT

SATURDAY MARKET

HANG KENH CARPET FACTORY

TAM BAC BUS STATION

TEXTILE FACTORY

CEMENT WORKS

BACH DANG

SAO DEM HOTEL

TO HIEU

TON DUC THANG

To Saigon

To Hanoi

DETAIL

POST OFFICE

KHUBA HOTEL

DUYEN HAI HOTEL

HONG BANG HOTEL

HISTORY MUSEUM

HAIPHONG TOURISM

HOTEL DU COMMERCE

HUU NGHI HOTEL

ARTEX SHOP

VID BANK

BACH DANG

HAI QUAN

THANG NAM

QUANG MINH HOTEL

MINH KHAI HOTEL

NHA KHACH

DIEN BIEN

VIETNAM TOURISM

AIRLINES AGENT

NGUYEN TRI PHUONG

DIEN BIEN PHU

0   .5 mi
0   .5 km

© AVALON TRAVEL PUBLISHING, INC.

The North

TOURING HAIPHONG

Haiphong Tourism office displays pictures of Thailand's Pattaya Beach and Krabi under its glass tabletops, and if you ask about Haiphong, you'll receive a glowing report about the beach resort of Doson, 22 kilometers away. There are only a few places to see in Haiphong. A couple of hours in a cyclo will get you round most of them, or simply walk. If you're going to take a cyclo, why not go in style? Several hotels—the Bach Dang in particular—have luxury cyclos with padded red seats, plush armrests, front suspension, fringed sunroofs, even headlights. All that's lacking is a karaoke machine up front. The imperialist-model cyclo will take two passengers, albeit slim ones, and costs about $1.20 an hour, not much more than the regular ratty cyclos with wooden boards for seats that bang you around from teakettle to breakfast time. The suspension-model supercyclos, incidentally, are used for VIPs or for family members on marriage negotiation visits. Haiphong's streets are exceedingly quiet—the only things that seem to move along them regularly are cyclos. A suggested cyclo route starts on Dien Bien Phu Street to the History Museum and the cathedral; then carry on to the Municipal Theater and Hang Kenh Carpet Factory, and visit Du Hang Pagoda. A good place to finish is the street market near Haiphong railway station.

Phu Street, formerly known as Avenue Paul Bert and Avenue Marechal Joffre. Imposing here are the History Museum, the GPO, the Hotel du Commerce, and the cathedral. If your timing is right (Thursday, Saturday, and Sunday 1400–1600), the History Museum may be open. South of the cathedral stands the Municipal Theater, built in 1904 with materials imported from France. It has a bland exterior but a magnificent interior with seating for 400, opera galleries, and solid wood fixtures and banisters. Another architectural relic is the railway station with its vintage freight trains, including a coal-fired Dutch engine from the 1930s, all stoked up and ready to go.

Du Hang Pagoda: Two kilometers south of town, at 121 Hang Kenh St., this pagoda was built in the 17th century and renovated many times since. The pagoda, which houses half a dozen resident monks, is Vietnamese in style and contains brilliant woodwork, bronze statues, and a bonsai collection. An array of statues highlight a circular lotus pond in the peaceful gardens, an excellent place to reduce your blood pressure.

Hang Kenh Pavilion: This communal house at 53 Nguyen Cong Tru St. was once part of the village called Kenh; the village was long ago swallowed by Haiphong. The small traditional house features intricate woodwork and sculpture and is dedicated to 10th-century national hero Ngo Quyen. You can safely skip this one if your time is short.

The Port: You'll no doubt see a good part of scummy Haiphong Harbor en route to Hong Gai or Cat Ba. But if you have some extra time, take a walk down by the docks, or hire a boat and cruise around. In the harbor chug old wooden fishing boats, barges, and heavy ships, while crane arms perch like giant praying mantises over container ships.

Accommodations

Most tourist services cluster along Dien Bien Phu Street, including half a dozen hotels and a few souvenir shops. Scattered around the train station and southwest side of Haiphong are a few other hotels and some private minihotels. Hotels do not fall into convenient price-range categories, since a top-end hotel may also offer cheaper rooms.

Near the Ferry: Ben Binh Hotel, also known as Nha Khach Thanh Pho Haiphong, 2 Ben Binh, tel. 31/842260, has nine cavernous rooms—$10–15 downstairs, and $25 upstairs. The place is favored by government officials and army personnel. Entry is via a café opposite Ben Binh ferry dock.

Around Dien Bien Phu Street (DBP): Nha Khach, 107 DBP, tel. 31/842292, is actually on a side street south of DBP, near the History Museum. Rooms are $5 room, no bath. Also on a side street off DBP is **Minh Khai Trade**

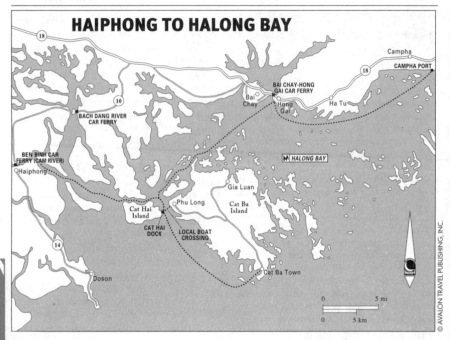

HAIPHONG TO HALONG BAY

© AVALON TRAVEL PUBLISHING, INC.

Hotel, 20 Minh Khai St., tel. 31/842443, with 20 rooms for $10 double in two opposing wings. South of the cathedral and close to Tam Bac River is **Thang Long Hotel,** 55 Tran Quang Khai St., tel. 31/841170—a privately run mini-hotel with 16 rooms for $10–12, a good deal with a/c, IDD phone, and hot water.

Duyen Hai Hotel, at 5 Nguyen Tri Phuong north of Dien Bien Phu Street, tel. 31/842134, fax 31/841140, has 35 rooms in the $12–18–30 range, most of them $30. **Thang Nam Hotel,** 55 DBP, tel. 31/842820, fax 31/841019, offers 19 rooms for $15–20, and you can bargain rates down in the off-season; there are some tennis courts attached to the hotel. **Dien Bien Hotel,** 67 DBP, tel. 31/842573, fax 31/842977, has 20 rooms—singles and doubles for $20, and some fancier models with fridge for $30.

Hotel du Commerce, 62 DBP, tel. 31/842790, fax 31/842560, features 35 large rooms for $18–25–35–40. Singles cost $5 less than doubles. Great atmosphere, good restaurant; this French classic is run by Vietnam

Tourism. Next door is the **Huu Nghi Hotel,** 60 DBP, tel. 31/823310, fax 31/823245, an 11-story high-rise with creature comforts including satellite TV. The 126 rooms here go for $50–85, suites for $155–300. **Quang Minh Hotel,** just off DBP at 20 Minh Khai St., tel. 31/823405, fax 31/823407, is a snappy eight-story high-rise with 30 rooms for $35–50. **Bach Dang,** 42 DBP, tel. 31/842444, has 21 rooms for $12–24–38 double. **Hong Bang Hotel,** 64 DBP, tel. 31/842352, fax 31/847510, has 28 rooms, mostly around $35, and some suites for $45. Rooms for drivers are $10–15. **Navy Guesthouse,** 27C DBP, tel. 31/823713, fax 31/842278, has 80 rooms for $30–55 and some suites for $100; this hotel is clean and comfortable. North of DBP is **Khuba Hotel** (Military Zone GH), at 2 Hoang Van Thu St., tel. 31/841341, with 45 rooms for $25–30 each.

Railway Station Area: Just to the left of the station is **Phuong Dong Hotel** (Orient), with 17 rooms for $13–15 with TV and hot water—great if you arrive late by train or want to leave early. It's run by Hanoi Railway Tourist Service Company. **KS Hoa Binh,** 104 Ly Khanh Thien St., tel. 31/846907, fax 31/846907, has 60 rooms in the $10–15–25 range. **Hoang Yen Hotel,** 7 Tran Hung Dao, tel. 31/842383, fax 31/842205, is an old French mansion with 20 rooms for $25–40–60–70. **Cat Bi Hotel,** 30 Tran Phu, tel. 31/846306, fax 31/845181, has 20 rooms with classy atmosphere for $20–40. **Phu Vinh Hotel,** 27 Cat Dai, Hai Bai Trung St., tel. 31/848381, fax 31/855579, is a good minihotel with 33 rooms for $15–35; the more expensive rooms include a shower and TV.

Tam Bac Area: Toward Sat Market you'll find some private minihotels. **Bongsen** (Lotus), 15 Nguyen Duc Canh St., tel. 31/846019, has doubles for $10 and its own restaurant. **Binh Minh Hotel,** 60 Nguyen Duc Canh St., tel. 31/845428, has 10 rooms for $15 double and a good restaurant, too. **Haitrang Hotel,** 40–42 Cat Cut St., tel. 31/845467, fax 31/845016, has 15 rooms for $18 s, or $20 d. A bit farther south is a private minihotel, **Sao Dem,** at 295 To Hieu St., tel. 31/844366, fax 31/840613, with eight rooms for $25 each. On the southern fringe of Haiphong is **KS Dulich Cong Doan** (Trade Union GH), 8 Ho Sen, tel. 31/846793; this is a large government-run place with 30 rooms for $5–14, but it's beset with plumbing problems.

Food

Street markets are good for snacks. Two lively areas are along the street in front of the train station and around Sat Market, with more than 1,000 shops housed in a six-story concrete structure built in 1992. Side streets nearby hold soup places, stalls, and local restaurants.

The dining room at the Hotel du Commerce serves crab soup, steamed fish, steamed snails with ginger, and grilled eel for reasonable prices. A good seafood place is **Hoa Bien Restaurant,** which is on Hoang Van Thu Street opposite Nguyen Du Park. A few private restaurants in the Tam Bac vicinity stand out, catering to Vietnamese wedding parties and to foreigners who can afford the bills. Asian and European food are served with a list of specialties. **Binh Minh Restaurant,** upstairs at 60

Nguyen Duc Canh St., tel. 31/845428, features an exotic menu with grilled pangolin, "brandy mixup pangolin's blood," grilled chopped snake, chicken stewed in Chinese herbs, and more conventional seafood dishes. **Quoc Hung,** at 50 Quang Trung, tel. 31/847639, near Binh Minh, is another private restaurant serving crayfish, squid, pigeon, eel, and beef. **Bongsen Hotel,** at 15 Nguyen Duc Canh St., tel. 31/846019, offers an extensive menu. **Haitrang Hotel,** 40 Cat Cut St., tel. 31/845016, has a fourth-floor rooftop restaurant.

Shopping

Artex Shop, on Dien Bien Phu Street, run by Haiphong Art and Handicraft Export Company, sells a range of mother-of-pearl inlay furniture, rattanware, ceramics, wood carvings, lacquerware, embroidery, and ready-made clothing. A bit farther east, at 48 Dien Bien Phu, **My Nghe Artshop** sells more of the same. Hotel lobby gift shops feature these items as well.

A major shopping thoroughfare is **Quang Trung Street,** which runs east of Sat Market along the banks of Tam Bac Canal. This is the busiest trading zone of Haiphong for clothing, hats, and housewares. At the west end of the enclosed canal here is Sat Market, and the east end of the canal is a large flower market.

At 128 Nguyen Duc Canh St. is **Hang Kenh Carpet Factory** (Tapis Hang Kenh) with a showroom and retail store at the front. Raw New Zealand wool is spun, dyed, woven, and cut by hand in this factory, which employs 500 workers. Using vertical looms, a team of weavers can take three months to produce a larger carpet by hand. Carpets range 1–100 square meters in size and sell for $60–100 per square meter; lower prices for commercial quantities. Designs vary from traditional Chinese and Vietnamese to modern patterns; carpets can also be woven to order. There are four carpet factories in Haiphong, employing 2,000 workers total. The first factory was established in 1929 by the French, using Chinese designs and mostly exporting to the French market. Today, Haiphong carpets are exported to Canada, France, Japan, Sweden, Australia, Italy, and Saudi Arabia.

Information and Services

Haiphong Tourism, at 15 Le Dai Hanh, tel. 31/842989, can arrange guides and car rentals. **Vietnam Tourism,** at 57 Dien Bien Phu, tel. 31/842432, fax 31/842674, arranges tours, cars, ticketing, and visa formalities. There is a 1995 tourist sheet map of Haiphong published by Haiphong Publishing House, but this may be hard to find. The Hotel du Commerce features a large map with old French street names painted on the wall, and it sometimes sells the same in printed form with corresponding Vietnamese street names. **Vietcombank,** 11 Hoang Dieu St., deals with foreign exchange; another place is **VID Bank** at 56 Dien Bien Phu St.; otherwise, try major hotels.

Getting There and Away

By Air: Cat Bi Airport lies five kilometers southeast of Haiphong, about a 10-minute drive from downtown. Flights from Haiphong to Saigon depart every Tuesday and Saturday, and other flights service Danang. There are several Vietnam Airlines ticket agents in Haiphong; the main office is near Cat Bi Hotel. Hanoi–based VASCO offers daily Squirrel Helicopter service between Hanoi's Gia Lam Airport and Haiphong's Cat Bi Airport. The helihop takes 25 minutes, costs $250 one-way per passenger. Maximum number of passengers is five. Inquire through VASCO's counter at the Metropole Hotel in Hanoi, tel. 4/8266919, ext. 8015. VASCO can also arrange custom flights over Halong Bay.

By Train: Four trains leave daily from Hanoi to Haiphong, taking 2–2.5 hours for the trip. Train HP1 departs Hanoi main station at 0550 and arrives Haiphong at 0755. Train LP3 departs Hanoi 1000, LP5 departs 1450, and LP7 departs 1745—all leaving from Ga Long Bien, the station near Long Bien Bridge. Express trains cost $4, foreigner price, for soft seat. You should be able to line up a train to Haiphong to connect with a Cat Ba ferry if you're headed that way. For example, take the 1000 train from Hanoi, arriving in Haiphong at 1230 and giving you an hour to connect with the 1330 ferry to Cat Ba Town. In the reverse

direction, traveling from Haiphong to Hanoi, train HP2 departs Haiphong at 1825, while LP4 departs 0620, LP6 departs 1030, and LP8 departs 1415. Minibuses are cheaper but not necessarily faster—traffic jams routinely clog the Haiphong–Hanoi road. You also get more legroom on the train.

By Boat: Ben Binh Pier on the waterfront can be reached by cyclo for $.50 from Haiphong railway station. The pier is divided into different sections. On the west end is a cross-river ferry, which cars and buses use for the route to Bai Chay. East of the ferry stretch two piers with boats to Cat Hai, Cat Ba, Hong Gai, Campha, and Dan Tien (for Traco Beach). Travelers congregate at a café opposite the Cat Ba ferry to while away the time before departure.

Boats leave from Haiphong for Hong Gai at 0630, 1100, 1330, and 1600. There may be another boat at 0900. The ride takes around 2.5 hours and costs $3. The ferry, a nasty rusting hulk, is loaded to the gunwales with passengers, squawking chickens, bananas, and sacks of produce. You're best off sitting on the roof. The vessel passes heavy shipping in Haiphong Harbor before threading its way through the choppy waters of the northern reaches of Halong Bay, so on a clear day you get an hour of limestone scenery into the bargain.

About 15 meters away from the Hong Gai ferry is the pier for ferries to Cat Hai and Cat Ba Islands, with departures usually at 0630 and 1330. There are two methods of getting to Cat Ba town. The best way is to take the direct ferry from Haiphong to Cang Cat Ba (Cat Ba Town port), costing $5 and taking about four hours. If the direct ferry is not available, you might consider taking a smaller ferry to Cat Hai Island. A ferry leaves 1230 from Haiphong, taking 2.5 hours for the trip at a cost of $2. From Cat Hai, you transfer to a small craft for the 15-minute run to Phu Long on Cat Ba Island, where you pick up a waiting bus to Cat Ba town—$2 for a one-hour ride—or take a moto. Total travel time from Haiphong is around four hours. There is an on-again, off-again high-speed boat from Haiphong to Cat Ba, cutting travel time to less than two hours. This boat, if still in service, is more likely to operate on weekends. The trip takes an hour and costs around $7 one-way.

By Road: Minibuses usually take about 2.5 hours for the run from Hanoi to Haiphong. There is a minibus depot south of the Opera House in Hanoi; cost is around $3 for the run. Buses from Hanoi's Gia Lam station on the east side of Long Bien Railway Bridge cost $2 to Haiphong.

In the other direction, Haiphong's Ben Xe Tam Bac (Tam Bac bus station), close to the Sat Market Building, dispatches buses and minibuses to Hanoi, Ninh Binh, Hadong, Thanh Hoa, Vinh, Ha Giang, Binh Minh, and other points. Check out the posted prices and expect to bargain: The minibus outfits will try and charge as much for the minibus as for the train. Ben Xe Ben Binh, on the north side of the Cam River, runs buses and minibuses to Bai Chay, Hong Gai, Campha, and Cai Rong. Ben Xe Lach Tray, to the southeast side of town, runs buses to Doson Beach.

Getting Around

There are a few Simson motos near the boat docks, but the most common form of transport is cyclos. Rent a cyclo for $.90 an hour, or $1.10 per hour for a fancy one from Bach Dang Hotel. A rented bicycle would be the ideal way to get around Haiphong, but rentals are next to impossible to come by, though this may change—try asking hotel staff. Arrange car rentals through hotels for destinations such as Doson or Bai Chay.

DOSON BEACH RESORT

Doson was established as an exclusive beach resort in 1886 by the French. The beach at Doson faces eastward, and half a dozen large hotels operated by Haiphong Tourism line the beachfront, north to south. Foreigner prices average $20–35 a room; hotels offer lower rates in the off-season (November 15–March 15) when the cold weather prohibits swimming and the place is deserted. The beaches are nothing special here—they verge on being scummy. Ho-

tels include Hoa Phuong, Van Thong, Hang Doi, and Hai Au. The Van Thong is a well-equipped 60-room hotel with satellite TV, a/c, and tennis court. At the southern tip of Doson is a French villa-hotel, the Van Hoa, with twin turrets. Built in 1938, it features commanding views and an above-average restaurant. Doson is also home to Vietnam's first and only casino, Hong Kong–invested and exclusively for foreigners—so you'll fit right in here.

Doson lies 22 kilometers south of Haiphong. To get there, take one of the hourly buses leaving from the Lach Tray bus station in southeast Haiphong for $.50. Or hire a car and driver for $20 for the day and split expenses with others.

CAT BA ISLAND

Cat Ba Island is the largest island in the Cat Ba Archipelago, consisting of more than 350 limestone outcrops adjacent to Halong Bay. Lying roughly midway between Haiphong and Hong Gai, the island falls under the administration of Haiphong City, while Halong Bay falls under the administration of Quang Ninh province. With an area of 356 square kilometers, Cat Ba encompasses forested zones, coastal mangrove and freshwater swamps, beaches, caves, and waterfalls. In 1986, the northeast side of the island was designated a national park, including a protected marine zone. Cat Ba Island supports a population of more than 20,000, most of whom live off fishing or farming in the south, in and around Cat Ba Town. To confuse matters, "Cat Ba" may refer to Cat Ba Island (Dao Cat Ba), Cat Ba Town (Pho Cat Ba), Cat Ba Town Harbor (Cang Cat Ba), or indeed any part of the island. To the west of Cat Ba Island is Cat Hai Dock on Cat Hai Island. Make sure you know where your boat is headed!

Cat Ba Town

Until the end of the 19th century, Cat Ba was home to Chinese and Vietnamese pirates, and the French maintained a customs station here. Both enterprises seem to linger—on landing or departure you may be hit with a $.20 "port tax." Experiences on Cat Ba vary. Some

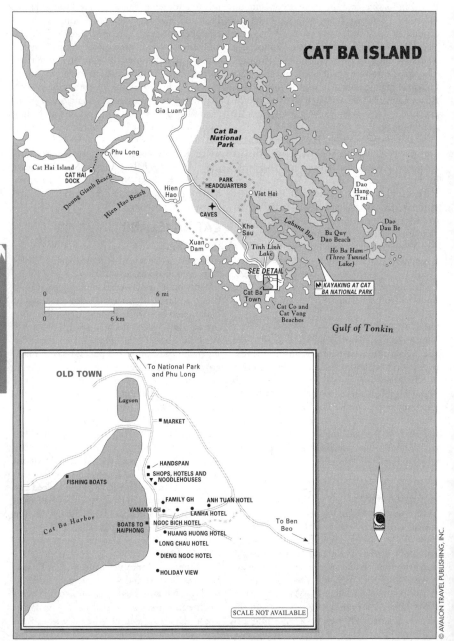

CAT BA ISLAND

Gia Luan

Cat Ba National Park

Phu Long

Cat Hai Island
CAT HAI DOCK

Doung Gianh Beach

Hien Hao

Hien Hao Beach

PARK HEADQUARTERS

Viet Hai

Dao Hang Trai

CAVES

Khe Sau

Lahuna Bay

Ba Quy Dao Beach

Dao Dau Be

Xuan Dam

Tinh Linh Lake

Ho Ba Ham (Three Tunnel Lake)

SEE DETAIL

Cat Ba Town

Cat Co and Cat Vang Beaches

KAYAKING AT CAT BA NATIONAL PARK

Gulf of Tonkin

0   6 mi
0   6 km

OLD TOWN

To National Park and Phu Long

Lagoon

MARKET

HANDSPAN

SHOPS, HOTELS AND NOODLEHOUSES

FISHING BOATS

FAMILY GH   ANH TUAN HOTEL

VANANH GH   LANHA HOTEL

BOATS TO HAIPHONG   NGOC BICH HOTEL

HUANG HUONG HOTEL

To Ben Beo

Cat Ba Harbor

LONG CHAU HOTEL

DIENG NGOC HOTEL

HOLIDAY VIEW

MOON

SCALE NOT AVAILABLE

© AVALON TRAVEL PUBLISHING, INC.

The North

travelers have found the islanders friendly; others have had rocks thrown at them and midnight visits from police checking documents. Nevertheless, on the Hong Gai/Bai Chay/Cat Ba triangle, it is Cat Ba that elicits the most interest. The town is small and ancient, easy to walk around, with clusters of fishing boats and inspiring sunsets across the harbor. A definite Chinese flavor remains to Cat Ba, particularly strong in the decrepit buildings on the northwest side. Chinese merchants and fisherfolk originally settled the town, but a mass exodus ensued in 1979 when hostilities broke out between the Vietnamese and Chinese. Then the tide turned somewhat as refugees were repatriated from Hong Kong holding camps. These returnees, having learned English at the Hong Kong camps, are involved with tourism on Cat Ba.

The town curves around a crescent-shaped bay, with an esplanade following the foreshore. You can check out the catch of the day in the early morning, see cuttlefish dried over hot coals, or stroll around the old town. You can also pay a boatman for a few hours' harbor touring, or just rent a boat yourself and row around.

It's a short hike from Cat Ba Town southeast over a trail and steps to sandy Cat Co Beach; from Cat Co you can hike farther along to rockier Cat Vang Beach.

Farther Afield

To explore the island further, you can rent a bicycle or a Russian motorcycle, or simply walk out into villages. You can easily reach Trung Trang and the national park by rented motorcycle (either self-drive or moto). Around the island you'll find other beaches and sandy coves, some accessible by boat. At the north end toward Phu Long are Duong Gianh and Hien Hao beaches.

Accommodations and Food

Cat Ba Town has seen a flurry of guesthouse and hotel construction—the place is still in progress. Prices are negotiable, generally higher in summer and lower in winter. Guesthouses and larger

hotels are strung along the wide boulevard close to the harbor and along the road leading east of town. Preferable are hotels with airy balconies, sea views, and a rooftop terrace. **Sunset Hotel,** tel. 31/888370, offers 10 rooms for $6–8 winter and $8–12 summer; **Huang Huong GH,** tel. 31/888274, has 12 rooms for $8–10; **Family GH,** tel. 31/888231, offers eight rooms for $7 each; **Van Anh GH,** tel. 31/888201, offers 14 rooms for $12–15. Other hotels include **Lanha Hotel, Ngoc Bich Hotel,** and **Anh Tuan Hotel.** Prices are $10 or so and the places are clean.

Restaurants along the esplanade serve palatable food, particularly seafood. In the market to the northwest end of town you can buy bread and fruit.

Cat Ba National Park

Cat Ba National Park (Vuon Quoc Gia Cat Ba), near Trung Trang, lies about 16 kilometers from Cat Ba Town and 12 kilometers from Phu Long. The park covers an area of about 200 square kilometers, of which two-thirds is a forested zone and one-third a marine zone. Park headquarters are at the small settlement of Trung Trang.

The park consists mainly of inaccessible terrain; you have to fight your way through thickets and up steep gullies to get anywhere. Many side trails branch off main trails in the park—mostly new forest, not old growth. On longer hikes you may see birds, including kingfishers and warblers, and perhaps a tree-dwelling possum with a long bushy tail. The park is home to rare wild white-headed langurs, which live on steep coastal cliffs. Hanoi's Biological Institute has identified more than 35 species of birds, 28 species of mammal (including wild boar, macaques, and deer), 20 reptile species, and more than 600 plant species within the park. The marine reserve supports dolphins, seals, and hawksbill turtles.

The designation "national park" is a grotesque misnomer when you consider that farming, logging, and fishing occur within park boundaries—as does poaching. When questioned about an animal trap close to a trail, one ranger responded that he had set it himself.

The park brochure describes different marine species found within the park, and then goes on to say, "most of them fetch high prices at market places." It seems that Vietnamese authorities just slap a national park label on stray bits of land to attract tourism.

Trung Trang Caves: Two kilometers south of Trung Trang park headquarters a set of caves open into the side of a limestone cliff. The entrances to the caves are visible from the road, about 50 meters up the cliff. You need a flashlight to explore the limestone caves. They are more than 300 meters long, and you can easily get lost without a guide—guides are available in Cat Ba Town.

There are a few rooms available at Trung Trang park headquarters for $4 a night; a hotel was under construction near the park. Otherwise, make a day trip from Cat Ba Town. To reach the national park, set out early by bus or moto or rented motorcycle from Cat Ba Town to Phu Long, and get off in Trung Trang. It would be a good idea to hire a guide—and to bring a flashlight. You can get off the bus two kilometers south of Trung Trang to visit Trung Trang limestone caves first. Securing a ride to Cat Ba Town in the afternoon after exploring the national park could present a problem. If there's no passing bus, the options include flagging down a passing moto or staying the night at the park and finding transportation the next morning on a bus returning from Phu Long.

Kayaking in Cat Ba National Park

As well as claiming most of Cat Ba Island, Cat Ba National Park covers a huge marine area. This part borders Halong Bay but is separate from it. In the marine zone of Cat Ba National Park lie some of the best karst spots of all. And the finest way to see them is in a kayak. There are lots of sea arches, caves, and grottoes that are accessible only by small boat or kayak—this depends on tides as well. To find these places you need a knowledgeable guide. Several well-known spots are Ba Quy Dao Beach and Ho Ba Ham (Three Tunnel Lake). You can reach the latter by kayak—you pass through several long tunnels that emerge into bright lagoons. It is preferable to have your kayaks loaded onto a "mothership" (a modified junk) so you can get to the key sites faster and save energy. Kayaks and guides come with an arranged tour package, which can be a day trip from Cat Ba or even something organized from Hanoi.

To go farther afield, you can club together with other travelers and rent a fishing boat from Cat Ba Harbor to view some of the beautiful karst islets in the direction of Halong Bay. Some islets offer fine sand beaches and sandy coves. Or charter a fishing boat from Cat Ba for an all-day ride north into Bai Chay, stopping at key points along the route. Suggested itinerary: Sail from Cat Ba Harbor to Ba Quy Dao (Three Peach Beach), then on to the grottoes of Me Cung, Tam Cung, Trinh Nu, Dong Tien, Sung Sot, and Bo Nau before anchoring at Bai Chay.

Getting There and Away

Getting there and away is a puzzle that also involves getting around and across Cat Ba Island. Be aware that once you're on the island transportation is either meager or nonexistent. You can catch a moto or an occasional bus—or walk. Approximate distances on the island are: Phu Long to Cat Ba Town, 28 kilometers (two morning buses, one-hour ride, cost $2 a head—or hire a moto); Phu Long to Trung Trang, 12 kilometers; Trung Trang to Cat Ba Town, 16 kilometers; Gia Luan to Trung Trang, six kilometers (motos only).

Cat Ba to Haiphong Ferries: Cat Ba Island lies 30 kilometers east of Haiphong. To get from Cat Ba back to Haiphong, catch the boat at the pier in Cat Ba Town Harbor. There are departures daily—at 0615 and 1300. Depending on the size of the ferry, it should take four hours or less to reach Haiphong.

Bai Chay to Cat Ba Town: No direct ferry links Bai Chay or Hong Gai to Cat Ba Town; you have to go via Cat Hai Island. You could take a boat from Hong Gai to Cat Hai and then transfer to Phu Long by small craft and continue by bus or moto to Cat Ba Town. Or you could transfer at Cat Hai to another vessel heading to Cang Cat Ba (Cat Ba Harbor), which takes 2.5 hours and costs $3.

While the ferries are awkward, renting a vessel for the trip is easier. The problem here is the possibility of rough seas on the open waters between Cat Ba and Halong Bay; a larger vessel is preferable in bad weather conditions. It's fairly simple to band together with other travelers to rent a vessel in Cat Ba Harbor for the trip to Bai Chay, setting off in the early morning, making touring stops at Halong Bay—visiting islands and grottoes—and arriving in Bai Chay by nightfall. Or you can take two days, touring Halong the first day, spending a night on the water in the midsection of Halong Bay, and continuing to Bai Chay the next day. From the reverse direction, from Bai Chay, quotes on boats range $40–100; a reasonable figure would be $60 split between 15 passengers. This also covers gas for the boat's return trip. Because the boat trip is not officially sanctioned, the captain may have to cover a $10 "fine" when docking at Cang Cat Ba. Negotiate carefully for a boat from Bai Chay. Captains might take a shortcut to the north end of Cat Ba Island and dump you at Gia Luan, where you'll be left to the mercy of stray moto drivers for a ride into Cat Ba Town.

HALONG BAY

With 3,000 limestone and dolomite islets sprinkled over an area of 1,500 square kilometers, Halong Bay offers a wonderland of karst topography. In recognition of this, in 1994 Halong was designated a UNESCO World Heritage Site. Legend has it that when the Vietnamese were under attack long ago, a dragon came to their aid, splitting mountains to impede the progress of the enemy. The limestone topography was created by the lash of the dragon's tail as it thundered down from the mountains to the sea; consequently, "Vinh Halong"—Halong Bay—means "Bay of the Descending Dragon." In geological terms, the mythical monster at work here is wind and water, weathering the porous limestone in the course of a few million years. This process created the bizarre limestone cathedrals, colonized by stunted and twisted vegetation. The romantic setting of rugged island peaks and bays dotted with sailing junks has inspired a whole genre of Vietnamese painting.

Depending on which kind of beer you drink, the islets resemble animals or other shapes. Some have been christened Head of Buffalo, Neck of Horse, Fighting Cock Rock, Elephant, Crocodile Rock, or Duck Island, while others

The North

CLIMBING THE KARST AT HALONG

Apart from sea kayakers and cavers, Halong Bay could attract another breed of sports fanatic: climbers. In December 1996, former world-champion climber Lynn Hill and fellow American climbers Paul Piana, Scott Milton, and Todd Skinner rented a fishing boat with crew to explore the pinnacles of Halong Bay. For some climbs, a basket-boat was launched from the fishing boat to carry Lynn Hill and climbing gear to the base of a sheer limestone wall, where she would start her climb. The American climbers spent a month exploring the bay, tackling several dozen more difficult routes on karst towers and overhanging stalactites.

Halong Bay is a maze of soaring karst limestone towers—composed of the same rock that has made Thailand's Krabi area the hottest climbing destination in Asia. Krabi boasts 25 separate climbing areas and more than 250 bolted routes (with names such as Primal Scream and Violence is Golden). But herein lies considerable contention: Some allege that the climbers are destroying the limestone and disfiguring the natural beauty of the area. As yet, there is nothing like this at Halong Bay; it's pristine climbing territory.

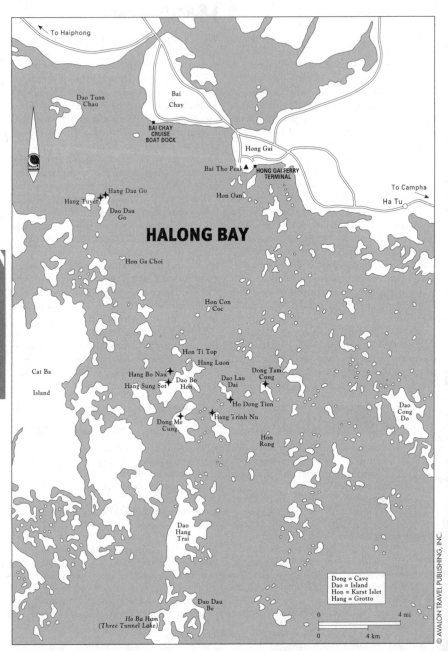

To Haiphong

Dao Tuan
Chau

Bai
Chay

BAI CHAY
CRUISE
BOAT DOCK

Hong Gai

Bai Tho Peak

HONG GAI FERRY
TERMINAL

To Campha

Ha Tu

Hang Dau Go

Hang Tuyet

Dao Dau
Go

Hon Oan

HALONG BAY

Hon Ga Choi

Hon Con
Coc

Cat Ba

Island

Hon Ti Top

Hang Luon

Hang Bo Nau

Hang Sung Sot

Dao Bo
Hon

Dao Lao
Dai

Dong Tam
Cung

Ho Dong Tien

Dong Me
Cung

Hang Trinh Nu

Hon Rong

Dao Cong
Do

Dao Hang
Trai

Dong = Cave
Dao = Island
Hon = Karst Islet
Hang = Grotto

0   4 mi

0   4 km

Dao Dau
Be

Ho Ba Ham
(Three Tunnel Lake)

© AVALON TRAVEL PUBLISHING, INC.

The North

are called Black Cloud Island, Teapot Island, or Riceball Peak. You can indulge in the fine sport of naming the features yourself, as the French did in their time. The fisherfolk of Halong navigate by these landmarks and can reel off every spot by name—Hon Ga Choi (Fighting Cock Rock), Hon Con Coc (Toad Island), Hon Rong (Dragon), Hon Rua (Tortoise), Hon Dua (Buddha Praying Island). To follow Vietnamese names, *hon* means karst peak or islet, *dao* means larger island, *hang* means grotto, and *dong* means karst cave.

Halong Bay allows you to see its geology from the inside—from grottoes with stalactites and stalagmites. This is a spelunker's paradise, with some very deep caves. Grottoes are prime places for shrines in Asia; Vietnamese and Asian visitors as well as locals pay their respects at Dau Go and Trinh Nu grottoes, among others. On a boat tour, you mainly view these karst grottoes. Otherwise, you relax on board, sunbathing, taking in the views, snapping off photos of the islands, eating seafood, or gazing at the sails of a junk heading off into the sunset. Sheltered sandy coves on the islands offer good swimming in summer. The beaches themselves are not the fine-sand variety, more often graveled or pebbly, or with sharp shells. Halong Bay holds great potential for snorkeling, diving, and kayaking. Bring your own equipment; rental possibilities are scarce.

SeaCanoe, which is based in Phuket, Thailand, has mounted some exploratory trips to Halong using inflatable kayaks. SeaCanoe offers four-day trips as well as custom journeys of up to several weeks on the water. Trips include sea kayaking instruction. Four-day packages cost $700 per person, starting and finishing in Hanoi. Tours are escorted by a wooden junk; you either sleep on the junk or at beach campsites. Mountain Travel Sobek in El Cerrito, California, United States, conducts 14-day kayak tours in the Halong Bay area.

Chartering a Boat

You can hire cruise boats for exploring Halong Bay in the mainland towns of Bai Chay or Hong Gai. Or you can charter a fishing vessel from Cat Ba Harbor to tour the far south of Halong Bay, though fewer boats offer this service here.

Rental boats anchor around the pier near the post office in Bai Chay or near the carferry crossing at the eastern end of town. These boats will motor into Hong Gai if needed. You negotiate directly with the captain. Available boats vary from classy yachts and modified junks to simple fishing boats. The most common rental craft is a converted 11-meter diesel fishing boat, which can hold up to 30 passengers. These roomy vessels have a covered deck, so you can sit under cover, on the roof, or on the open back deck. There should be a small galley and toilet facility on board.

Highly photogenic for daytrips are modified fishing junks with red canvas sails added (they rely on the motor, not the sails). **Quang Ninh Tourism,** tel. 33/846274, operating out

The North

JUNK SAILS

Fishermen at Halong mount fan-shaped Chinese junk sails on their boats, the same sort of sails once deployed by pirates in these waters. Junks have been used for centuries by the Chinese, Japanese, and Javanese for fishing and transportation, and often as living quarters; a junk commonly includes a deck, high masts, and several cotton sails.

Halong is one of the last places where junk sails are still handmade by families of sailmakers. Coarse cotton panels are sewn together with silk thread—every seam sewn by hand. To discourage rot and mildew, the completed sail is dipped in a liquid that comes from a beetroot-like member of the yam family. The sail is dipped and dried three or four times—a process that gives it its dark red-tan color.

The sails are braced flat by bamboo strips or battens. The bamboo must be treated for a quite different problem—bamboo parasites can literally shred the wood while at sea. Bamboo may be treated with Japanese lilac leaves, pounded into a paste with lime and seawater. Lacquering can also render bamboo less susceptible to borers.

of Halong Hotel in Bai Chay, can arrange for junks and rental yachts. Reconditioned junks work out to about $25 an hour, or $250 for the full 10-hour day. Boats vary in size, holding 8, 15, or 20 passengers.

There are a number of larger junks for hire in Bai Chay. The **Hong Ngoc Boat Group,** an outfit based in Bai Chay, commands more than 30 of these vessels, all going under the name Huong Hai. Its office is in Bai Chay, tel. 33/845042, www.halongtravels.com. Up to 10 of these vessels have been fitted out with hot showers and gourmet dining facilities—these boats rack up high bills. You can arrange to have kayaks brought aboard; they are launched from the mother ship for exploring. Groups book these vessels through an outfit called **Trails of Indochina,** in Hanoi, tel. 4/9715999, toi@fmail.vnn.vn.

Being on a vessel with sleeping cabins allows you to go for multiday trips—and take in a sunset on the water, a canopy of stars at night, and a Halong Bay sunrise. The captain can navigate at night because fisherfolk are active then, and they use lights to attract fish. Sleeping onboard leaves the way open for private island-hopping: If you want to explore Halong for two or three days, this is the way to do it. However, there are only a few spots in Halong Bay where tourist boats are allowed to park at night, so they tend to gather in larger numbers at these places, which can be disturbing (and noisy). Some groups arrange to camp out on beaches.

If you can spare the time and money, spend two full days exploring Halong. Day trips involve a full 10 hours on the water, starting at dawn. Charter cost depends on number of passengers, the season, the time, the distance, the route, position of the moon and stars, what the captain had for breakfast, and a few hundred other variables, but it usually all boils down to $4–5 an hour for the entire boat in winter, or $5–9 an hour in summer. It's cheaper to sail weekdays than on weekends. Sailboats cost more—$15 an hour and up. A two-engine boat that can hold up to 20 people should cost about $60 a day for 10 hours. To sleep overnight, if this appears possible, add $5 to the cost. So if you charter a boat for two full days and sleep onboard one night, you're paying for 20 hours and adding $5, which may total $65 in winter.

Food costs extra. Some boats charge an extra $4 per person if a cooked meal is supplied. Indicate whether you want the captain to arrange for meals. Find out if the boat has cooking facilities; most motorboats include rudimentary cooking facilities on board and an ice chest for drinks. You can buy bread, bananas, and other fresh food at the markets in Bai Chay before boarding. Take along bottled water. Bring along a bucket of seafood from the markets and ask the crew to cook it for you. You can also buy fresh fish, crabs, and prawns off fisherfolk en route—prices are high—and have it cooked on board.

Helitouring

Every Saturday a combination helicopter and boat tour is mounted to Halong Bay, organized through Hanoi's Metropole Hotel. The cost is $195 a person round-trip, with 25 people maximum. Departure is 0800 and return is 1500, just in time for high tea at the Metropole. The helicopter sweeps across Halong Bay for about 20 minutes, landing at the helipad near Giap's Villa in Bai Chay. Passengers then transfer to a vessel for a tour of Halong, with onboard seafood lunch. They are ferried back to the helicopter for the return trip. Custom helicopter tours from Hanoi can be arranged at any time.

Supplies

Apart from food and bottled water, you should take along a swimsuit in summer, and sunglasses and hat to ward off the fierce midday sun. Colder temperatures and drizzles predominate November 15–March 15; you'll need cold and foul weather gear. Take along garbage bags to pack your trash out; boat crew routinely heave bottles, cans, and plastic bags overboard. Help stop the practice before Halong Bay becomes a trash heap and the marine ecosystem breaks down permanently.

For grotto exploring you need a sturdy pair

of hiking shoes, long pants, and a good flashlight. Bicycle gloves will protect your hands from sharp limestone as you clamber up karst formations. Be careful: Sudden slips and falls in grottoes can result in injury. Take along a small medical kit to share among travelers to deal with cuts and scratches from sharp shells, coral, or limestone.

Hazards

A number of Westerners—myself included—have underestimated the extent of the karst grottoes. They ended up panicking as sunset approached and they hadn't the foggiest idea how to get out of the labyrinth and back to the boat, or indeed in which direction they left the boat. Moral: Take along a Vietnamese guide if the cave looks deep.

In the water, sharks will not trouble you, but watch out for pirates. Pirates used to hide out in Halong Bay, and it seems a few still do. Travelers have reported thefts from boats, so be wary of sampan-dwellers who may board and take off with valuables, both at night and in broad daylight. These same boat people make a practice of ripping up what little coral remains around Halong Bay and selling it to tourists—don't encourage them by buying any. Other travelers have reported petty theft by crew members, though generally this is not a problem.

Getting Around

As a point of reference, it helps to have a map with islands identified in Vietnamese. Quang Ninh Tourism publishes several decent maps of the whole coastline between Cat Ba and Campha. These also mark possible boat routes.

Don't let the captain control the itinerary; his idea of what's interesting may not match yours. To conserve gasoline, some captains will tell you a place takes two hours to get to and then motor very slowly, though the site may be only an hour away. A captain may dump you for hours at one site or spend hours eating lunch. Avoid Hang Dau Go Cave, a favorite with captains because it's close to Bai Chay, and it can consume several hours of your time as there are two grottoes there. Head for the Bo

Hon Island group first, and hit Dau Go when returning to Bai Chay. Get out your sextant, shoulder the parrot, hoist the mainsail—it's up to you to give some direction and keep the boat moving. If you've had enough of a cave, tell the captain to move on.

Approximate sailing times for an eight-hour trip might run thus: From Bai Chay about 60–90 minutes on the water to Bo Nau Grotto; from here you could easily spend 2.5 hours exploring the grottoes around Dao Bo Hon, and make a lunch stop; then 60 minutes back north to Dau Go and Tuyet grottos; and a final 40 minutes from there into Bai Chay. There are many variations for boat itineraries. You could skip Dau Go altogether, go straight out to Bo Hon Island, view that area, and then return to Bai Chay via the islands and port of Hong Gai.

Dau Go Island

On the north side of this island, about 40 minutes out from Bai Chay, are two deep grottoes—Hang Dau Go and Hang Tuyet. **Hang Tuyet** (Snow Cave) is also known as Hang Thien Cung (Celestial Palace). As a fairly recent discovery, it has thus far escaped the plague of graffiti and garbage. The large cave has a steep entryway. Be careful in here; you'll need a strong flashlight. Sparkling stalactites hang throughout the cave, glittering like diamonds.

Nearby **Hang Dau Go** (Hiding the Timber Cave) is the largest grotto in the Halong area. The first French tourists who clambered ashore in the late 19th century christened it Grotte des Merveilles. Its three large chambers contain numerous stalactites and stalagmites in the shapes of birds and animals. One chamber holds a freshwater pool. The grotto especially appeals to Chinese tourists, who love to take photos here and engrave their names on the walls.

Halong Bay has been the setting for some famous naval battles. On three separate occasions in the maze of channels between Haiphong and Halong the Vietnamese prevented the Chinese from landing. In 1288 Tran Hung Dao stopped Mongol ships from sailing up the Bach Dang River by placing steel-tipped bamboo stakes at high tide. The ships ran against them at low

© MICHAEL BUCKLEY

old French guns on Dragon Island, overlooking Halong Bay

tide and sank. General Tran Hung Dao supposedly hid the bamboo stakes in Hang Dau Go when preparing to fight the Mongols.

Bo Hon Island

Bo Hon lies about 1.5 hours from Bai Chay (one hour on a faster boat) and has seven of the best grottoes and caves in the Halong area within easy reach of each other. The French called the place Ile de la Surprise. Allow at least six hours to get out to the area, explore, and return to Bai Chay.

In a small islet off Bo Hon you'll find **Hang Bo Nau,** or Pelican Cave, apparently at one time frequented by these birds. This grotto has a deepwater entrance, so tour boats can dock up close. Hang Bo Nau consists of a short cave with no exit. From inside the grotto you can take a classic photo of the facing bay, framed by the mouth of the cave, with stalactites hanging like giant teeth. Bo Nau is a prime touring destination, and fishing families ply the area in sampans, letting loose children who beg for money and food in three languages and try to sell shells and coral pieces. The families also sell fresh fish and shrimp at high prices to tourist boats.

Bo Hon Island faces Bo Nau, and a five-minute cruise will put you into a wide semi-circular bay. The area holds a sea-level shrine and two caves high up on cliffs. One cave is not accessible directly from the shore. A set of steps ascends 50 meters to the other, called **Hang Sung Sot.** Hang Sung Sot is very deep, with sparkling white stalactites. A one-hour hike will take you through it.

If you continue eastward by boat around Bo Hon Island for about 20 minutes, you'll reach **Hang Luon,** a perfectly circular pool accessible by a cave entrance by boat. If your boat is too tall, transfer to one of the smaller fishing vessels that wait at the entrance. You can dive off the boat here into the calm water.

Bizarre rock formations jut from the sea to the north and east of Hang Luon. One resembles a tortoise, another a human head. Some guides call this a big-nosed Charles de Gaulle islet, but for American groups the name changes to George Washington. A nearby formation has limestone "bridges" suspended along its middle; east of the bridges lies a rock island that resembles a curved dragon's back rising out of the water.

Coming around the back of Bo Hon Island, a half-hour cruise will get you to a smaller island with a sea-level cave called **Hang Trinh Nu** (Virgin Grotto). You can scramble up to a back exit that opens onto two pretty coves at the back of the island. Watch out for sharp limestone when scrambling around here. Hang Trinh Nu is associated with a legend about a poor fishing family who rented a boat from a rich mandarin. When they could not pay what they owed him, the cruel mandarin demanded the hand of their exceptionally beautiful daughter. She refused to marry him, so he ordered his soldiers to seize her, but she escaped by boat and hid in Hang Trinh Nu. She ran out of food and died in the grotto—fishermen found her body and buried her here. One rock formation inside the grotto is said to resemble the woman; this has become a shrine, with offerings of incense, fruit, and money left for good luck.

Recent Cave Discoveries

Within range of Hang Trinh Nu are some pristine mid-1990s discoveries. Spurred by overcrowding at other caves, fishermen were offered rewards for blazing trails to new caves to ease the congestion. Locals have rights to charge entry if they set up walkways and illuminate the caves with generator lighting. Slightly west of Hang Trinh Nu is **Dong Me Cung** (Grotto of the Labyrinth), a deep cave with sparkling stalactites; the floor of the grotto is carpeted with sea-snail shells—apparently the detritus of picnic lunches left by fisherfolk who once inhabited this cave. Farther east of Hang Trinh Nu are some smaller cave complexes. **Ho Dong Tien** (Fairy Lake) takes its name from a shallow lake, completely enclosed within, where fairies are supposed to swim. Off to the side are large limestone chambers—the bedrooms of the fairies, of course. **Dao Lao Dai** is a water-approached grotto with big tunnels and chambers—it's of mild interest. Even farther east lies **Dong Tam Cung** (Three Palaces), which qualifies as the most spectacular cave at Halong Bay. There are three magnificent chambers here, well illuminated, with a fantasy landscape of limestone forms—great stalactites bunched together like cathedral organ-pipes or arrayed in fat Grecian columns.

Cat Ba Area

The coves around Cat Ba are riddled with oddly shaped karst formations. A well-known beach here is **Ba Quy Dao** (Three Peach Beach), so named because of three rock outcrops resembling peaches. You can easily visit these areas on a chartered boat originating in Cat Ba Harbor (Cang Cat Ba), on a day trip, or connecting from Cat Ba to Bai Chay. Note that choppy waters in Lanha Bay can make the trip difficult for smaller vessels.

Dau Be Island

One hour south of Hang Trinh Nu, or 3–4 hours out of Bai Chay, lies Dau Be Island, which has a small fishing settlement. To the western side of the island is **Ho Ba Ham** (Three Tunnel Lake), a deep grotto with three inland "lakes." You can reach it only at low tide in a small rowboat; locals will offer to take you through. The tunnels flood at high tide and become very dangerous, so pay attention to the time and the turning tide. Dau Be Island features sandy coves excellent for swimming and good diving spots with lots of coral. Unfortunately, the island seems to have been leased to Japanese companies engaged in pearl culturing, so it may be difficult to visit this part of the bay.

Hong Gai Area

You can visit Hong Gai by boat, coming in close to the fishing trawlers that form their own kind of floating market in the morning. You can arrange to alight here to check out the onshore market in Hong Gai. Nearby, tucked away in an alley, is Long Tien Pagoda, named after the illustrious dragon; it's guarded by statues of mythical warriors in elaborate coats of armor. A short way out from Hong Gai is Hon Oan, the island portrayed in the film *Indochine* as L'ile du Dragon. In the movie, plantation owners from the south came up to the impoverished north to recruit workers. Hopeful workers were ferried out to L'ile du Dragon by night, examined by the plantation owners, and

The North

HALONG BAY'S HIDDEN CAVES

Fishermen have explored every nook of Halong Bay. Or have they?

Karst islets may be hollowed out in parts of the interior. Some parts are accessible through grottoes and some can be explored by small boat at low tide. This is the way to enter Ho Ba Ham (Three Tunnel Lake) on Dau Be Island, and Hang Hanh Grotto, between Ha Tu and Campha. But there are probably many more tidal caves waiting to be explored.

Californian John Gray has been nicknamed "The Caveman" because of his insatiable craving for karst topography. In 1989, Gray set up the company SeaCanoe in Phuket, Thailand, to pursue his twin interests of karst caving and kayaking. He astounded the Thai tourist world by announcing he had found hidden tunnels in karst islets around Phuket, accessible by kayak at low tide. These tidal caves lead to pristine inland lagoons, or *hongs* (Thai for rooms), totally enclosed by sheer cliffs. The *hongs* had been spotted from aerial surveys, but the walls were too sheer to climb. Only birds and bats visited these saltwater lagoons. Gray was the first to launch a sea-level search for a way in.

Gray uses inflatable rubber kayaks of his own design. When the oarsman and passengers lie down in the boat, the overall height from the surface is negligible, thus enabling entry into a low tunnel. The *hongs* all differ—some are bare, some are full of mangrove trees and hanging vines, with lizards living in the vegetation.

Recently Gray turned his attention to other karst formations in Asian waters—Palawan in the Philippines and Halong Bay. Preliminary exploration at Halong Bay has revealed the presence of expansive *hong* systems, often interconnected by caves hundreds of meters long. Gray first started exploring in 1992 and set up SeaCanoe Vietnam for touring the area. He says it could take more than 20 years to uncover the secrets of the *hongs*. Around Halong Bay and Cat Ba are limestone labyrinths filled with caves, lagoons, arches, and rock gardens. Unfortunately, the cave systems at Halong Bay are deceptively dangerous—even slack tides create a difficult current. At new or full moons, a huge volume of water funnels through these caves, and the current may be impossible to swim or paddle against. Since the caves are carpeted with oysters, being cut to ribbons is a very real possibility. Gray has his work cut out for him at Halong Bay, so to speak.

shipped off; families were split up in the process at this slave market. In real Hong Gai history, thousands of laborers were brought to the area to work in the coal mines. Intolerable conditions sparked an uprising against the French overseers. The real Dragon Island lies farther south—it was too far out for the film crew of *Indochine* and is now occupied by the Vietnamese military. This island—Hon Rong—has a French bunker fortification on top of it, with a few heavy U.S. naval guns still in position but no longer functioning.

East of Hong Gai

Adjacent to Halong Bay stretches **Bai Tu Long Bay,** accessible from Campha, another coal-mining area, or Hong Gai. You can get to Campha by taking a minibus parked near the Hong Gai side of the Bai Chay–Hong Gai car ferry.

Far from the crowds, Bai Tu Long Bay waits to be explored. A full-day itinerary from Hong Gai eastward might take in Hon Oan, Hon Dua (Buddha Praying Peak), Hon Reu (Monkey Island), and Cua Ong Pagoda. **Hon Reu,** a soil island about four hours from Hong Gai, supports up to 100 monkeys. You must pay a $5 landing fee here to locals living on the island; the fee includes rice for feeding the monkeys, which are raised for traditional Chinese medicine.

Between Ha Tu and Campha, **Hang Hanh** is the spelunker's special—a tunnel of several kilometers accessible only on certain days of the month when the water level at the tunnel entrance is optimum. You'll need a small boat to reach the long grotto and a strong flashlight to pick out the rock formations and stalactites within. Hang Hanh is unique among the caves of Halong Bay in the diversity and size of its stalactites and stalagmites.

Although fishing and coal-mining constitute the major industries around Hong Gai and Campha, other curious industries have prospered on the inhabited islands east of Campha. Silicate (glass) is made on **Dao Quan Lan** by a Chinese joint-venture concern. At the midsection of this island is the port of Van Don, which in the 12th–14th centuries was a thriving exchange point for traders sailing junks from China, Japan, and Java. Trade with foreigners in gold, ivory, and precious wood was forbidden at the time, but smugglers abounded. Today, contraband is still trafficked in here, with beer, stereo systems, video players, and cigarettes brought in from China, Thailand, and Hong Kong.

Pearl prospecting thrives on **Dao Co To**. Off some islands lie rich abalone grounds—mother-of-pearl obtained from the shells is used in making Vietnam's lacquerware. On far-flung islets, daring climbers collect sea-swallow nests, highly prized for use in medicinal soup.

BAI CHAY

Bai Chay and Hong Gai serve as the twin jumping-off points for boat trips to Halong Bay, 165 kilometers by road from Hanoi and 60 kilometers from Haiphong. Officially, these two places are called Halong City West and Halong City East, but nobody refers to them by these names. Bai Chay and Hong Gai sit on facing slabs of land, connected by a car ferry that operates 24 hours. Should you stay in Bai Chay or Hong Gai? Most travelers choose Bai Chay, which is cleaner, offers a greater range of accommodations and facilities, features a strip of beach and—more to the point—offers the tour boats. Bai Chay saw significant expansion as a tour resort in the 1990s—with deluxe hotels springing up and karaoke salons proliferating. Even Bai Chay Beach has been "renovated" with sand brought in from outlying locations.

Hong Gai is an industrial coal-mining town, and boats must be summoned from Bai Chay for tours. Hong Gai is also more business-oriented, with banking, a post office, and a fair sprinkling of shops. Passenger ferries from Haiphong land in Hong Gai. To get to Bai Chay from Hong Gai, you go three kilometers west to a car ferry, make the five-minute crossing, and travel another two kilometers into Bai Chay. Land distance from Hong Gai dock to Bai Chay Post Office is about five kilometers.

Bai Chay is undergoing development as a major seaside resort, with a flurry of hotel and guesthouse construction. In summer you can swim at Bai Chay Beach or take a boat out to the nearby island of Dao Tuan Chau, which has small beaches and decrepit French villas, including one that served as a vacation retreat for Ho Chi Minh. This island features a solitary hotel that charges a ridiculous $25 a night for poor accommodations; a French company was considering building a high-class hotel. You'll find sandy coves on several of the karst islets around Halong Bay, and you can also swim off your tour boat.

Climate

The weather influences tourism at Bai Chay, Hong Gai, and Halong Bay. In the July–August high season, visitors pack hotels and Bai Chay Beach. Crowds taper off during the shoulder seasons of April–June and September–November. During the November 15–March 15 low season, rates drop for hotels and cruise boats. At this time, however, the weather becomes colder, foggier, and more prone to rain, reducing visibility in Halong Bay. However, there's less competition for boat rentals, and hotels charge less. The coldest months are January and February.

Accommodations

Bai Chay has more than 40 minihotels, as well as about 20 larger hotels and four luxury hotels. Rates vary with demand; a $10 room in summer costs $6 in winter. Rates also vary on weekends. A hotel that charges $8 for a room on weekdays might boost it to $12 on weekends. Demarcation lines are clear in Bai Chay: Near the car ferry loom the fancier hotels; two kilometers west of the car ferry, near the post office, is a cluster of budget minihotels; and west of that two

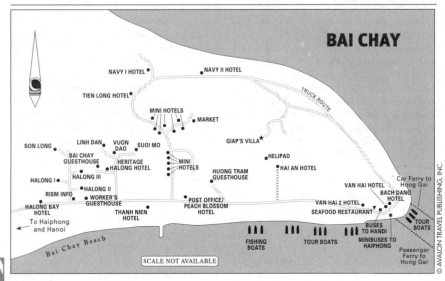

BAI CHAY

NAVY I HOTEL
NAVY II HOTEL
TIEN LONG HOTEL
TRUCK ROUTE
MINI HOTELS
MARKET
GIAP'S VILLA
SON LONG
LINH DAN
VUON DAO
SUOI MO
HELIPAD
BAI CHAY GUESTHOUSE
HERITAGE
HAI AN HOTEL
HALONG HOTEL
MINI HOTELS
HUONG TRAM GUESTHOUSE
HALONG I
HALONG III
HALONG II
VAN HAI HOTEL
Car Ferry to Hong Gai
BACH DANG HOTEL
RISM INFO
WORKER'S GUESTHOUSE
POST OFFICE/ PEACH BLOSSOM HOTEL
VAN HAI 2 HOTEL
HALONG BAY HOTEL
THANH NIEN HOTEL
SEAFOOD RESTAURANT
TOUR BOATS
To Haiphong and Hanoi
BUSES TO HANDI
Bai Chay Beach
FISHING BOATS
TOUR BOATS
MINIBUSES TO HAIPHONG
Passenger Ferry to Hong Gai
SCALE NOT AVAILABLE

© AVALON TRAVEL PUBLISHING, INC.

cul-de-sacs cater to group tours, with moderate prices. Watch out for touts on motorcycles in Bai Chay—there is a local mafia that try to direct you to their own hotel. Once you're staying at that hotel, you are considered their charges when it comes to boat rentals, which turn out to be exorbitant. Other captains will not deal with you because of possible trouble with the mafia elements.

Under $20: Vuon Dao (Peach Garden Street), leading north from the post office, has a string of minihotels—usually two- or three-story structures with half a dozen rooms. Most are private. Stroll the strip, check out the rooms, and take the one that suits. Rooms cost $8–14 and up for singles, doubles, or triples; prices may rise by 50 percent in high season. Hot water often is available; most places provide basic comforts such as slippers, mosquito nets, and towels; some establishments have air-conditioned rooms. The more than 15 minihotels in the area include **Phuong Vi,** tel. 33/846595; **Thu Thuy,** tel. 33/846295; **Viet Hoa,** tel. 33/846035; **Peace (Hoa Binh),** tel. 33/846009; **Rose,** tel. 33/846645; **Hai Ha,** tel. 33/846590; **Huang Ha,** tel. 33/846308; **Viet Phuong,** tel. 33/846493; **Suoi May,** tel.

33/846473; **Quoc Thanh,** tel. 33/846004; and **Sea Dragon,** tel. 33/845077.

On the alley to the east of Vuon Dao on a hilltop lies another cluster of minihotels—a bit quieter and offering good sea views. You'll find **Huong Tram GH** a good place offering rooms for $8–14 each; the upper-end rooms have fridge, TV, hot water, and sea views. Nearby are the following hotels: **Yen Ngoc Hotel,** tel. 33/846945, which has eight rooms for $8–10; **Hoang Thinh,** tel. 33/846944, which has eight rooms for $10–12; and **Hai Long Hotel,** tel. 33/846378, whcih has 25 rooms for $15 each.

Up the alley west of Vuon Dao, with hilltop views, are a few small places such as **Van Long Hotel,** tel. 33/846331, with 12 rooms for $8, and **Linh Dan Hotel,** tel. 33/846025.

Farther up Vuon Dao Street is **Tien Long Hotel,** tel. 33/846042. This four-story hotel has 47 rooms for $8–10. Around the back of the hill are the **Navy I** (also called Hai Quan) and **Navy II** hotels for naval personnel. The Navy also runs two colonial mansions with sea views—three rooms in each house. General Giap maintains a villa in this area, with helicopter access. No tourists allowed.

Near the minibus station and closer to the car-ferry crossing is **Minh Tuan Hotel,** tel. 33/8462000, with 14 rooms for $10 each.

$20–50: Down by the pier is **Thanh Nien Hotel,** tel. 33/846715, fax 33/846226, a concrete building with 11 rooms for $15 in winter, $22 in summer. At the junction of Vuon Dao and Halong roads is a building that is part post office and part the **Peach Blossom Hotel,** tel. 33/846205, with 25 rooms for $20–25, with fridge, TV, phone, and strange staff at the desk. West of the Peach Blossom, two cul-de-sacs with large hotels cater to group tours. **Worker's GH** (Nha Nghi Cong Doan), catering to coal miners and workers, rents rooms to foreigners for $25 and up, space permitting. **Suoi Mo,** tel. 33/846381, fax 33/846284, has 45 rooms for $26–55 and is run by Halong Tourist Company. **Phuong Dong Hotel** is an 18-room hotel with expansions under way. Standard rooms cost $25 and suites $45. The hotel is recommended for its business facilities. **Bai Chay GH,** tel. 33/846440, is a six-story hotel with 80 rooms for $15–25 apiece. **Vuon Dao,** tel. 33/846427, fax 33/846287, has 55 rooms for $35–55, and superior rooms for $60–90. There are two smaller places tucked up behind the group-tour hotels: **Doang Trang Hotel** ($6–20 for rooms) and **Linh Dan** ($15 a room).

In the second cul-de-sac west of the Peach Blossom Hotel is a cluster of hotels run by Quang Ninh Tourist Company. **Halong II,** tel. 33/846445, offers 40 rooms in two wings—an old French wing and a more modern wing. Prices range $40–45 for a room with fridge, phone, and other creature comforts. **Halong III,** tel. 33/846316, a modern five-story structure, offers 56 rooms for $35–45. Farther up the hill are tennis courts. **Son Long,** tel. 33/846319, fax 33/846226, has 50 bungalow-style rooms for $20 and up.

All by itself on a hilltop with commanding views, near the helipad, is **Hai An Hotel,** tel. 33/845514, fax 33/845512, with 40 rooms with a/c and hot water for $20–25–35. All rooms have sea views. This place is, however, a bit isolated—it's okay if you enjoy the exercise of going up and down steps to get there.

Close to the Bai Chay–Hong Gai car-ferry dock stands **Van Hai Hotel,** tel. 33/846403, fax 33/846115, with 76 rooms for $24–35–44. Rooms include a/c, bath, phone, fridge, and TV. The hotel offers a full range of amenities, including restaurant and souvenir shop, and is managed by Halong Tourist Company, which also runs nearby **Bach Dang Hotel** and **Van Hai 2 Hotel.** Both charge roughly the same prices as the Van Hai.

$100–200: Luxury hotels are recent additions in Bai Chay. They offer fancy restaurants and terrace cafés, health centers, and karaoke salons. **Halong I Hotel,** tel. 33/846320, fax 33/846318, is an old 1930s French building—it used to be a hospital. It was extensively renovated in the mid-1990s and now houses 23 rooms ranging $95–115 and one suite for $140–160. Catherine Deneuve stayed here during the filming of *Indochine.* The hotel features walkways and terraces overlooking the beach. Also overlooking the waterfront with terraces is **Halong Bay Hotel,** tel. 33/845209, fax 33/846856, with 42 rooms priced $70–110 for singles, $75–120 for doubles. The hotel has a swimming pool. Set back 1.5 kilometers from the beach is **Heritage Halong Hotel,** at 88 Halong Rd., tel. 33/846888, fax 33/846999, an eight-story hotel with 101 rooms, singles for $135–150, doubles for $150–165. The hotel has a business center, tennis courts, KTV disco, restaurants, and bar.

Food

There are times in Vietnam when you feel either you're not getting enough food or it's too bland. Not so in Bai Chay with its great seafood, very reasonably priced. You should always, however, establish prices before dining, especially if the restaurant lacks a menu. Try grilled whole fish, squid, prawns—all fresh, all good. The food is often cooked at the table on charcoal braziers and served with a garnish of lemon juice, salt, pepper, and spices. West of the post office try **Van Song Restaurant,** tel. 846084, with excellent seafood and friendly owners, serving fried squid and fish with tomato sauce, as well as pancakes. Close by are **Vinh Quang, Minh Binh** and **Thanh Hung** restaurants. On Vuon Dao Street, on the minihotel strip, you'll find Hoang Lan and Hong Minh restaurants. At the northern end of Vuon Dao Street are the markets, which offer fresh ingredients at food stalls.

Shopping

Souvenir stands line the seafront in Bai Chay and are scattered around Hong Gai. Buying items made of coral will encourage the destruction of coral reefs. Coal, on the other hand, is a different matter. The shops sell intriguing coal sculptures made by local artisans, often fashioned in the shape of animals such as eagles or lions. Starting price for a smaller sculpture is around $10.

Information and Services

Restaurants in Bai Chay act as informal traveler cafés. The owners of Van Song Restaurant can arrange boats and answer questions. Good maps of Halong Bay *(ban do Vinh Ha Long)* are sold in hotel lobbies in Bai Chay; you can also buy them down by the docks in Bai Chay. Boat captains own detailed marine charts unavailable to the touring public, but you might talk them into showing you a few once you're on board. **Quang Ninh Tourism,** tel. 33/846274, fax 33/846318, near Halong II Hotel, sells maps and offers pricey three- to eight-hour trips to the islands. You can arrange junk rentals here, as well as other transport rentals and guides. The desk at Halong Hotel can change U.S. cash; otherwise, the Foreign Trade Bank, east of the market in Hong Gai, can change other currencies and traveler's checks. There is a small post office in Bai Chay. Vietnam country code is 84; Bai Chay phone code is 33.

Getting Around

The most available form of transport is motos, which wait for customers at the bus and minibus stations and ferry crossing. There are a few metered taxis prowling the streets. Bicycle and motorcycle rentals are difficult to come by in Bai Chay—inquire through your hotel or guesthouse and see if staff members will part with their personal wheels for the day.

Getting There

It's best to board a traveler minibus from Hanoi to reach Bai Chay. You don't have to take a tour; just go as an extra passenger. The ride should cost about $4 one-way. Or you can take a one-way tour: Board a minibus, cruise Halong Bay, then get off in Bai Chay. Negotiate a reduction for a one-way ride, say, $21 instead of $25. You can hire cars or larger vehicles in Hanoi or Bai Chay; rates are calculated per 100 kilometers.

The 165-kilometer road trip from Hanoi to Halong Bay can be slow because of the poor condition of the road and several ferry crossings with long lineups. Added to this are two one-way bridges to cross. There are train tracks in the middle and bicycle lanes on either side. Only one lane of traffic can proceed at a time— the oncoming traffic waits its turn—and all traffic halts when a train comes through.

Buses from Hanoi's Gia Lam station, on the east side of Long Bien Railway Bridge, depart early in the morning and take five hours. The trip costs $1.50 one-way. Minibuses charging $3 depart from the area south of the Opera House in Hanoi. Bai Chay's bus station, near the car-ferry crossing to Hong Gai, offers five express departures daily to Hanoi (five hours) 0700–1400, and eight departures to Haiphong (two hours) 0700–1600. Minibuses are nearby. Unfortunately, foreigners are nailed with high fares from Bai Chay back to Hanoi because of a local $2 tax applied to foreign bus ticket sales. This means it costs $7, while if you stand on the highway and flag the departing bus down, it costs $5.

HONG GAI

Hong Gai lies in Vietnam's premier coal-producing area, with mines to the north of town and a setting straight out of the Industrial Revolution. For this reason, grimy Hong Gai does not attract much tourism. The coal mines once attracted the French, however: In 1882, Captain Henri Rivière and 600 men seized the mines for France. He was later ambushed and killed near Hong Gai by Black Flag pirates, who car-

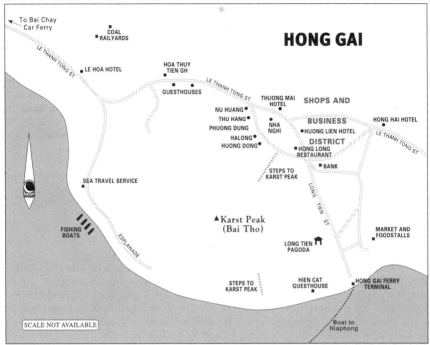

To Bai Chay
Car Ferry

LE THANH TONG ST

COAL
RAILYARDS

HONG GAI

LE HOA HOTEL

HOA THUY
TIEN GH

LE THANH TONG ST

GUESTHOUSES

THUONG MAI
HOTEL

NU HUANG

SHOPS AND

THU HANG
PHUONG DUNG

NHA
NGHI

BUSINESS

HONG HAI HOTEL

HUONG LIEN HOTEL

LE THANH TONG ST

HALONG
HUONG DONG

DISTRICT

HONG LONG
RESTAURANT

BANK

STEPS TO
KARST PEAK

SEA TRAVEL SERVICE

LONG TIEN ST

FISHING
BOATS

ESPLANADE

▲ Karst Peak
(Bai Tho)

LONG TIEN
PAGODA

MARKET AND
FOODSTALLS

STEPS TO
KARST PEAK

HIEN CAT
GUESTHOUSE

HONG GAI FERRY
TERMINAL

SCALE NOT AVAILABLE

Boat to
Hiaphong

© AVALON TRAVEL PUBLISHING, INC.

The North

ried his head from village to village as a symbol of France's defeat. The incident precipitated the decision of the French parliament to take over Tonkin and Annam as protectorates in 1883.

The town of Hong Gai wraps around a karst peak called Bai Tho, with sheer cliffs that plunge straight into the sea. Bai Tho means "Poem Mountain," so called because Emperor Le Thanh Tong scrawled a poem high up on the cliffs. There are several rough approaches where you can clamber up for a great view over Halong Bay. Or walk around the seaside esplanade in front of the karst peak, approachable from the west side only. The area around Long Tien Pagoda and the markets on the east side of the karst peak is busy; if you arrive early, you can see the fish catch unloaded. Offshore, the fishing fleet creates its own floating market. It's worthwhile strolling around the market and dock area; go ahead, wade in there and get your shoes slimy.

Accommodations and Food

More than 30 places vie for your trade in Hong Gai. Most guesthouses are run by Hong Gai Tourism. You'll find budget and moderate accommodations in half a dozen guesthouses at the north side of the peak. Rooms in this zone cost roughly $9–20 and are overpriced compared with Bai Chay hotels. The Government Guesthouse, up on a hill with views of the area, is reserved for official use. There are more small hotels and guesthouses in the market and business area closer to the main boat dock east of Bai Tho Peak.

Better deals in Hong Gai are the privately run minihotels. There is a strip of these lining Le Thanh Tong (LTT), the main east-west thoroughfare; these mostly have 5–8 rooms and cost $10–20. Here you'll find **Le Hoa Hotel,** at 107 LTT, tel. 33/824205; and **Hoa Thuy Tien,** 193 LTT, tel. 33/826297. Almost side by side are the following hotels.

Nu Hoang, 159 LTT, tel. 33/825689; Halong, 80 LTT, tel. 33/827497; Hai Van, 76 LTT, tel. 33/826279; and Phuong Dung Hotel, 78 LTT, tel. 33/828952. Other minihotels in the area include Thuong Mai, Huong Lien, and Thu Hang. About 150 meters east of the Hong Gai ferry terminal is a place bearing a sign that says simply, Resthouse. This is Hien Cat Guesthouse, tel. 33/827417, with five rooms for $8–15—a clean, family-run place with good views from the top floors. The owners can help arrange tour boats. In the business district, Hong Hai Hotel, 425 LTT, tel. 33/823527, fax 33/823436, is a posh state-run hotel with 47 rooms for $20–25–40–50.

It's about three kilometers from the coal rail yards to the car-ferry dock for Bai Chay, and half a dozen other hotels lie on this route, somewhat awkwardly placed when it comes to transport. These include the Thanh Long, Hoang Van, Huong Giang, Thang Ngoc, and Phuong Nam minihotels. Near the car-ferry crossing for Bai Chay is Khach San Hong Ngoc, 36 Le Thanh Tong, tel. 33/826330, with 18 a/c doubles for $22–28.

Dining mostly takes place in hotel restaurants. A reasonable restaurant in town is Hong Long, serving seafood and Chinese dishes. Other small eateries cluster around Hong Gai market.

Services

Hong Gai is very much the business and industrial end of things, with a downtown shopping center, banks, large post office, telecom tower, and so on. These are all grouped north or east of the main market. Rather inconveniently, an office of Vietnam Tourism and Haiphong Tourism is down by the Bai Chay car-ferry crossing at 2 Le Thanh Tong Street.

Getting There

Take the 1000 express train from Hanoi to Haiphong, a $.50 cyclo ride across town to the boat terminal (Ben Binh), and then board a boat to Hong Gai. In the reverse direction, three boats depart daily from Hong Gai to Haiphong, usually at 0600, 1100, and 1600;

the trip costs $4 and takes about 2.5 hours. Alternatively, take a minibus from Hanoi direct to Bai Chay or Hong Gai.

No direct boats service the Cat Ba Town–Bai Chay/Hong Gai route. Take a ferry from Hong Gai to Cat Hai Island, and transfer to Phu Long at the north end of Cat Ba Island. Another option is to hire a fishing vessel for the five-hour passage.

In Hong Gai, minibus transport is near the Bai Chay car-ferry crossing. An alternative to the car-ferry is a smaller boat that leaves from the minibus station and connects across the water with the minibus station in Bai Chay. Moto drivers wait at these places looking for customers.

THE FAR EAST

Campha and Cua Ong

About 40 kilometers east of Hong Gai lies the mining town of Campha, easily reached by minibus or ferry. Campha can serve as a base to explore islands off the coast; boat rentals are possible. However, the area is rather industrial, and it would be preferable to launch from more scenic Cai Rong on Cai Bau Island in Van Don Prefecture. Caoson Mine is the largest mining operator in Campha; the company has its own strip of beach with a guesthouse. Campha town itself hosts around 30 hotels and guesthouses, many of them privately run.

Thirty kilometers east of Hong Gai, and a short distance from Campha along the coast, stands Cua Ong Pagoda, dedicated to Tran Hung Dao, the 13th-century naval hero who not only took on the Mongols but also rounded up pirates. He is thus a protector of fishermen, and many come to pay their respects. Dragon pillars adorn the main pagoda interior; inside are statues of Tran dynasty generals. The pagoda overlooks the coal-loading port of Cua Ong. In ancient times, the site of Cua Ong (then called the Port of Suot) was a major maritime and road junction linking the Red River Delta with the northeastern border area. The pagoda is packed at festival times; patrons comes to make offerings and wishes at a series of small shrines leading to the main shrine at the hilltop.

There may be ferries running to Campha from Hong Gai. Minibuses from a depot near the Bai Chay-Hong Gai car ferry, on the Hong Gai side, depart regularly for runs to Campha, Cua Ong, Cai Rong, Tien Yen, and Mong Cai.

Cai Rong

A 15-minute ferry hop from Cua Ong is Cai Bau Island, where you can catch a moto into the main town of Cai Rong. Offshore diving is good from this area, and the scenery is in fact superior to that at Halong Bay. On this island you can see karst formations not only in the water but also on land. Though roads are rough, it is well worth hiring a moto and driver and heading off to explore the island coastline. There are a handful of hotels and guesthouses at Cai Rong, which makes it viable as a base. This beautiful area is little explored. You can hire small boats for offshore touring; you can also board the small ferries running to outlying islands as far as Co To Island. Schedules are irregular, so inquire at the docks. You can also charter a boat here for the trip back to Hong Gai or Bai Chay, which takes around five hours.

Tien Yen

Tien Yen is a fascinating small town with well-preserved Chinese–style shophouses. At the market you might see local Zao women wearing elaborate box–style headdresses coming into town from outlying villages to buy pigs or other goods. There is decent hotel accommodation in Tien Yen—the town caters to overnighters since it lies on the junction of routes to Lang Son and Mong Cai. **Thuy Tien Hotel,** tel. 33/876210, offers 25 rooms for $8–12. And there are three guesthouses strung along Quang Trung Street nearby.

Mong Cai

Mong Cai is a boring border town where smugglers amass large loads of Chinese cigarettes and beer. If your paperwork is in order, you may be able to enter or exit here. The Chinese town on the other side of the Beilun River is Dongxing. The bridge connecting the two sides was blown up in 1979 during cross-border warfare but was rebuilt in 1994. Mong Cai is well supplied with hotels and guesthouses because of frequent visits by Chinese tourists, traders, and smugglers. You won't have any trouble finding a place to stay, but why would you want to?

About 10 kilometers out of Mong Cai on the coast is **Traco Beach,** which commands a long stretch of white sand. Half a dozen large hotels and some guesthouses operate at Traco Beach—a major draw for vacationing Chinese. To the eastern end of the beach is a curious edifice—a huge Catholic cathedral put up by the French and later bombed by the Chinese in a cross-border war in the late 1970s. The cathedral received a direct hit, and only the steeple section survived, with its imposing external statuary of saints and mythical figures grimly hanging on. Locals have rebuilt the entire body of the church again, presumably in the interests of tourism (there are number of Chinese Catholics in Dongxing).

To get to Mong Cai, you can take a minibus from Hong Gai, a five-hour trip with five departures daily. There may also be ferries running up the coast near Mong Cai (to Dan Tien), connecting with Hong Gai. If you cross from Mong Cai into Dongxing, on the Chinese side, it's 180 kilometers from Dongxing to Nanning by road.

The Tonkinese Alps

Northwest of Hanoi, toward the Chinese border, lies the Hoang Lien Son Range, with Mount Fansipan, Vietnam's highest peak, elevation 3,143 meters. This range was christened the Tonkinese Alps by the French, who took a liking to the cool climate. Limestone largely comprises this northwest frontier where dramatic hills rise from the plains. From Hanoi to the northwest several routes will get you there, the most spectacular via Dien Bien Phu to Sapa. At Lao Cai, close by, you can cross into China and continue by rail to Kunming.

The northwest offers captivating mountain scenery; you can hike or trek into valleys around key towns. **Montagnards** inhabiting the valleys here include Tai, Hmong, Zao, and Muong groups. Some live in raised longhouses. Many still dress in traditional garb; intricate hand-embroidered clothing and silver jewelry are worn by the women. The best time to see minority people is on market day in the towns, when Montagnards hike in for days from surrounding areas. Thursday, Friday, Saturday, and Sunday offer the most animated markets; the big day is usually Sunday. To break the ice, you can buy something at a market—embroidery or clothing. If you want to take photos, you might have to hand over your precious lens for a few minutes to accustom them to it—let them look through the viewfinder.

Key destinations in the northwest include Dien Bien Phu and Sapa. Dien Bien Phu, toward the Lao border, is a small town that was the site of the Vietminh victory over the French in 1954. The village of Sapa remains the jewel of the northwest, a former French hill resort with splendid mountain scenery, a market thronged with people, and excellent hiking opportunities. But Sapa is not the only market where hilltribe members congregate. Other colorful markets are scattered through the northwest, including Bac Ha and Cancau. Right up on the Chinese border past Hagiang lie the towns of Xinman and Meovac. These remote towns take considerable effort to get to and most likely require permits and pay-offs along the way.

Route Notes

Most roads lead to Dien Bien Phu or Sapa, or both. You can travel round-trip to Dien Bien Phu, or continue up to Sapa and loop back to Hanoi. Sapa can also be approached directly from Hanoi by train via Lao Cai, or by road via Yen Bai. By jeep, allow at least four days for a round-trip to Dien Bien Phu. There is also a flight from Hanoi to Dien Bien Phu, which would be much faster. Allow at least six days for a loop from Hanoi via Dien Bien Phu to Sapa, or up to 10 days with longer stops; Sapa alone is worth two days. Or travel one-way to Sapa, cross the border at Lao Cai into China, and carry on to Kunming. Arrange your paperwork in Hanoi for this option. If coming in from China, it may be possible to join a tour going through Sapa back to Hanoi by jeep.

Hanoi–Lao Cai by rail is 295 kilometers, an 11-hour trip, with another 35 kilometers by bus to Sapa, another two hours away. By road, from Hanoi to Viet Tri to Yen Bai to Pho Rang to Lao Cai to Sapa, is 390 kilometers and takes 15–17 hours.

The circuitous route from Hanoi to Sapa via Dien Bien Phu is 750 kilometers and requires several days one-way. From Hanoi it's 75 kilometers to Hoa Binh, another 125 kilometers to Moc Chau, 120 kilometers to Son La, 90 kilometers to Tuan Giao, and 80 kilometers into Dien Bien Phu. From Dien Bien Phu it's 105 kilometers to Lai Chau, another 80 kilometers to Phong Tho, 86 kilometers more to Sapa, and 35 kilometers to Lao Cai at the Chinese border. From Lao Cai it's 355 kilometers to Hanoi via Yen Bai. To save time, you can skip Dien Bien Phu and head directly from Tuan Giao to Lai Chau.

A jeep can do 45 kph on a sealed road but only 25 kph on dirt. The road is paved from Hanoi all the way to Lao Cai, but blind corners are a hazard. Seasonal considerations are

THE TONKINESE ALPS

CHINA

To Kunming

To Ha Giang

Hekou

Phong Tho

Tam Duong

Bac Ha

M *BAC HA SUNDAY MARKET*

Lao Cai

Viet Quang

Sapa

M *HIKING IN THE SAPA REGION*

Mt Fansipan
(3,143 m) ▲

Binh Lu

Pho Lu

Pho Rang

Tuyen Quang

Thac Ba Lake

Yen Binh

Van Chan

Yen Bai

Red River

Red River

Viet Tri

Hanoi

Hoa Binh

Black River

Man Duc

M *MAI CHAU*

To Cuc Phuong
National Park

The North

Lai Chau

Tuan Guo

Than Uyen

2,913 m ▲

▲ 1,776 m

Mt Phu Luong
(2,985 m) ▲

Moc Chau

Hoang   Lien   Son   Range

Black River

Hat Lot

Son La

Dien Bien Phu

Thuan Chau

LAOS

0   25 mi

0   25 km

© AVALON TRAVEL PUBLISHING, INC.

HANOI–SAPA 4WD ITINERARY

Keep itineraries flexible. You can build in extra days along the route for extra payment. You may wish to spend more time, or less, in a particular place. If you're headed for Sapa, time yourself to arrive on Friday or early Saturday if possible, to catch the better part of the market. The following is a sample itinerary.

Day 1: Hanoi to Son La, 310 kilometers, 12–14 hours. With short stops at Man Duc and Mai Chau; overnight in Son La.

Day 2: Son La to Dien Bien Phu, 170 kilometers, seven hours. Stop in Tuan Giao; overnight in Dien Bien Phu. Alternate route: Son La to Lai Chau direct, 100 kilometers, nine hours.

Day 3: Half a day in Dien Bien Phu, and continue to Lai Chau, 105 kilometers, four hours. Overnight in Lai Chau.

Days 4/5/6: Lai Chau to Phong Tho to Sapa, 170 kilometers, nine hours. Very scenic. You might want to build in an overnight stop at Phong Tho before proceeding to Sapa. Phong Tho to Sapa is 86 kilometers, with three hours of spectacular climbing. Overnight in Sapa and spend extra days (Days 5/6) in Sapa.

Days 7/8: Long haul back to Hanoi via Yen Bai, 390 kilometers, The trip takes 15 hours, so it's best to break the journey overnight and carry on the next morning to Hanoi, when it will be easier to find a hotel room.

very important on this route—May–October, the road beyond Son La often washes out or becomes impassable because of monsoon damage or landslides. Recommended months for a 4WD trip on the Son La–Lai Chau–Sapa route are January and February.

Getting Around

Traveler cafés organize weekend tours to Sapa, with direct minibuses on the Yen Bai route. For longer trips, assemble a group of 3–4 passengers and rent a 4WD vehicle in Hanoi. It's much cheaper getting there by train or local bus, but you don't see a lot on the train and buses are notoriously uncomfortable. Another option, if you have the riding skills and mechanical know-how, is to rent a motorcycle.

Minibuses and Cars: Traveler minibuses usually take the direct route up, paralleling the railway to Sapa. The road is in better shape, so minibuses and cars can handle it. Especen charges $46–50 a person for a four-day minibus ride to Sapa, based on 5–10 passengers; for a four-day car ride, it's $60 a person based on four passengers, or $90 pp based on two passengers. A six-day trip via Dien Bien Phu to Sapa costs $320 for a car with a maximum of four

passengers. Old Darling Café, at 4 Hang Quat in Hanoi, offers a four-day trip to Sapa based on $60 a person, including transportation, meals, accommodations, and guide. The trip includes a couple of short hikes around Sapa. Old Darling Café also organizes longer hikes in the Sapa, Phong Tho, and Lai Chau regions.

4WD Vehicles: These remain the ideal vehicle for tackling rough mountain routes. You can stop where you want and take photos. With a 4WD you can be confident of taking the back route to Sapa via Lai Chau. Top of the line is a Toyota Land Cruiser, available from Vietnam Tourism, Vinatour, or TOSERCO for $45–50 per 100 kilometers. To cover the 1,150 kilometers from Hanoi to Dien Bien Phu to Sapa and back to Hanoi would cost a minimum $500 for the Land Cruiser. Negotiate a fixed price based on time and distance rather than a variable per/kilometer price. Also available are homegrown Mekong Land Cruisers, and the Land Cruiser II, a jeep version. A good sturdy vehicle is the Russian Gaz army jeep, renting for $300 for 5–6 days, or around $30 per 100 kilometers. This vehicle has two tanks, holding 40 liters of gasoline each, and two bucket seats up front with three gearshifts between them. In the back are three roomy seats and lots of luggage space at the rear. Especen charges $330 for a five-day round-trip in a Russian jeep from Hanoi to Dien Bien Phu; for a Land Cruiser, the trip is $530.

Before setting off, have the driver write down a rough itinerary. Pay half up front, the other half on completion. Jeeps work out to $30 per 100 kilometers, but it's better to negotiate the rate by the day—say, $50 a day. You should also negotiate how much extra to pay if you stay in a place longer, without driving; about $10 a day should suffice. Clarify other expenses also. You can cover the cost of the driver's lodging and food, which usually doesn't amount to much.

Motorcycle: You need a high-powered motorcycle for the hills and bad roads. A 125cc motorcycle can make it, but a 175cc Russian model is preferable. It's very tiring to motorcycle, bumping over rough roads for long distances. You must have tools and be able to improvise repairs—for example, when the headlight or muffler falls off because of vibration. You could ride a bike up to Sapa via Dien Bien Phu and then load it on the train back to Hanoi from Lao Cai. The bike costs $7, or roughly the cost of a hard seat.

Bus: Travel by bus in the northwest is slow, crowded, and uncomfortable. Usually only one bus a day travels in the direction you're headed, most likely leaving early, between 0500 and 0730. When it comes to viewing the landscape, bus travel is rather like riding in a submarine without a periscope, and you're so busy defending your turf you don't enjoy the trip. You do, however, meet lots of people, especially those who sit in your lap. Buses may not run daily, maybe every second day, or Tuesday, Thursday, Saturday, and Sunday. There is some jeep transport for short runs; another possibility is riding in postal vans.

Buses to the northwest leave from Hanoi's Kim Ma bus station. On the direct Sapa route you can take a bus to Yen Bai, stay the night there, then make your way north in stages to Lao Cai. For epic bus rides on the long route to Sapa, a bus departs from Hanoi for a two-day haul to Dien Bien Phu for $5, with an overnight stop in Son La. Hanoi to Son La takes 16 hours, if you have no breakdowns. From Dien Bien Phu, another three days of busing will put you in Sapa. Dien Bien Phu to Lai Chau is $3; Lai Chau to Sapa, $3, with an overnight stop in Phong Tho. Or skip Dien Bien Phu and head from Tuan Giao to Lai Chau. You could cover the entire route from Hanoi to Sapa for $12, but you might have to buy several seats for legroom, say, three seats bought for two people, which still makes the price less than $20.

Supplies

Take along a bag of nonperishable food in case the local fare of cabbage soup gets boring. You can buy fruit, biscuits, and small items along the way. Bring bottled water. Thermoses of hot water are supplied in truck-stop hotels; soak a thin towel with hot water—that's your shower. The hot water is purified; let it cool off and transfer it to a water bottle to drink the next day. Take cough and cold medicines along and water-purifying (iodine) tablets.

Do not underestimate the cold in the northwest, especially in winter. Sapa can hit freezing point. Although guesthouses supply quilts, rooms can still be clammy and cold; it's drafty and cold in jeeps and buses, especially when windows don't seal completely. Take a good sweater, waterproof jacket, toque, gloves, and thermal underwear. You can outfit yourself in Hanoi; try the Old Quarter for wool and silk goods. You can also buy Chinese-made parkas and army surplus gear on Le Duan Boulevard. Cigarettes make good gifts for drivers and wayward officials.

HANOI TO DIEN BIEN PHU
Hanoi to Son La

By jeep, you can cover the 320 kilometers from Hanoi to Son La in a day. The section from Mai Chau area all the way to Son La is a six-lane highway. However, drivers go slow on this part because of radar traps (was the highway designed to tempt racers?). Two hours out of Hanoi you reach Hoa Binh. An hour out of Hoa Binh you pass Man Duc (in Tan Lac District), a small town backed by karst peaks, with an interesting market. An hour's drive from here you can stop for spectacular views over Mai Chau Valley to the south. The route continues for another hour past tea plantations and terraced rice paddies to reach Moc Chau. Near Moc Chau, you strike an area inhabited by Hmong and Black Tai. Moc Chau, five hours from Hanoi by jeep, has several hotels, including a UBND Guesthouse. Unfortunately, as far as the eye can see on the Hanoi to Son La route, whole mountainsides have been stripped bare of trees.

Son La to Dien Bien Phu

Not much to see in Son La, a truck stop. The prison built in 1908 by the French to incarcerate revolutionaries still stands in the middle of town. The main place to stay is the **UBND Guesthouse** (People's Committee GH), tel. 22/852080, a large compound at the west end of town with a parking lot full of trucks and buses. The two-story hotel contains about 35 rooms. Rents run $20 for a double room, or $10 without bath. This government guesthouse typifies those along the route in larger towns. You get a bed with hard mattress, warm quilt, mosquito net, and Chinese thermos of hot water. Government guesthouses proliferate in the northwest, but foreigners may be allowed to use only the ones in the larger towns. Locals pay $.40 and up for UBND guesthouses, whereas foreigners pay $5 and up. For food, go out of the hotel to the main road and turn left—there are some small restaurants. Another place to stay is the **Trade Union Hotel** (Khach San Cong Duan), tel. 22/852244, costing $15 a room with two beds, $10 for three beds.

From Son La to Dien Bien Phu you'll see lots of minority villages—Black Tai, White Tai, Hmong, and Muong—some close to the road. You might also stray across a market. Black Tai (Tai Den) women wear black sarongs and tight-fitting blouses with rows of silver or metal buttons down the front, attached tightly to the neck. The blouses are usually bright green, blue, or purple. A woman coils her hair in a topknot, covering it with a black

turban embroidered with multicolored thread. After marriage, Black Tai women wear a silver hairpin. About 800,000 Black Tai and White Tai live in the northwest.

After Thuan Chau, the road starts climbing to cross Pha Din Pass at 1,300 meters before reaching Tuan Giao. At Tuan Giao, you can turn west along the rough, dusty road to Dien Bien Phu, or skip that and carry straight on to Lai Chau. White Tai villages lie along the route between Tuan Giao and Lai Chau. The White Tai (Tai Trang) women originally wore white skirts, but now they wear more practical garb, even denim.

DIEN BIEN PHU

Dien Bien Phu (Chief Frontier Post) is an isolated market town 480 kilometers northwest of Hanoi, famed as the site of the showdown between the forces of France and North Vietnam in 1954. It remains a pilgrimage site of sorts, for both Vietnamese and French, but a few things have changed since the big siege. The dirt track through the center of town has been paved, thatched roofs replaced with tiled roofs. Motorcycles and bicycles are common. Karaoke bars pump out Boney M songs ("Ra Ra Rasputin, Russia's greatest love machine"), video theaters do a brisk business, and market vendors sell Coca-Cola and Dien Bien cigarettes. In 1993, sleepy Dien Bien Phu was designated the capital of Lai Chau province because Lai Chau Town, the old capital, will be partly submerged when a hydropower station on the Black River begins operating. Along with the new status comes a change of name—from Dien Bien to Muong Thanh, but it's dubious whether anyone will heed this change.

The dust has not yet settled on Dien Bien Phu—the place is still under construction. The main drag, Be Van Dan Street, is lined on both sides with shacks and small restaurants. As you come in from the north side, a minihotel stands on the right; 300 meters south of that is the main market, set back from the road, and the bus station. At right angles to the market is a newer street, with new buildings going up. An-

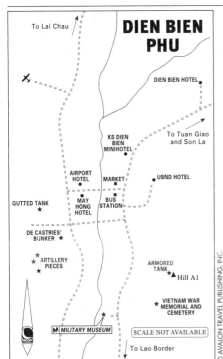

DIEN BIEN PHU

To Lai Chau

DIEN BIEN HOTEL

KS DIEN BIEN MINIHOTEL

To Tuan Giao and Son La

AIRPORT HOTEL

MARKET

UBND HOTEL

GUTTED TANK ★

MAY HONG HOTEL

BUS STATION

DE CASTRIES' BUNKER ★

★ ARTILLERY PIECES
★

ARMORED TANK
★ ▲ Hill A1

★ VIETNAM WAR MEMORIAL AND CEMETERY

★

M MILITARY MUSEUM

SCALE NOT AVAILABLE

To Lao Border

© AVALON TRAVEL PUBLISHING, INC.

lometers farther along the same road is a Lao village. Another 10 kilometers farther on the road reaches the Lao border.

Military Museum

This museum contains several large salons with displays of photos, documents, military hardware, and some statuary. One statue display shows a Vietnamese with an industrial bicycle—bringing supplies to the front. A large-scale model of the battlefield is shown up on one end of the museum: It is center stage for a mixed-media recreation of the fall of Dien Bien Phu, with video and synchronised popping lights. A souvenir shop at the museum sells Dien Bien stamps, French maps of the area, commemoration stamps and badges, General Vo Nguyen Giap's books on the battle, ethnic clothing and postcards, and some badly stuffed animals. There are photo cards of French President François Mitterrand, who helicoptered in for a visit in October 1993. Another illustrious visitor was General Vo Nguyen Giap, who returned in 1994 at the age of 83 for the 40th anniversary of the battle.

Cemetery

East of the museum is a large Vietminh war memorial and cemetery. A reconstruction of bunkers has been built close by to give an idea of fighting conditions. It is not clear what happened to fallen French soldiers. Under the Geneva Agreement, the dead from both sides were to be honored in a massive gravesite, but after a rift between north and south in 1955, the French were left where they'd fallen.

Battlefield Relics

To the north of the Vietminh cemetery is Hill A1, the former scene of fierce fighting. The Vietminh tunneled under Hill A1 and eventually blew up French bunkers with explosives. In this area you'll find an armored tank, bunker, war memorial, and tunnel complex. A few kilometers west of town you can see abandoned French tanks, howitzers, and artillery pieces. You can visit the rebuilt command bunker of General Christian de Castries, preserved as it

other two kilometers south is the Military Museum, also set back from the road on the right. Around the town lush fields of rice and corn flourish; rusted tanks and artillery pieces serve as playground equipment for local children.

Markets and Minorities

The central market at Dien Bien Phu is worth a browse. Ethnic groups shop here, among them colorful Hmong and Black Tai. More than a dozen ethnic groups live around Dien Bien Phu, the largest being the Black Tai, with more than 20,000 people. Other minorities include the Hmong, Nung, Cong, and Khomu groups. Some groups number only several hundred. You can organize day hikes to villages, such as the Hmong village of Noon Het to the south, or the Black Tai village of Na Nge to the east. The road leading to the Lao border to the southwest has a Xa minority village about 20 kilometers from Dien Bien Phu; three ki-

FRANCE LOSES AN EMPIRE

In 1954 the French made the fatal error of setting up a "fortress" from which to confront the Vietminh in the remote north at the valley of Dien Bien Phu. The base, supplied by aircraft, was picked by the French to guard Laos against Vietminh incursions and drive them back to the northern delta. Six battalions of French colonial troops were parachuted into Dien Bien Phu, and heavy equipment was also air-dropped there. The fortress was touted by the French as being impossible to assail.

The Vietnamese chose Dien Bien Phu for a decisive engagement. In March 1954, Vietnamese General Vo Nguyen Giap assembled more than 50,000 troops on the high ground surrounding 13,000 French troops in the valley. The French commander, Christian de Castries, created a series of heavily fortified strongholds surrounded by barbed wire. He named the strongholds after women (said to be his mistresses): Claudine, Françoise, Anne-Marie, Dominique, Eliane, Beatrice, Gabrielle. The assembled French colonial troops included Vietnamese, Algerians, Moroccans, Senegalese, and Foreign Legionnaires. But the French overestimated the strength of their air power and underestimated the Vietminh, who laboriously dragged artillery onto the high ground overlooking the valley with the help of more than 100,000 porters. Bad weather grounded French air power, and General Giap's howitzers and antiaircraft guns were able to pound the airstrip. French aircraft were reduced to dropping supplies from great heights to avoid the artillery, and the parachutes could not be guided with the necessary precision. Consequently, much of the ammunition intended for the French wound up instead in the hands of the Vietminh. The Vietminh approached the perimeter of the French fortress in tunnels, then burrowed underneath the French defenses.

One by one the French strongholds fell; finally, the French pulled back to the area around the airstrip. On May 7, 1954, the French surrendered. They'd lost more than 3,000 men; all the survivors were captured. The Vietminh losses were estimated at 20,000. An Asian guerrilla army had defeated professional French troops, including men from the Foreign Legion. "It was a victory for colonized countries all over the world," said General Vo Nguyen Giap. The defeat offered a lesson the Americans did not heed—the same simple tactical tunneling used at Dien Bien Phu largely won the Vietnam War of the 1960s.

was on May 7, 1954, when the red flag of Vietnam was raised over it in victory. In 1994, on the 40th anniversary of the battle, a low-key memorial to French soldiers who died at Dien Bien Phu was inaugurated. The memorial is unmarked: It is close to the bunker of General de Castries. The French strongholds, surrounded with barbed wire, were scattered around the command bunker, especially to the north in the direction of the airfield. The French airfield was positioned roughly where the present airfield lies—there used to be an auxiliary airstrip to the south. General Giap's command headquarters, with a rebuilt bunker, is eight kilometers away in Ban Muong Phan.

A huge statue ensemble of Vietnamese soldiers is sited atop a hillside overlooking Dien Bien Phu. Soaring 20 meters high and weighing more than 220 tons, this is Vietnam's biggest war memorial.

Accommodations

Hotels in Dien Bien seem to cater to the karaoke and taxi-girl crowd. There are more than a dozen hotels in town—possibly half of them open to foreigners. The best of the pack is the newer branch of **Muong Thanh GH,** across from the airport. The older **Muong Thanh Hotel,** farther into town at 25 Him Lam St., has gone to seed. **Airport Hotel** and **May Hong Hotel,** both on the road at the back of the market, both charge around $10 a room. **Khach San Dien Bien** is a privately owned minihotel with 30 double rooms in the $5–60–40 range. The hotel has its own restaurant; sound effects are courtesy of a karaoke bar next door. The cramped rooms allow only one person to maneuver in them at one time; however, this hotel is preferable to the nearby government-run **UBND Hotel.** Another possibility is **Dien Bien Hotel** on the road in.

Getting There and Away

Direct flights leave Hanoi for Dien Bien Phu on Tuesday and Friday for $130 round-trip, but bad weather can delay flights. A chartered jeep from Hanoi is the best way to reach Dien Bien Phu; arrange for one through agencies in Hanoi. A five-day round-trip in a Russian jeep might cost $330, based on 3–4 passengers; by Land Cruiser, probably more like $530. Buses wheeze into Dien Bien Phu from the direction of Son La or Lai Chau. An epic two-day run from Hanoi's Kim Ma bus station costs $5 a seat, but you'll probably want to buy several seats for legroom.

DIEN BIEN PHU TO SAPA
Dien Bien Phu to Lai Chau

From Dien Bien Phu to Lai Chau you proceed along a French-built road. Hmong and Tai minority villages line the route. In Lai Chau you can stay at cozy **Lai Chau UBND.** A bed in a four-bed room costs $5; a double with bath and TV is $15; a room with a single and double bed is $20. The hotel is near the Lai Chau suspension bridge and up a hill. At the base of the same hill is a place with a papaya tree and a blue sign that simply says Restaurant—the place is family-run, with hearty fare. Like Dien Bien Phu, Lai Chau makes a good base for hiking into the surrounding area.

On the fringes of Lai Chau is the province's only drug-rehabilitation center. Opium addiction represents a major problem among the Hmong in the mountainous regions of Lai Chau province. Provincial cadres have tried to persuade the Hmong to grow peanuts instead of poppies, but to no avail. Lai Chau province is home to more than 12,000 addicts.

Lai Chau to Sapa

The region between Lai Chau and Sapa harbors a few Hmong villages. Coiffures become more elaborate among Red Hmong women, who pile hair in a massive topknot. But big hair doesn't keep the sun out, so a conical hat may rest over the topknot. Hmong men often wear green pith helmets. Toward Phong Tho you encounter Zao villages. The women here may wear patterned pants and elaborate black headdresses with rows of coins jingling off them.

The Lai Chau–Sapa route is really spectacular. Try to arrange a stop at **Phong Tho,** four kilometers off the main road to Sapa on Route 4. Besides the primitive guesthouse here, Phong Tho offers fine opportunities for hiking, with Hmong and Zao hilltribes in the area. Phong Tho sits at the edge of the Hoang Lien Son Range, or the real Tonkinese Alps. From here the road snakes up to **Binh Lu,** another breathtaking location with a bowl of terraced rice paddies ringed by mountains. There is no guesthouse in Binh Lu, but it's an excellent place for hiking. From Binh Lu to Sapa more stunning scenery reels past during the three-hour jeep ride, with mountains and rolling hills winding up to Sapa. Take your time along here.

SAPA

Sapa is a magical combination of alpine landscapes, ethnic cultures, and bracing mountain air. This far-flung corner of Vietnam was "discovered" by a Jesuit missionary in 1918. In the 1920s the French—ever eager to duplicate parts of the Alps or the Pyrenees—decided to develop Sapa. They chased resident Hmong off the site and set up a cozy alpine resort serving a nearby mine. When the heat on the plains became unbearable, Sapa provided cool respite for French administrators. The town was dotted with French villa-estates with names such as The French Roses and The Pearls—rambling orchards, gardens, and sloping lawns amid pine trees. The French constructed a small hydroelectric station, hotels, a church, tennis courts, even an aerodrome.

This tranquil existence was rudely interrupted by Vietminh incursions, which forced the French to abandon their villas. Further

The North

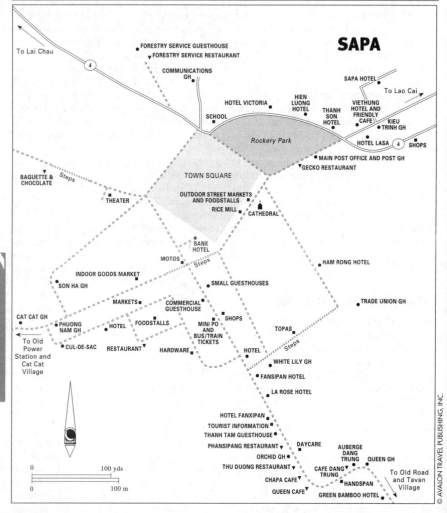

SAPA

To Lai Chau

FORESTRY SERVICE GUESTHOUSE
FORESTRY SERVICE RESTAURANT

COMMUNICATIONS GH

SAPA HOTEL

To Lao Cai

HOTEL VICTORIA

HIEN LUONG HOTEL

THANH SON HOTEL

VIETHUNG HOTEL AND FRIENDLY CAFE

KIEU TRINH GH

SCHOOL

Rockery Park

HOTEL LASA

SHOPS

MAIN POST OFFICE AND POST GH
GECKO RESTAURANT

BAGUETTE & CHOCOLATE

Steps

TOWN SQUARE

THEATER

OUTDOOR STREET MARKETS AND FOODSTALLS

RICE MILL

CATHEDRAL

BANK HOTEL

MOTOS

Steps

HAM RONG HOTEL

INDOOR GOODS MARKET

SON HA GH

SMALL GUESTHOUSES

MARKETS

COMMERCIAL GUESTHOUSE

TRADE UNION GH

CAT CAT GH

PHUONG NAM GH

HOTEL

FOODSTALLS

SHOPS

MINI PO AND BUS/TRAIN TICKETS

TOPAS

To Old Power Station and Cat Cat Village

CUL-DE-SAC

RESTAURANT

HARDWARE

HOTEL

Steps

WHITE LILY GH

FANSIPAN HOTEL

LA ROSE HOTEL

HOTEL FANXIPAN
TOURIST INFORMATION
THANH TAM GUESTHOUSE
PHANSIPANG RESTAURANT

DAYCARE

ORCHID GH

AUBERGE DANG TRUNG

QUEEN GH

THU DUONG RESTAURANT

CAFE DANG TRUNG

To Old Road and Tavan Village

CHAPA CAFE

HANDSPAN

QUEEN CAFE

GREEN BAMBOO HOTEL

0   100 yds
0   100 m

© AVALON TRAVEL PUBLISHING, INC.

damage to the buildings was caused in 1979 when invading Chinese held the area for a short while before being driven out by the Vietnamese Army.

Today, the town supports a population of about 3,300; the entire Sapa District has a population of 32,000. The forest canopy in the area provides a source of medicinal herbs such as ginseng and wild mushrooms, as well as wild honey. Orchards produce peaches, pears, and plums. The Hmong also grow opium in the surrounding hills. At 1,650 meters, Sapa enjoys bracing air—and bracing views overlooking the Muong Hoa River Valley, with its luxuriant vegetation and rice terracing. Facing the village, across a deep valley, soars Vietnam's highest peak, **Mt. Fansipan,** elevation 3,143 meters. Sapa is an excellent area for hiking through lush mountain valleys with minority villages.

Climate

It can get cold in Sapa. Every few years it even snows on the peaks nearby. Temperatures usually hover around 15–23°C, and up to 28°C in July, but can fall to zero in the winter (December–February). Sapa is gorgeous when the sun shines but mountain weather is fickle. The place could easily be socked in with low clouds and you might not see a thing for 4–5 days. Foggy days are common; it can grow damp and clammy. May–September is the rainy season, with heavy rain in July and August. At this time, trails and jeep tracks quickly turn to slush and are slippery and dangerous. The best time to tackle Mt. Fansipan is during the September–November dry season. The best time to admire the flora is in spring, March–May (when coastal areas are sweltering).

The Town

Downtown Sapa centers around the imposing cathedral overlooking the village green, now a kind of sunken soccer field where stray packhorses graze on weekends. The roadways around the cathedral are lined with food stalls, tiny shops, and impromptu market stalls. The cathedral was apparently wrecked in 1952 by French artillery firing at a nearby building that housed Vietminh troops. The 1920s French church has recently been restored; nearby is the abandoned French weather station. The town retains charming stone-paved cul-de-sacs and French villas, many undergoing renovation and rebuilding as Sapa finds new life as a tourist resort. Expansion has been rapid in this department—and the last people to be consulted on the changes are the hilltribe people who drift into town. There are hardly any shops selling hilltribe embroidery, so hilltribe members roam around selling clothing themselves.

Ethnic Groups

The Vietnamese actually represent a minority in the Sapa District, accounting for only 15 percent of the total population of 37,000. Vietnamese are highly visible, however, as they run most of Sapa's shops and stalls. Others are operated by Tay and Giay people. The

HOMO EKTACHROMO

Sapa has been open for tourism since 1993. At times in the weekend market it seems that foreigners outnumber the locals. In this frail balance, it's hard to judge whether tourism benefits the local economy or erodes local lifestyles. Camera-toting travelers form a distinct ethnic tribe themselves—the *Homo ektachromo* group. When foreigners are confronted by aggressive Hmong women hawking embroidered items, it's debatable who appears stranger to whom. While the Hmong will actually pose for photos, Red Zao women and certain other hilltribe people very much dislike having their photos taken—particularly close-ups. Back in the mid-1990s, young Red Zao men and women used to gather in Sapa's market area to check each other out in the early evening in the interests of matchmaking. However, so many foreigners used flash photography that the Zao decided to move along and meet elsewhere. You should respect their customs and right to privacy. If you pay people of the hilltribes in any fashion to pose for photos, this becomes a form of begging, which is definitely not to be encouraged.

Hmong and Red Zao live outside town in villages; there can be a lot of friction between shopkeepers who live in town and the hilltribe folks who drift in on weekends. Two minorities, the Hmong and Tay, interact well with foreigners. Others, such as the Red Zao, remain extremely shy and avoid foreigners. Less often sighted are the Xapho and Tai people. Minority women are much easier to identify than men because the women more often wear traditional dress.

The minority groups in Sapa engage in subsistence farming, mainly rice cultivation. With only one crop a year, shortages often occur, and rice must be imported from the Mekong Delta to feed families. Livestock is reared to provide food during rice shortages or money to buy necessities. Water buffalo, pot-bellied pigs, goats, chickens, and ducks are kept by local people. Other sources of income include foraging for wild mushrooms, ginger, and herbs in forests; hunting; and cultivating opium.

Minority peoples practice animism and ancestor worship, combining elements of Taoism, Confucianism, and Buddhism. They believe in the spirits of rice, the earth, wind, rivers, and mountains—altars to these spirits are often found at the bases of sacred trees. In spring, agricultural rites ensure a successful crop season.

Black Hmong: The biggest group in the area, the Black Hmong (Hmong Den), represent more than 50 percent of Sapa's population. The Hmong, of Chinese origin, are thought to have immigrated to Vietnam at the end of the 18th century. Easily identified by their dark blue or black clothing, Hmong women wear large heavy earrings, bracelets, and necklaces. Traditional jewelry is often made of old French silver piastre coins, which also figure as part of the bride-price in marriage contracts. Hmong women wear their long hair rolled inside a headband and go barefoot or wear plastic sandals. Clothing is woven out of hemp and dyed with indigo. Men wear simple black outfits. When courting, Hmong men play pan-pipes while performing a dance—to impress Hmong women with their agility. The Hmong engage mostly in farming; some cultivate opium poppies. Hmong interact more than other minority groups with foreigners and have taken full advantage of commercial opportunities, particularly selling hand-loomed clothing items.

Red Zao: With similar origins, and in the same linguistic family, the Red Zao (Dao Do) constitute 25 percent of the local population in the Sapa District, though they are less often seen in villages than the Hmong. Red Zao women wear black embroidered pants and loose tunic tops. They shave their eyebrows and a portion of the hairline and wear spectacular red headdresses. They tie their hair in a topknot; a red turban is pinned to this, with braided or beaded sections, pom-poms, or coins dangling off it. They also wear silver neck pieces and carry shoulder bags with red tassels. The reason that Red Zao dress stands out at Sapa's weekend market is partly due to matchmaking rituals. On market day, Red Zao men wear dark blue jackets similar to those of the Hmong but with an embroidered rectangular patch on the back and embroidered black turbans. Red Zao women put on their finest clothing—the more elaborate the headdress, the more pom-poms and bells and ornaments worn, the more marriageable the woman. Things build up to Saturday night, when Red Zao men and women check each other out in Sapa. As Red Zao villages are scattered, the market serves as a gathering place where villagers can size up prospective spouses. Red Zao villages are quite small, perhaps only 30–300 people, whereas Hmong villages tend to be much larger.

Tay and Giay: Constituting less than 10 percent of the area's population, the Tay and Giay (pronounced Zai) minority groups have similar customs, clothing, and language because of their southern Chinese origins. The Tay make up the largest minority group in Vietnam, inhabiting the valleys and lower mountain slopes of the northern border regions. Tay clothing is dyed with indigo. Women wear a below–knee-length dress split at the right side up to the armpit with five buttons and narrow sleeves. Giay women from the Tavan Valley area wear black pants; solid-color cotton tunics, usually pink, green, or blue; and checked woolen headscarves in plaid patterns. The Chinese–style cotton tunic has a high neck collar and is secured with buttons at the waist and upper torso. Many Tay and Giay people have integrated into mainstream Vietnamese culture through intermarriage. They've adopted Vietnamese dress and may live in villages of mixed ethnic groups.

Sapa Market

There's a market every morning in Sapa, but the place swells on Saturday and Sunday when people of the hilltribes converge on the town to buy and sell supplies and indulge in matchmaking rituals. Some walk for an entire day to get there; you may see exotic groups in the market that you won't find even by hiking far into the surrounding terrain. Packhorses graze on the village green as villagers visit the wonders of the video shows at Sapa cinema.

There are several market locations in Sapa. Up around the cathedral are street stalls, food stalls, and street vendors—this section is buzzing. The market spills over down a flight of stone steps at the town center, with cobblestone alleys radiating off them. Below that is a three-story concrete building housing an indoor market—which is pretty soulless but necessary in the rainy season.

Sapa market proceeds in ethnic waves. It starts around 0900 on Saturday and builds all day as Red Zao and Tay pour into town. The Saturday market is dominated by the Red Zao. Although it's particularly busy 0900–1200, the market continues all day, and eating and drinking go on well into the evening. On Sunday there's a changing of the guard; the Red Zao stream out of town, and the Hmong walk in with their wicker basketpacks. The market reaches a high point in the morning but continues till about 1400. The Sunday market sees mostly Hmong people who sell great embroidery. You can buy jackets for $15 and up, purses for a dollar, shawls, and ingenious infant-carry packs.

Accommodations

Electrical supply may be intermittent in Sapa. Hotels generally have hot water available, but this may only be at certain hours, so inquire. Another advantage of the arrival of electricity is heating in the hotels—often in the form of portable bar-heaters. Some hotels have the original fireplaces from French days. Hotels often double for other services, such as providing tour information and so on. Hotels have a sliding scale of rates for winter, summer, and weekends. A summer weekend is the most expensive time to visit (roughly April–August).

The best area to aim for, with great views over the valleys below and the mountains above, are the guesthouses to the southern side of Sapa, around a sidestreet called Dong Loi. There are quite a few that have balconies facing westward, which means you get sunshine as well as views of the mountains. One of these is **Chau Long Sapa Hotel,** 24 Dong Loi St., tel. 20/871245, with 60 rooms (and an extension

of 100 rooms) for $32–65. In the same vicinity are a dozen more hotels, all vying for the expansive views.

Family-Run Guesthouses: Your best bet in Sapa is a family-run guesthouse. There are several fine places available with lots of character. ⚐ **Auberge Dang Trung,** tel. 20/871243, fax 20/871282, has five-story block out the back with rooms going for $22–28. A number of the rooms have balcony views and fireplaces; hot water is available. This hotel includes an excellent upstairs café that functions as a traveler meeting point. Downstairs is an Internet café run by the hotel. The owner of the auberge, the affable Mr. Trung, is very knowledgeable about the area and can arrange guides and transport. He speaks French and English. His passion is orchid collecting: He keeps more than 200 specimens.

In the same vicinity are three more guesthouses: **Queen Hotel,** tel. 20/871301, with six rooms for $8; **Student GH,** tel. 20/871308; and the three-room **Orchid GH,** tel. 20/871238. Another fine family-run establishment is **Viet Hung Hotel,** tel. 20/871313, at the northern end of town. There are 12 rooms here for $5–6 in winter, $10 in summer. Mr. Hung will assist with tours, transport, ticketing, and so on, operating out of the ground-floor Friendly Café. You can rent a Minsk motorcycle here or book train and bus tickets.

With great views over the valley from a terrace is **Cat Cat GH,** tel. 20/871387, down past the market building. It's run by a superfriendly family who treat you just like one of their own. There are five rooms here for $5–10. Around the corner is **Son Ha GH,** tel. 20/871273, occupying an old French villa, with six rooms for $3–5 in winter, $10 in summer, $15 on summer weekends. The atmosphere is great, and there are views from the top deck. Opposite Commercial Guesthouse are some shops with a few rooms available upstairs—these include **Waterfall GH** and **Lotus House.** Also here is **La Rose Hotel,** tel. 20/871263, with 12 rooms (30 beds) for $5 a night.

Villa Hotels: Old French villas have been converted into hotels around Sapa. These places, however, seem to be lacking when it comes to attention in reception. But do drop in to check out the buildings. Near the post office, **Observatory Guesthouse** has six rooms; the largest room upstairs includes a fireplace—this building used to be connected with a French weather station. The **Trade Union GH** operates a total of 10 rooms in two wings for $5–6 d or t. The cavernous communal bathrooms feature vintage French plumbing—even bidets (which look great but, you should be warned, may not function). This hotel is set in what was obviously once a French orchard estate—you can make out the stone wall perimeter. The hotel occupies two wings of the original buildings. North of this is a brand-new villa, **Ham Rong Hotel,** tel. 20/871251, fax 20/871303, with 11 rooms, including three with fireplaces. Rooms cost $12–15 in winter and $15–18 in summer and include hot water and TV. **Communications GH,** tel. 20/871364, occupies an old double-story villa; and **White Lily Hotel** (Khach San Ke Hoach), tel. 20/871289, offers eight rooms for around $6 each.

Larger Hotels: A flurry of modern building has taken place throughout Sapa—with new multistory edifices catering to group tours. Some of these are karaoke specials catering to a Vietnamese crowd, including Hotel Lasa and Thanh Son Hotel. Some new additions, such as the Hotel Fanxipan, are downright eyesores—this one with white tiling all over the exterior. Others are not recommended because they lack hot water or heating (Bank Hotel, Post GH), lack windows (Sunrise Hotel), or because they're run-down and grubby (Fansipan Hotel) or exude a strange karaoke-charged atmosphere (Hien Luong Hotel).

More comfortable are some larger hotels on the fringes of town. At the southern edge is **Green Bamboo Hotel,** tel./fax 20/871214, with 17 rooms in two wings, for $20–25 winter and $25–30 summer. This cozy place is affiliated with the Rainbow Café in Hanoi and is where its tour participants lodge. The hotel has satellite TV and a bar, open late. At the northern end of town is **Forestry Service GH** (Nha Nghi Lam Nghiep Sapa), tel. 20/871230, with

11 rooms for $12–15 d or t (off-season rates may be lower); baths and hot water available—clean rooms, some with fireplaces. The Forestry Service runs its own small restaurant down the hill from the guesthouse. **Hotel Number 2,** on the west side of town, is a large hotel with clean rooms and modern amenities.

The 77-room **Victoria Sapa,** tel. 20/871522, victoriasapa@fpt.vn, www.victoriahotels-asia. com, is the last word on luxury in this neck of the woods. Within its precincts lie a heated indoor swimming pool, tennis courts, fitness center, a restaurant that can seat more than 100 people, and two bars. Prices range $85–100 for superior rooms and $150–180 for studios and suites. The Victoria Hotel group goes one step further on the luxury front by transporting guests in its own train cars, which are described as "extremely soft." (See the entry under *Getting There.*)

Food

Excellent vegetarian *(anh chay)* and other fare can be found in Sapa's market stalls. All have the same menu and offer good soups, spring rolls, tofu and peanut dishes, and delicious wild mushrooms. You can buy purified water here; Chinese beer is cheap because of Sapa's proximity to the border. For an extra buzz, try a hot lemon drink with honey produced by wild bees; the honey, said to be slightly toxic, is also available in bottles in Sapa market. You can wash down meals with Sapa plum wine, which, at little more than a dollar a bottle, can become addictive. On weekends dinner guests at the food stalls are mostly visiting tribespeople.

Vegetarian food is the specialty at **Café Dang Trung,** which features a balcony overlooking the valley. The place seats 20 and can get crowded. Near Café Dang Trung is a row of restaurants with quite palatable food—these include **Queen Café, Chapa Café, Thu Duong Restaurant,** and **Phansipang Restaurant.**

On Thac Bac Street to the northwest side of town is ⋈ **Baguette & Chocolate,** a bakery with fresh bread and pastries—great for breakfast and for arranging take-away picnics. The restaurant is part of a Hanoi-based training school for disadvantaged youth: In Sapa, some Black Hmong are trainees. Dining is low-key here: It's a quiet location, away from the market hustle and bustle. There's outdoor seating, and a fine indoor section. Upstairs is a minihotel with a few rooms.

Nightlife

Restaurants are the nightlife of Sapa. If pining for a proper pint of beer, try **The Red Dragon Pub,** south side of Sapa—a real English pub run by a real Englishman. And for the strangest pub in the north, go and see the bar at the **Green Bamboo** hotel on Friday and Saturday night, when it's Ethnic Night. Westerners quaffing beer mix with Black Hmong and Red Zao selling bracelets. The tiny bar serves as an impromptu arena. A Black Hmong man dances in a circle while playing pan-pipes, followed by a Hmong woman who plays a leaf-instrument similar to a harmonica. Next up might be Hmong and Red Zao women crooning renditions of love songs. Bizarre is the only word for it.

Services and Information

The tourist information office to the southern side of town sells booklets about Sapa—some of which are actually readable, detailing flora and fauna (especially birdlife), and describing hikes and walks. You can change dollars to dong in the marketplace or at the Bank Hotel. The rate here is lower than in Hanoi. Good sources of information and touring are Auberge Dang Trung, and the Friendly Café at Viet Hung Hotel.

Arranging Transport

Sapa has a stable of Russian jeeps, 4WD vehicles, and minibuses for hire—either for launching trekking day trips, for excursions to Bac Ha, or for going as far afield as Hanoi. A six-day/five-night Sapa–Hanoi trip works out at about $320 for four passengers, or $80 a head. This price is only for transport and gasoline; the driver covers his own costs on the road. The route goes via Dien Bien Phu and Mai Chau.

Adventure Touring: Outfits such as Hand-span and Topas can arrange adventure touring, from multiday treks with Hmong porters to mountain-biking forays.

Getting There

By Train: Travelers to Sapa usually take the train up to Lao Cai, and then make a 35-kilometer road run to Sapa on a connecting minibus. There are minibuses lying in wait at Lao Cai station when you disembark, but these can be pricey. An alternative is to take a moto over Coc Leu Bridge to the regular bus station and catch a ride to Sapa there. You can also club together and rent a private jeep. Or you can just hire a moto for the whole distance. Moto operators charge $6–8 for the haul; by regular bus the trip takes two hours and costs $2. The winding climb into the hills of the Hoang Lien Son Range to Sapa is magnificent, with sheer drops by the side of the road. But the road remains in poor shape, with rocks, rubble, and landslide debris; buses are prone to breakdowns.

You can also reach Sapa from Pho Lu station, which is an hour before Lao Cai. From Pho Lu, it's 75 kilometers up to Sapa, a trip of about four hours. Pho Lu (also called Bao Tang) is the jumping-off point for the highland village of Bac Ha. There is less frequent transport in Pho Lu—and it's not the best place to stay overnight.

Hanoi to Pho Lu is 262 kilometers by rail; on the same train, Hanoi to Lao Cai is 295 kilometers. Hanoi to Lao Cai costs $7.50 for a hard seat, $10 soft seat, or $16 hard sleeper. Train LC1 takes 11 hours, departing Hanoi around 2130 and arriving at 0740; another train, LC2, departs Hanoi 0510 and reaches Lao Cai at 1535. In the reverse direction, LC2 departs Lao Cai at 1800 for an overnight run, reaching Hanoi at an inconvenient 0400 hours (bide some time in nearby 24-hour cafés); LC4 departs Lao Cai at 0940, reaching Hanoi at 2020. The through train from Hanoi to Kunming (a two-night journey taking more than 30 hours), which runs twice a week, also stops at Lao Cai. Train LC5 leaves Hanoi at 2130 and arrives at Lao Cai at 0700 next morning; several hours are allowed for customs and immigration clearance at Lao Cai, and the train

The North

proceeds again at 0920 and reaches Kunming next day at 0600 hours. In the opposite direction, train LC6 leaves Kunming at 1445 and arrives Hanoi at 2020 the following day. Train schedules may fluctuate. Make sure you get the right station in Hanoi—the trains for Lao Cai do not depart from the main station, but from a minor station just north on Tran Quy Cap Street.

Victoria Express: The Victoria Hotel group tacks three deluxe cars onto the regular train to Lao Cai, running several times a week. There are two deluxe sleeping cars and a plush seating and restaurant car. The cars can accommodate 48 passengers: Cost is $50 round-trip weekdays, or $75 weekends in a four-bunk cabin, and more expensive in a two-bunk cabin. This comes as a kind of package deal—if you use the Victoria Express, you stay at Victoria Sapa Hotel. Contact the Victoria office in Hanoi at 33A Pham Ngu Lao, tel. 4/9330318, victoriaexpress@fpt.vn.

By Road: A variety of road routes lead to Sapa, most of them rough. A 4WD is recommended for these routes, although minibuses and wheezing local buses can handle the roads. Minibus tours from traveler cafés in Hanoi often opt for the direct 390-kilometer ride to Sapa, via Yen Bai, Pho Lu, and Lao Cai, roughly paralleling the rail line. You can cover this route in one long day of travel by private car, about 12 hours; there's little in the way of scenic highlights. A four-day round-trip jeep trip from Hanoi along this route costs $240; by Land Cruiser, as much as $400.

A direct bus to Sapa from Hanoi's Kim Ma station runs on Friday only, departing 0430 and arriving 2200 the same day; it returns to Hanoi on Monday. No news from any foreigner who has survived this epic journey—not recommended if you value your kidneys. You'd be better off tackling the bus route in stages. Take the first ride to Yen Bai and continue from there.

Definitely more rewarding if you can spare the time is a longer trip of four days or more from Hanoi via Dien Bien Phu to Sapa, a wild ride of 750 kilometers. Travel from Hanoi to Dien Bien Phu to Lai Chau to Phong Tho to Sapa, or the reverse. Excellent views and stops predominate along this route. A jeep or other 4WD vehicle is recommended, but you can also cover the ground in stages by bus.

Western motorcyclists have covered both road routes in two weeks, round-trip—and then sworn they'd never attempt the odyssey again. Their Russian motorcycles vibrated apart, and their nerves frayed from concentrating on potholes. Other motorcyclists have braved the Hanoi–Dien Bien Phu route to Sapa, and then loaded their bikes onto the train from Lao Cai returning to Hanoi. For those who like rodeo broncos, an even more rugged road route runs from Hanoi to Van Chan to Than Uyen to Sapa. The scenery, though beautiful, may jump up and down a lot, and focusing on it may present a problem. Buses even run along these stretches—every second day, if you're lucky.

Getting Around

On foot, mostly. A dozen or so moto drivers hang around the markets, ferrying heavy loads. Hire them if you want a head start on a longer hike; they also make runs to Lao Cai for hefty fees. Motos come equipped with sturdy racks and straps at sides and back, suitable for backpacks. Some guesthouses can arrange rental of a 4WD jeep to get you to a trailhead or farther afield—all the way to Hanoi. Sapa provides ideal terrain for mountain biking, with the emphasis on "mountain." Some foreigners have negotiated some trails by bicycle. If you're planning some paved road touring, you can rent a Minsk motorcycle from Friendly Café at Viet Hung Hotel for $8 a day. You can also rent jeeps or find a local guide here.

Getting Away

A bus departs for Lao Cai from the mini-post office area most mornings around 0600 and afternoons around 1400. You can buy advance tickets at the place next to the mini-post office, which will also arrange train sleeper tickets to Hanoi for a surcharge. The road run to Lao Cai is straight downhill, so it's fairly fast going—a bit longer than an hour if all's well with the engine. By moto, it's an hour. Train LC2 departs Lao Cai around 1700 and arrives in Hanoi at 0400; train LC4 departs Lao Cai around 0745, arriving in Hanoi at 1945.

There are other buses running from Sapa to Phong Tho and Lai Chau. Via Lao Cai, you can connect by bus to Pho Lu station, and Bac Ha highland village.

N HIKING IN THE SAPA REGION

You can embark on day hikes around Sapa by yourself. For overnight or longer hikes, where you face language problems and risk getting lost, you should consider hiring a guide/interpreter from a local guesthouse. Porters are also available. Locals along the trails will also act as impromptu guides, leading you through rice fields to the next village, with no payment expected. In theory you're not permitted to stay in villages without a guide, but some travelers have managed it. Villagers supply simple rice dishes; a small payment of $1–2 is expected for lodging. Consider taking along gifts, but be discreet so as not to encourage begging. The best way to break the ice with the Hmong is to buy something—a purse for a dollar, whatever. Pack out all litter and bury organic waste at least 20 meters away from any water sources. A disturbing development at Sapa is the setting up of roadblocks on the walks up to Cat Cat, Taphin, and Lao Chai, with a person charging a kind of "entrance fee."

Trails around Sapa are often steep and can get slippery when wet. For longer hikes, consider a kick-start in the form of a moto driver or jeep driver; he can drop you at a trailhead or take you partway along your route. The roads are atrocious, so motos can be hard on the system—your suspension and the bike's. Jeeps fare slightly better.

Old Power Station

This walk requires about 3–4 hours. You hike to Cat Cat village and the old power station, about three kilometers from Sapa, or about 1.5 hours downhill. From Sapa, take the road down past the concrete market building to the west. On a clear day, there are good views of Mt. Fansipan from here. Following the trail to the power station is tricky—the old power lines and pylons lead there. A few hundred meters past a villa you pass under power lines. Walk 100 meters and turn left down a side trail. Follow this trail till it arcs back under the power lines again; keep following the power lines as best you can. Eventually, this small trail leads to the Hmong village of Cat Cat. Beyond the village you'll find some small cascades within a bamboo forest and a few disused buildings that served as the French power station built in the 1920s. Several "grain robots" pound grain by means of an ingenious water-driven wooden contraption. You can hike farther westward from the power station toward Mt. Fansipan through meadows, but paths are not clear and you may need a guide.

Sinchai Village

Start off as for the old power-station hike—but follow the main trail past the power lines to

© MICHAEL BUCKLEY

Green Hmong tribespeople sort out crops on a roadway in northeast Vietnam.

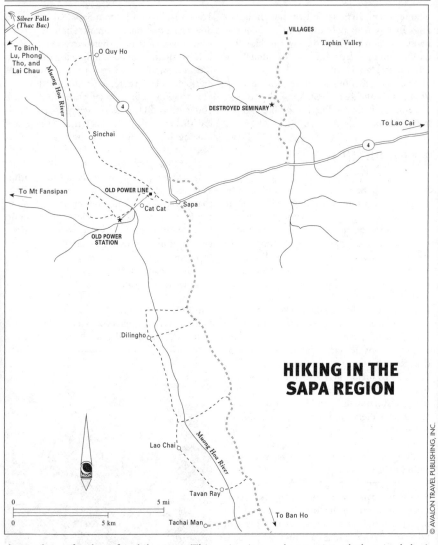

Silver Falls
(Thac Bac)

To Binh
Lu, Phong
Tho, and
Lai Chau

O Quy Ho

VILLAGES

Taphin Valley

Muong Hoa River

4

DESTROYED SEMINARY

To Lao Cai

4

Sinchai

To Mt Fansipan

OLD POWER LINE

Cat Cat

Sapa

OLD POWER
STATION

Dilingho

HIKING IN THE
SAPA REGION

Muong Hoa River

Lao Chai

Tavan Ray

To Ban Ho

Tachai Man

0   5 mi

0   5 km

© AVALON TRAVEL PUBLISHING, INC.

The North

the northwest for about four kilometers. This brings you to the large Hmong village of Sinchai, with a population of about 1,000. Along the way you witness the rhythms of rural life: Villagers harvesting rice or plowing with water buffalo. You may also see snippets of Hmong life: Someone dyeing clothing with indigo in huge vats, or playing a mouth organ (small piece in mouth, extension tube hanging below) made of brass and bamboo. Dogs in Sinchai can be a problem as they perform their guard duties. Continue past the village, and when the path diverges, take a right fork to climb out of the valley. There are majestic views of the rice paddies below. Eventually you make it up to the main road, Route 4, where you can either take a moto on to Silver Falls or take a ride back to Sapa (or walk the distance).

Silver Falls Trail

Silver Falls (Thac Bac), about 12 kilometers from Sapa on the Lai Chau route, lie just off the road a few kilometers south of Dinh Deo Pass. If you're driving along the route, stop for a view of the pretty falls. You can climb over rocks up toward the top of the falls. A few kilometers farther toward Lao Chai is Dinh Deo Pass—at 2,500 meters the highest point on the Sapa–Lai Chau route. There are stunning views over several valleys from Dinh Deo Pass; from there a short hiking trail leads to Quy Ho Lake, the source of Silver Falls.

Taphin Valley

Taphin Valley lies about 12 kilometers northeast of Sapa. The trail into the valley is accessible by jeep, but few vehicles attempt it, so the valley mostly sees foot traffic. You could, however, take a ride on Route 4 to the turnoff for Taphin Valley. The hike goes through some pleasant terrain and passes several Hmong and Red Zao villages. The very shy Red Zao usually keep a low profile and are reluctant to let foreigners take photos.

To reach Taphin Valley, head along the Lao Cai route for about five kilometers till you pass a kilometer stone that reads Pho Lu 69 kilometers. Take the dirt turnoff that appears soon after this marker stone; the turnoff lies between the marker and a bridge. Hike in about three kilometers on the Taphin Valley trail, past some Hmong villages, to the ruins of a large monastery. The seminary was destroyed by militant Vietnamese who suspected such a large place had a military connection. There are a small school and some Hmong houses in the vicinity. Take the road more or less straight ahead from here till you reach a fork, and then take the right fork. You will pass a Zao village nearby. If you keep hiking past the end of the dirt road—about 6–7 kilometers in from the Lao Cai road—you'll come to a valley with several villages. Local kids can direct you to a karst grotto in this area.

Tavan Valley

In this direction (south of Sapa) a two-day hike is preferable, with an overnight stay in a village. You may need a guide; obtain one at a Sapa guesthouse such as Auberge Dang Trung. To speed trailhead access, take a moto or jeep from the Sapa market down the dirt road south. Jeeps can run along here for about 15 kilometers. Otherwise, traffic down this way is mostly on foot or with packhorses.

If on foot, head past Auberge Dang Trung downhill from Sapa for about 12 kilometers, or about 2–3 hours. There are great views of mountain majesty and terraces laid out below in abstract patterns. Hike down to the Muong Hoa River on a trail and cross a bridge to the Hmong village of Lao Chai. If you pick your way over the rice paddies, you will reach the Giay village of Tavan Ray—look for a schoolhouse. In the vicinity you'll see ingenious bamboo plumbing and "grain robots," as well as bamboo bridges and small waterfalls. Farther down the valley is the Red Zao village of Ta-chai Man.

Mount Fansipan

At 3,143 meters, Mt. Fansipan is Vietnam's highest peak. Fansipan is not a distinct peak but a conglomerate. You'll need a guide from Sapa to make sure you've reached the right summit; a metal triangle marks it. Three routes lead to the top; the easiest ascent vaguely follows a riverbed from the foothills of Sapa. It's a minimum three days out to the summit and back; 4–6 days is preferable. You need a sleeping bag or blankets, tent, food, and good warm clothing. Some groups bring porters.

Along the way, when not cutting swaths through bamboo thickets, you might glimpse wild goats or monkeys. In this direction is Nui Hoang Lien Nature Reserve, an area of 30 square kilometers that encompasses Mt. Fansipan. Some 12 square kilometers of natural forest remains. Between 2,500 and 2,800 meters an elfin forest flourishes with gnarled trees covered in mosses, lichens, and flowering plants, particularly orchids. At higher elevations you'll come across dwarf rhododendron and bamboo. More than 150 species of birds have been spotted in the reserve. Some, such as the collared finchbill, the white-throated laughing-thrush, and the chestnut bulbul, are found only in the mountains of northwest Vietnam. On a clear day, views from the top of Fansipan are excellent.

MUONG HOUM

The Sunday market at the village of Muong Houm, about 80 km north of Sapa, is well worth the visit. You can arrange to drive there as a day trip from Sapa, leaving very early morning, visiting the market, and then hiking to villages of the region. There are at least a dozen ethnic groups at the market here, and you may not see some of them elsewhere. The drive up, past mist-shrouded rice terraces and through lush mountain terrain, makes the dawn departure worthwhile.

BAC HA

A popular side trip from Sapa is to the highland village of Bac Ha, about 75 kilometers away, where you can see Flower Hmong gathering at the big market on Sunday. A second market thronged by Flower Hmong, and not far from Bac Ha, is Can Cau Market, which takes place on a Saturday. During the week, nothing much happens in Bac Ha, but if you like quiet villages, this is the place to be. Various guesthouses run day trips from Sapa to Bac Ha for reasonable prices.

Using Bac Ha as a base, you can hike to Hmong villages, some of which lie only a few kilometers out. A good loop to try is to walk northwest past Sao Mai Guesthouse and continue in a clockwise direction. Eventually a five-kilometer circuit of dirt trails will bring you back into Bac Ha. Slowing down your progress will be Hmong hospitality—which may require you to knock back glasses of homebrew firewater.

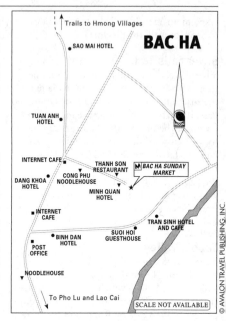 Sunday Market

On Sunday, the Hmong stream into Bac Ha from villages, using mangy horses to carry

goods. At the market there is trading in livestock and weaving materials, and a sit-down, open-air eating section. There are more than a dozen Montagnard groups inhabiting the area around Bac Ha, but Flower Hmong women stand out because of their flashy hemp-cloth costumes woven with floral designs. The costumes are hand-embroidered, and Hmong men apparently admire the handiwork—and size up prospective spouses from their skill in embroidery. The cloth section of the market is extensive, providing raw materials for costumes. Although there is a mundane dry goods section selling plastic buckets and pots and pans, walk around and you will soon find curious commerce in progress—such as a vendor presiding over a pile of tobacco, which is sold to customers right there by the bamboo bong-load (smoked on the spot). Lively parts of the market are the section trading pigs, buffalo, and dogs (don't ask), and a primitive foundry making knives.

Accommodations and Food

There are more than a dozen guesthouses—

basic, but comfortable enough. Guesthouses may double as noodlehouses. At the north end of town is **Sao Mai Hotel,** tel. 20/880288, with a few dozen rooms for around $20 each, popular with group tours. There are a number of other hotels around town, charging about $10 a room. The best choice is **Minh Quan GH,** which has a good atmosphere, balcony views (of the markets), and the price is right at $7 a room. Other options include **Tran Sin Hotel,** tel. 20/880240, with three rooms for $8 each; and **Anh Duong Hotel,** tel. 20/880329, with 13 rooms for $7 each. With much less character is **Dang Khoa Hotel,** tel. 20/881280, with 10 rooms for $6–8. Best places to eat are **Thanh Son Restaurant** (close to the markets), **Cong Phu Noodlehouse** (farther along the same road), and the dining room at **Tran Sin Hotel.** These places may serve good spring rolls, but don't expect gourmet meals in Bac Ha. On Sundays, when the market is in full swing, there are lots of open-air food stalls serving hot food.

Getting There

Travelers often make a round-trip from Sapa to Bac Ha on Sundays with traveler minibuses. These minibuses go via Cam Duong to Bac Ha. You can also arrange for the traveler minibus to drop you off at Lao Cai station on the way back from Bac Ha, and then continue by train back to Hanoi or on to China (an alternative is to be dropped at Pho Lu station, but since the train originates at Lao Cai, you would get reserved seats there). If you want to treat Bac Ha as a destination in its own right, the best approach is to get off the Hanoi train at Pho Lu station. There should be a bus connecting with the train and running up to Bac Ha—the buses wait at the station. If not, you will held to ransom by moto drivers for the winding uphill ride. Pho Lu is a dreary railway town with very limited facilities and transport—not a good place to stay overnight. There is a cheap, run-down guesthouse next to the railway station. There's also bus service running from Lao Cai to Bac Ha—the same bus stops at Pho Lu en route.

LAO CAI TO KUNMING

Lao Cai

Lao Cai sits right on the Chinese border on the route from Hanoi to Kunming. It's also the junction for getting to the town of Sapa. The Red River enters Vietnam at Lao Cai after covering 800 kilometers from its source 2,000 meters up on China's Yunnan Plateau and tracing a section of the China-Vietnam border.

Much of Lao Cai was destroyed in 1979 by the Chinese. The place is mostly under reconstruction, rejuvenated by resumption of cross-border trade and smuggling. The rebuilding plan for Lao Cai calls for two zones on either side of the Red River. On the southern bank is Lao Cai Town, with a market, bus station, and a few hotels—basically a main drag lined with shops. On the northern bank, arrayed along Nguyen Hue Street, are administrative offices with customs and immigration services and half a dozen hotels. Linking the two areas is Coc Leu Bridge, constructed in 1993 at a cost of $1.5 million to replace an earlier bridge destroyed by bombing. You can get around Lao Cai by moto—pick one up near Vietnam Immigration, outside the railway station, or near the bus station. An occasional jeep might wait near Immigration, too. It's about two kilometers from Coc Leu Bridge to Vietnam Immigration, and about four kilometers from Coc Leu Bridge to the railway station.

Accommodations: Most hotels in Lao Cai are situated on the north bank along Nguyen Hue Street. Here you'll find a slew of hotels: **Petrolimex, Xuat Nhap Khau (XNT) Hotel,** and **Hong Ha.** A good choice is **Song Hong Hotel,** tel. 20/830004, which offers 15 rooms for $10–12 with views of China across the river. **Post GH,** tel. 20/830006, has seven rooms and charges $12–15. **Hanoi Hotel,** 19 Nguyen Hue St., tel. 20/832486, fax 20/832488, is run by Hanoi Railway Tourist Company and offers nine rooms for $15–20 each. On the southern bank are **Thuy Son Minihotel** and the much larger **Duyen Hai Hotel,** tel. 20/822083, fax 20/820177, which boasts rooms with TV and hot water—all facing the Red River and China.

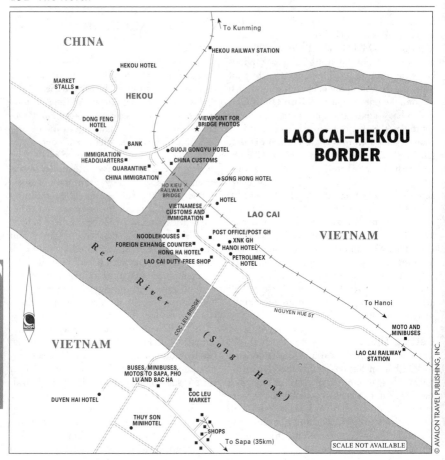

LAO CAI–HEKOU BORDER

There are 32 rooms. The higher you go in this five-story hotel, the cheaper it gets (there's no elevator); rooms vary from $20–25 for lower floors to $10–15 for upper floors.

Transport: Hanoi to Lao Cai is 295 kilometers by train (11 hours) and costs $7.50 hard seat, $10 soft seat, or $16 hard sleeper. There's an overnight train from Hanoi, LHC1, and a day train, LC3. You decide whether you want to see the scenery or get a night's sleep and be ready to carry on the next day. For the return leg, LC2 is the night train and LC4 the day train.

From Sapa to Lao Cai your choice is between a bus, minibus, or a moto for the 35-kilome-

ter run; there may be the odd jeep available. A bus or minibus takes two hours for the run and costs $2. Motos charge about $6–8 to Sapa. They're well equipped with racks and straps at side and back to accommodate backpacks. The road runs straight uphill, with big cliff drops.

China Border Crossing

The Ho Kieu Railway Bridge links China and Vietnam. The French-built narrow-gauge rail link from Kunming to Hanoi and Haiphong has been restored, giving landlocked Yunnan province access to a major seaport. Goods trains now run direct from Kunming to Hanoi, and facilities for direct passenger trains are in place. At the China border, the train passes over the narrow bridge. Pedestrians and bicyclists can also cross here. If the direct passenger trains are going through, you will of course have to allow for adjustments in the following information, which is based on the system of the two connecting trains. For through trains, customs and immigration formalities would take place at Lao Cai station. On the main street of Lao Cai, opposite the post office, is a foreign-exchange counter trading dollars to dong, and dong to Chinese renminbi. Opposite is a duty-free shop selling whiskey and 555 cigarettes.

Exiting Lao Cai: Don't give immigration here any excuse for fund-raising with incomplete paperwork. To exit at Lao Cai you go to customs first, hand over your form, proceed to Immigration for a stamp out, and then cross the bridge, check in at Chinese Immigration for a stamp in, go to Chinese Customs to fill out forms, and finally arrive at Chinese Quarantine to answer questions about cholera, plague, and yellow-fever inoculations. It takes more than an hour to finalize procedures between Vietnam and China if your papers are in order. There's a time difference of one hour between Lao Cai and Hekou, because Hekou runs on Beijing time. If the time is 0900 in Vietnam, it should be 1000 in Hekou.

Entering Lao Cai: Even if your paperwork is excellent, you can run into problems here. Some travelers report their one-month Vietnamese visa was reduced to seven days at Lao Cai. The Port of Entry official decides about registration on arrival and may choose to give you transit authority only. If this happens, you must head for Hanoi and get your visa extended.

Other travelers have reported irregularities with money declaration. One declared $3,200, the officers insisted on counting it, found $3,500, and fined the traveler $20 for the miscount. Another traveler came up $150 short at customs after officers asked him to count out all his traveler's checks and cash. If you arrive in Lao Cai from Yunnan with your visa stamped in for a month, and assuming you're still in possession of your cash and all your faculties, don't

be in any hurry to get to Hanoi—go and visit Sapa for some quiet relaxation.

Hekou

If coming from Vietnam and on the loose in Hekou, you'll need Chinese renminbi (RMB, People's Money). You'll find a bank near Immigration Headquarters. The bank will deal only with traveler's checks or U.S. cash. If you want to change dong to RMB you'll have to deal with money changers on the streets in the same area. There are several places to stay in Hekou: try the Soviet–style **Hekou Hotel** up on a hill, or the **Dong Feng Hotel** on the main street. Down by the border bridge is an eight-story pink hotel called **Guoji Gongyu.**

Down by the river on the way to Hekou railway station is a photo set-up with multicolored umbrellas and props. You can have your picture taken with Ho Kieu Bridge in the background, a memento of your crossing. Hand over your camera and a Chinese photographer will oblige you with a shot.

In Hekou you're in a little-visited part of Yunnan province. Roughly half of China's 50-plus minorities are represented in Yunnan; most live in border areas. You can explore this part of Yunnan by bus; the highway up to Kunming is in surprisingly good shape. Villages along the way hold Hmong; the women wear embroidered pastel dresses and leggings, the men Mao outfits.

KUNMING

Kunming, a boomtown with a fast-paced, free-market economy, is rapidly becoming the powerhouse of China's southwest. With increasing international air connections from its new airport to Bangkok, Hong Kong, and Singapore, Kunming is assuming an important role in trade routes through China and Indochina. Kunming is the gateway to the fascinating minority areas of Dali (Bai people) and Lijiang (Naxi). With the border south of Jinghong open into Laos, you could consider forging some trailblazer overland routes. You can obtain visas for Laos and Myanmar (Burma) in Kunming. A Vietnamese consulate has also been established in Kunming to facilitate travel. Vietnamese visas are normally issued in Hong Kong or Beijing; there's also a visa-issuing consulate in Nanning, which is connected by a new rail line to Kunming.

At an elevation of 1,890 meters, Kunming has a mild climate and a relaxing pace as Chinese cities go. Its wide boulevards are great for cycling. The main axis of Kunming is Beijing Road, a boulevard running almost five kilometers between Kunming North Station and Kunming South Station; this is intersected by Dong Feng Road, the main east-west axis. At the intersection of Dong Feng and Beijing roads sits the post office and Telecom building. The main commercial center of town is the quadrant north of Jinbi Lu and west of Beijing Lu. This part contains old streets, many retaining traditional green-and-red shuttered shop fronts now rarely found in China. Kunming is well-supplied for consumer goods and is an ideal place to stock up. You can, for example, buy well-crafted Taiwanese mountain bikes here.

Most accommodation is grouped toward the Kunming South Station. A ride in a three-wheeler from North to South Station costs less than a dollar; you can also hop on a 23 bus or take a metered taxi.

Accommodations

One of the best places to stay for budget travelers is **Camellia Hotel,** at 154 East Dong Feng, tel. 86-871/316-3000, offering dorm beds for $4 and rooms for $16–30 each. The hotel is huge, but many rooms are occupied by businesses. Another option is **Kunhu Hotel,** at 44 Beijing Rd., (toward Kunming South Station), tel. 86-871/313-3799. Rates run $5 a person in a three-bed room, $10 for a double room, $20 for a double with bath. You can rent bicycles here. At the northwest fringe of the city (a bit inconvenient for transport) is **Yunnan University Guesthouse,** a foreign-student hostel charging $5 a person in four-bed rooms; some carpeted rooms with hot water and TV are available for $14 and up.

There is no shortage of high-end accommodations in Kunming. **Holiday Inn Kunming,** at 25 Dong Feng East Rd., tel. 86-871/316-5888, fax 86-871/313-5189, is an 18-story building with 252 luxurious rooms for $80–115 and suites for $120–600. Aerial views from the nightclub on the top floor may prove worth the price of a drink there. To the southern end of Beijing Road is a cluster of mammoth 200- and 300-room hotels charging $50–80 for rooms and $150 and up for suites. These include the 17-story **Golden Dragon,** at 575 Beijing Rd., tel. 86-871/313-3015; the 19-story **King World Hotel,** 28 Beijing Rd., tel. 86-871/313-8888; the 18-story **Tea Gardens Hotel,** Yongping Road, tel. 86-871/313-9202; and the mega **Three Leaves Hotel,** 614 Beijing Rd., tel. 86-871/313-8644.

Food

A number of cafés around Kunming act as traveler hangouts—the owners maintain logbooks chock-full of information from backpackers passing through. These places will assist with bicycle rentals, train tickets, and bus transport up-country to Dali and Lijiang. Almost next door to the Camellia Hotel is **Jianje Café,** run by the helpful Luo family. At 262 Huan Cheng Nan Lu, opposite the Golden Dragon Hotel, is **Wei's Place,** run by Mrs. Wei—you can rent mountain bikes here. Around the corner from Wei's Place, near Kunhu Hotel, is a strip of small restaurants, including **Happy Restaurant** and **Yuelai Café.** These serve Western food: pizza, fruit salad, fried goat cheese. Kunming's foreign students hang out at Yunnan University—you can catch them at a back-alley den called **Journey to the East Café,** which has a good collection of Western books. In Kunming's old town a string of restaurants sells steaming bowls of across-the-bridge noodles, the local specialty. You can find these restaurants by exploring the alleys immediately west of Zhengyi Lu and north of Jinbi Lu. Lots of street-side eateries serve stir-fried food and clay steampots. For those who want to splurge,

VINTAGE RAIL SPUR

At the turn of the last century, the French attempted to reach the riches of Southwest China through Vietnam via railway. Hekou, Simao, and Mengzi were opened to French trade, and the port of Kwangchowan was leased to the French in 1898. The French wrangled a railway concession through Chinese territory, a narrow-gauge line that snaked from the port of Haiphong through Hanoi up to Kunming in landlocked Yunnan. Between 1902 and 1910 more than a third of the 80,000 Chinese and Vietnamese construction workers perished building the line over perilous terrain. The project turned into a white elephant—the rail spur cost twice the initial estimate, and the riches of China barely materialized.

Until the 1950s this was the only rail line into China's Yunnan province. The line fell into disrepair, and in 1979 the link was cut at Hekou because of fighting between the Vietnamese and Chinese. In 1997, the link was resumed for goods trains and passenger trains. Most of China's vast rail system is 1.435-gauge (standard gauge), while Vietnam's system is French-built meter-gauge (narrow gauge). The Hekou-Kunming line is vintage track for China, and a special narrow train is required on the route. The ride on the Chinese side must rank among Asia's finest rail journeys, with breathtaking views.

The Victoria Hotel group (with a four-star hotel in Sapa) has a deal with the Vietnamese railway authorities to tack some luxury cars onto the regular train for the Hanoi to Lao Cai run on this line. This includes a deluxe dining car. Normally the fare is tied in with stays at Victoria Hotel in Sapa.

The North

the Holiday Inn puts on a buffet breakfast and a buffet lunch.

Consulates

The **Vietnamese consulate,** on the 2nd floor of Kai Wah International Hotel, 157 Beijing Rd., tel: 86-871/352-2669, grants one-month Vietnamese visas for $50 in three working days or for $75 in one working day.

The **Lao PDR Consulate,** on the second floor of Building 3 at the Camellia Hotel, 154 East Dong Feng, tel. 86-871/317-6623, will issue a seven-day transit visa in one day for $28, but this most likely means you have to fly into Vientiane from Kunming. A better alternative is to try for a two-week visa—you should be able to forge your way across the land border into Laos at Ban Boten and carry on overland to Luang Prabang or onward through Laos to Thailand at Ban Huay Sai. **Myanmar Consulate-General** (Burma) is on the third floor of Building 3 at the Camellia Hotel, tel. 86-871/317-6609. The consulate issues a two-week visa for around $35, obtainable in three days. You may have to fly into Rangoon, which will

cost more than $230 one-way on CAAC; there seems to be only a flight every couple of weeks. The land borders into Myanmar (Burma) from Yunnan are open for locals, but the consulate will probably tell you these border crossings are off-limits for foreigners.

Hekou–Kunming Bus

You can make the trip from Hekou to Kunming by express bus, which takes 7–8 hours.

Rail Connections

Kunming is connected by rail to Chengdu (starting point for flights to Tibet) and to Nanning. Because of the rugged terrain of Yunnan, these rail journeys are among China's most spectacular. The Kunming–Nanning line is said to have been China's most arduous to build, with fully 30 percent of the 900-kilometer line composed of tunnels or bridges.

International Flights

Kunming International Airport is eight kilometers from the city. Departure tax on international flights is RMB90. Several carriers work the Kunming–Bangkok route. Yunnan Airlines, at 368 Tuodong Rd., tel. 86-871/312-1220, operates several flights a week; it is also the agent for Lao Airlines. China Southern Airlines schedules one flight a week. Thai Airways International schedules five flights a week to Bangkok; $160 economy one-way, $225 business class, flight time two hours. The Thai Airways office is at 32 Chun Cheng Rd. in the Panlong District. Thai Airways also flies twice weekly to Chiang Mai; $140 economy class one-way. Singapore Airlines flies from Kunming to Singapore twice-weekly for $402 one-way; the office is in the Holiday Inn, 25 Dong Feng East Rd., tel. 86-871/316-5888. Other connections from Kunming: daily flights to Hong Kong for around $195 one-way on China Southern Airlines or Dragonair (office in Golden Dragon Hotel); to Hanoi several times a week on Vietnam Airlines for $200 one-way; to Vientiane on Yunnan Airlines for around $150 one-way, flights once weekly.

Central Vietnam

The Vietnamese describe their country as a bamboo pole supporting a basket of rice at either end. The baskets of rice they speak of are the Mekong Delta in the south and the Red River Delta in the north—both important producers of the holy grain. But the skinny bamboo pole between the two plays a much lesser role, it appears.

Central Vietnam is a thin strip of land lying between a white-sand coastline to the east and mountain ranges to the west. It is a zone with a turbulent history, buffeted by stronger powers—as in north and south going at it during the Vietnam War. Economically, the central region lags well behind developments in the north and the south. This may be changing—not in the mountains, where ethnic unrest continues, but on the coast. Resort developers are snapping up large swaths of prime beachfront property to build megaresorts catering to visiting Asians, who can fly in direct to Danang from, say, Singapore. Resort building is continuing at a brisk pace along the coast, especially in the Danang to Hoi An strip, and the zone around Phan Thiet at Mui Ne. There were plans to build golf courses close to Phan Thiet, which is sure to attract Japanese vacationers. And Mickey Mouse to the rescue: There were plans to bring in the Disney troupes and build a Disneyworld Vietnam close to Phan Thiet—which is sure to boost the local economy.

And now for the weather report. Overcast, with a good chance of showers. Central Vietnam lies in a transitional climate zone between

Must-Sees

Look for **M** to find the sights and activities you can't miss and **N** for the best dining and lodging.

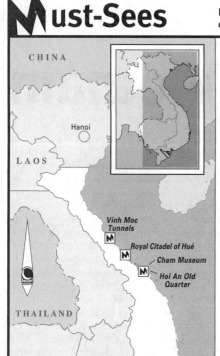

M Royal Citadel, Hué: The former seat of Hué's emperors, with remnants of palaces and temples and fortifications. This place has improved through the years as it is being fully reconstructed under U.N. auspices (page 161).

M Vinh Moc Tunnels, DMZ : It's hard to believe that this network of tunnels was home to more than 300 people during the American War. The extensive underground complex has been carefully preserved (page 177).

M Cham Museum, Danang: Houses the world's largest collection of Cham sculpture. Encounter a lost culture that is at once alien yet highly imaginative (page 184).

M Hoi An Old Quarter: Well-preserved old houses and pagodas are rare in Vietnam. Best explored on foot, this place has lots of both—which is why it is a World Heritage site (page 193).

M Mui Ne Beach: The resort hotspot of the central Vietnam, with sparkling white sands. Parked nearby are the biggest sand dunes in Vietnam (page 234).

north and south. That means that Hué and Danang see heavy rain September–February, often resulting in flooding. Hué in particular is susceptible to torrential downpours.

PLANNING YOUR TRIP

Not many travelers think of starting a journey in the center of Vietnam, although if you come in from Laos overland, that is where you will most likely arrive. The peculiar thing about

Central Vietnam is that it has no actual center—no hub such as Saigon in the south or Hanoi in the north. The twin gateways to central Vietnam are Danang and Hué, both on the dowdy side. For travelers, the real pearl is Hoi An, which has excellent food, good tailors, and terrific art on sale—and you won't get run down by motorcycles, either. Travelers barely pause on the overland route from Hanoi to Hué—many take an overnight bus or train. That's a pity because the area around

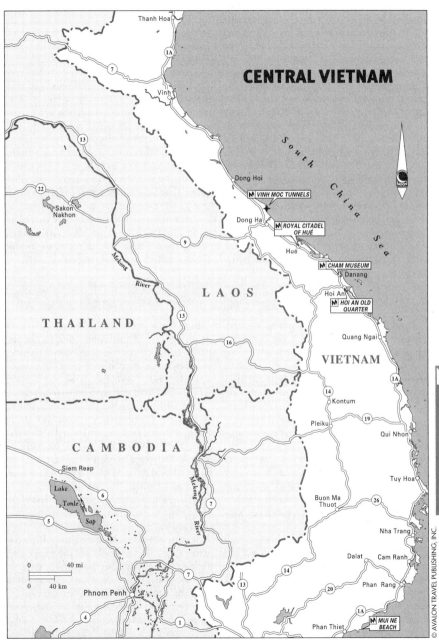

Central Vietnam

Ninh Binh has stunning karst scenery—well worth stopping for a few days before carrying on. Another point with great karst caves and grottoes is the World Heritage Site of Phong Nga caves, to the west of Dong Hoi—this area is harder to reach.

Between Hué and Saigon, travelers on the coastal route make at least 3–4 stops—Hoi An, Nha Trang, Mui Ne, and Dalat being the most popular. Open Tour operators include Sinh Café, TNK, and TM-Brothers, Dalat Toserco, and Delta Tour. Open Tour buses are inexpensive: They make the entire run from Saigon to Hanoi for less than $30. But where the companies make the real money is the extras—the hotels and restaurants they herd their customers into. A herd mentality pervades the Open Tour buses that ply this route—travelers spend all their time with other travelers and are unwittingly deposited at restaurants and guesthouses that the Open Tour bus operators have deals with (and some of the restaurants are real dumps). You might like to consider using the Open Tour buses for part of the distance but not the entire stretch.

Considerably more adventurous is to take the highlands route, starting at Hoi An and stopping at Kontum, Pleiku, Buon Ma Thuot, and on to Dalat. Though prone to landslides, the entire stretch of Highway 14 (also called the Ho Chi Minh Road) is sealed, which means travel times are fast and the ride is relatively smooth. But local transport is erratic and infrequent. One solution to that is to form a small group and rent a jeep for the journey. You can also mix mountains and beaches with a route going from Hoi An to Buon Ma Thuot, an then turning to the coast at Nha Trang, on to Mui Ne Beach, and eventually to Saigon.

Hué

Hué and Danang serve as twin gateways to central Vietnam. While Danang is the industrial, shipping, and air transport gateway, Hué is the cultural, religious, and educational heart. The landscape here—with its misty Perfume River and pagodas—is inspiration for poetry and painting. Hué has long been regarded as the "Third Capital" of Vietnam, after Hanoi and Saigon.

From 1802 to 1945, Hué served as Vietnam's political capital under the 13 emperors of the Nguyen dynasty. Emperor Gia Long, founder of the Nguyen dynasty, consolidated the country after several hundred years of civil war and began building Hué Citadel. This was the first time in Vietnamese history a single court controlled Vietnam from north to south. The emperors built the Mandarin Road, now Highway 1. It was dotted with relay stations, and communication was further expedited by a system of couriers. The dynasty was headquartered in the Imperial City, off limits to most mortals—only mandarins, princesses, and scholars lived here. In the finest Chinese tradition, the emperors constructed elaborate tombs, scattered around Hué.

In 1883 the French invaded Hué. Tonkin and Annam became French protectorates, but the French found it expedient to maintain the illusion of imperial rule. A rapid succession of emperors marked the early days of French presence as rulers either fled or were replaced by the French.

Hué still represents a third political force in Vietnam. During the Vietnam War of the 1960s, educated Hué citizens backed neither the South nor the North. During the Tet offensive of 1968, Vietcong and NVA forces marched into Hué and held it for 24 days. The soldiers used the Citadel, with its 10-meter-thick ramparts, as their base. During the occupation VC and NVA forces went on a rampage. Suspected sympathizers of the Saigon government were rounded up, then shot, beheaded, or buried alive. It is estimated that 3,000 residents of Hué were killed during those 24 days. You can still see symbols over doorways, indicating where residents were killed. In fierce door-to-door fighting, the Americans eventually ousted the North Vietnamese. An estimated 10,000 people died in Hué during the Tet offensive of 1968. Most were civilians.

THE MURDER OF HUÉ

In 1968, the city of Hué became a casualty of war. British journalist Gavin Young, who first visited Hué in 1965, returned in 1968 to survey the damage wrought by a fierce battle between the Vietcong and the Americans. He described parts of the city as resembling London after the Blitz. In his 1987 book, *Worlds Apart*, Young sums up his reaction:

Now, between them, in the name of the people's salvation, General Giap and the U.S. High Command have killed the flower of Vietnamese cities…. You can disguise it in whatever military terms you like, but in Hué murder has been arranged.

Young sketches the lines of bewildered refugees streaming from the city, Americans crouched in sandbagged strong points, tense ARVN troops fingering submachine guns and jets and helicopters screaming overhead, pouring napalm and bombs on the surrounding countryside.

We stepped through fragments of glass, pathetic muddied wrappings of Tet holiday gifts, filth and dead rats, to where a crowd of Vietnamese were passing under the great ornamental gate to the Citadel stormed by the U.S. Marines. They shuffled through quickly, holding their noses because here three rotting bodies of Vietcong soldiers lie as yet unburied. The Citadel's solid walls are punctured by shells, and the gate itself is riddled by everything from bullets to rockets. Inside the Citadel there seems to be no shop nor house that is not wholly or partially destroyed. The Americans used tanks here, after the air strikes. The Vietcong and North Vietnamese used rockets from the camouflaged foxholes you see everywhere.

Standing in the stench of Hué's streets, Young reflected on the damage: "And what has the battle of Hué meant? Tragically, it has symbolized the entire war." The United States regained Hué at the cost of destroying it. The North Vietnamese had attempted to indoctrinate Hué residents and had killed most of Hué's government officials. Neither side won any appreciable number of Hué hearts or minds.

In the process, the Imperial Palace was reduced to rubble. Today the monuments of Hué are on the United Nations's World Heritage list, so sites may one day be restored.

Today Hué is a quiet town of 350,000. While Saigon and Hanoi grow by leaps and bounds, places such as Hué crawl along. Few joint ventures are allowed, and there are few private hotels. Deliberate blocks placed by the central government insist joint ventures in Hué be "branches" of those in Hanoi or Saigon.

Getting Your Bearings

Hué is divided into north bank and south bank sections. The north bank is where the Citadel once stood—a huge walled area sealed by moats and enclosing the Imperial Palace. The north bank is now largely a residential area. Formerly the French quarter, the south bank is the commercial sector, with banks, hotels, restaurants, and transport terminals. Three bridges link the two banks over the Perfume River. Two are used by cars and buses; the third is a railway bridge, also used by pedestrians and bicyclists.

SIGHTS

Royal Citadel

Emperor Gia Long modeled the Royal Citadel on the Forbidden City in Beijing, China.

HUÉ

To Thien
Mu Pagoda

To An Hoa Bus
Terminal and Hanoi

To An Hoa Bus Terminal

Huang Giang (Perfume River)

RAILWAY BRIDGE (BICYCLE AND
FOOT TRAFFIC PERMITTED)

LE DUAN

THIEU QUANG PHUC

NGUYEN TRAI

HUONG SEN
RESTAURANT

HOANG

DINH TUYEN

MAI THUC LOAN

ONG TAO
RESTAURANT

BACH DANG

CHI LONG

DIEU DE PAGODA

MEXUNG
SHOPS

HUYNH THUC KHANG

DAO

HUNG

TRAN

DONG BA
MARKET

DONG BA
BUS
TERMINAL

THANH NOI HOTEL

MUSEUM OF ROYAL FINE ARTS

MILITARY MUSEUM

LAC THANH AND LAC
THIEN RESTAURANTS

THANH LOI HOTEL

ROYAL CITADEL OF HUÉ

N IMPERIAL PALACE

MIEU TEMPLE

9 URNS

THAI HOA PALACE

HIEN NHON GATE

ONG TAO II RESTAURANT

NGO MON
GATE

FLAG TOWER

PHU XUAN HOTEL

N

Central Vietnam

TRAIN STATION

BAO QUOC PAGODA

TU DAM PAGODA

To Danang

CAFE #3
LE LOI
HOTEL #5 LE LOI
LE LOI HOTEL

HO CHI MINH MUSEUM
QUOC HOC SCHOOL

NHA KHACH 18
MORIN HOTEL
BANK
POST OFFICE
NGO QUYEN HOTEL
BINH MINH HOTEL
HUE CITY TOURISM VILLAS
VIETNAM AIRLINES
DONG DA HOTEL

HUE HOTEL
INDOCHINE HOTEL
TRANG TIEN HOTEL
MANDARIN CAFE
THUAN HOA HOTEL
THANG LONG HOTEL
A DONG 2 HOTEL
IMMIGRATION OFFICE
KINH DO HOTEL
HOAN CAU HOTEL
BEN NGHE GUESTHOUSE
BANK
DZACH LAU RESTAURANT
MUNICIPAL THEATER

HUE CATHEDRAL

AN CUU BUS TERMINAL

SONG HUONG FLOATING RESTAURANT
BOAT RENTALS
TRANG TIEN BRIDGE
PHU XUAN BRIDGE

CENTURY RIVERSIDE INN
HUONG GIANG HOTEL
BOAT RENTALS
DAP DA BRIDGE
KYLIN HOTEL
A DONG GUESTHOUSE
NGOC ANH RESTAURANT
AM PHU RESTAURANT
ONG NEN RESTAURANT
RESTAURANT 20

NGUYEN THAI HOC
LE QUY DON
BA TRIEU
HUNG VUONG
HANOI
PHUONG
TRI
KIET
NGUYEN
BA
TRUNG
HAI
DONG
DA
LY THUONG KIET
NGO QUYEN
LE LOI
NGUYEN HUE
DINH PHUNG
PHAN CHU TRINH
DIEN BIEN PHU
BEN

250 yds
250 m

0
0

© AVALON TRAVEL PUBLISHING, INC.

IMPERIAL TOMB TOUR

This tour takes in the imperial tombs, scattered in the countryside 6–12 kilometers south of Hué. Actual cycling time is about two hours; be prepared for some uphill pushing. If you're in a tearing hurry, find a moto; if it's raining, adjust your route and switch to a boat. Start this tour on the south bank, where the old French quarter once was. The tree-lined avenues around Le Loi Boulevard are great places to wander. Along the waterfront was prime French real estate: in the north, the Customs House; between the two bridges, the Cercle Sportif, official residences, and colonial villas; to the south, the French-constructed railroad bridge.

Make your way to **Ho Chi Minh Museum** at the west end of Le Loi. The museum is pure propaganda—skip it if you wish. Nearby **Quoc Hoc School,** established in 1896, was attended at different times by Ho Chi Minh, General Vo Nguyen Giap, and Ngo Dinh Diem; it would have been a pretty rowdy class if they'd all attended at once. Quoc Hoc is now a coed high school.

Follow Dien Bien Phu Street for a side trip to **Bao Quoc Pagoda**—an important center of study. There are an estimated 500 monks and nuns in Hué, and upward of 100 small pagodas. Monks from different pagodas assemble here for instruction; Vietnamese students come to study in the tranquil gardens.

Nam Giao is not much to look at now, but it used to be the most sacred site in Hué. Built by Emperor Gia Long in 1802, Nam Giao was composed of three terraces—two square to represent the earth, and one circular representing the sky. As holder of the "mandate of heaven," the emperor would make sacrifices to the heavens here. The area was turned into a monument for fallen North Vietnamese after 1975—a controversial choice of statuary. From Nam Giao, it's downhill or flat to Khai Dinh Tomb, about 30–40 minutes by bike. You'll pass village life on quiet roads, forested zones, and farmed areas of sugarcane, rice, and vegetable plots. The countryside is the main reason for cycling through—you may find the imperial tombs disappointing.

It's hard to get excited about the mausoleums of Hué. The Hué emperors, believing they would be accorded as much splendor in their afterlives as in their present ones, spent their final days directing tomb construction. Some even threatened to execute artisans if their work was not up to standard. The tombs were copied from Chinese prototypes, but they do not match the craftsmanship or ostentation of the originals. In fact, the imperial tombs of Hué are quite dull and gloomy and exude a stagnant air.

Construction followed a formulaic design, although each emperor's deviated in details. The arrangement comprised five key elements: a brick courtyard with stone mandarin guards, horses, and elephants; a pavilion with marble

The ramparts, however, were built in the style of French military architect Sebastian de Vauban. The complex had fallen into neglect even before it was blown to pieces by the fighting of 1968 (it was damaged during fighting with the Vietminh in 1947). With much of the structural work made of wood, it fell prey to rain, typhoons, and termites, as well as thieves. The front gateway and several important structures within the Imperial Palace grounds have been restored; beyond these, it's mostly ruins in poor shape. Entry to the Imperial Palace area is $5. The north exit gates are not open, but you should be able to enter or exit by the east gate.

The Royal Citadel is composed of three walled enclosures, each within the other—a city within a city. The exterior moated enclosure (Kinh Thanh) encompasses six square kilometers—sufficient for housing the emperor, his family, administrators, bodyguards, and servants. Piercing the outer walls are 10 gates, each reached by a bridge across the moat. Toward the Perfume River is the Yellow Enclosure (Hoang Thanh), with six-meter-high walls about 2.5 kilometers in length. Within this lies the innermost walled section—the former Imperial Palace, or Forbidden Purple City—which is undergoing restoration under U.N. auspices as a World Heritage Site. A major restoration effort was mounted in 1995–1996.

tablets in praise of the emperor, inscribed by his son and heir; a temple for the worship of the emperor and empress; a lotus pond with a viewing pavilion; and, finally, a deep grave. During construction, the emperor used the viewing pavilion to direct operations; after his death, the temple at the site would be regularly visited by the emperor's widows. Although there were 13 emperors in the Nguyen dynasty (1802–1945), only seven reigned until their deaths, accounting for the low number of tombs in Hué.

Khai Dinh's Tomb, 10 kilometers from Hué, was completed in 1931 and was 11 years in the making. After the grandiose entryway with dragon pillars, the mausoleum itself is an anticlimax. The architecture is an ugly mix of European and Asian, with grimy rows of mandarin guards in the courtyard. Inside the main hall are colorful glass mosaic frescoes; a life-sized bronze statue of Khai Dinh, made in France in 1922, is positioned over the actual tomb.

At the village of Ban Lang, 12 kilometers from Hué, you can leave your bicycle behind and take a small ferry (bargain hard) across the Perfume River to **Minh Mang Tomb.** Out on the water you'll see fishing boats and sampans dredging for sand and rocks. Minh Mang is the finest of the imperial tombs. The attraction here is the harmonious garden with its frangipani and lotus blossoms. Minh Mang reigned 1820–1840; the tomb was constructed after his death

by his heir, Thieu Tri. The atmosphere is one of peace and tranquility.

Once back on the east bank, continue north. You could easily skip Thieu Tri and Dong Khanh tombs—they're not much to look at. **Tu Duc Tomb,** enclosed by walls, features pine woods and a lakeside pavilion with lotus blossoms where the emperor once fished, listened to music, and wrote poetry—between strenuous bouts of tomb building. Emperor Tu Duc went a bit overboard with the poetry, inscribing his own stones with praise of himself. Actually, he did this because he had no son to write the script, even though he had 104 wives and numerous courtesans. Tu Duc's Tomb was more of a pleasure garden than a tomb: The emperor used it as a second residence, where he indulged in extravagant 50-course meals of incredible delicacies. Tu Duc reigned 1847–1883; the mausoleum was constructed 1864–1867 by a force of 3,000 laborers. More recently, the lakeside pavilion has been restored with the help of UNESCO.

From here, you can make your way north to downtown Hué. However, if you're still up for more touring, you could hop over to the north bank. If you take a left at the Perfume River, you'll find some tiny boats to carry you across to **Thien Mu Pagoda.** You can put yourself and bike on the boat, visit Thien Mu, then return to Hué via the railway bridge.

The best parts to view are at the southern end, near the Perfume River. Approaching the Citadel you cross a moat by one of two gates, Nhon Gate or Quang Duc Gate. Inside the gates are two groups of cannons. The **Nine Cannons** were cast of brass in 1803. They're each five meters in length and are named after the four seasons and five elements. They've never been fired; their function is symbolic. Sandwiched between the two entry gates is the massive **Flag Tower.** The flag of the National Liberation Front flew here for 24 days in 1968.

Continuing north you come to **Ngo Mon,** or Royal Gate, where the ticket office is. This massive gate was built in 1834 during the reign

of Emperor Minh Mang. There are five entrances—in previous times, only the emperor was permitted to use the central one. The gate was extensively restored in the early 1990s; climb to the first level for expansive views. Golden Water Bridge, directly beyond the gate, was once reserved exclusively for the emperor's use. Crossing that, you come to **Dien Thai Hoa,** the Palace of Supreme Peace, where the emperor, seated on a raised golden throne, held official receptions and supervised important ceremonies. On the steps of the palace are nine stone stele, dividing the courtyard into areas of the nine mandarin ranks. Built in 1833, Thai Hoa Palace is one of the best-preserved

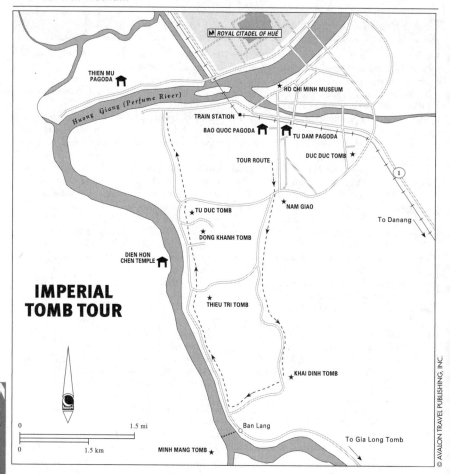

IMPERIAL TOMB TOUR

ROYAL CITADEL OF HUÉ

THIEN MU PAGODA

Huong Giang (Perfume River)

HO CHI MINH MUSEUM

TRAIN STATION

BAO QUOC PAGODA
TU DAM PAGODA

TOUR ROUTE

DUC DUC TOMB

TU DUC TOMB

NAM GIAO

DONG KHANH TOMB

DIEN HON CHEN TEMPLE

THIEU TRI TOMB

KHAI DINH TOMB

Ban Lang

To Danang

0   1.5 mi
0   1.5 km

MINH MANG TOMB

To Gia Long Tomb

buildings left in the complex, with magnificent red- and gold-lacquered pillars (repainted during mid-1990s restorations). There's a scale model of the entire site displayed inside the main hall. Behind Thai Hoa Palace are two huge bronze urns from the 17th century decorated with birds, plants, and animals.

From here, walk to the west side of the complex: This easily overlooked section provides the Citadel's main visual interest. In front of elegant Hien Lam Cac Pavilion are the spectacular **Nine Dynastic Urns.** Cast in bronze between 1835 and 1837, they stand two meters tall and weigh between 1,500 and 2,500 kilograms each. Each is dedicated to a different Nguyen emperor—the central and largest one to Gia Long. The urns are engraved with various designs—landscapes, wild animals, birds, the sun, the moon, the stars—symbolizing the power of the Nguyen dynasty. The craftsmanship is superb. The bronze urns are a must-see within the Citadel. A short distance north of the urns is **Mieu Temple,** Temple of the Generations, built in 1821. It contains altars for worship of 10 Nguyen sovereigns. The temple was restored in the mid-1990s with British assistance, gaining a reinforced concrete base.

Backtrack a bit to north of Thai Hoa Palace to the **Imperial Palace,** once reserved for the emperor, his concubines, and eunuch servants. Remaining buildings here are in very poor condition. The Hall of the Mandarins and the Royal Library have been partially restored. The government is investing several million dollars to restore Hué's monuments, so this phoenix may rise from the ashes yet. Financial and technical support has come from UNESCO; Vietnamese scholars traveled to the Oriental Museum in Paris to survey the original plans for construction of imperial buildings.

A good place to exit the Imperial City is by **Hien Nhon Gate** on the east. Here you'll find Ong Tao II Restaurant, set in a charming courtyard—an ideal place for a drink. If you exit from Hien Nhon Gate, you can continue walking east to the Imperial Museum.

Museum of Royal Fine Arts

This museum is at 3 Le Truc St., just east of Hien Nhon Gate. Housed in a former royal palace, the museum's collection of antique furniture, bronzeware, screens, ceramics, musical instruments, and royal clothing give you a real feel for the mandarin period. Exhibits are unlabeled. Also down this way is the **Military Museum,** with a few stray tanks and other military hardware in the courtyard.

Thien Mu Pagoda

Thien Mu is about three kilometers from downtown Hué, on the banks of the Perfume River. This Mahayana Buddhist temple is a peaceful place to spend time. It's the oldest monastery in Hué, dating from the 17th century. Near the front stands seven-tiered Phuoc Nguyen Tower, long the symbol of Hué. It was built in 1844, each level containing an altar dedicated to a different Buddha. Near the tower are several smaller buildings; one holds the temple's massive bell. Cast in the early 18th century, the bell weighs several tons. In another pavilion is a marble turtle; stele mounted on it chronicle the development of Buddhism in Hué.

Encased in glass at the front of the nearby temple is a brass statue of a Laughing Buddha, a figure with a fat, bare stomach reclining on a couch and laughing his bald head off. The Laughing Buddha is the nickname of 9th-century Chinese Zen master Poe-Tai Hoshang, who discovered the "Buddha within himself." This highly eccentric monk wandered blissfully through China without any worries. After his death he was worshipped throughout the Chinese world as a popular hero and a deity of good fortune. Three superb brass statues stand inside the temple: on the left the Buddha of the Past (Amitabha); in the center, the Buddha of the Present (Sakyamuni); on the right, the Buddha of the Future (Maitreya). There is also a smaller Laughing Buddha statue. The Laughing Buddha is sometimes associated with the Maitreya.

At the back of the temple are gardens and nurseries where the dozen monks who live here cultivate vegetables and trees. They collect orchids from surrounding woods to plant at the monastery; you'll see bonsai trees on display. In this area is a shelter displaying the blue Austin in which Thich Quang Duc, a 66-year-old monk from Thien Mu, was driven to Saigon

HUÉ ENTRY FEES

Entry fees to museums and historic attractions are rarely quoted in this book because they're usually a pittance. Not so in Hué. Each tomb in Hué charges a stiff $5 entry fee—the highest in Vietnam. Permission to use a still or video camera will cost another $5. The Imperial Palace also costs $5 to enter. In 1992 the entry price was $1.20, so the price has quadrupled. The Museum of Royal Fine Arts is an extra $2. Only foreigners pay these fees; no Vietnamese could possibly afford such luxury. The locals just pay a few thousand dong. Visit five tombs and you hit $25, a lot of money in Vietnam. To be more selective, the top tomb to visit is Minh Mang. Another possibility is Khai Dinh's Tomb. Most of the others are disappointing.

to immolate himself on a street corner on June 11, 1963, as a protest against repression under the Diem regime. Pictures of the scene gained international news coverage. The car is now revered as a sacred relic.

In May 1993, another immolation occurred outside Thien Mu Pagoda. The Buddhist layman's name was not released, and no reason was provided for the suicide. When the abbot of Thien Mu, Thich Tri Tuu, tried to organize a Buddhist funeral for the man, local government authorities intervened, claiming there was no proof he was a devout Buddhist. Several days later, Thich Tri Tuu was forced into a police car; six monks sat down in front of the vehicle in protest and a large crowd of supporters rallied around. The sit-down strike held up traffic for hours in what turned out to be the largest Vietnamese public protest since the Vietnam War. Eventually, the authorities and the abbot were forced out of the car. It was then overturned and burst into flames.

In November, the abbot and three other monks from Thien Mu were arrested and subsequently sentenced to three- and four-year prison terms after a closed trial without lawyers or witnesses. This imprisonment may be part of a wider issue; the monks were known supporters of Thich Huyen Quang, a dissident Buddhist exiled to a small village because of his protests against government attempts to control Vietnamese Buddhism.

Hué Cathedral

South of downtown Hué on Nguyen Hué Street is Hué Cathedral, completed in 1962. The cathedral is a curious blend of Asian and Western architecture—a recognizable European cathedral, but with an Oriental octagonal steel spire and Chinese-style eaves. The altar is made from marble quarried at the Marble Mountains near Danang.

Thuan An Beach

About 13 kilometers northeast of Hué, Thuan An Beach stretches for several kilometers and features a protected lagoon and South China

NORTH BANK TOUR

The sites mentioned here can be reached on foot, by bicycle, or by hired boat.

Start at Dong Ba Market, which can be reached by hired boat, by bicycle, or on foot directly over the Trang Tien Bridge. Or take a regular ferry from a landing to the east of the Century Riverside Inn, across Dap Da Bridge; you can load your bike onto the ferry. You can easily spend several hours at the market, with its profusion of women in conical hats engaging in just about every kind of food transaction known to Vietnam. Early in the morning country folk unload their produce at the market steps by the river, and fishermen from the coast bring in fresh seafood. The covered market features a large rice section.

From Dong Ba Market you can cycle or walk to the Citadel, park and visit, and then carry on to Thien Mu Pagoda several kilometers to the west. If you backtrack from the pagoda about 100 meters, you'll find a small boat that will deliver you to the south bank again for about $1. You can also ride back along the north bank, using the railway bridge to cross the Perfume River.

Sea frontage. Foreigners pay a fee to enter the beach. Get there by bus from Dong Ba Market, or hire a boat for a longer journey. If you want to stay overnight, check into the 12-room Tan My Hotel, tel. 54/866033—a string of villas with tropical gardens.

ACCOMMODATIONS

Hué is far enough north that hot water becomes a priority. It's often overcast or raining, and cold in winter. Hotels in Hué vary considerably; some, such as the Morin, have lots of character; others, such as the Dong Da, are impersonal concrete blockhouses. Hué hotels often fill up by late afternoon. Since you have no way of knowing which ones might be full, it's best to park your luggage and scour one particular zone. Be aware that a hotel charging $40 for a room may also have a $10 single tucked away—although the staff will show you the $40 room first, of course.

Under $20

Nguyen Tri Phuong Street: There is a large concentration of hotels situated on or close to Nguyen Tri Phuong Street, near the intersection with Hung Vuong Street. In the same area you'll find travel agents, cybercafés, and some bicycle-rental places. Just west of Binh Minh hotel is an alleyway that is packed with budget guesthouses, restaurants, and tour agents. Backpackers hang out here.

Binh Minh hotel/restaurant, at 12 Nguyen Tri Phuong St., tel. 54/825526, fax 54/828362, is a pleasant private minihotel with 22 rooms, charging $10–12 for a fan room and $15–25–45 for a/c rooms. Another private hotel is **Hoan Cau**, at 26 Ben Nghe St., tel. 54/824642, with rooms for $8–10 fan and $15–25 a/c. **Ben Nghe GH,** at 4 Ben Nghe St., tel. 54/823687, is a concrete two-story hotel, $5 s or d, $10 d with hot water. **Ngo Quyen Hotel,** 11 Ngo Quyen, tel. 54/823278, has 26 rooms in A and B blocks for $12–17–20; a few rooms for $6. **Hoanvu Hotel,** 16 Dong Da St., tel. 54/821666, fax 54/821561, is a private minihotel offering 20 rooms for $12–25.

Along Le Loi Street: On Le Loi West, close to the river and a five-minute walk from the train station is **Le Loi Hotel,** at 2 Le Loi St., tel. 54/822153, fax 54/824527. There are 150 rooms (two, three, and four beds) available in five different blocks. Prices vary with the plug-ins: fan, a/c, satellite TV, or hot shower. Most rooms fall in the range of $6–12 s, $8–25 d, $12–22 t; there are some deluxe rooms for $45.

Near Phu Xuan Bridge is **Nha Khach 18,** 18 Le Loi, tel. 54/823720. It offers one single for $5, four doubles for $10, and four doubles at $20 with bath. Almost opposite, **Hue Hotel,** at 15 Le Loi, tel. 54/823513, fax 54/824806, is run by Hué Tourism and has 12 rooms for $10–20–25.

At the east end of Le Loi are lots of budget/moderate guesthouses and hotels—some private and family-run—tucked down the side streets in the zone near the Century Riverside Inn. Near

Dap Da Bridge is **Cuu Long Hotel,** 80 Le Loi, tel. 54/828240, with eight rooms for $10–15 with a/c and hot water. **Trang Tien Hotel,** 46A Le Loi, tel. 54/822128, fax 54/826772, has 14 rooms for $10–15 s and $15–20 d. **Kylin Hotel,** at 58 Le Loi, tel. 54/826556, fax 54/826596, has 21 rooms for $20–30.

A great place for those on a budget is the family-run **Hoang Huong GH,** tel. 54/828509, with six rooms for $6–10, $4 for a dorm room. Although the street address is listed as 46/2 Le Loi, it's actually tucked down an unnamed dead-end alley running opposite the Century Riverside, past Hoa Hong I hotel. Also down this way is a minihotel called **Mimosa,** tel. 54/828068, with nine rooms for $8–15; and **Thanh Thuy GH,** tel. 54/824585, with six rooms for $6–10 s and $8–15 d. A larger hotel in the same alley is the **Phuong Hoang** (Phoenix), tel. 54/826902, fax 54/828999, with 30 rooms for $15–35.

North Bank: On the north bank of the Perfume River, close to the Citadel, is the 25-room **Khach San Thanh Noi,** 3 Dang Dung, tel. 54/822478, fax 54/827211. Also known as the Imperial Garden Hotel, this one indeed has pleasant gardens, even a small pool. Gets you away from the jungle downtown. The villa–style hotel charges $22–35 for a double; there are 50 rooms. **Phu Xuan,** at 27 Tran Hung Dao, tel. 54/827512, has 10 rooms for $20–25 each. Near Lac Thanh restaurant is **Thanh Loi,** at 7 Dien Tien Hoang St., tel. 54/824803, fax 54/825344, with 20 rooms for $6–12, some with a/c. Also down this alley, at 16 Dien Tien Hoang, is **Thuong Tu,** with 12 rooms for $12–15.

$20–50

In the Soviet concrete blockhouse class are the following three dowdy hotels. **Dong Da Hotel,** 15 Ly Thuong Kiet, tel. 54/823071, fax 54/823204, offers 37 rooms for $35–45 and a superior room for $60; this place is for the dance/karaoke set. **Thuan Hoa,** 7 Nguyen Tri Phuong, tel. 54/822553, fax 54/822470, is a blockhouse with a big extension at the back. The 65 rooms, mostly doubles and triples, cost $32–35, with a few singles at $20. **Kinh Do**

Hotel, 1 Nguyen Thai Hoc, tel. 54/823566, has 39 rooms. Doubles are $25, with a few for $35; there are half a dozen cheaper rooms in the $10–18 range.

To the west end of Le Loi is **Hotel 5 Le Loi,** at 5 Le Loi, tel. 54/822155, fax 54/824527, with 16 rooms in the $20–40–60 range. The hotel is in an elegant yellow mansion with large gardens—lots of character, and hot water on tap.

On Le Loi to the east is **A Dong I Guesthouse,** 1 Chu Van An, tel. 54/824148, fax 54/828074. This seven-room private hotel is in an alley opposite the Century Riverside Inn; rooms cost $20–25–30. There is a big cluster of minihotels in this area. Three streets west, at 7 Doi Cung St., is **A Dong 2 Hotel,** tel. 54/822765, with 15 rooms for $25–40. Another private hotel, **Hoa Hong I,** stands opposite the gates of the Century Riverside, at 46C Le Loi, tel. 54/824377, fax 54/826949. It features nine double rooms for $25–35–45. Around the corner on Pham Ngu Lao is the high-rise **Hoa Hong 2,** with 50 rooms for $30–55 and some suites for $60–90. Deeper down this street at 11 Pham Ngu Lao is **Dong Loi Hotel,** tel. 54/822296, fax 54/826234, with 30 rooms for $8–40; this is a pleasant, clean, and comfortable place with some balcony rooms.

$50–100

Close to the river is the **Saigon Morin Hotel,** 30 Le Loi, tel. 54/823526, sgmorin@dng.vnn. vn. This place features cavernous rooms: You can get lost in the bathroom. The Morin's 135 rooms go for $70–120, and 11 suites for $180–300. The Morin encloses a huge garden courtyard where (weather permitting) buffet dinners are served for guests; at night there may be live music. The hotel boasts a swimming pool and business center—and a hotel logo that looks suspiciously like the Golden Arches. **Century Riverside Inn,** 49 Le Loi, tel. 54/823390, fax 54/823394, has a total of 147 guest rooms and suites, with 64 standard rooms for $60–65; 22 superior garden-view rooms for $70–75; and 33 superior river-view rooms for $80–90. There are also some suites for $150 each. Add 10 percent tax to all calculations.

The hotel is five stories; the upper floors have views of the Perfume River. It features several restaurants, tennis courts, swimming pool, and a disco; the hotel arranges tour boats and "royal performances." The Century is a joint-venture hotel, part of the Century International Hotels chain, and affiliated with Century Saigon Hotel in Ho Chi Minh City.

Huong Giang Hotel, 51 Le Loi, tel. 54/823958, fax 54/823424, is a large three-story hotel near the Century, with standard rooms for $50–70; river-view rooms for $75–80; suites for $150. The Royal Suite goes for $200 a night. The hotel provides full facilities, including a conference hall, swimming pool, and tennis courts. Staff can arrange car rentals and dragon-boat tours; folk performances are held here, too.

FOOD, ENTERTAINMENT, AND SERVICES

Food

Hué is known for *banh khoai,* a crepe stuffed with bean sprouts, shrimp, and pork, eaten with salad, star fruit slices, and *nuoc tuong* (sesame and peanut sauce). A variation on this is *bun thit nuong,* which uses a noodle base. Wash it down with Huda, the local brew (a joint-venture Danish beer). For those with a sweet tooth, a sticky sesame-seed bar called *mexung* is handmade on the premises at 135 and 137 Huynh Thuc Khang St., to the east side of the Citadel, along Dong Ba Canal. Hué residents debate which shop produces the superior version. The families have been making the stuff for the last 40-odd years. **Phuoc Hung,** at 41 Tran Hung Dao St., also sells *mexung,* plus Chinese-type pastries. Street stalls occasionally have croissants.

Strung along Hanoi Street are a number of noodlehouses with cheap and tasty fare. They serve fried rice noodle soup (*pho tai*), dry noodles (*pho kho*), and soft-fried noodles. **Trung Lam** at 7B Hanoi, serves good soups; on the opposite side is **Quan An** at number 6. Nearby, at number 8, is **Phuoc Loc** restaurant, offering *banh bao* Saigon (stuffed

TOURING HUÉ

For touring Hué, it's a toss-up between biking and boating. You could load your bicycle onto a boat, head south, visit temples and tombs, and then cycle back. Vietnamese load bicycles onto boats all the time—it won't faze your boatman. Group tours often take a boat south on the Perfume River and then return by car. You cannot use cyclos to go touring around Hué because of the hills. Mix and match destinations using boat, bicycle, motorcycle, or car transportation. Only a few tombs can be reached directly by boat; most are accessible by land. In any case, the ride's the thing—the tombs are fairly dull.

One factor influencing your transportation decisions is the weather. Hué is cool and foggy, with very high rainfall. Rain is heavy August–October; the rainy season extends May–December. That leaves a dry season January–May.

Along the Perfume River
The Perfume River (Huong Giang) is named after a scented shrub that reportedly grows at its source. There's nothing perfumed about the river in Hué itself—still, a languid half-day on the river is one of the pleasures of Hué. It's easy to rent a small craft and visit tombs and other sites around Hué. A number of boats dock on the south bank of Hué between Trang Tien and Dap Da bridges. You could also try Dong Ba Market area. You can negotiate directly with boat owners or arrange a vessel through a hotel or tourist agency. A number of tour agents will put you in with a group for $4 a head, including some food. This, of course, does not include entry fees to attractions, which can run from $2 for Hon Chen Temple to $5 for Minh Mang Tomb. A whole boat for a five-hour trip is around $12–20, depending on the number of passengers (0800–1300, maximum 10 people); a fancier dragon boat is $20–25 per hour. The Huong Giang Hotel and Century Riverside Inn have "folksinging boats," on which you're serenaded as you drift along the Perfume River. Royal dishes are served on dragon boats as well—all for a price. Phoenix boats are even more expensive.

A sample itinerary follows this route: Trang Tien Bridge to Thien Mu Pagoda to Dien Hon Chen Temple to Tu Duc Tomb to Minh Mang Tomb to Trang Tien Bridge. Some tours skip Hon Chen Temple and may cover Tu Duc Tomb on land. Tours from Century Riverside Inn cover a three- to four-hour journey by boat to Minh Mang Tomb, then to Ban Lang on the east bank, where passengers transfer to a waiting car. Passengers then cover inland tombs by auto on the way back to Hué. A car for 4–5 people is $20; a minibus for seven people is $25. The tomb of Khai Dinh is two kilometers from the Perfume River.

If you want longer on the river, ask to add Gia Long Tomb, farther south on the Perfume River. The tomb is not often visited and will cost extra—add $5 more for an ordinary boat. Gia Long Tomb is about 16 kilometers from Hué. The tomb, built 1814–1820, was damaged by bombing during the Vietnam War and is today overgrown with bushes.

Another longer excursion by boat: Head east on the Perfume River to Thuan An Beach. At night on the river you can see people fishing with lanterns from sampans.

dumplings) as well as Chinese noodle soup. **Minh Y Restaurant,** at 10 Hanoi St., is a small Western-style restaurant great for breakfast. The menu features soup, omelettes, jam, bread, and cheese. At **Bun Bo Hué Restaurant,** 11 Ly Thong Kiet, you can find Hué-style soup.

North Bank Restaurants: Just off Tran Hung Dao Street is **Lac Thanh Restaurant,** at 6A Dinh Tien Hoang. This place is run by a deaf-mute family that communicates very well. They speak the language of food—lots of it, well prepared. Try the crab soup and pancake. The family will also assist with boat, motorcycle, and bicycle rentals. With exactly the same signs outside and exactly the same menu inside is **Lac Thien,** next door at number 6, where the servers often act deaf and mute, too (except when a mobile phone rings). It's all part of an ongoing restaurant war—both restaurants are excellent and equally crowded. And both claim to be "the real one." It appears that they may all be related—and there was a split in the family business—and not all family members are deaf-mute.

The more upscale **Ong Tao,** at 134 Ngo Duc Ke, tel. 54/822037, features excellent food. There is a small upstairs section on an open roof. This small private restaurant serves seafood and Hué specialties; it's also good for breakfast. **Ong Tao II,** tel. 54/823031, is a branch of this restaurant inside Hien Nhon Gate east of the Imperial Palace—no entry fee required. Ong Tao II has a very pleasant setting—orchard, rattan chairs, old crumbled walls—but the food is below par, so perhaps stick to the drinks. Northwest of the Imperial Palace is **Huong Sen,** 42 Nguyen Trai, tel. 54/823201, with a pavilion jutting into a lake for outdoor dining. Food is mediocre and can be pricey here; the full menu includes frog, eel, fish, and some vegetarian dishes.

South Bank Restaurants: The big concentration of budget eating spots is the string of café-restaurants opposite Hung Vuong Hotel. These include **Bistrot du Routard, Thien Huong,** and **Thuy Tien** cafés—they're open fairly late and are full of travelers, and hence make excellent listening posts for the latest on what's happening on the road ahead. A little way south at 14 Hung Vuong is **News Cafe Restaurant,** with vegetarian food and assorted newspapers.

Song Huong Floating Restaurant, tel. 54/823738, is moored near Trang Tien Bridge. The restaurant has a terrace and indoor tables and features a full menu; pricey for seafood. **Dzach Lau,** 23 Ben Nghe St., tel. 54/822831, has moderately priced crab, shrimp, fish, chicken, and beef dishes.

On the southeast side of town is **Ong Nen Restaurant,** and almost opposite, **Restaurant 20;** both started out serving specialty soups—eel soup, shrimp soup—but graduated to offering a full range of dishes. In the same area, on Nguyen Thai Hoc Street, is **Am Phu Restaurant,** which is busy and cheap. Down the street at 29 Nguyen Thai Hoc is **Ngoc Anh Restaurant,** which is more expensive and cleaner. It has a pleasant covered courtyard; specialties include eel with lemongrass and *chile,* and frog legs stewed with garlic.

The top floor of the **Huong Giang Hotel** has a restaurant with a good reputation. Elaborate royal dinners are served at the Century Riverside Inn and Huong Giang Hotel—the bill often over $100 for a small group.

Nightlife

Hué is quiet at night. Entertainment consists mainly of going to restaurants or cafés, though some hotels have dance floors. There's a possible venue for water puppetry shows near Phu Xuan Bridge, on the south side.

Night cruises on the Perfume River are heavily promoted—these 1.5-hour tours come complete with a crew of half a dozen Hué folk singers, who serenade you as you glide along. With luck, you can see locals night fishing by lantern-light from sampans. Some touring companies will arrange a night cruise for $35 for the boat (maximum 10 people).

The Century Riverside Inn and Huong Giang Hotel stage formal, imperial dinners and imperial song-and-dance ensembles for tourist groups. Two tourists dress as emperor and empress, and the rest of the party as mandarins. Ancient recipes of questionable authenticity are served. The complete package for 3–5 guests costs $100; for 6–10 it costs $160. Huong Giang Hotel has a curious price list: A royal dance performance is $170, and a round of folksongs $70 an hour for 10 or fewer guests. If the round of folksongs is sung on a dragon boat, it's $20 an hour extra for the boat. For a phoenix boat, it's $35 an hour extra. A "royal dinner" costs $100 for two guests, $140 for five guests, $200 for up to 10 guests.

Shopping

Conical hats made from palm leaves and bamboo are a Hué specialty. Hold one of these *non bai tho* (poem hats) up to the light to reveal stenciled designs such as a pair of birds or a short poem, proverb, or song hidden between the layers of palm leaves. There is a string of silk and souvenir shops opposite the gates of the Century Riverside Inn. Artists also sell their work directly at major sites such as Thien Mu Pagoda and the imperial tombs.

Information and Services

It's very easy to find highly educated Hué residents who speak good French or English, or both. Try the Centre de Français de Hué at 36 Le Loi. People in Hué are friendly and eager to practice their foreign-language skills. A good tourist map of Hué, in English and French, issued by the State Department of Cartography, should be available in sheet form.

A number of private and government-run outfits cater to individual tourists, renting bicycles, organizing Hué boat rides or DMZ tours, arranging guides, and, when all that's taken care of, fixing you up with train or minibus tickets to get out of Hué. The family at **Lac Thanh Restaurant,** across the river, rents bicycles and motorcycles and will assist with boats, guides, DMZ tours—and good food.

A few travel agents are found along the midsection of Huong Vuong Street, including **Sinh Café** (Open Tour buses). At 3 Hung Vuong, closer to the river, is the **Mandarin Café,** a popular hangout for travelers and a great place to swap notes. **DMZ Tour Office,** at 26 Le Loi St., tel. 54/825242, is a good tour agent.

ATC Hué, at 44 Le Loi (opposite the Century Riverside Inn), tel. 54/824500, arranges visa extensions, ticketing, accommodations, boat touring, royal dinners, and car rentals. Guides from larger hotels charge $15 a day for chaperoning a group of 10 people or fewer, $20 a day for more than 10 people.

The **post office,** at 8 Hoang Hoa Tham, is open 0630–2030. Vietnam country code is 84; the Hué area code is 54. The main bank for exchange is the **Bank of Industry** on Le Quy Don Street near the Municipal Theater. Another possibility is the **State Bank** at 6 Hoang Hoa Tham near the GPO.

Visa extensions are available at the **Entry/ Exit Control Office,** 45 Ben Nghe St., tel. 54/822131, open 0700–1130 and 1300–1700.

GETTING THERE AND AWAY
By Air

From Phu Bai Airport, 14 kilometers from town, there are scheduled flights to Hanoi and Ho Chi Minh City. The Vietnam Airlines office, 12 Hanoi St., can arrange bus service to the airport for a dollar. A three-wheel shuttle operates from Dong Ba Bus Terminal to the airport.

By Train

Trains run to Hanoi and Ho Chi Minh City several times daily. Hué to Hanoi is 688 kilometers. Foreign prices for Hué–Hanoi on Reunification Express trains are $20 hard seat, $23 soft seat, $33–37–40 hard sleeper, and $44 soft sleeper. These prices are 250 percent higher than local prices. Hué to Saigon is 1,038 kilometers and costs $29 hard seat, $35 soft seat, $50–55–60 hard sleeper, and $66 soft sleeper on an S7 train. On a CM5 train, prices are $40 soft seat, $55–60–66 hard sleeper, and $76 soft sleeper. A good compromise for price and comfort is soft seat. The reclining seat allows some latitude for sleeping. Like the bus trip, the train trip from Hué to Danang is spectacular. It takes four hours and costs $5. The Hué train station is at the west end of Le Loi Street.

Private Car and Minibus: You can club together with other travelers and rent a car for the 108-kilometer route from Hué to Danang for $25–40 one-way. Several travel agents arrange a $35 one-way trip by car or minibus for the route Hué to Lang Co Beach to Hai Van Pass to Danang (Cham Museum) to Marble Mountains to China Beach to Hoi An. Longer trips can also be arranged from Hué. A one-way trip from Hué to Saigon, passing Hoi An, Qui Nhon, Nha Trang, and Dalat in eight days, costs $400 for the minibus. A minibus to Hanoi costs $25 a person. The Open Tour, run by Sinh Café and Kim Café in Saigon, allows travelers brief sightseeing stops along the proposed route; contact Sinh at 8 Hung Vuong St., tel. 54/822121.

By Bus

An Cuu Bus Terminal, at the southern end of Hung Vuong Street, handles destinations to the south, with departures at 0500 for Qui Nhon, Buon Ma Thuot, Pleiku, Nha Trang, Dalat, and Saigon. **An Hoa Bus Terminal,** northwest of the Citadel, handles connections to the north, departing at 0500 for Dong Ha, Vinh, Khe Sanh, and Hanoi. Local buses leave from Dong Ba bus terminal at the east end of Tran Hung Dao.

GETTING AROUND

Cyclos lie in wait at the railway station, the bus stations, the market, and major hotels. There are also some motos for hire. Bicycles rent for about $1 a day—available from places along Hung Vuong Street or from various hotels (a deposit of $40 may be required by hotels). Motorcycles are harder to come by but should be rentable for $6 a day. Lac Thanh Restaurant is a good source of motorcycle and bicycle rentals. Cars can be rented here for around $20–35 a day 0700–1700, with a maximum 100 kilometers on the odometer; you can hire an air-conditioned 12-seat minibus for $40 a day, or a 24-seat coach for $60 a day. Boat rentals cost $15 per half-day with 4–6 people in a regular boat, and $25 a half-day for a dragon boat with folk singing.

North of Hué

DONG HA

Heavily damaged in the 1970s, Dong Ha now supports a population of 60,000. It became the main town in the province by default. In 1972, NVA troops poured across the Demilitarized Zone (DMZ) and laid siege to Quang Tri, once the provincial capital, and in four months of heavy fighting, American planes and South Vietnamese artillery reduced Quang Tri to rubble. After the war, all provincial government offices were moved to Dong Ha.

Dong Ha is basically a truck stop. At the junction of Route 9 and Highway 1 (called Le Duan here) there's a desultory collection of food shacks and small hotels, a market, bus station, gas station, post office, and Quang Tri Tourism Office. Ramshackle noodlehouses and bars with taxi girls complete the picture. Strung out along Highway 1 are a dozen hotels, with rates ranging $7–25 a night; there are other hotels deeper into Dong Ha.

Farther into town, several kilometers west along Route 9, you come to another center—a roundabout with railway tracks to one side, some discarded U.S. tanks, a tank retriever, and a 105mm howitzer. The roundabout was once the site of a French defense bunker. Facing the tanks are the main post office and Party Headquarters building. About three kilometers west on Route 9 is Dong Ha's best hotel, the **Dong Truong Son Hotel,** in the $20–30 range; it's not well situated. Enjoy a good view of the DMZ area from the top-floor restaurant.

Quang Tri Tourism, tel. 53/852266, fax 53/852639, is on Le Duan Boulevard at the intersection of Highway 1 and Route 9. The company arranges cars for touring the DMZ for $45 a day and issues permits in a few minutes for $5 a person—quite a tidy sum of money, since the names of all in a group are often entered on a single permit. The permit restrictions appear to be greater in the Khe Sanh area. You may be able to dodge permit requirements if you have a local guide with you.

Up to eight guides are available at Quang Tri Tourism. They speak several languages between them: Russian, English, French, Lao, and Thai. Guides are $10 for the day—they tell fascinating stories about the area. Sometimes the clients do the guiding—more than 200 American veterans visited in 1993. One vet broke down and cried at a site close to the Lao border, where his camp was overrun by NVA

infantry. A dozen of his friends were killed by fire from four Russian tanks. The vet left joss sticks in memory of his friends, offered prayers, and took photos.

THE DMZ

The 75-kilometer stretch of road from Hué to Dong Ha was dubbed *La Rue Sans Joie* (Street Without Joy) by French Foreign Legionnaires. They took a beating along this narrow strip at the hands of the Vietminh and secured the road only in 1953—a year before leaving

TOURING THE DMZ

The most popular day trip out of Hué is to the former Demilitarized Zone (DMZ). Many hotels and guesthouses and travel agents in Hué organize trips to the area. These tours cover a lot of ground and are well worth the $15 or so per person. The countryside varies from bombed-scarred wasteland to luminous green rice paddies; along the way you get an earful of DMZ history and visit Vietcong tunnels and Montagnard villages. The DMZ visit is an experience—it gives you real insight into how the Vietnamese people suffered during the war.

For this excursion wear your worst clothes and take a flashlight. If you enter Vinh Moc Tunnels you'll get covered in muck. The following is a sample itinerary. Leave Hué around 0700, and take 90 minutes to drive to Dong Ha. After a stop in Dong Ha to obtain permits and pick up a local guide, the minibus heads north for the first leg of the tour, over the Hien Luong Bridge to Vinh Moc Tunnels. By around 1300 the minibus is back in Dong Ha for lunch, and then it departs for the second leg—west along Route 9 toward the Lao border, stopping at various sites, and finishing at Khe Sanh. By 1900, you should be back in Dong Ha, and in Hué by 2030.

Assuming a minibus is shared by 6–10 people, expenses work out to $55–60 for the minibus, $10–15 for a DMZ guide, $5 a person for a DMZ permit, and a few bucks for extras such as entry tickets. Sharing expenses, it breaks down to $12–15 a head. You can also arrange a two-

day tour with an overnight stay in Dong Ha. This requires $85 for transportation, $20 for a guide, and $10 per person for a permit. In addition to the previous itinerary, this tour takes in Ashau Valley, including Hamburger Hill and parts of the Ho Chi Minh Trail, and visits hilltribe villages. Other hotels in Hué also organize DMZ tours but charge more. A full-day tour from Dong Da Hotel is $60 for 1–2 people; $70 for 3–4; $96 for 5–8; and $120 for 9–10.

You can also take a bus to Dong Ha; stay overnight there. Find a moto driver to be your guide for about $10 a day. Two Western motorcyclists heading south from Hanoi toured the Dong Ha area, including the road to Lao Bao, by picking up a local guide. It's necessary to have a local guide to keep police at bay. In any case, it would be unwise to go by yourself in this area—there's still a lot of live ordnance around. If you're coming from Hanoi and don't want to backtrack from Hué, you can use Dong Ha as a base for touring the area. However, it will be difficult to put a group of travelers together in Dong Ha. You can wait at Quang Tri Tourism Office to join a minibus of Hué travelers coming through.

If you're planning to leave Vietnam by the Lao Bao border, you might consider taking in a DMZ tour along the way—it makes the trip more interesting. You just hop aboard the regular DMZ tour from Hué, which drops you near Khe Sanh about midday. From there, take a moto for the last 20 kilometers to the border.

Central Vietnam

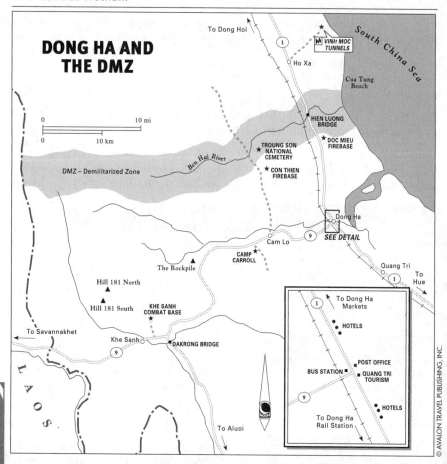

DONG HA AND THE DMZ

To Dong Hoi

To Dong Hoi

1

Ho Xa

VINH MOC TUNNELS

South China Sea

Cua Tung Beach

HIEN LUONG BRIDGE

DOC MIEU FIREBASE

TROUNG SON NATIONAL CEMETERY

0   10 mi

0   10 km

Ben Hai River

DMZ – Demilitarized Zone

CON THIEN FIREBASE

Dong Ha

9   SEE DETAIL

Cam Lo

The Rockpile

CAMP CARROLL

Quang Tri

1   To Hue

Hill 181 North

Hill 181 South

KHE SANH COMBAT BASE

To Savannakhet

Khe Sanh

DAKRONG BRIDGE

9

L A O S

To Aluoi

1   To Dong Ha Markets

HOTELS

POST OFFICE

BUS STATION   QUANG TRI TOURISM

9

HOTELS

To Dong Ha Rail Station

© AVALON TRAVEL PUBLISHING, INC.

Indochina. In July 1954, the Geneva Conference called for a line drawn at the 17th parallel, partitioning North Vietnam from South Vietnam. This area became known as the DMZ. In the 1960s, the Americans came up with the concept of building a "fence" to keep out the North. In 1967 the United States erected the McNamara Wall at the 17th parallel—a zone of mines, fences, firebases, and high-tech military gadgetry. The dividing line was the Ben Hai River, supposedly demilitarized for five kilometers on either side. Invading North Vietnamese simply walked around the west end.

In a bleak irony, the Demilitarized Zone saw some of the war's most intense battles. The legacy: mountains of scrap metal, live ordnance, and chemically defoliated areas. Since the war, millions of pieces of live ordnance have been dug up throughout the zone—at a cost of more than 5,000 dead and maimed. The zone from Dong Ha to Ben Hai River is only now beginning to be reused as farmland. Scrap-metal hunters abound in the DMZ; some use sophisticated metal detectors. The scrap goes to smelting factories in the north and south and is turned into reinforcing rods, plates, and girders for use in structures such as bridges. Other scrap is turned into ingots for export to Korea, Japan, and Taiwan. Top dong is paid for brass, followed by aluminum and steel. The larger DMZ leftovers—tanks, bulldozers, Armored Personnel Carriers—have now disappeared, leaving locals to forage deeper for shell casings and chunks of shrapnel. This is a risky business, as mines still infest the area. Impoverished families scavenge for scrap metal, including unexploded bombs, mortar rounds, and deadly white-phosphorous shells. Casualties often occur when farmers try to defuse live shells themselves instead of contacting military experts.

DONG HA TO VINH MOC

Heading north from Dong Ha, you stop at Doc Mieu firebase. There's not much to see here except for red earth dented with bomb craters. Stick close to your guide, and watch out for live materiel. Never touch *anything* lying around the DMZ—there are lots of nasty things left over from the war.

From Doc Mieu, Highway 1 heads to Hien Luong Bridge, spanning the Ben Hai River 22 kilometers north of Dong Ha. The bridge was bombed in 1967; the present bridge was completed in 1974. It was formerly controlled by the police, not the army, and mail still went through. On the north side of the bridge a statue of a soldier stands next to a pillar marked with the dates July 20, 1954, the date that Vietnam was divided into two at the Geneva Conference, and April 30, 1975, the fall of Saigon, marking the reunification of North and South.

Not usually included in tours because the area is heavily mined is Con Thien firebase, a former Marine base attacked by the NVA in 1967. There's not much here anyway—the remains of trenches, bunkers, ammunition boxes, and bits of camouflage netting. Close by is Truong Son National Cemetery, the largest war cemetery in Vietnam. Row after row of white tombstones mark the 22,000 Vietnamese killed in DMZ battles. Truong Son Cemetery is 17 kilometers west of Highway 1.

⋈ Vinh Moc Tunnels

Across the 17th parallel you continue through surprisingly verdant rice paddies, with water buffalo and cows roaming around. About seven kilometers north of Ben Hai River you turn off Highway 1 and drive another 14 kilometers along a dirt track to the fishing village of Vinh Moc.

After heavy bombardment of the area in the 1960s by U.S. airplanes and offshore naval vessels, the 1,200 villagers of Vinh Moc went underground. They constructed three kilometers of tunnels 1966–1968, emerging only to work in the fields or fish. Later the tunnels were used by the Vietcong to keep supplies rolling to offshore Con Co Island. One guide claims one square meter of ground at Vinh Moc was subjected to 9.6 tons of American bombs 1966–1972, although how such a precise figure was arrived at is not clear. Another statistic easier to grasp: 17 children were born in Vinh Moc Tunnels during the Vietnam War.

These tunnels are much better preserved than their southern counterpart (Cu Chi Tunnels, outside Saigon). Upon arrival at Vinh Moc you're ushered into a small museum displaying photos and models of the simple instruments used to dig the tunnels. There's a $2 entry fee for the museum, the tunnels, and the loan of a flashlight. The entrance to the tunnels is close to the museum; you exit above the nearby beach. Unlike Cu Chi Tunnels, the ones at Vinh Moc have been only slightly modified, with retimbered exits. This means you may have trouble getting around. If you suffer from claustophobia, do not venture into the tunnels. The tunnels can be quite slippery—your clothes may get covered in mud.

The tunnels dug in the red clay here are arrayed on 15-meter, 20-meter, and 25-meter levels. The water table is only a few meters below the deepest level. Apart from family dwellings, the tunnels previously contained a clinic, conference room, and warehouse; electric lighting was even installed in 1972. There are six exits to the sea, and seven to the air. You exit overlooking a surfing beach. Prepare to be hounded by enterprising youths selling soft drinks.

DONG HA TO LAO BAO

From Dong Ha, you now head west toward the Lao border along Route 9. Dong Ha to Khe Sanh is 57 kilometers, about two hours with stops. Khe Sanh is only 18 kilometers away from the Lao Bao border crossing into Laos. The road up to Lao Bao was built by the French and improved by the Americans and is in quite good shape. Here is a complete contrast in scenery from the Vinh Moc route; you'll see rolling hills on the way to Khe Sanh.

When American troops arrived here in 1965, they built camps, hospitals, command and logistics centers, and military firebases bearing names such as Sharon and Ann. The firebases were an attempt to set up a string of strongholds along the DMZ. This area, just south of the 17th parallel, saw some of the bloodiest battles of the Vietnam War. Heavy fighting rocked Khe Sanh in 1968 and Hamburger Hill in 1969.

Today there's not a lot to see. Scrap-metal foragers have hauled off remaining pieces of military hardware. Camp Carroll was once the headquarters of U.S. operations, but there's little to see except for some overgrown trenches. The camp is three kilometers south of Route 9. The Rockpile—a huge mound of rocks—was a U.S. lookout with an artillery base nearby.

South of Dong Ha

Dakrong Bridge, completed in 1976, is about 60 kilometers from Dong Ha. Just before the bridge is a checkpoint where permits may be requested; police are looking for goods smuggled across the Lao border. West of the bridge are several Bru Van Kieu hilltribe villages with wooden and thatched housing. Cottage industries include traditional rattan collecting and, more recently, amassing scrap metal for resale. The Bru sort through artillery and cluster bomb casings and load these onto trucks several times a month.

Farther to the south, across Dakrong Bridge, is a feeder of the **Ho Chi Minh Trail,** now overgrown with jungle. The famous trail is a dud as a sight. Scenery is quite ordinary, and the whole purpose of the trail

was to be inconspicuous. Impeding the evolution of trekking routes are two factors: the huge amount of unexploded ordnance hidden along the trail, and uncertain security in the Central Highlands.

Minority villages are scattered along the route south, from Dakrong Bridge to **Aluoi**—once a U.S. Special Forces base—and eventually on to Hué. Somewhere south of Aluoi in the Ashau Valley is Hamburger Hill; American forces fought a fierce battle with NVA troops here in May 1969, resulting in heavy losses for the Americans. More than 200 died in a single week. Hamburger Hill today is just a name. Even returning American vets cannot pinpoint the exact location, any more than Vietnamese can pinpoint the exact course of the Ho Chi Minh Trail. A better reason to venture farther down the Aluoi route is to visit minority villages. This part of the itinerary is not included in day trips from Hué but is featured on the two-day trip. With a 4WD vehicle it's possible to travel the 65 kilometers from Dakrong Bridge to Aluoi, and then continue another 60 kilometers into Hué.

Khe Sanh

The rich, reddish soil around Khe Sanh is used for cultivating coffee, manioc, jackfruit, and pineapples. About 10,000 people live in the Khe Sanh area. Hilltribe women smoke long-stemmed pipes and wear embroidered skirts.

Khe Sanh is a strategic spot 75 kilometers southwest of Dong Ha that once controlled Route 9 to Laos. In a hill area three kilometers north of Khe Sanh town, the Americans maintained a large combat base with an adjacent airstrip. A plaque inscribed in English and Vietnamese reads: The Area Of Tacon Pont Base Built By U.S. And Saigon Puppet. There's nothing left of the base except bits of barbed wire and scraps of metal, and holes dug by locals looking for scrap metal. To attract tourism, the government plans to rebuild the base, foxholes and all.

Khe Sanh is a famous battleground. Soon after it had been turned into a marine stronghold in the mid-1960s, NVA infantry converged on it. The specter of another Dien Bien Phu hung over Khe Sanh. To hold the combat base, American troops had to garrison the hills dominating the valley. In early 1967, a fierce exchange of fire occurred on Hill 861, Hill 881 South, and Hill 881 North—all areas held by the NVA. By late 1967, an estimated 20,000–40,000 NVA troops had converged on Khe Sanh and dug in.

The 77-day siege of Khe Sanh began in January 1968. Refusing to back off, U.S. General William Westmoreland turned the siege into a showdown, with massive aerial and ground attacks on the surrounding area and the buildup of U.S. and ARVN troops to a force of more than 6,000. In April 1968 U.S. Army troops reopened Route 9 to the base, ending the seige. The cost was 248 American dead. Although they lost an estimated 10,000 troops, the North Vietnamese claimed the real objective of Khe Sanh was to distract American attention while the NVA launched the 1968 Tet offensive. The Americans, on the other hand, believed Tet was a diversion for Khe Sanh.

Khe Sanh was subsequently determined to be of no strategic importance, and the United States quietly pulled out of the combat base in July 1968. Before withdrawal, American troops destroyed the base entirely to leave nothing for Vietnamese propaganda purposes.

Lao Bao Crossing

Khe Sanh is 20 kilometers from the Lao Bao border crossing into Laos, which is slated to become a fast overland route for goods carried from Vietnam to Thailand. Trucks can cover the 350 kilometers from Dong Ha to Savannakhet in Laos in a full 12-hour day of driving. The Lao Bao crossing has been open to foreigners since the beginning of 1994. Several have even bicycled the route from Thailand into Vietnam. You can pick up a Lao visa in Danang. (More description of the route is given in the *Laos* section of this book.) An international bus runs three times a week from Danang to Savannakhet. It costs about $15 from the Lao side or $33 from the greedier Vietnamese side.

THE NORTH COAST

There is little to recommend the thin strip of country north of Hué to Vinh and Thanh Hoa. Consider the facts: The Hué-Vinh strip, in places only a few hundred kilometers wide, was subjected to saturation bombing during the Vietnam War, and it remains one of the poorest parts of the country. Highway 1 is in very bad condition here, sometimes disappearing into mud and potholes. To make matters worse, the area suffers some of the worst weather in Vietnam—typhoons, floods, hot dry spells. Most travelers speed through by train or plane. Traveling by a bus along this stretch is not recommended, but traveler minibuses can be arranged from Hué to Hanoi. An Open Tour bus manned by two drivers can cover the 660 kilometers from Hué to Hanoi in a long overnight trip. Approximate distances on this route are: 75 kilometers to Dong Ha, 95 kilometers to Dong Hoi, 198 kilometers to Vinh, 138 kilometers to Thanh Hoa, 60 kilometers to Ninh Binh, and 95 kilometers to Hanoi.

Dong Hoi

Dong Hoi is a fishing port 170 kilometers north of Hué. It was wiped off the map by U.S. bombing during the Vietnam War because of its position just north of the 17th parallel. Foreigners stay at the **Phuong Dong** or **Hoa Binh** hotels, with overpriced rooms. **Dong Hoi Tourist Office** is near the hotel.

Phong Nha Caves

Phong Nga Caves are 50 km northwest of Dong Hoi, or about an hour by car. In 2003, Phong Nga-Khe Bang National Park was inscribed as a World Heritage site. The park is home to myriad karst peaks and underground caverns. The huge grottoes here were known to the colonial French, but it was not until 1990 that explorers from the British Royal Geographic Association set about probing further and mapping the extensive cave system.

Much remains to be explored at Phong Nga, and very little indeed is open to the touring public. If you're expecting something on a par

scenery on Nam Song River, near the Phong Nga caves

with Halong Bay, you'll be (deeply) disappointed. Phong Nga has some great scenery, but every step of the way has been planned for you by the local tourism authorities—you get the idea that you are being processed through a large mill, with money being extracted at every turn. The place is set up for Vietnamese tourists, who are prone to tossing garbage, stubbing out cigarettes in the caves, and worse.

You are not free to roam around at Phong Nga. On arriving at Son Trach village, a fee of $8 will be extracted for the one-hour boat ride up the Son River to the caves, winding past karst peaks. When you reach the caves, there are two choices: Hike up to a dry cave, or take the boat into the wet cave. To reach the dry cave, there are concrete stairs all the way, and vendors keen to sell you drinks most of the way too. Nothing really special in the dry cave, though the views from the top ridge are good. The spectacular part is the lower grotto, which is entered along the Son River: Your boatman will row you in, probably a few hundred meters. The cave is garishly lit, revealing wondrous stalagmite and stalactite formations. You can get off to investigate the various "rooms" within the main cav-

ern. The caves were used as grotto-sanctuaries by the Cham and as a field hospital for northern troops during the Vietnam War.

During November and December, access to the grotto may be closed because of flooding. There are minihotels at Son Trach village, or you can stay in Dong Hoi, with many hotels strung along Highway 1.

Vinh

Vinh is another town on this strip of coast leveled by repeated aerial bombing by both the French and the Americans. With East German assistance, the town has been rebuilt in the drabbest style imaginable. Parts look like East Berlin on a wet Sunday.

Because it's halfway between Hué and Hanoi, traveler minibuses tend to break the journey in Vinh; other minibuses carry on overnight straight through. Vinh features not much in the way of sights, apart from a dowdy Military Museum and an Army Museum, but 15 kilometers northwest of town is **Kim Lien village,** the birthplace of Ho Chi Minh. Eighteen kilometers northeast is Cua Lo Beach. There's a 48-room hotel out in this direction called Cua Lo Hotel.

A concrete wasteland of sorts, Vinh is nevertheless brimming with hotels. In fact, Highway 1 along here consists entirely of hotels on one side (grim apartment blocks on the other). Low-end hotels include **Tra Bong** (no TV), **Quang Trung** (no hot water), **Phuong Hoang, Bong Sen,** and **Ben Thuy.** There's also **Ngan Ha** (Military) hotel on Le Loi St., tel. 38/849897; and **Nha Khach Vat Tu,** at 28 Nguyen Thi Minh Khai, tel. 38/847422, fax 38/843162, with 19 rooms for around $15 apiece.

More upscale is a private minihotel, **Hong Ngoc,** at 86 Le Loi, tel. 38/841314, fax 38/841229, with 20 rooms in the $15–25–35–40 range; satellite TV, bar; it will arrange car rentals (and this six-story hotel actually has an elevator!). Also with satellite TV is the **Friendship Hotel** (Huu Nghi), at 41 Le Loi, tel. 38/842492, fax 38/842813, with 75 rooms in the $25–35–40 range and some suites for $90. In the same boring-but-functional high-rise class

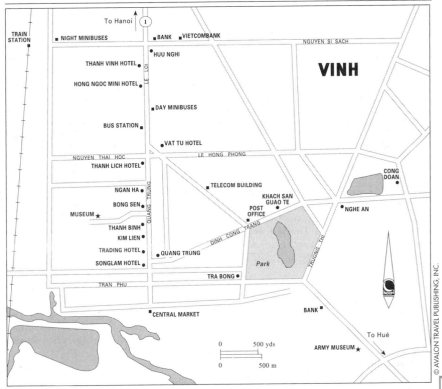

is **Kim Lien Hotel,** at 12 Quang Trung St., tel. 38/844751, fax 38/843699, with 79 rooms for $25–35–45–57. Arrayed along Le Loi are the following smaller hotels: **Khach San Thanh Vinh,** 9 Le Loi, tel. 38/847795, with 18 rooms for $25–40; the **Trading Hotel** (Thuong Mai), 10 Quang Trung, tel. 38/8930211, fax 38/830393, with 40 rooms for $30–40 and a fridge, phone, and TV in every one. To the eastern side of town is a rum bunch of hotels—**Khach San Giao Te,** with satellite TV, and rooms for $10–20–30; farther east is a concrete monstrosity with furry carpets, **Nghe An Guesthouse,** on Phan Dang Luu, tel. 38/846124, with 30 rooms for $20 apiece; yet farther east is the derelict **Cong Doan Hotel.**

Vinh is about 365 kilometers from Hué and 290 kilometers from Hanoi. Reunification Express trains stop here. Express buses depart from

Vinh bus station on Le Loi early morning for Ninh Binh, Hanoi, Hué, Danang, and other destinations. You can pick up minibuses along Highway 1, though these are likely to be overcrowded. If headed for Hanoi from Vinh, you might want to consider a stop in Ninh Binh to check out the great karst landscapes there.

From Vinh there is a turnoff westward on Route 8 leading to a border crossing at Cau Treo (Keo Nua Pass) and on to Lak Sao in Laos.

Thanh Hoa

Thanh Hoa, capital of the province of the same name, marks the northernmost point of central Vietnam. Thanh Hoa was the cradle of the Dong Son culture, which flourished in the first millennium B.C. along the Ma, Lam, and Red River valleys. Excavations in these areas have unearthed large engraved bronze drums, statues, jewelry, and other artifacts. A number of finds were made in the village of Dong Son, just west of Thanh Hoa. About 40 kilometers northwest of Thanh Hoa near the town of Vinh Loc is the site of Ho Citadel, built in 1397—only the massive gates remain. About 15 kilometers southeast of Thanh Hoa you'll find Sam Son Beach, a three-kilometer stretch of fine white sand. There are several hotels in Thanh Hoa on Highway 1. The town also serves as an express train stop. The area around Ninh Binh, 60 kilometers north of Thanh Hoa, features majestic karst scenery, especially near Tam Coc and Bich Dong.

Danang

The road from Hué winds 108 kilometers south to Danang, passing spectacular Lang Co Beach and Hai Van Pass. The latter marks the northern limit of the former Kingdom of Champa that once extended along the coast as far south as present-day Vung Tau. Danang served as center of the kingdom. Near Danang are the ruins of My Son, and in Danang itself is the excellent Cham Museum.

Danang succeeded Hoi An as the most important port in central Vietnam during the early 19th century. The French, seeking to open Vietnam to trade, mounted a naval attack on Danang in 1858, opening the way for almost a century of French domination. Under the French, Danang was known as Tourane. Vestiges of French presence appear in the colonial architecture of the cathedral and the former bank, town hall, and courthouse.

On March 8, 1965, another landing force hit Danang as the first American marines waded ashore at Red Beach to secure an airfield. Danang developed into one of the biggest U.S. military bases in Southeast Asia. Nearby China Beach, an R&R spot for U.S. troops, has become well known in the West because of the American TV series of the same name.

Today, Danang is Vietnam's third-largest city, with a population of around 1.1 million. An idle sailing ship waiting for a gust of wind, Danang is slated to become the major gateway to central Vietnam. Banking on the China Beach name, officials hope grandiose plans to develop Danang are realized. The Americans left behind a gigantic airbase near China Beach capable of receiving large commercial jets. And Danang's beaches are much closer to Hong Kong and Taiwan than the islands of Thailand or the Philippines. Cruise ships ply the coast, stopping at Saigon, Danang, and Haiphong, then continue to Hong Kong. Danang's deep-sea port can accommodate four 20,000-ton ships at a time. This port is of great interest to landlocked Laos. A land border opened in 1994 at Lao Bao has allowed container trucks to rumble up and down Highway 9 from Savannakhet in Laos through Lao Bao on to Dong Ha and down Highway 1 from Dong Ha to Danang. Some independent travelers have used the same route. This shortcut is slated to link Thailand, Laos, and Vietnam for trade and tourism.

Joint ventures were being negotiated for resort hotels around China Beach. Under construction was **Indochina Beach Hotel,** a Hong Kong–Vietnamese venture for a 260-room hotel and villa complex. The American BBI group has signed a joint-venture deal to build a $250 million luxury resort and business center next to **Non Nuoc Resort Hotel.** The complex was to feature a total of 1,200 rooms in four new hotels, a golf course, and a conference center. It was scheduled for completion in the year 2005. Another American firm, DeMatteis Construction, was planning to build a resort with a five-star hotel, townhouses, offices, and a marina at Bac My An Beach outside Danang. Other joint-venture hotels in Danang are with a Hong Kong company (80-room hotel) and a Thai company (120-room hotel), making up for Danang's lack of international standard accommodations.

Danang is a port city. Unless you enjoy looking at container vessels and rusty hulks, consider using it simply as a base for trips to the

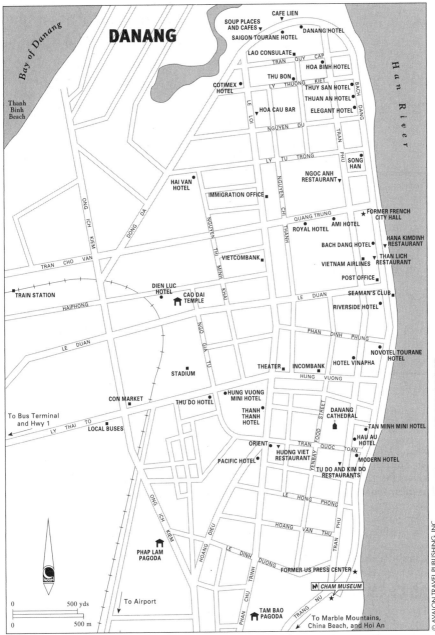

DANANG

Bay of Danang

Thanh Binh Beach

Han River

CAFE LIEN
SOUP PLACES AND CAFES
SAIGON TOURANE HOTEL
DANANG HOTEL
LAO CONSULATE
TRAN QUY CAP
HOA BINH HOTEL
THU BON
LY THUONG KIET
COTIMEX HOTEL
THUY SAN HOTEL
THUAN AN HOTEL
BACH DANG
HOA CAU BAR
ELEGANT HOTEL
LE LOI
NGUYEN DU
LY TU TRONG
SONG HAN
PHU
HAI VAN HOTEL
NGUYEN CHI
IMMIGRATION OFFICE
NGOC ANH RESTAURANT
FORMER FRENCH CITY HALL
QUANG TRUNG
AMI HOTEL
THANH
ROYAL HOTEL
HANA KIMDINH RESTAURANT
BACH DANG HOTEL
VIETCOMBANK
THAN LICH RESTAURANT
NGUYEN MINH KHAI
VIETNAM AIRLINES
POST OFFICE
DONG DA
ONG ICH KIEM
DIEN LUC HOTEL
CAO DAI TEMPLE
NGO GIA TU
LE DUAN
SEAMAN'S CLUB
RIVERSIDE HOTEL
TRAIN STATION
TRAN CHO VAN
HAIPHONG
LE DUAN
PHAN DINH PHUNG
NOVOTEL TOURANE HOTEL
STADIUM
THEATER
INCOMBANK
HOTEL VINAPHA
HUNG VUONG
CON MARKET
HUNG VUONG MINI HOTEL
THU DO HOTEL
THANH THANH HOTEL
To Bus Terminal and Hwy 1
LY THAI TO
LOCAL BUSES
FOOD STREET
DANANG CATHEDRAL
TAN MINH MINI HOTEL
ORIENT
HAU AU HOTEL
PACIFIC HOTEL
HUONG VIET RESTAURANT
TRAN QUOC TOAN
MODERN HOTEL
YEN BAY
TU DO AND KIM DO RESTAURANTS
LE HONG PHONG
ONG ICH KIEM
HOANG VAN THU
TRAN PHU
HOANG DIEU
LE DINH DUONG
PHAP LAM PAGODA
FORMER US PRESS CENTER
CHAM MUSEUM
PHAN CHU TRINH
To Airport
TAM BAO PAGODA
TRANG NU
To Marble Mountains, China Beach, and Hoi An

0   500 yds
0   500 m

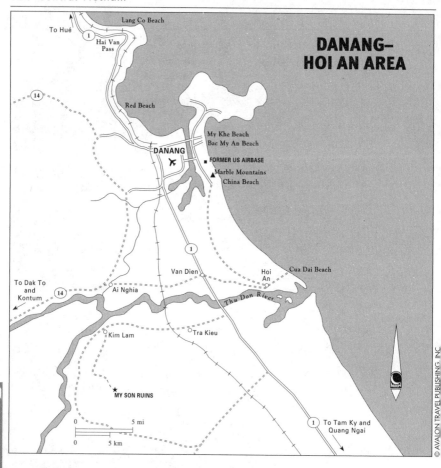

DANANG–HOI AN AREA

To Hué
Lang Co Beach
Hai Van Pass
Red Beach
My Khe Beach
Bac My An Beach
DANANG
FORMER US AIRBASE
Marble Mountains
China Beach
Van Dien
Hoi An
Cua Dai Beach
To Dak To and Kontum
Ai Nghia
Thu Don River
Kim Lam
Tra Kieu
MY SON RUINS
0   5 mi
0   5 km
To Tam Ky and Quang Ngai

© AVALON TRAVEL PUBLISHING, INC

Central Vietnam

Marble Mountains, China Beach, Hoi An, and My Son. Danang may assume an important role as the gateway to central Vietnam—it is an international entry/exit point with the same powers as Saigon or Hanoi for customs and immigration. International cruise ships stop here, and flights have started up direct from Bangkok to Danang, with direct links to Hong Kong on the agenda.

CHAM MUSEUM

This museum was set up by the French, who shipped off a number of exhibits to France;

other pieces were stolen and sold to art collectors overseas. Nevertheless, the Cham Museum houses the world's largest collection of Cham sculpture, with more than 300 sandstone pieces housed in a building constructed in 1915 by the Ecole Française d'Extrême-Orient and expanded in 1935. The second-largest collection of Cham sculpture is at the Musée Guimet in Paris. .

There is little English captioning at the Cham Museum. You can buy some literature from a kiosk at the front gate, but it doesn't help much. The museum has four musty rooms named after the original sites where the displayed Cham sculptures were found—My Son, Tra Kieu, Dong Duong, and Thap Mam. These also denote sculptural styles of the following periods: My Son 8th–9th century, Tra Kieu 7th–10th century, Dong Duong 9th–10th century, and Thap Mam 12th–13th century. Since former Cham sites have been razed or extensively damaged during wars, the museum represents the last bastion of Cham culture.

Patrons to the museum encounter a culture at once alien and highly imaginative. The larger pieces here are stupendous—the Goddess Uma, the bust of Shiva, Vishnu backed by 13 *nagas,* the Tra Kieu altar with its *Ramayana* scenes, and the giant Dvaraparas and Dhamapala. There are friezes, lintels, altarpieces, and inscribed stones. Masterful sculptural skills are shown in the fluid forms of the celestial dancers, the *apsaras,* sculpted in stone in a piece in the Tra Kieu Room. Several pieces are associated with Cham fertility cults, including rows of breasts on the altar ornaments and pedestal bases in the Thap Mam Room. Also in the Thap Mam Room are mythical animals, varying from *garuda* (bird-man) to *makara* (aquatic monster) to *gaja-simha* (elephant-lion).

A gift shop sells small-scale replicas in sandstone, marble, and terra-cotta. Outlets in the Marble Mountains and gift shops around town also sell replicas. There are some shops opposite the museum entrance. The museum is open daily 0700–1800; no closures for lunch, but it's been known to close earlier than posted if no tourists are clamoring for entry. Entry is $2.

ACCOMMODATIONS

Although Danang has more than 60 hotels, it's estimated that only a third meet international standards. A number of hotels are not accessible to foreigners. Most of the hotels open to big noses are listed below, but times change—suddenly a Vietnamese hotel comes of age, and the plumbing is deemed up to scratch, and the doors are flung open to foreigners. Groups of hotels often fall under the same management: the Song Han and Hoa Binh hotels are run by Danang Shipchandler Company, while Dan-

ang Tourism runs the Hai Au, Phuong Dong, Hung Vuong, Danang, and Riverside hotels. New luxury additions in Danang include the Novotel Tourane Hotel and the Saigon Tourane Hotel.

Under $20

At the northern tip of Danang is a strip of hotels facing a traveler café. Previously called Danang 1, 2, and 3 buildings, these hotels used to house U.S. troops, which might explain the dance bar, Hoang Gia, next door. This area is three kilometers from the bus station or railway; you can reach the hotel strip by cyclo, or pay a bit more for a moto. Remember that cyclos and motos receive a commission from the hotel for delivering you to the doorstep.

Danang Hotel, (old wing) at 5 Dong Da, tel. 51/823258, fax 51/821039, has 60 rooms, ranging from basic $6 rooms to $15–25 a/c rooms with hot water. In between, rooms differ by $2 and $3 increments. The place is clean, quiet, and efficient, and will store luggage. **Danang Hotel,** (new wing) 3 Dong Da St., tel. 51/821986, fax 51/823431, is a completely renovated section; it features 114 rooms ranging $25–75; facilities include a restaurant and bar.

Harmony Hotel, at 6 Dong Da St., tel. 51/829146, fax 51/829145, has 21 rooms for $15–25; car and motorcycle rentals available. Around the corner, fronting the river, is **Thuan An Hotel,** at 14 Bach Dang St., tel. 51/820527, with 12 rooms for $7–12. Next door is a concrete nightmare, the 21-room **Thuy San Hotel,** at 12 Bach Dang, tel. 51/835005; rooms go for $15–20 apiece. Farther south is Tan Minh minihotel, at 142 Bach Dang, tel. 51/827456, fax 51/830172, with 10 rooms for $15–25.

Hai Van Hotel, 2 Nguyen Thi Minh, tel. 51/821300, has 40 rooms ranging from $10 fan rooms to $15–20 with a/c and hot water. **Hung Vuong Minihotel,** 95 Hung Vuong, tel. 51/823967, offers 10 rooms in a French–style building, $8 s and $12–15 d with a/c and hot water. Favored by backpackers, **Thu Do Hotel,** at 107 Hung Vuong, tel. 51/823863, features 35 rooms for $5 s and $6–12 d. **Thanh Thanh Hotel,** 54 Phan Chu Trinh, tel. 51/821230, has

44 rooms in the $5–12 range; seedy, with taxi girls about. **Hotel Vinapha,** 80 Tran Phu St., tel. 51/825072, has 16 rooms for $8 with fan, or $15–18 with hot water. There's a big hotel near the bus station called **Khach San Dien Bien.**

$20–50

The following hotels are on the waterfront with views of the Han River. The **Elegant Hotel,** at 22A Bach Dang St., tel. 51/892893, fax 51/835179, offers 26 rooms for $35–45 standard, $45–55 first class, $65–75 superior, $120–140 for a suite. The hotel has a business center and travel agent. **Hai Au Hotel** (Seagull), 177 Tran Phu, tel. 51/822722, fax 51/824165, has 28 rooms for $32–55 s; $5 extra for doubles. The 90-room **Bach Dang Hotel,** 50 Bach Dang, tel. 51/823649, fax 51/821659, charges $20–44–64 s, $5 extra for doubles; the rooms have a/c, fridge, TV, phone, and other creature comforts. **Song Han,** 36 Bach Dang, tel. 51/822530, fax 51/821109, rents 49 rooms, $22–25–40 single or double. To the southern end of town is **Modern Hotel,** at 182 Bach Dang, tel. 51/820550, fax 51/821842, with rooms for $25–40 standard, $45–50 deluxe, and $60–65 for a suite.

Just off the river at 7 Quang Trung St. is **Ami Hotel,** tel. 51/824494, fax 51/824407, with 17 rooms in the $22–30 range, and a few cheaper deals possible.

At the north end of town is **Hoa Binh Hotel** (Peace Hotel), 3 Tran Quy Cap, tel. 51/823984, fax 51/823161, with 25 rooms in the $25–50 range, single or double; popular with group tours. A rather bland hotel up this way is the **Cotimex Hotel,** at 8 Le Loi St., tel. 51/894501, fax 51/823470, with 52 rooms for $40–65. The hotel has a parasol antenna (satellite TV).

In central Danang you'll find the following hotels. **Pacific Hotel** (Thai Binh Duong) at 92 Phan Chu Trinh, tel. 51/822137, fax 51/822921, is an eight-story hotel with more than 40 rooms for $15–28 s, $25–40 d, $35 t. The Danang Tourism Company operates from here. **Orient Hotel** (Phuong Dong), 93 Phan Chau Trinh, tel. 51/821266, fax 51/822854, is a six-story hotel popular with group tours; it features 36 rooms for $39–43 s, $49–53 d, or $65 t. **Dien Luc Hotel,** 37 Haiphong St., tel. 51/821864, fax 51/823263, offers 27 rooms in the $26–55 range; doubles run $28–60.

$50–100

Riverside Hotel (Tiensa), on the waterfront at 68 Bach Dang, tel. 51/832592, fax 51/832593, hosts 22 rooms for $55–85 first class, $80–95 superior, and $100–120 deluxe. It is run by Danang Tourist Company, which naturally will assist with travel arrangements. **Royal Hotel,** at 17 Quang Trung St., tel. 51/823295, fax 51/827279, is a luxury-class hotel with 28 rooms from $80–90 deluxe to $135–145 suite. The elegant rooms feature satellite TV, minibar, and room safes; facilities include a VIP nightclub. New in Danang is the four-star **Novotel Tourane,** a 10-story tower with 217 rooms, a pool, and fitness center.

FOOD

Most eating in Danang takes place in hotels (expensive), or on the streets at noodlehouses (cheap). The Orient Hotel features a top-floor restaurant, and Bach Dang Hotel has a pleasant but pricey restaurant near the waterfront. Down the street is **Thanh Lich Restaurant,** at 42 Bach Dang St., popular with foreign businesspeople—French and Vietnamese food. Some of Danang's best restaurants line Tran Phu Street—**Ngoc Anh,** at 30 Tran Phu, tel. 51/822778, expensive; **Tu Do,** at 172 Tran Phu, tel. 51/21869, moderate; and **Kim Do,** at 174 Tran Phu, tel. 51/821846. Near Phap Lam Pagoda on the south of town is a small vegetarian place, **Quan Chay.** It's at 484 Ong Ich Khiem Street and closes around 1800.

For waterfront dining or drinking, try **Hana Kim Dinh,** at 7 Bach Dang St., tel. 51/830014, with Western and Vietnamese seafood dishes—not cheap, but stylish. The Hana Kim Dinh has a bar, terrace restaurant, and a top-floor banquet room; live music is sometimes performed.

In the café line, **Café Lien,** 4 Dong Da St., tel. 51/820401 (opposite Danang Hotel), has reasonable food and excellent gossip. Nearby is **Free Time,** an American–style pub-bistro. For classier decor, try **Hoa Cau** (Areca Flower Café), at 358 Le Loi St.—a bar with live piano music on weekends. There are many cheap noodlehouses farther west. A bit farther south, there's a string of soup shops on Ly Tu Trong, between Tran Phu and Nguyen Chi Thanh. Parallel to Tran Phu Street at the southern end is a popular street for noodlehouses, called Yenbay Food Street.

SERVICES AND INFORMATION
Traveler Cafés
Café Lien, at 4 Dong Da St., opposite Marble Mountain Hotel, is the prime foreign hangout in Danang. It's run by a good-humored family and serves palatable food. Lien can fix you up with just about anything—Hondas or bicycles, cars to My Son, minibus rides down the coast. She'll even take care of baggage during your absence. Moto drivers hang around this area offering guide services.

Tourist Information
Danang Tourism appears to go by many different names—Dana Tours, Quangnam Danang Tourist Service Company, Danang Tourist Company, Danang Travel Service—but operates out of one address—92 Phan Chu Trinh (the ground floor of the Pacific Hotel), tel. 51/821423, fax 51/821560. The office displays an array of brochures about Monaco, Club Med in the Maldives, and Colorado—but nothing on Danang (for good reason). There are guides on hand who speak English, French, German, and Russian; a tour guide costs $10–15 a day. The staff will arrange a car or minibus if you need one. Otherwise, Danang Tourism staff are deeply involved in the study of local newspapers; they perk up only when a cruise ship pulls into port and they smell big bucks.

Maps
A tourist map of Quang Nam province and Danang City is issued by the State Department of Cartography. Destination information in

Vietnamese and English makes this map useful for excursions out of Danang.

Communications
The **GPO** is at the corner of Bach Dang Street and Le Duan Boulevard, with mail, telex, fax, and phone services. There's a foreign mail service counter at 62 Bach Dang Street. Vietnam country code is 84; the Danang area code is 51. **TNT** courier service has an office in Danang, tel. 51/821685.

Banks
Vietcombank, on Le Loi, is open 0730–1100 and 1300–1530 Mon.–Fri.; 0700–1000 on Saturday. The bank charges a 1.2 percent fee for converting traveler's checks to U.S. dollars, with a minimum $2 charge; if you change $200, you get $197.60. There's an **Incombank** on Ly Thai To Street.

Shopping
There are silk shops in the area of Pacific and Orient hotels, and both hotels have souvenir shops. Try the **Cham Museum art gallery** for figurines, paintings, and other souvenirs. There are some gift shops opposite the museum.

Health Care
A Western-run clinic is **Family Medical Practice,** at 50 Nguyen Van Linh St., Hai

Chau District, tel. 51/582699; www.vietnam-medicalpractice.com.

Immigration Services

Danang Immigration Office, at 71 Le Loi St., handles emigration and immigration formalities, possibly including visa extensions.

GETTING THERE AND AWAY

By Air

Danang International Airport is seven kilometers from the city. A moto ride into town costs around $1.50, by taxi several times that price. There are connections from Danang to Ho Chi Minh City for $80, and to Hanoi for $85 daily, and twice-weekly flights to Qui Nhon, Nha Trang, Buon Ma Thuot, and Pleiku. Although Danang is supposed to be an international entry and exit point, flights are usually routed through Saigon or Hanoi from places such as Frankfurt, Paris, Bangkok, or Sydney. There is a direct connection several times a week from Danang to Bangkok and to Hong Kong. Other direct links are expected to Taipei, Tokyo, and Seoul. Vietnam Airlines booking office for domestic flights is at 35 Tran Phu St., tel. 51/821130.

By Rail

Danang is roughly the midway point between Hanoi and Saigon on the Reunification Express line. By express from Danang to Hanoi is 20 hours; to Saigon, about 22 hours. The ride to Hué from Danang costs $5 for a soft seat and is spectacular. The four-hour trip passes along the coastline. In the other direction, to Nha Trang, is an equally scenic four-hour trip.

By Bus

The Danang long-distance bus station is two kilometers west of town, at 8 Dien Bien Phu St.—the western continuation of Le Thai To Street. Buses depart to Vinh, Hué, Haiphong, Hanoi, and the Central Highlands, Nha Trang, and Ho Chi Minh City. Another express bus station operates out of 52 Phan Chu Trinh St., next to Thanh Thanh Hotel. Bus stations in Danang are bristling with vicious cyclo drivers who latch onto foreigners because they can make commissions by taking them to particular hotels. Keep walking when you first get out of a bus until the cyclos thin out. Then negotiate.

By Private Car and Minibus

A number of hotels can arrange cars. The run to Hué is worthwhile: Get together with a few travelers and rent a car for the day, stopping at Hai Van Pass. You'll pass great viewpoints over Lang Co Beach, with a clear blue lagoon on one side and a strip of beach facing the South China Sea on the other. Lang Co is a fishing village—it's possible to stay overnight at the **Lang Co Hotel,** tel. 54/874426, with 20 rooms for $8–20, and a reasonable restaurant. The hotel is a bungalow-style place within walking range of the beach.

Café Lien in Danang rents cars for $35 per day round-trip to Hué; a one-way run to Hué is $20. Café Lien will also coordinate lifts for traveler share-taxis or minibuses. Saigon-based private minibus operators returning from the Saigon-to-Hué run drop in here to line up riders heading south. This early morning departure for Nha Trang costs $15 a person; other destinations are negotiable.

GETTING AROUND

Cyclo and moto transport is abundant and drivers will literally stalk you. It's cheaper to hire cyclo or moto operators by the hour—about $.70 an hour for a moto driver, or $6 a day.

From Café Lien, opposite Marble Mountain Hotel, you can rent 50cc and 70cc bikes for $5 a day or $3 per half-day. Good bicycles cost $1 a day; $.50 for an older model. Car rentals through Café Lien are $15 for the day around Danang including Hoi An, $25 round-trip to My Son, and $30 round-trip to My Lai. Danang Hotel rents bicycles. Car rentals are widely available through hotels in Danang or through Danang Tourism.

River Trips: If you can assemble a larger group, Dana Tours will rent you a boat (parked on the waterfront south of the Novotel Tourane Hotel) to cruise up and down the Han River and beyond. You might also want to consider longer boat trips—to reach My Son or Hoi An via skeins of canals.

EXCURSIONS FROM DANANG

To explore the China Beach–Hoi An–My Son triangle of sites you can base yourself either in Danang or Hoi An. Travelers prefer Hoi An because of its more pleasant atmosphere and because of its concentration of traveler cafés, tour agents, and transport rentals. Staying at China Beach is another option, though an expensive one.

Local transportation is exasperatingly slow and may drop you short of your destination. You can get rides from local pickups and three-wheelers to the Marble Mountains and China Beach from a depot a block west of Con Market in Danang. A better alternative is to hire your own car for half a day or a full day, splitting expenses with others. Or hire a moto, or rent a motorcycle or bicycle. Pack a picnic lunch, water bottle, and swimsuit, and a flashlight for the Marble Mountains. Some travelers stash their packs at a hotel in Hoi An or Danang, and spend several days on motorcycles exploring the area. If you don't want to ride your own motorcycle, you can hire a moto driver for about $6–7 per day to go to Hoi An and Marble Mountains/China Beach. A one-way trip by moto to Hoi An with no stops is about $2. Motos charge around $8 to go to My Son Cham Ruins.

Hoi An, 30 kilometers from Danang, is a great town worth several days; the Marble Mountains and China Beach are worth up to a day; My Son, 70 kilometers away, demands an entire day because of bad roads. If your time is short, you can set out early from Danang on a moto or motorcycle and get to the Marble Mountains in 20 minutes. You can see the Marble Mountains and China Beach in the morning, visit Hoi An during the afternoon, and be back in Danang by nightfall. If you have more time, consider staying in Hoi An a few days, and taking a boat from Hoi An to Danang.

My Khe Beach

The R&R beach featured in the *China Beach* TV series is actually My Khe Beach, about six kilometers from Danang. However, in the interests of promotion, the beach farther south has been called China Beach to draw people to the government hotel there. My Khe Beach is rarely visited by tourists but has its own large hotel fronting the sands. This is the 42-room **My Khe Beach Hotel,** tel. 51/836125, fax 51/836123, with rooms from $18–40 s and $24–48 d; several villas are available. There are some seafood restaurants just north of the hotel. Directly south of My Khe is **Bac My An Beach,** with accommodation at the luxury-class **Furama Resort Hotel,** a Hong Kong joint-venture project featuring a mix of contemporary Asian and French colonial architecture on the site of the former U.S. Air Force PX. In addition to 200 luxury rooms, Furama Resort also boasts three pools, two restaurants, bars, fitness centers, and a business center.

Danang to the Marble Mountains

To get to the Marble Mountains, follow Tran Phu Street south past the Cham Museum till you cross **Nguyen Van Troi Bridge,** originally constructed by U.S. Marines. Farther south you can see the gigantic former U.S. airbase from the roadside. After the war, scrap-metal foragers frequented the recycling works just down the road. Set back from the road is **Peace Village,** funded by the East Meets West Foundation. The foundation was established by Le Ly Hayslip, author of *When Heaven and Earth Changed Places,* made into the motion picture *Heaven and Earth* directed by Oliver Stone. The foundation seeks contributions from the U.S. and Vietnamese governments, as well as corporations, organizations, and individuals. Contributors include Walt Disney Corp., the San Diego Medical Center, and the University of California. Peace Village has a primary school, pharmacy, and artificial-eye lab. Le Ly Hayslip came back from the United States to initiate several projects, including a Victims of War Center for the homeless and poor in her place of birth, Xa Hoa Qui village, and an orphanage near Danang.

Central Vietnam

The Marble Mountains

About 12 kilometers out of Danang you'll find rows of marble shops. Turn left; about 200 meters along is a parking area with food stalls and a set of steps leading to **Tam Thai Pagoda.** Entry charge to the zone is $4. The many marble shops in this area sell gravestones to the locals and souvenirs to the tourists. Watch out for extortionists who act as "free" guides—they'll demand you buy a marble Buddha or elephant after the tour is over. Children pursue visitors through caves and pagodas pushing drinks and marble figurines. Beggars also hang about on the Marble Mountain circuit. The marble shops have some curious souvenirs—Uncle Ho images engraved in flat marble, depictions of Jesus Christ, and assorted nudes. The marble comes in a variety of colors—red, white, green. You can see craftspeople at work in the shops lining the road to China Beach.

The Marble Mountains comprise a cluster of limestone crags, several with marble quarries. The peaks are named after the five elements: Thuy Son (Water), Tho Son (Earth), Kim Son (Metal), Hoa Son (Fire), and Moc Son (Wood). Thuy Son is the peak most often identified as Marble Mountain. It is the most "developed" peak—a pilgrimage site with Buddhist sanctuaries. Shrines originally associated with Cham worship dot the area. During the Vietnam War the Vietcong used the area as a base for harrying troops at the nearby American airbase.

Your pilgrimage begins at one end with a steep set of marble steps and finishes at the other down another steep set of steps. The two sets of steps are about 300 meters apart on the China Beach road. Marble shops are cunningly placed to entice you along the way. Park your transport at the west end of the road to China Beach; if you have a driver, arrange to meet at the east-end steps, near Linh Ung Pagoda.

Climb the set of 120-odd steps toward Tam Thai Pagoda. Before you reach the small pagoda, turn to the left for a spectacular view over the entire valley. From here you can see other peaks, and marble quarries, and a Cao Dai temple at the base of Moc Son Peak. Tam Thai Pagoda stands on the site of a former

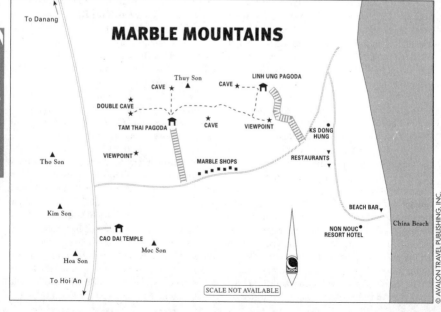

Cham temple; the present pagoda was first constructed in 1825 and rebuilt through the next century. Inside you'll find statues of Sakyamuni Buddha and the bodhisattva Quan Am. Around the back of the pagoda, on a trail westward, is an intriguing double cave, called **Hoa Nghiem Cave,** featuring a half-marble, half-concrete statue of Quan Am at least two meters high. A side cave leads to a massive bell-shaped cave pierced by five crater-sized holes at the top. The skylights were caused by U.S. bombing in 1968, when the cave served as a VC field hospital. There's a large meditating Buddha halfway up the walls of the cave, plus a number of shrines and animal-shaped stalactites.

Off the path to the east of Tam Thai Pagoda you travel through an ancient archway pockmarked by bullets; nearby is a long, narrow cave called **Dong Van Thong** with a standing Buddha inside. Continue along the path to reach a viewpoint overlooking China Beach. The path eventually leads to **Linh Ung Pagoda.** The original pagoda was constructed on this site in 1825 but was destroyed by the Americans in 1968. The present Chinese–style structure went up in 1993–1994. Linh Ung is an active temple with images of Sakyamuni and Quan Am inside. The statues guarding the main entrance represent Hell (on the left) and Heaven (on the right). The columns of entwined dragons and tree decorations on the side of the temple, as well as the rooftop dragons, are made of broken beer bottles and crockery. To one side of the pagoda is a huge stucco Buddha in meditation posture, shaded by a tree high on a rock. Around the statue nine panels show scenes from the life of Buddha, from birth to enlightenment to preaching to death.

China Beach

Non Nuoc (China Beach) lies about 15 kilometers from Danang, only one kilometer or so from the Marble Mountains. You can get there by moto or rented car. By bicycle, it's a 1.5-hour trip one-way on pleasant roads—a full day trip from Danang. There's also a local bus running from Danang. The beach is a glorious five-kilometer stretch of white sand—pristine for the

moment, and great for walks. Swimming is a different story, marred by a wicked undertow. Red flags set up near Non Nuoc Resort Hotel warn swimmers—heed them. A hotel lifeguard is usually posted near the flags.

The surf at China Beach is entirely wind-driven. The water may be glassy and flat or feature one-meter waves. March–August is the main season for swimming, and the beach is crowded. It's very hot May–July; the area is colder the rest of the year, and more prone to typhoons, but you'll have the beach to yourself. Because of wind conditions, surf is up around the typhoon season.

In October 1993 Vietnam's first surfing competition occurred at China Beach, with $50,000 in prizes drawing more than 30 international surfing pros. The contest was the brainchild of David Garcia, a Californian who surfed in the area during his tour of duty before spending two years in captivity in Laos. "Surfer Dave" pitched the idea of a surfing contest to various sponsors and the Vietnamese government. It eventually gained the support of Prime Minister Vo Van Kiet; the surf complied with three-meter typhoon-driven waves. Day-glo-clad surfers amazed the locals with their nautical acrobatics; four young Vietnamese surfers also took part in the contest. The **Vietnam Surf Pro** may become a regular event.

China Beach Hotels: Set back from the beach is **Khach San Dong Hung,** tel. 51/836066, a minihotel with 16 rooms for $8–15. It has a café-restaurant; there are several other restaurants close by. Right on the beach is **Non Nuoc Resort Hotel,** tel. 51/836217, fax 51/836335. This resort sprawls across a large compound and features a concrete main building with restaurants, foreign exchange office, souvenir shop, and conference hall, as well as several outlying buildings. It boasts around 100 rooms, with price tags of $25–42 single and $30–48 double. The hotel was on the dilapidated side, though an American company was planning to renovate it. The hotel has tennis courts, and rents out umbrellas, beach chairs, inner tubes, and swimsuits for beachgoers. There are three restaurants: Some seafood is

Central Vietnam

served at outdoor tables for $1–3 a dish. Down the way is the **Beach Bar,** a couple of thatched huts selling beer and beach souvenirs. Car and bicycle rentals available.

A few kilometers along the beach is **Indochina Beach Hotel,** which was expected to feature 60 rooms of three-star quality; another 200 rooms in villas were under construction.

My Son Cham Ruins

The early Cham site of My Son is about 70 kilometers southwest of Danang. Getting there is most of the adventure: The ruins themselves are humdrum, though set in lush rolling terrain. My Son is a group of brick edifices thought to be where the remains of Cham kings were kept after cremation. The temples and towers that once stood here were dedicated to kings who had the status of deities. Stele found at the site indicate the sanctuary was active between the 4th and 13th centuries. Methods of construction mystify experts. Some theorize the Cham structures were built using a firing process: Dried bricks were laid, vegetable resin used as adhesive, and the entire structure set afire from the outside for several days to seal the brickwork.

My Son may once have been an impressive sight: Now there's little to see. Perhaps reconstruction would improve the odds: My Son was designated a World Heritage Site in 1999, and if complete reconstruction of the razed Royal Citadel at Hué is any indication, My Son may yet be resurrected from the ashes. After French archaeologists carefully began restoring the site, the Americans came along and blew it to bits. The Vietcong began using the ruins as a base; it was declared a free-fire zone by the Americans in the late 1960s, and masterpieces of Cham architecture were leveled by B-52s. The director of Guimet Museum in Paris, repository of many Cham and Angkor pieces, wrote a terse letter of protest to Richard Nixon, but the damage had been done.

The best pieces from My Son are in the Cham Museum in Danang. What remains at the site are some building shells with broken columns, decapitated Buddhas, and the odd sculpted lintel or bas-relief. One building has been turned into a barred storeroom containing sculpture. The rest of the place is damaged beyond recognition, or reclaimed by the jungle. Scattered around the site are a few lichen-covered lingas and rows of yoni bases. You can step over stones across a creek to reach a second site where very little remains except a yoni base. There are good views of the area from here. My Son makes a great picnic site in a romantic jungle location, but do not stray from the ruins as there may be mines and unexploded ordnance about.

Getting to My Son: Because of the rough trail, a rented car, minibus, jeep, high-powered moto, or rented motorcycle is the way to travel. No special permits are needed to visit the site. Take food and water along, as little is available along the way. By car or jeep it takes about two hours to reach My Son; a car rental should cost $25–35. You can organize a small group from either Danang or Hoi An for a car or minibus.

Overland, head south along Highway 1 till you cross a bridge spanning the Thu Bon River. About two kilometers past the bridge, turn right and proceed to the village of Tra Kieu. Tra Kieu, 40 kilometers from Danang, marks the site of the first capital of Champa, but there's nothing left except traces of Cham Citadel ramparts. You can look out over the area from the Catholic church (also çalled the Mountain Church) built over the foundations of a Cham tower.

From Tra Kieu, it's still about 28 kilometers to My Son. Continue to the village of Kim Lam and turn south. Along this part the road turns to dirt—or, if it's been raining, mud. If there's any mud, a car may not make it along the last bit. About three kilometers short of the ruins is a river. You pay $5 to enter the ruins, which includes a short minibus ride from the river. Be aware: There may be mines in the area. Do not stray from proper paths, and use a local guide if the way is not clear.

A longer approach is by boat from either Hoi An or Danang. Smaller boats can get within eight kilometers of My Son. From

Hoi An, it takes about 3–4 hours to reach the area. That's followed by a two-hour walk to the ruins; however, if you bring a bicycle on the boat from Hoi An, you can ride in on the potholed route much faster. Some-times local moto operators wait on the route, charging rip-off prices. Departing My Son you could take the boat back to Hoi An, or continue by boat to Danang—this would make a long day.

Hoi An

Hoi An is an ancient port town on the Thu Bon River, no longer bustling with interna-tional trade but certainly getting a new lease on life by attracting tourism. Hoi An has a ter-rific ambience: Traditional architecture, great cafes and restaurants, some of the best deals in Vietnam for custom tailoring and buying artworks—and you can walk around without being bowled over by a motorcycle or getting your ears blown out by a truck airhorn. Other Vietnamese towns have a lot to learn from Hoi An. In fact, Hoi An has been so successful at attracting tourism that it is in danger of turn-ing itself into a theme park. The main indus-try in town is tourism, with chunks of its old quarter given over to hotels, cafés, restaurants, and souvenir shops. In 1999, Hoi An became a World Heritage Site, which may assist in pre-serving its traditional values—there are certain U.N. guidelines that go along with the designa-tion. One of the things that U.N. assistance got up and running was a homepage for Hoi An. It's www.hoianworldheritage.org and provides a wealth of information on the town.

Hoi An Prefecture spreads across 60 square kilometers, is home to 75,000 inhabitants, and consists of six mainland villages and Cham Is-land. The first inhabitants of the Hoi An area were the Champa, who occupied the area from the 2nd to 15th centuries. From the 15th to 19th centuries, under Vietnamese rule, Hoi An attracted foreign trade, with vessels coming to buy silk, fabrics, tea, pepper, and Chinese med-icines. Chinese traders would sail south in the spring, and then stay in Hoi An for three or four months waiting for the wind to change di-rection and blow them back home in summer. Other ships came from Japan, Portugal, Spain, India, the Netherlands, France, and Britain.

On old marine maps, Hoi An shows up as Faifo, Faiso, Haiso, or Cotham. It developed into one of the most important trading ports in Southeast Asia. By the early 19th century, Hoi An trade declined partly as a result of inter-nal conflicts, mostly because the mouth of the Thu Bon River silted up, rendering the sea ap-proach too shallow. The port of Danang gradu-ally usurped Hoi An.

Hoi An is one of the rare places in Vietnam where you'll find genuine Vietnamese architec-ture. The Old Quarter, though heavily influ-enced by Chinese styles and lined with French row houses, still has vestiges of native architec-ture. Much of the country was destroyed dur-ing wars, but Hoi An survived, even through the traumatic 1960s and 1970s.

ⓜ OLD QUARTER

Along Hoi An's waterfront, from the Japa-nese Covered Bridge to the main market, lies its historic Old Quarter, featuring well-pre-served old housing and pagodas. This section of town is protected against development and is slowly being restored with help from inter-national experts. Local authorities will try to talk you into buying a ticket that entitles you to visit a combination of museums, assembly halls, and old houses—five in all, for $5; an extra fee is charged if you need a guide. How-ever, you can do better by making individual self-guided visits to sites of interest, which usually charge a $1 entry fee per site (others are free or ask for a donation).

Ask about lantern festivals: several times a month, Hoi An's Old Quarter is closed off to traffic and lanterns are hung up everywhere, with street performers providing atmosphere.

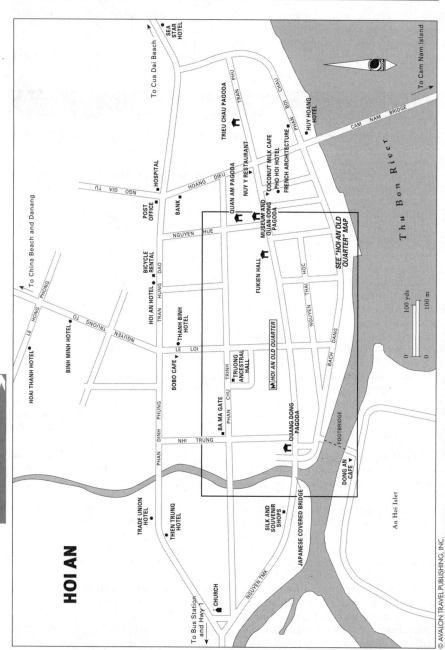

HOI AN

Central Vietnam

To China Beach and Danang

To Cua Dai Beach

SEA STAR HOTEL

TRIEU CHAU PAGODA

TRAN PHU

HOAI THANH HOTEL

LE HONG PHONG

NGUYEN TRUONG TO

BINH MINH HOTEL

HOSPITAL

NGO GIA TU

HOANG DIEU

QUAN AM PAGODA

NUY Y RESTAURANT

COCONUT MILK CAFE

PHO HOI HOTEL

FRENCH ARCHITECTURE

PHAN BOI CHAU

HUY HOANG HOTEL

CAM NAM BRIDGE

To Cam Nam Island

POST OFFICE

BANK

NGUYEN HUE

MUSEUM AND QUAN CONG PAGODA

Thu Bon River

HOI AN HOTEL

BICYCLE RENTAL

TRAN HUNG DAO

FUKIEN HALL

HOC

SEE "HOI AN OLD QUARTER" MAP

THANH BINH HOTEL

LE LOI

NGUYEN THAI HOC

BACH DANG

0   100 yds
0   100 m

BOBO CAFE

TRINH

TRUONG ANCESTRAL HALL

PHAN CHU

HOI AN OLD QUARTER

BA MA GATE

FOOTBRIDGE

PHAN DINH PHUNG

QUANG DONG PAGODA

DONG AN CAFE

NHI TRUNG

An Hoi Islet

TRADE UNION HOTEL

THIEN TRUNG HOTEL

SILK AND SOUVENIR SHOPS

JAPANESE COVERED BRIDGE

NGUYEN TH XI

CHURCH

To Bus Station and Hwy 1

© AVALON TRAVEL PUBLISHING, INC.

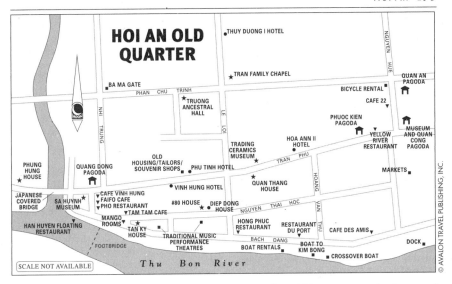

HOI AN OLD QUARTER

THUY DUONG I HOTEL

TRAN FAMILY CHAPEL

BA MA GATE

PHAN CHU TRINH

TRUONG ANCESTRAL HALL

NHI TRUNG

LE LOI

QUAN AN PAGODA

BICYCLE RENTAL

CAFE 22

PHUOC KIEN PAGODA

HOA ANN II HOTEL

YELLOW RIVER RESTAURANT

MUSEUM AND QUAN CONG PAGODA

TRADING CERAMICS MUSEUM

TRAN PHU

OLD HOUSING/TAILORS/SOUVENIR SHOPS

PHU TINH HOTEL

PHUNG HUNG HOUSE

QUANG DONG PAGODA

VINH HUNG HOTEL

QUAN THANG HOUSE

HOANG

MARKETS

JAPANESE COVERED BRIDGE

SA HUYNH MUSEUM

CAFE VINH HUNG
FAIFO CAFE
PHO RESTAURANT

#80 HOUSE

DIEP DONG HOUSE

NGUYEN THAI HOC

VAN THU

MANGO ROOMS

TAM TAM CAFE

HAN HUYEN FLOATING RESTAURANT

TAN KY HOUSE

TRADITIONAL MUSIC PERFORMANCE THEATRES

HONG PHUC RESTAURANT

RESTAURANT DU PORT

CAFE DES AMIS

FOOTBRIDGE

BACH DANG

BOAT RENTALS

BOAT TO KIM BONG

DOCK

CROSSOVER BOAT

NGUYEN HUE

SCALE NOT AVAILABLE

Thu Bon River

© AVALON TRAVEL PUBLISHING, INC.

Museums

Hoi An Market sells everything from larvae to lug wrenches. If you go early in the morning you can see the fresh seafood arrive at the dock. To relieve hunger pangs, try the string of open-air cafés along Nguyen Hue Street. Opposite the cafés is the entrance to **Hoi An Historical and Cultural Museum.** The museum occupies the site of former Quan Am Pagoda and features artifacts, old maps, photos, and information on history, culture, and architecture in Hoi An; English captions provided. Adjoining the museum is **Quan Cong Pagoda.** You enter from the museum through a small courtyard with goldfish in a rock pond. To the sides of the main altar in the pagoda are two full-scale horse statues and two fierce guards. General Quan Cong is the seated figure with the red face and beard. He was a talented general of the 3rd century Three Kingdoms period in China. The Chinese–style exterior of this pagoda is photogenic, especially from the direction of Tran Phu Street.

Two other small museums are found westward along Tran Phu Street. The **Trading Ceramics Museum,** at 80 Tran Phu, offers a display of old Hoi An ceramics. The 15th and 16th centuries were the golden age of Vietnamese ceramics, which were exported to Japan and parts of Southeast Asia. These ceramics included wares from Bat Trang in the north, Hai Hung (blue and white ceramics), and Binh Dinh (celadon wares); in the 17th century, Vietnamese ceramics suddenly disappeared from the market. Near the Japanese Covered Bridge is **Sa Huynh Museum,** with exhibitions from the earliest period of Hoi An history.

Phuoc Kien Pagoda

The Chinese clans in old Hoi An established community halls to assist traders, depending on their origins—Fukien, Canton, Chaozhou, Hainan. These self-governing clans ran their own schools, hospitals, cemeteries, and temples. The temples were an eclectic mix of Buddhism, Taoism, Confucianism, and other imports from China. Phuoc Kien Pagoda, opposite 35 Tran Phu, is the former Fukien Community Hall. Phuoc Kien is the Vietnamese rendition of "Fukien." The temple dates to the late 17th century; it's been extended and renovated through the past 300 years.

This pagoda is dedicated to Thien Hau, goddess of the sea and patroness of sailors and fisherfolk; Thien Hau also retains elements of the Taoist Queen of Heaven. You enter the pagoda

FULL MOON RISING

In 2000, Hoi An revived an old custom called the Night Festival, taking place around the 14th day of each lunar month (the time of a full moon). For this event—scheduled for early evening—Hoi An reverts for one night to the way it looked 600 years ago. No motor traffic is permitted; televisions are turned off. Residents cut fluorescent lights, and illumination is provided by silk and paper lanterns hung from buildings. Events are staged on street corners in the Old Quarter by Hoianese in traditional dress—music and poetry recitals, games of Chinese chess. So the town appears to be the set for a Chinese historical drama—its narrow streets festooned with lanterns glowing red or yellow—hanging from restaurants and shops, reflected in the water near riverside cafés.

through a triple arch. To the right a large mural depicts a boat being tossed about on a stormy sea, with Thien Hau and an assistant with a lantern coming to the rescue. To the left is a battle scene showing a Fukien general.

Inside you'll find a series of altars. At the back sanctuary are glass cases containing two statues of Thien Hau, made in Fukien. On either side of Thien Hau stand her helpers, also in glass cases: on the left, a blue-skinned figure who can see great distances; on the right, a red-skinned emaciated being who can hear great distances. When either of these gentlemen sees or hears fisherfolk in distress, he tells Thien Hau. That was back in the 17th century—one would hope the fisherfolk have radios by now. To the east side of the courtyard is a large-scale model of a 17th-century Chinese war junk. The original vessel held about 100 people.

Behind the main altar, through a courtyard, is a set of wish-granting statues: the god of prosperity on the left, and on the right 12 midwives. Infertile women come here to pray for pregnancy. One of the central figures in this group, clothed in pink, apparently decides if a child will be born male or female. To ensure a successful visit, temple guardians sell small red plastic disks

engraved with characters to promote all kinds of positive results—from auto, air, and boat safety to peace in the family. Ceramic statues bringing prosperity, longevity, and happiness are also sold. Toward the front of the temple you'll notice large gold Chinese characters on the walls—the east side bears the characters for happiness, the west side for longevity, while the center represents prosperity but has no characters.

Heritage Housing

Continuing west along Tran Phu you'll see moss-covered roofs, some concrete buildings, and some French–style buildings with shutters. There are half a dozen houses in Hoi An recognized as heritage pieces—they even get a certificate to prove it. Although repaired and remodeled, these houses retain their original character, family heirlooms, and furniture, and often the original family.

Drop in at **Quan Thang House** at 77 Tran Phu for a cup of tea. They'll show you around for a $1 fee—and will talk you into buying souvenirs. Half-a-dozen family members live there now; on the wall hangs a portrait of the great-great-grandfather, a Chinese merchant and traditional medicine practitioner. The house is about 300 years old, but of course wood doesn't last that long—it's been replaced gradually. Wooden pillars are ingeniously mounted on marble bases to prevent rotting; ornate woodwork features dragons or unicorns on finials.

On Nguyen Thai Hoc, next door to number 80, you'll find another classic, **Diep Dong Nguyen House.** Diep Dong Nguyen is marked on the building; a lattice doorway and bold calligraphy on the exterior. Diep Dong Nguyen House was once a dispensary for Chinese medicine. This place doesn't seem keen on visitors, but if you get past the door, the interior features antique furniture, porcelain, and lanterns. **Tan Ky House,** 101 Nguyen Thai Hoc, features Chinese and Japanese influences in its structure. Visitors welcome. This elongated house has a shop front entrance on Nguyen Thai Hoc Street, and a storage and dock entrance in back on Bach Dang Street. The interior living quarters are grouped around an open courtyard.

There are three kinds of timber in the 200-year-old structure—timber from the jackfruit tree poses a problem as it attracts termites. Fine carvings decorate the woodwork; some are inlaid with mother-of-pearl.

The **Japanese Covered Bridge** is a Hoi An landmark. The curved bridge has a green-and-yellow tile roof, two guardian dogs on the east side, and two guardian monkeys to the west side. The bridge is vintage 16th century, most likely constructed by the Japanese community to link the Chinese quarter with the Japanese quarter. A small Japanese-style pagoda that protects sailors is built into the north side of the bridge. The chapel is normally locked—you can get in if you buy a ticket, but there's not a lot to see.

Over the Japanese Covered Bridge is **Phung Hung House,** at 4 Nguyen Thi Minh Khai St., the mansion of the Phung Hung family for eight generations. The wooden structure has elements of Vietnamese, Chinese, and Japanese styles, contructed using 80 columns of ironwood with marble bases. The structure is held in place with large wooden nails. The four-sided roof is made of Yin and Yang tiles, named after the way the tiles lock together. Another interesting feature of the house is a flood provision: A square opening on the ceiling allows hauling of belongings to the second floor. The last major flood hit Hoi An in 1998. The Phung Hung family welcome tourists and sell souvenirs and T-shirts from a boutique at the front. In the same area, on both sides of the bridge but especially on the west side, other shops sell silk, art, souvenirs, and marble carvings. There's also an art gallery in a French two-story building near the bridge.

A short way east of the Japanese Covered Bridge is **Quang Dong Pagoda,** or the Assembly Hall for Maritime Commerce. This pagoda was open to all Chinese traders or seamen, and it is dedicated to Thien Hau. It's a small Chinese-style temple, with a lintel-gate, a rockery courtyard, and lucky animals depicted in statuary—a lion and a phoenix mounted on turtles, and dragon-coiled columns inside. Strolling eastward along Tran Phu you'll come across some ancient buildings formerly used for cotton mills, weaving workshops, or furniture making, and now adapted for other uses.

Last stop for tea: The **Tran Family Chapel,** near the corner of Phan Chu Trinh, is entered from Le Loi Street. A small donation is expected. The ancestral chapel is maintained by eight members of the Tran family, who live in the house nearby. The Tran family is seeking funds for renovation of the chapel, which is 200 years old and was last restored in the 1930s after a fire. With some houses occupied continuously for seven generations, ancestor worship is big in Hoi An. The altar holds wooden boxes containing the tablets of Tran family ancestors arranged in order from oldest to newest generations, with Chinese characters chiseled in the tablets to summarize their curricula vitae. The annual gathering of the Tran clan in December draws up to 100 relatives.

VICINITY OF HOI AN

Hoi An is a great base to explore the Marble Mountains and China Beach by rented car, motorcycle, bicycle, or moto. Boat trips around Hoi An are pleasant. Tour agents organize trips for groups out to My Son Cham Ruins; you may need to assemble a small group.

Most sights in the vicinity of Hoi An can be approached by bicycle. A popular ride is to head for **Cua Dai Beach,** about five kilometers east of Hoi An—a great beach for a swim or run. The white sand here is expansive; the water is slightly surfy. You can catch the sunrise if you're out there by 0500 or so—it's worth it because the water is cooler, and all the fishing boats come in to unload the night's catch. Alternatively, you can go when all the locals go, around 1600, to have a dip before dinner. There are thatched drink stands grouped at one section of the beach, with tables and chairs, and serving seafood; some also sell crabs. The only drawback is the children who pester you to buy coconuts or rice biscuits. An alternative way to reach Cua Dai Beach is to hire a boat at Hoi An Market area and pack your bicycle aboard the boat. The trip by boat from Hoi An to Cua

BOAT TRIPS

You can hire a boat for a few hours from the waterfront to explore the Thu Bon River and the area around Hoi An. Go to the boat dock near the market and bargain—$3 for a few hours is standard. A regular boat runs out to **Kim Bong village** on **Cam Kim Island**—a 10-minute ride costing $.10. Kim Bong is a village of woodworking and boat-building families. Handcrafted boats vary from simple fishing models to vessels the size of Noah's Ark. Families also carve statues and furniture, some incorporating marble from the Marble Mountains.

Long-distance boats travel to **Cham Island** and Danang. Cham Island lies about 20 kilometers off the coast. A motorboat leaves the Hoi An Market docks early in the morning for the island and returns in the afternoon. Cham Island has several fishing villages and is famed as a source of swallows' nests, used in gourmet soups. Access to the island is restricted and requires a permit.

From Hoi An, boats can sometimes make it out toward My Son and into Danang. This trip is not sanctioned by authorities, either.

Dai should take 2–3 hours and costs $6. At the other end, you bid the boatman goodbye, and leave the return trip to your trusty bicycle.

Another recommended bike ride is across the bridge east of the markets, and over to Can Nam Island—there's pleasant countryside here. Other side trips reached easily by bike are to pagodas and sites around Hoi An. The oldest pagoda in the area is **Chua Phuc Thanh,** dating from the 15th century. The ride offers more to look at than the temple. To get there follow Nguyen Truong To Street north out of Hoi An, and then turn left and follow a path for half a kilometer. At the opposite end of the spectrum is **Chua Long Thuyen,** a Vietnamese pagoda, with a main hall built in 1993. Take the first dirt track to the right after the bus station and gas station west of Hoi An, and then continue for about 400 meters through rice paddies and loads of graveyards. Garish and fanciful, the pagoda features broken beer-bottle and porcelain decoration, and a multicolored lotus tower at the back. The low concrete wall around the pagoda is painted in the form of two dragons who come head to head to form a gate.

ACCOMMODATIONS

In an effort to preserve the character of Hoi An, city hall will not entertain the idea of building new 10-story hotels—and you have to give it credit for that. Character hotels are the restored older-style buildings, complete with period furniture. Along Tran Phu Street, there are a handful of these places, such as Phu Thinh Hotel (at number 144) and Vinh Hung (at number 143).

Finding accommodation can be tight. **Hoi An Hotel,** at 6 Tran Hung Dao, tel. 510/861445, fax 510/861636, is a rambling compound with a total of 80 rooms (and a big swimming pool). Management is brusque and may tell you the cheap rooms are full, even if they aren't. In the main building are 30 rooms, ranging $12–30 s, $10–46 d, $25–60 t, $20–70 with four beds—with private bath, hot water, and a/c. Other rooms in outlying buildings run $15–27 with private bath and no a/c, $10–17 with toilet, and $8–16 with shared toilet. The hotel will rent cars and bicycles. Managed by Hoi An Tourist Service Company, it serves as a de facto tourist information headquarters.

Run by the same outfit is **Hoi An II Hotel,** at 92 Tran Phu St., tel. 510/861331, in the Old Quarter. It offers only seven rooms, $4 a bed in a four-bed dorm, $8–10 double rooms, and $12 a/c rooms, most with common bath, but good location, small, and friendly. Three more minihotels are arrayed along Tran Phu Street. **Pho Hoi,** at 7/2 Tran Phu, tel. 510/861633, has 20 rooms in a musty old villa for $10–25 apiece. **Phu Thinh,** a minihotel at 144 Tran Phu, tel. 510/861297, has 15 rooms for $12–25; this place is family-run, with a garden. **Vinh Hung Guesthouse,** at 143 Tran Phu, tel. 510/861621, fax 510/861893, charges $15–30 a room. This 12-room private minihotel is in an older converted mansion. The lobby and higher-end rooms have traditional lacquered furniture; the lower-end rooms just have moldy walls. At 1 Le Loi St. is **Thanh Binh Hotel,** tel. 510/861740, with 15 rooms for $10–12 without windows, $15–20 with. At 11 Le Loi is **Thuy Duong I** minihotel, tel. 510/861394, with 12 rooms for $10–15–20–25.

A hotel with a great location, at 73 Phan Boi Chau, is **Huy Hoang,** tel. 510/861453; the 20 rooms here go for $20–40, and there are good river views from the top back deck of the building. To the eastern fringe of town is the comfortable and popular **Sea Star Hotel,** (Sao Bien) at 15 Cua Dai St., tel. 510/861589, with 15 rooms for $12–18–25–30; they'll take good care of you here. Nearby is the **Cua Dai Hotel,** tel. 510/862231, with 16 rooms for $20–30 each in a converted mansion.

When the downtown hotels are full, you have to go farther afield for accommodation. Out near the bus station, to the west side of town, are **Thuy Duong 2 Hotel,** 68 Huynh Thuc Khang St., tel. 510/861394 (near the Cao Dai Temple), with 14 rooms for $10–20; and a little farther west is **My Lan Hotel,** 87 Huynh Thuc Khang St., tel./fax 510/862126, with 30 rooms for $10–25. To the north of town is the characterless **Hoai Thanh Hotel,** at 23 Le Hong Phong, tel. 510/861242, fax 510/861135, which has 43 large rooms for $20–30–40; it's clean and has windows, and it is used by group tours. To the northwest fringe are some last-resort hotels: **Thien Trung,** at 66 Pahn Dinh Phung, tel. 510/861720, with 16 rooms for $10–12 fan or $15–20 a/c; and the dowdy **Trade Union,** at 50 Phan Dinh Phung, tel. 510/861899, with 12 rooms for $10–15.

Life Resort Hoi An, at 1 Pham Hong Thai, tel. 510/914555, has rooms going for $95 to over $200. This is run by a Dutch hotel group.

Cua Dai Resort Hotels

Because major hotels cannot be built in Hoi An (they would ruin the symmetry), joint-venture hoteliers have shifted their attention to the Cua Dai Beach area. On the road out to the beach, by a river, is **Hoi An Riverside Resort,** tel. 510/864800, hoianriver@dng.vnn.vn. This place, connected with silk entrepreneur

Khai (from Hanoi) is very attractively laid out, with sumptuous rooms for $140–200. Right on the beach is **Victoria Hoi An Resort,** tel. 510/927040, victoriaha@dng.vnn.vn, with 100 rooms, pool, spa, and other creature comforts, going for $150–300. Not to be outdone by these private upstarts, Hoi An Tourist Service Company jumped in there and created **Hoi An Beach Resort,** tel. 510/927011, with 70 rooms going for $60–120.

FOOD

Great news on the gastronomic front—Hoi An is the place to satisfy your stomach, if not your soul. You can get Vietnamese, Western, and vegetarian fare. Restaurants are usually family-run, use fresh produce from the market, and offer a cozy atmosphere—better thought of as café-bistros. You can arrange cooking lessons at some restaurants.

You could eat your way up and down the main streets of Hoi An, and most of the fare is really good, if not outstanding. There are semioutdoor venues such as **The Cargo Club** patisserie and tea room. There are innovative places such as **Mango Rooms,** which has an entire menu based on mango—including mango spring rolls, mango salad, mango shakes, and seafood with a mango-tomato-garlic sauce (wash that down with some mango cocktails). Along the waterfront hosts a string of restaurants with great ambience that serve excellent seafood.

Hoi An Specialties

Hoi An has its own special dishes. *Cao lau* is a bowl of thick noodles in a dark rich broth, topped with herbs, bean sprouts, slices of pork, and crunchy croutons, and served with a crispy rice pancake—delicious! A number of small eateries along Tran Phu Street serve *cao lau.* The secret of *cao lau* is that it must be made with water from Hoi An's own well to get it right. *Hoi An loanh thanh* is a special wonton soup. White Rose is fresh shrimp wrapped in rice paper with garlic, lemon, and chili sauce, fashioned to resemble a rose. For *Hoi An pancake,* you're supplied with all the elements—

Central Vietnam

rice paper, egg, bean sprouts, slivers of raw banana, and lettuce. Assemble the pancake, then dip it in sauce, and add chili sauce.

In the market area is **Café 22,** at 22 Nguyen Hue, tel. 510/861603, run by the Ly family. This friendly café serves snacks and full meals. You can get vegetarian food, banana pancakes, fruit salad, hamburgers, and a great *cao lau* soup. They can whip up a seafood extravaganza if you let them know ahead of time. For a very reasonable price you get clams, prawns, crab with roe sauce, ginger fish, squid, and spring rolls—all excellent.

Nuy Y (Mermaid) Restaurant, 2 Tran Phu, serves Hoi An pancake and special sauce, *mi quang* (noodle soup and seafood), prawn fritters, pizza laced with garlic, and pasta. The squid is especially good; this restaurant serves wonderful guacamole in season. Nearby is **Coconut Milk Café,** featuring coconut milk, beer, yogurt, and mineral water.

Along the midsection of Tran Phu, between Nguyen Hue and Le Loi streets, is a concentration of eating houses. **Number 42 Restaurant** specializes in *cao lau;* opposite, at number 31, is **Fukien Restaurant.** To the east is **Yellow River Restaurant** (Hoang Ha), at 38 Tran Phu St., tel. 510/861053, with superb cuisine Hoianese—this tiny place serves seafood, hotpot fondue, *cao lau,* and Vietnamese pancakes, all at reasonable prices with a great atmosphere. Farther west is **Cao Lau** at 87 Tran Phu; and at 104 Tran Phu is **Faifoo Restaurant.** Phew!

Toward the Japanese Covered Bridge are three cafés with sidewalk tables. **Café Vinh Hung** has a big drink list, *cao lau,* Vietnamese soup, breakfast, seafood, and banana pancakes. Nearby is **Faifo Café,** for breakfast and vegetarian, omelettes and avocado sandwiches; on the corner is **Thang Long,** with great seafood. **Han Huyen** floating restaurant, tel. 510/861462, has a pleasant setting—the extensive menu includes deer, sea cucumber, and steamboat. Opposite that, across a bridge, is **Dong An Café.**

Seafood

A number of bistros along Bach Dang Street serve excellent seafood. The plum place is **⋈ Hong Phuc Restaurant,** at 86 Bach Dang, tel. 510/862567, which is famed for its fish wrapped in banana leaf. The fish comes with an incredible sauce of garlic, lemongrass, pepper, and lime. Equally tasty is squid with *chile,* garlic, and sesame. If you want to find out culinary secrets, sign up for an afternoon cooking class, where you learn how to make four dishes (cost is $10).

Café des Amis, 52 Bach Dang, tel. 510/861360, near the market, is owned by Kim, who once cooked for French officers; this two-story restaurant is run by his family. Food is eclectic—French, Chinese, Vietnamese. There's no menu; you ask for, say, a vegetarian or seafood theme. Kim likes a challenge: One customer requested "something different, maybe escargot," and Kim came up with 10 courses, including three different types of escargot. A gastronomic experience! The ambience, the music, the flavors, and the textures are just right. Save some space for the excellent chocolate flan. Book ahead—meals are pricey, about $5 a person.

OTHER PRACTICALITIES
Nightlife

There's very little here. However, of genuine note are the performances of traditional music and drama at two small places—72 Nguyen Thai Hoc St. and 92B Bach Dang Street. Inquire in advance about evening showtimes. **Tam Tam Café,** at 110 Nguyen Thai Hoc St., tel. 510/862212, is on the first floor of a beautifully renovated merchant house. This French-run venue sports a grand bar and a pool table and stays open late.

Shopping

Hoi An has a slew of souvenir shops strung out along Tran Phu and Le Loi streets. The stock is high quality: Shops sell silk paintings and sketches of Hoi An street scenes, pottery, marble carvings, and other handcrafted items. One of the specialties of Hoi An is silk-and-synthetic lanterns of various shapes and sizes. Though these are designed to be used with electric lights,

600 years ago, Hoi An streets were lit only by lanterns (there are sometimes lantern festivals in Hoi An that commemorate this).

At 108 Nguyen Thai Hoc St. is **Kim Bong** traditional carpentry shop, selling mother-of-pearl inlaid boxes, among other items. There are a number of reputable tailors in town—you can get made-to-order clothing fashioned in a few days. Travelers say the quality of tailoring here is equal to (or higher than) that in Hanoi or Saigon. There are some excellent tailors along Le Loi Street. Try **Thu Thuy** at number 60 Le Loi, or **Phuong Huy** at 13 Le Loi. Both specialize in Chinese and Vietnamese silks and cotton. They also deal in synthetics, so if you want to be sure, use a lighter for a litmus test: If you burn a thread of pure silk it will smell like burnt hair, and if touched will turn to ash; if it has any synthetics, the thread will shrivel up into a hard ball and give off a plasticky smell.

And what about a new pair of shoes while you're at it? You can have shoes custom-made in Hoi An.

Services

Traveler Cafés: Lots of hangouts. **Café 22** offers great food and will arrange car rentals and minibus rides; Kim at **Café des Amis** can arrange boat trips and has traveler logbooks. **Hoi An Hotel** houses the Tourism Service Company, but staff there is not much help.

Moneychanging: You can change U.S. cash and traveler's checks at the bank at 4 Hoang Dieu St., open Monday to Thursday 0700–1100 and 1300–1600, closed Thursday afternoon to Sunday. If the bank is closed, try changing U.S. cash at hotels or a jeweler's shop.

Getting There and Away

By Bus and Minibus: Traveler buses and minibuses on the Saigon–Hanoi route stop in Hoi An; buses are not permitted in the Old Quarter, so a minibus shuttle is usually arranged if you're connecting by bus. Many hotels, cafés,

and travel agents will arrange long-distance transport—you can easily find ticket agents along Tran Phu Street for minibuses going to Hué or Danang, or overnight to Nha Trang, Dalat, or Saigon. Sinh Café at 61A Phan Chu Trinh St. arranges links with the Saigon Sinh Café buses.

For public transport, express buses do not pull into Hoi An. Take a moto to the Highway 1 junction for $.30 and wait there to flag down an express bus for traveling along the coast to Hué, or down south to Quang Ngai. Try hitching too—sometimes it's faster than a bus. A moto costs $2 one-way to Danang.

Hoi An bus station mostly offers red-and-yellow Renaults on rice runs. The Renault van takes up to two hours to run the circuitous route from Hoi An to Danang, which involves unloading furniture and loading cases of drinks and tires. Another option is to take a jeep with an elongated back section.

By Boat: A boat trip from Hoi An to Danang takes about 4.5 hours. The trip is frowned upon by authorities in Danang, so the boat might drop you short of the city. Ask at Café des Amis about organizing a group for a boat. Prices operate on a sliding scale: $10 for two people, $15 for four, and $20 for six. Only small vessels can make the trip—the boat goes along the Thu Bon River and turns up toward Ai Nghia.

Getting Around

Hoi An is easily covered on foot. A different perspective is from the water—rent a boat near the market; the boaters will approach you. Bicycle rentals run about $1 a day, with a small extra charge to keep the bike overnight. Rent via hotels and guesthouses; there are also sidewalk rental places along Tran Phu Street and elsewhere. Several places rent Honda 50cc and 70cc motorcycles—$5 for one person, or $6 for two people on the same bike. Various cafés, hotels, and tour agents will arrange car or minibus trips to China Beach and My Son.

Central Highlands

The Central Highlands are on the Cao Nguyen Plateau between the coast and the Annamite Mountain Range. The plateau is sparsely populated by minority groups; economic activity centers around coffee, tea, cassava, and rubber tree plantations, the lumber industry, and cattle raising. Lush tropical forests are interspersed with farmed areas. The towns here have a frontier feeling to them—they're still under construction. Settlers come from overpopulated regions of Vietnam; the unemployed in the large cities are encouraged to move here and work on farms or forestry projects. The latter have not always been successful, and there has been friction between the settlers and minority ethnic groups, whom the Vietnamese discriminate against. Montagnard groups in the Central Highlands include the Ede (also Rhade or Raday), of Cham origin; the Jarai, Bahnar, Rongao, and Sedoun, also of Cham origins; and the Mnong, of Cambodian origin.

People here are becoming increasingly Vietnamized. They're losing the battle to maintain traditional life, language, and customs under increasing pressure from government authorities. These societies used to be matriarchal, but since 1975 that has changed.

Vietnamization means building new housing with tile or corrugated rather than thatched roofs, and wearing Vietnamese clothing instead of handwoven ethnic dress. Traditional wear is brought out for wedding parties, festivals, and ceremonies.

Resistance to Vietnamization started as armed warfare. After 1975, a band of Montagnards called Front Unifié de Lutte des Races Opprimées (FULRO) waged guerrilla war in the highlands. Though backed by France and the United States, they were largely defeated by 1980. FULRO guerrillas based in Cambodia's Ratanakiri province are still active, staging cross-border raids.

A major obstacle to Vietnamization is the suppression of religious practices. The Montagnards are mostly Christian but retain strong elements of animism. Harvest festivals may culminate in the sacrifice of a buffalo, chicken, or pig; to celebrate good harvests fermented rice wine is consumed from a common clay vat through long bamboo straws. The Ede and Bahnar/Jarai stage tomb-leaving ceremonies at local burial vaults to honor the souls of the dead. In the interests of tourism, the powers that be organize ethnic ceremonies out of season and advertise ethnic song and dance to order, phoning ahead to demand villagers appear arrayed in ethnic costume.

The Central Highlands lacks tourist infrastructure. Finding an English menu is tough, but most likely you will be able to find an English-speaking local as a guide. Pleiku and Buon Ma Thuot were both U.S. bases during the Vietnam War and many Montagnards learned their English during this period.

PLEIKU

Pleiku is a town of 40,000 people in an area inhabited by Jarai and Ede minority peoples. Pickings are slim in Pleiku. The market features a large basketry section; you might also check out the local museum. Out of town, within a 50-kilometer radius, are Montagnard villages, as well as tea and rubber plantations, scenic spots, and former battlefields. Gai Lai Tourism organizes trips to all these destinations. Of greater interest are journeys to a Jarai burial vault at **Plei Mrong** village, 37 kilometers to the northwest of Pleiku and five kilometers short of Yaly Falls; a Bahnar spirit house at **Dektu** village, 35 kilometers out; and an elephant ride at **Nhon Hoa** village, 65 kilometers to the south. If you make an appointment through Gia Lai Tourism, the Montagnards will no doubt don ethnic dress. Order an elephant in advance to avoid disappointment; a two-day notice may be required. Gai Lai Tourism organizes ethnic song-and-dance performances for outrageous sums of

CENTRAL HIGHLANDS ROUTE NOTES

The most common road route is the highland bypass from Qui Nhon to Pleiku on Route 19, continuing on Route 14 to Buon Ma Thuot, and then traveling along Route 26 to Nha Trang. To speed your passage, consider throwing in a plane ride—say, from Hanoi or Danang to Pleiku, or from Buon Ma Thuot to Saigon. Weather could well be adverse, considerably affecting road conditions. Although this route is paved, parts may be impassable during heavy rains. In Buon Ma Thuot, April–May and September–November are the months of light rain, June–August brings hard rain, and December–March is the dry season. The Central Highlands are actually not that high—the place is still humid and hot. Pleiku is at 780 meters, Kontum 525 meters, Buon Ma Thuot 450 meters.

To give an idea of distances on this route, from Danang it's 130 kilometers to Quang Ngai, a further 154 kilometers to Binh Dinh at the junction of Highway 1 and Route 19, 140 kilometers from there to Pleiku, another 50 kilometers to Kontum (backtrack to Pleiku), 197 kilometers from Pleiku to Buon Ma Thuot, and another 160 kilometers to Ninh Hoa at the junction of Route 26 and Highway 1. From there it's 33 kilometers into Nha Trang.

Route 19 is a good sealed road, so the trip from Qui Nhon to Pleiku takes about 4–5 hours. The road climbs from rice paddies through scenic hill terrain. On hilly Route 14 from Pleiku to Buon Ma Thuot are coffee and gigantic rubber tree plantations, as well as peanut, pepper, and cassava farms. These crops are often dried along the roadsides. A lot of development is in progress on this route, with new farms and housing. The area looks like a medieval Breughel canvas—strips of color, patches of farmland, laboring farmworkers. You should be able to cover the route in five hours, though a crawler bus might take seven. Buon Ma Thuot to Nha Trang on Route 26 is rough and hilly but scenic. The 190-kilometer route can be covered by bus in about six hours.

A longer, rougher route proceeds from Saigon through Chon Thanh, Dang Boa, Buon Ma Thuot, Pleiku, Kontum, Dak Pek, Phuoc Son, and Hoi An. Although Buon Ma Thuot to Pleiku is plain sailing, the other two legs are formidable—sections may be passable only by motorcycle. At one time these routes were considered dangerous because of bandit activity, but this is apparently no longer the case. Route 14 south, from Saigon to Buon Ma Thuot via Dang Boa, can be accomplished in stages—it's possible to cadge rides in coffee trucks. The route is fair from Saigon as far as Dang Boa, and then in very poor condition from Dang Boa to Buon Ma Thuot. It takes an estimated 14 hours to cover this route—if you're lucky and if there's no waiting time between rides. The route from Buon Ma Thuot to Dalat is currently inaccessible to motor vehicles. Kontum to Hoi An on Route 14 north is extremely rough, although attempts are being made to upgrade the road. From Kontum, it's 150 kilometers to Dak Pek, a further 70 kilometers to Phuoc Son, and a final 125 kilometers to Hoi An.

---

money. If you plan your own trips you won't see the song and dance, but you can save a lot of money. Find your own moto driver and head off from Pleiku.

As you head north on the road to Kontum, village visits can be combined with such scenic stops as **Bien Ho,** a lake eight kilometers from Pleiku, and 40-meter-high **Yaly Falls,** 42 kilometers from Pleiku west of the main Pleiku-Kontum road. Police are sensitive about foreigners in the areas outside Pleiku and Kontum. You'll also hear rumors of tourists being robbed by tribespeople. Consult other travelers for the current wisdom. If in doubt, bring a local guide along to do the talking.

Accommodations and Food

Dining is largely confined to hotel restaurants and the market area. **Pleiku Hotel,** 124 Le Loi, tel. 59/824891, fax 59/824891, has 40 rooms—12 musty cubicles for $12 each, regular rooms for $17–27, rooms with a/c and fridge for $32–37. The hotel has a souvenir shop full of sad, stuffed creatures, including a

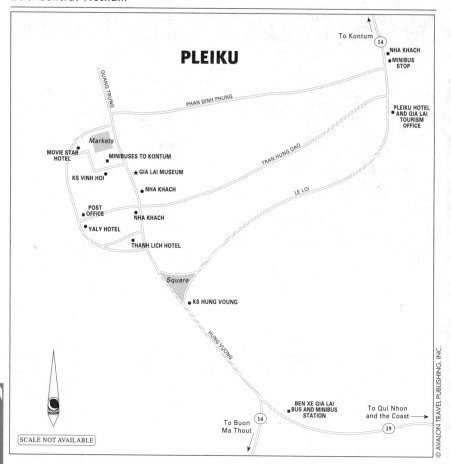

PLEIKU

To Kontum

NHA KHACH

MINIBUS STOP

PLEIKU HOTEL AND GIA LAI TOURISM OFFICE

QUANG TRUNG

PHAN DINH PHUNG

Markets

MOVIE STAR HOTEL

MINIBUSES TO KONTUM

KS VINH HOI

★ GIA LAI MUSEUM

TRAN HUNG DAO

• NHA KHACH

LE LOI

POST OFFICE

NHA KHACH

• YALY HOTEL

THANH LICH HOTEL

Square

• KS HUNG VOUNG

HUNG VUONG

BEN XE GIA LAI BUS AND MINIBUS STATION

To Qui Nhon and the Coast →

To Buon Ma Thout

14

19

SCALE NOT AVAILABLE

© AVALON TRAVEL PUBLISHING, INC.

tiger and a leopard. The Gia Lai Tourism Office is here, along with a passable restaurant.

Thanh Lich Hotel, at 86 Nguyen Van Troi, tel. 59/824674, has 20 rooms for $6; on the seedy side. The 30-room **Khach San Vinh Hoi,** at 39 Tran Phu, tel. 59/824644, is right near the central market, and thus noisy. The **Movie Star Hotel** (Khach San Dien Anh), 6 Vo Thi Sau St., tel. 59/824626, has a good restaurant and car rentals. The hotel offers 20 rooms: six doubles for $10 each; a four-bed room for $15; the remainder for $20–25 d with TV, $30 d with fridge. **Yaly Hotel,** opposite the post office at 89 Hung Vuong, tel. 59/824843, has 54 good

rooms in the $20–40 range, half with air-conditioning. Close to the bus station is very clean **Hung Vuong Hotel,** tel. 59/824270, with 25 rooms for $10–25. Several guesthouses in Pleiku do not seem to accept foreigners—the two Nha Khachs on Quan Trung Street, and one more north of Pleiku Hotel.

Services and Information

Gia Lai Tourism Office, 124 Le Loi, in the Pleiku Hotel, tel. 59/824891, is, for a change, actually helpful. The staff run half-day (three-hour) and full-day (six- to eight-hour) tours to surrounding villages and scenic spots. If you're a small group of 1–2 people, they might set you up with motorcycle guides. The price is still expensive—$18 for a half-day trip, which breaks down to $6 for the motorcycle plus $12 for the guide and organizing fee. The tariff is $26 per day for one person with a motorcycle guide, $38 for two motorcycles and drivers. Organization fees vary $20–40 depending on group size; guides are $12–18; a car for 100 kilometers $30; elephant ride $50; folk-music performance $70; folk music and rice-wine drinking hits the jackpot at $100.

Getting Around and Away

Vietnam Airlines staffs an office in the Yaly Hotel. The airport is 25 kilometers from Pleiku, or 40 kilometers from Kontum. Thrice-weekly flights leave Pleiku for Danang, Ho Chi Minh City, and Hanoi. The bus station, Ben Xe Gia Lai, schedules buses and minibuses to Buon Ma Thuot, to coastal destinations, and farther afield to Hanoi or Saigon. Minibuses to Kontum run from the central market. For getting around Pleiku, rent a moto for around $6 a day, or hire a car through a larger hotel or Gia Lai Tourism.

KONTUM

Kontum, a frontier town of 35,000, lies about 65 kilometers north of Pleiku. The old town of Kontum was destroyed in 1972 when hundreds of B-52s leveled the area during a major battle between North and South Vietnamese troops. A new town arose from the ashes—it's still under construction, with the paint barely dry, so expect changes. Bahnar, Sedoun, and Jarai minority groups inhabit the surrounding villages. The main pursuits around Kontum are of the farm and forest variety—the cultivation of coffee, tea, and cassava on a large scale. Cattle raising is also on the increase. The nearby forests provide lumber and medicinal plants such as ginseng; furniture is fashioned from sandalwood and rattan.

Catholic Relics

Heard about missionaries with huge plantations in remote places such as the Congo? Kontum conjures that bygone era, with its large seminary on the east side of town. The French seminary dates from the 1850s and must have been self-sufficient. It is an impressive three-story building with a chapel above a sweeping staircase, classrooms, and place to park vehicles below. The upstairs section houses a hilltribe museum. Out front is a bust of Martial Jannin Phuoc (1867–1940), the seminary's first pastor. There were once as many as 30 priests and 35 nuns here. The last French citizen left in 1975, but by that time their work was completed— Kontum province is 80 percent Catholic.

To the east of the seminary stands a grotto with a shrine of Mary; directly south is a convent with maroon walls dating from the 1930s—a few Vietnamese nuns live here. An orphanage run by nuns looks after about 200 minority kids—well worth dropping in for a visit.

A nearby wooden Montagnard church features a Gothic interior and plaster walls; it was built by the French in 1913, and the wood columns were hauled in by elephants. Sunday Masses held 0530–0630 and 1630–1730; 0700–0800 for Montagnards only. Outside the church is a statue of Kuenot, the 19th-century French bishop who established the community here, and a scaled-down version of a Montagnard house, used as a shrine for festivals such as Christmas and the end of harvest in May. West of the Montagnard church is a Vietnamese church, Tan Huong, with medieval-looking bas-reliefs on the outer walls.

Villages

Montagnard villages lie within easy walking distance of town. Go east on Nguyen Hue Boulevard past the Montagnard church till you reach a fork, and then veer right to a Bahnar village about 600 meters farther on. From here you can walk northward through another Bahnar and Jarai village on a path that goes back to Nguyen Hue Boulevard. There's another mixed village—Bahnar, Jarai, Rongao, Sedoun—about 400 meters south of Nguyen Hue Boulevard. The villages are primitive, with wooden houses on stilts sheltering pigs and chickens beneath. You can see villagers

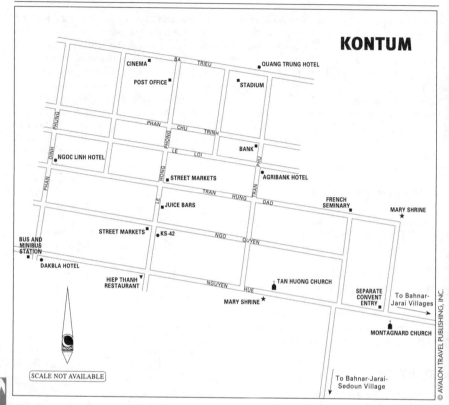

KONTUM

CINEMA ■
BA TRIEU
QUANG TRUNG HOTEL ●
POST OFFICE ■
STADIUM ■
PHAN CHU TRINH
PHONG
LE LOI
PHAN DINH PHUNG
NGOC LINH HOTEL ■
BANK ■
PHU
AGRIBANK HOTEL ■
STREET MARKETS ■
LE HONG
TRAN HUNG DAO
FRENCH SEMINARY ■
JUICE BARS ■
TRAN
MARY SHRINE ★
STREET MARKETS ■
KS-42 ●
NGO QUYEN
BUS AND MINIBUS STATION ■
DAKBLA HOTEL ■
HIEP THANH RESTAURANT ▼
NGUYEN HUE
TAN HUONG CHURCH ✝
MARY SHRINE ★
SEPARATE CONVENT ENTRY ■
To Bahnar-Jarai Villages
MONTAGNARD CHURCH ✝

SCALE NOT AVAILABLE

© AVALON TRAVEL PUBLISHING, INC.

To Bahnar-Jarai-Sedoun Village

drying corn or cassava, weaving cloth on han-dlooms, or carrying loads of wood in wicker baskets. Sometimes the load is scrap metal—around Kontum and Pleiku there is a lot of war materiel recycling.

Accommodations

Try **Family Hotel,** at 55 Tran Hung Dao, tel. 60/862448, with rooms for $10. **Quang Trung Hotel,** at 168 Ba Trieu, tel. 60/862249, charges $16 for a fan room and $18 with a/c—excel-lent value. The three-story building houses 30 rooms. **Agribank GH,** tel. 60/862853, has 20 rooms for $10–15. The low end is a three-bed fan room; the high end a double room with a/c and TV. **Khach San 42,** at 42 Le Hong Phong, tel. 60/862461, offers doubles for $12 but no bath—a "short-time" place, with taxi girls. **Ngoc Linh Hotel,** on the west side of Tran Hung Dao Street, tel. 60/864560, offers 17 doubles for about $17 and some dorm rooms for $6 apiece. On Phan Dinh Phung Street is **Dakbla Hotel,** tel. 60/863333, fax 60/864407, with 43 rooms for $14–30—this is about as classy as accommodation gets in Kontum.

Food

Hiep Thanh Restaurant, 129 Nguyen Hue, tel. 60/825262, is one of the best in town—and the most expensive, charging around $5 a head for a good feed. In the market area is **Song Huong Restaurant.** A number of juice bars line Le Hong Phong Street. Depending on the season, oranges, mangoes, jackfruit, pineapple, and bananas are available in the Kontum re-gion. Near the bus station, **Dakbla Restaurant**

offers basic fare such as *com* and *pho* dishes in a hygienic environment.

Getting There

Buses and minibuses run to Pleiku, Buon Ma Thuot, Binh Dinh, Qui Nhon, Quang Ngai, and even as far afield as Hué, Hanoi, Nha Trang, and Saigon, though not on a daily basis. Because the road north of Kontum is too rough, Kontum is a round-trip from Pleiku. You might consider skipping Pleiku on the way in but stopping there on the way back.

Getting Around

This is mostly on foot or by moto. You can get hold of a car or jeep through some of the hotels. Also inquire at Kontum Tourist and Trade Company, 218 Tran Hung Dao St., tel. 60/862222.

Excursions from Kontum

Minority groups are not city folk—if you want to see them, you have to get out of town. You can organize a 60-kilometer trip to the crossroads of Indochina, the meeting point of the Lao, Cambodian, and Vietnamese borders northwest of Kontum. A dirt road goes up Highway 14 through Dak Mot, and on toward the Lao border on Route 18 past a military base to the town of Ngoc Hoi (the entire district here is also called Ngoc Hoi). The border villages out of Kontum may require permits, but this is more likely a fund-raising scam by the local constabulary. Hiring a jeep from Kontum will cost upward of $40 for a full day of driving, plus $10 to rent a policeman, plus extra for a guide. Bargain hard for price and timing.

On the way to the border zone you pass scrap-metal dumps. The area around Dak To and Tan Canh was a battlefield, and some rusted tanks are still lying around. The Dak To area contains villages inhabited by Bahnar, Jarai, Sedoun, and Rongao. The farther west you go, the poorer the villagers, with grubby malnourished kids living on earthen floors. Jarai, Sedoun, and Bahnar villages feature a large, distinct structure with a towering thatched roof—the *rong*, or communal spirit

house, where men gather to sing and drink. Another distinctive feature is a Bahnar-Jarai burial vault, a wooden structure with two long poles at either end—buffalo hooves and skulls hang from it.

BUON MA THUOT

Buon Ma Thuot, population around 65,000, is the largest town and unofficial capital of the highlands. The area specializes in coffee and lumber. Vietnam's finest coffee comes from this region, although the brewing process is not yet perfected in the local cafés. The French introduced coffee and rubber trees to the area in the 1930s, with large rubber plantations operated by Michelin. Sericulture was introduced in the 1990s, and there were plans for large-scale mulberry plantations in an effort to turn Buon Ma Thuot into one of the silk-weaving centers of Vietnam.

The center of Buon Ma Thuot is a dusty traffic circle with a T-34 tank mounted on a block of concrete in the middle, one of the sacred vehicles that rolled in to liberate the area in 1975. In March of that year, NVA troops mounted an all-out attack on Buon Ma Thuot that turned into a rout of South Vietnamese forces, paving the way for the final assault on Saigon. Apart from the bizarre landmark tank, there's not a lot to see in Buon Ma Thuot. The surrounding countryside holds the real interest.

Minority Museum

This small museum focuses on the Ede, the dominant cultural group in the area. There are displays of musical instruments, wooden jewelry, costumes, weaving, baskets, models of Ede longhouses, and some moth-eaten stuffed animals. Pictures of the Liberation round out the tacky display. At the current rate of Vietnamization, the entire Ede culture may end up in the museum. Open Tuesday, Thursday, and Saturday 0700–1100 and 1400–1700.

The Ede appear to have originated in Malaysia or Indonesia. They live in houses on stilts, with pigs and chickens scurrying around under the floor. Most have been converted to

THROUGH THE HIGHLANDS ON A MINSK

by Patrick Morris

With tanks full and fingers crossed, the three of us roared out of Saigon. We were riding Russian 125cc Minsk motorcycles, purchased with cash dollars in Saigon. On the map of the Central Highlands, thick red lines promised roads of some sort, and we decided to tackle them by motorcycle. Along for the ride were fellow American Alan and a young Londoner named Steve.

We chose the Minsks because they have sufficient power for mountain regions and are easily and cheaply repaired. None of us had licenses; supposedly you need a license in Vietnam only when riding a 150cc bike or higher. It is useful, however, to possess ownership papers—even forgeries—in case you're stopped by police. I even took the further precaution of procuring green government plates before leaving Saigon to avoid harassment.

Making an awful racket on our sputtering Minsks, we rode from Saigon to Nha Trang, and the next day to Tuy Hoa. There we turned off Highway 1 up a dirt road that gradually rises from a humid valley onto the cooler highlands plateau, emerging in lush rubber-tree plantations. Scenery along the route is mostly scrub mountain ranges with occasional forest and hill-tribe villages. By nightfall we reached a small town named Ayun Pa. We were instant celebri-ties, mobbed within 10 minutes of our arrival. Iced lemonade was poured and we were offered a shampoo at the beauty salon in front of the hotel. We were then led to $2 fan rooms with mosquito nets. We took bucket showers and re-tired exhausted to wood-slat beds that threat-ened to collapse with every movement.

From Ayun Pa to Route 14 the road be-comes paved, passing through beautiful tree plantations. After a couple of hours Alan fell behind. We waited and waited, then finally turned around. We found Alan banged up on the side of the road, a man working on his bike. Alan showed us the scrapes he sustained when the handlebars fell off his bike. Like the for-mer Soviet Union, a Minsk has been known to fall to pieces without warning. The stranger remounted the handlebars and left, refusing to accept payment for his assistance.

As we neared Pleiku, an older man with a shock of white hair pulled up alongside me on a scooter. He asked where I was from and if I would visit his family. Weary and dusty, I tried to defer by saying I was too filthy, to which he quickly retorted, "Yes, you are filthy, but you are civilized!" He called himself Professor Lee. We ended up staying overnight at the professor's house, listening to his rantings, while his son sang Lionel Ritchie numbers.

Traffic on all roads as far as Pleiku was light to nonexistent. One to two hours of rain, some-

Catholicism or Protestantism, but they retain traces of animist worship of spirits of the for-est, streams, and hills. In festivals celebrating good crops, villagers drink wine from a large vat through bamboo-stem straws.

The stair leading to one Ede longhouse has a pair of wooden breasts at the top, symbolizing the power of women. The Ede are traditionally matriarchal, but since 1975 and Vietnamization, they're becoming less so. Another matriarchal group is the Mnong, with about 50,000 people living around Buon Ma Thuot. They speak a language similar to Khmer, have no written script, and live in houses flat to the ground. The Mnong are famed elephant catchers, using do-mesticated elephants to round up wild pachy-derms. They practice elephant spirit worship.

Accommodations

Buon Ma Thuot has a rum bunch of hotels. Happy hunting grounds are along Ly Thuong Kiet and Ha Bai Trung streets, which between them have a cluster of more than 25 hotels. On Ly Thuong Kiet, cheaper hotels range $7–15 a room. Typical of these is **Khach San 43**, at 43 Ly Thuong Kiet, tel. 50/852250, featuring 20 rooms at $7 each, no bath. One of the better hotels in town, **Tay Nguyen Hotel,** at 106 Ly Thuong Kiet, tel. 50/852250, features rooms for $25–30. The hotel is clean—a rare find in

times heavy, occurred almost daily in the afternoon. Confident now that we'd made it this far, in Pleiku we threw caution to the wind and rode to the old U.S. base at Plei Mei, then caught a trail for the few kilometers toward the Cambodian border. But lots of attention from villagers spooked us and we went back.

From Pleiku past Kontum to Dak To the road is paved, scenic, and rolling. Dak To to Dak Ngoi is dirt with rocks. The road from Dak Ngoi to Dak Pek winds through lush mountain passes. Dak Pek is a small town situated in a valley. Here we stayed in unnamed dormitories for $4. The hotel manager told me not to bother locking my Minsk, because "Dak Pek have no thief." The rural Vietnamese and Montagnards were very friendly—one Montagnard worked two hours fixing my friend's wheel and flatly refused to accept money. The children were shy, running away terrified when the motorcycles approached a hilltribe village.

We saw very little traffic along this section, mostly other motorcycles and the odd logging truck. We encountered no police problems in two weeks of motorcycling, and we were stopped only once by frontier soldiers at an outpost on the way to Phuoc Son. The soldiers insisted we take a bath in a nearby stream, then harassed us with family photos, and foisted bitter tea and plates of food on us.

Dak Pek to Phuoc Son is incredible terrain. Two steep mountain passes make an all-rock road barely passable on a motorbike. One stream crossing was a meter deep. A van would never make it and it would be totally impassable in the rainy season. We saw rainforest with waterfalls the entire 70 kilometers. It took us a whole day to cover this section of the route over mountain passes strewn with loose rocks and dirt. In Phuoc Son the cinema provided our hard beds—$5 with fan. Meals were delivered by eager staff. Out of Phuoc Son we found 10 kilometers of paved road, then a good dirt road mostly downhill or flat to Hoi An.

Apart from rough roads we had no problems and covered a lot of ground. I found the people along this route—especially the Montagnards—far friendlier and more hospitable than those along the more touristy Highway 1. The most important thing I've learned about traveling in Vietnam is to keep smiling. The Vietnamese are just becoming accustomed to foreigners, so it helps to be friendly and patient.

Patrick Morris is director of VeloAsia Cycling Adventures, an outfit based in Berkeley, California, that runs bicycle tours to Vietnam and other parts of Southeast Asia. The Minsk journey he described was undertaken in times when the roads were rougher and the permits more difficult to get. The whole route is paved now and can be negotiated more quickly.

these parts. The upper-end rooms have a/c and hot water. Along Hai Ba Trung are the following hotels. **Hong Kong Hotel,** 30 Hai Ba Trung, tel. 50/852630, is a small budget joint with $7 rooms. **Khach San UBND** is the People's Committee Guesthouse at 5 Hai Ba Trung, tel. 50/852407; the 33 rooms here range $15–30. A recommended private hotel is **Bach Ma (White Horse),** at 61 Hai Ba Trung, tel. 50/853963, with 22 comfortable rooms for $20–40.

Around the corner is **Cao Nguyen Hotel,** Phan Chu Trinh Street, tel. 50/851913, which offers 32 deluxe rooms for $20–50. The **Thang Loi** (Victory) at 1 Phan Chu Trinh, tel. 50/852322, is near the tank in the center of town and has 36 rooms for $45–65, which is rather overpriced, but the rooms do have satellite TV—and great tank views. South of the post office on Doc Lap Street are **Bao Dai Villas,** tel. 50/852177, with a/c rooms for $25. Finally, out near the bus station if you're arriving late or trying to make an 0500 departure, there's **Banme Hotel,** tel. 50/852415, with 52 rooms for $17–30.

Food

Next door to Hong Kong Hotel is **Bo Ne Restaurant,** which serves a sizzling steak-and-egg breakfast for under $1. This place has a peculiar selection of animals marinating in jars

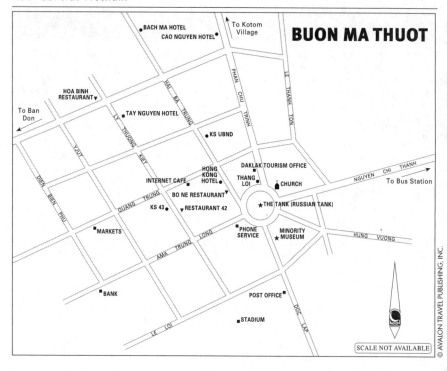

BUON MA THUOT

SCALE NOT AVAILABLE

© AVALON TRAVEL PUBLISHING, INC.

of rice wine—$1 a shot for wine with deer or monkey fetus. Other jars contain pickled birds, lizards, boa constrictors—there's even a jar full of dead bees. **Quan To Nu** (Restaurant 42), 42 Ly Thuong Kiet, has passable food; **Khach San 43** hotel (opposite) has a restaurant; and there's also **Hoa Binh Restaurant** near Tay Nguyen Hotel. Scattered around town are other eateries—it's best if you can pick up a "food guide" to help with ordering. **Ninh Hoa,** on Ly Thuong Kiet Street, serves spring rolls; **Kim Hue** on Hoang Dien Street serves frog and duck.

Services and Information
Daklak Tourism Office (Dulich Daklak), 3 Phan Chu Trinh, tel. 50/852108, offers guides, car rentals, and high-priced services. The office will arrange elephant rides with a two-day notice—$50 for two hours on an elephant, $90 extra for logistics. Other tour enticements: a ride in a dugout canoe for $30; witnessing a

wine-drinking ceremony for $80, dancing optional. Daklak Tourism has a Toyota four-seater, minibus, and small bus.

Find a moto driver; they are much cheaper in lining up deals than the tourism office. The language barrier is not a big problem in the highlands, as some older folk worked with U.S. forces before 1975.

Getting There
By Air: The daily flight from Saigon on a 34-seat light plane can be overbooked, so reserve well ahead. A one-way flight costs $45, and this short flight avoids an 18-hour road trip—another reason for its popularity. There are also connections twice-weekly from Buon Ma Thuot to Danang and Hanoi. Buon Ma Thuot airport is 10 kilometers out—take a moto to or from town for $2.

By Bus: Buon Ma Thuot bus station three kilometers east of town has up to 25 departures

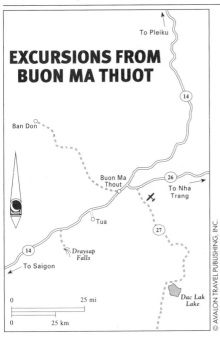

EXCURSIONS FROM BUON MA THUOT

To Pleiku

14

Ban Don

Buon Ma Thuot

26

To Nha Trang

Tua

27

14

Draysap Falls

To Saigon

Dac Lak Lake

0   25 mi

0   25 km

© AVALON TRAVEL PUBLISHING, INC.

daily; most leave in the early morning. The buses vary from good Hungarian Icarus models to crawlers that seem incapable of making it over the next hill—let alone to Haiphong, Vung Tau, Hué, Saigon, or the other far-flung destinations advertised. Several buses a day travel to Pleiku and a number of points along the coast. Danang buses will stop in Pleiku.

Getting Around

Use motos. Moto plus driver runs about $5 a day, or you can give the moto driver $5 and take it yourself.

Excursions from Buon Ma Thuot

About two kilometers north of Buon Ma Thuot is **Kotom,** a wealthy model village of immaculate longhouses with tiled roofs, hedgerows, electricity, and big motorcycles in the driveways. A paved road leading to Kotum provides easy access. The Catholic middle-class Ede residents of this ritzy strip appear to have received a large transfusion of money from official sources.

Tua, another Ede village on the tourist circuit (read: well-off model village), is 13 kilometers southwest of town on the road to Saigon. To reach mediocre **Draysap Falls** continue down the same road and turn left at the 20-kilometer marker. Follow a rough trail for seven more kilometers—about 20 minutes on a motorcycle.

An excursion to **Ho Lak** (Dak Lak Lake) is recommended. This area lies about 60 kilometers to the south. The route passes through pretty valleys and countryside. A few small ferry crossings can be found on this route. Ho Lak is ringed by mountains; on the lake you can see dugout canoes; in the villages you pass geese herders and basket makers. A good viewpoint in the area is the burned-out Bao Dai villa. Boat and elephant races are staged here every spring; cranes and storks coat the place during migratory visits.

The village of **Ban Don** lies 55 kilometers northwest of Buon Ma Thuot, or about two hours by moto. Local buses also make the trip. A rather ordinary town, it has been chosen as a model tourist circus because elephants can be ordered into the village from nearby jungles on 48-hour notice. Adding to its improvised attractions is Ban Don's very own skein of bamboo bridges—which are for tourists. Authorities may insist on a permit to visit Ban Don, but this is pure fund-raising. Ban Don offers an eclectic mix in its small population of 300 people, including Ede, Jarai, Lao, Khmer, Bahnar, Thai, and Mnong peoples. The Mnong are renowned as elephant trainers; some practice their craft around Ban Don. None of the minority peoples wear traditional costume except at weddings or festivals. There are some Ede longhouses and Lao–style houses in the area. You can stay in a basic bungalow at the village, or stay at bungalows at Yakdon National Park farther out.

Occasionally, an elephant and mahout saunter through the village, but you are unlikely to see elephants—except if some are ordered for rides. There are very few elephants left in Vietnam. During the Vietnam War, the pachyderms suffered major setbacks: Domesticated elephants and water buffalo used by the Vietcong to move supplies were attacked and slaughtered by U.S. pilots and ground troops. Wild elephants were adversely affected by the ecological warfare waged by the United States. In 1980 there were an estimated 1,500–2,000 elephants in Vietnam, mainly living in the forests of the Central Highlands. By 2005 that number had dwindled to fewer than 500; the decline was due to destruction of natural habitats and illegal hunting. The species is now endangered. Although protected under Vietnamese law, tuskers have come into increasing conflict with farmers encroaching on forest land. The only hope for the remaining population of wild elephants is the creation of a national park protection zone.

Twenty or 30 kilometers out of Buon Ma Thuot on the route to Ban Don you can visit perfectly good Ede villages engaged in the farming of peanuts, coffee, or pepper, and they don't require any permit nonsense.

Quang Ngai to Nha Trang

QUANG NGAI

Quang Ngai, the capital of the province of the same name, is a dull town on Highway 1 about 130 kilometers south of Danang. Twelve kilometers to the east is the site of the My Lai massacre, now an on-site museum and memorial. If you keep going along the same road to the coast, there are fishing villages at fine-sand **Bien Khe Ky Beach.** It's simple to reach the **My Lai Memorial** site—you could spend a few hours there and carry on without stopping in Quang Ngai.

Accommodations and Food

With the discovery of off-shore oil near Quang Ngai, a number of high-rise hotels have sprouted in this obscure town to accommodate an influx of petroleum fortune-seekers. On the north side of town is the best in town: the **My Tra Hotel,** tel. 55/842985, fax 55/842980. This high-rise sports rooms with river views; there is a fair-sized swimming pool and tennis courts—otherwise, concrete has been used with abandon. Rooms run $30–40, and two suites for $105 each. Close by is **Petrovietnam Hotel,** 1 Quang Trung St., tel. 55/822664, run by Quang Ngai Tourism Company, which also maintains offices here. The Petrovietnam is a vast, soulless concrete structure with a restaurant, dance floor, and souvenir counters; 38 rooms in the $10–25 range for a double. **Quang Ngai Hotel,** 62 Quang Trong, tel. 55/822757, offers 16 clean double rooms with

bath for $20 each—it's also known as **Cong Doan** or **Trade Union Guesthouse.**

Closer to town on Phan Boi Chau is a cluster of hotels; if you don't get into one, walk over and try the next one. **Nha Khach UBND Quang Ngai,** 50 Phan Boi Chau, tel. 55/822873, a large compound opposite the church, features several wings, with a total of 45 rooms in the $8–22 range. Official guests lodge here so you might have trouble getting in; good tucker in the dining room. **Khach San Vietnam,** 41 Phan Boi Chau, tel. 55/823610, has 10 rooms at $8 each. **Khach San Kim Thanh** at 19 Phan Boi Chau, tel. 55/823471, is a private 20-room hotel; $6–12 single, $15–20 hot water and a/c. In the same area is **Hotel 502.**

Near the market a budget hotel, **Hotel #1** (Khach San So I) at 42 Nguyen Nghiem, tel. 55/83609, has 20 rooms at $5; friendly management. Try the central market for good food stalls. Otherwise, most eating takes place in hotels—try the **UBND Quang Ngai** dining room.

Getting Around and Away

Buses run to destinations north and south on Highway 1, as well as to the Central Highlands, from Lien Tinh Ben Xe on the south side of Quang Ngai. Quang Ngai railway station is three kilometers west of town; Reunification Express trains stop here. For car rentals in Quang Ngai, inquire at the hotels. Prices average $25 per day with driver. You can find motos near the market and at the bus terminal and other strategic sites, including the turnoff to My Lai.

To Danang

MOTOS

To My Lai

MY TRA HOTEL

Tra Khuc River

SONG TRA HOTEL

QUANG NGAI

QUANG NGAI HOTEL

To Rail
Station

CHURCH KS VIET
NAM
KS KIM THANH
PHAN BOI CHAU
POST OFFICE
HOTEL 502
NHA KHACH
UBND QUANG
NGAI

Markets

QUANG TRUNG

NGUYEN NGHIEM
HOTEL #1

To Qui Nhon

LIEN TINH
BEN XE (BUS
STATION)

SCALE NOT AVAILABLE

© AVALON TRAVEL PUBLISHING, INC.

MY LAI

The rural district of Son My was the site of the My Lai massacre in 1968. To get there, turn east from the bridge over the Tra Khuc River and proceed 12 kilometers along a dirt road, passing through villages and rice paddies. On the same road, farther east past the My Lai site, is Bien Khe Ky Beach with a long stretch of sand. There are motos at the bridge over the Tra Khuc River; hiring a moto for 2–3 hours should cost under $4. A guide posted at the My Lai Memorial site will show you around;

no permits or permissions needed, though a donation is expected.

The Massacre

On March 16, 1968, three companies of U.S. infantry entered the Son My District by helicopter to search for Vietcong. The area was believed to be a Vietcong stronghold; several U.S. soldiers had been killed by mines in the area a few weeks earlier. Under the orders of Lt. William C. Calley, the first platoon moved into the village of My Lai and shot and bayoneted unarmed civilians, killed livestock, blew up underground bomb shelters, and torched dwellings. Women were raped, dead animals tossed into wells to poison the water. Up to 150 villagers were herded into a ditch and cut down by machine-gun fire. Calley's platoon accounted for about 350 deaths; more than 500 Vietnamese were killed in the operation by the three infantry divisions combined, mostly in My Lai hamlet itself. At no point did U.S. troops come under fire. The only U.S. casualty that day was an American soldier who shot himself in the foot to escape involvement in the massacre. The remaining villagers were forced into camps.

It was not until eight months later that *New York Times* reporter Seymour Hersh managed to confirm the story and place it before the world. The resulting uproar had a demoralizing effect on the U.S. military and was a turning point in the American public's perception of the war. The cover-ups reached every level of the U.S. Army command. Military justice was farcical—of all those involved, only Lieutenant Calley endured court-martial and conviction. Found guilty of murdering 22 civilians, he was sentenced in 1971 to life imprisonment. He spent only three years under house arrest before being paroled.

The Memorial

My Lai has become a pilgrimage spot for both Americans and Vietnamese trying to heal the wounds and come to grips with the atrocities. Visiting My Lai is a moving, humbling experience—a reminder of the insanity of war. Every

M

Central Vietnam

THE COAST ROAD

Highway 1 was originally engineered by the Vietnamese imperial government more than 200 years ago—it was then called the "Mandarin Route" and was about 1,150 kilometers long, connecting Hanoi, Hué, Saigon, and Phnom Penh. Under the present government the road has been extended, stretching more than 2,000 kilometers from Lang Son on the Chinese border to Camau at the tip of the Mekong Delta. The World Bank recently announced plans to lend Vietnam $158 million to rebuild the most heavily traveled sections of Highway 1, so improvements may be on the way.

From Danang south to Phan Thiet is an 800-kilometer coastal stretch sometimes within sight of the railway and Highway 1. The coastal plains support rice farmers and fine harbors and beaches offer bases for fishing. Beach areas are undeveloped and unspoiled, with simple fishing villages reminiscent of those in Thailand in the 1960s. Unspoiled often also means inaccessible—many lie hidden off the main road. The most developed beach is Nha Trang and even that is low-key.

Minibus drivers heading down the coast cover the trip in stages. From Danang it's 130 kilometers to Quang Ngai, 175 kilometers farther to Qui Nhon, 188 kilometers to Tuy Hoa, then 88 kilometers to Ninh Hoa, 32 kilometers to Nha Trang, another 105 kilometers to Phan Rang, 150 kilometers to Phan Thiet, and a final 198 kilometers to Saigon. The railway largely parallels the road. Key junctions on the coast road are at Binh Dinh (17 kilometers from Qui Nhon, marking the turnoff to Pleiku), Ninh Hoa (turnoff to Buon Ma Thuot), and Phan Rang (turnoff for the Dalat route to Saigon).

year on March 16, there is a special memorial gathering at the site.

The My Lai Memorial is built on the site of the former village, with gardens, reception halls, and a museum. At the far end lies an irrigation ditch bearing a plaque stating that GIs killed 170 villagers. Near the ditch is a model of a family bomb shelter and coconut trees scarred with artillery holes. To one side, a large mosaic wall completed in 1988 by a group of Hanoi artists shows a *Guernica*-like mosaic of screaming figures, whirling helicopters, blazing guns, and dripping tears of blood.

Toward the reception halls is a statue group of Vietnamese villagers displaying sorrow and anger. The statue was sculpted by Ho Thu, husband of Vo Thi Lien, a massacre survivor. Vo Thi Lien was 11 years old at the time. She traveled in Europe in 1970, at age 13, to denounce the United States. "I tell you this story," she said, "so peace may be restored in my country. So I can go to school and meet my friends and relatives again."

The museum at My Lai is small but devastating—this place will leave a lump in your throat.

Through photos and eyewitness accounts, the museum re-creates the events that took place that day. Some pictures have English captions; others are captioned in Vietnamese only. Ronald Haeberle, a U.S. Army photographer present for the first hour of the carnage, had three cameras along—he turned over some official film and kept the rest. The photos appeared in a Japanese source, and later in *Life* magazine and *Newsweek*. The Vietnamese lifted the photos from these sources and enlarged them for the museum. His photographs show people before and after being shot. There are testimonials from half a dozen survivors and from two Vietnamese interpreters who were there for the first hour of the shooting. Paintings in the museum depict the events. There's also a heart-wrenching display of some personal effects of villagers killed that day—teacup shards, a child's crayon, a Buddha statue from a destroyed family shrine.

In the reception hall at My Lai are several dozen thick guest books, filled with comments from Vietnamese and foreign visitors. Among the foreign entries, the most poignant come from Vietnam vets. One group came to My Lai in 1992 to build a U.S.-funded health center, with vets contributing medicines and a solar power system on the roof. One vet wrote, "By coming back to Vietnam to build this clinic I have helped heal the deep psychological wounds that have plagued me for 21 years." In 1993, Hugh Thompson, one of the nine helicopter pilots at My Lai on March 16, revisited the site:

On my first trip to My Lai, I was filled with pain and anger. On my second trip 25 years later, I am filled with sorrow and pain. I wish I could have prevented more death. Please forgive all former helicopter pilots. I hope all worlds can learn to live in peace.

SA HUYNH BEACH

Sixty kilometers south of Quang Ngai is Sa Huynh, one of the few places along this coastal stretch with some facilities—seaside restaurants and a small hotel. If you're driving through, this is a pretty spot to break the journey. The beach is fringed with coconut palms and rice paddies; the town is known for its salt marshes and salt-evaporation ponds.

QUI NHON

Qui Nhon, the capital of Binh Dinh province, is a port town with a large fishing fleet. If you're traveling by car or minibus, it's a possible pit stop on the Saigon-to-Hué route; by public transportation, it's a disaster—you'll be dropped off way to the west of the town.

There's little to see in Qui Nhon. To make matters worse, the locals are rude, unfriendly, and ready to rip off the unwary. You can visit the museum **Bao Tang Binh Dinh;** three small salons offer ethnic and natural history through models of thatched housing, Cham artifacts, war memorabilia, and a few artillery pieces. Two Cham works stand out—an impressive Brahma statue from Thap Doi, and a *garuda* statue from Duong Long.

The two Cham towers in Qui Nhon are nothing to get excited about. The twin towers of Thap Doi are at the northern edge of town, down an alley near 906 Tran Hung Dao St., three kilometers from Qui Nhon center. Most of the tower statuary has been hauled off; one of the towers has been completely rebricked and reconstructed on a new stone and concrete base, so it's hardly a Cham ruin—wait till it grows some moss.

There are some other Cham towers around Qui Nhon, such as **Thap Duong Long,** about 30 kilometers northwest, and **Thap Banh It,** 20 kilometers north, and the remains of **Cha Ban** and **Canh Tien,** 27 kilometers north. None are as impressive as the ruins in Phan Rang or Nha Trang.

The beach at Qui Nhon looks pleasant enough—white sand, fishing boats—but it contains raw sewage and other pollutants. Close to the war memorial by the beach, stalls serve snacks. At the east end of the beach, past Qui Nhon Tourist Hotel, is a small enclosure with monkeys and sad black bears. It's free, which is what you wish you could say about the animals. In the center of Qui Nhon, **Long Kanh Pagoda** features a large standing Buddha in front, presiding over an industrial wasteland.

Accommodations

Under $20: No shortage of accommodations in Qui Nhon. In town is a slew of hotels with similar prices, mostly under $15 a room. **Dong Phuong Hotel,** 39 Mai Xuan Thuong, tel. 56/82915, has fan rooms for $6 s, $8 d, and $12 t, and a/c rooms for $7–15, popular with backpackers. **Huu Nghi Hotel,** 210 Phan Boi Chau, tel. 56/822152, offers $6 rooms. **Binh Dinh Guesthouse,** 399 Tran Hung Dao, tel. 56/822012, is run by the Binh Dinh Investment Bank and has 15 rooms: $5–6 no bath, $9 with toilet, $12 with a/c and hot water; $15 with TV.

The **Peace Hotel** (Hoa Binh) on Tran Hung Dao, tel. 56/822900, offers 62 rooms for $6 s and $9 d. Right opposite is the **Nha Khach 264,** tel. 56/821611. Next door, on the corner of Dao Duy Tu and Tran Hung Dao, is **Saigon Hotel,** with 15 double rooms at $15 each. **Agribank Hotel,** at 202 Tran Hung Dao, tel. 56/822245, has 16

QUI NHON

To Hwy 1 and Dieu Tri Train Station

VIET CUONG

BUS TERMINAL

LAMBROS TO DIEU TRI

South China Sea

PHAN DINH PHUNG

XUAN THUONG

MAI

DIEN ANH HOTEL

BINH DINH GUESTHOUSE

TANU BINH

VIETINCOMBANK HOTEL

NHA KHACH 264

CAO VAN

PEACE HOTEL

SAIGON HOTEL

DONG PHUONG HOTEL

ANH THU MINI

TRAN

NGOC LIEN RESTAURANT

POST OFFICE

STADIUM

HUU NGHI HOTEL

AGRIBANK HOTEL

VIETCOMBANK

1 THANG

OLYMPIC HOTEL

LONG KHANH PAGODA

CHURCH

TRAN HUNG DAO

TANG BAT HO

LE LOI

CENTRAL MARKET

PHAN BOI CHAU

TRAN BINH TRONG

CAR RENTAL OFFICE

LE HONG PHONG

HAI BA TRUNG

CAR RENTAL OFFICE

NGUYEN TRAI

HAI HA MINI HOTEL

BINH DINH TOURISM

QUI NHON TOURIST HOTEL

DO LINH

DIN

TRAN PHU

BINH DINH MUSEUM

NGUYEN HUE

WAR MEMORIAL

City Beach

0   100 yds

0   100 m

© AVALON TRAVEL PUBLISHING, INC.

Central Vietnam

rooms for $9 s and $12–15 d. **Anh Thu Mini,** 54 Mai Xuan Thuong, tel. 56/821168, is a drive-in hotel with 10 rooms for $11–15 each. **Olympic Hotel,** near the stadium, tel. 56/822375, features 30 rooms in the $7–15 range.

Vietincombank Hotel, 257 Le Hong Phong, tel. 56/822779, has 20 rooms in the $15–20– 25 range. **Dien Anh Hotel** (Movie Star Hotel), 312 Phan Boi Chau, tel. 56/822876, offers 19 rooms for $18 each, with a/c and hot water; it's run by Binh Dinh Video Company.

$20–50: Near Qui Nhon Beach are two more expensive hotels. **Hai Ha Mini Hotel,** tel. 56/821295, charges $25 for each of its

seven double rooms. **Qui Nhon Tourist Hotel,** 8 Nguyen Hue, tel. 56/822401, features more than 50 rooms in a large modern compound; $22–30 for doubles.

$100–200: A big step up, in terms of quality and pricing, is **Life Resort Quy Nhon,** on Bao Dai Street, tel. 56/840132, with rooms going for $100–155. This is part of the Life Resorts chain in Vietnam, owned by Hotel Projekt of Holland.

Food

There are no decent restaurants. **Ngoc Lien Restaurant,** at 268 Le Hong Phong, is reasonable;

the area around it has lots of eateries. Otherwise, try foraging in hotel dining rooms. Qui Nhon is a fishing port so some seafood is served. About three kilometers southwest of town is **Ganh Rang Restaurant** on the waterfront.

Services and Information
Binh Dinh Tourism Office is in the same compound as the Qui Nhon Tourist Hotel. The **Vietcombank** is at 148 Le Loi Street.

Getting There and Away
Highway 1 is eight kilometers west of Qui Nhon at Phutai; the railway is 10 kilometers west at Dieu Tri; Phu Cat Airport is 35 kilometers north of Qui Nhon. Motos and lambros shuttle passengers from Qui Nhon back to road or rail junctions. A lambro is $.50 to Dieu Tri, a moto $1. Both are available from the area in front of Qui Nhon bus station, Ben Xe Binh Dinh, on Tran Hung Dao Street.

Buses depart Qui Nhon at 0500 to Hanoi, Saigon, Nha Trang, Dalat, Danang, and Hué. If you don't want to get up at this unearthly hour, or if the bus station doesn't offer an express to the destination of your choice, consider heading out to Phutai on Highway 1 and flagging down a passing express bus. Although there's a rail spur into Qui Nhon, it's used only by local trains. Study Reunification Express timetables in a hotel in Qui Nhon before heading to Dieu Tri to catch a train. There are twice-weekly flights from Phu Cat Airport to Danang and Ho Chi Minh City.

Getting Around
Try the hotels for rentals—otherwise, stick to cyclos or motos. Car and minibus rentals are available from the Limited Responsible Tourist Car company at 79 Le Hong Phong, tel. 56/823066. You can hire a car and driver for about $25 a day. Another place for rentals is Central Vietnam Traveling, at 176 Le Hong Phong, tel. 56/821199. This agency offers motorcycle rentals—Honda 50cc for $6 a day, 100cc for $8 a day. If you rent for a two-day period, you keep the motorcycle overnight. A Toyota Land Cruiser is about $30 per 100 kilometers of driving; a four-seat car is $28 for 100 kilometers.

TUY HOA
There is no reason to visit Tuy Hoa except to sleep there. You can't miss the main hotel, the **Huong Sen,** which has doubles for $15 and suites for $25–35. The hotel includes a vast restaurant that is always empty but charges outrageous prices. A guesthouse in Tuy Hoa is also open to foreigners, charging $15 a night. A good restaurant is **Phong Lan,** at 156 Tran Hung Dao, with great noodle soup. Tuy Hoa is so boring the arrival of a plane is enough to cause hysteria. In 1955 after the Geneva Accords, the Vietminh withdrew north of the 17th parallel, so President Diem dropped into Tuy Hoa for a visit. More than 50,000 peasants turned up, mobbing the field when his small plane arrived, almost trampling him. The U.S. Information Service photographed the frenzied welcome as proof that the peasants and townspeople were overjoyed to be rid of oppressive communism.

DAI LANH BEACH
About 35 kilometers south of Tuy Hoa is Dai Lanh, a picturesque fishing village with red-tile roofs. There's a high vantage point to the north, Mui Dai Lanh (known to the French as Cap Varella), with sweeping views. Dai Lanh Beach extends along Highway 1; at the southern end it becomes a sand dune area that connects with the 30-kilometer Hon Gom Peninsula, another scenic area. Sheltered in here is Vung Coco, one of the nicest beaches on the coast. The area around Hon Lon Island off the coast is good for diving—somewhat marred by the local custom of "fishing" by using explosives. There are no facilities as yet in these areas. Accommodations are scarce in these parts, but you can stay at Tuy Hoa, or just travel the extra 85 kilometers from Dai Lanh to Nha Trang.

About 40 kilometers north of Nha Trang—and 10 kilometers east off Highway 1—lies **Doclet Beach,** a beautiful stretch of white sand with shallow waters. You can get there by rented car or motorcycle from Nha Trang on a day trip, or plan to spend the night at the **Doclet Hotel,** with bungalows for $7.

Nha Trang

Established as a port town in the 1920s, Nha Trang now has a population of 315,000 and serves as capital of Khanh Hoa province. Fishing is the major industry. Although Nha Trang is one of the most developed of all the beaches in Vietnam, beach "infrastructure" is largely confined to the rental of umbrellas, deck chairs, and inner tubes. In contrast to Thailand's coastal regions, there is little in the way of diving equipment rental or sailboarders. Some prefer it this way—no personal watercraft or parasailing to disturb the tranquil setting. But give them time—the personal watercraft will blot the horizon yet. Nha Trang is pleasant for cycling, with wide boulevards and little traffic.

For a beach, Nha Trang has distinctly unbeachy architecture. The hotels lining the strand look more like museums or hospitals. For this you can partly blame the French, who put up some of the early models, and partly the lack of imagination among the Vietnamese. Building 15-story concrete hotel blocks right next to the beach is the latest trend. Just hope that the sewage from these new hotels does not empty into the sea (it probably does).

SIGHTS

Cham Towers

On the north side of Nha Trang, across Xom Bong Bridge, are the best-preserved Cham towers in central Vietnam, the sanctuary of Po Nagar. The towers were constructed between the 7th and 12th centuries. In the 9th century, warriors believed to hail from the Srivijaya kingdom of Sumatra ransacked the temple, plundering a lingas of precious metal. Later, marauding Khmers removed a gold lingas and other items. In the 16th century Nha Trang was the last stronghold of the Cham before they were overrun by powerful Viet forces from the north. Today, only four of the sanctuary's original eight towers remain. The octagonal pillars that formed the original entrance have been completely rebricked. Though there is a

lot of obvious new brick and concrete reconstruction on the north tower, the lichen-coated sections are clearly original masonry. The towers all face eastward. There are magnificent views of the surrounding area from the hill—a quiet and relaxing place.

A small on-site museum displays early plans of the site, as well as photos of French excavations. But the site itself is no museum: These smoke-stained towers are still used for spiritual purposes. Pilgrims make a circuit of the shrines, the main object of devotion the Uma statue in the north tower.

Three of the towers shelter lingas—phallic sculptures symbolic of Shiva and royalty, and popular objects of devotion in Cham art. A lingas is usually coupled with a yoni, representing the female organs and symbolizing fertility. The lingas and yoni structure has spouts and drains for carrying water away in ceremonies. As you approach from the entrance gate you'll see the first tower, sheltering a small lingas on a solid base. The tower is in bad condition. The next tower encases a meter-high stone lingas on a lotus base. At the back, the northwest tower harbors a small but exquisite yoni and lingas; two elaborate ceremonial fans stand behind the altar.

The main shrine is the north tower, which originally sheltered a gold lingas. The precious lingas was stolen by the Khmers; in its place, a statue of Uma was constructed in the 11th century. The 23-meter-high tower is a masterpiece of Cham art; its richly decorated roof remains relatively intact. At the entrance to the tower stand two huge sandstone pillars covered with inscriptions describing offerings to the goddess within; above the entrance doorway are three carved *apsaras* (celestial dancers). The Uma shrine is of the "wish granting" variety—patronized not only by Cham Hindus, but also by Chinese and Vietnamese Buddhists. The shrine is considered a source of miraculous cures and attracts its share of beggars. Visitors make offerings of fruit, flowers, incense, and

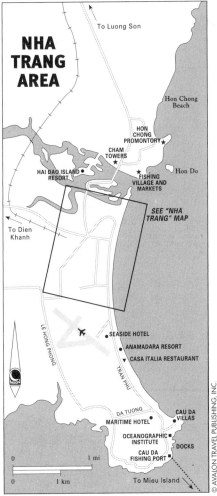

NHA TRANG AREA

To Luong Son

Hon Chong Beach

HON CHONG PROMONTORY ★

CHAM TOWERS ★

HAI DAO ISLAND RESORT ●

FISHING VILLAGE AND MARKETS ●

Hon Do

SEE "NHA TRANG MAP"

To Dien Khanh

LE HONG PHONG

TRAN PHU

SEASIDE HOTEL ●

ANAMADARA RESORT ●

CASA ITALIA RESTAURANT ▼

DA TUONG

MARITIME HOTEL ●

CAU DA VILLAS ●

OCEANOGRAPHIC INSTITUTE ■

DOCKS

CAU DA FISHING PORT ■

To Mieu Island

0   1 mi

0   1 km

Additional costumes and jewelry are kept in a glass wardrobe near the back of the interior. The head is a copy—the original was lopped off and now sits in the Guimet Museum in Paris.

Uma's ceremonial clothing covers an extraordinary figure—with legs crossed and breasts bare, and carved neck and shoulder decorations. Uma is a 10-armed deity: Four arms attached at the back of the statue hold the ritual implements of dagger-gong, arrowhead-tusk, disk-conch, and spearhead-bow; four arms rest at the sides; and two arms protrude from the front of the statue, palms resting on the knees. Above Uma's serene face looms a fierce stone guardian with fangs. Dragons are carved on either side of the headpiece. The entire statue sits on a lotus pedestal above a meter-high stone yoni-base, sheltered by four ceremonial parasols. To the left and right stand small elephant statues.

Hon Chong Headland

Due east of the Cham towers are fishing villages. A lot of boats move in and out of the surreal-looking bay by Xom Bong Bridge. A slippery fish market opens early in the morning. West of the Cham towers is **Hai Dao Island Resort,** a ramshackle collection of cabins connected to the mainland by footbridges. Cockfights are sometimes staged here. To the northeast of the towers is **Hon Chong Promontory,** where hundreds of boulders are balanced on top of one another. The massive boulder at the tip of the promontory is called Chong Rock. Various legends are associated with this boulder, which is said to bear the imprint of a large hand. There are shrimp farms in the vicinity and various lookouts, one with a refreshment stall.

To the west of the Cham Towers, some tour agents in Nha Trang mount river trips along the Nha Trang River, with stops at fishing villages, Coco islet, and other sites.

Yersin Museum

At the north end of Tran Phu Boulevard behind Nha Trang's Pasteur Institute is a small but fascinating Yersin Museum, open 0730–1100 daily except Sundays and holidays. All

candles; some prostrate themselves before the Uma statue while an attendant hits a large brass bowl with a soft mallet, producing an eerie reverberating sound.

Uma is believed to be the female state of Shiva, called Po Nagar (goddess mother) by the Cham. The Uma statue here is made of a large piece of black stone. The face is painted brown, with red lips and black eyebrows and hair. The head supports a jeweled crown and the body a bright yellow embroidered and sequined coat.

M Central Vietnam

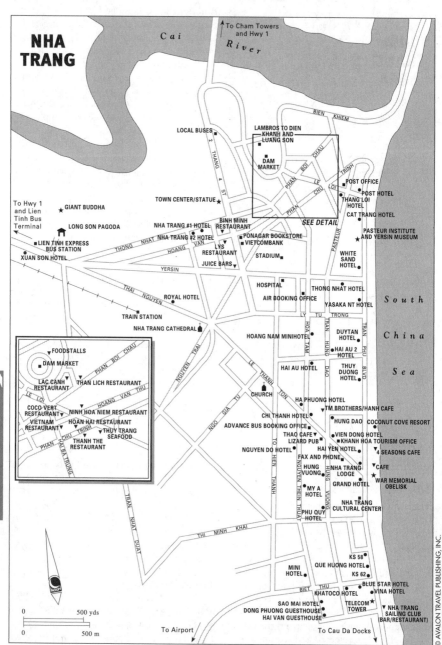

NHA TRANG

To Cham Towers
and Hwy 1

Cai River

LOCAL BUSES

LAMBROS TO DIEN
KHANH AND
LUANG SON

DAM MARKET

BIEN KHIEM

POST OFFICE
POST HOTEL
THANG LOI HOTEL
CAT TRANG HOTEL

TOWN CENTER/STATUE

SEE DETAIL

To Hwy 1
and Lien
Tinh Bus
Terminal

GIANT BUDDHA

LONG SON PAGODA

LIEN TINH EXPRESS
BUS STATION

XUAN SON HOTEL

NHA TRANG #1 HOTEL
NHA TRANG #2 HOTEL

BINH MINH
RESTAURANT

PONAGAR BOOKSTORE
VIETCOMBANK

PASTEUR INSTITUTE
AND YERSIN MUSEUM

WHITE SAND HOTEL

LYS RESTAURANT

JUICE BARS

STADIUM

THONG NHAT

HOANG VAN

YERSIN

HOSPITAL

AIR BOOKING OFFICE

THONG NHAT HOTEL

YASAKA NT HOTEL

South

China

Sea

THAI NGUYEN

ROYAL HOTEL

TRAIN STATION

NHA TRANG CATHEDRAL

LY TU TRONG

HOANG NAM MINIHOTEL

HOA TAM

TRAN HUNG DAO

DUYTAN HOTEL

HAI AU 2 HOTEL

TRAN PHU BLVD

HAI AU HOTEL

THUY DUONG HOTEL

NGUYEN TRAI

LE THANH TON

CHURCH

HA PHUONG HOTEL

TM BROTHERS/HANH CAFE

CHI THANH HOTEL

HUNG DAO COCONUT COVE RESORT

ADVANCE BUS BOOKING OFFICE

THAO CAFE
LIZARD PUB

VIEN DONG HOTEL
KHANH HOA TOURISM OFFICE

NGO GIA TU

NGUYEN DO HOTEL

HAI YEN HOTEL

4 SEASONS CAFE

TO HIEN

FAX AND PHONE

NGUYEN THIEN THUAT

HUNG VUONG

NHA TRANG LODGE

GRAND HOTEL

CAFE

WAR MEMORIAL
OBELISK

MY A HOTEL

PHU QUY HOTEL

NHA TRANG
CULTURAL CENTER

TRAN NHAT DUAT

THI MINH KHAI

KS 58

QUE HUONG HOTEL

KS 62

MINI HOTEL

BIET THU

KHATOCO HOTEL

BLUE STAR HOTEL
VINA HOTEL

TELECOM TOWER

SAO MAI HOTEL
DONG PHUONG GUESTHOUSE
HAI VAN GUESTHOUSE

NHA TRANG
SAILING CLUB
(BAR/RESTAURANT)

To Airport

To Cau Da Docks

Detail inset

FOODSTALLS

DAM MARKET

PHAN BOI CHAU

LAC CANH
RESTAURANT

THAN LICH RESTAURANT

LE LOI

COCO VERT
RESTAURANT

NINH HOA NIEM RESTAURANT

VIETNAM
RESTAURANT

HOAN HAI RESTAURANT

CHU TRINH

HAI BA TRUNG

THANH THE
RESTAURANT

THUY TRANG
SEAFOOD

MOON

0   500 yds

0   500 m

captions are in French, but a guide should be on hand to explain pictures. The site of the museum is Yersin's former library and office.

Alexandre Yersin (1863–1943) left France in 1890 as a ship's doctor. In Hong Kong, in June 1894, after six exhausting days of research, he isolated a plague bacillus, now called *Bacillus yersinia pestis*. In 1895 Yersin journeyed to Nha Trang and established a laboratory at the present site of the Pasteur Institute. He also began a cattle farm on the outskirts of Nha Trang for the manufacture of serums and vaccines. Serum was sent as far away as China and India, and his lab became known as a center of medical research and treatment of domestic animal diseases. In 1902 he went to Hanoi to establish a university of medicine; once this task was completed, he returned to Nha Trang to conduct further research.

Yersin was a Renaissance man. Apart from pioneering medical research, he was an explorer, botanist, biologist, and entomologist, and he was interested in photography and astronomy. He explored the Dalat area and recommended siting a hill station there; he voyaged to Stung Treng in Cambodia and overland to Phnom Penh. In his later years he devoted much time to the cultivation of tropical plants, namely orchids. Yersin introduced to the area coffee, cocoa, rubber, coconut, and quinine trees— another medicinal connection as quinine was used at the time to treat malaria. However, he did not introduce the "coca-cola" plant as indicated on the museum's leaflet.

Yersin led a simple life in Nha Trang, devoting himself to research and his other interests. He rode a battered bicycle and lived next to a fishing village. He used his powerful telescope to warn fishermen of approaching typhoons. He died at the age of 80 and is buried outside Nha Trang; his medical library and personal effects were bequeathed to the Pasteur Institute.

It was on Yersin's recommendations that his laboratory in Nha Trang and Dr. Albert Calmette's laboratory in Saigon were upgraded to the level of Indochina Pasteur Institutes, the first established outside Paris. Pasteur Institutes later appeared in Hanoi and Dalat, and microbiology labs opened in Hué, Vientiane, and Phnom Penh. The Pasteur Institutes in Vietnam continue producing vaccines and conducting research, but the budget is limited and the equipment old. Work continues now at Pasteur Institutes on a greater riddle—AIDS—though here it's probably limited to testing the Vietnamese for the presence of HIV infection.

Pagodas and Churches

On the northwest side of Nha Trang is **Long Son Pagoda,** an active temple featuring an unusual red brass Buddha on a wooden lotus pedestal. On top of a hill behind the pagoda is a massive white Buddha on a lotus throne. Embedded in the octagonal base are seven stucco likenesses of Buddhist martyrs, monks, and nuns who died protesting the repressive Diem regime. Several immolated themselves. The white Buddha was built in their memory in 1963.

On the other side of the tracks, east of the railway station, is **Nha Trang Cathedral,** complete with stained-glass windows and French Gothic lines. It was built in the 1930s; daily Masses are held early morning and late afternoon.

RECREATION

Marine pursuits are the chief draw in Nha Trang—lazing around the beach soaking up the rays, taking a day trip by boat to outlying islands. Assuming, of course, there are no typhoons. A smattering of other sights include the Cham towers to the north of Nha Trang. Skip the Oceanographic Institute to the south. It may once have been a center of marine study, but today it offers only a motley collection of stuffed and pickled sealife and a few live specimens. Displays are poorly presented, and half the tanks are empty (perhaps the creatures escaped?).

Nha Trang Beach

Nha Trang's palm-fringed beachfront stretches for five kilometers. Hop on a bicycle, cruise along Tran Phu Boulevard, and pick your spot. Beachfront cafés provide shelter and drinks; a number of places rent beach umbrellas and

VISITING THE ISLANDS

Day-tripping to offshore islands by chartered fishing boat is popular in Nha Trang. You can swim and snorkel, dine on seafood aboard the boat, and visit a beach and fishing village. Some operators include the infamous "floating bar," which means cheap liquor is provided on a water-borne bamboo bar while clients attempt to stay afloat using life-preservers.

Weather permitting, chartered boats leave at 0900 from Cau Da dock at the southern tip of Nha Trang. Deals vary: Most itineraries include a full-day boat trip, taking in 3–5 islands: **Hon Tre, Hon Mun, Hon Mot, Hon Tam,** and **Hon Mieu.** Adapted fishing boats can carry 20–30 people; trips generally operate on a minimum of 10 people and maximum of 30. The full-day trip, 0900–1700, usually costs around $7 per person. Operators will provide hotel minibus pickup, with transport from Nha Trang to Cau Da dock.

You can also make your own trips to the islands from Cau Da. It's easy, for example, to take a small ferry from Cau Da dock to Bai Mieu fishing village on Mieu Island. Most likely, you can also arrange your own small boat to reach some of the other islands from the Cau Da dock area.

The choice for operators is a toss-up between Mama Hanh, Mama Linh, or Captain Cook. They can be a rough bunch around Nha Trang and competition for boat traffic is fierce, so once you've chosen, try not to switch allegiances. Operators offer attention-grabbing perks—some guarantee one kilo of seafood per person or will arrange vegetarian fare on request. Most boat operators will make some attempt to provide masks, snorkels, and even fins, but quality and size varies—make discreet inquiries about equipment (there may be an extra charge of $2 for fins). Some boats will arrange onboard massage for $3 a person. There are about 6–8 companies in Nha Trang running the boat trips. Among these are Hanh Café, Nam Long Co., My A Tour, and Khanh Hoa Tourism. Many hotels around town make bookings.

Try to direct the itinerary. Some operators are lazy and drop anchor in dull locations for long periods. On the way back to Cau Da, boats sometimes stop to visit an "aquarium" on Hon Mieu. This place is actually a fish-breeding tank and is deadly boring.

deck chairs. The "civilized" end of the beach is from Hai Yen Hotel northward; south of that, the beach is more pristine. Roving vendors sell fruit and seafood; others offer beach massages. The water is slightly surfy in Nha Trang. Watch out for the rip tide—this is the Pacific Coast. The beach drops off very quickly, and soon you're out of your depth and in an undertow. Typhoons are a problem at Nha Trang, as elsewhere along the coast—those coconut trees can bend right over when there's a good wind in progress. The typhoon season is roughly October–mid-December. The high season at Nha Trang is in July and August, when Vietnamese vacationers arrive in droves.

Islands near Nha Trang

Hon Tre (Bamboo Island) has beaches and sandy coves where fishing communities live—you can see people repairing nets. They use a basket boat *(thung chai)* to commute between the fishing boats anchored offshore and the beach. The *thung chai* is made of woven bamboo strips covered with tar; it's puzzling how these round coracles are steered.

On **Hon Tam,** a resort has been set up, with a small hotel, beach umbrellas, kayaks, and personal watercraft. The tour boats drop in here on their rounds.

Only one square kilometer, **Hon Mun** (Black Island) harbors some of the most pristine coral reefs and marine life in the area—somehow it has managed to escape the dynamite fishing that has destroyed many nearby coral reefs. The World Wide Fund for Nature, based in Switzerland, is lobbying to establish Hon Mun as a marine park.

Vietnam is gifted with a 3,200-kilometer coastline, harboring a diverse range of marine resources, but these habitats are under severe

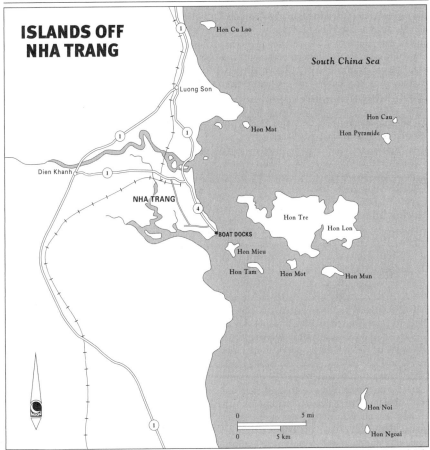

ISLANDS OFF
NHA TRANG

Hon Cu Lao

South China Sea

Luong Son

Hon Cau
Hon Mat
Hon Pyramide

Dien Khanh

NHA TRANG

BOAT DOCKS

Hon Tre
Hon Lon

Hon Mieu

Hon Tam
Hon Mot
Hon Mun

Hon Noi

0   5 mi
0   5 km
Hon Ngoai

© AVALON TRAVEL PUBLISHING, INC.

threat. Many coral reefs have been destroyed by dynamite fishing, coral mining, overfishing, pollution, and coastal development. The local government turns a blind eye to these practices; the Marine Resource Protection Department does not even have a patrol boat.

Outlying Islands

To the north of Nha Trang is **Hon Cu Lao,** an island off the coast with a monkey-rearing farm. The island has a very shallow approach with sharp, broken coral. There's a $2 landing fee; a bag of popcorn to feed the monkeys costs another $2. Some tour operators in Nha

Trang will arrange car and boat transportation to reach the island, usually for $15 a head. Up to 100 monkeys live on the island, bred for export to Malaysia and Singapore and destined for use in traditional medicine.

Another traditional medicine ingredient highly sought after in Nha Trang is the swallow nest, which, consumed in soup, is reputed to be therapeutic—some claim it's an aphrodisiac. Off the coast of Nha Trang are a number of small islands—**Hon Cau, Hon Pyramide, Hon Noi, Hon Ngoai**—where sea swallows *(salanganes)* make their nests. Both the male and female birds secrete a gel-like substance in their saliva that is used to build nests on a cliff crevice or in a cave. The bird chews, retches, and smears its spit to mold a small cup-shaped nest. The nests are usually white, though rarer varieties are orange and red. When the nest is completed, the female lays two white-and-blue speckled eggs. The nests are collected only twice a year, in spring and fall. Nest harvesting is a precarious venture. Harvesters rappel down rock faces to reach the nests, steering clear of the poisonous snakes that feed on swallow eggs. The motivation for risking life and limb is the high return on nests—they can fetch up to $2,000 a kilogram on the open market.

Marine Sports

Nha Trang has little in the way of the sporting hardware associated with beach resorts in Thailand. Sailboarding equipment can be rented at the southern end of the beach in the vicinity of the airport; try Nha Trang Sailing Club for rentals. You can also rent fishing tackle and boats through Khanh Hoa Tourism. Diving equipment is limited—you can rent reliable French equipment at the **Blue Diving Club at Coconut Cove Resort,** opposite Hai Yen Hotel at 40 Tran Phu Blvd., tel. 58/825390. Cost is on a sliding scale depending on how many in your group, but two dives averages out at about $50–60 per person, including lunch and drinks. The foreign dive masters here offer instruction for PADI diving courses, and for those who want to test the waters there is a "try-a-dive" program. Coral around Nha Trang is often broken and unspectacular—a victim of dynamite-fishing and boat anchors. Some of the better dive spots are the northeast side of Hon Tre, the area around Hon Mun, and the south side of Hon Lon.

ACCOMMODATIONS

Prices for hotels vary with the season: They go up at least 20 percent in the main holiday season, August–September, and around Tet, in February. Not all hotels in Nha Trang accept foreigners. Some cater to the rampant population of taxi girls in town; others employ guards who

will wave you away with a gun, usually from exclusive villas for officials. Pricing is slippery in Nha Trang—the same hotel may have budget and moderate ranges in different wings. Most of Nha Trang's hotels are arrayed down or within a few blocks of Tran Phu Boulevard. Building along Tran Phu has gone high-rise, overshadowing the beach with concrete monsters such as Nha Trang Lodge Hotel—a sort of Waikiki Syndrome. The north end is closer to the business and commercial district of Nha Trang.

Under $20

In Town: Near the commercial district is the dull **Nha Trang #1 Hotel,** 129 Thong Nhat, tel. 58/822347, offering 50 rooms for $8–18–25. **Nha Trang #2 Hotel,** nearby at 21 Le Thanh Phuong, tel. 58/822956, has 30 rooms for $10–15–20. A better place to be is in the Dam Market area. Here you'll find **Tulip Hotel,** 30 Hoang Van Thu St., tel. 58/821302, fax 58/829893, with $10 fan rooms and $12–18 a/c rooms. This 15-room hotel is clean and well run. At 5A Phan Chu Trinh St. is **Van Can minihotel,** tel. 58/826383, with eight rooms for $8–12. If you arrive late or want to depart early, try **Xuan Son Hotel,** opposite the bus station, 99A Duong 23/10, with 14 rooms for $3; cars for rent.

Private Minihotels: For budget travelers, privately run hotels are the best deal, since they're clean, secure, family-run, and eager to assist with travel arrangements. Two blocks west of Nha Trang Beach is **Huong Nam minihotel,** 13B Hoang Hao Tham St., tel. 58/826792, with six rooms for $6–12. **Chi Thanh,** 17B Hoang Hoa Tham, tel. 58/822092, has 10 rooms for $8–12. Opposite Hanh Café is **Ha Phuong Hotel,** at 30 Hoang Hoa Tham St., tel. 58/829015, fax 58/829015, with 10 rooms for $10–12.

Nguyen Do Hotel, at 4 Nguyen Thien Thuat St., tel. 58/825064, offers a handful of rooms for $5–8. **My A Hotel,** 9 Nguyen Thien Vuong St., tel. 58/826195, fax 58/824214, has 36 rooms for $5–10–15. One street away, **Phu Quy minihotel,** 54 Hung Vuong St., tel. 58/810609, has 12 rooms for around $10 with bath; very clean and efficient. Down the road, down an alley off Hung Vuong Street, at 12/8 Hung Vuong, is **Hung Vuong Hotel,** tel. 58/824505, with nine rooms for $10 apiece.

Farther south, near the Khatoco Hotel, is a cluster of minis. **Blue Star Hotel,** 1B Biet Thu St., tel./fax 58/826447, has 11 rooms for $12–15. **Sao Mai,** 99 Nguyen Thien Thuat St., tel. 58/827412, is a private minihotel with 10 rooms for $8 fan to $14 a/c. **Dong Phuong,** 103 Nguyen Thien Thuat St., tel. 58/825986, has 30 rooms for $8–10 fan and $15–20 a/c; there is a pleasant café at the front. **Hai Van,** 115A Nguyen Thien Thuat St., tel. 58/825139, offers 14 rooms for $10 each.

Beachside Guesthouses: Huu Nghi Hotel, 3 Tran Hung Dao St., tel. 58/826703, fax 58/827416, maintains 65 rooms priced $10–23. **Rang Dong Hotel,** 18 Tran Hung Dao, tel. 58/822771, fax 58/824053, offers 25 rooms for $6–10. Westward at 5 Le Thanh Ton St. is **Nam Long Hotel,** tel. 58/827423, fax 58/824991, with 25 rooms for $12–22–25.

Naval Hotel (Hai Quan), 58 Tran Phu, tel. 58/822997, is a characterless block with 70 rooms charging $12–15–20. You can rent bicycles here.

Cat Trang Hotel (White Sand Hotel), 14 Tran Phu St., tel. 58/822896, fax 58/824204, is a modern villa with 20 rooms for $17–24. **Cat Trang II,** in the same area at 9 Yersin St., tel. 58/822896, has 25 rooms for $15–18–27; this place features a garden. **Thong Nhat,** 5 Yersin St., tel. 58/822966, fax 58/825221, has 55 rooms for $8–25 single or double, and some three- and four-bed rooms. Staff are helpful with rentals and travel arrangements. **Khach San 62,** at 62 Tran Phu, tel. 58/821395, has lots of character, lots of taxi girls. The hotel has 31 rooms—$6 d with fan, $8 t with fan, $10 s a/c, $14 for three people. A colonial–style villa restaurant near the gates serves food. At the southern end is **78 Guesthouse** (Nha Khach 78), at 78 Tran Phu, tel. 58/826342, offering 36 rooms for $8 fan, $12 a/c, and $15–25 superior. There are a few private minihotels tucked away in this vicinity, including **Thanh Binh minihotel,** 84 Tran Phu, tel. 58/825203, with six rooms for $10–20. Right next door are **Quang Vinh Hotel,** tel. 58/822536, with $10 rooms, and **Thanh Ngoc Hotel,** tel. 58/825194, with five rooms for $10–12.

$20–50

Beach, North End: The magnificent **Post Hotel** (Nha Khach Buu Dien), at 2 Le Loi St., tel. 58/821252, fax 58/824205, lies just a step away from the post office—very convenient for postcards. There are 20 rooms wired with satellite TV and IDD phones; they go for $26–28 for singles or doubles, $32–42 for triples and quadruples. **Thang Loi** (La Fregate), 4 Pasteur St., tel. 58/822241, fax 58/821905, features 55 rooms along with a 150-seat restaurant and 100-seat conference hall. Rooms range $20–30–38; some cheaper rooms available.

Beach, Midsection: The strip from the Duy Tan Hotel to Que Huong Hotel contains the greatest concentration of hotels. **Duy Tan Hotel,** at 24 Tran Phu, tel. 58/822671, fax 58/825034, is a Soviet–style blockhouse with 86 rooms for $25–50. A businessperson's hotel.

Vien Dong Hotel, 1 Tran Hung Dao, tel. 58/821606, fax 58/821912, has 103 rooms: 31 "third-class" rooms for $25–38; 66 rooms for $33–50; and some suites for $60–85. Vast grounds contain a small pool, deck chairs, tennis courts, and billiard tables—visitors are welcome.

Hai Yen Hotel, 40 Tran Phu, tel. 58/822828, fax 58/821902, has 107 rooms and good facilities, though furniture is somewhat sparse and drab. There are about 10 fan rooms for $6–12; 30 a/c rooms for $20–25; and first-class rooms for $30–44 with satellite TV; suites run $56–100 with sea views.

Grand Hotel, 44 Tran Phu, tel. 58/822445, fax 58/825395, offers 60 rooms. Several at the back cost $9–15, but most are $20–45, and deluxe suites run $70. The more expensive rooms—20 of them—are in a classic old French structure that may have once been an office building; cheaper rooms in outlying wings.

Khatoco Hotel, 9 Biet Thu St., tel. 58/823724, fax 58/821925, has 22 rooms for $30 s and $40 d; there are also two suites for $60 each. Rooms come equipped with phone, hot water, fridge, and a/c. The Khatoco is a modern building run by Khanh Hoa Tobacco Company. The hotel employs spiffy receptionists in yellow and white *ao dais* and runs its own cyclos.

Cau Da dock area: About three kilometers from central Nha Trang you'll find two upmarket hotels. **Maritime Hotel** (Hang Hai), 34 Tran Phu, tel. 58/821969, fax 58/821922, has 60 rooms for $25–40–60, and rents cars, bikes, and a motorboat. Disco on weekends.

A classic place to stay is **☒ Cau Da Villas,** tel. 58/822449, fax 58/821906. The five villas here sit among trees and shrubs on a small promontory with superb views of the South China Sea. The place was built in the 1920s as the summer romping ground of playboy Emperor Bao Dai. Today, it lies a bit derelict: Musty rooms go for $30; for a seaside view (windows!), it's $40–50 a room. The place is a short hop away from a private beach and tennis courts. Boat rentals available from a private marina.

$50–100

Nha Trang Lodge Hotel, 42 Tran Phu Blvd., tel. 58/810500, fax 58/828800, is a 14-story block with 121 rooms going for $50–75 standard, $95 superior, and $145 suite. Facilities include business center, restaurants, disco, and karaoke lounge. This is the shape of things to come on the waterfront as Nha Trang grows into a mini-Waikiki. **Que Huong Hotel,** 60 Tran Phu Blvd., tel. 58/825047, fax 58/825344, has 52 deluxe rooms for $50–60, and several suites for $85–100.

$100–200

Ana Mandara Resort, Tran Phu Boulevard, tel. 58/829829, fax 58/829629, is a French joint-venture resort that boasts 16 villas with a total of 68 rooms scattered over pristine beachfront. Doubles start at $140, and go from there through the roof to $300. Facilities include pool, tennis court, gym, and business center. An outdoor pavilion serves gourmet local dishes; boats can be hired for island excursions.

FOOD

Market Fare

Dam Market has superb fresh produce, with a number of food stalls at the back of the markets on the northeast side. This place is a feeding frenzy. For vegetarian stalls, look for Com Chay signs—you point at dishes of cauliflower, bean sprouts, or whatever else is in season, and assemble your meal. Meat dishes abound too, and you can buy excellent fresh fruit and fruit juices at the stalls. Here be dragons and durians—in February and March you can savor *thanh long,* or dragonfruit. This oval fruit is magenta, with a smooth skin sprouting green petals. Inside, the pulpy and translucent white flesh is scattered with thousands of black crunchy seeds. The succulent flesh is a good thirst-quencher in juices but rather bland if eaten alone. Much tastier is another bizarre fruit—the spiny soursop *(mang cau xiem),* a longish fruit with a spiky, dark green exterior and a milky interior.

Restaurants

Seafood, naturally, is the specialty of Nha Trang. Seafood platters with squid, shrimp, lobster, and fish are available for quite reasonable prices. Near Dam Market is **Lac Canh,** at 11 Hang Ca, tel. 58/821391. It's always crowded, with lots of beggars hanging around the outdoor seating. Meat and seafood dishes are served; you can cook at the table with charcoal braziers. Try the delicious tuna steaks. **Thanh Lich,** around the corner at 8 Phan Boi Chau, tel. 58/821955, features similar fare and fewer beggars.

The area around the markets is full of excellent restaurants. **Hoan Hai,** at 6 Phan Chu Trinh, tel. 58/823133, serves delicious marinated beef, vegetarian dishes with tofu, and possibly the best spring rolls in Nha Trang. At **Ninh Hoa Nem** restaurant, you can roll your own food. There are only two dishes here—pork and beef *nem,* and the waitress and other customers will gladly instruct you on the correct etiquette.

Also in the area is **Thuy Trang Seafood,**

at 9A Le Loi, near Thang Loi Hotel. **Vietnam Restaurant,** 23 Hoang Van Thu, tel. 58/822933, is popular with travelers and serves a great hot and sour fish soup. **Thanh The Restaurant,** at 3 Phan Chu Trinh St., tel. 58/821931, serves seafood and Vietnamese dishes, as well as Western fare. Two other places to try in the neighborhood are **Van Canh Restaurant** and **Coco Vert Restaurant.**

At 64 Hoang Van Thu St., **Binh Minh,** tel. 58/821861, serves good food at reasonable prices. Almost right opposite is **Lys,** 117A Hoang Van Thu, tel. 58/822006. If you fancy swallow saliva, you can order swallow-nest soup for $10 at Lys or Binh Minh. Across town at **Khatoco Hotel Restaurant,** swallow-nest soup costs $25; another specialty served in this classy venue is braised sea cucumber.

Pizza has hit the beach in Nha Trang. For fine beachside dining, go to **Casa Italia,** right at the southern end of Tran Phu Boulevard, near Ana Mandara Resort, tel. 58/828964. The restaurant is run by an Italian and features a large menu of pizza, pasta, and steak. There's seating both indoors and under pine trees near the beach.

Cafés

At the intersection of Yersin and Nguyen Trai streets, several juice-bar cafés sell delicious concoctions of crushed fruit, ice, sugar, and condensed milk—called *sinh to* in Vietnamese. The cafés are called **Banana Split 58** and **Banana Split 60.** These two have some kind of turf war going on and try to poach customers (try standing right between the two cafés!). The places have identical menus, identical food, and identical signs out front—and they're both open until well into the evening. Among the exotic fruit offerings are jackfruit, soursop, sapodilla, star apple, custard apple, and dragonfruit. You can also sample durian or coconut ice cream, banana splits, and fresh yogurt. The cafés are great for snacks and breakfast, serving bread and cheese, good coffee, and Lipton tea. Sit back and watch the ice-cream wars rage.

Nha Trang includes a sprinkling of seaside cafés. Opposite the Hai Yen Hotel is **Four Sea-**sons Café** and **Coconut Cove Resort.** Others along this strip serve seafood, snacks, and beer, but the best place to lounge and soak up the sun is **Nha Trang Sailing Club,** at 74 Tran Phu Blvd., tel. 58/826528, a bar-restaurant with a back terrace—about the only café with beach-compatible architecture and good beach views. Alfresco dining in wicker chairs on the deck is the key attraction. This place fills the nightlife void in Nha Trang, so it's popular with round-eyes late at night, sometimes staying open till 0400 hours.

SHOPPING

Down by the Cau Da dock area lurk vendors of shell and coral items. These include shell jewelry and grotesque kitschy shell collages. There is a large souvenir shop on Tran Phu Boulevard, almost opposite Nha Khach 24, selling lacquerware and pieces inlaid with mother-of-pearl. If you wish to encourage the destruction of coral reefs, there are pieces fashioned from coral. Numerous items made of shell are also found here. Some may be fashioned with shells washed up on the beach, but many more are likely harvested from the sea—the creatures inhabiting them are destroyed in the process. All species of sea turtle are highly endangered.

SERVICES AND INFORMATION

Traveler Cafés

Hanh Café at 5 Tran Hung Dao, tel. 58/827814, is a good place to bump into fellow travelers. The café arranges bicycle and motorcycle rentals, boat trips to the islands, and minibus transport to Saigon, Dalat, and Hué. They work with Kim Café in Saigon. At **Thao Café,** 46 Le Thanh Ton, tel. 58/823772, you can get breakfast, a motorcycle rental, or minibus service to the highlands or Saigon.

Tour Agents

A number of places will assist with Nha Trang boat rides, traveler minibuses to Dalat, buses up and down the coast, and so on. They can also organize tours to the Central Highlands—

you must put together your own group of 6–8 passengers for a minibus tour of, say, four days and three nights for $40–50 a head. Apart from Hanh Café and Thao Café, here are some agents: **My A Tour,** at 10 Hung Vuong, tel. 58/826195, has connections with Sinh Café in Saigon and offers a wide selection of booking services. **Nam Long Tour,** 52 Tran Phu Blvd., tel. 58/824494, offers boat trips and visa services.

Tourist Information

Khanh Hoa Tourism, tel. 58/822753, fax 58/821912, is the provincial tourist authority; the office is on Le Thanh Ton Street near the gates of Vien Dong Hotel. The organization runs a lot of hotels in Nha Trang, such as the Vien Dong, Hai Yen, Thong Nhat, and Thang Loi. Staff can arrange vehicle rentals—$25 a day for a car, $30 for a minibus. Guides cost $10 a day. The Hai Yen hotel sells sheet maps of Nha Trang, as do other hotels, but the maps are most likely out of date.

Hoang Yen Tourism, 26 Tran Phu, tel. 58/822961, offers boat trips, guides, transport, and long-distance minibuses for groups of 8–10 people. Like Saigon, Nha Trang has an official information line—dial 108 for info on rail and air travel, car rentals, and cultural and sporting events. Sounds too good to be true? The hot line will even arrange a wake-up call.

Services

Vietcombank, 17 Quang Trung St., will change major currencies in cash or traveler's checks. The main **post office** is at the north end of Nha Trang on Le Loi Street. The **fax and phone center** is a few kilometers south at 50 Le Thanh Ton St., half a block from the beach. For **TNT Express** courier service, call tel. 58/821043. Nha Trang area code is 58.

Visa Extensions

Agents can handle visa extensions—$20 for a one-month extension through Thong Nhat Hotel. A one-week extension costs $15. Extensions usually require a day to process.

GETTING THERE AND AWAY

By Air

There are six flights a week from Nha Trang to Ho Chi Minh City ($60), four flights a week to Hanoi ($130), and sometimes a flight to Danang ($50). Nha Trang Airport is right near the beach. Vietnam Airlines office in Nha Trang is at 86 Tran Phu St., tel. 58/821147. There's another airline booking office at 12B Hoa Tam, tel. 58/823797.

By Rail

Nha Trang to Saigon on CM6 or CM7 train is $17 soft seat, $23–27 hard sleeper, and $30 soft sleeper. Nha Trang to Hanoi on the same trains costs $50 soft seat, $70–80 hard sleeper, and $95 soft sleeper. The CM6 express has no hard seats—it's the most expensive Reunification Express train; other trains are cheaper.

By Bus

Nha Trang is on the Saigon-to-Hué traveler minibus and bus route. It's easy to sign up for transport with private operators, who will pick you up at your hotel. Sign up at least a day before your intended departure. Some private minibus transport originates in Nha Trang. From Hanh Café, for instance, you can arrange a ride to Dalat or to Hoi An. If you can rustle up a few people, you can arrange your own itinerary through the Central Highlands on the route to Hué. Nha Trang to Hoi An/Hué is around $20 a head, taking 12 hours; to Dalat $8, five hours; to Saigon $15–18, 10–11 hours.

Lien Tinh Express bus station is on the west side of Nha Trang near Long Son Pagoda. Crack-of-dawn departures head north to Qui Nhon, Quang Ngai, Danang, Hué, Vinh, Hanoi; to Central Highlands destinations Buon Ma Thuot and Pleiku; and south to Dalat, Phan Rang, and Saigon. There's an advance bus booking office on Le Thanh Ton, near Vien Dong Hotel. You can also buy advance tickets through a hotel travel agent. If you want to catch a bus later in the day, head out to Highway 1 and flag down a passing express bus. You can take a moto or lambro to

SAIGON–NHA TRANG BIKE ROUTE

This round-trip route, including rest days in Dalat and Nha Trang, takes about 15 days, with five days for each leg of the route. If you want to dawdle, take longer rest stops and allow 20 days for the route. On a motorcycle, the route can easily be accomplished in half the time.

Saigon–Dalat Leg

On this route, from Saigon it's 60 kilometers to Dau Giay, a further 90 kilometers to Suoi Thien, then 38 kilometers to Bao Loc, and a final 119 kilometers to Dalat. To avoid heavy traffic out of Saigon and to avoid getting lost, try to have a travel agency or traveler café take you and your bicycle by minibus the 60 kilometers to Dau Giay, the junction of Highway 1 and Route 20. From here, ride 90 kilometers to **Suoi Thien,** where you can stay at **Suoi Tien Guesthouse,** run by Saigon Tourism, for $6 bungalow, $10 d, or $25 for a four-bed room. Suoi Tien to Bao Loc is only 38 kilometers but mostly uphill with a steep grade. In **Bao Loc,** stay at **Seri Hotel,** $35 a room; or **Bao Loc Hotel,** $10 with fan. Bao Loc to Dalat is 119 kilometers. Start early—it's a long ride with great views. The undulating terrain rises from Bao Loc at 850 meters to Di Linh at 1,010 meters; it's a little steeper from Di Linh to Dalat at 1,475 meters. The last 10 kilometers or so is straight up. Rest in Dalat—there are some great bike rides in the vicinity.

Dalat–Nha Trang Leg

From Dalat it's 116 kilometers to Phan Rang, and a further 110 kilometers to Nha Trang. From there you can backtrack to Phan Rang. From Dalat center, follow Hung Vuong Road out of town to the east. This road, actually Route 20, is not used by cars because it's potholed and in poor shape, but that's less of a problem for cyclists; the lack of motor traffic makes the ride pleasant. Dalat to Phan Rang is 116 kilometers downhill on winding mountain roads, with spectacular scenery. Stay at **Ninh Chu Beach,** six kilometers northeast of at Phan Rang, instead of Phan Rang. Phan Rang to Nha Trang is 110 kilometers, with no stop permitted in Cam Ranh Bay. With a headwind, the ride takes maybe 10 hours, with a tailwind seven hours—you'll get one or the other depending on the season. After a rest in Nha Trang, take the same route back to Phan Rang. If short of time, cut Nha Trang out of the itinerary.

Phan Rang–Saigon Leg

From Phan Rang it's 42 kilometers to Cana Beach, a further 123 kilometers to Phan Thiet, then 120 kilometers to Long Khan, and a final 78 kilometers to Saigon. In Cana Beach, stay at **Khach San Cana,** $10 double, $15 for three; or **Haison Hotel,** $10 for two. In Phan Thiet, try **Phan Thiet Hotel,** $17–20, no hot water; or **Vinh Thuy Hotel,** $26–36. Cyclists will be pleased to know the coastal strip from Phan Rang to Phan Thiet is one of the most arid regions in Vietnam. The next leg is Phan Thiet to Long Khan, 120 kilometers inland near Xuan Loc. Stay at **Hotel Hoa Binh,** $20 double. The last 78 kilometers into Ho Chi Minh City is very busy with traffic; if it becomes a problem, flag down a passing bus and load your bike onto the roof.

Highway 1. Go to Dien Khanh, seven kilometers to the west if headed for Dalat or Saigon; or Luong Son, eight kilometers north of Nha Trang if traveling north. Three-wheel lambros operate as shuttles to these Highway 1 junctions, connecting to Dam Market. A bit north of Dam Market on 2 Thang 4 St. is a local bus station with battered Renault vans that run to destinations mostly within 100 kilometers of Nha Trang—about all a Renault engine can take without overheating.

GETTING AROUND

The easiest way of getting around Nha Trang is by rented bicycle. Motos and cyclos patrol the streets. Cyclo drivers can be on the aggressive side—their radar picks you up, they lock on, and relentlessly pursue you down the street.

Car Rentals: A number of places rent cars and minibuses—four-, eight-, 12-, or 24-seat vehicles—for $25 and up. Hotels can arrange this transport too.

Motorcycle and Bicycle Rentals: A number of bicycle and motorcycle rental operators can be found around Hai Yen and Vien Dong hotels, along Tran Phu, Le Thanh Ton, and Tran Hung Dao boulevards. Bicycles can be rented for $1 a day; motorcycles cost $5 for 50cc, $7 for 70cc, and $10 for 125cc models. Rent a car, motorcycle, or bicycle on Tran Hung Dao near Hung Dao Hotel; around the corner next to the tourist office on Le Thanh Ton is a motorcycle and bicycle rental outlet; the Vien Dong and Hai Yen Hotels also rent bicycles. Farther north on Tran Phu Boulevard, there's a bicycle and motorcycle rental place opposite Thuy Duong Hotel; Hoang Yen Tourism and Thong Nhat Hotel both rent bicycles for $1 a day.

Taxis: Several companies prowl the streets, including Khanh Hoa Taxi, tel. 58/810810, Nha Trang Taxi, and Vietcombank Taxi Company.

South of Nha Trang

CAM RANH BAY

Up until the early 1990s, 20–30 Russian warships, including submarines and an aircraft carrier, were based at Cam Ranh Bay. The two U.S.-made runways were home to 40 naval and military aircraft, including Tu-95 naval reconnaissance aircraft and a squadron of MiG-23 fighters. About 7,000 Russian sailors and their dependents called Cam Ranh home, though it never developed the raucous atmosphere once associated with the American naval bases in the Philippines.

After the Americans pulled out of the Philippines, the Russians began to pack up and leave Cam Ranh Bay, and, in 1992, the Russian press reported that the last major battleship had sailed back to Vladivostok. However, in 1993 a Russian guided missile cruiser was sighted in the South China Sea. The Russians admitted the cruiser was indeed stationed at Cam Ranh Bay, claiming it was required to protect Russian merchant ships from pirates. Vietnam probably wants Russian cruisers in the area to deflect Chinese claims of sovereignty to the Spratly Islands and to ensure security for joint Russian-Vietnamese oil and gas explorations off the coast. There is a large signal intelligence station at Cam Ranh capable of monitoring the movements of the Chinese South Sea Fleet. The Russian Cam Ranh agreement with Vietnam was effective until 2000.

PHAN RANG

Phan Rang is hell on wheels—noisy, dirty, unpleasant. It's strung out along Highway 1, with trucks and buses barreling through day and night, spraying everything with dust and diesel fumes as drivers hit their air horns. In the midst of all this is a busy market, with a temple to one side. The 100-year-old temple has a pink exterior and bright red interior and is dedicated to the deified Chinese General Quan Cong. A statue of black-bearded Quan Cong sits at the back of the temple; lining the way to

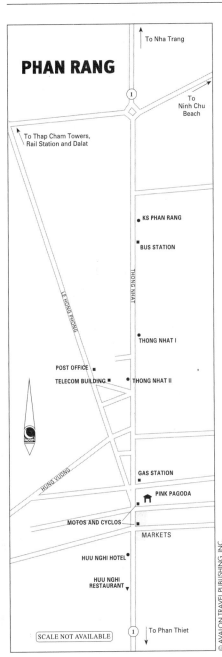

PHAN RANG

To Nha Trang

To Ninh Chu Beach

To Thap Cham Towers, Rail Station and Dalat

KS PHAN RANG

BUS STATION

THONG NHAT

LE HONG PHONG

THONG NHAT I

POST OFFICE
TELECOM BUILDING

THONG NHAT II

HUNG VUONG

GAS STATION

PINK PAGODA

MOTOS AND CYCLOS

MARKETS

HUU NGHI HOTEL

HUU NGHI RESTAURANT

SCALE NOT AVAILABLE

To Phan Thiet

© AVALON TRAVEL PUBLISHING, INC.

the altar are Quan Cong's weapons, mounted on long poles. The main sight of Phan Rang, **Thap Cham Towers,** is six kilometers to the northwest; an equal distance to the east is **Ninh Chu Beach.**

Accommodations

Hotels line Highway 1, most run by Ninh Thuan Tourism. Don't expect anything fancy; try to get rooms away from the highway. At the south end of town is **Huu Nghi Hotel,** 354 Thong Nhat, tel. 68/822606, a three-story hotel with 21 rooms, half of them $10 double, the rest $12–24. **Thong Nhat II,** at 194 Thong Nhat, tel. 68/822942, features seven rooms for $6 s or $8 d. **Thong Nhat I,** tel. 68/825406, just up the street at 99 Thong Nhat, is a four-story building with doubles for $33–40. **Khach San Phan Rang,** 13 Thong Nhat, near the bus station, tel. 68/823057, has 17 rooms—$4 s or $9 d; triples available. **Ninh Thuan Hotel,** 1 Le Hong Phong St., tel. 68/827100, has 24 rooms for $20–40 with satellite TV.

Food

Eateries are along the main drag, Thong Nhat. There are a few others on Le Hong Phong, such as **Quan An** restaurant at number 18. The second-floor dining room at **Huu Nghi Restaurant,** about 100 meters south of Huu Nghi Hotel on Thong Nhat, is the best in town, serving such delicacies as wild boar tongue, calf heart, grilled sparrow, and grilled mud fish. If those don't turn your crank, choose from regular fare such as chicken and beef. A specialty on the menu is gecko *(dông)*—eaten raw with vegetables, grilled, or roasted with green mango. Gecko is a popular specialty in Phan Rang restaurants. The lizards are dipped in batter and pan-fried, or sliced into slivers and served with a green mango salad. Escher-like piles of squirming geckos are sold by the kilo at Phan Rang's market.

Transportation

Highway 1 passes right through town. Phan Rang bus station is at the north end of town. The train station is six kilometers out on the

Dalat Road at Thap Cham. You can find motos and cyclos around Phan Rang bus station and close to the market.

VICINITY OF PHAN RANG
Thap Cham Towers

Thap Cham Towers (Po Klong Garai) consists of three towers and a brick platform from the 13th century. The towers are a mix of old lichen-covered brick and brand-new graffiti-covered brick; despite the rebricking and concrete ornaments, the site is impressive. The two smaller towers have nothing inside. The largest tower houses bats and features a lintel supporting a dancing six-armed Shiva, guardian deity of the site. The door to this tower may be locked—if so, ask the gatekeeper for the keys. Inside is a small Nandin, or bull statue: On ceremonial occasions, Cham descendants offer herbs to this statue. Farther in you'll find a *mukha*-lingas altar (stylized phallus, symbol of Shiva the Creator) under a conical parasol, surrounded by a wooden frame. The face painted on the lingas represents the head of Shiva; the setting in a yoni base allows water to drain away in ceremonies. Cham living in the Phan Rang area and around the province hold an annual festival at these towers.

From the towers there are commanding views over the entire valley. If you look past the entrance booth for the towers, you can see extensive rail yards with hangarlike buildings. Thap Cham was a strategic base for the French and heavily defended as the junction of the north-south line and the line to Dalat. The railway from Thap Cham to Dalat operated 1930–1964, when it was shut down by Vietcong attacks. The French line used a *crémaillère* (pothook) system of switchbacks. Though the Dalat station still exists and the track is good for about 15 kilometers out of Dalat, there are at present no plans to reinstate the service.

Thap Cham Towers are six kilometers from Phan Rang, on the Dalat Road, near Thap Cham rail station. You can visit Thap Cham en route to or from Dalat if you have your own transportation; otherwise, if leaving Phan Rang, get a moto to drop you at the towers, then flag down a vehicle heading to Dalat. If arriving by rail on the route to or from Saigon, you can exit at Thap Cham station, walk over to the ruins, and then board another train. To reach Thap Cham Towers by road from Phan Rang, take the Dalat Road until you cross the railway tracks; close by is a six-kilometer marker stone. Turn right after the stone and you'll see the towers about 400 meters away on a cactus-covered hilltop.

Other Cham towers in the Phan Rang vicinity are in very poor condition. **Thap Po Rome** is about 15 kilometers southwest of Phan Rang—named after the last king of Champa, who ruled in the 17th century. Another group of decayed towers called **Hoa Lai** (Yan Bakran) lie 16 kilometers north of Phan Rang, off the road to Nha Trang. Some Cham descendants live in the village of **Tuan Tu,** about five kilometers south of Phan Rang. The men wear white turbans with red tassels hanging over the ears and a white costume; the women wear head-scarves. There are intermittent Cham festivals in the Phan Rang area, centering around Thap Cham Towers.

Ninh Chu Beach

The ride out to Ninh Chu Beach, about six kilometers from Phan Rang, is well worth it. On the way you'll see lots of rice paddies, grape trellises, cacti hedgerows, and salt pans. Set back from the beach is a hill with large rock formations and several small temples. The beach is fringed with coniferous trees, not palms, an indicator of the region's aridity. Ninh Chu features a long, narrow, white-sand beach and a fishing village with basket boats *(thung chai).*

There are two hotels in the area. The three-story **Huong Bien Hotel,** tel. 68/823216, is in the middle of nowhere, 1.5 kilometers back from the beach on the road to Phan Rang. The 18 rooms run $20 each; there may be cheaper deals. A better place, **Ninh Chu Hotel,** tel. 68/823823, sits on the beach and features bungalows and a café-restaurant with outdoor tables and umbrellas; there are also a few beach huts to recline under. Five concrete bungalows with corrugated roofs and balconies stand nearby; there are two sides to each bungalow, so a total of 10 units are available, costing $16 d or $17 t. Plans were in the works for a four-story hotel at Ninh Chu.

CANA BEACH

About 35 kilometers south of Phan Rang, and 123 kilometers north of Phan Thiet, lies Cana Beach, a great stretch of white sand strewn with boulders. The water is a beautiful turquoise; onshore, the area has been colonized by prickly pear cacti. **Haison Hotel,** tel. 68/864589, has doubles for $10. **Khach San Cana,** tel. 68/864554, is $10 d and $15 t; taxi girls hang around the hotel. Both hotels include bland but adequate restaurants.

PHAN THIET

Phan Thiet is an old Cham outpost of 75,000 people that supports a large fishing fleet and is famous for *nuoc mam,* or fish sauce. The un-pleasant smell of fish and fish sauce permeates the downtown area, since the Phan Thiet River cutting through the center of town is packed with boats. Phan Thiet has a beachfront a few kilometers to the east of town, but a bigger draw is the sand dunes at Mui Ne Beach, 22 ki-lometers east of town. Local buses ply the route during the day from Phan Thiet bus station. There are half a dozen places to stay in town, not all receptive to foreign faces. **Phan Thiet Hotel,** at 40 Tran Hung Dao, tel. 62/821694, costs $17–20 a room; no hot water. Toward the seashore is the more isolated **Vinh Thuy Hotel,** tel. 62/822394, with more than 60 a/c rooms in the $26–36 range. Phan Thiet lies right off Highway 1, almost 200 kilometers from Saigon. The nearest train station is at Muong Man, 12 kilometers to the west.

Because of its relative proximity to Saigon, Phan Thiet has been "developed," with major money poured into the Ocean Dunes Golf Club and high-end beach resorts. Closer to town is **Pansea Beach Resort,** with 50 bungalows, res-taurant, pool, and fitness center; recreational

activities include sailboarding, snorkeling, and golf. About 12 kilometers outside Phan Thiet on a secluded beach is **Coco Beach Resort,** with bungalows built in traditional style and outfitted with minority handicrafts—from bedspreads to wall hangings; the hotel offers water sports and a pool. And nine kilometers outside Phan Thiet is **Victoria Phan Thiet Resort,** tel. 62/847171, with 50 thatch-roofed bungalows set in tropical gardens. Rates are more than $100 for bungalows in low season; $140–180 for bungalows in high season; and $220 for a family villa.

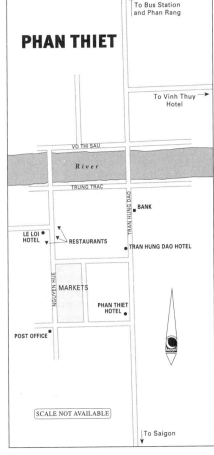

PHAN THIET

To Bus Station and Phan Rang

To Vinh Thuy Hotel

VO THI SAU

River

TRUNG TRAC

BANK

LE LOI HOTEL

RESTAURANTS

TRAN HUNG DAO HOTEL

NGUYEN HUE

MARKETS

PHAN THIET HOTEL

POST OFFICE

SCALE NOT AVAILABLE

To Saigon

Central Vietnam

⋈ MUI NE BEACH

From simple fishing village to tourist hotspot—Mui Ne has developed into a major stepping stone on the coastal route from Saigon to Hué. Lying 22 km east from Phan Thiet, Mui Ne is essentially a string of resorts along the beachfront. Sand, sand, and more sand. After lazing on the sand, you can tackle its sand dunes, a few kilometers away—the biggest in the country. As the sand can get hot, it's best to climb early or late in the day. You can indulge in sand-sledding here. Partially protected by the dunes, Mui Ne sees a lot less rainfall than Phan Thiet. Between August and April, the wind whips up the waves—attracting surfers. Several operators offer sailboarding and kite-surfing rentals.

There is some budget accommodation at Mui Ne in the form of family-run guesthouses, offering rooms for around $10–15. But most accommodation here falls in the midrange and luxury category. Stylish places such as **Mui Ne Sailing Club, Blue Ocean Resort,** and **Bamboo Village Beach Resort** charge $40 and up for a room or bungalow. Some have beachfront restaurants, a garden and pool area, and a whirlpool tub. High-end resorts charging $80 and up include **Seahorse Resort** and **Sanctuary Resort.**

Dalat

Dalat is an entire French town—railway station, cathedral, schools, shops, villas—plunked down in the Vietnamese highlands. With its pine forests, rolling hills, and tranquil lakes, the area could pass for anyplace in France—which explains its appeal to the French.

At 1,475 meters in elevation, Dalat provides a cool respite from the heat. In 1897 the first explorer of the area, Alexandre Yersin, recommended this French settlement as a retreat for those suffering from the tropical climate of the lowlands. Governor Paul Doumer established a research center for agriculture and meteorology. Within 15 years, the town was established; in 1933 it was linked by rail to the coast. Land grants were made to French, Chinese, and Vietnamese to develop the area. Tea, coffee, and rubber plantations flourished, along with intense vegetable cultivation. By the 1940s the hill station of Dalat was slated to become the administrative nerve center for the whole of French Indochina and was called Le Petit Paris. Building in Dalat continued during World War II after Vichy-appointed Governor-general Jean Decoux concluded an agreement accepting the presence of Japanese troops in Vietnam. In March 1945 the Japanese learned of Decoux's tardy plans to rebel and overthrew him, imprisoning his administrators and troops. At the conclusion of the war, Indochina fell into turmoil.

Dalat is now a resort town, a favorite with honeymooners and droves of tourists tramping through the former French villas. The Vietnamese wax poetic about Dalat and rave on in awestruck detail about every waterfall and valley, but in fact the scenery is nothing special. The deforestation around Dalat doesn't say much for wilderness conservation, and neither do the stuffed animals parked at various scenic spots. If you're looking for a place to exercise your lungs, however, the hills around Dalat are great for hiking, biking, or breathing in that pine-scented air. Or shoot a few rounds of golf. Dalat market has excellent and varied fresh produce, which means dining out in Dalat is great. It's a good spot to rest up for a few days and stretch those muscles atrophied from minibus rides.

Dalat is not known for clement weather. It's in the mountains, so rain could put a damper on your visit.

Getting Your Bearings

Dalat centers on Xuan Huong Lake, with the downtown area at the northwest side and exclusive villas on the south side. The heart of downtown Dalat is Hoa Binh Square, adjacent

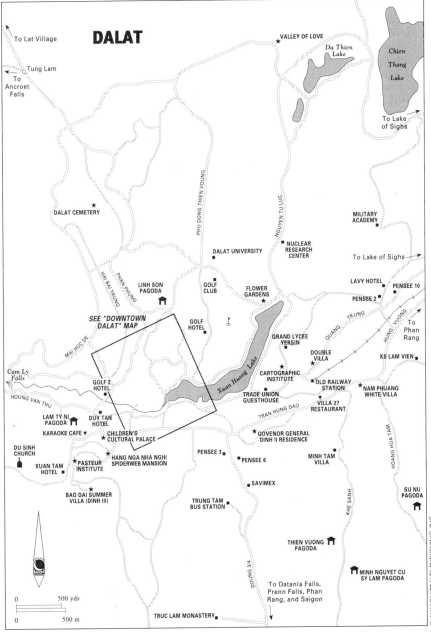

DALAT

To Lat Village

Tung Lam
To
Ancroet
Falls

VALLEY OF LOVE

Da Thien
Lake

Chien
Thang
Lake

To Lake
of Sighs

DALAT CEMETERY

MILITARY
ACADEMY

PHU DONG THIEN VUONG

DALAT UNIVERSITY

NGUYEN TU LUC

NUCLEAR
RESEARCH
CENTER

To Lake of Sighs

PHAN PHUNG

MAI BAI TRUNG

LINH SON
PAGODA

GOLF
CLUB

FLOWER
GARDENS

LAVY HOTEL

PENSEE 10

PENSEE 2

SEE "DOWNTOWN
DALAT" MAP

MAI HOC DE

GOLF
HOTEL

GRAND LYCEE
YERSIN

QUANG   TRUNG

HUNG VUONG

To
Phan
Rang

Cam Ly
Falls

Xuan Huong Lake

DOUBLE
VILLA

KS LAM VIEN

GOLF 2
HOTEL

CARTOGRAPHIC
INSTITUTE

OLD RAILWAY
STATION

NAM PHUANG
WHITE VILLA

HOUNG VAN THU

TRADE UNION
GUESTHOUSE

TRAN HUNG DAO

VILLA 27
RESTAURANT

LAM TY NI
PAGODA

DUY TAN
HOTEL

KARAOKE CAFE

CHILDREN'S
CULTURAL PALACE

GOVENOR GENERAL
DINH II RESIDENCE

HOANG HOA TAM

DU SINH
CHURCH

HANG NGA NHA NGHI
SPIDERWEB MANSION

PENSEE 3

PENSEE 6

MINH TAM
VILLA

XUAN TAM
HOTEL

PASTEUR
INSTITUTE

SAVIMEX

SU NU
PAGODA

BAO DAI SUMMER
VILLA (DINH III)

TRUNG TAM
BUS STATION

KHE SANH

THIEN VUONG
PAGODA

MINH NGUYET CU
SY LAM PAGODA

DOUNG 3/4

To Datanla Falls,
Prenn Falls, Phan
Rang, and Saigon

0   500 yds

0   500 m

TRUC LAM MONASTERY

© AVALON TRAVEL PUBLISHING, INC.

Central Vietnam

to the cinema; steps lead down from here to the Central Market. Motos, taxis, and lambros cluster round the top or bottom of the steps. With its narrow alleys and hilly streets, downtown Dalat is best negotiated on foot. However, if going around the south side of the lake, a bicycle or moto is desirable. A classic navigation landmark on the south side is the mini-Eiffel—the telecommunications tower near the post office.

Dalat features some long-winded street names. There's Duong 3 Thang 4, or Duong 3/4, which runs south of Dalat and turns into Highway 20. The figure 3/4 refers to April 3, 1975, the date of the Liberation of Dalat by NVA forces. The cinema is called Rap Chieu Bong 3/4. Leading off the cinema is a street called Duong 3 Thang 2, referring to the February anniversary of the 1930 founding of the Communist Party.

To really get into Dalat, you have to get out of it—get above it all into the pine forests, with great views and classic villas. The two recommended tours are best done by bicycle, motorcycle, or moto with some walking involved. (See the sidebars, *Dalat Zen Tour* and *Dalat Villa Tour*.) You can complete both tours in one long day, back-to-back, but they're better attempted on separate days. Actual cycling and walking time for each tour is around 1.5 hours, so allow at least three hours with stops to complete each tour.

SIGHTS

Bao Dai Summer Villa

Past the Pasteur Institute lies Dinh III, or Bao Dai Summer Villa. The 1930s villa is set in beautiful grounds, with gardens and views. The 25-room villa was the private residence of Bao Dai, the last emperor of Vietnam, who abdicated in 1945. Inside were rooms reserved for Empress Nam Phuong, Prince Bao Long, and Princess Phuong Mai. You can see photos of them on the walls, plus remaining pieces of family furniture. Upstairs, in the royal living quarters decorated with bright yellow, is a large couch used by the emperor and empress

for consultations with their three daughters and two sons.

Bao Dai was born in 1913 and was crowned in 1925 after the death of his father, Emperor Khai Dinh. Groomed by the French as the puppet emperor of Vietnam, Bao Dai was dispatched to Paris for an education, where he acquired a fondness for French girls and tennis. Back in Vietnam in 1935, the playboy emperor spent his time in leisure pursuits—chiefly chasing women and hunting—oblivious to the intrigues of the Vietminh. His main palace was in Hué, but he kept villas in various parts of the country. He came to Dalat to hunt, play tennis, fish, and ride horses.

Bao Dai abdicated in 1945 at the request of the Vietminh, allowing Ho Chi Minh to be crowned new "emperor." In 1946, Bao Dai fled to Hong Kong. When the French attempted to regain control of Vietnam after the war, they required Bao Dai to resume his imperial duties, but he fled instead to Europe, shifting from city to city, hiding in cinemas by day and cabarets by night. Comically, Bao Dai was eventually found and returned to Vietnam in 1948, but he quickly slipped back to Europe, claiming he would not wear the crown until true unity and independence prevailed in Vietnam. In 1952, it was said Bao Dai received an official stipend of $4 million a year, much of it squirreled away in Swiss bank accounts as insurance against hard times ahead. By the time of the 1954 Geneva Conference, Bao Dai lived in permanent exile in a luxurious Cannes château with his wife and five children. He kept a Vietnamese mistress in Paris and maintained a steady diet of French courtesans. Much of his time was spent at casinos in Monte Carlo, where he squandered extravagant sums of money. He never returned to Vietnam: He died in Paris in 1997.

After a lengthy rash of anti-Bao Dai propaganda, there's now a documentary video on sale in Dalat about the life of the emperor, titled *Riding You to the Palace*. It was produced by Saigon Films for Dalat's centennial. In the communist era, it's odd that this video should be subtitled, *A Sketch of an Unforgettable Epoch of Our History*.

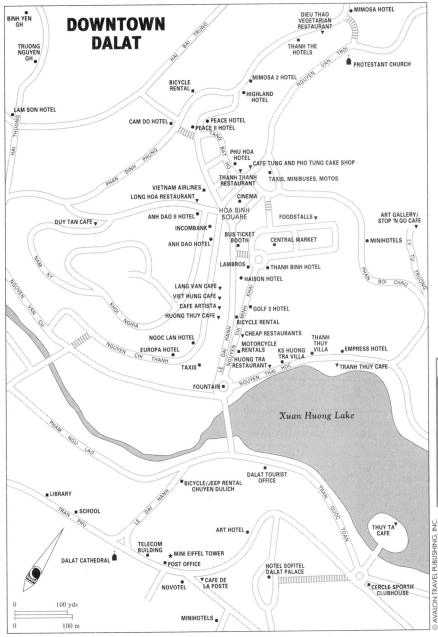

DOWNTOWN DALAT

BINH YEN GH

TRUONG NGUYEN GH

DIEU THAO VEGETARIAN RESTAURANT

MIMOSA HOTEL

THANH THE HOTELS

PROTESTANT CHURCH

HAI BA TRUNG

NGUYEN VAN TROI

MIMOSA 2 HOTEL

BICYCLE RENTAL

HIGHLAND HOTEL

LAM SON HOTEL

CAM DO HOTEL

PEACE HOTEL
PEACE II HOTEL

PHU HOA HOTEL

CAFE TUNG AND PHO TUNG CAKE SHOP

TAXIS, MINIBUSES, MOTOS

HAI THUONG

PHAN DINH PHUNG

TANG BAT HO

THANH THANH RESTAURANT

VIETNAM AIRLINES
LONG HOA RESTAURANT

CINEMA

DUY TAN CAFE

ANH DAO II HOTEL

HOA BINH SQUARE

FOODSTALLS

ART GALLERY/ STOP 'N GO CAFE

INCOMBANK

BUS TICKET BOOTH

CENTRAL MARKET

MINIHOTELS

LY TU TRUONG

ANH DAO HOTEL

NAM KY

LAMBROS

THANH BINH HOTEL

PHAN BOI CHAU

KHOI NGHIA

HAISON HOTEL

LANG VAN CAFE
VIET HUNG CAFE
CAFE ARTISTA
HUONG THUY CAFE

GOLF 3 HOTEL

BICYCLE RENTAL

NGUYEN VAN CU

NGOC LAN HOTEL

CHEAP RESTAURANTS

THANH THUY VILLA

NGUYEN CHI THANH

EUROPA HOTEL

TAXIS

MOTORCYCLE RENTALS

KS HUONG TRA VILLA

EMPRESS HOTEL

LE DAI HANH

NGUYEN THI MINH KHAI

HUONG TRA RESTAURANT

NGUYEN THAI HOC

TRANH THUY CAFE

FOUNTAIN

Xuan Huong Lake

PHAM NGU LAO

DALAT TOURIST OFFICE

BICYCLE/JEEP RENTAL CHUYEN DULICH

LIBRARY

TRAN PHU

SCHOOL

LE DAI HANH

TRAN QUOC TOAN

THUY TA CAFE

ART HOTEL

DALAT CATHEDRAL

TELECOM BUILDING

MINI EIFFEL TOWER

POST OFFICE

HOTEL SOFITEL DALAT PALACE

CERCLE SPORTIF CLUBHOUSE

NOVOTEL

CAFE DE LA POSTE

MINIHOTELS

0   100 yds
0   100 m

Central Vietnam

© AVALON TRAVEL PUBLISHING, INC.

DALAT ZEN TOUR

Apart from a surfeit of French villas, the Vietnamese also inherited a taste for French bread—and poetry and art. As one Vietnamese source phrased it, "The Americans left us Coke, but the French left us poetry." Hanoi and Saigon dominate the art market in Vietnam, but it's towns such as Dalat and Hué that are said to inspire the best poetry. So put on your beret, hop on your bike, tuck a baguette under your arm, and set off in search of inspiration.

Starting point for this tour is the Eiffel Tower—the telecommunications tower on the south side of the lake. The mini-Eiffel was completed in 1995 and flies the red flag. Proceed past a traffic island with a statue of Jesus holding a lamb. If the door's open, it's worth looking inside **Dalat Cathedral** at the stained-glass windows imported from Grenoble and woodcarvings of the crucifixion. The cathedral was completed in 1942. Services are held at 0530 and 1700 daily, and at 0530, 0700, and 1600 on Sunday.

This neck of the woods is Catholic Corner, what with the cathedral, Jesus statue, and the former St. Paul of Nazareth School. Dalat at one time was home to three churches, a seminary, two convents, and Catholic schools. An unusual educational facility was the Eau de Vie, a religious order of reformed French prostitutes who set out to reform other prostitutes around the world. Apart from the French influence, Catholicism was bolstered here by an influx of North Vietnamese Catholics after the 1954 partition.

Spiderweb Mansion
Continue past an elementary school and *thu vien* (library) housed in a yellow building. You pass a Bauhaus-like villa, and a three-story pink guesthouse villa, not for foreigners. Farther west is **Dalat Children Cultural Palace.** Catering to children ages 5–15, it organizes movies, music performances, and camping trips. The Children's Palace was designed by Hang Nga, a Vietnamese architect and sculptor with a flair for the bizarre. Trained in Moscow, Hang Nga first came to Dalat in 1983, fell in love with the architecture and mountain air, and decided to settle here. She lives just up the hill from the palace at Spiderweb Mansion on Huynh Thuc Khang Street. It's easy to spot—look for a towering giraffe. Hang Nga has had trouble convincing the Vietnamese authorities to accept her ideas, but being the daughter of a former prime minister helps. When you visit Spiderweb Mansion you can see why she needed special permits—this place actually displays imagination. The garden features wrought-iron spiderwebs, huge stone mushrooms, and a stack of futuristic-looking treehouses—go see this wild and wacky place.

The Last Emperor
Past the Pasteur Institute lies Dinh III, or **Bao Dai Summer Villa.** The 1930s villa is set in beautiful grounds, with gardens and views. The 25-room villa was the private residence of Bao

The villa is open 0700–1200 and 1330–1700; there's a $1 entry fee and extra charge for camera or video. The villa has art deco features, but the interior is now quite modest considering the extravagant tastes of its former occupant. It's likely that many personal effects of the emperor have been removed.

Other Sights

As a resort town, Dalat will in the future become a base for hikers and bicyclists, as well as rafting trips on the Da Nhim River. At present, sporting amenities are few. You can ride ponies at a few locations around town—the Valley of Love, Lake of Sighs—but they're mainly for photos, with ponies led by a noose.

Offering innovative day trips is **Dalat Adventure Sport,** at 183 Phan Dinh Phung St., tel. 63/829422. This French-run outfit offers torrent descents of waterfalls—rappelling down them, in fact. It may introduce paragliding and rafting in the future.

Dalat Palace Golf Club, tel. 63/821201, offers 18 holes on 55 acres designed and landscaped by a Thai company; an international championship was held there in 1993. Visitors and walk-in players are accepted: You must pay greens fees and use a caddie. The original golf

Dai, the last emperor of Vietnam, who abdicated in 1945. (For more information, see *Sights*.)

Poets and Eccentrics

Head downhill for the next stop—**Lam Ty Ni Pagoda.** The sole monk here, Thuc Vien, looks after the pagoda. When he joined the temple in 1968, there were two other resident monks, but since 1975 Vien has lived alone, with a dog to keep him company. Not that he's short on visitors—he receives at least a dozen a day. The brown-robed monk welcomes you to visit his amazing **Divine Calmness Bamboo Garden** on the wonderful way toward drifting rosy clouds. He created the garden himself, and just about everything around it, as he will explain exuberantly. Thuc Vien has not only mastered half a dozen languages but has also developed his own elliptical variations of them—he can run you round in circles in English, French, Vietnamese, Thai, or Khmer, with a good dose of surrealism and Zen mixed in. Thuc Vien is a published poet and an accomplished calligrapher of Vietnamese and Chinese script. He will sell you a copy of one of his own books for $6. A profusion of papers, painting, wood creations, and calligraphy fill his workspace. The "business monk" has made sales internationally, with paintings ranging $50 and up. He will run you off a piece of calligraphy or art for a "donation"—in cash U.S. dollars. Be wary of a monk with a cell phone. Less Zen, more money these days.

For a chance to see the interior of one of Dalat's fine villas, visit the mansion converted into a karaoke café along Tran Phu Street. Continue eastward, past the Dalat Children's Cultural Palace, take a left, and go down the hill. Just after you cross a small bridge, take a narrow alley to the right; this cobblestone alley runs through a section of town that looks as if it were lifted straight out of China. It ends near the town fountain.

For a finale, why not drop in on one of Dalat's leading poets? Carry on around to Ly Tu Truong Street—a fair way in, on the right, is Duy Viet's house. He lives here, has his art gallery here, and runs the **Stop'n Go Café.** Apart from being a Dalat poet and calligrapher, Duy Viet's career has included stints as Dalat's town deputy and as a journalist in Saigon. Duy Viet looks like a bohemian—dressed in beret and scarf, chain-smoking. He welcomes travelers to the kitsch and clutter of his gallery and café. He keeps log books for travelers, which are filled with poetry and calligraphy in 20 languages, plus sketches and photos of famous Vietnamese painters, singers, and poets who've passed through. You say stop and I say go, go, go—the name Stop'n Go Café derives from a haikulike stanza written by Duy Viet:

The world is an inn
The nature is mystical
Human beings are travelers
Stop'n Go

course on the site is Vietnam's oldest, established in the 1930s.

Off the northeast tip of the golf course you'll find **Dalat Flower Gardens**—with a modest showing of roses, camellias, lilies, and orchids. Dalat's temperate climate supports many species of flowers, including a large array of orchids. Buy cut flowers at the central market. For train buffs, there's a 1.5-hour run from Dalat station to the village of **Trai Met,** about 10 kilometers from Dalat; the journey winds through vegetable farms. A diesel engine hauls a small wagon with open seating twice daily for $5 per person round-trip. Or you can hire the locomotive for

a custom trip. Get out and explore Trai Met, where there's a Buddhist temple.

If you haven't had your fill of pagodas and churches in Vietnam by now, Dalat can provide healthy doses of both. **Truc Lam Pagoda,** a short distance south of Dalat, is an active monastery built 1993–1994. About 50 monks and 50 nuns live here. Visitors are allowed to attend meditation sessions but are not allowed to stay overnight. The monastery is situated on top of a hill with imposing lake views—well worth motoring out here. **Linh Son Pagoda,** at 120 Nguyen Van Troi, is an active pagoda run by a dozen monks. Built in 1942, it's the center of

Central Vietnam

DALAT VILLA TOUR

In 1930 there were an estimated 400 villas in Dalat; by 1953 more than 1,000. A favorite of rich French fleeing the stinking heat of Saigon summers, Dalat in 1944 had 5,600 French inhabitants out of a total population of 25,000. Dalat was spared the ravages of the Vietnam War—it was not bombed or mined and the villas are largely intact, with the French plumbing still in place. The villas are scattered, with the most exclusive ones near the former Governor-general's residence, on the south side of the lake.

Colonial Dalat can be explored by bicycle (some uphill walking required), moto, motorcycle, or car. If on a bicycle, allow at least three hours to cover the sights. A good place to start is **Thuy Ta,** a café perched right over the lake. You can still make out the old French name at the back—La Grenouillère (The Froggery). There's a diving platform out the back; drinks are served under umbrellas on the sundeck. Just down the way is a place that under French ownership was the **Cercle Sportif** clubhouse, dating from 1931. It is now a disco. The stadium, completed in 1942, is still there; the nearby buildings are used for gymnastics and karate training.

From here you have to push your bike all the way up to the **Governor-general's residence,** at the top of a hill—look for the Dinh II Hotel sign. The residence was built 1933–1937. Vichy-appointed Governor-general Jean Decoux used the residence as a summer workplace May–October each year. The residence is open in theory all day, as it's also a hotel, but staff may disappear for lunch. If the building is closed you won't be missing much. The interior is uninspiring, with bland furniture, a Chinese lacquer screen, random souvenir cases, and a stuffed bear—presumably one bagged in a big game hunt around Dalat when the area was still home to big game. The residence has 25 rooms, but the upstairs section is a hotel and official guesthouse, so no touring is permitted. The gardens, with wattle trees, weeping willows, roses, cacti, and bougainvillea, are more interesting, and free. Dinh II offers excellent views over Dalat.

Exclusive Villas

Proceeding east from Dinh II, you wheel along through pine forests and on to a strip of Dalat's more exclusive villas—more than a dozen of them. These 1940s villas were renovated in 1992 and are rented to tour groups from France and Hong Kong. Some of the French have even returned on nostalgic vacations to villas they once occupied. The area was developed by DRI, U.S.-managed but fronted by a Hong Kong company; the staff received Swiss training. The restaurant in the area is Villa 27; you can stop by and look at the interior.

Farther along Hung Vuong Street, high on a hill, is **Nam Phuong White Villa,** a white three-story French villa with gray shutters and beautiful grounds with rose gardens and palms. You might be able to gain access to the grounds. Empress Nam Phuong, wife of Bao Dai, died in 1963. Far-

Buddhism in Dalat. Vietnamese tourists flock to **Thien Vuong Pagoda,** about four kilometers from town to the southeast. The pagoda, constructed in 1958, is pretty dull, but one building houses three massive standing Buddhas made of gilded sandalwood; the figure in the center is the historical Buddha, Sakyamuni. Reached by a path opposite is **Minh Nguyet Cu Sy Lam Pagoda,** dedicated to the bodhisattva Quan Am.

Churches are the landmarks of Dalat. On the south side of town is the towering spire of **Dalat Cathedral;** on the north side is the pink facade of **Domaine de Marie Convent.**

In 1942, 300 nuns occupied the convent, and a handful of Vietnamese nuns still live there. Up on a ridge above Mimosa Hotel is a **Protestant church** built in 1940. Near Cam Ly Falls stands a church with a twist—a small **Montagnard church,** constructed in 1968, that incorporates elements of animist worship. Another large former convent in this area—**Couvent des Oiseaux,** southwest of Dalat—is now a school for ethnic minorities. Past Couvent des Oiseaux, along Huyen Tran Cong Chua Street, is **Du Sinh,** a small church built in 1955 in Sino-Vietnamese style.

ther east, past Khach San Lam Vien, is **Dinh I,** the former workplace of Emperor Bao Dai.

Continue through villa land, go down Tran Quy Cap Street, and turn left onto Quang Trung Street to view more quaint villas, some converted for use by official bodies. Toward the railway station is a **double villa.** This double-turreted stone castle is reminiscent of a building style found in Provence, in the south of France. Painted Cambodian *apsaras* are emblazoned outside on the stone wall. At the time of my visit, the double villa housed half a dozen families—some involved in breeding pigs, others in the production of rice wine. It's close to Dalat's old railway station.

Ghost Station

Gare de Dalat (corrupted to "Ga Dalat" in Vietnamese) is a classic—a ghost station with a stopped clock out front. The russet-roofed station is an imaginative piece of French architecture completed in 1938. The Swedish-built crémaillère, or cog railway, ran 1933–1964 down to Thap Cham junction outside Phan Rang. It was put out of commission by Vietcong attacks. A small part of the line has been revived for tourism, and a diesel locomotive runs 10 kilometers out to the village of Trai Met once a day. Tea is served in a kiosk inside Dalat station, where the halls once echoed with departure announcements. A Swiss company is considering repair of the line.

Push on to the **Cartographic Institute.** The building with the distinctive sloping roof was originally the French Geographic Institute, established in the 1940s to produce maps for military purposes. The Cartographic Institute today produces maps of Vietnam, including some excellent topo maps (one of Dalat itself), but few of these top-secret works seem to find their way onto the general market.

Past the Cartographic Institute is **Grand Lycée Yersin**—named in honor of Alexandre Yersin, the French medical researcher who recommended Dalat be set up as a hill station. The curved brick building with the tower was completed in 1935. Formerly a French secondary school, today it's a Vietnamese school for teacher trainees—who are only too pleased to practice their foreign-language skills.

From the *lycée,* make your way down Yersin Street to the **Trade Union Guesthouse.** This French structure is rather dull: It used to serve as offices for the French colonial administration. Out the back are some chalets designed by Hang Nga, Dalat's foremost architect. Farther on, you'll reach **Xuan Huong Lake,** which is named after an 18th-century poetess whose works ridicule pompous officials and praise free love. The lake, created by the French in 1919 with the construction of a small dam at the west end, used to be called Grand Lac. You can stop for a drink at Thuy Ta Café (expensive), or continue riding around the lake to the north side to Thanh Thuy Restaurant, where you can sit outside. Thanh Thuy rents rowboats and swan-shaped pedal boats.

ACCOMMODATIONS

Because of its abundance of colonial buildings, Dalat offers a great range of hotels, villas, mini-hotels, and guesthouses. However, not all are open to foreigners (those that are must obtain "foreigner-dealing licenses"). At last count about 50 hotels were sanctioned for foreigners. By more than coincidence, a large number are operated by Lam Dong Tourism, the official touring arm. However, private hotels increasingly are on the rise—these are recommended because the owners try a lot harder, with better services and better standards of cleanliness. Unfortunately, many of these private hotels are restricted to Vietnamese patrons only. Keep an ear to the ground—places get declassified or reclassified; other hotels are being built or renovated. Not all hotels are listed here.

Because of Dalat's high elevation nights can be cool, so hot water is an important consideration. Some hotels supply hot water for several hours a day with wood-fired heaters; others use electrical systems. It's difficult to classify some Dalat hotels. A moderate hotel such as the Duy Tan may feature a main block with

$25 rooms and another block with dormitory rooms for $7 a bed.

Under $20

Backpackers congregate in half a dozen hotels around the center of Dalat. **Phu Hoa Hotel,** 16 Tang Bat Ho St., tel. 63/822194, has 32 rooms in the $5–10–15–20 range (no baths in lower-end rooms, while upper-end rooms are bigger and have baths, balconies, and bigger beds). Good value; irregular hot water supply.

Mimosa Hotel, at 170 Phan Dinh Phung, tel. 63/822656, is often frequented by traveler minibus tours and offers 55 rooms for $7–20; hot water on tap. Close to the Mimosa are dowdy **Thanh The I Hotel,** at 118 Phan Dinh Phung, tel. 63/822180, with 20 rooms in the $5–7–12 range; and **Thanh The II** at 90 Phan Dinh Phung, tel. 63/822780, with 14 rooms in the same range. A better deal is the **Cao Nguyen Hotel,** at 90 Phan Dinh Phung, tel. 63/823738, with 13 rooms for $5 s or $9 d, including hot water. The 18-room **Cam Do** at 81 Phan Dinh Phung, tel. 63/822732, charges $12–18 for singles and doubles. The nine-room **Peace Hotel** (Hoa Binh), 67 Truong Cong Dinh St., tel. 63/822787, charges $8–20; you can rent mountain bikes and motorbikes here. Down the hill is **Peace Hotel II.**

Near the Central Market, **Thanh Binh Hotel,** at 40 Nguyen Thi Minh Khai, tel. 63/822909, offers a total of 41 rooms for $7–10 s or $12–20–25 d. **Hoa An Hotel,** on the same street, has 12 rooms for similar prices. Nguyen Chi Thanh Street, leading south of Anh Dao Hotel, features a few small guesthouses. About a kilometer to the southwest of Dalat is **Lam Son Hotel,** at 5 Hai Thuong St., tel. 63/822362, fax 63/822661; the 14 rooms go for $8–10 s or $10–15 d.

Private minihotels offer good deals in Dalat. One of these is the 13-room **Binh Yen Hotel,** at 7/2 Hai Thuong St., on the northwest side of town, tel. 63/823631, with TV and hot water included in the $8 s or $10 d room tariff. Another place in this area is **Truong Nguyen GH,** at 74 Hai Thuong St., tel. 63/821772, with 14 rooms for $15–25.

Another cluster of minihotels with good prices is found at the quieter south end of town, on a street leading off Tran Phu near the Sofitel Dalat Palace.

$20–50

Private hotels are cleaner and offer much more in the way of services—the owners try a lot harder. Often the family lives in the same building, which means the place is also more secure. Private hotels include the following three (there are more). **Europa** (Chau Au), 76 Nguyen Chi Thanh St., tel. 63/822870, fax 63/824488, offers 15 very clean rooms for $20–35, some with views. **Art Hotel** (Hoang Hau), 8A Ho Tung Mao St. (near the post office), tel. 63/821431, fax 63/822333, is a 10-room private hotel with modern artwork gracing the white walls (which can be refreshing after staring at moldy water-stained walls elsewhere in Dalat). The large rooms have hot water, fridge, TV, and views at the back and go for $15–40. **Xuan Tam Villa,** tel. 63/826036, fax 63/820871, has 19 rooms for $30–42, some with views. It's on the southwest side of town, near the Pasteur Institute.

Government-run hotels in the Central Market area include nondescript **Haison Hotel,** 1 Nyugen Thi Minh Khai, tel. 63/822379. Block A, the better choice, features $25–35 s, $30–40 d, $40–45 t, and $45–50 for a four-person room. Block B has $10–30 s, $15–35 d, $25–40 t, $30–45 for four-person rooms, and $45 for a five-person room. **Anh Dao II,** at 7 Duong 3 Thang 2, tel. 63/822482, offers large doubles for $20–30, expensive for the facilities. **Anh Dao Hotel,** at 50 Hoa Binh Square, tel. 63/822384, is one of Dalat's premier hotels. It has 27 clean and renovated rooms in the $30–55 range. **Ngoc Lan Hotel,** at 42 Nguyen Chi Thanh, tel. 63/822136, has 28 rooms and charges $15 and up per room.

On the north side of Xuan Huong Lake is **Hotel Trixaco,** at 7 Nguyen Thai Hoc, tel. 63/822789. This 14-room mansion charges $35 for an upstairs room with a/c and hot water. In the same area is **Thanh Thuy Hotel,** at 5 Nguyen Thai Hoc, tel. 63/822262—a great villa-restaurant with six rooms for $25–

35. Close by, **Khach San Huong Tra** offers 25 rooms—six in a white building overlooking the lake for $30 each; the rest in another section for $15. The Huong Tra has its own restaurant building facing the lake.

West of central Dalat is **Duy Tan Hotel,** 83 Duong 3 Thang 2, tel. 63/822216, offering mediocre rooms for $20–25–30 in one wing and $7–12–17 in another. To the southeast, on the outskirts of Dalat, is **Khach San Lam Vien,** at 20 Hung Vuong, tel. 63/822507. From a distance this place looks like a hospital—the blockhouse has 66 rooms in two wings, in the $20–25 range. Russians from Vung Tau like this place. You need some form of transportation to commute into town.

To the north of Dalat, by the golf course, is **Golf Hotel,** 11 Dinh Tien Hoang, tel. 63/824082, fax 63/824945, with 36 rooms for $35–60. If you stay at the Golf Hotel you get a 30 percent discount on green fees at the Dalat Palace Golf Club. Angled for the businessperson is **Lavy Hotel,** at 2B Lu Gia St., tel. 63/825465, fax 63/825466, with 37 rooms for $35–55.

$50–100

On the south side of the lake is the **Novotel Dalat,** at 7 Tran Phu, tel. 63/825777, fax 63/825888. This is a former colonial hotel from 1907, featuring 144 guest rooms, including 12 suites. Superior rooms are $40–55, deluxe $50-65, suites $85, extra charge for extra bed. The hotel was extensively renovated and is now run by the French group Accor.

$100–200

Dalat's top-rated hotel is the **Hotel Sofitel Dalat Palace** at 12 Tran Phu St., tel. 63/825444, fax 63/825666. Sofitel is the five-star trademark of Accor, the world's biggest hotel group. The Palace caters to golfers mainly and offers 43 rooms $170–200 d and suites $300–450. The deluxe colonial hotel was originally built in 1922 and has been magnificently restored to its former glory—no expense has been spared on the period decoration here. Several hundred imitation French paintings (produced in Saigon) grace the walls and halls. The

place looks like a cross between an art gallery and a golf course. Most rooms come with fireplaces; modern comforts such as satellite TVs, IDD phones, and minibars have been added. The hotel has a business center, two restaurants, several bars, tennis courts and a garden café. There are sweeping views of Xuan Huong Lake from the landscaped grounds.

Classic Hotels

Sleeping with History: Dinh II, the former Governor-general's residence at 12 Tran Hung Dao, tel. 63/822092, has eight rooms upstairs—six for $35 each, and two for $45. The spacious rooms feature oversize bathrooms. There are also two villas attached. Book through Lam Dong Tourism, 4 Tran Quoc Toan St., tel. 63/822125, fax 63/828330.

Southeast of Dinh II is **Minh Tam Villa,** at 20A Khe Sanh St., tel. 63/822447. Formerly the summer residence of notorious Madame Nhu (Tran Le Xuan), sister-in-law of President Diem, the villa was constructed in 1936. Larger-than-life Madame Nhu, nicknamed the "Dragon Lady" for her fiery rhetoric, took off for a conference in Europe in 1963. Shortly thereafter, Diem was killed, and Madame Nhu never came back. There are beautiful rose gardens on the grounds of the villa. Large crowds of visiting Vietnamese and Asian tourists descend daily in tour buses. Rooms go for $25–40; some bungalows are set back from the main hotel building.

Villas: The enticing villas around Dalat are mostly owned and operated by Lam Dong Tourism; foreigners make reservations through agents with advance bookings, but walk-ins are possible. Try approaching Lam Dong Tourism, tel. 63/822496; with hard bargaining you might be able to secure a villa for under $15. However, you might need some form of transportation, as villas are not centrally situated.

Near Dinh II are 10 classy French villas, renovated and upgraded by DRI; try the office at 25 Tran Hung Dao St., tel. 63/822203, fax 63/821241. Each villa is composed of 4–5 rooms, with bathroom facilities. There are about 35 rooms altogether, going for $20–30 s or $30–40 d. The villas are often assigned to group tours from France or Hong Kong and can accommodate 50 people. A typical place is **Villa Hotel 28,** at 28 Tran Hung Dao, tel. 63/822764, with eight rooms going for $25.

Volunteer Youth Company (VYC) is a private chain that manages the prestigious Omni Hotel in Saigon. VYC runs a total of 40 rooms sprinkled around Dalat, mostly in newer houses, but some in older villas. Toward the northeast fringe of town you'll find **Pensée 2,** 2 Lu Gia St., tel. 63/822933, with 20 rooms at $15 each. Close by, **Pensée 10,** at 10 Phan Chu Trinh, tel. 63/822937, offers six homey rooms for $15 each. In the direction of Dalat bus station is **Pensée 3,** at 3 Duong 3 Thang 4, tel. 63/822286. This is also the head office for VYC in Dalat. It's a two-story newer house with gardens, featuring seven doubles for $25 each. Rooms have bidets and garden and forest views; a bar is downstairs. Nearby **Pensée 6,** at 6 Duong 3 Thang 4, tel. 63/822378, has four double rooms for $20 each. South of that is **Savimex,** at 11B Duong 3/4, tel. 63/822640, with $25 rooms. It's a hotel for businesspeople, run by a rival Saigon agency.

Lots more villas are scattered around the hills of Dalat. Out at 1 Yersin St. is **Dalat Trade Union Tourism Hotel,** tel. 63/822173, fax 63/825329, with 85 rooms in several wings—one wing is a huge French villa with rooms for $30–50; there are also some modern chalet rooms for $35 each. Somewhat run-down are two more villa-hotels in this vicinity, to the southeast side of Dalat: the Forestry Tourist Company's **Green Hotel,** 16 Hung Vuong St., tel. 63/822417, with eight doubles for $15 each; and **Dalat Railway Tourism Hotel,** 1 Quang Trung St., tel. 63/822667, with several old villas on the grounds—there are 20 rooms, with a tariff of $10 each.

Tree Houses: M Hang Nga Nha Nghi, also called Spiderweb Mansion, at 3 Huynh Thuc Khang, tel. 63/822070, is the wacky creation of architect Dang Viet Nga. She has constructed a series of tree houses around her original villa—there's not a straight line in the place. She offers five rooms in the pink mansion for $10–15 with shared bath. Rooms in the chalet are $30.

The chalet has wild decor, lights set in a cave-type ceiling, a fireplace, and an upstairs den with mirror and bed. Dang Viet Nga's masterpiece is a four-story tree house near the giraffe. The nine self-contained tree-house rooms go for $35–85 and feature round beds and zany windows. Each room is presided over by its own sculpted animal: The tiger room goes for $75, the kangaroo room for $40.

FOOD

Street and Market Food

The **Central Market** (Cho Dalat) features stalls for fresh produce, fruit and flowers, processed food, consumer goods, and clothing. There are a few juice bars down this way. A dazzling array of fruit grows in the temperate zone around Dalat, including strawberries, plums, cherries, apples, and avocados. Candied fruit and jam are made in Dalat.

Upstairs at the back of the markets is a large food-stall area, an excellent place to dine. Dalat provides excellent fresh vegetables—the French introduced European varieties. At the food stalls you'll find an abundance of vegetables—yams, squash, spinach, beans, peppers. There are half a dozen vegetarian stalls here; look for Com Chay signs. The vendors fashion tofu to resemble prawns or pork chops, though it's dubious whether this simulation appeals to a true vegetarian. For a change from the usual restaurant fare, try the delicious carrots in the produce market. Buy the carrots, take them over to a restaurant, and order them sautéed or however. Wash down your meal with a glass of Dalat mulberry wine; other liqueurs are also produced locally.

At the foot of the steps leading down to the market is another makeshift food stall area: At night women preside over cauldrons of hard-boiled quail eggs and snails, cooking for customers at narrow tables.

Noodlehouses

Tang Bat Ho, an alley that runs off the Phu Hoa Hotel, is hardly used by street traffic. At night, it's Soup Alley; inside and outside eateries serve Hué soup and other regional specialties.

Restaurants

Along Nguyen Thi Minh Khai Street, leading down from the Central Market to Xuan Huong Lake, a string of small restaurants serve cheap, hearty fare. These include **Nhu Ngoc Restaurant,** opposite the Haison Hotel; farther south are **Mimosa Restaurant** and **Huynh Lien Restaurant.**

Up at the top of the steps near the cinema is **Thanh Thanh Restaurant,** at 4 Tang Bat Ho St., tel. 63/821836, which has an elegant interior. It's small, cozy, clean, and offers good dining at reasonable prices. Particularly tasty are the soups: mustard vegetable, cauliflower, crab, and asparagus. Around the corner, the family-run **Long Hoa Restaurant,** 6 Duong 3 Thang 2 St., tel. 63/822934, does a brisk business and is popular with travelers. **Anh Vo,** 15 Truong Cong Dinh, tel. 63/823175, is a good restaurant in the center, with lots of vegetarian dishes; staff is fluent in French and passable in English. Other restaurants in this central area may disappoint—**Shanghai** is mediocre, and **Do Yen Restaurant** is overpriced.

Phan Dinh Phung Street is the "Chinatown" of Dalat, with naturally more Chinese influence in the cooking. At 98 Phan Dinh Phung is **Dong A Restaurant,** tel. 63/821033, with good food but mediocre service. Farther north is **Hoan Lan Resto** on the ground floor of the Thanh The I Hotel at 118 Phan Dinh Phung. Toward Mimosa Hotel is **Dieu Thao Restaurant,** a small, cheap vegetarian place next to 142 Phan Dinh Phung.

For French food in classic French surroundings, try **Le Café de la Poste,** which is near the post office, of course. The café is affiliated with the luxury Hotel Sofitel Dalat Palace across the way. Farther to the east is **Villa 27 Restaurant and Bar** at 27 Tran Hung Dao St., tel. 63/822743. It's on the south side of the lake, past the former Governor-general's residence. At night there are a fireplace and a piano bar—drinks are $2. Villa 27 is also open for breakfast—you can get French bread, juice, tea, and two eggs for $3. Of course, it's the ambience you pay for, since the same fare would cost a lot less at the Central Market.

Cafés

Cafés have a lot of character in Dalat. They're the social hub of the town, functioning as rendezvous points, gossip and rumor mills, and nightclubs. To savor the taste of local tea and coffee, try **Le Ky Café,** at 249 Phan Dinh Phung, near the Mimosa Hotel; it's a small wholesale outlet with a few tables. For tea freaks, Bao Loc tea, produced close to Dalat, is considered one of the finest in Vietnam. Artichoke tea, made from the root of the plant, reputedly restores liver and diuretic functions. Just what you need after one of those long bus rides.

On the south side of the lake, near the post office tower, is **Le Café de la Poste,** which is run by the Sofitel Dalat Palace and is a posh place to have a drink—expensive, but comfortable if you have a lot of postcards to write. A daytime or sunset venue for drinks is **Thuy Ta Café** by the lakeside—an upscale joint with a relaxing sundeck run by Dalat Tourism. It even serves carrot juice. You can eat breakfast here; other meals should be ordered in advance at tel. 63/822288. On the north side of the lake is **Thanh Thuy Café,** which rents pedal boats to cruise the lake.

In town, near the back of the cinema, is **Café Tung.** Old men gather here to shoot the breeze; the place was famed as a hangout for intellectuals in the 1950s. Café Tung serves only drinks, but if you need a snack, grab one at **Pho Tung Cakeshop,** at 1 Nguyen Van Troi. Pho Tung sells delicious coconut and marzipan cakes and other pastries; you'll find small sidewalk cake stalls a few blocks west on Truong Cong Dinh Street.

Perched on a ridge along Nguyen Chi Thanh Street is a string of cafés with views—**Lang Van Café, Café Artista, Viet Hung Café,** and **Huong Thuy Café.** These places serve ice cream, iced coffee, and filtered coffee, and they provide dark corners for Vietnamese couples to grope in. Even more romantic is **Duy Tan Café** on Nam Ky Khoi Nghia, featuring secluded open-air tables on several levels high above the street. Duy Tan is a karaoke café where tuneless patrons commit vocal atrocities on songs such as "Country Roads." Fortunately, the karaoke is contained inside.

SERVICES AND INFORMATION

Tourist Information

Lam Dong Tourism Office, at 4 Tran Quoc Toan St., tel. 63/822125, is the provincial tourism authority. It is also known as Dalattourism. The office arranges transportation, guides, and permits for Lat Village. You can pick up maps of the Dalat area here. If you come across the bridge from downtown Dalat, Lam Dong Tourism occupies the second house on the hill to your left, overlooking the lake. The office advertises "tours to inner country including forbidden areas"— roughly translated, this means that the people at Lam Dong Tourism made the area forbidden so you'd have to visit them to get the permits.

There's a second office, **Chuyen Dulich,** at 9 Le Dai Hanh St., tel. 63/822479. As you come across the bridge the office lies to your right, not far along the road. This office provides transportation rental—bicycles go for $1.50 a day, a U.S. jeep $25 a day, other vehicles also arranged. A guide is $15 a day.

Another agent in Dalat is **Phuong Nam Tourism,** 6 Ho Tung Mau, tel. 63/822781, conducting tours to the highlands and coast. It arranges trekking, climbing, camping, hunting, and visits to ethnic groups and old battlefields.

Post Office

The GPO is at 14 Tran Phu, on the south side of the lake, with a telecommunications building nearby. Look for a mini–Eiffel Tower to guide you to the vicinity. Fax and IDD facilities available here. Vietnam country code is 84; the Dalat area code is 63.

Banks

Incombank (Ngan Hang Cong Thuong), 46–48 Khu Hoa Binh, next to Anh Dao Hotel, charges 1.2 percent commission for changing traveler's checks to dong, and 2 percent commission to convert traveler's checks to U.S. cash.

GETTING THERE AND AWAY

By Air

There is intermittent air service from Dalat to Ho Chi Minh City, with flights for $45 one-way. There may be flights also to Hué. At present only light aircraft can land at Lien Khang airstrip, 30 kilometers south of Dalat. Taxi transfer into Dalat should be under $10. A Vietnam Airlines office is at 5 Truong Cong Dinh St., tel. 63/822895, in the main square.

By Bus

The main bus station, Ben Xe Trung Tam, is four kilometers south of Dalat; you can get there by moto or take a lambro from the foot of the Central Market steps. The bus station has minibuses, Peugeots, express buses, regular buses, and share-taxis to points north and south. The bus station is out of town, but you can still get bus pickup in town, an important consideration if the damn thing departs at 0500. A ticket booth is open 0600–2100 at the top of the main steps, north of Haison Hotel; you buy a ticket in advance here, and on the appointed morning either wait at the booth or arrange for hotel pickup. Buses leave at very early hours. They circle the cinema area before 0600 (not legal after this), then head out. Some buses, such as those to Nha Trang, depart only 0500–0700. For Saigon there's hourly service 0500–1500 by bus or minibus. The run takes about 6–7 hours.

By Traveler Minibus

To avoid the rigors of local buses, travelers should keep an eye out for traveler minibuses plying the coast. If you're heading south, you might be able to find a seat on a minibus coming back from Hué. There are also minibuses running the Saigon–Dalat route. Inquire around Mimosa Hotel. To Nha Trang, it costs about $7 a person by traveler minibus. By comparison, a packed public minibus from the bus station to Nha Trang costs about $2.50.

GETTING AROUND

By Rental

You can arrange car and minibus rentals for getting around town through major hotels or through Lam Dong Tourism. The area at the top of the steps above the Central Market has taxi rentals, old Peugeot 203s and 404s, and small buses and lambros. At the bottom of the steps are lambros that run back to the bus station and to a few short-run destinations around Dalat.

By Moto

Motos cost $7 a day or $1 an hour. Lots of motos are available near the top of the steps close to the Central Market. Dalat is hilly: A Honda 50cc carrying two people is going to crawl up a hill and will overheat easily, so try to get something with more power, such as a 125cc or 175cc moto. If you want to drive yourself, offer a moto driver $5–7, commandeer the moto, and take off—agree on a meeting spot to return the bike. A deposit may be required. You can also rent motorcycles from some guesthouses, including the Peace Hotel.

By Bicycle

No cyclos traverse Dalat because of its hills. But you can rent a bicycle from several places. The first priority, because of the gradients, would be to find a mountain bike with gears. There are a few around; again, try the Peace Hotel, or see the Thanh Van Hotel (about four kilometers to the north), which has a fleet of mountain bikes. In a parking lot near the Haison Hotel is a booth where you can rent a Chinese bike for $1.50 a day or $.80 half day. For a Vietnamese bike it's $1 a day or $.50 half day. At Chuyen Dulich, on the southeast side of town over the bridge, you'll find similar deals; perhaps half a dozen bikes for rent. Just north of Cam Do Hotel, next to 99 Phan Dinh Phung, is a tiny rental place with bikes going for $1 a day. The bikes have no gears, so expect to walk the bike at times. For really long climbs, put yourself and the bike on a minibus. This is the case when going to Prenn Falls—it's all downhill to get there and all uphill on the way back.

EXCURSIONS FROM DALAT

Adventure Touring

Several outfits in Dalat offer adventures such as mountain biking, hiking, hybrid bike-and-hike

THE DALAT ROUTE

From Nha Trang to Saigon there are two routes: following the coast via Phan Rang and Phan Thiet, or swinging west from Phan Rang and going via Dalat. The Dalat route is definitely more inspiring, climbing from the arid coast at Phan Rang to pine forests at 1,475 meters in Dalat. Dalat is 110 kilometers from Phan Rang and 310 kilometers from Saigon. From Dalat a forest zone extends about 20 kilometers to the south, gradually giving way to fruit orchards and tea plantations.

The largest town on the route is Bao Loc, known for its silk industry. About 25 kilometers from Saigon, at Bien Hoa, you can turn off to Vung Tau Beach Resort. (Information on distances, road conditions, and accommodations along the route can be gleaned from the sidebar, *Saigon-to-Nha Trang Bike Route*.)

tours, multiple-day trekking, and bird-watching tours. But the one to go for is canyoning. For this you abseil down a waterfall: an action-packed day of rappelling, swimming, slipping, and sliding on the Datanla River, about five kilometers south of Dalat. This will set you back $20, equipment included: They'll even throw in some lunch. Inquire at **Phat Tire Ventures,** 73 Truong Cong Dinh St., tel. 63/829422, www.phattireventures.com. The competition is an outfit called **Hardy Dalat,** 66 Phan Dinh Phung, tel. 63/836840, www.hardyadventuretours.com.

Moto Mystery Tour

A number of spots around Dalat can be visited by hiring a moto guide for around $10 a day. Guides carry small picture books of the sights; you agree to an itinerary, hop aboard, and head off. A mixed bag of sights is a good idea. Guides usually head for Lien Khuong Falls (about 28 kilometers south of Dalat), Truc Lam Pagoda, a silkworm-breeding village, an incense factory, the Crazy House (Hang Nga Spiderweb Mansion), and a handful of other spots. Well worth the money, and logistically sound. You could also organize a similar tour in a hired car, pooling together with others.

Beauty Spots

If you've ever seen the Swiss Alps or the Rocky Mountains in North America, Dalat's much-vaunted scenic spots won't impress. These "beauty spots" become crowded with Vietnamese vacationers on weekends, making them even less attractive. **Cam Ly Falls,** two kilometers west of central Dalat, is just a trickle, with ragged flower gardens and some poorly stuffed animals as photo props; more impressive is the **Montagnard church** nearby. **Datanla Falls,** five kilometers south on the Saigon Road, is a minor cascade with a short forest hike down to the ravine where the falls are. **Prenn Falls,** 15 kilometers down the Saigon Road, is larger, but still another backdrop for honeymoon and family photos with all kinds of props, as well as restaurants large and small. If you want to see real waterfalls, go 50 kilometers south to **Thac Pangour Falls** on the route to Saigon; the thundering falls are seven kilometers in from the highway along a bad road.

Dalat is sprinkled with lakes once surrounded by wilderness but now encompassed by thin woods. Still, the trees provide sufficient cover for Vietnamese couples intent on romance. You can bike the five kilometers out to the **Valley of Love:** Take Phu Dong Thien Vuong Street north past the golf course and Dalat University, then continue past vistas of farmland and a towering Quan Am statue. The Valley of Love is an area around Da Thien Lake with a tourist circus of souvenir stalls, paddleboat, canoe, and motorboat rentals, and pony rides.

From here you can cycle back straight south along Nguyen Tu Luc Street into Dalat via the **Flower Gardens,** or, if you're feeling energetic, take a longer loop out eastward, skirting the south end of Chien Thang Lake toward the **Lake of Sighs.** The unremarkable Lake of Sighs (Ho Than Tho) is about five kilometers east of Dalat; Montagnard cowboys with plastic guns and Texas-style boots conduct pony tours on lakeside trails. The name of the lake is of uncertain origin—one theory is that it's named after the sighs of the women courted by the handsome young men from the nearby military academy.

Lat Village and Lang Bian Mountain

The original inhabitants of the Dalat area, the Lats, were pushed back to outlying villages. Lat Village is about 10 kilometers outside Dalat, or half an hour by car. You can combine a visit to the area with a hike up Lang Bian Mountain. There are nine hamlets in the area, populated by Lat, Koho, and Ma tribes living in impoverished conditions in thatched-roof houses. The villagers grow rice, coffee, and potatoes, and they produce charcoal. Lat Village has two small Christian churches.

Nearby Lang Bian Mountain has a series of peaks ranging 2,100–2,400 meters. In 3–4 hours you can hike to viewpoints up the mountain—one place, used as a U.S. base, has views of Ancroet Lakes. The dual Ancroet Lakes were created as part of a hydroelectric project. Also in the area is 15-meter-high **Ancroet Falls.** The Ancroet area, populated by Montagnards, lies about 15 kilometers northwest from Dalat and is reached by a separate route.

Getting There: Because of associations between the Americans and the Montagnards during the war, permits may be required for Lat Village—one of the last places to require a permit in Vietnam. The $5 permit takes 20 minutes to process from Lam Dong Tourism Office. Along with the permit comes a guide and transportation—a guide for a group of fewer than 10 is $10, more than 10 is $15. For 1–2 people it's $5 for a guide. The police station guide is "same price but different mind." To climb Lang Bian, it's $5 more for the guide. The tariff is $10–20 for a car for the day, or $30 for an a/c minibus; you can also hire a car from the back of the cinema. By bicycle, Lat Village is little more than an hour from Dalat, but be aware that foreigners attempting to visit Lat Village by themselves have been fined by police.

The Big Chicken

If you can't afford the Lat Village circus or don't want to deal with permits, then this is just the thing for you—the village of the big chicken, **Lang Ga.** Moto drivers will take you to a genuine Montagnard village 18 kilometers south of Dalat on the Saigon route in about half an hour. Look for the 18-kilo-meters marker stone; the village is about 500 meters off the highway. In Lang Ga villagers will walk around beating their breasts yelling "Montagnard," just to make sure you don't get them mixed up with the Vietnamese. The locals indeed look darker than Vietnamese, but their way of life is quite ordinary—subsistence farmers grow coffee and papayas, and they live in wooden housing with corrugated roofing. Women in the village use hand looms to create unusual weavings: There's a small thatched hut selling this garish stuff near the highway.

Towering over the village is a concrete rooster in a crowing stance, mounted on a rock base with an odd rockery waterway behind it. The symbolism of the three-meter-high bird is unclear: According to one version, the big chicken was presented to villagers by government officials after they succeeded in resettling the Montagnards here.

Although Lang Ga is 18 kilometers out, it's easy to reach by bicycle. The first 12 kilometers is straight downhill from Dalat, then it's flat highway. So getting there is quick, but going back you have to walk the bike. If you're too tired, wave down a bus or minibus and stick the bike on the roof.

Saigon

Like Shanghai or Bangkok, Saigon comes imbued with its own myth—you have a vision in mind already. You've seen it on television, you've seen it in movies: the city of war, the city of sin, the city of changing fortunes. Saigon is busy and brash, the commercial hub of Vietnam, the industrial muscle of the nation. It's a city of economic contrasts, too. At temple festivals you'll see women in shimmering silk *ao dais* float by filthy ragged beggars.

Little is known of Saigon's early history, and the origins of the city's name are uncertain. In the 15th century Saigon was little more than swampland in a forest wilderness, an area under the Khmer sphere of influence. The Cambodians hunted in this area, then called Prei Nokor.

Slowly it grew into a small market town; as forest was cleared and rice paddies were carved out, it became an outpost on the eastern flank of the Angkorian Empire.

As the Khmer and Cham empires shrank, the Vietnamese advanced from the north. In the early 17th century, on the condition they be allowed to settle the south, the Vietnamese agreed to help the Khmers fight the Thais. Fully in control by 1680, the Vietnamese allowed 3,000 refugee Chinese Ming soldiers to settle the area of Bien Hoa. A few years later the Chinese started a market at Cholon. Eventually, the Khmers were pushed back to the Mekong Delta.

Saigon continued to grow as Vietnamese

© MICHAEL BUCKLEY

Must-Sees

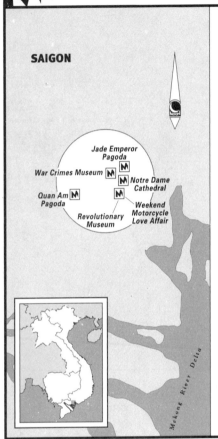

SAIGON

Jade Emperor
Pagoda

War Crimes Museum

Notre Dame
Cathedral

Quan Am
Pagoda

Revolutionary
Museum

Weekend
Motorcycle
Love Affair

Mekong River Delta

M Revolutionary Museum: Charts Ho Chi Minh's victory and the demise of the puppet government in the south. The building alone is worth a trip, as it used to be the mansion of the French governor of Indochina (page 259).

M Notre Dame Cathedral: The icon of the city, this twin-towered Gothic structure is a prominent landmark. Go inside to see the stained-glass windows, imported from France (page 259).

M War Crimes Museum: Documents American atrocities in the 1965–1975 period. Politics gets dirty: There are no clean wars (page 262).

M Quan Am Pagoda, Cholon: A fog of incense pervades this Chinese-style temple. It is dedicated to the Goddess of Mercy (page 266).

M Jade Emperor Pagoda: A strange fertility shrine of sorts, visited by women. Home to a bizarre collection of carved deities and wooden panels (page 267).

M Weekend Motorcycle Love Affair: Thousands of throbbing motorcycles converge near the Hotel de Ville on Saturday and Sunday nights. Take a ringside seat to witness Saigon-style courtship rituals (page 282).

settlers arrived from the north, spreading out along the delta waterways and clearing forest. The settlement became the administrative center of the region, a trade base and tax-collecting center. Gia Dinh, a small fort housing the area governor and his administrators, was built. In the 17th century, factions of the Nguyen clan were crushed by a peasant revolt led by the Tay Son brothers, who captured Gia Dinh. In 1788 Nguyen Anh, with the help of the French Jesuit missionary Béhaine and an army of French mercenaries, recaptured

Gia Dinh. In 1790 Nguyen Anh conscripted a force of 30,000 laborers and set about building a large Citadel in Gia Dinh, in the area between what is now the zoological gardens and Reunification Hall. The octagonal Citadel was based on a French military design; at its center lay the Royal Palace. When Nguyen Anh proclaimed himself Emperor Gia Long and moved the court to Hué, the trappings of royalty were transported north, with Saigon serving as a base for governing the southern third of the country.

Saigon

SAIGON
(HO CHI MINH CITY)

To Cu Chi Tunnels
and Tay Ninh

TAN SON NHAT AIRPORT

CONG HUA

HOANG VAN THU

MEKONG TRAVEL HOTEL

CHAINS FIRST HOTEL

GARDEN PLAZA HOTEL

DONG PHUONG

CACH MANG THANG TAM

TAN BINH DISTRICT

LE DAI HANH

THUNG KIAT BLVD

HUONG LO 2

HUONG LO 14

GIAC LAM PAGODA

LAC LONG QUAN

DISTRICT 10

AN VUONG

NGUYEN TRI

GIAC VIEN TU PAGODA

BINH THAI

DISTRICT 11

BA HAM

3 THANG 2 BLVD

DISTRICT 5

HUONG VUONG BLVD

DISTRICT 6

NGUYEN CHI THANH

LO HAU GIANG BLVD

HUONG VUONG BLVD

HOTEL EQUATOR

To Mein Tay Bus Terminal and Mekong Delta

BINH TIEN

DISTRICT 8

SEE "CHOLON" MAP

To Can Giuoc

Saigon

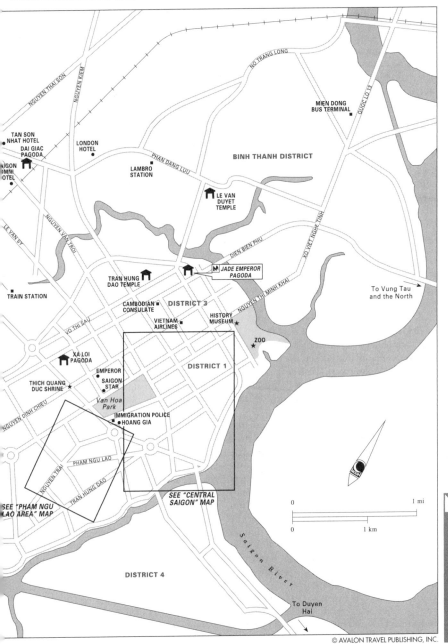

NGUYEN THAI SON

NGUYEN KIEM

NO TRANG LONG

MIEN DONG
BUS TERMINAL

QUOC LO 13

TAN SON
NHAT HOTEL

DAI GIAC
PAGODA

LONDON
HOTEL

PHAN DANG LUU

BINH THANH DISTRICT

SAIGON
OMNI
HOTEL

LAMBRO
STATION

LE VAN SY

NGUYEN VAN TROI

LE VAN
DUYET
TEMPLE

DIEN BIEN PHU

VO VIET NGHE TINH

TRAN HUNG
DAO TEMPLE

JADE EMPEROR
PAGODA

To Vung Tau
and the North

TRAIN STATION

CAMBODIAN
CONSULATE

DISTRICT 3

VO THI SAU

VIETNAM
AIRLINES

HISTORY
MUSEUM ★

NGUYEN THI MINH KHAI

ZOO ★

XA LOI
PAGODA

EMPEROR

DISTRICT 1

THICH QUANG
DUC SHRINE ★

SAIGON
STAR

NGUYEN DINH CHIEU

Van Hoa
Park

IMMIGRATION POLICE
HOANG GIA

PHAM NGU LAO

NGUYEN TRAI

TRAN HUNG DAO

SEE "PHAM NGU
LAO AREA" MAP

SEE "CENTRAL
SAIGON" MAP

0   1 mi

0   1 km

DISTRICT 4

Saigon River

To Duyen
Hai

Saigon

© AVALON TRAVEL PUBLISHING, INC.

By 1800 Saigon had a population of 50,000. In 1835 a peasant revolt at Gia Dinh was put down by Emperor Minh Mang, who razed the Citadel. A fort about a quarter of its size was constructed in its place. The emperor and his successors blamed French missionaries for peasant uprisings, and when French and Vietnamese priests were executed, the French used this as an excuse to invade the country. In 1859 a French force of eight battleships and 2,000 troops started up Saigon River. The French used explosives to breach the walls and capture Saigon. During counterattacks by the Vietnamese, the fort was destroyed. The bulk of the population was moved out to the country, leaving perhaps 25,000 residents. Shortly thereafter, the French established the colony of Cochinchina, with Saigon as its capital.

Using forced labor, the French built a new city of boulevards and buildings in what is now Central Saigon. Public works such as the post office and governor's palace were initiated. Notre Dame Cathedral was completed in 1883, built upon the site of the former Citadel's arsenal. There were hotels and villas for businessmen and administrators; canals were filled in to make roads. Towering tamarind trees lined the boulevards and palms graced the villas—now rain-stained and moldy from years of neglect.

The population of Saigon has fluctuated with its changing fortunes. In 1962 the city's population was only 1.2 million; by the late 1960s it had swelled to more than three million. After 1975 the population decreased as ethnic Chinese fled the country. The population of Saigon now exceeds five million residents. Many new arrivals come from the countryside—the average income in Saigon is more than four times higher than in rural areas. Most Saigon residents seem to own either a bicycle or a motorcycle, making this a tricky place for pedestrians.

Today Saigon is the major manufacturing and distribution center of southern Vietnam. Industries include shipbuilding, leather tan-

ning, and the manufacture of bicycles, textiles, and traditional handicrafts.

Name Game

People are schizoid about the name of this city. It's been called Gia Dinh, Ben Nghe, Ben Thanh, and half a dozen other names. After 1975, the communists tried to put their stamp on the place by changing the name from Saigon to Ho Chi Minh City, although nobody attempts to use such a tongue-twister in real life. In Vietnamese, it's Thanh Pho Ho Chi Minh; in French it's Ho Chi Minh Ville, sometimes shortened to Ho-ville. In English print, the city often turns up as HCMC, or HCM City, which is shorter, but not any easier to pronounce or comprehend.

Ho Chi Minh City hasn't stuck, even with officialdom—it's Saigon Tourism you'll see on the sign, not Ho Chi Minh City Tourism. Because of the failure of the general populace to embrace the name Ho Chi Minh City, the authorities have compromised, dubbing the central district Saigon.

Ho Chi Minh City now refers to the greater metropolitan area, comprising 12 *quan*— urban districts—and six suburban districts. Ho Chi Minh City is one of the three independent municipalities in Vietnam, the others being Greater Hanoi and Greater Haiphong. Central Saigon refers to Districts 1 and 3, the downtown business core with high-rise hotels and landmark French buildings such as the old Hotel de Ville (City Hall) and Notre Dame Cathedral. District 3 is an exclusive zone of government offices, renovated French villas, and tree-lined streets. Districts 5 and 6 are Saigon's "Chinatown." These are commonly referred to as Cholon, although officially this name does not exist. Cholon used to be separated from Saigon but grew until it melded into it. The Chinese presence is evident in Districts 8, 10, and 11 as well.

Hazards

Saigon, more than any other part of Vietnam, harbors an unpleasant assortment of rip-off artists. The place has more than its share of prostitutes, child beggars, aggressive cyclo drivers, con artists, and punks on Suzuki Crystal bikes who specialize in high-speed purse-snatching. The street kids are mostly orphans or runaways, called *bui doi* (dust of life) by the Vietnamese. They eke out a living selling newspapers, lottery tickets, cigarettes, postcards, photocopied guidebooks, flowers, fans, chewing gum—the list goes on. Many target tourists and can be very persistent. Child beggars will lock on to your clothing or your leg, releasing their grip only upon payment in dong. You should discourage such ransom activity. Prostitutes have been known to lure customers off the streets, deliver a knockout, and then take off with all valuables. Cyclo drivers occasionally attack and injure foreigners in arguments over prices. Be aware that some cyclo drivers may also be involved in drug dealing and other fringe activities. Merchants are fond of ripping off tourists—always carefully negotiate prices be-

forehand, and never pay for anything until the vendor has supplied the goods.

PLANNING YOUR TIME

Allow at least 1.5 days to see the main sights of Saigon—colonial architecture at the heart of the city (Notre Dame Cathedral, the Revolutionary Museum, the Hotel de Ville), plus the stark War Crimes Museum, and Jade Emperor Pagoda. Take in the bustling markets and pagodas of Cholon if you have more time. Add an extra day if you want to go on the Cu Chi tunnels and Cao Dai Temple day trip (highly recommended). Getting around is similar to the situation to Hanoi, except that cyclos are not popular for touring in Saigon. Public buses exist, but they are not much used by travelers, who mostly resort to using moto-drivers or hired cars, rented by the day. Renting a bicycle is another option, but dealing with the heavy motorcycle traffic can be hazardous, especially at roundabouts.

Sights

COLONIAL SAIGON

Colonial Saigon can be explored by bicycle, motorcycle, taxi, or classic French automobile. Cyclos are a leisurely way of getting around—and you will go the long way round, because cyclos were banned from 50 streets in the city center in mid-1995 to ease traffic congestion. If on a bicycle or motorcycle, watch for one-way streets, and be wary of rush-hour traffic—the boulevards can be thronged, making it difficult to turn at major intersections.

Casting yourself back to 1930s and 1940s Saigon is easy. The grand colonial edifices still stand—dwarfed, it's true, by newer high-rises—but nonetheless providing sufficient illusion for the time traveler. In fact, Saigon functions as a large outdoor museum of French colonial architecture, most of it plain and ugly. The buildings also serve as navigation landmarks, particularly the cathedral and the Hotel de Ville.

Norman Lewis described 1950 Saigon in *A Dragon Apparent:*

A French town in a hot country.... Its inspiration has been purely commercial and it is therefore without folly, fervour or much ostentation. There has been no audacity of architecture, no great harmonious conception of planning. Saigon is a pleasant, colourless and characterless French provincial city, squeezed onto a strip of delta-land in the South China Seas. From it exude strangely into the surrounding creeks and rivers 10 thousand sampans, harbouring an uncounted native population.... The better part of the city contains many shops, cafés and cinemas, and one small, plain cathedral in red brick. Twenty thousand Europeans keep as much as possible to themselves in a few tamarind-shaded central

CENTRAL SAIGON

To Zoo and History Museum →

SAIGON TRADE CENTER

TON DUC THANG
DO DUAN BLVD
CHU MAN TRINH
NGUYEN DU
MAC DINH CHI
HAI BA TRUNG
NGUYEN THI MINH KHAI

SAPA RESTAURANT
PHAROS RESTAURANT
CAMARGUE RESTAURANT

THAI VAN LUNG
VAN SAC
HAI BA TRUNG
LE LOI

APOCALYPSE NOW BAR

MUNICIPAL THEATER
HOTEL CONTINENTAL

UNITED STATES CONSULATE

FRENCH CONSULATE

PARK HYATT

LE BEAUJOLAIS RESTAURANT
ASIAN HOTEL
XUANTHU BOOKSTORE
SAIGON TOURIST
VIETNAM TOURISM
VIETNAM AIRLINES INTERNATIONAL BOOKINGS

BUFFALO BLUES BAR
STAMP AND COIN MARKET
DONG KHOI
NGUYEN DU

GOODY ICE CREAM CAFE
THANH NIEN RESTAURANT
DIAMOND PLAZA BUILDING

NOTRE DAME CATHEDRAL
GENERAL POST OFFICE ★
MARY STATUE ★

METROPOLITAN BUILDING
MERLION RESTAURANT
VY RESTAURANT

WEEKEND MOTORCYCLE LOVE AFFAIR
HOTEL DE VILLE
SAIGON CONNECTION CAFE

LAO CONSULATE/ LAO AIRLINES

QUAN AN NGON

REVOLUTIONARY MUSEUM

★ FOUNTAIN
NAPOLI CAFE

PASTEUR
DE RHODES
ALEXANDRE
LE DUAN
VAN THUYEN
NAM KY KHOI NGHIA
NGUYEN THI MINH KHAI

EMBASSY HOTEL
EMBASSY FOOD STREET

ALTERNATE ENTRANCE

MAIN ENTRANCE
REUNIFICATION HALL ★

Van Hoa Park

To Airport →

LE MEKONG RESTAURANT
WAR CRIMES MUSEUM
LE QUY DON SCHOOL
INTERNATIONAL HOTEL

TRANG CONG CHUA

Saigon

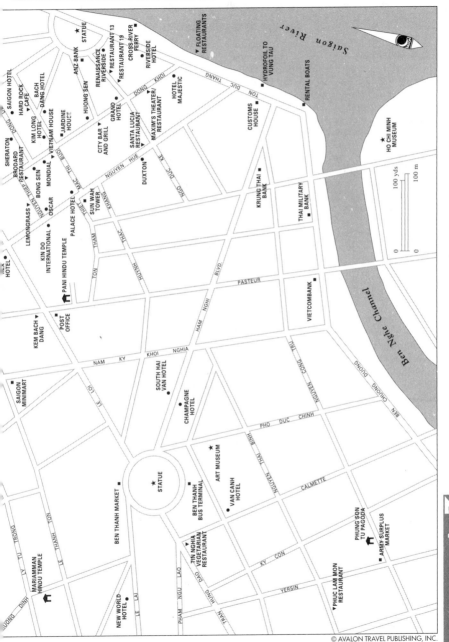

Saigon River

FLOATING RESTAURANTS

HYDROFOIL TO VUNG TAU

STATUE

ANZ BANK

RENAISSANCE RIVERSIDE

RESTAURANT 13

RESTAURANT 19

CROSS-RIVER FERRY

RIVERSIDE HOTEL

SAIGON HOTEL

HARD ROCK CAFE

BACH DANG HOTEL

HUONG SEN

KIM LONG HOTEL

VIETNAM HOUSE

JARDINE HOUSE

GRAND HOTEL

HOTEL MAJESTIC

RENTAL BOATS

SHERATON

BRODARD

CITY BAR AND GRILL

MAXIM'S THEATER/ RESTAURANT

SANTA LUCIA RESTAURANT

CUSTOMS HOUSE

LEMONGRASS

BONG SEN

MONDIAL

OSCAR

DUXTON

HO CHI MINH MUSEUM

KIN DO INTERNATIONAL

PALACE HOTEL

SUN WAH TOWER

KRUNG THAI BANK

THAI MILITARY BANK

IXA HOTEL

PANI HINDU TEMPLE

0   100 yds

0   100 m

PASTEUR

VIETCOMBANK

KEM BACH DANG

POST OFFICE

NAM KY   KHOI NGHIA

HAM NGHI BLVD.

Ben Nghe Channel

SAIGON MINIMART

SOUTH HAI VAN HOTEL

CHAMPAGNE HOTEL

PHO DUC CHINH

NGUYEN CONG TRU

CALMETTE

STATUE

BEN THANH BUS TERMINAL

ART MUSEUM

VAN CANH HOTEL

BEN THANH MARKET

MARIAMMAN HINDU TEMPLE

NEW WORLD HOTEL

LE LAI

TIN NGHIA VEGETARIAN RESTAURANT

PHUNG SON TU PAGODA

ARMY SURPLUS MARKET

KY CON

PHUC LAM MON RESTAURANT

VERSIN

Saigon

© AVALON TRAVEL PUBLISHING, INC.

HONORED FRENCH

Not all the French were rubber-plantation slave drivers. A few are actually honored with street names. Near Reunification Hall is Duong Alexandre de Rhodes, named for the 17th-century French Jesuit who introduced romanized script into Vietnam. This is in fact the original French name for the street; during the 1980s, the street was renamed after national Vietnamese hero Thai Van Lung, but in 1995 it was decided to restore the name Alexandre de Rhodes. Thai Van Lung is still on the map—the name simply bumped another street off the map farther east.

Duong Pasteur is a nod to Louis Pasteur, who established medical research institutes around the world to fight disease. Duong Pasteur features a Pasteur Institute (Vien Pasteur) at the north end. Two other Saigon streets with French names are also related to Pasteur—Rue Calmette and Rue Yersin, both named for protégés of Pasteur. Dr. Albert Calmette established a research lab in Saigon in 1890, and Dr. Alexander Yersin set up a lab in Nha Trang in 1895. These were the first Pasteur Institutes established outside Paris. There are also a Rue Pasteur and Rue Yersin in Nha Trang. Another Pasteur protégé, Marie Curie, is also honored in Vietnam. Marie Curie School has changed little since its founding in 1918. The archway still bears her name, though Ecole Marie Curie has been changed to Truong Marie Curie. At 159 Nam Ky Khoi Nghia, the high school is attended by 1,000 students studying English and French.

streets and they are surrounded by about a million Vietnamese and Chinese.

Saigon has little in the way of native architecture, barring pagodas and Chinese–style shophouses. The city was largely built by the French. When the French captured Saigon in 1859, the area was swamp and marshland. They set about filling in canals, draining marshlands, and building roads, tree-lined boulevards, an opera house, court, arsenal, customs houses, cinemas, and schools. For entertainment, the French introduced exclusive sports clubs, glitzy casinos, and sleazy opium dens. Down by Saigon River lay the offices of the shipping and communications company Messageries Maritimes. At 74 Hai Ba Trung St. sat the state opium factory.

Saigon of the 1930s was cleaner and leafier than it is now—the French took great pride in their manicured lawns and botanical gardens—now the zoo area. They planted the tamarind trees that shade Saigon boulevards and break up the monotonous architecture. The French left behind their cars, too. In among the throng of cyclos and motorcycles plying the streets you might stray across a Citroën Traction, the 1930s classic French car with running boards. Traces of the French presence linger in the food as well. Sitting in a café you can crack open a BGI—a joint-venture French beer not far removed from the original beers of French Indochina—and indulge in a baguette with pâté.

Hotel de Ville

The Hotel de Ville, at the northern end of Nguyen Hue Boulevard, still serves as Saigon's City Hall. With its ornate gingerbread facade, the Hotel de Ville looks like the town hall of a French town. Considerable debate raged over its design and location before it was finally completed in 1908. Today it's called the People's Committee Headquarters, but neither the people nor visitors are allowed to see the interior, where crystal chandeliers hang.

If you want to walk around this area, park your transport in the garage at number 155 near the Rex Hotel, used by taxis, tour buses, motorcycles, and bicycles. The original iron grillwork exterior is still intact and is possibly of German origin.

Big French stores such as Les Grands Magasins Charner once lined Nguyen Hue Boulevard, then Boulevard Charner. Its motto: "We supply you with every requisite for colonial life, at the lowest prices." Little has changed in this corner of Saigon, except for the addition of a large statue of Ho Chi Minh cradling a child, on the strip of greenery facing the Hotel de Ville. A few red flags flutter from the building.

Revolutionary Museum

The Revolutionary Museum, at 65 Ly Tu Trong, used to be the mansion of the French governor of Cochinchina; under President Ngo Dinh Diem, it was known as Gia Long Palace. This is one building where you can see the interior. The neoclassical building itself and the grounds actually hold greater interest than the museum displays, which you'll see repeated in many military museums in Vietnam.

Downstairs are former ballrooms with high ceilings; a grand sweeping staircase leads to the upper salons. Downstairs you'll find random displays from the 1850s to 1940s, including some pictures of old Saigon; memorabilia upstairs recalls the 1940s–1960s and Vietnam's struggle against the French and Americans. Of interest here are displays of propaganda leaflets urging GIs to hurry home.

Outside, a parked Huey UH-1 helicopter overlooks landscaped lawns and gardens. Under the helicopter is a bunker with six meeting rooms and a tunnel leading to Le Thanh Ton Street and Reunification Hall. It was built in the 1960s under the Diem regime. Also on the grounds are artillery pieces, two small planes, and a Russian tank used in the 1975 assault on Saigon. The Revolutionary Museum is open 0800–1130 and 1330–1630, closed Monday. Free entry. Opposite the museum is a tranquil park and a café serving refreshments.

Because of the one-way streets here, you go against the grain to reach the museum. If on a bike, you can either get off and walk it to the museum, or loop around the block north of the museum, circling past the Palais de Justice.

Cercle Sportif

From the museum, circle up Rue Pasteur, turn left on Nguyen Du, and loop around the back of Reunification Hall to Nguyen Thi Minh Khai Street. Step inside a north entrance, and you'll find ghostly traces of French presence in a dilapidated sports club, once the Cercle Sportif. The French set up a chain of Cercle Sportif clubs in Indochina; these clubs, of course, were exclusively French, with no Vietnamese allowed. Today the old Cercle Sportif building is part of a Vietnamese youth recreation club. You can still make out the Cercle Sportif logo, a C entwined with an S inside a circle, carved in wood at the former clubhouse entrance. The clubhouse overlooks tennis courts and a small outdoor café. Farther back is a vintage full-length swimming pool, surreally framed by Grecian columns; trellised areas and plants shelter wicker chairs. There are two wading pools here, and a place still known as the Cercle Gym, housing the Cercle Cafeteria. Adjacent **Van Hoa Park** used to be Jardin de la Ville; it was turned over to the public by the French governor in 1869.

East of the Cercle Sportif is **Le Quy Don School,** formerly the French school Lycée Chasseloup-Laubat. The school was featured in the movie *The Lover.*

Notre Dame Cathedral

Notre Dame is a Gothic cathedral with twin brick towers tipped with iron spires and flying buttresses, all faithfully reproduced in tropical Vietnam. All the parts were shipped from France. The cathedral was built 1877–1883. It's a prominent Saigon landmark often featured on postcards. Services are held here six times on Sunday and several times during the week. Go inside to view the stained-glass windows; the cathedral is open 0700–1100 and 1430–1630 weekdays. The cathedral overlooks a statue of the Virgin Mary in a small square once known as Place Pigneau de Béhaine, named after an 18th-century missionary who lobbied for French military intervention in Cochinchina.

Facing onto the same square to the east is the **General Post Office,** built in the 1880s. It looks pretty much the same today, apart from a red flag waving outside, a couple of big antennae sprouting on the rooftop, and, inside, a large Ho Chi Minh portrait presiding over the proceedings. Go inside to see the large glass dome and long vaulted ceiling. On the outside, little plaques bear the names of distinguished French: Descartes, Voltaire, Ampere.

Municipal Theater and the Hotel Continental

On Dong Khoi Street a few blocks southeast of Notre Dame Cathedral lies the Municipal Theater, also known as Saigon Concert Hall. Originally built in the early 1900s, it was renovated in the 1940s. After 1956, the building housed the lower division of the National Assembly. Today the theater is used as a venue for traditional theater, gymnastics displays, and rock concerts. The interior is not as elaborate as the exterior suggests. Although there are plush red chairs and fancy wrought-iron banisters, there's hardly anything in the way of ceiling decoration. For bike or motorcycle parking, go to the back of the theater to the east side.

Facing the Municipal Theater is the Hotel Continental, a French hotel that has been restored to its colonial grandeur. The hotel was originally constructed in 1885 by the Societé des Grands Hotels Indochinois, part of a chain of elegant hotels also found in Hanoi, Hué, Vung Tau, and Phnom Penh. The sidewalk terrace outside the Continental was a popular rendezvous spot for highbrow French society. In the 1980s, the terrace bar was glassed in and transformed into an air-conditioned Italian restaurant. Graham Greene featured the terrace in his novel *The Quiet American*. Somerset Maugham described it in *The Gentleman in the Parlour* (1930):

> *Outside the hotel are terraces, and at the hour of the aperitif, they are crowded with bearded, gesticulating Frenchmen drinking the sweet and sickly beverages…. It is very agreeable to sit under the awning on the terrace of the Hotel Continental, and with an innocent drink before you, read in the local newspaper heated controversies upon the affairs of the colony.*

The "heated controversies" included how to treat domestics (should one hit them?) and how many hours to spend in siesta (two or three?). Beyond domestic worries, the French tended to business affairs and the pursuit of leisure. After work a round of absinthe, a visit to a restaurant, the theater, and possibly a trip to a casino, brothel, or opium den. Their decadent lifestyle led to another big problem—large unpaid tabs.

Along Dong Khoi

Dong Khoi Street is a classy shopping thoroughfare with antiques, jewelry, Parisian fashions, and perfumes. During the French era this was Rue Catinat, an exclusive shopping area and haunt of spies, French police inspectors, and Annamese beauties. It was also the site of occasional terrorist café bombings. During the Vietnam War, the street became Tu Do (Freedom Street)—a red-light district—and was renamed Dong Khoi (General Uprising) Street after 1975.

Though it's seen better days, Dong Khoi Street still has an exclusive air about it, with art galleries, gift shops, lacquerware shops, and a few cafés. On the east side of Dong Khoi art shops sell hand-painted reproductions of famous canvases. For insight into this curious industry, go past the Dong Khoi Hotel and turn east on Ngo Duc Ke; here you'll find a whole workshop of oil artists—some 20 of them—busy touching up their Monets, Gauguins, Van Goghs, and Picassos. Everything down to that Mona Lisa smile or Gauguin breast is copied from art books by graduates of the Fine Arts School of Ho Chi Minh City. A canvas that takes a week to copy starts out at $80–100, while a six-week effort may yield a hefty $600. Custom-made canvases can also be ordered.

The hotels along Dong Khoi are mostly operated by Saigon Tourist. The outfit makes select renovations, often in joint ventures. A classic that was renovated in 1997 is the **Dong Khoi Hotel,** at 8 Dong Khoi, which back in the 1920s was called the Saigon Palace. The lobby features the original spiral marble staircase; the rooms have cavernous bathrooms. Down by the Saigon River the **Hotel Majestic** has also seen extensive renovations. This old French hotel at 1 Dong Khoi is known in Vietnamese as the Cuu Long, or River of the Nine Dragons. The fifth-floor bar affords great views of Saigon River.

WARTIME SAIGON

THE UNWILLING WORKING FOR THE UNABLE TO DO THE UNNECESSARY FOR THE UNGRATEFUL

inscription on a U.S. Army–issue Zippo lighter;
Saigon, 1970

Charles de Gaulle told John F. Kennedy that Vietnam was "a bottomless military and political swamp." He forgot to mention the moral quagmire. American soldiers who fought in Vietnam paid a double price for a dumb and immoral foreign policy: They fought the war and then weathered the stigma of defeat and disfavor at home. Faced with these unpleasant truths, a number of Vietnam vets have returned to Vietnam as a healing process, to lay to rest the uneasiness that has plagued them since the war. The Vietnamese, for their part, had trouble understanding exactly why the Americans interfered in their affairs. Still, they treat returning U.S. veterans the same as any other tourists—they bear no grudge. It's really the Vietnamese who should be bitter

© AVALON TRAVEL PUBLISHING, INC.

THE WARTIME SOUVENIR SHOP

In 1993 two shops opened on either side of the gates at the War Crimes Museum, each called Wartime Souvenir Shop (that signage has since been removed, but it sums up the trade here very succinctly). Apart from the standard stock of T-shirts, the proprietors sell a rather bizarre collection of souvenirs. How about a flower vase made from a 40mm cartridge, burnished to a bright gold? Or a pair of Ho Chi Minh tire-tread sandals? Perhaps a green NVA pith helmet or NVA campaign and victory badges? Other items on sale include lighters made from M-16 cartridges and small oil lamps the Vietcong recycled from M-79 cartridges and used to illuminate tunnels. There's even a set of Vietnam in Wartime postcards, one featuring a Vietcong woman in full combat gear, striking a heroic pose.

You can also buy U.S. flashlights, watches, compasses, and field glasses. And there's a range of rusted U.S. dog tags with name, religion, and blood type embossed on each one. Authentic? Probably not. Certainly morbid.

U.S. army-issue Zippo lighters cost $5–20 depending on "quality" and whether or not they work. Many antique and souvenir shops in Saigon, as well as shops at Dan Sinh army surplus market, carry Zippos. Some feature a poignant, prayerful, military, romantic, or obscene slogan; others bear engravings such as nude women, Peanuts cartoon characters Snoopy and Lucy, or the bearded Zig Zag rolling-papers man.

During the Vietnam War, aluminum cans discarded by U.S. soldiers were turned into hand grenades by the Vietcong. This came as a shock to American troops, who began to be more careful about what they threw away. The Vietnamese are still transforming those cans. At the Wartime Souvenir Shop and on the streets of Saigon, you can buy tanks, Huey helicopters, F-4 Phantom jets, F-111s, and Cessnas made of old Coke, Tiger, or Heineken cans. These origami-in-metal pieces sell for a dollar and feature painstaking detail—the helicopter doors are even detachable.

War materiel is recycled in the oddest places. Once, when I mentioned the war, my cyclo driver, a former ARVN soldier, pointed at his bicycle bell—a large brass cylinder struck with a small handlebar-operated device, like a gong. I took a closer look: The bell was made from a 105mm shell case, cut off at the bottom.

about the whole thing, but they're not. Life goes on.

ⓜ War Crimes Museum

To take a shattering leap back to the wartime 1960s and 1970s, visit the War Crimes Museum, open daily, including holidays, 0730–1145 and 1330–1645, on Vo Van Tan near the intersection of Le Quy Don. After new relations were established with the United States, the name of this place was changed to "War Remnants Museum," and by the time you get there, it may have changed again. Who knows? The official HCMC City Map of 2000 calls it the "Museum of Aggressive War."

To get there from downtown Saigon, take Pasteur Street north and turn left on Vo Van Tan. The museum is on the grounds of a French villa that once housed the U.S. Information Service. The villa is not used for displays—these are in four salons close by. This small museum is grisly, horrifying, sobering, and deeply disturbing. Few English captions accompany the pictures on the walls, but the photos speak for themselves—the My Lai massacre, victims of antipersonnel weapons such as napalm and Agent Orange, deformed babies. A series taken from the *Chicago Sun-Times* shows a Vietnamese POW being pushed from an American helicopter. This raises the ethical questions regarding war crimes: Where does "normal" war end, and where do war crimes begin?

There is a photo parade of the guilty, from Lyndon Johnson to Richard Nixon, pictures of U.S. and European antiwar demonstrations, a display of eight medals sent to the museum by American vets in 1990. On display are American infantry weapons used in Vietnam. And in one salon is a picture of General Giap greeting former Secretary of Defense Robert McNamara in November 1995, after he announced the whole war was a terrible mistake. There used to be a Chinese atrocity wing in this museum, related to the border wars of 1979. After Vietnam normalized relations with China, the display was discreetly removed. In the meantime, two Wartime Souvenir Shops popped up, selling Zippo lighters, war memorabilia, cobra wine, T-shirts, water puppets, and other odd items.

Around the grounds you'll find an array of captured weaponry—M-41 tank, 175mm howitzer, M-113 flamethrower, A37B light bomber, U17A observation aircraft, and a few Huey helicopters. There's also a French guillotine, brought to Vietnam in the early 1900s. As late as the 1950s it was hauled around the provinces to publicly decapitate Vietminh resistance fighters in the French colonial manner. After normalization with the United States, exhibits at the War Crimes Museum were rearranged and modified, and the authorities decided to take another crack at the French by putting up a replica of several cells of the notorious French prison of Condao, complete with models of "tiger cages" and pictures of torture methods. These same prisons were taken over by the South Vietnamese regimes and used to torture captured North Vietnamese—strangely enough, the exhibits focus more on the Diem Regime era rather than the French era.

The War Crimes Museum is an odd place to stage entertainment, but as the biggest tourist draw in Saigon, it's somehow logical. There are 20-minute water puppetry performances in a small on-site theater and performances of traditional Vietnamese music in another salon.

American Haunts

From the War Crimes Museum, head east until you reach an odd traffic circle. American civilians once occupied apartments around the circle, an exclusive residential zone. In the middle of the circle stands a shaft of concrete. At first glance this appears to be a piece of Socialist sculpture—there's a surreal flight of stairs to one side. Apparently there was once a statue of a sacred tortoise mounted on top of the concrete pillar, but it was blown up by disgruntled Vietnamese. Around the traffic circle are lots of open-air cafés where you can sit and contemplate the damage. Inside the derelict area a set of fountains have been installed, turned on for photo opportunities on special holidays.

Vietcong terrorists sometimes turned Saigon into a battlefield, bombing businesses patronized by Americans. Despite these attacks, Saigon was one of the safest places to be during the Vietnam War, and its legendary bars, restaurants, and hotels were the dreams of GIs in the field. Some of the places they frequented still thrive. The Rex Hotel was used by U.S. officers, as was the Majestic; war correspondents gathered to watch the war on the roof of the Caravelle Hotel; Maxim's nightclub was the same overpriced dive it is today.

The American Consulate

On Le Duan Boulevard, Vietnamese mill around the entrance of the U.S. Consulate, queuing up to apply for U.S. visas or immigration papers. Déjà vu of sorts: The present cream-and-green consulate building was constructed in 1999 in the same walled compound as the old wartime embassy. The six-story American Embassy of wartime days was completely demolished and turned into a garden area that adjoins the present U.S. Consulate.

The Americans moved the embassy to this site in 1967 after the previous location was blown up by a 100-kilogram car bomb. But the new fortresslike building on Le Duan was not enough to stave off an attack: A 17-man Vietcong commando unit stormed the embassy on January 31, 1968. The commandos, dressed as South Vietnamese soldiers,

Saigon

were killed, along with five American marines and MPs.

The U.S. Embassy closed on April 30, 1975, when the last of the staff boarded a helicopter from the roof as Saigon fell around their ears. The last chopper lifts were hectic. Thousands of Vietnamese who had worked for the Americans had been promised a lift out, but the United States reneged and they were left behind. The furious Vietnamese sacked the embassy. In *All the Wrong Places,* English writer James Fenton recounts,

> *The place was packed, and in chaos. Papers, files, brochures, and reports were strewn around.... One man called me over to a wall safe and seemed to be asking if I knew the number of the combination. Another was hacking away at an air conditioner, another was dismantling a refrigerator.*

In their rush to get out, American embassy staff left behind files on those who worked for them, making it easy for the north to identify collaborators.

Although the embassy was razed in the late 1990s, a few relics were salvaged—including the set of portable stairs leading up to the last chopper. Those were removed to Washington, D.C.'s, Smithsonian Institute.

Military Museum

The main target of Vietcong tanks rumbling through the capital was not the U.S. Embassy but the gates of the Presidential Palace, three blocks to the west. Americans remember the last helicopter leaving the U.S. Embassy, but for the Vietnamese the key image is that of tanks smashing down the palace gates. The tanks then rolled onto the lawn, formed a semicircle, and fired a salute.

The Vietnamese point of view on the war is presented at the Military Museum, just north of Central Saigon (District 1). There's a big 1975 section on the fall of Saigon, complete with scale models, maps with lights indicating strategic campaign points, and data on the American imperialist aggressors and their southern puppets. The Vietcong infiltrated the capital well before the final attack, dressed in Saigon Army uniforms. They stayed in Cholon, where the Chinese—always shrewd businesspeople—were already manufacturing North Vietnamese flags. The real Saigon Army soldiers stripped off their uniforms and fled, leaving mounds of clothing, boots, and weapons on the streets. Others dressed in Vietcong–style black pajamas.

Apart from its centerpiece battle-plan model, the museum displays photos and small arms. Most signs are in Vietnamese, with scattered English captions. Although the museum covers some events from 1945 on, most cover the period 1973–1975, including a garbled 15-minute video on campaigns of that era. Some pictures document the use of bicycles, which were very important to the military success of the North Vietnamese. They moved tons of supplies along the Ho Chi Minh Trail in caravans of modified and reinforced bicycles. These "steel horses" could each carry up to 200 kilos of supplies, even through deep mud. If the Americans bombed a bridge, NVA troops simply ferried their bicycles across and carried on.

In the museum's outer courtyard lie rusting leftover hardware—a jeep, 85mm guns, small planes. There are an incongruous bonsai nursery and an art gallery—regular art downstairs, revolutionary art upstairs. For $500 you can buy a canvas showing the Fall of Saigon; for $200, a Cu Chi Tunnels painting. The Military Museum is open 0830–1130 and 1330–1600, closed Monday; entry is free.

Puppets

When the American imperialists left, their South Vietnamese puppets were crushed— sent to reeducation camps for the next 6–7 years. But some puppets have never fallen out of favor with the North Vietnamese—water puppets. Right across the street from the Military Museum is the **History Museum.** Enter the grounds of the zoological gardens, $1; go into the History Museum, $1; then find the **water puppet theater,** another $2 for entry. The 20-minute shows are intended to delight children—but will please all ages. Shows start when the puppeteers ascertain the audience has enough kids—usually once an hour, on the hour. Small model water puppets are sold here, too. This is one of the few places you can see water puppets in Saigon (you can also see shows at the War Crimes Museum). There are special performances for children at festivals in other temporary sites, but no fixed venue as in Hanoi.

The History Museum is open daily 0800–1130 and 1330–1630, including Sundays and holidays. Interesting displays include the Cham sculpture section, with a superb standing bronze Buddha; the ethnography section, with displays of Central Highlands costumes and village models such as those from the Kontum-Pleiku area; a display of pieces from Funan, Oc-Eo, and Han Chinese periods; and the Buddha sculpture section, with superb Buddha and Avalokitesvara statues from East Asia. Under the French this 1928 structure was known as Musée Blanchard de la Brosse, set in what were once the finest French botanical gardens in Southeast Asia. Saigon's motley zoo collection has since been added to the flora, making this a zoological gardens—a relaxing place to pass time and chat with the locals. It's best to stick to the flora side; the animals look rather forlorn. Despite the ravages of war, the gardens present a great variety of plant species.

CHOLON PAGODAS

In 1978 the government launched an assault on capitalist practices in Saigon, primarily targeting the wealthy Chinese business community in Cholon, the "Chinatown" of Saigon. The following year China engaged Vietnam in a vicious border war in the north, and a quarter of Vietnam's ethnic Chinese fled the country—the first of the "boat people." Most of the exodus was from Saigon and Cholon, where every shop and house was ransacked for valuables and gold and many Chinese stripped of their wealth. In the 1980s Cholon was a ghost town. Cautiously, ethnic

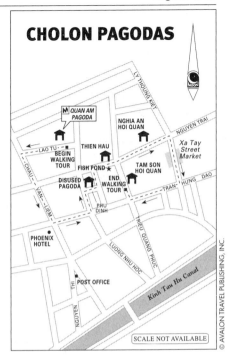

Chinese have been returning since the normalization of relations with China in 1991 and the relaxation of foreign investment laws. Now it appears Cholon is once again becoming the economic powerhouse of the city, with high rents, thriving hotels, nightclubs, and department stores in District 5. The vice of gambling is back, too: Saigon Race Track in District 11 reopened in 1989; horse races are held four times a week.

The pagodas of Cholon once served as congregation halls for different Chinese communities depending on their origins—Fukienese, Cantonese, and so on. The communities fragmented in the 1970s and 1980s, and most pagodas were abandoned or fell into disrepair. Nevertheless, Cholon's pagodas are the finest in Ho Chi Minh City. A few have been restored, are active, and serve as showpieces for tourism. Other pagodas have been transformed—one has been turned into a local sports club, with weightlifting and bodybuilding hardware.

Saigon

BIG MARKET

Cholon means "Big Market," and the area is certainly bustling. Especially in District 5, windows display luxury goods imported from China and Thailand, and the boulevards are jam-packed with commuters on brand-new motorcycles and cyclos loaded with goods. Riverside warehouses are piled high with dried fish and sacks of rice; outdoor markets are thronged with customers. The largest market in Cholon is **Binh Tay Market,** off Hau Giang Boulevard in District 6. A courtyard-type block contains open-air and covered stalls, mainly in wholesale trade. The market is vast and colorful and sells everything from spices to silk; it's an ideal place to ramble for an hour or two. On the south side, there are many foodstalls.

An Duong Market opened in late 1991 near the intersection of An Duong Vuong Boulevard and Su Van Hanh Street in District 5. This market shows the confidence of the Chinese community in the new Cholon—it was built with a $5 million investment from almost a hundred Cholon businessmen. The five-story market complex has 24,000 square meters of commercial space. The top two floors comprise a Taiwanese hotel and office complex; the lower floors offer retail space, with the first floor for clothing. The basement houses many small restaurants—a good place to dine on a budget.

Ⓜ Quan Am Pagoda

Quan Am Pagoda, at 12 Lao Tu St., is the most active pagoda in Cholon. Hawkers here sell incense sticks, paper offerings, and captive birds to a steady stream of devotees. About 25 nuns and monks are based at the temple, and several live on the premises. In front of the main altar is a white ceramic statue of Quan Am, known in Chinese as Guanyin, the Goddess of Mercy. There are also red wedding dresses and elaborate funeral chariots on display. The roof is richly decorated, with Chinese legends rendered in ceramic tiles.

Clear your lungs of incense and walk south toward the Phoenix Hotel. In the distance you'll spot a yellow building, the post office. It bears a Buu Dien sign, but you can still make out the old French PTT sign. In the open area before the post office is a statue of Dinh Phung, a Vietnamese hero famed for fighting the French.

Pleasure City

At a disused pagoda on a corner, turn onto tiny Phu Dinh Street, a tiny neighborhood street with old architecture and lots of local cafés. Halfway along, at number 7, is the house seen in the French movie *The Lover.*

It is now a small café (you can get a better idea of the original architecture by looking at number 9 or number 15). The Chinese shophouse looks rather bland and innocent now, difficult to imagine as a trysting place in a steamy affair between a Chinese man and a French schoolgirl. But remember the context: Cholon in the 1930s, '40s, and '50s was rife with opium dens, mahjong joints, and gambling joints such as the Grand Monde Casino. Cholon had a reputation as a place for business and pleasure, often conducted in the same hotel. The City of Pleasure appears to be reviving, with seedy karaoke, nightclubs, and taxi dancers in major hotels catering to Asian businessmen.

Goddesses and Generals

Thien Hau Pagoda, at 710 Nguyen Trai, honors Thien Hau, the goddess of the sea and protectress of sailors and fisherfolk. Thien Hau also retains elements of the Taoist Queen of Heaven and is a popular deity in Hong Kong and Taiwan. The pagoda was constructed in the early 19th century and is one of the largest and busiest in the city. It was once the focus of the Cantonese community. Recently restored, it now serves as a showpiece for Saigon Tourism. Inside the front gate are two enormous in-

SAIGON RIVER BOAT TOURS

Since Saigon is a port, cruising the city gives you a different perspective. The simplest trip to make on the river is a cheap ferry-hop to the east banks of the Saigon River—there's a crossing near the Riverside Hotel. And if you want to follow the Saigon River all the way to the sea, consider taking a hydrofoil trip to the coastal resort of Vung Tau—there are several daily departures from a terminal at the foot of Ham Nghi Boulevard. It's a pleasant trip, proceeding past heavy port shipping and on through flat countryside.

At night you can take dinner cruises on the Saigon River, which is a good idea because you can't see the black scum and polluted water then. Saigon Tourism arranges boats for a two-hour dinner-dance trip along the Saigon River to Thanh Da Island at a cost of $15 a head. Boats depart several times weekly from the lobby of the Hotel Majestic. Three separate programs are performed on different nights. One is song and dance, the second traditional music, the third a traditional wedding ceremony.

Canals around Saigon are black and scummy. Ramshackle houses balance on stilts along the banks of tributaries, and you might get a glimpse of boats with leg-rowers. There are a few commuter boats along the canals, though foreigners rarely use them. Cholon's Ben Tay Market can be reached along the Saigon River by regular or rented boat along Ben Nghe Channel. The boat drops you short of the market; then you walk up. Since you've already seen the scum, no need to take the boat back—use the bus or other transportation back to town.

cense urns; huge incense spirals burn for hours. The principal temple image is a gilded Thien Hau; a model boat lies nearby. More interesting visually are the intricate ceramic friezes on the temple roof, best viewed from a small courtyard. Opposite the temple is a run-down old fishpond, formerly connected with temple ceremonies. Although Thien Hau Pagoda is busy all day, there are special services on Sunday at 0600 and 1600.

One block to the east is **Nghia An Hoi Quan Pagoda**, at 678 Nguyen Trai. The temple was built by the Chaozhou Chinese congregation. After passing a carved wooden boat shading the entrance, you come to the larger-than-life red horse of Quan Cong, a revered Chinese general. The statue of Quan Cong is encased in glass and bears a red face, long beard, and green costume. He's flanked by two assistants, a general and a mandarin.

Continue to **Tam Son Hoi Quan Pagoda**, at 118 Trieu Quang Phuc St., a Fukienese pagoda that has fallen into neglect. It's dedicated to Me Sanh, Goddess of Fertility—childless mothers patronize a statue at the back. The temple was built in the 19th century in Sino-Vietnamese style and is pleasantly uncluttered.

SAIGON PAGODAS

Saigon has upward of 200 pagodas. Most are either run-down or humdrum; the best are found in Cholon. A pagoda is a community center of sorts and often a repository for small funerary jars, each containing the ashes of the deceased with a photo and nameplate. Newer pagodas, such as Xa Loi and Vinh Nghiem, are of more interest at festival time, when they're ablaze with incense and thronged with devotees and beggars. Some of the following pagodas are on the fringes of Saigon.

Phung Son Tu Pagoda

At 338 Nguyen Cong Tru St., Phung Son Pagoda lies south of Ben Thanh Market, close to the Army Surplus market in District 1. This Chinese–style pagoda was built by the Fujian community in the 1940s and is very similar in style to Cholon pagodas. Fierce warrior statues guard the entrance doors. The temple is dedicated to Ong Bon, guardian of happiness and virtue.

🄼 Jade Emperor Pagoda

You'll find the small Jade Emperor Pagoda at 73 Mai Thi Luu St., off Dien Bien Phu Street.

Built in 1900, it's home to a bizarre collection of superbly carved wood deities—some Buddhist, some Taoist. Presiding at the main altar is Ngoc Hoang, the Taoist Emperor of Jade. The wooden panels in a side chapel, the Hall of the Ten Hells, show the thousand tortures awaiting evildoers. Near the main entrance, to one side of the temple, a chamber holds many small ceramic figures of mothers and children cloaked in red—a fertility shrine of sorts, visited by women.

Dai Giac Pagoda

Dai Giac Pagoda is at 112 Nguyen Van Troi, near Saigon Omni Hotel. Dai Giac is cluttered with kitsch—more like a Chinese amusement park than a pagoda. Inside are Buddha and Quan Am statues in glass cases, a few lion statues, a magnificent brass gong, a huge black drum made of porcelain with mother-of-pearl inlay, and funerary urns bearing photos of the departed. In the courtyard is a huge Laughing Buddha made of wood, and a grotto with a Quan Am statue. To the north side of Dai Giac a six-level pagoda features an exterior coated in pieces of broken porcelain; linked to the pagoda are monks' quarters.

Vinh Nghiem Pagoda

Vinh Nghiem Pagoda is also on Nguyen Van Troi, just south of Thi Nghe Channel. Here there are two buildings—the main temple and a seven-story pagoda. The latter contains funeral urns and is open only on holidays and at festival time, when the place is packed. The temple was completed in the early 1970s with assistance from the Japan-Vietnam Friendship Association, which explains the Japanese architecture. The interior walls bear scrolls with scenes from the *Jataka Tales*. The temple's large bell was a gift from Japanese Buddhists, presented during the Vietnam War.

Xa Loi Pagoda

Xa Loi Pagoda, at 89 Ba Huyen Quan Thanh St. off Dien Bien Phu Street in District 3, is a large modern concrete structure with a large, newish Buddha backed by a neon halo. In the courtyard below is a stucco Quan Am. Xa Loi was the headquarters of militant Buddhists during their struggle to overthrow the Diem regime. In August 1963 thousands demonstrated to protest religious persecution; on August 21 special forces attacked the pagoda, and martial law was declared.

Thic Quang Duc Shrine

This shrine is named for a 66-year-old monk from Hué who immolated himself on June 11, 1963. A photograph of the monk in flames made front-page news around the world. About 30 monks and nuns followed his example, protesting the Diem regime and U.S. involvement in Vietnam. Diem's sister-in-law Madame Nhu made jokes about barbecued monks and said, "Let them burn—we shall clap our hands!" This shrine lies at the corner of Nguyen Dinh Chieu and Cach Mang Thang Tam streets, a few blocks south of Xa Loi Pagoda. The car used to drive the monk to the immolation site is in Thien Mu Pagoda in Hué.

Giac Vien Tu Pagoda

On the outskirts of Saigon in District 11, the Vietnamese–style Giac Vien Tu Pagoda is dedicated to Emperor Gia Long. The accumulation of 300 years of incense burning imbues this place with a striking atmosphere. There is a profusion of carvings—Buddhist, Taoist, and Confucian deities and mythical figures. The most significant is a large gilded statue of Amitabha, Buddha of the Past. After a body is cremated, the ashes are transported in a funeral carriage to the pagoda. Numerous funerary jars are on view in the first chamber. Twenty monks are attached to the temple, and half live on the premises. The temple is hard to find—it's about 200 meters off Lac Long Quan Street. Get there by moto or rental car.

Giac Lam Pagoda

Giac Lam Pagoda, at 118 Lac Long Quan St. in Tan Binh District, was built in 1744. It is believed to be the oldest pagoda still standing in Saigon. It's quite similar in architecture and atmosphere to Giac Vien Tu Pagoda. The two pagodas are a few kilometers apart; a visit to one or the other should suffice. Giac Lam is large and has darkened halls with carved jackwood statues. Senior monks wear yellow robes; novice monks wear brown robes.

OTHER SIGHTS
Additional Museums

The **Art Museum** (Bao Tang My Thuat), in a mansion at 97A Pho Duc Chinh St. in Central Saigon, displays revolutionary art and sculpture, as well as artifacts from the Oc-Eo civilization.

The **Ho Chi Minh Museum** occupies the old French customs house, known as Dragon House Wharf, at the confluence of the Saigon River and Ben Nghe Channel. The French transport company Messageries Maritimes once had its headquarters here. The museum celebrates the exploits of Uncle Ho, who left Saigon at the age of 21 aboard a French freighter from this wharf. Signing on as a galley boy, he departed in 1911 on an extended journey through Europe, Africa, North America, and Asia and did not return to Vietnam until 1941. A visit to the museum is compulsory for legions of Saigon schoolchildren, who have their photos taken with a statue of Uncle Ho in the background.

Museums in Ho Chi Minh City are usually open Tuesday–Sunday 0800–1130 and 1400–1700.

Reunification Hall

Reunification Hall, or Thong Nhat Conference Hall, is one of those take-it-or-leave-it destinations. Some like it, some hate it. On entry you get a brochure; there's also a crackly revolutionary film thrown in along the line. A cross between a museum and conference center, the rambling Reunification Hall exudes a sterile atmosphere and displays appalling taste in architecture and furnishing. Sometimes the place is closed for state occasions; otherwise, it's open 0730–1030 and 1300–1600 daily. There are two entrances and exits: The main gates are on Nam Ky Khoi Nghia; there is a side entrance on the south side of the grounds at 106 Nguyen Du Street. Visitors must take a guided tour; the English of the guides may be poor.

The hall was formerly the site of Norodom Palace, the residence of the French Governor-general of Indochina, built in 1868. The Governor-general spent little time there, as his principal seat was in Hanoi. After the Geneva Conference in 1954 and the installation of President Ngo Dinh Diem, the place was renamed the Presidential Palace. In 1962, two South Vietnamese Air Force pilots turned their firepower on the palace in an attempt to assassinate Diem. The president and his family escaped to the cellar, but the palace was largely destroyed. Diem had the place razed and ordered construction of a new palace (which he did not live to see through because of his assassination in December 1963).

The present building was thrown up in the early 1960s—designed by Paris-trained architect Ngo Viet Thu, who combined Western and Oriental architectural elements within a Chinese structural framework. On October 31, 1966, the Thieu-Ky administration inaugurated the new presidential palace. Thieu lived and worked there for the next eight years. In early April 1975 another renegade pilot bombed the new palace, damaging part of it. On April 30, 1975, NVA tanks smashed down the gates of the palace. The NVA took control of Saigon, arresting President General Duong Van Minh and his cabinet. A short career for General Minh: He'd become head of state only two days before. After a period of reeducation, Minh was allowed to emigrate to France in 1983.

The hall has been preserved as it was on April 30, 1975. Various rooms are decorated with lacquered paintings and filled with dowdy 1960s furniture. More interesting are the basement and the rooftop. President Nguyen Van Thieu had a bombproof bunker built in the basement of the hall; from here he conducted government affairs until April 1975, when he fled. The bunker was the nerve center for conducting the war: You can view military maps, field radios, and banks of U.S. telecom gizmos. The president's Mercedes is parked near the kitchen. On the rooftop is a helipad with

Saigon

a Huey helicopter parked on it. This makes a macabre photo-op: Group tours are sometimes permitted to line up for pictures, pretending it's 1975 and they're scrambling for the last chopper out. In this area are a small coffee shop and a video salon with a longish scratchy documentary with excerpts from a French television documentary. The video shows events leading up to the fall of Saigon—from the Vietnamese Communist point of view, of course.

Parked on the manicured grounds of Reunification Hall are some stray bits of hardware from the war. Near the main gate is a Soviet tank—supposedly the one that smashed down the same gate on April 30, 1975, although there seem to be an awful lot of tanks around laying claim to this honor. It appears that at least two NVA tanks smashed down the gates. Tank 843 rammed the side gate, and Tank 390 crashed through the front gate (the commander of Tank 843 raced up to the fourth-floor balcony to grab the main trophy—which was the South Vietnamese flag). Parked on the northeast side of the grounds is an American F-5E jet that was flown by South Vietnamese pilot Nguyen Thanh Trung. On April 8, 1975, double-agent Nguyen made a radical departure from his scheduled bombing run: He suddenly banked and left his squadron's formation in midair, turned back—and dropped two bombs on the palace before defecting northward.

Hindu and Muslim Temples

Saigon's eclectic mix of temples includes a few mosques and Hindu temples. Like the ethnic Chinese, Hindus and Muslims were persecuted by the revolutionary government and most, including the spiritual leaders, fled Vietnam. Still, there are a dozen mosques around Saigon. At 66 Dong Du St., off Dong Khoi, is **Saigon Central Mosque,** built by South Indian Muslims in 1935. The spotless blue and white structure features four minarets and is a tranquil retreat in the heart of the city; excellent Indian food is served at lunch hour.

Within a few blocks of Ben Thanh Market stand two Hindu temples. To the northwest of the market is **Mariamman Temple,** at 45 Truong Dinh Street. This century-old site is dedicated to the goddess Mariamman; it was taken over in 1975 and turned into a josstick factory. To the northeast of Ben Thanh Market is **Pani Hindu Temple** (also called Sri Thenday Litthapani), at 66 Ton That Thiep. This temple—more than a century old—was disbanded after 1975, but in early 1993 the government returned the temple to Saigon's tiny Hindu community. Hindu adherents of several nationalities come to this sacred shrine. You enter through a colonnaded interior courtyard with a small shrine guarded by horse statues, and an ornate door with bells mounted on it. If the walls look bare, it's because a lot of the statuary went missing—the central statue has been replaced by a picture. Framed pictures of Indian deities and important figures grace the walls—Shiva, Vishnu, Ghandi, Nehru. On the roof are towers with detailed Hindu sculpture.

Accommodations

Saigon has the largest selection of hotels in Vietnam. The scene is constantly changing—Saigon is like one huge construction zone. Accommodations vary from small homey guesthouses to luxurious suites. High-end hotels provide in-house movies, minibar, IDD, room safe, and individual air-conditioning control; facilities often include health club, business center, and restaurants. Major hotels charge 10 percent government tax and 5–10 percent service charge on top of listed prices; others include those charges in the tariff. Larger hotels will accept Visa, Master-Card, Diners Club, American Express, and JCB cards, but will surcharge up to 4 percent for using a credit card.

The two prime tourist accommodation zones are in District 1: Central Saigon appeals to business travelers, and Pham Ngu Lao is backpacker headquarters. However, the lines are becoming blurred as major hotels rise away from the downtown core. A burgeoning area for business visitors is District 3. Asian businesspeople and tourists, particularly Taiwanese, stay in Cholon in District 5.

PHAM NGU LAO

Under $20

Pham Ngu Lao is Saigon's version of Bangkok's Khao San Road—a rabbit warren of travel and transport agencies, cafés and bars, hotels and guesthouses, bicycle and motorcycle rentals, photo shops, secondhand bookstores, souvenir shops, and money changers. Add Western pop music and backpackers quaffing 333 beers under sidewalk umbrellas, and you've got the picture.

Family-run guesthouses often hang out signs that say simply Room for Rent (Phong Cho Thue) to avoid paying taxes. There are more than 70 guesthouses and minihotels in the Pham Ngu Lao area, and more on the way. There have been reports of thefts in some of the cheaper hotels—use your own padlock on the door whenever possible. Family-run places tend to be more secure.

Because of the great number of guesthouses, what follows here is just a sampling—you will find many more if you poke around the area, particularly around De Tham and Bui Vien streets and the alley between De Tham and Nguyen Thai Hoc streets. Things to look for in a guesthouse: quietness, windows, hot water, security, luggage storage for out-of-town trips, and a lounge or bar area downstairs where you can get a cold drink if need be—late at night when everything outside is locked or closed. Some guesthouses have a kind of "curfew"—they are reluctant to open the doors after 2300 hours—inquire whether late nights are a problem.

The **Liberty 3** (Que Huong), at 187 Pham Ngu Lao, tel. 8/8322657, offers upscale rooms, including a/c in the upper range. **Sinh GH,** 185/4 Pham Ngu Lao, tel. 8/8324877, offers rooms for $6–12—it's down an alley off the main street. **Le Le Room for Rent,** 269 De Tham, opposite Kim Café, tel. 8/8322110, has 24 rooms for $15–19. A few doors down at number 265 is another Room for Rent, tel. 8/8331512, charging $15 triple. At 254 De Tham is **Ngoc Dang GH,** tel. 8/8332019, with nine rooms for $6–10 fan, or $16–18 a/c. **Quyen Thanh,** 212 De Tham, tel. 8/8322370, fax 8/8324946, is a 14-room hotel with prices ranging $18–20 for rooms with fridge, TV, and a/c.

At 70 Bui Vien St. is **Guesthouse 70** (Phuong Lan), tel. 8/8330569, featuring seven rooms with shared bath for $9–18; family lounge downstairs. Next door at number 72 is **Guesthouse 72** (Le Van Tam), tel. 8/8330321, with five rooms for $7–10. **Minh Chau GH,** 75 Bui Vien, tel. 8/8331288, is a good deal with $8 fan rooms with hot water, or $10–15 a/c rooms. There are lots of other guesthouses along Bui Vien Street, often simply known by number—as in 54 Bui Vien, or 97 Guesthouse. At 58 Bui Vien is **Minh Phuc,** tel. 8/8360537, with $7 fan rooms or $14 doubles.

PHAM NGU LAO AREA

SCALE NOT AVAILABLE

© AVALON TRAVEL PUBLISHING, INC.

On the west side of Pham Ngu Lao, down an alley off the markets, is **Coco Loco Guest-house,** tel. 8/8322186—a family setup with superclean rooms. This guesthouse is a great value and often full—the seven rooms go for $10–12 each. "Room for Rent" signs are springing up in this area as fast as families can convert their houses into guesthouses—rooms go for $5–10, but fancier ones might cost $20. Tucked down an alley directly east

of the market is a bunch of hotels, including **Nhat Thai,** 373/10 Pham Ngu Lao (which means a side-alley), tel. 8/8360184, with good rooms for $11.

At the back of Pham Ngu Lao, toward New World Hotel, is **Le Suong,** 94–96 Le Lai, tel. 8/334137, a six-story hotel with 20 rooms for $5 s, $7 d with fan, and $10–12 d a/c. **A Chau,** 92B Le Lai, tel. 8/8331814, offers 10 rooms— $6 s or $7 d, with shower and fan.

$20–50

Down an alley close to Chua An Lac Pagoda is **Linh Linh,** 175/14 Pham Ngu Lao, tel. 8/8361851, a spotless boutique hotel—good rooms for $20–25 with a/c and hot water. **Giant Dragon Hotel,** 173 Pham Ngu Lao, tel. 8/8353268, fax 8/8353279, is a character-less high-rise hotel with 34 rooms for $30–70. **Hanh Hoa Hotel,** 237 Pham Ngu Lao, tel. 8/8360245, fax 8/8361482, offers 11 rooms for $20–50–60.

To the west side of Pham Ngu Lao, **Top Minihotel** (KS Thienh Dien), at 61 Do Quang Dau, tel. 8/8353281, offers 10 rooms for $40–50–60. **Le Canari** (Hoang Yen), 83A Bui Thi Xuan, tel. 8/391348, is an airy, clean minihotel featuring eight rooms for $18–25. At the back of Pham Ngu Lao, on Le Lai Street, are the following hotels. **Palace Saigon Minihotel,** 82 Le Lai, tel. 8/8331353, has nine rooms, all with shower and TV, for $25 s or $35 d. **Hotel Le Lai,** at 76 Le Lai St., tel. 8/8291246, fax 8/890282, is an eight-story building with 46 rooms for $23–47 s, $30–54 d, $36–61 t, and $69–94 for a suite. A bit farther to the north of Pham Ngu Lao is **Hoang Gia,** 12D Cach Mang Thang Tam St., tel. 8/8294846, fax 8/8225346, a nine-story hotel with 42 rooms for $30–50.

$50–100

There has been a flurry of joint-venture hotel building and renovation in this area. **Vien Dong Hotel** (Far East), at 275A Pham Ngu Lao, tel. 8/8393001, fax 8/8332812, has 109 double and triple rooms for $63–100. Hotel facilities include a restaurant and ABC Karaoke Bar on the first floor. Nearby is **Liberty 4,** with rooms for $25–60 and good views from the ninth-floor restaurant.

$100–200

The **New World Saigon,** at 76 Le Lai, tel. 8/8228888, fax 8/8230710, is Vietnam's largest hotel. This is a joint-venture project with Hong Kong's New World Development Company. There are 544 rooms in the 14-story building, with doubles for $185–210, executive floor suites for $250–500, and the Presidential

Suite for $850. The hotel boasts six restaurants, business center, an Olympic-size pool, flood-lit tennis courts, even a jogging track and a golf driving range.

Hotel Mercure Saigon, 79 Tran Hung Dao, tel. 8/8242525, fax 8/8242533, is run by the French Accor group. This four-star hotel has 104 rooms with every conceivable creature comfort known to Vietnam, including electronic safe, minibar, and satellite TV—there's even a phone installed in the shower so you won't miss a call. Rooms range $90–110 for standard and superior singles; $120–140 for deluxe; for double occupancy add $30 to the single price. The hotel features a restaurant, nightclub, and business center.

The **Metropole Hotel** (Binh Minh), 148 Tran Hung Dao, tel. 8/8322021, fax 8/8322019, has 94 spacious rooms with a/c, minibar, IDD, room safe, and satellite TV. Costs range $95 standard, $120 deluxe, and $120–150 suite. It's run by Saigon Tourist, and facilities include a business center, swimming pool, and a sky bar on the seventh floor.

CENTRAL SAIGON

Most of the hotels around the downtown core in District 1 are owned and operated by Saigon Tourist, sometimes as joint ventures. The Saigon Tourist hotels include the Rex, Caravelle, Majestic, Continental, Huong Sen, and Bong Sen. You can spot the top hotels—look for satellite dishes on the roof. Special permission is needed for these larger satellite dishes, capable of receiving StarTV.

Under $20

Budget and moderate hotels are hard to find around Central Saigon, and may not be great value, either. The following minihotels are tucked into the downtown area: **Viet Phuong,** at 105 Dong Khoi, tel. 8/8295429; **Khach San 69,** 69 Hai Ba Trung, tel. 8/8291513; and **Phong Cho Thue,** 26 Dong Du St., tel. 8/8230164. **Van Canh Hotel,** 184 Calmette, tel. 8/8294963, has 13 rooms for $5–10–20 single, an additional $2 for doubles.

Saigon

$20–50

Hai Van Hotel, 69 Huynh Thuc Khang St., tel. 8/8291274, fax 8/8291275, charges $22 s and $30 d. **Champagne Hotel,** at 129 Ham Nghi Blvd., tel. 8/8292672, fax 8/8230776, has 38 rooms for $27–42. **Orchid Hotel,** 29A Thai Van Lung St., tel. 8/8231809, fax 8/8292245, has 32 rooms for $40–55.

Ben Thanh Minihotel, 14 Ho Huan Nghiep, tel. 8/8230656, is down by the waterfront. The sliding rate scale works this way: $68 for a room on the first floor, $36 on the second floor, $32 on the third, and $25 on the fourth. There's no elevator, but the rooms have a/c and hot water.

Along Nguyen Hue and Dong Khoi boulevards is a cluster of hotels catering to businesspeople. Some are colonial structures newly renovated and upgraded. Renovation is an ongoing process, so be aware that price jumps can occur. **Saigon Concert Hotel,** right inside the back end of the Municipal Theater, at 7 Lam Son Square, tel. 8/8291299, fax 8/8295831, is as old as the venerable French theater. The 25 rooms cost $35–40 double. **Saigon Hotel,** 45 Dong Du St., tel. 8/8299734, fax 8/8291466, has 103 rooms for $25–50; $60–80 for a suite. **Huong Sen,** at 70 Dong Khoi, tel. 8/8291415, fax 8/8290916, charges $40–66, with 53 singles and doubles. Under the same management is **Bong Sen** (Lotus) at 117 Dong Khoi, tel. 8/8291516, fax 8/8299744, with 134 rooms for $45–65 and $65–140 suite. **Bach Dang Hotel,** 33 Mac Thi Buoi, tel. 8/8251501, fax 8/8230587, is a good businessperson's hotel with 16 large rooms for $40–80 and suites for $100; it has a bar and restaurant.

$50–100

The **Grand Hotel,** at 8 Dong Khoi, tel. 8/8235871, is an old French hotel that was extensively renovated in 1997 with the addition of a high-rise wing. Despite the renovations, the old-wing rooms are preferable—they are cavernous, with high ceilings and French windows. An internal courtyard features a pleasant pool. Room prices start at $85.

Asian Hotel, 146 Dong Khoi St., tel. 8/8296979, fax 8/8297433, has 47 rooms for $55–80 s and $70–95 d. Facilities include a business center. The **Mondial,** 109 Dong Khoi, tel. 8/8296291, fax 8/8296324, charges $50–85 s and $65–100 d; with 40 rooms run by Vietnam Tourism, this hotel has been renovated and a business center added.

The **Riverside Hotel,** 18 Ton Duc Thang St., tel. 8/8224038, fax 8/8298070, has 45 rooms for $60–115, and suites for $115–250. Rooms at the **Palace Hotel** (Huu Nghi), 56 Nguyen Hue Blvd., tel. 8/8292860, cost $40–50 s, $55–60 d, $60–75 deluxe, and up to $140 for a suite. Facilities include a small pool and two restaurants. **Embassy Hotel,** 36 Nguyen Trung Truc St., tel. 8/8231981, fax 8/8295019, has 94 rooms and suites in the $40–70 range, and up to $120 for suites. This Hong Kong-financed hotel features its own nightclub with karaoke.

Hotel Continental, 134 Dong Khoi, tel. 8/8299201, fax 8/8290936, is a classic French hotel completely renovated in the 1980s at a cost of several million dollars. This hotel is notable for its location and links with the past: It featured as a setting in the Graham Greene novel, *The Quiet American.* The hotel has somehow slipped from being quiet into being comatose—something to do with slipshod management by Saigon Tourist. What could have been a five-star hotel is definitely not. Rooms range $60–130.

Norfolk Hotel, 117 Le Thanh Ton, tel. 8/8295368, fax 8/8293415, has 47 rooms going for $85–95 s and $150–220 a suite; add $15 for double occupancy. All rooms offer full facilities and StarTV reception. The Norfolk is an Australian joint-venture hotel, with a seventh-floor business center, and conference and secretarial services.

$100–200

A cut above the rest for reasons of location, history, and prestige are the following hotels. Down by the waterfront is the 120-room **M Hotel Majestic** (Cuu Long), at 1 Dong Khoi, tel. 8/8295515, fax 8/8291470, www.majesticsaigon.com.vn, which has a quality that many other hotels in Saigon lack: character. The hotel dates to the 1920s—and major renovations have retained that French colonial feel to the place, keeping the original French marble fittings. The fifth-floor Sky Bar has original marble floors and provides great views over the Saigon River. To cool off, you can take a plunge in the courtyard pool; to heat up, try a sauna. Rates start at $130 for a room and rise to over $500 for a suite.

Kim Do International, at 133 Nguyen Hue Blvd., tel. 8/8225914, fax 8/8225913, is a 135-room hotel with a host of facilities including health club, business center, and top-floor bar. Rooms are $120–200; executive suites cost $300–480. The **Caravelle** (Doc Lap), at 18 Lam Son St., tel. 8/8234999, fax 8/8243999, is a nine-story hotel with an art deco lobby; rates are $120 for standard rooms and up to $800 for a deluxe suite. This relic from the 1950s was renovated in a Hong Kong joint venture: The package includes a towering high-rise wing next door. The rooftop bar of the old wing is a great place for looking over Central Saigon.

The **Rex** (Ben Thanh), at 141 Nguyen Hue, tel. 8/8292185, fax 8/8296536, offers 207 guestrooms in several wings. Rates are $80–105 standard rooms, $110–200 for suites, and $450 for an executive suite. The Rex sprawls over an entire city block, encompassing the Rex Cinema; to the northwest at 146 Rue Pasteur an annex features tennis courts and a café. The Rex is a friendly place—outsiders are welcome to visit the rooftop bar and the legendary dance hall, both relics from the days when the building served as the U.S. Army's Bachelor Officer's Quarters.

The **Sheraton Saigon,** at 88 Dong Khoi, tel. 8/8272828, www.sheraton.com/saigon, is composed of two towering blocks containing 382 hotel rooms and 98 serviced apartments. Rooms range $155–175, and $260–370 for suites. The place has eight bars and restaurants, with the Signature Restaurant on the 23rd floor providing 360-degree views of the city—probably the best spot to look down on Central Saigon. The bar up on the 23rd floor is one of Saigon's hotspots, with live music.

The **Duxton,** 63 Nguyen Hue Blvd., tel. 8/8222999, fax 8/8241888, offers 198 rooms for $180–210, and royal suites for $350. Opened in 1996, the hotel is strategically situated but doesn't exude much atmosphere. With lavish karaoke and massage facilities—and an excellent sushi restaurant—this hotel caters to the Japanese market.

Oscar Hotel, 68A Nguyen Hue Blvd., tel. 8/8231818, fax 8/8292732, is an 11-story hotel with 109 rooms. Rates are $115–200 for standard and superior rooms, and $380–530 for a suite. Amenities include a health club and a business center with multilingual staff.

Confusingly, right next door to the Riverside Hotel is **Renaissance Riverside Hotel,** 8–15 Ton Duc Thang St., D1, tel. 8/8220033, rsvn.rrhs@hcm.vnn.vn, with rates $105–185, and suites for $330. You have to wonder how many clients end up in the wrong Riverside. The Renaissance Riverside has 350 rooms and a majestic sunken swimming pool on the rooftop (at the 22nd floor)—with stunning views over the Saigon River below.

A bit farther north along the river is the 283-room **Legend Hotel,** at 2A Ton Duc Thang St., tel. 8/8233333, www.legendhotelsaigon.com. Rooms are $180–200, and suites $350–850. The hotel has all the creature comforts, but lacks flair with a boxy design.

NORTH OF THE CATHEDRAL

An alternative to accommodations in the downtown core is District 3, north of Notre Dame Cathedral—still within reach of sights and amenities. This area was an exclusive residential zone under the French and still maintains that aura.

$20–50

At **Emperor** (KS Hoang De), 117 Nguyen Dinh Chien, tel. 8/8231251, fax 8/8230515, rates for the 47 comfortable rooms are $28–60. **Liberty** (Que Huong), 167 Hai Ba Trung, tel. 8/8294227, fax 8/8290919, has 60 rooms. Rooms cost $20–40 but are not the greatest value. **Dee's,** an eight-room minihotel at 223A

Hai Ba Trung, tel. 8/8231522, charges $20 s, $25 d, and has two rooms for $30 each.

$50–100

Saigon Lodge, 215 Nam Ky Khoi Nghia, tel. 8/8230112, fax 8/8251070, offers 94 rooms for $77–99 standard and deluxe, $121–143 suite, and $330 penthouse.

International Hotel, 19 Vo Van Tan, tel. 8/8290009, fax 8/8290066, has 50 rooms and a business center. This Hong Kong joint-venture hotel charges $80–110 for rooms, and $135–160 for a suite.

$100–200

Saigon Star, 204 Nguyen Thi Minh Khai, tel. 8/8230260, fax 8/8230255, is a Hong Kong joint-venture hotel overlooking Van Hoa Park; rooms run $99–120 and suites $150–180. Nearby is **Sol Chancery Saigon,** 196 Nguyen Thi Minh Khai, tel. 8/8299152, fax 8/8254484, with 96 spacious rooms for $107–180, and full facilities, including business centers.

Over $200

Hotel Sofitel Plaza Saigon, 17 Le Duan Blvd., D1, tel. 8/8241555, fax 8/8241666, sofitelsgn@hcmc.netnam.vn, is host to 280 rooms and 12 suites and has a rooftop swimming pool. French flair and striking design combine to make this one of the top luxury hotels of Saigon. Rooms start out at $200 and shoot up to a staggering $1,500 for the Presidential Suite.

CHOLON

West of Pham Ngu Lao, in Cholon (District 5), hotels cater mainly to Asian visitors, particularly Taiwanese. Some Westerners regard these accommodations as cheaper alternatives to downtown sites; some just like to get away from the tourist ghettos. On the eastern fringe of District 5 is the stylish Hotel Equatorial.

$20–50

Phoenix Hotel (Phuong Hoang), 411 Tran Hung Dao, tel. 8/8551888, fax 8/8552228, has 70 rooms for $11 fan, or $22 s/d a/c. **Cholon Tourist Minihotel,** at 192 Su Van Hanh, tel. 8/8257089, fax 8/8255375, features rooms for $25–30. Nearby at number 174 is **Cholon Hotel,** with a similar price range. **An Dong Hotel,** 9 An Duong Vuong, tel. 8/8352001, has 25 rooms from $28 s to $38 d. Rates at the 90-room **Tokyo Hotel** (Dong Kinh), 106 Tran Tuan Khai, tel. 8/8355352, fax 8/8352505, range $15–25–40. The sixth floor features a dance hall and karaoke lounge. **Hanh Long Hotel,** 1027 Tran Hung Dao, tel. 8/8350251, fax 8/8350742, has 48 rooms with satellite TV and IDD. Saigon Tourist manages this nine-story hotel.

$50–100

Arc En Ciel Hotel, 52–56 Tan Da, tel. 8/8552550, fax 8/8550332, includes 91 rooms. Rates are $33–55 standard for singles or doubles, $38–60 superior, and $66–88 suite. The Arc En Ciel features Volvo nightclub and karaoke lounge on the second floor and a rooftop garden café. **Regent Hotel,** at 700 Tran Hung Dao, tel. 8/8353548, fax 8/8357094, offers 37 rooms for $40–75.

$100–200

Hotel Equatorial, 242 Tran Binh Trong St., D5, tel. 8/8390000, fax 8/8390011, occupies an odd spot between downtown Saigon and Cholon. This very stylish hotel straddles an entire block—it has a business center, fitness center, a bevy of restaurants, bars and lounges, and a beautiful pool and garden on the fourth floor. There are 334 well-designed rooms; standard and deluxe rooms range $130–175; suites go for $250–350; the Senator Suite is $600–720; and the Presidential Suite costs $1,000 a night.

AIRPORT VICINITY

$20–50

Not far from the airport is **Dong Phuong I,** 311 Nguyen Van Troi, tel. 8/8442088, fax 8/8440895, with 31 rooms for $30–45. This place is run-down, as is its sister hotel, **Dong Phuong II,** on Hoang Van Thu Boulevard.

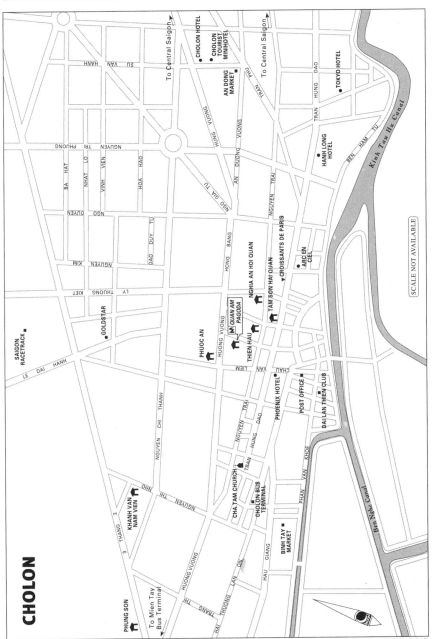

CHOLON

To Central Saigon

CHOLON HOTEL

CHOLON TOURIST MINIHOTEL

AN DONG MARKET

TOKYO HOTEL

HANH LONG HOTEL

SU VAN HANH

BA HAT

NGUYEN TRI PHUONG

NHAT LO

VINH VIEN

HOA HAO

HUNG VUONG

AN DUONG VUONG

NGO GIA TU

NGUYEN TRAI

TRAN HUNG DAO

TRAN PHU

Kinh Tau Hu Canal

BEN HAM TU

CROISSANTS DE PARIS

L'ARC EN CIEL

NGO QUYEN

DAO DUY TU

HONG BANG

NGHIA AN HOI QUAN

TAM SON HAI QUAN

NGUYEN KIM

LY THUONG KIET

GOLDSTAR

QUAN AM PAGODA

THIEN HAU

HUONG VUONG

VAN LIEM

CHAU VAN

PHOENIX HOTEL

POST OFFICE

DAI LAN THIEN CLUB

SAIGON RACETRACK

LE DAI HANH

PHUOC AN

CHI THANH

NGUYEN TRAI

HUNG DAO

NGUYEN

PHAN VAN KHOE

Ben Nghe Canal

KHANH VAN NAM VIEN

3 THANG 2

NGUYEN THI

HUONG VUONG

CHA TAM CHURCH

TRAN

CHOLON BUS TERMINAL

BINH TAY MARKET

PHUNG SON

To Mien Tay Bus Terminal

HAI THUONG LAN ON

TRANG TRI

HAU GIANG

SCALE NOT AVAILABLE

Saigon

© AVALON TRAVEL PUBLISHING, INC.

At 200 Hoang Van Thu Blvd., **Tan Son Nhat Hotel,** tel. 8/8241079, offers 25 doubles for $25–50. The place is in good shape; it was once a guesthouse for government officials. Farther east, in the Phu Nhuan District, is **London Hotel,** 216 Phan Dang Luu, tel. 8/8443344; its 23 rooms go for $20 s and $40–45 d. **Hotel l'Arc de Triomphe** (Khach San Khai Hoan Mon), is not far away at 135A Phan Dang Luu, tel. 8/8447941, fax 8/8447940, with 20 rooms in the same price range. **Starhill Hotel,** 14–16 Hoang Viet, tel. 8/8443623, fax 8/8444627, offers 36 rooms for $25–40.

$50–100

The Tan Binh District features some nondescript but functional hotels and two superluxury hotels—the Saigon Omni and Garden Plaza Hotel. A short distance from the airport is **Mekong Travel Hotel,** 243A Hoang Van Thu, tel. 8/8442986, fax 8/8442981. It offers 88 rooms equipped with IDD, satellite TV, and electronic safes. Rates are $65–85. Helpful staff at the Mekong Hotel business center will arrange visas, visa extensions, translation, and typing. Confusingly, there's another place called the Mekong Hotel nearby.

Chains First Hotel occupies a quiet side street at 18 Hoang Viet St., tel. 8/8441199, fax 8/8444282. It's a joint-venture hotel with two large wings. There are 89 rooms in the new wing; these run $65–85 for a standard room, and $100–125 for a suite. The old wing, a brick blockhouse across the street, provides 38 rooms for $35–65. Chains First has sports facilities, several restaurants, and a pool.

$100–200

Garden Plaza Hotel, 309B Nguyen Van Troi, tel. 8/842111, fax 8/8424363, charges $100–250 for rooms. This large hotel opened in 1997. **Saigon Omni Hotel,** 251 Nguyen Van Troi St., tel. 8/8449222, fax 8/8449200, is a vast hotel with prices to match. The 248-room hotel was completed in 1994 and features two wings. Room rates vary from $140 for a standard room to $220 for a deluxe room. A junior suite is $300. On the seventh floor of the main wing, an executive floor features rooms for $260–350. Prices go through the roof for the two Club Suites—$500 apiece—and the Continental Suite—$800 a night. There are 18 executive apartments listed for $200 a day for a minimum three-month stay. Omni facilities include a Vietnamese and a Thai restaurant, pool and sauna, business center, and three ballrooms.

Food

Food in Saigon is mainly Vietnamese, Chinese, and Western, although the city offers the odd Indian, Thai, or Japanese restaurant. The best Chinese food is found in Cholon; in Central Saigon, Vietnamese and Western food are the main fare. Vietnamese food is cheap and the best value for the money—Western food is expensive.

RESTAURANTS

Budget Dining

Bakeries: French bread is widely available and best consumed fresh, in the early morning. Sandwich assembly is easy—baguette vendors with mobile carts set up on many street corners. Large bakeries include **Givral's** bakery at 169 Dong Khoi and **Brodard's** boulangerie at 11 Nguyen Thiep. Also try **Nhu Lan Bakery** at 66 Ham Nghi Boulevard. In Cholon, try **Croissants de Paris,** a bakery and tearoom at 274 Tran Hung Dao, west of Arc En Ciel Hotel.

Sidewalk Noodles: Amazing culinary improvisation artists appear daily along certain avenues, such as Ngo Duc Ke, on the side west of Nguyen Hue Boulevard, and the side streets off Pham Ngu Lao. Pull up a sidewalk kindergarten stool and dive into a heaping bowl of noodles or beef soup. Areas close to produce markets are excellent places to find food stalls—try the area west of Ben Thanh Market.

At **An Dong Market** in Cholon is a basement section with small restaurants.

Street food-stall perches make great vantage points for observing street life—you blend in and watch everything flow past. You'll hear the jangle of bicycle bells as schoolgirls in white *ao dais* drift past, or the tock-tock of kids hitting wooden bowls, patrolling the neighborhood taking soup orders. But the strangest sight may be the slow-motion monks of Saigon. These saffron-robed acolytes make alms rounds in the Pham Ngu Lao area with a slow-motion gait that allows shopkeepers plenty of time to think about whether to contribute.

Embassy Food Street: The food center, a place where you can browse through a selection of cheap eateries, is an idea that has worked well in Bangkok, Hong Kong, and Singapore, but it is new to Saigon. Embassy Food Street, at 39 Nguyen Trung Truc St. near the corner of Nguyen Du, tel. 8/8231981, has stalls with Vietnamese, Taiwanese, and Singaporean fare. It also features Malaysian barbecue and grilled *sate,* Hong Kong–style seafood, Indian curries, and Muslim food. The center is affiliated with the nearby Embassy Hotel. The stalls are a great value; you have a choice between common seating and mini–air-conditioned rooms.

Roll Your Own: To the southwest of Pham Ngu Lao, along Nguyen Cu Trinh Street, is a string of inexpensive *bo bay mon* (beef seven kinds) restaurants—look for a laughing cow logo. For assembling your own meal, you're supplied with rice paper, lettuce, mint leaves, herbs, slivers of star fruit, pineapple, raw banana, bean sprouts, and cucumber. You order one of the seven beef dishes, which are cooked on a charcoal brazier at your table. When the beef is done, roll everything up, and dip in sauce. It's delicious! There are *bo bay mon* restaurants at 91, 93, 109, and 127 Nguyen Cu Trinh.

Vegetarian: It's difficult to find vegetarian food in Saigon. Most Vietnamese and Chinese restaurants, however, have a special vegetable section on the menu, with offerings such as braised tofu, sautéed straw mushrooms, and stir-fried vegetables. Food stalls, especially near markets, are another source of vegetarian fare. In the Pham Ngu Lao area there are several fine vegetarian restaurants down an alley named after a small temple on it—Chua An Lac. Down this alley, which leads off Pham Ngu Lao at the Giant Dragon Hotel, you'll find Cay Bo De vegetarian restaurant and three other restaurants with vegetarian selections on the menu: Quynh Giao, Zen, and Thanh Huyen. Near Ben Thanh Market, at 9 Tran Hung Dao Blvd., is **Tin Nghia Vegetarian Restaurant,** run by Vietnamese Buddhists. Staples in this cheap, tiny place are tofu, mushrooms, and vegetables.

Central Saigon

Quan An Ngon, at 138 Nam Ky Khoi Nghia, tel. 8/8257179, is an extremely popular place—so busy that you may well have to battle to land a table at lunch or dinner. The place trades on one very simple idea: the market foodstall. Every Vietnamese remembers the tasty food from market stalls, and this courtyard restaurant brings all those flavors home by setting up "stalls" that sizzle in the background, preparing noodles and other market-style dishes. You can browse by the stalls first, then order what looks good. This is a gastronomic experience: The dishes are spiced just right, and the juices are amazing. A good sign at this restaurant is that it is mostly packed with Vietnamese, not foreigners—an indication of the reasonable prices charged. You can eat well here for around $5 a head. The success of Quan An Ngon has inspired a number of copycat restaurants in Saigon, but none comes close to the original.

The area near the south end of Dong Khoi offers a number of popular restaurants. On Ngo Duc Ke several restaurants serve Vietnamese food and seafood at very reasonable prices. Try **Restaurant 19** or **Restaurant 13.** Right at the east end of Dong Du and Thi Sach streets on a corner is **Restaurant 333,** with similar food and prices. **Lemongrass,** at 4 Nguyen Thiep, tel. 8/8220496, serves excellent Vietnamese food—elegant dining with bamboo decor. Tucked in behind the mosque on Dong Du is a no-frills Indian *halal* ("lawful" for Muslims) restaurant serving curry fish, chicken, squid, goat, beef, and vegetarian fare. The family restaurant is busy at lunch; it is popularly known as "The Mosque."

Forgoing fancy decor but serving healthy portions at the right price are **Givral Restaurant** and **Brodard Restaurant**, two 1960s–style eateries on Dong Khoi. **Givral,** at the corner of Dong Khoi and Le Loi, tel. 8/8292747, has wonky tables—drop in for a coffee or a full feed. The fare includes spaghetti, steak, and seafood. **Brodard,** at 131 Dong Khoi, has a similar price range. Both places operate separate cake shops: Givral's bakery is to one side of the restaurant, Brodard's is down the road from the restaurant at 11 Nguyen Thiep, between Nguyen Hue and Dhong Khoi.

Napoli, at 75 Nguyen Hue, tel. 8/8225616, serves a full range of pizza and pasta and offers home delivery. **Santa Lucia,** a trattoria at 14 Nguyen Hue, tel. 8/8226562, makes thincrust pizza—service is good at this popular lunch venue.

A cluster of restaurants at the intersection of Nguyen Du Street and Nguyen Thi Minh Khai sell French food for midrange prices. Right on the corner is **Merlion,** at 172 Pasteur, tel. 8/8231799; nearby is **Ami Jean Pierre** at 170 Pasteur, tel. 8/8224015. Down a driveway at 164 Pasteur, you'll find **VY Restaurant,** tel. 8/8296210. VY has fancy decor and a patio section where fresh fish and shrimp are grilled. The restaurant calling card claims you catch your own dishes. At 26 Thai Van Lung St. is **Sapa** restaurant and bar, tel. 8/8295754, with a Western menu—the house specialty is fondue. The upstairs section is pleasant. On the same small street here are several other restaurants, including **Pharos** and **Why Not?**

Luxury: Vietnam House, 93 Dong Khoi at the corner of Mac Thi Buoi, tel. 8/8291623, is a classy place serving fine Vietnamese food. On the menu are dishes as varied as grilled beef with lemongrass and lotus roots with shrimp. A bar and small restaurant occupy the first floor; the main dining area is upstairs. Great decor in an old mansion, and great service. Other

choices for Vietnamese food are **Mandarin,** 11A Ngo Van Nam St., tel. 8/8229783, and **Ancient Town,** 211 Dien Bien Phu St., tel. 8/8290625. Close to Vietnam House, **City Bar and Grill** at 63 Dong Khoi, tel. 8/8298006, serves French nouvelle cuisine.

Other recommended French restaurants are **Le Beaujolais,** 211 Dong Khoi, tel. 8/8222342; **La Cigale,** at 158 Nguyen Dinh Chinh, tel. 8/8443930, with downstairs piano bar; and **L'Etoile,** at 180 Hai Ba Trung, tel. 8/8297939, in a refurbished villa. For a rambling renovated colonial villa serving excellent French food, visit **Camargue,** at 16 Cao Ba Quat, tel. 8/8243148—this place can be pricey, but try the set lunch. There's an airy upstairs bar, open at night.

Chez Guido, on the ground floor of Hotel Continental, tel. 8/8299252, serves excellent pasta, pizza, and seafood. For dessert, try Norman pancakes, mousse, or poached pears with amaretto ice cream.

North of the cathedral, **Thanh Nien Restaurant,** at 11 Nguyen Van Chiem, tel. 8/8225909, is an excellent place for Vietnamese cuisine. The restaurant has a bamboo garden patio and offers nighttime piano entertainment in the bar. It's owned by the same manager as **Goody Ice Cream** on Hai Ba Trung—you can walk through from one place to the other. **Le Mekong,** at 57 Dong Du St., tel. 8/8295045, is an elegant French joint-venture restaurant in a beautifully restored villa near the War Crimes Museum. Open for lunch and dinner.

South of Pham Ngu Lao is one of Saigon's top-rated Chinese restaurants, called **Phuc Lam Mon,** at 1A Tinh Van Can, tel. 8/8223681. The restaurant specializes in wild game and seafood and has an "advanced karaoke complex" with private rooms to help ease digestion. There's a branch of **VY Restaurant** nearby at 105 Yersin St., serving French food.

Just south of the Pham Ngu Lao area is **Indochine Restaurant** (Dong Duong), at 32 Pham Ngoc Thach St., tel. 8/8239256, with elaborate decor of rattan and wicker—this place serves good Vietnamese and Chinese cuisine.

CAFÉS

Pham Ngu Lao

Cheap and down-to-earth are Pham Ngu Lao sidewalk cafés. There are more than 20 small cafés where travelers congregate under sidewalk umbrellas to eat, drink, swap tales, play pool, or sign up for day trips around Saigon or for minibuses up-country. Unlike those downtown, these cafés stay open late at night, so Westerners and Vietnamese alike patronize them in the evening.

The main concentration of cafés is around the intersection of Pham Ngu Lao and De Tham. On Pham Ngu Lao are **Long Phi Café, Café 215,** and **Lotus Café;** on De Tham are **Saigon Café, Kim Café, Sinh Café, La Goulue, 333 Bar, Shanti Indian Restaurant,** and **Lucky Restaurant.** Cafés offer full menus with mediocre Western food, coffee, beer, juices, and fruit salad. The Pham Ngu Lao cafés are excellent for breakfast—try **La Goulue** at 197 De Tham. **Paris Deli,** 31 Dong Khoi St., offers great pastries.

Ice Cream Cafés

You know a city has arrived when the ice cream machines roll in from Rome and pizza home delivery begins. Both are happening in Saigon, though you may have trouble recognizing the results.

Goody Ice Cream, at 133 Hai Ba Trung north of the cathedral, has installed Italian technology and serves snacks, ice cream, and drinks at Italian prices. Some items, however, would never appear on the menu in Italy: fruit ice cream with orange juice, orange and lemon floats, *cocco bello* (ice cream served in young coconut), and a dish called "coffee sunk"—one scoop of coffee ice cream sunk between two scoops of vanilla. In season, Pisa serves exotic items such as custard apple *(mang cau)* ice cream. The owner insists the café uses only fresh milk and boiled water and that everything is safe.

A few blocks away is **Napoli Café,** at 5 Pham Quoc Thach St., with a menu similar to Pisa's. It's open early morning to late night and is good for breakfast as well as snacks. **Ciao Café,** at 72 Nguyen Hue Blvd., tel. 8/8251203, serves ice cream, pizza, and cake. **Saigon Connection Café,** at 114 Le Thanh Ton opposite the Norfolk Hotel, has the atmosphere of an American diner. The place is air-conditioned and clean; the music is '50s and '60s American. On the menu is a sundae served in a real pineapple base, and a dish called "fried ice cream"—a kind of fried sandwich with chocolate chip ice cream. Hamburgers and other items are available.

For cheaper ice cream try **Kem Bach Dang,** with two facing cafés at 26 and 28 Le Loi at the intersection of Rue Pasteur. Because of its proximity to a cinema, the place is packed with Vietnamese patrons.

Rooftop Cafés

Panorama 33, on the 33rd floor of Saigon Trade Center, affords terrific views over all Saigon. Matching the giddy elevation, drinks are sky-high, of course. Afternoon tea set is $4.50 a head. Panorama 33 is the highest place in Saigon—that is, until the completion of the 60-story Bitexco financial tower, designed by U.S. architects.

Major downtown hotels have rooftop bars or restaurants, and sometimes even a small pool. The craziest and coziest bar is **Rex Rooftop Café,** both a rooftop and garden café. It's a great place to relax at sunset, lounging around in wicker chairs high above the hubble and bubble of Saigon. You can order snacks or full meals; dining is outdoor on a terrace and can be pricey. There is sometimes live entertainment on a podium under the revolving Rex Crown, with traditional music combos. Otherwise, you'll hear twittering birds from the rooftop aviary. Bonsai trees, half-dead fish, plaster statues of elephants, and other high-kitsch artworks occupy the terrace. There's a small pool off to one side.

The **Caravelle** (old wing) features a restaurant and bar on the ninth floor—a breezy place with wicker furniture. You can drop by for a drink. This was the tallest building in Vietnam during the 1970s, when war correspondents used to gather on the roof to watch the

Saigon

fighting. There's no elevator to the very top; you must walk up one more flight of stairs from the restaurant. Other rooftop bars include the **Palace Hotel**, with a 15th-floor bar and a small pool on the 16th floor; the rooftop bar and disco at the **Century Saigon Hotel;** and the Huong Sen and Bong Sen rooftop bar-restaurants. The **Sheraton** has a 23rd-floor bar with high-flying views, often with a live band—open after 1600. Drinks are $7 and up.

Nightlife

Saigon nightlife is subdued, mainly revolving around restaurants and cafés. There's an unofficial curfew: Bars close at 2300, though some hotels remain open until 0100 or 0200. Foreigners tend to end up in common areas when it comes to nightlife. In the Pham Ngu Lao area nightlife means sitting at cafés, which serve beer and stay open late; there are several rowdier bars—Allez Boo and Backpackers Bar. In Central Saigon, entertainment centers in a select number of venues—many around Dong Du Street or Thai Van Lung/Thi Sach streets. You can also indulge in the fine sport of cyclo racing to get from one part of town to another: Cyclo drivers hurtle down one-way streets the wrong way without any lights, which certainly gets the adrenaline going.

Locals visit movie theaters, take in performances at the Municipal Theater, hang out at cafés, or croon over karaoke machines. On Saturday and Sunday nights thousands of young Vietnamese take to the streets. Dong Khoi and Nguyen Hue boulevards come alive with Honda hordes cruising the streets. If you stroll in the garden square in front of the Hotel de Ville, it's easy to meet people.

Traditional Music

Keep an eye out for traditional music and dance performers. Artists from the Saigon Conservatory of Music may appear at venues such as the Rex Rooftop Café, Maxim's, or Madame Dai's. Also check for scheduled performances at the **Conservatory of Music** at 112 Nguyen Du Street. The most intriguing of the music recitals is a performance on the *dan bau,* a single-string lute unique to Vietnam. The single steel string is manipulated to produce a haunting sound. Other wonders include the two-string

vertical violin and the bamboo xylophone. Sometimes seen are Vietnamese dance performances, including folk dances originating from rural traditions and sensuous Cham dances revived from centuries past.

Night Cruising

Saigon features some real floating restaurants: boats that go on short cruises along Saigon River, leaving the bright lights of Saigon behind. The boats usually depart between 1900 and 2000 for a one- or two-hour trip; you dine aboard. There's only a minimal charge for the cruise, but food and drinks are expensive. The best part is the cruise; the food is mediocre. Some boats have live bands onboard, and several decks crowded with diners; others are commandeered by private Vietnamese groups for wedding banquets or birthday parties.

Four of the floating restaurant cruise-boats are strung along the Saigon River between Dong Khoi Street and Ham Nghi Boulevard. These include **Siren Floating Restaurant; Ben Nghe Tourism Boat,** cruise 1900–2130 with additional departure 1630–1830 on Sundays and holidays; and **Tau Saigon Floating Restaurant,** cruise 2000–2115. **Saigon Tourist** operates a longer cruise/dinner/cultural show combination, 1730–2130 on Tuesday, Thursday, and Sunday for $15. Another departure runs 1900–2000, costs $5, and features the cultural show alone.

Weekend Motorcycle Love Affair

On Saturday and Sunday nights there's an exuberant parade of scooters and motorcycles in a clockwise circuit of Dong Khoi and Nguyen Hue boulevards. The whole town center is throbbing as hundreds of young Vietnamese tour the boulevards in an Asian version of *Saturday Night Fever*—although the busier night in Saigon is Sunday. Young women are decked out in tight jeans and T-shirts or silk *ao dais;* young men show off shiny new Hondas. In the squares near the Hotel de Ville, riders congregate for a rest or to chat up the opposite sex. This marriage of youth and motorbikes is known as *chay long rong* (living fast).

Expensive motorbikes and cell phones are vital components of the urban Vietnamese teenager's self-image, to the extent that a teenage girl will drop a boyfriend in favor of one who has a later-model Honda. The motorcycle is an essential part of courtship rites. It is the ultimate symbol of freedom and opportunity—the freedom to move around at will, the opportunity to find intimate privacy.

There is considerable fallout from these attitudes: Combining a cell phone with a motorcycle in motion is not a stable idea, because one hand leaves the handlebars. And seeing teenagers weaving at breakneck speeds through heavy traffic is not uncommon in cities such as Saigon and Hanoi. Take a closer look at the traffic and you will see slower, more cautious motorcyclists of all ages—from an entire family squeezed onto a motorcycle (parents, two kids, baby on mother's lap) to a grandmother returning from the market with bags of shopping dangling.

"Nothing symbolises the massive economic and social shift of the last decade better than the increase in two-wheeled vehicles," reports Charles Melhuish, a transportation specialist at the Asian Development Bank. He is referring to the dramatic transition from bicycles to motorcycles in cities such as Saigon and Hanoi—a transition that happened in Vietnam faster than in almost any other country. During the period 1990–2005, the number of motorcycles on the roads in Vietnam soared from fewer than 500,000 to more than 10 million. Annual sales worth $2 billion make Vietnam the world's fastest-growing motorcycle market, and the third-biggest in the world after China and India.

This rapid increase has led to a daunting parking problem for motorcycles. Millions of motorcycles have been sold, but no special parking facilities have been constructed to keep pace with those sales. The result is that motorcyclists clog up the sidewalks with parked motorbikes, and police wage a constant battle trying to keep the streets clear of those same parked motorcycles.

Another unpleasant side effect of all those motorcycle sales is pollution—and noise. With chaotic road rules, Vietnamese motorcyclists resort to using the horn to announce their presence—and hope that others will give way. This practice, used by cars and motorcycles alike, has turned Saigon and Hanoi into very noisy cities. Very few motorcyclists wear helmets, because they say a helmet is too much trouble and it reduces visibility. Colonel Tran Dao, of the Hanoi Police Department, informed a seminar in 2004 that during the previous seven years, 30,000 people had died in traffic accidents, while another 94,000 had been injured. He calculated that the casualty rate was increasing about 300 percent a year.

Central Saigon

Under the Americans, Rue Catinat, or Dong Khoi Street, became Tu Do, or Freedom Street. Bars, nightclubs, and strip joints crowded the south end, and names such as Bluebird and Papillon flashed in neon. The same area now appeals to young Vietnamese and foreigners, and it still has its share of sleaze, with beggars, pickpockets, and assorted pushers on patrol. In 1992 a string of bars along Dong Du Street—Good Morning Vietnam, Cyclo Bar, Apocalypse Now—recalled Tu Do Street in the days of the Vietnam War. The authorities became concerned about the proliferation of taxi girls and drug-dealing cyclo drivers; one day in 1993 the bright yellow police jeeps arrived to confiscate all the stereos and close down the bars. In the 1993 mop-up, police closed 45 nightclubs around Saigon.

Maxim's theater-restaurant is a Saigon institution surviving from the U.S. era, its plush red decor intact. The theater is at 15 Dong Khoi St., tel. 8/8225554. Maxim's is open 1100–2300; the floor show starts around 1900. In the 1960s Maxim's was reserved for American officers—the loose women within were said to be untouchable for less than a month's pay. Banking on nostalgia, Maxim's still charges outrageous prices for drinks. Watch your wallet in this place; surcharges are common. Theater acts seem stuck in the 1960s. Some performances are so bad they'll have you rolling in the aisles. Crooners do lip-sync numbers, artists play traditional Vietnamese instruments, others perform sundry song-and-dance routines. The food—Vietnamese, Chinese, and European—is touted as the best in Saigon but is in fact mediocre and pricey. The chef relies on the fact that the lights are low and your taste buds will be numbed by sound effects.

The famous, or infamous, **Apocalypse Now** is on Thi Sac Street, close to the intersection with Dong Du. It's not hard to find—cyclo drivers cluster round the bar, drawn like moths to a flame. On the wall at Apocalypse Now is a large poster from the movie of the same name, autographed by Martin Sheen. The bar does a brisk trade in Apocalypse Now T-shirts ($5 apiece). The patrons are mostly Westerners; the place is smoky (and not just from cigarettes), and when the staff cranks up mesmerizing lyrics by The Doors, Saigon of the '60s is not too far away. If you're feeling blue, ask for a shot glass of Apocalypse Whiskey, a medicinal Chinese concoction—the pickled cobra sits coiled in a glass jar of rice wine behind the counter. Cobra wine is surprisingly smooth and mellow.

Karaoke Clubs

Karaoke has taken Saigon by storm. Karaoke lounges are intended primarily for Asian visitors or rich Vietnamese, and they can be sleazy, with private rooms ostensibly for karaoke singing but including a "karaoke hostess." Drinks can be very expensive. There are several nightclub complexes in Saigon.

Cholon Clubs: Cholon nightlife targets Asians, especially Taiwanese. Karaoke is the keyword here. Activity revolves around hotels with karaoke, discos, and massage parlors. The Arc En Ciel Hotel operates **Volvo Nightclub** on the second floor; **Hotel Tokyo** has a dance hall on the sixth floor; and **Dai La Tien Nightclub** features a dance floor and karaoke rooms.

Shopping

The main areas for antiques, paintings, and handicrafts are Dong Khoi Street and Nguyen Hue Boulevard, as well as side streets running off these. You can wander along and comparison shop. Specialty shops abound in Saigon—there's even an entire shop devoted to Swiss Army knives and Maglites at 31 Ham Nghi Boulevard.

ANTIQUES AND ARTS

Antiques

The market for antiques is dwindling. Items are often faked to look older or are honestly sold as copies. This includes old porcelain, clocks, and items of silver, jade, or ivory. If the product in question was a genuine antique, you might have trouble getting it out of the country without a government permit. Vestiges of the colonial past are part of the antique trade: Vendors sell overpriced banknotes, coins, and stamps from French Indochina.

Painting

Art galleries along Dong Khoi Street and Nguyen Hue Boulevard display original works by Vietnamese artists. The selection includes fine watercolors, oil paintings, gauche, and paintings on silk, often depicting Vietnamese rural scenes, landscapes, cityscapes, portraits, and abstract themes. The Military Museum art gallery has some interesting "revolutionary" painting. Fine arts students make excellent copies of Western art in oil, working from art books. If you ever wanted to get your hands on a Gauguin, Modigliano, or a Picasso—it's all here. Paintings can be custom-ordered; just bring the artwork in print form and a student will copy it. Galleries

CLASSIC IMAGES OF THE WAR

Hoang Van Cuong is a former UPI photojournalist whose pictures of war-torn Vietnam ran in newspapers around the world. After the fall of Saigon, Hoang worked as a farmer in the Mekong Delta for nine years. He was then arrested and forced to serve six years in reeducation camps. While in detention, he kept his negatives hidden and now continues to print again and sell photos to tourists.

Hoang Van Cuong has opened a private antique museum at 64 Dong Du St.—with more than 1,000 antiquities on display, particularly ceramics. The first floor of the museum features 600 black-and-white photos from the Vietnam War. His family has been in the antique business for generations and he's keeping the tradition alive. Featured in a lot of Western media, including the BBC, Hoang has achieved untouchable status. He says he's lived through so many close calls he's no longer afraid of consequences. At his country home, Hoang Van Cuong was constructing a memorial to the 200 journalists killed during the war.

to check include **Espace NK,** at 218A Pasteur, exhibiting contemporary art, and **Art Gallery Particulier,** at 43 Dong Khoi, with private collections of famous Vietnamese artists.

Handicrafts

In the Dong Khoi Street and Nguyen Hue Boulevard area are a number of shops packed to the ceiling with handmade goods. Major hotels also include gift shops selling local crafts. You can buy hand-painted silk pictures and greeting cards, embroidered clothing articles, wood carvings, lacquerware items, ceramics, statuettes, jewelry boxes, seals, and *non la* (conical hats). Larger items for sale, if you can figure out a way to transport them, include bamboo and rattan items, carved wood furniture, and ceramic elephants. Be aware that wood and lacquerware can crack when removed to cold, dry climates. At the History Museum, in the back of the water-puppet theater, you can buy handmade wooden puppets. If you're attracted to a particular handicraft, you can go straight to the source. There are several lacquerware factories around Saigon, for example, where you can learn about the intricate production process.

CLOTHING

Ao Dais

Unique to Vietnam are silk *ao dais,* the graceful billowing dresses worn by Saigon women. You can buy one of these ready-made, or custom-order it at a tailor's. Like dresses, *ao dais* come in a great variety of forms, from bright solid colors to flamboyant hand-embroidered patterns. Tailors who specialize in *ao dais* and *cheong sams* include **Thanh Chau,** at 244 Dinh Tien Hoang St., Q1, tel. 8/8231031, and **Tram Huong,** 212A Tran Quoc Thao, Q3, tel. 8/8443934.

Message T-Shirts

From street vendors you can buy message T-shirts—reading Miss Saigon, Tintin in Vietnam, or Ho Chi Minh—for a few dollars. Direct from the relevant bars you can buy Apocalypse Now or Hard Rock Café Saigon T-shirts for $5. T-shirts vary in quality; some are made of flimsy material that will disintegrate after a few washes. Look for hand-embroidered T-shirts. These cost around $3—a great value.

MARKETS

The largest food market in Saigon is **Ben Thanh.** The landmark building was constructed by the French in 1914 and looks little changed. Under the cupola is a vast array of food, hardware, electronics, and fabric stalls embracing 11,000 square meters. It's well worth strolling in the area around the market. The side streets are bustling with activity too, presenting great photo opportunities, particularly around Tet when everybody is buying miniature trees. Out in Cholon is **Binh Tay Market,** a huge food and consumer goods center, and **An Duong Market,** a large clothing and retail venue. You can buy *ao dais* here.

Dan Sinh Army Surplus market is at 104 Nguyen Cong Tru St., near Phung Son Tu Pagoda, south of Ben Thanh Market. Clothing, housewares, and new and used army goods are sold here. Some of the vendors sell U.S. Army–issue goods: everything from fungicidal foot powder to dog tags and field glasses. Some are real, most cleverly copied. Zippo lighters—probably not originals—sell for $10–20 if working, $5 if not. Other army-surplus items are Chinese or Russian and include gas masks and stretchers. On a more practical note, the

market sells compasses and webbing and lacing (good for fixing a backpack). Small hammocks go for $4 and mosquito nets for $3–7, depending on size and quality. Other items of interest are gloves, socks, and jackets, useful if traveling to the Central Highlands or the mountainous north. A flak jacket might be a wise investment if you're heading to Cambodia.

The **Thieves Market** runs along Huynh Thuc Khang and Ton That Dan streets—it used to be the place stolen U.S. Army goods were sold. It then became a black market for electronic goods, but the trading is now quite open. The market sells a great range of consumer and luxury goods, some still smuggled in by Vietnamese sailors and visiting overseas Vietnamese.

Services and Information

Traveler Cafés
Your finest source of information in Saigon is any one of the traveler cafés strung along Pham Ngu Lao. Just sit down at one of these sidewalk cafés and find someone who's come from the direction you're headed; maybe offer to buy a cold beer. The cafés serve decent food and are usually open 0800–2200. The café owners run tours and may have traveler logbooks recounting recent voyages in Vietnam.

Pham Ngu Lao Street in District 1 features a string of traveler cafés—combination restaurants, cafés, travel agents, meeting points, amusement halls, and pubs. These cafés handle visa extensions, day trips, bicycle and motorcycle rentals, guides, and traveler minibuses to Hué. For day trips and longer trips, the big cafés are Sinh Café, Kim Café, and 333 Bar. Saigon Café and Lotus Café also dabble in tours. These cafés do a roaring trade—in the morning outside Sinh Café there might be half a dozen minibuses about to take off for various day trips, with an organizer standing outside with a mobile phone directing traffic.

The two original cafés stand almost side-by-side: **Kim Café,** 270 De Tham, tel. 8/8398177, fax 8/8298540; and **Sinh Café,** a few doors along on De Tham Street, tel. 8/8251842, fax

8/8222347. Both cafés have their own travel agencies, with a knowledgeable English-speaking staff. They will also organize Open Tour bus or minibus tickets to points north. Other agents on Pham Ngu Lao include **Long Phi Café,** at 171 Pham Ngu Lao, tel. 8/8323124; and **333 Bar,** on De Tham, tel. 8/8331231, fax 8/8251550. **Fiditourist** has a branch at 199 Pham Ngu Lao, tel. 8/8322324.

Tourist Information
Saigon Tourist Travel Service, 49 Le Thanh Ton (corner of Dong Khoi), tel. 8/8295834, fax 8/8224987, is the official arm, but not a friendly one. This outfit is money-hungry—if the staff smells money, information is forthcoming; if not, you'll get a pair of glazed eyeballs that will quickly disappear behind a newspaper. Saigon Tourist runs more than 50 hotels and 45 restaurants. **Vietnam Tourism,** in the Mondial Center at 203 Dong Khoi St., tel. 8/8290776, fax 8/8290775, is not much better, though the brochures are glossier. Both agencies sell overpriced tours. Saigon Tourist, for example, charges a whopping $30 a person for a Cu Chi Tunnels tour, and $60 a head for a day trip to Vung Tau. Out in Cholon is **Cholon Tourist,** the official agency catering to ethnic Chinese tourists.

Saigon

SAIGON AIRLINE OFFICES

The following is a listing of airline offices in Saigon. Frequency of flights may vary with season and demand.

Aeroflot, 4G Le Loi at the corner of Nguyen Hue, tel. 8/8290076; flies to Moscow once a week

Air France, 130 Dong Khoi, tel. 8/8290981; flies to Paris three times weekly

Asiana Airlines, 34 Le Duan, tel. 8/8222663; flies to Seoul twice a week

British Airways, 114A Nguyen Hue, tel. 8/8292262

Cathay Pacific, Jardine House, 58 Dong Khoi St., tel. 8/8223203; flies to Hong Kong daily

China Airlines, 132 Dong Khoi St., tel. 8/8251387; office in the Hotel Continental; flies to Taipei four times a week

China Southern Airlines, 52B Pham Hong Thai St. (facing north side of New World Hotel), tel. 8/8291172; flies to Guangzhou twice weekly

Eva Air, 127 Dong Khoi, tel. 8/8224488; flies to Seoul

Garuda, 106 Nguyen Hue Blvd., tel. 8/8293644, fax 8/8293688; flies to Jakarta and Singapore several times a week

Japan Airlines, 115 Nguyen Hue, tel. 8/8219098

KLM, 244 Pasteur St., tel. 8/8231990; flies to Amsterdam

Korean Airlines, 79 Le Thanh Ton St., tel. 8/824879; flies to Seoul twice weekly

Lao Airlines, 93 Pasteur St., tel. 8/8226990; handles flights to Vientiane

Lufthansa, 132 Dong Khoi, tel. 8/8298529; office in the Hotel Continental; flies to Frankfurt twice weekly

Malaysia Airlines, in Continental Hotel, 132 Dong Khoi, tel. 8/8242885; flies to Kuala Lumpur daily

Pacific Airlines, 77 Le Thanh Ton St., tel. 8/8290844; flies to Taipei and Kaohsiung (Taiwan), and Macau

Philippine Airlines, 4A Le Loi, tel. 8/8292113; flies to Manila

Qantas Airlines, 114A Nguyen Hue, tel. 8/8238844

Singapore Airlines, 29 Le Duan, tel. 8/8231588; frequent flights to Singapore

Thai International, 65 Nguyen Du St., tel. 8/8223365; in the Officetel Building near the GPO; flies to Bangkok daily

United Airlines, ground floor of Sofitel Plaza Hotel, 17 Le Duan, tel. 8/8234755; flights to San Francisco via Hong Kong

---

Unofficial private operators offer services identical to state-run Saigon Tourist at a fraction of the price. Through travel agents, guides are about $10 a day. Freelancers operate from street corners. Moto and cyclo drivers know the city well and can arrange for half-day or full-day tours. Some cyclo and moto operators are former soldiers or translators who worked with the Americans—they speak good English, and now, after years in reeducation camps, find conditions changing in their favor. They're conversant with American idioms and slang. Hiring a guide with a motorcycle is a good way to see Saigon.

Miniguide to Saigon
Because things tend to chop and change (particularly with restaurants and clubs) you should

supplement your information diet with two slim magazines: *Time Out,* which comes as a weekly addition to *Vietnam Investment Review,* and *The Guide,* a monthly addition to *Vietnam Economic Times.* Both of these give up-to-the-minute listings for both Saigon and Hanoi. You should be able to buy them separately from vendors.

Maps and Books
Sheet maps of Saigon are available in numerous places, particularly from the street vendors around Dong Khoi Street and Nguyen Hue Boulevard. If you intend to use one of these maps, buy a magnifying glass as well—there's a lot of detail squished into a tiny space. The best sighted is a larger sheet map produced in 2000 by HCMC Publishing House; this map is

Saigon

actually readable with the naked eye, but it does have a lot of Chinese characters all over it. Check out the up-country destination maps from the sidewalk vendors; there's a good selection, and who knows when you'll see these maps again. The Cartographic Mapping Institute of Hanoi publishes a superior scale map of Saigon with the Canadian company International Travel Maps.

Saigon offers few English-language books, the result of government import bans on foreign material. You'll do better at a bookstore in Bangkok Airport than in the entire city of Saigon. You might try the **Xuanthu Bookshop** (Fahasa) at 185 Dong Khoi St., just north of the Hotel Continental. There are Fahasa branches all over Saigon—one of the largest is at 40 Nguyen Hue Boulevard. At 201 Dong Khoi is **Le Anh Bookshop,** with secondhand English and French books. A charming bookstore with dusty tomes lining the shelves is off 26 Dong Khoi St. at 20 Ho Huan Nghiep. It's just called "bookstore" and sells Vietnamese, French, and English books. It also doubles as a café. Out on Le Duan Street toward the zoo is **Sterns Books,** with a reasonable stock of English titles. At 28 Dong Khoi St. is **Bookazine,** specializing in imported magazines and books.

Most reading material is sold by street vendors in the Dong Khoi and Nguyen Hue area who peddle outrageously expensive photocopied booklets. From the street vendors, and in major hotel lobbies, you can get a range of Western magazines and newspapers—*International Herald Tribune, Bangkok Post, Paris Match, Le Figaro, L'Express, Le Monde, Sydney Morning Herald, Time,* and *Newsweek.* Some are simply left behind by hotel guests and recycled. Check dates. To get around import restrictions, secondhand bookstores in the Pham Ngu Lao area sell books left behind by travelers. If you want some good novels to read, there are several secondhand places on De Tham Street, such as **The Cat** (Con Meo) at number 243.

Fax, Phone, and Email

For IDD information, consult the Ho Chi Minh City Telephone Directory. It gives country codes for direct dialing, time differences, and full details on rates in U.S. dollars. The Saigon area code is 84-8. By looking at the column for the first minute of an overseas call, you can figure out approximate fax rates. Hotels may add a surcharge when sending faxes. A fax is about $5 a page to the West (Australia, North America, Europe). Most hotels can place IDD calls, as can the GPO. Overseas calls from Vietnam are expensive—a fax is cheaper. Phone cards in various dong denominations are available—buy one from a post office.

Some useful numbers: Police, 113; Fire, 114; Ambulance, 115. For telephone inquiries, dial 116. **Ho Chi Minh City Post and Telecom** has an information service—dial 108 for run-downs on air and rail tickets and schedules, hotels, restaurants, law consultation, tourist information, and even storytelling for children, or so the phone book claims.

Help yourself to addresses in the **Ho Chi Minh City Telephone Directory**—white pages and yellow pages in one fat volume. This tome is produced annually as a joint-venture project. Most major hotels possess a copy. Since the Vietnamese language uses a roman alphabet you can dig out most of the information yourself. It takes a while to steer through the listings—the thin residential section, for example, lists people by *first name,* followed by family name in alphabetical order. The limited number of Vietnamese first names is the reason for this anomaly. This section is followed by a white page business directory, given first in Vietnamese, then in English. Some fax numbers are also provided with company listings. At the back is a yellow pages classified index.

Cybercafés: There are a number both in the business district downtown and around backpacker-ville (Pham Ngu Lao area). Hotel business centers cater to the email-dependent.

Satellite TV

Permits are needed for larger satellite dishes in Saigon. Luxury hotels such as the Norfolk, Saigon Omni, New World, and Dainam have satellite dishes that can pick up StarTV (BBC) and CNN, as well as Chinese and Malaysian TV—a total of around 10 channels. The New

World Hotel lists 17 channels, but some of those are in-house movie channels. Increasingly, smaller hotels are gaining access to satellite programming.

Post Office and Courier

The **GPO,** facing Notre Dame Cathedral, has *poste restante,* plus EMS, DHL courier counter, and IDD phones. Down the street, at the corner of Nguyen Du and Hai Ba Trung, is the parcel shipping section. Be aware that sending parcels requires a lot of form-filling, soul-searching, and goods inspection. At the north side of the GPO is **Federal Express,** at 1 Nguyen Hau St., Q1, tel. 8/8290747, fax 8/8290477; deliveries to the United States take 2–3 days. **TNT Vietrans Express** has an office at 406 Nguyen Tat Thanh St., Q4, tel. 8/8725520.

Photography and Film

Kiosks selling film are found along Nguyen Hue Boulevard. Print film can be processed quickly at labs in the Nguyen Hue area; prints make great gifts for Vietnamese friends. You can have digital images processed in photo shops, and you can have images burned to CD at Internet cafés also.

Banking and ATMs

ATMs are in enough locations around Saigon that you don't need to use a bank at all. The ATMs are operated by Vietcombank, Sacombank, the ANZ Bank, and others. Ensure that the ATM carries Plus and Cirrus symbols.

Changing traveler's checks in Saigon is easy, unlike in other parts of the country. Hotels usually offer exchange counters, and there are a number of bank branches that will convert traveler's checks to dong. Several of these branches are found around Pham Ngu Lao; others are in Central Saigon.

The main banking area in Central Saigon lies to the south near Ben Nghe Channel. In this area you can witness the wonders of economic progress—people in suits unloading dirty sacks of dong from sparkling new cars. Banks either employ a staff of hundreds to count the dong, or use dong-counting machines. Banks charge

1–2 percent commission for converting traveler's checks to dong. Some charge no commission but offer a lower rate of exchange; yet others charge a minimum $1 fee. Conversion rates are slightly lower for cash U.S. dollars than for traveler's checks; rates depend on the size of the notes offered—higher for larger bills. You can convert U.S.-dollar traveler's checks to U.S. cash for 1–2 percent commission. Insist on clean bills with no rips or tears, as older wrinkled bills may be rejected by hotel staff. Visa, MasterCard, JCB, Diners Club, and American Express are coming into use in Saigon. You can get Visa cash advances, but expect a 4 percent commission (minimum $5 charge) on transactions.

Banks are usually open 0730–1200 and 1300–1630 Monday–Saturday, although they usually only open in the morning on Saturday. The main foreign exchange bank is **Vietcombank,** at 29 Ben Chuong Duong Street. Here you can exchange dollars to dong (for .5 percent commission) and convert U.S.-dollar traveler's checks to U.S. cash (for a 1.2 percent commission). **Thai Military Bank,** down the street at 11 Ben Chuong Duong St., has a 1 percent commission for dollars to dong, with a minimum $1 charge. **Vietnam Agribank,** 7 Ben Chuong Duong, charges 1 percent for converting U.S. traveler's checks to cash.

In the shopping mall of the New World Hotel is the **Hongkong Bank,** which has a functioning ATM. Another ATM machine functions at the ANZ Bank, near the waterfront. Other foreign banks with branches in Saigon include **Banque National de Paris** and **Credit Lyonnais;** rep offices include **Deutsche Bank,** Britain's **Standard Chartered Bank,** and **Internationale Nederlanden Bank.** More foreign banks, including American ones, are standing in line waiting for licenses. A number of Thai banks have opened, including **Bangkok Bank,** at 117 Nguyen Hue Blvd., and **Krung Thai Bank,** at 33 Ham Nghi Blvd.

Business Services

Major hotels in Saigon offer their own business centers with fax and IDD facilities, workstations, computers, photocopiers, equipment

Saigon

rental, and secretarial and translation services. There are also some independent operators. **Lotus Business Centre,** 71 Hai Ba Trung, Q1, tel. 8/8223053, fax 8/8298348, offers word processing, secretarial services, office space rental, and consulting services. **Saigon Business Centre,** 49 Dong Du St., tel. 8/8298777, fax 8/8298155, offers telecommunications services, desktop publishing, short-term office and workstation rental, mailing address and mail forwarding, and even mobile phone rental.

Health Care

Health facilities are poor. You are best off going to a Western-run clinic. A good one is **Family Medical Practice** in the Diamond Plaza Building, 34 Le Duan St., Q1, tel. 8/8227848, www.vietnammedicalpractice.com. At the same address is **Family Dental Practice.**

The **Emergency Center** at 125 Le Loi, tel. 8/8292071, has a 24-hour casualty section with English- and French-speaking doctors and a well-stocked pharmacy. In Cholon, **Cho Ray Hospital,** at 201 Nguyen Chi Thanh Blvd., tel. 8/8554137, has a 10th-floor section with English-speaking doctors for foreigners. It's $25 per night in the foreign ward; this facility has a good reputation. Bring a donor if you're likely to need blood, as certain blood types are in short supply. Emergency evacuation from Vietnam (normally to Singapore) can be arranged through **International SOS** (also known as OSCAT/AEA) at 65 Nguyen Du St., Q1, tel. 8/8298424, fax 8/8298551, emergency tel. 8/8298520. This clinic has contacts with expatriate doctors and provides consultation, pharmacy, and dental services.

Rest and Recreation

Major hotels have fitness centers and health clubs with gym and sauna. Some feature tennis courts and swimming pools. The Rex, the Palace, and other large hotels allow nonguests to use their swimming pool for a fee. The finest tennis courts in town are those at the larger hotels, such as the Rex. Top-rated hotel health clubs are in the Equatorial, Omni, and New World—these allow drop-ins for about $12 a day and have pools.

Saigon Hash House Harriers stage runs on Sunday and sometimes Saturday. Up to 50 runners take part—a great way to meet expatriates and locals. Get information at Apocalypse Now Bar or the Norfolk Hotel.

Accompanying the headlong rush into capitalism are some decadent bourgeois pastimes. Billiards is very popular, with many parlors in Saigon. A round of golf at the country club? This can be arranged at **Song Be Golf Resort,** about 20 kilometers north of Saigon. The last word on capitalist enterprise, this resort is a multinational development with Olympic-sized pool, tennis courts, hot tub, and bowling alley. Membership fees start at $25,000. There's another course about 20 kilometers east of Saigon—contact Saigon Tourist for details. **Saigon Race Track** (Phu Tho) dates from 1932. As the South Vietnamese government began to crumble in the mid-1970s, the track's owners closed it down, and the new government left it shuttered as part of its crackdown on gambling. In 1989 Vietnamese-Chinese businessman Philip Chau proposed to reopen the track, with taxes collected on track earnings. It was soon up and running. On a good day at Phu Tho as many as 10,000 enthusiasts show up. The maximum wager is $2, and the wager-placer must pick both first- and second-place horses. The track is north of Cholon in District 11; races are staged on Saturday and Sunday afternoons.

Getting There

BY AIR

Tan Son Nhat Airport is 12 kilometers from downtown Saigon. The large, modern airport features adequate facilities—gift and duty-free shops, café, tiny post office, and IDD calling booths.

Entry Formalities

If you are entering Saigon on an international flight, the authorities sometimes ignore the visa you already have and force you to fill out paperwork for another visa. There's no charge for this visa, but it costs $2 for passport photos. If you don't happen to have any handy, that's all right; a photographer waits in the wings. Then the authorities keep the new paperwork. Mysterious, huh?

On arrival you fill in the usual customs declaration form and entry/exit card, which you keep with you, to be surrendered on departure. Confusion reigns about how much money to declare. Only currency above $3,000 must be declared, and nobody's going to check the form when you depart anyway. Officials are also in the habit of handing out a small cardboard folder that hotels are supposed to stamp. Since there's no special prize or punishment for this effort, the best thing to do is lose it.

Transfers into Saigon

The airport is 12 kilometers from the Hotel de Ville. A drive downtown takes 15–30 minutes by car, depending on traffic. Cab fare should be about $5–7, but drivers will probably ask for more. Keep walking, keep talking—you can bring the price down. Major hotels charge $10–15 for airport transfer. A moto costs $3 to or from the airport.

Airline Offices

Airline offices in Saigon are mostly clustered around the Hotel de Ville and on the boulevards radiating off it—Dong Khoi, Le Thanh Ton, Le Loi, and Nguyen Hue. Right in front of the Hotel de Ville is Vietnam Airlines international booking office, 116 Nguyen Hue, tel. 8/8292118; for flight information, tel. 8/8443179. Vietnam Airlines flies on a number of international routes, including Bangkok, Vientiane, Kuala Lumpur, Singapore, Hong Kong, Manila, Seoul, Osaka, Jakarta, Paris, Berlin, Frankfurt, Vienna, Amsterdam, Moscow, Dubai, Sydney, and Melbourne. There is also a flight from Saigon to Los Angeles, but this requires a carrier change in Taipei or Manila. Vietnam Airlines is the agent for Royal Air Cambodge for flights to Phnom Penh and direct from Saigon to Siem Reap. Vietnam Airlines handles the Hong Kong–Saigon and Bangkok–Saigon legs of flights in a joint service with airlines such as Qantas and Cathay Pacific.

More carriers than the ones listed here are waiting to offer flights into Saigon. Qantas Airlines has a rep office at 24 Ly Tu Trong, tel. 8/8394720. Japan Airlines flies from Osaka to Ho Chi Minh City five times weekly. United States airlines negotiating for services include United, Northwest, Delta, and Continental. Canadian Airlines International is working on a route from Toronto via Paris to Ho Chi Minh City. Fares on some of these direct routes are expensive, so shop around. Asiana Airlines, for example, quotes a one-way fare of $400 from Ho Chi Minh City to Seoul, or $700 round-trip, while Singapore Airlines offers a one-way flight from Ho Chi Minh City to Singapore for $237. If you can't find any direct flights at the right price, your best bet is to fly to Hong Kong or Bangkok and proceed from there.

BY LAND

You can travel by road from Saigon to Phnom Penh, but if you're conscious of time and safety you should fly. One-way flights take 30 minutes and cost $50; you can pick up a Cambodian visa on arrival. For cheaper travel, try the $5 bus ride that takes an entire day to cover the 248-kilometer route. Your paperwork needs to be in order for the crossing; otherwise, you may be turned back. The Moc Bai land border is open 0630–1800. The road on the Cambodian side is paved and has few military checkpoints; it's considered one of the safest in the country. To smooth your passage however, carry packs of cigarettes—either Marlboro or 555 brand.

Phnom Penh to Saigon

You must possess a valid Vietnamese visa. Vietnamese visas take 2–5 working days to obtain in Phnom Penh—best arranged through an agent. It's advisable to carry small U.S. dollar bills for transportation and other expenses. There are several junctions along the way where money changers will approach you; at a ferry crossing over the Mekong you can trade dollars or riels for Vietnamese dong.

By Taxi: You can charter a taxi from Phnom Penh to the border or all the way to Saigon. Assemble your own group and negotiate with a driver. An alternative is to join Cambodian passengers in a share-taxi to Bavet on the Cambodian side of the border, walk across to Moc Bai on the Vietnamese side, and then take a Vietnamese share-taxi to Saigon. A share-taxi to Bavet costs $5–10 a person, with six or more passengers jammed into the car. The main departure point for share-taxis to Bavet is a depot just over the east side of Monivong Bridge, at Street 369, in the Chbampao Market area. Taxis leave 0600–1300. You can reach Monivong Bridge by moto. Make sure your share-taxi takes you all the way to the border—some stop a few kilometers shy. Once on the Vietnamese side, the share-taxi to Saigon costs under $10 per head. There are also motos waiting on the Vietnamese side; a moto ride into Saigon should be under $5. By car, it takes about three hours to the border, half an hour for paperwork, and another two hours to Saigon.

By Bus: A bus leaves at 0530 daily except Sunday from Phnom Penh. The ticket office is near the intersection of Street 182 and Street 211, close to Nehru Boulevard; it's open 0500–1000 and 1400–1700. A sign here simply says Ticket Office. Buy tickets one day in advance. It costs $5 for a regular Cambodian bus, or $12 for an a/c Vietnamese bus. The buses alternate so that only one leaves each day. If all goes well, the bus should arrive in Saigon by 1500. However, greedy Vietnamese police are prone to disassembly of the bus in search of contraband, and major delays can be caused by negotiating "taxes" on smuggled goods. One way to avoid this circus is to get off the bus at the Vietnamese border and change to a share-taxi for the final leg.

Getting Around

Before the mid-1980s, traffic in Saigon consisted almost exclusively of bicycles. Now the motorcycle rules. There were only a few thousand motorcycles in the early 1980s; by 1994 the figure eclipsed one million. No license is required for motorcycles under 150cc. In this age of motorcycle madness, you'll see some remarkable things in the traffic: 10-year-olds as well as grandmothers riding Hondas, schoolgirls with baseball caps and billowing *ao dais,* and hooligans on high-powered bikes. Hardly anyone bothers with the dismal bus system.

Metered Taxis

There are numerous taxi-company operators in Saigon—response time is often less than five minutes if you call a taxi. Vinataxi, tel. 8/8222990, runs a fleet of yellow metered Toyotas. The meter runs in dollars, and payment is accepted in dong, dollars, or both. The meter runs at around $.50–.70 a kilometer. If you get 3–4 people together for a taxi ride, it's actually cheaper than a cyclo, and you ride in air-conditioned comfort. Airport Taxi, tel. 8/8446666, is an outfit with 200 white Japanese and Korean cars, including limousines. This company regards Tan Son Nhat Airport as its turf and will menace any yellow cabs out this way. Other taxi operators include Cholon Taxi, tel. 8/822666; Festival, tel. 8/8454545; Saigon

SAIGON TOUR COMPANIES AND AGENTS

Numerous agencies in Saigon will handle visas, paperwork, ticketing, transportation rentals, tours, guides, hotel reservations, day-trip packages, and upcountry travel. Some of the agencies in Central Saigon (District 1) are listed here.

Ann Tourist, 58 Ton That Tung, Q1, tel. 8/8332564, fax 8/8225626; efficient, reliable agency with good guides

Atlas Travel, 41 Nam Ky Khoi Nghia, tel./fax 8/8298604

Cam On Tour, 62 Hai Ba Trung, Q1, tel. 8/8222166, fax 8/8298540

Eden Tourist, 106 Nguyen Hue Blvd., tel. 8/8293651, fax 8/8230783

Exotissimo Travel, 7 Mac Thi Buoi, tel. 8/8251723, fax 8/8251684; runs some innovative adventure tours

Fiditourist/Sunimex, 71 Dong Khoi, tel. 8/8296406, fax 8/8222941; guides, interpreters, motorbike rentals, visa extensions

New Indochina Travel, 4F Yoco Bldg., 41 Nguyen Thi Minh Khai, tel. 8/8227905, fax 8/8227904, stavn@hcm.fpt.vn; the STA rep for Vietnam—very reliable and efficient

Oil Services Co. (OSC), World Travel and Tour Service, 65 Nam Ky Khoi Nghia, tel. 8/8296658, fax 8/8290195

Peace Tours, 60 Vo Van Tan, tel./fax 8/8294416

Saigon Tours, 95 Hai Ba Trung, tel. 8/8294253, fax 8/8297215; visas, land packages, service for business travelers

Sinhbalo Adventures, 43 Bui Vien St., tel. 8/8367682, sinhbalo@hcm.vnn.vn; run by the man who started the original Sinh Café in Saigon—and then abandoned it in favor of guiding adventure tours

Vidotour (VTS), 58 Ngo Duc Ke, tel. 8/8291438, fax 8/8231278; comprehensive services, upscale market

Voiles Vietnam, 17 Pham Ngoc Thach, Q3, tel. 8/8296750, fax 8/8231591; French-run outfit offering cruises on a junk and diving on the coast

Volunteer Youth Company (VYC), 178 Nguyen Chu Trinh St., tel. 8/8399428, fax 8/8330399; runs Saigon Omni Hotel and several private hotels in Dalat

---

Tourist, tel. 8/8222206; Star, tel. 8/8651111; and Ben Thanh Taxi, tel. 8/8422422.

Motos and Cyclos

You can hire a moto for only a little more than the cost of a cyclo, and moto drivers don't snap back at you. Moto drivers are not always easy to find, however. A moto will get you across town for $.50; by the hour, motos cost a dollar or so. Few moto drivers wear helmets—and neither do passengers.

In mid-1995 authorities in Ho Chi Minh City banned cyclos from 50 streets in the city center to reduce traffic congestion. An estimated 40,000 cyclos operate in the city. Another possible reason for keeping cyclos out of the city center is that they are extremely aggressive toward tourists.

You can put yourself and the bicycle on a cyclo—that's how you get the bike home after an accident. Even a motorcycle can be loaded onto a cyclo. Cyclo drivers will sometimes try to manhandle you into their carriages. Bargain with cyclo drivers but in a friendly manner—don't push them too far, or they might turn nasty. One traveler related how he paid an inflated price for a one-way cyclo journey, and then refused to hire the same cyclo for the return journey. When he started walking away, the cyclo driver attacked him with a metal bar. Many cyclo drivers carry weapons of some kind (usually a knife or crowbar) under their seats.

Always negotiate the destination and full price before setting out on a cyclo. Make sure the driver knows where he is taking you. Saigon cyclo drivers are notorious for *really* taking their customers for a ride, charging foreigners 15–20 times the local rate. Make sure you're negotiating in dong rather than dollars. Cyclo drivers are quick to capitalize on misunderstandings. If you hold up two fingers indicating 2,000 dong, the driver may choose to interpret it as $2 (after you arrive, of course). The best way to avoid this kind of argument is to pay up front in dong. With whole dollars there's no change, and with dong you can bargain smaller increments. Cyclos can be hired for about $3.50 for a full day, or around $1 per hour. A trip across town costs around $1, which is still an inflated foreigner price. To get an idea of prices, the luxury Norfolk Hotel sets rates of $1.30 per hour per person, and $4 for half a day—and this is for plush white cyclos with sunroofs.

Two-Wheel Rentals

Motorcycle Rental: A number of guesthouses and private operators in the Pham Ngu Lao area rent motorcycles. Rates are around $6 a day. At 101 Dong Khoi is a motorcycle rental outfit with 50cc, 70cc, and 90cc bikes for $6 a day each; nearby Fiditourist, at 71 Dong Khoi, also rents bikes. Use designated motorcycle parking in Saigon to ensure your motorcycle is not stolen. If renting overnight, put the machine right inside your hotel gates or compound. It's a double whammy for motorcycles—if it's stolen, you may have to pay for it; if it's in an accident, you may have to pay for the damage. Clarify liabilities before renting. There is usually nothing in the way of insurance.

Bicycle Rental: Many bicycle-rental agencies operate in the Pham Ngu Lao area. Bike rentals cost about $1 a day, depending on bike quality and other factors. Chinese-made Forever and Phoenix brands are solid and sturdy. There are other rentals around the Dong Khoi area. Saigon Tourism rents bikes, but they're expensive at $3 a day. Some places want your passport as a deposit, but avoid leaving such a valuable document. Some just want a $10 deposit and charge $40 if the bike is stolen. Sinh Café requires a passport or $50 deposit for rental of a Chinese bike.

Vehicle Rental

Numerous agencies around Dong Khoi or Pham Ngu Lao can arrange a car and driver, or 15-seat minibus and driver, or something even larger.

Rental depends on the condition of the car (Russian or older models are cheaper), the kilometers racked up on the odometer, the number of proposed passengers, and whether the vehicle has air-conditioning. Some agencies quote a flat rate to save the half hour on the calculator. Kim Café, for example, offers custom car trips for a flat $25–30 for four passengers, including driver and gas. Daily rental is usually based on an eight-hour day; if you exceed that, overtime rates apply. Make bookings at least one day in advance. Some agents have accident damage insurance but no theft protection. They require you to leave a passport or cash for a deposit.

Here's a sampling of rates. A non–air-conditioned four-seat Volga or Peugeot is $25 a day and $.12/km; overtime $2/hour; overnight an extra $5.50 to cover the driver's expenses. An a/c four-seat Toyota for one day is $35 plus $.13/km; overtime $3/hour; if the vehicle is out overnight, it's an extra $7. An a/c Toyota 12–15-seat minibus starts at $37 a day, plus $.18/km; a 50-seat bus runs $55 a day.

Classic Wheels

Saigon Tourist and several of the major hotels rent chauffeur-driven Citroëns. A 1938 Citroën Traction 15 is the ideal luxury touring vehicle, with lots of legroom in the back. This is the gangster model, with running boards, dashmounted gearstick, and a windshield that can be winched open for ventilation. Via Sunimex and Hoang Minh shop, at 103 Dong Khoi St., you can hire a 1960s Chevrolet Nova 400—open top, white exterior, red interior—for $20 an hour with driver and guide. A few vintage cars along Pham Ngu Lao are available to rent. The owner of 333 Bar collects cars. He rents a gray Mercedes for $40 a day, and a VW convertible and black Citroën for $30 a day each. Many of Saigon's nonmetered taxis are classic autos too—1950s-vintage Peugeot 203s, Peugeot 305s, old Renault Dauphins. There is another class of taxi, referred to as "wedding taxis," used by married couples on their wedding day. These include spacious Dodges, Ford Falcons, even U.S. Army jeeps. However,

QUASAR KHANH AND THE BAMBOO BICYCLE

Bamboo is strong enough for use as construction scaffolding and for furniture, so why not use it for a bicycle? That's what Quasar Khanh did. He reinvented the bicycle by using a bamboo frame reinforced with metal braces, supports, and moving parts, and some rattan wrapping frills. He calls this whimsical device the Bambooclette—it looks like a piece of mobile furniture. He has several models in production. There's the regular model with picnic basket up front (made of bamboo, of course). Khanh also has a sports model and a mountain-bike model—a bike with simpler and more forceful bamboo design; he even has one with full suspension (front and rear) on it.

The bicycles, handmade by Khanh at his Saigon home, are exported to Europe and the United States and have been sold to celebrities including rock star Bono of U2, fashion model Kate Moss, and the prime minister of Italy.

Born Nguyen Manh Khanh (Quasar is an adopted name) in Hanoi in 1934, Khanh moved to France with his family at the age of 15. He made a name for himself in the field of women's fashion, getting involved in the miniskirt craze, designing eye-catching looks for his model-wife, Emmanuel. Khanh was an *enfant terrible* who turned the fashion world on its ear, hanging out with jet-setters such as Vidal Sassoon. He also started an inflatable furniture fad and was involved in several controversial engineering projects in Paris. He invented the Cube Car, a huge cube of plexiglass and metal on wheels—15 of these absurd-looking cars were produced and are held by collectors.

In 1994, Khanh decided to move back to Saigon to have a hand in the country's economic transformation. Apart from bamboo bicycles, his energy has been directed into designing a bridge to span the Saigon River. The problem of bridges (or lack of them) has plagued Saigon's planners for more than a decade. A tantalizing swath of undeveloped land lies across the river from downtown, but to put a conventional bridge in place would close down the busy port, reducing shipping access. The bridge would need a 40-meter clearance—but this in turn would require a ramp almost a kilometer long and snarl up traffic. Khanh has a model that provides the solution: a bridge with spiral ramps at both ends. He envisions a futuristic city of high-rises fanning from the bridge, connected at different levels with elevated streets and walkways.

Vietnamese planners have found Khanh's solution too radical (and how dizzy will drivers be by the time they work their way up the spiral ramps?), so it's on the back burner. In the meantime, he's working on the Hydrair Surface Effect Ship—a kind of high-speed hydroplane that can deliver fish from Vietnam to Japan overnight.

THE CLASSIC CARS OF SAIGON

by Hans Kemp

Imagine a society where cars have been frozen in time, where private car ownership was suddenly banned, where the country isolated itself from the rest of the world and prevented aging autos from being snapped up as collectors' items. This is exactly what happened in Saigon. In the 1950s, this city was the jewel in the crown of the French Asian Empire; money flowed, and both expatriates and locals spent heavily on cars—first on French models, then on other European cars such as Mercedes, Volkswagen, Fiat, and MG.

During the American occupation, the money continued to pour in, bringing a generation of Fords and Dodges to the streets. Then came 1975. With Saigon overrun by the North Vietnamese, ownership of a car became a capitalist sin. Owners either "sold" them to the state or stashed them in remote barns. Private cars disappeared from the streets for a decade.

When the Hanoi leadership committed itself to a market-oriented economy in the mid-1980s, Saigon's automotive classics were dusted off and cautiously brought out of hiding. Unfortunately, plunderers also began scouring the country looking for classic treasures, intent on shipping them abroad for huge profits.

Some Saigon classics have been put to work as taxis, including a number of Peugeot 203s from the 1950s. Some of the drivers date to the 1950s too—Mr. Ngoc has been driving his 1952 Renault 4 since he bought it more than 40 years ago. Among the taxis operating out of a bus station on the outskirts of Ho Chi Minh City is another French classic, a 1930s Citroën Traction Familiale. Looks are less important here than capacity, and the already long chassis of the vintage Citroën has been chopped and extended to accommodate 12 passengers. Other Citroëns are parked within the bus station compound, alongside custom-enlarged American cars—their bigger wheels and truck suspensions bumping up the profits.

Other vintage automobiles are maintained by collectors for private use. "People say I'm crazy to buy old cars," says Mr. Dong. "If I have the money I buy a car and not a house, whereas nowadays a house would be a better investment." Mr. Dong's collecting began

most couples now prefer newer Japanese cars for their wedding day.

Your Own Wheels

If you're buying your own motorcycle to head up-country, try the vicinity of New World Hotel, along Ly Tu Trong Street, with scores of motorcycle shops. These mostly sell brand-new Hondas imported from Japan or Thailand, but they also showcase a few Russian motorcycles. The model favored by the Vietnamese, the Honda Dream II, sells new for up to $2,800. A Russian Minsk 125cc costs $500. Opposite the New World Hotel

is a string of stalls selling motorcycle helmets and accessories. You might also try to buy a motorcycle from a fellow traveler—check the notices posted at Kim and Sinh cafés. Officially you need some sort of license if operating a motorcycle over 70cc, but the police don't seem to care.

If you're staying longer in Saigon, or want to ride around the Delta or the countryside, consider buying a bicycle: for around town, a bike with a wire basket up front; for longer touring, a model with racks and a water-bottle cage. On Le Thanh Ton near the New World Hotel two small shops sell 10-speeds, and two other shops

in 1988 when he stumbled across a Volkswagen Kharman Ghia convertible on a visit to a local hospital. "I found it in a shed, along with discarded towels, blood, mice, and ants." A French doctor gave it to the hospital in 1975, but the hospital director thought it beneath his dignity to be driven around in a car with only two doors. The battery was dead, so the VW was shoved into a corner of the hospital grounds and used as a rubbish dump. "There is only one like this in the whole of Vietnam," Dong smiles. "I bought it for only $60, though many times more has been spent on repair and maintenance."

Mr. Dong couldn't have found a better car. Foreign visitors adore it, and by renting it out Dong was able to earn enough to buy a mid-1950s Mercedes 190. Later he bought a six-cylinder Citroën Traction 15 from an old woman who'd inherited it from her father. "I used to be brought to school in a car like this," says Dong, whose father was the chief accountant for IBM in the days before 1975.

Another avid collector is Mr. Huynh Van Mui, who runs a tailoring shop opposite the Hotel de Ville. He has been in business for more than 40 years. "I had three cars before '75," says the white-haired tailor, "one for business, one for the family, and one for myself. Now the Rolls and the Mercedes are gone, but I could never part with my MGA." He bought the car in 1961 from a catalog in Hong Kong with 30 ounces of gold, and although times are tough, no way will Mr. Huynh sell his pride and joy.

Mr. Pham loves American cars. The drawers of his desk are filled with old brochures and magazine ads of every model available in the 1960s. "Plymouth is out to win you over," extols an ad clipped from an old *Playboy*. Under the photographic gaze of Uncle Ho, Mr. Pham's desk is soon covered with his paper collection. The only real car he owns is parked outside his office—a 1957 Dodge badly in need of work. Pham dreams of having enough money to restore it to its original state.

Pristine American models are sometimes sighted cruising the streets of Saigon. A young couple may hire a spacious American car for a wedding day cruise around town, although today these "wedding taxis" are increasingly Japanese models. Other U.S. cars sighted include shiny Mustangs and a Chevrolet Nova 400. It's not hard to imagine this 1965 classic with GIs crammed into the red seats, cruising the bars of downtown Saigon.

sell mountain bikes. Low-end prices range from less than $60 for a Thai bike or a Peugeot made in Vietnam to $70 for a gearless Chinese-made Forever. High-end prices for Taiwan-made 10-speeds or pseudomountain bikes range $130–230 depending on quality. Even higher-end are bikes fitted with real Shimano components.

Boat Rentals

You can hire a boat to cruise up and down the Saigon River and its tributaries for around $5–10 an hour from the docks near the foot of Hai Ba Trung Street.

Saigon

Getting Away

BY AIR

The Vietnam Airlines domestic office is at 15 Dinh Tien Hoang, tel. 8/8299980. You can book flights directly here, or via travel agents such as ATC, 63 Ly Tu Trong St., tel. 8/8230234. Tan Son Nhat Airport is the busiest in the country, with scheduled domestic departures to the Central Highlands towns of Dalat, Buon Ma Thuot, Pleiku; Nha Trang and Qui Nhon on the coast; and points north such as Hué, Danang, Haiphong, and Hanoi. There's also a flight to Phu Quoc Island in the southwest. Sample fares from Saigon: to Dalat, $25; Nha Trang, $45; Danang, $85; Hué, $90; Hanoi, $160; Haiphong, $150—foreigner prices all. Be sure to reconfirm your ticket. Flights are continually overbooked and schedules altered. The booking system, allegedly computerized, doesn't seem to work very well, as passengers often fail to materialize. So if the plane you want is overbooked, go to the airport on standby and chances are you'll still be able to board.

The only options in domestic carriers are Pacific Airlines and Vietnam Air Service Company (VASCO). VASCO operates light planes and helicopters on a charter basis, with regular flights to Con Dao Islands and Cantho. Contact VASCO at 27B Nguyen Dinh Chieu St., or use Vietnam Airlines as the booking agent. Pacific Airlines flies from Saigon to Hanoi and Haiphong; the outfit has an office in the same building as Vietnam Airlines domestic (14 Dinh Tien Hoang, tel. 8/8241139) and another office downtown at 77 Le Thanh Ton, tel. 8/8290844, near the Hotel de Ville.

BY RAIL

Saigon Railway Station is about six kilometers from the Hotel de Ville, about a 15-minute drive. You can get advance tickets from travel agencies. Most hotels have rail schedules; you can also get the information by phone by calling 108. Foreigners pay premium prices on trains—much more than locals.

Saigon is the end of the line; from here you can go only north along the coast to Hué and Hanoi. Sample fares from Saigon to Hué, a distance of 1,038 kilometers, on an S7 train: $29 hard seat, $35 soft seat, $50–55–60 hard sleeper, and $66 soft sleeper. From Saigon to Hué on a CM5 train, prices are $40 soft seat, $55–60–66 hard sleeper, and $76 soft sleeper; no hard seats. Train travel is more comfortable and more expensive than bus travel, but not much faster.

BY ROAD
Traveler Minibuses and Buses

A number of Saigon outfits can arrange up-country tours by car or minibus. You can arrange a custom trip with your own small group or join other travelers. If accompanying others, you don't have to complete the trip; just bail out wherever you want. Traveler cars and minibuses are more comfortable than Vietnamese bus or minibus transport, and the logistics will be simpler. Weighed against this is the higher price and the fact that you're traveling with other Westerners who'll all take out their cameras at every stop. There are sign-up boards for traveler vans heading up the coast at cafés on Pham Ngu Lao. Usually as many as 10 passengers per minibus are required; for cars, four passengers.

Express Minibus: Pham Ngu Lao cafés offer only transport on minibuses (no tours). Direct to Dalat costs $7 a person (six hours), and express to Nha Trang runs $12–15 (nine hours). Sometimes the rider is put in with a touring group. Vietnamese agencies offer the same service to popular destinations. Addresses keep changing, so inquire at your hotel desk about possibilities. A minibus office at 39 Nguyen Hue Blvd. arranges rides to Dalat, Vung Tau, Nha Trang, and the coast. Vietnamese minibuses are packed to the maximum, and you won't see much along the way.

CONSULTATES IN SAIGON

Most embassies and consulates are in Hanoi. However, because of frequent land/air connections or other reasons of expediency, some are based in Saigon. A few consulates of note are:

Australia, 5B Ton Duc Thang, Q1, tel. 8/8296035

Canada, 235 Dong Khoi St., Q1, tel. 8/8245025

China, 39 Nguyen Thi Minh Khai, tel. 8/8292457

France, 27 Nguyen Thi Minh Khai, Q1, tel. 8/8297231

Germany, 126 Nguyen Dinh Chieu, Q3, tel. 8/8291967

India, 49 Tran Quoc Thao, Q3, tel. 8/8294498

Japan, 13 Nguyen Hue, Q1, tel. 8/8225314

Netherlands, 29 Le Duan, Q1, tel. 8/8235932

New Zealand, 41 Nguyen Thi Minh Khai, Q1, tel. 8/8226907

Russia, 40 Ba Huyen Thanh Quan, tel. 8/8392936

Singapore, 65 Le Loi, tel. 8/8225173

United Kingdom, 25 Le Duan, Q1, tel. 8/8232604

USA, 4 Le Duan, Q1, tel. 8/8229433

Regional Consulates

The **Cambodian Consulate,** at 41 Phung Khac Khoan, Q1, tel. 8/8292751, issues a one-month visa for around $30 (through an agent). Visa issue is possible same day or next day. If you fly into Phnom Penh or Siem Reap you can get a one-month visa at the airport for $20; if crossing by land from Vietnam or along the Mekong route to Phnom Penh, you must get your Cambodian visa in Saigon.

The **Lao Consulate,** at 93 Pasteur St., Q1, tel. 8/8297667, issues a two-week to one-month visa for $50 and up, depending on nationality; it takes up to a week to process, unless you want to pay a surcharge, in which case it's ready in two working days. There are also Lao consulates in Danang and Hanoi.

The **Consulate-General of Thailand** is just up from the Rex II annex at 77 Tran Quoc Thao St., Q3, tel. 8/8222637. Visa issue takes two working days and costs $15.

Open Tour Bus: Sinh Café and several others offer an Open Tour bus ticket from Saigon to Nha Trang or farther up the coast all the way to Hanoi. The tickets cost $35 one-way Saigon to Hué (you can get out at various stepping stones en route to stay overnight or longer), plus $22 from Hué to Hanoi. Buses make short sightseeing stops along the route. The idea is that you buy, for example, Saigon to Hanoi, then get off at major stops such as Nha Trang or Hué and rejoin the bus when you feel like it. These private buses are particularly useful if trying to move around in the Tet period, when most transport shuts down. You should be aware that an Open Tour ticket involves more than a simple bus ride. The driver may pull into your destination late at night, driving into the courtyard of his chosen hotel. So your ticket comes with attached restaurant and hotel coercion deals. There's no obligation for you to use these places, but there's certainly a strong suggestion that you should.

Bus Terminals

The two main bus terminals are Mien Tay, with buses to the south, and Mien Dong, with departures to the north. Try to buy express bus tickets a day in advance by having your hotel desk or an agent phone ahead. Bus stations are all on the fringes of Saigon, so allow time to get out to these places if you anticipate a 0500 departure. Some stations are up to 10 kilometers out of town. Arrange a taxi to get to the station, or find a regular lambro shuttle for a few thousand dong. The lambro is slower because of frequent stops. Some regular buses also connect the outlying terminals with Ben Thanh Bus Terminal near Ben Thanh Market in Central Saigon. Ben Thanh Bus Terminal also runs buses to Cu Chi.

Some of the bus terminals on the fringes of Saigon are huge and serve as bases for other transportation such as minibuses, old Citroën share-taxis, Renault vans, and other mobile wonders. Bus travel is cheap: You can make it all the way from Saigon to Hanoi in less than 50 hours for $20, although your kidneys will never be the same. You may be a few inches shorter by the time you arrive, too—buses and minibuses crowd those passengers in. Although presumably there's no foreign markup, the ticket sellers routinely gouge big noses, especially on the minibus runs.

Mien Tay Bus Terminal: Ten kilometers southwest of Central Saigon on Huong Vuong Boulevard, this sprawling terminal handles departures to the Mekong Delta and points south. There are buses to Vinh Long, Cantho, Phung Hiep, Camau, Long Xuyen, Chau Doc, and Rach Gia. Timing depends on ferry crossings along the route: three hours to Cantho, 12 hours to Camau. Buses go to Mien Tay from the Ben Thanh Market area; you can also hop on a lambro from the east side of Pham Ngu Lao.

Cholon Bus Terminal: No express buses run to Mytho from Mien Tay terminal, just regular buses. It's more convenient to take a Mytho bus from Cholon bus terminal (Ben Xe Khach Cholon) in District 5, a lot closer to Central Saigon. Other departures from this terminal go to My Thuan, Caibe, and Long An.

Mien Dong Bus Terminal: This station is on Quoc Lo 13, about six kilometers northeast of Central Saigon; follow Xo Viet Nghe Tinh Street all the way out. You can take a bus from the Ben Thanh Market area, or a moto. The station handles most departures to the north, to Vung Tau, Dalat, Buon Ma Thuot, Hué, Danang, and the coast road to Hanoi. Express buses leave around 0500.

Other Bus Stations: Tay Ninh bus terminal in Tan Binh District west of the airport has departures to Tay Ninh, Cu Chi, and other points northwest of Saigon.

Saigon to Phnom Penh

To enter Cambodia by road you can either get a Cambodian visa in Saigon or pick one up on arrival at the border post (have a passport photo and $20 in U.S. cash at hand). If you plan to cross into Cambodia and then return to Saigon, you'll need a reentry stamp for your Vietnamese visa.

Taxi to Phnom Penh: A share-taxi is $30 to the Moc Bai border, only $7.50 when split between four people. You can arrange a ride through a traveler café such as Sinh Café. Or try Saigon's Mien Tay bus station on the western outskirts of town, or negotiate with a downtown taxi driver if you have your own small group. Once over the border you can arrange another share-taxi for about $5–10 a person—just crowd in with the locals. Depending on immigration holdups, the full trip from Saigon to Phnom Penh should take 7–8 hours.

Bus to Phnom Penh: Cambodian buses (non a/c) cost $5 and leave Thursday, Friday, and Saturday from an old Mercedes-Benz dealership at 145 Nguyen Du, around the corner from Hoang Gia Hotel. The Vietnamese a/c bus leaves from the same area on Monday, Tuesday, and Wednesday, and costs $12. You can buy tickets for both buses at the garage next to the Rex Hotel, 155 Nguyen Hue Blvd., tel. 8/230754; one-day advance purchase recommended. The seller must see your Cambodian visa before issuing the ticket. No buses on Sunday or holidays, which means no buses for 3–4 days around Tet. The trip takes about 9–10 hours. Buses leave at 0530 and arrive around 1500 or 1600 in Phnom Penh. However, if there are delays because of contraband spot checks, the trip could take 12 hours or longer.

A much more interesting alternative to the bus trip is to go by land and water through the Mekong Delta to Chau Doc, and then arrange to travel north up the Mekong to Phnom Penh. Several outfits can arrange the journey, including Saigon Tourism and Victoria Chau Doc Hotel (which runs its own boat).

BY WATER

A great river journey is to take the hydrofoil from Saigon to the beach resort of Vung Tau. The trip takes only an hour (as opposed to several hours by car) and costs $10 one-way. En route you pass by Saigon port shipping on the Saigon River; then the hydrofoil cruises through rural areas and emerges into the South China Sea. Two modern hydrofoils are run by Vina Express, a Singapore–based shipping company. There are two daily return services from Saigon to Vung Tau—you could leave Saigon in the morning and be back the same night. In Saigon, the hydrofoil leaves from a jetty at the foot of Nguyen Hue Boulevard, near the old Customs House. Buy tickets 30 minutes before departure or make advance purchases. In Saigon, contact Vina Express at the jetty booth, tel. 8/8297892 or 8224621; in Vung Tau, contact the jetty booth opposite Hai Au Hotel, tel. 64/856530, or book via Petro House, tel. 64/852014.

EXIT FORMALITIES

On exit you surrender your customs form, though nobody seems to check it. If you have a paper visa, you surrender this, too. International departure tax is $14; no domestic departure tax. When boarding a domestic or international flight, you have to pass through Heimann scanners, the same kind used at Bangkok Airport. They say "Film Safe" but it's still advisable to divert film around them.

VIETNAMESE VISA MODIFICATIONS

The following stamp additions to your Vietnamese visa are handled by either Ho Chi Minh Department of Immigration and Foreigners Affairs, 161 Nguyen Du St., tel. 8/8297107, or the Immigration Department, 254 Nguyen Trai St., tel. 8/8391701. Travelers usually have the paperwork handled by an agent to expedite delivery, but you can try it yourself if you don't mind a bit of aggravation.

Visa Extension: There's a sliding fee scale for extensions depending on whether a week, two-week, or longer extension is requested. Extensions are best handled through agents; the average cost is around $20 for two weeks or $40 for a month.

Reentry Visa: If you wish to reenter Vietnam after visiting Cambodia, you need a Vietnamese reentry stamp, in effect turning your Vietnamese visa into a double-entry visa. This costs about $25.

Saigon

The South

The south is blessed with the most consistently balmy weather in Vietnam, though some find it too humid. "Balmy" is a word that could equally be applied to the religious faiths of the south—such as the Cao Dai sect, with its synthesis of half a dozen creeds.

The most striking feature of the south is the lush Mekong Delta—a tropical wonderland of deep-green rice fields, fruit orchards, floating markets, and more coconuts than you'd ever want to contemplate. The delta is where the Mekong River meets the South China Sea. Here it is called Cuu Long or "River of the Nine Dragons"—an oblique reference to the perceived number of branches of the mighty river as it fans out on its final approach to the sea—after its long trip down from the Tibetan plateau. Water life in the delta is brisk, with floating markets and floating fish-houses. The market towns of Vinh Long and Cantho are easily accessible from Saigon and make great bases for exploring surrounding channels and islands by small boat—the best way to see this fertile region.

The Mekong Delta is one of Vietnam's premier rice-producing areas and the source of a lot of its fresh fruit. This is nothing short of miraculous when you take in the fact that parts of the delta were devastated in a deliberate strategy of "ecocide" during the American War—whereby whole riverbanks were stripped bare of foliage.

Must-Sees

Look for M to find the sights and activities you can't miss and ⍬ for the best dining and lodging.

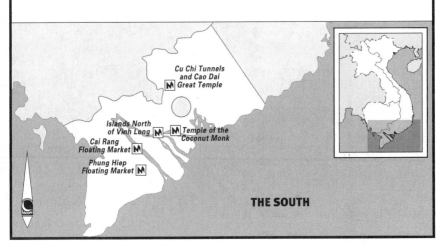 **Cu Chi Tunnels and Cao Dai Great Temple:** These two sights make up the top day trip from Saigon, which has you crawling through Vietcong tunnels and staring at dragon-coiled columns. Watch out for Divine Agents (pages 305 and 307).

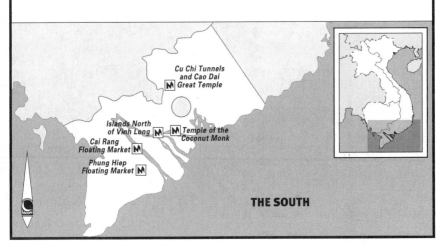 **Temple of the Coconut Monk, Mytho:** Getting there is more than half the fun. See the zany temple of a monk with a mission—to unite north and south (page 325).

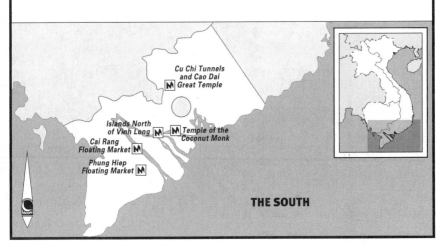 **Islands North of Vinh Long:** Fruit orchards abound in this region, and a boat trip is the best way to get to them. You can see—and sample—unusual varieties (page 326).

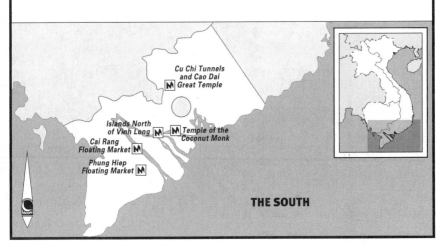 **Cai Rang Floating Market, Cantho:** Boats loaded with pineapples, coconuts, and rose apples converge in dawn trading. Make a special effort to see this spectacle (page 329).

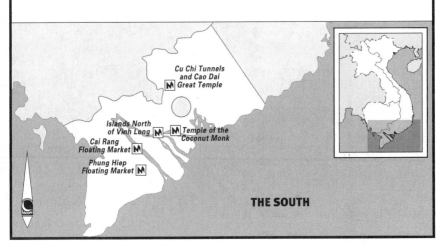 **Phung Hiep Floating Market, South of Cantho:** Busy river life can be witnessed at the market at the confluence of seven rivers. See stand-up rowers perform a balancing act as they steer through the maze of boats (page 331).

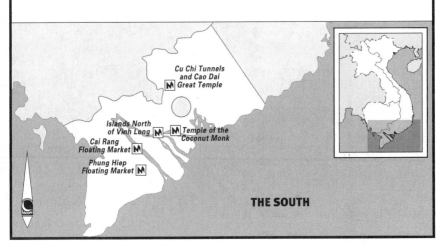

Cu Chi Tunnels
and Cao Dai
M Great Temple

Islands North
of Vinh Long **M** **M** Temple of the
Coconut Monk
Cai Rang
Floating Market **M**

Phung Hiep
Floating Market **M**

THE SOUTH

More than half the mangrove swamps in the Mekong Delta were destroyed by the American military through use of chemical poisoning, defoliants, and napalm in an attempt to flush out Vietcong soldiers. That the region has recovered its lushness speaks volumes about the resilience and resourcefulness of the Vietnamese people.

PLANNING YOUR TIME

Most travelers use Saigon as a base for round-trip explorations of the south. Popular sites

outside Saigon include Mytho, a riverine town 70 kilometers southwest; the beach resort of Vung Tau 115 kilometers southeast; and Cu Chi Tunnels and Cao Dai Great Temple to the northwest. Numerous Saigon tour agencies package these destinations as day trips or overnight journeys. You can also ride tourist vans one-way to these destinations, and then take off on your own.

A number of traveler cafés on Pham Ngu Lao in Saigon organize cheap day trips by minibus, usually venturing out 0900–1800. The day trip

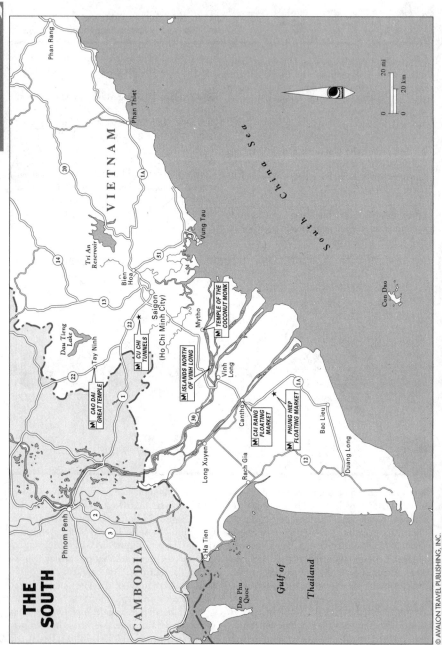

to Cu Chi and Cao Dai Great Temple is $6 a head; a Mytho day trip costs $7. Popular tour operators include Delta Tours, TNK Tour, TM-Brothers, and Kim Café. Farther afield, you can join a two-day trip to the Mekong Delta for $20, or a three-day trip for $30.

As far as your own transport goes, bicycling is not a good option as you will most likely be run off the road by larger vehicles. However, mountain biking is a great way of getting around places such as Cantho to see the sights (you can rent a mountain bike there). If you have excellent motorcycle skills and are attuned to Vietnamese road "rules," you might consider renting a 125cc motorcycle in Saigon for around $5 a day and heading off into the Delta for four days or longer. This way you have lots of legroom and have no trouble getting to hotels that are far from bus stations. However, you should bear in mind that roads are narrow in the delta and erratic traffic maneuvers by Vietnamese drivers can be highly hazardous to your health. You have to watch the bike—always pay for parking and lock the bike in a hotel courtyard (or your room) at night. Delta roads are in quite good condition, and being on a bike allows for plenty of photo stops. Like pedestrians, motorcyclists gain entry to ferries faster than travelers using other modes of transport. A little-explored option for your own transport in the delta is to go kayaking. In a water-based culture, this makes a lot of sense, but it might be difficult to find a place to moor for the night—or places to sleep.

Northwest of Saigon

Saigon's most popular day trip is to Cu Chi Tunnels and the Cao Dai Great Temple at Tay Ninh. Although you can reach these areas by public transportation, the logistics are complicated. For $6, a minibus from a traveler café will take care of all the driving and directions. Tours generally leave Saigon at 0900, reach Tay Ninh for the 1200 Cao Dai service, and then leave at 1300 for Cu Chi Tunnels. You're usually back in Saigon around 1800 or 1900. The Cao Dai Great Temple stop is short—if you'd like to spend more time at Tay Ninh, for a small extra fee the tour bus will drop you at the Cao Dai Temple, and then pick you up the next day. In the interim you can spend more time at the temple and visit Black Lady Mountain, overnighting in Tay Ninh.

M CU CHI TUNNELS

Cu Chi Tunnels are near the village of Ben Suc, about 75 kilometers northwest of Saigon and about 40 kilometers from the town of Cu Chi. The tunnels were part of an underground network that zigzagged from the southern tip of the Ho Chi Minh Trail near the Cambodian border to the Saigon River. Most Vietcong tunnels in the Cu Chi area have been sealed, but a few passageways were doubled in width and height to accommodate Western tourist bodies.

There are actually two tunnel locations, both in the direction of Ben Suc village. Backpackers usually go to Ben Dinh, where the entry price is $1.50. They're shown a short video, given a garbled spiel about the tunnels, and allowed to crawl through a 50-meter passage. Swanker tourists head for Ben Duoc, about five kilometers away, where a $3–4 entry price pays for a more articulate translator, a superior Saigon Tourist video, and wider tunnels. Insecticide is sprayed daily and the tunnels are cleared of any crawlies such as snakes or scorpions (tiny bats like the tunnels, too).

The Vietcong used to crawl on their bellies through the dark, dank tunnels, but visitors can walk through them (albeit hunched over). After scrambling through the tunnels for a claustrophobic, sweaty 15 minutes, you'll wonder how anybody could last a day in the tunnels, let alone a year. The Vietcong carried on much longer than that—people got married and women gave birth down here. Below ground was a complete system of kitchens, rudimentary clinics and operating rooms, meeting rooms, and sleeping chambers with bamboo beds. The network also incorporated storage chambers for weapons and rice, drinking wells, ventilation shafts, false tunnels, and booby-trapped passages.

The Vietnamese spent decades digging in the reddish-brown laterite clay in this area—the tunnels were all built with simple hand tools. Up to 50 kilometers of tunnels were constructed by the Vietminh fighting the French 1948–1954. Between 1960 and 1965, their successors, the Vietcong, added an astonishing three-level network four times as big, bringing the total to more than 200 kilometers. The deepest layer of tunnels lay 8–10 meters underground. Up to 16,000 guerrillas could live in the tunnel complex at any one time, though 5,000–7,000 was the normal complement.

The soil at Cu Chi was perfect for tunneling—the clay was sticky, allowed some air penetration, did not crumble, and proved remarkably stable. The Vietcong employed ingenious camouflage to conceal tunnel exits, entrances, and ventilation holes.

A question that immediately springs to mind is what did the Vietcong do with all the dirt collected from all that digging? The Vietnamese, intimate with the lay of the land, never left earth from the tunnels in mounds or near a tunnel site. Instead, it was smuggled out in small quantities and recycled into house basements or other structures, poured into streams, and dumped in recent bomb craters.

The tunnels were key to Vietcong success, providing a stronghold close to Saigon. Against superior American firepower and technology, the Vietcong had the element of surprise. By the time U.S. troops arrived they faced an army of moles: Vietcong could pop up a trapdoor, fire away, and be back down the hatch before the U.S. soldiers could react.

Nor was it easy to destroy the VC "subway." United States forces declared Cu Chi a free-fire zone and dropped 50,000 tons of bombs on the region, but the tunnels continued to operate. Blowing gas or pumping water into the tunnels proved ineffective, as each section of an important tunnel could be sealed off by the Vietcong. The United States formed squads of "tunnel rats"—slim, small-bodied men who probed tunnels—and sniffer dogs were also used. These rat squads only partially uncovered the mysteries of the underground labyrinth. Among the visitors to Cu Chi have been U.S. veterans who come back to see this incredible network with their own eyes.

The Cu Chi Tunnels area is the most accessible and commercial yet (dubbed "Cong World" by a visiting Western reporter). After crawling around in the tunnels, you can move over to a nearby firing range, where you can empty an AK-47 or M-16 rifle at targets of paper tigers or water buffalo. Souvenir shops sell war-related paraphernalia—you can buy a genuine pair of rubber sandals once worn on the Ho Chi Minh Trail. Attendants at the shops wear black pajamas and rubber sandals, just as the Vietcong did.

TAY NINH

Tay Ninh, 96 kilometers northwest of Saigon and 62 kilometers from the town of Cu Chi, is a staging point for excursions to the Cao Dai Great Temple, Long Hoa Market, and Black Lady Mountain. You can reach all these sites by moto—it's a good idea to hire a moto or car for a half day or full day, as it's hard to find transport around Tay Ninh.

The main attraction is the Cao Dai Great Temple. If you have more time on your hands and want to stretch your legs, visit Black Lady Mountain (Noi Ba Den), about 15 kilometers northeast of Tay Ninh. The 900-meter peak is a sacred site, with a few cave temples perched on its flanks. It's a striking sight, as there's no major peak within a 100-kilometer radius. Caves on the mountain were used as a base by the Vietnamese fighting both the French and the United States. Walking up the mountain to the main temple complex and back again should consume a leisurely two hours; climbing to the peak and back requires about six hours. Hire a moto for half a day from Tay Ninh and ask the driver to wait for you.

Basics

Tay Ninh is a small town. The cleanest place to stay is **Anh Dao Hotel,** tel. 66/827306, a three-story hotel with a/c and TV in 18 rooms for $15–20 apiece; good restaurant. Cheap and seedy accommodation at the labyrinthine **Hoa Binh Hotel** runs $5 for fan rooms and $10 for a/c. This run-down socialist palace is a short-time hotel, with rooms rented hourly, and taxi girls and cockroaches hanging about. There are a few other hotels around town in the $10–20 per room range. Food stalls and small restaurants are strung out along the main drag of Tay Ninh. Buses leave Tay Ninh hourly 0600–1300 for Saigon—the trip takes three hours, with frequent stops. Buses to Tay Ninh depart Saigon from Tay Ninh bus terminal on the northwest fringe of the city.

N CAO DAI GREAT TEMPLE

The Temple

From the outside, the Cao Dai Great Temple is already bizarre, combining the lines of a French baroque church with pagoda-like steeples. Inside you enter a realm described by Graham Greene as "a Walt Disney fantasia of the East, dragons and snakes in technicolour." Greene himself took the faith very seriously and at one point considered conversion to Cao Daism.

It is perhaps odd, then, that the figure of Graham Greene has not yet found its way into the Cao Dai pantheon. One of the fascinating aspects of Cao Daism is belief in Divine Agents, or patron saints—whose spirits make "contact" at seances through a temple medium using a planchette. Among the Divine Agents contacted in the past are Jesus Christ, Confucius, Lao Tzu, Moses, St. John the Baptist, Joan of Arc, William Shakespeare, Rene Descartes, La Fontaine, and Louis Pasteur. Among the leading lights contacted from the 20th century are Vladimir Lenin, Charlie Chaplin, and Winston Churchill. Greene died in 1991, so perhaps it is too early for him to be inducted into the Cao Dai hall of fame.

The three guiding spirits of the Cao Dai faith are featured in a mural in the temple vestibule:

poets, prophets, and revolutionaries. The figure holding the inkstone is Sun Yatsen (instrumental in the fall of China's Manchu dynasty); writing in French is Victor Hugo (who had a hand in starting the romantic movement in France); at the right is 15th-century Vietnamese poet Nguyen Binh Khiem, famous for his prophecies. On the other side of this wall are three statues mounted on lotus buds and raised on a three-step dais. The central figure is Ho Phap, a symbol of justice, flanked by statues of cardinals. Draped around Ho Phap is a seven-headed serpent: The top three heads symbolize love, joy, and bliss; the lower heads symbolize jealousy, anger, hatred, and uncontrollable desire.

The dragon, symbolizing the force of intellect, is a dominant temple feature. Down the nave are two rows of dragon-coiled pillars supporting a lofty vaulted ceiling dotted with clouds and inlaid with flying dragons. The lotus, symbolizing purity, is another prominent motif. Piercing the walls are open lattice-work windows composed of a striking lotus design. Each lattice window encloses a Cao Dai eye set in a triangle, just like the one on the U.S. dollar bill.

While Cao Dai worshippers wear white, Cao Dai priests wear red, blue, or yellow robes—red symbolizes Confucianism, blue Taoism, and yellow Buddhism. Separating the inner sanctuary from the main temple are three curtains, one each in red, blue, and yellow. Suspended from the ceiling is a pediment featuring Divine Agents. There are eight small figures here—at top left is Lao Tzu, the founder of Taoism; below him the bodhisattva Quan Am. In the middle, from top to bottom, are Sakyamuni Buddha, Ly Thai Bach (Ly Tai Pe, the spiritual pope), Jesus Christ, and Cuong Thai Cong (a mythological figure). To the right, at the top is Confucius; below is Quan Cong, a deified Chinese general.

Smooth, tiled flooring leads up nine broad steps to the main altar. The inner sanctuary sits on an octagonal base with 12 steps, enclosed by eight dragon pillars, with a flying dragon embedded in the ceiling. In Taoism the octagon symbolizes creation and the celestial regions. An octagonal table supports a huge

CAO DAI GREAT TEMPLE

THE DIVINE EYE

INNER

OCTAGONAL BASE WITH 12 STEPS

MAIN ALTAR

YELLOW CURTAIN

SANCTUARY

RED CURTAIN

PEDIMENT FEATURING DIVINE AGENTS,
HANGING IN FRONT OF BLUE CURTAIN

CHAIRS FOR POPE AND
SIX CARDINALS

OPEN LATTICE-WORK WINDOWS WITH
LOTUS-ENCLOSED EYE DESIGN

MEN'S PULPIT

WOMEN'S PULPIT

DOORS

WOODEN DOORS

DRAGON-COILED COLUMNS

STATUE OF HO PHAP

MURAL OF GUIDING SPIRITS
IN CAO DAISM

DRUM TOWER

WOMEN'S ENTRANCE

MEN'S ENTRANCE

ORCHESTRA (UPSTAIRS)
AND VIEWING AREA

© AVALON TRAVEL PUBLISHING, INC.

globe, on which is painted the all-seeing all-knowing Divine Eye, symbol of Cao Dai or the Supreme Spirit. Only high priests are allowed to approach the octagonal table during the emotionally moving service. Offerings of fruit, flowers, incense, candles, tea, and wine are made to the Divine Eye.

The Compound

The Cao Dai Great Temple is set in a large compound of residences, administrative buildings, schools, and gardens. There are a few places where you can sit down for a quiet cup of tea. A short walk south of the main temple is the Temple of the Divine Mother, smaller in scale than the Cao Dai Great Temple. It is here that important figures are given last rites. Three kilometers south of the Cao Dai Great Temple is Long Hoa Market, with mostly food and poultry on sale and lively trading in progress.

Conduct

Scanty attire upsets the Cao Daists. Cover your arms and legs—perhaps bring some loose pants

THE STRANGE SECT OF CAO DAI

What do Winston Churchill, Joan of Arc, Jesus Christ, Confucius, Moses, St. John the Baptist, Charlie Chaplin, and Louis Pasteur have in common? They are all Divine Agents, adopted as patron saints by the Cao Dai sect. This faith is a synthesis of Buddhist, Confucian, Taoist, and Christian beliefs, with a dash of Islam thrown in. Cao Daism copies its organization from the Roman Catholic Church, with cardinals, bishops, archbishops, and a pope, though there is no pope at present.

The sect was founded in the 1920s by Ngo Van Chieu, a civil servant blessed with a series of visions, including several of the Divine Eye. The messenger in the visions was Ly Tai Pe, a literary figure from the Tang dynasty, who maintained that previous revelations of the Supreme Spirit—Confucianism, Buddhism, Christianity—took place at a time when people had little contact with each other because of deficient means of transportation. As a representative of the Supreme Spirit, Ly Tai Pe announced the time had come to reorganize the world's disparate religious elements and form the Universal Religion of the Age of Improved Transport, thus achieving a harmonious whole. The Supreme Spirit was henceforth to be known as Cao Dai, symbolized by a giant eyeball.

In the 1930s and 1940s the Cao Dai sect gained a steady following, and the Great Temple—the equivalent of the Vatican—was constructed at Tay Ninh. The Cao Daists were estimated to number 1.5 million, and they fielded a private army of 20,000 tolerated by the French because the sect was anti-Vietminh. In 1943 the Cao Dai's pope, Ngo Van Chieu, died and was succeeded by Pham Cong Tac, who suffered under the French and was deported to the Comoros Islands. In 1946 he returned. In 1950 writer Norman Lewis visited Tay Ninh and glimpsed Pope Pham Cong Tac, an encounter described in his book *A Dragon Apparent*:

His Holiness, Pope Pham-Cong-Tac, whose name means "the Sun shining from the South," awaited us, beneath the golden parasol, attired in his uniform of Grand-Marshal of the Celestial Empire. He was carrying his Marshal's baton, at the sight of which, according to Cao-Daist literature, all evil spirits flee in terror.

Physically, the Pope looked hardly able to support the weight of his dignity. He was a tiny, insignificant figure of a man, with an air of irremediable melancholy. His presence was, in any case, overshadowed by the startling architectural details of the cathedral, for the design of which he himself had been responsible.

The last Cao Dai pope, Pham Cong Tac suffered again under the Diem regime and was forced to flee to Cambodia. Because the Cao Dai Army was incorporated into the South Vietnamese Army, and because the Cao Daists refused to support the Vietcong, the sect was disbanded after the 1975 takeover by the north. All Cao Dai lands were confiscated and the sect's leadership broken up. In 1985, however, many of the temples were returned to the Cao Daists. The sect today has several million followers in Vietnam and is particularly strong in the Mekong Delta region, where smaller temples are modeled after the Cao Dai Great Temple. There are an estimated 1,000 Cao Dai temples throughout southern Vietnam.

Although it first appears a weird religion, Cao Daism follows the same basic precepts as other religions, with common goals of peace, justice, and harmony. Among its key practices are ancestor-worship, spirit contact through séances and mediums, and vegetarianism; Cao Daists believe in a cycle of reincarnation similar to that found in Buddhism. Like other religions in Vietnam, Cao Daism is restricted in its practices by a watchful government.

and a jacket to slip on before going into the temple. Remove shoes and hats before entering; men enter to the right, women to the left. You may walk around the temple before the service—women are supposed to walk clockwise around the temple, men counterclockwise. During the service you're restricted to the back top gallery, near the orchestra. Photography from this point is permitted—the popping of flashbulbs seems an accepted part of the ceremony and doesn't faze anyone.

Getting There

The Cao Dai Great Temple lies 100 kilometers from Saigon, four kilometers east of Tay Ninh at the village of Long Hoa. Services are held daily at 0600, 1200, 1800, and midnight, and last about 45 minutes. The best plan is to arrive 30 minutes before the noon service so you can tour the entire temple and take in the service as well. Most tours permit only about an hour at the temple. If you wish to stay longer, take one tour in, stay overnight in Tay Ninh (you can reach the temple from Tay Ninh by moto), and hop back on the tour bus the following day. For full control of your itinerary, hire a car from Saigon for about $40 a day, which works out to $10 each for four passengers.

Southeast of Saigon

VUNG TAU

Vung Tau is an old port town 115 kilometers southeast of Saigon, developed under the French as a seaside resort called Cap Saint Jacques. It served as a rest center for French officers and later for Australian and American troops on R&R during the Vietnam War. Next came the Russians—they're still here, drilling for gas and oil at rigs 60 kilometers off the coast. The Russians have lots of company these days; BP, BHP, Petrofina, Total, and the Japan-Vietnam Petrol Association (JVPC) are also exploring these waters.

Apart from oil, gas, and fishing, the main industry in Vung Tau appears to be prostitution. There are large numbers of bamboo brothel shacks around, mainly catering to groups of men from Taiwan, Hong Kong, and China, who tour the minibrothels chaperoned by a state tour guide in the air-conditioned comfort of a government-owned bus. Then the town is plastered with AIDS-awareness posters.

Vung Tau is a town of about 100,000. The population swells in July and August when Vietnamese vacationers arrive in droves. The commercial end of Vung Tau is at Front Beach, or Bai Truoc, where you'll find banks, businesses, high-end hotels, nightlife, and shopping. Foreign oil workers and businessmen base themselves here; tour groups lodge here because of better hotels. There's a weird energy when the oil workers mix with the karaoke crowd.

Beaches

Front Beach is a joke—thin, short, crowded, hemmed in at the north end by an embankment and at the south by fishing boats and freighters. A few kilometers south of Front Beach is a rocky cove with a few umbrellas sticking out of it—this "beach" is called Bai Dua. There are several hotels and guesthouses in the area, and good cafés. Around the corner, near the Jesus statue, is a tiny, rocky, sandy beach called Bai Tam—there are umbrellas here, but no cafés. About three kilometers north of Front Beach is Bai Dau, a paltry strip of sand; some budget accommodations are out here.

The best place for swimming is Back Beach, or Bai Sau, with a six-kilometer stretch of sand; the beach offers budget- and moderate-priced hotels and run-down cafés and is a magnet for backpackers and budget travelers. The French called the place Plage Au Vents—it can get extremely windy, causing a bad riptide.

Right up the northern end of Back Beach is a place called Paradise Beach, which has been signed over to a Taiwan developer who is busy promoting Taiwan group-tour antics, such as every watersport known to Asia.

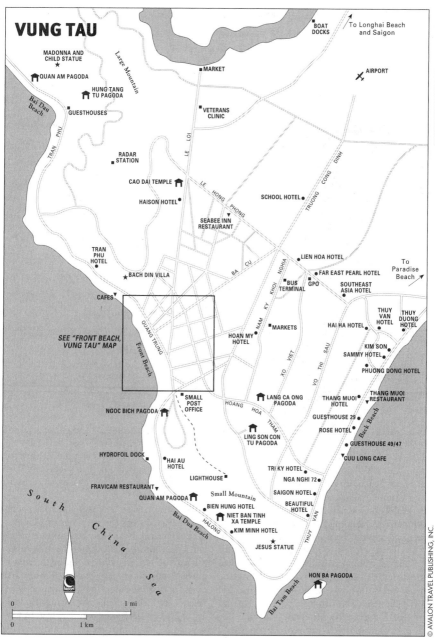

VUNG TAU

MADONNA AND CHILD STATUE ★

QUAN AM PAGODA

HUNG TANG TU PAGODA

GUESTHOUSES

Large Mountain

TRAN PHU

Bai Dau Beach

RADAR STATION

CAO DAI TEMPLE

HAISON HOTEL

LE LOI

LE HONG PHONG

VETERANS CLINIC

MARKET

BOAT DOCKS

To Longhai Beach and Saigon

AIRPORT

SCHOOL HOTEL

TRUONG CONG DINH

TRAN PHU HOTEL

BACH DIN VILLA ★

CAFES

SEE "FRONT BEACH, VUNG TAU" MAP

Front Beach

QUANG TRUNG

BA CU

NAM KY KHOI NGHIA

SEABEE INN RESTAURANT

LIEN HOA HOTEL

FAR EAST PEARL HOTEL

BUS TERMINAL

GPO

SOUTHEAST ASIA HOTEL

HOAN MY HOTEL

MARKETS

HAI HA HOTEL

THUY VAN HOTEL

THUY DUONG HOTEL

KIM SON HOTEL

SAMMY HOTEL

PHUONG DONG HOTEL

XO VIET

VO THI SAU

To Paradise Beach →

NGOC BICH PAGODA

SMALL POST OFFICE

HOANG HOA THAM

LANG CA ONG PAGODA

LING SON CON TU PAGODA

THANG MUOI HOTEL

THANG MUOI RESTAURANT

GUESTHOUSE 29

ROSE HOTEL

Back Beach

GUESTHOUSE 49/47

CUU LONG CAFE

HYDROFOIL DOCK

HAI AU HOTEL

LIGHTHOUSE

FRAVICAM RESTAURANT

QUAN AM PAGODA

Small Mountain

BIEN HUNG HOTEL

NIET BAN TINH XA TEMPLE

KIM MINH HOTEL

TRI KY HOTEL

NGA NGHI 72

SAIGON HOTEL

BEAUTIFUL HOTEL

THUY VAN

JESUS STATUE ★

Bai Dua Beach

HALONG

South China Sea

HON BA PAGODA

Bai Tan Beach

0   1 mi

0   1 km

© AVALON TRAVEL PUBLISHING, INC.

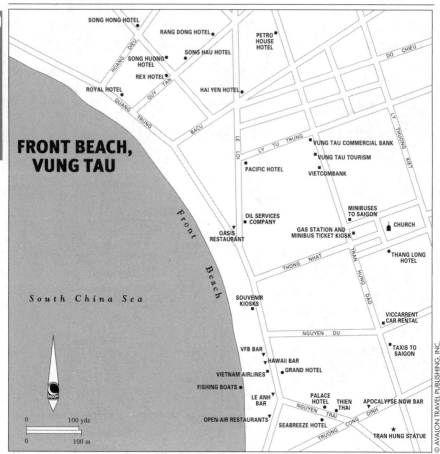

FRONT BEACH, VUNG TAU

South China Sea

Front Beach

SONG HONG HOTEL
RANG DONG HOTEL
PETRO HOUSE HOTEL
SONG HAU HOTEL
SONG HUONG HOTEL
REX HOTEL
HAI YEN HOTEL
ROYAL HOTEL
DO CHIEU
HOANG DIEU
QUY TAN
QUANG TRUNG
BACU
LE LOI
LY TU TRUNG
LY THUONG KIET
VUNG TAU COMMERCIAL BANK
VUNG TAU TOURISM
PACIFIC HOTEL
VIETCOMBANK
MINIBUSES TO SAIGON
CHURCH
OIL SERVICES COMPANY
OASIS RESTAURANT
GAS STATION AND MINIBUS TICKET KIOSK
THANG LONG HOTEL
THONG NHAT
TRAN HUNG DAO
SOUVENIR KIOSKS
VICCARRENT CAR RENTAL
NGUYEN DU
VFB BAR
TAXIS TO SAIGON
HAWAII BAR
GRAND HOTEL
VIETNAM AIRLINES
FISHING BOATS
LE ANH BAR
PALACE HOTEL
THIEN THAI
APOCALYPSE NOW BAR
NGUYEN TRAI
CONG DINH
OPEN-AIR RESTAURANTS
SEABREEZE HOTEL
TRUONG
TRAN HUNG STATUE

0   100 yds
0   100 m

MOON

© AVALON TRAVEL PUBLISHING, INC.

The White Villa

The White Villa, or Bach Dinh, to the north of Front Beach, was built in the 19th century as a summer palace for Indochina Governor-general Paul Doumer. It was later used by other luminaries, including South Vietnamese presidents Ngo Dinh Diem and Nguyen Van Thieu. The villa is perched on a hillside amid tranquil grounds of frangipani and bougainvillea; there are a slew of cafés at the base and along the coast here: Café Eva, Café Bach Dinh, Café Villa Blanche. You can hike past the villa up to a peak overlooking the bay. The villa features elegant stairwells and wood fittings, and art nouveau touches outside up near the roof. Upstairs is a small room of artifacts from Baria and another room full of moth-eaten furniture from France.

Downstairs is an engrossing museum of objects salvaged from the wreckage of a Chinese junk that sank near Con Dau Islands in the late 17th century. Relics from the junk form a microcosm of Qing dynasty life at the time—pottery, porcelain, earthenware, bronze artifacts, and stoneware. The bronze section is fascinating, with small bronze cannons, locks and keys, kettles, nails, sundial watch, Chinese coins, small mirrors, and beard tweezers.

TOURING VUNG TAU

Vung Tau has a motley bunch of sights—you might as well get a moto, rented motorcycle, or bicycle and polish the lot off in one long loop around the headland. You can start anywhere on the circuit described—the Vung Tau Grand Prix. Some sections along the coast are paved with four lanes—a favorite for local motorcycle racers bent on shortening their lifespans.

From Back Beach, head south round the headland, past the island pagoda of Hon Ba, which is accessible at low tide. Coming round the headland, you'll see a Rio-style giant Jesus with arms outstretched; there's a trail leading to the statue from Back Beach. This incongruous 30-meter statue was erected by the Americans in 1971 and is complemented by a smaller Mary statue.

On a hill to the west side of the headland is Niet Ban Tinh Xa, a large temple built in 1971. Niet Ban is Vietnamese for Nirvana, a concept embodied in a 12-meter-long reclining Buddha statue; the temple also features a massive bronze bell. Farther around the headland is a trail leading up to a French lighthouse, dating from 1910, which affords a panorama of the entire peninsula. There's a military base up this way, so photography is touchy. Head north to the White Villa, and perhaps take a trip north to Bai Dau to see the giant Madonna and Child statue. On the way back, you can cut across to the Cao Dai Temple, and then take Le Hong Phong Street to Back Beach.

There are also large pottery storage jars, stone seals, pieces of sail cord—even charred pieces of dried fruit. Entry to the museum is $1; open 0700–1130 and 1330–1700.

Bai Dau Shrines

Bai Dau, the beach to the far north, now boasts a giant Madonna and Child statue, erected in the mid-1990s, providing competition for the giant Jesus statue. The statue is visible from a long distance. It's set back from the beach; there's a winding walkway area with manicured gardens and bougainvillea trees, punctuated by garish Catholic statuary depicting crucifixion scenes. There's a small church here. Also in the vicinity is a Quan Am Pagoda with a giant statue of Quan Am—the bodhisattva of compassion, a kind of Buddhist version of the Madonna.

Cao Dai Temple

There are lots of Cao Dai temples around Saigon and the Mekong Delta and as far north as Danang, but the Vung Tau Temple stands out for its architecture. It has an imposing location at the head of a huge flight of stairs at the north end of Le Loi Boulevard. At the front door are two guardian statues and two dragon-coiled columns; over the door is a painting of a hand with the scales of justice held over a globe of the world, while above floats the eye of Cao Dai.

The temple interior matches that of the Cao Dai Great Temple at Tay Ninh in detail, though not in size. There are several rows of dragon-coiled columns, and flying dragons are embedded in the ceiling. Up front is a beautiful altar with the eye of Cao Dai mounted on a board. If you can find someone with a key, you may be allowed to view the interior—try the residence at the back. There is a small turnout for services at 0600, 1200, 1800, and midnight.

Whale Pagoda

Closer to Back Beach is Lang Ca Ong Pagoda (Dinh Than Thang-Tam), a small temple built in 1911 with a maritime theme—pictures of boats and a couple of real wooden longboats. The main altar is enclosed by six dragon columns, the two up front topped by a phoenix with popping lights for eyeballs. Behind the altar is a glass case with whale vertebrae and bones. This temple is dedicated to the whale, a deity of Vung Tau fisherfolk. Whale worship derives from ancient Cham customs, in which the whale is considered a friend and benefactor.

Con Dao Islands

About 180 kilometers off the coast of Vung Tau is the Con Dao archipelago, a group of 14 islets with unspoiled beaches, coconut groves, coral, and crystal-clear water. The largest island, at about 20 square kilometers, is Con Son, which is partially forested with teak and pine trees. There is one dive operator on Con Son, called Rainbow Divers, www.divevietnam.com. And there is a lot more under the water here than at Nha Trang: The coral reefs off Con Dao are the finest found in Vietnamese waters. Possible sightings include sharks, rays, turtles, and that fabulous creature, the dugong. Families of dugongs (also known as the "sea-cow," and the Siren of Greek mythology) have been sighted in April and May, drawn to the area to feed on seagrass. Sea turtles lumber ashore to lay eggs February–July.

Under the French, Con Son was a top security prison known as Poulo Condore, where opponents of French colonialism were held in appalling conditions. Part of the prison system has been turned into a museum. Though few travelers make it this far, there are accommodations on Con Son. Local authorities want to turn the island into a resort spot with the development of a national park, marine reserve, bird sanctuary, and beaches. The fastest way to get to the islands is by light aircraft operated by Vietnam Air Service Company (VASCO), with connections from Saigon to Con Dao. The island is also served by intermittent boat service (about 13 hours from Vung Tau).

Front Beach Practicalities

A lot of the hotels at Front Beach are run by the National Oil Services Company of Vietnam (OSC), with offices at 2 Le Loi, tel. 64/859863, fax 64/852834. In addition, OSC maintains a dozen expensive villas for rent or lease in the Front Beach area; some are used by foreign businesses. The OSC issues its own map of Vung Tau and area, but it's hard to find.

Under $20: The north end of Front Beach has some rooms in the $10–20 range, formerly favored by visiting Russians. Don't expect wonders in the plumbing department. In this category are **Rang Dong Hotel,** at 5 Duy Tan, tel. 64/852133; next door is **Song Hau Hotel,** tel. 64/852601; along Truong Vinh Ky Street are **Song Hong Hotel,** tel. 64/852137; and **Song Huong Hotel,** tel. 64/852491. **Thang Long Hotel,** at 45 Thong Nhat St.,

tel. 64/852175, near the church, has lower-priced accommodations.

$20–50: Pacific Hotel, 4 Le Loi, tel. 64/852391, fax 64/852239, has 32 rooms. **Grand Hotel,** 26 Quang Trung St., tel. 64/852469, fax 64/852088, has 70 rooms, tennis courts, fitness center, and several restaurants; cheaper rooms are available. **Hai Yen Hotel,** 8 Le Loi, tel. 64/52571, has 24 doubles. **Rex Hotel,** 1 Duy Tan St., tel./fax 64/859862, features 84 rooms, several restaurants and bars, tennis courts, and business facilities. **Diamond Hotel,** 8 Tran Nguyen Han, tel. 64/859236, fax 64/859237, has about 50 rooms for $40 apiece, as well as a disco-karaoke setup. **Palace Hotel,** tel. 64/852265, fax 64/859878, is owned by OSC; it has 105 a/c rooms, including eight suites and three apartments, and conference halls. A notch up, in the $35–60 price range, is the **Seabreeze Hotel,** across from the Palace Hotel, 11 Nguyen Trai St., tel. 64/852392, fax 64/859856, an Australian joint-venture hotel with a pool and full facilities.

$50–100: Royal Hotel, 48 Quang Trung St., tel. 64/859852, fax 64/859851, has 52 rooms. Single prices are standard $46, deluxe $65–75, suite $95, sea-view suite $120; for doubles add $10. The hotel features in-house video, restaurants, and a business center—popular with foreign businesspeople. **Petro House Hotel,** 89 Tran Hung Dao, tel. 64/852014, fax 64/852015, is the classiest place in Vung Tau, a beautifully renovated older building, furnished in colonial style. The 75 rooms go for $50–60 standard, $80–185 suite; swimming pool, fitness center, French restaurant, and comprehensive range of business services.

South of Front Beach: Near the hydrofoil dock is **Hai Au Hotel,** 100 Halong St., tel. 64/852178, fax 64/859868, a six-story waterfront hotel with full facilities. It has 52 rooms, ranging $25–35 for standard rooms; 10 deluxe rooms $40 each; eight suites $55–100. The hotel features a business center and disco. It's jointly run by the OSC and Vietcombank, so currency exchange isn't a problem. About a kilometer south of Hai Au Hotel is a strip of guesthouses at Bai Tam Huong Phung. Down this way is the larger **Kim Minh Hotel,** at 60 Halong St., tel. 64/856192, fax 64/856439, with 42 rooms for $35–65 each.

North of Front Beach: Near Bach Dinh Villa is **Tran Phu Hotel,** at 42 Tran Phu, tel. 64/852489, with 15 large, pleasant rooms for $12–22.

Restaurants and Bars: There are half a dozen seafront seafood places opposite the Grand Hotel featuring alfresco dining—a magnet for Front Beach diners. For breakfast, try the upstairs section of **L.A. Café.** The **Oasis Restaurant,** at 1 Le Loi, has sharp decor and serves Western food at reasonable prices, including seafood, pizza, Italian food, steak sandwiches, and Western breakfast. For high-class dining there's a French restaurant, **Ma Maison,** at Petro House Hotel, 89 Tran Hung Dao, tel. 64/852248. Nearby is a good Vietnamese restaurant, **Sao Mai.** In a building jutting into the South China Sea south of Hai Au Hotel is another classy place—**Fravicam Restaurant,** tel. 64/856320, specializing in seafood with Chinese and Vietnamese–style cuisine.

There is a small strip of rowdy bars along the Front Beach waterfront. These include **Le Anh Bar, VFB Bar,** and **Hawaii Bar**—patrons here are besieged by beggars and bar girls. Hotels such as the **Rex** and the **Hai Au** have their own discos, and karaoke cafés proliferate in the area. Expatriates and oil workers frequent the **Apocalypse Now Bar,** at 438 Truong Cong Dinh, east of the Seabreeze Hotel. There's a bar with pool tables and a bulletin board for Hash House Harriers. The bar features an upside-down helicopter painted on the ceiling, with the swishing ceiling fan serving as the chopper's blades.

Bai Dau Beach Practicalities

Bai Dau Beach, to the north of Front Beach, is a bit remote, but a paved road leading in this direction is making it more accessible. The beach is not recommended—small and thin, with a few run-down pagodas and a motley bunch of eateries. There are plenty of accommodations in guesthouses occupying former villas—a dozen are strung along Tran Phu Street, catering mainly

to Vietnamese. Some are basic, with shared bath costing $4–8; others have private baths and even air-conditioning, for up to $15. The places are so low-key they often have no name. They just use the street number, so you'll see Nha Nghi 19, Nha Nghi 78, and Nha Nghi 66. Some villas, such as **Nha Nghi Mytho** at 47 Tran Phu, offer ocean views. At 65 Tran Phu is a guesthouse charging $10–12 for a room with a view. Fronting the main beach are several larger concrete structures. These include **Thuy Tien Hotel,** 96 Tran Phu, tel. 64/832625; **Savimex,** at 180 Tran Phu, tel. 64/858553; and **Khach San Haideng,** at 194 Tran Phu, tel. 64/858536, near the giant Quan Am statue. Rooms here go for $16–25.

Food: Try **69 Cay Bang,** a seafood restaurant on the waterfront at 69 Tran Phu St.—the setting and the food are excellent.

Le Hong Phong Practicalities

Without a beach in sight is Le Hong Phong Street, which stretches across the north end of Vung Tau. Hotels here range from budget- to moderately priced and cater more to the Asian karaoke visitor. **Haison Hotel,** 27 Le Loi, tel. 64/852955, contains 30 rooms going for $8–10–15 in a white concrete building with zero character. **School Hotel** (Khach San Truong), at 156 Truong Cong Dinh, tel. 64/859964, has 15 rooms for $8–25. **Lien Hoa Hotel,** 50 Le Hong Phong St., tel. 64/859604, fax 64/852225, has 21 rooms for $25–30–35 d a/c. **Far East Pearl Hotel,** at 28 Le Hong Phong, tel. 64/858871, fax 64/859838, offers 30 rooms in the $30–35 range, as well as a fancy restaurant. **Hoan My Hotel,** at 30A Nam Ky Khoi Nghia, tel. 64/858118, is a karaoke dive with 16 rooms in the $15–22 range. **Hai Ha Hotel,** at 1 Le Hong Phong, tel. 64/859793, fax 64/859792, has 45 rooms for $20–30 d with a/c. **South East Asia Hotel,** at 8 Le Hong Phong, tel. 64/859412, is a Chinese-run place with 45 a/c rooms for $25–42. It exudes a strange atmosphere.

Food: The western end of Le Hong Phong features cafés with signs in Cyrillic script catering to Russians who live in concrete high-rises in the area. For a restaurant, try **Seabee Inn**

The South

(Ong Bien Quan), at 283 Le Hong Phong, with French, Chinese, and Vietnamese food, and a small garden out back.

Paradise Beach Area

At the northern tip of Back Beach is an area known as Paradise Beach, which is a resort created primarily for Taiwanese visitors, who indulge in parasailing, sailboarding, and other marine sports. At night, it's karaoke-ville, with popping lights and nightclubs. Paradise Beach seems to be owned by the management of the resort—it's a private piece of sand. At the northern tip of Back Beach are some larger hotels that are big on karaoke and massage and cater more to Asian visitors. These include **Thuy Duong Hotel,** at 4 Thuy Van St., tel. 64/852635, fax 64/852807, with standard rooms for $30–35 and suites for $40–50; and **Sammy Hotel,** at 18 Thuy Van St., tel. 64/854755, fax 64/854762, with 120 rooms in the $50–70 range and suites for $80–100.

Back Beach Practicalities

Back Beach features budget- and moderately priced hotels and is a growth area, with new hotels going up.

Under $20: There are a few family-run guesthouses in the midsection of Back Beach. **Guesthouse 29,** at 29 Thuy Van, is a café-restaurant-motel right on the beach with nine rooms at $5–8–10. **Guesthouse 47** has about half-a-dozen rooms each for $5–6. **Rose Hotel** (Khach San Mini Rose), at 39 Thuy Van, rents 14 rooms for $10–12 each. **Dang Gia Trang Hotel,** at 38/22 Thuy Van St., tel. 64/859249, offers 16 rooms for $10–15–25; it is managed by Phung, who is helpful with touring information. **Thang Muoi Hotel,** 6 Thuy Van St., tel. 64/852665, features roomy doubles and triples for $10, billiard tables, small pool, and a Thai massage parlor.

$20–50: Saigon Hotel, at 72 Thuy Van St., tel. 64/852317, fax 64/859472, is a secure, comfortable place—120 rooms with a tariff of $15–25–40. Gardens and bicycle rental. **Thuy Van Hotel,** tel. 64/859518, fax 64/859519, has 100 rooms going for $20 s and $30 d, plus 10

bungalows at $5 each. **Phuong Dong Hotel,** 2 Thuy Van, tel. 64/852158, includes 54 rooms in the main building, three villas, and 10 beach bungalows. Rooms are mostly $30, with four rooms priced at $45. There are four rooms in each of the villas, with a tariff of $30 per room; negotiable monthly rate for an entire villa. Tennis courts, small pool (why do they always look so big in brochures?), and karaoke lounge. Caters mainly to Asian visitors. **Beautiful Hotel** (Khach San My Le), at 100 Thuy Van St., tel. 64/852177, fax 64/853175, has 90 rooms going for $35 standard, $50–75 deluxe and $85 for a sea-view suite. The hotel is set up for business guests, with conference facilities.

Food: Apart from hotel bars, there is a string of small cafés along the middle of the beachfront. The tiny **Cuu Long Café,** at 57 Thuy Van, serves simple fare, seafood, and drinks, and functions as a kind of traveler café. It rents bicycles for $1 a day; will also arrange motorbikes and guides. The largest venue along Back Beach is **Thang Muoi Restaurant,** opposite the hotel of the same name.

Services

The general **post office,** on the corner of Le Hong Phong and Xo Viet Nghe Tinh, has fax and EMS service counters. Vietnam country code is 84; the Vung Tau area code is 64. **Vietcombank** at 27 Tran Hung Dao, in Front Beach, is open 0700–1130 and 1330–1700; closed Thursday afternoon and Sunday; traveler's checks accepted. **Vung Tau Commercial Bank** (Ngan Hang Thuong Mai), at 59 Tran Hung Dao, has similar hours but only accepts cash. **International SOS** (also known as OSCAT/AEA) has a clinic for foreigners with a resident Western doctor at 1 Le Ngoc Han, Vung Tau, tel. 64/858776, fax 64/858779. This facility has been set up to work with oil companies: Patients can be helicoptered out to Saigon if need be.

Getting There and Away

Vietnam Airlines maintains a booking office at 27 Quang Trung, Front Beach, tel. 64/859099.

VETERANS CLINIC

Completed in 1989, the Veterans Clinic on Le Loi Boulevard was the first building constructed by Americans in Vietnam since the end of the war in 1975. Although the clinic is dedicated to general medicine and obstetrics, sick travelers are welcome here, providing they have hard currency.

The 14-room primary health care facility, known as the Friendship Clinic, was the first project of the Veterans Vietnam Restoration Project (VVRP). The VVRP sends over teams of American vets on humanitarian aid projects. Veterans have helped thousands of Vietnamese and in the process have themselves experienced significant healing.

Since the Vung Tau project, VVRP has completed six additional projects in Vietnam, building medical clinics, adding wings to hospitals, supplying medical and alternative energy technology, and delivering much-needed medical equipment and supplies. In 1994 VVRP helped set up a facility near Saigon to house Vietnamese amputees being fitted for artificial limbs. The limbs are provided free by another American NGO, Vietnam Assistance for the Handicapped.

By far the most pleasant way to get to Vung Tau—though by no means the cheapest—is to take a hovercraft, departing Saigon in the morning or the afternoon. The modern 120-seat vessel leaves from a dock at the foot of Nguyen Hue Boulevard. The trip takes a little more than an hour and costs $10 one-way. There's a return trip every afternoon, so you can make a round-trip from Saigon in the same day. Or you can stay overnight in Vung Tau and return the following afternoon. You can usually just roll up at the docks (at either end) and buy a ticket 30 minutes before departure. Next-day and advance ticket purchase is possible. For bookings, contact Vina Express at the ticketing booth opposite Customs House in Saigon, tel. 8/8297892 or 8/8224621; in Vung Tau, contact the jetty in front of Hai Au Hotel, tel. 64/856530, or book through Petro House, tel. 64/852014.

By road, Saigon to Vung Tau is 115 kilometers. Taxis and minibuses take less than two hours, whereas buses can take three or more hours. The bus terminal in Vung Tau is at 52 Nam Ky Khoi Nghia Street. Other transport leaves from the church area on Tran Hung Dao Street in Front Beach. A kiosk in a gas station near the church handles minibus tickets to Saigon, with departures every half hour. Taxis leave one block south, closer to the Tran Hung Dao statue. From Saigon you can catch a bus to Vung Tau from Van Thanh or Mien Dong bus terminals, or hook up with a traveler minibus.

Getting Around

There are plenty of cyclos around, useful for shorter trips. There are also some motos. Many find a rented bicycle or motorcycle preferable for getting around. You can rent a bicycle at Back Beach through some hotels, such as Nha Nghi 72; for motorcycle rentals try Thang Muoi Hotel or Cuu Long Café. For shuttling between Front Beach and Back Beach, take Hoang Hoa Tham Street—it's only a few kilometers.

Vungtau Taxi Company, Viccarrent, and other operators run fleets of taxis in Vung Tau—common enough around Front Beach. You can rent cars through major hotels or through a touring company such as Viccarrent at Front Beach. The Baria-Vung Tau Tourist Corporation, at 33 Tran Hung Dao, tel. 64/856445, fax 64/856444, arranges minibuses and transport, mostly for group tours.

LONGHAI BEACH AND VICINITY

Superior to the beaches at Vung Tau are those at Longhai, about 40 kilometers east or an hour by moto. The road out of Vung Tau is the same as the Saigon route—about 20 kilometers out, you veer off on a right fork leading to Longhai Beach. There is no direct bus from Vung Tau to Longhai, but there is a Saigon-Longhai direct connection. You can easily reach the beach from Vung Tau as a day trip, or spend a few days in the area. Longhai echoes the shape of Vung Tau, sited at the tip of a peninsula. The

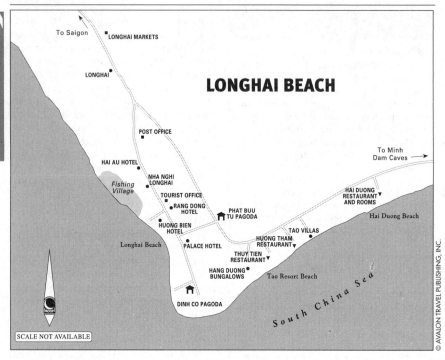

To Saigon
LONGHAI MARKETS

LONGHAI

LONGHAI BEACH

POST OFFICE

To Minh
Dam Caves

HAI AU HOTEL

NHA NGHI
LONGHAI

Fishing
Village

TOURIST OFFICE

RANG DONG
HOTEL

HAI DUONG
RESTAURANT
AND ROOMS

PHAT BUU
TU PAGODA

Hai Duong Beach

HUONG BIEN
HOTEL

TAO VILLAS

Longhai Beach

PALACE HOTEL

HUONG THAM
RESTAURANT

THUY TIEN
RESTAURANT

HANG DUONG
BUNGALOWS

Tao Resort Beach

South China Sea

DINH CO PAGODA

SCALE NOT AVAILABLE

© AVALON TRAVEL PUBLISHING, INC.

main activity in Longhai is fishing; there are also salt pans in the area.

Longhai Beach

Longhai town is strung along Longhai Beach (Huong Bien) to the west. Here are cafés, juice bars, and the offices of Longhai Tourist Corporation, which runs several of the hotels in town. Longhai Tourism (tel. 64/868401) deals in guides, accommodations, transportation, and information. To the north end of Longhai Beach is a fishing village with shanty housing. The beach is poor because of scummy garbage and smelly fishing detritus. Fishermen here catch sea snakes, which sets you wondering. The south end of Longhai Beach is much cleaner, palm-fringed, and better suited to swimming.

Though Longhai Beach has half a dozen hotels, they can be crowded on weekends or holidays, especially around Tet. Several kilometers north of town near the central market is **Longhai Hotel,** with 18 rooms in the $15–

20 range and one a/c suite for $30. Closer in, **Hai Au Hotel** has a seedy and derelict air to it—massage and steam bath, 15 fan rooms for $8, and two rooms (no bath) for $6. **Nha Nghi Longhai,** tel. 64/868312, has 40 rooms, most of them $10 fan rooms, and 10 doubles at $15 each. **Rang Dong Hotel,** tel. 64/868356, has 20 rooms, $20–22 d and $25 t. **Huong Bien Hotel,** tel. 64/868430, rents 10 rooms and five bungalows for $15 d.

The **Palace Hotel,** tel. 64/868364, features terraced areas with gorgeous frangipani trees. On the top floor is a dome with a small dance floor; great views from the open rooftop. The hotel features vintage Chinese furniture and wall decorations of unicorn, dragon, and tortoise designs. There's a restaurant and across the street are tennis courts. A total of 18 rooms at $20–25 d a/c, with fridge, TV, and bath; some rooms have sea views.

Blowing away all the competition is **Anoasis Beach Resort,** tel. 64/868227, anoasisresort@hcm.vnn.vn, www.anoasisresort.com.vn. This resort is sited on a huge area of deserted coastline amid pine-studded hills. It boasts not only a private beach but a huge swimming pool and two tennis courts. The resort has 27 spacious luxury bungalows, and three oceanside villas with their own hot tubs. Depending on size, daily rates for bungalows range $120–180 in peak season, less on weekdays; villas run $255.

Other Beaches

Around the headland to the east, beaches become cleaner and more secluded. Close to town is a beach with a set of bungalows facing it— **Hang Duong Bungalows,** a large compound with its own restaurant and 20 wooden bungalows. The bungalows contain only a bed, but the price is right—$4 single, $5 with two beds.

There are two dozen kiosks on the way in, selling souvenirs and drinks; you can also rent deck chairs. Farther east, Tao Resort Beach has sand dunes and is rocky in parts. **Tao Villas**—two of them—have three rooms each for $20, no phone. Hai Duong Beach, about six kilometers from the Palace Hotel, includes a restaurant, a few thatched huts, and a few cheap rooms for rent. There was a hotel under construction. A few kilometers east are mountain caves once used by Vietcong Generals Minh and Dam. The caves are dull, but the mountain hike is good. Farther east, along a dirt road, are more beaches and fishing villages. Along this coastline, 55 kilometers from Longhai, is Ho Coc Beach, with several minibus tours coming in from Saigon to visit. The beach is remote; at present, amenities are scarce. There are a few guesthouses, and some hot springs not far away.

Mekong Delta

RIVER OF THE NINE DRAGONS

As the Mekong River enters Vietnam from Cambodia it splits into two channels, which the Vietnamese call the Tien Giang (Upper River), and Hau Giang (Lower River). The river continues to divide as it traverses the soggy delta, a fertile area of almost 50,000 square kilometers. By the time it empties into the South China Sea, it has seven branches, or mouths. Two others have silted up through the years, but because nine is an auspicious digit, the Vietnamese name for the river is still Cuu Long, or River of the Nine Dragons.

Streams and canals linked to the Nine Dragons are the main streets and irrigation canals of the delta. Rich silt deposited by the Mekong and its tributaries created the delta, an area that holds a fifth of Vietnam's population and supplies half its rice crop. Surplus rice from the south has traditionally supplied the rice-poor north or been shipped abroad. Other crops include coconuts, sugarcane, and fruit. Fishing is also a major industry. With a profusion of tropical fruit in the delta, there are bound to be some exotic varieties. A unique species of vegetation lining the delta's canals is the water coconut palm. The fruit of the palm *(dua nuoc)* hangs close to the ground and at first sight resembles a husky pinecone. Edible, transparent, fleshy pieces are embedded in the rough segments of the water coconut and are revealed only after the fruit is cracked open. Another variety found in the Ha Tien area is called *thot lot,* with blubbery, opaque pieces embedded in three sides of a small, purplish brown coconut. Instead of cutting this coconut in half for you to eat, the vendor slices off the sides. The coconut contains no milk; its flesh is served in a glass with ice and sugar.

With its extensive reed beds, lakes, and mangrove forests, the delta is home to many species of rare birds, among them kingfishers, red-headed cranes, and eastern saurus cranes.

The delta also seems to be a breeding ground for unusual religions. Besides an eclectic range of Buddhist temples, Catholic churches, and Islamic mosques, there are many Cao Dai temples in the delta. Hoa Hao Buddhism emerged in the delta area, with a large number of devotees around Chau Doc.

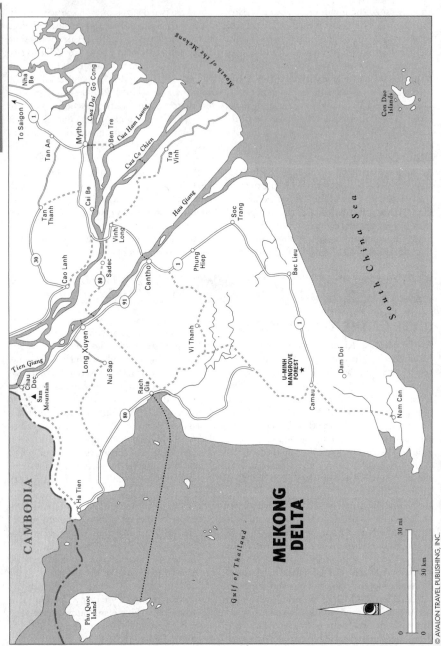

MEKONG DELTA

© AVALON TRAVEL PUBLISHING, INC.

TOURING THE DELTA

Because of the logistics involved with bus and minibus travel in the delta (waits at ferry crossings, long transfers from bus station to hotel), many opt to take the traveler café tours originating in Saigon. This solves the problem of bus station transfers, hiring boats and so on, but it does not leave you much flexibility to do your own thing. To give yourself that flexibility, you could also assemble your own group, custom-design an itinerary, and run the show yourself—with a car or minibus rental.

An innovative touring method in the delta would be to hire your own boat. However, it appears difficult and expensive to achieve this. Coming down to earth, a number of traveler cafés along Pham Ngu Lao in Saigon offer low-priced delta day trips as well as overnight and extended trips by car or minibus. You can add your name to sign-up lists in places such as Kim Café, Delta Tours, TM-Brothers, or Sinh Café. The quoted price includes transportation and guide, with prices depending on group size, route, and duration. Food, accommodations, and boat fees are usually extra.

A typical three-day delta tour may run like this. Day 1: Saigon to Caibe floating market, Vinh Long, Sadec, Long Xuyen, and Chau Doc. Stops en route might include a visit to a flower nursery in Sadec or a rice-noodle factory. Day 2: Visit floating houses and fish farms in Chau Doc, temples at Sam Mountain, visit stork garden, and drive to Cantho to sleep. Day 3: Cantho to Cai Rang floating market, cruise around Cantho, and then back to Saigon.

The Delta Experience

With the delta on Saigon's doorstep you would think the place would be overrun with tourists. Not so. This sprawling "rice bowl" is little traveled, yet it offers a wealth of sights and experiences for those who care to explore. If you make the effort you'll be amply rewarded. The delta is a region of extraordinary energy and market commerce, with burgeoning markets, floating markets, fruit orchards, and more coconuts than you'd want to contemplate. The delta is a relaxing place, with good food (seafood!), pleasant river trips, cheap boats, and friendly people.

You're never far from water in the delta, and boats in some districts are the main mode of transportation. Intriguing in the backwaters are the floating markets, which have disappeared in other parts of Asia.

Getting Around the Delta

By Bus: Mien Tay bus station, nine kilometers from Saigon center, runs buses to many delta destinations, including Vinh Long, Cantho, Tra Vinh, Long Xuyen, Chau Doc, and Rach Gia. Cholon bus station, five kilometers from Saigon center, runs buses to short-haul destinations such as Mytho, Caibe, and An Huu (close to My Thuan suspension bridge).

Few bridges span the silt-brown Mekong, so most traffic proceeds across the river by car-ferry. Bus travel in the delta can be slow because of ferry crossings. These crossings can be bottlenecks, with long lines of trucks and cars. You may wait several sailings before getting on; the crossing itself can take half an hour. So you lose about an hour to gain perhaps one kilometer. The opening of the My Thuan Bridge spanning the Mekong near Vinh Long has considerably reduced travel time to the delta. The 1,560-meter cabled-stayed bridge opened in May 2000: It is the first of its kind in Vietnam, and it was funded by the Australian government, which also backed the building of another bridge on a quite different part of the Mekong—the Friendship Bridge between Laos and Thailand.

By Boat: Boats are by far the best way to see the delta. If you assemble a small group you can charter a boat and cover quite a lot of ground. A larger boat for a whole day should cost less than $30, which, split between five passengers, is quite reasonable. You'll need to hire small

MEKONG DELTA ROUTE NOTES

It's easy to tour the delta by yourself, but because of the high cost of hiring boats for sidetrips, it is preferable to join a small group from Saigon.

Although you can do two- or three-day round-trips to the delta from Saigon, it's also possible to do a one-way trip, ending in Chau Doc, and then carrying on past a Mekong river border checkpoint all the way up to Phnom Penh. The river trip is a lot more interesting than the road trip from Saigon to Phnom Penh—and it's short. Chau Doc to Phnom Penh takes maybe six hours. For this exercise, you should have a Cambodian visa in advance (it is possible to be stamped in at the border). Book through Saigon Tourist in Saigon or Victoria Chau Doc hotel. Both run boats on the Chau Doc-to-Phnom Penh route. Saigon Tourist is the budget choice, but its boat goes only half the distance—the boat goes as far as Highway 1 in Cambodia, where you are tranferred to a minibus for the final stretch into Phnom Penh. Victoria Chau Doc's boat must be chartered and will cost around $250 for the whole boat (minimum four passengers). There are other boat tour operators in Chau Doc that make the full run to Phnom Penh. Check out www.transmekong.com.

Distances in the Mekong Delta look like this:

Saigon to Mytho, 70 kilometers; Mytho to Vinh Long, 70 kilometers; Vinh Long to Cantho, 32 kilometers; Cantho to Long Xuyen, 61 kilometers; and Long Xuyen to Chau Doc, 55 kilometers. Delving deeper into the delta might require 7–10 days. Not many venture to the further reaches of the delta, so expect to be treated like a Martian in places such as Ha Tien.

Some travelers make motorcycle tours of the delta. This doesn't mean you have to keep to roads; a boat captain won't bat an eyelid if you load a motorcyle onto the roof of a riverboat. A local did, however, bat an eyelid when an Australian couple moored alongside his sampan in kayaks. The couple flew the kayaks into Saigon and paddled along the Mekong for a few weeks. They packed the folding kayaks onto a local ferry for the run back to Saigon.

For some reason, travelers seem to give up on travel in the delta by themselves and opt for group tours in minibuses. That's fine, but what if you discover a really interesting place and you've got only two hours on your fixed-tour itinerary? If your time is limited, minibus tours are good—you can travel faster and get priority at ferry crossings. But if you're looking for interaction and want to mix with the locals, tackle it yourself.

vessels to explore around Cantho, Vinh Long, or Mytho. The Victoria Hotel group runs its own boats on the Cantho to Chau Doc route and the Chau Doc to Phnom Penh run. Minimum four passengers—and not cheap. Saigon Tourist runs a three-day package in the delta that gives an option of a trip part-way along the Mekong and minibus on to Phnom Penh.

Much cheaper are the regular passenger vessels that ply the delta. For these, departure information may be elusive—the authorities do not like foreigners traveling by public boat. A larger wooden boat, called a *dò,* can carry about 60 passengers and freight, with the emphasis on freight. Freight covers the floor and the top deck of the boat. Some loads look dangerous, as if this were Noah's Ark or the last boat out. There's very little

in the way of safety equipment—only a few life buoys are provided. More to the point might be fire-fighting equipment, since passengers sometimes cook onboard with charcoal braziers.

The *dò* is an enclosed boat with the captain up front, engine at the back, and passenger section in the middle. Wooden benches run the length of the boat on either side, and there are wooden slide-up window slots. There's a rudimentary cooking area and toilet near the engine. There may be a small upper deck, used for sleeping, on top at the back of the boat; overnight passengers sleep on mats on the floor in the main section of the boat, or string up hammocks. At night the captain uses searchlights to warn approaching vessels and lights a front shrine with incense and candles. Nice and cool out there at night.

Although goods—bananas, bicycles, dried coconut, live ducks, baskets—are scattered all over the roof of the boat, you're not supposed to sit up there. However, once the vessel leaves port and you're past police checkpoints you can ride on the roof—which is very pleasant, with panoramic views. Destination and intermediary points for the boat are painted on a chalkboard at the departure point. The approximate departure time may be posted, but usually the boat leaves when full.

Delta Hubs: A chalkboard at a delta boat terminal lists destinations and departure times. For these boats there appears to be no exact departure time or advance tickets—boats leave when full. The story changes from hour to hour, so keep asking, and asking, and asking about departures. Tickets are dirt-cheap—a day trip by boat is about $1, overnight $2. Cantho is a major boat junction because of its central location; other boat hubs are Ben Tre, Long Xuyen, Chau Doc, Rach Gia, and Tra Vinh. Journeys vary from a great five-hour trip through canals from Tra Vinh to Ben Tre to a full-day excursion from Ha Tien to Chau Doc. Trips run faster downstream.

MYTHO

Mytho, 70 kilometers southwest of Saigon, is a market town of about 100,000 on the banks of the Tien Giang, or lower Mekong. The town was under Khmer domination till the 17th century, when advancing Vietnamese forces took over. The French gained control of the area in 1862.

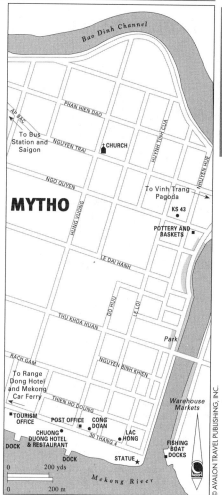

In Town
Both sides of Bao Dinh Canal are active market areas. On the east side, toward the Mekong, are fish markets and warehouses. The west side is a honeycomb of food vendors and food stalls, with a dizzying array of flowers and fruit. The outer sections toward the water sell mainly food, fish, and produce; farther inland are stalls selling hardware and household goods; at the north end is a section with ceramics and basketry.

Temple pickings are slim around Mytho—to the east is Vinh Trang Pagoda, with 30 monks and 20 nuns. Go across a bridge to the north; at the first fork across the bridge take the left and ask—the pagoda is about a kilometer from here. There's a small Cao Dai temple to the west of Mytho.

To the Islands
There are excursions from Mytho around the four small islands in the center of the

The South

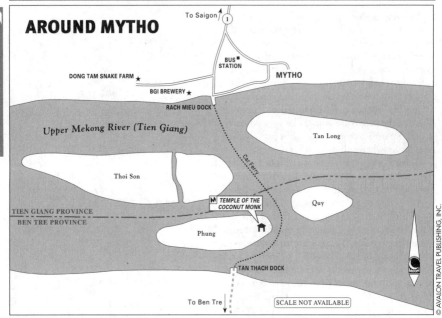

AROUND MYTHO

To Saigon

BUS STATION

MYTHO

DONG TAM SNAKE FARM

BGI BREWERY

RACH MIEU DOCK

Upper Mekong River (Tien Giang)

Tan Long

Thoi Son

TIEN GIANG PROVINCE
BEN TRE PROVINCE

TEMPLE OF THE COCONUT MONK

Quy

Phung

Car Ferry

TAN THACH DOCK

To Ben Tre

SCALE NOT AVAILABLE

© AVALON TRAVEL PUBLISHING, INC.

Mekong—Tan Long (Dragon), Phung (Phoenix), Quy (Tortoise), and Thoi Son (Unicorn). The islands are inhabited, with walkways and waterways between fruit orchards. Tan Long, known for its longan orchards, can easily be reached by a five-minute boat ride from the dock at the southern tip of Le Loi Boulevard in Mytho, near Cuu Long Restaurant.

It's a good idea to rent a boat for a longer period; smaller boats offer access to orchards via channels that crisscross the islands. Some of the tighter canals are lined with water coconut palms; kingfishers and other bird species live in the groves. A full day's excursion of 5–7 hours by boat is recommended, taking in fruit orchards and the Temple of the Coconut Monk.

A trip to three islands for five hours should cost around $20 for the boat, but the rental is made trickier by the fact that Tien Giang Tourism seems to have a monopoly on the trade. There's a police box down by the junction of the Tien Giang River and Bao Dinh Canal, where officials scan the water searching for local fishermen taking foreigners out

for a spin. You may have to smuggle yourself out; our crew took us north on foot, where we crossed a bridge to the east bank, walked another 10 minutes, transferred to a boat, and were then told to lie flat until we reached open water. The boatman dropped us on Tan Long Island and told us to follow the guide to the south side of the island where the boat would pick us up again—a strategy necessary because of a police box on the northeast side of the island. Other complications include crossing over to Ben Tre Province. Fishing boats will not go straight across to Phung Island to reach the Temple of the Coconut Monk; instead, they take the long way round down the coast and cut through a river on Thoi Son Island.

Dong Tam Snake Farm

Dong Tam Snake Farm is about 10 kilometers west of Mytho. You can bicycle there in an hour. Small boats can get within several kilometers of the farm; the boatman can drop you off and wait while you walk to the farm. Entry fee is $1. The place is no big deal as a sight, with concrete enclosures harboring various venomous snakes. Antivenin serum is made on the premises. There are also monkeys and other small animals that look suspiciously ready for illegal traffic. A shop on-site sells snake wine (snake pickled in rice wine), as well as other snake pills and potions—including bottles of Cobratonic "for insomnia, rheumatism and neurasthenia," and Cobratox, an ointment made from dried cobra-venom, menthol, and eucalyptus "for rheumatism, arthritis, myositis and neuralgia."

Temple of the Coconut Monk

The Mekong Delta is a breeding ground for unusual religions, among them Cao Daism and Hoa Hao Buddhism. Even more unusual is the congregation surrounding the coconut monk of Phung (Phoenix) Island. The cross-river ferry acting as a bridge over the Mekong near Mytho passes by the temple, but it's worth actually visiting the site for a closer look. Rent a boat in Mytho for the trip; if you go directly it takes about 30 minutes from Mytho, and if you skirt around other islands it can take 1.5 hours. You might also be able to arrange boat transportation from the Ben Tre province side.

The coconut cult was initiated by Nguyen Thanh Nam (1909–1990), who studied in France for seven years and then returned to Vietnam to marry. In 1945 he left his wife and daughter to lead the life of a monk, and is said to have meditated at Sam Mountain for a lengthy period. Thereafter he created the temple at Phung Island—between 1969 and 1975, worship was in full swing, with up to 3,000 devotees. Although the area around it saw fighting and bombing during the war, Phung Island was left alone—a sanctuary of sorts. One of the visitors, taking a break from covering the war, was celebrated photographer Tim Page, who took some of the only pictures that remain of the cult in action. Page and others would come down from Saigon for a weekend of meditation. The coconut monk was periodically imprisoned by the South Vietnamese and, after the 1975 takeover, by the communists. After 1975, the temple was

closed, and its followers dispersed. The coconut monk died in obscurity in Ben Tre province in 1990.

The front of the Phung Island temple is constructed in the shape of a grotto for meditation, with a throne for the coconut monk. Above is a tower with a metal map showing Hanoi and a small bridge linking it to Saigon—the monk advocated peaceful reunification of north and south, which did not go down too well with the South Vietnamese government at the time. Nearby is another tower, with an Apollo rocket that can be hoisted up and down. Facing the throne is a dais with nine dragon-coiled pillars raised over lily ponds. The dais is large enough to seat several thousand followers.

The coconut cult appears to have been a mix of Buddhism, Cao Daism, and Catholicism, with a healthy dose of coconuts. The role of the coconuts is not clear, but the monk is said to have lived on a diet of vegetables and coconuts during meditation. According to some sources, the monk at one point ate only coconuts—if you believe this, you must be, well, bananas. Certainly there is no shortage of coconuts in Ben Tre province, which grows more coconut palms than any other province in Vietnam. Since none of the pictures on display shows the coconut cult in action, you're left to wonder what kind of rituals took place here, pondering the connection between the throne, the followers, the coconuts, and the movable Apollo rocket.

Accommodations

Songtien Hotel, at 101 Trung Trac St., tel. 73/872009, run by Tien Giang Tourism, is a dowdy place, but there are not a lot of choices for Mytho. This seven-story hotel has 38 rooms in the $7–20 range; the high end includes a/c, hot water, and TV. Down by the Mekong is the most pleasant hotel option in town, the **Chuong Duong Hotel,** tel. 73/870875. Rooms go for $20–30 with river views. **Rang Dong Hotel,** at number 25, 30 Thang 4 St., tel. 73/874400, offers clean a/c rooms for $12, superior rooms for $18–24; some rooms have Mekong views.

Food

Chi Thanh Restaurant, 279 Tet Mau Than St., tel. 73/873756, is popular with Vietnamese—lots of locals eating here. **Ngoc Gia Trang,** 196 Ap Bac St., tel. 73/872742, is a nice garden restaurant with good set menu. On the south side of town are the more expensive **Cuu Long Restaurant** and **Chuong Duong Café.** At 60 Nam Ky Khoi Nghia is **Cay Me Restaurant** (close to Rang Dong Hotel), serving local food at good prices. At 44 Nam Ky Khoi Nghia is **Hu Tieu** restaurant, with great noodle soup with pork. There is a vegetarian branch of the same restaurant at number 24 (same street). A classy garden restaurant is **Trung Luong,** reached by boat up the Bao Dinh Canal. About three kilometers north on the route to Saigon, this is the place to order bat, rat, or grilled snake if you are so inclined.

Services and Information

Mytho is fairly well set up for tourism because it's the closest delta destination to Saigon. **Tien Giang Tourism,** at 65 April 30 St., tel. 73/873184, fax 73/872154, offers guides at $7 a day, as well as boat and car rentals. The staff are willing to answer questions. For an inexpensive local guide, pay a boatman—he knows where to go. **Ngan Hang Cong Thuong Bank,** on the west side of town, handles most transactions.

Getting There and Away

The easiest way to get to Mytho is by bus or hired vehicle from Saigon: This may take several hours to cover the 70 kilometers because of traffic holdups. Mytho bus station is about three kilometers from the town center on the Saigon Road. There are connections here to Vinh Long, Cantho, Chau Doc, and other delta destinations, also buses to Tay Ninh and Vung Tau.

Getting Around

Tien Giang Tourism offers car and boat rentals. Cyclos are easy to find. You can rent bicycles from cafés on Trang Truc Street, also from Cuu Long Restaurant and Chuong Duong Café on the south side.

VINH LONG

Vinh Long faces the Co Chien River (a Mekong tributary) to the north side; rivers and canals on the other three sides make it virtually an island. Most of the tourist action takes place at the northeast promontory.

Vinh Long has been one of the key points for the spread of Christianity in the Mekong Delta, which explains the Catholic church and seminary in town, the church on nearby Bin Hoa Phuoc Island, and the spectacularly sited church at Caibe.

In Town

The market in Vinh Long is very active. It covers about one square kilometer and features a wide range of fruit and vegetables, some from the fruit orchards on the opposite banks. The market also offers a curious trade in animals; it hops with fish, snakes, turtles, eels, and frogs. There are bins filled with live eels, large frogs tied together, fish unloaded at the docks at the crack of dawn, and bicycle runners delivering live geese and chickens for killing, cleaning, and cooking.

Down by the Co Chien River to the west of Cuu Long B Hotel is a small military museum with a Phantom fighter, Huey helicopter, and tanks.

Islands North of Vinh Long

Take a half-day or longer trip out to the town of Caibe and come back through the islands north of Vinh Long. You need about 4–5 hours to cover the distance; allow time for stops. The trip is best accomplished in the early morning, when you can catch a floating market at Caibe. It takes about 1.5 hours to reach Caibe by boat, with the floating market operating roughly 0600–1100. If you miss the market, try the fixed market near the bridge in Caibe. There's a Catholic church with a spectacular location at the head of the river. The church is open on Sundays.

On the return route you can stop at various orchards for rambutan, uglifruit, rose apple, jackfruit, pomelo, and longan on Binh Hoa Phuoc and An Binh islands north of Vinh

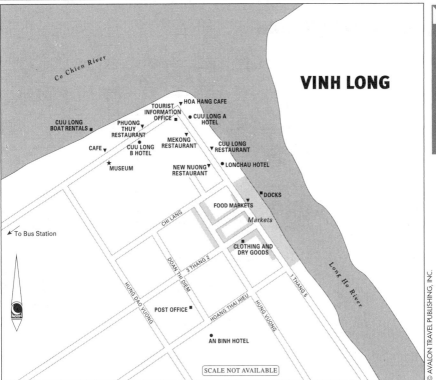

VINH LONG

Co Chien River

HOA HANG CAFE
TOURIST INFORMATION OFFICE
CUU LONG A HOTEL
CUU LONG BOAT RENTALS
PHUONG THUY RESTAURANT
MEKONG RESTAURANT
CAFE
CUU LONG B HOTEL
CUU LONG RESTAURANT
MUSEUM
NEW NUONG RESTAURANT
LONCHAU HOTEL
DOCKS
FOOD MARKETS
Markets
To Bus Station
CHI LANG
CLOTHING AND DRY GOODS
DOAN THI DIEM
3 THANG 2
1 THANG 5
Long Ho River
HUNG DAO VUONG
POST OFFICE
HOANG THAI HIEU
HUNG VUONG
AN BINH HOTEL
SCALE NOT AVAILABLE

© AVALON TRAVEL PUBLISHING, INC.

Long. Some orchards are open to boat tourists—reach these via waterways and footpaths. Tea is provided at the orchard manor, and some kind of donation may be expected. In Binh Thuan hamlet are a bonsai nursery and longan orchard run by Mr. Giao. Binh Hoa Phuoc Island features a settlement midway along the large channel cutting through it; you can see a church and school here. Plying the waterways are barges laden with husked rice or fruit.

Cuu Long Tourism has a mafia stranglehold over boat rentals in Vinh Long. Any independent operator seen hiring a boat to foreigners is stopped and fined. Cuu Long Tourism arranges larger boats for $25 for three hours, or $35 for four hours. These boats are usually covered to keep you from roasting. Bigger is not necessarily better, as some canals are very shallow and can be negotiated only by smaller craft.

Accommodations

The **Cuu Long Hotel** chain monopolizes the Vinh Long waterfront, with three hotels of 20–25 rooms each arrayed along First of May Street. **Cuu Long A,** tel. 70/822494, has 21 rooms for $38–45–55, with some rooms overlooking the river. Nearby is **Longchau Hotel,** tel. 70/823611, with ratty rooms for $8–14 each; either a double bed or two singles. Rats and prostitutes are in evidence. **Cuu Long B,** also called Vinh Tra, tel./fax 70/823357, has 25 a/c doubles for $15–30 and a quiet garden set back from the Mekong; the hotel has tennis courts. To round out the Cuu Long monopoly, there are Cuu Long Restaurant and Cuu Long Tourism. Cuu Long Tourism runs a set of villas, known as **Truong An Tourist Villas,** about four kilometers from Vinh Long town.

Two non-Cuu Long hotels are the **An Binh**

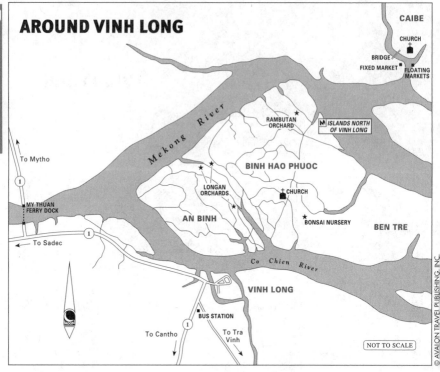

AROUND VINH LONG

CAIBE
CHURCH
BRIDGE
FIXED MARKET
FLOATING MARKETS

Mekong River

To Mytho

RAMBUTAN ORCHARD

ISLANDS NORTH OF VINH LONG

MY THUAN FERRY DOCK

BINH HAO PHUOC

To Sadec

LONGAN ORCHARDS

CHURCH

AN BINH

BONSAI NURSERY

BEN TRE

Co Chien River

VINH LONG

BUS STATION

To Cantho

To Tra Vinh

NOT TO SCALE

© AVALON TRAVEL PUBLISHING, INC.

Hotel, on Hoang Thai Hieu Street, and **Thai Binh Hotel,** close to the bus station, which is four kilometers out of town.

Food

There's a pleasant bunch of cafés along the waterfront promenade—try the **Hoa Nang Café,** which is attached to Cuu Long A Hotel. This is the top hangout bar in the evening. **Phuong Thuy** floating restaurant, serving European and Asian food, is popular with travelers. The Cuu Long hotels include dining rooms—the premier venue is Cuu Long A Hotel. Food stalls are in the market.

Services and Information

This town has not one but *two* tourist information offices—**Cuu Long Tourism** and, almost opposite, a place called **Tourist Information Office.** They're both after your business for guides but will also answer questions. They even have a few maps on the walls. The Tourist Information Office has two bikes for rent at $2 a day each; Cuu Long Tourism, tel. 70/823616, can arrange cars, minibuses, and boats.

Getting There and Around

Vinh Long bus station is four kilometers southwest of town, with links to Tra Vinh, Cantho, and other delta towns. A smaller station closer to town operates buses to Sadec. Use cyclos for getting around town. Near Phuong Thuy Restaurant you can hire a boat to visit the islands around Vinh Long. There may be a speedboat service from Caibe (close to Vinh Long) to Cantho.

CANTHO

Cantho, population 330,000, is the largest town in the delta by virtue of its central posi-

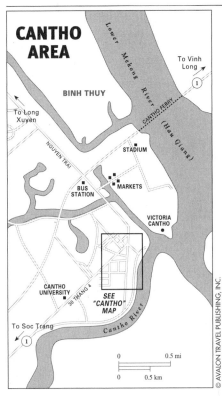

CANTHO AREA

To Vinh Long

Lower Mekong River (Hau Giang)

BINH THUY

To Long Xuyen

CANTHO FERRY

STADIUM

NGUYEN TRAI

BUS STATION

MARKETS

VICTORIA CANTHO

CANTHO UNIVERSITY

30 THANG 4

SEE "CANTHO" MAP

Cantho River

To Soc Trang

0   0.5 mi

0   0.5 km

© AVALON TRAVEL PUBLISHING, INC.

tion and its location near the Hau Giang, or lower Mekong. Cantho is a major transport center at the junction of numerous canals and roads; it also has an airport. The town has a university and a teacher training college.

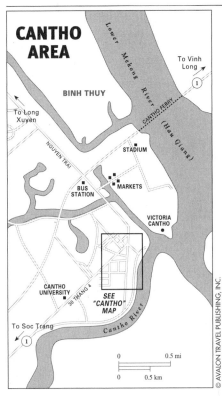 Cai Rang Floating Market

The main attraction from Cantho is a series of floating markets. Cantho is a good base for exploring river life: The area, with its lush canals, is known for its durian, orange, and mangosteen orchards. You can investigate by boat but also by bicycle if you can get a rental (a mountain bike would be preferable). The main place to target is Cai Rang floating market, which is very busy in the morning—get there at the crack of dawn if you can (this makes for better photo opportunities). Stand-up rowers in small craft mingle with much larger rice barges. You will see vessels

entirely filled with pineapples or melons or rose apples. If you're there at the crack of dawn, you may well be interested in a bit of market trading yourself—as in buying fresh fruit and hot baguettes from roving vendors in small boats. On organized tours, boat hire for trips close to Cantho is $15 for three hours for a group.

Accommodations

A surprising number of hotels are in Cantho, varying from guesthouse-type to towering edifices. In fact, Cantho has the best range of hotels in the delta. The following listing is for only a few of those. **Quoc Te** (International Hotel), 12 Hai Ba Trung, tel. 71/822079, costs $10 d for a basic room, $23–36–43 for more elaborate rooms. Car and boat rentals available. **Hau Giang Hotel,** 34 Nam Ky Khoi Nghia, tel. 71/821806, includes 35 a/c rooms. **Hoa Binh Hotel,** at 5 Hoa Binh Blvd., tel. 71/820536, has 22 fan and a/c rooms. A slew of quite passable hotels are strung along Chau Van Liem Boulevard—**Phong Nha, Tay Do I, Tay Do II, Asia Hotel,** and **Khach San 27.**

To the northern end of Cantho, isolated from the other hotels, is **Victoria Cantho,** tel. 71/810111, www.victoriahotels-asia.com. The hotel, built in French colonial style, features 92 rooms and a large pool set in tropical gardens facing the river. The hotel has two restaurants and full business center. Room rates are $135–150 and suites are $250. A free shuttle boat runs from the dock at the Ninh Kieu Hotel to Victoria Cantho.

Food

A good choice for dining in Cantho is **Nambo,** at 50 Hai Ba Trung, tel. 71/823908. The restaurant serves simple Vietnamese and European fare—pizza, sandwiches, salads, and desserts—but the ambience is what sets this place apart. It is housed in a restored colonial villa, with polished wood floors, rattan furniture, and wooden ceiling fans. Dining on the upstairs balcony affords a fine view of the waterfront. Nearby is **Mekong Restaurant,** at 38 Hai Ba Trung, a long-running traveler hangout that offers Vietnamese and Chinese dishes

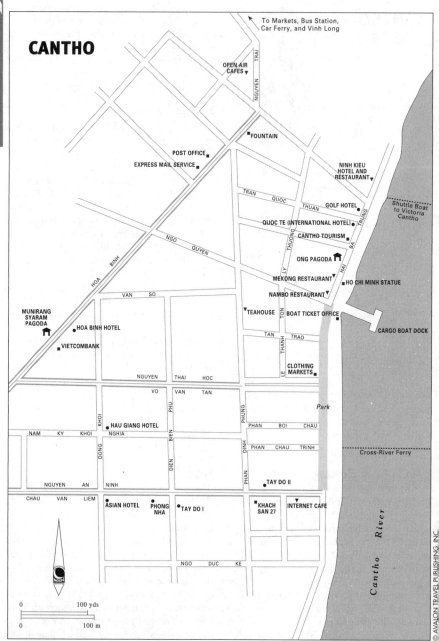

CANTHO

To Markets, Bus Station, Car Ferry, and Vinh Long

OPEN AIR CAFES

FOUNTAIN

POST OFFICE

EXPRESS MAIL SERVICE

NINH KIEU HOTEL AND RESTAURANT

TRAN QUOC THUAN GOLF HOTEL

Shuttle Boat to Victoria Cantho

QUOC TE (INTERNATIONAL HOTEL)

CANTHO TOURISM

NGO QUYEN

HOA BINH

ONG PAGODA

MEKONG RESTAURANT

HO CHI MINH STATUE

NAMBO RESTAURANT

MUNIRANG SYARAM PAGODA

VAN SO

TEAHOUSE

BOAT TICKET OFFICE

HOA BINH HOTEL

VIETCOMBANK

CARGO BOAT DOCK

TAN THANH TRAO

CLOTHING MARKETS

NGUYEN THAI HOC

VO VAN TAN

PHONG

Park

KHOI

HAU GIANG HOTEL

NGHIA

PHU BIEN DIEN

PHAN BOI CHAU

NAM KY KHOI

DONG

PHAN CHAU TRINH

Cross-River Ferry

NGUYEN AN NINH

PHAN DINH

TAY DO II

CHAU VAN LIEM

ASIAN HOTEL

PHONG NHA

TAY DO I

KHACH SAN 27

INTERNET CAFE

Cantho River

NGO DUC KE

0   100 yds

0   100 m

for very reasonable prices. Cantho is a market town: Some pretty strange things pop up on menus at restaurants around town, such as snake sausage, stewed tortoise, and tossed eel.

Services

The government-run **Cantho Tourism Company** is at 20 Hai Ba Trung, tel. 71/821852. Staff can organize boat trips or bicycle day trips. **Cantho GPO** is quite large, with fax and IDD sections; express mail service nearby. **Vietcombank** is at 7 Hoa Binh Boulevard.

Getting There and Away

Buses from Saigon take about four hours to reach Cantho, a distance of 165 kilometers. The Cantho bus station is 1.5 kilometers northwest of town. It may be possible to charter a boat going from Cantho to Chau Doc. The trip takes about five hours. Inquire as to what may be running at the time—these boats are prone to breakdowns. The Victoria Hotel group runs its own speedboats on the Cantho to Chau Doc route, and onward to Phnom Penh. There are no scheduled runs for the Cantho to Chau Doc secction: The boat must be chartered, or you join an existing charter. It's possible to go from Chau Doc all the way to Saigon by speedboat, but a charter would be very expensive. Cantho has a busy boat terminal with a ticket office at the dock, near the Ho Chi Minh statue. There's a chalkboard listing destinations. Destinations are likely to be Phung Hiep and points south and southwest in the delta.

SOUTH OF CANTHO

Highway 1 runs from Cantho along a poor road through Phung Hiep, Soc Trang, and Bac Lieu to its southern terminus in Camau. Organized tours to Camau make a few stops now and then along the route from Cantho—at Phung Hiep floating market, Soc Trang bat sanctuary, perhaps the bird garden at Bac Lieu. Soc Trang bat sanctuary is actually a Cambodian temple with a number of fruit bats hanging around in nearby trees. Those in tours may spend a day or more in Camau, taking in mangrove swamps, Damdoi bird sanctuary, and fish and shrimp breeding grounds.

Phung Hiep Floating Market

Floating markets are sprinkled around the delta. The one at Phung Hiep is busy because it lies at the confluence of seven rivers. Dozens of boats gather here to trade. Stand-up rowers—mostly women—steer longboats loaded to the gunwales with fruit and vegetables. It's quite a balancing act. A red-mouthed betel-nut vendor shouts her wares, another propels a load of papayas through the water, another sells baguettes. The floating market at Phung Hiep is best viewed in the early morning, 0600–0930. There's a small dock where you can rent a rowboat and rower for about $1.50 an hour, putting you right in the center of the floating market. Another vantage point for watching the busy river life is from the bridge to the north of the floating market—from here you get an unparalleled view of commuter boats, large craft moving pottery upriver, and stand-up rowers with crossed oars.

Phung Hiep is 35 kilometers south of Cantho, one hour by road or 3–4 hours by boat. Because there are no hotels in Phung Hiep it's best to get there as early as possible from Cantho by road, see the sights, and try to make it back to Cantho by boat. A small hired boat should cost under $10 for the four-hour trip; there's also a regular passenger boat from Phung Hiep to Cantho.

Camau

Camau is the largest town on the Camau Peninsula, at the tip of Indochina. Because the area is rugged, remote, and marshy, it has the lowest population density in southern Vietnam—and possibly the highest mosquito density.

Camau sits in the middle of U-Minh Forest, the largest mangrove habitat outside the Amazon. The area was an ideal hiding place for Vietcong during the Vietnam War. Trying to flush out the Vietcong, the Americans dug canals to drain the swamps and poured down a rain of napalm and herbicides to destroy the covering foliage. Locals have replanted the forest in pursuit of timber and charcoal. Unless you're keen on mangrove swamps and mosquitoes, this area has little to recommend it.

Camau has half a dozen surly hotels that accept foreigners. Make sure you're well supplied with mosquito netting. You can reach Camau by road from Cantho (180 kilometers) or directly from Saigon's Mien Tay bus station (350 kilometers); there's also an epic 30-hour boat journey from Saigon to Camau. You can get around Camau by cyclo or moto; there are also river-taxis near the market. You can hire boats by the hour.

EAST OF CANTHO

Tra Vinh

Tra Vinh is a small town with little to see, but the locals will certainly enjoy looking at you—you may end up the main attraction. There are a few pagodas in the vicinity; **Ong Met Pagoda,** in town, is home to about 30 monks and a Khmer school. Five kilometers to the southwest of town is a rice-paper factory; two kilometers north is a coconut garden.

Tra Vinh has a handful of hotels. **Khach San Cuu Long,** at 999 Nguyen Thi Minh Khai St., tel. 74/862625, offers 17 rooms for $18–30. **Tra Vinh Palace Hotel,** at 3 Le Thanh Ton, tel. 74/864999, has rooms for $20–35. One of the better restaurants in town is **Binh Ky,** at 4 Tran Phu St., with good Vietnamese and Chinese food.

An interesting boat route runs from Tra Vinh to Bai Xan to Mocay to Ben Tre, taking five hours, for $1. The journey moves off the wide rivers and cuts through narrower sections with extensive coconut groves. The daytime boat trip leaves from Long Binh Bridge, 1.5 kilometers from Tra Vinh. There are occasional boats to Saigon from Tra Vinh, taking 14 hours.

Ben Tre

Ben Tre is small. There's a dock area with a riverside market; farther back is Truc Giang Lake with the main hotel facing it. Out of town are a sugarcane factory, whiskey factory, sawmill, and brickyards.

Dong Khoi Hotel, near the lake at 16 Hai Ba Trung, tel. 75/822240, offers 25 rooms. A basic fan room is $6; a/c rooms are $16–30–33 for singles, a few extra dollars for doubles. The Dong Khoi also features a large restaurant. There are two other hotels in Ben Tre, including the **Hung Vuong Hotel,** by the river.

Ben Tre Tourist Company, 65 Dong Khoi St., tel. 75/829618, lies about 400 meters west of Dong Khoi Hotel. It charges $50 a day for a car and $10 a day for a guide. The tourist company arranges trips to floating markets, fruit orchards, and a stork farm.

There are boats from Ben Tre to Tra Vinh, Thuoi Thuan, Camau, Song Doc, and other southern destinations.

NORTHWEST OF CANTHO

Sadec

On the outskirts of Sadec more than 150 families operate private nurseries; flowers, shrubs, and young trees are grown here in large quantities. These are shipped all over Vietnam, especially around Tet in February. The nurseries are about four kilometers from the center of the city; just wander through the gardens, and someone will show you around. Best time to view the blooms is December. By the river are numerous home factories, where young men churn out noodles using flour, water, rice, and sunshine.

Sadec's claim to fame is that it was where French writer Marguerite Duras lived: She wrote about it in her coming-of-age story, *The Lover*. The old villa where she grew up is still there. To go see it, proceed along Hung Vuong Street from the post office and turn right at Tran Phu Street, go over a bridge, turn left for one kilometer to a nurseries village, follow a small path for about 800 meters, and you will see the Duras villa. Some scenes in the movie *The Lover* were filmed on location in Sadec: Old French villas that appeared were filmed at the market along Sadec River.

Bong Hong Hotel, about one kilometer from the post office, tel. 67/861301, has a/c rooms for $18–25. **Khach San Sadec,** at 108 Hung Vuong St., tel. 67/861430, has $7–10–15 fan rooms and $20–25 a/c rooms. It's run by Dong Thap Tourism, which is based in the hotel. Nearby is a good restaurant, **Cay Sung,** at 4 Hung Vuong St., tel. 67/861749.

Long Xuyen

Long Xuyen, population 250,000, is the uncharming capital of An Giang province and was formerly a stronghold of the Hoa Hao sect. The faith began in 1939 in the village of Hoa Hao in Chau Doc province. A breakaway Buddhist sect, it emphasizes simplicity and discourages temple building and ritual worship.

Until the mid-1950s the Hoa Hao constituted a major force in the region, even maintaining its own army; even today there are believed to be 1.5 million adherents in the delta.

Long Xuyen is one of the black holes of the delta—nothing to see, lousy food, and overpriced hotels. Since the Hoa Hao are not keen on temples, you'll have to settle for **Long Xuyen Catholic Church** on Hung Vuong Street. The cathedral, completed in the 1970s, is one of the largest in the delta. Along Le Minh Nguy On Street are two pagodas, **Dinh Than Pagoda** and **Quan Thanh Pagoda.** Organized tours

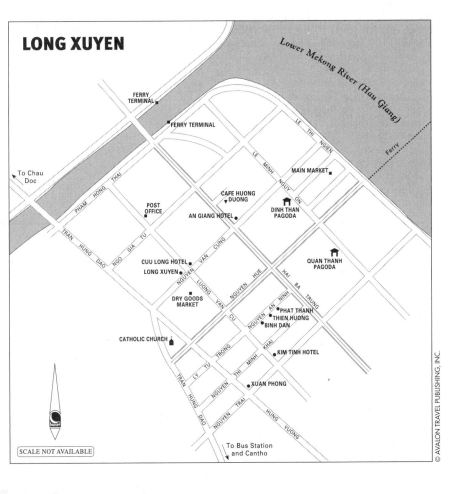

LONG XUYEN

passing through Long Xuyen usually focus on the market. You might also want to visit **Tong Duc Thang Museum,** with artifacts from the Oc-Eo civilization.

Long Xuyen features half a dozen smaller hotels. The cheapest include the **Binh Dan, Thien Huong,** and **Phat Thanh** hotels, all on Nguyen An Ninh Street, with rooms for under $5. Not much more expensive are **Kim Tinh Hotel,** tel. 76/853137, and **Song Hau Hotel,** tel. 76/852979. **An Giang Hotel,** at 40 Hai Ba Trung, tel. 76/841297, has 16 rooms for less than $15. **Long Xuyen,** at 17 Nguyen Van Cung St., tel. 76/852927, offers almost 40 rooms for less than $20 each. The 24-room **Cuu Long Hotel,** at 21 Nguyen Van Cung, tel. 76/841365, fax 76/843176, has doubles for $15–20 and up. There's nothing really worth recommending in the food line, although a busy place to try is **Café Huong Duong,** at 20 Phan Dinh Phung St., down a market alley north of An Giang Hotel. It serves large dishes of fresh food.

Long Xuyen bus station lies several kilometers to the south of the town. From Long Xuyen there are connections to Saigon, Vinh Long, Cantho, Chau Doc, Camau, Ha Tien, and Rach Gia. You might consider private minibuses for some of these runs—minibuses stop near the Catholic church on Hung Vuong Street. Boat transport may be available to Chau Doc and Nui Sap.

Chau Doc

Chau Doc is an attractive town of 80,000 on the banks of the Hau Giang, by the Cambodian border. Until the mid-18th century, Chau Doc was part of Cambodia. Today it supports the largest Khmer population in the delta—the ranks of the Khmer were swelled by refugees escaping persecution under the Pol Pot regime. Chau Doc also has the largest Cham contingent in the delta, and a sizable Chinese community. The Chau Doc area is additionally the seat of the Hoa Hao religion, with a concentration of devotees.

You can hire a local boat to visit Chau Doc's floating houses around Con Tien Island. The going price is about $4–6 for one boat (takes

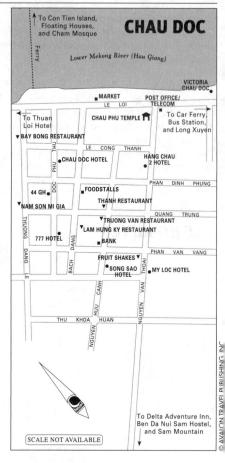

up to six people) for a two-hour tour, taking in river life and a visit to a Muslim Cham village. Hundreds of floating houses around Chau Doc are built on empty metal drums, with suspended metal nets (sometimes up to five meters deep) beneath them. A family lives on the floating house and fattens up the fish by throwing handfuls of cooked mush through a trapdoor; when they're fat enough, the fish are "harvested"— taken to a vessel that can hold thousands of kilos belowdecks for transport to Saigon. Ingeniously, this wooden vessel keeps the fish alive in water trapped below deck, although by this stage many fish are bloated, red-eyed, and half-dead.

Chau Doc features a large market along the river, offering produce and Thai black-market goods smuggled in through Cambodia. About one kilometer to the southeast of town is a ferry crossing that takes you to Chau Giang Mosque, which serves the Muslim Cham community. From here you can hop on a Honda and ride another 15 kilometers to Tan Chau District, famed for its silk industry; the market offers imported Thai goods.

About five kilometers southwest of Chau Doc is Nui Sam, or Sam Mountain—so named because it resembles a king crab, or *sam*. The site draws pilgrims and tourists who visit several pagodas at the foot of the mountain. Although the pagodas date from the 19th century, they were extended and rebuilt in the 20th century. **Tay An Pagoda** contains a display of more than 200 statues. Nearby **Chua Xu Temple** has a revered statue of Lady Xu, enshrined in a new multi-tiered pagoda; patrons donate old sequined costumes as a gift here in the hope of having wishes fulfilled. Close by is the tomb of Thoai Ngoc Hau (1761–1829), a former local mandarin buried here with his two wives. Thoai Ngoc Hau is revered as the person responsible for building the Chau Doc Canal.

The short hike to the top of the mountain rewards you with panoramic views of the delta—duck farms, rice paddies, and cigarette smugglers struggling to cross the vast delta wetland into Cambodia. En route you pass **Chua Phuc Dien Tu,** a pagoda that backs onto a cave and contains a shrine dedicated to Quan Am. Lining the staircase are loads of cafés where you can slake your thirst on the climb.

Chau Doc Hotel, at 17 Doc Phu Thu St., tel. 76/866484, is popular with backpackers; there are 36 rooms here: fan rooms for $8 and a/c for $15. The **Tan Tai** and **Thai Binh** hotels are substandard dumps. Two other budget possibilities are **Nha Khach 44,** at 44 Doc Phu Thu St., tel. 76/866540, with 19 rooms for $5–8, and **Hotel 777.** South of Thai Binh hotel is **My Loc Hotel,** 51 Nguyen Van Thoai, tel. 76/866455, with rooms for $8–12. In the center of town is **Tai Thanh Hotel,** at 86 Bach Dang St., tel. 76/866147; 20 rooms for $5–10 apiece. About a

kilometer south of town, near Chau Giang ferry terminal on Le Loi Street, is **Hang Chau Hotel,** 32 Le Loi St., tel. 76/866196, fax 76/867773, with a/c rooms for $14–28—this place has a noisy nightclub. To the northern end of town by the river is **Thuan Loi Hotel,** at 18 Tran Hung Dao, tel. 76/866134, with 19 rooms for $7–15; rooms at the top have views. **Thanh Tra Hotel,** at 77 Thu Khoa Nghia, tel. 76/866788, has two rooms from $8 fan to $14 a/c. Facing the river is **Victoria Chau Doc,** 32 Le Loi St., tel. 76/865010, victoriachaudoc@hcm.vnn.vn; this 93-room hotel charges $80–95 for rooms and $150 for a suite. Constructed in French-colonial style, it features a swimming pool near the river. Farther out from town is **Victoria Nui Sam,** another one in the Victoria chain. The Victoria group operates its own boats between its hotels in Chau Doc and Cantho, and between Chau Doc and Phnom Penh.

Foodwise, the best bet is to roam the market area. There are food stalls attached to the markets on Quang Trung Street. Close by are several reasonable restaurants: **Truong Van,** at 15 Quang Trung St., and **Lam Hung Ky,** at 71 Chi Lang St.

Chau Doc bus station is two kilometers from town, along Le Loi Street; it has connections to Long Xuyen, Cantho, and Vinh Long. There is a rough dirt road to Ha Tien, sometimes tackled by motorcycle. A smoother ride is a boat route along canals. Other boats from Chau Doc may run to Rach Gia and other delta hubs.

GULF OF THAILAND
Rach Gia

Rach Gia, the capital of Ken Giang province, is a deepwater fishing port on the Gulf of Thailand with a population of 125,000. Major industries include fishing, fish-sauce production, and smuggling from Thailand. The population includes a number of ethnic Chinese and Khmers. The center of town is an island at the mouth of the Cailon River. Rach Gia is a rather ramshackle place with widespread prostitution—many hotels serve as brothels.

There are a number of pagodas in and around

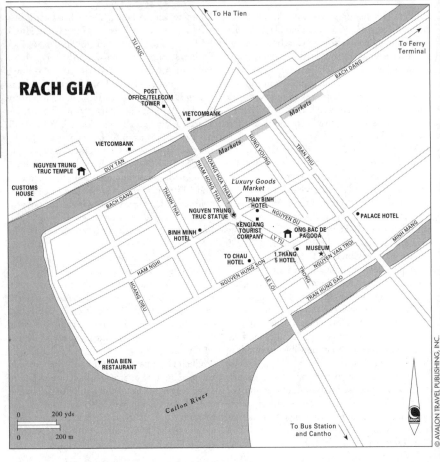

RACH GIA

© AVALON TRAVEL PUBLISHING, INC.

Rach Gia. On the mainland north of town off Quang Trung Street is **Phat Lon Pagoda.** This airy Khmer Hinayana Buddhist pagoda features Cambodian and Thai-style sculptures and is home to 30 monks. Closer to the Cailon River is a temple dedicated to Nguyen Trung Truc, who led resistance against the newly arrived French in the 1860s. One raid resulted in the burning of the French warship *Esperance.* Nguyen Trung Truc turned himself in after the French took his mother and a number of civilians hostage and threatened to kill them. The resistance fighter was executed in Rach Gia's marketplace in 1868. A statue of Nguyen Trung Truc stands at the

center of town. This part of town is modestly scenic, with fishing boats dotting the canal.

Not far from this is the Chinese-style **Ong Bac De Pagoda** on Nguyen Du Street; to the south of town is **Tam Bao Pagoda,** which features trees pruned in the shape of dragons and other animals. Rach Gia has two **markets:** a luxury goods market along Hoang Hoa Tham Street, and a main market area on the northeast side of the island, running along Bach Dang Street.

About 12 kilometers north of Rach Gia (and 30 kilometers southwest of Long Xuyen) lie the **ruins of Oc-Eo,** a powerful trading port from the 1st–6th centuries A.D. Oc-Eo was part of the Funan Empire, trading with India and China, and possibly even with Persia and the Roman Empire. The site was unearthed in the 1940s. There is little to see here now—just a pile of stones and potsherds. The site is reached via the town of Tan Hoi, where you hire a boat for a one-hour journey to Oc-Eo. You can see artifacts from the area at Saigon's History Museum and Art Museum, Hanoi's Art Museum, and Long Xuyen's Tong Duc Thang Museum.

Accommodation and Food: Most hotels are on the island; some hotels do not accept foreigners or do not want to deal with them. Fan rooms in Rach Gia's budget hotels go for $5–10, while a/c rooms are $12–18. At 38 Nguyen Hung Son St. is **1 Thang 5 Hotel** (May 1 Hotel), with 18 rooms for $7–14. It is run by Kengiang Tourist Company, as are a number of hotels in Rach Gia. At 48 Pham Hong Thai St. is **Binh Minh Hotel,** tel. 77/862154, with 20 rooms for $8–12. **Palace Hotel,** at 41 Tran Phu St., tel. 77/866146, is an 18-room, privately run place with rooms for $22–27 and a few cheaper singles. **To Chau Hotel,** at 4 Le Loi St., tel. 77/863718, has 30 rooms for $8–12 fan and $15–25 a/c.

Rach Gia is famed for its seafood, served laced with *nuoc mam* and black pepper. There are a dozen restaurants on the island serving good Vietnamese and Chinese dishes; on the western end of the island is **Hoa Bien Restaurant,** which has views.

Getting There: Express buses to Rach Gia leave Saigon's Mien Tay station, taking about eight hours for the trip. Rach Gia bus station is six kilometers south of town (take a lambro for 20 minutes), with connections to Cantho, Long Xuyen, and Ha Tien. On the north side of Rach Gia is another express bus office at number 33 on 30 Thang 4 St., with departures to Ho Chi Minh City, Ha Tien, and Cantho. Regular boats run from Rach Gia's Mui Voi ferry terminal to Chau Doc, Long Xuyen, and Tan Chau.

Rach Gia to Ha Tien

The road from Rach Gia to Ha Tien is rough but scenic. It passes many duck farms and affords glimpses into canal life. The scenic coastline between Rach Gia and Ha Tien comprises a number of fine beaches and caves to explore. On a promontory 30 kilometers from Ha Tien is Chua Hang Grotto, with an entrance behind the altar of a pagoda set against the base of the hill. Next to the grotto is Duong Beach, with fine sand and crystal-clear water. Offshore is Father-and-Son Island. A bit farther along the coast, 25 kilometers from Ha Tien, is Hang Tien Grotto, accessible only by boat. Another 10 kilometers toward Ha Tien is Mo So Grotto, with tunnels that are accessible on foot during the dry season and by boat during the rainy season.

Ha Tien

Ha Tien faces the Gulf of Thailand, lying only seven kilometers from the Cambodian border. During the Pol Pot era the town was subjected to harassment by the Khmer Rouge and tens of thousands of people fled. The Khmer Rouge massacres of Vietnamese in places such as Ha Tien eventually led to Vietnam's 1978 invasion of Cambodia.

Today Ha Tien is a town of 100,000 thriving on fishing and items made from mother-of-pearl and tortoiseshell (fans, combs, boxes, glasses frames). Around the town are limestone crags and caves, making this an area quite unlike other parts of the delta. There are a few pagodas in town, but more interesting are the cave temples outside town. Using a hired moto or other transport, you can visit **Thach Dong Caves** and **Mui Nai Beach** in the same excursion. About three kilometers from town is Thach Dong, or The Grotto that Swallows the Clouds, which shelters a Buddhist sanctuary dedicated to Guanyin. Continuing along the same scenic dirt road westward for another two kilometers, you reach Mui Nai, which is a thin strip of black sand fringed by coconut palms. There are fishing boats and a few seafood shacks. In the fruit department, Mui Nai offers the purplish brown coconut called *thot lot.*

About 15 kilometers off the coast of Ha Tien are the secluded beaches of **Hon Giang Island,** which you can reach by boat. The inhabitants make a living by harvesting sea-swallow nests, a delicacy prized for medicinal soup.

You enter the fair city of Ha Tien via a floating toll bridge. It's a picturesque town and quite easy to walk around. If you need transport, it's mostly found at the west end of the bridge—motos, lambros, and cyclos. Right here are two hotels—**To Chau** (cheap and nasty), and **Dong Ho** (reasonable). **Dong Ho Hotel,** on Ben Tran Hau St., tel. 77/852141, has a total of 20 rooms: fan rooms for $5–7 and a/c rooms for $12–15; nice views from the rooftop over the town—this is the best deal for a place to stay. Another option is the nearby private hotel **Kim Thanh,** at 940 Tuan Phu Dat, tel. 77/852656, with rooms for $8–12.

Khach San Dulich, farther south, has more expensive rooms with baths. There's also **Khai Hoan Hotel,** 239 Phong Thanh St., tel. 77/852254, and **Phuong Thanh Hotel,** tel. 77/852152, with rooms for $8, some with baths.

For dining, try **Xuan Thanh** (airy, lots of windows, good seafood) and **Hoa Hiep** restaurants, as well as the nearby market area.

Buses to Ha Tien leave from Cholon's Mien Tay terminal and take about 10 hours for the trip. There are departures from Ha Tien to Rach Gia, Cantho, and other delta destinations. There's also a regular boat from Ha Tien to Chau Doc, departing at the crack of dawn from the terminal near the floating bridge. It, too, takes about 10 hours for the trip and most of the time parallels a dirt road (used by hardy moto voyagers). The boat trip should cost about $2, although the captain will most likely want $5 from a foreigner.

Phu Quoc

The 16-island archipelago of Phu Quoc lies about 40 kilometers west of Ha Tien in the Gulf of Thailand. It is governed from Ha Tien as a district of Ken Giang province. The major island—Phu Quoc—is 48 kilometers long and covers an area of 1,320 square kilometers. Lying only 15 kilometers off the Cambodian coast, the island is disputed territory—also claimed by the Cambodians. Phu Quoc Island boasts lush tropical forest and mountain zones. The main activities are fishing and *nuoc mam* pro-

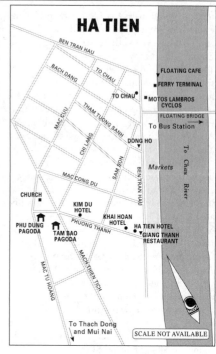

duction; about 18,000 inhabitants live mainly in the town of Duong Dong, on the west side of the island.

The main attraction at Phu Quoc is the pristine beaches, especially in the south (there's one called Kem Beach—Kem meaning "ice cream"). Marine sports focus on deep-sea fishing and snorkeling. There's also bird-watching at a rainforest in the north of the island. Hotels on the island offer rooms for about $15–20 a night. You can get a local guide and motorbike for around $7–15 a day. Visit November–May; January and February are the best months.

There are flights from Saigon to Duong Dong on Phu Quoc about four times a week; the flight takes 50 minutes and costs around $65 one-way. The entire moto population of Phu Quoc will be waiting for your arrival—choose carefully, as your moto may end up being your guide as well. There is also a boat service to Duong Dong and Cay Dua from Rach Gia, taking 8–12 hours for the trip.

Cambodia

ប្រជុំ កាហ្វេ   Le Grand Café

Introduction

The Four Horsemen of the Apocalypse—Conquest, War, Famine, and Death—have ridden roughshod over Cambodia. During the 1970s Cambodia suffered from the twin horrors of war and famine—the invading Vietnamese called it "a land of blood and tears, hell on earth."

Cambodia is hardly the place to go for a relaxing holiday. Visiting the country is a humbling experience—you wonder how people can possibly manage to even crack a smile after what they've been through. And yet they have the widest smiles and must be the friendliest people in Indochina. Their willingness to start anew speaks volumes for the resilience of the human spirit. Here's a country starting from scratch, rebuilding its traditions, culture, laws, government, and economy. The gruesome past is still around. Every month hundreds of people are maimed by land mines; Cambodia has the highest number of amputees per capita of any country in the world.

Cambodia flies the world's only flag with a

building on it—the triple towers visible from the causeway at Angkor Wat. All political factions of all inclinations (even the Khmer Rouge) have depicted Angkor Wat on their version of the Cambodian flag. The Angkor Wat towers are the national logo, also found on Cambodian money, the national beer label, as a backdrop to TV newsreaders, and the official seal on the Cambodian visa.

Angkor is also the brand name of a number of products and services, though the Cambodians draw the line at foreigners' using the logo. The Cambodian government filed an official complaint against a Thai company for using "Angkor Wat" as a brand name for its fish sauce, citing this use by a non-Cambodian company as an "illegal and unfriendly act." The Foreign Affairs Ministry argued that Angkor Wat is the symbol of Khmer national identity. And so it is: Angkor is the cornerstone of Khmer culture, symbol of national pride and past greatness, and inspiration for painting, sculpture, and woodcarving.

Angkor is also a symbol for hope, because it is Angkor that draws tourists, and foreign exchange generated from tourism can help rebuild the economy. Angkor casts its spell over all who visit. Despite the risks of travel, or perhaps because of them, Cambodia is an extraordinary adventure.

THE LAND

Cambodia occupies an area of 181,035 square kilometers and borders Laos, Thailand, and Vietnam. The country is divided into 20 provinces. To the north is the Dangrek Range; to the west, the Cardamom Mountains; to the southwest, the Elephant Mountains. The Mekong courses 500 kilometers through Cambodia. The country's second-longest river is Tonle Sap River, which connects the Mekong to Lake Tonle Sap.

Cambodia has a tropical monsoon climate, with high humidity. March–May is very hot with occasional rain; June–October is the monsoon season; November–March is the cooler dry season.

THE PEOPLE

Cambodia's population is estimated at 13 million. The Khmers constitute 90 percent of the population. The remainder is composed of hilltribe groups, Cham, Vietnamese, Chinese, and Thais. The breakdown is 80 percent rural and 20 percent urban. The largest city is Phnom Penh, with about 1.5 million people.

Language

Khmer, the official language, is a nontonal language of the Mon-Khmer family, enriched by Pali and Sanskrit. French is the second major language, closely followed by English. Russian, Vietnamese, and Chinese are also spoken in Cambodia. Literacy rate is a low 38 percent, a legacy of the Pol Pot years.

Religion

Theravada Buddhism was almost annihilated under the 1975–1979 reign of terror of the Khmer Rouge, but it has since been reinstated as the national religion of Cambodia. Minority groups adhere to other religions such as Catholicism (mainly Vietnamese), Taoism and Confucianism (Chinese), and Sunni Muslim (Cham).

GOVERNMENT AND ECONOMY

A coup in 1996 resulted in a virtual dictatorship of the Cambodian People's Party (CPP) under leader Hun Sen. King Sihanouk has a symbolic role as constitutional monarch.

The national flag consists of three white Angkor towers set on a red background,

Khmer-style Buddha seated on *naga* Mucilinda

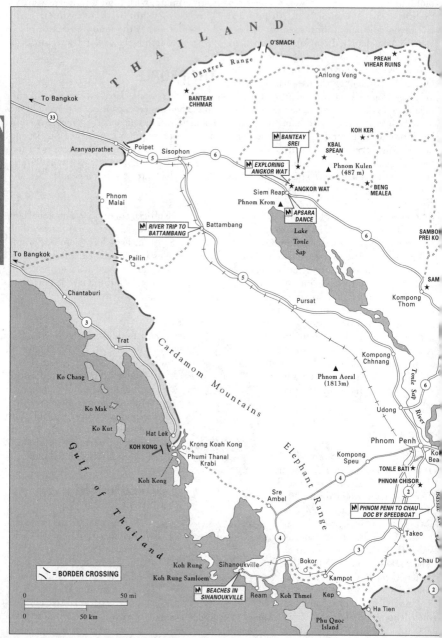

edged with blue trim, based on the royalist Sihanouk design.

Economy

Agriculture employs about 75 percent of the workforce. Top exports are timber, rubber, cane furniture, and garments. The shadow economy in Cambodia is impossible to track but is clearly quite large. There is illegal mining and logging near the Thai border, and a lot of smuggled goods pass through central Cambodia. Per capita income is $260. The unit of currency is the riel; US$1=4,000 riel.

TOURISM IN CAMBODIA

At the beginning of the 1900s, Europeans were afflicted with Angkormania. Colonial exhibitions in France featuring Khmer statuary and models of Angkor structures were very popular. In 1906 a Khmer dance troupe wowed audiences all over Europe. There were near-riots when people demanded entrance to the performances of sacred and sensual dance. Sculptor Auguste Rodin compared the dancers to Greek nymphs. In 1907 the Siamese ceded the Angkor region to the French, and in 1908 the first car forged through to Angkor from Saigon. In 1922 the Marseilles Colonial Exhibition featured a recreation of the central towers of Angkor Wat; the same exhibition appeared in Paris in 1931. In the 1920s travel agencies led trips to Angkor, and motor traffic was so busy that laws were enforced for parking and speed limits. For added thrills, globetrotters and colonial visitors could roam around ruins on elephant-back.

Cambodia was extremely popular with tourists between the two world wars, when it could be reached from both Bangkok and Saigon. Through the 1960s about 60,000 tourists a year visited Cambodia; in the early 1970s civil war made the country inaccessible. The tourist flow did not resume again until 22,000 UNTAC personnel arrived in 1992. In 1994 about 178,000 tourists passed through Pochentong Airport in Phnom Penh. In the year of the coup, 1997, the overwhelming direction of travel was out of Cambodia, not in-bound.

But with tourist confidence restored after the complete demise of the Khmer Rouge guerrilla group, figures soared. In 2004, there were 900,000 tourists, generating an income that accounted for a fair slice of the national budget. Cambodia has potential for much higher tourism figures, considering that neighboring Thailand sees more than eight million visitors a year. Except that Thailand has a formidable network of air links, transport, roads, hotels, and tourism personnel—and Cambodia has a sparse and spotty infrastructure. But the Thais are helping build that up, and the Asian Development Bank allotted $136 million for tourism-related programs.

The situation in Cambodia has become much more stable, but areas up-country remain insecure, and land mines mean some regions are dangerous. Keep an ear to the ground and an eye on the news for developments.

HIGHLIGHTS

Travelers find the Cambodians amazingly hospitable: If you like adventure and don't mind people waving guns in your face, this is the place to be. There are no Holiday Inns or Pizza Huts or McDonalds in Cambodia, and up-country you'll most likely be the only foreigner around.

Cambodia's special hazards include bandits, soldiers seeking handouts, mines, and unexploded ordnance. Even in really peaceful times, the Ministry of Tourism has been unsure how to promote Cambodia, or, indeed, what to do to ensure that tourists actually survive the trip. The basic strategy has been to set up a kind of "Khmer Triangle" to guarantee three safe havens for tourists—Phnom Penh, Angkor, and Sihanoukville—and then pray that nobody disappears in the triangle. Naturally, they advise tourists to travel by air to these three destinations. The Interior Ministry says units of special tourist police have been established at Phnom Penh, Siem Reap, and other parts of the country in a setup similar to a successful tourist protection program in Thailand.

Most visitors indeed do stick to the traveler trinity of Angkor, Phnom Penh, and Sihanoukville. But there's a lot more to see in Cambodia—and with the threat of insurgency lifted in 1999, the place is wide open. You are limited only by the threat of mines (in remoter areas) and sporadic banditry (particularly in the northeast). More adventurous options include renting a motocross bike and heading off along red dirt roads. To help smooth the path, an excellent guidebook is *Adventure Cambodia* (Silkworm Books, Bangkok, 2001). The authors, Matt Jacobsen and Frank Visakay, toured backwoods Cambodia by motocross bikes to come up with this tome, which carries 50 maps— alone worth the cost of the book (good maps of remoter Cambodia are extremely difficult to find). The book is not just for motorcyclists; anyone getting off the track in Cambodia could make use of the information.

Phnom Penh

Traces of the city's former splendor are visible at the Royal Palace, enclosing the Silver Pagoda. The National Museum houses the world's finest collection of Khmer artifacts. The proud achievements of the Khmer culture are offset by the horrors of the Tuol Sleng Holocaust Museum.

Siem Reap

The small gateway town to Angkor Wat is a good place for rest and relaxation, with good food. Around town are quiet rural areas and forested zones; within reach is Lake Tonle Sap, with fishing activity and floating houses.

Angkor

Angkor is fabulous! The Angkor region casts its spell over all who visit—the stuff of dreams.

This is the top archaeological site in Southeast Asia, and it's worth 3–10 days or more. It was declared a World Heritage Site in 1992. The romantic ruins are a wonder of the eastern world, with 70 sites sprawled over an area of 200 square kilometers. Giant tree roots drape over sandstone Buddha faces, banyan trees sprout over cloister roofs, and lines of celestial nymphs appear on 100-meter friezes. Angkor Wat and Angkor Thom are the star sites. Transportation options here include bicycling, motorcycling, and driving.

Sihanoukville

This is a port and resort town on the Gulf of Thailand, with several sandy beaches and good seafood. It's earmarked for major development, with an offshore island casino resort.

River Trips

A key attraction in Cambodia is its wild jungle terrain and forests. A fast boat runs from Phnom Penh up the Tonle Sap River and across Lake Tonle Sap to a dock near Siem Reap. You can take river trips of several days up the Mekong northeast to Stung Treng and exit to southern Laos. Ratanakiri, in the northeast, is a hilltribe area; it's possible to ride elephants here.

Festivals

In mid-April is Cambodian New Year, with three days of celebration at the peak of the hot season. At full moon in October or November is a festival celebrating the reversal of the current of the Tonle Sap River, with boat racing, processions, and games. The biggest venue for the celebration is Phnom Penh.

Introduction

Phnom Penh

In the 1950s and 1960s Phnom Penh was one of the finest cities in Southeast Asia. The riverine city's yellow-ocher buildings, squares and cafés, and frangipani-lined boulevards give it the atmosphere of a French provincial town. The city is situated at what the French called les Quatre Bras (the Four Arms), where two arms of the Mekong meet the Bassac and Tonle Sap tributaries. The city's original name, Chaktomuk, means Four Rivers.

After years of dislocation and disarray, Phnom Penh has regained some of its eccentric charm, with groomed gardens along main boulevards and a well-kept waterfront promenade. Seen from the river, palm trees and pagoda-like spires of Khmer royal buildings rise over French-era shophouses and villas. In the back alleys, the picture is not so bright: scum and garbage strewn down side streets and vacant lots, amputee-beggars, squatters, prostitutes, lawlessness, blackouts. Welcome to Cambodia. Sanitary conditions are poor because of

Must-Sees

M Silver Pagoda: The only accessible part of the Royal Palace, this is the royal chapel. The floor is made of tiles containing real silver (page 355).

M National Museum: Harbors an astonishing wealth of Khmer stone, bronze, and wooden sculpture. Pass through these doors to witness the passage of a great civilization (page 361).

M Tuol Sleng Genocide Museum: A former detention center, now used to document Khmer Rouge atrocities. Chilling and disturbing (page 365).

M Beaches in Sihanoukville: Kick back and catch some rays at Ochateal, with dazzling white sand and clear waters. You can take day trips out to pristine islands (page 392).

M Phnom Penh to Chau Doc by Speedboat: Cruise along a stretch of the Mekong in style, like early French explorers. And it won't cost much, either (page 395).

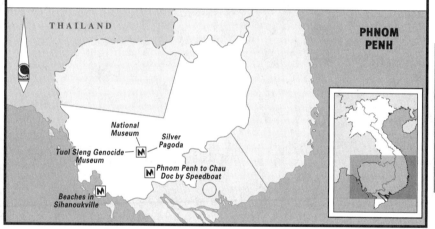

PHNOM PENH

THAILAND

National Museum

Silver Pagoda

Tuol Sleng Genocide Museum

Phnom Penh to Chau Doc by Speedboat

Beaches in Sihanoukville

destroyed water and sewage facilities: Up to 20 percent of all households do not have toilets. When the first monsoon rains hit, the streets are flooded: The sewer system doesn't function, and there's no money to repair water-pumping machinery. There is a chronic lack of education facilities and teachers. Forty-five percent of Phnom Penh's population is under the age of 15, and there are roving bands of street kids, many from the provinces.

Phnom Penh has witnessed rapid—and bizarre—changes of fortune. After Angkor fell to the Siamese in the 15th century, Cambodian King Ponhea Yat founded a new capital at Chaktomuk. This city was soon abandoned as well, and from the mid-17th to mid-19th centuries the Cambodian capital was in Udong, 40 kilometers northwest of Phnom Penh. King Norodom moved the capital to Phnom Penh in 1866. The city is largely a French creation—even the Khmer–style buildings and temples were built under French supervision. Wide boulevards and stately mansions were constructed in the French colonial era, and Phnom Penh quickly became an important commercial center. The city was—and still is—the only major port on the Mekong above the delta; it is navigable by ships of up to 7,000 tons. From Phnom Penh, smaller vessels can navigate upriver to Siem Reap or Kratie.

Phnom Penh

PHNOM PENH

To Battambang

To Udong
(Routes 5,6,7)

Chruoy Changvar
Peninsula

CHRUOY CHANGVAR
(JAPANESE) BRIDGE

Tonle Sap

A CHA XAO ST

47

BAYON HOTEL

HOLIDAY
INTERNATIONAL
HOTEL

CHEZ LIPP
RESTAURANT

FRENCH
EMBASSY

CALMETTE
HOSPITAL

BRITISH EMBASSY

LE SOLEIL
VERT GH

70

CONCORDE
HOTEL

BOENG
KAK GH

CLOUD 9 GH

GH

*Boeng Kak
Lake*

WAT PHNOM

51

SEE "CENTRAL
PHNOM PENH" MAP

BOAT TERMINAL

SISOWATH QUAY

SAMDECH SOTHEAROS BL

NATIONAL
MUSEUM

SILVER

NORODOM BLVD

*Central
Market*

63

MONIVONG BLVD

RAILWAY
STATION

CHARLES DE GAULLE BLVD

181

JULIANA
157

161

169

ORIENTAL

182

SHARE-TAXIS
TO SIHANOUKVILLE

SAIGON BUS

POCHENTONG
BLVD

171

211

NEHRU BLVD

KROM
BLVD

KAMPUCHEA

MAO TSE TUNG BLV

To Pochentong Airport and
Sihanoukville (Routes 3,4)

PHNOM PENH
UNIVERSITY

RUSSIAN EMBASSY
ROYAL PHNOM PENH
PRAYUVONG BUDDHA FACTORY
WAT THAN
EUROPEAN DENTAL CLINIC
JAPANESE EMBASSY
THAI EMBASSY
BAN THAI RESTAURANT
ACCESS MEDICAL SERVICES
CCC
PHNOM PENH GARDEN HOTEL
LAOTIAN EMBASSY
HUA NAM RESTAURANT
VIETNAMESE EMBASSY
INDIAN EMBASSY
BASSAC RESTAURANT
VIETNAM TOURISM
SYDNEY INTERNATIONAL HOTEL
IMC CLINIC
TUOL SLENG HOLOCAUST MUSEUM
CHINESE EMBASSY
Russian Market
OLYMPIC STADIUM
Markets
Olympic Market
BUS STATION
DANG KOR MARKET
PARIS II
INTERCONTINENTAL HOTEL
SHARE-TAXI RANK / BUS STATION
THE OASIS RESTAURANT
MARTINI BAR

NORODOM BLVD
PREAH SIHANOUK BLVD
MAO TSE TUNG BLVD
MONIVONG BLVD
MONIRETH BLVD
VIMEAN SOUR

Tonle Bassac

MONIVONG BRIDGE

To Saigon (Route 1)
To Tonle Bati and Takeo (Route 2)
To Choeung Ek

1 mi
1 km

© AVALON TRAVEL PUBLISHING, INC.

GETTING YOUR BEARINGS

Direction finding in Phnom Penh is completely chaotic: The map is full of streets designated only by numbers. An address may be rendered 112 Rue 106, 112 Street 106, 112 106 Street, or No. 112 Street 106. To avoid confusion, the French-ordered system of 112 Street 106 has been adopted for this guide. Reference is also made to landmarks—for example, "north of Wat Phnom" or "east of Central Market." Sometimes Phnom Penh addresses cover all bases—providing street number, street junction, and local landmark. An example is La Paillote Hotel, Marché Central-No.234, Rue 130-53. The hotel address translates as 234 Street 130 at the corner of Street 53, near the Central Market.

Even-numbered streets generally run east-west, with low numbers starting from the north; odd-numbered roads run north-south, with low numbers starting from the east. Thus you'd expect to find Street 19 running north-south at the east side of Phnom Penh. Easy, huh? The only snag is that half the streets are dead ends, anarchically numbered in semisequential fashion. Boulevards are named, but on these long wide roads you need to know the junction of two streets to get your bearings, or else you could be a kilometer or two off. Phnom Penh stretches some seven kilometers from north to south, and five kilometers from east to west. The designation "Eo" in an address stands for *étage zéro*, French for ground floor. Thus 4 Eo Street 118 means the ground floor at number 4 on Street 118.

In the 1970s and 1980s the Lon Nol regime, the Khmer Rouge, and the Vietnamese wiped King Sihanouk's royalist names off the map. After the triumphant return of Sihanouk in 1991 and his crowning in 1993, boulevard names began to revert from the revolutionary and Communist heroes imposed by the Vietnamese to the royalist names of the 1960s. This process is ongoing and can be very confusing. Some businesses use the old boulevard names, not having the time, money, or inclination to change signs or business cards.

It's best to navigate by landmarks, as even locals are hazy about the location of certain streets. Key landmarks include Wat Phnom, Chruoy Changvar Bridge, Central Market building, the Royal Palace, National Museum, Hotel Sofitel Cambodiana, and Independence Monument.

Here are some name changes for boulevards:

Name from 1980s	Post-1993 Name
Achar Mean Blvd.	Monivong Blvd.
Quay Karl Marx	Sisowath Quay
Lenin Blvd.	Samdech Sothearos Blvd.
Sivutha Blvd.	Preah Sihanouk Blvd.
Tousamouth Blvd.	Norodom Blvd.
Achar Hemcheay Blvd.	Charles de Gaulle Blvd.
Kampuchea Vietnam Blvd	Kampuchea Krom Blvd.
USSR Blvd.	Pochentong Blvd. (a.k.a. Russian Federation Blvd.)
Keo Mony Blvd.	Mao Tse Tung Blvd.
Pokambor Blvd.	Monireth Blvd.

In the late 1960s prosperous Phnom Penh had a population of perhaps 600,000. Almost two-thirds of the population consisted of Vietnamese and Chinese merchants and workers. The Chinese, Vietnamese, and Khmer ethnic groups occupied their own distinct neighborhoods. Business and trade congregated in streets of their own, with sections devoted to basket-making and silversmithing. By 1975, swollen with refugees from civil war, the city had a population of more than two million.

On April 17, 1975, Phnom Penh became a ghost town, emptied out by the Khmer Rouge within 48 hours. During the 1975–1979 reign of terror, the city's inhabitants were mostly soldiers and prisoners. By 1978 there were only 15,000–30,000 people in the city. The Khmer Rouge painted over all signs in Phnom Penh—traffic signs, advertising signs, markers of any kind. Wrecked cars lay where they were abandoned in 1975. All shops and hotels were closed. A number of buildings were blown up or demolished, including the Catholic Cathedral and the National Bank. Up to two-thirds of the city's houses were damaged. The plumbing system was destroyed.

People started streaming back to the city shortly after the Vietnamese takeover in January 1979; more than 100,000 returned in that year alone. The current population is around 1.5 million.

Phnom Penh was the main base of operation for UNTAC in 1992–1993. The place was swamped with U.N. personnel. Thousands of white UNTAC Land Cruisers, jeeps, and trucks created traffic jams on Phnom Penh's boulevards. After UNTAC came a rush of businesspeople—Thai bankers and Japanese businessmen—to make deals in the fragile peace under the new coalition government. The Japanese funded a major renovation of the Phnom Penh port. Phnom Penh, like the rest of Cambodia, is in a boom-or-bust situation. If peace reigns, tourists and businesspeople come in and the economy does well.

PLANNING YOUR TIME

You need at least 1.5 days to cover the main sights: the National Museum, Silver Pagoda, Tuol Sleng Genocide Museum—and perhaps the Killing Fields memorial if you have more time. Exploring at night is somewhat limited by a mugging factor. Individual travelers often hire a moto driver for the day to get around Phnom Penh. Another option is for several travelers to team up and hire a car with driver. Others take in the sights on an organized tour by minibus, arranged through hotels. You can stroll around some areas—such as the pleasant waterfront of Phnom Penh, near the Royal Palace.

Sights

The city's most exclusive real estate is toward the Tonle Sap River, with French villas and institutions in the north, and the Royal Palace, Silver Pagoda, and other traces of the former royal city to the south. Options for touring include walking, bicycling, or hiring a cyclo or motorcycle. If bicycling, watch out at uncontrolled intersections—traffic is chaotic in peak hours. Apart from the more formal sights described here, the markets around Phnom Penh hold the greatest visual and people-watching interest. If you get a case of "museum feet," hop on a bicycle and explore the boulevards.

THE ROYAL PALACE

Since the return of King Norodom Sihanouk in November 1991, the palace has been closed to public viewing. The gates are thrown open for three consecutive days in early November, when the compound becomes a kind of fairground. The rest of the year the palace is off-limits, although it is possible to peek at the palace from various side gates. It occupies a huge block between Streets 184 and 240, facing Samdech Sothearos Boulevard.

The Royal Palace was built in stages in the

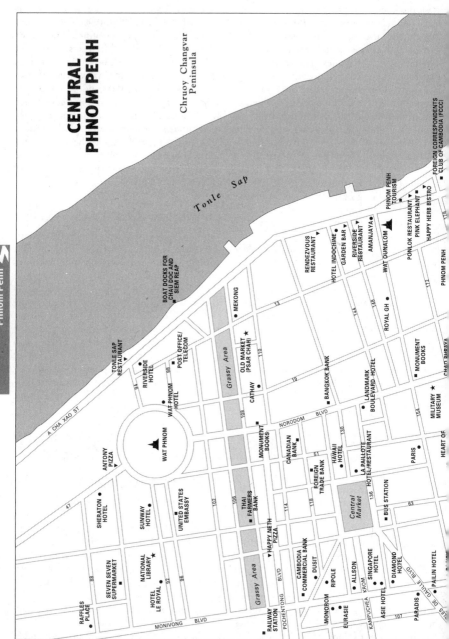

CENTRAL PHNOM PENH

Chruoy Changvar Peninsula

Tonle Sap

Phnom Penh

© AVALON TRAVEL PUBLISHING, INC.

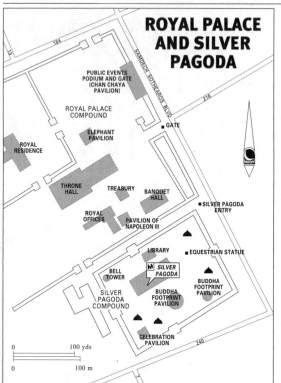

ROYAL PALACE AND SILVER PAGODA

PUBLIC EVENTS PODIUM AND GATE (CHAN CHAYA PAVILION)

ROYAL PALACE COMPOUND

ELEPHANT PAVILION

ROYAL RESIDENCE

GATE

THRONE HALL

TREASURY

BANQUET HALL

SILVER PAGODA ENTRY

ROYAL OFFICES

PAVILION OF NAPOLEON III

LIBRARY

EQUESTRIAN STATUE

BELL TOWER

SILVER PAGODA

SILVER PAGODA COMPOUND

BUDDHA FOOTPRINT PAVILION

BUDDHA FOOTPRINT PAVILION

CELEBRATION PAVILION

SAMDECH SOTHEAROS BLVD.

0   100 yds

0   100 m

© AVALON TRAVEL PUBLISHING, INC.

Depending on the mood of the guards, you might be able to peek through the gates. Buildings at the palace include the Royal Residence (Khemarin Palace), built in 1930; an Officers' Club, built in 1958 for officers of the royal guard; and Phochani Hall, built in 1913 for performances of royal dance. The Throne Hall, topped by a four-headed tower (inspired by Angkor's Bayon Temple), was completed in 1917 under King Sisowath. The glazed tiles on the layered roof were added in 1993 during a German-funded renovation project.

The hall, once used for coronations, is now employed for traditional ceremonies and official receptions. In the center are thrones for the king and queen, and seats for court officials. The walls are decorated with *Ramayana* murals. The king and queen were once ferried around for royal processions in sedan chairs or gilded wooden chariots, and sometimes by elephant. An elephant-mounting pavilion is just north of the Throne Hall; elephants were previously stabled within the grounds.

From the barred gate along the alley entryway to the Silver Pagoda you can see an ornate gray French pavilion. This was originally presented by Emperor Napoleon III to Empress Eugenie during the Suez Canal opening celebrations in 1869. The prefabricated summer house was then dismantled and packed off to Cambodia as a gift to King Norodom. Erected at the Royal Palace in 1876, the structure was renovated by a group of French volunteers in 1990. The Royal Offices stand just behind this building, built in 1948 and used as a residence by the regent. Beyond you can see the outlines of the Throne Hall.

early 20th century over the site of Banteay Kev, a 19th-century citadel. A number of the present buildings were built in concrete under French supervision, emulating previous Khmer–style wooden structures. Between 1970 and 1979 the palace was looted and sustained considerable damage. The most accessible feature of the Royal Palace is Chan Chaya Pavilion (Pavilion of Dancers), which fronts Samdech Sothearos Boulevard. Built in 1913, it served as a public events podium, a venue for music and dance performances on special occasions, and for speeches by the king. King Sihanouk put the podium to royal use again for the celebration of the 40th anniversary of independence in 1993. Under the pavilion is the main entrance gate to the palace, which is closely guarded.

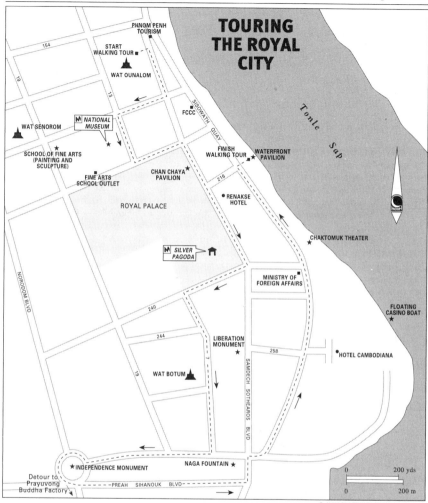

TOURING
THE ROYAL
CITY

© AVALON TRAVEL PUBLISHING, INC.

SILVER PAGODA

The Silver Pagoda is the royal chapel, situated within the Royal Palace grounds but walled off in a separate enclosure. The pagoda was built in 1962, replacing an earlier 1892 version. After suffering damage and neglect in the Pol Pot era, it is cracked and peeling. The temple is intermittently closed because of restoration work, ongoing since 1993. The Silver Pagoda takes its name from the estimated 5,000 silver tiles covering the floor of the main temple. Each tile is made from a kilogram of silver. Although plundered by the Khmer Rouge, the Silver Pagoda contains some superb Buddha statuary; a few artifacts from the royal collection are displayed in glass cases.

Near the central dais in the main temple is a standing Buddha, made of pure gold and weighing in at 75 kilograms. The Buddha isn't simply

TOURING THE ROYAL CITY

The southern sector of Phnom Penh close to the Tonle Sap River exudes a strong royal Khmer presence, with a wealth of Cambodian traditional architecture. The city was once rich in temples—many were destroyed under the Khmer Rouge, but some are being reconstructed. This tour starts at Wat Ounalom, opposite the Phnom Penh Tourism Office.

Wat Ounalom is a Mahanikai Buddhist temple and highly respected institute of learning, with 50 monks in residence; before 1975 there were 500 monks here. This is the residence of the supreme patriarch of the Mahanikai sect. The temple was founded in the 15th century; a large number of its buildings were destroyed under Pol Pot, including the library. The temple has since been partially restored. The compound contains two residences, and a three-floor building that functions as a temple; the interiors are stark and bare. On the ground floor is a marble Buddha from Myanmar (Burma)—smashed by the Khmer Rouge, but pieced together again in 1979. On the second floor is a brass statue of the patriarch of Cambodian Buddhism, Somdech Huot Tat, who was murdered by the Khmer Rouge. The statue, made in 1971, was flung into the river, but it was retrieved in 1979. On the third floor the walls depict scenes from the Jataka Tales.

From Wat Ounalom you can skirt round past the **National Museum.** The museum is notable not only for its outstanding exhibits but also for its superb traditional-style architecture. To do justice to the place, you really

need to spend several hours. In this area is the Ecole des Beaux Arts (School of Fine Arts), where students often work on reproductions of famous Khmer artifacts. The souvenir and gift shops in the surrounding blocks are especially good for paintings, wood sculptures, and crafts. The School of Fine Arts has its own retail outlet.

Back on Samdech Sothearos Boulevard you can cruise past **Chan Chaya Pavilion,** which doubles as a front gate to the Royal Palace and a public events podium. Above the pavilion is a huge portrait of King Sihanouk. The Royal Palace is closed to the public—what you glimpse through the gates is about it, unless you arrive in November when the palace is thrown open for three days. At the southern end of the palace grounds, you can drop in and visit the **Silver Pagoda.** Skirt the walls of the palace and head south to Wat Botum.

Buddhas and Bayon Heads

Wat Botum is known as the "Temple of the Lotus Blossoms"—the original site was a small island surrounded by a lotus-filled pond. This temple is the center of the Thammayut (royalist) sect of Buddhism in Cambodia. The royalist sect has been revived since the return of Sihanouk; about 85 monks now live at Wat Botum. In July 1992, more than 150 bonzes (monks) were ordained here. At the front of the temple is an unusual cluster of stupas with Bayon-style four-headed tops; the ceremonial stupas hold the ashes of members of the royal family.

life-sized—it conforms to the vital statistics of King Norodom. The image was made in 1907 in the royal workshops, inlaid with more than 9,000 precious stones, including diamonds studded on the forehead and palms. Companion statues include a silver and a bronze Buddha.

On the central dais sits a crystal Buddha image, copied from Pra Keo, the Emerald Buddha, at Bangkok's Grand Palace. The Emerald Buddha is regarded throughout Southeast Asia as a powerful talisman, imbued with miraculous powers. The inspiration for the Silver Pagoda is believed to be Bangkok's Wat Pra Keo. In Khmer, the Silver Pagoda is known as Preah Vihear Keo Morakot because it houses the Emerald Buddha knockoff.

At the rear of the dais is a standing Buddha made of Italian marble. Right at the back of the pagoda is a large marble Buddha in the Earth Witness pose, a gift from Myanmar (Burma). Beside it is a litter used for coronations—it was carried by a dozen men. More coronation regalia and dozens of smaller statues are displayed here.

Opposite Wat Botum in a park is the **Liberation Monument,** carved from Angkor marble by the staff of the School of Fine Arts in 1989 to commemorate the 1979 liberation of Phnom Penh by Vietnamese troops. Proceed south and turn onto Preah Sihanouk Boulevard to see some of the best-preserved colonial mansions and manicured gardens in Phnom Penh. Over the boulevard to the west is the **Independence Monument,** looming like a kind of Cambodian Arc de Triomphe. Also called the Victory Monument, this Khmer-style *prasat* (tower) was built in 1958 to commemorate independence from France, but it has since assumed the role of a war memorial. Wreath-laying ceremonies honor the dead. Like the towers of Angkor Wat and the four-headed spires of the Bayon, the monument is a national logo.

From the Independence Monument you can detour about 300 meters south to the **Prayuvong Buddha Factory.** In the grounds of Wat Prayuvong, a neighborhood of workshops produces statuary and "spare parts" used in repairing temples smashed by the Khmer Rouge. The workshops turn out stupas and Buddhist artifacts, including gaudy concrete Buddhas, Bayon heads, *nagas,* and mythological figures. You can walk around the various workshops and watch the artisans at work.

High Tea
Back on Preah Sihanouk Boulevard, head east past the *naga* fountain and along Samdech Sothearos Boulevard to the **Hotel Cambodiana.**

The Cambodiana is a peculiar structure: It looks as if the architect decided at the last minute to cap a European building with a pseudo-Khmer tile roof. Drop into the foyer to see the huge wooden model of the Bayon. A small gift shop sells books on Cambodia. High tea at the Cambodiana is held 1500–1700—stuff yourself with sandwiches, pastries, fruit, and drinks for around $5; live classical music will ease your digestion. A plunge into the swimming pool will set you back $5. Khmer–style roofing also caps the nearby Ministry of Foreign Affairs, which looks like a converted wat, and Chaktomuk Theater.

Waterfront Pavilion
Locals turn out for a stroll at the end of the day past the tiny slope-roofed pavilion fronting the Tonle Sap River, opposite the Royal Palace Gates. At sunset impromptu picnickers frequent the place; police pursue food vendors up and down Sisowath Quay. Cyclo drivers arrive for river baths, and roving photographers work the crowds. This is an excellent place to mingle. There are two shrines for offerings of garlands of jasmine and coconuts spiked with incense sticks and lotus buds. North of the pavilion are many sidewalk vendors. For drinks, try a beer stall on the banks of the Tonle Sap. For a more refined drink, the Foreign Correspondents Club of Cambodia (FCCC) top-floor bar is a colonial-era throwback, with swishing fans and elegant furnishings. The bar affords great views over the river.

Phnom Penh

In the courtyard of the Silver Pagoda compound are four large stupas (shrines) built by the Norodom family. The original temple arose during the reign of King Norodom—the stupa to the northeast is dedicated to him, and there's an equestrian statue of the king nearby. Actually, it's a statue of Napoleon III with Norodom's head. Three other stupas in the compound are dedicated to Norodom royal family members; the stupa to the southwest commemorates Sihanouk's favorite daughter, who died of leukemia in 1953. The others honor Sihanouk's father, King Norodom Suramarit, and the 19th-century king, Ang Duong. Also in the courtyard is a bell tower, a library that once contained manuscripts on palm leaves, and a pavilion used for celebrations by the royal family. There are two Buddha footprint pavilions—one footprint is made of bronze and comes from Sri Lanka.

Running the length of the walls enclosing the compound are 600 meters of covered galleries. Starting at the east gate and proceeding in a clockwise direction, the galleries depict

TOURING THE FRENCH QUARTER

Might as well go straight to the heart of Phnom Penh: step right up and meet Madame Penh herself. She's the revered figure encased in a tiny shrine on the top of **Wat Phnom,** the temple on the hill overlooking the city from the north end of Norodom Boulevard.

Wat Phnom is the oldest temple in town. Legend has it that in the 14th century a wealthy widow, Madame Penh, discovered four statues of Buddha in a tree trunk that washed up on the riverbank. It turned out that these Buddhas originally came from Laos and were miraculously carried downstream by a flood. With the help of villagers, Madame Penh built a small pagoda to house the images. Phnom means "hill," so this is the hill of Madame Penh. The name was later transferred to the settlement that grew up around the hill.

Madame Penh looks very Buddha-like herself—big eyebrows, big earlobes, and earrings. The residents of Phnom Penh make offerings of fruit, flowers, incense, and money at this small shrine. They come to this and other small temples on the hill to pray for protection on journeys, success in exams or the lottery, or healing from sickness.

The eastern stairway is the most dramatic approach to this sacred area. There are two huge five-headed *nagas* sliding down the stairs here, beggars and bird sellers line the steps (aggressive child beggars are rife). Purchased birds are released for luck or merit making, and are quickly recaptured. At the top of the steps is the main temple; out back is the tiny Madame Penh shrine, and to the south side a massive stupas. The stupas is said to contain the ashes of Ponhea Yat, the post-Angkorian king who made Phnom Penh his capital.

Eventually Madame Penh's pagoda was replaced by larger temples, built in 1806, 1894, and 1926. The main temple houses a resplendent seated Buddha. The exterior features painted Angkor *apsaras* in relief; a series of frescoes on the life of Buddha cover interior walls. Worshippers make their rounds, leaving incense at various shrines or offering food for blessing before it's taken home to the family table. The Chinese and Vietnamese residents of Phnom Penh have constructed a shrine off to the side. Raw meat and eggs are sometimes placed in the mouths of two lion statues here, near a burner for Chinese–style paper money.

On the north slope of Wat Phnom once stood a mini-zoo with elephant rides. Now there's a white elephant in the form of an enormous *chedi* (stupas) scuttled halfway through construction when it was discovered the foundations were only 10 meters deep, instead of 25. Amid charges of fraud, corruption, and graft, plans for a 50-meter-high *chedi* were abandoned after a million dollars had been spent on the project, intended to house a sacred bone of the Buddha. There are plans to turn the site into a museum for Buddhist scriptures. On the south slope is a plaque inscribed "Traite Franco-Siamois 1907 Battambang-Siem Reap-Sisopon, Consul de France 1903," commemorating the French-orchestrated return of Siem Reap and Battambang provinces to Cambodia; the French had ceded these same territories to the Thais in 1867. Opposite Wat Phnom to the northeast is a building that served as UNTAC Headquarters from 1992 to 1993.

French Villas

Proceeding from Wat Phnom north on Street 47 (a.k.a. Rue de France or Vithei France) you encounter a string of villas—the old French residential area, with structures under renovation for use by companies like TNT and Castrol. Some villas here are in great condition, others decayed and crumbling. Turn right on Street 80 toward the Tonle Sap River and follow the banks up to the bridge.

Chruoy Changvar Bridge was built in 1965 and destroyed 10 years later. Until 1993 the initial spans jutted out from both sides of the Tonle Sap. Enterprising stall vendors set up impromptu restaurants at the very edge of the Phnom Penh side of the blown-up bridge, and motorcyclists would run out for an afternoon snack. The bridge was reconstructed with Japanese aid and reopened in 1994 as the Cambodian-Japanese Friendship Bridge. It leads to fishing villages, farmland, and a popular strip of restaurants on the Chruoy Changvar Peninsula.

Due west of the bridge, along Street 72 is the **School of Fine Arts** where Khmer dance and music are taught. It might be possible to drop in and observe children being trained in the delicate Khmer dance movements; there are sometimes rehearsals of longer Ramayana pieces here. To one side is an acrobatic ring where young students train for trapeze, acrobatic, and juggling acts.

Returning to the big roundabout to the east, you will notice a bizarre piece of statuary mounted on a dias in the middle of a park at the roundabout. It is the **Knotted Gun**—a huge handgun made from melted-down firearms—and the barrel tied in a knot. Knot for Use is the message here: the statue was erected by Phnom Penh officials to symbolize a crackdown on gun use and stiffer firearms laws. An odd way to get your message out, but then you have to allow for the fact that this is Cambodia, where people sleep with handguns under the pillow, just in case.

Back on Monivong Boulevard is the **French Embassy** compound where foreigners took refuge after the Khmer Rouge takeover of Phnom Penh on April 17, 1975. Some 800 foreigners and 600 Cambodians crowded onto the grounds; meanwhile, Phnom Penh's entire population was forced into the countryside. The French vice-consul was informed that if he did not expel all the Cambodians within 48 hours, the foreigners would forfeit their lives: the Khmer Rouge recognized no diplomatic privilege. Only Cambodian women married to foreigners could remain, and a number of marriages were hastily arranged to safeguard some of the Cambodian women. The Cambodians left the embassy quietly—very few survived. Within two weeks, the foreigners were driven in trucks to the Thai border and released. Among those released was a Cambodian child born on the embassy grounds—the child's mother gave him to a young French couple when she was forced to leave the compound. After terms as an orphanage, ammunition dump, and a place for squatters, the embassy compound was returned to the French in 1991, when diplomatic relations were restored. The building was completely gutted and restored, with the addition of landscaped gardens, and the embassy reopened with a champagne toast to Bastille Day in 1995.

From the French Embassy, head south. You might want to detour to Boeng Kak Lake, accessed from Street 86. Here you pass a mosque and the Cambodian Islamic Institute. There are some cheap guesthouses and shanty dwellings fronting the lake. The northern part of Boeng Kak Lake contains a large shantytown district with taxi girls called Tuol Kork.

(continued on next page)

Phnom Penh

TOURING THE FRENCH QUARTER (cont'd)

The Royal

Moving south, you'll reach the Royal Hotel on palm-lined Street 92. If on a bicycle, you may have to dismount and wheel your bicycle as it's one-way traffic here. The Royal was originally constructed as part of a chain of flashy hotels by the Societé des Grands Hôtels Indochinois. It was the best-known tourist hotel in Phnom Penh in the 1920s and 1930s—well-heeled travelers motoring up to Angkor or en route to Bangkok or Saigon would stay here. In the 1970s it was the preferred residence of journalists covering the war. In the early 1990s the hotel served as an elaborate brothel, with a bar full of Vietnamese taxi girls. Singapore's DBS Land group, which owns the Raffles Hotel, signed a $25-million deal to renovate and expand the 200-room hotel.

The **Bibliothèque Nationale** (National Library), built in 1924, is not much to look at and has very few books. What is remarkable is that it has any books at all. When the Khmer Rouge moved into Phnom Penh they intended to wipe out recorded history. They tore up books to make cigarettes and hurled volumes into the street. Some 20 percent of the collection was destroyed. Pigs were raised at the front of the library to supply meat to Chinese experts staying next door at the Royal.

After the Khmer Rouge were ousted in 1979, people returning to Phnom Penh took cartloads of books to their homes—some to read, some to sell, some to use as wrapping paper. The library reopened in 1980 with bare shelves. It had to rely on foreign donations in the form of books, equipment, and training. Today, there are fewer than 200,000 titles—139,000 in Khmer, 23,000 in French, and 17,500 in English. Library staff hope to access works written in Khmer by importing microfilms of French collections.

Cross the road to Street 96, and continue past the Ecole Française and you'll reach a premises on the corner that used to be the Cercle Sportif, the French sports club, with tennis courts, gym, and swimming pool still in operation when it mutated into the International Youth Club. Then the site was purchased by the Americans: to be turned into the new U.S. Embassy.

The Waterfront

Continue east on Street 96. Skirting Wat Phnom, take the road to the south of the wat, which passes between two children's parks, and turn left on Street 108. This district is part of the former French administrative area, with huge grassy strips in the middle of wide boulevards. The architecture is a study in contrasts—finely refurbished colonial mansions with satellite dishes on the rooftops juxtaposed with colonial edifices now blackened by charcoal and smoke.

At the far east end of Street 108 used to be a busy dock area—the action all moved further north. There are lots of warehouses for rice and other products in the strip along the waterfront. Many of these commercial enterprises were previously run by Chinese and Vietnamese—their presence is still apparent in the area. You can still see large loads of rice, bags of coconuts, or sacks of charcoal being transported around by cyclo or motorized three-wheeler.

To see more port activity, hire a sampan or other vessel. Boat rentals are available north of Chruoy Changvar Bridge. A covered boat is a good idea to keep you and your camera sheltered from the harsh sun. A one- or two-hour boat trip offers a unique perspective of the Royal Palace and other waterfront landmarks.

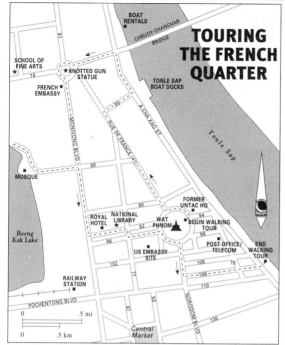

TOURING THE FRENCH QUARTER

BOAT RENTALS
CHRUOY CHANGVAR BRIDGE
SCHOOL OF FINE ARTS
★ 70
★ KNOTTED GUN STATUE
FRENCH EMBASSY
TONLE SAP BOAT DOCKS
TOURING THE FRENCH QUARTER
MONIVONG BLVD
80
A CHA XAO ST
RUE DE FRANCE (T)
Tonle Sap
86
MOSQUE
90
FORMER UNTAC HQ
94
Boeng Kak Lake
ROYAL HOTEL
NATIONAL LIBRARY
92
WAT PHNOM
BEGIN WALKING TOUR
98
96
US EMBASSY SITE
POST OFFICE/ TELECOM
END WALKING TOUR
102
106
78
RAILWAY STATION
108
110
POCHENTONG BLVD
53
67
NORODOM BLVD
130
0   .5 mi
0   .5 km
Central Market
© AVALON TRAVEL PUBLISHING, INC.

178 and 184. It was designed by French archaeologist and painter George Groslier and constructed in traditional style by Cambodian craftsmen in 1917–1918 as an annex to the Ecole des Beaux Arts. The museum first opened in 1920. During the Pol Pot era, the museum was left derelict and bats moved in. Some two million of them. An Australian bat expert identified three species of bats living in the rooftop of the museum, including a tiny critter responsible for pollinating durians. The Australian government, the Australian National Gallery, and Australian corporate sponsors worked to document the National Museum collection, train staff, introduce modern management and marketing techniques, and take on the bats. Because the bats consumed huge numbers of insects, a solution was settled upon: to build a secondary ceiling below the roof, preventing bat guano (and lice) from falling on museum exhibits—and visitors. Work was completed at a cost of $500,000 but apparently failed in its objective to keep the bats away from the exhibits. Every month, three truckloads of bat guano were removed from the museum roof and sold as fertiliser. But the lingering musty odor of bat guano and the potential damage to exhibits from acidic droppings became too much for the museum overseers. They finally evicted the bats and sealed the roof off.

After periods of chaos and bat occupation, the museum is on its feet again. The museum is small, but harbors an astonishing wealth of Khmer stone, bronze, and wooden sculpture. The imposing wooden doors to the museum, which weigh more than a ton, were made by teachers and students from the Ecole des Beaux Arts. Passing through these doors you can witness the passage of a great civilization—as great as that of ancient Egypt,

episodes from the Reamker. The murals are in bad condition from water damage and neglect—a Polish government group is restoring them.

The Silver Pagoda used to be under the control of the Ministry of Culture, but it is now under the aegis of the palace. Entry fees and opening times chop and change—you have to negotiate with guards at the eastern entry gate. Because of restoration work, entry is not guaranteed—you might have to try several times before you get in. Guards may charge $2 to enter the grounds. It should be open daily except Monday, 0730–1130 and 1430–1700. Remove your shoes when entering the Silver Pagoda; an attendant may require you to deposit your camera at the entrance.

NATIONAL MUSEUM

The National Museum is housed in a magnificent russet pavilion on Street 13 between streets

Phnom Penh

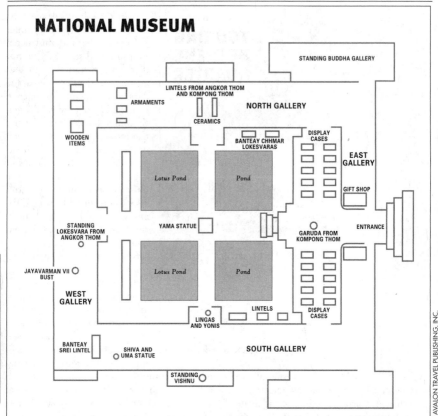

NATIONAL MUSEUM

Greece, or China. A set of galleries arrayed around four lotus ponds, the National Museum is a tranquil and relaxing place.

The museum is open daily 0800–1130 and 1400–1730; possibly closed on public holidays. Lunch hours tend to be flexible if you push your case. Entry fee is $2; an English- or French-speaking guide costs $2 for a one-hour tour, $10 for groups. There are brief labels in Khmer and French and sometimes in English; if you want more details, hire a guide. Scaled-down copies of well-known Khmer pieces are on sale at the museum gift shop, the pieces most likely created by students at the adjacent School of Fine Arts. A number of handicraft shops in the area also sell these artifacts.

The description here of the museum's exhibits may not be precise for a number of reasons. Major pieces may be on tour to Paris, New York, or Tokyo, under special arrangement with the museum. The museum's collection will undoubtedly change as renovation proceeds, and there are special exhibitions staged. In 2001, there was an exhibition of stolen statuary that had been returned to Cambodia from abroad.

There are more than 400 works in the collection, including massive stone heads from Angkor brought to the museum as late as 1994 for protection from theft. A conservator from the Australian National Gallery, who decided to tackle a flooding problem in the basement, came across 120 unopened crates in the dusty light. Boxes of rare artifacts were rushed by road from ancient temple sites around the country by the Ecole Française d'Extrême Orient for safekeeping as civil war escalated in 1970, and they were never unpacked. As the museum's collection is documented and photographed, and computer records are compiled, more of Cambodia's treasures may surface. In 1992 a special exhibition of 35 stone and bronze pieces was arranged in Australia, which led to pledges by the Australian government for assistance at the National Museum.

Of special interest at the National Museum are pieces from the Angkor region, moved to this location for safekeeping. If you're going to Angkor, a visit to the museum before (and after) will bring the place to life. Angkor has hardly a single Buddha head left in place, as most have been looted. Small objects are likewise nowhere on display at Angkor, but in the east gallery of the National Museum you'll find display cases filled with exquisite smaller pieces. These include delicate bronze oil lamps and incense holders, some shaped like lotuses, as well as jewelry, silver spittoons, bronze spoons, fine bronze Buddhas, heads, hands, fragments, and such rarities as a small quartz linga from Angkor Thom. The National Museum itself is not immune from headhunters—during the confusion of the 1970s, several pieces were stolen.

The museum is arrayed around a beautiful garden courtyard. At the center of four ponds is a seated statue, originally from the Terrace of the Leper King at Angkor Thom. French archaeologist Groslier noticed marks on the head of the statue and had it removed to Phnom Penh. A concrete copy was left at Angkor Thom, but even that was subsequently decapitated (a few times) by daft art thieves. The sandstone statue in the National Museum is one of the most celebrated images in Khmer art. While some identify the statue as Yama (Judge of the Dead in Hindu legend) or a naked ascetic (possibly an incarnation of Shiva), others speculate it's a likeness of Yasovarman I, the Angkor king who reigned 889–910 and reputedly died of leprosy.

Large sculptures in the courtyard galleries are arranged haphazardly. The south gallery contains pre-Angkor pieces, including a rare 6th-century eight-armed Vishnu from Takeo, and a few colossal lingas on yoni bases. The west gallery features sculpture and lintels from the 9th- through 13th-century Angkor period and the 13th- through 14th-century Bayon period. In the north gallery are wooden pieces from the 15th–19th centuries, some 16th-century armaments, and a display of ceramics.

Some Angkor-related pieces to look for include the following (again, bear in mind that these and other prime pieces could be out of the country for special exhibit abroad).

Banteay Srei Pediment

In the southwest corner of the museum is one of the finest examples of Khmer narrative sculpture before Angkor Wat. It is a 10th-century pediment—a large sandstone triangular decoration above a doorway—from Banteay Srei. Only six such pediments are known to have survived: Four are at Banteay Srei, northeast of Angkor; the fifth is here; the sixth was removed by the French and sits in the Musée Guimet in Paris. The National Museum piece shows a scene from the great Hindu epic, the *Mahabharata,* with Bhima battling Duryodhana.

A footnote here: The Musée Guimet in Paris holds one of the finest collections of Khmer artifacts in the world, second only to Phnom Penh's National Museum. Many large pieces were floated down the Tonle Sap River and removed to Paris in the late 1800s and early 1900s for "safekeeping" by artist-explorer Louis Delaporte and others. The Musée Guimet showcases Asian art from Tibet to Cambodia. When the museum reopened in 2001 after a $50 million face-lift, the front entrance unveiled a 13-ton Khmer *naga* statue, reassembled from sections—and not seen on display since an exposition in 1878. Makes you wonder how on earth a 13-ton statue could make its way from Angkor to Paris in the 1870s.

Shiva and Uma

Close to the Banteay Srei pediment is a small sandstone image of Shiva with his consort

Phnom Penh

Uma, believed to have been sculpted in the 10th century. The statue once presided over the south sanctuary of Banteay Srei Temple; a French army officer removed the image to Phnom Penh in 1914. Uma's head was lopped off and stolen from the National Museum during the 1970s. Earlier photographs of the complete piece reveal that the missing head resembles Shiva's, but on a smaller scale.

Jayavarman VII

Near the center of the west gallery is a magnificent sandstone bust of Jayavarman VII, the great

Uma's head was stolen in the 1970s.

© NATIONAL MUSEUM, PHNOM PENH

Angkor king who ruled 1181–1218. The statue comes from Siem Reap and is sculpted in 12th- and 13th-century Bayon style. Jayavarman's eyes are downcast; the arms are missing, but presumably the king is sitting in a meditative pose. Portraiture was one of the great achievements of the Khmers. In the same area is a portrait head of a younger-looking Jayavarman VII, found in 1958 at Kompong Svay, 105 kilometers east of Angkor. A kneeling statue in this area, with a headdress made up of rings of lotus petals, is thought to depict one of Jayavarman VII's wives. Another huge piece in this part of the museum is a two-meter-high standing Lokesvara from the Gate of the Dead at Angkor Thom, dating from the 12th–13th centuries.

Coming back to the portrait head of Jayavarman VII, found in 1958: This is perhaps the best-known icon of Khmer art. In January 2000, another spectacular find was made in the same area of Kompong Svay, where the head had been found. Looters abandoned a large sandstone piece—

heads of Lokesvara at the Bayon

© MICHAEL BUCKLEY

either because it was too heavy or did not look valuable enough, or both. French archaeologist Christophe Pottier, from the EFEO (Ecole Française d'Extrême Orient), came across it. Although it resembled a boulder, hauled upright the 150-kilogram stone more resembled a human torso seated in a meditation posture, albeit without arms or legs. Pottier took a cast from the neck area and went to the National Museum. The cast matched one head perfectly—the portrait head of Jayavarman VII. Staff are still deciding whether to reunite body and head. At least they now have that choice.

Woodcarving

Most elaborate woodwork from Angkor has completely disappeared, including the wooden structures of the Royal Palace. At the northwest corner of the museum is a small section with wood (particularly teak) items from the 15th–19th centuries. These give an idea of the considerable skills of Khmer woodcarvers. Items on display include a royal boat, wooden temple ornaments, and weaving looms. Also in the north gallery is a display of armaments, and ethnology and ceramics sections.

Angkor Thom Lintel

At the center of the north gallery are two sandstone lintels (decorative elements used above doorways). One is an 11th-century piece from Kompong Thom, depicting a battle between Krishna and the *naga* serpent-king Kaliya. The second lintel, from Angkor Thom, also depicts a scene from Hindu mythology. Both lintels reflect the perfection of sculptural techniques and fluid florid forms in sandstone that prompted several early Western theorists to conjecture the Khmers had borrowed elements from Italian sculpture—in fact, they predated it.

Banteay Chhmar Lokesvaras

At the northeast side of the courtyard are two reconstructed walls with bas-reliefs that feature a 10-armed Lokesvara and a six-armed Lokesvara. These were looted stone-by-stone from Banteay Chhmar, intercepted in Thailand, and returned in 2000 to Cambodia and reas-

VISIONS OF VISHNU

On your far right as you enter the National Museum is a fragment of a huge bronze head of Vishnu (assuming that the piece is not on international tour somewhere). Undoubtedly one of the greatest bronzes in Southeast Asia, the Vishnu figure was cast using the lost-wax method—an achievement on par with the casting skills of the ancient Greeks or Romans. The original statue is estimated to have been six meters long; it presumably showed the four-armed Vishnu reclining on the serpent Ananta, pondering the future of the new world about to be born. The facial features were once inlaid with precious metal and gems.

Chinese chronicler Zhou Daguan, who visited Angkor in the 13th century as envoy to Timur Khan, left the only description of the original Vishnu, which functioned as a fountain: "At the center of the Eastern Lake stands a stone tower, with dozens of stone chambers. In it lies a recumbent bronze Buddha, from whose navel flows a steady stream of water." Zhou Daguan mistook the type of statue (it's not a Buddha) and the location (not the eastern lake but the western)—which is probably just as well since it foiled treasure hunters for centuries.

Incredibly, the location of the fabled statue was finally divined in a dream. Following the advice of a Siem Reap resident who had a vision of Vishnu in a dream, French archaeologists excavated an island-temple in the Western Baray Reservoir, reaching the head of Vishnu in 1936.

sembled here. These Lokesvara bas-reliefs are extremely rare in Angkorian art. A 32-armed Lokesvara and a faded 20-armed Lokesvara remain on-site at Banteay Chhmar ruins in far northwest Cambodia.

⊠ TUOL SLENG GENOCIDE MUSEUM

This chilling place has been dubbed "Auschwitz on the Mekong." Tuol Sleng and Auschwitz are indeed remarkably similar and remarkably

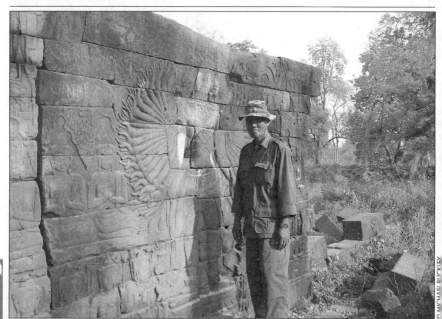

A 32-armed deity Lokesvara is depicted in this ancient bas-relief at Banteay Chhmar.

sickening. Genocidal purges targeting those with racial, religious, or other differences are no different today—witness the "ethnic cleansing" in Bosnia, Tibet, and Rwanda. What stands out in Cambodia is the sheer scale of the operation. More than 1.5 million people were slaughtered under Pol Pot's genocidal regime. And not one of those former Khmer Rouge leaders responsible has been brought to justice (they claim they did not know what was going on).

Tuol Sleng, also known as Security Prison 21 (S-21), is a former high school transformed into a detention and interrogation center. Cambodians and their families accused of being "traitors" were brought to S-21. An estimated 14,000–20,000 inmates passed through Tuol Sleng and were tortured to death or killed by summary execution, either here or at Choeung Ek. Mass graves are in the school grounds. This insane program of extermination extended to former Khmer Rouge cadres and functionaries—and even to the executioners themselves. Incoming prisoners were numbered and photo-graphed on arrival. They were violently coerced into writing elaborate confessions of lifelong allegiance to the CIA, KGB, Vietnamese, or all three. The Tuol Sleng manual revealed the sole purpose of torture was to extract these absurd confessions of foreign allegiance. With meticulous efficiency, the confessions were carefully filed away with the black-and-white snapshots of the victims. Then the "traitors" were put to death at Tuol Sleng, or taken to Choeung Ek and executed.

Into the Compound

When the invading Vietnamese entered Phnom Penh in 1979, they captured Tuol Sleng, the instruments of torture, and the archive in a fairly intact state. With assistance from East German experts, the Vietnamese turned the building into a holocaust museum.

The compound consists of four buildings of similar size. Signs are posted in English, including a translation of the stark S-21 Security Regulations. Building A consists of three sto-

AMPUTEES

Cambodia has more than 40,000 amputees, more per capita than any other country in the world. There are three facilities for amputees in Phnom Penh, and 15 or so other centers around Cambodia. Half a dozen foreign aid groups in Cambodia are involved in manufacturing prosthetics and wheelchairs. Eventually, Cambodia aims to be self-reliant in the production and fitting of limbs. Cambodia Trust established a national school of prosthetics and orthotics at Phnom Penh's Calmette Hospital in 1994 to train Cambodians to fit artificial limbs.

Those with amputations below the knee are fitted for prostheses and wait two weeks for limbs. Those with amputations above the knee must wait a month for a fitting. Artificial arms are also available. Since rice growing is a major activity in Cambodia, a prosthetic limb must withstand long periods of submersion in water. The Jaipur limb is a fully mobile prosthesis made from locally available materials. It was designed by an Indian doctor for agricultural work. The Vietnam Veterans of America Foundation (VVAF) has established a clinic to produce the prostheses and train Cambodians as skilled technicians in the Jaipur limb system.

In the southern section of Phnom Penh on Norodom Boulevard is Wat Than, an unusual temple compound. In one corner lies a temple, with residences for several dozen monks; other parts of the grounds are used as a rehabilitation center for the disabled. Several NGOs set up a program in the 1980s to work with amputees: This was then turned over to local directors. There are workshops for teaching tailoring, furniture making, and secretarial skills to amputees. Wheelchairs are improvised from wooden chairs mounted on bicycle wheels. A small shop sells carpentry items, tailored clothing, and handicraft items made by those disabled by mines; you're welcome to visit the shop and browse.

ries with 20 cells. Ten cells were used for interrogation of high officials, who were chained to beds. Nearby are the graves of the last 14 victims, found tortured to death when the Vietnamese took the building in 1979. Another seven prisoners were found alive—they had survived because they had mechanical skills useful to their captors. Some had worked turning out busts of Pol Pot.

Building B contains rooms and rooms of black-and-white photos of those arrested and tortured, from the record-keeping archives of the Khmer Rouge. These pictures are haunting. The victims are men and women, young and old: They stare back at the camera—some defiant, some wide-eyed with terror, some with blank looks, resigned to their fate. Thousands of stark snapshots overlook the same rooms where the victims were most likely tortured. The Khmer Rouge often took pictures both before and after torture, with gruesome results.

The most shocking pictures are not displayed on the walls, as two Western photographers restoring the negatives found out. From 6,000 negatives of S-21 inmates, the Photo Archive Group selected 100 to make high-quality prints to be housed in archives in Cambodia and abroad.

On the ground floor of Building C, former classrooms were divided by brick partitions into single cells. The second floor contained wooden cells; the top floor was for mass detention. Barbed wire was installed on the third floor to prevent inmates from jumping off to commit suicide. In Building D are artists' renditions of tortures carried out at Tuol Sleng—mostly captioned in Khmer, and occasionally in French. Paintings show mass detention in Building C, single-cell inmates, use of the courtyard for water torture, and Khmer Rouge soldiers bayoneting babies and dashing them against coconut trees. A few photos depict the expulsion of the population from major urban centers. Some material is clearly Vietnamese propaganda to justify its invasion of Cambodia—a map details some 6,000 acts of aggression by Pol Pot and company against Vietnam 1975–1978.

Building D contains a large framed photograph of the "skull map." This room used to contain a huge wall map of Cambodia fashioned out of human skulls and bones, with rivers painted blood-red. This macabre skull map was of questionable taste, showing a lack of respect for the dead. The intention was to show physical evidence of Khmer Rouge atrocities. The skulls were assembled in the shape of a map of Cambodia by the Vietnamese for their own propaganda purposes. In 1994, King Sihanouk proposed the bones and skulls of Khmer Rouge victims in the museum be cremated. Buddhists believe cremation is necessary to lib-erate the soul. Sihanouk contributed money for the cremation ceremony and to build a stupa for the ashes. The deputy director of Tuol Sleng Museum said, "If we keep the display of bones it goes against our Buddhist belief, but if we cremate them we lose the evidence of Khmer Rouge crimes." In the end, the skull map was disassembled and the skulls were stacked behind glass cases in the last room of the museum. A symbolic stupa shrine is found here.

Tuol Sleng Museum is on the southern side of Phnom Penh off Street 350; the entrance is on the eastern side of the compound. The museum is open daily 0700–1130 and 1400–1700; a $2 contribution is expected upon entry. A one-hour movie about the Khmer Rouge era is shown in the morning (around 1000) and the afternoon (around 1500). Visitor books are kept by the museum custodians—you might want to read the comments and add your own.

SHOOTING RANGES: "WAR DISNEY"

First-time shooters will have their choice of high-grade automatic weapons, promises Victor Chao, owner of a 48-lane shooting range that opened in Phnom Penh in January 1998. The Marksmen Club, just beyond Pochentong Airport, offers for rent more than three dozen kinds of guns, including a Beretta, a 1911 Colt .45, a Smith and Wesson, Makarov WZ63s inherited from the KGB, and lots of AK-47s.

Victor Chao is a middle-aged Taiwanese businessman who opened Manhattan Disco at the Holiday International Hotel back in 1994. Chao had problems in the nightclub, whose eclectic dance-floor patrons—expats, soldiers, bodyguards, police officers, and Chinese businessmen, all mingling with attractive women—didn't always coexist peacefully. So he created his own paramilitary group of bodyguards, called the Eagles. From there he developed a passion for marksmanship. He says the shooting range is open to everyone who has the money (about $40 for a day trip), regardless of whether they are commandos, would-be Rambos, retired generals, or wide-eyed tourists.

Ranges such as Chao's would normally be available only for commandos and special-forces troops in other countries because of safety requirements and gun restrictions. The AK-47, for example, is illegal in the United States, but one can be bought for less than $20 at a gun market in Cambodia. Chao elaborates on the machine-gun culture (his remarks are somewhat exaggerated, and they refer to paramilitary types): "For Cambodians, you know, machine guns are part of their lives. They go to sleep with one every night."

Chao has dubbed his shooting club "War Disney." His rationale for opening the club is somewhat dubious. "We wanted to create another tourist attraction in Cambodia besides Tuol Sleng and the Killing Fields, which basically depress people—you know, put them into deep depression. We wanted to create something a bit more entertaining." A few kilometers beyond Chao's club is a government-owned shooting range at Kambol, catering to police, soldiers, and the odd backpacker. There are a dozen or so guns for hire there. Chao claims his range is superior—with more weapons on offer, and better safety and insurance measures.

A follow-up to Tuol Sleng is a trip to the Killing Fields at Choeung Ek, 15 kilometers southwest of Phnom Penh.

MILITARY MUSEUM

This small museum is of specialized interest and offers little English labeling. It's on Norodom Boulevard near the corner of Street 172. A $2 entry fee includes a guide who escorts you round the exhibits. There are several salons inside the main building. One shows the fight against the French in 1951, with U.S., French, and Chinese military hardware displayed. Another section concerns the Vietnamese fight against the Khmer Rouge in 1979. There are three sculptures from Angkor Wat, intercepted from smugglers on the Thai border. A large painting depicts the construction of Angkor.

The Khmer Rouge received the bulk of their supplies from the Chinese. In the courtyard is captured Chinese and Russian equipment: a MiG-19 seized at Pochentong, half a dozen Russian T-58 and Chinese T-59 tanks, a dozen artillery pieces, a Chinese truck, and an army boat used on the Tonle Sap.

Accommodations

UNDER $20

A popular area of cheap guesthouses fronts Boeng Kak Lake. To the north end is **Le Soleil Vert,** with 15 wooden rooms for around $3 apiece; in the same price range farther south is **Boeng Kak GH,** with two wings, and **Cloud 9 GH,** also with two wings—rooms with fan for $6. These places are a bit hard to get to but have their own small restaurants. **Sok Sin Guesthouse,** in a lane between Calmette Hospital and the French Embassy, features a dozen fan rooms for $5 each. Also at the northern end of town is **The Last Home,** at 47 Street 108, with rooms for $3–8 (but not much in the way of windows).

Downtown, the main backpacker hotel is the **Capitol,** at 14 Street 182 (at the corner of Street 107), tel. 23/724104. On the ground level is a restaurant and café; above are several floors of rooms (56 in all) for $3–5 s without bath or $8–10 d with bath. The Capitol Restaurant is the place to meet other travelers and to arrange cheap taxis or visa extensions. Also run by the owners of the Capitol is the low-priced and seedy 20-room **Happy Guesthouse,** next door with paper-thin walls. Around the corner on Street 111 is family-run **Guesthouse 20,** with a few rooms available for $5 each. The **Naga Guesthouse,** at 48 Street 111 near the corner of Street 232, offers double rooms in the $15–40 range.

Phnom Penh Villa, at 17A Street 178, tel. 23/824397, offers rooms for $15–20 in a large mansion with a garden café. At 76 Street 172 is **City Lotus Guesthouse,** tel. 23/362409, fax 23/426268, with 10 comfortable rooms in the $10–15 range. In the area close to the Tonle Sap River are some sleazy Chinese-run hotels and guesthouses—some of the smaller ones are massage parlors and short-time places. **Hotel Indochine,** near the Tonle Sap River at Street 144, tel./fax 23/427292, is family-run and secure, and has a great location; there are 10 rooms for $10–30. Right next door is **Sunshine Hotel,** with rooms for $15–30. But the best of the lot in this area is **Royal GH,** 91 Street 54, tel. 23/854806, with rooms for $5–12, and an overflow annex around the corner. Farther west is the **Cathay Hotel,** 123 Street 110, at the corner of Street 19, tel. 23/722471, fax 23/426303, with 23 rooms for $10 and up, with a/c, hot water, TV, and fridge.

$20–50

Midrange hotels are concentrated along or near Monivong Boulevard in the section near the Central Market. Most were built or renovated for the U.N. trade and offer creature comforts such as air-conditioning, hot water, satellite TV, phone, minibar, and so on. You can often negotiate 20–30 percent discounts

CAVEAT LECTOR

The information contained here can change instantly—street names revised, phone numbers altered, hotels or restaurants closed, and new ones opened. Cambodia has seen tremendous upheavals through the 1990s. When 20,000 foreign soldiers and U.N. workers came in, businesses mushroomed—and many hotels and restaurants folded when they left. Then just as tourist traffic was picking up again, the coup of July 1997 caused many Cambodians, and foreigners resident in Cambodia, to flee the country. However, with the complete demise of the Khmer Rouge in late 1998, a level of stability and confidence was achieved, and foreigners—including hoteliers and restaurateurs—gravitated back. With these swift changes of fortune, any practical information for Cambodia is highly volatile.

in the following hotels, particularly for longer stays. Rates may not include government tax and service charges.

Wat Phnom Area: The superb 31-room **Bayon Hotel,** at 2 Street 75, tel. 23/427281, fax 23/427378, offers singles for $30, doubles for $45, and deluxe rooms for $55–60. There is partial French management, and the restaurant, serving French and European cuisine, is excellent.

A few Chinese-run hotels are found near the river. One possibility in this area is **Mekong Thmey Hotel,** 35 Street 108, tel. 23/60087, with 29 double rooms for $30–40 with fridge, phone, and bath.

Central Phnom Penh: There are a number of hotels in the Central Market area. The **Pailin** on Monivong Boulevard, tel. 23/422475, has 81 renovated rooms for $33–66. On the opposite corner is the **Paradis,** tel. 23/422951, with 102 rooms for $45–60. **Hawaii Hotel,** near the market on Street 130, tel./fax 23/426652, offers 33 rooms for $30–40. Near Cambodia Commercial Bank is **Dusit Hotel,** at 2 Street 120, tel./fax 23/427209, with 40 rooms for $20–30 and suites for $65; this place is a good value and has a small business center and travel agent. **Asie Hotel,** at Monivong and Street 136, tel. 23/427825, fax 23/426334, rents 135 rooms with satellite TV for $25–60. **Singapore Hotel,** 62 Monivong, tel. 23/425552, fax 23/426570, has 25 rooms for $25 s or $40 d with all mod cons. To the east side of the Central Market is **La Paillote,** on Street 130 at the corner of Street 53, tel. 23/722151, fax 23/426513—an old building with 24 rooms for $30–80. **Regent Hotel,** 7 Street 109, tel. 23/427651, fax 23/427649, has 21 rooms for $35 s or $40 d. In the same area are Neakpean and Mittapheap Hotels, catering to the karaoke crowd.

Renakse Hotel, 40 Samdech Sothe2ros Blvd., tel. 23/722457, fax 23/428785, is right opposite the Royal Palace. It's run-down, but the location and price are right, and it has a big garden. There are 30 rooms in this building, used as a government building in the 1950s. Prices are $27 s and $30 d, with a/c and hot water but no TV or phone. **Hotel Pasteur,** at 60 Street 51 near the corner of Street 174, tel. 23/424746, fax 23/426727, has 16 quiet rooms for $35–55. Nearby, with slightly higher prices, is **International House,** at 35 Street 178, tel. 23/62159. **Chinatown Hotel,** 46 Street 214, tel. 23/423445, fax 23/427641, offers 20 rooms for $30 s or $40–65 d with a/c, TV, fridge, and phone. More on the fringes, southwest along Charles de Gaulle Boulevard, is a string of hotels—**Oriental, Sangkar, Borei Thmei** and **Vimean Suor.**

South of Preah Sihanouk Boulevard: At 100 Preah Sihanouk Blvd., west of Independence Monument, is **Beauty Inn,** tel. 23/722676, fax 23/721677; this is a minihotel offering 29 rooms with all modern conveniences for $20–25. **Sydney International Hotel,** on Street 360, tel. 23/427907, features a lobby decor of Foster's cans and a model of the Sydney Opera House; it offers 45 rooms with full facilities for $21–50.

$50–100

Along the waterfront is the **FCCC,** tel. 23/724014; www.fcccambodia.com, which offers a dozen attractive rooms at reasonable prices—about $70, including breakfast. Rooms have a balcony overlooking the river. The FCCC started out by creating the best bar in town, then a great restaurant, and expanded into the guestrooms.

Allson, on Monivong at Street 128, tel. 23/362008, fax 23/362018, offers 67 rooms for $80 and up. The Singapore-managed hotel has room safes, satellite TV, IDD, and minibar. **Monorom,** 89 Monivong, tel. 23/426149, fax 23/426073, is an older hotel with 63 rooms; singles $35–45 (no TV), doubles for $55 with fridge and TV. **Holiday International Hotel,** on Street 84 near Calmette Hospital, tel. 23/427402, fax 23/427401, has 60 rooms for $70–90 apiece and suites for $120; small pool; renowned for its casino and its hot nightspot, the Manhattan Disco.

A short way south of the Independence Monument is the **Green Hotel** at 145 Norodom Blvd., tel. 23/426055, with 35 rooms going for $65–75. Near the corner of Streets 57 and 398 is **Phnom Penh Garden Hotel,** tel. 23/427264, fax 23/427345, with 22 rooms for $60 s and $80–120 d.

Regent Park Hotel, at 58 Samdech Sothearos, tel. 23/427674, fax 23/61999, charges $80 a day, $500 a week; there are 44 spacious rooms, with long-term service apartments available.

Wat Phnom Hotel, just east of Wat Phnom, tel. 23/426286, has 47 rooms for $50–110. The **Riverside,** by the river east of Wat Phnom, at the corner of Street 94, tel./fax 23/427565, charges $70–90 a room.

$100–200

The **Ⲝ Amanjaya,** at 1 Street 154, tel. 23/214747, fax 23/219545, www.amanjaya. com, is right by the waterfront. This is the city's premier boutique hotel, with 21 spacious rooms (average 55 square meters in size) that go for $95 deluxe to $125 panorama, and $155–195 for suites. Emphasis is on tasteful decor, with hardwood floors, silk fabrics, rosewood furniture, and Khmer sculptural motifs and

artwork. The harmonious design of the rooms makes this place stand out. The location is unbeatable: A number of rooms have a terrace overlooking the waterfront.

The **Sharaton Cambodia** is a seven-story luxury hotel with 112 rooms, on Street 47 west of Wat Phnom, tel. 23/360395, fax 23/360393. The **Sunway Hotel,** on Street 92 near Wat Phnom, tel. 23/430333, charges $160–240 for rooms.

Diamond Hotel, 184 Monivong, tel. 23/427221, fax 23/426637, has 86 rooms for $70–90 s and $120 d. The **Juliana Hotel,** at 16 Street 152, tel./fax 23/366070, has 50 rooms for $120–140 apiece. Within easy reach of downtown, this is a low-rise resort hotel nestled amid lush gardens. The Thai-managed **Royal Phnom Penh** is at the south end of Samdech Sothearos Boulevard, tel./fax 23/60036. The hotel features 40 rooms for $120–150 single or double; there were plans to add another 300 rooms with a high-rise wing and a pool, making this a resort. The hotel has a good restaurant, the Bassac, and a nightclub.

Inter-Continental Hotel, at 296 Mao Tse Tung Blvd., tel. 23/424888, fax 23/424885, phnompenh@interconti.com, has 354 rooms along with seven bars and restaurants. Rather bland architecture; rates are $170 for standard rooms, and up to $1,500 for suites.

OVER $200

Hotel Cambodiana, 313 Sisowath Quay, tel. 23/426288, fax 23/426392, packs in a whopping 300 rooms—$170 s, $200 d, and $280–400 for a suite, plus taxes. Facilities include pool, tennis court, sauna, business center, and conference rooms. In the lobby is a wooden scale model of the Bayon at Angkor.

The top-rated hotel in Phnom Penh is **Hotel Le Royal,** on Street 92 near Monivong, tel. 23/981888, fax 23/981168, raffles.hlr. ghda@bigpond.com.kh. There are more than 200 rooms here: The hotel occupies an entire city block. The original hotel (the front wing) first opened in 1929 as part of a French chain—and played host to royalty, dignitaries, and journalists in its heyday. After falling on hard times, the hotel was purchased by the Raffles Hotel Group and underwent extensive renovation, completed in 1997. Three wings were added as part of this deal—a major investment by Raffles. In the middle of the four wings is a 25-meter pool; the hotel has its own spa with hot tub. Tariff runs $260–300 for rooms and $400–2,000 for suites.

Food

If you have a craving for Western luxury foodstuffs, minimarts are scattered around town. **Seven Seven Supermarket,** on Street 90, is very popular for a wide range of dishes. Also try the **International House** minimart, at 35 Street 178, or **Lucky Market,** on Preah Sihanouk Boulevard. Minimarts may have in-house bakeries or delis where you can assemble your own food.

Caution: Many businesses and restaurants are in the habit of supplying customers with a glass of water with ice—double peril—as a way of making you feel at home. The water is almost certainly not filtered, and the ice may be suspect, especially if it's broken or crushed ice. Stick to bottled water. However, if you are in a Western-run restaurant, you will be given "drinking ice," which should be okay—these ice cubes are smooth and rounded, and each has a hole in the middle.

Budget

Market areas are great for cheap food stalls, and at breakfast you can put together baguettes, cheese, and fresh fruit. There's a string of bakeries along Kampuchea Krom Boulevard just off Monivong, all offering freshly baked baguettes. Arm yourself with a baguette, find the nearest place selling café au lait, and take a seat. Sandwich cart vendors with pâté and other selections roam the streets.

One of the best bakeries is at the Hotel Cambodiana's *boulangerie*—on the menu are banana bread, coconut cake, and mouthwatering mango cake. Wicked French pastries tempt those with a sweet tooth. Also try the **French Bakery,** on Preah Sihanouk Boulevard.

East of the Independence Monument on Samdech Sothearos Boulevard is a cluster of Thai places serving Issan food, including **Eid** and **Chiang Mai** Restaurants. A bit pricier is **Green House,** at 50 Sihanouk Blvd., with Thai and Western food, snacks, ice cream, and sandwiches. Around the corner, south of Sihanouk Boulevard, is **Mahop Thai Restaurant.**

Khmer food—minced frog and other specialties—is available from eateries along Monivong Boulevard south of Red Cross Street, not far from the Capitol Hotel. Here you'll find **Asia Soup, Beef Soup,** and **Paris Pizza** (Italo-Franco-Khmer food). A very popular Khmer restaurant is **Dararasmey,** at 292 Street 214. The sidewalk tables here are always packed. On the menu are smoked fish with mangoes, fried eel, grilled frog, and a hotpot that is cooked with a charcoal brazier at the table—you add meat, mushrooms, noodles, and greens.

Moderate

To the east side of the Central Market is **La Paillote,** with great French food and excellent desserts. At 76 Street 172 is **City Lotus Restaurant,** serving Indian, Malaysian, and Singaporean spicy dishes—vegetarian and nonvegetarian, plus some Western selections. Try **Royal India** for great tandoori chicken and samosas—it's at 310 Monivong Boulevard. The **Green Room,** at the Pailin Hotel, **Great Wall Restaurant,** at Hotel Paradis, and the **Allson Hotel** all offer buffet lunches for about $7. **Chao Phraya Restaurant,** on Norodom Boulevard at Street 172, serves Thai buffet lunch for $6; the dinner buffet, at $12, features an assortment of barbecued crab, shrimp, lobster, chicken, duck, sushi, and Thai salads. The restaurant is in a stylish 1930s building that served as the Health Service Office in French days.

© MICHAEL BUCKLEY

Fried insects make a crunchy snack. Buy them from a street vendor in Phnom Penh.

Battling it out for top pizza honors are Happy Herb Bistro and Happy Neth Pizza, one a renegade offshoot of the other. **Happy Neth Pizza,** 295 Pochentong Blvd., tel. 23/60443, serves pasta and three sizes of pizza. **Happy Herb Bistro,** at 345 Sisowath Quay, tel. 23/62349, dishes up 17 varieties, including a double-happy Happy Herb pizza, and an extremely happy version. Both parlors offer free delivery (and this is a dedicated service—they even delivered when tanks prowled the streets during the 1997 coup). Not far from Happy Herb's is **Ponlok Restaurant,** serving Asian food. Ponlok can be pricey, especially for seafood. Also facing the waterfront strip in this vicinity are the **Rendez-Vous Café, Riverside,** and **Garden Bar** restaurants; the food is nothing special, but ambience is good, with sidewalk tables and chairs.

Along Preah Sihanouk Boulevard near Street 63 is **Phnom Kiev** (Khmer and French). **California Restaurant** serves hamburgers, tacos, Tex-Mex, and ice cream. **Cactus,** almost opposite, serves Thai and Western dishes. **Red,** at 56 Sihanouk Blvd., tel. 23/360676, is a bistro serving French food at reasonable prices. At the south end of Monivong is **Long Beach Family Restaurant,** serving American food; dishes are $4–8. Farther west at 139 Monireth Blvd. is **Café Mogambo,** tel. 23/360432, a small and cozy place serving American, Mexican, English, and Australian fare.

The **Foreign Correspondents Club of Cambodia** (FCCC), at 363 Sisowath Quay, tel. 23/427757, has several restaurants and exudes a grand colonial atmosphere. There's the second-floor restaurant with views of the National Museum—this cozy place serves mostly Western dishes for $5–10 apiece. Views in the other direction, overlooking the Tonle Sap River, are afforded from the adjacent bar with its open balconies and swirling fans. This is the place to hang out for sunset drinks (and beyond) (see the *Nightlife* section). Above the bar, one more floor up, is another great drinking spot with a small restaurant attached.

North of Wat Phnom: On Monivong Boulevard are two reasonably priced restaurants. **Chez Lipp** serves Khmer-French cuisine, including frog legs, pepper steak, and soufflé. Right opposite, next to the Pasteur Institute, is **Calmette Restaurant,** which is popular with

Cambodian customers for soups. Up this way is the **Restaurant Khmer,** at 24 Monivong Blvd., tel. 23/428439, open daily and serving Khmer specialties—some recipes come from Sihanouk's palace, where the restaurateur's mother once worked. And for those looking for more familiar food, there's **Antony Pizza,** right at the north side of Wat Phnom; the owner, who is from Marseilles, makes 20 varieties of pizza in his hand-built wood-fired oven. Farther north, patronized by the upwardly mobile and those with mobile phones, is **Casablanca,** tel. 23/724339, at the junction of Street 47 and Street 84; this place serves Moroccan food amid appropriate accompanying decor.

Upscale

Hotel Cambodiana boasts five restaurants with Asian and Western specialties. L'Amboise is a French restaurant with cellar; Dragon Court serves Chinese food. There are lunch buffets for $9–15 in several of the restaurants, and afternoon tea with French pastries from the hotel's own boulangerie.

Nightlife

A curfew and siege mentality permeates nights in Phnom Penh—foreigners tend to gather at a handful of exclusive bars and cafés that originally sprang up to serve the U.N. trade. The setup smacks of French imperialism—segregated nightlife with foreigners frequenting exclusive clubs and locals congregating at disco and karaoke places or the local movie house. Embassies sometimes generate their own nightlife. The **Center Culturel Français,** at Street 184 off Monivong Boulevard, screens French films several times a week. Otherwise, all quiet on the Phnom Penh front. Most people, deprived of electricity, are soundly snoring in readiness for an 0500 wakeup.

Because guests are reluctant to venture out at night, the management in upper-end hotels attempts to provide nightlife with in-house bars or discos. The **Cyclo Bar** at the Hotel Cambodiana sometimes stages revues. A rare treat, if you can find out where performances are being held, is classical Khmer dancing.

Muggers are abroad at night. In the past, when mugging has gotten out of hand, the army and police have resorted to setting up checkpoints around the city to stop people and check for illegal weapons. If you're out after 2000, travel in a group and carry enough cash for the evening's expenses but no more. Avoid walking; use a moto or cyclo. Make sure you're aware of the route back to your hotel—cyclos can easily get lost. Cyclos do not have lights and can be dangerous when creeping down the wrong side of the road, with you up front facing oncoming traffic.

The presence of highly paid U.N. staff resulted in rampant prostitution in Cambodia (some say UNTAC stood for "UN Transmission of AIDS in Cambodia"). In Phnom Penh the prostitutes are often Vietnamese. Around Phnom Penh are scores of places with taxi dancers and karaoke booths, such as the Pacific Nightclub and Boss KTV, both on Monivong Boulevard.

Phnom Penh by night can be dangerous— armed bandits are on the loose. Several foreigners and diplomats have been pinned down by crossfire when robbers armed with machine guns tried to hijack expensive vehicles at night, and security guards fired back. Travelers have also been known to be stopped by police demanding money.

The disco and karaoke hot spot in town, favored by visiting Asians, is the trendy **Manhattan Club** in the Holiday International Hotel in the northern sector of Phnom Penh. The club stays open till 1 or 2 in the morning; drinks are expensive here—a cover charge is applied. Another disco operates at the back of the **Hong Kong Center** on Samdech Sothearos Boulevard. The infamous **Sharkys Bar** is a hostess disco in the downtown east side. It stays open until 0200 or later.

Heart of Darkness is a popular upscale

dance-bar with crafty neo-Angkorian decor—the place is buzzing late at night (it stays open until 0200). It is on Street 51 and sells a great pub T-shirt. Strung along Street 51 in the same vicinity are rival bars, including **Walkabout** and **Soho2 Bar.** The **Irish Rover,** at 78 Sihanouk Blvd., is an Irish pub that serves salads and sandwiches; look for a shamrock sign. **Atmosphère,** at 141 Norodom Blvd., serves draft beer and French food.

An excellent venue for a drink, snack, meal, game of billiards—even a movie—is the **Foreign Correspondents Club of Cambodia** (FCCC), at 363 Sisowath Quay, tel. 23/427757. The FCCC is an accredited organization but you don't have to be a member—anyone can use the facilities. The airy, high-ceilinged top-floor Continental Café serves drinks, and a small restaurant section offers spaghetti, steak, and other dishes for $5–10 each. There are special photography exhibits; in the past, these have included showings by Tim Page and Roland Neveu. Foreign movies are regularly screened at the FCCC and special-topics panels are arranged. The FCCC is a cozy place with great views across the Tonle Sap River—perfect for sunset gazers.

Casino

Moored off the Hotel Cambodiana is a 12,000-ton floating vessel with five floors of casinos and dozens of blackjack, baccarat, and roulette tables. The entertainment complex is run by Ariston, a Malaysian company that made a multimillion-dollar secret deal with the government. In the hold of the ship is a pirate theme park where those weary of the roulette tables can experience the thrill of buccaneers roaming the seven seas in search of buried treasure. The floating casino can accommodate up to 1,000 customers at a time.

Shopping

Clothing

Khmer multipurpose *kramas* (checked scarves) made of silk or cotton are a good purchase. Souvenir T-shirts bear such designs as Angkor Wat, Bayon faces, and Holiday in Cambodia. Also watch for clothing made from Khmer silk—elegant fashion reflects French- and Khmer-inspired designs. **La Boutique,** at 36 Sihanouk Blvd., sells locally made clothing in Western designs and handicrafts of cotton and silk.

Handicrafts

Handicrafts can be found at the Russian Market on the south side of the city and at a number of shops in the National Museum vicinity, especially along Street 178. For handicrafts available through NGOs, try **Khemara Handicrafts,** at the Cooperation Committee of Cambodia on the first floor of 25 Street 360, selling silk bags and clothes; and **Wat Than Handicrafts,** south end of Norodom Boulevard, selling tailored clothing and wooden items made by victims of land mines. **Apsara Rehab Craftshop,** on Norodom Boulevard just south of Independence Monument, sells attractive handcrafted silk and leather items made by craftspeople with disabilities in Phnom Penh. Among the offerings are wallets, purses, shoulder bags, and cosmetics bags. **Wat Than Giftshop,** at the southern end of Norodom Boulevard, sells Khmer silk handicrafts, gifts, furniture, and clothing made by disabled victims of land mines.

Shops sell silver opposite the Hotel Cambodiana and along Monivong near the Diamond Hotel. Silver boxes and jewelry are often made of alloys, sold by weight. Silver boxes were originally made to hold the elements of betel-nut chewing; often they bear animal designs.

Angkoriana

In 1993 the government approved stiff penalties for trafficking in antiquities. Do not buy stolen Khmer artifacts, sculpture, or bronzes. Quality reproductions are widely available in

GECKO WINE, TOAD WINE

At markets around Phnom Penh, vendors of traditional medicines and herbs sell bags of ganja, and all kinds of dried and skinned life forms, including geckos. The lizard is being hunted to extinction in rural Cambodia to feed the insatiable appetite in China and Vietnam for gecko wine and other potions.

Gecko wine is made by preserving a gecko in a liter of white wine for six months. In China and Vietnam, gecko wine is sought as a curative for asthma, coughs, and breathing ailments, and for improving muscle tone.

The word gecko comes from the Malay *gekok,* in imitation of its cry. In some villages in Takeo province, the cry of the gecko is hardly heard any more, nor kids repeating it. A Vietnamese businessman came to catch geckos in the province in the 1980s, recruiting young boys to roam around with bamboo sticks and cages to hunt and seize the reptiles. The dried geckos were brought back to Vietnam by boat. In Battambang during the 1970s the Khmer Rouge ordered people to catch geckos for export to China. Geckos are now found only in remote parts of Cambodia, in the far north and northeastern provinces. Lizard traders must move farther afield to capture them.

Unlike gecko wine, which is believed to have originated in China and Vietnam, another variant, toad wine, is an ancient Khmer recipe. Toads are dried, fried, crushed, and mixed in white wine, along with herbs and black sugarcane. Toad wine is believed to cure sexually transmitted diseases such as syphilis and to promote good appetite and sound sleep. The stoutlike toad wine is much cheaper than beer or whiskey. Buckets of live toads can be seen at Phnom Penh markets.

It's not pretty to contemplate the impact on the environment if toads and geckos disappear from Cambodia. Both creatures spend a good deal of time catching harmful insects that destroy crops. And geckos consume prodigious quantities of mosquitoes, so their disappearance would not help in the fight against malaria.

Phnom Penh, especially in the block around the National Museum. The National Museum gift shop sells heavy concrete copies of famous Khmer sculptures. Wooden, concrete, bronze, and marble copies of Buddhas, *apsaras,* and Angkor statuary are made at the School of Fine Arts—they're sold in nearby shops and at a Fine Arts retail outlet south of the National Museum. Khmer painting mostly depicts *apsara* dancers at Angkor Wat. For a touch more class, an art gallery at 20 Street 9, close to Green House Restaurant, mounts exhibitions of contemporary Khmer paintings and drawings.

Markets

Most of the markets around Phnom Penh are of interest to locals and deal in electronic goods, housewares, or food. The most popular are the Central Market, Russian Market, and Olympic Market.

The **Central Market,** also called the New Market, or Psah Thmay, was constructed by the French in 1937. You can't miss it—a huge, yellow art deco building between Norodom and Monivong boulevards. Four arms radiate off the domed hall. The central area is dominated by gold, silver, and jewelry merchants who also trade in currency. A large section of the market features food and household goods. You can buy supplies for up-country travel here, such as hammocks and mosquito netting. There is army surplus gear for sale, too. The main area of interest for foreign shoppers is on the east side of the market, toward Street 53. Here you'll find stalls selling T-shirts, *kramas,* garments, fabrics, paintings, and handicrafts, and kiosks selling maps, phrasebooks, temple rubbings, and postcards. Bargain hard. The Central Market has an engrossing (or grossout?) food section, selling everything edible, including things you didn't even know were edible—such as tarantula kebabs and fried grasshoppers. Dragon fruit and other exotica can be found here.

The **Russian Market,** also known as Psah Tuol Tom Pong, is south of Mao Tse Tung Boulevard off Street 155. The Russian Market is the place to go for tailor-made clothing, sarongs, fake and genuine antiques, handicrafts, jewelry, and souvenirs. It's great for food stalls (found within the market). Nearby is a furniture market.

Services and Information

TOURIST INFORMATION

The people at **Phnom Penh Tourism,** 313 Sisowath Quay, tel. 23/24059, are pretty useless unless they smell money. The place is set up for group tours, not individual assistance. The office organizes day trips around Phnom Penh, often advertised through the Hotel Cambodiana. You might inquire about performances of classical dance. The General Directorate of Tourism, also known as Cambodia Tourism, on Monivong Blvd. at the corner of Street 232, tel. 23/25607, organizes tours and arranges vehicle rental.

Traveler Cafés

The café under the **Capitol Hotel** is backpacker headquarters, a good source of information on who's been where and when. The food is terrible but the information is fresh. Staff at the Capitol will also arrange visa extensions, rent bicycles, and provide taxis for trips to Choeung Ek, Tonle Bati, and Udong. The **Foreign Correspondents Club of Cambodia (FCCC) bar** at 363 Sisowath is the meeting spot for journalists, photographers, businessmen, and expatriates. The FCCC sponsors Wednesday evening "talks"—a good venue for reporters and others interested in what's happening in Cambodia.

Maps and Books

The biweekly *Phnom Penh Post* prints an up-to-date map in the center of the newspaper; however, the entries on the map are mostly paid advertising, so many details are missing. The best available map of Phnom Penh is a large foldout city map produced by Point Maps and Guides. It gives a three-dimensional overview, pinpointing larger buildings with amazing accuracy. Phnom Penh Tourism provides outdated, overpriced, and unwieldy maps of the capital; these are also sold at the Central Market. English-Khmer and French-Khmer phrasebooks are available at stalls on the east side of the Central Market. The booklets and dictionaries are sold mainly to Cambodians learning English or French, but they're useful for foreigners too.

At 111 Norodom Blvd. is **Monument Books,** Cambodia's largest bookshop, stocking books and magazines from around the world—extensive title selection on Indochina and Southeast Asia. Supermarkets and minimarts stock some magazines and books. Try International House Minimart. The Hotel Cambodiana and Hotel Le Royal each have a small bookstore and gift shop.

Media

It's important in Cambodia to keep tabs on what's happening. The best source of information is the *Phnom Penh Post,* published every two weeks, and *Le Mékong,* a French paper issued monthly. Other publications include the *Cambodia Daily, Cambodia Times* (English), and *Cambodge Soir* (French). You can buy Bangkok English newspapers and international magazines at supermarket stands and gift shops. There's satellite TV reception in Phnom Penh—hotels can pick up Hong Kong–based StarTV (BBC World Service) and Australian ATVI. Canal France International (CFI) TV is retransmitted from the French Cultural Center. The Thai company Shinawatra operates Channel 5 in Phnom Penh, and there are two

Phnom Penh

NGOS

There are more than 100 foreign and 50 Cambodian nongovernmental organizations (NGOs) in Phnom Penh. These aid agencies cover a wide range of educational, medical, archaeological, and other fields. NGOs will be delighted if you volunteer—Cambodia needs your skills. Working for an NGO, you'll see a totally different side of Cambodia. For more information, approach the relevant NGOs directly, or visit the Co-operation Committee for Cambodia (CCC), 25 Street 360, tel./fax 23/26009, which acts as a liaison between organizations. The CCC stocks reports and publications on NGOs in the capital and up-country.

channels on Khmer TV. On radio, you can pick up Radio France Internationale (RFI), the BBC, VOA, and Radio Australia.

COMMUNICATIONS

Fax and Phone

The main post office offers a 24-hour section with IDD phones and fax machines. Fax and IDD calls are expensive. To reduce charges, some strategies are to use NetPhone systems, use a phone card (available at various dollar values for both international and in-country calling), or place a collect call. You can place IDD calls through hotels, though these tend to surcharge.

Because regular phone lines are intermittently down in Phnom Penh, mobile phones are useful—but only to contact other mobile phone users. Businesses in Phnom Penh specify up to five different phone numbers on their calling cards—local phone, IDD phone, fax number, mobile phone numbers. Mobile phones have nine-digit numbers, while regular Phnom Penh numbers are five or six digits. The Cambodia country code for phone/fax is 855. Phnom Penh area code is 23; for Siem Reap, 63; for Sihanoukville, 34. Mobile phones (also called "hand phone") use prefixes such as 011, 012, or 016 depending on the network. Because calling is deliberately made difficult between networks, some Cambodians carry 3–4 mobile phones, each with a different network number.

Email and Internet

Cybercafés are found all over the city. Some have faster lines than others. A number of them offer CD-burning services for digital cameras. The company PIC online (www.online.com.kh) has WiFi hotspots around Phnom Penh, accessible with prepaid cards: these include Phnom Penh Airport, the FCCC, K-West Café in the Amanjaya Hotel, Lucky Burger on Monivong, and larger hotels such as the Cambodiana, Inter-Continental, Le Royal, Imperial Garden, and Sunway.

Post Office and Courier

The main post office is on Street 102 at the corner of Street 13 near Wat Phnom. The post office is open 0700–1800 seven days a week; the fax and phone section is open 24 hours. Mail is expensive from Cambodia—it all goes airmail, even packages of several kilos. You might be better off sending mail to a drop-off point in, say, Bangkok, and posting it from there later. For example, a 1.5-kg package to Canada costs $45 airmail; to Bangkok, the same package would be $17. Courier services in Phnom Penh include **DHL,** 28 Monivong Blvd., tel. 23/427726; **Transpeed Cargo** (agents for FedEx), 19 Street 106, tel. 23/426931; **UPS,** 8 Street 134, tel. 23/66323; and **TNT,** 139 Monireth Blvd., tel. 23/424022.

PHOTOGRAPHY AND FILM

There are photo shops on Monivong Boulevard in the area near the Central Market. Although brand-name film—Agfa, Kodak, Konica, Fuji—can be purchased in Phnom Penh, check the expiration date and storage conditions. Film may have water streaks from exposure to humidity and high temperatures. Print film can be processed quickly; snapshots make fine gifts for Cambodian friends.

MONEY AND BUSINESS

Banks

Banks charge 2–5 percent to convert U.S. traveler's checks to U.S. cash. The **Canadia Bank** on Street 118 charges 2 percent; the nearby **Foreign Trade Bank of Cambodia** charges only 1 percent commission but will not accept large traveler's checks without proof of original purchase. Banks are clustered around the central core, near the Central Market. In this area is the **Cambodia Commercial Bank** at the corner of Monivong and Pochentong boulevards. Foreign banks in Phnom Penh include **Siam City Bank, Bangkok Bank, Thai Farmers Bank, Standard Chartered, Banque Indosuez,** and **Singapore Banking Corporation.** Diamond Hotel has a money-changing office. You can change cash U.S. dollars into riel with the gold and jewelry merchants inside the Central Market. Be aware that lots of fake U.S. dollars circulate in Cambodia. When paying for hotels or restaurants in Phnom Penh, you can use U.S. dollars, Thai baht, or Cambodian riel.

Credit Cards: The Commercial Bank of Cambodia doesn't charge a commission for cash advances for Visa credit cards. You might also try Bangkok Bank. Thai Farmers Bank wants $10 to process Visa cash advances; it will advance up to $800 a day.

Business Services

The FCCC at 363 Sisowath Quay, tel. 23/427757, fax 23/427758, has a business center, open 0730–2300, with secretarial services, Khmer typing, and computer equipment rentals. Major hotels have business facilities, and there's a 24-hour business center on Monivong Boulevard near the Eurasie Hotel with fax machines, IDD phones, and photocopiers. Global Business Center, at 378 Sihanouk Blvd., offers equipment rentals and secretarial services.

CASH AND THE KHMER ROUGE

Part of Pol Pot's mad vision was of a society without money. During his rule, the country reverted to the barter system—the only nation to do so in recent history. To emphasize the point, the Khmer Rouge blew up the National Bank in Phnom Penh (although in the late 1980s, it was rebuilt on the same site, on Norodom Boulevard).

At first the Khmer Rouge wavered on the question of money; in 1975, they had a batch of bills printed up, apparently in China. The bills—depicting Khmer Rouge mortar and machine-gun crews, factory workshops, rice harvesters, the towers of Angkor Wat, and Bayon–style sculpture—were never circulated. However, invading Vietnamese troops arriving in 1979 looted thousands of sets of these banknotes from the treasury of Cambodia. The bills then found their way back to Vietnam for sale to collectors.

The Khmer Rouge bills were not the only useless notes floating around. Currency issued under Lon Nol in the early 1970s and the money printed by the Vietnamese-backed Heng Samrin regime is now used for other functions—a kind of historic wallpaper. During these unstable times, Cambodians reverted to hoarding wealth and trading in small bars of gold.

In 1993, the Khmer Rouge proclaimed their newfound admiration for the "market" by coming up with a brand new idea: money. In their section of "liberated Cambodia," the Khmer Rouge issued banknotes of 5, 10, 50, and 100 riels bearing the signature of Khmer Rouge leader Khieu Samphan. Pol Pot envisioned setting up a monetary economy in the "liberated areas," using agricultural banks to hold the surplus earning of farmers.

In early 1995, French-educated economist Sar Kim Lemouth—said to have been responsible for Khmer Rouge finances—defected to the government. He claimed ignorance of the rebel finances, which are reputed to include accounts in Beijing, Hong Kong, Switzerland, and Bangkok (the stashes are yet to be unearthed). The Khmer Rouge bankrolled its military campaigns through the sale of millions of dollars' worth of gems, timber, and Angkorian artifacts to Thailand.

Khmer Rouge 10-riel note

HEALTH CARE

IMC Clinic, at 83 Mao Tse Tung Blvd., mobile tel. 015/912765, is a 24-hour primary and emergency health-care facility with international standards. There's also a **European Dental Clinic** at 195A Norodom Blvd., tel. 23/362656. In the Hotel Cambodiana is **Raffles Medical Clinic,** which is set up for guests but can be used by visitors for a fee. This clinic will tend to wounds and perform minor surgery; it also can arrange vaccinations for Japanese encephalitis, typhoid, and so on. Another possible facility for medical problems is the **Tropical and Travellers Medical Clinic,** at 88 Street 108 (southwest of Wat Phnom), tel. 23/366802, with a British doctor in residence. For buying medicines such as doxycycline, **Raffles Pharmacy,** at 57 Preah Sihanouk Blvd., is well stocked. **International SOS** (also known as AEA International) will arrange emergency evacuation from Cambodia to Singapore. It's at 161 Street 51, Sang-Kat Boeung Peng, Khon Doun Penh, tel. 23/216911, fax 23/215811.

REST AND RECREATION

The **Hotel Cambodiana** charges nonguests $5 to use its pool. The price includes towel and drink (you're not permitted to bring your own drinks). There are poolside showers, and you can leave your bag with an attendant. The **International Youth Club,** at the western side of Wat Phnom, has a pool, gym, and tennis court. The entry fee works out to about $5 a day on weekdays and $10 on a Saturday or Sunday. Considerably cheaper is the pool at the **Olympic Stadium,** charging $2. For runners, Phnom Penh offers a chapter of the Hash House Harriers.

Getting There

BY AIR

There are two international arrival points by air in Cambodia: at Siem Reap (Angkor) and Pochentong (Phnom Penh). Pochentong Airport received a major face-lift in 1994, but all this handiwork received a severe setback during the July 1997 coup, when the airport was the scene of heavy fighting. Government soldiers and vandals stripped the facility of all its fittings, including air-conditioning units. The entire stock of duty-free liquor—estimated at more than half a million dollars' worth—disappeared. More alarmingly, so did important technical equipment, including the sophisticated landing guidance system, originally donated by UNTAC and particularly useful for guiding landings in heavy rain. Officials are still debating whether this lack of equipment caused the crash of a Vietnam Airlines Tupolev-134B in poor weather on September 3, 1997. The plane crashed in a rice field, about 160 meters from the tarmac, and exploded—killing all but two of the 66 people aboard (and after the plane crashed, dozens of Cambodians looted from the dead passengers). The plane had the necessary avionics to use the ground equipment and fly by instruments in poor weather—but it seems that essential navigation equipment was missing from Pochentong Airport at the time. Speculation continues as to whether the crash was caused by pilot error, tower error, or simply mechanical failure on the vintage Soviet jet. The moral of this story: Flying Russian aircraft in the rainy season and trying to land at Pochentong is not a wise combination.

In late 1997, all night flights in and out of Pochentong were suspended because of the necessity for the pilot to make visual contact with the airstrip and rely on manual guidance systems. At one point, lights on the runway were also stolen, although these have since been replaced. Rainy-season landings are particularly hazardous—and not just for the passengers; in September 1997, an airport official said a

Kampuchea Air Lockheed Tri-Star circled the airport for almost an hour, and flew very low right over the terminal on its last attempt, causing people in the tower to dive for cover. Apparently, looters even took the movable stairs that are rolled out to assist deplaning passengers. One stairway set was later discovered in an orchard, where it was being used as a ladder to pick mangoes from trees.

Thai Airways International flies Phnom Penh to Bangkok daily for $140 one-way. Bangkok Airways charges $250 round-trip, $125 one-way. SilkAir to Singapore is $300 round-trip, five times weekly; Dragonair to Hong Kong, twice weekly, $350 round-trip; Lao Airlines to Vientiane, $150 one-way, once a week; Vietnam Airways to Saigon daily for $50 one-way, to Hanoi once a week, $155 one-way; Malaysia Airlines to Kuala Lumpur, $260 round-trip, three times a week. There are also flights to Taipei on Transasia Airways, and Aeroflot has a few flights a month to Moscow via Dubai.

Entry and Exit Formalities

Customs and immigration are relaxed on arrival and departure. Export of Khmer artifacts is forbidden. International departure tax is $10, domestic departure tax is $4.

Transfers into Phnom Penh

Pochentong Airport lies eight kilometers southwest of Phnom Penh. An entire taxi should cost $5–8, depending on the number of passengers. You can also jump onto a moto for a cheap ride—say $1 or $2. In the reverse direction, a taxi from the Capitol Hotel costs $3.

Airline Offices

Thai Airways International is at 19 Street 106, tel. 23/427211; Dragonair is at the same address, tel. 23/417665. SilkAir is in the Pailin Hotel on Monivong Boulevard, tel. 23/724852. Lao Airlines is at 58 Sihanouk Blvd., tel. 23/426563. Malaysia Airlines is in the

Phnom Penh

Diamond Hotel, tel. 23/426688; Air France in the Hotel Cambodiana, tel. 23/426426. You'll find Aeroflot in the Allson Hotel, tel. 23/362008. Vietnam Airlines is at 35 Sihanouk Blvd., tel. 23/364460.

BY LAND

There are a number of land routes into Cambodia: The main ones are from Bangkok overland to Poipet and on to Siem Reap (Angkor), and the land route from Saigon to Phnom Penh. Two rougher crossings are open from Thailand to Cambodia at the border points of Pailin and O'Smach. For the Bangkok-Poipet-Angkor route you do not need visas in either direction—you pick them up at the border crossing. However, if crossing from Cambodia to Vietnam, you need to have a Vietnamese visa in advance.

Saigon to Phnom Penh by Bus: Daily buses ply Route 1 from Phnom Penh to Saigon, a distance of 248 kilometers. Your paperwork must be in order to cross. Coming from Vietnam, you can pick up a Cambodian visa at the border, but it would be preferable to get it ahead of time in Saigon. Going the other way, you need to have your Vietnamese visa ahead of time. There are two species of bus on the Phnom Penh–Saigon route. The nonairconditioned Cambodian crawler costs $5; the a/c Vietnamese bus is $12. Buses leave Phnom Penh on alternate days at 0530 except Sunday and holidays, departing from a ticket office near the intersection of Street 182 and Street 211, close to Nehru Boulevard. The office is open 0500–1000 and 1400–1700; buy tickets one day in advance. In Saigon, buy tickets at the garage next to the Rex Hotel at 155 Nguyen Hue Boulevard. Buses heading east from Cambodia are frequently stopped for contraband checks on the Vietnamese side, turning what should be a nine-hour trip into a 14-hour odyssey. Grandmothers tuck cigarettes under their belts, young women hide goods in overhead racks, the driver and crew hoard goods in the roof and under the floor panels. Vietnamese police try to take a cut of this booty or confiscate the lot—a great introduction to avarice, greed, bad tempers, and another day in

bullet boat on the Mekong

© MICHAEL BUCKLEY

Vietnam. Sometimes they take the whole bus apart. It would be prudent to cover the Vietnamese sector by share-taxi: If heading east from Phnom Penh, get off the bus at Moc Bai and continue by taxi.

By Share-Taxi: Share-taxis run as far as the border from each side; a through taxi costs a lot more. A share-taxi from Phnom Penh to Bavet runs $5–10 a person, with six or more passengers jammed into the car. The main departure point for share-taxis to Bavet is a depot east of Monivong Bridge at Street 369 in the Chbampao Market area. Taxis leave 0600–1300. On the Vietnamese side, you pick up a share-taxi to Saigon for less than $10 per head, or $30 for the whole taxi. Motos also wait on the Vietnamese side; a ride into Saigon should be about $5. By car, it is about a three-hour trip to the border, half an hour for paperwork, and another two hours to Saigon. From the Saigon end, a share-taxi is $30 to the Moc Bai border.

Try Mien Tay bus station on the western outskirts of town or negotiate with a downtown taxi driver if part of a ready-made group. On the Cambodian side in Bavet, you can arrange another share-taxi for $5–10 a person.

BY RIVER

In 2001, the Tonle Mekong river crossing opened to foreigners, opening a route from Chau Doc to Phnom Penh along the Mekong. This is a much more interesting route than going by road, and it's actually faster because you start from deep in the delta (at Chau Doc). While Cambodian immigration will stamp you in on the spot (you need to present a passport photograph), you need a Vietnamese visa in advance to cross here. There are several boat companies plying the full Chau Doc–Phnom Penh route. The Victoria Chau Doc Hotel operates its own speedboats on the route.

Getting Around

Although Phnom Penh features some green city buses donated by a Parisian council, most people get around the city on foot, cyclo, bicycle, or motorcycle. Foreigners and dignitaries sometimes use taxis. At night it's not advisable to walk; hire a moto to get around from point to point.

By Boat

You can rent a sampan for a few hours and travel along the Tonle Sap and Bassac rivers to small villages. A longer trip will take you out to Ko Dach, a weaving village north of Phnom Penh. The Hotel Cambodiana operates larger wooden cruise boats for half-day excursions and sunset viewing of the Royal Palace. There have been several instances of cruise boats sinking.

By Taxi

Major hotels and travel agents can arrange taxis for about $20–30 a day. It's also possible to hire minibuses. Numerous taxis wait near the gates of Hotel Cambodiana. Taxis not attached to hotels are usually operated by private citizens who own a car and want to make extra money. Some of the lower-priced hotels can arrange deals—the Capitol can get a taxi for $20 a day. Share-taxis, which lurk at various depots around Phnom Penh, are also available for private hire at similar rates. *Tuk-tuks* can also be rented by the half-day or day.

By Cyclo

Cyclos are the most common method of getting around; most destinations around town run $.50–1. You can hire them by the hour, half-day, or the day. Cyclo drivers don't speak much English. It may be your responsibility to follow maps and supply directions. You're up front—just provide the appropriate left or right turn hand signals to direct the driver. Be aware that certain boulevards in Phnom Penh are blocked to bicycles, cyclos, and motorcycles: They're not allowed on Norodom Boulevard between Independence Monument and Street 114.

Phnom Penh

At the floating villages, boats are the main way of getting around.

By Moto

Motos are not much more expensive than cyclos; a ride across town is a dollar or less. Prices may rise slightly at night because of the danger factor and the fact you can't bargain as hard since you have no other transportation choice. By the hour a moto is maybe $1, for the entire day, maybe $6. Motos are mostly offered by private owners making an extra buck. Just stand on a street corner and wave a hand, and someone will pull over. The only credentials a moto operator needs, it seems, are a baseball cap, a frayed collar, broken tail and signal lights, an ability to knock down customers to get their attention, and a poor sense of direction. A moto driver who speaks a fair amount of English or French is great for touring and up-country destinations. One big caveat with motos—occasionally bandits shoot moto drivers to get their motorcycles. Stealing vehicles is big business in Phnom Penh, the cause of a lot of shoot-outs.

By Two-Wheel Rentals

A bicycle or motorcycle is a good way of getting around, but very few places rent them. The Capitol Hotel peddles ratty rental bicycles, and nearby Street 107 sells new bicycles. Try hotel staff at other budget hotels in this area too. If riding a motorcycle or bicycle, be wary at intersections and roundabouts—turns can be difficult in chaotic peak hours.

Motorcycle rentals in Phnom Penh are not recommended because the risk of theft is too high. Even in broad daylight, robbers will shoot a Cambodian off a motorcycle to steal it. Around the corner from the Capitol are two motorcycle rental places at numbers 413 and 417 Monivong, near the Hong Kong Hotel. Motorcycle rentals are $15 a day for a Honda 250cc at 417 Monivong; at 413 Monivong a Honda Dream 100cc is $8 a day, a 250cc Honda Rebel $15 a day. If your bike is stolen, you have to pay the cost of a new one: The Honda 250cc is worth $2,000, the 100cc Dream $1,200. If there's an accident, you pay for the repairs. Your passport—or $750—is required as a deposit. It might be preferable to get a moto driver for the day, or ask one if you can use his bike.

Gasoline is sold by roadside entrepreneurs

in old soft-drink bottles. Sometimes they sell cigarettes and lighters too. Cambodian drivers drop by to light up a cigarette and refill the gas tank. Makes sense, doesn't it?

Tour Companies

There are more than 45 travel agencies around Phnom Penh. They can arrange tours around town or up-country, provide air tickets, arrange taxis and minivans, and assist with visas and other paperwork. Some maintain good contacts in Vietnam or Laos and can arrange tours and visas for those countries. Travel agents include:

Angkor Voyages, Champs Elysées Hotel, 183 Street 63, tel. 23/427268, fax 23/427268

Apsara Tours, 29 Street 150, tel./fax 23/426705

Bopha Angkor Tourism, 797B Monivong Blvd., tel. 23/427933

Diethelm Travel, 8 Sothearos Blvd., tel. 23/426648, fax 23/426676

East-West Group, 170 Street 114, tel./fax 23/426189

Eurasie Travel, 97 Monivong, near Monorom Hotel, tel./fax 23/423620

Khemara, 134 Preah Sihanouk Blvd., tel. 23/427434, fax 23/427434

Naga Travel, Renakse Hotel, Samdech Sothearos Blvd., tel. 23/426288

Orient Express Tours, 19 Street 106, tel. 23/426248, fax 23/426313

Peace Travel, 246 Monivong Blvd., tel. 23/424640, fax 23/426533

Skylink, 124 Norodom Blvd., tel. 23/427010

Thai Indochina Supply, 4 Street 118, tel./fax 23/427143

Transindo (Transair), 16 Monivong, near the French Embassy, tel. 23/426298, fax 23/427119

Getting Away

By Air

Domestic flights leave several times daily for Siem Reap, and 3–4 times a week to Battambang, Koh Kong, and Sihanoukville. Less frequent flights depart for the northeast destinations of Stung Treng, Ratanakiri, and Mondulkiri. Domestic flights cost around $40–55 one-way; the flight to Angkor is $55 one-way, $110 round-trip. Domestic schedules are erratic, and flights may be suspended. Domestic departure tax is $4.

By Fast Boat

There's fast boat service to Siem Reap ($25 one-way) in the northwest, and to Kompong Cham ($10) and Kratie ($25) in the northeast. The service is operated by several companies using 50- to 80-seat riverboats with onboard video from Malaysia. Among the operators are Golden Sea Shipping and Soon Lee Express. The boats are usually reliable, though some have sunk en route (causing a big flap among the passengers who lost luggage), others have been fired upon when running past unofficial

"checkpoints," and some have been held up by bandits—and passengers relieved of their valuables. The fast boats leave from a dock about 500 meters north of Chruoy Changvar Bridge. You can book tickets through hotels, or pick them up at jetty booths. Slow cargo boats run to Siem Reap and to Stung Treng but aren't recommended because of checkpoint dangers.

By Rail

Trains run to Battambang in the north and Kampot and Sihanoukville in the south. These are freight trains, and passengers are a secondary consideration.

By Land

Excellent bus service to Sihanoukville is offered by several Malaysian companies near the Central Market. These employ comfortable a/c buses that make the run in record time.

Collective taxis operate on set routes, packing in passengers and departing when full. The fare is around $5 a person for a day's run. The record seems to be nine passengers—four in

PHNOM PENH EMBASSIES AND CONSULATES

Phnom Penh has over 20 embassies and consulates. These include:
Australia, 11 Street 254, tel. 426254
China, Issarak Blvd. at Street 163, tel. 426271
France, north end of Monivong Blvd., tel. 426278
Germany, 76 Street 214, tel. 426381
India, 777 Monivong Blvd., tel. 425981
Japan, 75 Norodom Blvd., tel. 427161

Laos, 15 Issarak Blvd., tel. 426441
Malaysia, 161 Street 51, tel. 426167
North Korea, 39 Street 268, tel. 427224
Russia, Samdech Sothearos Blvd. at Street 312, tel. 422081
Thailand, 4 Monivong Blvd., tel. 426182
U.K., 29 Street 75, tel. 427124
U.S.A., 27 Street 240, tel. 426804
Vietnam, Monivong Blvd. at Street 436, tel. 425481

the front (plus driver) and five in the back. Not comfortable, but better than a wooden bench on a bus, and faster too. Bus and share-taxi depots are usually situated near a market partway in the direction of travel. There are several depots near the Central Market: Northwest of the market you'll find share-taxis to Battambang; southwest of the market is a minibus station to Udong, Kompong Speu, and Battambang, plus share-taxis to Kompong Cham. West of the Capitol Hotel is a depot with share-taxis to Kampot and Sihanoukville. At Dang Kor Market, to the southwest of town, share-taxis run to Takeo. At Chbam Market, southeast of town across Monivong Bridge, share-taxis run to Koki Beach, and to Bavet at the Vietnamese border.

Visa Shopping

Vietnamese Embassy: You can get a Vietnamese visa directly from the embassy, or through an agent such as the Capitol Hotel. Processing takes about five working days (the embassy is open Saturday morning); two photos required. Cost is around $50 for a one-month dual-entry

visa. A faster visa costs more. Longer visas are obtainable—a three-month multiple-entry visa costs $80.

Lao PDR Embassy: The embassy is open Monday–Friday 0800–1130 and 1400–1700, and Saturday 0800–1130. A seven-day transit visa direct from the Lao Embassy takes one working day. A 14-day tourist visa requires three days and costs $25–35, which is much cheaper than in Bangkok. For this visa you need to submit your original passport and three photos. If these visas are not available through the embassy, try an agent—who will also try to talk you into a travel package. Visas via agents run $25–80 and take 2–4 days.

Thai Consulate: The Royal Thai Consulate is open Monday–Friday 0830–1200. You can receive a 30-day tourist visa for $10 in three working days; a 60-day visa runs $15.

Cambodian Visa Extensions

Extensions cost $30–35 for one month, $50 for two months, and $60 for three months. Go through a travel agent or hotel staff.

Excursions from Phnom Penh

Around Phnom Penh are a number of destinations within day-trip range—nothing special, but a chance to get into the countryside and receive a blast of oxygen after the fetid air of Phnom Penh. With the exception of Choeung Ek, the sites described here are picnicking destinations, popular with the weekend escape crowd. Travel agents offer packages to sites, leaving early in the morning. You can also arrange your own taxi or moto.

Choeung Ek

There are killing fields all over Cambodia, skull-and-bone cairns that stand as stark memorials to Khmer Rouge atrocities. At Choeung Ek, 15 kilometers to the southwest of Phnom Penh, an estimated 17,000 people were killed, most clubbed to death to save ammunition. Many were taken from the interrogation center at Tuol Sleng. There are more than 120 mass graves in the area; half have been disinterred. A stupa-like tower of glass panels was erected in 1988 to house the grisly remains, with shelf after shelf of skulls—an unnerving sight. Be sure to read the moving visitor book here. Moto drivers charge $4–5 for a round-trip to Choeung Ek; a taxi should cost about $10, which can be split among several passengers.

Koki Beach

Koki Beach, about 12 kilometers east of Phnom Penh on the Saigon route, is a popular weekend and public holiday destination. Residents of Phnom Penh decamp to the river and rent huts raised on stilts for a day of picnicking, talking, or romance. Cafés here sell grilled fish and chicken. Don't expect much in the way of a beach, though there is a strip of sand and it is possible to swim. Most visitors rent a stilt hut to take a nap, ward off the heat, or counter the floodwaters of the monsoon season. You can hire a boat to tour the lake; waterborne vendors come alongside to sell food. Crowded on weekends, with lots of food vendors, but nothing much happening during the week. Share-taxis run to Koki Beach from a stand near Chbam Pao Market on the east side of Monivong Bridge; you could also take a moto.

Mekong Trips

Phnom Penh Tourism and the Hotel Cambodiana organize trips to a tourist trap called **Mekong Island,** which is actually Oknhatey Island, about an hour by boat from Phnom Penh. The island is a theme park with ersatz Cambodian culture packaged for the tourist masses—a model village, handicraft production, zoo, traditional dance and music ensembles, and restaurant. The trip costs around $25 and includes lunch and show. Another, longer trip organized by Phnom Penh Tourism is to **Koh Dach,** a silk-weaving village northeast of Phnom Penh. A boat ride up the Mekong to Ko Dach takes three hours round-trip. You can also visit fishing villages and see river life along the way. Hire your own vessel, or join a group through a travel agent.

Udong

Udong, 40 kilometers northwest of the capital along Route 5, is the site of an ancient capital, with a cluster of kings' tombs. This is another popular picnic site, affording great views of the surrounding area. Udong was the seat of Cambodian kings 1618–1866. Almost all the buildings of the former royal city were razed when Lon Nol launched air strikes against Khmer Rouge hideouts in the 1970s; other sites were later blown up by the Khmer Rouge. A Khmer Rouge prison was situated here. A memorial to the victims was erected in 1982, with torture devices and bones from mass graves on display, as well as murals depicting Khmer Rouge atrocities. To reach Udong, hire a taxi for $20, or take a motorcycle.

Tonle Bati

About 33 kilometers south of Phnom Penh on Route 2 is a turnoff that leads several kilometers to Tonle Bati. This is a popular picnic

A huge strangler fig has invaded the ruins of Ta Prohm.

© MICHAEL BUCKLEY

spot, with a lake and two temples, Ta Prohm and Yeay Peau. A taxi from the Capitol Hotel should cost around $15. On weekends the place is full of food stalls and picnic paraphernalia. Soldiers and amputee beggars demanding money sometimes try to stop cars coming into the area.

Twelfth-century **Ta Prohm Temple** looks similar to a minor Angkor temple. Some attribute the handiwork to King Jayavarman VII, who ruled in Angkor from 1181. According to legend, the temples were built by Ta Prohm. While traveling through Tonle Bati, an Angkor king fell in love with Yeay Peau, the beautiful daughter of a fisherman. The king passed three months with her and she became pregnant. Upon leaving, the king gave her a ring with instructions to send the child she bore to Angkor. When her son, Prohm, duly presented the ring at Angkor, he was welcomed at his father's palace and given an education. The king later sent him back to govern Takeo province.

Prohm built a temple similar to those he'd seen at Angkor, and named it after himself. For his mother, he built Yeay Peau Temple.

Phnom Chisor

About 20 kilometers south of Tonle Bati is a hilltop ruin dating from the Angkor period. The turnoff to Phnom Chisor is 55 kilometers south of Phnom Penh; the temple is about four kilometers from Route 2. The main sanctuary—what's left of it—is an 11th-century structure dedicated to Brahma. This spot is isolated, so do not go alone. Bring a guide. The temple is reached by a staircase on the northern side of the hill. From the top are expansive views over the countryside—you can see two other temple ruins to the east. Leave the hilltop by the southern staircase.

Takeo

The town of Takeo is 75 kilometers south of Phnom Penh on Route 2. It can also be reached by Route 3; this way is 87 kilometers from Phnom Penh, but the road is in better shape. This is stretching the limits of a day trip from the capital because travel time alone is six hours round-trip by taxi. About 20 kilometers east of Takeo is the modern village of **Angkor Borei**, which is thought to have been the site of Vyadhapura, the last capital of the Funan Kingdom. South of town is a hill called **Phnom Da.** Statues discovered in caves at Phnom Da by French archaeologists are displayed at Phnom Penh's National Museum. The Phnom Da style was identified as the first stage of pre-Angkorian art. On top of Phnom Da is a small building made from heavy basalt blocks.

Sea Route to Thailand

During the French colonial era the area along the Gulf of Thailand was renowned for its seaside resorts and mountain spas. These resorts were largely destroyed during the civil war, when they were first occupied and then blown up by the Khmer Rouge. These resorts have been revived. The road to Sihanoukville is the smoothest in the country—it was engineered by the Americans. Sihanoukville is a major stepping stone on the sea route by a series of hops along the Gulf of Thailand to the coastal town of Ban Hat Lek.

KAMPOT

Kampot is a small town on the Tuk Chhou River, five kilometers inland from the sea. Fishing and farming are the main activities; durians and melons grow in abundance. To the south end of town is a large dusty traffic circle with three hotels arrayed around it—**Phnom Kieu, Phnom Kamchay,** and **Tuk Chhou.** Each has its own restaurant; Tuk Chhou offers a seedy nightclub. Also on the circle is **Prachummith Restaurant,** close by is **Amar Restaurant.** To the south near the river is the GPO and telecommunications building. At the north end of town, about 1.5 kilometers away, is the central market, with food stalls. All Kampot transportation is concentrated within range of the market—cyclos, motos, taxis, trucks, and buses. The railway station lies farther north. There's nothing of interest in Kampot except to walk around town and look at crumbling French-built blue-shuttered shop fronts. Previously, Kampot was a stepping-stone to Bokor and Kep.

You can reach Kampot by irregular plane service from Phnom Penh. It's also possible—but not advisable—to get there by share-taxi. It takes about five hours to cover the 150 kilometers from Phnom Penh to Kampot. From Sihanoukville it's 105 kilometers to Kampot by a treacherous dirt road. The train from Phnom Penh to Kampot, when it runs, takes seven hours.

Vicinity of Kampot

Kep, 25 kilometers southeast of Kampot, is easily reached by moto on a day trip. The resort was founded in 1908; in colonial days, Kep-sur-Mer was a favorite vacation spot for French administrators and Cambodian aristocrats. Sihanouk maintained a private offshore island to entertain guests. The French constructed villas, residences, hotels, and a handful of public buildings. In the 1970s the Khmer Rouge methodically dynamited every single one. This is an eerie place to visit—Cambodian fishermen huddle in the shells of palatial French villas, cooking over open fires. The beaches at Kep are hardly suited to swimming—most are pebbly or hard-sand strips with coconut palms. The tiny main beach is deserted during the week, but since Kep is closer to Phnom Penh than Sihanoukville, it's deluged on weekends. A restaurant and food stalls near the beach sell fresh crab. Facilities are limited, with only a few guesthouses in operation. You could stay with locals.

About 40 kilometers west of Kampot, reached by a rough winding road, is the former French hill station of **Bokor.** Sitting at

WATER CORRIDORS FROM PHNOM PENH

Using Phnom Penh as the hub, three water border crossings are possible. In the southwest is a sea route via Sihanoukville to Thailand. Also in the southwest is a route along the Mekong to Chau Doc in Vietnam. And in the northeast is another route along the Mekong that crosses into southern Laos. (A fourth major border crossing route, in the northwest, is described in the *Angkor* chapter.) This is also possible mostly by water.

These border crossings can be done by land in two cases, but this is not as scenically interesting, and you miss out on river lifestyles. Some destinations, such as Sihanoukville and Kep, are beach resorts—and can thus be targeted as round-trips from Phnom Penh. For round-trips, you might want to consider a flight one-way to Stung Treng, for instance, and take the boat back (or the reverse routing).

1,080 meters in the Elephant Mountains, the resort was known for its mild climate, forest, gurgling streams, waterfalls, and panoramas of the Gulf of Thailand. The resort now lies in ruins, but they are interesting ruins. Best way to get there is by motocross bike, rented from Kampot. You can see a destroyed French casino and French church—two ruins of Biblical proportions. Popokvil Falls are close to the access road to Bokor.

The Khmer Rouge razed all the buildings at the hill resort of **Kirirom** in the Elephant Mountains. At 700 meters in elevation, Kirirom once provided a cool respite from summer heat for the Phnom Penh elite. With forests of rare pine trees and a rich stock of wildlife and fauna, Kirirom was selected in 1995 as the centerpiece of a 35,000-hectare national park straddling Kompong Speu and Koh Kong provinces. Kirirom lies about 115 kilometers southwest of Phnom Penh off Route 4, on the way to Sihanoukville. Don't expect a real national park—logging concessions are granted within the park confines.

SIHANOUKVILLE

Because the Mekong was long Cambodia's major thoroughfare, the coastal region never developed as a trade center. With the Vietnam War, however, Cambodia was forced to look for alternate routes. A road was built from Phnom Penh to the coast with American aid in the 1960s. Sihanoukville was founded in 1964 by its namesake, underwent a name change under the Khmer Rouge to Kompong Som, and reverted to its original name upon the return of the king in 1991.

Sihanoukville is two entities: port and resort. This deepwater port in the Gulf of Thailand was developed with Soviet aid to circumvent the need to pass through Vietnam's Mekong Delta. Fishing is a major activity in Sihanoukville, with a cannery north of the main port. The national beer maker, Angkor Brewery, operates from Sihanoukville. Container-loads of Angkor Beer have sailed out of Sihanoukville bound for Japan, Canada, and even the United States (heading for Long Beach, California, where a 50,000-strong resident Cambodian community lives). There were plans to build an oil refinery, and international companies are exploring along the Gulf of Thailand for offshore oil and gas.

The port was undergoing a $5 million facelift thanks to a dramatic rise in shipping activity. Renovations include the construction of a new container terminal, repairs to 1950s-era waterfront warehouses, installation of new cranes and cargo-handling equipment, and the purchase of new tugboats. With the new facilities, Sihanoukville could become an important transit stop for inter-Asia cargo. The town is receiving a massive transfusion of foreign investment funds and has been earmarked for major tourist development. Sihanoukville is slated to become Casino City. There were plans for a $400 million casino resort on Naga Island off the coast, complete with an international airport. The Tourism Ministry says casinos will

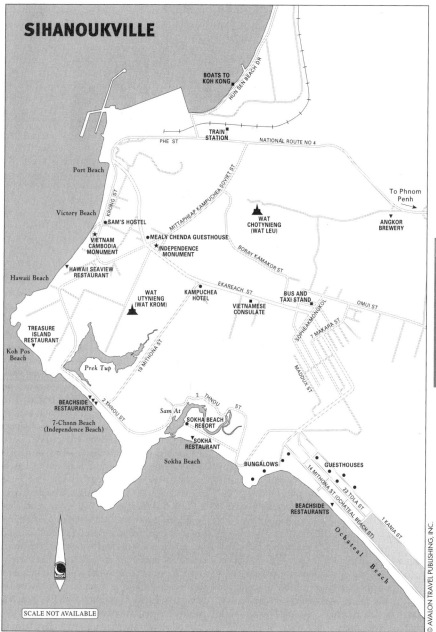

SIHANOUKVILLE

BOATS TO KOH KONG
HUN SEN BEACH DR
TRAIN STATION
PHE ST
NATIONAL ROUTE NO 4
Port Beach
KRONG ST
MITTAPHEAP KAMPUCHEA SOVIET ST
To Phnom Penh
Victory Beach
SAM'S HOSTEL
WAT CHOTYNIENG (WAT LEU)
ANGKOR BREWERY
VIETNAM CAMBODIA MONUMENT
MEALY CHENDA GUESTHOUSE
INDEPENDENCE MONUMENT
BORAY KAMAKOR ST
HAWAII SEAVIEW RESTAURANT
Hawaii Beach
EKAREACH ST
BUS AND TAXI STAND
OMUI ST
WAT UTYNIENG (WAT KROM)
KAMPUCHEA HOTEL
VIETNAMESE CONSULATE
SOPHEAKMONGKOL
7 MAKARA ST
TREASURE ISLAND RESTAURANT
Koh Pos Beach
Prek Tup
19 MITHONA ST
MADDUX ST
BEACHSIDE RESTAURANTS
2 THNOU ST
2 THNOU ST
Sam At
SOKHA BEACH RESORT
7-Chann Beach (Independence Beach)
SOKHA RESTAURANT
Sokha Beach
BUNGALOWS
GUESTHOUSES
14 MITHONA ST (OCHATEAL BEACH ST)
23 TOLA ST
1 KANIA ST
BEACHSIDE RESTAURANTS
Ochateal Beach

Phnom Penh

SCALE NOT AVAILABLE

© AVALON TRAVEL PUBLISHING, INC.

Phnom Penh

be restricted to foreign passport holders, and that strict controls will be implemented to prevent criminal activities. The government plans to levy a 1 percent gaming tax for distribution to worthy cultural and welfare organizations and causes. In the 1950s and 1960s several casinos operated in Cambodia.

Being There

Sihanoukville is scattered over a wide area. There is a downtown section with shops, restaurants, and banks; all local transport piles up near the central market. The deluxe buses coming in from Phnom Penh will drop passengers in Sihanoukville town; from here you would have to proceed by moto to the beaches, or on foot around town. The town maintains some links with the outside world: Cambodia Samart telecommunications group has an office in Sihanoukville with mobile phones and satellite hookup. Try the post office for IDD calls too. The Cambodia country code is 855; Sihanoukville area code is 34. There are several banks in Sihanoukville town, including the Cambodian Commercial Bank. There's a Vietnamese Consulate where you can process visas—and take time out on the beach to wait out the processing!

Beaches

As a beach resort, Sihanoukville has it all over Kep. There are several long stretches of white sand with palm trees, and coves of white sand with scattered fishing villages. Starting from the eastern side, **Ochateal** is a wide stretch of powdery sand favored by visitors, a lot of whom stay in hotels nearby. The beach is busy with foodstalls and roving vendors, but it is so long that quiet sections can easily be found. The water at Ochateal is clear and unpolluted, but it's not clear for how much longer as this part of Sihanoukville was being "developed," with new resorts on the horizon and a golf course in the works. To the western side of Ochateal lies tiny **Serendipity Beach,** with a few bungalows right at the beachside. The next cove along is **Sokha Beach,** with white sand running 1.5 kilometers, fringed by fir trees. Unfortunately, Sokha Beach Resort lays full claim to the beach, telling casual visitors to keep away, except for public-access sections at the periphery. The next cove to the west commands a strip of sand that is very popular with locals on weekends. Farther west, tiny **Koh Pos Beach** is public, but you would not be welcomed by the seafood restaurant that appears to lay claim to the beachfront for diners. And then the sand runs out: Toward the port area, the beaches turn rocky and narrow. Don't bother with **Victory Beach.**

Offshore Islands

At Koh Pos Beach you can arrange a boat to visit offshore islands such as **Kos Pos Island,** which lies a few kilometers out. This would be a half- to a full-day trip offering possibilities for snorkeling and diving if you have your own gear. You can also rent fishing boats at the fishing dock to the north of Sihanoukville. Boats usually cost around $20 to Koh Pos, perhaps $30–40 to go to more-distant islands. More expensive is to arrange a trip through Pet's Pub in Sihanoukville—an Australian rents out diving and snorkeling gear and fishing rods and runs an aluminum-hulled boat to the islands, launching from Hawaii Seaview Restaurant. The charge is $100 a day for the boat (holds more than 20 people).

On a faster boat you can venture farther to pristine beaches, diving locations, and picnic spots. About three hours out by boat is **Koh Rung,** with the area's best diving. **Koh Rung Samloen,** the island to the south of this, has clean beaches. To the southeast is the **Bay of Ream,** with good diving and snorkeling—and a fledgling marine park.

Accommodations

Accommodations are widely scattered in Sihanoukville; restaurants are often attached to hotels or owned by hoteliers. It is far preferable to be out near the beaches in Sihanoukville, such as Serendipity or Ochateal.

Sihanoukville Town: In town is a slew of hotels in the $15–40 range, but these are far from the beaches. A number of hotels here are Chinese-run and angled for business travelers who are partial to karaoke machines. Among these are Thai San, Colap II, Kompong Som, Koh Thas, Soriya, and Victory hotels. On Ekareach Street you'll find **Star Hotel,** tel. 34/320148, with 19 rooms for $15–20, including a/c and hot water; **Semsak Hotel,** tel. 34/320096, with 20 rooms for $13–15. In the

vicinity is **Mohasal Hotel,** tel. 34/933488, with 19 rooms for $15–20.

Serendipity Beach: This is a great location because the guesthouses are quite close to the beach, not removed as they are at Ochateal Beach. Rooms range from $5 for a room with shared bath to $30 for private bungalows. Down this way are bungalows at **Coasters, Cloud Nine, Diamond, Eden** and **Roneth.** Cheaper deals can be found farther back from the beach. Among the best of the bungalows are those at Coasters, with views of the ocean and islands. Coasters has a handful of bungalows charging $10–25 a room, and a prime restaurant location right near the sand.

Ochateal Beach: Lining the road about 150 meters back from the beach is a string of guesthouses: **Golden Sand, Holiday, Sunshine, Crystal, Romny, Susaday, Jasmine,** and others. **Villa Orchidee** offers rooms for $20–40 with hot shower and satellite TV, and a sunset terrace. Nearby is **Les Feuilles,** a restaurant and hotel, with a/c rooms with satellite TV for $25. There are many more midrange places at Ochateal, and a few budget offerings farther back from the beach.

Sokha Beach: Sokha Beach Resort, tel. 34/935999, fax 34/935888, www.sokhahotels.com, lays claim to the entire beach. The sprawling high-end complex charges $80 for a standard room and up to $1,000 for a suite (including breakfast). The place has 186 rooms and a large pool close to the beach. The resort is not exactly friendly: It posts signs to keep outsiders off the beach, although there is a small public zone at the east end. Not that you might want to bathe there—Sokha Beach Resort rents personal watercraft and banana-boats—both lethal for casual swimmers.

Victory Beach: Sam's Hostel, on a hill overlooking the last beach before the port, is a pleasant place with wooden rooms for $3 dorm, $4 no bath, and $6 with shower. Sam is a Cambodian cook; her fish dishes are excellent. Up this way is **Mealy Chenda GH,** tel. 34/933472, a backpacker's palace with large rooms for $5–10; the family-run restaurant on the top deck has great views over the water and serves excellent food—drop in for food even if not staying here.

Food

Beachside restaurants serving seafood are the places to be. You can find good ones at Serendipity Beach. Strung all the way along Ochateal Beach are foodstalls, with restaurants farther back under the shade of trees. The foodstalls are lit up with candles at night. As you move farther west along the coast, **Treasure Island Restaurant** at Koh Pos Beach serves seafood and seems to have rights over the beach here. If you buy food from the restaurant, you can sit in one of it open-air pavilions. A great venue serving seafood right near Victory Beach is **Hawaii Seaview Restaurant,** tel. 34/933659—it has indoor and outdoor sections.

Getting There

By Air: There are several flights a week from Phnom Penh to Sihanoukville for $40 one-way, $70 round-trip. There may be flights connecting Sihanoukville direct to Koh Kong.

By Road: Sihanoukville is 230 kilometers from Phnom Penh on Route 4. This highway, constructed by USAID in the 1950s, was rebuilt by the United States and is the best paved road in the country. The best way to get there is to take an air-conditioned bus that runs from the area of Phnom Penh's central market. Two Malaysian companies—DH Cambodia and GST Co.—run 3–4 buses each way daily. Cost is around $5 one-way; the buses have tinted windows and a hostess delivering drinks. The ride is supersmooth (for Cambodia).

A taxi to Sihanoukville costs $20 from Phnom Penh's Dang Kor Market and takes about three hours one-way. If you must travel this route by taxi, depart early: Avoid travel by road after dark.

By Rail: The slow goods train from Phnom Penh via Kampot takes at least 12 hours to reach Sihanoukville—not a practical option.

By Sea: Those crossing from Thailand come via the town of Hat Lek by small boat and transfer at Koh Kong (Cambodian side) for a fast boat to Sihanoukville. The fast boat costs about $12 one-way. On occasion, foreign cruise ships have docked in Sihanoukville.

Getting Around

Local transportation is clustered round the market downtown. Motos are the best way to get around Sihanoukville. It's possible to rent motorcycles or bicycles through hotels. You can rent small boats from Koh Pos Beach and the fishing docks to the northwest to visit offshore islands. Pet's Pub on the north side of Sihanoukville town arranges motorcycle rental and dive-equipment rentals.

Vicinity of Sihanoukville

The country's first national park, **Preah Sihanouk National Park,** was established in 1995 at Ream, 20 kilometers east of Sihanoukville. The park covers 21,000 hectares of forest and beaches and embraces a marine zone. There's a visitor center at the park. Ream is a port with a naval base.

THAI MARINE BORDER CROSSING

Travelers regularly enter Cambodia by sea from Trat province, crossing to Koh Kong in Cambodia. Both Cambodia and Thailand will stamp you in on the spot. Take a small boat from Ban Hat Lek at the tip of Thailand to the Cambodian side and carry on. From Ban Hat Lek, 10-person long-tail boats run for an hour through mangroves to reach the area of Koh Kong. From there you can take a daily large speedboat to Sihanoukville.

Mekong Route to Vietnam

While the land route from Phnom Penh to Saigon is dull, the boat route is a blast. Follow in the soggy footsteps of French explorers of the Mekong who used this water route, and in the footsteps of 1930s French tourists who took the Saigon to Phnom Penh boat en route to Angkor. Scenery combined with fishing and other activity on the riverbanks makes this trip well worth it. If you charter a whole boat, you can even arrange some stops at villages along the way. Several variations of the water route exist—one is to travel along the Mekong and turn down a channel to Chau Doc; another route goes from Phnom Penh along the Bassac River directly to Chau Doc.

Phnom Penh to Chau Doc

Boats regularly ply the Mekong between Phnom Penh and Chau Doc. Your paperwork must be in order to cross here. While it is possible to get a Cambodian visa at the Tonle Mekong border post, you cannot get a Vietnamese visa on the spot—this must be obtained in advance. A trip by 24-seat speedboat leaves from downtown Phnom Penh every afternoon and takes about five hours to get to Chau Doc; the cost is $15. More expensive is the Victoria Hotel speedboat from Phnom Penh to Chau Doc (see the *Chau Doc* entry under *Mekong Delta* in *The South* chapter in the *Vietnam* section for details on Victoria Chau Doc Hotel). A number of companies compete for the Phnom Penh to Chau Doc route: Some companies will try to sell you short by offering a combination land-and-boat ride. The first leg is by minivan from Phnom Penh to Neak Luong, where transfer is made to a boat for the shorter river ride to Chau Doc. All of which defeats the purpose of the trip, which is to see the river—at its most scenic closer to Phnom Penh.

Chau Doc to Cantho

From Chau Doc, it may be possible to continue by speedboat to Cantho. The boat companies can fold overnight—or their boats might be out of commission for some reason. You will have to resort to scanning websites to see what is currently up and running, and what the prices are. Try these: www.transmekong.com and www.travelmekong.net. TransMekong has a larger rice barge called *The Bassac* for group tours in the delta. Tu Trang Travel operates a fleet of about 20 boats in the Mekong Delta.

Cantho to Saigon

You can make it from Cantho to Saigon on the water, but companies do not seem interested in covering this route. You could try to hire your own speedboat—a very expensive option unless shared. High pricing on boats is apparently due to the cost of gasoline. Otherwise, you would have to resort to travel by bus.

In the reverse direction, from Saigon to Phnom Penh, you can join a two- or three-day Mekong Delta trip from Saigon (many agencies offer these) and finish in Chau Doc. From Chau Doc, you take the morning speedboat to Phnom Penh.

Land Border Crossing

The only reason to travel along Route 1 is to get to Saigon: The landscape is dull. Route 1 from Phnom Penh to Saigon is in excellent shape, sealed for rapid troop movement when Vietnam occupied Cambodia 1979–1989. The border crossing point is at Bavet on the Cambodian side and Moc Bai on the Vietnamese side. Your paperwork needs to be in order for the land crossing. To exit Cambodia you need a valid Vietnamese visa. Money changers offer poor rates at the border, so you're better off carrying small U.S. bills to pay for any transportation or other expenses.

The Bavet-Moc Bai border is in theory open 0630–1800 daily, which means you need to leave Phnom Penh early. At Neak Luong, 60 kilometers from Phnom Penh, you must catch a ferry across the Mekong; traders will change dollars into Vietnamese dong at reasonable rates here. Once in the border town of Bavet

CHARTING THE MEKONG

In the mid-19th century, the British and the French competed for the new China trade. Europeans saw China—rich in silk, tea, and textiles—as a kind of El Dorado. The British were expanding along the Yangzi from Shanghai on China's east coast; the French thrust into China came through Indochina. By this shortcut the French hoped to beat the competition to Yunnan province.

Very rough terrain lay between China's southwest and the seaports on the coast of French-dominated Vietnam. Could the Mekong serve as a trade route between the port of Saigon and landlocked Yunnan province? The French organized an expedition to find out. Leading the expedition were Captain Ernest Doudart de Lagrée and his deputy, Lieutenant Francis Garnier. Doudart de Lagrée was the first French resident in Cambodia; Garnier was a 27-year-old naval lieutenant. In the grand tradition of the time the Frenchmen set off in 1866 on what was to be a two-year journey. The six principal explorers set off in an expedition that was imperially motivated and semiscientific in nature, with cartographer, artist, botanist, and geologist aboard.

The explorers and their native bearers left Saigon in June 1866, detouring via Lake Tonle Sap to Angkor Wat, rediscovered by Henri Mouhot in 1860. The expedition mapped the ruins of Angkor and returned to the Mekong. They then proceeded upstream to Laos, apparently consuming large amounts of alcohol to counter the effects of mosquitoes, disease, and the inhospitable climate and terrain. They traveled up past the Kratie rapids to the Laos-Cambodia border, where sandbars impeded their progress. They then encountered Khong Phapheng Falls, which posed a major obstacle to boat transport. Garnier stumbled across the ruins of Wat Phu, an Angkor-era temple complex in southern Laos. The expedition finally reached Vientiane in April 1867, a year after setting out.

At this point the expedition had established that the Mekong was not a viable trade route, but, obsessed by a maniacal drive, Garnier persuaded the group to forge on. Two weeks later they were in Luang Prabang, the royal capital of Laos. Then they pushed north into China, where Doudart de Lagrée collapsed and died in Yunnan from fever and fatigue. Garnier led the group down the Yangzi River to Shanghai and back to Saigon. Of the 9,960 kilometers covered on the expedition, more than 5,000 kilometers represented uncharted territory. The explorers had discovered abandoned Khmer ruins, encountered remote hilltribe groups, and forged through virgin jungle.

The report of the expedition is a landmark work on Indochina and one of the finest of its genre. Garnier's two-volume *Voyage d'Exploration en Indochine* was published in Paris in 1873. This lavishly illustrated collection of details unfolded the mysteries of the Mekong. The first volume describes the voyage and is illustrated with engravings; the sec-

you can walk through to Vietnamese customs and immigration. Clearing both sides takes about half an hour. Phnom Penh to Saigon by taxi requires 6–7 hours. A bus ride can consume 9–14 hours depending on police checks on the Vietnamese side.

ond volume comprises technical appendices, with observations on history, geography, meteorology, archaeology, anthropology, and language. There were also two magnificent folios: an atlas with extensive maps and plans of areas previously unseen by European eyes, and a pictorial record of peoples, landscapes, and ruins provided by expedition cartographer and artist Louis Delaporte.

In his grand opus Garnier expounded the theory that France should not wait to fulfill its imperial destiny, but should act immediately. Debate raged at the time in France on the ethics of expansionism in foreign places, viewed by some as a waste of funds.

Garnier then took matters into his own hands. He'd given up on the Mekong as a navigable route, focusing instead on the Red River as a route from China to ports on the Gulf of Tonkin. Enter Jean Dupuis, a gunrunner who'd met Garnier along the Yangzi. Dupuis sold weapons to a warlord in Yunnan and needed an alternative route to the Yangzi. After a successful experiment on the Red River, the governor of Cochinchina, Admiral Dupré, deployed French warships near Haiphong as a gesture of support for Dupuis.

Dupuis transported weapons to Yunnan in March 1873 and returned two months later to Hanoi with a cargo of tin and copper. When mandarins who controlled the salt monopoly in Hanoi blocked the departure of Dupuis with a cargo of salt, Garnier joined forces with Dupuis, stormed Hanoi Citadel, and declared the Red

River open to trade. Within a month their forces had conquered the entire region between Hanoi and the sea, including Haiphong. On December 21, 1873, under attack outside Hanoi by Black Flag mercenaries fighting for the Vietnamese, Garnier led a charge and was cut down by a hail of bullets. He was 35 years old. His exploits came to symbolize the glories of imperialism.

The French withdrew from Tonkin, but, concerned that colonial powers such as Britain or Germany might seize the coal mines at Hong Gai, Captain Henri Rivière followed in Garnier's footsteps. He was killed near Hong Gai by Black Flag forces who paraded his head from village to village. In 1883 the French set out to take Tonkin a third time, and by the end of the year had more than 20,000 men in Tonkin. Not content with the Red River trade route, the French built a railway concession between Hanoi and Kunming, completed in 1910. The line cost a fortune, and the fabled riches of China barely materialized.

The source of the Mekong remained one of the world's last great geographical mysteries. In April 1995, a Franco-British expedition led by Michel Peissel announced his discovery of the source in the mountains of Kham, Tibet, at the 4,975-meter head of Rupsa Pass. However, this claim was refuted by the Chinese Academy of Sciences, which in 2001 identified the source as lying at a glacier in Kham at 5,224 metres. Because the latter site is farthest from the sea, it is now accepted as the true source.

Mekong Route to Laos

Accessible by boat is the Kompong Cham–Kratie–Stung Treng route, leading to a border crossing into Laos. Malaria is a risk in this area. You should carry your own mosquito netting and repellent. To reach the far northeast the best option is to take boats along the Mekong; you can also fly into Stung Treng. A long sleek cigar-shaped vessel plies the route from Phnom Penh all the way to Stung Treng if the water levels are sufficient (usually September–January). This is known as a "bullet boat," but some travelers refer to it as the "flying coffin." Because of sometimes-fierce air-conditioning and blaring videos, you are better off being on the roof of this vessel, though you can get fried by the sun. A bullet boat carries 50 passengers inside and another 20 on the roof. If water levels recede, the bullet boat will cease service at Kratie and a smaller, slower wooden vessel will make the run.

Kompong Cham

Kompong Cham is a river port on the west bank of the Mekong, 145 kilometers from Phnom Penh. Typical of Cambodian riverine towns, it has its complement of French shophouse architecture—and taxi girls. Best choice for a place to stay is the **Mekong Hotel,** overlooking the river, with rooms for $10 and up. It's possible to reach Kompong Cham by bullet boat in less than five hours. By road, a bus or share-taxi on Route 7 requires about three hours. Kompong Cham lies in a zone of rubber plantations with rich, red earth. You can visit Chhup Rubber Plantation, reached across the long bridge over the Mekong. There are a few shrines and temples around Kompong Cham, including **Wat Nokor** and **Prey Nokor.** The town of Kompong Cham and the surrounding province of the same name were a former base of the Cham people, renowned as skilled fishing folk. They settled riverbanks east and north of Phnom Penh and along the shores of the Tonle Sap. During the Pol Pot era, the Cham were persecuted because of their Sunni Muslim religion and their unique language and customs; only a third of the Cham in Cambodia survived. They're gradually regaining their confidence, reestablishing themselves in their old neighborhoods, and rebuilding mosques.

Kratie

Farther north on the Mekong is Kratie, a fishing and logging town. The citizens of Kratie appear to have perfected the art of doing nothing—life proceeds at a very tranquil pace. Some French colonial buildings survive near the waterfront. The Mekong is navigable year-round from Phnom Penh to Kratie. Boat trips are faster when the river runs high September–January; in other seasons the captain has to navigate around obstacles, and the going is slower. There may be air service to Kratie. About 30 kilometers north of Kratie is the site of the ancient capital of Sombor, which lies close to the Mekong. In the vicinity is a viewing area for Irrawaddy dolphins: You can hire a boat to go out to the middle of river to increase your chances of sighting the elusive mammal.

Stung Treng

Stung Treng is the capital of the province of the same name. The town lies 485 kilometers north of Phnom Penh and 210 kilometers south of Pakse in Laos. It's only 40 kilometers from the Lao border, where travelers make a water border crossing up the Mekong (you must have a valid Lao visa). Stung Treng is perched on the banks of the Sekong River, not far from the Mekong. Sights around town are few—a couple of rapids and waterfalls. You can rent a boat for trips along the Mekong. Stung Treng's market is brimming with goods that come in by road, river, or plane, down from Laos, across from Vietnam, or up from Phnom Penh. Thai, Chinese, and Vietnamese goods all find their way here.

You can reach Stung Treng by bullet boat from Phnom Penh September–January. As water levels recede, smaller craft make the run from Kratie to Stung Treng, negotiating minor rapids and flooded forest. There's also a rough truck route from Kratie to Stung Treng; share-taxis cost $4 per person for the six-hour run. On paper there are several flights a week from Phnom Penh to Stung Treng; round-trip $90. A handful of guesthouses in Stung Treng await you. The **Riverside GH,** not far from the river, charges $5 a room: it has a pleasant rooftop restaurant. The **Sekong Hotel,** tel. 074/973762, lies close to the river and charges $3–5 for fan rooms or $6–15 for rooms with bath; the hotel has seen better days. The downtown 50-room **Sok Sambath Hotel** charges $5–10 for a fan room and $15–25 for a/c rooms. For food, try the Riverside GH rooftop bar. The **Sunn Thai** restaurant, close to the markets, serves decent Khmer food.

If heading north of Stung Treng for Laos, ask about fares on a long-tailed boat. The cost of hiring the whole boat to the Lao border should be around $30–40. After exiting Cambodian customs, the boatman will take you across the Mekong to Lao immigration to be stamped in. From here, you can proceed farther upstream with the same boatman, who will drop you at the south side of Don Khone island. Another option is to disembark at Lao immigration and proceed by road to Ban Nakasang, where you can transfer to a small ferry to reach the northern end of Don Det island.

Ratanakiri

Bordering Vietnam's Central Highlands are the remote provinces of Ratanakiri and Mondulkiri, both with thickly forested hilly terrain, hilltribe people, and abundant wildlife. Commercial enterprises in the region include logging, gem mining, and rubber plantations. A fertile basalt plateau with red dusty soil lies between the Se San and Srepok rivers. Mondulkiri is virtually cut off, roads impassable. The provincial capital of Sen Monorom is best reached from Vietnam; Ratanakiri is accessible by air from Phnom Penh.

Over 80 percent of Ratanakiri's population of 72,000 is classified as hilltribe people, mainly Jarai, Krung, Brou, and Tampuan. The 12 ethnic minority groups are collectively called Khmer Loeu (highlanders), a name coined by Sihanouk in the 1940s. Some of these groups are found across the borders in Vietnam's Central Highlands or in southern Laos.

The recent history of Ratanakiri is not a happy one. During the Vietnam War the province of Ratanakiri was devastated by American carpet bombing because it formed part of the Ho Chi Minh Trail. The Khmer Rouge used Ratanakiri as their main base of operations in the early 1970s; when they came to power in 1975, the Khmer Rouge wiped out at least half the tribal population. Because the area is so remote and the infrastructure so weak, the highlanders today have little access to education or health care. Deaths result from malaria, diarrhea, and childbirth complications. There is a high incidence of malaria in both Ratanakiri and Mondulkiri provinces.

Most highlanders in Ratanakiri are animist and practice slash-and-burn agriculture. They farm rice and grow vegetables, and raise water buffalo and cows. They also hunt, using crossbows with poison-tipped bamboo arrows. Sacrifice to the numerous animal spirits of the forest is common and regularly performed for any special event such as marriage, the construction of a new thatch-roofed hut, or a move to a new village location. At these events a feast is held, a pig sacrificed, and large quantities of rice wine are consumed. At these gatherings the spirits are believed to take possession of certain individuals, who in a trance lose their own personality and take on that of the spirit, acting out a particular animist trait. Priestesses regarded as spiritual healers contact ancestral spirits and relay dreams.

Highland women enjoy as much freedom as men. They're free to divorce a husband who is cruel, and decisions on childbirth are the exclusive domain of women. If an unmarried woman finds herself pregnant, she is not disgraced—the man responsible, if not willing to marry, must reimburse the woman's family. The going rate is four buffalo, some pigs, a few chickens, and rice wine. Abortions are common after 4–5 children, with herbal potions used to end an unwanted pregnancy.

Although some hilltribe people don Khmer dress, others retain traditional wear. Krung tribeswomen wear sarongs, go bare-breasted, and smoke long-stemmed pipes. Brou tribeswomen have large pierced earlobes and wear earrings sculpted from chunky ivory tusks. Their faces are tattooed and they wear bead necklaces and brass anklets.

Ban Lung, population 10,000, is the principal town in Ratanakiri province and lies 155 kilometers east of Stung Treng. There should be direct flights into Ban Lung from Phnom Penh for $55 one-way; there may also be interprovincial flights from Stung Treng to Ban Lung. Another connection to look into is a direct Phnom Penh–Mondulkiri flight. The hotel in Ban Lung charges $5 a room; the town has a post office and bank. You can get to Ban Lung for about $5 on a truck from Stung Treng. The trip takes 5–7 hours, but the road may be washed out in the May–November monsoon season. In parts of Ratanakiri, the only conveyances that move during the rainy season are oxcarts and elephants.

Angkor

With a retinue of bearers, eccentric French naturalist Henri Mouhot hacked his way through the Cambodian jungle in January 1860 in search of beetles and butterflies. Though his interest lay more in insects than antiquities, he spent three weeks exploring the ruins of Angkor. He arrived by way of Lake Tonle Sap, where, he noted, fish were so abundant they impeded the progress of his boat. As a collector, Mouhot was entranced by butterflies the size of soup plates lazing on the stones. He was also intrigued by the stones themselves. In his diaries he claimed Angkor's ruins were grander than those of ancient Greece or Rome. He raved about a monument equal to the temple of Solomon, erected by some ancient Michelangelo. The sight of the ruins, he wrote in his diary, made the traveler

forget all the fatigues of the journey, filling him with admiration and delight, such as would be experienced in finding a verdant oasis in the sandy desert. Suddenly, and as if by enchantment, he seems to be transported from barbarism to civilization, from profound darkness into light.

Must-Sees

Look for **M** to find the sights and activities you can't miss and **ℕ** for the best dining and lodging.

M River Trip to Battambang: Get to see river life and fishing activity as you cross the top of Lake Tonle Sap and pass by floating villages. This trip is very different from taking a bus (page 418).

M *Apsara* **Dance:** Nightly performances of this sensuous choreography are staged at various dinner-dance venues in hotels and restaurants around Siem Reap. The food is mediocre, but the dance is divine (page 421).

M Exploring Angkor Wat: Large and classical, this awesome site is the world's largest temple, with the world's longest bas-relief panels. On the second terrace are friezes of celestial dancers (page 428).

M South Gate of Angkor Thom: Of the five gates leading to Angkor Thom, this one is in the best condition, with rows of demons and gods on either side. At the other gates, a lot of statuary has been stolen (page 436).

M The Bayon: This mysterious structure has archaeologists baffled. Huge four-headed towers are the key feature—the faint smiles of the stone faces seem to change with the time of day and the play of light (page 436).

M Leper King Terrace: A hidden inner wall reveals superb multitiered friezes, which have been restored. These are among Angkor's finest artworks (page 443).

M Ta Prohm: This temple has been left abandoned to kapok trees, strangler figs, and giant creepers. It has a romantic and poetic air to it (page 444).

M Preah Khan: A labyrinth of hallways and pavilions, vestibules, cloisters and courts, and collapsed masonry, this austere temple complex is definitely spooky (page 446).

M Banteay Srei: With its pink sandstone walls and exquisite carvings, Banteay Srei is an architectural jewel. Close by is **Kbal Spean,** with bas-reliefs sculpted in a river bed (page 449).

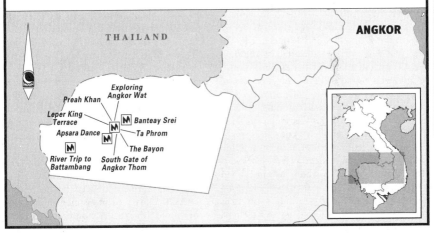

THAILAND

ANGKOR

Exploring Angkor Wat
Preah Khan
Leper King Terrace
Apsara Dance
Banteay Srei
Ta Phrom
The Bayon
River Trip to Battambang
South Gate of Angkor Thom

LOUIS DELAPORTE

illustration by Louis Delaporte as in Francis Garnier's *Voyage d'exploration en Indochine*, 1873

Angkor

Mouhot was not the first European to visit Angkor. A long line of traders, missionaries, and travelers had passed this way before him in the 17th, 18th, and 19th centuries. In fact, Mouhot's visit was inspired by the travels of French missionary Charles-Emile Bouillevaux, who visited in 1854. For some reason, the reports of others had gone unnoticed by the West. Mouhot, traveling under the auspices of England's Royal Geographical Society, was the most publicity-conscious of the visitors. He died in Laos in 1861 from a malarial fever; his diaries and travel correspondence were published posthumously in 1863 in a magazine called *Le Tour du Monde*, triggering European interest. More writings, focusing as much on natural wonders as on archaeology, appeared in a book *Voyage in Siam* in 1868. Englishman John Thompson took the first photographs of Angkor in 1866, and the ruins

exercised a powerful hold on the 19th-century European imagination. The image of ruined temples emerging from thick jungle vegetation became part of colonial romanticism—the lost city rediscovered.

It was not until after World War II, when archaeologist Bernard Groslier made aerial surveys of the area, that the full extent of Angkor was realized. Angkor comprises 70 monuments scattered over an area of 200 square kilometers. The complex of tombs, temples, palaces, moats, reservoirs, and causeways was built over a period of 400 years; only Egypt's Nile Valley can compare to this array of monuments.

There is nothing like Angkor in Southeast Asia. Only two monument complexes come close: 9th-century Borobodur in Indonesia, and 11th-century Pagan in Myanmar (Burma). The French could not imagine the Khmer kings were responsible for such monu-

mental work. Theories as to who constructed Angkor's monuments varied from the ancient Romans to Alexander the Great. Indeed, the structures echo styles from other monumental ruins. Angkor Wat is built in classical Indian style, with elements of the Java ziggurat of Borobodur, and yet the numerous bas-reliefs have a strangely Egyptian character. The columns and arches at Preah Khan Temple evoke those of the Greeks and Romans, while the pyramid of Phimeanakas resembles those of the Maya at Tikal, Guatemala.

The inspiration for Angkor architecture comes from a unique mix of Hinduism and Buddhism. The early rulers of Angkor promoted various Hindu sects, mainly dedicated to Shiva and Vishnu. Shiva was initially the most favored deity, but by the 12th century, Vishnu had replaced him. At the same time the kings encouraged Buddhist scholarship; Jayavarman VII introduced Mahayana Buddhism

as the court religion by the end of the 12th century. Layered onto these concepts was the tradition of deification of kings in sculptural form. This mix resulted in Angkorian structures that have no parallel, such as the fantastic South Gate of Angkor Thom and the bizarre Bayon.

Angkorian Architecture

French archaeologist Bernard-Philippe Groslier, who devoted his life to the documentation and preservation of Angkor, tried to convey its importance to his fellow countrymen through this comparison:

Imagine that within the city limits of Paris, between La Défense and the Place de la Nation, you found thrown together Versailles, the Place de la Concorde, the Louvre, the Place des Vosges and the palace of Fontainebleau and, surrounding these, the cathedrals of Notre Dame, Chartres, Reims, Amiens, Bourges and Strasbourg—flanked by all the churches built in Paris before the nineteenth century.

Angkor is astounding and complex in scope—how were these colossal structures built? The caste system of the Khmers was similar to the hierarchy extant in ancient Egypt and Mexico when the Pharaohs and Maya erected their pyramids. There was a line of kings, a class of priests and merchants, and a cast of thousands of slaves (captives of war), laborers, masons, sculptors, and decorators. Artisans, including architects, belonged to the lower echelons of society. They remain anonymous—nothing is known of the stone masons and sculptors who worked for the Angkorian kings.

Wooden buildings in the Angkor area have not survived. The use of brick or stone was reserved for sacred temples and monuments. Architects must have worked with priests on the design of such buildings: A number are temple-mountains representing the paradise of Mount Meru, center of the universe in Hindu-Buddhist cosmology. Rigidly geometric and symmetric patterns radiating in concentric circles compose the ground plans of a number of Angkor buildings. The effect is similar to a mandala, or sacred diagram of the cosmos, with Mount Meru at the center. To translate these concepts into three-dimensional form, Angkor's architects probably worked from wax models.

Early Angkor buildings were made of large bricks, with a mortar of vegetable–based adhesive. From the 10th century on, sandstone foundations were laid, and laterite was used in walls. Laterite is a red, porous material that is actually a kind of iron-bearing soil. It is easily quarried, cut into large blocks, and then left to harden upon exposure to the air. Angkor Wat and Angkor Thom rest on laterite foundations; the temples were mostly fashioned from sandstone quarried at Phnom Kulen, 45 kilometers northeast of Angkor. The sandstone exhibits a wide range of coloration, from gray to pinkish, yellowish buff to greenish. The sandstone was floated down the Siem Reap River and dragged to the building site using ropes, rollers, and winches. A bas-relief in the west inner gallery of the Bayon depicts the hauling and polishing of sandstone. The roughly dressed blocks were perfectly fitted, smoothed off, and the surfaces decorated with bas-reliefs. Some stones were held in place with bronze clamps while others relied entirely on gravity.

Signature in Stone

At the time of construction, temples at Angkor most likely bore the names of the kings who built them and the gods to whom they were dedicated. The name "Angkor" surfaced in the 16th century—the place was called Anjog, Onco, Anckoor, Ongcor, Angcor, and Vat Nokor by Western explorers. Angkor is believed to be a corruption of the Khmer *nokor* (*nakhon* in Thai, and *nagara* in Sanskrit), meaning the royal city of the Khmer Empire. Wat was added because of a Siamese monastery established on the grounds by Buddhist monks in the early 19th century, when the area fell under the Kingdom of Siam. Angkor Thom means "Great City."

The designation "Angkor" has several layers of meaning. Geographically, it refers to the 200-square-kilometer plain between Lake Tonle Sap and Phnom Kulen, the abode of the *devarajas* (divine kings). It also refers to the Khmer capital city, as well as to the A.D. 802–1431 period when the Angkor kings reigned. In addition, to art historians, Angkor denotes an art style prevalent 802–1175; work roughly 500–800 is considered pre-Angkorian art, while art 1177–1230 is classified as post-Angkorian or Bayon art. Angkor art is further subdivided into nine styles; the 1100–1175 period is called the Angkor Wat style.

Because no palm-leaf or parchment books survive from the Angkor period, inscribed stones are the primary source of information. Most of these stele have now been deciphered. They bear lines in Pali, Sanskrit, or ancient Khmer script praising the king. Sometimes they provide inventory information; some offer insight into daily Angkor life. A Sanskrit inscription at Preah Khan lists property belonging to the temple—a set of gold dishes weighing more than 500 kilograms; 35 diamonds; 40,620 pearls; 4,540 precious stones; 876 Chinese veils; 512 silk beds; 523 parasols.

In the 19th century, the French asked the locals what the names of Angkor's temples were. The old temple with the big mango tree? That was Prasat Svay, the Mango Tree Temple. The old temple in the forest? Banteay Prei, the Forest Temple. The one with fine bas-reliefs, and niches inset with statues of beautiful women? Banteay Srei, the Citadel of Women. The one with the stone lion statue? Prasat Sing, the Temple of the Lion. Unfortunately for archaeologists, there were lots of forests, fine bas-reliefs of women, and stone lions. Another EFEO (Ecole Française d'Extrème Orient) expedition numbered the monuments, but talking about a magnificent temple as Monument 497 did not win many hearts. Some of Angkor's lesser ruins are still identified by number.

Eyewitness at Angkor

Angkor, the capital of the Khmer Empire, was undoubtedly as splendid as any European city. And larger, too: At its zenith, Angkor may have hosted 750,000 citizens. It was built between the 9th and 14th centuries as the administrative and religious center of the powerful Khmer Empire. Bas-reliefs such as those at the Bayon and Angkor Wat provide clues about life at Angkor, but the only detailed eyewitness account comes from Zhou Daguan, an envoy from China. Daguan reached Cambodia by boat and land and stayed a year, 1296–1297. At this time, Indravarman III had just ascended the throne. The Khmer Empire was past its zenith but still powerful. Zhou Daguan was the Chinese envoy from the Mongol court of Timur Khan, his mission to induce the Khmer court to pay homage to the court of the Khans (a tribute exacted from sovereigns all over Asia). There is no mention in his writings of whether he was successful.

On his return to China, Daguan jotted down some impressions. Fragments from his *Notes on the Customs of Cambodia* date from the early 14th century. The manuscript is short, with occasional apologies for forgetting place names and other details. Surviving fragments were partially translated by Jesuit missionaries in Peking and published in Paris in 1789. A more complete French version was published in 1819; French scholar Paul Pelliot issued the best-known translation in 1902.

Brief as they are, the notes nevertheless bring Angkor to life. Zhou Daguan describes a glittering city of palaces and pagodas, palanquins and elephants, concubines, celestial dancers, and slaves. Life revolved around the Royal Palace and the temples of Angkor. Villagers were pressed into service for temple construction or maintenance tasks. The king's family held all the important posts of state, but if a commoner were chosen for office, the king offered his daughter as a royal concubine. A hierarchy of ministers, generals, astronomers, and other functionaries could be identified by their insignia. Daguan was not admitted to the grounds of the Royal Palace, where, by his estimation, the king lived with five wives and about 3,000 concubines.

Daguan exposed some darker sides of life at Angkor. Slaves were treated badly, chained at the neck. Serious criminal offenders could be punished by burial alive; for lesser offenses, the accused lost their hands, feet, or noses. Still, for this visitor, Angkor seemed like paradise on earth. Zhou Daguan wrote,

Chinese sailors coming to the country note with pleasure that it is not necessary to wear clothes, and, since rice is easily had, women easily persuaded, houses easily run, furniture easily come by, and trade easily carried on, a great many sailors desert to take up permanent residence.

It could not last. Weakened by huge construction projects and vast territorial gains that needed governing, Angkor went into decline. Its intricate irrigation system fell into disrepair, and crops failed. The Cham sacked Angkor in 1177. Siamese armies ravaged the area with attacks in 1353, 1393, and 1431. Finally, Angkor was abandoned. Well, not entirely—parts were occasionally used by

DEVARAJAS: DIVINE KINGS

The Angkor period is generally designated as the 630-year stretch from 802 to 1431. In 802, Jayavarman II ascended to the throne and established a line of *devarajas* (divine kings); in 1431 the Siamese overran Angkor. Except for a brief period in the 10th century, kings continuously occupied the plains of Angkor.

The Khmer kings adopted the Hindu trinity of Shiva, Brahma, and Vishnu, and each became the focus of cult worship. In Shiva cults, the spirit of the king was embodied in the statue of a giant sacred phallus, sheltered in a temple built by the king for that purpose.

Angkorian rulers frequently changed names during their reigns. Names were adopted from gods or denoted a king's special quality. Thus Indravarman means "He Who Enjoys the Protection of the God Indra," Jayavarman is "Protected by Victory," and Udayadityavarman denotes "Protected by the Rising Sun." Relying on site inscriptions, French scholars developed a chronology of Khmer art and Khmer kings using each king's most common name. Recurring names were sequenced I, II, III, and so on. Precise chronology of rulers is, at best,

guesswork, and archaeologists contradict each other. Thirty-odd kings ruled between 802 and 1431; a dozen of the most significant are mentioned here. Some kings reigned only briefly—succession was often contested, and foul play occasionally befell monarchs.

Shivaite Jayavarman II, 802–850, built a temple at Phnom Kulen, 45 kilometers northeast of Angkor Wat. Indravarman I, 887–889, also a Shivaite, was a usurper who established his capital at Roluos, to the east of Angkor Wat. Yasovarman I, 889–900, built his capital of Yasodhapura at Phnom Bakheng, near Angkor Wat, and constructed the East Baray and the brick temple of Lolei at Roluos. The empire of Yasovarman I stretched from the south of Laos to the Gulf of Siam. Jayavarman IV, 928–942, was a usurper who moved the capital to Koh Ker, 70 kilometers northeast of Angkor.

Rajendravarman II, 944–968, built East Mebon and Pre Rup Temples. Although he was Hindu and employed Brahman advisers, he also relied on Buddhist ministers. His chief Brahman adviser, Yajnavaraha, oversaw construction of the beautiful sandstone temple of Banteay

subsequent Khmer kings, including a 50-year stretch in the mid-16th century.

Much is missing today. No wooden buildings have survived, and all the residential compounds have disappeared. In 1431 the conquering Siamese killed, looted, and destroyed, carrying off thousands of slaves, stripping the palaces and temples of their statuary and ornaments encrusted with precious stones, and removing the gold coatings from towers and rooftops. Gone are the wooden palaces and dwellings with their terra-cotta roof tiles; gone are the sumptuous carpets and furnishings, Chinese pottery and ceramics, bronze weapons and cult objects, jewelry and utensils, silk beds and parasols. What remains are the huge sandstone blocks that could not be carted away. Some artifacts—statuary, jewelry, ritual objects—are on display at the National Museum in Phnom Penh. The rest—the vast kingdom peopled by

priests, celestial dancers, astronomers, ministers, and generals, and the court of Angkor with its banquets, music, dancing, rich tapestries and paintings, merchants coming and going—is left for you to conjure. In the haunting contrast between past grandeur and present decay lies the perverse pleasure of ruins.

The Plumbing Puzzle

Contrary to the design of most great cities, which grow on the banks of substantial bodies of water, Angkor lies inland some distance from a major river or port. Why was this site chosen for a capital? And how did the city sustain itself? The answer lies in the city's proximity to Lake Tonle Sap. The Khmer Empire depended on the annual flooding of the Great Lake for rice harvests and an abundant supply of fish; Lake Tonle Sap is one of the world's richest fishing grounds.

Srei. After about 950, important structures were built of sandstone, while brick was reserved for secondary sites. Jayavarman V, 968–1001, built the sandstone temple-mountains of Takeo and Phimeanakas, which became classic models.

Suryavarman I, 1002–1050, extended Cambodian rule into Siam. He is credited with the building of far-flung Preah Vihear sanctuary on today's Cambodian-Thai border and Phimai sanctuary in northeast Thailand, both as part of a royal highway that stretched from the Angkor region to the borders of Myanmar (Burma). He also acquired the region of Louvo (Lopburi) in Siam. Udayadityavarman II, 1050–1066, ordered the construction of the West Baray and the great temple of Baphuon.

Suryavarman II, 1112–1152, was one of the greatest Angkor kings. He was a Vishnuite responsible for the building of Angkor Wat, Chau Say Tevoda, and Thommanon, and probably also undertook Wat Phu in southern Laos. Under his rule the Khmer Empire expanded into present-day Malaysia, Thailand, Myanmar (Burma), and Vietnam. In a disastrous attempt to conquer north Vietnam, his armies were decimated by fever on a march through jungles and mountains.

Jayavarman VII, 1181–1218, embarked on a grand building binge, constructing Angkor Thom (the Bayon, walls and gates, Royal Palace), Neak Pean, Ta Som, Ta Prohm, Preah Khan, and Banteay Kdei, among other works. Jayavarman VII designated Mahayana Buddhism as the kingdom's main faith; some temples were possibly dedicated to Lokesvara, the bodhisattva of compassion. During his reign the boundaries of the empire extended from Pagan in Myanmar (Burma) to the Vietnam coast, and from the vicinity of Vientiane in Laos to the Malay Peninsula.

After Jayavarman VII the Khmer Empire declined, and no stone building of any significance was constructed. His sons and heirs reverted to Shivaism, and Indian Brahmans gained great influence at the court. Inscriptions give the names of five kings who reigned after Jayavarman VII. All were unable to prevent the rise of the Thai kingdom of Sukothai; increasingly violent attacks by the Siamese led to the collapse of Angkor in the 15th century.

Initially, researchers believed the Khmers established a sophisticated system of reservoirs and canals for irrigation at Angkor, enabling them to grow 3–4 rice crops a year. The reservoirs, the theory went, filled in the monsoon season and were used for irrigation during the dry season. The reservoirs could hold millions of gallons of water, making Angkor a hydraulic society par excellence.

However, this view is now being challenged. Water is never once mentioned on stone inscriptions at Angkor sites. Zhou Daguan, a 13th-century visitor, did not describe Angkor's plumbing except to mention bathing. Bathing was undoubtedly popular—the Chinese delegation took great pleasure in observing women bathing nude several times a day, "covering their sex with their left hand." Some geographers argue that the barays and canals were only for urban use—for bathing, ritual ceremonies, drinking, transport, beautifying the landscape, and perhaps for supplying fresh fish.

Using remote sensing equipment and satellite images to study land formations, engineers have found little evidence of extensive irrigation. Researchers calculate the combined storage capacity of all Angkor reservoirs is sufficient to irrigate only a paltry 400 hectares of rice fields—hardly enough to support a population estimated at up 750,000. The large moats around Angkor's monuments could not have been used for irrigation because there were no outlets into the fields. The annual flooding of Lake Tonle Sap is instead credited as the major water supply for rice growing. If Angkor's plumbing was instead for urban use, it was also an easy target for enemy saboteurs. A recent theory is that after Angkor's elaborate reservoirs and canals fell into disrepair, the pools became stagnant breeding grounds for mosquitoes, causing an outbreak of malaria.

Australian archaeologist Professor Roland Fletcher believes that Angkor was abandoned after it simply outgrew itself and burned out. As the city grew in population, this created a huge demand for rice, which meant that more and more land had to be cleared for rice fields. Eventually, Professor Fletcher says, river flows were destabilised—an event that would have torn apart the canal system and caused unpredictable flooding and damage to roadways.

Several Western experts have lobbied to restore the canals and reservoirs of Angkor, or at least raise the water table, to stabilize the monuments by hydraulic pressure and thus prevent further collapse.

Saving Angkor

Since 1989 UNESCO has coordinated international efforts to restore the monuments of Angkor, with half a dozen international agencies providing financial and technical aid. Looking forward to a more stable political situation, in December 1992 UNESCO adopted Angkor as a World Heritage Site, simultaneously placing Angkor on the World Heritage in Danger list. In October 1993, at a Tokyo conference hosted by Japan and France, funds were pledged to preserve the ruins and promote Angkor as a special tourist destination. A Japanese survey identified as a key priority supporting the foundations of Angkor Wat, the Bayon, Baphuon, and Preah Khan. Angkor was formally accepted onto the World Heritage List in 1996.

From 1870 to 1970, Angkor survey and restoration work was conducted exclusively by the French. Louis Delaporte participated in the French expedition to survey the Mekong in 1866–1868, with an initial stop at Angkor in 1866. He returned to Angkor in 1871 to compile extensive maps and sketches. Delaporte removed more than 100 of Angkor's finest statues to Paris, where they are now housed in the Guimet Museum. His published survey results appeared in *Voyage au Cambodge: l'architecture khmère* in 1880, and he returned to Cambodia

again in 1882–1883. In Paris he organized colonial exhibitions of Khmer art and architecture, featuring three-dimensional building replicas taken from moldings of smaller sites.

In 1898 the EFEO began clearing jungle, mapping sites, and making inventory lists as a prelude to restoration. Such prominent French archaeologists as Henri Marchal, Henri Parmentier, George Coedes, and Bernard Groslier made major commitments to preserving Angkor. Using local work teams, the French cleared vegetation, installed hidden drains to prevent water damage, and reconstructed a number of temples with anastylosis—the process of disassembling a structure, then reassembling it using the original methods and materials on top of a new concrete foundation. French restoration work ceased when they were driven out in 1970 by the Khmer Rouge.

Miraculously, Angkor survived the Pol Pot era largely intact. The Khmer Rouge lit fires in the galleries, used Angkor Wat as an ammunition dump, fired at bas-reliefs for target practice, and hacked off heads of numerous Buddha statues to sell on the international market to help finance their war efforts. With a few exceptions they did not dynamite entire structures, as they did with wats in other parts of the country. Buddha images were singled out for destruction—a large Buddha next to the Bayon was dynamited. But mostly Angkor was left alone, because as a cornerstone of Khmer culture, it served as inspiration for the Khmer Rouge too. Pol Pot extolled the independent greatness of Angkor as a model to be emulated, and the Khmer Rouge flag featured the triple towers of Angkor.

Western experts are sharply critical of the Indian-led efforts to restore Angkor's monuments in 1986, under the Vietnamese-installed regime. Archaeologists maintain the chemicals used to clean monuments of mold and lichen actually damaged the stonework by stripping the protective patina. Indian teams also used concrete with great abandon to reinforce structures, in some cases replacing original stone pillars with crude concrete replicas, even though the originals could have been restored. Concrete ages at a different rate than sandstone, creating a jarring two-tone effect over time.

A highly contentious issue is exactly how to restore Angkor's monuments. Debate has raged since Mouhot rediscovered Angkor in 1860. Some advocate complete restoration, rebuilding buildings according to their original designs; others are from the "do no harm" school and believe the ruins should be left as ruins—the only goal being to prevent further decay. Water damage occurs during the annual monsoon when the reddish laterite foundation stone turns soft and spongy. The stone is further ravaged by lichen, algae, mold, acidic bat droppings, insect nests, thick jungle growth, and fumes from logging trucks.

Tourism could save Angkor by providing funds for repair and maintenance. In the past, Angkor Tourism restricted access to high-paying group tours; in 1992, UNTAC personnel visited in large numbers, paving the way for independent travelers. However, too much tourism could create the same problem that has plagued the Acropolis in Greece—large numbers of people trampling through can damage the buildings.

Conservation efforts at Angkor are coordinated through the UNESCO international campaign to safeguard Angkor. The EFEO has returned to Cambodia, offering technical advice and restoring the Elephant Terrace. An eight-year, $5.6 million EFEO project will rebuild and restore 11th-century Baphuon, using advanced computer technology to graphically visualize the reconstruction. The EFEO dismantled, labeled, and stockpiled the stones of the Baphuon before departing in the 1970s. Now, it must reassemble them. Other restoration groups include the United Nations Development Programme (UNDP), restoring Angkor Wat moat; World Monuments Fund, working on Preah Khan restoration; and a Japanese government team restoring part of the Bayon. The Archeological Survey of India and Japan's Sophia University are also involved in restoration projects.

Art Heists

After centuries of plunder, Angkor has been stripped to its stone structures and heavy stone sculptures. Now these, too, are under threat, from a new breed of treasure hunters. Since 1970, there has been a phenomenal incidence of statuary theft from Angkor sites. The Cambodian government does not have the people and resources to prevent theft, and corrupt officials may in fact be involved in the trade. Even well-guarded sites are subject to looting. In early 1993 thieves armed with machine guns launched an attack on the Angkor Conservancy in Siem Reap. They shot one of the guards, fired a rocket-propelled grenade at a storeroom door, and made off with 11 valuable pieces worth up to half a million dollars on the open market. Down the road, at Sihanouk's villa, a 100-kilogram statue as tall as a human was stolen from the courtyard. The rare 9th-century piece, a female divinity who'd lost her head to previous plunderers, had stood in the courtyard only a few months before. The same week, five stone heads were reported stolen from the northern gate of Angkor Thom, worth $3,000–4,000 in Thailand.

Local officials say these pieces, like most Khmer sculptures, were smuggled into Thailand. Moving a 100-kg statue across the border requires considerable logistics and a sophisticated level of organization. In early 1995 a truck loaded with rice was intercepted at Aranyaprathet on the Thai border; five Khmer artifacts were hidden under the grain, including a Shiva linga, a Buddha image, and a stone *garuda* carving. Other pieces have been seized on the Thailand-Cambodia border. There is little doubt the Khmer Rouge were involved in the lucrative trade; a 1994 attack on a Khmer Rouge base in Anlong Veng in northern Cambodia revealed a huge stone piece stolen from Angkor Wat.

In the mid-1970s Khmer sculpture began to appear at leading auction houses and in private art collections in the West. Thailand is not a signatory to the United Nations' 1970 convention against antiquities trafficking; Cambodia is. Although Thailand stringently protects its own cultural heritage, it allows Bangkok dealers to trade in Burmese and Cambodian pieces. Unethical Western buyers have even been able to place orders for pieces of their choice through black market dealers in Bangkok or Singapore.

Few pieces seized in Bangkok find their way back to Cambodia—a major source of friction between the two countries. The Cambodian Ministry of Culture is still trying to recover 13 artifacts seized from a Bangkok antique dealer in 1990 and held in storage at Bangkok's National Museum. The French government is more obliging. In 1994 a 10th-century four-headed statue of Brahma was smuggled into Thailand, then cut into four pieces, each with one face. When a Thai dealer offered one piece for auction in France, the French National Museum became suspicious, seized it, and returned the piece to Cambodia. Another piece, a bust of Shiva from Phnom Krom, turned up at New York's Metropolitan Museum of Art.

Under UNESCO guidance Cambodian authorities are now training special forces to police Angkor's ruins and document missing pieces for identification. The National Heritage Protection Authority of Cambodia was set up to prevent trafficking in statuary.

PLANNING YOUR TIME

You could spend an entire week in Angkor, sunup to sundown, and still not see it all, but at the very least, you need three full days. Angkor and Siem Reap are the kind of places you have to tear yourself away from. Siem Reap itself is slow-paced and relaxing, with reasonable restaurants and lots of countryside. It's a good place to sit on the front porch, swap tales with other travelers, and watch the geckos climb the walls. If your time is short, concentrate on the two main complexes, Angkor Wat and Angkor Thom. Opinions vary on the rest; everybody seems to have a personal favorite.

It's not difficult to organize a trip—in Siem Reap, you can hire motorcycle guides to visit the ruins, or rent your own motorcycle and cruise around. You can also head off on rented bicycles. With a small group of 3–4 you can rent a vehicle and guide for the day from Angkor Tourism in Siem Reap—it's cheaper than a package tour and allows greater flexibility.

Escorted tours to Angkor are organized by a host of agents in Phnom Penh and Bangkok. Tours originating from Bangkok entail more logistics and middlemen, so prices escalate. From Phnom Penh an Angkor tour of two days and one night is about $220 a person, including flights, hotel, food, guide, and local transportation. Such a short tour will probably prove unsatisfactory; between flights you'll spend only one full day at the ruins.

The soundest advice on touring Angkor is, in a word, *variety.* Avoid concentrations on a series of temples in the same style, as you may become blasé and won't be able to remember one from the other later. Angkor Wat is very different in style from Angkor Thom, and the jungle-locked ruins of Ta Prohm and Preah Khan are worlds away again. For a different perspective, hike up to a viewpoint, or visit an artificial lake such as Neak Pean. With more time you can spend a day at the ruins, and then take a day to visit the rural areas around Siem Reap.

Expect to spend at least half a day at **Angkor Wat,** the world's largest temple, or make several visits. The cluster of sites at **Angkor Thom** is another must-see, and will again easily consume at least half a day. The spectacular **South Gate** is the best-preserved entry to Angkor Thom. The central temple, **the Bayon,** is small in scale, but bizarre, mysterious, and imaginative—the favorite of many visitors. North of the Bayon are fine friezes at the **Leper King Terrace.**

A hike up **Phnom Bakheng** affords fine sunset views of Angkor Wat and gives you a sense of jungle and forest vegetation. Another hilltop is Phnom Bok, away from the main ruins to the east, on a red-dirt road; this area might be inaccessible, however and could be dangerous.

For jungle-locked ruins, **Preah Khan** and **Ta Prohm** are romantic and spooky sites, covered by centuries of vegetation. The French left Ta Prohm untouched to give an impression of how Angkor looked in the 19th century, with tree roots and foliage winding through the stonework.

To get an idea of the waterworks in the Angkor region, visit the ceremonial bathing sites of

Neak Pean and Sra Srang, or make an excursion to the West Baray for boating or swimming.

For a look at rural living, take a road in any direction from Siem Reap and you're in the countryside. Best excursions are 13 kilometers east to **Roluos**, where you can view village life; or 15 kilometers south to **Lake Tonle Sap** to see floating houses sitting over fish-holding pens.

Touring Strategies

Angkor Archaeological Park consists of 70 ruins in an area of 200 square kilometers, although the key ruins are clustered in a zone of about 60 square kilometers. The French engineered routes of hard-packed earth around the Angkor area in the 1920s to facilitate visits by car. Several roads were later paved and dubbed *le Petit Circuit* (the Little Circuit) and *le Grand Circuit* (the Grand Circuit), but there are really no set patterns. You can mix and match, or come up with your own routes.

Start early. The heat of the day can get to you even by 0900. Fortunately there are well-shaded sections, especially around the Bayon, and if you move along by *remork* or bicycle you get some breeze. It's a good idea to take a siesta in a cool spot: Find a food stall selling noodles 1100–1400, or just go back to town and rest. Dawn and dusk add special magic to Angkor. Angkor Wat at the break of dawn is awesome. A little later, at the Bayon, it's misty and mysterious, with the sun filtering through the forest canopy, illuminating enigmatic smiling faces; the chirping of birds breaks the silence. The last glows of the setting sun over Angkor Wat are dramatic, viewed from either the causeway or the viewpoint of Phnom Bakheng. Then sound the frogs and cicadas, the birds and bats.

Angkor Wat is overwhelming. The mind cannot take it in at one visit. Neither will your camera—attempts to fit Angkor into a standard lens viewfinder are frustrating. Angkor can monopolize your time, consuming half a day or more. You're better off making several visits to Angkor Wat. Drop in and walk down the causeway to get acquainted, then take off

to smaller ruins up north such as the Bayon, and maybe return to Angkor Wat in the late afternoon to take in a bit more.

Limiting factors on routes are available time, hot spells, transportation, and road conditions. The best road conditions are found going north from Angkor Wat to Preah Khan on the northern axis, and east from Baphuon to Ta Prohm on an eastern axis. Other roads may be potholed, slowing progress. Some ideas for routes follow, but you can chop, change, or add destinations to suit.

In a car or by *remork* you can cover the Little Circuit in an hour of actual travel time; by bicycle, you'll need 2.5 hours for the same route. From the Grand Hotel to the west entrance of Angkor Wat is seven kilometers. For the following routes, the start and finish point in Siem Reap is the Grand Hotel.

Northern Axis: Siem Reap (Grand Hotel), Angkor Thom (South Gate, Bayon, Baphuon, Leper King Terrace), Preah Khan, back south to Angkor Wat west entrance, Phnom Bakheng (sunset), Siem Reap. Distance: 29 kilometers.

Little Circuit: Siem Reap, Angkor Wat west gate, Bayon, Victory Gate, Takeo, Ta Prohm, Sra Srang, Angkor Wat east entrance, Siem Reap. Distance: 30 kilometers.

North and East Axes: Siem Reap, Angkor Wat west entrance, Bayon, Preah Khan, back to Leper King Terrace, Victory Gate, Chau Say Tevoda, Takeo, Ta Prohm, retrace route to Elephant Terrace, Angkor Wat again, Siem Reap. This erratic route is designed to take advantage of the best road conditions, especially if cycling. Distance: 38 kilometers; if Preah Khan is eliminated, 32 kilometers.

Grand Circuit: Siem Reap, Angkor Wat, Angkor Thom (South Gate, Bayon, Baphuon, Leper King Terrace), Preah Khan, Neak Pean, Sra Srang, Angkor Wat east entrance, Siem Reap. Distance: 40 kilometers.

Combination Circuit: Siem Reap, Angkor Thom (South Gate, Bayon, Leper King Terrace), Preah Khan, Neak Pean, Sra Srang, Ta Prohm, Victory Gate, Elephant Terrace, Angkor Wat west entrance, Siem Reap. Distance: 45 kilometers.

When to Visit

November–March is the peak touring season, with dry conditions. April–July is sizzling hot; August–October is the rainy season. Some like to see the ruins in the mist and rain—roman-tic, if somewhat slippery. The reservoirs around Angkor are fuller, and the lush vegetation off-sets the reddish sandstone. At this time Angkor is also devoid of crowds.

Siem Reap

Siem Reap is the gateway town to the ruins of Angkor, 250 kilometers northwest of Phnom Penh and 15 kilometers north of Lake Tonle Sap. With a population of about 70,000, the town has a relaxing frontier air to it: There are few phones, and the electricity and water sup-ply is erratic. Running through the center of town is the polluted Siem Reap River. Traces of the French presence have survived in a small quarter of colonial buildings to the southwest side—the rest of Siem Reap was badly dam-aged by bombing and civil war. In the early 1970s, during the Pol Pot era, people were fed to the crocodiles in Siem Reap. There is a "kill-ing fields" memorial to victims of the Khmer Rouge to the northwest of town, at Wat Thmey, with grisly skulls filling part of a pagoda.

In 1979 the province was the scene of heavy fighting between the Khmer Rouge and the Vietnamese army. In 1993, the Khmer Rouge massacred Vietnamese fishing families at Lake Tonle Sap, precipitating an exodus of Vietnam-ese to the Mekong Delta. To safeguard Angkor, the government stationed 900 troops, ringing the entire zone of ruins.

Since the demise of the Khmer Rouge, life has returned to normal around Angkor: farm-ers transporting goods in oxcarts, village women clad in sarongs cycling to market, Buddhist monks in flowing orange robes out for morn-ing strolls, kids lolling about on the backs of water buffalo in green fields. For tourists, this is a chance to see rural life. For locals, tourism is seen as a return to normalcy after years of sav-age war and upheaval. New hotels, guesthouses, and restaurants started appearing in Siem Reap in the 1990s, catering first to visiting UNTAC troops and later to the Angkor-bound tourists who arrived in their wake. Since 2002, there has been an incredible building boom in Siem Reap, with many more guesthouses, mega-group-tour hotels and five-star hotels on the way.

Angkor Conservancy

Incredibly, there is no on-site museum housing Khmer artifacts at Angkor, though land has been set aside for such a project. In the mean-time, thousands of pieces rest at Angkor Con-servancy, several kilometers to the north of Siem Reap. Anything movable at Angkor has disap-peared. Even the heads of the larger stone stat-ues have been hacked off by treasure hunters. To guard against art theft, virtually all smaller Angkor statuary, wood items, and artifacts have been removed to museums, particularly to the National Museum in Phnom Penh.

You need special permission from the Ministry of Culture in Phnom Penh to visit Angkor Con-servancy, which was established by the French in 1907 when Siem Reap province was restored to Cambodia by the Thais. From 1953 to 1970 Angkor Conservancy was jointly operated by the French and Cambodian governments. With the exception of a period during World War II, the French at Angkor worked steadily, at times di-recting more than 1,000 employees. In 1972 the civil war forced the French to leave.

Angkor Conservancy is a warehouse for about 10,000 sculpture fragments and artifacts from the Angkor region. Fresh concrete heads are stocked here, destined to replace ones removed from the Angkor area by bandits. Museum staff also remove heads before bandits can get to them. There are two floors of statuary at Ang-kor Conservancy. On the ground floor are the larger Buddhas, Vishnus, and lintels; the upper floor houses smaller Buddhas, hand fragments, stone animals, and large wooden Buddhas.

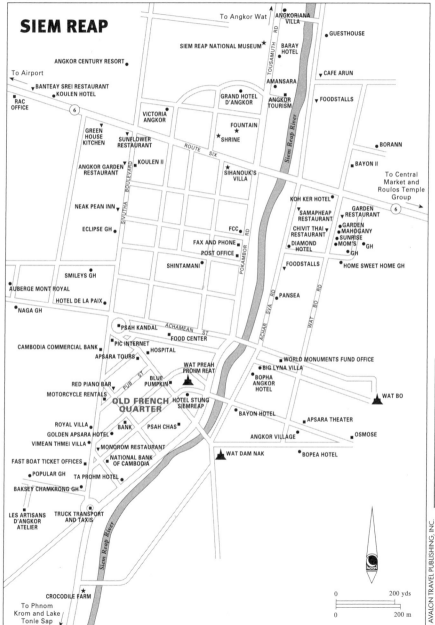

SIEM REAP

To Angkor Wat

ANGKORIANA VILLA

GUESTHOUSE

SIEM REAP NATIONAL MUSEUM

BARAY HOTEL

To Airport

ANGKOR CENTURY RESORT

CAFE ARUN

BANTEAY SREI RESTAURANT
KOULEN HOTEL

AMANSARA

RAC OFFICE

GRAND HOTEL D'ANGKOR

ANGKOR TOURISM

FOODSTALLS

VICTORIA ANGKOR

FOUNTAIN

SHRINE

BORANN

GREEN HOUSE KITCHEN

SUNFLOWER RESTAURANT

ROUTE SIX

KOULEN II

BAYON II

ANGKOR GARDEN RESTAURANT

SIHANOUK'S VILLA

To Central Market and Roulos Temple Group

NEAK PEAN INN

KOH KER HOTEL

GARDEN RESTAURANT

ECLIPSE GH

FCC

SAMAPHEAP RESTAURANT

GARDEN MAHOGANY
SUNRISE
MOM'S   GH

CHIVIT THAI RESTAURANT

FAX AND PHONE

DIAMOND HOTEL

POST OFFICE

SHINTAMANI

FOODSTALLS

HOME SWEET HOME GH

SMILEYS GH

PANSEA

AUBERGE MONT ROYAL

HOTEL DE LA PAIX

NAGA GH

PSAH KANDAL

ACHAMEAN ST

FOOD CENTER

CAMBODIA COMMERCIAL BANK

PIC INTERNET

HOSPITAL

APSARA TOURS

WORLD MONUMENTS FUND OFFICE

BIG LYNA VILLA

RED PIANO BAR

BLUE PUMPKIN

WAT PREAH PROHM REAT

BOPHA ANGKOR HOTEL

MOTORCYCLE RENTALS

OLD FRENCH QUARTER

HOTEL STUNG SIEMREAP

WAT BO

ROYAL VILLA

BAYON HOTEL

APSARA THEATER

GOLDEN APSARA HOTEL

BANK

PSAH CHAS

OSMOSE

VIMEAN THMEI VILLA

ANGKOR VILLAGE

FAST BOAT TICKET OFFICES

MONOROM RESTAURANT

NATIONAL BANK OF CAMBODIA

WAT DAM NAK

BOPEA HOTEL

POPULAR GH

TA PROHM HOTEL

BAKSEY CHAMKRONG GH

LES ARTISANS D'ANGKOR ATELIER

TRUCK TRANSPORT AND TAXIS

Siem Reap River

Angkor

CROCODILE FARM

To Phnom Krom and Lake Tonle Sap

0   200 yds

0   200 m

© AVALON TRAVEL PUBLISHING, INC.

MONUMENTS OF ANGKOR

To Phnom Bok ▲

Phnom Bok ▲

Roluos River

BANTEAY SAMRE ▲

TA SOM ★

EAST MEBON ★

East Baray (dry)

GRAND CIRCUIT

PREAH NEAK PEAN ★

LITTLE CIRCUIT

🕌 TA PROHM ★

CHECKPOINT

🕌 PREAH KHAN ★

🕌 THE BAYON ★

BENG THOM

Phnom Bakheng ▲

ANKOR WAT 🕌 ★

ZOO

Siem Reap River

LANDMINE MUSEUM ■

PROPOSED TOURISM DEVELOPMENT ZONE

CHECKPOINT

CHECKPOINT

CHECKPOINT

ANGKOR TICKET BOOTHS ■

WAT THMEY/KILLING FIELDS MEMORIAL 🕌

ANGKOR CONSERVANCY (STORAGE BUILDING) ■

GRAND HOTEL ●

SIEM REAP

CENTRAL MARKET ■

To Kompong Thom →

ROLUOS VILLAGE

LOLEI ★

PREAH KO ★

BAKONG ★

6

WALL

WALL

WALL

WALL

West Baray

WEST MEBON ★

BOAT RENTAL ■

AIRPORT ✈

To Puork Silk Farm →

To Sisophon ↓

To Puork ↓

6

0 _____ 3 mi
0 _____ 3 km

© AVALON TRAVEL PUBLISHING, INC.

Unfortunately, the pieces are not safe even here—the place has been broken into several times.

Landmine Museum

Cambodia's tragic recent history tends to be glossed over by visitors to Angkor. To bring the Khmer Rouge era back into sharp focus, pay a visit to the Landmine Museum, on the Siem Reap River, reached by a turn-off before the Angkor ticket booths. Authorities have tried to close this museum down several times because they think it will scare tourists away. The displays of mines and other wartime paraphernalia were set up by former child-soldier Aki Ra, who was press-ganged into fighting for the Khmer Rouge. The museum depends on donations. Western volunteers will show you round the place. A number of kids who have lost limbs to land mines live on the premises or nearby: Donations to the museum go to supporting their education. If a sufficient audience materialises, the kids stage a show (perhaps one night a week) dubbed "land-mine theater," which recounts the horrors of the Khmer Rouge and tells their personal stories.

Zoo

A pathetic cluster of cages and concrete compounds north of the Landmine Museum houses a motley collection of Cambodian wildlife and birds. The animals are kept in disgusting condition—endangered species such as the milky stork and the greater adjutant have had their wings clipped to prevent them flying away; an otter paces around a bare concrete enclosure with no water. If you like animals, steer clear of this depressing minizoo.

EXPLORING THE COUNTRYSIDE

If you spend a week or so in Angkor, it's best to pace yourself: one day at the ruins, one day off. Otherwise you'll suffer from cultural overload and may become templed-out. You need Time Out. Siem Reap presents a great opportunity to rove around the Cambodian countryside. You can witness facets of rural life unchanged from those depicted on temple walls at Angkor Wat 800 years ago. Roads can be rough in these areas, sometimes just dirt tracks. Taking a local guide along is highly recommended. A guide doesn't cost much and can take you around the villages and show you how palm sugar and palm wine are brewed. Moto drivers can often double as guides.

The West Baray

To reach the West Baray, head northwest from Siem Reap along Route 6. Go past the airport road and take the next turnoff to the right: This leads to a parking area at a dam at the south side of the West Baray. The West Baray reservoir was part of the elaborate Angkorian irrigation system, although researchers are not sure of its exact function. Originally, the West Baray and East Baray were two gargantuan artificial lakes. The West Baray is a 2- by 8-kilometer rectangle enclosed by an earth dike. Though it may have been used for irrigation, recent evidence indicates it was more likely a mooring place for royal barges, a fish-breeding site, or simply a place for bathing.

The East Baray is now dry. The West Baray, first constructed in the 11th century, was partially restored in the 1950s with foreign-aid funds. Today it's about two-thirds full. The West Baray is fed by the Tonle Sap River; a small dam has enlarged the rice-growing potential of the area with water carried through a network of irrigation canals. The West Baray is also used for fish breeding. You can go for a swim along the southern section (hire an inner tube). Situated in the West Baray is a small island—you can hire a boatman to motor out to a sanctuary called the **West Mebon** in about 15 minutes. The boatman charges a few dollars for the round-trip. There are a few people living on the island. Much of the original stonework has collapsed here, though two towers on the east entrance to the temple have survived. It was here that a large bronze statue of Vishnu was discovered in 1936. It now sits in the National Museum in Phnom Penh.

Roluos Group

The ruins of Roluos are 13 kilometers east of Siem Reap along Route 6. The ruins are of mild interest compared with the splendors of central Angkor, but the trip to Roluos gives you a chance to experience village life. Stop at the central market, a short distance east of Siem Reap, on the way out or back. The market is always engrossing, a great place for watching people. Cambodian women are partial to sarongs with blinding colors and patterns, which makes the place quite bright. This is most likely a reaction to the Pol Pot years, when everybody was forced to wear black. Up-country a common form of transportation is the bicycle-hauled wooden chariot. This workhorse can carry several passengers, a few hands of bananas, a score of chickens, or a mountain of vegetables—sometimes all at once.

If you're on a moto, ask the driver to take you on red dirt back roads to get to Roluos. A beautiful back road starts around the back of the markets. While Route 6 is busy with traffic, the back roads are rural and serene. Along the way you might see buffalo-drawn carts, men catching frogs, women husking rice, or kids climbing sugar-palm trees.

The Roluos Ruins are among the oldest Khmer monuments in the Angkor area, dating to the 9th-century reign of Indravarman I. Two key temple sites remain, **Bakong** and **Preah Ko**. The latter consists of six brick towers or *prasat*s, arranged in two rows; the site is bounded by walls, with sandstone lintel decoration. Bakong is a five-step brick pyramid with sandstone doorways. At the corners of the first three levels stand elephants hewn from single blocks of stone. Next to the ruin is an active Buddhist monastery. From here, you can continue south to the village of Roluos, which lent its name to the ruins.

Puork Silk Farm

About 15 kilometers to the west of Siem Reap, on Route 6, there's a sign on the right pointing to Puork Silk Farm, lying a short distance off the road. This facility is part of the atelier Les Artisans d'Angkor, providing employment opportunities for young disadvantaged Cambodians. Here you can witness the fascinating cycle of the silkworm, collection of raw silk, dyeing, and creation of weavings by hand-loom. There is an on-site shop selling silk scarves and clothing items.

Getting there is half the fun: Leading from the town of Puork (just beyond the silk farm) is a red-dirt road that goes back to Preah Khan Temple, in the northern Angkor Ruins. To find this road, go to Puork central markets. The road starts at the east side of the markets, but it heads directly north for a while, then swings east. Eventually, it comes out at a turnoff that leads to Preah Khan Ruins. If you're on a dirt-bike, this is a beautiful road, but a dusty one. Bullock carts use this for ferrying goods around.

Lake Tonle Sap

Head south on Route 29, following the river by moto or rented bicycle. Just south of town on the left is a crocodile farm. There's not much to see here, just concrete and crocodiles. About 12 kilometers from Siem Reap is **Phnom Krom,** a hill with an 11th-century temple. From the ruins are expansive views over Lake Tonle Sap. A few kilometers farther along is Lake Tonle Sap, the Great Lake. A glance at the map will show how it came by this name—it's an enormous freshwater sea.

Lake Tonle Sap fills with water during the monsoon season, but by February it shrinks to a fraction of its former size, becoming one of the richest fishing grounds in the world, yielding as much as 10 tons of fish per square kilometer. The main fishing season is February–May. When the waters recede, fish are prevented from escaping with nets and bamboo traps. Some are caught in the branches of trees, or in the mud, and simply picked up. Fishing families live in temporary huts that can be dismantled and moved forward as the water recedes. When the fishing season is over, fishing families return to their villages.

The flooding of the Tonle Sap covers the area with a rich mud ideal for growing rice. Farmers have developed unique deepwater rice strains that grow with the rising lake to keep the grain above the water. Under Pol Pot, large parts of the flooded forest around Tonle Sap were sacrificed to expand the area for rice fields. During the war much of the rice seed stock was lost, and deepwater rice cultivation declined.

Coming from Siem Reap you reach a boat dock on the shores of Lake Tonle Sap. It's a scummy area, with boats loading and unloading goods, fish drying in the sun, and assorted video cafés. The lake itself is peaceful and uneventful, but hidden dramas abound. If you hire a boat for an hour, or row out yourself, you can reach floating houses suspended over huge bamboo fish-holding pens. Families here fatten up the fish in the pens; some houses are rigged with trapdoors that open so feed can be dropped. A fish pen may be three meters deep and hold thousands of fish. You don't realize how many fish there are until feeding time, when you see them thrashing around in the water. This kind of "fish farming" is also practiced in Vietnam's Mekong Delta.

Because the lake keeps shrinking and expanding, a species of fish has evolved here that can survive several hours out of water, flopping overland in search of deeper pools. This species, known as *hock yue,* or elephant fish, is considered a delicacy in Asia. Another highly prized delicacy is the sand goby, or *soon hock,* a greenish gray, troutlike specimen. One company ships the fish live to Phnom Penh, where they're held in tanks. For transportation to restaurants in Singapore and Kuala Lumpur, the fish are placed in tanks filled with ice and a mild sedative. In a semi-inert state they're air-freighted in plastic bags pumped with oxygen. They must reach their destination within 16 hours. In a Singapore restaurant, a single sand goby, cooked with ginger, chili, tomato, and mushrooms, is worth $40–60, depending on its size.

Preak Toal Bird Sanctuary

Tonle Sap was declared a UNESCO Biosphere Reserve in 1997. One of the reasons for that is it harbors some of the most important breeding grounds for large waterbirds in all of Southeast Asia. The birds flock here for the abundant fishing, of course. To the northwest side of the lake lies Preak Toal Bird Sanctuary. In the mating season (February is a good month), you can

see great flocks of ibis and stork. But you have to time it right: You won't see much in the rainy season. Birds breed in the February–April period: Sightings are best December–April.

More than 100 species of birds have been spotted at Preak Toal—15 of those endangered species. On a good day you might see these birds: brahminy kite, greyheaded fish-eagle, purple heron, spot-billed pelican, purple swamphen, Indian shag, oriental darter, blue-tailed bee-eater, storkbilled kingfisher, black-headed ibis (more than 500 pairs nest here), Asian openbill (more than 2,000 pairs) and painted stork (1,000 pairs in season—the largest colony in Southeast Asia. Other species spotted include the masked finfoot, lesser adjutant, greater adjutant, greater coucal, and milky stork.

Preak Toal is not easy to get to. It takes about 75 minutes by boat to get there from Chong Kneas, the main boat dock close to Siem Reap. The initial destination is the floating Environmental Research Station at Preak Toal, from which a naturalist will guide you (for a fee) through swamp forest to see the birds. The tour from the Research Station is by small vessel and lasts about four hours. You can arrange all this from Siem Reap through OSMOSE, a tour office there (cost around $50 a head), or you could just motor out to Preak Toal and pick up the guide there. Preak Toal Research Station hosts a small exhibition space and has laminated field-guide sheets for identifying birds likely to be seen. There's one glitch here: The birds are most likely to be seen in greater numbers at dusk or dawn—and by the time you get out of Siem Reap, and across the lake, it could be 0900 already. Solution: Get under way from Siem Reap before dawn, and eat breakfast en route. You might be able to make it out there by 0800 that way, which would give you a better chance to sight the birds. Another option is to stay overnight at the Environmental Research Station, which has a few rooms going for $10 each. And you don't have to go back to Siem Reap after this trip: Preak Toal lies on the route to Battambang by river. You could get aboard one of the chartered tourist boats coming through, or else attempt to board a local ferry for Battambang (which originates from Chong Kneas).

◪ RIVER TRIP TO BATTAMBANG

A super boat ride to consider in this region is Siem Reap to Battambang. This costs around $15 one-way and allows you to see lifestyles at floating villages and along the riverside up close. From Chong Kneas dock (the dock closest to Siem Reap), the boat crosses a section of Lake Tonle Sap and proceeds through Preak Toal floating village. The route continues along down narrow Sangker River for 3–6 hours to reach Battambang (the boat takes longer in the dry season because of low water). Inquire closely about your proposed boat: Some have ended up jammed into an uncomfortable open wooden boat (no shelter from the harsh sun); others have traveled in style on a sleek double-deck boat with deck chairs and drinks aboard. From Battambang you can pursue a road route to Phnom Penh—or head for Thailand via the Poipet border crossing, or take the rougher road west to the Pailin border crossing into Thailand.

ACCOMMODATIONS

For the following section, particularly the upper-end hotels, pricing is not exact since some hotel prices include all taxes (and breakfast), while other rates quoted may be subject to 10 percent VAT. Payment by credit card may also incur extra charges. Group tours negotiate lower rates than those posted, and you can possibly get lower rates through Internet booking online (check the hotel website). Rates drop in the April–September off-season when there are few guests around.

Under $20

Siem Reap boasts scores of guesthouses, charging $5–30 a room. Prices fluctuate with seasonal demand. Fan rooms in guesthouses are generally under $10, while air-conditioned rooms go for $15–20. Check for a mosquito net in your room. The owners can arrange moto drivers, guides, and boat ticketing.

Rock-bottom for guesthouses are the $1–4 specials. These are guesthouses that virtually give away the rooms and make their profit elsewhere. They sell boat tickets at a slight markup, peddle marijuana and special "soup," and ask patrons to eat only at their guesthouse. These guesthouses include **Eclipse, Naga, Big Banana GH, GH46,** and **Popular GH,** all on the west side of town.

A step up in amenities and room size are guesthouses such as **Sweet Dreams, Home Sweet Home GH,** and **Ivy GH,**—with en suite bathroom and hot water, and even breakfast. East of the main bridge off Route 6 is a cluster of recommended family-run guesthouses, charging $6–10 for a room. In a row here are **Mom's GH, Sunrise, Mr. David's GH,** and **Mahogeny.** On the opposite side of the street is **Garden House,** run by the family of a retired doctor (there's a small pharmacy at the front of the house). Farther south near Wat Bo is **Big Lyna Villa,** tel. 63/964807, in a converted mansion—a pleasant place with great balcony upstairs, charging $15 for a fan room.

Along Route 6, the airport road, signs simply read Guesthouse or bear a number—GH 108, GH 361—there are about a dozen places on the airport road. Some of these seem to be devoted to the Japanese backpacker trade. An exception is **Earthwalkers,** which is a friendly place with lush garden. To the south edge of Siem Reap, near the river, is **Rasmei Angkor GH,** with cheaper rooms in a colonial-type mansion.

Along Sivutha Street you'll find the following hotels. **Royal Villa,** 13 Sivutha, tel. 63/639114, with garden, 13 rooms at $20 each. **Vimean Thmei Hotel,** 12 Sivutha (opposite Monorom Restaurant), tel. 63/963494, fax 63/380102, offers 21 rooms for $10 fan and $15–20 a/c. **Baksey Chamkrong GH** on Sivutha offers seven a/c rooms for $20 with bath, and three fan rooms for $10 each. **Green Garden Home,** 51 Sivutha, features nine rooms for $8–12–15. A cluster of guesthouses is found around this area in the old French quarter, with rooms for $5–20. These include the **Reaksmey Chan-**

reas Hotel, **Psar Chas GH,** and **Phkay Proeuk Villa.** Toward the central market on Route 6 is **Ban Thai,** with a/c rooms for $15 and a restaurant serving Thai and Western food. **Freedom Hotel,** near the markets, tel. 63/963473, has 50 rooms for $12–25—a bland, boxy place, although comfortable enough with doubles featuring a/c, hot shower, and balcony.

On the southern edge of town, **Golden Apsara Hotel** rents 17 a/c rooms for $15–20; there are a few cheaper fan rooms. In the same price range, nearby, is **Golden Angkor Villa,** tel. 63/380120, with 22 rooms.

$20–50

On the airport road is **Secrets of Elephants,** tel. 63/964328, run by a Frenchman. This charming place is full of artistic character: It is a converted mansion with four rooms upstairs and four downstairs. Rates are $25–35 with breakfast included. Another hotel with character is **Auberge Mont Royal,** tel. 63/964044, with 30 rooms for $35–55 and rooftop breakfast restaurant. It is on the western side of Siem Reap. **Neak Pean Inn,** 53 Sivutha St., has 13 rooms for $35–40, with a/c, satellite TV, and fridge.

On the southern edge of town, **Hotel Stung Siemreap,** tel. 63/913074, has 33 rooms in the $35–45 range with satellite TV and a/c. The hotel is a renovated French mansion in the old French quarter. The **Bayon Hotel,** tel. 63/911769, features 44 rooms for $30–35 single, $35–40 double, and $45–50 triple. Rooms include a/c, private bath, fridge, and minibar.

In the center, the Thai-managed **Diamond Hotel,** tel. 63/913130, fax 63/910020, has 27 bungalow-style doubles for $35. **Bopea Hotel I,** tel./fax 63/380027, lies east of Wat Dam Nak; it has 28 doubles for $25 with a/c— this hotel is favored by Japanese groups. To the west of Siem Reap, **Koulen Hotel** offers 12 double rooms with a/c, fridge, and bath, for $30. With a bar and dancing this place is noisy. To the north of town, the **Baray Hotel** has 12 a/c rooms for $40. **Angkoriana Villa,** a short way north, offers similar rates—this family-run place is a good value, with five a/c rooms for $25 each.

$50–100

In the Wat Bo vicinity, the motel-like **Bopha Angkor Hotel,** tel. 63/964928, has 30 a/c rooms with satellite TV, for $40–70. By the Siem Reap River is **Ta Prohm Hotel,** tel. 63/380117, fax 63/380116, with 58 luxury rooms for $80–90 and several suites for $120–130. Rooms include all mod cons: fridge, minibar, satellite TV.

Route 6 leading to the airport is full of dreary group-tour hotels that cater to Japanese, Koreans, French, and others. They have all amenities, but lack atmosphere. **Bantei Srei Hotel,** tel. 63/913839, has 55 rooms for $55 and up. **City Angkor Hotel,** tel. 63/637301, fax 63/380035, has 114 rooms for $85–110; this place has a pool, a business center, and souvenir shop.

$100–200

In a class all of its own is ▪ **Angkor Village,** tel. 63/965561, fax 63/965565, welcome@ angkorvillage.com, www.angkorvillage.com. This place takes its inspiration from traditional Khmer designs—from monks' residential quarters near pagodas. Angkor Village's wooden pavilions are beautifully set in lush gardens. The wooden pavilions, furniture, and decoration were all handmade by local craftsmen. This harmonious place is a gem. There are 36 a/c standard and deluxe rooms and three apartments, with prices ranging $100–180. At the center of the complex is a breezy restaurant serving Khmer and French food. The boutique hotel has its own small pool screened by palm trees. Angkor Village was designed and is run by a French-Cambodian architect couple. Check the Angkor Village website for 360-degree panoramas—not just of their rooms but of a dozen ruins at Angkor.

Designed and run by the same owners is **Angkor Village Resort and Spa,** at the northeast side of Siem Reap, tel. 63/963561, www.angkorvillage.com, with sterling rooms going for $170 each. All rooms have a view of the amazing 200-meter "serpentine pool." This is the longest pool in Siem Reap, but not in a straight line. It is five meters wide and ingeniously winds through the resort cottages and lush tropical gardens. Other waterworks of note: The hotel features an excellent spa.

Near the post office is the **Shintamani,** tel. 63/761998, fax 63/761999, www.sanctuaryresorts.com, with rooms in the $150 range. This boutique hotel features a clever compact design, with 18 rooms, each with free WiFi. It has a small pool and spa. Falling under the same management is **Hotel de la Paix,** tel. 63/761998, www.sanctuaryresorts.com, which offers 107 spacious rooms including nine rooftop spa suites with private terraces, and six courtyard rooms with large private gardens and outdoor bathtubs. Standard deluxe rooms go for $165; the others are $240.

FCC Angkor, Pokambor Avenue, tel. 63/760280, http://fcccambodia.com, has a handful of well-designed rooms set around a courtyard, going for $120–140 and a suite for $330. There is a small pool and the separate Visaya Spa. Up front is the FCC Angkor Restaurant and Bar, which was the first structure built here (the hotel was tacked on later because of demand).

Preah Khan Hotel, tel. 63/766888, fax 63/766889, www.preahkhanhotel.com, has 140 rooms from $90 standard to $140 deluxe and $250 suite. Features of note: a casino, plus large-scale elephant statues at the swimming pool.

Nokor Phnom Hotel, on Route 6 leading to the airport, tel./fax 63/380106, has 92 rooms for $110 standard and $150 suite.

Over $200

With the return of peace and stability to Cambodia after the complete demise of the Khmer Rouge in 1999, there has been a flourish of building of four- and five-star hotels. And many more are on the way. **La Résidence d'Angkor,** in Wat Bo vicinity, tel. 63/963390, fax 63/963391, www.pansea.com, features 55 deluxe rooms for $340 apiece. The hotel is run by the Pansea Orient-Express Hotels group, and has a super swimming pool. The hotel is built in Khmer style with lots of wood and marble.

Angkor Palace Resort and Spa, off the airport road, tel. 63/760511, www.angkorpalaceresort.com, has a whopping total of 270 rooms tucked away amid luxuriant gardens on a property of 11 hectares. A deluxe room goes for $325, a suite for $600, and villas for $800–1,550.

Victoria Angkor, tel. 63/760428, fax 63/760350, www.victoriahotels-asia.com, offers 120 rooms for $285–320, and 10 suites for $400–440. Each room has a balcony setting facing the interior courtyard with its excellent pool, set among tropical gardens. Other facilities of note are a French restaurant and White Lotus Spa. The hotel, though built in 2003, is constructed in the French colonial style of the 1930s. In keeping with the vintage theme, a 1931 Citroën C6 limousine is parked near the front and is available for touring or special occasions.

Angkor Century Resort and Spa, at the northwest side of Siem Reap, tel. 63/963777, www.angkorcentury.com, has 190 rooms. Tariff is $220 superior room, $250 deluxe, $380 executive suite, and $800 for century suite. The hotel has a large pool.

Doyen of the hotels is the **Grand Hotel d'Angkor,** tel. 63/981888, www.raffles.com. The French Empire lives on at the Grand, originally constructed in 1929 for the French tourist trade, and renovated and extended in the mid-1990s in a $30 million face-lift undertaken by Singapore's DS Land (which owns the Raffles Hotel in Singapore). The Grand reopened for business in January 1998. It contains 131 art deco rooms with wicker furniture and Khmer objets d'art. The Raffles group is aiming at high-end customers—rooms at the Grand start at $360 a night for a double, including two meals, and rise to $510 for a studio suite. An exclusive two-bedroom villa costs $1,900 a night. There are several wings to the hotel; the Grand offers satellite TV, a 35-meter swimming pool, business center, health services (including fully equipped spa), gift shop, retail shops, air-conditioned restaurants, bar, tennis courts, and other amenities. If dropping in, check the tiny teak elevator, carefully restored to its original state—and still working.

Sofitel Royal Angkor, tel. 63/964600, fax 63/964610, www.sofitel.com, runs 240 rooms—most of them go for $280. The hotel has some innovative design features with a pool surrounded by tropical gardens, and an outdoor restaurant. Angkor Spa is beautifully sited among the gardens. The Sofitel has a 24-hour business center and dataports in all rooms. Parked out front is a vintage yellow Rolls-Royce left behind by the film crew of *Two Brothers*.

In the same vicinity, **Le Meridien Angkor,** tel. 63/963900, fax 63/963901, www.lemeridien.com, offers 223 rooms for $300 and suites for $430–540. The hotel has a small pool and spa.

Near the Tourist Information Office is the exclusive **Amansara,** tel. 63/760333, fax 63/760335, www.amanresorts.com. The original main building, constructed by a French architect in 1962, functioned as the royal guesthouse of Sihanouk, hosting visiting ambassadors and celebrities—it lay in ruins when Amanresorts took over the property in 2002. Thoroughly rebuilt and renovated, the resort has a retro feel to it, along with a note of Zen simplicity. Twelve modern suites feature twin bathrooms and a small water garden. Rates are $700–825 a night, which includes several meals and guided tours of the ruins, plus all the house wine you can drink. With the hefty price tag comes a high staff-to-guest ratio, great attention to detail, and access to highly knowledgeable staff—guides for the ruins, savvy in-house spa director. Mick Jagger stayed here. So did Gwyneth Paltrow.

FOOD

Might as well start with breakfast—and at the **Blue Pumpkin,** you'll get a mouth-watering one. This is the premier bakery in town, with scrumptious fresh-baked baguettes, breads and croissants, tasty pastries, fresh juices, and coffee. And home-made ice cream and sherbet. Because the Blue Pumpkin has a WiFi zone, it is a favorite with foreigners resident in Siem Reap. The restaurant has some outdoor seating.

The variety and quality of food in Siem Reap is impressive. It's close to Lake Tonle Sap, so there's a lot of fish on the menu. In cheaper restaurants, a meal runs $1–3; in more expensive restaurants expect to pay perhaps $2–8. Closer to markets you will find open-air foodstalls serving Khmer food, including *loclac,* a plate of sliced beef spiced with lemon and black pepper. Along with clusters of foodstalls, there are a few indoor venues with a similar atmosphere: One is simply called **Food Center** and is just east of Psah Kandal (market) up an alley. You sit in the middle—and go to the different vendors to order dishes, which vary from Khmer fish dishes to fresh fruit juices. This is terrific value: You shouldn't experience language problems because you can point out what you want. More upmarket for Khmer dishes is **Viroth's,** at 246 Wat Bo St., behind La Residence d'Angkor hotel. Viroth's has a stylish terrace garden with covered open-air seating.

Happy gourmet hunting grounds at night are in the old French Quarter to the north of Psah Chas. There is a string of converted colonial villas with cosy upstairs dining. Upstairs you get breezy views and can avoid the approaches of street vendors. The restaurants are packed into a small zone, so it's easy to wander around and make your choice—which could be Khmer, Thai, Chinese, Italian, French, or Vietnamese.

The hotels around Siem Reap have their own restaurants, all on the expensive side. A good choice here would be **Angkor Village,** near Wat Bo, with a beautiful setting among lush gardens. And near the post office, the **FCC Angkor** upstairs restaurant has an extensive menu of international and local fare in a stylish atmosphere. The **Grand Hotel d'Angkor** and **Sofitel Royal Angkor** feature elegant dining and bars.

Picnic Catering: Several places will provide food to go for picnics at the ruins. A good place to try is the Blue Pumpkin. The Chivit Thai Restaurant will package Thai food, given notice. The Grand Hotel d'Angkor provides customized picnic hampers—for a hefty fee.

NIGHTLIFE
Khmer Dance, Apsara Dance
The Grand Hotel, Sofitel Royal Angkor, Angkor Village, and other hotels stage *apsara* and

folk dancing at night. You won't see this elsewhere in Cambodia on a regular basis—not even in Phnom Penh. The hotels in Siem Reap offer a dinner-dance package, with buffet around 1830 or 1930, followed by a one-hour smorgasbord of Khmer dance at around 1900 or 2000. The three venues mentioned charge around $20 a head for the dinner-dance soirée. The Grand stages its performances in an outdoor setting in the park opposite the hotel (this draws a large local viewing audience, standing beyond the perimeter!). Angkor Village stages performances in its Apsara Theatre, a striking Khmer-style, wooden two-story building. There's one lazy concession to the 21st century: air-conditioning. Group-tour buses pull in here—the place can seat 130. You can get half-price admission at the Angkor Village venue by asking for a performance-only ticket. Charging considerably less than the hotel venues—around $10 a head—are restaurant venues where dance is staged: at Koulen II Restaurant, Bayon II, and Chao Praya Restaurant. Performances take place nightly, although some are staged three times a week.

There are several dance troupes around Siem Reap. Les Enfants d'Angkor, supported by a French NGO, is a troupe made up of orphaned Cambodian children ages 10–18. Another resident troupe is Borann Vicheth Troupe. Performances last an hour, with a repertoire of classical and folk dances. Among the folk dances you might see are the Coconut Dance (sound effects provided by dancers clapping together halved coconut shells—this dance is performed at weddings in southeast Cambodia), the Fish Trap Dance (real fish traps are used as props in this romantic interlude), and the spectacular Bamboo Dance (bamboo poles are smashed together low on the ground and the barefoot dancers nimbly sidestep them, seeming to risk serious ankle injury). But the highlight of the evening is the seductive, slow-motion dancing of the *apsara,* with its sensual hand-gestures. A bonus: Live music for the dance programs is provided by the *pinpeat*—the small traditional Khmer orchestra.

Bars and Pubs

There is nightlife of sorts at **"Pub Street"**—a cluster of restaurants and bars in the area just north of the Old Market (Psah Chas). Patrons linger long over dinner and stoke up with a few drinks. Here you'll find Soup Dragon, Temple Bar, Buddha Lounge, the Red Piano Bar, and others. Or you could try Only One Bar, whose bar is fashioned out of a full-sized Khmer river boat. Some venues stay open till midnight. Locals amuse themselves with karaoke and taxi-dancing bars on the edge of town. Guesthouse gates are often locked for security reasons at 2200. Larger hotels such as the Grand Hotel d'Angkor offer satellite TV, which includes the StarPlus movie channel and CNN programming.

SHOPPING

There's a large cottage souvenir industry at Siem Reap, with stalls near the ruins and in town. Most of the items are also for sale in Phnom Penh. For handicraft items, go to Psah Chas (Old Market), which lies in the old French quarter down by the river. Stalls here carry a wide variety of handmade goods, including papier-mâché dance masks. North of this is another market, Psah Kandal, also stocking handicraft items and clothing.

Angkoriana: Try Les Artisans d'Angkor—an atelier at the southwest fringe of Siem Reap. This large workshop provides employment for disadvantaged youth: The artisans make excellent replicas of Khmer statuary in stone, wood, and other materials—and that includes sandstone pieces weighing up to 100 kilos. The pieces copy famous Khmer statuary, such as the portrait head of Jayavarman VII. Other fine crafts produced here are lacquerware and silk items (from the atelier's own silk farm at Puork). The Grand Hotel d'Angkor, Ta Prohm, City Angkor, and Sofitel Royal Angkor include gift shops selling Angkor kitsch, as well as postcards, books, and newspapers. Rice-paper prints made from charcoal rubbings of bas-reliefs of Angkor temples are inexpensive and come close to the original artwork. Opposite Ta Prohm Hotel is Sila Angkor, a small shop with a stock of Angkor kitsch.

Film: You can buy E6 and print film in Siem Reap: try the section of road on Route 6 just east of the main bridge; you can find one-hour photo places here that develop print film and burn CDs. Hotel gift shops also sell film—at higher prices.

SERVICES AND INFORMATION

Maps and Books

Monument Books, at 278 Psah Chas Market, offers a big selection of books and magazines and maps. Monument Books has branches at FCC Angkor and some other hotels.

Telecom Services

Don't expect wonders from the post office, on the west side of Siem Reap River. If you prod the staff, they might shell out a few stamps— a postcard from Angkor, if it makes it back home, will certainly have tremendous snob-appeal value. Next door, Cambodia Samart Communications has a satellite dish and a mobile IDD phone. You can phone home from here, though it's expensive. The office is open 0800–1800. Satellite dishes are sprinkled around hotels in Siem Reap—this links them to Phnom Penh and provides fax and IDD capabilities. The Cambodia country code is 855, and the Siem Reap area code is 63. Satellite TV, also operating off dishes, can pick up StarTV, CNN, and BBC. There are a few phone boxes where you can use a phone card to make calls to Phnom Penh or internationally. You buy the card for $10, $20, $50, or $100, and feed it into the apparatus. Using a NetPhone connection is much cheaper.

Email and Internet

Because of the large number of tourists drawn to Angkor, there are good cybercafés—especially in the area around the old market. Rates are more expensive than in Phnom Penh. A number of these cafés handle NetPhone calling as well as CD-burning for digital cameras.

PIC Online has a good Internet café south of the Hotel de la Paix. PIC offers WiFi connections through a prepaid Internet card. Hot spots around Siem Reap are found at the Blue Pumpkin Bakery, FCC Angkor, Raffles Grand, and the Sofitel. Consult www.online.com.kh for more details on WiFi hotspots.

Banking

You can easily deal in U.S. dollars in Siem Reap, or exchange traveler's checks (rate may not be as good as in Phnom Penh); credit-card use is limited. There is a branch of **Cambodia Commercial Bank** on Sivutha Boulevard; in the same vicinity are the **National Bank of Cambodia** and the **First Overseas Bank.** The Cambodia Commercial Bank will convert U.S. traveler's checks to U.S. cash for a 2 percent commission. The bank is open 0800–1500 daily.

Pools, Massage, and Spas

In recent years, a more stable Angkor has attracted high-end guests, particularly the Japanese, who demand pampering facilities such as pools and spas. Catering to these demands, four- and five-star hotels in Siem Reap are tacking "Resort and Spa" onto their hotel names—whether they just have a gym with some weights, or whether they have a full-blown spa facility.

Pools: Cooling off is a constant battle in Siem Reap. Some favor air-conditioned environments, but a superior method of climate control is to jump into the pool, of which there are quite a few in Siem Reap, though they're not always accessible to nonguests unless paying a premium. You might want to ask about a pool and spa combination: at some hotels, if you pay for a two-hour spa treatment, you are given free access to the pool. Hotels that are specifically designed around the pool are Victoria Angkor and La Residence d'Angkor. Both have well-thought-out designs. The swim-up bar at the Sofitel Royal Angkor is a stand-out, while the long pool at the Grand Hotel is on a majestic scale. For sheer ingenuity, however, the prize goes to Angkor Village Resort, which has a 200-meter pool that winds through the lush tropical gardens among the guesthouse cottages.

Massage and Spas: After a hot dusty day at the ruins, climbing near-vertical steps at Angkor Wat or laboring up Phnom Bakeng—and driving around in the stifling heat—you may need to indulge in some restorative massage. There are an awful lot of foot-massage places downtown advertising "traditional Khmer massage." There is actually no such thing—it has been lifted and adapted from Thai massage techniques. High-end hotels in Siem Reap have done similar—imported training and beauty products from Thailand and turned it all into spas for the Angkor-weary. Four- and five-star hotels in Siem Reap usually offer in-house massage and treatments; others have spa facilities attached to a gym. The Sofitel's Angkor Spa is a sumptuous structure with a wide range of treatments—including a rice body polish and Khmer white mud wrap. One of the spa's very first guests was actress Angelina Jolie, who visited every night during the filming of *Tomb Raider* in 2000. She again was a regular when she returned to Siem Reap to adopt a Cambodian child. Other high-end spas can be found at the Grand Hotel, Shintamani, FCC Angkor, Victoria Angkor, La Residence d'Angkor, and Angkor Village Resort.

GETTING THERE

By Air

Siem Reap is an international entry and exit point for Cambodia, with visa-on-arrival issued for $20 in U.S. dollars only (have a passport photo handy). Siem Reap International Airport can accommodate the Airbus-320, which is a 150-passenger plane. The 50-minute Bangkok Airways flight, on an ATR-72 turboprop or a smaller Boeing jet, is scheduled several times daily and costs about $240 round-trip (one-way fare is half that). Since Bangkok Airways flies round-trip to Phnom Penh from Bangkok also, it might be possible to negotiate an inbound flight to Angkor and an outbound flight back via Phnom Penh if you want to see more of Cambodia. Bangkok Airways may also operate a Bangkok–Sukothai–Siem Reap flight (but reverse direction does not stop in Suko-

thai). There are regular air connections from Phnom Penh to Siem Reap, but boat and road travel are much cheaper and you get to see more along the way.

Other international carriers winging into Siem Reap are Vietnam Airlines (daily flights from Saigon and Hanoi), Lao Airlines (direct flight to Luang Prabang, and flights several times a week from Pakse, linking to Vientiane), SilkAir (several times a week from Singapore), and Malaysia Airlines (connection to Kuala Lumpur). The Hanoi to Siem Reap flight takes less than two hours and costs $200 one-way—which is pricey for individuals (the flight is mostly filled with Korean and Japanese group tours who do not pay this price per person).

The airport at Siem Reap lies eight kilometers northwest of town. The larger hotels maintain airport representatives who will arrange taxis. If arriving on your own, you can transfer to town for $2 by car, or take a moto. Moto drivers may offer free rides to a guesthouse (where they get a commission); then they'll try to line you up for moto tours of Angkor. On departure from Siem Reap Airport, passengers' bags and personal effects may be searched for Angkorian statues and artifacts.

By Boat

Westerners can take the boats from Phnom Penh up the Tonle Sap River and across Lake Tonle Sap, arriving at Chong Kneas dock, which is 15 kilometers south of Siem Reap (transfer to moto or taxi for the land leg). Timing depends on the direction of the Tonle Sap River. There are several speedboats—preferable are the Malaysian models. From Phnom Penh it costs about $25 to Siem Reap, and the journey takes 5–7 hours. The boat is seasonal and runs when waters are high, November–February: Some boats have experienced trouble, running aground on sandbars. If the water is low, and the large speedboat cannot approach the dock near Tonle Sap, passengers are transferred to smaller craft. In drier seasons, the speedboats used are smaller. Less regular and more elusive to book are cargo

TOURING ANGKOR

TA SOM ★

NEAK PEAN ★

GRAND CIRCUIT

★ PREAH KHAN M

East Baray (dry)

EAST MEBON ★

PRE RUP ★

THOMMANON ★

SEPEAN THMA (BRIDGE)

TAKEO ★

CHAU SAY TEVODA ★

CIRCUIT

★ TA PROHM M

BANTEAY KDEI ★

LITTLE

VICTORY GATE

GATE OF THE DEAD

Siem Reap River

★ PRASAT KRAVAN

CHECKPOINT

NORTH GATE

PREAH PALILAY ★

LEPER KING TERRACE ★ M

ELEPHANT TERRACE ★

PHIMEANAKAS ★

BAPHUON ★

★ THE BAYON M

BENG THOM ★

SOUTH GATE

BAKSEI CHAMKRONG ★

ANKOR WAT

★ ZOO

WEST GATE

▲ Phnom Bakheng

CHECK POINT

FOODSTALLS

CHECKPOINT

1 mi

1 km

0

0

Angkor

© AVALON TRAVEL PUBLISHING, INC.

boats departing Phnom Penh for Siem Reap. A double-deck cargo boat takes anywhere from 18–26 hours, with passengers stringing up hammocks or sleeping on deck. You need to bring your own food. One traveler reported a journey of 36 hours, though the first 12 hours were spent in Phnom Penh with propeller troubles. The cost is $5–8.

By Land

Buses run the Phnom Penh to Siem Reap route and other parts of the north. Preferable would be express or VIP buses, which offer a fair degree of comfort and guarantee some degree of speed. Fares are low—around $5 for the trip. Share-taxis run all the way in stages from Phnom Penh via Battambang and Sisophon to Siem Reap. By road from Bangkok to Siem Reap takes about 12 hours. Minibuses ply the route daily, running from Bangkok's Khao San Road to the Old Market of Siem Reap for about $12 one-way. The border crossing point is Aranyaprathet (Thai side) to Poipet (Cambodia). The road is superb on the Thai side but uncertain on the Cambodian side—expect delays there.

By Rail

You can take a train from Phnom Penh to Battambang, but few pursue this option because it's so slow. In any case, you still need to get from Battambang to Siem Reap by boat or by road. But stay tuned: The Eastern and Oriental Express was inquiring about extending its services to Cambodia. E&O runs a high-end train from Bangkok to Singapore. The track from Bangkok to Phnom Penh via Poipet and Sisophon is in place, but the Cambodian section of the track would have to be considerably upgraded to take the heavier Orient Express train.

GETTING AROUND

There are plenty of motos and *remorks* around town—just flag one down. The *remork*—a motorcycle-pulled chariot—is a cool way to get around. Under your own steam, you can cover Siem Reap on foot or by bicycle. Between the Red Piano bar and the Blue Pumpkin bakery is a road in the old market area with a string of bicycle rentals, including some mountain bikes. Another location with rentals is on Route 6 west of the main bridge.

Angkor Wat

Angkor is not orchestral; it is monumental. It is an epic poem which makes its effect, like the Odyssey and like Paradise Lost, by the grandeur of its structure as well as by the beauty of the details. Angkor is an epic in rectangular forms imposed upon the Cambodian jungle.

Arnold Toynbee, East to West

Occupying an entire square kilometer, Angkor Wat is the world's largest temple and the best-preserved of all Angkorian temples. This masterpiece of Khmer design is contemporary with the major Gothic cathedrals of Europe. Angkor Wat's central tower soars 65 meters, equivalent in height to Notre Dame Cathedral in Paris. Angkor Wat is estimated to contain the same cubic volume of stone blocks as

Egypt's pyramid of Cheops. And every stone surface at Angkor is carefully dressed, carved, and decorated.

Angkor Wat is a three-tier pyramidal structure symbolizing Mt. Meru. In Hindu cosmology, Mt. Meru is a holy mountain composed of seven terraces, upon which 33 gods are enthroned, all surrounded by an ocean. Hindu epics describe Mt. Meru as the navel of the world—a vast peak with flanks of gold, crystal, ruby, and lapis lazuli.

The building of Angkor Wat began around 1120 under King Suryavarman II—the king actually lived to see the work completed about 30 years later. Suryavarman II dedicated Angkor Wat to the Hindu deity Vishnu, with whom he identified as divine king. As part of the Vishnu cult, sacred lingas and Vishnu

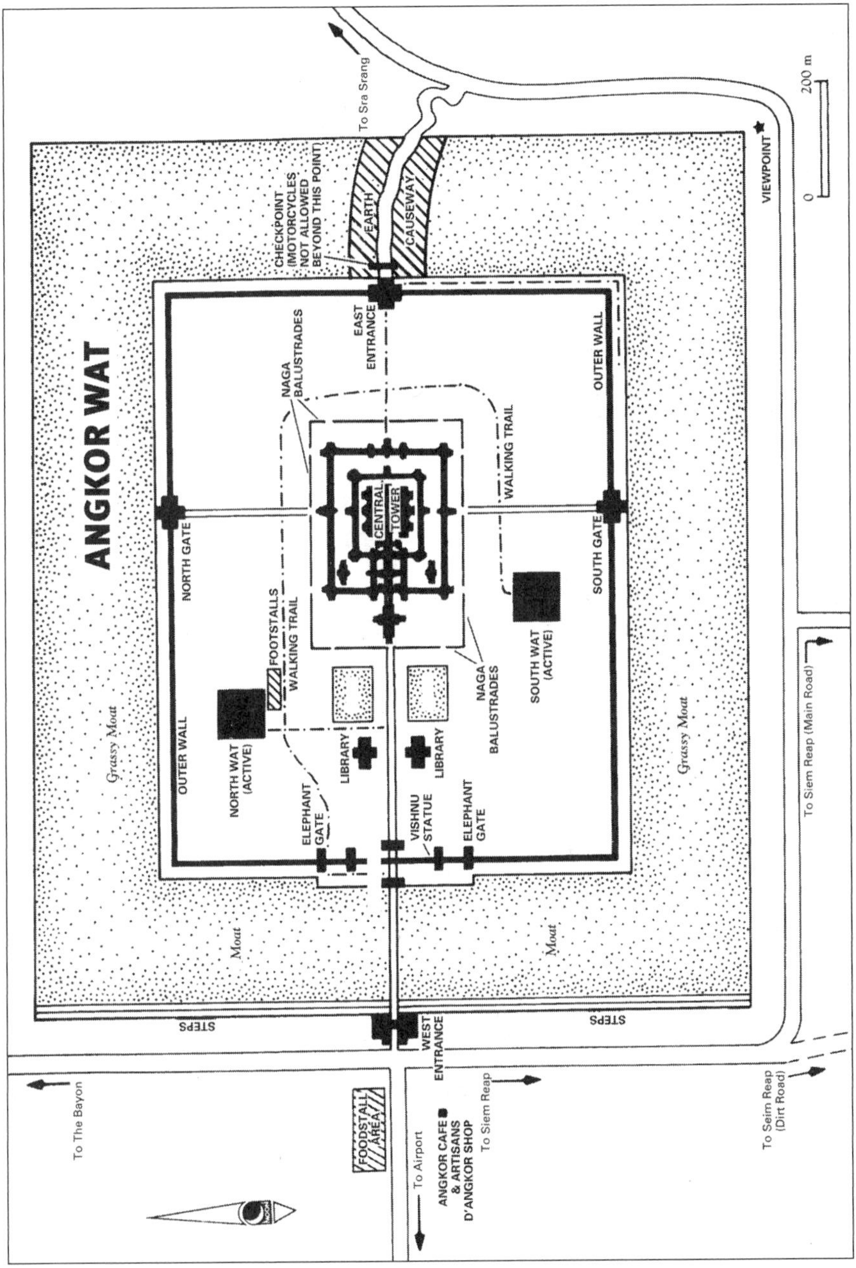

ANGKOR WAT

To Sra Srang

To The Bayon

VIEWPOINT

0   200 m

CHECKPOINT
(MOTORCYCLES
NOT ALLOWED
BEYOND THIS POINT)

EARTH

CAUSEWAY

EAST
ENTRANCE

NAGA
BALUSTRADES

OUTER WALL

Grassy Moat

NORTH GATE

CENTRAL
TOWER

WALKING TRAIL

SOUTH GATE

Grassy Moat

FOOTSTALLS
WALKING TRAIL

NORTH WAT
(ACTIVE)

OUTER WALL

ELEPHANT
GATE

LIBRARY

VISHNU
STATUE

LIBRARY

ELEPHANT
GATE

NAGA
BALUSTRADES

SOUTH WAT
(ACTIVE)

Moat

Moat

STEPS

STEPS

WEST
ENTRANCE

To Seim Reap
(Dirt Road)

To Siem Reap (Main Road)

To Siem Reap

To Airport

FOODSTALL
AREA

ANGKOR CAFE
& ARTISANS
D'ANGKOR SHOP

Angkor

© AVALON TRAVEL PUBLISHING, INC.

ANGKOR WAT GROUND PLAN

NAGA BALUSTRADES

NW CORNER PAVILION

LIBRARY

SECOND TERRACE

QUINCUNX TERRACE

CENTRAL TOWER

EAST ENTRANCE

TERRACE OF HONOR

Basin

GALLERY OF A THOUSAND BUDDHAS

FRONT TOWER

FIRST TERRACE

BROKEN TOWER

LIBRARY

Basin

SW CORNER PAVILION

NAGA BALUSTRADES

0   50 m

© AVALON TRAVEL PUBLISHING, INC.

statues were sheltered in sanctuaries at the temple; a large Vishnu statue remains near the front entrance. Suryavarman II was one of Angkor's greatest kings, extending the Khmer Empire into present-day Malaya and Thailand, invading Myanmar (Burma) and parts of Vietnam, and sending emissaries to the imperial court of the Khans in Peking. Under Suryavarman, Angkor reached its zenith. Toward the end of his reign, Suryavarman's forces suffered a major defeat in North Vietnam, and the king lost a number of his territories.

Because it faces westward, Angkor Wat is thought to have served as a funerary temple for the king. Site inscriptions support this theory, and the first terrace bas-reliefs are meant to be viewed in a counterclockwise direction, which indicates a mausoleum—clockwise circumambulation is the norm for temples. Otherwise, archaeologists are in the dark. We do not possess the keys to Angkor's grandeur—we stumble along blindly through the colossus, not sure how it functions, how it all fits together.

◪ EXPLORING ANGKOR WAT
Entrances

There are two ways into or out of Angkor Wat—the west or front entrance, and the east or back

ON PILGRIMAGE AT ANGKOR

Even after it was abandoned in the 15th century, Angkor continued to operate as a pilgrimage site. Under the Siamese, Buddhist monks later occupied part of the site, which explains why Angkor Wat is the best-preserved temple in the entire region—the monks cleared away encroaching jungle. Angkor is on the pilgrimage circuit not only for Cambodians and Buddhists from neighboring countries but also for visiting Indians, since the temple is consecrated to Hindu deities. There are two small monasteries on the grounds of Angkor Wat, the North Wat and South Wat; at dawn, orange-robed monks stroll about the ruins.

Since a lot of Angkor's freestanding statuary has been looted or removed for safekeeping, there are only a few areas of interest for pilgrims. The first is the huge eight-armed Vishnu statue to the south side of the second causeway entrance tower. Joss sticks and other offerings are left here. Cambodians often come to consecrate food, which is then presumably taken off and eaten. Another popular site is the top sanctuary, where pilgrims *sompeah* the statues and the courtyard is smoky from burning joss sticks.

entrance. It's seven kilometers from the Grand Hotel north to the front entrance of Angkor Wat, where there's a parking lot for cars and tour buses, and a food stall area. Opposite the front entrance to Angkor Wat is an air-conditioned place called Angkor Café, serving food and drinks; there is an attached shop for Les Artisans d'Angkor, selling carvings, silk, and handicrafts.

The Causeway

The western approach to Angkor Wat is guarded by Khmer-style lions and seven-headed cobras (called *nagas*) with hoods outspread. A majestic 220-meter causeway, paved with large stone slabs and lined with colossal *naga* balustrades (which also encircle the entire temple), leads across a moat to the temple. The temple complex is bounded by a laterite wall, representing the earth; this is enclosed by a square moat more than five kilometers long, symbolizing the oceans. The moat is 1.3 kilometers long from north to south, 1.5 kilometers from east to west, and 200 meters wide. The few meters of water in the plant-choked moat teem with frogs and are also home to lolling water buffalo and herons, who use it as a wading pool. The moat serves as a cooling-off spot for local kids, too. Boat racing in the moat has been revived for the November Water Festival, a celebration of victory in a naval battle against the Cham dating to the 12th century.

Farther along you reach a second entrance, a triple-tower entryway. This leads to a second section of the causeway about 350 meters long. The regal approach here is breathtaking. On the spot, and in three dimensions, the perspective is grander than anything words or photos can convey. Closer to the temple, to the left and right of the causeway, are two small isolated buildings, thought to have been libraries housing sacred scriptures on palm leaves. On the left is a pool that reflects Angkor's towers at sunset. Ahead loom the triple towers of Angkor Wat; two more are hidden out of view at the back.

A cruciform terrace stands in front of the principal entrance to Angkor Wat. The terrace probably served as a review stand for the king; ritual dances may have been performed here. Called the Terrace of Honor, this area features steps flanked by Khmer lions. There may have once been 300 stone lions guarding staircases and entryways at Angkor Wat.

First Terrace

There are three rectangular terraces at Angkor, each rising above the other in pyramid fashion. The first terrace, measuring 200 meters by 180 meters, is four meters from ground level; the second, 115 meters by 100 meters, rises six meters above that; and the third, 60 meters by 60 meters, is another 13 meters up.

ANGKOR WAT'S BAS-RELIEFS

Girdling the walls of Angkor Wat's first terrace are eight panels of bas-reliefs displaying scenes from Khmer historical events and the Hindu epics Ramayana and Mahabharata. The two-meter-high panels cover 1,200 square meters of sandstone carving—the longest continuous bas-relief in the world. This mind-boggling work of art must have been undertaken by innumerable sculptors working in teams. Bas-relief sculpting varies considerably in quality; panels were sculpted in various eras by different craftsmen. Some sections have been damaged; others have acquired a glossy sheen—the result of either lacquer coating or centuries of pilgrims rubbing their hands over the figures. Some panels may originally have been painted or gilded.

The panels essentially depict the battle between good and evil—keeping these forces in balance produces harmony. A prominent figure is four-armed Vishnu, shown quite large (the larger the figure on the bas-reliefs, the more important). Vishnu the Preserver was summoned whenever troubles arose in heaven or on earth. He is credited with at least 10 incarnations, among them Krishna and Rama. The righteous Rama was specifically incarnated to destroy evil demons.

The galleries at Angkor Wat are meant to be read in a counterclockwise direction, a circumambulation signifying a mausoleum. If you don't have the time or inclination to walk around the entire building, the most striking section is panel 4, Churning the Sea of Milk.

In the **West gallery, panel 1** depicts the civil war that is the main subject of the Hindu epic the Mahabharata. An army of Kauravas, advancing from the left, meets Pandavas with pointed headdresses attacking from the right. In the upper part of the panel lies Bhima, the leader of the Kauravas, struck down by arrows. In the center is Arjuna, leader of the Pandavas, in his war chariot. The **southwest corner pavilion** shows scenes from the Ramayana and the life of Krishna.

South gallery, panel 2 features two images of Suryavarman II, the builder of Angkor Wat. He is first shown on an upper tier, seated on a low throne, giving his court instructions. Further along he appears with sword in hand, shaded by 15 ceremonial umbrellas, riding an elephant in a triumphal procession and readying his troops for battle. Other commanders also appear on elephants. Bringing up the rear are musicians and Brahman priests carrying holy fire. The figures with raffish headgear are probably Siamese mercenaries.

South gallery, panel 3: the left tiers show people proceeding toward 18-armed Yama, the Hindu Judge of the Dead here riding a buffalo, with his two assistants. On the upper tier the good advance to the leisurely pursuits of the 37 heavens, in celestial palaces filled with angelic *apsaras*. On the lower tier the wicked are cast into the realm of the 32 hells, where they are starved, bludgeoned, sawn in half, shackled, savaged by wild animals, or spiked with nails, among other tortures.

East gallery, panel 4 is a famous 50-meter-long panel depicting the Hindu legend, Churning the Sea of Milk (see below). The east entrance to Angkor Wat is located between panels 4 and 5. **East gallery, panel 5** depicts war between demons and gods for possession of the ambrosia *amrita,* the essence of life. Four-armed Vishnu is victorious over the demons. This panel is poorly executed and was left unfinished.

In the **North gallery, panel 6** shows Krishna advancing to attack the demon-king Bana. A wall of fire blocks his progress but is extinguished by Garuda, the mount of Vishnu. Bana (multiple arms, mounted on rhinoceros) is captured, but upon the intervention of Shiva, Krishna spares his life. On the far right, thousand-headed Krishna kneels in front of Shiva.

North gallery, panel 7 displays another battle between gods and demons, with a procession of 21 deities in the Brahman pantheon riding their traditional mounts. This panel is poorly executed, but if you continue to the **northwest corner pavilion** there are some finely wrought bas-reliefs of Ramayana scenes.

In the **West gallery, panel 8** depicts the Battle of Lanka from the Ramayana. Evil is personified by the demon-king Ravana (10 heads, 20 arms) who has abducted the beautiful Sita, consort of Prince Rama, and taken her to Sri Lanka. Assisted by the monkey army of Hanuman, Rama launches an attack on Lanka to rescue Sita. Ravana and Rama fight near the center of the panel: Rama stands on the shoulders of the monkey king Sugriva, while Ravana rides in a chariot drawn by mythical lions; monkey warriors fight giant demons nearby.

Cambodia's Creation Myth: Churning the Sea of Milk

Every culture has its legends of the origin of the species. The Hindu creation myth Churning the Sea of Milk is shown in the bas-relief panel at the East gallery (panel 4) of Angkor Wat. In Hindu mythology, 13 precious things including the elixir of immortality were lost in the churning of the cosmic sea. Finding them again required a joint dredging operation between gods and demons. Assisting in this endeavor was the giant serpent Vasuki, who offered himself as a rope to enable twirling of a "churning stick." The serpent was yanked back and forth in a giant tug-of-war that lasted for a thousand years.

In the bas-relief panel, the front end of the serpent is being pulled by 91 surly-looking *asuras* (demons), anchored by the 21-headed demon king Ravana; on the right are 88 almond-eyed *devas* (gods) pulling on the tail, anchored by monkey-god Hanuman. The central pivot, or churning stick, is a complicated piece of imagery. Vasuki has wrapped himself around Mount Mandara, represented by a tower. At one point Mount Mandara started to sink, and had to be propped up by a giant tortoise, an incarnation of Vishnu. The Sea of Milk, or the Ocean of Immortality, is represented by innumerable fish and aquatic creatures, torn to shreds as they swim close to powerful air currents near the churning stick.

Directing operations at the center is the large four-armed figure of Vishnu, closely associated with Angkor Wat's builder, Suryavarman II. The smaller figure above Vishnu is Indra, god of the sky. The actions of the gods and demons cause Vasuki to rotate the tower-mountain and churn the sea into foam, like a giant cosmic blender. This releases a seminal fluid that creates a divine ambrosia, *amrita,* the essence of life and immortality. Many other treasures are also flung up. Born of this action are *apsaras*, or celestial dancers, a purely Khmer innovation. The seductive *apsaras* promise a joyful existence for those who attain the ultimate incarnation; it is assumed that higher incarnations will be male in form.

According to Angkorologist Eleanor Mannikka, who has been studying the place for over 20 years, the bas-relief has a practical function in marking the number of days between the winter and summer solstices. Mannikka maintains that the 91 *asuras* mark the 91 days between the winter solstice and spring equinox in March, while the 88 *devas* represent the 88 days to the summer solstice after the equinox period. Mannikka says this is just one of the hidden cosmological meanings coded at Angkor Wat, and that the temple is remarkably attuned to the movement of the sun and moon.

Thus on the third terrace you are 23 meters above ground level.

The main feature of the first terrace is the massive gallery of bas-reliefs. Viewing the gallery is time-consuming and distracts from the main fare—the uppermost sanctuary. It's best to view the first-terrace gallery after you've climbed to the top of Angkor and come back to earth. Walking the entire length of the gallery, you traverse 750 meters.

Consolidating the grand entry to Angkor Wat is a series of cruciform courtyards. One of these is the Gallery of a Thousand Buddhas, which contained many images from the period when Angkor was Buddhist. Scarce few remain today, though there's a large standing Buddha with open palms. This section may have once been used for the ritual ablutions of priests.

Second Terrace

A flight of steps takes you to the second terrace, where galleries and staircases are adorned with baluster windows with seven twisted stone columns. The interior walls and niches of the second terrace gallery are decorated with the ethereal forms of more than 1,700 stone *apsaras* (celestial dancers) and *devatas* (goddesses). Sculptors evidently spent long hours crafting these bas-reliefs—they're the finest Angkor has to offer. The figures face straight ahead with feet in profile. Framed by elaborate floral decoration and arranged in coquettish groups of two or three, they link arms and strike seductive poses, rather like models on a catwalk.

These bare-breasted angels were most likely modeled on the king's entourage of dancers, and they are the height of Khmer chic. The king of Angkor maintained a bevy of dancers as part of his royal harem. Hindus considered dancing a sacred act, and female dancers devoted their lives to performing to please the gods. At Angkor dance was both sacred and sensual: Through the medium of dance the women communicated with the divine world, guaranteeing fertility for the land and well-being for the people. While the men were out hunting, women at the court of Angkor evidently spent long hours grooming, styling their hair, preen-

ing, and adjusting their jewelry and girdles. The bas-reliefs display the elaborate coiffures—hair knotted on the crown and braided or bejeweled (36 hairstyles have been identified)—and the fantastic fashions at the court of Angkor, with jeweled crowns, skirts, hip girdles, and upper-arm bracelets. The king's dancers were often spoils of war—when the Siamese invaded, they took Khmer dancers back to the Thai court.

In the 1950s under Sihanouk's patronage, an *apsara* dance was created, with costumes and jeweled headpieces based on these bas-relief carvings—though with more modest apparel. The *apsara* is danced by five or seven women (odd numbers are auspicious) wearing multispired crowns and garlands of frangipani. The chorus sings of the delight of being surrounded by beautiful flowers in a garden. In the 1950s and 1960s tourists were treated to performances of *apsara* dancing at Angkor Wat itself. In November 1994, for the first time in decades, *apsara* dancers performed again at Angkor Wat under the full moon during the Water Festival. Light was provided by 600 youths bearing torches.

Quincunx Terrace

Dizzying steps lead from inner courtyards to the third terrace. It is believed that only the king and high priests ascended to this terrace. The temples at Angkor were not designed to accommodate devotees—pilgrims were restricted to open ground-level courtyards. Steps to the third terrace are steep and best tackled sideways in a zigzag pattern; the south stairway has concrete steps and a handrail.

The third terrace is in the shape of a quincunx—a square platform supporting five towers, one in each corner and one in the center. The central tower soars to a height of 65 meters. Here you get a closer look at the flower-shaped towers, an innovation in Khmer architecture at the time. The tower spires feature eight stories and a crown, and are actually square, although multiple projections make them look octagonal. They display the curved outline of a sprouting bud. Four more partially destroyed towers sprout from the corners of the second terrace.

Originally, the central or uppermost sanctuary probably held a great image of Vishnu, which has long since disappeared. Now the central sanctuary features standing Buddhas set into niches, some seated, some freestanding, and one reclining. These images are in poor condition, added by Buddhist monks who once lived in the area. A passageway behind the freestanding Buddha in the south section leads to the hollow core of the central tower, now occupied by bats. This entrance was walled up after the sacking of Angkor by the Siamese in the 15th century. Inside the central core French archaeologists discovered a 30-meter vertical shaft with a cache of gold objects at the base.

You can walk all around the top terrace for great views of Angkor and the surrounding terrain. On the western perimeter is a seated stone Buddha, sheltered by a *naga*. The statue gazes over the causeway—lone sentinel to the theft and destruction of statuary at Angkor Wat.

Angkor's Back Door

You can approach Angkor Wat from the east side along a dirt road through the forest. However, there is a checkpoint here where you must park a motorcycle and walk the last 300–400 meters, passing through a slab of Angkor's old wall. The east entrance leads directly to the bas-relief panel Churning the Sea of Milk. This back-door route to Angkor Wat was probably used for delivering building materials and supplies to the temple. It appears to have also been the elephant docking bay; in the center of the back gallery is a stairless section probably used by Khmer royalty for mounting and dismounting elephants. Making allowances for elephant arrival and departure is a curious feature of Khmer architecture found elsewhere at Angkor Wat and Angkor

Thom. Elephants draped in ceremonial colors transported royalty; the pachyderms were valuable as "tanks" in pitched battle, too.

AERIAL VIEWS

Phnom Bakheng

An aerial view of the Angkor region is the attraction at Phnom Bakheng, 1.3 kilometers north of Angkor Wat. The ideal time to visit is toward sunset, when lighting is dramatic; dawn is also good. Although Phnom Bakheng is a temple-mountain, the emphasis today is more on the mountain than the temple. You hike to the summit of the 65-meter peak up steep steps once lined with guardian lions; a few remain near the top. At the summit are half-demolished ruins of a pyramid dedicated to Shiva: Phnom Bakheng was the 9th-century center of King Yasovarman's city, Yasodharapura. Numerous small towers that once stood in the area have vanished.

Because of its strategic position, the hill once served as a camp for troops. Today, elephants lumber to the top bearing Japanese tourists bound for a splendid sunset view. On a clear day, from the top you can see the West Baray, Phnom Krom (to the southwest), and parts of Angkor Wat. From this position, you'd need a long lens and a tripod to take effective pictures.

Hot-Air Balloon

Due west of the main entrance to Angkor is a tethered hot-air balloon with caged passenger basket, offering a 10-minute ride for $11. Poor value, and the balloon never gets airborne—it is attached by a cable to the ground. It takes 15 passengers about 200 meters up so they can fire off pictures at Angkor Wat. You can do similar from Phnom Bakheng for free.

Angkor

Angkor Thom

Angkor Thom (Great City) encloses an area of nine square kilometers, and at its peak may have held a population of more than 100,000, living in tiled or thatched houses. The building of the citadel dates to around the year 1200. Angkor Thom enclosed the Royal Palace (now vanished) and a handful of major temples; the complex was bounded by walls and a moat (now mostly dry) and pierced by five gates. The city was surrounded with rice fields, which provided food; these were irrigated with reservoirs, which also supplied drinking water.

While Angkor Wat is Hindu in inspiration, Angkor Thom resonates with sculpted images expressing the Mahayana Buddhist ideal of Lokesvara (compassion), Prajnaparamita (wisdom), and the Buddha (enlightenment). Although still incorporating Hindu elements, Angkor Thom is a three-dimensional representation of Buddhist cosmology. Temple ground plans reveal a mandala-like base, with radiating symmetrical forms.

Numerology played a part in the design. The Khmer consider odd numbers auspicious, so a *naga* is likely to be five-headed, seven-headed, or nine-headed. Angkor Thom features five gates; the king of Angkor had five wives at the time of Zhou Daguan's visit in 1296. One wife lived at each of the cardinal points of Angkor Thom, with a fifth in the central palace. A sacred number in Mahayana Buddhism is 108. Rosary beads used in counting meditation are 108 in number—the devout were supposed to recite the name of Buddha 100 times; the extra eight beads were provided in case the user became forgetful or lost some. The gods and demons at each gate of Angkor Thom number 108. At the Bayon it's no accident there were once 54 towers with four heads each, for a total of 216 heads—double 108.

A stone motif that runs through Angkor Thom is a four-headed deity, most likely derived from Mahayana Buddhism. It's found at the gates to Angkor Thom, and at entrances to a handful of major temples such as Preah Khan

and Ta Prohm. At the Bayon the four-headed motif comes into its own in a stunning and bizarre design. The motif is the one most often featured in Angkoriana—in statuary, paintings, and on banknotes.

The four-headed motif is the trademark of Jayavarman VII, regarded as the last great king of the Khmer Empire. After Cham legions sacked Angkor in 1177, Jayavarman VII not only set about rebuilding Angkor Wat, he also built Angkor Thom, incorporating previously built works such as Baphuon and the pyramid of Phimeanakas. He embarked on a frenzy of slapdash building, throwing up the outer wall and five monumental gates of Angkor Thom, constructing roads and stone bridges and hundreds of hospitals, monasteries, and pilgrim rest houses throughout the empire. For these enterprises he received support from his favorite wife, Jayadevi, who taught Buddhism in the monasteries.

Capping all these achievements, he created the masterpiece of the Bayon, the last great temple constructed at Angkor. In the process, Jayavarman VII used up an enormous amount of sandstone. The building frenzy virtually exhausted the quarries of Phnom Kulen, which may explain why no more large temples were built of sandstone after his reign. Jayavarman VII quite likely exhausted his country and its population, too. After him the empire declined, ravaged by internal conflict and by war with the Siamese.

Jayavarman VII was a complex figure. It seems he was a humble monk who was twice denied the throne, and who then became the greatest of all Angkor kings. When Suryavarman II died, Jayavarman VII was off fighting a campaign in Champa and his half brother took the throne. Jayavarman VII then withdrew to Preah Khan Temple in Kompong Svay, about 105 kilometers to the east of Angkor. A rebellion broke out in 1166 and his half brother was killed by a usurper who subsequently seized the throne, denying Jayavarman VII a second

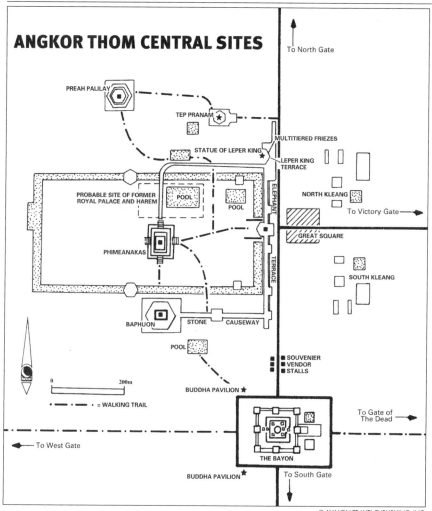

ANGKOR THOM CENTRAL SITES

To North Gate

PREAH PALILAY

TEP PRANAM ★

MULTITIERED FRIEZES

STATUE OF LEPER KING ★

LEPER KING TERRACE

PROBABLE SITE OF FORMER ROYAL PALACE AND HAREM

POOL

POOL

NORTH KLEANG

ELEPHANT

To Victory Gate

PHIMEANAKAS

GREAT SQUARE

TERRACE

SOUTH KLEANG

BAPHUON

STONE   CAUSEWAY

POOL

0   200m

= WALKING TRAIL

BUDDHA PAVILION ★

■ SOUVENIER
■ VENDOR
■ STALLS

To Gate of The Dead

To West Gate

THE BAYON

BUDDHA PAVILION ★

To South Gate

© AVALON TRAVEL PUBLISHING, INC.

Angkor

chance at rule. In 1177 this Khmer king died in battle when the Cham fleet came up the Mekong and across Lake Tonle Sap. Jayavarman VII took up the fight against the Cham, destroyed their fleet, and forced them to retreat. He then ascended to the throne in 1181, in his late 50s.

Stele and temple inscriptions praise Jayavarman's deeds, and Bayon bas-reliefs depict the entire story of the battle against the Cham.

From these sources, we know more about Jayavarman VII and his reign than about any other Khmer king. He fought against the Dai Viet, wreaked vengeance on the Cham Empire, advanced into Laos, and reached the borders of Myanmar (Burma). Yet other parts of his life remain obscure. His date of birth and death are uncertain—the latter is variously given as 1201 or 1218—and it is not known how he viewed Mahayana Buddhism. Surviving portrait heads of Jayavarman VII show him in a meditative pose with a facial expression that is at once humble, pious, scholarly, and ponderous. His hair is slicked back into a small chignon on top of his head. Jayavarman VII left some of his own thoughts, chiseled in stone: "He suffered more from his subjects' infirmities than from his own, for it is the people's pain that makes the pain of kings and not their own."

 SOUTH GATE

There are five gates to Angkor Thom. The South Gate, several kilometers north of Angkor Wat's west entrance, is the best preserved. The south approach over the moat to Angkor Thom is a causeway of the giants, guarded by two magnificent balustrades of mythical figures and a four-headed portal. On the left balustrade are 54 celestial *devas* involved in a tug-of-war with a nine-headed *naga;* on the right are 54 underworld *asuras* engaged in a similar struggle. Together they total the sacred number of 108. The demons grimace and pull faces; the sterner-looking gods wear conical headdresses. The dual balustrades of gods, demons, and *nagas* are most likely a three-dimensional representation of the Hindu creation myth, Churning the Sea of Milk, which is depicted in more detail in a bas-relief at the back of Angkor Wat.

A number of heads in the balustrade lineups are copies—you can tell by the lack of lichen growth on the pale concrete substitutes. This configuration of 108 statues is repeated at two other gates—the North Gate and the Victory Gate. If you look at the balustrade from the side, you'll see that it forms part of a stone causeway or bridge over the grassy moat of Angkor Thom. The moat was probably once stocked with crocodiles to discourage enemy advances.

The South Gate's stone portal is 23 meters high. The inner section is large enough to admit with ease a fully caparisoned royal elephant. On either side of the archway are sentry-box niches, once lined with wood. The imposing tower-gate is crowned with four heads facing the cardinal points; 13th-century Chinese chronicler Zhou

The South Gate of the Bayon was specially designed to accommodate elephants.

Daguan mentions a fifth head on the portal, made of gold, in the central position. At the lower half of the gate on each side is a sculpted three-headed elephant, the mount of the Hindu deity Indra. Indra appears at the center of the elephant holding a thunderbolt, framed by an *apsara* on each side. The three elephant trunks, which appear as pillars, pluck lotuses.

Tall trees line the avenues to the Bayon. Among the 80-odd species of trees found in the Angkor region are a number that have died out in other parts of Cambodia. The trees shelter a great variety of bird and insect species. Among the insects are droning cicadas, and bird species include the vernal hanging parrot (green), the lesser racket-tailed drongo (with a very long black tail), the black-crested bulbul (with a yellow body), and the spotted dove. You are more likely to hear these birds rather than see them.

THE BAYON

At whatever hour one walks around the Bayon, and particularly by moonlight on a clear evening, one feels as if one were

Angkor

THE BAYON

* ELEPHANT-BACK BATTLES
  BETWEEN KHMERS AND CHAMS

LINGA

EAST ENTRANCE
(MAIN ENTRANCE!)

* PROCESSION OF JAYAVARMAN VII
  ON ELEPHANT-BACK

Pool (Dry)

OUTER GALLERY

INNER GALLERY
BAS-RELIEFS

SEATED BUDDHA
WITH NAGA HOOD

* BEST BAS-RELIEF PANELS ON OUTER GALLERY

0   50 m

LIBRARY

LIBRARY

OUTER GALLERY

NORTH ENTRANCE

* NAVAL BALLES BETWEEN
  KHMERS AND CHAMS

* SCENES OF DAILY LIFE
  (COOKING, MARKETS)

TOP TERRACE

CENTRAL TOWER

TOP TERRACE

SOUTH ENTRANCE

OUTER GALLERY

* BAS-RELIEFS OF JUGGLERS
  AND WRESTLERS

OUTER   GALLERY

WEST ENTRANCE

Angkor

© AVALON TRAVEL PUBLISHING, INC.

BAYON BAS-RELIEFS

The bas-reliefs at the Bayon are less refined but livelier than those at Angkor Wat. They depict historical events and mythical stories and offer rare glimpses into daily life at Angkor. There are two series of bas-reliefs, one at the outer gallery and one at the inner gallery. The galleries are meant to be read in a clockwise direction, starting from the east entrance. The amount of carving at the Bayon was staggering: It is calculated that more than 11,000 figures were carved in bas-relief around the temple—much of that work has fallen victim to damage.

Outer Gallery

The magnificent outer gallery depicts land and sea battles between Cham and Khmer. The best parts are on the east and south sides with two- and three-tier panels. If your time is short, you could just cover the section from the east entrance to the south entrance, and then enter the Bayon from the south side. While the east and south sections are in good condition, others have either collapsed, suffered water damage, disappeared beneath moss or lichen, or are too dark to make out. Some panels were never completed.

The east gallery depicts battles between the Khmer and their historic enemy, the Cham. The Cham are easily identified by distinctive headgear, which looks like an inverted lotus. Troop commanders, including Jayavarman VII (identified by umbrellas with insignias), are mounted on elephants. Musicians accompany cavalry and foot soldiers; oxcarts bringing up the rear carry military provisions.

As you turn the corner at the south gallery, two- and three-tier bas-reliefs show naval battles between Cham (with headdress) and Khmer (no headgear); one boat makes a 90-degree turn in stone at the corner. In 1177 the Cham sailed across Lake Tonle Sap to sack Angkor; warriors are armed with javelins, bows, and shields. Corpses are thrown overboard, sometimes to the crocodiles. These panels record something else quite remarkable: They show species that are today extinct or highly endangered. On the naval battle panels, below the waterline you can see some elephant fish, giant catfish, and Siamese crocodiles—all of which are rare in Tonle Sap today. One panel shows dancing saurus cranes—very rarely seen today—while a golden peafowl is shown in another panel (now thought to be extinct). The lower panels record everyday life—a woman removing lice from another's hair, a patient in a hospital, an archer hunting, fishermen on Lake Tonle Sap, a cockfight, cooking, and market cameos. Palace scenes depict wrestlers, chess players, sword fighters, and princesses partying with their suitors. Farther along the south gallery, the battle between Cham and Khmer resumes—this time, in 1181, the Khmer are victorious, and Jayavarman VII sits in the palace surrounded by celebrating subjects. The military chronicle continues around the outer gallery, though bas-relief quality deteriorates and the north gallery is heavily damaged. Sections of the northwest gallery were unfinished: One fascinating detail at the northwest side shows jugglers and acrobats on wheels—a sort of Khmer Cirque du Soleil.

Inner Gallery

These sections are punctuated by jutting cells and other obstacles. If you persist you can follow the panels, again proceeding in a clockwise direction from the east entrance. Some panels are eroded and hard to make out; the better-preserved sections are to the east side. The bas-reliefs are mostly drawn from Hindu legends, but these Khmer picture books in stone also offer accurate detail of the common people of the time, with vignettes showing a fisherman casting his net, a man climbing a coconut tree, and scenes of temple construction.

visiting a temple in another world, built by an alien people, whose conceptions are entirely unfamiliar.

Henri Marchal, Guide Archéologique aux Temples d'Angkor

If Angkor Wat is classic and grand, the Bayon is wild and erratic. Who could've conjured this fantastic structure, and then—even more incredible—fashioned it from stone? Like Stonehenge or the Pyramids, the bizarre Bayon baffles with its design, its mysterious structure, its aura. The structure is simply amazing. What at first appears to be a random pile of masonry actually consists of massive stones shaped into fluid sculptures, without apparent use of cement or mortar.

The Bayon was once even more elaborate, the central tower apparently covered in gold leaf. Zhou Daguan described it in the 13th century:

At the center of the Kingdom rises a Golden Tower flanked by more than twenty lesser towers and several hundred stone chambers. On the eastern side is a golden bridge guarded by two lions of gold, one on each side, with eight golden Buddhas spaced along the stone chambers.

Oddly enough, Zhou Daguan failed to mention the massive heads on the Bayon towers.

The importance of the Bayon was not realized until the early 1900s, when French archaeologists cleared 10 square kilometers of land at Angkor Thom. This made it possible to sketch accurate maps for the first time, and it was discovered that the Bayon lay at the exact center of Angkor Thom. French archaeologists surmised the Bayon was built over the foundations of an earlier structure, resulting in dark galleries, deep courtyards, and towers crowded next to one another. Some parts were walled over, the original sculptures left intact within. Hidden below the upper terrace, Henri Parmentier in 1924 discovered a fine pediment of Lokesvara, the bodhisattva of compassion. This indicated the Bayon was Buddhist, and not, as previously thought, Hindu. The discovery of a large Buddha statue within the central sanctuary of the Bayon confirmed this.

Disorder in the construction of the Bayon is reflected in the numerous architectural changes. It seems that after the Cham sacked Angkor in 1177, Jayavarman VII decided the Hindu deities had failed, so he switched allegiance to Mahayana Buddhism. However, he made no attempt to alter existing Hindu elements. The Bayon was caught in the middle—the foundations are Hindu, but the superstructure is Buddhist. It is estimated that the Bayon took 20 years to build. Jayavarman VII's son and grandson reverted the use of the temple to Hindu (Shivaist) worship, with Brahmans from India gaining great influence over the Angkor court. Heads and faces on statues were destroyed and replaced with Hindu gods.

A Japanese government team working on restoration at the Bayon estimates that more than 200,000 blocks of stone were used for the building. Some of the larger blocks weigh 300 kilograms and must be moved by crane in the Japanese project. For the original construction, it would have been possible for four men to carry a piece like this with a sling, but that would not explain how such blocks reached the heights of the central tower. Reassembling pieces left behind by French archaeologists is proving a giant jigsaw puzzle for the Japanese—it has taken the Japanese group four years just to restore a small library building at the Bayon (restoration can only proceed six months of the year because of the rainy season).

Entrances

The square outer gallery of the Bayon serves as its walls. You can approach it from four entrances; inside is an inner enclosure, another gallery of bas-reliefs. The original main entrance was the east side—the best-preserved bas-relief sections are here. A good plan is to have your driver drop you at the east gate, and then meet you later by the north gate.

The pillars at the east entrance bear beautiful tapestry-like bas-reliefs of three *apsaras* in triangular formation, dancing on a bed of lotuses. These flying *apsaras* are often featured on temple rubbings. The arched leg position is associated with flying. It may also be associated with the bow and arrow, a symbol of the Buddhist path—the flexed leg carrying the body weight symbolizing the bow; the other leg, pulling up against the body, symbolizing the arrow.

Near the north gate is small display pavilion, built by the JSA (Japanese government team for Safeguarding Angkor). The pavilion details extensive work by the JSA at the Bayon through the years.

Meditating at the Bayon

In the early morning, mist rises over the fan palms, birds sing, and shafts of sunlight filter through the surrounding forest to illuminate the enigmatically smiling lichen-encrusted heads of the Bayon towers. Those smiles are perfect for contemplation, and meditating at the Bayon is a pursuit of visiting monks. Like Angkor Wat, the Bayon is a pilgrimage site. Around the perimeter of the Bayon, on the other side of the road, lie several pavilions housing large stucco Buddhas. Pilgrims make the rounds, leaving joss sticks. Right at the top terrace of the Bayon is an interior hollowed-out shell with a Buddha and candles—there's a small shrine here. Other seated Buddhas are positioned at various points in the building.

portrait head of Jayavarman VII

Lower Levels

The first and second levels of the Bayon comprise two square galleries with bas-reliefs; at the third level is a large circular terrace. The lower levels are a chaotic jumble of passages, steps, and galleries, and dim walkways with low ceilings. When Henri Mouhot discovered Angkor, the local nickname for the Bayon was the "hide-and-seek sanctuary." You'll need a flashlight to explore this underworld—you may stray across the odd linga or Buddha statue. Watch your footing, as flights of stairs are not safe, and there are sudden drops and gaps in masonry. In one part there is a deep internal shaft, possibly a well. In some areas, ladders have been installed to reach the upper levels.

Top Terrace

After playing hide-and-seek with the Bayon heads on the lower galleries, you come out on the circular top deck of the Bayon, where the bizarre design is fully revealed. Here you come face-to-face with myriad giant heads topped with lotus crowns. There were originally 54 towers with four heads each; 37 towers remain. The heads, ranging 3–4.5 meters in size, feature eyes downcast under lowered lids. The faces flicker the famous "smile of Angkor"—a Sphinx-like expression that seems to communicate much.

Early French adventurers found the all-seeing heads threatening, sinister, oppressive, even blood-curdling—odd when you consider the serene expressions, the traces of compassion, wisdom, contentment, even divine humor. Time has added further decoration to the mysterious heads—the brownish stone is splotched with moss, gray lichen, green fern growth, and bat dung. The 43-meter-high central tower, topped with four heads, is home to a colony of bats. This central tower once housed a large Buddha—probably stolen—which has been since replaced with a smaller one. Offerings of incense are left here.

The use of a circular shape is rare in Khmer art—in fact, everything you see on the terrace is unique, as this is the only Buddhist mountain-temple in Cambodia. Archaeologists are unsure if the heads are meant to represent Buddha, Brahma, Shiva, Lokesvara, or Jayavarman VII. Brahma is often depicted as a deity with four heads, representing deliverance, compassion, tolerance, and piety. Several French archaeologists concluded the Bayon heads are a combination: Jayavarman VII deified in the pose of Buddha or Lokesvara. Lokesvara is the bodhisattva of compassion in Mahayana Buddhism. Some manifestations of Lokesvara bear multiple heads—between 3 and 11—and a forest of arms. In one form, he boasts 11 heads—said to have burst from the original head as a result of contemplating the suffering of human beings. Portrait heads of Jayavarman VII today found in museums in Phnom Penh, Bangkok, and Paris bear an uncanny resemblance to the Bayon heads, with broad forehead, long earlobes, downcast eyes, wide nostrils, and thick, slightly curled lips.

The development of the personality cult—depicting real individuals in the form of a Hindu deity in sculpture—was common with the earlier kings of Angkor. Jayavarman VII may have raised the *devaraja* cult to new heights, transferring the cult to Buddhism and considering himself as an embodiment of a bodhisattva. Through such sculpture, the king could be connected to the power and compassion of the deity. The real story behind the heads may never be known—and perhaps this piece of sorcery is better left that way. As Rose Macaulay says of the Bayon towers in her book *Pleasure of Ruins,* "All is now desolate, fantastic, and ambushed with ghosts; the erroneous opinions of archaeologists twitter among them like bats."

NORTH OF THE BAYON

Baphuon

A few hundred meters north of the Bayon is Baphuon, which is undergoing extensive restoration by the French. The entryway to Baphuon is unusual—a sandstone causeway supported by short columns. This leads to a shell of a sanctuary, originally constructed by Udayadityavarman II in the mid-11th century. Baphuon was once one of the grandest of Angkor's temples, now fallen on hard times. In 1995 the EFEO returned to Cambodia to continue the reconstruction of Baphuon begun in the 1960s. The eight-year, $5.6 million project will rebuild and restore Baphuon; advanced computer technology will be used to graphically visualize the

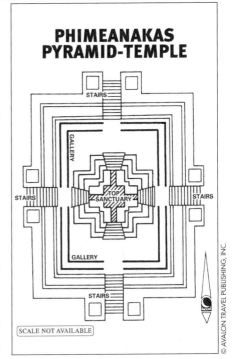

PHIMEANAKAS PYRAMID-TEMPLE

STAIRS

GALLERY

STAIRS · TOP SANCTUARY · STAIRS

GALLERY

STAIRS

SCALE NOT AVAILABLE

© AVALON TRAVEL PUBLISHING, INC.

reconstruction, including the return of innumerable stones to their original location.

Phimeanakas

Phimeanakas (Celestial Palace) is a three-terrace pyramid of rough-hewn sandstone blocks. It has little decoration, but Khmer lions stand guard at the corners of the terraces and the entrance stairs. Though Phimeanakas lies within the former Royal Palace walls, it was built in the late 10th and early 11th centuries before the palace was constructed. The pyramid was developed by several Khmer kings. At the top of the pyramid is a destroyed temple. The steps to the top are very steep; there are guardrails installed on the north staircase to assist upward progress.

Phimeanakas looks eerily like the jungle-locked pyramids of the Maya at Tikal, Guatemala—a lost world suddenly revealed. Odd rituals were performed at the temple on top of the pyramid. Phimeanakas is legendary as

THE SOVEREIGN COMES FORTH

Adjoining the pyramid of Phimeanakas was the Royal Palace, which, having been constructed of wood, has not survived. The palace, it is believed, was once arrayed in five great courtyards, with separate areas for the king's wives and concubines. The only description of this structure extant is in the manuscript of Chinese envoy Zhou Daguan. No stranger to opulent palaces, Zhou Daguan was nevertheless astonished by the splendors of Angkor. Although he was not permitted to enter the grounds of the tightly guarded palace, he described the exterior as it appeared in the year 1296:

> The Royal Palace, as well as official buildings and homes of the nobles, all face the east. The Royal Palace stands to the north of the Golden Tower [the Bayon] and the Bridge of Gold; starting from the gate its circumference is nearly one and a half miles. The tiles of the central dwelling are of lead; other parts of the palace are covered with pottery tiles, yellow in color. Lintels and columns, all decorated with carved or painted Buddhas, are immense. The roofs, too, are impressive. Long colonnades and open corridors stretch away, interlaced in harmonious relation. In the chamber where the sovereign attends to affairs of state, there is a golden window, with mirrors disposed on square columns to the right and left of the window-trim, forty or so in number. Below the window is a frieze of elephants.

During his stay at Angkor, Zhou witnessed the Khmer sovereign Indravarman III venture forth from his palace several times, along with an entourage from the palace harem. With an Arthurian touch, Indravarman III bore the sacred golden sword of office, which he'd wrested from his brother-in-law to claim the throne. Here is Zhou's description:

> When the Sovereign leaves his palace, the procession is headed by the soldiery; then come the flags, the banners, the music. Girls of the palace,

the site where the Khmer king had nightly union with the serpent goddess in the shape of a beautiful woman. Chronicler Zhou Daguan recounts:

> Every night this naga-spirit appears in the shape of a woman, with whom the sovereign couples. Not even the wives of the King may enter here. At the second watch the King comes forth and is then free to sleep with his wives and concubines. Should the naga-spirit fail to appear for a single night, it is a sign that the King's death is at hand. If, on the other hand, the King should fail to keep his tryst, disaster for the kingdom is sure to follow.

Phimeanakas restoration work is funded by an Indonesian team. A team is also working on excavating the possible site of the former palace and harem, just north of Phimeanakas. You can walk through this area to get to the temple ruin of Preah Palilay.

Elephant Terrace

The Royal Palace was not bounded by a wall but by the raised Elephant Terrace. From this vantage point, according to chronicler Zhou Daguan, royal family members could watch parades, games, and processions on the Great Square. The venue was apparently also used to dispense justice and oversee audiences for affairs of state. The Elephant Terrace may date from the 11th-century reign of Suryavarman I, with later renovations by Jayavarman VII. The terrace takes its name from a frieze featuring life-sized elephants and an elephant hunt. There are a few three-dimensional elephant trunks at the bases of stairs. Interspersed along the massive frieze are garudas and lions, a mythical five-headed horse, and demons and dancers. Much of this

three or five hundred in number, gaily dressed, with flowers in their hair and tapers in their hands, are massed together in a separate column. The tapers are lighted even in broad daylight. Then came other girls carrying gold and silver vessels from the palace and a whole galaxy of ornaments, of very special design, the uses of which were strange to me. Then came still more girls, the bodyguard of the palace, holding shields and lances. These, too, were separately aligned. Following them came chariots drawn by goats and horses, all adorned with gold; ministers and princes, mounted on elephants, were preceded by bearers of scarlet parasols, without number. Close behind came the royal wives and concubines, in palanquins and chariots, or mounted on horses or elephants, to whom were assigned at least a hundred parasols mottled with

gold. Finally the Sovereign appeared, standing erect on an elephant and holding in his hand the sacred sword. This elephant, his tusks sheathed in gold, was accompanied by bearers of twenty white parasols with golden shafts. All around was a bodyguard of elephants, drawn close together, and still more soldiers for complete protection, marching in close order.

The Sovereign was proceeding to a nearby destination where golden palanquins, borne by the girls of the palace, were waiting to receive him. For the most part, his objective was a little golden pagoda in front of which stood a golden statue of the Buddha. Those who caught a glimpse of the King were expected to kneel and touch the earth with their brows. Failing to perform this obeisance. . . they were seized by the masters of ceremonies, who under no circumstances let them escape.

area has been cleared and restored by the EFEO, which is also restoring Baphuon. Opposite the Elephant Terrace is a vast open area—the Great Square. Pavilions for dancers who entertained the king probably once stood here. Farther back are the ruins of the north and south *kleangs,* thought to have been either storehouses or centers for visiting envoys to the capital.

Leper King Terrace

The terrace to the north, attributed to Jayavarman VII, is known as the Leper King Terrace. High-tech anastylosis restorations in the 1990s have resulted in an assembly of multi-tiered friezes—at a hidden inner wall—with row upon row of seated figures. Kings, sword in hand, are surrounded by courtiers and dancers; the lower tiers feature five- and nine-headed *nagas.* The friezes are stunning works of art, on a par with those at the Bayon.

Some archaeologists believe Khmer aristocracy were cremated on the Leper King Terrace. The place derives its current name from a kneeling statue atop the terrace. This may or may not be a representation of Yasovarman I, the founder of Angkor, who may or may not have died of leprosy. In any case, the statue is a copy. Archaeologist George Coedes noticed some saw marks on the head of the original and had the statue removed to Phnom Penh's National Museum for safekeeping. The substitute at Angkor is made of concrete, but it was still convincing enough to fool a bandit who lopped its head off. Behind the Leper King Terrace is a path leading to a small temple, Tep Pranam, with a 4.5-meter-high statue of Buddha. Only the base and the entrance portico of Tep Pranam remain. The temple is attributed to Yasovarman I; monks and nuns live in the area. Farther back is another ruin, **Preah Palilay,** built by Jayavarman VII. This is a small but impressive pyramidal temple ruin surrounded by hundreds of blocks of stone—beheaded statues, *nagas,* lintels, broken pieces. This makes an excellent picnic site.

North Gate

The North Gate of Angkor Thom features a monumental causeway with four-headed portal and 108 mythical figures, like the South Gate, but facing northward. A few of the heads are made of concrete, replacing those either stolen or considered in danger of theft. Beyond the North Gate lies the great temple of Preah Khan on the Grand Circuit.

Victory Gate

The Victory Gate lies to the east, with a four-headed portal and 108 mythical figures facing eastward. However, the Victory Gate does not lie true east from the Bayon. At true east is a gate that is no longer used—the Gate of the Dead. This gate lies 500 meters south of the Victory Gate and is reached by a narrow forest trail—you can approach it by moto, or simply walk along the top of the wall to get there. The crumbling four-headed gate is a great picnic site; there are still some *asuras* and *devas* scattered around. Another way of reaching the Gate of the Dead is by motorcycling along a dirt path directly east of the Bayon. You can also motorcycle or bicycle out to the far west of Angkor Thom to the West Gate, in a similar overgrown state. Beyond Victory Gate to the east is the jungle-locked temple of Ta Prohm.

Outer Temples and Sites

LITTLE CIRCUIT

The route comprising the sites of Victory Gate, Thommanon, Chau Say Tevoda, Spean Thma, Takeo, Ta Prohm, Banteay Kdei, and Prasat Kravan was called *le petit circuit* by the French. About 1.5 kilometers east of Angkor Thom's Elephant Terrace, along a drive with tall trees, you come to **Victory Gate,** or the east gate of Angkor Thom. About 500 meters beyond are two small facing temples called **Thommanon** and **Chau Say Tevoda.** The temples are similar in plan and style and are believed to be the early 12th-century work of Suryavarman II. Thommanon is in better condition, with some fine decoration on exterior walls, particularly carvings of female divinities.

About 200 meters east of Thommanon you cross a bridge over the Siem Reap River. The bridge is made of wood and steel, but closer examination reveals that the supports are sandstone. **Spean Thma,** an early Khmer bridge, is more clearly viewed from a path to the side of the road, where you'll see other sandstone arch supports and Khmer masonry. Continuing east you'll come to **Takeo,** a five-tiered pyramid dating from the late 10th century. Entry to the temple is from the south side. Takeo was the first temple built of sandstone in the central Angkor region. Each of its five towers was laid out in a cruciform pattern, but they were never finished. The temple is dedicated to the Hindu deity Shiva and is devoid of decorative reliefs or sculptures.

⋈ Ta Prohm

The great temple of Ta Prohm was constructed by Jayavarman VII in 1186 to house an image of his mother in the likeness of the goddess Prajnaparamita. In Mahayana Buddhism, Prajnaparamita is the personification of wisdom, and mother of all Buddhas. She is depicted in Khmer statuary with 11 heads and myriad arms. A 12th-century Sanskrit inscription from Ta Prohm tells of Jayavarman's victories over the Cham and provides other curious details. The place functioned as a vast monastery, with 39 sanctuaries, 566 stone dwellings, and 288 brick dwellings. Housed in these dwellings were 18 abbots, 2,740 monks, and 2,817 other residents, including 615 dancers. Some 70,000 men and women

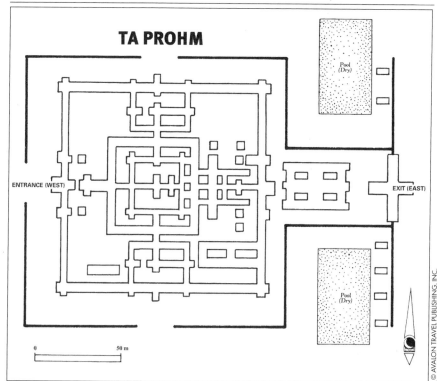

TA PROHM

Pool (Dry)

ENTRANCE (WEST)

EXIT (EAST)

Pool (Dry)

0   50 m

© AVALON TRAVEL PUBLISHING, INC.

Angkor

from surrounding villages were pressed into service at Ta Prohm.

The main entry to Ta Prohm is at the west side, with a fine four-headed tower similar to those at the gates of Angkor Thom. The central temple is approached by a forest path of 400 meters. To the side, remains of stone mythical creatures lie scattered about. Passing through an entrance pavilion you reach the central shrine, surrounded by dense jungle. Light filtering through the branches of tall trees provides an ambience similar to that of a Gothic novel.

French archaeologists left Ta Prohm to the elements—to the giant fig, kapok, and banyan trees, with their fantastic roots wrapped around walls and towers. The flora adds an element of mystery to the ruins. Guy de Pourtales describes the haunting phenomenon in 1931:

The tree roots flow over the roofs, tumbling in all directions like a flow of lava, sometimes breaking the stones apart, sometimes holding them together. Here and there, the jungle respects a facade, frames a row of columns without destroying it. And, in places, it even cements together with its powerful creepers a porch that was on the point of collapsing, props up a crumbled archway and grasps pillars or an emblature in its strong arms....

Some of the trees may eventually have to be felled to prevent destruction of stonework; other trees actually hold masonry in place.

The inner temple is a series of galleries, halls, and passages, with some entrances blocked off. If you keep to worn paths you can work out where to go, discovering a frieze, bas-relief, or the odd statue set in a niche. To exit, move through Ta Prohm's east gate (turn right and head to the roadway), or retrace your steps back to the west entrance.

Other Sites

On the route back to Siem Reap you can make a few more stops if time permits. First check out the temple of **Banteay Kdei,** accessible from its east gate, which lies opposite **Sra Srang.** Farther south is **Prasat Kravan** (Cardamom Sanctuary), which is unusual for its row of five brick towers, built in the 10th century, and brick bas-reliefs depicting scenes from the myth of Vishnu. From here you pass a back entrance to Angkor Wat—it's possible to take a side trail for a few hundred meters to view the colossus from the back. The main road skirts the mighty moat of Angkor Wat and heads south back to Siem Reap.

GRAND CIRCUIT

The grand circuit contains a number of sites in 12th-century Bayon art style, including Preah Khan, Neak Pean, Ta Som, East Mebon, Pre Rup, Banteay Samre, Banteay Kdei, and Sra Srang. The bold hand of Jayavarman VII is at work here—the inspiration for construction is Buddhist, or a mix of Hindu and Buddhist. You can view Angkorian plumbing features at Neak Pean and Sra Srang. There's a fair bit of ground to cover on this route; by motorcycle this isn't a problem, but by bicycle the going can be slow. From the Bayon it's about 10 kilometers to Neak Pean, and from there it's another 12 kilometers to Sra Srang. Because some of these temples lie farther out, they're targets for art thieves.

ⓜ Preah Khan

Preah Khan (Sacred Sword) was designated the temporary Khmer capital by Jayavarman VII after the sacking of Angkor in 1177 by the Cham and before the completion of Angkor Thom. Preah Khan was evidently dedicated to Jayavarman VII's father (while Ta Prohm was dedicated to his mother). A stone stupa at the center of the complex may have been a tomb for Jayavarman VII's father. A two-meter stele discovered at the site gives fine detail about Preah Khan and its founding: This piece of engraved stone was removed to the Conservation d'Angkor for safekeeping. The stele's Sanskrit inscriptions glorify Jayavarman VII; they also enumerate the staff at Preah Khan. Temple maintenance required the services of 98,840 men and women from neighboring villages, as well as 444 chefs, 4,606 footmen, and 2,298 servants. The Buddhist temple itself housed upward of 15,000 monks, dancers, and members of the Khmer hierarchy. The stele goes on to describe 515 divinity statues and 18 major annual festivals.

Preah Khan lies 3.3 kilometers north of the Bayon. There are three ways to enter or exit—from the west gateway, the east gateway, or the north gateway (you can use several: A good plan is to have your driver drop you at the west gate and meet you when you exit at the east gate, or vice-versa). On the way in or out, be sure to drop in at the World Monuments Fund Exhibition Pavilion, with displays and information about the site. It's on the walk in from the west side.

From the west gateway, you walk in almost 400 meters from the roadway to reach the main temple: it's a pleasant jungle walk, with chirping birds and droning cicadas for company. The long entryway is lined first with stone boundary posts and then with a row of serpent-restraining deities—22 on each side—backed by a portal. This assembly indicates a royal city—the same portal and rows of deities are found at Angkor Thom's gates. Like Angkor Thom, Preah Khan features a moat and four entryways. The original main entrance was from the east but only the west entrance is used today, though you can view another set of serpent-restraining deities from the roadway at the north entrance to Preah Khan. The statues at the north entrance are in poor shape, and many heads have been stolen.

The central temple at Preah Khan is a labyrinth of hallways and pavilions, vestibules, cloisters, and courts—with dead ends, blocked

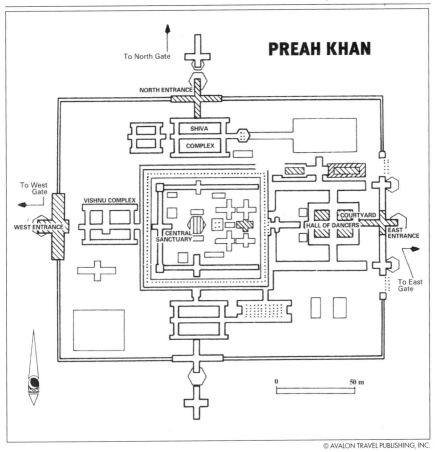

PREAH KHAN

To North Gate

NORTH ENTRANCE

SHIVA
COMPLEX

To West
Gate

WEST ENTRANCE

VISHNU COMPLEX

CENTRAL
SANCTUARY

COURTYARD

HALL OF DANCERS

EAST
ENTRANCE

To East
Gate

0   50 m

© AVALON TRAVEL PUBLISHING, INC.

passages, and collapsed masonry. In 1989 a freak hurricane struck the place, adding to the chaos. Scrambling through the ruins imparts the thrill of discovery that early French adventurers must have experienced. Or perhaps the feeling here is that of archaeology turned spooky—which is sure to send shivers up the spine. In this jumble of stone, finding bas-reliefs and small sculptures requires a good flashlight and the services of a guide. To the east side of the complex is a courtyard where doorway lintels are decorated with finely sculpted friezes of *apsaras*—hence it has been dubbed the Hall of the Dancers. Live performance of dance are sometimes staged in the temple at this site.

The foliage is being cleared under the auspices of the World Monuments Fund. Hanging tenaciously onto stone walls is a species dubbed the *fromageur* or "cheese tree" by the French. This refers to the towering 50-meter strangler fig and silk-cotton trees that slip over the stones like molten cheese. The surreal effect could come straight from a Salvador Dali painting with melting clocks, a metaphor for the persistence of memory.

Out back is the shell of a unique two-story pavilion, with supporting rounded columns that look positively Grecian. This is the only known example of two-story Khmer architecture. The function of the building is obscure—it may have been a library, or it may have housed the sacred sword for which the temple was named. Jayavarman II left his successor a sacred sword, passed on to future kings. Since Preah Khan was built to shelter a statue of Jayavarman VII's father, it was a logical place to keep the king's sword.

If you continue for the exit to the east gateway, check out the two immense and beautiful *garuda* bas-reliefs on the wall as you step out of the main complex. The half-man half-bird of prey is the protector of Preah Khan, and 72 such bas-reliefs are studded into the outer laterite wall. A little farther east lies a Dharamsala, or rest house, completely restored to its original condition in 1999. Concrete and metal rods have been used to prop up the place, but it's the most complete-looking of this type of building in the Angkor region.

Neak Pean

Continuing north and then east from Preah Khan there's a narrow road in deteriorating

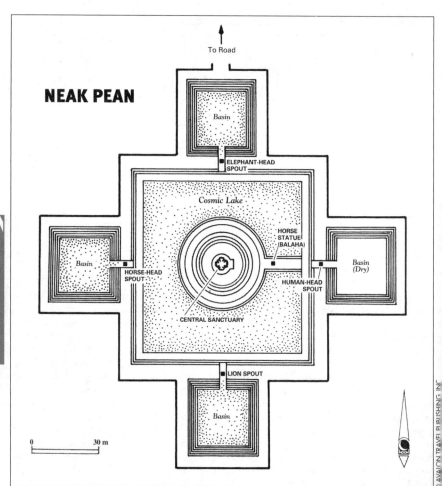

condition. It leads seven kilometers to the entrance for Neak Pean, set back a few hundred meters south of the main road.

Neak Pean is an enchanting replica of a Himalayan paradisal mountain lake, Anavatapta, from which magic healing waters flow. It's built in the shape of a large square pond enclosed by four smaller ponds. In the middle of the inner pond is a stone tower-island dedicated to the bodhisattva Lokesvara. Ringing the base of the tower-island are two seven-headed serpents with entwined tails: This motif gives the sanctuary its name, "Coiled Serpents." The heads of the serpents are separated to allow entry on the east side. Lotus-petal designs decorate the base of the island, while a blooming lotus design surrounds the top.

Off to the side in the water is a stone horse with figures clinging to its sides. The horse is identified with Balaha, an incarnation of Lokesvara. According to legend, Lokesvara metamorphosed into a horse to rescue shipwrecked merchants off the coast of Sri Lanka; they clung to the horse's tail to be carried ashore.

Construction of Neak Pean is attributed to Jayavarman VII. The cosmic lake was most likely the site of important ceremonial rites, perhaps affiliated with the Preah Khan Temple. The four side pools enclosing the central pond were probably used by pilgrims to anoint themselves with lustral water. Originally the side pools were connected to the center pond. Water flowed through different spouts—in the shape of an elephant (north), Khmer head (east), Khmer lion (south), and horse (west). Trees and plants have invaded the site, and bas-reliefs are hard to make out, but Neak Pean still retains its aura. The pools are now mostly dry, filling up only at the end of the rainy season. Monks occasionally come to Neak Pean to bathe. Otherwise, it's the exclusive domain of small fish and brilliant orange or blue dragonflies.

Other Sites

A few kilometers farther along the road is **Ta Som,** a small unrestored temple built by Jayavarman VII; the temple has some fine sculpture on lintels and doorways—right out the back

is a four-headed portal buried under a giant fig tree. The **East Mebon** and **Pre Rup** were both built in the latter half of the 10th century by Rajendravarman II, and they are almost identical in style. The East Mebon sits at the center of what was once the East Baray, a large reservoir, now dry and planted with rice. The East Mebon is a weathered pile of rubble with stone elephants at the corners. Pre Rup is a brick ruin, believed to have been the focus of cremation ceremonies. From a turnoff between the East Mebon and Pre Rup a 400-meter detour to the east leads to **Banteay Samre,** a 12th-century temple painstakingly restored by the French. The main shrine is well preserved, with bas-reliefs depicting scenes from Vishnu and Krishna legends.

Heading south back on the Grand Circuit, you can stop at Banteay Kdei and Sra Srang, at the junction of the Little Circuit. **Banteay Kdei** (Citadel of the Cells), a small unrestored temple, features a four-headed entryway at the east side; visible in the temple is a Buddha statue in meditation posture. Fallen blocks of stone lie scattered about. Across the road from the Banteay Kdei's east entrance is **Sra Srang,** a large artificial lake with a landing terrace. The lake is surrounded by greenery and provides an illusion of calm, majesty, and immensity. On the landing terrace are *naga* balustrades flanked by Khmer-style lions. A building used to sit in the middle of the lake, but it is now just a heap of stones. Sra Srang (the name means "Royal Bath") is a serene spot, especially when bathed in soft sunset light.

NORTH OF ANGKOR
Ⓜ Banteay Srei

Banteay Srei is a bewitching miniature temple 30 kilometers northeast of Angkor Wat, reached by a rough dirt road running past rural villages. Because of its remote location, the temple poses a major security problem: It is a target for art thieves. In January 1995 an American woman and her Cambodian guide were killed by gunfire in the area. They were in a five-car convoy heading to Banteay Srei Temple;

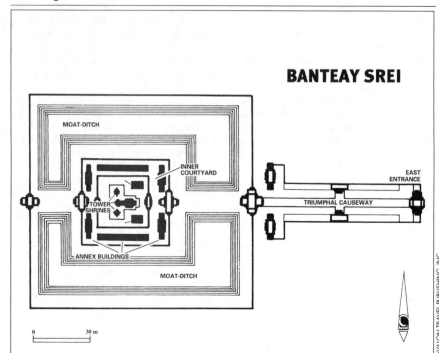

BANTEAY SREI

MOAT-DITCH

INNER
COURTYARD

EAST
ENTRANCE

TOWER
SHRINES

TRIUMPHAL CAUSEWAY

ANNEX BUILDINGS

MOAT-DITCH

0   30 m

© AVALON TRAVEL PUBLISHING, INC.

gunmen fired automatic rifles and rocket-propelled grenades at the group. Another tourist was seriously injured. A dozen other tourists escaped, and several armed police in the convoy fled. Eleven suspects, identified as bandits with Khmer Rouge backgrounds, were later arrested. Subsequently, tourist authorities placed Banteay Srei off-limits, but then allowed travelers to venture out in a group ($25 for a car) accompanied by a police motorcycle outrider (who asked $70 for the trip—the equivalent of three months' wages). Since the previous lot of police fled when under attack in 1995, it's dubious what kind of protection this would be anyway—but Japanese tourists love the armed escorts—and will pay through the nose for them. By 2001, things were back to business as usual—no police escort required—and the tour buses were trundling through.

Banteay Srei was discovered by the French in 1914, but the site was not cleared until 10 years

later. The temple was restored in the 1930s by archaeologist Henri Marchal. This was the first temple in the Angkor region to be restored by the process of anastylosis—removing and repositioning each block—a method developed by the Dutch at Borobodur in Java. Banteay Srei is small, but the bas-reliefs, pediments, lintels, and statues are the finest in the Angkor region. This jewel of Khmer art is remarkably well preserved. The temple is unusual in that its building was not sponsored by royalty but by the king's chief Brahman adviser, Yajnavaraha. The temple was founded by two Brahman brothers at the royal court in 967 A.D., according to an inscription at the site. Banteay Srei decoration is virtually intact, with a wealth of symbolism. For archaeologists it's a rich source of detail on how Angkorian temples were constructed.

A triumphal causeway with stone boundary posts leads to the inner sanctuary, enclosed by a moat-ditch and triple walls. The sanctuary

THE MALRAUX HEIST

The most contentious heist of Khmer statuary took place at Banteay Srei in 1923. A French couple in their early 20s, André and Clara Malraux, scandalized Clara's relatives—first by marrying, and then by squandering her inheritance. After a visit to Guimet Museum of Oriental Art in Paris, the Malraux hatched a harebrained scheme to find an unclassified Khmer temple and make a fortune selling Khmer relics to American museums. André came across an article by Henri Parmentier on a 1916 visit to Banteay Srei, and he decided this was the temple. Malraux even lined up buyers in New York.

Joined by a friend, Louis Chevasson, André and Clara Malraux set sail for Cambodia aboard the SS *Angkor* in 1923. In the Angkor area they hired several local guides (one of whom later turned out to be a police informer), a dozen coolies, horses, and four oxcarts of equipment. After several days of hacking through jungle, they reached Banteay Srei. Malraux later wrote in *The Royal Way*,

> *Something inhuman brooded over all these ruins and the voracious plants which now seemed petrified with apprehension: a presence of supernatural awe guarded with its dead hand these ancient figures holding their lonely court among the centipedes and vermin of the forest.*

The place was enclosed by dense overgrowth; snakes slithered over the surfaces, monkeys chattered in nearby treetops. Working feverishly, the trio managed to hack off four large blocks of sandstone comprising a beautiful bas-relief. These pieces were slung into the oxcarts.

Back in Siem Reap, they loaded their treasure, an estimated 400 kilograms of it, onto a river steamer in boxes labeled Chemical Products, and headed for Saigon. In Phnom Penh they were arrested. Clara fell seriously ill and was allowed to return to France, smuggling with her the head of a Khmer *apsara* in a hatbox. Chevasson was sentenced to 18 months in prison, while Malraux received three years. French literary luminaries rallied to André's defense. His lawyer argued that if two young men were to be imprisoned for taking stone from Banteay Srei, should not the same penalty be meted out to various governors, high commissioners, and administrators who'd done the same thing? Banteay Srei was not classified as a historical site, and no court had ruled on this issue before. The judge reduced Malraux's conviction to one year, suspended, and Chevasson's to eight months, suspended. The bas-reliefs, meanwhile, were sequestered at the museum in Phnom Penh, and later returned to the temple walls of Banteay Srei (they were put back in due place by Henri Marchal when he completed restoration of the temple—using for the first time in Cambodia the technique of anastylosis that he learned from the Dutch in Java).

André became an eloquent spokesman for the commoner in Indochina. He returned to France, picked up Clara, and went back to Saigon in 1925 to start up *L'Indochine,* a newspaper that dared to criticize the colonial administration. The French powers responded by intimidating any printer who handled the newspaper, effectively shutting it down after two months of operation. Undaunted, the Malraux sailed to Hong Kong to buy ancient wooden type from Jesuit missionaries. With this type they printed a biweekly broadsheet, *L'Indochine Enchainée—Indochina in Chains.* In 1926, the Malraux decided they could agitate more forcefully by returning to France. André wrote a trilogy of Asian novels—*The Conquerors (Les Conquérants), The Royal Way (La Voie Royale)*—a fictionalized, heroic retelling of the Banteay Srei expedition and the Phnom Penh trial—and *Man's Fate (La Condition Humaine),* which earned him the prestigious Prix Goncourt in 1933.

Angkor

consists of a courtyard with three sandstone *prasats,* or tower shrines, on a single raised plinth. The tallest *prasat* is 10 meters high. A combination of red sandstone, gray lichen, green moss, and fern growth give the towers peculiar coloration. Guarding the entrance stairs are sculpted kneeling figures of human torsos, originally bearing monkey or lion heads. Most of the heads have been hacked off by treasure hunters. Some figures are copies; the originals are in the Phnom Penh National Museum. The inner sanctuary is dedicated to Shiva and a Shiva linga was the main image of worship in the central *prasat.* A statue of Shiva and Uma presided over the southern *prasat;* this statue was taken to Phnom Penh in 1914 by a French army officer and now rests in the National Museum. Set in niches on the central towers are harmonious sculptures of male and female divinities.

To either side of the tower-shrines are two small library buildings featuring beautiful triangular pediments with scenes from the Hindu epics of Indian literature, the *Mahabharata* and the *Ramayana.* Projecting from the lower corners of each pediment are five-headed *nagas,* held by the jaws of lion-headed figures. Enclosing the assembly of central towers and libraries is a brick wall; between this and an outer wall are six long annex buildings, which may have been rest houses for meditation or part of a monastery. Think of Banteay Srei as a large piece of sculpture: Almost every surface of red sandstone at Banteay Srei is carved with floral garlands, geometric patterns, demons, coiled *nagas,* or mythical figures. The mask-like head of Kala—a demon that devoured its own body—is a common motif over doorways, where it serves as a temple protector. The carvings are amazingly fluid—at first it's hard to believe they're fashioned in stone. Right at the back of Bantei Srei is an entry tower with another fine carved lintel.

River of a Thousand Lingas

Fifteen kilometers farther north of Banteay Srei, you reach a parking lot with food stalls. Park your vehicle here and take a 45-minute sweaty hike up to **Kbal Spean.** The most astonishing feature of Kbal Spean is the River of a Thousand Lingas. This sacred river is named after the series of lingas carved into riverbed rock, lying about 15 centimeters below crystal-clear water. The lingas are about 25 centimeters square and 10 centimeters deep, arranged in a perfect grid pattern. Between the lingas are some well-preserved statues of *apsaras* and Vishnus carved in underwater sandstone. One of the largest lingas is carved just before a 10-meter waterfall. At one point on the river, the rock rises above the water to form a natural bridge, Kbal Spean, which is covered with sculpture—bulls, frogs, Vishnu lying on the serpent Ananta, and innumerable lingas. The lingas were possibly part of fertility rites: carved to sanctify the waters irrigating the Angkor plain.

Depending on seasonal flow of water, the reliefs may appear above waterline, at the surface, or just below the surface, with water cascading over them. The area was not discovered until 1968 when French archaeologist Jean Boulbet from the EFEO stumbled across it. He found an inscription from an Angkorian master carver. Proud of his handiwork, the carver boasted of working on a thousand lingas. Hence the area's more prosaic name, River of a Thousand Lingas. Unfortunately, not long after its "discovery," the zone fell into Khmer Rouge hands, and looters have been at work, hacking off heads of reliefs above waterline. The area has been accessible to foreigners only since 2000.

Phnom Kulen

About 40 kilometers northeast of Siem Reap is Phnom Kulen, a holy mountain that is the mythical birthplace of Cambodia. Phnom Kulen is where sandstone was quarried for the building of the monuments of Angkor; the stone floated on rafts down the Siem Reap River. Past kings are said to have performed mystical rites at Phnom Kulen, and the king's spirit was said to reside on the mountaintop, from which he could communicate with the gods. Several early Angkor kings were crowned on this mountain.

A few small temples are scattered around Phnom Kulen. The key temple boasts a 900-year-old reclining Buddha—the largest in Cambodia. The reclining Buddha is, incredibly, carved right out of the top of a massive boulder, with a temple enclosure sheltering it. This and the attached temple grounds are very popular with pilgrims and picnickers. Another key attraction at Phnom Kulen is a cascading set of waterfalls. The lower falls plummet about 15 meters into a large pool with a beautiful jungle setting.

Phnom Kulen has several riverbed sculpting efforts, very similar to those at Kbal Spean. In fact, the name River of a Thousand Lingas is confusingly applied to both zones.

Access to Phnom Kulen is controlled by some military mafia: Foreigners are charged a ransom of $20 a head to visit. Phnom Kulen is not part of the Angkorian Ruins, so your Angkor pass is no use here.

Services and Information

TOURIST INFORMATION

Travel Agents

Near the Grand Hotel, government-run Angkor Tourism handles guides and transportation in cars and minibuses for organized groups. Staff are not interested in assisting individual travelers unless guides and rentals are requested. Branches of Phnom Penh agents stationed in Siem Reap include Diethelm Travel, tel. 63/963524, and Bopha Angkor Tourism, in the Bantei Srei Hotel, tel. 63/913839. The larger hotels have their own travel and touring desks.

Guides

Angkor Tourism has about 40 guides on tap. The majority speak English or French, although some also speak Japanese, Thai, Chinese, and Khmer. Angkor Tourism guides are expensive at $15–20 a day, and will expect to be shuttled around in the comfort of a hired car ($20–35 a day for the vehicle). A motorcycle guide is $2–3 a day, plus $6–7 a day for a motorcycle. A moto guide is a bonus for a number of reasons: backup in the event of mechanical failure or a flat tire, another eye on the bike to prevent theft, reduced likelihood of problems if stray soldiers are encountered. And finally, some guides speak quite reasonable English and can point out features you may not notice. Assess the guide's level of English and the vehicle's condition before departing.

Guidebooks

French archaeological specialists such as George

Coedes and Henri Parmentier have published detailed guides to Angkor. Photocopied versions of their works are peddled in gift shops in Phnom Penh and around Siem Reap. These guides may be well out of date, the author describing statuary long ago stolen, beheaded, or removed to a museum. Best of the current crop is *Ancient Angkor,* by Claude Jacques and Michael Freeman (River Books, Bangkok, 1999)—an excellent tome on all counts: lucid text, great photos by Michael Freeman, and wonderful maps. Use this one as your guide to Angkor.

Even detailed guidebooks sometimes appear inadequate when confronted with the sheer majesty of the buildings, and a lot of questions go unanswered. Of course some prefer mysteries to remain mysteries, allowing the imagination to run riot. It is possible to take perverse pleasure in the shattered grandeur, the crumbled dreams, the tree roots run amok, the jumble of towers and walls.

PHOTOGRAPHY AND FILM

At Angkor it's best to bring five times more film along than you think you'll need. A sturdy tripod is invaluable for sunrise and sunset shots, and for close-ups of bas-reliefs. Angkor Wat is extremely difficult to photograph because of the sheer scale of the place, and results can be very disappointing. You'll have more success at the Bayon, where the stonework at least fits into the viewfinder. The Bayon's gallery bas-reliefs are also easier to photograph because they're not covered by a projecting or overhanging roof—those at Angkor Wat are, and so require a flash. Wide-angle lenses are also very useful at Angkor.

The most photographed sections of Angkor are the gateways to Angkor Thom, which benefit from wide-angle lenses. Avoid the harsh midday sun, which results in washed-out pictures. The best light is in early morning, since most temples face eastward. Angkor Wat, on the other hand, faces west, so the best light is in the late afternoon. Angkor monuments look very different depending on blue or gray skies, dusk or dawn, new or full moon. Patience is required for dramatic lighting conditions, which can make or break a photograph. It's wise to scout locations for the best angles and vantage points.

Other Practicalities

CONDUCT

Angkor is a series of sacred temples, so appropriate behavior should be observed. Khmer visitors may be on pilgrimage and may resent having their photos taken. Similarly, do not disturb monks by hounding them for photographs. Under no circumstances remove debris or artifacts from temple sites, or places where restoration is in progress. Travelers' bags are checked on exit at Siem Reap Airport to prevent theft of statuary and artifacts.

SAFETY

Although the following section may sound daunting, life in Siem Reap and Angkor is quite simple, and if you exercise common sense your trip will be smooth—and very special. Just avoid visiting the ruins alone, especially those farther out.

Heritage Police

A special Heritage Police force of 350 men, trained by the French government, was established in 1997. Part of their training includes motorcycle pursuit of statue-jackers. The force's primary mission is to guard Angkor itself and prevent theft of statuary. Sometimes soldiers with AK-47s appear in and around the ruins, especially at the Bayon, Angkor Wat, and at Ta Prohm. More soldiers materialize when a visiting dignitary tours the ruins—you can tell how important the visitor is by the number of escorts. Occasionally bored policemen put on a special security show for a VIP, all in the interests of fund-raising. The perimeter of the Angkor region is guarded by government troops. Government soldiers can be a problem—depending on when they were last paid, and if they've been drinking.

In the early days of tourism to Angkor, when the dreaded Khmer Rouge still roamed the area, tourists sometimes heard the sound of distant gunfire around Angkor. An American woman was overheard at Angkor Wat: "That's not thunder. Do you think they're bombing the airport?" Her companion turned and listened intently. "No honey, I think they're bombing where we were yesterday." At night, sporadic gunfire was explained by guesthouse owners as "people hunting birds" (nocturnal hunting would not account for the bullet that grazed the head of a Portuguese tourist sitting in his room at the Grand Hotel, however).

Mines

The Siem Reap area is heavily mined. According to Cofras, a French mine-clearing firm, more than 1,000 land mines and 7,000 unexploded shells were removed from the fields and forests around the temples of Angkor in 1994. Although the main tourist areas are believed to be mine-free, this is not the case at more remote temples and in outlying village areas. Be careful. Use a guide, keep to the major ruins, stick to well-trodden paths, and do not venture into areas with long grass. There have been no reports of death or injury to tourists resulting from land mines or unexploded ordnance, but as one traveler put it, "Who's going to tell you that last week they blew up a Parisian?" Out at

Bantei Srei, I saw a man step into mined jungle beyond the temple perimeter to attend to the call of nature. His wife sighed: "Oh darling, you're so brave!" And I was conjuring up the newspaper headlines: *American Tourist Explodes*. Even a mundane act such as emptying a bladder becomes an exciting event in Cambodia.

Loose Rubble

Ruins are unstable. There may be sharp drop-offs, steep stairs, loose or broken masonry, crumbling galleries, or piles of rubble. It's rather like a giant construction zone. Tread carefully, and don't venture into dark areas without a flashlight.

Other Hazards

Poisonous snakes exist—some cobras, and the small, emerald green tree snake. This variety, called *hanuman* by locals, drops on its victims from above and can be deadly. Avoid long grass, which may also harbor mines. Malaria is a hazard—Lariam, also known as mefloquine, is the best drug for the Siem Reap area. To prevent bites use a repellent, cover exposed flesh at sundown, and sleep under a mosquito net.

CHECKPOINTS AND ENTRY FEES

There are checkpoints on the three roads leading to Angkor Wat. The major checkpoint used by visitors is the one 4.5 kilometers north of the Grand Hotel on a paved road. Here there are six tollbooths that issue photo-ID passes for Angkor. Hand in a passport-sized photo, and the ID is laminated on the spot (if you don't bring a photo along, there's a Polaroid option on the spot). The charge is $20 for one day, $40 for three-day passes, and $60 for seven-day passes. The ticket specifies an expiration date, which will be monitored around the ruins. Once past the checkpoints you can go anywhere you want.

Previously, money from the tickets went into deep pockets of soldiers manning the checkpoint. Later on, the money went into the pockets of the Ministry of Tourism and corrupt officials. Recycled tickets became big business.

Today, the show is run by the oil company Sokimex, and the money goes into the pockets of those in high places. A portion of the funds generated supposedly goes to APSARA.

GEARING UP FOR TOURISM

Mass tourism has yet to arrive at Angkor, though the potential is certainly there. There are no entry signs, billboards, ticket booths, or restaurants. Just the odd DANGER!! MINES!! skull-and-crossbones sign. There's not even a museum or visitor information center. It's all very casual. In the heady 1920s and 1930s, hordes of foreign tourists arrived by boat from Saigon, or motored in from Bangkok.

One of the sad realities of life in Cambodia today is that the infrastructure was better in 1930. In 1930, you could catch a floatplane from Saigon or Bangkok and land right in the moat of Angkor Wat, and then tour the area by car, horse, or elephant. Visitors could stay in the Hotel des Ruines, opposite Angkor Wat's main entrance. According to a French guidebook of 1930, "just before sunset one can see from the Hotel clouds of bats that leave the towers of Angkor Wat by millions in the cool of the evening, circling around them and finally dispersing in all directions in search of food and water."

In 1968 more than 70,000 visitors toured Angkor, mostly French and American. Two luxurious hotels were constructed opposite the main causeway to Angkor Wat. Evening performances by traditional Cambodian dancers on the causeway were commonplace—afterward, hotel guests could stroll around by moonlight. The hotels were destroyed by the Khmer Rouge. From the early 1970s until the early 1990s there was hardly any tourism. Then, spurred by UNTAC, visitors began to come back again. An estimated 187,000 people visited in 2000—up to 1,000 a day at the ruins in peak months. According to UNESCO, the maximum yearly capacity for the site is around 500,000–700,000 tourists.

In November 1994, dance was revived on-site at Angkor. The following year, in December 1995, an international *Ramayana* festival

Angkor

drew troupes from all over Asia and India. In December 1996, an Asian half-marathon was staged at the ruins and, by the light of the full moon, a three-day national dance festival was staged on the cruciform terrace fronting Angkor Wat. Illuminated by spotlights, dances varied from classical to folk, with troupes drawn from all the provinces of Cambodia. In November–December 1997, a *Ramayana* dance extravaganza was again staged at Angkor with international participants from Laos, Vietnam, and India attending (other Asian nations declined because of safety concerns after the July 1997 coup). A millennial performance was staged in December 2000.

Angkor Wat bas-reliefs provided the inspiration for choreography of *apsara* dances. Put the ruins and the dancers together and you have an unbeatable tourist attraction. There's a highly controversial plan to stage light and sound shows at Angkor, like those staged at Egypt's pyramids. The $40 million project is backed by the Malaysian company YTL, which plans to relate the history of Angkor and its mighty kings with shows (three nightly, hosting up to 500 people per sitting) proposed in English, French, German, and Japanese. So far, these initiatives have not gotten off the ground.

Along with a new influx of tourists, cottage industries have appeared around the ruins. Enterprising food and drink vendors set up stalls every morning outside Angkor Wat, the Bayon, and other key sites. Beggars occupy strategic gateways at Angkor Wat and the Bayon waiting for tour buses to unload, hawkers sell souvenirs at roadside stalls, and tribes of urchins push Angkor Wat and Bayon T-shirts, rubbings of Angkor bas-reliefs, wooden cowbells, crossbows, joss sticks, rolls of film, musical instruments, and other paraphernalia. But mostly they sell cold drinks. The cold drink brigade can be very persistent. "Cold drink, mister?" "You buy cold drink, madam?" At some sites, these kids will not leave you in peace until you're holding a cold drink in your hands. In any case, you won't suffer from dehydration at Angkor. Many kids try to earn pocket money by acting as guides. There is only one escape route: Vendors are not allowed to sell anything within the precincts of each ruin—and you may notice that the kids will stop at the gates. However, it appears that the kids with connections in high places (those with a father in the police force, for example) can venture in and sell in the ruins. And some ruins are exceptions to the general no-sell-inside-the-ruins rule: Phnom Krom, the primo sunset-viewing point, is a veritable sea of vendors at that time. Touts are becoming more numerous, soliciting for guesthouses and motorcycle tours.

SELLING OUT AT ANGKOR

After surviving centuries of monsoon rains, invading armies, French museum collectors, Khmer Rouge insurgents, and art thieves, Angkor now faces possibly its greatest threat—greed and corruption associated with boosted tourism. There appears to be little or no control over rampant hotel building in Siem Reap. Land prices in Siem Reap have shot up so much in the last few years that residents have been forced out to new satellite towns under construction nearby.

Opposition to rapid development has been mounted by the World Monuments Fund, by UNESCO, and by APSARA (Authority for the Protection of the Site and Management of the Region of Angkor). As part of meeting World Heritage guidelines, APSARA was created by royal decree by King Sihanouk in early 1995 to act against inappropriate development. According to APSARA, there are three zoning areas. The World Heritage Site of Angkor is fully protected, with very limited building allowed (some low-key restaurant facilities). Along Route 6 is a corridor of land where buildup of larger hotels and restaurants is allowed. Little or no development is allowed along the Siem Reap River, but just east of Angkor Conservancy and 700 meters east of Siem Reap River is a proposed 560-hectare hotel ghetto zone, bordering the fully protected Angkor ruin zone. To the northwest of Angkor Conservancy toward the airport is another zone where international hotel groups are vying to begin building four- and five-star hotels—and casinos and golf courses.

GETTING AROUND
By Car
Angkor Tourism handles taxi and minibus transportation for organized groups. A car runs $35–45 a day with driver, plus an extra $15 for a guide. A minibus seating 10 costs $65 a day including driver, plus $15 for the guide. Travel agents can also arrange cars in Siem Reap, and there are privately owned vehicles obtainable through guesthouses—ask around.

By *Remork*
A breezy alternative to a taxi, and cheaper (around $10 a day) is a motorcycle-pulled chariot called a *remork*-moto, or *remork* for short. Other locals call it a *tuk-tuk*. A *remork* is ideally suited to touring around Angkor because it takes two in comfort and has space for camera bags and water bottles. Many travelers prefer these chariots to taxis because of the open views and the breeze. You can also get in and out of them faster for photo stops. Some larger versions can take 3–4 passengers. The most exclusive hotel in town, the Amansara, keeps its own fleet of black *remorks* for guiding guests around the ruins.

By Motorcycle
A motorcycle with driver costs around $6–7 a day. Sitting on the back of a moto for long periods is not comfortable compared with a *remork* chariot. Don't worry about finding a moto driver: He will find you. The policy on independent travelers' renting their own motorcycles varies. Sometimes it is possible, but mostly it seems impossible (except for foreigners working in Siem Reap). Another large obstacle: The contract for renting a good motorcycle may specify that if it is stolen or damaged, you forfeit $1,800. If you want to tour longer distances, the best rental option is a Honda Motocross 250cc—a wonderful bike to use up-country because it just floats over the bumps. You should clean the chain every few days be-

cause the fine red dust in this region gets in and clogs it up. Other road hazards include occasional sand or water patches, stray cows and water buffalo, plus craters and potholes—especially on the more isolated northern route where roads are gouged by monsoon rains.

By Bicycle
Bicycles cost $2 a day from guesthouses and vary from gearless to 18-speed mountain-bikes (but most likely the gear system will be shot). Check that the wheels actually roll unobstructed, and that both brakes are working. Cycling is a great way to see the ruins as long as you avoid the midday sun. Some sections around the Bayon are sheltered by forest—with serene cycling through the woods. Park your bike near a food stall and perhaps tip someone to watch it while you're gone. Count on progress of 10–12 kilometers per hour on a bicycle. The roads are usually flat, sometimes with a slight grade.

It's about 11 kilometers from the Grand Hotel to the Bayon, requiring an hour of pedaling. You should start early if you want to cover a bit of ground. Allow 2.5 hours actual cycling time to cover the Little Circuit; taking in stops and a midday siesta means a full day of biking. Looping around the Grand Circuit is possible by bicycle, but you have to move quickly to cover the ground, and road conditions are poor. It's a long way between temples on the Grand Circuit, and you may spend more time in the saddle than at the sites. Getting up to Preah Khan Temple on the Grand Circuit is a 30-minute round-trip from the Bayon on a good road.

By Elephant
Yes, for cash U.S. dollars, you can ride an elephant around the Bayon (mornings), or up Phnom Bakheng (hilltop sunset spot). The dozen working elephants here also commute between the two spots at certain times of day. The elephants are saddled with a traditional–style howdah carriage, harking back to the era 10 centuries ago when these pachyderms were the mounts of kings—or generals in battle. For lots

of cash U.S. dollars you can even arrange customized rides and give the elephants a bath.

By Helicopter

You can fully comprehend the grand scale of Angkor only from the air. And if you have a grand wallet, you can do that. Check on Helicopters Cambodia via this website: www

.angkorscenicflights.com. This NZ-affiliated company operates short flights toward Angkor. Longer flights are customized to visit remote sites such as Koh Ker and Beng Mealea ruins to the northeast of Angkor, Banteay Chhmar to the northwest, and Preah Vihear up by the northern border with Thailand. All of this is ultraexpensive, of course.

Around the North

Apart from the Angkor region, travel in the north is limited by the presence of land mines, poor roads, sporadic banditry, or a combination thereof. One of the best ways to get around up-country is by motocross bike but these cannot be rented in Siem Reap (they can be rented in Phnom Penh). Some towns are little more than transport transit points.

BATTAMBANG

Battambang is the second-largest city in Cambodia, with a population of perhaps 80,000. Due to its position near the Thai border, the town has profited from large-scale black market trading. Fishing is secondary. Dengue fever is a big problem in the area and theft is rampant—motorcycles, cars, generators, and medical supplies all go missing. Facilities are primitive, electricity and water limited. Some areas enjoy electricity only a few hours a day.

Basics

Prices for Battambang hotels range from $5–10 a room at the **Samakai Hotel** to $10–25 a room at the **Paris Hotel.** Two hotels by the river offer $12–20 rooms—the **Victory** and **Angkor.** Near the Victory is a large swimming pool. **Sarika's Restaurant** serves good Thai food, steak, and pizza.

Getting There

There are three flights a week from Phnom Penh for $45 one-way. There is road access from Siem Reap—a bumpy ride. There is also a boat from Siem Reap to Battambang if water

levels are high enough. Westerners have been allowed to ride the train from Phnom Penh to Battambang and sometimes even farther up to Sisophon. Riders may have to sit on the roof of a carriage for this 12- to 17-hour trip because the train interior is packed with goods; female passengers ride inside. It can get pretty hot on the roof. The train leaves Phnom Penh at 0630 every few days and in theory arrives at Battambang at sunset. Express buses, regular buses, and share-taxis all make the run from Phnom Penh to Battambang. An excellent way of getting from Battambang to Siem Reap (or the reverse) is to go by boat: The trip takes about five hours (longer when water levels are lower), costs $12–15 a person, and is highly recommended for scenery viewed en route along a river and then across part of Lake Tonle Sap.

OTHER KEY POINTS
Thai Border Crossing

The border at Poipet on the Cambodian side and Aranyaprathet on the Thai side is regularly used by minivans running from Siem Reap to Bangkok. The full route takes about 12 hours, including time for border formalities. On the Cambodian side, some stretches of roadway are choppy; on the Thai side, it's smooth going. Poipet is turning into a kind of Cambodian Las Vegas, with 10 glittering casinos in the strip between the Thai and Cambodian border posts. Busloads of Thais stream into the casinos daily. It is forbidden for Cambodians themselves to visit the casino tables.

BATTAMBANG

To Sisophon and Poipet ←

PROVINCIAL HOSPITAL ■

SIEM REAP FERRY DOCK ■

FRENCH CULTURAL CENTER ■

JIN HUA INTERNATIONAL HOSPITAL ■

VIETNAMESE CONSULATE ■

5

■ TAXI STAND

WAT PEAPAHD

WAT BO KNONG

MONOROM GUESTHOUSE ●

CANADIA BANK ■

ROYAL HOTEL ●

PSAH NATH ■

WAT BOVIL

5

INTERNET CAFE ■

CHAYA HOTEL ●

KHEMARA HOTEL ●

LONG HENG HOTEL ●

CCB BANK ■

GOLDEN RIVER HOTEL ●

WAT KANDAL

TRAIN STATION ■

PRESIDENT AIRLINES ■

ROAD #2

ROAD #1

ROAD #3

ROAD

WAT TAHM RAI SAW

WAT PACHHAA

WAT SANGKER

TEO HOTEL ●

POST OFFICE ■

Sangker River

To Phnom Penh

ODA HOTEL ● TA DAMBONG STATUE ★

CLINIC ■

DEPARTMENT OF TOURISM ■

Angkor

© AVALON TRAVEL PUBLISHING, INC.

WAT KAMPHENG

SCALE NOT AVAILABLE

To Pailin

MINEFIELDS AND MINDGAMES

by Gary McFarlane

"**Y**ou've got to trust the de-miners. If you don't trust their work you might as well quit before you start because the stress will kill you."

I was talking with Commander Roar Holm, Chief Engineer, Norwegian People's Aid (NPA), about the attitude needed to enter a minefield. Faith, I suppose, would also help.

Last week I was in Saigon eating ice cream. Now I'm standing in a Cambodian minefield and my legs won't work. How do I get myself into these things? While riding through Sisophon on a mountain-bike tour, I'd been distracted by the sight of a Norwegian flag topping an official-looking building, then lured in by thoughts of pasta, newspapers, and a shower. At dawn the next morning I found myself accompanying the Norwegian De-mining Team into a minefield outside Poipet.

The minefield layout was simple: Mines could be anywhere. Mine variety is impressive: the undetectable Vietnamese homemade N0M Z2B, packed with grease oil and chicken bones to promote infection; the German-made POMZ; Chinese 72As; and the Valmara 69 jumping mine, infamously known as a Bouncing Betty, which, when triggered, devastates a 20-meter kill zone.

As we entered the minefield thoughts of becoming a statistic dogged every step I took. Where Roar stepped, I stepped. Exactly. I didn't see much of the area, staring at my feet the whole time. At one point, after stopping to take a photo, I looked up to see Roar 20 meters away, with no obvious trail between us. I knew he'd walked through, I'd been assured the area was clean, but still I hesitated badly. I was sweating. The first steps were the worst. Frightened into silence, I continued. A piggyback would've been nice.

When we came to the live area all work stopped, resuming only after I'd cleared the vicinity. Red-and-white striped poles designated between regions "clean" and "live." Red skull-and-crossbones signs (DANGER!! MINES!!) emphasized the areas to avoid. The safe areas were meterwide paths marked by orange tape crossing from one section to another. Excessively careful to step directly in the middle of the path, nervously forgoing the cleared edges, brave enough to no longer follow exact footsteps, I tiptoed along this checkerboard pattern of safety.

Stopping beside a tree jutting into the path, Roar pointed at three stakes in the ground at the tree's base. "That's where we found mines, placed where people are most likely to take cover. On the other side there," he pointed to the far side of the tree where uncut brush accentuated the orange tape, "we'll find at least three more."

As I walked away from the tree, a stray branch knocked my hat off. I froze while it settled in the dirt behind me. On the path. Realistically, a falling hat doesn't carry the force needed to set off a landmine. Try telling that to a tight sphincter.

Time for lunch. Two of the de-miners took me in their vehicle to the Thai border town, Aranyaprathet, for a meal—an illicit crossing for me. As our chosen restaurant was out of cheesecake, I settled for Thai fried rice. As we crossed back into Cambodia a border guard offered to sell me his Colt revolver. Cool souvenir but not a good idea. I spent the afternoon watching the detonation of live mines, safely tucked in behind a hillock outside the 100-meter "safe zone." Funny, I didn't feel all that safe.

Banteay Chhmar

About 70 kilometers north of Sisophon near the Thai border is the temple of Banteay Chhmar, built by Jayavarman VII as a memorial to his son and four generals killed in the war against Cham invaders in 1177. The story of the battle is engraved on stone walls surrounding Banteay Chhmar in a style similar to that of Angkor's Bayon Temple.

The forest-covered temple is both in a remote zone and close to the Thai border: The only thing that saved it from looting was the presence of the Khmer Rouge. However, by the end of 1998, the Khmer Rouge had melted away—and a squadron of Cambodian soldiers descended on Banteay Chhmar. In early December 1998, a *National Geographic* reporter and accompanying photographer stumbled across looting in progress: the dismantling of an entire outer wall at Banteay Chhmar. Their guide hustled them out of the area, saying it was extremely dangerous. The *National Geographic* reporter noticed that stones had been marked in pink for reassembly.

In late December, Claude Jacques walked into an antiquities dealership at River City in Bangkok and was astounded to come face-to-face with an inscribed stone. He recognized it instantly because some time back he had worked on deciphering the Sanskrit text carved on it. Jacques is the world's foremost expert on Khmer epigraphy. Known to French archaeologists as Inscription K227, the stone came from Banteay Chhmar. Claude Jacques informed Thai police and the artifact was promptly seized. On January 7th, 1999, more ominous news: Thai police intercepted two trucks carrying 117 stone pieces—which the drivers admitted came from Banteay Chhmar. Reassembled, the pieces formed a 12-meter-long wall with beautiful reliefs of multiarmed Lokesvaras—a style peculiar to Banteay Chhmar.

Alarmed by this news, Claude Jacques and aides traveled to Banteay Chhmar on a special UNESCO mission. Jacques was horrified by what he saw: hacked-off bas-reliefs, missing statuary, pediments missing. But the most extraordinary part was that entire walls had gone missing. Jacques called it looting "on an industrial scale": By using modern power tools, thieves had assaulted what was previously thought invulnerable—a massive stone section of the ruins. It is the largest heist of Khmer artifacts in modern history. Although the 117 stones intercepted in Thailand were returned to Cambodia in 2000, that represents perhaps only a quarter of the booty taken. And this is a black eye for Cambodia—the statue-jackers, fingered by several sources, were corrupt Cambodian government soldiers.

Since the heist, Banteay Chhmar has been adopted by the World Monument Watch, providing some funding for protection. The best protection would be to open the site to tourists—and there are plans for that. But a formidable obstacle is that the road leading to the ruins is itself a ruin. It needs to be upgraded considerably. UNESCO plans to install guard stations around the ruins to prevent further looting. There are six other smaller satellite ruins in the Banteay Chhmar area, which could provide a circuit for tourism. There is a guesthouse at Banteay Chhmar across the road opposite the main entrance. Banteay Chhmar can be reached in about six hours from Siem Reap by 4WD vehicle.

Kompong Thom

The town of Kompong Thom lies 165 kilometers northwest of Phnom Penh on Route 6 and is a transit point for onward journeys to Angkor. About 35 kilometers northeast of Kompong Thom is **Sambor Prei Kok,** the 7th-century capital of the Chenla Empire. The temples have been vandalized, but some brick terraces with sandstone ornamentation remain. **Preah Khan,** 104 kilometers due north of Kompong Thom, is a large sandstone temple dating from the 11th and 12th centuries.

Beng Melea and Koh Ker

Two major ruins within day-trip range of Siem Reap are Beng Melea and Koh Ker. They can be combined in a single day if you start at the crack of dawn. Beng Melea, about 60 kilometers northeast of Siem Reap, is a sprawling ruins with collapsed doorways and lintels. It gives a feeling for the way the French explorers found these sites, although the site is being cleared of encroaching vegetation. The temple predates Angkor Wat and is built in a similar style, probably by the same king. However, the stone used is poorer quality, which has led to numerous collapses. Beng Mealea appears to have been a key point on an ancient road between Angkor Wat and Koh Ker temple. From Koh Ker, the road went north to Preah Vihear temple and other points. Constructed by Jayavarman IV in the 10th century, Koh Ker served briefly as the capital. The great brick temple here has been severely damaged.

Anlong Veng and O'Smach

An adventurous border crossing route is to proceed from Siem Reap northward to Anlong Veng, the last stronghold of Pol Pot. You can drop by and see Pol Pot relics, such as the toilet seat he used. A rough road leads west from here to the border crossing of O'Smach, leading into Thailand. The nearest big town on the Thai side is Surin. Once in Thailand, you might want to consider going east to Preah Vihear ruins, which are better approached from that Thai side.

Preah Vihear

The Angkor-period temple complex of Preah Vihear lies in disputed territory on the Thailand-Cambodia border in the Dangrek Range. Built in the early 11th century during the reign of Suryavarman I, the mountaintop complex was constructed on four different levels, each connected by stairways. Walls and doorways are decorated with a profusion of carvings. The best structures are those at the summit. In 1962 the International Court of Justice awarded the area to Cambodia. However, the temple complex is perched on top of a 700-meter cliff that is more accessible from Thailand.

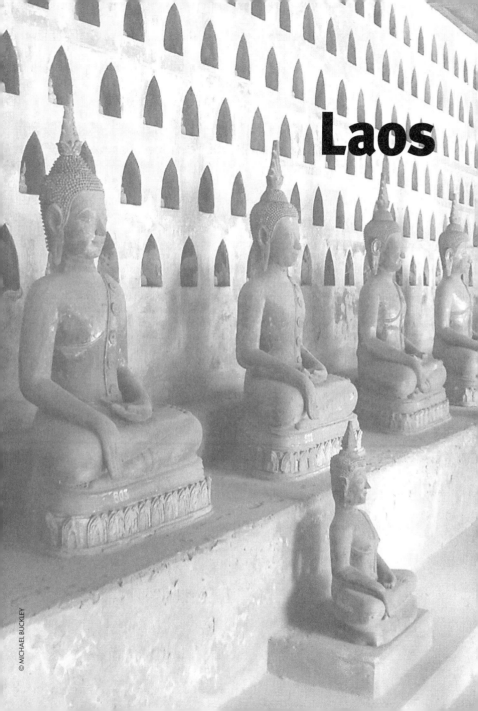

Laos

Introduction

To many Westerners Laos is so obscure that without a detailed map of Asia, they couldn't tell you where it is—much less anything else about it.

Laos dropped out of the news after the Pathet Lao takeover in 1975. And therein lies its charm. The country's isolation, for reasons of war and politics, has preserved an older, slower, and more traditional way of life: Old Asia, Asia without the crowds. This is the perfect antidote to the frenzied pace of Bangkok—or New York or London, for that matter.

Laos is one of the poorest countries in the world. Yet people do not go hungry here, and you rarely see beggars when traveling around the country—a tribute to the fact that the Lao social fabric has its own social welfare system woven in. This is a culture in which relatives and neighbors provide support for each other. Laos is very sparsely populated—mostly rural, with a patchwork of hilltribes, especially in the wild northern provinces. Health care in the provinces is mostly of the herbal kind, augmented by rare visits from health officials. Buddhist practices

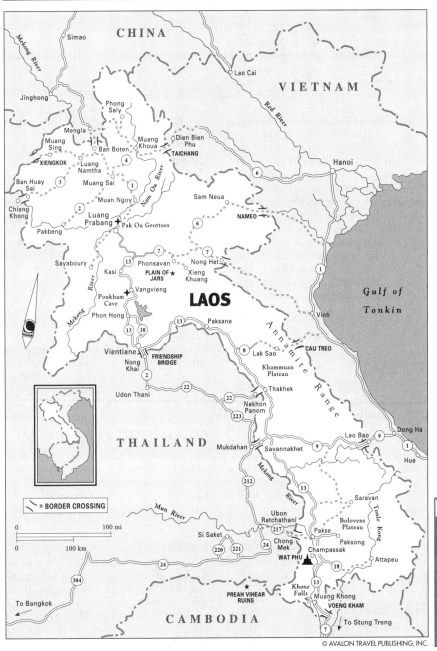

© AVALON TRAVEL PUBLISHING, INC.

form a significant part of the Lao social fabric. These practices are ingrained in Lao life: At the crack of dawn in Vientiane, Luang Prabang, and other towns, barefoot orange-robed monks file out of the monasteries to collect food donations from the locals. The Lao Buddhist calendar is studded with festivals, often lasting 4–5 days, with lively temple fairs.

As Laos moves ahead with modernization and foreign investment, its fragile social fabric is at risk. There is considerable controversy in Vientiane over how to handle increased exposure to Western influence. Laos favors controlled tourism: Although the authorities have announced relaxation of travel restrictions, Laos caters primarily to high-priced escorted tours. These tourists have little impact on the local culture and are taught about Lao customs and culture before arranged encounters with locals. Laos is in a unique situation when it comes to tourism because of its unspoiled natural environment and unexposed ethnic cultures. Here customs and ceremonies are meaningful, and rural hospitality is genuine. By carefully regulating tourism, Laos hopes to keep it that way.

THE LAND

Laos has an area of 236,800 square kilometers. It is landlocked, sharing borders with Thailand, Cambodia, Vietnam, Myanmar (Burma), and China. The Mekong meanders 1,800 kilometers through Laos, forming the major part of its borders with Myanmar (Burma) and Thailand; to the east, the Annamite Range separates Laos from Vietnam. Laos is mostly mountainous, especially to the north and east, with villagers living in isolated valleys.

The climate is hot and humid, tropical and temperate, with monsoon activity May–October and a cooler dry season November–February—the best time to visit. February–May is the hot dry season, with occasional rain.

THE PEOPLE

With about 5.5 million inhabitants living in an area the size of Britain, Laos is the most sparsely populated country in Asia, with a scant 17 people per square kilometer. About 80 percent of the population is rural—mostly hill-tribe groups and riverine farmers. Vientiane, the capital, has a population of only 150,000. Population estimates for other towns are hard to come by because of refugee exoduses and returns. Three "urban" centers are Luang Prabang, Savannakhet, and Pakse—each with no more than 50,000 people.

Language

Lao is a tonal language of the Thai language family. The Vientiane dialect is the standard. Because of exposure to Thai media, many Laotians can understand Thai, but the reverse may not be true. Other languages spoken in Laos include French, English, Chinese, Vietnamese, and Russian. The literacy rate is estimated at only 57 percent.

Religion

Theravada Buddhism suffered severe setbacks under the Pathet Lao but is now making a comeback as the country's main faith. The hill-tribe groups follow shamanist practices and animist beliefs. A small number of Laotians are Protestant or Catholic, perhaps 80,000, mainly living in the towns. No figures are available for those professing no religion.

GOVERNMENT AND ECONOMY

The Lao People's Revolutionary Party is directed by the Party Congress, which meets every 4–5 years to elect party leaders and discuss policy. The national flag is a white circle centered on a blue stripe, sandwiched between two horizontal red stripes.

Economy

Major industry includes timber, garments and textiles, beer, detergent powder, and agriculture, with rice, maize, tobacco, sugarcane, coffee, and cotton the major crops. Opium production is a major source of foreign exchange. Major exports are garments and textiles, timber, and electricity. There is tremendous potential in energy production, as the Mekong has yet to be fully tapped. Per capita income is around $330. The currency unit is the kip; US$1=10,500 kip.

TOURISM IN LAOS

From 1975 to 1989, Laos was largely closed to tourism. In 1994, an estimated 146,000 tourists visited Laos—and half of those were from Thailand. In 2000, the number of visitors was over 670,000. Laos is not prepared for any great expansion in tourism; there are few hotels and little infrastructure for travelers in the way of service personnel, guides, and so on. Liberalization of travel regulations in the 1990s made the country more accessible to individual travelers.

Laos has a stable political situation, and there are no gun-waving guards or militia about the place. There are, however, residual insurgency problems, and certain roads are not considered safe because of bandits and Hmong rebel groups. In May 1994, a convoy of Ministry of Agriculture trucks carrying diesel fuel to Xieng Khuang province was ambushed; six people were killed, including an Australian. The attack was the first involving the death of a foreigner since 1981. In mid-1996 near Kasi, a Frenchman was killed by gunfire when traveling in a car. Since the late 1990s there have been sporadic reports of bombs going off in restaurants and other public places in Vientiane and several other towns. In 2000, a dozen foreigners were injured when either a bomb or a grenade went off at the Khopchaideu, a popular restaurant and bar in Vientiane. This was hushed up by authorities, who claimed it was an explosion from a gas tank used for cooking. The injured foreigners were quickly evacuated to hospitals in Thailand.

In February 2003, at least 12 people were killed, including two Europeans on bicycles, when gunmen attacked vehicles on Route 13 just five kilometers north of Vangvieng. The mystery attackers behind this and other shoot-outs or bombings have not been identified—and it appears that not a single bomber or insurgent has ever been captured, which is

very odd given the length of time this has been going on. The finger is constantly pointed at a Hmong separatist group, but this group has yet to announce itself, which is again very odd.

Tourism is a Pandora's box for Laos—it can generate desperately needed foreign exchange, but it can also devastate the fragile Lao culture. Laos looks nervously at what happened in neighboring Thailand, where rampant tourist development created severe social problems and pollution. Luang Prabang, with a population of only 25,000, could easily be inundated by tourists. The town may find itself in a situation similar to Thailand's Chiang Mai, not far across the Mekong. While Chiang Mai farmers increased their incomes by selling food and handicrafts to tourists, selling food soon led to selling drugs, and the quality of handicrafts began to deteriorate. Dance events were performed purely for tourists, out of sync with the Buddhist calendar and therefore meaningless. Competition for tourist dollars diminished rural trust and turned a self-reliant society into a begging culture. Farmers became lazy—they didn't want to return to the fields to plant rice. Some gave up farming and migrated to the cities, accelerating the development of problems there.

Besides the social problems that come with tourism, protection of the environment and historic sites is a key concern. Thus, the Lao national tourism authority prefers working with tour operators and tour groups rather than individual travelers. Tourism in Laos is at present directed toward group tours that have the least impact on locals—they stay for only a short period and spend a lot of money. With controlled tourism, Laos hopes to promote cultural awareness—cultural interaction where tourists come to look at weaving and traditional culture but not look down on it.

HIGHLIGHTS

Devoid of beaches or outstanding historical attractions, Laos's main draw is its laid-back lifestyle and *bo pein nhang* (never mind, take it easy) attitude. As J. B. Priestley put it, "a good holiday is one spent among people whose notions of time are vaguer than yours." Laos offers great natural beauty, with as-yet-unspoiled mountain, plateau, and river regions.

Vientiane

There's little to see in the capital apart from a handful of temples—Wat Pra Keo Museum, Wat Sisaket, and That Luang. Vientiane, however, is a great place to bicycle or walk around, with wide boulevards and little traffic. The top day trip from Vientiane is to Nam Ngum Lake, where underwater logging takes place.

Vangvieng

This tiny town lies midway between Vientiane and Luang Prabang, and it has shot to prominence as not only a convenient stop to break the road journey, but also as an adventure sports mecca. Set in an entrancing karst landscape, Vangvieng offers tubing, caving, kayaking, rafting, and hilltribe trekking.

Luang Prabang

The old capital offers the major cultural attractions of the Palace Museum and Wat Xieng Thong. Luang Prabang is considered one of the best-preserved traditional cities in Southeast Asia, with a number of 16th-century temples, as well as colonial and traditional timber houses still standing (for these reasons the town was inscribed on the U.N. World Heritage List in 1995). There is an excellent day trip to Pak Ou Caves on the Mekong. Luang Prabang is a laid-back town with little traffic, eminently walkable, with lots to see. Worth at least three days.

Lolo hilltribe dress

Other Sites

To the northeast is the overrated Plain of Jars. Pakse, in southern Laos, is a departure point for Wat Phu, an abandoned Khmer temple worth a day's excursion. Wat Phu is not as impressive as the Khmer ruins in Thailand, and it's not even remotely comparable to the ruins of Angkor Wat. However, farther south lies a real gem—the region of Siphandon, or 4,000 islands, which straddles the Mekong at the border with Cambodia. Travelers have been known to pass a week or more at Siphandon, lying in hammocks among the coconut palms by the Mekong.

River Trips

Laos's real attraction for future tourism could well be its primeval forests and pristine environment. There is a network of 19 National Biodiversity Conservation Areas (NBCAs) in Laos: Some allow entry to trekking, kayaking, or boating groups. There is great potential for white-water rafting trips. Stretches of the Mekong are lined with stands of giant bamboo and primary-growth forest, particularly between Ban Huay Sai and Luang Prabang; on the lower section of the Mekong near the Cambodian border are thundering rapids. Mekong tributaries such as the Nam Ou, snaking from Muang Khoua in the north to Muang Ngoi and on to Luang Prabang wind past sugarloaf peaks and spectacular limestone gorges. Several Thai–based kayak companies such as SeaCanoe and Paddleasia have conducted exploratory tours in Laos. Based in Vangvieng is Wildside, run by an Australian rafter, who uses inflatable kayaks on a 12-kilometer stretch of the Nam Song River. He was planning to offer multiday runs, as well as kayaking in other parts of the country such as the far south. In the rainy season, when the water is rougher, Wildside offers white-water rafting on the Nam Song River. There are plans to stage white-water rafting near the southern border of Laos, near the mighty Khong Phapheng Falls, and there is a kayak trip from Siphandon in Laos to Stung Treng in Cambodia.

Hilltribe Trekking

Visitors can jungle-trek and ride elephants in the Bolovens Plateau area. Trekking is still in its early stages in Laos, and expenses can run high. There are numerous hilltribe groups in the mountain areas of northern Laos—in the hard-to-reach provinces of Phong Saly, Udomxai, and Luang Namtha. The best place to see people of the hilltribes is at markets, which draw villagers from outlying areas—one of the best is at Muang Sing on the Lao-China border, northwest of the capital Luang Namtha. Hilltribe-trek tours are conducted from both Luang Namtha and Muang Sing.

Festivals

Laos has preserved traditions that have long disappeared from other parts of Asia. This is most obvious in its festivals, of which there are many. The biggest celebrations are Pimai, or Lao New Year, in April—with three official days of holidays—and the Water Festival at the end of the rainy season in October—with longboat racing. Some tours to Laos are specifically timed to take in special festivities.

Vientiane and Southern Laos

Vientiane's Revolutionary Museum, housed in an old French palatial building, is a monument to the achievements of communism. These days, however, Marxist ideology has been firmly sidelined—young Laotians pursue capitalism ardently. Vientiane is as cosmopolitan as Laos gets. You can catch glimpses of new Japanese cars and motorcycles, satellite dishes, minimarts, and even discos—signs of things to come. Young Laotians, at least in Vientiane, are copying the carefree lifestyles of swinging Thailand, promoted by Thai television and magazines. The new revolution here is led by Toyota, Honda, and Mitsubishi: With the opening of the Friendship Bridge, hundreds of Japanese cars, pickups,

Must-Sees

Look for M to find the sights and activities you can't miss and ℕ for the best dining and lodging.

VIENTIANE AND SOUTHERN LAOS

LAOS

Poukham Cave — M — Kayaking the Song River

M Wat Sisaket

THAILAND

Wat Phu M Ruins

M Khone Falls

M Wat Sisaket: Oldest surviving temple in Vientiane, and easily the most impressive. The temple has an intriguing design: Cloistered galleries contain hundreds of seated and standing Buddhas (page 475).

M Poukham Cave, Vangvieng: Inside this enormous cavern is a blissful reclining Buddha statue. Outside (nearby) is a blissful swimming hole (page 498).

M Kayaking the Song River, Vangvieng: A fun day that novices can handle. You kayak right into caves—and you will get very wet (page 500).

M Wat Phu Ruins, Champassak: While not in the same league as Angkor, these Khmer ruins give reason enough for a splendid hike up to a mountain ridge. The way is perfumed by frangipani trees (page 510).

M Khone Falls, Mekong Islands: The widest cataract in all of Southeast Asia. The Mekong turns nasty here—you can get in close to thundering torrents (page 512).

and motorcycles are crossing over from Thailand. This influx has led to the deployment of traffic police at main intersections in Vientiane during "rush hour," and the introduction of a road-safety campaign to combat a jump in the number of traffic accidents.

Vientiane means either "Citadel of the Moon" or "Citadel of Fragrant Trees." It became the capital of Laos under King Settathirat in 1563. The king constructed a palace and two wats—That Luang and Wat Pra Keo—and

fortified the riverine town. Vientiane steadily expanded and prospered until it was abandoned after the Siamese sacked it in 1827. In 1866 the French found the ruins of Vientiane overgrown by jungle, with little more than a fishing village remaining. Because of its position on the Mekong, favorable for shipping, the French initiated the building of large colonial structures and wide boulevards at the turn of the century. Until the late 1930s there were no cars in Vientiane.

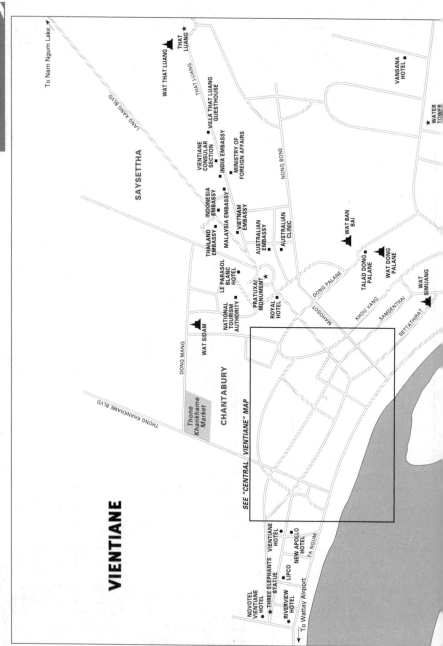

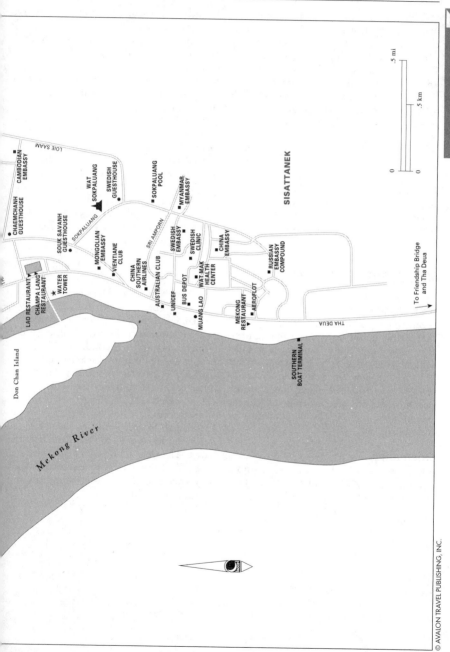

.5 mi

.5 km

0

0

To Friendship Bridge
and Tha Deua

SISATTANEK

THA DEUA

LOIE SAAM

CAMBODIAN
EMBASSY

CHAEMCHANH
GUESTHOUSE

WAT
SOKPALUANG

SWEDISH
GUESTHOUSE

SOUK SAVANH
GUESTHOUSE

SOKPALUANG

SOKPALUANG
POOL

MYANMAR
EMBASSY

MONGOLIAN
EMBASSY

VIENTIANE
CLUB

SRI AMPORN

SWEDISH
EMBASSY

SWEDISH
CLINIC

CHINA
EMBASSY

CHINA
SOUTHERN
AIRLINES

AUSTRALIAN CLUB

UNICEF

BUS DEPOT

WAT MAK
HEALTH
CENTER

RUSSIAN
EMBASSY
COMPOUND

MUANG LAO

MEKONG
RESTAURANT

AEROFLOT

WATER
TOWER

LAO RESTAURANT

CHAMPA LANG
RESTAURANT

Don Chan Island

Mekong River

SOUTHERN
BOAT TERMINAL

Today Vientiane is a laid-back town of 150,000 strung along the lazy Mekong. Architecture is a mix of Buddhist temples, French colonial buildings, Chinese shophouses, and Russian blockhouses. The French left in 1953, and in some quarters there appears to have been no repair since then: Dilapidated French villas once occupied by a single family are now shared by half a dozen Lao families. The Russians left too—in some places you'll see hammer-and-sickle neon lights that no longer function. Office buildings sorely in need of a coat of paint preside over traffic circles swirling with dust. The winds of change are blowing, however—French villas are undergoing renovation for use as businesses and small hotels, catering mainly to investors and visitors from Thailand.

PLANNING YOUR TIME

One day would suffice to cover visits to Wat Sisaket, Wat That Luang, and Pratuxai Monument. You may not even need that long: Your best plan in boring Vientiane is to figure out the fastest escape route. However, if you like relaxing over a glass of beer, a popular sunset pursuit is to hang out at cafés and food stalls along the banks of the Mekong, lingering over beer or fresh juice. Getting around Vientiane is easy: on foot, by bicycle, or with rented vehicle and driver.

Orientation

Vientiane actually refers to three entities. Vientiane City has a population of 200,000, there are 240,000 people in Vientiane Prefecture, and Vientiane Province contains 360,000 inhabitants.

Vientiane is a city of villas and boulevards. Street signs are mostly in Lao script—or occasionally French—but getting around is easy. Points of reference are more often landmark statues, monuments, or prominent wats rather than streets.

Nam Phu Square, arrayed around a fountain, is the center of town. A bit farther north is That Dam, a large stupa stranded in a traffic circle. Legend has it a seven-headed dragon lurks beneath the black stupa, ready to rise to protect the city in time of dire need. Vientiane's answer to the Arc de Triomphe is Pratuxai Monument, at the northeast end of Lane Xang Boulevard. If you continue along the axis from the Presidential Palace past Pratuxai, you reach That Luang. This huge stupa is the most sacred site in Vientiane and often appears in illustrations as an icon for the city.

Two other landmarks are the statue of King Sisavang Vong, in a traffic circle near Wat Simuang, and the Three Elephants Statue, on Luang Prabang Road. Erawan, the three-headed elephant, comes from Hindu mythology. In Laos, it was a former royal symbol, adopted by Lao kings in keeping with the Kingdom of Lan Xang, or Land of a Million Elephants.

Out in embassy land, along Tha Deua Road, addresses are based on kilometers from the Presidential Palace. Thus Tha Deua KM4 is four kilometers down Tha Deua Road from the palace, Tha Deua KM5 is five kilometers, and so on. Tha Deua Road stretches about 20 kilometers to the Tha Deua foot-passenger crossing opposite Nong Khai.

Sights

Vientiane does not possess the wealth of traditional sites common in other Asian capitals; Vientiane's original wats and sacred sites were mostly destroyed by the Thais in 1827. Modern touches such as the Revolutionary Museum are little more than crude propaganda—the museum features photo displays chronicling the revolutionary struggle, plus military hardware. If you're in Vientiane during a festival, there will be lots of action on the streets; otherwise, Vientiane is not the place for temples or nightlife—Bangkok is the place for that. Visitors come to Vientiane to slow down. Get yourself a fresh coconut or beer, kick back, chill out, and watch the sun go down over the Mekong.

Wat Sisaket

Wat Sisaket is the oldest surviving temple in Vientiane, and easily the most impressive. It was built in 1818 by King Chao Anou and survived the Thai incursions of 10 years later. The temple is active, with about 20 monks attached who live in *kutis* to one side.

Wat Sisaket has an intriguing design—a central temple with a Thai–style five-tiered roof, enclosed by a square cloister, a courtyard with covered passageways facing the temple. The cloister galleries contain more than 300 seated and standing Buddhas; set in niches behind them are several thousand smaller silver and ceramic Buddha images. The count of Buddhas large and small at Wat Sisaket is estimated to exceed 6,000. During Lao New Year, the Buddhas are ritually cleansed—water is poured over them. At the end of Buddhist Lent, the larger Buddha statues in the courtyard are "fed"—Laotians make a circuit of the temple, placing sticky rice in the hands of each of the larger statues.

On the walls of the galleries are Jataka murals depicting stories from the life of Buddha. Most are damaged, and restoration work is

© MICHAEL BUCKLEY

Rows of Buddha statues are backed by niches with more statuary at Wat Sisaket.

Vientiane & Southern Laos

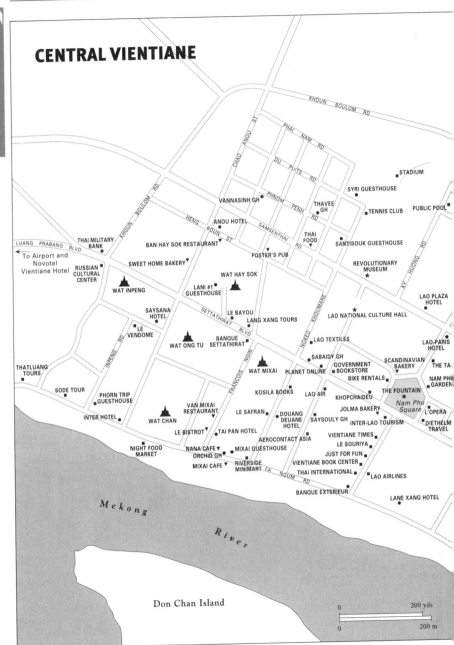

CENTRAL VIENTIANE

KHOUN BOULOM RD

CHAO ANOU ST

PHAI NAM RD

DU PUITS RD

STADIUM

SYRI GUESTHOUSE

PHNOM PENH

THAVEE GH

VANNASINH GH

TENNIS CLUB PUBLIC POOL

HENG BOUN ST

ANOU HOTEL

SAMSENTHAI

THAI FOOD

KHOUN BOULOM RD

LUANG PRABANG BLVD

THAI MILITARY BANK

BAN HAY SOK RESTAURANT

SANTISOUK GUESTHOUSE

KY HUONG RD

← To Airport and Novotel Vientiane Hotel

RUSSIAN CULTURAL CENTER

SWEET HOME BAKERY

FOSTER'S PUB

REVOLUTIONARY MUSEUM

WAT INPENG

WAT HAY SOK

LANI #1 GUESTHOUSE

LAO PLAZA HOTEL

SAYSANA HOTEL

SETTATHIRAT

LE BAYOU

LANG XANG TOURS

LAO NATIONAL CULTURE HALL

INPENG RD

LE VENDOME

WAT ONG TU

SETTATHIRAT BLVD

BANQUE SETTATHIRAT

NOKEO KHOUMANE

LAO TEXTILES

LAO-PARIS HOTEL

THATLUANG TOURS

FRANCOIS NGIN

WAT MIXAI

SABAIDY GH

PLANET ONLINE

GOVERNMENT BOOKSTORE

BIKE RENTALS

SCANDINAVIAN BAKERY

THE TA

NAM PHU GARDEN

SODE TOUR

KOSILA BOOKS

LAO AIR

KHOPCHAIDEU

THE FOUNTAIN

Nam Phu Square

PHORN TRIP GUESTHOUSE

VAN MIXAI RESTAURANT

LE SAFRAN

DOUANG DEUANE HOTEL

JOLMA BAKERY

SAYSOULY GH

INTER-LAO TOURISM

L'OPERA

INTER HOTEL

WAT CHAN

LE BISTROT

TAI PAN HOTEL

AEROCONTACT ASIA

VIENTIANE TIMES

LE SOURIYA

DIETHELM TRAVEL

NIGHT FOOD MARKET

NANA CAFE

MIXAI GUESTHOUSE

JUST FOR FUN

ORCHID GH

RIVERSIDE MINIMART

VIENTIANE BOOK CENTER

MIXAI CAFE

FA NGUM RD

THAI INTERNATIONAL

LAO AIRLINES

BANQUE EXTERIEUR

LANE XANG HOTEL

M e k o n g

R i v e r

Don Chan Island

0   200 yds

0   200 m

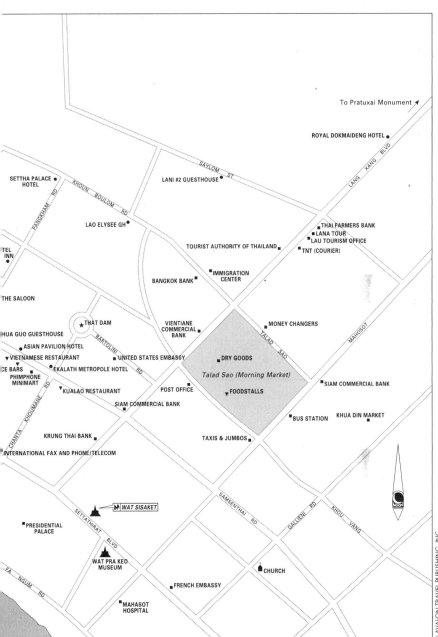

To Pratuxai Monument

ROYAL DOKMAIDENG HOTEL

LANG XANG BLVD

SAYLOM ST

SETTHA PALACE HOTEL

LANI #2 GUESTHOUSE

KHOUN BOULOM RD

PANGKHAM RD

LAO ELYSEE GH

THAI FARMERS BANK
LANA TOUR
LAU TOURISM OFFICE

TOURIST AUTHORITY OF THAILAND

TNT (COURIER)

TEL INN

IMMIGRATION CENTER

BANGKOK BANK

THE SALOON

THAT DAM

VIENTIANE COMMERCIAL BANK

MONEY CHANGERS

HUA GUO GUESTHOUSE

MAHOSOT

BARTOLINI

TALAD SAO

ASIAN PAVILION HOTEL

VIETNAMESE RESTAURANT

UNITED STATES EMBASSY

DRY GOODS

Talad Sao (Morning Market)

CE BARS

PHIMPHONE MINIMART

EKALATH METROPOLE HOTEL

SIAM COMMERCIAL BANK

KUALAO RESTAURANT

POST OFFICE

FOODSTALLS

SIAM COMMERCIAL BANK

CHANTA KHOUMANE RD

BUS STATION

KHUA DIN MARKET

KRUNG THAI BANK

TAXIS & JUMBOS

INTERNATIONAL FAX AND PHONE/TELECOM

WAT SISAKET

SAMSENTHAI RD

GALLIENI RD

KHOU VANG

SETTATHIRAT BLVD

PRESIDENTIAL PALACE

WAT PRA KEO MUSEUM

CHURCH

FA NGUM RD

FRENCH EMBASSY

MAHASOT HOSPITAL

Vientiane & Southern Laos

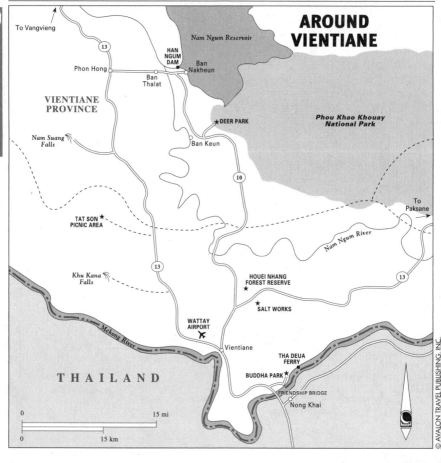

To Vangvieng

AROUND
VIENTIANE

Nam Ngum Reservoir

13

HAN
NGUM
DAM

Ban
Nakheun

Phon Hong

Ban
Thalat

**VIENTIANE
PROVINCE**

*Phou Khao Khouay
National Park*

★ DEER PARK

*Nam Suang
Falls*

Ban Keun

10

To
Paksane

TAT SON
PICNIC AREA ★

Nam Ngum River

13

*Khu Kana
Falls*

13

HOUEI NHANG
FOREST RESERVE
★

Mekong River

★ SALT WORKS

WATTAY
AIRPORT
✈

Vientiane

THA DEUA
FERRY

THAILAND

BUDDHA PARK ★

FRIENDSHIP BRIDGE

0   15 mi

Nong Khai

0   15 km

© AVALON TRAVEL PUBLISHING, INC.

being funded by UNESCO. To one side of the
compound is a raised library building with a
Burmese-style roof; the scriptures were spir-
ited off to Bangkok. Wat Sisaket is open to the
public Tues.–Sun. 0800–1130 and 1400–1630,
closed on public holidays.

Wat Pra Keo Museum

Down the road is Wat Pra Keo Museum. From
the rooftop decoration showing three elephants
in gold, you can tell this wat was originally constructed as a royal temple. It was built in the
16th century by King Settathirat to house the
Emerald Buddha, Pra Keo. The Thais carted off

the Emerald Buddha in 1778—it now resides at
the Grand Palace in Bangkok—and razed the
temple in 1827. Between 1936 and 1942, the
structure was completely rebuilt by the French,
supposedly faithful to the original, though it's
impossible to tell. The temple was again restored
in 1993, this time with a German grant.

Wat Pra Keo is now home to a small but superb collection of Buddhist and other statuary
from the 17th and 18th centuries, most of it inside the building, some labeled in French and
Lao. Along the outer galleries of the *sim* (temple) are larger Buddha images, including some
bronze Lao-style Buddhas in the attitude of

Calling for Rain. Inside is a copy of Pra Bang, the most revered Buddha image in Laos; a stone Buddha said to be the oldest in Laos; and a collection of stone stele and wooden lintels and door carvings displaying Burmese, Indian, and Khmer influences.

The temple is surrounded by a garden. Almost opposite the entrance, sheltered by a pavilion, is a small jar flown in by helicopter from the Plain of Jars in Xieng Khuang province. Visitors throw money in the jar for luck. The museum is open Tues.–Sun. 0800–1130 and 1400–1630.

Revolutionary Museum

This museum was renamed the Lao National Museum sometime in the late 1990s, but don't let that fool you: Most of this musty place illustrates the Pathet Lao struggle for power against the French and American imperialists. The motley collection of exhibits and pictures is captioned in Lao and sometimes in English. On the ground floor are geographical and cultural exhibits (pottery, ethnology, ancient times); a jar airlifted in from the Plain of Jars; and dinosaur paintings (based on digs 120 kilometers east of Savannakhet in southern Laos). The upper floor is mainly devoted to evidence of brutality by the French and American imperialists, a collection of photos from Pathet Lao campaigns, and displays of weaponry used in the Pathet Lao struggle. Revolutionary relics such as revered leader Kaysone Phomvihane's kettle, briefcase, and chest expander are on display. Finally, there's an exhibit on the achievements of communism since the 1975 Pathet Lao takeover. The museum occupies a classical French colonial structure built in 1925 for the Résident Supérieur, the highest-ranking French official in Laos. It lies at the center of town, on Samsenthai Road. Hours of opening are irregular—it seems the bored staff close the place down when they feel like it. Try 0800–1130 and 1400–1630.

That Luang

To the northeast of town is Vientiane's most sacred shrine, That Luang. This is a massive stupa, or *that,* surrounded by a square cloister pierced by an entrance on each side. The stupa was built by King Settathirat in the mid-16th century—a modern statue of the seated king faces toward the city near the main entrance to That Luang. The area was sacked by the Thais in 1827 and by Chinese bandits in 1873. In 1900, and again in the early 1930s, the monument was restored by the French, though not to Lao liking. That Luang is a national emblem; its squarish structure is uniquely Lao and sets the standard for stupas in other parts of the country.

The brick-and-stucco stupa was designed for pilgrims to climb, so there are stairways around each level—devout Buddhists are meant to contemplate the features of the stupa as they ascend. The square base of the stupa is a mix of Lao, Indian, and Khmer styles, featuring several hundred sacred boundary stones; there is a small offering pavilion at each side. The second level is surrounded by a lotus-petal wall with 30 smaller stupas representing the 30 Buddhist perfections. The top level leads to the spire, a tall structure meant to resemble an elongated lotus bud, crowned by a stylized banana flower and parasol. It represents the flowering of the beautiful lotus from a murky lake bottom: the triumph of knowledge (enlightenment) over ignorance. Originally the spire was covered with gold leaf; in the mid-1990s, the spire was repainted a brilliant gold to replicate this.

Though it's Vientiane's most important historical site, That Luang usually tends to disappoint the casual visitor. All that changes, however, at festival time. Adjacent to That Luang is a large parade ground that comes to life in mid-November with the That Luang Festival. The weeklong festival starts with offerings to the monks in the cloisters that surround That Luang, swings into gear with fairground entertainment, and culminates with a candlelit procession around the stupa.

That Luang was originally surrounded by four wats. Two remain and are still active— Wat Luang Nua, the north wat, and Wat Luang Tai, the south wat. Wat Luang Nua is the more important of the two, with a glittering gold facade. To the east lies That Luang markets; to

Vientiane & Southern Laos

CYCLING VIENTIANE

The following tours can be accomplished by bicycle, cyclo, motorcycle, or even on foot. The tours are intended as a rough guide only; if you see something interesting along the way, take a tangent! Use designated bike-parking areas in places like markets; impromptu bike-repair stands around Vientiane are marked by a hanging inner tube or tire. Avoid the killer midday sun—both tours are best attempted in the morning, when it's cooler and there's more activity.

TOUR 1

Vientiane is a great place for bicycling, with spacious boulevards and none of the frantic traffic of Thailand. Not yet, anyway. This is one of the last Southeast Asian capitals where pedestrians and bicyclists still rule the roads.

For breakfast, or to stock up on picnic supplies, head for the south side of the markets, opposite the GPO. There are lots of French bread vendors, and you can buy processed cheese, spam-pâté, mandarins, fried bananas in batter, and soup. Or stop at a minimart like Phimphone and buy real cheese; eat with the market bread. It's a good idea to carry a bottle of purified water when cycling in Vientiane—stores don't always carry water, and the treacly soft drinks they do stock will only increase your thirst.

Vientiane is a cluster of distinct neighborhoods; this tour takes in a few of them. Start outside the gates of the **Presidential Palace,** the most exclusive turf in town, located on a power axis facing Vientiane's version of the Champs Elysées. Kilometer-counting for areas around Vientiane starts from here. You won't be allowed into the palace—you won't be allowed to even photograph the palace—but at least you can peer through the gates at this stucco, belle epoque mansion with its French garden. Formerly the site of the Royal Palace, the building is now used for official state receptions and as a guesthouse for VIPs. The area around the Palace features some of the classiest villas in Vientiane—the palace was the focus of the traditional administrative area, and later the center of French colonial life. Former French villas in this zone vary: some (west of the palace) have been superbly renovated for use by government ministries or foreign investors; some are run-down and occupied by half-a-dozen families; others are slated to be torn down to make way for Thai banks, hotels, and other developments.

First stop: Wat Sisaket and Wat Pra Keo. The more interesting of the two, architecturally, is **Wat Sisaket**—drop in for a quick look. Nearby, the French tricolor flies over the **French Embassy** compound; this huge enclosure is a French ministate with French school, French club, and so on. On a building facade to the east of the embassy you can still make out "école de Médecine." Diagonally opposite the rear of the French Embassy is a Catholic church, with masses every morning at 0630 in Lao, and services at 0700, 0830, and 1600 on Sunday.

City Pillar

The main offering at **Wat Simuang,** along tree-lined Settathirat Boulevard, is young coconuts, followed by bananas, incense, flowers, and candles—which explains the stock of roadside vendors here. Wat Simuang functions as a wish-granting shrine: coconuts and bananas are offered if a wish has been fulfilled. The city foundation pillar, a sacred stone wrapped in cloth and festooned with popping lights, forms the centerpiece of the altar inside the main temple. The stone—probably of Khmer origin—was positioned here in the 16th century, when King Settathirat established Vientiane as his capital. In front of the altar is a small Buddha imbued with magical powers, frequently consulted by Lao people to answer troublesome questions. Wat Simuang is one of the "powerhouses" of Vientiane—packed at festival time, with coconuts strewn all over the floor and the smell of incense thick in the air.

Past Wat Simuang, on a traffic-island park, is a statue of King Sisavang Vong, who died in 1959. Curiously, this Russian-made statue survived the Pathet Lao takeover. Further down the road you can make a quick side trip—take the trail behind the **water tower,** which leads to a narrow bridge to Don Chan Island. From the bridge you can see extensive fruit and vegetable farming on the island, supplying Vientiane's markets.

Back on dusty Tha Deua Road you'll find some exclusive real estate: ambassadorial residences, clubs, private guesthouses for visiting VIPs. Past Vientiane Club and the Prince's Palace, where official government guests are hosted, you come to a Lao gas station. Turn left just past the station, pulling into a more rustic neighborhood featuring basket weaving and coconut grating.

Forest Wat

Follow the road up to a fork and turn right. A short way along the road is a yellow-and-white triple archway, the entrance to the forest temple **Wat Sokpaluang.** Set in the leafy grounds are three *sims;* about 25 monks and 10 nuns live in residences scattered through the forest and gardens. The peaceful location is ideal for meditation; the abbot conducts courses in *vipassana* meditation. Tucked into a corner of the wat is a primitive but effective herbal sauna—a tiny six-seater box on a second level of a hut, with a 10-gallon drum under burning wood. The sauna is run by nuns and is open all day; a few of the monks and nuns speak English and French. Payment is by donation; there's a teahouse attached.

Some like it cool—down the road is Sokpaluang swimming pool. Open 1300–1900 weekdays except Mon., and 1000–1900 Sat., Sun.; entry $1. The pool has changing rooms, umbrella shelters, drinks, and even swimsuit rentals. Outside and around the corner is a small "traditional medicine sauna" offered by one of the locals. An optional ride involves going farther south to the Swedish part of town (Swedish school, Swedish guesthouse, Swedish Embassy), where you're bound to find more in the way of saunas—and yes, there's a largish operation at Wat Nak Health Center, with Finnish sauna 1630–2130 and Lao traditional sauna 1430–2130.

After visiting the Sokpaluang District, you can retrace your route back to Khou Viang Street, or loop right around and back to the same street. Khou Viang is very pleasant—a narrow road lined with tamarind trees. These trees have bean pods that the locals like to chew on, but which will make you pucker up like you've never done before. Khou Viang is elevated—it was once part of the old city wall, an earthen fortification with moats on either side. Remnants of the moat are used for growing crops like watercress.

Khou Viang leads right to **Talad Sao,** the morning market, with four cavernous two-story buildings—more like a department store. Talad Sao offers mostly consumer goods and hardware, but there's a section in the building to the north where weavings, Lao cotton, basketware, wood and ceramics, and souvenirs are sold. Oddities include old Soviet cameras, Lao music tapes, jars of herbal medicines, and marijuana, which is sold in the tobacco section. You can call it a day here (there's always tomorrow) or head off on the next tour.

TOUR 2

Start this ride on Lane Xang Boulevard, Vientiane's answer to the Champs Elysées. There at the end looms—can it be?—the Arc de Triomphe. Well, not quite, but they tried. Pratuxai (Victory Gate) Monument was built in the 1960s to honor those who fell in civil wars. Set in a star of radiating boulevards (fashioned after l'Étoile in Paris) the monument is nicknamed "the vertical runway." During construction, the project ran out of cement, so hundreds of tons of the stuff were diverted from a U.S. aid package, meant for an extension for B-52 bombers at Vientiane's Wattay Airport.

Pratuxai is a mix of French and Lao design elements, with Byzantine-like spires cast in U.S.-aid concrete; the interior is popular with local graffiti artists. You can clamber up the concrete steps for a bird's-eye view of the town from the top battlements. There's a small café at the base of the monument, and bike parking for a token fee. The monument is open 0800–1700.

This tour is short. To get your quota of exercise, ride a few kilometers out to That Luang, the

(continued on next page)

CYCLING VIENTIANE (cont'd)

great stupas. Then ride back to Pratuxai Monument, and on to Talad Thong Khankhame—the largest produce market in Vientiane, and much cleaner than Talad Sao. Poking around produce markets always reveals some weird variety of flora or fauna. The market is more active in the morning, although it's open all day. Food stalls serve up cheap Lao food as well as exotic offerings like bat kebabs, or frog or deer meat. Some consumer goods are sold here; lining the road opposite the markets are basketry shops, with ingenious variations on packaging. Use the market's designated bike parking.

A fitting end to a day's hard touring is a cold drink by the Mekong. One popular spot is Mixai Café, which serves draft Lao beer in plastic tumblers—or bottled beer or other drinks if you prefer. Spicy Lao food is available too. For a quieter place, head in the other direction, past the Riverview Hotel, where you'll find small waterfront huts serving young coconuts, juice, bottled Lao beer, and maybe green papaya salad or barbecued chicken. A mortar and pestle is used to grind up green papaya or green banana, which is then mixed with chiles, garlic, lime, and other condiments. Spicing is done to order: if you're not keen on chiles, order a dish without them. The stalls are great vantage points for catching those last rays over the Mekong.

---

the north is the National Assembly Building and the Unknown Pathet Lao War Memorial; to the northwest is a Pathet Lao museum (open only to VIPs) with a few tanks, trucks, guns, and aircraft visible within the compound.

You can easily bicycle out to That Luang: It's three kilometers from central Vientiane, or about two kilometers from Pratuxai Monument. That Luang is open 0800–1130 and 1400–1630; closed Monday and public holidays.

Other Sights

Vientiane is a 40-wat city. Most, though they date from the 16th century, were destroyed by the Thais and then rebuilt in the 19th and 20th centuries. The wats are not so interesting for their architecture, but more for the fact that they're active and the center of festivals. Apart from Wat Sisaket and Wat Simuang, the most important is **Wat Ong Tu**, which was once connected with Lao nobility. It sits on an axis with four other wats radiating from it—Wat Inpeng to the west, Wat Hay Sok to the north, Wat Chan to the south, and Wat Mixai to the east. With such a tight cluster of wats, there is a lot of dawn activity along Settathirat Boulevard as monks file out to collect alms. Buddhist practices do not permit women to stand higher than monks: Women kneel when offering food to the monks, whereas men stand. Both men and women offering food often dress in traditional sash.

Wat Ong Tu (Temple of the Heavy Buddha) is an important center of learning, with a Buddhist Institute that attracts monks from all over Laos. The main temple here has exquisite carved wooden doors and windows depicting scenes from the *Ramayana;* inside is a huge bronze Buddha from the 16th century. Those are the original parts; the rest of the temple largely dates from a restoration in 1996. Some other temples of note: **Wat Chan** houses a large seated bronze Buddha with panels of sculpted wood from the original site; **Wat Inpeng** offers an elaborate wood-and-mosaic facade; at **Wat Mixai** there are some goofy-looking *yaksha* statues—Bangkok-style temple guards—near the front gates.

If you're in town during a festival, you'll find that the grounds of key wats become fairgrounds, filled with shooting galleries, food and drink vendors, and carnival games such as trying to throw a hoop over the neck of a live duck among a group of penned ducks. Elaborate presentations of food and gifts to the monks take place at key wats during festival time.

Accommodations

UNDER $20

A number of guesthouses are clustered close to the Nam Phu (fountain) area. Prices range from $4 (for a room with little more than a bed in it) to $10 for a decent room, and $18 for a room with bath and a/c. A good guesthouse with a central location is **Saysouly GH,** 23 Manthatulath Rd., tel. 21/218383, with budget and more comfortable rooms and great atmosphere; it occupies an old villa. On Settathirat Boulevard, close by, is **Sabaidy GH.** There is a string of guesthouses in this vicinity, or just off the boulevard. **Hua Guo GH,** 359 Samsenthai Rd., tel. 21/216612, is Chinese-run and a bit weird, but the price is right: $8–15 for a room, with hot showers available. There are 13 rooms. **Settha GH,** 80 Samsenthai Rd., tel. 21/213241, fax 21/215995, is opposite Lao Plaza Hotel, with a dozen or so rooms for $16 double with a/c. It's part of the Hong Kong Restaurant complex, which falls under the same management.

Pangkham GH, near Nam Phu Square, 72/6 Pangkham Rd., tel. 21/217053, fax 21/216382, has 12 rooms at $10 (no window) to $20 (windows and a/c). There are several more guesthouses in this vicinity to choose from.

Down by the Mekong is a good hotel called **Orchid Guesthouse,** with rooms for $10–17 each, and a rooftop viewpoint. **Inter Hotel,** at 24–25 Fa Ngum Rd., tel. 21/215137, has 15 rooms for $10–20; and **Mixai Guesthouse** at 30/1 Fa Ngum Rd., tel. 21/216213, has eight basic rooms at $8 fan or $12 a/c. **Phornthip Guesthouse,** at 72 Inpeng Rd., is small and clean; it charges $8–14 for a room.

Near the stadium is **Santisouk Guesthouse,** at 77 Nokeo Khoumane St., tel. 21/215303, with 15 rooms upstairs; downstairs is Santisouk Restaurant. The rooms cost $10–12 s and $15 d, with huge bathrooms, sometimes shared between several rooms. **Vannasinh GH,** on Phnom Penh Rd., tel./fax 21/222020, has 23 rooms from $10 fan to $20 a/c double—this place is often full.

Closer to the morning market is **Lani Guesthouse 2,** 286 Saylom St., tel. 21/213022, offering seven rooms that go for around $15 apiece. Also out this way is **Lao Elysee GH,** 168/5 Khoun Boulom Rd., tel. 21/213619, fax 21/215628, with 12 rooms for $12–20 apiece. Nearby is **Say Lom Yen GH,** on Say Lom Rd., tel. 21/214246, with fan rooms for $6–8 and a/c rooms for $12.

Near the southern end of town, **Thienthong GH,** off Sokpaluang near Wat Nak, rents rooms for $15–20.

Vientiane Hotel, opposite the New Apollo on the west side of town, tel. 21/212928, has 45 uninspiring rooms; $10 fan, $15 a/c, $20–22 with fridge. To the south side of town near a small lake is **Souk Savanh GH,** with 22 rooms $3–6 a bed—run-down, but popular with visiting Indians and Pakistanis.

Right out west, past Wat Khounta and down an alley off Luang Prabang Road, is a French joint-venture villa-hotel called **Auberge du Temple,** tel. 21/214844, with eight tastefully furnished rooms for $10–20. The Auberge has a garden-side place for breakfast.

$20–50

Hotel rates are subject to government tax of 10–11 percent plus a service charge of 10 percent. You can bargain discounts of 10–25 percent for longer stays. Extra beds added to the room run $7–10. Some hotels include breakfast in the tariff.

Asian Pavilion, 379 Samsenthai, tel. 21/213430, fax 21/213432, used to be the Hotel Constellation, which was the pre-1975 roosting place for foreign gunrunners, opium dealers, gold smugglers, spies, mercenaries, and journalists. In the 1960s it was run by Maurice, a gentleman of Corsican, Vietnamese, Chinese, and Lao extraction. Renovated under a Thai joint venture, the hotel still retains some of its old atmosphere. Today the Pavilion offers 43 rooms, ranging from $26 standard and

$45 superior to $60 for a suite; an extra bed is $10. **Ekalath Metropole,** on Samsenthai Road near That Dam, tel. 21/213420, has 32 rooms; $10 fan, $20–22 s and $28 d a/c. Inside the hotel is Melody Club disco. **Holiday Day Inn,** on Pangkham Road, tel. 21/214792, fax 21/22984, has 18 nicely furnished rooms for $25–30. There are a couple of single rooms for $15 each. **Lao-Paris Hotel,** at 100 Samsenthai, tel. 21/213440, fax 21/216382, features 18 rooms in the $25–40 range. **Douang Deuane Hotel,** on Nokeo Khoumane Road, tel. 21/222301, fax 21/222300, is Thai-managed; it has 30 rooms with TV, a/c, and hot water for $22–28.

Lani **Guesthouse 1,** 281 Settathirat Blvd., Hay Sok, tel. 21/215639, fax 21/216103, is down an alley near Wat Haysok—great location, with a beautiful garden. The guesthouse includes 11 rooms in the $25–30 price range. **Anou Hotel,** 3 Heng Boun St., tel. 21/213630, fax 21/213635, has 48 rooms costing $18 and up. It's possible to rent some single rooms for under $18; double rooms run $16–25; suites are $28–35. The hotel has a restaurant and a disco—Anou Cabaret—that is one of the most popular in town. **Saysana Hotel,** Chao Anou St., tel. 21/213581, features 34 rooms for $20–25 each—a good deal for the price. The hotel has its own restaurant and bar. **Syri GH,** Chao Anou Quarter, near the stadium, tel. 21/212682, fax 21/217251, is nice and homey; it's family-run with 14 rooms $15–17 s without bath, and $20–30 d with bath.

Near Pratuxai Monument is **Le Parasol Blanc,** on Sidamdouan Road, tel. 21/216091, fax 21/214108. The hotel has a lounge and restaurant in a restored colonial mansion; accommodation is in bungalows set in pleasant gardens with a small pool; the restaurant serves European food. There are 34 rooms—$30 s or d; the hotel also rents bikes and cars. Farther east along That Luang Boulevard is the family-run **Villa That Luang,** 307 That Luang Rd., tel. 21/413370, with 11 rooms in the $20–30 range.

On the west side of town is the moderately priced **Senesouk GH,** at 100 Luang Prabang Rd. KM2, tel. 21/215567. **Mekong Apartment Hotel** is a large Chinese-run concrete block on Luang Prabang Road, tel. 21/212938, fax 21/212822. There are 92 rooms, of which 27 are standard rooms and 65 are furnished apartment rooms with kitchens, baths, air-conditioning, satellite TV, and IDD phones. There are single, double, and triple rooms available; standard rooms are $35–45 a day, or $600–700 a month; furnished apartments are $25–40–60 a day or $350–550–650 a month.

On the eastern fringe of Vientiane, and somewhat isolated, is **Vansana,** 9 Phonethan Rd., tel. 21/413171, fax 21/413171; a multi-story hotel, it offers satellite TV, swimming pool, and lush gardens. Its 45 rooms cost $25 s or $35 d.

To the southern end of town are several moderately priced places: **Chaemchanh GH** at 78 Khou Viang, tel. 21/312700, with five rooms for $11 fan/share toilet; $15 s a/c, private toilet; $22 d; it also has five $33 apartments with kitchen. The guesthouse has a nice garden. **Oudomphone GH,** 22/241 Dongpalane Rd., has eight rooms in the $20–25 range. **Muong Lao (China Hotel),** at Tha Deua KM3, tel. 21/216287, is parked near the Mekong and charges $20 for rooms or $40 and up for suites. It has a Thai-Lao restaurant.

Riverview Hotel, Fa Ngum Road, tel. 21/216244, fax 21/216231, sited on the western edge of town close to the Mekong, has 32 rooms for $35–44 s, $44–48 d, $56 t, and $80 for a suite. There's a strange collection of kitsch in the lobby.

$50–100

The most stylish luxury hotel in Vientiane is **⚑ Settha Palace Hotel,** at 6 Pangkham Rd., tel. 21/217581, settha@laonet.net. It occupies a huge French colonial building that has been completely renovated. The 29 rooms go for $80 standard or $96 deluxe. This joint-venture with Belmont hotel group has its own swimming pool and a London taxi parked out front.

Lane Xang Hotel, Fa Ngum Road, tel. 21/214102, fax 21/214108, is right near the Mekong; it's centrally situated with a good pool, sauna, tennis court, restaurant, and disco. Decor leaves a lot to be desired, but you can't expect too much from Russian architecture. This dowdy place used to be government-run, but it was privatized in 1992. The hotel has 40 rooms for $42 s or $54 d; an additional 20 apartments go for $70–80 apiece.

Tai-Pan Hotel, 22/3 François Ngin St., tel. 21/216907, fax 21/216223, is a clean, comfortable, efficient businessperson's hotel with Thai management. There are 36 rooms equipped with satellite TV, IDD phones, and other amenities; a business center; and a sauna and fitness center. Rates are $54–75 for rooms, $85–165 for suites.

The **Royal Hotel** (Dokmaideng), on Lane Xang Boulevard, tel. 21/214455, fax 21/214454, is just south of Pratuxai Monument. It has a/c rooms and suites, satellite TV, a business center, swimming pool, and a nightclub with a dance floor and karaoke lounge—obviously angled for Chinese visitors. The Royal charges $80–90 for singles or doubles and $130 for a suite.

Several luxury hotels lie on the airport road. The **New Apollo,** at 69 Luang Prabang, tel. 21/213244, fax 21/214462, charges $70–90 for rooms, but discounts them to $40–50; the hotel's key attraction is its hostess nightclub.

Novotel Vientiane, Thanon Luang Prabang KM2, tel. 21/213672, fax 21/215448, is one of Vientiane's best. It attempts French-style architecture, but the Singapore architect didn't quite bring it off. The Novotel, run by the French Accor hotel group, offers 233 rooms (including nine suites), 24-hour room service, a business center with Internet access, conference room, health and sports facilities (gym, tennis, small pool), and several restaurants and cafés. Prices are $45 for an economy room, $90–110 for standard and deluxe rooms, and $140–220 for a suite; discounts may be available. Rooms come equipped with a/c, IDD, satellite TV, and a host of other creature comforts.

$100–200

The seven-story, 142-room **Lao Plaza Hotel,** 63 Samsenthai Rd., right downtown, tel. 21/218800, fax 21/218808, is a joint-venture hotel with rooms for $100–200 and suites $200–400. In terms of atmosphere: not much. The Lao Plaza Hotel joins the bevy of concrete monstrosities built along Samsenthai Road, including the Lao National Culture Hall. Where do they find the architects for these buildings? Graduates from Moscow?

Food

Bakeries

For breakfast or snacks, try the markets— the south side of Talad Sao, or **Khankhame Produce Market**—where you can get French bread and trimmings, plus fruit and juice. Bakeries are excellent places for breakfast. Top of the line is the **Scandinavian Bakery** in Nam Phu Square; it serves excellent sandwiches, croissants, and drinks. Around the corner on Settathirat Street is **Healthy and Fresh,** another excellent place. Down by the Mekong is the French-run **Nana Café,** which is good for breakfast (and also provides traveler information). At 109 Chao Anou is **Sweet Home Bakery,** and nearby is **Liang Xiang Bakery,** which sell croissants, pineapple pie, coconut

buns, doughnuts, and hamburgers. Both have street-side outdoor seating—a good place to meet other travelers. There is a string of small bakeries in this area.

Street Fare

Chao Anou Street is part of Vientiane's unofficial Chinatown. Street vendors and noodle-houses in this area—as well as along Khoun Boulom and Heng Boun roads—sell rice noodles and other noodle dishes. For a sit-down venue, try **Nang Souri Noodle Shop** (Green Hole in the Wall) at 12 Heng Boun, a shop-house restaurant serving Chinese and Thai food. Khoun Boulom Street, on the strip north of Settathirat one block west of Chao Anou,

DINING LAO-STYLE

Some of the restaurants listed in this section serve Lao food as well as European dishes. You can special-order traditional Lao food in advance from places such as **Le Souriya** or **Nam Phu Restaurant** (Lao food takes a long time to prepare and does not keep well). Since these venues tend to offer menus written only in Lao script, most travelers will need a food guide to translate; a guide should also know the best places to go. An upscale restaurant specializing in Lao food is **Kualao Restaurant,** a block south of That Dam at 111 Samsenthai Road.

For cheap Lao food, **Talad Dong Palane** night market, on Dong Palane Road to the southeast of Talad Sao, has food stalls serving roast chicken, stir-fried vegetables, and spicy green papaya salad. Several Lao restaurants are on Luang Prabang Road, to the west side of town, including **Nokkeo Restaurant** and **Somchan's Pub and Restaurant.**

features vendors with Vietnamese fare, including spring rolls and barbecued kebabs. On the east side of Khoun Boulom, toward the Mekong, is a string of roast duck restaurants.

All along Fa Ngum Boulevard facing the Mekong are thatched huts where you can sit at a small table on a plastic chair and order fresh young coconut, Lao beer, or a shot glass of Lao whiskey. You can also order *tam som* (spicy green papaya salad), sticky rice, rice noodles, and barbecued chicken from the food stalls. Foreigners and locals alike gather at these food stalls in the late afternoon for ritual sunset watching.

Self-Catering
Vientiane has a number of minimarts, mainly angled at the expatriate community, featuring canned and frozen goods imported from Thailand. You can find French cheese, New Zealand butter, and fresh Thai milk; cheaper are items such as yogurt and canned juices. **Phimphone Minimart** on Samsenthai has a good selection; there's a branch down the way

next to the Hotel Ekalath Metropole. Other minimarts include **Laophanit,** on Khoun Boulom, and **Foodland** on Chao Anou.

Thai Food
With the influx of Thai businesspeople, Thai eateries have sprung up in Vientiane. Thai food is invariably cheaper than Western dishes. A place with a sign reading **Thai Food** on Samsenthai is popular—it's west of the Revolutionary Museum. **Van Mixai,** down the road from Wat Mixay on François Ngin Street, serves cheap, fiery Thai dishes. On Luang Prabang, past the Russian Cultural Center, is **Thai Food Garden** with excellent dishes—look for an oxcart outside. Combining Thai and Western is **Just for Fun** on Pangkham Road near Vientiane Book Center. It's open for breakfast, lunch, and dinner, and it offers a good selection of dishes. Among the vegetarian offerings are fried bean curd with sweet peanut sauce, and lemongrass fried with spicy vegetables. The restaurant also sells cookies, cakes, brownies, a full range of herbal teas, and 10 kinds of coffee, including French roast, Lao, Viennese. Just for Fun is a fund-raiser for a weaving cooperative.

Other Inexpensive Options
The place for good and inexpensive Vietnamese food is **PVO Restaurant** at 344 Samsenthai, tel. 21/214444; it has excellent Vietnamese sandwiches and also rents bicycles and motorcycles. Pricier—but still affordable—are some places on the west side of town. **Noorjhan,** at 366 Samsenthai, serves good Indian food—curries, samosas, chapatis, *masala dosa*—at fair prices. **Ban Hay Sok Restaurant,** across from Anou Hotel, offers Chinese food. On the ground floor of the Inter Hotel is a place that serves sizzling platters of steak and fries—honest portions at reasonable prices.

Nam Phu Square
This area is known for its upscale restaurants. Right next to the fountain is **L'Opera,** tel. 21/215099, a branch of a Bangkok restaurant. L'Opera has Italian pizza and wines, an Italian

chef and management, and, of course, Italian opera. The restaurant boasts the only Italian ice-cream machine in Laos; stop by for a gelato takeaway. Also facing the fountain is **Nam Phu Restaurant,** tel. 21/216248, a long-established venue with an interior of whitewashed walls and dark timber, and tables of smoked glass with varnished rattan. This lowkey place has a selection of fine French dishes including frog's legs Provençale and steak *au poivre vert.* The French-speaking proprietor waits on the tables herself. You can special-order Lao dishes in advance.

French Cuisine

For a reasonably priced place with good atmosphere, try the small and intimate **Le Bistrot** on François Ngin Street. One of the premier venues for French food is **Le Cote d'Azur,** at 63 Fa Ngum, offering fine Provençale food. **Arawan Restaurant,** 474 Samsenthai, offers a range of French dishes: coq au vin, lobster thermidor, *crab farcie,* and filet mignon, as well as appetizers, soups, salads, cheeses, and wines. Next door, owned by the same family, is a charcuterie selling delicacies imported from France—

wines, cheeses, and pâtés. **Le Vendôme,** near Saysana Hotel, has French ambience, French food, French management, and French prices. In an old mansion, it offers a range of pizzas from a wood-fired oven. The interior is decorated with Lao and Thai antiques; there are breezy tables on a shaded verandah. On Nokeo Khoumane Street are several French places—**Le Safran,** toward the Mekong, and **La Terasse.** In between is the **B-52 Bar.**

Garden Restaurants

A good place for breakfast is the garden of **Le Parasol Blanc;** the interior dining room, in a beautiful old mansion, is known for its European cuisine. **Lani Guesthouse 1** also has tables in a garden setting that are great for breakfast.

Water Views

To the south, fronting the Mekong, is the pricey **Mekong Restaurant** at Tha Deua KM4, tel. 21/312480. A vast venue, it serves international and Asian food, and caters to large groups. This air-conditioned place is popular with expatriates and upper-income Lao people.

Nightlife

In the early 1970s, before the Pathet Lao took over Vientiane, the city had a high-flying nightlife that catered to CIA agents, Air America pilots, French advisers, and hippies on the overland trail. Exotic bars such as the White Rose, the Purple Porpoise, the Green Latrine, and le Rendezvous des Amis sprang up. Paul Theroux summed up the nightlife in his 1975 book, *The Great Railway Bazaar:* "The brothels are cleaner than the hotels, the marijuana is cheaper than pipe tobacco, and opium easier to find than a glass of cold beer." Marijuana is still cheaper than tobacco (it's used as a cooking spice for soup by the locals), but the brothels have been turned into guesthouses (the women exiled to an island in Nam Ngum Lake for re-education), and the opium dens are gone.

Vientiane is quiet at night. The era of complete austerity under the Pathet Lao has been relaxed—Stalin is dead and has been replaced by Madonna, at least with the younger set. You can join them at the **Anou Cabaret**—the hottest disco in town, attached to the Anou Hotel—or at the **Vienglaty,** on Lane Xang Boulevard near Talad Sao, featuring live bands. There are half a dozen other dance venues around Vientiane, mixing Western disco and Lao *lam wong* dance music. Otherwise, entertainment mostly focuses on major hotels (which usually have a bar or disco) and a few popular watering holes. Hotel soirées may feature traditional music—one venue is the **Saysana Hotel restaurant,** 1800–2100; the Saysana also has a disco. **Salongxay Restaurant** at the Lane Xang Hotel has similar digestion-easing music; the hotel also features a nightclub. The downstairs bar

MOVIE NIGHT IN VIENTIANE

The Lao PDR has no film industry to speak of. A black-and-white movie called *Red Lotus* was shot in 1988 by the State Cinematographic Company, but since then only propaganda efforts have appeared. Therefore, only imports are viewed in Vientiane. There are two snags: strict government censorship, and a stipulation that all dialogue must be rendered in Lao. Because dubbing and subtitling in Lao is prohibitively expensive, exhibitors must provide translations of the screen dialogue for readers to speak *live* over the PA system during projection. At the Odeon Rama cinema on Talad Leng Road in the Chanthabouly District, four readers sit hunched in a little booth next to vintage Russian projectors. As the film is projected, the original dialogue must be switched off when a character speaks, with Lao dialogue simultaneously substituted. Although popcorn is sold in the lobby, Laotian filmgoers prefer munching on black watermelon seeds. Film offerings are largely limited to recent Thai and Chinese films. No Westerns are allowed: Government censors apparently don't like gunfights.

and lounge at **Le Parasol Blanc hotel** often features live piano music. At the **Royal Hotel** there's a 1,000-square-meter dance floor and a Karaoke Television (KTV) salon with 16 private karaoke rooms where, the hotel brochure claims, you can "yell your joyfulness and seek the spiritual communication."

Embassy staff have created their own nightlife: movies, video rentals, in-house bars, and so on. The French have Le Centre, on Lane Xang Boulevard, and the Aussies the Australian Club, near the embassy. These places are usually for members only, but if you have the right passport, you may be able to get in.

To the western side of Nam Phu, on Settathirat Boulevard, is the highly popular **Khopchaideu Restaurant.** Housed on the grounds of an old French mansion, this place is a food garden, pub, Internet café, and ritzy restaurant all rolled into one—it has a wide appeal and a great ambience. Check out Nam Phu, the fountain at the center of town, if close to here—it may be lit up. The fountain was out of action for many years, but it was restored to working order in 1991, courtesy of a Swedish joint venture. It lights up in full gushing majesty sometimes at night—especially at festival times or holidays.

Shopping

An excellent map for finding shops is enclosed in the back flap of *The Vientiane Guide,* issued in Vientiane; you might be able to obtain the map separately. The map is annotated with fine detail on which section of town sells what. Textile, clothing, and handicraft shops are mainly situated along Samsenthai, Pangkham, and Settathirat roads. Some shops specialize, others carry a full range of Lao handmade products. The northernmost building of the Morning Market (Talad Sao) stocks cotton goods, modern weavings, basketry, silverware, and handicrafts. There's an excellent range of textiles, and a great array of silverware, including betel

nut trays, opium pipes, and silver bowls. Inquire what percentage silver is used. Visitors should note that exporting antiques and Buddha images is strictly banned in Laos.

Textiles

Vientiane sells a wide range of silk and cotton fabrics in attractive designs and colors. These are mostly handmade by loom and are fashioned into scarves, shawls, *sinhs,* small bags, pillowcases, slipcovers, and wall hangings. Pure silk is expensive, so weavings often consist of cotton or a blend of silk and polyester. Hilltribe embroidery is usually sold at the textile shops. You might also find some antique textiles—family heirlooms of hilltribe origin, up to 150 years old. There are also replicas of ancient designs.

Lao Textiles, at 84 Nokeo Khoumane, housed in an old French villa, designs hand-woven silks for major couturiers in Europe and North America. The shop sells fabrics and museum-quality wall hangings; prices are high. Lao Textiles was founded in 1990 by textile designer Carol Cassidy, who arrived in Laos as a weaving consultant for the United Nations. Cassidy uses a Macintosh computer to interpret traditional colors and designs; her master weavers then use handlooms to transform these designs into fabrics for fashion and decor. Working with and training local Lao weavers and dyers, Cassidy is producing wall hangings, fashion accessories such as shawls and scarves, and custom furnishing fabrics. In the process, she has revived sericulture and the art of weaving, abandoned in decades of warfare. Everything at Lao Textiles is handmade, and, remarkably, all the work is done on the premises—spinning of the silk, dyeing, and weaving. Lao Textiles is thus much more than a shop—it's a representation in miniature of the entire Lao textile-weaving process. Staff is pleased to show you around.

The UNICEF-supported **Art of Silk,** on Manthaturat Street opposite Samsenthai Hotel, offers a variety of textiles, clothing and accessories, and antique weavings. Operated by the Lao Women's Union, the Art of Silk preserves old textiles and trains weavers in traditional techniques. Upstairs is a small museum of old textiles.

To the west side of town, north of Luang Prabang Road and near Wat Oupmoung, is the factory and salesroom of **Lao Cotton,** supported by the United Nations to preserve weaving skills and develop contemporary products. Lao Cotton has a wide range of cotton fabrics and ready-made articles, including bed linen, table linen, and upholstery items. There is a small Lao Cotton shop on Settathirat Boulevard near the fountain, and another branch on Sokpaluang Road, opposite the Swedish Guesthouse.

Clothing

There are many Vietnamese tailors north of Nam Phu Square, on Pangkham and Samsenthai roads. You can hand over a piece of clothing and have it copied; all material purchased from Talad Sao should be preshrunk before dressmaking. **Lao Vilai Fashions,** at 24 Samsenthai, has designer-created fashions for women using Lao cotton. It exports to Europe.

Handcrafted Goods

Talad Sao is a good place to look for handmade goods. Opposite Talad Thong Khankhame, the market northwest of town, is a large basket-ware section. Along Pangkham Road are a number of shops selling woodcarvings, silver ornaments, and cotton and silk goods. Two of these are **Kanchana Boutique,** near That Dam, and **Lao Phattan Art and Handicraft,** opposite Lao Airlines. At 18–20 Settathirat is **Somsri Handicrafts,** with a selection of crafts and antiques upstairs. **Nang Xuan,** at 385 Samsenthai, features a selection of old opium pipes and hilltribe jewelry. **Phonethip,** at 55 Saylom St., offers handicrafts and ceramics. Furniture items made of rattan, bamboo, and teak can be found in Vientiane, or you can custom-order them from workshops on the fringes of town. An excellent place for colonial-style furniture is **Mandalay,** a shop on François Ngin Street, opposite the Taipan Hotel; it's run by a Frenchwoman. In addition to furniture, she sells Burmese crafts and small copies of Angkorian friezes.

Services and Information

Communications services are poor in Laos, but changes are coming rapidly to Vientiane. In 1992, the Lao government permitted foreign newspapers, IDD, private fax machines, and satellite dishes for the first time. In 1993, the government signed a telecom and broadcasting deal with Thai giant Shinawatra; in 1994, the Lao Information and Culture Ministry issued a small-circulation weekly newspaper, the *Vientiane Times*—the country's first English-language newspaper since 1975.

TOURIST INFORMATION

Don't bother with Lao National Tourism Authority; its only function, it seems, is to attend to the issuing of documents or research ways of boosting tourism. There's a dearth of information about current conditions in Laos. Aerocontact Asia is a tourism promotion and development company at 23 Manthaturat Rd., tel. 21/217294, which publishes a magazine called *Discover Laos* every few months; it's a good source of current news and events, with up-to-date hotel listings. Lao Airlines publishes its own in-flight magazine, *Dok Champa,* which sometimes features illuminating articles and carries a good map of Vientiane. You might bag one at the Lao Airlines office. A French-run café that provides traveler information is Nana Café, down by the Mekong on Fa Ngum Road, near François Ngin Street.

Maps

The Lao National Tourism Authority distributes a large, detailed map of Vientiane, printed in China; it might be available from Vientiane Book Center or the Lane Xang Hotel shop. Map street names are given in both English and Lao script; the reverse side carries a bilingual map of Vientiane Prefecture. In the back flap of *The Vientiane Guide,* available at Vientiane Book Center, is an oversized sketch map of Vientiane issued by the Women's International Group. This map has excellent annotations for those interested in shopping; you might be able to buy it separately from *The Vientiane Guide.*

The State Geographic Service, on a side street to the west of Pratuxai Monument, has topographical maps of a number of regions in Laos, plus some town plans. The maps are plastered all over the walls, so you just point to the relevant map and the clerk will trot off and attempt to find it. Some of the maps are taken from French aerial surveys and are quite accurate, if a bit outdated.

Books

Vientiane Book Center, at 25 Pangkham Rd., tel./fax 21/212031, caters to English and French speakers, stocking some international magazines and travel books. The bookstore is a good source of information on travel conditions; check the notice board. It sells *The Vientiane Guide,* an annual tome written in Vientiane by the Women's International Group; it also sells some Lao-English dictionaries and phrasebooks, as well as artifacts. Two blocks west is Kosila Books, with a smaller selection of material.

The Novotel and Lane Xang hotels each have a small book counter. You might try the gift shops of other major hotels in Vientiane. At the corner of Manthurat and Settathirat roads is the government bookstore; it's more for Laotians learning English, but it stocks some posters, maps, folk tapes, and children's books. This place may also have some foreign news magazines for sale.

Satellite TV

Satellite dishes abound in Vientiane. A regular dish can pick up StarTV, which includes BBC World Service; a large dish picks up CNN. Satellite dishes are provided to the Lao market by Samart Group, the largest dish maker in Thailand.

VIENTIANE EMBASSIES

Foreign embassies in Vientiane are roughly grouped in two areas: to the east of Pratuxai Monument, around That Luang Boulevard; and to the south end of town, around the Sokpaluang area. There are more than 20 foreign embassies in Vientiane. These include:

Australia, Nehru Street, Wat Phon Xay area, tel. 21/413610

Cambodia, Saphathong Nua area, tel. 21/314952

China, Wat Nak Street, Sisattahanak area, tel. 21/315103

France, Settathirat Boulevard, tel. 21/215258

Germany, 26 Sokpaluang, tel. 21/312111

India, That Luang Road, tel. 21/413802

Indonesia, Phon Kheng Road, tel. 21/413910

Japan, Sisangvone Road, tel. 21/212623

Malaysia, That Luang Road, tel. 21/414205

Mongolia, Tha Deua KM2, tel. 21/315220

Myanmar (Burma), Sokpaluang Road, tel. 21/312439

Russia, Thaphalanxay area, tel. 21/312219

Sweden, Wat Nak, Sokpaluang area, tel. 21/315018

Thailand, Phon Kheng Road, tel. 21/214582

U.S.A., Bartolini, That Dam area, tel. 21/212580

Vietnam, That Luang Road, tel. 21/413400

COMMUNICATIONS

Fax and Phone

International phone, fax, and telex service is available on Settathirat, near Nam Phu Square, in a set of restored villas. The telecom section is open 0800–2200 daily. Fax is expensive. The phone system has been greatly expanded since 1990, and it is chaotic: Various aid projects have resulted in many kinds of phone lines, so the numbers keep changing as the streets are dug up and new systems are laid by the Australians, Japanese, Germans, and French. In this mixing and matching, phone numbers are notoriously unreliable. Cellular phones have made an appearance, prompted by Thai businessmen. The country code for Laos is 856; the city code for Vientiane is 21. For the international operator, dial 16.

Post Office and Courier

The general post office (PTT) is on the corner of Lane Xang Boulevard and Khou Viang. It's open 0800–1700 weekdays, 0800–1600 Saturday, and 0800–1200 Sunday, and handles mail, *poste restante* (general delivery), and local phone calls. The post office stocks large stamps with flora and fauna and other eye-catching designs—worth a visit if you're a collector. Try to have stamps on envelopes canceled in front of you. Contents of packages must be inspected before they are sealed. The post office offers Express Mail Service (EMS). Commercial courier service in Vientiane is handled by **DHL,** at 52 Nokeo Khoumane Rd., tel. 21/216830; by **TNT,** on Lane Xang Boulevard, tel. 21/214361; and by **Federal Express** (close to GPO). A **UPS** office also operates in Vientiane.

MONEY AND BUSINESS

Banks

The Thai baht has become the coin of the realm in Vientiane, partly because it's easy to shift funds back and forth over the Mekong in baht. There has been a frenzy of Thai bank building in Vientiane, with half a dozen top banks now installed: **Bangkok Bank, Siam Commercial, Thai Military, Thai Farmers, Krung Thai, Bank of Ayudhya.** Thai banks give a slightly better rate than Lao banks for U.S. cash to kip, but a slightly worse rate for traveler's checks to kip.

The **Banque pour le Commerce Extérieur Lao,** at 1 Pangkham Rd., charges no commission on traveler's checks to kip. It charges 1.4 percent for converting U.S. traveler's checks to U.S. cash, so a $100 traveler's check nets $98.60 cash; Thai banks charge 2 percent for the same conversion. The Banque Extérieur is the agent for Visa in Vientiane, but it charges 4–6 percent commission on Visa withdrawals. Try the Thai banks if you need a cash advance on a credit card. **Diethelm Travel,** near Nam Phu Square, is the American Express agent in Vientiane.

For fast changing, or changing when banks are closed, try the private money changers who deal in cash: one near Nam Phu, two more to the north side of Talad Sao Market. Higher-denomination U.S. bills fetch a slightly higher rate.

Business Services

Computers specialist shops are near the intersection of Chao Anou and Settathirat roads. Photocopy shops are easy to find downtown; one-hour film processing is available. Business hours for shops and offices in Vientiane are roughly 0800–1200 and 1400–1700; Saturday 0800–1200; closed Sunday.

HEALTH CARE

The Australian and Swedish embassies both operate clinics for embassy staff, but they may be consulted by other foreigners on a paying basis. The Australian clinic is in the Australian Embassy Compound, tel. 21/413603; on weekends or after hours, call 21/312343. The Swedish clinic is near the Swedish Embassy, tel. 21/315015. Both clinics are normally open mornings only; on weekends or after hours, call 21/312343 or 21/217010. There's also the International Clinic, Mahosat Hospital Compound, Settathirat Boulevard, tel. 21/214018.

REST AND RECREATION

Swimming Pools

Lane Xang Hotel pool is $1, open 0800–1800. Approach it from Settathirat Boulevard; there's a bar nearby in the garden. Near the stadium is a public pool charging $.50;

closed Monday, otherwise open Tuesday–Friday 0730–1100 and 1300–1600, plus Saturday–Sunday 0600–1700. To the southeast is **Sokpaluang Swimming Pool,** open 1300–1900 Tuesday–Friday and 1000–1900 Saturday–Sunday; it has changing rooms, umbrella shelters, drinks, and swimsuit rental.

Sauna

In the Sokpaluang area are a number of saunas—some attached to wats, some private. Herbal saunas are provided at Wat Sokpaluang and Wat Sri Amphorn; Wat Nak Health Center offers a Finnish sauna. Some hotels, such as the Royal, also offer saunas. For a quite different experience, visit Ajaan Amphone's Herbal Sauna, just one block north of the Taipan Hotel in Vientiane. Ajaan Amphone's place has separate steam chambers for men and women. The sauna is very popular with Lao women, who apply mixtures of tamarind and turmeric to their skin. If interested, you can undergo the Shaolin massage, which includes heated vacuum cups that will leave red welts the size of tennis balls on your back. Otherwise, stick with the lemongrass aroma of the steam bath. Once you get into the sauna habit, you will start to notice saunas all over Laos, even in such far-flung regions as Muang Sing.

Other

Vientiane Golf Club has a six-hole course at KM6. There is a small pro shop with golf supply rentals and sales, and a clubhouse. Vientiane Hash House Harriers organize a run every Monday at 1700, open to all. The Hash venue is posted each week at the Australian Embassy Recreation Club and a few other locations.

Getting There

Visa-on-Arrival

Laos joined ASEAN in mid-1997, designated 1999 "Visit Laos Year," and eased up somewhat on visa formalities. The result of all this is that a $30 visa-on-arrival (valid for two weeks) may be available in Vientiane—either at Wattay Airport or the Friendship Bridge (and no other land entry points). However, you should always check ahead to see if you can get a visa-on-arrival—or get the visa beforehand. The $30 for the visa-on-arrival must be paid in U.S. cash. A single extension of up to two weeks is permitted. There are some restrictions, though it's doubtful that they'll be paid much attention. You are supposed to have a return air ticket or a visa to enter a third country (because Thailand requires no visa on entry, you could claim that as your forward destination). You are also required to know an individual or organization to contact in the Lao PDR (you can make one up). You are supposed to have a confirmed hotel reservation in the Lao PDR (again, you can make one up). And you must have proof of sufficient funds for your visit.

BY AIR

International and domestic arrivals and departures are from Vientiane's Wattay Airport, three kilometers west of town. As Laos opens up, there may be more direct flights into the country. For the moment, Bangkok serves as the main staging point for international flights to Vientiane. Air France, for example, routes passengers through Bangkok, where they transfer to a Lao Airlines B-737 flight to Vientiane. Eva Air does the same with its Vientiane–Bangkok–Taipei flight. Bangkok to Vientiane takes an hour; ticketing is jointly operated by Lao Airlines (mostly weekday flights) and Thai Airways International (weekends). The price is $100 one-way, but you can sometimes get special fares. Lao Airlines in Bangkok is at 491/17 Ground Floor, Silom Road, tel. 21/236-9822; Thai Airways is at 485 Silom Rd., tel. 21/233-3810.

If you're bumped from a Bangkok-Vientiane flight, an alternative is to fly north to Udon Thani. From Udon Thani Airport there's a Thai Airways express bus to the office in Nong Khai, 53 kilometers north. From here, you can cross by land into Vientiane. There are also twice-weekly flights from Chiang Mai to Vientiane.

Flight information for Laos is unreliable. Services fluctuate depending on traffic volume and the airworthiness of Russian turboprops used on some runs. There are two return flights a week from Hanoi to Vientiane—one on Tuesday on Lao Airlines, and the other on Thursday on Vietnam Airlines. The tariff is $90 one-way on both airlines. In Hanoi, Vietnam Airlines is agent for both airlines; in Vientiane, Lao Airlines serves as agent for both. There are also connections to Saigon/Ho Chi Minh City on Lao Airlines for $140 one-way.

Lao Airlines flies to Vientiane via Pakse to Siem Reap (Angkor, Cambodia) several times a week. There are flights from Vientiane to Phnom Penh once or twice a week, for around $125 one-way; flights may go to Saigon first. Another route, flown by Malaysia Airlines, goes Kuala Lumpur–Phnom Penh–Vientiane. SilkAir flies from Singapore to Vientiane three times a week. From China, there's a flight from Guangzhou via Kunming on China Southern Airlines once a week—$280 one-way from Guangzhou and about $150 from Kunming. The Kunming-Vientiane fare seems to change often, but the trip is only 1.5 hours by air, so you shouldn't pay too much. On paper there is a flight from Vientiane via Luang Prabang to Jinghong in Yunnan, but this could prove elusive. Other dark horses include a five-hour flight from Vientiane to Beijing—$338 one-way, $475 return on Saturday—and highly irregular flights to Rangoon.

Transfers into Vientiane

Bargain hard; it's not far from Wattay Airport into town. Metered taxis charge $5, and a jumbo should cost $3 for the 10-minute ride.

Drivers often try to charge $7. In the reverse direction, fares are much lower.

Airline Offices

Lao Airlines, 2 Pangkham St., tel. 21/212051, 21/212052, 21/212053, or 21/212057, fax 21/212065, handles most international and domestic bookings, including arrangements for other carriers such as Air France, which does not fly out of Vientiane, though you can make Bangkok bookings through Vientiane. Almost opposite Lao Airlines is the office of Thai Airways International, tel. 21/216143. Not far off is Lao Air Bookings, at 43/1 Settathirat Blvd., tel. 21/216761; this is a Lao Airlines, Vietnam Airlines, Malaysia Airlines, and SilkAir agent handling international tickets. SilkAir has an office in the Royal Hotel (just south of Pratuxai Monument), tel. 21/214455. Malaysia Airlines occupies an office on the first floor of the Lao Plaza Hotel, Samsenthai Road, tel. 21/218816. China Southern Airlines has an office at Tha Deua KM3; the Aeroflot office is at Tha Deua KM4.

BY LAND

There is an overland overnight bus running from Hanoi to Vientiane priced at $27 and taking as many hours. The scenery on this route is drab, and in any case most of it is at night, but the price is right.

Overland routes to Vientiane are common from Thailand: The access town to Laos is Nong Khai, a relaxed town along the Mekong with pleasant riverfront guesthouses and restaurants. Nong Khai offers a full range of accommodations, from the budget Mekong Guesthouse to the upscale Mekong Royal Holiday Inn. There are a few guesthouses in Nong Khai that handle Lao visas—some are routed via courier back to Bangkok, others go over the Mekong to Vientiane for approval, but mostly the information is faxed in and faxed back, and you can pick up the visa at the Friendship Bridge. To reach Nong Khai from Bangkok takes 12 hours by overnight train and costs $14 for a regular sleeper. You can also get there by

air-conditioned bus, or travel by air to Udon Thani and then take a bus. Thai bus companies run direct a/c luxury buses from Bangkok into Vientiane over the Friendship Bridge for around $20.

Roughly 60 percent of arrivals in Laos come overland at Nong Khai. There is a passenger ferry that crosses directly from Nong Khai to Tha Deua, but this is only for locals. Foreigners are required to cross a few kilometers from Nong Khai at the Friendship (Mittaphab) Bridge, with a link to Tha Naleng. From the Thai side, you can reach the bridge by *tuktuk* for $1 a person, and then take a minibus across the bridge for $.50. At the Lao side of the bridge, you must change transport; there's direct bus and taxi service from the Lao side into Vientiane, a distance of about 20 kilometers. The cost is about $2 for a whole jumbo. A fleet of metered taxis sits at the Lao immigration side of the bridge waiting for customers for the Vientiane run. Traffic moves on the left in Thailand, on the right in Laos. This must have posed an interesting design problem for the bridge engineers. The resolution: bridge traffic moves on the left.

Thai Immigration and Customs is at the south end of the bridge; Lao Immigration and Customs is at the north end, at Tha Naleng. Immigration checkpoints are open every day 0800–1730, with a small "overtime" service fee charged 1200–1400 and on Saturday afternoon and Sunday. Immigration formalities are very simple—you get a Thai exit stamp, a Lao entry stamp, and a customs declaration form. As you come off the north end of the Friendship Bridge there's a crossover where left-handed traffic moves to the right-hand side of the road. Right-hand traffic from Laos approaching the bridge moves to the left-hand side.

Vientiane and Nong Khai are only 30 kilometers apart. Tour agents shuttle papers back and forth for visas and so on, and they can thus arrange advance railway tickets in Nong Khai (for sleepers to Bangkok) and have these sent via courier back to Vientiane. If you want to buy an advance rail ticket from Vientiane, go to a travel agent next to the Inter Hotel, but be warned that on Fridays, Saturdays, and Sundays, most trains are fully booked for sleepers. Chances are better for travel on weekdays. If you can't get a sleeper on the train, a good choice would be to buy a ticket (sold in Vientiane) from Udon Thani to Bangkok. Because that's a domestic flight, it's considerably cheaper. You take regular transport across the Friendship Bridge, and get to the Thai Airways office in Nong Khai; it runs a shuttle van direct to Udon Thani in time to catch the night flight to Bangkok.

Getting Around

There are no motorcycle-taxis in Vientiane—use jumbos for longer distances (either shared with Laotians on fixed runs, or hired individually), and *tuk-tuks* or cyclos for short distances. Vientiane is small: You can cover the ground by bicycle or on foot.

A number of metered taxis have been introduced in joint-venture operated fleets; these are replacing older, nonmetered taxis. Fare is 250 kip or 10 baht per kilometer, with a charge of $8 to the Friendship Bridge. Taxi hire is $60 for an entire day. Still in use, the older nonmetered taxis with no air-conditioning are much cheaper.

For car rentals, inquire through hotels. A car and driver from Le Parasol Blanc hotel is $40 a day in town (0800–1900) and $50 a day out of town.

Nissan Motors, on Settathirat near the fountain, has 80cc Yamaha scooters for $8 a day (0800–1700). Le Parasol Blanc rents motorcycles for $10 a day.

Motorcycle rentals run around $5 a day. There are several places to hire from; try the tailor shop near the Scandinavian Bakery at Nam Phu Square (it also rents bicycles). A place opposite Hua Guo GH rents Honda 250cc motocross bikes for $20 a day (reduced prices if it's a longer rental).

Bicycle rentals cost around $2 a day, though some hotels charge more. Costing $2 a day are rentals from Lao-Paris Hotel and Phimphone minimart, near Nam Phu; Kanchana Boutique, the handicraft shop opposite Ekalath Metropole Hotel; Inter Hotel; and Syri GH, renting to guests only. Le Parasol Blanc charges $4 a day. Chinese bikes, if you can get them, are sturdier.

If you're interested in buying a bike, Chinese and Taiwanese pseudo-mountain bikes are for sale near the central markets—they come complete with derailleurs and back rack for $150. An increasing number of Laotians are using them around Vientiane.

Tour Agents

Because of logistical problems, some travelers prefer to use the services of travel agents, but this increases prices considerably.

Getting Away

There are flights from Vientiane to Muang Sai for $49 (one-way); Luang Namtha, $57; Phonsavan (Xieng Khuang, Plain of Jars), $32; Luang Prabang, $40; Ban Huay Sai, $64; Thakhek, $49; Savannakhet, $54; Saravan, $86; and Pakse, $95. Frequency varies from daily to weekly. Flights to other locations may be available—check with Lao Airlines. Return fares are double one-way fares.

The bus terminal near the Morning Market (Talad Sao) runs a frequent service south to Tha Deua and points in and around Vientiane Prefecture; north to Thalat (Nam Ngum Dam), Vangvieng, Kasi and Luang Prabang; and to Thakhek. Another bus station out by That Luang Market has some buses running to the far south, including departure to Savannakhet (takes 12 hours, departs 0530, costs $11), and Pakse (18 hours, overnight trip, costs $14). There may be cargo boats to

Savannakhet. You can take a cargo boat from Vientiane about halfway to Luang Prabang; from the stopping point, you will have to hire a long-tail speedboat to complete the run to Luang Prabang.

Leaving Laos

For information on flight arrivals and departures, call tel. 21/212066. International departure tax is $5. Get rid of all Laotian kip notes before leaving—the currency is useless outside Laos. Use Thai baht for last-minute money needs. Export of antiques and Buddha images from Laos is strictly forbidden.

Visa Shopping

A **Vietnamese** visa is obtainable only through agents (unless you're applying with an invitation) and requires three working days. Costs range $110–150, depending on which agent you deal with. Telex to Vietnam is said to be expensive, but that doesn't account for the $100 markup over the cost of the same visa in Bangkok. If you're applying directly for an invitation visa, the visa section is in a building east of the embassy along That Luang Boulevard.

If flying into Cambodia, you don't need a visa; you can get one on arrival at the airport. If you want to play it safe, the embassy in Vientiane issues a one-month **Cambodian** visa for $20 in one day. You need three photos. The embassy is open 0730–1130 and 1400–1700, plus Saturday 0730–1130.

A **Thai** visa runs 400 baht or $16 for a 60-day tourist visa; 500 baht or $20 for a 90-day nonimmigrant visa. A visa for **Myanmar** (Burma) costs $20; you apply yourself. A 30-day **Chinese** visa costs $20 and gives you two months' leeway to get there; it's issued in four working days. It's worth mentioning that **Mongolian** visas are readily dispensed in Laos, though they may start running immediately.

Excursions from Vientiane

Check a map of Laos and you'll find three areas called "Vientiane." They are Vientiane City, Vientiane Prefecture, and Vientiane Province. The following excursions can be mounted as day trips from Vientiane or included in onward trips toward Vangvieng or points north.

East of Vientiane

About 25 kilometers east of Vientiane and three kilometers east of the Friendship Bridge on the banks of the Mekong is **Buddha Park,** also known as Wat Xieng Khuan. Here you'll find bizarre reinforced concrete statues of Buddhist and Hindu deities and mythological figures. You can crawl around inside a 3-D representation of hell—scramble to the top for an overview of the kitsch. The park was built in the 1950s by eccentric monk Bunleua Surirat, who had a large following in Laos and northeast Thailand. When the Pathet Lao moved into Vientiane in 1975, the monk repaired across the Mekong, where—with the help of donations—he built a bigger, even wilder version of concrete kitsch at Wat Khaek in Nong Khai, Thailand. Since the monk had abandoned the original site, the Lao authorities opened it as a public park. You can get there by jumbo from Vientiane or on a rented motorcycle.

Back past the Friendship Bridge is another tasteless theme park—the **National Ethnic Cultural Park.** Here the concrete kitsch consists of dinosaurs. The place is a combination of minizoo and ethnic museum of traditional housing. There are sometimes live performances of song and dance at an outdoor theater here.

North of Vientiane

About 90 kilometers north of Vientiane is Nam Ngum Reservoir. You can make a round-trip or overnight trip up Route 13 north to Phon Hong, turning right to Nam Ngum Reservoir, and then coming back along scenic Route 10 to Vientiane. Options include renting your own motorcycle, hiring a car and driver, or taking local buses. Taxis charge about $30 round-trip to the lake. A regular bus departs early from

Vientiane's Morning Market Station direct to Nam Ngum Dam; otherwise, there are five buses a day running to Ban Thalat, from where you can take a pickup to the dam.

If you have your own transport, there are a few picnic stops along the way to Nam Ngum on Route 13. Past KM16 there's a turnoff leading to **Khu Kana Falls,** about 10 kilometers along a gravel road. Two other picnic spots are **Tat Son,** with a turnoff at about KM22 and a 15-kilometer journey down a dirt road, and **Nam Suang rapids and waterfall** off KM40. The falls are impressive only during the rainy season. North of that, at KM52, is a market where Hmong people sometimes visit. At about 65 kilometers from Vientiane is Phon Hong; turn right at Phon Hong, and there's another market at **Ban Thalat,** selling forest animals such as deer, rodents, and spiny anteaters (pangolins). There's no accommodation at Ban Thalat, but if you head east across a narrow bridge, you'll find the **Electricity of Laos Guesthouse** (sign in Lao only) with doubles for $7—this place was built for foreigners working on the dam at Nam Ngum Reservoir.

South of Nam Ngum Reservoir, on Route 10 back to Vientiane, you can make a detour. About two kilometers south of Ban Khoun, turn east and go about 400 meters to a **Zoological Gardens.** There is a small collection of species here, including the Asiatic jackal and the palm civet. Continue south, and about five kilometers before the junction of Route 10 and Route 13, there's a turnoff to **Houei Nhang Forest Reserve,** open daily –1700, with a nature trail leading in from the parking lot. The trail is a leisurely two-hour loop, with points of interest—mainly plant and insect life—explained by a guide.

Nam Ngum Reservoir

East of Ban Thalat you cross a narrow bridge and roll into **Ban Nakheun,** with a dock, a few hotels, and a smattering of seafood restaurants. This is the largest settlement on the banks of the reservoir. Not far to the south is Nam Ngum Dam, which dams the Ngum River. The dam is the pride of the nation: The 150-megawatt hydroelectric plant provides much of the electricity for the Vientiane Valley, and power exported to Thailand is an important source of foreign exchange. Thailand buys power via high-voltage lines stretching as far across the Mekong as Udon Thani.

Nam Ngum Reservoir is home to the strangest loggers in the world. They log *underwater.* The forested hillsides here were intentionally flooded to create a lake. It was not until much later that Laotians realized the value of the drowned hardwood trees. After determining that submergence underwater had no harmful effect on the quality of the timber, a Thai-Lao joint venture figured out a system for retrieving the wood. Barges scout the lake's surface, divers locate the lumber, then an underwater hydraulic chainsaw is lowered, sometimes to a depth of 25 meters. The diver cuts the tree, and the log is delivered to the surface with a hook and a winch. Slow and painstaking, but in Laos there's no particular rush. The logging operation is a fair way out from Ban Nakheun—you have to hire a boat for 3–4 hours to get there and back.

Countless small islands dot the reservoir. You can arrange a scenic cruise, but you'll have to bargain hard with the boatmen. Fishing, swimming, and picnicking are the major Nam Ngum pursuits. Among the islands are the **Island of the Men** and the **Island of the Women,** where reeducation camps once were. In 1975 the Pathet Lao rounded up prostitutes and petty criminals in Vientiane and banished them to a 15-year reeducation stint here.

For accommodations at Ban Nakheun, there's a floating hotel (actually a converted barge) with 10 rooms for $13 each; there's a restaurant upstairs. This is a peculiar kind of naval architecture: The original hull has been overbuilt and is supported by pontoons. Next door is a floating restaurant with fresh fish below deck. There are half a dozen seafood restaurants in the vicinity. About 15 minutes away by boat, on **Don Dok Khonkham Island,** is a great two-story mansion with $7 rooms. This family-run place has its own small restaurant, but you might think about taking supplies out if planning to stay a couple of days.

Lao Pako Resort

Something of a groundbreaker in this neck of the woods is Lao Pako ecoresort, on the banks of the Nam Ngum River about 50 kilometers from Vientiane. It was built and is operated by a German couple and is popular with expatriates on weekends and holidays. Lao Pako offers "an environmentally friendly experience." You can river raft, take boat tours, visit local villages, or just relax and unwind. The place is self-sufficient, with its own restaurant and bar. Low-rise building construction is almost entirely from native materials using local techniques—with built-in European creature comforts. Access to Lao Pako is via the town of Som Sa Mai; from there it's about 25 minutes by local boat to the resort. Accommodation ranges from $3 dormitory beds to $15 private bungalows. Inquire at Burapha agency in Vientiane for bookings (14 Fa Ngum Rd.).

Vangvieng

On the road to Luang Prabang is Vangvieng, a picturesque area with karst formations, caves, and waterfalls. Although it is 160 kilometers north of Vientiane, Vangvieng lies in Vientiane Province. The Vangvieng area is inhabited by Hmong and Yao tribespeople. Vangvieng has ballooned as a backpacker destination, with other species of tourists starting to lock on. Because land prices have been pushed up in the "tourist" area, locals have decamped to a satellite village a few kilometers north. The markets and the bus station have moved to this vicinity.

Vangvieng has shot to prominence as an adventure sports mecca. Activities include caving, kayaking, tubing (or combinations of those three sports), mountain biking, rock-climbing on karst, and hilltribe trekking. In the wet season, rafting can be added to the list. Otherwise, the main activity in Vangvieng is hanging out by the river with a beer and watching the sun go down.

CAVING

There are more than 30 caves in the Vangvieng area—varying from small to very large and deep. More will surely be discovered. You need a powerful flashlight to explore (locals use burning bundles of brush to illuminate the caves). Some caves are hazardous: You stand a chance of getting lost inside, in which case you're best having a guide along.

Poukham Cave

If you cross the temporary bamboo bridge near the Thavansouk Hotel, you can walk or bicycle about six kilometers out to Poukham Cave. You pass pretty rural countryside, and there are several turnoffs en route leading to other caves, but the jewel is Poukham. Its interior is amazing: a huge cavern where shafts of light focus on a reclining Buddha statue sheltered within. Near the entrance to this area is a watering hole that is excellent for swimming or for diving: Although it appears to be small, it is very deep.

Tham Chang

An easy cave to get to from Vangvieng is Tham Chang, about two kilometers to the southeast of the town, accessible by a foot trail over a bridge past Vangvieng Resort Hotel. These caves are illuminated, and there's an entry fee. Nearby is an excellent swimming hole with crystal-clear water.

Tham Pou Kham Caves

About seven kilometers to the northwest of Vangvieng are Tham Pou Kham Caves. You can motor farther afield 15 kilometers up Route 13 to Ban Kokxian; west of this village is a series of small caves, including **Tham Xang** and **Tham Hoisung.** The karst scenery here is striking. The caves are hard to find: You might want to take a guide with you—ask around in Vangvieng. Watch out for leeches.

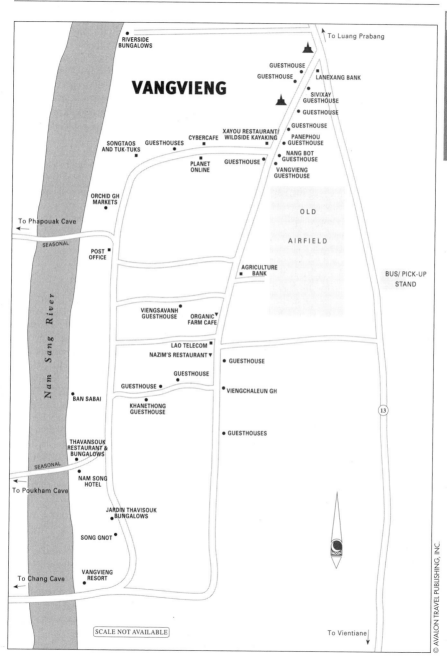

© AVALON TRAVEL PUBLISHING, INC.

KAYAKING THE SONG RIVER

Several outfits in Vangvieng run kayaking day trips on the Nam Song River. An outfit called Wildside, operating from the Xayoh Pub, uses inflatable kayaks: Cost for the day trip is $10. Other outfits have similar charges. The day trip is highly recommended: You get drenched, you get thrown around, you get lost in the dark—and you'll have a great time, prompted by the wacky antics of the guides. An inflatable kayak seats two (singles are available): The inflatables and passengers are piled onto a *songtao* and trucked 12 kilometers upstream, where you launch. Guides ride in fiberglass whitewater kayaks to carry out minor rescue maneuvers if called for.

You encounter mild rapids on this trip, which involves stops to hike and explore some terrific caves. The first one bores straight through a mountainside—you scramble right through the other side. The locals apparently use this as a shortcut when transporting logs. Reached farther downstream is Tham Nang Savanh, a cave that involves kayaking in (wet season) or swimming in (dry season), then clawing your way until you surface in a massive cavern. The guide here snaps on a powerful flashlight to pick out strange limestone formations high on the ceiling. This clammy cave was one of many where Lao people sought sanctuary from devastating aerial bombardment by the Americans during the 1970s.

In the rainy season, when the Nam Song runs faster, Wildside mounts rafting trips. Wildside also runs multiday camping trips with a mix of activities (kayaking, caving, trekking) and has pioneered rock-climbing on the karst cliffs around Vangvieng.

TUBING

Numerous places in Vangvieng rent inner tubes, along with a three-wheeler ride three kilometers upstream on the Nam Song to the put-in point. Ask at the rental place for a kayak dry bag to keep camera and valuables (money) high and dry. The put-in point is Phoudindeng, where a mulberry farm runs an engrossing restaurant serving mulberry tea, mulberry dishes, and mulberry wine. Load up with a few drinks and launch your tube to begin a pleasant 2–3 hours of floating past villages where women are washing clothes, and kids and water buffalo happily splash around. You can stop for a rest or picnic en route. Several tubers can lock together on the water to make a single large vessel. Turn off your mind, relax, and float downstream: Various substances are offered along the way by locals to make your trip a pleasant one. At the other end, tubers all congregate at small riverside bars with bamboo shelters and deck chairs to drink beer and party. You can reach this part of the river on foot from Vangvieng—a great place to watch the sunset.

PRACTICALITIES
Accommodations

It seems that every second house in Vangvieng is a guesthouse, restaurant, or tour-guide office—or is going to become one of these three. There are more than 50 guesthouses in Vangvieng. Places such as the **Siripangna GH**, **Chanthala GH,** and **Sivixay GH** all charge $5 a room. A good room with bath and fan would run about $10. Although there are many guesthouses around town and tucked down side streets, the ones with real atmosphere are places close to the Nam Song River. Along the river, from north to south, are the following. **Riverside Bungalows,** tel. 020/5523426, has 15 bungalows, ranging from $5 (basic), $5–9 (fan with bath), and $8–12 (a/c with bath). **Vangvieng Orchid GH,** tel. 020/511172, is a large concrete structure with a dozen rooms facing the river with balconies—the other rooms face away from the river. Rooms are a bargain at $5 each. The **Ban Sabai** is connected with Wildside and has superior rooms at $25–35. To the south end of Vangvieng, a well-run guesthouse with good restaurant is **Thavansouk GH,** with bungalow accommodation ranging $10–35 for a double. Right opposite is **Nam Song Resort,** charging $30 a double: This place seems largely derelict for some reason. Farther south is **Jardin Thavisouk Bungalows,** with spotty bungalow accommodation for $9; close by is **Song Gnot Guesthouse. Vangvieng Resort,** the first resort hotel in these parts, has fallen on hard times: Room charges have plummeted to $10 a bungalow and the place appears derelict.

Food

There are a number of fine places to dine in Vangvieng. For great river views, try the **Sunset Restaurant,** attached to Thavansouk Guesthouse. The main north-south strip of Vangvieng has a string of restaurants offering pizza and blaring DVD movies at night; guests relax on cushions—or lie down. For excellent vegetarian fare, try the **Organic Farm Café,** which is a branch of the mulberry farm: This place offers dishes such as Lao salads and soups, and mulberry pancakes. **Phoudindeng Mulberry Farm,** three kilometers north of town, is a great place to dine, with vegetarian dishes and odd brews such as mulberry green tea.

Services and Information

Though a village, Vangvieng is packed with tourists. So there are several banks that will actually change traveler's checks, and there are a number of cybercafés.

TRANSPORTATION

Getting Around

Bicycle rentals are easily found in town. You can also find mountain bikes. Honda motorcycles can be rented for $5 a day. Three-wheelers and *songtaos* are the common method for venturing farther afield from Vangvieng.

Getting There and Away

One of the reasons that Vangvieng's tourist traffic has ballooned is that it is the perfect spot to break up the long road trip between Vientiane and Luang Prabang (or vice versa). Vientiane to Vangvieng is about four hours by bus or pickup; from Vangvieng to Luang Prabang, allow six hours. There are a number of departures daily on these routes—it's best to plan on starting early in the morning. You can also rent your own motorcycle in Vientiane for the trip to Vangvieng (there were no motorcycle rentals available in Luang Prabang at the time of writing). Another (slow) approach to Vangvieng is to hire a boat at Nam Ngum Dam and then cross to the northern tip of the reservoir, where you can transfer to road transport. Buses or pickups arriving in Vangvieng touch down at the edge of the abandoned airfield to the west of town. From there you can either walk the remaining two kilometers into town or take a three-wheeler.

Southern Laos

Vientiane is the hub for routes leading to and from southern Laos. You can get around on your own using the express buses from Vientiane: Overnight buses ply long routes for very reasonable fares. There are a number of border crossings into Vietnam or Thailand operated by bus companies. If you prefer to go on a tour (much more expensive) through one of the agencies in Vientiane, make sure you know exactly what's included and what isn't. Usually the airfares, ground transport, and guide are included. Another option is to arrange a tour once you're on the spot in, say, Pakse or Savannakhet. Jeep rentals range $25–50 a day, including driver;

guides are $5–10 a day. Described in the following section are routes out of Vientiane that eventually lead to southern border crossings with Thailand, Vietnam, or Cambodia.

ROUTE 8 TO VINH

Between Paksane and Thakhek lies Route 8, which turns off northeast, snaking toward the Vietnamese border. For the moment, paperwork at the Cau Treo border post seems easygoing. You can cross here at Keo Nua Pass and carry on to the concrete nightmare of Vinh. It's a sort of shortcut to Hanoi, because you could clip straight through from Thailand, streak past Thakhek, hurdle Keo Nua Pass, and rumble into Vinh, on the route to Hanoi.

In theory, you can have breakfast in Vientiane and dinner in Vinh if all goes well. Take a bus from Vientiane to Paksane and Lak Sao (eight hours), and then get a jumbo for the last 1.5-hour haul to the Cau Treo border, about 40 kilometers away. From the Lao side, walk 15 minutes to the Vietnamese side, fill in papers, pay a $2 levy, and thumb a lift—you should make it to Vinh by nightfall.

For those in less of a hurry, **Lak Sao,** along Highway 8, is the only sizable town of the area. It may have one sight of interest: the zoo. Lak Sao sits on the edge of **Nakai Nam Theun forest reserve,** which (along with Vietnam's Vu Quang reserve) is gaining a reputation as something of a lost world. The dense wet evergreen forest has yielded some remarkable discoveries of mammalian species long thought extinct. Some unusual species may be on view at Lak Sao Zoo, including the extremely rare Owston's palm civet, a sleek marsupial-like animal with distinctive dark and light bands across its body.

THAKHEK AND KHAMMOUAN PLATEAU

Thakhek was founded in 1911 as a French outpost. Its old name is Khammouan. There's not a lot to see around Thakhek, but the town is the gateway to the spectacular karst scenery of the Khammouan Plateau. Seven kilometers south of town is **Wat Sikhotaboun,** built on the banks of the Mekong by King Chao Anou in the 19th century. It was restored in 1956, and a large wall was thrown up around it in 1970 by King Sisavang Vatthana. Eight kilometers north of Thakhek is **"the Great Wall,"** a 15-kilometer stretch of rocky wall constructed by a 9th-century kingdom.

About 50 kilometers to the east of Thakhek on Route 12, near the town of Mahaxai, are striking limestone formations accessible by boat along the Xe Bang Fai River. The Khammouan Plateau is replete with karst-limestone landscapes, including its own "stone forest" similar in appearance to the famous one near Kunming in China's Yunnan province. Numerous caves lie in this area. Because of that large concentration of karst, the Khammouan Plateau is a prime candidate for adventure sports: rafting, kayaking, caving, and climbing. But with little tourism infrastructure, this will have to wait. The Hinboun River has cut a path through rugged limestone mountains, at times with sheer-sided gorges with 400-meter cliffs on both sides. This is all set in pristine forest with a labyrinth of cave networks.

One way into Khammouan is to turn off Route 13 at Vieng Kham, which lies between Paksane and Thakek. Take a *songtao* for a few hours to get to Khoun Kham, and another *songtao* to reach a tiny ecolodge called Sala Hinboun, which lies inside the Phou Hinboun NBCA. Sala Hinboun is right by the Hinboun River—from the lodge you can hire a wooden boat to proceed through pristine forest to spectacular **Khonglor Cave.** You will need headlamps to see this wonder. The cave is very deep. Getting there is half the fun—this trip will take most of the day, going through stunning scenery. Wildside Asia mounts a four-day trip to this area. There is apparently an ancient temple in a hidden valley that is accessible only by passing through a swimming cave. The temple is a mystery and is yet to be surveyed by archaeologists.

The Thais would like to develop the Khammouan Plateau as an access point to Vietnam. There's been talk of building a bridge over the Mekong from Nakhon Phanom to Thakhek, and then improving the road to connect Thakhek to Vinh in Vietnam. Thakhek is only 240 kilometers from Vinh along Route 8, compared with the 540-kilometer journey from Savannakhet to Danang along Route 9. The port of Cua Lo near Vinh, however, can carry ships of only 3,000–5,000 tons, whereas shipping at Danang can take 15,000–20,000 tons. Also on the drawing board was a hydroelectric plant at Thakhek to tap the Mekong.

There are several guesthouses in Thakhek, and more under renovation in anticipation of increasing trade. Ferries across the Mekong to the Thai town of Nakhon Phanom operate frequently during the day. You can reach Thakhek by road from Vientiane in 7–9 hours.

SAVANNAKHET

Savannakhet is a trading town of 45,000. There is very little to see here. Most people visit the place because it happens to be on the way, or gets in the way. Recently, Savannakhet has found itself in the way quite a lot, as it's a key town on a fast overland route from Thailand through Laos to the Lao Bao border crossing into Vietnam. Chinese- and Vietnamese-made goods stream across the Mekong to Thailand from Savannakhet; trucks loaded with lumber from Khammouan province bank up for kilometers on the outskirts of town; from Savannakhet, the lumber moves to Thailand or Vietnam. More activity can be seen at the well-stocked central market in the northeast part of town.

Trading in Laos in the French colonial era was largely in the hands of resident Chinese and Vietnamese, which explains the yellow Catholic church and the Chinese temple in town. These communities were disrupted in 1975, when many residents fled across the Mekong. Since then, a number have returned. There are now large Chinese and Vietnamese trading communities and ornate Chinese-financed hotels; the Chinese school is said to be the best in town.

North of Savannakhet is the top sacred site of the area: **That Ing Hang.** The 16th-century Lao-style stupa is nine meters high and was most likely built at around the same time as Vientiane's That Luang. Some resident monks live in temple buildings nearby. To get there, go along Route 13 north for 12 kilometers, then turn east for three kilometers.

There's a Jurassic-period site, about 120 kilometers east of Savannakhet, where a French-Lao team is digging for dinosaur bones. The results of these excavations may show up in a museum in Savannakhet.

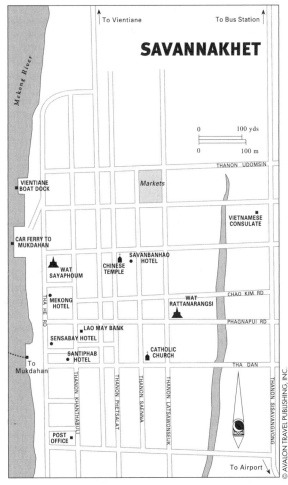

SAVANNAKHET

Accommodations and Food

Savannakhet is well supplied compared to other provincial capitals. It has 24-hour electricity, cable TV, and foreign newspapers in hotel lobbies. There are a dozen hotels in and around the town, including the 47-room, Chinese-run **Nanhai Hotel.** Toward the river are three cheaper hotels: the **Sensabay, Santiphab,** and **Mekong,** with rooms for $4 fan and $7 a/c. Near the post office is the **Phome Vilay Guesthouse** with rooms for $4. In town is the **Savanbanhao Hotel,** which houses the head office for Savannakhet Tourism and charges $7–14. To the northeast of town is **Phone Praseuth Hotel** with rooms for $20, complete with all creature comforts; across the street is a full-sized swimming pool with a $1 entry fee. Apart from hotel restaurants and local noodlehouses, the eating options are slim. The one restaurant of note is **Rung Tip,** serving Lao and Thai dishes. The restaurant has a disco too.

Transportation

By road there are connections during the dry season from Vientiane to Savannakhet (12 hours), and from there to Pakse (six hours). An overnight cargo boat plies the route from Vientiane to Savannakhet with irregular departures in the rainy season only (May–November).

Group tours generally fly into Savannakhet, go overland to Pakse, and fly back to Vientiane from Pakse—or the reverse. There are daily one-hour flights from Vientiane to Savannakhet on Yun-7 turboprops, costing $54 one-way. On Sunday, the same flight continues to Saravan. Three days a week, the flight goes to Pakse first, stopping at Savannakhet on the route back to Vientiane.

Thai Border Crossing

You might want to consider flying to Savannakhet, exploring the south, and exiting to Thailand from either Savannakhet or Pakse. Or exit to Vietnam from Savannakhet via the Lao Bao border to Dong Ha. For entry or exit here, your paperwork must be in order. Some group tours approach Savannakhet directly from Thailand. There is frequent ferry service between Savannakhet and Mukdahan on weekdays, and half-day on Saturday. On the Thai side, Thai immigration issues an entry stamp for Thailand valid for 30 days.

SAVANNAKHET TO LAO BAO

East of Savannakhet along Route 9 is a road exit to Vietnam via the Lao Bao border. The Vietnamese Consulate in Savannakhet may issue visas valid for this crossing; once you have a Vietnamese visa, you must also fix up Lao paperwork to travel this route and exit at Lao Bao—try Savannakhet Tourism for the stamps. From the reverse direction, on the Vietnam side, Lao visas valid for Lao Bao entry are issued at the Lao Consulate in Danang. At the time of writing, such visas were available only in Danang, not from the Lao visa offices in Hanoi or Saigon. Route 9 is a rough road, and it may be difficult to traverse during the May–November rainy season. Travelers have reported some trouble with Lao and Vietnamese border officials at Lao Bao, including demands for large U.S. bills. A wait of several hours at the border is not uncommon. Presumably the border guards are used to making deals, as this is a smuggling point for rare animals, lumber, and motorcycles from Laos to Vietnam.

Savannakhet to Dong Ha is 350 kilometers. It's 170 kilometers from Savannakhet to Xepon, and 80 kilometers more to Lao Bao; from there, it's 100 kilometers to Dong Ha. There is international bus service running several times a week from Savannakhet to Danang—it costs $12 from the bus station (in the reverse direction it costs $33). Assuming you have transport lined up on the Vietnamese side, you can cover the route in 12 hours of driving. A chartered vehicle from Savannakhet to Lao Bao costs a minimum $150. You can take a local bus as far as Xepon, but transport after that is uncertain. On the Vietnamese side, from Dong Ha it's 75 kilometers—or 1.5 hours of driving—to Hué. On both the Lao and Vietnamese sides of Route 9 are remnants of the Vietnam War because of proximity to the former DMZ. From the town of Xepon, 170 kilometers to the east of Savannakhet, you can arrange visits to parts of the Ho Chi Minh Trail, if you like looking at scrap metal and downed planes. In the Xepon District is a village on the roadside with the skeleton of a U.S. Army helicopter; next to it is a large stone statue of Vietnamese and Pathet Lao soldiers advancing with AK-47s. Many of the houses in the area are partly built of scrap metal; bomb shells and spent fuel canisters still litter the landscape.

Another 80 kilometers from Xepon brings you to the border at Lao Bao; from there it's about 100 kilometers east to Dong Ha. About 20 kilometers east of the Lao Bao border is the former battlefield of Khe Sanh, which technically requires a Vietnamese permit to visit. Tours in the DMZ can be arranged in Dong Ha through Quang Tri Tourism.

THE BOLOVENS PLATEAU

The scenic Bolovens Plateau sits astride the border of Saravan and Champassak provinces; the main towns are Paksong and Saravan. The plateau is home to such obscure southern Laos ethnic groups as the Alak, Katu, Suay, Tahoy, Ngai, and Suk. Its climate and red volcanic soil are ideal for the growing of cardamom, arabica coffee, and tea—crops first introduced by the French in the 1920s and 1930s. Durian and other fruit trees also fare well here. You can reach the plateau by road from the towns of Saravan or Pakse, or by driving between the two. You can travel overland from Savannakhet to Saravan, and then make your way to Paksong and eventually Pakse. With stops, this takes several days. Although Savannakhet to Pakse on the direct road is only 250 kilometers, roads in the region are atrocious—full of broken bitumen and potholes. A 4WD vehicle is therefore preferable. Saravan to Paksong is about 4–5 hours; from there it's 2–3 hours to Pakse.

Saravan

Like a number of towns on the Bolovens Plateau, Saravan was leveled during the Vietnam War, and the only reminder of French colonial influence is the post office. Because the town is being reconstructed, guesthouses are hard to come by. The lowlight of Saravan is its daily market, which is stocked with wildlife to be smuggled across the border into Thailand—destined for the cooking pot or Chinese medicine store, or sold to animal collectors and foreign zoos. Thailand turns a blind eye to this profitable and illicit trade in endangered species. Fauna on sale in Saravan includes pythons, wild pigs, mynah birds, and monkeys; less offensive is a great variety of jungle fruit and vegetables. At Lake Bua, 14 kilometers east of town, is a crocodile breeding area. There's an airfield at Saravan, with weekly flights from Vientiane via Savannakhet on Sunday. One-way fare to Saravan from Vientiane is $86, from Savannakhet, $32.

Tha Teng

On the road between Saravan and Paksong you can visit several Alak and Katu villages. At roughly the midway point on this route lies the village of Tha Teng, with several Alak villages close by. The Alak live in thatched huts; under rice storage huts they store wooden coffins for each member of the household. Both Alak and Tahoy shamans in this area perform buffalo sacrifices on special occasions.

Paksong

Paksong is a small market town about 60 kilometers northeast of Pakse, originally a French hill resort and favored for its mild climate. The area is known for its fruit and vegetables. It takes 2–3 hours to get there from Pakse depending on the type of vehicle, so day-tripping from Pakse is possible. Another way of reaching Paksong is to take a share-taxi from KM2 outside Pakse, costing about $4 one-way. On this route you gain elevation on a dirt road, driving past fruit orchards, tea and coffee plantations, stands of teak, and numerous species of flowers. At higher elevations on the Bolovens Plateau you'll see grazing cattle.

A few kilometers west of Paksong are **Tadphan Falls,** with a 130-meter drop, and **Tat Lo Falls,** with a 10-meter cascade. Right near Tat Lo Falls is accommodation at **Tat Lo Resort** in chalets and bungalows, plus an open-air dining room and sitting area. About 15 rooms are available, costing $15–20 a night, with a few at $30 overlooking the falls. The resort is operated by Sodetour; you can book through the office in Pakse. Swimming in the deep pool at the base of Tat Lo Falls is safe. The resort lodge arranges elephant rides, usually an hour's worth, but a longer ride can be arranged to a local Alak village.

PAKSE

Pakse, on the banks of the Mekong, is the main town of southern Laos and the capital of Champassak province. The area had strong links with the Khmer Empire through the centuries. The town was established by the French as an administrative post in 1905, and it is still a small place, with a population of around 50,000. More refugees fled Champassak during the post-1975 era than from other Lao provinces because it developed a reputation for repressive and Stalinist policies. Even viewing Thai television was banned. Today Pakse welcomes joint ventures and foreign tourists—though few reach southern Laos—and Lao refugees are welcomed back to their former homes.

One of the major activities around Pakse appears to be the transport of timber across the border to Ubon Ratchathani in Thailand. Although the Lao government sets a strict quota on logging, it seems Khmer logging companies take logs from Laos, haul them back to Cambodia, and sell them to Lao middlemen, who then sell them to Thai companies. Lacking sufficient manpower, the authorities in Pakse are said to be powerless in cracking down on this laundering of logs.

Pakse Market

Talad Dao Heuang, the fresh food market, lies at the east side of town, just off Route 13. Markets are the best places to people-watch, although it's more likely you will be the center of attention. While you're poking around, do some shopping yourself; you'll need supplies if heading off to Wat Phu or out of Pakse for a day trip. If you are on a bicycle or a hired

moto, you can make a good circuit out of the market trip: Drop in and see Boun Oum Palace first, continue to Talad Dao Heuang, then carry on south to the Japanese-funded bridge across the Mekong (great views), and return to Pakse westward along the road by the shores of the Mekong.

Champassak province is famed for its handwoven silks and cottons. Eleven kilometers northwest of Pakse (take the Russian bridge up Route 13) is **Saphay,** with a weaving marketplace. Saphay sits right on the Mekong, so it's a pleasant spot. Take a jumbo or sidecartaxi, or find a local with a motorcycle.

Boun Oum Palace

The rambling palace that dominates Pakse is sited on a prime piece of land overlooking the Sedon River. The building was confiscated in 1975; the authorities couldn't decide whether to turn the place into a socialist cultural center or a tourist hotel. In the end the tourists won: Thai contractors were allowed to renovate and run the place. The 60-room hotel has function rooms to handle 150 people, as well as a fitness center, sauna, and disco with karaoke. The interior has echoes of its original opulence, with teak fittings, tile floors, and a parquet-tiled ballroom.

The palace is definitely haunted and cries out for explanation, so here's the ghost story. Construction of the palace was begun in 1968 by the Prince of Champassak, Boun Oum, a descendant of the royal family that once ruled southern Laos as a separate kingdom. The prince led a guerrilla struggle against the Japanese in World War II and later served as prime minister in Vientiane. By the early 1960s, three princes—Boun Oum, Souphanouvong, and Souvanna Phouma—ruled jointly in Laos, but they were in effect locked in combat. Prince Boun Oum developed into a staunch anticommunist who battled the Pathet Lao.

Opinions about the character of Prince Boun Oum vary according to the source. Some thought he was cruel; by some accounts, he killed people who disagreed with him and appropriated peasant lands, including the land on

PAKSE

Sedon River

To Savannakhet

To Airport

FRENCH BRIDGE

RUSSIAN BRIDGE

JASMINE
ADAM INTERNET
CHAMPASSAK PALACE HOTEL
(FORMER BOUN OUM PALACE)

WAT LUANG
LAO CHALEUN
SOUKSAMLANE HOTEL
AUBERGE SALA CHAMPA
HOTEL PAKSE

WAT THAM FAY

CHAMPASAK PLAZA
SHOPPING CENTER

13

To Bus Station,
Champassak,
Paksong, Bolvens
Plateau, and
Saravan

SMALL BOAT HIRE
SODETOUR
CHURCH
POST OFFICE

TALAT DAO HEUANG
(MAIN MARKET)

0   200 yds
0   200 m

Mekong River

To
Mekong
Bridge

© AVALON TRAVEL PUBLISHING, INC.

which the palace was built. But he had his good points; he threw great parties at traditional festivals, where the rice wine flowed and he allowed himself to be the butt of ribald jokes. On one point, everyone—including the prince—agreed: He was a large, fat, ugly, overbearing aristocrat. The prince had a weakness for pretty women, whom he invited to sing during festivals. "Powerful Prince, you are enormously fat, you are ugly, you are old, and yet you ask me to speak to you of love," they would sing. And the prince would laugh loudly, and sing back through an intermediary, "You are right to say that, pretty maid. It's true that I am old and fat and ugly. But I am like a tough old elephant who will leave you ivory when it dies." Boun Oum Palace was constructed as a large harem—intended to house the ugly prince's many girlfriends.

In 1975, with the Pathet Lao about to take over, the prince fled Pakse with the "ivory" in tow: He departed in style for Thailand with

five elephants and a cavalcade of trucks reputed to contain priceless artifacts. He left behind only the unfinished palace. The prince died in Paris in 1980 at the age of 72. Under the relaxation of restrictions in Laos, his surviving sons and daughters have been invited back to visit.

Renovating the palace has given local authorities a few headaches. At the top of the central building, on the fifth level, is a small dome that commands a great view of town; it used to be a casino. The small concave ceiling of the dome bears elaborate frescoes of tigers, elephants hauling teak logs, and *Ramayana* figures. There have been a few changes—if you look closely, you'll see that the royal mahouts riding the elephants have been given hammers and hard hats. Elsewhere in the palace, hammer-and-sickle emblems were painted over royal crests; after Laos dropped Marxism, the hammer-and-sickle emblems were themselves painted over, though there may be the odd one still left.

Accommodations

Rock-bottom accommodation costs $3 at places such as **Sabaidy GH,** which has dorm-type rooms in a pleasant atmosphere. Budget guesthouses such as the **Lao Chaleun** and **Lankham** charge $5 for fan rooms and $10 for rooms with bath. Hotels with more creature comforts such as the Chinese-managed **Sang Aroun Hotel** charge $15 and up for a room.

Recommended for its efficiency and service is the French-run six-story **Hotel Pakse,** tel. 31/212131, info@paksehotel.com. The 65 rooms here range from $14 economy to $19 superior up to $24 deluxe and $30 panorama (top-floor views). Prices include breakfast; the hotel has a good restaurant serving Lao, Thai, and Western food. Under Boun Oum, this hotel site was a cinema and casino—the hub of Pakse. It was totally renovated in 2003 to become the hotel.

On the main street in Pakse is **Auberge Sala Champa,** with 15 rooms for $20–30, bar and terrace, and advance-order dining. This is a former colonial French hotel and exudes an air of old Asia, but it is not the best value for money. Isolated on the southeast edge of town, near the stadium, is the **Champa Residence,** tel. 31/212120, which has a pleasant courtyard garden and its own dining room and gift shop. The 45 rooms are decorated with marble and teak and have satellite TV and hot water, and go for $30–35 a night.

The **Champassak Palace Hotel,** tel. 31/212263, palace@cscoms.com, was the former Boun Oum Palace. The hotel is overpriced and undermanaged (Vietnamese management—services are spotty), but it has history on its side—and a derelict charm. It's on the banks of the Sedon River, with 60 well-appointed rooms and suites (musty rooms in old wing and less musty rooms in new wing), all featuring a/c, TV, and cavernous bathrooms. Prices range $20–45.

Food

A fine place to dine is the **Hotel Pakse,** in the center of town. In this vicinity are a few small restaurants serving Chinese, Thai, or Viet-namese food. **Jasmin Restaurant,** east of the French Bridge, serves passable Indian dishes: There are other al fresco spots here, while if you continue eastward you'll find **Ketmany Restaurant,** serving Lao and Western food. **Adam Internet** is good for fresh juices.

Services

The **Tourism Authority of Champassak** is along the Sedon River, toward its confluence with the Mekong. The **BCEL bank** is just south of the French bridge. Several cybercafés are found in town: A good one is **Adam Internet,** on the main east-west road.

Getting There

Pakse Airport is a convenient two kilometers from town, over the old French metal bridge to the west. A ride into town in a jumbo should cost $2–3. A one-way Vientiane-Pakse ticket is $95—an expensive proposition if you double that for a round-trip. If you plan an exit from Pakse through Chong Mek to Thailand, you can save on the return airfare. There are intermittent flights on light aircraft from Pakse to Saravan, Savannakhet, Attapeu, and Muoang Khong.

You can reach Pakse by overnight VIP bus, which should be comfortable if it has the advertised 32 seats and hence lots of legroom—and the chance to catch some sleep. However, some unscrupulous operators will try to sell you short—and put you on a crowded bus with no legroom. Be sure to inspect the bus before you board, or it could be a rough trip. The VIP bus leaves Vientiane around 2000 and arrives Pakse at 0600, and costs $15. The VIP bus terminal in Pakse is downtown near the hospital.

Chong Mek Border Crossing: If your paperwork is in order, you can exit or enter Thailand from Pakse via Chong Mek. Pakse is far easier to reach by land from Thailand's Ubon Ratchathani than from Vientiane. You need a valid Lao visa to enter here. If entering Thailand without a visa, you'll get 15–30 days stamped into your passport.

To exit Pakse to Thailand, first take the bridge across the Mekong. On the other side you may have to walk several kilometers to find jumbos or *songtaos,* which park across a narrow bridge. Jumbo and *songtao* drivers ask for high prices to Chong Mek, so bargain hard. Chong Mek is 40 kilometers west of the Mekong, about an hour's drive in a *songtao* on a good road. The Lao side of the Chong Mek crossing is open 0730–1130 and 1330–1630; you can change kip to baht at an informal bank.

Once on the Thai side, you switch from driving on the right side to the left side of the road. It's 75 kilometers through Pibun to Ubon Ratchathani, about two hours by *songtao.* In contrast to Laos, Thailand has an excellent travel infrastructure: good roads, fast a/c buses, express trains with sleepers, and roving vendors in smart uniforms dispensing beer and seafood. From Ubon you can travel to other parts of Laos by bus; the train line runs westward to Korat and Bangkok.

If your timing is right, you can catch an overnight train from Ubon to Bangkok. There are three rapid trains in the late afternoon, taking 11 hours to cover the ground. There's also an afternoon plane from Ubon to Bangkok. You can make it all the way from Pakse to Bangkok overland in less than 24 hours for less than $20—including $14 for a sleeper from Ubon.

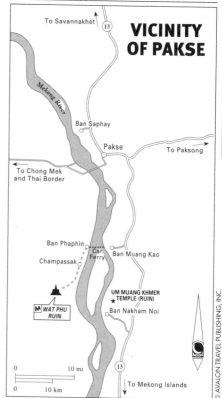

VICINITY OF PAKSE

To Savannakhet

Mekong River

Ban Saphay

Pakse

To Paksong

To Chong Mek and Thai Border

Ban Phaphin

Champassak

Car Ferry

Ban Muang Kao

WAT PHU RUIN

UM MUANG KHMER TEMPLE (RUIN)

Ban Nakham Noi

0   10 mi
0   10 km

To Mekong Islands

© AVALON TRAVEL PUBLISHING, INC.

Getting Around

You can easily cover Pakse on foot or by rented bicycle. Moto drivers are another option. Motorcycle sidecar-taxis take a maximum load of three passengers—two in the sidecar and one sitting behind the driver on the motorcycle. A moto or a sidecar-taxi will get you to Saphay weaving village. Car rentals can be arranged through hotels. You can also hire boats from Pakse for a day trip to Champassak or arrange a one-way boat to Champassak.

VICINITY OF PAKSE

The bus terminal is out of town to the east; at KM2 are share-taxis to Paksong and Saravan. Local transport to Paksong and Saravan can be slow, and accommodations in either place are limited or nonexistent. The other

land option is rented transport: Sodetour and Lane Xang Travel rent jeeps, fat-tired pickups, and minibuses at exorbitant prices—to the tune of $.50 per kilometer. You can use Pakse as a base for visiting the market town of Paksong or sites to the south, such as Wat Phu. In this direction, boat transport can be hired to go part way.

Um Muang Ruins

The Khmer ruins of Um Muang are 44 kilometers south of Pakse. There are two sanctuaries here built at roughly the same time as Wat Phu, plus an assortment of sandstone *nagas* and lingas. This minor site is dilapidated and moss-covered and not as impressive as Wat Phu, but it depends how you like your ruins—Um Muang gives you the thrill of discovery because the site has not been cleared of encroaching jungle. The ruins are approached from Ban Nakham Noi. You can get there by road from Pakse by turning at Ban Thang Beng, but the more interesting approach is to travel to Ban Nakham Noi by boat and hike in half an hour to the ruins. Local kids will act as guides on the jungle trail. You can either hire a boat from Pakse or pick up a local boat for about $14 round-trip from Ban Muang, the riverside village to the north. It might be possible to squeeze in a trip to both Wat Phu and Um Muang Ruins if you line up your transport the right way—both Um Muang and Champassak can be reached by boat.

About 27 kilometers east of Route 13 on the road to Attapeu is the village of Ban Phapho, where young elephants are trained for hauling hardwoods and rice, and for other hard labor. There are up to 90 pachyderms in the elephant school.

CHAMPASSAK AND WAT PHU

The ruins of Wat Phu, 42 kilometers south of Pakse, are reached via the village of Champassak. Wat Phu, an outpost of the Khmer Empire, is not as impressive as Angkor Wat in Cambodia or Khmer sites in Thailand. However, it makes for a great hourlong boat trip down the Mekong—which runs very wide here—and there's a good hike up a mountain to view the top sanctuary. Allow a full day for the excursion and a minimum of three hours at the site. It will take at least an hour to hike to the top and back.

Champassak

Champassak is an agricultural village strung for several kilometers along the banks of the Mekong. Prince Boun Oum began building another of his rambling mansions at the edge of town; it's unfinished and considerably more modest than the one in Pakse. In town are a couple of French–style houses, formerly owned by the prince's brothers. There are a handful of guesthouses and restaurants in Champassak, some with Mekong viewpoints.

Wat Phu Ruins

Wat Phu's history is sketchy. Apparently an outpost of the far-flung Khmer kingdom based in Angkor Wat, this "lost city" lay abandoned in the jungle until French explorer Francis Garnier stumbled across it in 1866. Unlike Angkor Wat, however, Wat Phu was never really "abandoned"—it continued as a place of worship through the centuries. Little is known about the history of the temple. Locals told Garnier that the temple had been built by "another race." Inscriptions found by archaeologists suggest the mountain was already an important place of worship in the 6th century when the Cham ruled the area. The temple complex appears to have been built in the 12th century—the handiwork of Khmer King Suryavarman II, who also initiated work on Angkor Wat. At some point, possibly in the late 13th century, the temple switched from Hindu to Buddhist; in the 14th century the Lao conquered the area.

The temple is the focus of thousands of Buddhist and Hindu pilgrims from Laos and northeast Thailand who converge here for a full moon festival in February every year. Pilgrims leave offerings and participate in football, boat racing, and boxing competitions, as well as singing and dancing. Water buffalo are sacrificed during the three-day festival; another buffalo sacrifice takes place in June to appease the earth spirit of Champassak.

At present the temple complex is in bad shape with collapsed walls and mossy blocks of stone scattered around. Encroaching vegetation and the ravages of unchecked monsoons are also evident. Since declaring the place a World Heritage Site in 2001, UNESCO has been involved in reconstruction of the complex; experts estimate the project will cost at least $6 million and take six years. The method of reconstruction is known as anastylosis—also used at Angkor Wat—which involves taking apart the main sanctuary and staircase, numbering the pieces, building a new concrete base, and reassembling the structures piece by piece. An underground drainage system would also be installed to counter the considerable damage of the annual monsoon.

The Wat Phu Temple complex is strewn up 1,400-meter-high sacred Mt. Phu. At the base of the mountain are two large reservoirs that collected rainwater to irrigate surrounding rice fields. There are two decayed wooden pavilions down this end, both of 20th-century vintage. The larger pavilion in the center was constructed for the Lao king to lodge in and to observe ceremonies. The second pavilion is now used to collect minimal entry fees (there are extra charges for still and video cameras); the site is officially open 0800–1630, but there are no fences.

Past the entry gate you proceed along a triumphal causeway once lined with *nagas,* lions, and other guardians—virtually nothing remains of these. Up ahead, there's a pair of sandstone ruins thought to have functioned as housing for pilgrims—women to the left, men to the right. The buildings are shells. The walls are still standing, but the roofs have collapsed, resulting in a jumble of sandstone blocks. You can make out some lintel decoration on the doorways.

From this point you start to climb a long, stone-laid slope, passing through a gateway with several *Plumeria* trees. *Plumeria rubra acutifolia,* a species of frangipani, is a tropical flower with a heavy fragrance also found in Vietnam and other parts of Asia and sometimes called the "temple tree." Although the frangipani blossom is the national flower of Laos (called *dok champa*), the tree originally comes from Central America; *Plumeria acutifolia* trees are found as far afield as Tahiti and Brazil.

Up the mountain is the main sanctuary, a small sandstone structure with the ruins of a library and a gallery attached. Bas-reliefs on the temple's columns and lintels depict major themes of Hindu mythology: the Churning of the Sea of Milk, scenes from the *Ramayana,* and the cosmic sleep of Vishnu. Behind the sanctuary, carved into a large boulder, is a Trimurti consisting of Brahma (at left), Shiva (standing at center), and Vishnu (kneeling at right). Other less-elaborate rock carvings in the area—those of a *naga,* elephant, and crocodile—may once have been associated with human sacrifice.

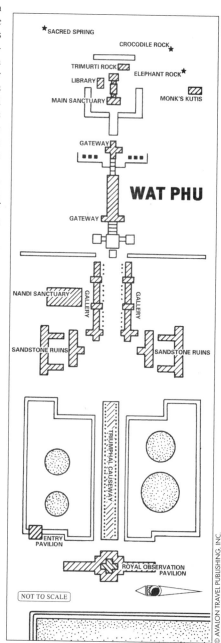

Behind the temple is a mountain cliff. A spring at the base of the cliff was channeled by a system of stone pipes to the inner sanctuary to anoint a sacred Shiva linga, or stone phallus. The sanctuary is now linga-less: The sculpted piece disappeared long ago. Water from the spring is considered sacred—or, at the very least, good luck—so Laotians sprinkle it on themselves. The top sanctuary affords serene views over the valley, which the few resident monks up this way have plenty of time to contemplate.

With a guide, it's possible to hike farther up Mt. Phu, itself perceived as a linga by the Khmers. Hiking to the top may require camping out overnight.

Getting There

There are several ways of reaching Wat Phu. The intermediate point to aim for is the village of Champassak, 34 kilometers south of Pakse; from there it's another eight kilometers to the ruins. Pakse to Champassak is downstream, so tour groups may take a rented boat on the outbound journey—1.25 hours downstream, half an hour longer upstream. At Champassak, tours rendezvous with a jeep that covers the last eight kilometers to the ruins. On the return trip, the jeep crosses the Mekong by small ferry at the village of Ban Phaphin, five kilometers north of Champassak, to the village of Ban Muang Kao; then you drive back to Pakse. Take picnic supplies (bananas, bread, bottled water) because there's very little in Champassak.

On your own, you can take a *songtao* to the river crossing near Champassak (or farther on to the ruins if you arrange it with the driver). You can hire a bicycle in Champassak for the last leg to the ruins. There's an irregular ferry service to Champassak. Consider staying in Champassak overnight to make the best of this trip.

MEKONG ISLANDS

At the southern tip of Laos, about 150 kilometers south of Pakse, the Mekong reaches a breadth of 14 kilometers—the greatest width of the river in its entire 4,200-kilometer course from Tibet to Vietnam. Swollen by tributaries,

the Mekong here splits to create a maze of channels; the area is known as the 4,000 Islands, or "Si Phan Don." The number of islets varies with water level, and this optimistic figure counts sandbars that appear during the dry season. The area has become a hot spot for travelers intent on resting up in a hammock for a couple of days—or even a week or more. Walking and bicycling are relaxing here, but swimming in the area cannot be recommended as there is a slight chance of picking up schistosomiasis, which is caused by tiny flatworms that burrow through the skin and enter the bloodstream. If that one sounds nasty, consider the fact that opisthorchiasis (liver flukes) may also be contracted from swimming in contaminated waters around Don Khong or from eating raw fish.

Khone Falls

The major attraction of the Mekong Islands is the spectacular set of cascades toward the Cambodian border. A 10-kilometer chain of cascades and rapids south of Don Khong is loosely referred to as Khone Falls. There are in fact two impressive falls in the area. Off Don Khone Island are **Khong Phapheng Falls,** among the largest in Southeast Asia. The falls are about 22 kilometers south of Muang Khong along Route 13. The falls can be viewed from several perilous vantage points just below Ban Thakho; watch local fishermen perform daring stunts on the rocks near the falls. To the west of Don Khone Island is **Li Phi Falls,** another roaring torrent. The best way to get there is to hire a small boat from Don Det or Ban Nakasang for a one-hour round-trip costing $6 or so. The boat goes through fast-flowing channels and requires a skilled boatman. Islands in this area are renowned for the cultivation of coconut, bamboo, kapok, and hardwoods. Another approach for viewing the falls is by foot on Don Khone Island: Walk westward past Wat Khone Tai.

Irrawaddy Dolphins

Rare freshwater Irrawaddy dolphins come upriver to spawn January–March; they're unable to pass the rapids, so the only place you might catch a glimpse of these rare mammals is at the

MEKONG ISLANDS

southern end of Don Khone Island. You can hire a boat here to reach offshore islands; viewing is best in the late afternoon. Don't get your hopes up, though: There are estimated to be fewer than 50 members of this endangered species left. The main habitat of the dolphin is the area above Stung Treng in Cambodia. The dolphin is threatened by indiscriminate use of explosives for fishing in Cambodia and by the use of gillnets in Laos. Dolphins are considered re-

incarnate beings, with many stories about dolphins coming to the rescue of fishermen and saving them from drowning or crocodile attacks. Thus Lao fishermen do not intentionally trap dolphins for food or sport, but if a dolphin becomes entangled in a net, the fisherman may be reluctant to cut it free because of the $20 cost of replacing the net. The net traps the dolphin underwater and it drowns. On the Cambodian side, where lawlessness prevails,

RUNNING THE MEKONG

By the time the river spat him out, Mick O'Shea was in very bad shape. After nine gruelling days of white-water kayaking in the Mekong gorges, he let down his guard, misjudged a set of rapids—and plunged straight into a "hole," where he suddenly found himself fighting for his life. Locked in a deadly spin cycle in the hole, he tried to cartwheel out—but he could not escape. Fearing that he would lose consciousness, he bailed out of the kayak and surfaced—but took a mouthful of water instead of air. Dazed and disoriented, he swirled along until he managed to latch onto a rock to regain some strength. But he was hypothermic in the frigid waters, and his kayak had been swept away—with all his camping supplies, food and photography records.

"I owe my life to a Tibetan family," says Mick. "Miraculously, there were a few huts by the side of the river. The grandmother who opened the door was astonished—but she realised I was in great distress. The family sat me down by the fire and gave me warm clothing and hot tea. If they hadn't been there, I don't know if I would have survived the night. I was shaking violently with hypothermia."

Next day, another stroke of luck: While hitching a ride with a truck, Mick sighted a tiny red dot in a canyon far below—his abandoned kayak. He retrieved the kayak, hooked up with his support team, and returned to thank the family who saved him. Then he launched back into the Mekong and was immediately flipped upside-down. "The Tibetan grandmother was screaming at this point, and praying and crying," says Mick. "She was convinced I was going to die."

The source of the Mekong lies at 5,224 meters in eastern Tibet. From this snowbound location, the river gathers momentum, roaring through the Mekong gorges—dropping more than 4,500 meters in elevation through Tibet and China (over a distance of some 1,800 kilometers) before turning tamer and more placid in Laos. "I figured the only chance of running the upper Mekong is in April, when the flow is lower," says O'Shea. But this means frigid waters and an unusual kayaking hazard—in the form of avalanches crashing into the river. Once inside the sheer-walled Mekong gorges, there is little way of scouting ahead for cascades, rapids, whirlpools, eddies—or waterfalls. And there may be no way out. "It was the scariest thing I've ever done," said Mick. "It pushed me to the absolute limit."

O'Shea took some crazy risks on the expedition. He was by himself in the Mekong gorges for a week with no support crew in sight. His sole link with the outside world was a satellite phone—but connections often failed because of the high walls of the gorges. He was riding along on doses of adrenaline—and sheer luck. Luck with reading the rapids, luck with officialdom. O'Shea had to wrangle with hard-nosed Chinese officials—intent on charging extortionate permit fees. There were shortfalls with funding from sponsors. And then there were high altitude and blizzards to deal with at the start. In the last decade, a number of expedition attempts have been made on sections of the Mekong gorges—but O'Shea became the first to power through the entire stretch, which cleared the way to run the entire Mekong from source to sea—a distance of 4,800 kilometers.

After five months of paddling, O'Shea finally reached the Mekong Delta in Vietnam—where he had to smuggle himself past Vietnamese authorities because he mistakenly took a branch of the Mekong that he did not have an official permit for. But he finally reached the sea—the end of the river, and the realization of a dream. The 29-year-old Australian expedition kayaker first laid eyes on the Mekong as a young backpacker: He returned to start the very first kayaking and rafting tours in Laos. Meanwhile, he was plotting a Mekong first descent—the project consumed two years of complex logistics and fund-raising. Based in Laos, O'Shea continues to pioneer new kayak routes in Asia as adventure and ecotourism developer for the company Wildside. Find out more from the man himself—you can read his Mekong first-descent expedition dispatches at www.wildside-asia.com.

fishermen use explosives, which are strictly banned in Laos. In an effort to halt this deplorable practice, the Lao government banned the import of fish from Cambodia.

French Relics

Seething Mekong activity in this vicinity will explain the presence of an old French rail line built across Don Khone and Don Det islands. The five-kilometer line—the only section of railway track in Laos—was built to bypass the treacherous rapids and facilitate transport of French cargo boats between Pakse and Phnom Penh around the turn of the century. The line

has concrete piers at either end; an old customs house sits next to a railway bridge at the main town of Ban Khone, with a rusted locomotive and boiler. The aqueduct-style bridge is a great sunset viewpoint. Little of the French track is left—most has been ripped up by locals and put to use elsewhere—but you can still make out where the track went. You can hike or bicycle along the former railway track, which passes through rice fields, forest, and small villages.

Accommodations

Don Khong, the largest of the islands at 16 kilometers long and eight kilometers wide, is inhabited year-round and is used as a base for exploring the region—to visit nearby waterfalls and rapids, or to go fishing. Reached by ferry from Hat Xai Khun, the main village on Don Khong is Muang Khong, a former French settlement about 130 kilometers from Pakse. It is reached by car ferry from Hat Xai Khun. Muang Khong has a market, a few cafés, and wats. Near the pier are several guesthouses. Accommodations at **Auberge Don Khong** can be booked through Sodetour in Pakse or Vientiane; rooms run about $30 a night. In the vicinity of the ferry landing are several cheaper guesthouses.

Farther south, reached by boat from the town of Ban Nakasang, are the smaller islands of Don Det and Don Khone. These have a cluster of bungalows overlooking the water—very simple family-run accommodations among the coconut palms, with cooking at a restaurant on the premises. There are other family-run restaurants in the vicinity. This is a great place to witness the laid-back rural Lao lifestyle—with rice fields, water buffalo, and fishing. Basic bungalows on Don Det and Don Khone start at a dollar or so. The **Auberge Don Khone** has eight superior bungalows with bathroom, at $25 a night.

Getting There

The 150-kilometer run from Pakse to Khong Phapheng Falls takes about five hours one-way along Highway 13, often accomplished by *songtao*. You can break the journey by detouring slightly to Champassak. It's also possible to get a ferry from Pakse to Champassak and onward to Muang Saen (on the west side of Don Khong). Ferries do not run daily: Check for timing.

If you want to travel in style, Sodetour runs a 34-meter-long steel-hull barge converted into a wooden floating hotel with 10 separate air-conditioned staterooms, each with two beds and private bath. The vessel, the *Vat Phou,* is self-contained, with its own restaurant and sundeck. Passengers board the *Vat Phou* in Pakse and take two- to four-day cruises to Don

Khong Island, stopping at sites such as Champassak en route. From Don Khong Island, passengers head for Khong Phapheng Falls by car. The cost is prohibitive, around $650 a person for a three-day tour. Some passengers are recruited from Vientiane and fly into Pakse; others cross from Thailand at Chong Mek to join the boat tour.

Cambodian Border Crossing

The Mekong Islands sit right on the Cambodian border. The border at Voeng Kham on Route 13 south, leading to Stung Treng, permits foreigners to cross as long as their paperwork is in order (relevant visas obtained in advance). Relations are testy between the Cambodians and the Lao at this border zone. There are rumors of anti-Lao resistance groups operating in the area, and of illegal loggers hard at work.

Proceeding south to cross the border: You can reach the Lao border checkpoint either by road or by small boat from Don Khone. By road, take a *songtao* along Route 13 to the Lao border town, complete paperwork there, and hire a long-tailed boat to cross the river to the Cambodian border checkpoint. At both checkpoints, the officials collect a "stamp fee" of $1–2. The same long-tailed boat hired will then take you downstream for an hour or so to reach Stung Treng. The long-tailed boat is worth about $30 or so for the entire boat—and can be split among 4–6 passengers. If coming from the other direction, from Stung Treng, you might talk the boat driver into to taking you through Cambodian and Lao immigration and then proceeding upriver to the south side of Don Khone, from where a hike overland is required to reach the bridge linking to Don Det—where bungalows can be found. The other choice is to disembark at Lao immigration and proceed by road from this point—if the target is Don Det, then the point you want to reach by land is Ban Nakasang, where a local boat makes the short crossing to the islands.

Luang Prabang and Northern Laos

Luang Prabang is the splendid old capital of Laos, featuring a cluster of shimmering royal temples, remnants of the faded grandeur of the Lao monarchy. Luang Prabang is jewel-like: tiny and compact. The "setting" is what gives it a jewel-like aura: The town is encircled by peaks and camouflaged by palm trees and dense tropical foliage. From a distance, only golden-spired stupas can be seen—flashes of gold among the greenery. The town is sited on a tongue of land at a strategic junction of the Mekong and Khan rivers. Originally, ramparts to the south and west sealed off the land approaches. At the heart of Luang Prabang is

Must-Sees

Look for **M** to find the sights and activities you can't miss and **M** for the best dining and lodging.

M Palace Museum: Memorabilia and artworks bring the royal Lao lifestyle into sharp focus. This was the home of the last king of Laos, who disappeared (page 523).

M Saffron Circuit: At the crack of dawn, the streets are a blur of orange, as monks go on their alms-gathering rounds. This ritual is seen all over Laos, but not in these numbers (page 526).

M Pak Ou Grottoes: The top day trip from Luang Prabang is to these grottoes, which shelter a large collection of Buddhist statuary (page 536).

M Muang Ngoy: The town itself is pretty, but on the river trip up the Nam Ou tributary from Luang Prabang, there is spellbinding karst scenery. It seems to get better the farther north you venture (page 540).

M Kayaking the Namtha River: From Luang Namtha, multiday kayak or rafting trips can be mounted. This is the way to enter really remote parts of the north (page 543).

M Hilltribe Trekking: Ecofriendly tours, accompanied by an official ethnic guide, can be arranged at Luang Namtha. You stay in villages en route (page 543).

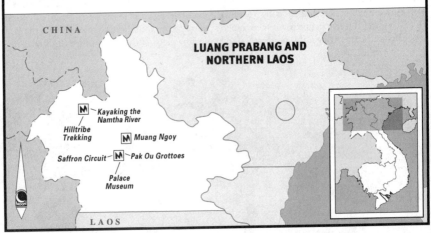

Mt. Phousi, a high rocky outcrop with forested slopes, dotted with sacred shrines and stupas.

Luang Prabang has long been the site of local kingdoms; in the 14th century, the first kingdom of Laos, Lan Xang, was established here by King Fa Ngum. The kingdom lasted 200 years before the royal seat was transferred to Vientiane. When the kingdom of Lan Xang split up on the death of King Souligna Vongsa in 1694, Luang Prabang was one of three independent kingdoms created. The city-state has seen its share of invasions; the place has been sacked

and rebuilt, and many older wooden structures have disappeared without trace. Luang Prabang's natural beauty and its golden temples are well-preserved because of the town's isolation. Although it flourished as a trading post among the people of upper Laos, Thailand, Vietnam, southern China, and Myanmar (Burma), there was little contact with non-Asian countries until the French arrived in the mid-19th century. Under French rule, a commissariat was established in Luang Prabang, which led to a spate of French residential

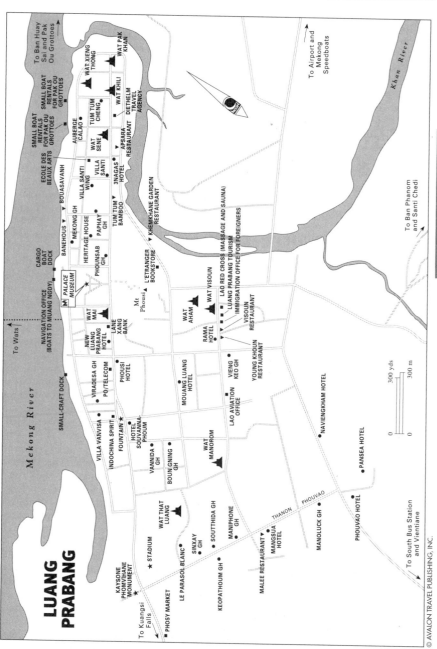

Luang Prabang & N. Laos

LUANG PRABANG

To Ban Huay Sai and Pak Ou Grottoes

To Wats

Mekong River

SMALL BOAT RENTALS FOR PAK OU GROTTOES

SMALL BOAT RENTALS FOR PAK OU GROTTOES

WAT XIENG THONG

WAT PAK KHAN

WAT KHILI

ECOLE DES BEAUX ARTS

AUBERGE CALAO

TUM TUM CHENG

DIETHELM TRAVEL AGENCY

APSARA RESTAURANT

WAT SENE

VILLA SANTI WING

VILLA SANTI

3NAGAS HOTEL

BOUASAVANH

BANEHOUS

MEKONG GH

HERITAGE HOUSE

PAPHAY GH

TUM TUM BAMBOO

KHEMKHANE GARDEN RESTAURANT

CARGO BOAT DOCK

PHOUNSAB GH

L'ETRANGER BOOKSTORE

NAVIGATION OFFICE (BOATS TO MUANG NGOY)

PALACE MUSEUM

Mt Phousi

WAT MAI

LANE XANG BANK

WAT AHAM

WAT VISOUN

LAO RED CROSS (MASSAGE AND SAUNA)

LUANG PRABANG TOURISM

IMMIGRATION OFFICE FOR FOREIGNERS

VISOUN RESTAURANT

RAMA HOTEL

NEW LUANG PRABANG HOTEL

VIRADESA GH

PO/TELECOM

PHOUSI HOTEL

MOUANG LUANG HOTEL

VIENG KEO GH

YOUNG KHOUN RESTAURANT

LAO AVIATION OFFICE

NAVIENGKHAM HOTEL

SMALL-CRAFT DOCK

VILLA VANVISA

INDOCHINA SPIRIT

FOUNTAIN

HOTEL SOUVANNA-PHOUM

VANNIDA GH

BOUN GNING GH

WAT MANOROM

PANSEA HOTEL

KAYSONE PHOMVIHANE MONUMENT

STADIUM

WAT THAT LUANG

SINXAY GH

SOUTTHIDA GH

MANIPHONE GH

MANGSUA HOTEL

THANON PHOUVAO

MANOLUCK GH

PHOUVAO HOTEL

To South Bus Station and Vientiane

LE PARASOL BLANC

PHOSY MARKET

To Kuangsi Falls

MALEE RESTAURANT

KEOPATHOUM GH

To Airport and Mekong Speedboats

Khan River

To Ban Phanom and Santi Chedi

0   300 yds

0   300 m

© AVALON TRAVEL PUBLISHING, INC.

building. The Lao monarchy endured in Luang Prabang, surviving right up until 1975.

The present population of Luang Prabang is only 30,000—even fewer in the downtown area. Luang Prabang works its charm on visitors: It has the aura of a place caught in a time warp, with orange-robed monks making their rounds, market and Mekong commerce, women cycling along with parasols to ward off the midday sun. The days of Luang Prabang's isolation, however, are numbered. Transport to the town has improved dramatically with a paved road snaking in from Vientiane and plans for a larger airport. On the drawing board was a road linking Luang Prabang all the way to the Chinese border.

Preserving Luang Prabang

In December 1995, the entire town of Luang Prabang, including its Mekong shoreline, was inscribed on the UNESCO World Heritage Site List. The UNESCO report identified 33 temples and 111 historic Lao-French buildings for specific restoration, citing Luang Prabang as the best-preserved traditional town in Southeast Asia—a kind of outdoor museum. The UNESCO plan for Luang Prabang guarantees preservation of the town's heritage and limits new building developments. To preserve the town's character, zoning laws restrict advertising billboards and decree that no concrete eyesores or out-of-character buildings can be constructed (which means no plague of photo-finishing shops or fast-food outlets will be visited upon the place). Power and telephone lines must be buried. However, U.N. guidelines have been clearly flouted in recent construction in Luang Prabang and authorities seem not concerned about facing off with UNESCO.

Under World Heritage Site plans, Luang Prabang's temples are being painstakingly restored, with particular attention to artwork damaged by monsoon rains and tropical humidity. Temples were the center of the Lao universe and, until the French arrived, were the only structures allowed to be constructed of brick. The French led indolent lives in Luang Prabang, and it remained an idyllic trading backwater.

In 1907 the French finally got into gear, with a spate of colonial building in Luang Prabang that lasted until 1925. The French administration used styles developed in Vietnam—but instead of simply transplanting European architecture, they adapted designs to better suit the climate: wooden houses with internal corridors to provide cool air circulation. There are temple-inspired designs and remarkable blends of Lao-French architecture. Not so inspiring are the French public buildings: the former customs house, post and telegraph office, school, hospital, and gendarmerie. To build these, the French imported Vietnamese laborers who established their own quarter at the south side of the peninsula, constructing two-story Chinese shophouses to live in.

There are three zones for preservation under the UNESCO plan: the old quarter (in the palace vicinity, along the peninsula), a peripheral building zone, and natural zones along the Mekong River banks. The old quarter, with the former royal palace and royal wats, is fully protected, with stringent building restrictions; no new building is permitted in this area. In the peripheral zone, new building is permitted but must be "in character." Integral to its status as a World Heritage Site is the protection of Luang Prabang's Mekong shoreline and natural areas, especially those on the northern bank of the Mekong, with the natural protection zone.

Paradoxically, designation as a World Heritage Site will undoubtedly lead to a substantial boost in tourism, which places a heavy demand on hotel resources. Here lies a riddle: How can Luang Prabang preserve its traditional character and yet expand its hotel offerings? The solution is to convert existing colonial mansions for use as guesthouses: In the old quarter, the number of guest rooms in new hotels is limited to fewer than 15. Beautifully restored colonial villas such as Auberge Calao and Villa Santi stand out in fulfilling these guidelines; the Paphay Guesthouse preserves a traditional Lao timber house. Outside the fully protected zone, larger hotel construction is permitted, subject to design approval. An eye-catching design is used at Mouang Luang Hotel, completed in 1996; this hotel draws its inspiration from Luang Prabang temples.

Limited photography and other details on the different styles of architecture can be found at **Heritage House,** itself a Lao heritage building. This place offers training and advice on restoration techniques and heritage protection for residents. Heritage House is signposted deep down an alley just east of the Palace Museum.

PLANNING YOUR TIME

Expect to stay at least two days to cover the key sights—the temples of Wat Xieng Thong and Wat Mai, plus the Palace Museum. Plan a crack-of-dawn wake-up call if you want to witness legions of orange-robed monks collecting alms. Getting around Luang Prabang is easy on foot, and it is the best way to soak up the local atmosphere. Or you can tour by rented bicycle—this is a pleasant place to cycle. For reasons that are not quite clear, motorcycle rental may not be permitted for visitors to Luang Prabang. Another transport option is to get several people together and hire a jumbo *(tuk-tuk)* by the half day or full day to go farther afield to, say, Kuangsi

Falls. Set aside an entire day if you want to tackle the popular trip to Pak Ou Grottoes, reached by rented boat from Luang Prabang.

Festivals

Usually 2–5 days should suffice to see Luang Prabang, but if it's festival time, plan to stay longer—if you can find a hotel room. Because of its previous links with royalty, Luang Prabang festivals are elaborate, sometimes lasting a week or longer. The place is packed around festival times, especially at Pimai (Lao New Year) and for the annual boat racing in August. For Pimai, people from all over the province make a beeline for Luang Prabang for four days of fun and festivity. Pimai kicks off with the crowning of Miss New Year, who is paraded through town; the following days see the ceremonial washing of Buddha statues, construction of small sand stupas in wats as symbolic requests for prosperity in the coming year, processions of monks, a candlelit tour of Mt. Phousi, *baci* ceremonies, folk singing and circle-dancing, fairgrounds, and fireworks. During the August boat races, temple longboats are raced by people living in the vicinity of each wat.

Luang Prabang & N. Laos

Sights

Luang Prabang is small: You can easily cover it without assistance from a tour agency. Tour offices in Vientiane quote prices such as $250 for two days/one night, or $350 for three days/two nights, but you can do better on your own. You can cover Luang Prabang on a rented bicycle. Oddly enough, there are no cyclos in Luang Prabang. Other transport options include renting a motorcycle, taking a sidecar-taxi, boating, or simply hiking. For trips out of town, consider using a rented motorcycle, hiring a jumbo, or renting a car from a larger hotel. Rented motorcycles are a blast for open-air rides. Navigation using wats as landmarks is effective; pick the closest wat to your desired destination to get started.

Old Quarter Heritage Buildings

The UNESCO World Heritage Site List cited

Luang Prabang as a town not only of temples but also of Lao-French historic housing. Opposite Wat Mai, in the Ministry of Culture and Information building, is a small display of heritage housing. Under the French, the building was once the library, and, before that, the Gendarmerie, with construction dating 1920–1925. This part of town is the former French administrative center; the Lane Xang Bank is a renovated French colonial building. On the same side of the street as the bank, and near it, is a single-story Vietnamese-style mansion dating from 1923 that is now home to several shops. If you proceed east from the Palace Museum, you'll come across Chinese–style shop fronts, a few colonial mansions such as Villa Santi (former homes of royalty and aristocracy), and an odd mix of French and Lao styles at Wat Khili.

Mount Phousi

To get your bearings on Luang Prabang—and get some exercise—head for Mt. Phousi at the heart of Luang Prabang. It's an excellent place at sunset and it's great for picnics. The wats here are small; it's the views you go for. You can approach or leave the peak from several directions via steep staircases. A round hike from the Khemkhane Garden Restaurant direction can be done as a side trip on a bike tour. Or start from the Khemkhane side, viewing Pra Puttabat, Tham Phousi, and That Chomsi, and emerge opposite the Palace Museum; from there you can walk east past Wat Sene to Wat Xieng Thong. Or, if you have a few hours, you can take a longer hike across the other side of the Mekong.

Mount Phousi is a 150-meter-high rocky out-crop with forested slopes. In the 18th century it was covered with monasteries; several small monasteries continue to operate. Opposite the royal palace, on the lower slopes of Mt. Phousi, is the abandoned temple of **Wat Huak,** with a carved wood facade and excellent interior murals depicting visits by foreign diplomats. The wat is locked, but an attendant can be persuaded to open up on token payment. Up about 300 winding steps, at the summit of Mt. Phousi is **That Chomsi,** a gold-spired stupa on a rectangular base constructed in 1804 and restored a century later. This is a prime viewpoint and the focus of a candlelit procession during Pimai in April. A Russian antiaircraft gun is positioned on a ridge up here. Down the hill is **Tham Phousi,** a rock shrine with a fat Buddha image in a cave.

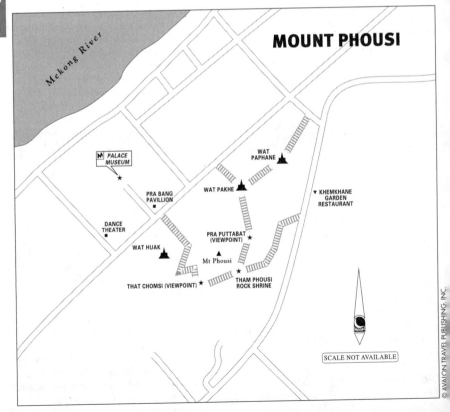

MOUNT PHOUSI

Mekong River

PALACE MUSEUM

WAT PAPHANE

PRA BANG PAVILLION

WAT PAKHE

KHEMKHANE GARDEN RESTAURANT

DANCE THEATER

PRA PUTTABAT (VIEWPOINT)

WAT HUAK

Mt Phousi

THAT CHOMSI (VIEWPOINT)

THAM PHOUSI ROCK SHRINE

SCALE NOT AVAILABLE

A second fine viewpoint is at **Pra Putta-bat,** which features an enclosure containing a giant Buddha footprint. You must find one of the monks nearby to open the sanctuary. The original wooden temple on this site dates back to the 17th century, with the present structure erected in 1959. Back down at the base of Mt. Phousi on the northeast side are two wats; one, **Wat Paphane,** has a classic carved and painted facade.

Palace Museum

The Palace Museum is open at erratic hours; the best bet is Monday–Saturday 0830–1100; there's a token entrance fee. Although there's absolutely nothing sacred about the king anymore, the museum has a dress code for Lao and foreign visitors: no shorts, T-shirts, or short dresses. You must leave any cameras or bags at the front reception area.

The Royal Palace was built 1904–1909, with later extensions and renovations. It's surrounded by a high fence and extensive gardens. Although occupied by Lao King Sisavang Vong, the building was commissioned by the French colonial administration, which explains the mix of French and Lao architecture. This effect was intentional—meant to cement the relationship. At the front entrance, high up on the front of the building, is Erawan, the three-headed elephant symbolizing the three kingdoms of Laos. The pillars below bear French fleur-de-lys emblems, and you sweep up steps made of Italian marble. Inside are French mirrors and Czech chandeliers alongside traditional Lao lacquered and gilded furniture.

You proceed on a counterclockwise tour through the main halls and rooms of the palace. The palace was meant to dazzle, and the king's former audience room, used for receiving foreign envoys, certainly does that. The room is to the right of the entry hall; the walls are covered with paintings of traditional festivals and daily life in Luang Prabang, painted in 1930 by French artist Alix de Fautereau. The vivid, Gauguin-style murals bring to life an era of village feasts and elephant parades. In the same room are two gilded and lacquered

screens depicting scenes from the *Ramayana,* created by Lao master craftsman Thit Tanh, and three French-made busts of Lao monarchs. In the former Throne Room magnificent glass-mosaic murals on reddish walls depict Lao legends and festivals. The mosaic decoration was commissioned by Sisavang Vatthana, the glass imported from Japan. By contrast, the royal residential area is surprisingly modest, even spartan. It has been preserved as it was the day the royal family was sent into exile. On the tour through these quarters you can see an old gramophone with a Pablo Casals record on the turntable, and the king's bedroom, with elephant motifs carved on the bed frame.

The Palace Museum includes a small but impressive collection of royal Lao artifacts (*Ramayana* dance masks, musical instruments, royal seals and medals, porcelain) and Buddha statues (many brought in for safekeeping by monks from wats or stupas abandoned or destroyed). Even the palace was not the safest place to stash priceless Buddhas. In 1910 the French government sent a specialist to Laos to select articles from the royal collection for the Louvre Museum. A treasure of gold and bronze Buddha statues, works in silver, and other decorative objects was loaded onto a boat that subsequently sank without trace in the Mekong River.

The last room of the palace tour is the former queen's reception room, where oil portraits of the last king, Sisavang Vatthana, and the queen and crown prince, painted by a Russian artist in 1967, gaze down from the walls. In the same room is a hodgepodge of diplomatic gifts from foreign heads of state, including items from Mao Zedong, Norodom Sihanouk, Leonid Brezhnev, and Lyndon Johnson. Among the gifts on display is a piece of moon rock collected by an Apollo mission and donated by President Richard Nixon in December 1973 to the people of Laos. The caption reads, "It is given as a symbol of the unity of human endeavor, and carries with it the hope of the American peoples for a world of peace"—a rather absurd gesture after almost 10 years of carpet bombing of Laos by U.S. aircraft. A more practical donation from the

THE KING WHO DISAPPEARED

When King Sisavang Vong died in 1959, he was succeeded by his son Sisavang Vatthana, who set about modernizing the palace—and that's where the trail abruptly ends. Given the sorry history of Laos, and the fact that the Pathet Lao spent years battling Royal Lao forces, the Palace Museum is very odd indeed. A museum brochure claims that the last king offered the palace to the Pathet Lao shortly after 1975, and that "the palace was then converted into a national museum, the main aims of which are to preserve the palace and the royal collection and inform the public of the history of the former monarchy."

On one wall is a composite photo portrait of the former monarchy: king, queen, three princes, and two princesses. Official guides are either unable or unwilling to inform the touring public about the palace's last resident, the last king of Laos, Sisavang Vatthana. Ask a guide what happened to the king and you'll draw a blank. First there's the question of whether he was ever even a real king, as the official version has it he was never crowned. Then you have to try to establish if he's alive or dead—some seem to think he's still alive somewhere.

The disappearance of the king is a taboo topic in Laos: The Laotians have never been publicly informed of his fate. After the Pathet Lao takeover in 1975, the king remained in the palace for several years as an "adviser." But with simmering insurgency in the jungles close to Luang Prabang, the monarchy became a symbol of the resistance, so, in 1977, the king, queen, and crown prince were shuffled off to the far north, where the Pathet Lao once convened in hidden caves. Locals say the king went to a seminar "to study Marxism"—a polite way of saying he was dispatched to a Pathet Lao reeducation camp. When pressed for details by Paris-based journalists in 1989, Communist Party Chief Kaysone Phomvihane said the king had died of natural causes. "It happens to all of us," explained Kaysone, who would not divulge any further details. Queen Kham Phuoy apparently also died in the north. No word was ever given on the fate of Crown Prince Vongsavang, though he is presumably dead, too. The other princes and princesses went to live in the United States and France.

U.S. government was a white Ford Edsel, the king's favorite car, which rests in a garage at the back of the palace, along with two Lincolns, a Citroën, and a speedboat, all from the 1950s and 1960s. You need a separate "Car Ticket" to get into the garage: Ask at the front reception. The vehicles bear the royal three-elephant crest on the side and back. Near the east gate are two Shell pumps where these extravagant vehicles were refueled.

Right near the front gate of the palace is the **Pra Bang Pavilion,** which has been specially built to house the Pra Bang, the sacred standing Buddha image that gives Luang Prabang its name (City of the Great Buddha). The pavilion, completed in 2002, stands as the biggest Lao architecture project in traditional style in Luang Prabang. It is proof that the ancient arts have not been lost—although those arts have certainly changed. While wood is certainly used in this structure, most of it—including supporting pillars—is made of concrete. Ingeniously, craftsmen have concealed the concrete material by gluing tiny glass mosaic pieces to the surface.

Whether the Pra Bang statue housed within is the original or not is open to question (the original is rumored to rest in a bank vault in Vientiane). The image has both hands held palm out in the attitude of Dispelling Fear, stands 83 centimeters tall, weighs around 50 kilograms, and is reckoned to be 90 percent pure gold (other accounts say it is merely bronze coated in gold). The image is reputedly from the 1st century A.D., made in India, presented to the King of Ceylon, then to the King of Cambodia, and eventually finding its way into the hands of Lao King Fa Ngum, founder of the kingdom based in Luang Prabang. In 1778, the Thais invaded Laos and carted the image back to Bangkok. It was then determined, however, that Pra Bang and the Emerald Buddha—taken from Vientiane at the same time—did not see eye to eye; legend has it that if both occupy the same city, misfortune will befall the place. So the Thais kept the Emerald Buddha, and about 60 years later packed Pra Bang back to Luang Prabang, where it remains a source of spiritual protection for Laos.

While near the front of the palace, check out the theater to the west side for timing for traditional Lao performance, held several times a week.

Wat Xieng Thong

Every so often, Laos serves up a spectacular feast for the eyes and soul; this is definitely one of them. Wat Xieng Thong has richly decorated chapels and a magical aura about it—the stuff of Oriental fairy tales. The temple was easily reached by boat from the royal palace, as both sites enjoyed Mekong access. At the temple Lao kings were crowned and cremated, and royal ceremonies held. Some ceremonies endure: A temple longboat is housed in a shed to the north side for use at Lao New Year in April and the annual boat-racing festival in August.

Wat Xieng Thong was built by King Settathirat in 1560 and remained under royal patronage for four centuries. The temple survived raids by intruders and has been kept in immaculate condition. Present upkeep is the responsibility of monks. The temple is active, with monks' residences scattered throughout the

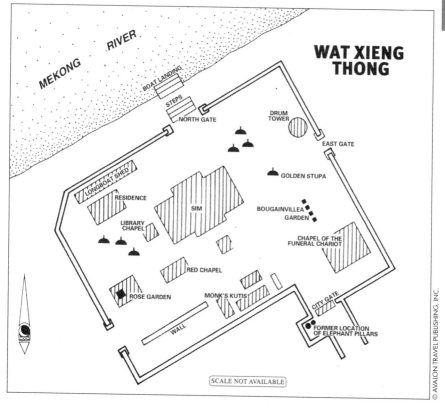

WAT XIENG THONG

MEKONG RIVER

BOAT LANDING
STEPS
NORTH GATE
DRUM TOWER
EAST GATE
LONGBOAT SHED
RESIDENCE
GOLDEN STUPA
SIM
BOUGAINVILLEA GARDEN
LIBRARY CHAPEL
CHAPEL OF THE FUNERAL CHARIOT
RED CHAPEL
ROSE GARDEN
MONK'S KUTIS
CITY GATE
WALL
FORMER LOCATION OF ELEPHANT PILLARS

SCALE NOT AVAILABLE

compound, sited among tranquil banyan and palm trees and bright bougainvillea blooms.

Wat Xieng Thong takes its name from a *bodhi* tree, or *thong,* standing on the site. The rear of the main temple is encrusted with colored glass pieces in a red background, depicting the *bodhi* tree. The *sim* is pure Luang Prabang style, with low-sweeping roofs; inside, gold-stenciled wooden pillars support a ceiling decorated with dharma wheels. The walls bear rich frescoes. The *sim* houses a huge seated Buddha in Earth Witness pose, fronted by smaller seated and standing Buddha images. Near the *sim* are three small chapels. To the north is the Library Chapel, built in 1828, which houses the *Tripitaka,* or Theravada Buddhist sacred texts. This chapel is normally locked. Directly south of the *sim* is the tiny stucco White Chapel, sheltering a gold standing Buddha with both palms out. To the southwest is the Red Chapel, containing a rare bronze reclining Buddha with graceful lines that dates from the construction of the temple. A red exterior with glass-inlay mosaic depicting village life was added in the late 1950s.

A similar style of mosaic is found in the interior of the Chapel of the Funeral Chariot—the mosaic here was never completed. It's hard to believe that anything so dazzling—and with such sensuous carvings—could be a garage for a funeral chariot, but that's what this chapel is. Inside is a 12-meter-high gilded wooden hearse enclosing a 12-sided royal funerary urn of the king; up front is a seven-headed *naga* prow, and the entire assembly is mounted on the chassis of a six-wheel truck. The golden hearse was fashioned by Lao master sculptor Thit Tanh to transport the urn of King Sisavang Vong to the stadium next to Wat That Luang for cremation in 1959—the last elaborate funeral rites enacted for a Lao king. The sumptuous exterior chapel panels are sculpted in wood with gold-leaf overlay and show episodes from the *Ramayana* with erotic overtones. In the late afternoon, if the sun is out, the chapel is bathed in a gorgeous light that really brings the sculpted figures to life.

Near the west gate is a 1990s addition:

A small pavilion set in a rose garden houses a seated Buddha in the Earth Witness pose. Wat Xieng Thong has four entrances (at the south or city gate there used to be hitching posts for royal elephants); atop the plain brick east gate are two small guardian lion statues; at the north side, outside the temple, two pairs of large white cat statues guard the steps down to the Mekong River.

Wat Mai

Next to the palace is Wat Mai, a temple inaugurated in the 18th century. It took more than 70 years to build and was once home to the supreme patriarch of Lao Buddhism. The wooden *sim* is built in classic Luang Prabang style, with a magnificent five-tiered roof and pillars with gold patterns stenciled on black. The dazzling exterior wall bears gold stucco bas-reliefs recounting the legend of Pravet, the last incarnation of the historic Buddha, amid a profusion of village scenes; the top band depicts scenes from the *Ramayana.*

On the grounds of the wat are some "elephant pillars": posts painted in red. At Lao New Year, several royal elephants draped in ceremonial blankets were tethered at this site; an ear of each elephant was lifted up and a sermon was whispered into it before the elephants took part in a procession. The ceremony continued until the early 1970s; there used to be elephant hitching posts also at Wat Xieng Thong and Wat Visoun.

Saffron Circuit

If you're up early, you'll catch the most impressive sight of Luang Prabang: long lines of orange-robed and barefoot monks on their alms rounds on the main streets and back alleys of Luang Prabang. "Early" means at dawn—around 0500–0600. Announced by the beat of a large drum, the monks proceed out of wats to the far east side of town, closer to Wat Xieng Thong, and walk toward the Palace Museum, then turn toward the Mekong, walk along the Mekong banks, and complete the "circuit" back to their monastery. Locals offer sticky rice as well as other food and necessities to the monks.

© MICHAEL BUCKLEY

Early in the morning, monks go out on their rounds, collecting donations of food.

The long line of monks creates a swirl of orange, accentuated by the soft morning light. Within an hour, the monks complete their rounds and melt back into the monasteries—and the streets become quite ordinary again. Although this alms-giving ritual can be seen in numerous parts of Southeast Asia, it's particularly striking in Luang Prabang because of the density of temples on the peninsula and the concentration of monks (there are more than 500 in Luang Prabang). You'll be most welcome at the wats—many of the monks are studying English or French, so it's easy to make friends. If you're in Luang Prabang during a festival, it will most certainly be centered around one or more of the wats.

Other Temples

Of the 40-odd wats around Luang Prabang, the best-preserved and most lavish are those lying due east of the Palace Museum, from Wat Mai to Wat Xieng Thong. These wats were formerly associated with royalty; the villas and residences of royal Lao family members were also along this strip, as were the residences of the French in the colonial days. Villa Santi, now a small hotel, was the residence of a real princess; it was returned to her family in 1991. Down this way is **Wat Sene,** with a Thai-style *sim* with a yellow-and-red roof, built in the 18th century with later restorations. A side temple encloses a large standing Buddha and a drum.

Those interested in Lao art, architecture, or Buddhism might want to explore the wats further. Each wat has its own character and features. **Wat Khili** presents an unusual blend of French colonial and Lao temple architecture. **Wat Visoun** features a *sim* with a high ceiling, a collection of Buddha statues, and a 35-meter-high Lotus stupa called the "melon stupa" because of its shape. **Wat Manorom** is noted for its large armless bronze Buddha, reckoned to weigh several tons and reputedly cast in the 14th century.

monks returning to Wat Mai after collecting alms

Hiking Across the River

There are good views of Luang Prabang from the other side of the Mekong—you can ramble along the foreshores here 2–5 hours through villages and derelict wats. This side of the river is ideal for hiking because there's hardly any motor transport—even motorcycles disappear. Cross the Mekong by small craft at the landing at the back of the Palace Museum. There's no regular service: The boatman waits till there are half a dozen passengers and then goes. The locals pay about $.30; for you the price is double or triple. You can hire the entire boat for $2 for the crossing.

Once across the river, walk to the right to **Wat Xieng Mene,** in a village of the same name. The wat has an elaborate gilt door. Two kilometers from the village in the forest is the **royal cemetery** with sculptures of royal family members who could not be cremated: victims of contagious diseases, or children who died as infants. It's hard to persuade local guides

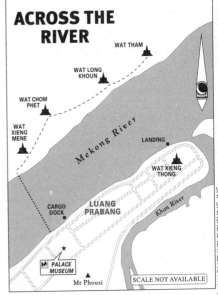

ACROSS THE RIVER

MARKET AND MEKONG BIKE TOUR

Visitors to Luang Prabang tend to focus on the temples, glossing over the town's other charms, such as Mekong bustle and market life. Touring by rented bicycle or motorcycle, or with a sidecar-taxi, is the easiest way to get a glimpse of local activity. If on a bicycle, park in designated areas when visiting markets.

Start this tour at the foot of Thanon Kitsirat Settathirat, where a flight of stairs leads down to a small-craft loading area. It's very busy here in the early morning, with boats coming in from outlying areas and boats headed upstream for Muang Ngoy or Ban Huay Sai.

From here go southwest to the **Kaysone Phomvihane Memorial**, with a bust of the revered revolutionary parked at a roadside shrine. Continue westward a bit and you will come across **Phosy Market**, the largest food market in Luang Prabang. Stalls are piled high with produce. Luang Prabang is closer to Kunming than Bangkok, and in the markets Thai consumer goods are starting to give way to Chinese goods. You can find Chinese soap, bicycles, Mao caps, thermoses, and American baseball caps made in China. Photo opportunities always abound at markets—not inside, since the markets are covered and you need a flash, but outside where huge loads are stacked onto motorcycle sidecars.

From Phosy Market, backtrack a bit and continue past the stadium to **Wat That Luang**, where the nation's penultimate king rests. King Sisavang Vong's ashes are interred inside the large gold stupa at one end of the compound. Locals often come to leave offerings.

Head eastward back into town, swing south and east and you'll come to a crossroads. From this direction you're treated to a striking view of **Mt. Phousi**, with the gold spire of **That Chomsi** rising high above. As you ride toward Mt. Phousi, to the left is **Wat Aham**, with two banyan trees in the grounds—an important spirit shrine. A pleasant place to take a breather is **Khemkhane Garden Restaurant**, overlooking the Khan River. An option here is to leave your bike at the restaurant and head off for a foot tour of Mt. Phousi. You can climb a set of stairs near the restaurant, hike to That Chomsi, and return via Tham Phousi and Pra Puttabat to **Wat Paphane**, then walk back along the road to the restaurant.

From Khemkhane Restaurant, carry on round to **Wat Pak Khan**, also known as the Dutch Pagoda because its wooden doors are carved with costumed figures said to be 18th- and 19th-century Dutch explorers. A short distance from here is **Wat Xieng Thong**, the most stunning of Luang Prabang's many wats. Around the corner, along the river, are some excellent open-air places serving drinks and snacks, and sometimes serving up a Mekong sunset as well. For great views, try the dining terrace of the **Auberge Calao**, or the pleasant atmosphere of **Banehous Restaurant**.

to visit this place, because they're terrified of ghosts. From Wat Xieng Mene, you can walk up to destroyed **Wat Chom Phet**, a peaceful spot with expansive views. The walking trail continues to **Wat Long Khoun**, which, though small, is the principal active wat on this bank. It has seen a lot of reconstruction, but faded 18th-century grandeur may be detected in the murals, some of which show foreign traders.

From this point there's a forest trail to **Wat Tham**, an abandoned wat in a deep limestone cave, with stairs cut out of stone. You need a flashlight to explore. The cave-temple was a storage depot for statuary from destroyed wats around Luang Prabang, and it is stacked with rotting Buddha images. There are several other caves nearby. Wat Tham is almost directly opposite Wat Xieng Thong. If you can find a villager with a boat, you can cross the Mekong here for a small fee, but you'll most likely have to backtrack to the Wat Long Khoun area to find a boat.

Adventure Touring

Outfits such as White Elephant Adventures and Tiger Trail can arrange mountain-biking trips around Luang Prabang. These one-day sorties take you on some great road and off-road trails, and might throw in a boat ride or two, plus lunch. Riding in the hills around Luang

Prabang is a blast. Give it a whirl. Rafting and other adventure-tour options are also offered by these outfits. Multiday trips are possible.

Boat Touring

The royal way to see Luang Prabang is to cruise the river—see the waterfront docks, visit Wat Xieng Thong, tour the opposite bank of the Mekong, and explore the Khan River. Boats cost around $5–10 an hour and can be hired from docks along the Mekong. Most travelers save their shekels for the boat ride along the Mekong to Pak Ou Grottoes (see *Excursions from Luang Prabang*).

Practicalities

ACCOMMODATIONS

Luang Prabang has an acute shortage of accommodations. New hotels are being built, but they may not be able to keep pace with the projected tourist influx. The problem is how to keep hotel building from disfiguring the tiny town. The solution is to convert existing colonial mansions for use as lodging—which is why, under U.N. auspices, newer accommodations (both budget and luxury) are restricted to 15 or fewer rooms in the oldest part of town. Hotels built before these regulations came into force are not affected—the Phousi Hotel, for example, has more than 100 rooms. Another constraint is electrical supply: Although power is supplied from the Vientiane area, hotels need their own generators to fight blackouts.

Under $20

The best guesthouses in Luang Prabang are small, intimate, family-run affairs. These places will take very good care of you. Hot showers are usually available; some places rent bicycles and help with touring logistics. Refer to the map of Luang Prabang to pinpoint locations, as street references are unreliable, and the street names change with every different map consulted. Toward the Mekong, you will find many guesthouses tucked away down alleys.

Paphay GH, facing Wat Paphay, tel. 71/212752, is a Lao timber house with simple guest rooms—very clean, run by very friendly folk. Down the same street is **Heritage GH,** tel. 71/252537, with $10 rooms; it's well-run and housed in old French building. **Phounsab GH,** tel. 71/212595, offers 11 rooms for $7–12; good management and rents bicycles. **Mekong GH,** at 57 Choumkhong, close to the Mekong, has five rooms for $8–10 double; the place is operated by a former pilot with the Royal Lao Air Force. Nearby is **Chaliny GH,** tel. 71/252377, with rooms for $5 apiece; it's clean and pleasant. **Villa Vanvisa,** tel. 71/212925, is a simple French villa with five rooms for $10 each; also sells Lao traditional weavings and antiques. **Viradesa GH,** in the same area (no phone), offers 12 rooms for $5–9 apiece; there's also a dorm room, and the guesthouse sells handicrafts. **Vannida GH** at 97/4 Souvannaphoum Rd., tel. 71/212374, is a large colonial mansion containing 13 mildewy rooms with shared toilet facilities for $8 s or $10 d. Large dining hall downstairs and a garden area for drinks. A short way off, at 109 Souvannaphoum Rd., is **Boun Gning GH,** tel. 71/212274, which is a clean, family-run place with 16 rooms for $9–14.

With a pleasant location overlooking the Nam Khan River is **Khemkhane Garden Restaurant,** with several bungalows for $15 d. **Rama Hotel,** near Wat Visoun, tel. 71/212247, has 33 rooms for $7–10; there's a loud nightly disco below with music till 2400. **Vieng Keo GH,** around the corner, tel. 71/212271, has eight rooms for $7 s or $12 d. On the southwest fringe of town is **Sinxay Villa,** on Phou Vao Street, tel. 71/212587, a concrete villa with a handful of doubles for $15 each.

$20–50

A really great place in this price range is the 10-room **Tum Tum Cheng Guesthouse,** right near Wat Xieng Thong, tel. 71/253224.

There is a choice of fan or a/c, and shared balcony with cushions and candlelight. Cost is $35–50. Close to Wat Sene is **Saynamkhan GH,** tel. 71/212976, with 14 rooms for $25–30. **Phousi Hotel,** right downtown on Thanon Kitsirat Settathirat, tel. 71/212192, fax 71/212719, charges $28–40 d, $56 for a family room. A comfortable hotel with an excellent location, it is otherwise uninspiring; exchange rates at the hotel are good. The hotel has several wings with a total of 100 rooms. Close by is **New Luang Prabang Hotel,** tel. 71/212264, fax 71/212804, with 15 a/c rooms for $30 d; this hotel combines Lao and Western architecture, but the mix looks odd, and the atmosphere is bland. **Manoluck,** 121 Phou Vao St., tel. 71/212250, fax 71/212508, is a modern hotel with Lao–style design elements offering 30 a/c rooms with bath for $40 d or s. **Muangsua Hotel,** Thanon Phou Vao, tel. 71/212263, offers 17 rooms—$20 s with a/c and hot water, $25 d, $35 t. The hotel also rents a minibus; there's disco here on weekends.

Close to the stadium is **Le Parasol Blanc,** tel. 71/252124. The 30 rooms here go for $44–50 each. This well-designed boutique hotel has a pool, but not the kind you swim in; it's a kind of lotus pond, with an al fresco restaurant overlooking it.

Auberge Calao, near Wat Xieng Thong, tel./fax 71/212100, is a deluxe villa with five rooms with bath and a/c for $45 apiece. The upstairs rooms have balconies. Auberge Calao was originally the home of French trader Monsieur Doré and his Lao wife (who appear in a 1904 photo hanging on the wall). The colonial mansion was extensively renovated in 1993 in a Canadian-Lao joint venture (which explains the name "Calao"). There's a great double terrace with bamboo shading overlooking the Mekong.

Villa Santi (formerly Villa de la Princesse) on the main east-west road, tel./fax 71/212267, has 10 a/c doubles and one single in the $55 range—in a beautifully restored colonial villa with a small garden. Lao antiques provide interior decor for the 120-year-old mansion. The boutique hotel is connected with Princess Kampha, daughter of the crown prince, who disappeared along with the king in 1977. Royal property was confiscated in the 1970s, but in 1991 the government returned the villa to the princess. She renovated it with her husband, Santi Inthavong, the manager of Lana Tour. Villa Santi stages Lao folk dances and *baci* (welcoming) ceremonies for group tours, and it serves excellent Lao food. Around the corner from Villa Santi is a second hotel under the same management, constructed with classic Lao temple roofing. This wing has 14 rooms; doubles run $40–45.

$50–100

Upscale boutique hotels are trendy in Luang Prabang. On the road running along the Mekong is **Sala Prabang Boutique Hotel,** tel. 71/252460, www.salalao.com, with garden-view rooms for $50 and Mekong view rooms for $60. Prices drop about 25 percent in the May–September off-season. The hotel is housed in a renovated colonial mansion. **3Nagas,** tel. 71/253888, www.3nagas.com, has only seven rooms, all of them huge and furnished with wood, silk and traditional weavings. Tariff is $90 for superior rooms and $120 for suites.

Mouang Luang Hotel, on Boun Khong Road, tel./fax 71/212790, features 35 a/c rooms with bath for $55, and two suites. Out the back is a lawn with a small pool. The hotel, completed in 1996, draws its inspiration from Luang Prabang temples, with layered sweeping roofs on the outside, and on the inside, royal-style teak furniture with handwoven silk upholstery and traditional carved wood panels on the walls—all made by local artisans. Staff dress in traditional Lao costumes; the restaurant serves Luang Prabang specialties on its varied menu. Although one of the top-rated hotels in Luang Prabang and boasting excellent facilities, this place has a humdrum location. The **Hotel Souvannaphoum,** tel. 71/212200, fax 71/212577, is a converted mansion with 20 balcony rooms for $55 d or $50 s, three junior suites, and two grand suites for $75–80. Rooms—and bathrooms—are cavernous but otherwise unremarkable. The place was formerly a residence of Prince Souvanna Phouma. It's run by Inter-Lao Tourisme and contains a garden restaurant, L'Elephant Blanc, featuring classical Lao cuisine. Another rambling restored villa complex with royal connections is **Satri House,** tel.253418, with just seven large rooms. It was the residence of Prince Souphanouvong when he was growing up. It is decorated in colonial style.

The French-managed **Pansea Hotel** at the southern edge of town, tel./fax 71/212194, is a modern hotel with 67 rooms—$60 d with a/c, hot water, and minibar. The Pansea has the largest swimming pool in Luang Prabang, not counting the Mekong, of course. Close by the Pansea is the **Phouvao Hotel,** run by the same group—an extension of sorts.

FOOD

Luang Prabang has a number of culinary specialties. Watercress grows around waterfalls and is used in salads; a river moss from the Khan River is mixed with sesame; soups are flavored with spicy or bitter-hot herbs. At market stalls you can find excellent *tam som* (green papaya salad), ground as you watch. A place called **Han Somtam Khaem Khong** serves Luang Prabang's most deadly spicy *tam som*—the place is close to Wat Nong. Locals also make tamarind jam and pineapple jam, and their own moonshine liquor, *lao lao.*

Markets are a great source of fresh and tasty food and good places to hunt for breakfast. Markets are humming 0800–0900; here you can find French bread and Spam-pâté, and sometimes crude croissants, coffee, and fresh orange juice. Look for small pineapples and finger bananas to supplement your breakfast rations.

Talking of breakfast: Along the main east-west road of Luang Prabang, just east of the Palace Museum, are two fine bakeries—the **Scandinavian Bakery** and **Luang Prabang.** In the same vicinity is a slew of restaurants popular with travelers, turning this strip into a kind of Pub Street. Farther east on this road, closer to Wat Xieng Thong, is a string of upscale restaurants such as Café Ban Vat Sene.

Ironically, it is difficult to find good Lao food in Luang Prabang—the explanation is that it takes a long time to prepare. However, there are some places where you can find a Lao menu. One of the best is **Tum Tum Bamboo,** along the main east-west road opposite the Scandinavian Bakery. This place dishes up great Lao food: If you want to find out the cooking secrets, you can sign up for $20 and be taken market shopping and be shown how to prepare Lao recipes at a cooking school close to Wat Khili.

Overlooking the Mekong, on the strip between the Palace Museum and Wat Xieng Thong, are several thatched and wooden structures that serve drinks, snacks, and tasty main dishes; here you'll find the **Banehous** and **Bouasavanh** restaurants, which are popular traveler hangouts.

There's a cluster of family-run restaurants in the vicinity of the Rama Hotel, with meals for about $3–5 a head (not including beer). **Yong Khoune Restaurant** and **Visoun Restaurant** have selections of Chinese and Lao dishes; **Luang Prabang Restaurant** serves European and Lao. Cheaper is **Chandavan Restaurant** near Vieng Keo Hotel, with Lao food.

For real atmosphere, **Khemkhane Garden Restaurant** has thatched cottages perched over the Nam Khan (Khan River), a tributary of the Mekong. The tariff is roughly $4 a head for a meal, or just have drinks—very pleasant.

Farther north on the Nam Khan is **Apsara,** tel. 71/212420, a restored mansion-restaurant and bar, serving French and Lao specialties—atmosphere and presentation are good. Near Wat Nong is **L'Elephant Brasserie,** with spacious seating and an eclectic menu.

The classiest place to sample Lao food is **Villa Santi,** where a Lao fixed evening meal costs $8 a head. It's best to book ahead because the place could be packed with a group tour: There may be performances of traditional dance staged here. The **Mouang Lao Hotel** has a decent restaurant offering a wide range of Lao and Western dishes. Other hotels in town have mediocre dining rooms and bars, but **L'Elephant Blanc** restaurant at the Hotel Souvannaphoum is worth a try. On the west side of Luang Prabang is **Malee Restaurant,** quite a few notches down in decor but no loss at all in the food department—and considerably cheaper. Malee

LUANG PRABANG'S CULINARY DELIGHTS

by Jeffrey Alford and Naomi Duguid

In Luang Prabang, you're in for a treat: The local food is a distinctive branch of Lao cuisine, with sour and bitter flavors in some dishes. Try *ohlam,* a category of slow-cooked dishes with simmered dill, vegetables, and meat or fish; and *larp,* a pounded seasoned paste of fish or meat dish eaten with sticky rice. Luang Prabang offers good-tasting sticky rice, plenty of steamed vegetables, a distinctive warm salad of lettuce, herbs, and egg, as well as delicious grilled fish and meat, generally served with one of the many hot-tasting relish-cum-salsas called *jaew.* You can find much of this in the small night market between the river and the post office, as well as in restaurants specializing in Luang Prabang food. You'll also find Chinese and French restaurants, somewhat pricey and generally good. Try eating noodle soup from vendors near Talad Phosy or other markets; you'll also want to taste the small, lettuce-wrapped flavor packets sold by street vendors and generically known as *miang.*

serves a good range of Lao dishes, including spicy eggplant soup, chicken salad with lemongrass, and curried fish dishes.

NIGHTLIFE

Nightlife in Luang Prabang mostly centers on restaurants and dining and lingering over Beer Lao at cafés and hangouts. A night market extends along the main east-west street, near the Palace Museum: It sells mostly cloth, clothing, and handicrafts. The Palace Museum Theater, to the west side of the compound, stages traditional Lao performances, including *baci* ceremonies, folksongs, *Ramayana* dance episodes—check on when these are on. Several hotels such as Villa Santi stage dance shows, packaged with dinner.

SHOPPING

Luang Prabang is a good place to shop for silver items and textiles. Silk and cotton *sinhs* are sold for $5–20 depending on design and quality; textiles, embroidery, and bags make good purchases too. Silver jewelry and other items are sold by weight, though quality craftsmanship is a factor: Silver ornaments are often purchased by Hmong hilltribes as portable wealth. Larger hotels—the Phou Vao, Phousi, and Villa Santi—have higher-priced gift shops.

Strung out east of the Palace Museum are a number of souvenir shops: A few of them sell high-quality textiles and handicrafts. Down by the Mekong, near Villa Santi, is a silversmithing shop with items made on the premises; opposite Wat Mai is a woodcarving place. The night market close to the Palace Museum is a good place to browse for items.

SERVICES AND INFORMATION
The Tourist Trade
Luang Prabang Tourism Office, tel. 71/212198, may stock maps of Luang Prabang. There are several travel agents in town. **Lane Xang Travel,** tel. 71/212793, is on Visounnarat Road; **Diethelm Travel** is opposite Wat Sene; **Inter-Lao Tourisme** can be contacted through Hotel Souvannaphoum; **Lana Tour,** tel. 71/212267, operates from Villa Santi. Also in Luang Prabang are **Southern Lao Travel** and **Lao Travel Service.** Travel agents can arrange tours, cars, and guides, and can arrange extended trekking trips or boat trips up-country. Guides cost $5–9 a day (negotiable).

Books
L'Etranger Bookstore stocks used English and French paperbacks and has a teahouse upstairs. It is south from Mt. Phousi.

Bank
Lane Xang Bank is right near Luang Prabang Tourism. Rates are higher for cash than for traveler's checks, and not as good as rates in Vientiane for traveler's checks, but comparable

for cash. The bank is open 0830–1530. Hotels such as the Phousi offer much the same rates for U.S. cash as the bank.

Communications

The general post office handles mail and IDD calls. The country code for Laos is 856 and the area code for Luang Prabang is 71.

Health Care

The Lao Red Cross runs a traditional Lao herbal sauna costing $2 a person, or $4 for a massage. Shower first, and bring your own towel. The sauna and massage section is set back off the road near the Lao Red Cross, opposite Wat Visoun; it's open 1700–1930 daily, plus 0900–1100 on Sunday.

Getting There and Away

By Air

Round-trip fare from Vientiane is $90; one-way is $45. There are usually at least three flights a day on this route. Sometimes extra charters are added. The flights are mainly on ATR-72s, which seat 70 passengers and take about 30 minutes for the trip. En route, if you crane your head out a porthole, you'll see Nam Ngum Reservoir, peppered with islands.

Luang Prabang is emerging as an air hub with connections by light aircraft to Phonsavan, Muang Sai, Luang Namtha, and Ban Huay Sai. Flights are irregular: The airlines chop and change with passenger or freight demand, so inquire closely about schedules. International connections: On Bangkok Airways, there are flights directly from Luang Prabang to Thailand's Chiang Mai airport, a 1.5-hour flight, and also to Bangkok. A neat connection is from Luang Prabang to Siem Reap (Angkor) running several times a week on Bangkok Airways. The airline may also operate a direct route to Sukothai. There's a possible flight from Luang Prabang to Jinghong in Yunnan (most likely originating in Vientiane).

Luang Prabang International Airport is three kilometers from the town by car; transfers take 10 minutes. In a jumbo it's $.75 for locals and double that for foreigners. There's a Lao Airlines office (tel. 71/212172) in Luang Prabang—be sure to confirm reservations.

By Boat

Traveling upstream on the Mekong from Vientiane to Luang Prabang can be accomplished part-way by regular ferry; from the stopping point, you would most likely have to hire a long-tailed speedboat to complete the journey. There are occasional cargo boat departures from Luang Prabang to Vientiane, a distance of more than 400 kilometers downstream, taking two days. There are no timetables for these boats. Hang around the landings and keep asking where the boat is going and when. There is a fast boat service by eight-person long-tail speedboat from Luang Prabang to Vientiane: The trip takes about eight hours.

There are various docks along Luang Prabang's Mekong shoreline. At the back of the Palace Museum is a large cargo boat dock for boats to Vientiane or Ban Huay Sai. There's a concrete driveway for heavy cargo loading, and cars can be driven directly onto the boat. There are frequent departures during the rainy season, when the Mekong runs high; the boats take passengers for extra income. The slow boat to Ban Huay Sai takes at least two days, with an overnight stop in Muang Pakbeng, and costs around $10. If you want to take in Mekong scenery, the slow boat will give you ample time—maybe too much time. The slow boat is windowless and stuffy, and facilities are basic.

Small covered craft to Muang Ngoy and Ban Hat Sa leave from the dock nearby, adjacent to the Navigation Office. You can rent boats here, too. In high-water season only, small craft run to Ban Hat Sa in Phong Saly. The first day, the boat navigates the Nam Ou past Muang Ngoy and overnights at Muang Khoua; the second day, the boat carries on to Ban Hat Sa, with passengers transferring to 4WD vehicle for the last 20 kilometers into Phong Saly, the capital.

For trips to Pak Ou Grottoes, boats can be rented near Wat Xieng Thong. You could also inquire through your hotel to arrange a boat.

Ban Don Dock, six kilometers north of Luang Prabang, is for long-tail departures. Out of character for Laos, six-person long-tail boats imported from Bangkok cover the 320-kilometer route to Ban Huay Sai in a mere six hours, as opposed to the regular slow-boat pace of 2–3 days. The long-tail boats are not allowed to dock in Luang Prabang itself because they're noisy and travel at dangerous speeds. Passports and papers are checked at Ban Don, and also at Muang Pakbeng, the midway point. For a hefty fee you can charter a speedboat to Ban Huay Sai, or try to join assembled passengers for the run. The advantage of chartering the boat is that you can tell the captain to stop along the route—pulling in at Pak Ou Grottoes, Muang Pakbeng, and so on. Ever since a Thai passenger died when a boat crashed in 1992, passengers have been required to wear crash helmets and life jackets. Actually, the crash-helmet visor serves to protect the faces of passengers from the sting of spray churned up at 70 kilometers per hour.

By Road

The paved 420-kilometer road linking Luang Prabang with Vientiane is one of Asia's most scenic, winding through karst scenery after Vangvieng. The distance can be covered in one day (about 9–10 hours) if you leave Vientiane early. The presence of Lao military has eased the threat of banditry (or is it Hmong insurgency?), but debate rages over whether the road is entirely safe or not. It's best to travel in daylight hours. Bus stations in Vientiane are about five kilometers out of town. You need to transfer by *tuk-tuk* five kilometers to the South Bus Station to head for Vientiane, and a similar transfer to the North Bus Station headed for Muang Sai. Long-distance buses ply routes from Luang Prabang north to the Chinese border and southward all the way to Pakse.

Getting Around

Three different maps of Luang Prabang will show three different sets of street names. The best way to navigate is by wats, whose names are fixed. You can pinpoint your destination by naming the nearest wat—some streets or neighborhoods are actually christened after a prominent wat.

There are no cyclos in Luang Prabang. Options include touring on foot, or by boat, bicycle, motorcycle, sidecar-taxi, or jumbo. Some hotels rent cars. Luang Prabang is small and flat, so a bicycle can easily cover the ground; you can rent bicycles from guesthouses and hotels, although some hotels will rent only to their own guests, and the police have put the screws on rental outlets in town. The Phousi Hotel rents mountain bikes, though they're not always in prime condition. Bicycle rentals run $2–4 a day. At the time of writing, it was not possible to rent motorcycles because of police policy on foreigners. This may change—look around. Motorcycles are very useful for out-of-town trips, such as to Kuangsi Falls.

Motorcycles with sidecars are a common way of getting around Luang Prabang. Sidecar-taxis cost $.30 for most destinations around town, or $.75 for longer hauls; you can hire one by the hour for $1.50. You can also hire jumbos or three-wheelers for around $2 an hour. These vehicles congregate near markets and boat docks. A variety of small boats, including speedboats, can be rented from docks along the Mekong.

on a mountain biking day trip from Luang Prabang

Excursions from Luang Prabang

N Pak Ou Grottoes

The top trip from Luang Prabang is a full day's excursion by boat along the Mekong to the Pak Ou Grottoes at the confluence of the Nam Ou River, about 25 kilometers upstream from Luang Prabang. On the way you can stop in the village of Ban Sang Hae, where moonshine whiskey is made. Just as interesting as the destination is the trip along the Mekong; the river runs wide, cutting a swath through jungle-clad banks and limestone gorges. There are times, on a slow boat headed down the river, when you are completely alone—not even a village in sight.

Boats for hire from the small-craft dock north of Luang Prabang Tourism Office include open long-tails (speedboats), open longboats (slow boats), and covered wooden longboats. It's a long trip in the harsh sun, so unless you have an umbrella, a covered boat is preferable. Long-tails are twice as fast, but the Mekong scenery whips by you. Covered boats

take two hours to get to Pak Ou Grottoes and 1.5 hours back (downstream), so you need to hire a boat for at least six hours. Assemble a group to split expenses; the boats can easily hold 10 or more passengers. Boats are expensive: $20 for an open longboat, $25 for a long-tail, $30 on a larger covered boat. Negotiate timing and itinerary.

About 20 kilometers—or 90 minutes—out of Luang Prabang along the Mekong is **Ban Sang Hae,** a village engaged in the production of rice whiskey. In the rainy season, the villagers grow glutinous rice, which is fermented in water and yeast in the dry season—a process that takes 10–15 days for each batch. This under-the-table whiskey, or *lao lao,* sells for $.75 a liter or $1 a bottle in Luang Prabang. This firewater is best drunk over ice, with a dash of lime and soda, or Coke if you prefer.

Pak Ou Grottoes are sacred caves tucked into limestone cliffs and filled with hundreds of gilded and wooden Buddha statues. Many of the images are in the distinctive Lao stance of Calling for Rain. Cave temples have been of religious significance throughout Asia from the earliest days of Buddhism, creating unique places for Buddhist monks and hermits to dwell and worship; the Pak Ou Grottoes were once occupied. Now candles and filtered light illuminate the caves, pervading them with an aura of holiness. The lower cave, Tham Ting, is reached by a series of steps from the Mekong. From here, you climb to the upper cave, Tham Phum, which is deeper and darker and requires a flashlight to explore. There are picnic shelters for lunch between the lower and upper caves. The caves are thought to be the home of guardian spirits, and the site was once inhabited by monks. The king of Laos used to visit here once a year; today, at Lao New Year, hundreds of pilgrims wend their way out from Luang Prabang.

"Pak Ou" means mouth of the Ou River. After stopping at the grottoes, you can detour up the Nam Ou tributary.

Nam Ou River Trips

The banks of the Nam Ou are much closer than those on the Mekong, and this brings in karst canyon walls closer too. The Nam Ou tributary provides a great ride—this route is used by small craft heading to Phong Saly province. You can combine a trip on the Nam Ou with a return trip on the Mekong: Go from Luang Prabang up the Nam Ou tributary to Muang Ngoy, then overland via Muang Sai to Pakbeng, where you join the Mekong again. From Pakbeng you can return along the Mekong to Luang Prabang, or forge westward to Ban Huay Sai. The options on this route include taking scheduled leaky local wooden craft and bumpy *songtaos* or putting together your own group and hiring boats and vans (which allows you to stop where you want). River conditions must be favorable for the trip up the Nam Ou (a nonstarter in the dry season); the round-trip circuit from Luang Prabang takes 2–4 days, with overnights possible in Muang Ngoy, Muang Sai, and Pakbeng. The land sections of this trip are dull, but on both rivers the scenery is spectacular.

Santi Chedi

About three kilometers east of Luang Prabang is a forest wat, Pra Phon Phao, famed as the abode of meditation master Saisamut, who died in 1992. The gold-spired Santi Chedi, or Peace Pagoda, was constructed in the 1970s and 1980s and completed in 1988. The octagonal yellow stupa has three floors and a view terrace at the top. The exterior features beautifully carved wooden shutters and doors; inside, on the ground floor, are hellish comic-strip frescoes showing the fate awaiting adulterers, murderers, and thieves—scenes that appear to spring straight out of Dante's *Inferno*. (In the Buddhist system of reincarnation, there are half a dozen realms for rebirth, among them the realm of the Hungry Ghosts and the realm of the Hells. Because Buddhism predates Christianity, Christian representations of Hell may well have been copied from Buddhist versions.)

The upper floors contain frescoes with peaceful episodes from the life of Buddha. Make your way through to the top cupola for views of Luang Prabang. Santi Chedi is open daily 0800–1000 and 1300–1630. You can bicycle out there or take a sidecar-taxi. A little way out of Luang Prabang to the southeast you come to a fork in the road; the left fork goes to Santi Chedi, the right fork to Ban Phanom.

Village Visits

Head out of Luang Prabang in any direction and you'll strike villages. Some travel outfits can arrange long treks through village areas: Lane Xang Travel arranges a three-day trek through Hmong, Lao Theung, and Khamu villages. Or just rent a motorcycle and cruise out there. You should also be able to find local jumbos or *songtaos* going to outlying villages; these vehicles usually connect to market areas in Luang Prabang.

You can combine visits to scenic sites with village visits en route. The best picnic and waterfall spot around town is **Kuangsi Falls,** 30 kilometers to the south of town. The impressive falls are multitiered and accessible by forest trails—you can hike right to the top of the falls. In a nearby village are water-driven rice mills, and about 10 kilometers short of the falls are several villages engaged in the spinning of raw cotton. Another waterfall destination is the pristine **Tad Se Falls**, about 15 kilometers southeast of Luang Prabang.

Closer to town, the villages of higher interest are those specializing in a particular craft. **Ban Phanom**, three kilometers southeast of town, is an ancient weaving village—people working handlooms under the houses turn out cotton and silk shawls and *sinhs*. Visitors are led to the village tourist trap, a circular area where the village women practically leap into the air with hard-sell tactics.

Four kilometers west of Luang Prabang is the village of **Ban Chan,** which produces ceramic storage jars and pots. The village can be reached by boat along the Mekong, or by road and a short boat hop. Right near the airport is the village of **Hat Hien,** whose inhabitants use simple implements to make knives and metalware. Take a dirt track just before reaching the main terminal building; the village is 500 meters down this road. This is not a quiet place. The air is filled with the din of sledgehammers striking metal, supplemented by the odd plane overhead and intense heat from bellows-operated foundries.

Northern Laos

The most difficult part of Laos to reach, and the least explored, is the far north, leading to the Chinese border. This zone is known for its opium cultivation—part of the notorious Golden Triangle at the intersection of Myanmar (Burma), Laos, and Thailand. In a new twist—adding China to the equation—there are plans to develop the region as a trade route known as the "Golden Growth Quadrangle," with emphasis on economic growth not dependent on poppies. While the far north holds nothing in the way of historic sights, it is certainly the most intriguing in terms of ethnic groups. The provinces of Phong Saly (22 ethnic groups), Udomxai (23 ethnic groups), and Luang Namtha (39 groups) have the country's greatest diversity of hilltribes. The best place to see these people is at the markets.

At present, travel to this region is difficult and slow; most locals rely on boat transport. Road travel is rough and can be dangerous, although the roads are being upgraded. There is intermittent air service from Vientiane to Luang Namtha, $57; and to Muang Sai, $49. There are also air connections from Luang Prabang to Luang Namtha, Muang Sai, and Ban Huay Sai. Inquire closely about air connections in the region—what appears on the Lao Airlines timetable does not necessarily agree with what appears on the runway.

A glance at the map will reveal that between the key points of Ban Huay Sai (Thai border), Luang Namtha/Ban Boten (China border), Pakbeng, and Luang Prabang, there are a number of possible rough-and-ready overland and river routes (or combinations of these). The easiest route is Ban Huay Sai to Luang Prabang along the Mekong, but there are adventurous alternatives. From Luang Prabang, for example, you could cruise up the Nam Ou tributary to Muang Ngoy, continue overland to Muang Sai and Pakbeng, then along the Mekong to Ban Huay Sai. Also consider round-trip routings using Luang Prabang as a launching pad. You could fly to Luang Namtha or Ban Huay Sai and make your way back to Luang Prabang along road and river routes. Go for the journey and river scenery—the provincial capitals, such as Muang Sai and Luang Namtha, are uninspiring. Here is a brief description of "stepping stones" along the way.

Ban Huay Sai, Thai Border

The easiest route to tackle in the north is the Ban Huay Sai to Luang Prabang boat trip. This presents some of the most scenic sections of the Mekong in Laos. You can enter or exit Thailand at Ban Huay Sai; the Thai town across the Mekong is Chiang Khong. It's possible to pick up a Lao tourist visa in Chiang Khong at guesthouses—the cost is around $70. The ride from

Luang Prabang west to Ban Huay Sai takes at least two days by cargo boat—the boats stop along the river at night because of the danger of rocks and reefs. Boat service may be infrequent, and the boats themselves are windowless and stuffy, with very basic facilities. You might persuade the captain to let you sit on the roof once you're out of sight of officialdom.

A more expensive alternative is a long-tail boat, which takes a mere six hours to cover the distance. The scenery is majestic, with limestone cliffs, monsoon forest, stands of giant bamboo, and fishing villages. You get to see the many moods of the Mekong, which run the gamut from serene to surging currents. The midway point is Pakbeng, a collection of wooden housing with a few wats and guesthouses. The trip lasts about seven hours downstream from Ban Huay Sai to Pakbeng. It takes a skilled boatman to navigate the Mekong: At times limestone outcrops and rocky reefs emerge above the water, and low water exposes huge sandbanks. When the river narrows—sandwiched between limestone cliffs—the currents are especially tricky, and sometimes whirlpools form as different currents collide.

Other road and river routes to and from Ban Huay Sai may be hazardous because of smuggling activity and banditry. Another possible Mekong river trip leads from Ban Huay Sai to Xiengkok, on the Burmese border, by speedboat—a trip of about five hours upstream. From Xiengkok you can continue 75 kilometers by rough road to Muang Sing ethnic market, near Luang Namtha. However, because of opium-smuggling activity close to the Myanmar (Burma) border, parts of this route could be dangerous. Also considered dangerous because of sporadic banditry is the road route from Ban Huay Sai to Ban Boten. Smugglers use this route to deliver luxury cars from Thailand to China, driving from Ban Huay Sai direct along Route 3 to Luang Namtha and then on to Ban Boten border crossing.

While the cars head north toward China, the town of Ban Huay Sai sees a brisk trade in Chinese goods; it's an important commercial center along the Mekong, as is its counterpart in Thailand, the town of Chiang Khong. Barges come downstream all the way from Yunnan in China. Ban Huay Sai has a checkered past as part of the opium and heroin route to Chiang Mai in Thailand; the area is known for its poppy fields. Sapphires are mined in the area, and timber is exported through the town to Thailand. You can hike up a set of stairs lined with *naga* balustrades to the top of Wat Chom Khao Manirat for a view of the town. For an unusual experience, inquire about a place called Gibbon Experience, which is a canopy walkway about 70 kilometers from Ban Huay Sai. You stay in a treetop house and look for gibbons. Three-day trips out this way cost $70.

Facilities in Ban Huay Sai are limited but extend to a bank, post office, and a dozen guesthouses. A number of guesthouses are clustered close to the Mekong boat crossing point: These also serve as restaurants. There's a Lao Airlines office in Ban Huay Sai; in theory, there are daily flights to Luang Prabang.

Border formalities: On the Thai side, at Chiang Khong, there are no visa problems—you are simply stamped in or out. On the Lao side, you need a valid Lao visa. If you weren't able to arrange this in time in Bangkok, you can pick up a 15- or 30-day Lao visa right in Chiang Khong for about $70. Depending on the political mood at the time, the passport (in theory) either (a) goes across to Ban Huay Sai for the necessary visa, or (b) is spirited all the way back to the embassy in Bangkok. If exiting Laos at Ban Huay Sai, you can take a ferry to Chiang Khong in Thailand (a bridge spanning the Mekong was under construction here). Chiang Khong is 137 kilometers from Chiang Rai, one of Thailand's largest trekking centers; from Chiang Rai, it's 197 kilometers to Chiang Mai, with excellent connections to other parts of Thailand. There are comfortable air-conditioned express buses running to Bangkok from Chiang Rai and Chiang Mai, and a rail-link with sleepers operating from Chiang Mai.

Pakbeng

Pakbeng is a laid-back port town midway between Ban Huay Sai and Luang Prabang.

The town hosts a ramshackle collection of wooden huts strung out along a winding slope that leads down to the Mekong docks. Town offers some good views of the Mekong, and as port towns go, it's not bad. There are several wooden guesthouses in Pakbeng, toward the top of the hill, with basic rooms with mosquito net and common toilets for around $4. Here you can find **Phuvien GH** and, next door, **Nang Mime GH.** There's a small day market farther down the hill, and some restaurants with basic fare. Top end of Pakbeng is **Luangsay Lodge,** an ecostyle cluster of 16 pavilions with a vista of forest and river, and the bonus of being rodent-free.

You might want to overnight in Pakbeng if you're on a boat headed to Luang Prabang. There's also the option of getting off a cargo boat here and proceeding on a fascinating overland-and-boat route through Muang Sai and Muang Ngoy to Luang Prabang. Long with larger cargo boats passing through Pakbeng, there are small wooden covered craft that originate here—and you can also hire longtail speedboats. If leaving or arriving by boat, check in with your passport at the "customs" shack down by the waterfront.

Muang Sai

This dreary frontier town is the capital of the province of Udomxai and is a strategic junction in the north. Confusingly, the town is also known by the name of "Udomxai." The town is little more than an elaborate intersection with four roads radiating at the compass points. At the junction in the middle of town is the bus terminal and the main market; to the north, past the Kaysone statue, is the Immigration Police Office and a bank; to the west is the post office. There are more than a dozen concrete-monstrosity hotels and guesthouses, mostly on the north road and to the east across a bridge. The guesthouses on the east side are cheaper and quieter. The larger hotels at the center of town tend to cater to the Chinese karaoke crowd, with prostitutes imported from Yunnan province in southwest China (there is a large contingent of Chinese construction workers in town). Muang Sai is reached by rough *songtao* pickup ride from Pakbeng (about 140 kilometers, six hours), from Muang Ngoy (120 kilometers, five hours), or Luang Namtha (117 kilometers, five hours). These pickup rides are around $4–5 a person, or you can charter the whole pickup. Muang Sai has an airstrip, and there are (on paper anyway) frequent connections to Luang Prabang and twice-weekly flights to Vientiane. More irregular are flights to Ban Huay Sai.

Muang Khoua

This riverine town to the northeast near the Vietnamese border can be reached in a few hours by pickup truck from Muang Sai. Muang Khoua has an entrancing setting, enclosed by lofty karst peaks: There's great hiking in the area. It lies at the confluence of two rivers, and a suspension bridge across one provides majestic views. The elaborate bridge is for foot and two-wheel traffic only. A great trip by small wooden boat proceeds from Muang Khoua to Muang Ngoi along the Nam Ou River. This may not be a regular commuter ride; you might have to team up with others and split the cost of the boat.

Muang Ngoi

Watch the name confusion with Muang Ngoy. Sited along the Nam Ou, Muang Ngoi is an excellent place to experience Lao village life. You become part of the village because the guesthouses are family-run. Several attractions around town: a hike out to a waterfall and a hike to a series of caves. There is a small monastery to one end of the town: Monks do the alms rounds at the crack of dawn.

Muang Ngoy

Muang Ngoy (also known as Nong Khieo) is a pretty village with classic karst backdrops. The village has its own concrete bridge spanning the Nam Ou river. Muang Ngoy acts as a major transfer point by road or river: The village can be visited as a stepping-stone on a foray into the north, or as a destination in its own right as a round-trip from Luang Prabang.

Water levels must be high enough to make the journey up the Nam Ou tributary—inquire in advance. If they are, it is a don't miss trip. There are lots of guesthouses to choose from in Muang Ngoy.

It can take a full day for the trip from Luang Prabang upstream on the Nam Ou—the pilot must plot a course around sandbars and through minor rapids. Generally, 6–7 hours should be enough for a covered boat to make the trip; by speedboat it's only two hours. If you have hired a boat yourself, you can arrange stops at Pak Ou Grottoes and various villages along the way. You can get to Muang Ngoy by scheduled covered wooden boat from Luang Prabang, with departures near the Navigation Office at the back of the Palace Museum. There are also long-tail boats on this route. After overnighting in Muang Ngoy, you can hop in a *songtao* heading westward to Muang Sai, about 120 kilometers away. From Muang Sai you can carry on by *songtao* to Luang Namtha, or head southward to Pakbeng. At Pakbeng, you join the Mekong, with routes back to Luang Prabang, or west to Ban Huay Sai.

Phong Saly

When the water levels are high enough, in the June–October rainy season, you can ride the Nam Ou tributary all the way up to Ban Hat Sa, 20 kilometers south of Phong Saly, and transfer to a 4WD jeep for the final stretch to Phong Saly, the capital of Phong Saly province. This would most likely be a two-day journey by covered wooden boat, with an overnight at Muang Khoua. By speedboat, however, it's considerably faster. It's also possible to travel on a rough road from Muang Sai to Muang Khoua, and then take a boat from Muang Khoua to Ban Hat Sa. A Chinese-engineered road was under construction from Muang Sai to Phong Saly. At present, Phong Saly does not lie on any connecting routes: It's an in-and-out trip (or you can diverge at Muang Ngoy on the way back). However, if the Chinese border to the west of Phong Saly is opened to foreigners, Phong Saly would be a fast route into Yunnan.

The town itself can disappoint if you're in search of ethnic groups: Most minority people live outside town, which requires hiking for a few days. There's a small ethnology museum in Phong Saly with background information on ethnic traditions and costumes. Phong Saly has a bank, post office, several guesthouses, and a larger, Chinese-built hotel.

Muang Sing Market

Muang Sing was once the largest opium market of the Golden Triangle—a trade sanctioned by the French. Today it's a magnet for hilltribe groups such as the Thai Lu, Shan, Hmong, Mien, Lolo, and Iko, shopping for produce, meat, hardware, and textile supplies (some stalls in the market sell traditional textiles). Because of the ethnic mix, the market is among the most fascinating in northern Laos and well worth the visit. Get there early. The hilltribe folk drift into town in predawn hours: At the crack of dawn, the market is bustling. The main Morning Market is at the northwest edge of town, along a narrow single street. It is mostly for food: People of the hilltribes sell everything from wild mushrooms to bootleg whisky—mundane transactions to the hilltribe eye, but an exotic swirl of color and movement to the Western eye. After selling their wicker basket-loads of ginger or sweet potato, they stock up on batteries, candles, and cloth—things they cannot grow—and head for the hills, where the real working day begins. By 0900, the market is pretty much all over.

If you want to see the hilltribes in their own environment, you must hike to the villages out of town. You can also rent a bicycle in Muang Sing and proceed by a combination of bike and on foot. There are several basic guesthouses in town with rooms for $2 apiece, allowing you to base yourself here and explore the area for a few days.

You can reach Muang Sing by truck from Luang Namtha in about two hours: There are usually several trucks a day. An adventurous onward route is to travel by truck from Muang Sing to Xieng Kok, a Lao village 75 kilometers to the southwest, right on the Mekong at the Myanmar (Burma) border. There is a lively

MUANG SING

To Adima Guesthouse and Chinese Border

To Morning Market and Bus Station

SAONGDEUANE GUESTHOUSE

BICYCLE RENTAL

EXHIBITION HALL ■

● SINGTHONG GUESTHOUSE

● DAN NEUA GUESTHOUSE

● TAILUE GUESTHOUSE

MUANGSING GUESTHOUSE ●

● VIENGPHONE GUESTHOUSE

BANK ● VIENGXAY GUESTHOUSE

● SENGKATYIVONG GUESTHOUSE

SINGXAY GUESTHOUSE

CHAMPADAENG GUESTHOUSE

POST OFFICE ■

Markets

THAI DAM EMBROIDERY

KAYSONE MONUMENT ★

BUNGALOWS

TRADITIONAL HERBAL SAUNA/MASSAGE/ MUONGSING VIEW ■ RESTAURANT

SING CHAREAN GUESTHOUSE

PHODIU GUESTHOUSE

0   100 yds

0   100 m

To Luang Namtha

To Xieng Kok

© AVALON TRAVEL PUBLISHING, INC.

Luang Prabang & N. Laos

in Thailand to Ban Huay Sai, take a long-tail up to Xieng Kok, and then pickup truck to Muang Sing.

Ban Boten, China Border

As long as your paperwork is in order (valid visas), you can cross the China-Laos border at Ban Boten, which lies about three hours by truck from Luang Namtha. You can also reach Ban Boten directly by road from Muang Sai. At present there are no facilities in Ban Boten, although a border town of some sort will most likely spring up. The nearest large towns are Luang Namtha on the Lao side, Mengla on the Chinese side.

There are plans to link the components of the Golden Growth Quadrangle—Thailand, Laos, China, and Myanmar (Burma)—with a ring road. The new ring road, still some years away because of opium armies and unruly minorities, would connect Chiang Rai in Thailand with Jinghong, China, for the purposes of trade and tourism. The road through Laos is in very bad shape: The projected route goes from the Thai town of Chiang Rai to Chiang Khong, across the Mekong at Ban Huay Sai, along Route 3 to Luang Namtha, then crosses via Ban Boten to the Chinese town of Mengla, and runs to Jinghong. Completing the ring road, from Jinghong the road arcs south to Kengtung in Myanmar (Burma), then to Tachilek, crossing the Thai border to reach Mae Sai and Chiang Rai.

Even without proper roads, the Lao border point of Ban Boten sees a brisk trade in luxury automobiles delivered from Thailand to China. Hundreds of luxury cars, shipped into Thailand from Bahrain and the Gulf states or the United States, are driven to Chiang Khong, ferried across the Mekong to Ban Huay Sai, and driven to Ban Boten. Traders spend about $1,000 on "handling charges" to get the cars through Thailand. On the Chinese side, taxes can exceed 200 percent of the value of the car, though less costly arrangements can be negotiated with border officials.

Roads on the Chinese side are in good condition. Chinese tourists from Kunming take

market held at Xieng Kok twice a month (inquire when exactly) with Lao and Burmese tribespeople gathering. From Xieng Kok, the next day you can arrange a long-tail boat from Xieng Kok downstream on the Mekong to Ban Huay Sai, a journey of about four hours. There is a kind of monopoly on pricing for foreigners on the long-tail boats: The drivers generally want to see $22 for the ride, which is a lot for Laos, and you can be sure that locals do not pay that princely sum. One side of the Mekong here is Laos, the other Myanmar (Burma)—the long-tail stops at both banks to pick and drop passengers. You can also get to Muang Sing by the same route: Cross over from Chiang Khong

trips by road through the area, crossing south of Mengla. Phong Saly province is in fact more accessible from Mengla than from Luang Prabang. If trade flourishes at the Laos-China border, and if road transport is upgraded, this area may develop as a crossing point into China's Yunnan province. Boat routes are also being developed. Small cargo boats ply the Mekong between Jinghong and Ban Huay Sai (Chiang Khong); passenger boats also make the run.

LUANG NAMTHA

Luang Namtha is the capital of the province of the same name, but lest this conjure visions of a grand metropolis, be assured that the town is just a trading post with a cluster of wooden and concrete buildings. It caters to trade between China, Thailand, and Laos. Luang Namtha is a staging point. It is divided into two sections separated by a gap of seven kilometers. To the south is old Luang Namtha with the airfield and not much else; seven kilometers from the airfield is the main new town, with a market, bus depot, post office, bank, travel agent, and a dozen guesthouses. Old Luang Namtha was severely bombed during the Vietnam War, which explains the building of new Luang Namtha. New Luang Namtha is built on a Soviet model of sweeping boulevards (which see very little traffic).

Most of the things to see lie outside town. With a hired mountain bike and a half-decent map, you can easily mount your own loop-tour of Luang Namtha environs. Cycle directly north on the main road of Luang Namtha, turn east to get to the village of Ban Nam Dee, where there is a turnoff to a small waterfall. Backtrack to the main road, go southeast to the village of Ban Nam Thoung, and you will strike a beautiful dirt road leading through villages to Ban Phong. From Ban Phong you can proceed to the Boat Landing Guesthouse for a drink, and then complete the circuit back into town.

Kayaking the Namtha River

Wildside, near Manychan Guesthouse, arranges one- to three-day hiking, kayaking, and rafting trips downstream on the Namtha River. You can arrange trek and kayak combinations, too. Rafting depends on whether the water level is high enough. You probably won't see much in the way of wildlife on a trip like this, but there is the chance of sighting birds and butterflies, and the scenery is grand. It is unusual in Laos to be able to mount a kayak foray that actually gets you somewhere: The trip from Luang Namtha could be one-way—you could proceed downstream all the way to Pak Tha, which is close to Ban Huay Sai. From there you have a number of options: crossing over into Thailand, or making your way along the Mekong to Luang Prabang.

Hilltribe Trekking

Through the Luang Namtha Tourism Office (tel. 86/211534) you can arrange one- to three-day hiking and river trips. Some are only trekking; others are combination boat-trek tours. Prices range from $10 for day trips to $35 for three-day treks with village homestays. Guides trained by a foreign NGO group lead hikes along the edge of the 222,400-hectare Nam Ha National Biodiversity Conservation Area (Nam Ha NBCA).

A two-day hike costs $25 a person, including transport to the starting point, all food, and overnight stay in a Khmu village. The trek winds past cultivated rice fields near villages, while other sections meander through remnants of old-growth forest, with an arabesque of lianas and gnarled strangler figs or thickets of bamboo. You will hear birdcalls and see a number of bright butterflies, but don't expect to see wildlife on this hike: Centuries of hunting has made wildlife very reclusive and wary (tours conducted by river in this NBCA result in more bird sightings). Instead you will see a lot of domestic animals—pigs, chickens, turkeys, and yapping dogs—belonging to villagers. Getting to know the hilltribe folk and their simple lifestyle is a major part of the hike. In a Khmu village where you stay the night, part of the trek fee is given to develop the area. You dine in a thatched Khmu hut raised on stilts; typical fare is sticky rice, meat, and vegetables eaten with the bare hands. You will invariably be offered the local firewater—*lao hai*—made

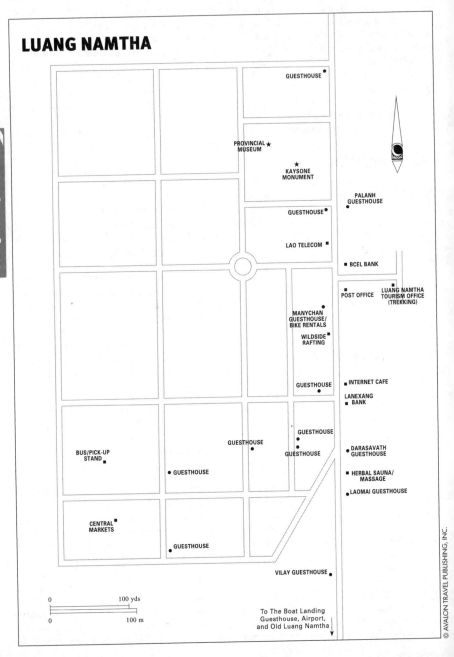

LUANG NAMTHA

GUESTHOUSE

PROVINCIAL ★ MUSEUM

★ KAYSONE MONUMENT

PALANH GUESTHOUSE

GUESTHOUSE

LAO TELECOM ■

■ BCEL BANK

POST OFFICE ■   LUANG NAMTHA TOURISM OFFICE (TREKKING)

MANYCHAN GUESTHOUSE/ BIKE RENTALS

WILDSIDE ■ RAFTING

GUESTHOUSE   ■ INTERNET CAFE

LANEXANG ■ BANK

GUESTHOUSE

GUESTHOUSE

GUESTHOUSE   ■ DARASAVATH GUESTHOUSE

BUS/PICK-UP STAND ■

■ HERBAL SAUNA/ MASSAGE

● GUESTHOUSE

● LAOMAI GUESTHOUSE

CENTRAL ■ MARKETS

● GUESTHOUSE

VILAY GUESTHOUSE ●

0   100 yds

0   100 m

To The Boat Landing Guesthouse, Airport, and Old Luang Namtha

Luang Prabang & N. Laos

© AVALON TRAVEL PUBLISHING, INC.

from fermented rice and spices. This is kept in a large earthen jar: Everyone gathers round the jar and drinks through long bamboo straws. Gracious hilltribe hospitality requires that you get sozzled before leaving the hut.

Practicalities

Almost everything you need in new Luang Namtha is on the north-south boulevard to the east side of Luang Namtha. In the midsection of that boulevard is **Manychan Guesthouse,** which serves terrific fruit shakes and serves as a traveler rendezvous point of sorts. The guesthouses around town charge about $10 a room. More upscale is the **Boat Landing Guesthouse,** tel. 86/312398, http://theboatlanding. com. This 10-room ecotourism lodge is near the airfield and charges $28–45 for beautiful bungalows close to the river. The design is well thought-out, taking full advantage of its natural setting. The lodge can arrange mountain-bike touring. The Boat Landing website is a mine of information about Luang Namtha. One problem with this place is that it is a long way from town: Management can call in a *tuk-tuk,* or you can rent a bicycle to solve this.

Ground transport to Muang Sing, Ban Boten, Muang Sai, and Ban Huay Sai leaves from the market area. Planes from Luang Namtha to Luang Prabang and Vientiane can be booked at Lao Airlines, whose office is at the airfield to the far south of town. Only 17-seater light planes operate to Luang Namtha, so seats are at a premium.

THE PLAIN OF JARS

The Plain of Jars is a plain with a lot of big jars on it—worth a few hours of your time to figure out what the heck all those jars are doing there. How did they get there? Who made them? Why? Nobody knows.

Is it worth flying up from Vientiane to look at a stack of old jars? Well, if you want a preview, go to Wat Pra Keo or the Revolutionary Museum in Vientiane; each has a jar airlifted from the plain. For a visit to the Plain of Jars, you must weigh several factors: the expense in-

volved, the fact that the jars are overrated, and the fact that this is a remote and little-visited area. If you like to get right off the track and into the surrounding countryside, then the area holds interest; the jars alone do not. You can, however, use the Plain of Jars as a stepping-stone from Vientiane to Luang Prabang or vice versa, because there are plane and road connections to both. Also consider the Plain of Jars as a stepping-stone on two border exits to Vietnam: one due east at Nong Het, and the other beyond Sam Neua at Nameo border crossing.

The tiny gateway town to the Plain of Jars is **Phonsavan** (population 8,000), the capital of Xieng Khuang province, to the northeast of Vientiane. Flying into Phonsavan you can see the bomb-scarred terrain of Xieng Khuang Plateau (this province was heavily bombed during the Vietnam War era and was off-limits for tourism until quite recently). Teams of American MIA searchers were allowed to scour the zone starting in 1993—what's remarkable is that they're allowed in at all after all the destruction wrought by U.S. bombing.

During the Vietnam War, the Xieng Khuang Plateau became a strategic battleground. On one side were U.S.-backed royalist forces, and Hmong fighters under General Vang Pao; on the other side were the Pathet Lao, supported by the North Vietnamese Army (NVA). For the Vietnamese, the plateau was the rear flank of Hanoi; by 1972 the NVA had seven divisions in Laos supporting the Pathet Lao. American B-52 bombing of the plateau had a devastating effect on villages in the area; in addition to direct bombing, B-52s returning from raids on Hanoi jettisoned bomb loads over Laos en route to the U.S. air base at Udon Thani in Thailand.

Villages around Phonsavan use scrap metal from bomb casings and downed U.S. planes for building materials and household items. Scrap metal is taken to small warehouses in Phonsavan and later melted down as a source of cheap metal.

Logistics

Take a few supplies from Vientiane; availability is limited in Phonsavan. That's why you'll see

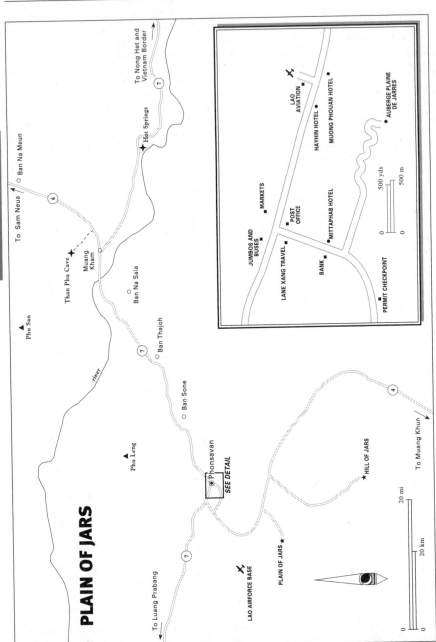

PLAIN OF JARS

To Luang Prabang

To Sam Neua

To Nong Het and Vietnam Border

Ban Na Meun

Phu San

Than Phu Cave

Muang Kham

Hot Springs

Ban Na Sala

Ban Thajoh

river

Phu Leng

Ban Sone

Phonsavan

SEE DETAIL

LAO AIRFORCE BASE

PLAIN OF JARS

HILL OF JARS

To Muang Khun

20 mi

20 km

0

Detail inset:

LAO AVIATION

HAYHIN HOTEL

MUONG PHOUAN HOTEL

AUBERGE PLAINE DE JARRES

MARKETS

POST OFFICE

MITTAPHAB HOTEL

JUMBOS AND BUSES

LANE XANG TRAVEL

BANK

PERMIT CHECKPOINT

500 yds

500 m

0

0

© AVALON TRAVEL PUBLISHING, INC.

passengers loading up on French bread at the airport in Vientiane: Baguettes are not made in Xieng Khuang, and they make nice gifts for local hosts. Plain of Jars Mineral Water, however, is available. Bring lots of cash. The bank in Phonsavan gives a similar exchange rate to those in Vientiane but deals only in cash. Bring a jacket if you're visiting December–February, as temperatures can fall to 0°C overnight in Xieng Khuang province at that time of year. Xieng Khuang Plateau sits at an elevation of 1,000 meters, which means the weather is mild.

Transport is a headache in Phonsavan; you'll more than likely be held for ransom by local tour companies because there aren't many options for local transport. Roads—even in the dry season—require 4WD vehicles in some areas, and buses are prone to breakdowns. In the rainy season the roads are often impassable. It would be wise to hook up with a guide in Phonsavan. Guides cost about $5 a day, regardless of group size. Regulations are strict here: The place is still back in the communist era, more remote, with fewer visitors. If you're wandering around by yourself, you must be a spy. Authorities are also sensitive about exploding foreigners—there's a lot of leftover ordnance lying around. A guide should be aware of danger areas.

Another reason for the heightened security lies just west of the Plain of Jars: a huge new airbase, destined to be the headquarters of the Lao Air Force. Vientiane is considered too close to Thailand for a strategic base.

Authorities are vigilant about paperwork in Phonsavan. Your papers may be checked at Phonsavan airfield and at the checkpoint on the road to the Plain of Jars.

Phonsavan Market

Phonsavan is the base for exploring the area. There's little to see in this frontier town except for the market. Besides the food stalls, fresh vegetables, and rice, the market sells dry goods—mainly household goods from the Vietnamese border such as thermoses and blankets. Look closely and you'll find spoons of aluminum recycled from U.S. planes. On sale,

too, are *sinhs,* Hmong necklaces, opium in the form of a black fudge sold by Hmong tribespeople, and all kinds of mysterious herbs and potions that are local remedies for anything from fatigue to impotence.

The Plain of Jars

There are eight sites with jars in the area around Phonsavan, with a total of perhaps 200–300 intact jars. Most are concentrated at two sites. The main site is about 12 kilometers from town on a gravel road; it takes about 20 minutes by jeep or maybe half an hour by jumbo from the markets. The site is fenced off, with a pavilion at the entrance charging a $1.40 entry fee, extra for a still or video camera. Unfortunately, the jars have recently been numbered in white lettering in order of size starting with 001 for the really big one down to fragments numbered at around 290. Look for round lids to the rimmed jars too—there are several lying around.

The jars stand 1–2.5 meters high, with diameters ranging .5–2 meters. Some weigh in at the size of cars—600 kilograms to six tons. Some archaeologists speculate masons in ancient Laos found a way to produce a cement that looks exactly like stone, like the fabled medieval alchemists who turned lead to gold. The material looks like gray sandstone covered with lichens. Some jars appear to have been chiseled from granite or limestone. Other theories run the gamut from extraterrestrial activity to the Land of the Giants. Similar urns have been found in Central Sulawesi, Indonesia, and are also of unknown origin. The jars may be connected with the Dongson culture of the Bronze Age, which flourished in the Thanh Hoa area of Vietnam's Red River Delta.

As to the function of the jars, theories vary from funerary urns to rice storage to wine fermentation vessels. Some jars required lids, which suggests there was a reason to open and close them. The most plausible theory is that the larger jars were used as sarcophagi for aristocracy, and the smaller jars for those of lesser rank. The fact that human bones have been found in some of the smaller jars adds weight

© MICHAEL BUCKLEY

at the Plain of Jars

to this theory. The cave at the site could have been where cremations took place or where the jars were fired. There are no stone quarries in the vicinity, so how the jars were transported is a puzzle. Some kind of civilized society was responsible for the jars, but this culture disappeared without a trace.

An even greater mystery is just how all these jars survived saturation bombing by the U.S. Air Force. According to the guides, only a few were shattered by bombs. Considering the Pathet Lao maintained their headquarters in the cave next to the site, it seems odd the area survived unscathed.

The Hill of Jars

A secondary jar site about 20 kilometers south from the Plain of Jars is reached over a rough dirt road. It takes about 50 minutes to get there by jeep, which will give you some idea of road conditions. This one is a Hill of Jars, sited on a nice slope overlooking valleys. There are more than 50 pieces here. Several jars are longer than two meters, with larger pieces resting on the ground rather than upright. This area is more remote; follow your guide.

Accommodations and Food

Just around the corner from the airstrip is the main drag. Phonsavan is still under construction, with most of the hotels built since the 1990s. A good choice is **Kong Keo GH,** tel. 61/211354, with rooms $3–6. It has a communal area with a fire-trough made out of a bomb casing. The owner, Mr. Kong Keo, is very knowledgeable about the region and can arrange touring and onward transport. Right near the airfield are three hotels: **Muong Phouan,** with rooms going for $7–11. Next door, and a few notches down in quality and price, is **Vieng Thong GH.** Farther west is **Hayhin GH,** with basic rooms for $5. To the west of this are the post office and the markets. There are several other basic guesthouses along the main drag here, including **Seng Mixay GH** and **Vanhaloun Hotel.** About two kilometers from the airfield is **Phu Doi Hotel** (Mittaphab Hotel), Vietnamese-run and charging $10–15 for a room with outside bathroom. The classiest place in town, requiring taxi service, is the **Auberge Plaine de Jarres,** also known as the French Hotel, with 16 rustic cabins for around $50 each, with hot water, shower, fireplaces, and a generator till 2100. This chalet resort is about five kilometers from the airfield, out of town on Mt. Pupadeng. It has great views and its own dining hall. For food in Phonsavan, try the hotel dining rooms—the Muong Phouan is good—or the food stalls in the markets.

Getting There

By road, you can detour from Route 13, forking to Route 7, where the going gets rough. That means you could include Phonsavan as part of a Vientiane to Luang Prabang trip. Another option is Vientiane to Phonsavan and then exit to Vietnam via the Nong Het or Nameo border crossings.

The plane flying from Vientiane to Phonsavan is a Yun-12 Chinese light turboprop, a type that has yet to receive international certification—a comforting thought. The plane seats 17 passengers, but three seats may be taken up by passenger baggage, so that means 14 passengers. The flight consists of 40 minutes of aerial terror—the terror factor depending on weather, visibility, and thermals. Concentrating on the scenery is a good idea; the plane passes over mountain terrain, including the highest peak in Laos, Mt. Phu Bia, at 2,850 meters. The locals seem to take it all casually—at the other end, in Phonsavan, you walk off the plane to find water buffalo eating grass near the runway. Return airfare from Vientiane is $65. A second airfield accommodating larger aircraft, Yun-7s and ATRs, opened in early 1995. There is a twice-weekly flight from Phonsavan to Luang Prabang, making it possible to loop by air from Vientiane to Phonsavan to Luang Prabang and back to Vientiane, or make a Vientiane–Phonsavan–Luang Prabang one-way trip and then proceed to Luang Namtha or points in the northwest by air, boat, or truck.

Getting Around

Several tour outfits in town handle travelers, who are largely forced to band together to see the sights farther out of town. This means hiring a jeep or minibus with guide. **Xieng Khuang Travel** operates a regular taxi on good roads. The charge is $48 round-trip to Nam Het, the trading town on the Vietnamese border. **Lane Xang Travel,** with an office near the markets, maintains jeeps. A jeep is $25 a day, including driver; a guide is $5 a day extra. Set schedules: $33 round-trip south to Muang Khun; $30 east to Tham Piu Cave and the hot springs. Negotiate your itinerary carefully. Once you've agreed on the route, the driver is very reluctant to change plans. Hidden extras include food for the crew, site entry fees, and paperwork if necessary.

There's a transport depot near the markets with jumbos for rent. Although small buses run to local towns, the authorities may decide you're not allowed to use them—regulations can change, however. Some travelers have been able to commandeer a jumbo to reach the main site of the Plain of Jars, but others have been told jumbos cannot be rented for this purpose. No bicycle or motorcycle rentals are available.

VICINITY OF PHONSAVAN
Route 4 South

The old capital, formerly known as Xieng Khuang and now called **Muang Khun,** is 35 kilometers south from Phonsavan on Route 4. The village was destroyed by U.S. bombing, its temples reduced to rubble. A forlorn-looking Buddha statue presides over the rubble. There were plans to rebuild the temples, as well as a 30-meter stupa that overlooks the town. The town has been rebuilt since 1975, and the population is now around 10,000. You can secure accommodations in Muang Khun; ask a guide to arrange it. The town is a dead-end of sorts because the road south of Muang Khun is in very bad shape. There are four buses a day to Muang Khun from Phonsavan, but authorities may block your use of local transport—you're expected to go by jeep.

Along Route 4 south are lots of villages. Villagers are poor and there is evidence of malnutrition, with cases of goiter; malaria is also a problem. The people live in thatched huts on stilts, some supported by bomb casings; casings are also used for fences and pig troughs. No mystery here—the bombs were dropped by American warplanes during saturation bombing raids in the 1960s and 1970s. Most of the Lao in Xieng Khuang province fled; an estimated 8,000 civilians were killed by U.S. bombs, and entire towns were razed.

The bomb casing used to support a hut is half a CBU, or cluster bomb unit. This is composed of a "mother bomb" with a pea-pod casing containing 150 tennis-ball sized bomblets. At a predetermined altitude, the CBU casing splits open, releasing the bomblets. Each anti-personnel bomblet contains several hundred steel pellets—some detonate upon hitting the ground; others, insidiously, fall to earth to detonate only when something or someone comes in contact with them. Up to a dozen people a month are killed or injured by bomblets.

Route 7 East

Route 7 east leads 115 kilometers to the town of Nong Het, close to the Vietnamese border, where it's possible to exit Laos into Vietnam if your paperwork is in order. The road out this way is sealed and in good shape, which means you can cover a lot of ground quickly. The major junction along the way is Muang Kham, at the intersection of Route 6 and Route 7. From Phonsavan, it's 53 kilometers to Muang Kham, and then 62 kilometers on to Nong Het, which is 25 kilometers short of the Vietnamese border. The trip from Phonsavan to Nong Het takes about eight hours by local bus, three hours by taxi, or 4.5 hours by jeep one-way, so it's a very full day trip to reach Nong Het, with a suggested stop at Tham Piu Cave near Muang Kham. The route features lush bamboo, banana, fir, and spruce trees, and villages of Hmong (Meo) and Thai Dam (Black Thai) people. Heading out of Phonsavan on Route 7 you pass the villages of Ban Sone, 12 kilome-

ters out; Ban Thajoh, 30 kilometers; and Ban Na Sala, about 45 kilometers. Sunday could be market day in one of the villages.

You can stop at the villages and wander around. Villagers sometimes approach tourists to sell embroidery, bugs, or fighting beetles. There are food stalls at **Muang Kham,** a bit more than an hour from Phonsavan by car. From Muang Kham, your transport can drop you a little way north on Route 6 at the trailhead for **Tham Piu Cave.** A half-hour hike (take a guide) gets you to the cave. On March 8, 1968, two U.S. T-28 fighter-bombers swooped in from Thailand and fired rockets into Tham Piu Cave, which served as an air-raid shelter. More than 300 villagers were killed in the rocket attack; the interior of the cave is littered with rubble, a stark war memorial.

About 18 kilometers east of Muang Kham are some hot springs off Route 7. The springs are quite ordinary, with hot water piped 200 meters from the springs into a miniresort enclosure with four standard bathtubs. You can take a bath for $.60, but entry to the area is a rip-off $3.50. The compound was built as a retreat for high-ranking officials; huts rent for $5–20.

Nong Het is a trading town with lots of commerce. Vietnamese goods flow across the border. It's 25 kilometers shy of the actual border crossing.

Route 6 Northeast

An alternate border crossing into Vietnam lies at Nameo, which is in the northeast, beyond the town of Sam Neua. Sam Neua can also be reached by a rough road from Luang Prabang. Not much to see at Sam Neua—the place is revered because caves in the area sheltered the Pathet Lao leaders when the chips were down.

Know Vietnam, Cambodia & Laos

The Land

GEOGRAPHY

Vietnam

Encompassing 332,000 square kilometers, Vietnam is roughly the size of Italy or Japan. The S-shaped peninsula of Vietnam faces the South China Sea, which the Vietnamese, none too keen on China's presence in the area, call the Eastern Sea. To the north and west, Vietnam is bordered by China, Laos, and Cambodia. The majority of the population is concentrated in two fertile delta areas where rice is intensively cultivated: the Red River Delta in the north and the Mekong Delta in the south. In between lies a long, narrow coastal plain. The Vietnamese describe their country as a bamboo pole supporting a basket of rice at either end. From north to south, Vietnam stretches about 1,800 kilometers, with its width varying from as little as 60 kilometers in the center to as much as 600 kilometers along the northern border with China.

Vietnam has 3,200 kilometers of coastline, stretching from the Gulf of Tonkin to the Gulf of Thailand. The coastal and marine environment harbors rich biodiversity and resources. Marine habitats remain under severe threat because of unregulated practices such as dynamite fishing, overfishing, and coral mining.

Numerous islands lie off the coast. These, together with the Con Dao archipelago, are recognized as Vietnam's. However, other island groups are contested. Phu Quoc Island is claimed by Cambodia. Cambodia and Thailand both claim islands in the Gulf of Thailand; China asserts sovereignty over the Paracels. Spratly Islands are contested in whole or part by China, the Philippines, Malaysia, Brunei, Indonesia, and Taiwan.

The flashpoint of the region is the Spratlys. Taiwan has built a meteorological station there, Vietnam plans to build lighthouses and fishing harbors, and China is surveying the place for oil. Territorial waters around these islands may be a lucrative source of undersea oil, fishing, and other resources. Both Vietnam and China have issued statements claiming sovereignty over the Spratlys and the Paracels, and there have been naval skirmishes in both areas. Official Vietnamese maps must show the Paracels and Spratlys.

In terms of geography, history, and culture, Vietnam falls into three divisions: the north, which the Vietnamese call Bac Bo; the center, Trung Bo; and the south, Nam Bo.

The North: The Red River, descending from China's Yunnan Province, courses through North Vietnam before emptying into the Gulf of Tonkin. It joins several other tributaries near Hanoi, creating a skein of rivers that feed the 15,000-square-kilometer Red River Delta. The Red River is unruly. Dikes built to contain it require constant raising to keep pace with river sedimentation. Flanking the delta is a region of spectacular karst topography with grottoes, caves, and sheer cliffs formed from porous limestone. Sugarloaf peaks rise dramatically from valley floors, similar to parts of southern China or the south of Thailand. Wind and water act on the limestone most dramatically at the islets comprising Halong Bay. Vietnam shares a 1,150-kilometer mountainous border with China to the north. In the northwest, the Hoang Lien Son range near the Chinese border features Vietnam's highest peak: Mt. Fansipan, elevation 3,134 meters.

The Center: The main features of this area include the coast and highlands. The palm-fringed tropical coastline with white-sand beaches supports fishing villages. The soil here is dry, rocky, or saline, so the area is not conducive to farming. The Central Highlands, however, do contain plateau areas such as the Pleiku Plateau and Dac Lac Plateau, with rich volcanic soil ideal for growing tea and coffee. Stretching 1,200 kilometers along the western flank of Vietnam is the Truong Son Range in the Central Highlands, which forms Vietnam's border. Vietnam shares a 1,650-kilometer northwestern border with Laos and a

930-kilometer western border with Cambodia. Parts of the Cambodian border are a subject of dispute between the two nations.

The South: The prominent feature here is the 50,000-square-kilometer Mekong Delta, an alluvial fan formed by branches of the Mekong River. The Mekong courses down from China, through Laos and Cambodia, into Vietnam, and empties into the South China Sea. The Vietnamese call it Cuu Long, or River of the Nine Dragons—a reference to the number of Mekong tributaries, which is actually seven. The Mekong does not pose a great flood threat: When the Mekong swells in monsoon season, it backs up into Tonle Sap Lake in Cambodia. Irrigation in the delta is achieved through an ancient system of canals. Another feature of the delta is swamp and marshland areas: the Plain of Reeds near the Cambodian border, and U-Minh Mangrove Forest, near Camau at the tip of the peninsula.

Cambodia

Covering 181,035 square kilometers, Cambodia is roughly the size of England and Wales combined. During the last few centuries its borders have shrunk because of encroachment by Thailand and Vietnam.

To the southeast side of the country lie the central plains, a vast, flat agricultural area. Cambodia has three densely forested mountain ranges—the Dangrek Range on the northern border, the Cardamom Mountains to the west, and the Elephant Mountains, southwest of Phnom Penh. In the Cardamom Mountains, Phnom Aoral, elevation 1,813 meters, is the country's highest peak. In the southwest, 340 kilometers of coastline along the Gulf of Thailand gives Cambodia access to the ocean.

The Mekong River courses 500 kilometers across the country. It enters Cambodia from Laos over a crashing set of cataracts at Khong Phapheng; there are more rapids around Stung Treng and Kratie. At Phnom Penh the Mekong joins two tributaries, the Bassac and Tonle Sap. The Tonle Sap River, coursing for 100 kilometers, links the Mekong to Lake Tonle Sap, the largest freshwater lake in Southeast Asia. The

lake supports huge stocks of fish and aquatic life. An annual phenomenon is the enlarging of Lake Tonle Sap from 2,600 square kilometers to 10,400 square kilometers at the height of the June–October rainy season. In June, swollen by monsoon rains, the Tonle Sap River reverses direction and proceeds northward to Lake Tonle Sap. The lake acts as an overflow reservoir for the Mekong. The area around Lake Tonle Sap is flooded. In November, after the rains subside, the river changes course again and flows once more—together with the Bassac and Mekong rivers—to the sea. It maintains this course for the November–May season, and then the cycle starts anew. By February, the shrinking lake becomes one of the richest fishing grounds in the world. As floodwaters recede, fish are trapped by nets or bamboo traps—or simply caught in branches of trees. Flooding also covers the area in rich mud, ideal for growing rice. Farmers have developed unique deepwater rice strains that grow with the rising lake to keep the grain above water.

Cambodia has suffered terrible ecological damage. Deforestation has had drastic effects: Waterways are beginning to clog up, and fish are dying from siltation in the Tonle Sap River. Before 1970, more than 70 percent of Cambodia was forested; the cover is now down to 40 percent or less. Although the government placed a ban on the export of logs or sawn wood, it offered forest concessions to investors allowing the export of processed timber such as veneer furniture. The government awarded a 30-year renewable lease to Samling Corporation on a 800,000-hectare concession—Sarawak–based Samling is one of the world's logging giants. There are two areas of virgin rainforest in Cambodia: to the west, bordering Thailand, and to the northeast, bordering Vietnam. In the west, forest areas formerly under Khmer Rouge control were being ravaged for teak and mahogany logs, which are sold to Thailand. One of the great ironies of Cambodia is that the best deterrent to further deforestation is the presence of land mines.

In the 1980s and 1990s, gem mining in former Khmer Rouge–controlled zones created a lunar landscape. Trucks operating 24 hours a day removed earth and took it across the Thai border, where it was panned and valuable gemstones removed: The Khmer Rouge levied a 45 percent tax on all gems removed. To the southwest, under government control, intensive shrimp farming has ravaged mangrove forests on Koh Kong.

Laos

Laos stretches 1,000 kilometers from China to Cambodia, with the Mekong River forming its westerly border with Thailand and Myanmar (Burma), and the Annamite Range dividing it from Vietnam. From east to west, the country ranges 150–500 kilometers in width; total land area is 236,800 square kilometers. Laos is about half the size of Thailand, or two-thirds the size of Vietnam, and is 30 percent larger than Cambodia. The principal geographical features are mountains and the Mekong: Tributaries of the river rise in the mountains and flow through deep valleys. More than 75 percent of the country is rugged and mountainous.

In the north, heavily forested mountain ranges and plateaus are intersected by deep valleys. The nation's highest mountain, Mt. Phu Bia (2,850 meters), lies at the edge of the Xieng Khuang Plateau, which includes the Plain of Jars. Running along the eastern border of Laos is the rugged Annamite Range, with peaks ranging 1,600–2,700 meters in elevation. In the center of the range is the Khammuan Plateau, with sparsely forested limestone terraces, gorges, and grottoes. Farther south is the basalt-covered 10,000-square-kilometer Bolovens Plateau, rising over 1,200 meters. In this area the people cultivate coffee, tea, rice, and other crops.

The Mekong delineates Laos's northwest border with Myanmar (Burma) and traces a good deal of the Lao border with Thailand (as agreed under a treaty between the Siamese and French in 1893). The Mekong traverses more than a third of its length in Laos. Together with 15 major tributaries, it drains Laos with nearly 2,400 kilometers of waterways and provides abundant fishing resources—an important staple food for the Laotians. Major Mekong tributaries include the Nam Ou and Namtha in the north, and the Nam Ngum in Vientiane province. Because of rocky stretches or rapids, perhaps only a third of these waterways are navigable, some only in high water. The Mekong River Valley and surrounding floodplains constitute the country's wet-rice lands, with the largest valley sections near Vientiane and Savannakhet.

About 45 percent of Laos is forested. Tropical rainforest grows on mountainsides exposed to heavy rainfall. At higher elevations, monsoon hardwood forest is found, while sheltered mountainsides host deciduous trees. In the north are mixed forests, with subtropical pine and evergreen oak.

In addition to widespread bombing, in 1965–1966 the U.S. Air Force dumped an estimated 700,000 liters of herbicides on the eastern side of Laos, on the Ho Chi Minh Trail; the defoliants contaminated drinking water. Despite the enormous damage, Laos still retains much of its original forest—among the last untouched tropical rainforest in Southeast Asia.

CLIMATE

Vietnam

Vietnam has a tropical monsoon climate with wet and dry seasons. The country straddles different climatic zones: tropical in the north, subtropical in the south. Because of climactic fluctuations, there's no best time to visit the country as a whole, although November–April is the dry season in the north, Central Highlands, and south. Among the best times to visit some major cities: Hanoi, October–January; Hué and Danang, February–April; Saigon, Dalat, and the Mekong Delta, December–March.

Avoid peak monsoon periods as mountain roads may be impassable, and flooding may impede progress on the plains. Stifling heat and humidity strike in summer (June–August in the north and center, March–May in the south). If conditions are not conducive to travel in one part of the country, consider going elsewhere.

The North

There are two distinct seasons in the north: a cold dry winter November–April, and a hot rainy summer May–October. Seasonal changes are similar to those in the south of China. In winter, the average temperature is 22°C. In January, the coldest month, the average temperature dips to around 16°C; it can be chilly in Hanoi; and it can freeze at higher elevations in the mountains. In February and March, there is fine rain or continuous drizzle along the north-central coast and up to 100 kilometers inland, encompassing Hanoi. Called *crachin* by the Vietnamese, this phenomenon is often accompanied by fog and mist. From May to October the weather is hot and humid with heavy rainfall. Peak times are July and August, when the temperature soars to 33°C. The occasional devastating typhoon or tropical storm may strike at this time.

Central Highlands

Weather patterns in the highlands resemble those in the north more than the south. The highlands experience cooler temperatures, with conditions depending on altitude. At 1,475 meters, Dalat is the coolest place; the annual average temperature is 19°C, rainfall around 2,000 millimeters. Dalat's dry season lasts December–March. Pleiku, elevation 780 meters, has an annual average temperature of 22°C, and rainfall of almost 2,500 millimeters a year. Other parts of the Central Highlands get up to 3,300 millimeters of rainfall per year. The rainy season is April–September, peaking June–August. The dry season is November–April.

Central Coast

Conditions are erratic in the center, which has a transitional climate between that of north and south. Around Hué and Danang, it rains almost without interruption September–December; flooding can be a problem. Avoid these areas in September and October, which see the most rainfall. Hué is one of the wettest places in Vietnam, with an annual average rainfall approaching 3,000 millimeters. The best time to visit Hué and Danang is February–April, when rain is less frequent. Temperatures can reach 35°C in June on the coast, and typhoons can be a problem between July and November. Nha Trang is farther south, so it's drier; typhoons may strike here October–December.

The South

With a subtropical climate similar to Thailand's, southern Vietnam stays evenly hot throughout the year and sees the greatest number of sunny days. The thermometer hovers around 27°C. The dry season runs November–April; lower humidity December–February makes this the best time to visit. The hottest months are March and April, with stifling heat and unpleasantly high temperatures reaching 35°C. The rainy season runs May–October and is characterized by midafternoon storms.

Cambodia

Cambodia has a tropical monsoon climate with two periods of rainfall. The sequence of seasons is hot, bloody hot, light rain, and heavy rain. There is high humidity throughout, sometimes up to 90 percent. Overall, Cambodia is a sweaty place.

Hot Season: The northeast monsoon blowing in from China brings the "mango rains" in March, the first showers of the season. March, April, and May are deadly hot, with April the cruelest month. Humidity reaches 90 percent, and the thermometer can hit 35°C. Higher elevations and coastal regions afford the only respite from high heat and humidity.

Rainy Season: From early June to early October the southwest monsoon arises over the Indian Ocean and brings heavy rains and high humidity. The streets of Phnom Penh flood at this time. Rainstorms occur in the afternoons; the wettest months are August and September. The southwest monsoon accounts for roughly 75 percent of total annual rainfall. Rainfall varies considerably from area to area.

Cool Dry Season: November to March is "cool" and dry, and obviously the best time to visit, though it's somewhat dusty. December–February sees milder temperatures; January is the "coolest" month.

CLIMATE CHART

All temperatures in degrees Celsius. Rainfall measured in millimeters.

	Jan.	Feb.	Mar.	April	May	June	July	Aug.	Sept.	Oct.	Nov.	Dec.
Hanoi												
Max:	21	21	23	28	32	33	33	32	31	29	26	22
Min:	14	14	17	20	23	26	26	26	24	22	18	15
Humidity percentage:	68	70	76	75	69	71	72	75	73	69	68	67
Rain:	20	30	40	80	200	240	320	340	260	100	50	25
Danang												
Max:	26	27	29	31	33	33	33	22	32	30	29	27
Min:	17	18	19	22	24	25	25	25	24	22	20	18
Humidity percentage:	86	86	86	85	81	77	78	77	84	85	86	86
Rain:	95	30	10	15	45	40	95	115	440	530	225	210
Saigon												
Max:	32	33	34	35	33	32	31	31	31	31	31	31
Min:	21	22	23	24	24	24	24	24	23	23	23	22
Humidity percentage:	61	56	58	60	71	78	80	78	80	80	75	68
Rain:	15	5	10	50	220	330	310	270	340	260	120	60

Phnom Penh											
Max:	31	32	34	35	34	33	32	32	31	30	30	30
Min:	21	22	23	24	24	24	24	25	25	24	23	22
Rain:	7	10	40	77	134	155	171	160	224	257	127	45

Vientiane											
Max:	28	30	33	34	34	33	32	31	31	31	30	30
Min:	14	17	20	23	24	24	24	24	24	22	19	15
Rain:	10	20	40	100	260	260	310	305	300	110	20	5

Luang Prabang											
Max:	28	30	32	39	34	34	32	32	32	31	30	29
Min:	14	16	19	23	24	25	24	24	24	23	20	16
Rain:	10	15	25	100	165	150	235	300	170	75	25	10

Laos

The climate in Laos is hot and humid, with three distinct seasons: hot dry season, monsoon season, and cool dry season.

The **hot dry season** runs mid-February–April, with the thermometer approaching 40°C, broken only by the occasional shower or "mango rain." April–May sees an increase in humidity and a buildup of rain.

The **monsoon season** can be May–November, with heavy rains and cloudy days, and temperatures averaging 25°C in the highlands and 29°C in the lowlands. The rains fall mainly at night, and heavy downpours are often accompanied by storms. Laos experiences an average of three storms per week in May and June and two per week July–September. Humidity is high in this season. Rivers run high, roads turn to mud, and there's often flooding. By mid-October the rain eases off. Rainfall in Laos varies with location and elevation: Vientiane and Savannakhet get 1,500–2,000 millimeters of rainfall a year, while Luang Prabang and Xieng Khuang see 1,000–1,500 millimeters a year. The mountains of the southeast, bordering Vietnam, may receive more than 3,000 millimeters.

November–February, the **cool dry season,** is the best time to visit. In November there's reduced humidity; temperatures may dip as low as 15°C in December and January, and down to freezing in mountain areas such as the Xieng Khuang Plateau or the Bolovens Plateau.

Flora and Fauna

VIETNAM

Originally, Vietnam was covered in dense forest. Much of the forest cover has been stripped, a process that has accelerated since 1945. From 1945 to 1975, intense warfare and extensive use of defoliants devastated the forest cover and its wildlife residents. The American war against Vietnam marked the first time that military technology was employed to destroy the environment of an entire country. During this strategy of "ecocide," it is estimated that the Americans dropped more than 85 million liters of defoliants, affecting a quarter of South Vietnam, stripping bare an estimated 10,000 kilometers of land. The most devastated areas were the Ho Chi Minh Trail, the riverbanks in the Mekong Delta, along the demilitarized zone, and around U.S. bases and airfields. The north was riddled with craters, in addition to being shattered by seven million tons of bombs. In the Mekong Delta, more than half the mangrove swamps were destroyed by chemical poisoning and napalm.

Since 1975, population growth and rampant use of resources for rebuilding and firewood has further reduced woodland areas. Forest cover is now estimated at less than 20 percent of the total land area, down from more than 40 percent in the early 1940s. Reforestation projects cannot keep pace with losses from cultivation and logging operations. Further loss of forest lands may lead to catastrophic soil erosion, mud slides, flooding, and changing climate patterns. These changes, combined with heavy monsoons, may prove an ecological disaster much worse than war.

Preservation

An attempt to shore up further loss of woodlands through the creation of national parks has proved to be a halfhearted solution. National parks and forest reserves in Vietnam are poorly managed and too small to sustain breeding populations of endangered species. The two largest parks are in the north: Cuc Phuong and Cat Ba national parks. Ethnic minority groups live within both park boundaries and often hunt wild animals. Other smaller national parks include Ba Be Lakes in the north, Cat Tien Reserve and Bach Ma National Park in the center, and Con Dao Islands in the south. There is a sprinkling of forest preserves, including U-Minh Mangrove Forest in the south, the former French hill stations of Tam Dao and Bavi in the north, and Bach Ma in the center. Cuc Phuong was the first national park, established in 1962 with the help of the World Wildlife Fund (WWF). The WWF maintains an office in Hanoi and is advising on the creation of more nature reserves.

Flora

With wide variation in elevation and climate zones, Vietnam's flora is diverse. At higher elevations in the mountainous northwest are rhododendrons, orchids, needle trees, and rare dwarf bamboos; on the central coast in extremely dry areas you can find cactus plants and pines; in the humid south are zones with tropical fruit trees; and in the far south are mangrove swamps.

Fauna

Many species of wildlife face decline and probable extinction in Vietnam in the near future because of loss of forest habitat, widespread hunting and poaching, and an illegal traffic in wildlife. Tigers, for example, are sought for their skins and for other body parts used in Chinese traditional medicine. The government does very little to prevent this kind of traffic.

At present Vietnam's wildlife is diverse and includes species extinct in other parts of Asia. In the early 1990s a small herd of one of the rarest large mammals in the world—the Javan rhinoceros—was discovered in Vietnam. The one-horn rhino, believed to have been wiped out during the war, was discovered in the swamps and thickets of Cat Tien Reserve, to

VIETNAM'S UNIQUE SPECIES

In 1992, in the dense rainforests of northern Vietnam, British biologist John MacKinnon stumbled across the skull of a goatlike creature mounted on a post in a hunter's house. It took him only a moment to realize he was looking at an animal unknown to modern science. Subsequent analysis of the specimen's DNA showed this was not only an unknown species but in fact a new genus, now called *Pseudoryx*. The creature has been christened *Pseudoryx nghetinhensis*, meaning false oryx of Nghe Tinh, the former name of the province where it was found. The common name is Vu Quang ox, or *sao la*. David Hulse, head of the World Wildlife Fund, hailed the find as "the biological equivalent of discovering a new planet."

giant muntjac

The *Pseudoryx* skulls were discovered in Vu Quang forest reserve, near the Laotian border to the northwest of Vinh. Although it bears superficial similarities to the Arabian oryx of the antelope family, genetic analysis revealed the creature is more closely related to the ox. The world's newest creature may actually be one of the oldest: The Vu Quang ox most likely separated from its closest cattlelike relatives 5–10 million years ago. The creature is thought to be similar to a long-extinct species that once lived in India. Only three other new genuses of large land mammal were documented in the 20th century.

The Vu Quang ox has large eyes; straight, sharp horns; and a brownish head patterned with white patches. It developed a narrow concave hoof for negotiating steep, slippery mountain terrain. The ox weighs about 100 kilograms when fully grown. In June 1994, a live specimen

Vu Quang ox

of the Vu Quang ox caused a sensation when it was displayed at a forestry institute in Hanoi.

In July of 1994 villagers captured a second specimen in the Vu Quang forest reserve. However, in October, the Vietnamese press reported both captive oxen had died of respiratory and digestive ailments; their keepers knew little of the animal's diet and habitat.

Two new species of primitive deerlike creatures have also been found in north Vietnam. A Vietnamese biologist on the track of the Vu Quang ox found instead the skull of what is believed to be a new species: the slow-running deer, or *Quang khem*. Another variety now named the giant muntjac was discovered; a live specimen is held by a Laotian military group. The giant muntjac is twice as heavy as the common muntjac; the deerlike creature's large canine teeth were probably used in fights between males before it evolved elaborate antlers.

This "Lost World"—the wet evergreen forest of the Vu Quang region—has since yielded even more astounding mammalian discoveries. In April 1997, a team led by biologist Alan Rabinowitz discovered a live specimen of a dwarf barking deer, believed to be genetically different from the giant muntjac. The team was told of a long-snouted yellowish pig, and George Schaller acquired the partial skull of a male. This was identified as the Vietnamese warty hog *(Sus bucculentus),* not seen by scientists since it was identified in 1892, from two skulls collected in southern Vietnam.

Vu Quang forest reserve may hold other life forms unknown to science, from fish to plants. This region is so remote even local Tai and Hoa tribes rarely venture into it. The World Wildlife Fund proposes the area be set aside as a nature reserve. So far the Vietnamese government has expanded the reserve from 16,000 to 60,000 hectares and shut down logging in the park. Vu Quang reserve abuts the 365,000-hectare Nakai Nam Theum National Conservation Area in Laos. There are proposals to link the two, creating a large jointly managed reserve.

Know Vietnam, Cambodia & Laos

the southwest of Dalat. The Javan rhino can weigh up to 1,500 kilograms and is the rarest of the five existing species. Only 50 other individuals survive in a reserve in Java. More than 50 species of mammals live in Vietnam. Among the larger species are the Indian elephant, Himalayan black bear, rhinoceros, clouded leopard, tiger, wild buffalo, antelope, deer, wild boar, and tapir. There is a variety of simian species, including the world's last Delacour's langurs.

Two species of crocodile inhabit Vietnam, estuarine and Siamese, as well as two species of python, reticulated and Indian. These reptiles are found in the U-Minh Mangrove Forest, a huge mangrove swamp at the southern tip of the peninsula. Poisonous snakes include the king cobra, krait, and pit viper.

Very little marine life is protected, though there's a small marine reserve at Cat Ba National Park in the north harboring dolphins and hawksbill turtles, and another at Con Dao Islands National Park.

The prospect for birds is brighter. Many largely escaped the ravages of the Vietnam War by simply relocating. More than 600 species are found in Vietnam. Unusual birds include white-winged wood duck, the osprey, and the crested Argus pheasant, associated with the legendary phoenix. The eastern saurus crane, regarded as a symbol of longevity and good luck, made an auspicious return to the Mekong Delta. The cranes completely disappeared during the Vietnam War years, but returned in the late 1980s from breeding grounds in Cambodia. A preserve in the Mekong Delta has been established to protect them. Several other bird sanctuaries are scattered around the Mekong Delta, particularly in the U-Minh Mangrove Forest zone.

CAMBODIA

Flora

The flat central plains of Cambodia are primarily agricultural, used for growing rice and other crops. The transitional plains are mostly covered with savanna grasses. Cambodia's coastal strip supports evergreen and mangrove forests. In the southwest, primary-growth forest in the Cardamom and Elephant ranges contains hardwood trees such as teak, with pine forests at higher elevations. Forested areas harbor a profusion of lianas and orchids. In the northern mountains, trees soar above an undergrowth of vines, palm trees, bamboo thickets, and ground plants. Palm trees and bamboo are the main source of village building materials; the sugar palm tree is also used to make wine, vinegar, and medicine.

Fauna

Cambodia has extensive mammal, reptile, bird, and insect life. Among the larger mammals are elephants, Malaysian sun bears, tigers, clouded leopards, barking deer, pangolins, and monkeys. The rarest mammal is the *kouprey* ("jungle cow"), first identified in 1939. It was declared Cambodia's national animal in 1963 and has not been seen since. The *kouprey* is a bovine with large lyre-shaped horns and a long dewlap drooping from the neck. The *kouprey* is now thought to be close to extinction, its numbers depleted by mines and guerrillas hunting for meat. It was once found along the Dangrek Range on the northwestern Cambodian border, and it may also inhabit territory in Mondulkiri. The most remote part of Cambodia, and hence the area with the most abundant wildlife, is to the northeast, in Ratanakiri and Mondulkiri provinces.

There are numerous reptile species in Cambodia, including crocodiles and several species of poisonous snake (kraits and cobras). Among the birdlife of Cambodia are herons, cranes, storks, wild duck, pelicans, cormorants, pheasants, and egrets. Cambodia's rivers and lakes teem with fish. Some are unusual: The elephant fish, in Lake Tonle Sap, is a species that flops overland to deeper pools as floodwaters recede. In the Mekong waters at the Laos-Cambodia border in the northeast lives the endangered freshwater Irrawaddy dolphin, threatened by indiscriminate use of explosives for fishing. Marine life abounds around Cambodia's offshore islands on the Gulf of Thailand.

There is little protection of wildlife in Cambodia—stuffed wild animals are on sale at

TIGERS IN TROUBLE

By 1900, after a millennium of tiger-hunting, perhaps 100,000 tigers remained in the wild, ranging from the Caspian Sea in the west to Sumatra in the east to Siberia in the north. Trophy hunting and habitat destruction eliminated the Bali tiger more than 40 years ago; the Caspian and Javan cats disappeared in the 1970s and 1980s. The Indochinese tiger may well be next. Wildlife experts believe that fewer than 6,000 tigers are left today, and that the majestic cat is headed for extinction within the next 10 years.

The two largest tiger subspecies remaining today are the Bengal tiger (estimated population 3,000–4,000, mostly found in India), and the Indochinese tiger (no more than 1,600 remaining—the figure could be much lower). The Indochinese tiger ranges across the Indochinese Peninsula from Myanmar (Burma) to Malaya. Cambodia has 100–300 Indochinese tigers; there may be 100–200 left in Vietnam; the number remaining in Laos and Myanmar is not known; there are up to 500 individuals around Thailand, especially in the Thailand-Myanmar border region. Tigers are more likely to be found in remote border areas. Tigers were a casualty of the Vietnam War—during the 1970s hundreds of tigers were killed by Vietnamese troops forced into remote areas and by the Khmer Rouge. In Cambodia, you can imagine what impact the laying of millions of mines has had on tigers. In both Vietnam and Cambodia environmental degradation and poaching continue to take their toll.

Despite laws protecting tigers, poaching is rampant. Tiger products—including skin, bones, kidneys, lungs, and penis—are on sale in wildlife markets along the borders of Cambodia, Vietnam, and Laos and are dealt openly in Phnom Penh and Poipet. The sale of a tiger skeleton can net the equivalent of 10 years' income for a Cambodian farmer.

Despite a ban on tiger hunting as a sport by most of the tiger-range nations by 1970 and despite the outlawing of the trade in tiger skins, tigers are killed in alarming numbers. The parts once discarded—bones, blood, and body parts—are now the most valued. Behind the booming trade in tiger parts is the market for ancient Chinese medicines and potions. The Chinese exhausted their own tiger bone stockpiles in the late 1980s, which is when conservationists began to notice an increase in tiger poaching.

The insatiable appetite of the Chinese for animal parts used in aphrodisiacs and traditional medicines remains the greatest threat to many endangered species in Asia. There is heavy traffic in snakes, frogs, lizards, turtles, geckos, and monkeys. In Hong Kong, Korea, China, Taiwan, and Chinatowns across the globe, apothecaries do a steady trade in tiger wines, balms, and pills. These are valued by the Chinese and other Asian peoples who believe tiger-bone potions cure rheumatism, whiskers provide strength, and tiger-penis soup boosts a flagging libido. Tiger parts are also used in the treatment of typhoid and dysentery. By the time tiger bones, claws, eyes, penis, and whiskers reach Taiwan, the value can increase exponentially. A study by the monitoring arm of the World Wildlife Fund revealed that a tiger penis can sell for $1,700 in Taiwan and powdered tiger bone for $135–500 a gram. A single tiger can yield as much as 10 kilograms of bones.

---

markets around the country. In early 1995 the country's first national parks were established. Preah Sihanouk National Park, at Ream about 20 kilometers east of Sihanoukville, covers 21,000 hectares abutting the coast and includes a marine zone with two islands and a coral reef. Kirirom National Park, straddling Kompong Speu and Koh Kong provinces, covers 35,000 hectares in a pine forest zone. In other parts of the country, the government was planning to

establish seven national parks, 10 wildlife sanctuaries, and three multiple-use zones. However, a number of the proposed parks lie in territory that may well be riddled with mines.

LAOS
Flora

Vegetation in Laos is a rich mix of tropical and subtropical, with an abundance of flowering species such as orchids. Monsoon forests consist of several layers: Towering to 30 meters are hardwoods such as teak or Asian rosewood; below is grass and bamboo undergrowth, especially along riverbanks.

A great variety of fruit trees and tropical palms are found in Laos. On plateaus, grassy savanna is the main feature.

Fauna

With such copious forest cover and a sparse human population, Laos has plentiful wildlife. Huge swaths of forest—still untouched by humans—shelter myriad species of flora and fauna. There are both resident and migratory birds, thought to number up to 500 species, including pheasants, partridges, ducks, songbirds, and hawks. The reptile population includes king cobras, banded kraits, vipers, lizards, and crocodiles. Larger mammals include wildcats, bears, leopards, tigers, wild cattle, macaques, gibbons, and flying squirrels. Exotic Laotian species include the pangolin, a kind of scaly creature that feeds on ants and termites; several species of civet, a nocturnal possumlike creature; pygmy slow loris, a nocturnal primate with large eyes and thickly furred body; lesser panda; snub-nosed langur; and raccoon dog.

For centuries, wild Asiatic elephants have been caught and domesticated for use in warfare, carrying freight, and hauling logs. For many years Lao hunters and even forestry officials have used antlers taken from the Vu Quang ox and the giant muntjac as hat racks or parts of ceremonial altars—oblivious to the fact these trophies represented species unknown to science. It was only in 1992 that British and Laotian fieldworkers under contract to New York's Wildlife Conservation Society managed to take blood samples from a live specimen of a giant muntjac in a menagerie owned by a Lao military group; it is said to be double the weight of the previously known species of muntjac. Remote Nakai Nam Theum National

Frangipani is the national flower of Laos.

Conservation Area up on the Vietnamese border is regarded as a kind of lost world, with recent discovery of a new species of wild pig.

Another giant found in Laos is aquatic—the *pla buk,* or giant catfish. This monster of the Mekong grows up to three meters long, can weigh up to 300 kilograms, and takes 6–12 years to attain full size. The world's biggest scaleless freshwater fish is found only in the Mekong River. Little is known about its life cycle. The females are said to live in Cambodia's great lake, Tonle Sap, swimming north to meet male fish in Dali Lake in China's Yunnan province. The flesh is considered a delicacy in Laos and Thailand; fishermen trap the catfish in Bokeo province April–June as it heads for spawning grounds in China. Dam construction in southwest China, blasting of rapids to clear the way for commercial navigation, and overfishing have reduced the number of giant catfish to the endangered level. Another rare river species is the freshwater Irrawaddy dolphin, found in the southern Mekong bordering Cambodia. The dolphin is

WILDLIFE TRAFFICKING

The brisk trade in rare species from Laos continues, with most animals going to Thailand, China, and South Korea, where there's a high demand for certain species for the cooking pot and for use in traditional medicine.

Laos is not a signatory to the U.N. Convention on International Trade in Endangered Species (CITES). The exact size of the trade in rare and endangered species in Laos is hard to gauge, but in Saravan in the nation's center is a large wildlife market with monitor lizards, pythons, mynah birds, red-leaf monkeys, and other species from the Bolovens Plateau. Some species are on the CITES endangered list. Saravan is a great staging point on the smuggling route to Bangkok.

not captured for food or sport as it is considered a reincarnated human; however, the species is threatened by gillnetting in Laos and explosives fishing in Cambodia. The Mekong is a biological gold mine—many species of Mekong fauna are still unknown to science.

Preservation

In the 1990s, Laos established a network of National Biodiversity Conservation Areas (NBCAs) designed to protect wildlife and prevent logging; 19 are scattered through the country. They cannot be called national parks because villagers continue to live—and hunt—within the boundaries as they have done for centuries. But it's to be hoped that the NBCAs will put a stop to excessive logging, with a view to replacing that with ecotourism projects.

Vietnam History

Excavations show the Red River Delta, the cradle of Vietnamese culture, was inhabited as far back as 5000 B.C.; stone implements have been discovered in limestone cave dwellings. The Vietnamese people trace their origins to a tribal group known as the Lac Viet, or Dongson culture. The group may have been of Mongolian origin, migrating from southern China and settling in the north of Vietnam at the beginning of the Bronze Age. Large bronze drums unearthed in the Dongson area indicate sophisticated knowledge of mining and casting. The bronze drum was the symbol of the Au Lac Kingdom, which probably reached its zenith in the 3rd century B.C., when Co Loa near Hanoi became its citadel.

Chinese Rule

The Red River Delta's early history is dominated by China, which regarded the place as an unruly province. The Han dynasty annexed north Vietnam in the 2nd century B.C. and named it Annam, or "pacified south." The Chinese rigorously imposed their own model on the Vietnamese. They introduced ancestor worship and Confucianism, established schools to spread Chinese script, and levied high taxes to support a system of mandarin rule. The north remained part of China for close to 1,000 years, but the Chinese failed to assimilate the Vietnamese. Chinese rule was repeatedly challenged. Vietnamese rebels have acquired legendary status, women warriors figuring prominently among them. Around A.D. 40, the Trung sisters organized nobles to drive out the Chinese. Their rebellion was crushed two years later, and the sisters committed suicide by throwing themselves into a river.

More successful was the rebel Ngo Quyen, a military genius who took on the soldiers of the Chinese Tang dynasty in A.D. 939 at the battle of Bach Dang River. A flotilla of armed Chinese junks was attempting to reinforce the Chinese garrison in Hanoi. Ngo Quyen laid iron-tipped bamboo stakes in the riverbed: Chinese vessels were impaled on the stakes at low tide and ambushed by a Vietnamese army. This decisive engagement laid the foundation for an independent state in the north. A new emperor, Dinh Bo Linh, ascended the throne in A.D. 967. To remain independent, the Vietnamese paid tribute to the Chinese—an arrangement typical of Chinese relations with other parts of Southeast Asia.

Other Kingdoms

In the south, other kingdoms flourished. In the Mekong Delta area, the Indianized Funan culture ruled from the 1st to 6th centuries A.D. Funan's wealth was based on maritime trade; its largest port city was Oc-Eo. Oc-Eo's trade links reached as far as Rome, Persia, India, Myanmar (Burma), and China. Archaeologists have unearthed artifacts from the site that include Roman coins, Indian rings, and Burmese jade. The Funan kingdom mysteriously collapsed, usurped by the pre-Khmer Chenla Empire in the 7th century A.D.

The Lost Kingdom of Champa

Along the coast, another great maritime empire, the Kingdom of Champa, was taking shape.

The Cham constitute one of the oldest ethnic groups in Indochina. Records of the Kingdom of Champa stretch back to the 1st century A.D. The people are described as having dark skin, deep-set eyes, turned-up noses, and frizzy hair; they dressed in sarongs, like the Malays. The origin of the Cham is lost in time; they're most likely seafarers who arrived by boat from the Indonesian archipelago. The Cham speak a Malay-Polynesian language; stele from the Cham dynasties were inscribed in both Sanskrit and in similar-looking Cham script. The Indianized culture of Champa was almost completely extinguished by Viet conquest.

At the peak of their prosperity in the 10th and 11th centuries, the Cham controlled an area from north of Hué to the Mekong Delta, carving out a kingdom situated between the Khmer and the Viet. Their economy was based on agriculture, ocean fishing, and maritime trading. Their principal exports appear to have been slaves (prisoners of war) and sandalwood; the latter was in great demand for temple building throughout Southeast Asia. The Cham themselves did not indulge in extensive temple building. They constructed brick-and-sandstone towers for Hindu worship, with the main sites at My Son and Tra Kieu (now largely destroyed). Crumbling Cham towers are today scattered along the central coast of Vietnam; the best extant examples are in Nha Trang and Phan Rang.

In Danang is a Cham Museum with a fine collection of Cham sculpture, reflecting contacts with Java and later Cambodia. A recurring image in Hindu Cham art is that of Uroja, the mother figure who gave birth to Champa. Uroja means "breast" in the Cham language and was represented in sculpture by breast or nipple motifs. The Cham were also ardent worshippers of Hindu lingas and yonis.

The civilization made a great impression on Marco Polo with its advanced use of agriculture and irrigation and its encouragement of the arts and sciences. He visited in the year 1285, seven years after Kublai Khan attacked the kingdom and exacted a yearly tribute of elephants and aloe wood from the aging Cham king. Polo reported:

In this kingdom no girl may marry without the King having seen her first. If he likes her, he marries her himself. Those who prove agreeable to him he retains for some time, and when they are dismissed, he furnishes them with a sum of money, in order that they may be able to obtain, according to their rank in life, advantageous matches. The King had 326 children and at least 150 of his sons were well trained in the arts of war. The kingdom abounds in elephants. There are also many forests of ebony of a fine black which is worked into various handsome articles of furniture. Every year the King sends elephants and sweet-scented wood as a tribute to the Great Khan.

In the 16th century, the Dominican friar Gabriel de San Antonio visited the Cham and returned with a more macabre account. He found the civilization brilliant, but unbalanced; like the Aztecs, they sacrificed humans. On certain days, San Antonio reported, the Cham sacrificed hundreds of people. The gall of the dead was collected and sent to the Cham king, who bathed in it to gain immortality.

Apart from this bloodletting, the Kingdom of Champa was weakened through several centuries of warfare with both the Khmer and the Viet. In 1471, the Viet raided and captured the Cham capital of Vijaya. An estimated 60,000 Cham troops were killed, and an equal number captured and carted off into slavery. The Kingdom of Champa was reduced to a tiny area centered on Nha Trang, which lingered for another 250 years. In 1720, the last remnants of the Kingdom of Champa were surrounded by powerful Viet forces. The king and his subjects fled south to the Mekong Delta, at that time controlled by Khmers. Although the Cham had in the past battled the Khmer, they preferred Khmer rule to the Viet's because of a shared Indic tradition. By 1820 the Mekong Delta, too, had fallen under the control of the Viet. While some Cham remained, other groups moved farther up the Mekong to settle east of Phnom Penh in the province of Kompong Cham and along the shores of the Tonle Sap.

For hundreds of years the Cham were devout Hindus; Islam was introduced in the 18th and 19th centuries, most likely by traders from India and Indonesia. In contrast to the Cham in Vietnam, who remained only partly Islamicized, the Cham in Cambodia widely adopted Sunni Islam customs and maintained links with other Muslim communities in Thailand and Malaysia. The Cambodian Cham, numbering perhaps 400,000, prospered, settling in 200 towns and villages. Cambodia served as a haven for the Cham for the next couple of centuries. But during the Pol Pot era, the Cham were branded "recent immigrants" and marked for expulsion or death. Up to two-thirds of the Cham community was wiped out in the post–1975 era; Cham were killed, starved to death, or driven out of the country. A small group fled to Laos, where they now prosper in Vientiane. Today there are an estimated 80,000 Cham descendants in Vietnam, 165,000 Cham in Cambodia, and 250 in Laos. Other small communities exist in Thailand, Malaysia, and southern China.

VIETNAMESE DYNASTIES

From the 10th century onward, Vietnam was ruled by a series of imperial dynasties with administrative structures copied from the Chinese. The emperor ruled through the Mandate of Heaven, mediating between the heavens and the earth. Nine ranks of mandarins controlled the armed forces, justice, finance, and public works. The system was elitist and totalitarian, and it often did not endear itself to the people, who were at times heavily taxed or coerced into labor projects.

Ngo Dynasty (939–965)—Co Loa (Vinh Phuc)
Dinh Dynasty (968–980)—Hoa Lu (Ninh Binh)

Early Le Dynasty (980–1009)—Hoa Lu
Ly Dynasty (1010–1225)—Thang Long (Hanoi)
Tran Dynasty (1225–1400)—Thang Long
Ho Dynasty (1400–1407)—Dong Do (Hanoi)
Post Tran Dynasty (1407–1413)
Under Chinese rule (1414–1427)
Later Le Dynasty (1427–1524)—Dong Kinh (Hanoi); *claimed nominal rule until 1788*
Mac Dynasty (1527–1592)
Northern Trinh (1539–1787)—Hanoi; *by the mid-17th century, Vietnam was divided into feuding clans in the north and south*
Southern Nguyen (1558–1778)—Hué
Quang Trung (1787–1792)
Tay Son Dynasty (1802–1945)—Hué, Saigon, Hanoi; *the Tay Son brothers ruled from Hué and Saigon citadels in the south and Hanoi Citadel in the north*
Nguyen Dynasty (1802–1945)—Hué

Ly Dynasty (1010–1225)

The Ly dynasty period consolidated Vietnamese independence in the north. The Kingdom of Dai Viet, as it became known, became a formidable military power, invincible from attacks by the Chinese, Cham, and Khmer. Buddhism flourished, the nation's first university (the Temple of Literature in Hanoi) was founded, and embankments for flood control were built along the Red River.

Tran Dynasty (1225–1400)

By the year 1225, three kingdoms occupied the territory of present-day Vietnam. The Dai Viet Kingdom, centered in Hanoi, occupied the north; the Kingdom of Champa, centered in Vijaya, occupied the central coast; and the Khmer Empire, at Angkor, covered the south of Vietnam as well as present-day Cambodia. In the late 13th century, Mongol emperor Kublai Khan invaded Vietnam three times in an attempt to drive south to control the spice routes of Indonesia. Setting aside their differences, the Viet and Chams joined forces to repulse the khan's forces—making Vietnam one of only two nations (the other was Egypt) ever to defeat the Mongols. Military hero Tran Hung Dao repeated a successful tactic by embedding steel-tipped bamboo stakes in the Bach Dang River to sink the Mongol fleet. The last great battle took place in 1287 in the Red River Valley, where the Vietnamese routed Mongol troops.

Spurred by this victory, the Viet themselves became expansionists, turning on the Chams. The conflict between these two kingdoms dragged on for several centuries. Having exhausted their resources in the campaign against the Cham, the Vietnamese were victimized by the Ming dynasty Chinese, who reestablished direct rule in the early 15th century. The Chinese suppressed Vietnamese culture and language and plundered Vietnam's resources: precious stones, elephant tusks, rare woods, and spices—for export to China.

Later Le Dynasty (1427–1524)

The harsh rule of the Ming dynasty sparked another great revolt in 1418, led by wealthy landowner Le Loi, whose forces finally defeated the Chinese in 1426. Two years later, China recognized Vietnam's independence. Le Loi declared himself Emperor Le Thai To and established his new capital at Hanoi. The Later Le dynasty is viewed as a golden age in Vietnamese history, as Vietnam tried to break away from Chinese civilization. The Vietnamese language gained favor with scholars, although Chinese remained the language of the elite.

In this period the Vietnamese began expanding south, crushing the Kingdom of Champa in 1471. In the mid-15th century Angkor fell to the Thais, and the Khmer capital was reestablished at Phnom Penh. The Khmers asked the Vietnamese for help against the Thais. The Vietnamese agreed in return for the right to settle the area of Saigon.

Trinh and Nguyen Dynasties

As Vietnamese settlers moved south from the capital of Hanoi, the ruling Le dynasty lost control. In 1620 the Nguyen family broke from the empire and established their own dynasty, ruling from Hué. By the mid-17th century Vietnam was divided into north and south

at the 18th parallel, controlled by two clans, the Trinh and the Nguyen. Feuding between them continued into the 18th century. The southern Nguyen clan extended Vietnamese control through the Mekong Delta, administered from the citadel at Gia Dinh (Saigon). By the early 18th century, the Viet controlled the territory from the Chinese frontier to the Gulf of Thailand.

During the period of the Trinh and Nguyen dynasties, the first contacts were made with Western traders. In the early 16th century Portuguese sailors set up a trading colony at Faifo (Hoi An). In the early 17th century the Dutch were allowed to establish trading posts in the north. Interest in trading with Vietnam dropped off by the late 17th century, but foreign missionaries remained. Among them were Franciscan missionaries from the Philippines and Jesuits expelled from Japan. The first French to visit Vietnam were missionaries who dabbled in politics. In fact, both the Trinh and the Nguyen clans negotiated military supplies through missionaries—the Portuguese and French supporting the south, the Dutch supporting the north.

Tay Son Rebellion

In 1765 three brothers from a merchant family (dubbed the Tay Son rebels) precipitated a popular revolt against corrupt landlords and mandarins in central Vietnam. The Tay Son revolt quickly spread south, crushing the Nguyen clan in Saigon in 1783. The royal family was executed, with the exception of Prince Nguyen Anh, who fled to the French mission in Ha Tien. In the north, the Tay Son overpowered the Trinh clan, bringing the entire country under the aegis of the Tay Son brothers by 1787.

Quang Trung, the brother who ruled in the north, decisively stopped yet another Chinese advance in 1788, routing a 200,000-strong army near Hanoi. This feat is one of the most celebrated in Vietnamese history, adding Quang Trung's name to the roster of heroes. Quang Trung introduced land reform, a fairer system of taxation, and a new system of edu-

ROUGH JUSTICE

After assuming power in 1802, new Emperor Gia Long ordered his soldiers to exhume the body of the last of the Tay Son brothers and urinate upon it in front of the deceased's wife and son. Mother and child were subsequently torn apart by elephants.

Such rough justice was common in Vietnam's past. Under the mandarin system, trampling by elephants was the fate of adulterous women. Thieves were beheaded with swords, as were foreign missionaries who incurred the wrath of the emperor. The emperor's word was final, as he ruled with the Mandate of Heaven.

This legal system was bolstered by Confucian ethics—the mandarins kowtowed to the emperor, and ordinary folk prostrated themselves to the mandarins. The despotism, corruption, and flaunted wealth of some of the Nguyen dynasty emperors and mandarins did not endear them to the average Vietnamese, who railed against social injustices.

When, as a convenience, the French initially retained royal rule, ordinary Vietnamese resented the mandarins even more, considering them collaborators with the French. As part of their "civilizing mission," the French introduced the Napoleonic code, claiming they'd eliminated backward forms of justice. However, dissidents in the French colonial era could be sentenced to 10 years, life imprisonment, or even death for as little as distributing anti-French leaflets. The French also imported the guillotine to behead political offenders in public and established notorious penal colonies, including Poulo Condore in the South China Sea.

cation. After this promising start, he died in 1792, leaving the north in great confusion.

Nguyen Dynasty

Meanwhile, the exiled Prince Nguyen Anh was befriended by Pierre Pigneau de Béhaine, an 18th-century Jesuit missionary who dreamed of building a French empire in Asia. Pigneau de Béhaine negotiated a treaty on Nguyen Anh's behalf with Louis XVI in 1787 for military assistance. Louis XVI soon changed his mind, but the undaunted Pigneau de Béhaine recruited a force of 400 French deserters in India and sailed back to Vietnam in 1789 on two ships loaded with weapons. Nguyen Anh built up the French-trained army of mercenaries, pushing back the Tay Son rebels in 1799 and finally defeating them in 1801. A year later, after subduing the far north, Nguyen Anh proclaimed himself Emperor Gia Long, ruling from Hué. This was the first time a single court controlled Vietnam from north to south. This called for a change of name: A combination of the names Annam (north) and Viet Thuong (south) resulted in the new Viet Nam.

Gia Long ushered in the era of the last Vietnamese dynasty, the Nguyen dynasty (1802–1945), with its capital in Hué. Gia Long embarked on a series of ambitious projects. He built the Mandarin Road connecting Hanoi to Saigon, and star-shaped citadels in provincial capitals along the designs of French military architect Vauban. The Nguyen dynasty headquartered itself in Hué's Royal City, off-limits to most mortals; only mandarins, princesses, and scholars lived there. In return for their military assistance, French merchants were allowed commercial concessions and thus gained a foothold in Vietnam.

FRENCH COLONIAL ERA

Gia Long's successor, Emperor Minh Mang, reversed the policies of his father, drawing trade concessions to foreigners and issuing an imperial edict in 1825 outlawing Christian proselytizing. Christianity interfered with Confucian ethics maintained by the court as a system of ruling the peasants. The Vatican was opposed to ancestor worship (one of the cornerstones of Confucianism) and the polygamy the emperor practiced. Both of Minh Mang's successors, Thieu Tri and Tu Duc, were anti-Christian. Emperor Tu Duc ordered the execution of 25 European priests, 300 Vietnamese priests, and thousands of Vietnamese Catholics from 1848 to 1860.

The French used these attacks as a pretext for unleashing a military campaign against

THE HIGH LIFE

The French have a reputation as poor colonizers: repressive, racist, self-interested. In Vietnam they imported their lifestyle lock, stock, and barrel. Here, the French lifestyle could be maintained at lavish levels. Among the consequences: A bevy of domestic servants was cheap. Upon arrival in Haiphong or Saigon, the French began assembling domestics: cook, amah (nanny), coachman, laundry boy, rickshaw driver, gardener, errand boy, and assorted other coolies. In the days before electric fans, the French even employed human fan wavers. Since the French favored white—wearing everything from white drill suits to white cork hats—there was plenty of work for the laundry boy. Hitting domestics was common; whipping and beating plantation employees was standard.

Liberated from domestic worries, French settlers and civil servants tended to business affairs and the pursuit of leisure. After a short work day with a long siesta, the evening was free for socializing at cafés, restaurants, or the theater. For the more decadent, perhaps a visit to a casino, brothel, or opium den. By the 1920s, Indochina was the most profitable of all French overseas possessions. As it became richer from trade, further refinements arrived. In the major cities, the French set up exclusive clubs such as the Cercle Sportif, with a pool, tennis courts, and dining area. Journalist Howard Sochurek describes the scene in 1950:

In the private homes, the French traditions were carried on. If you went to dinner, it was always formal. You dressed in a white jacket and black trousers. The generals and the top military of course observed this very strictly. So if you attended a dinner thrown by de Lattre it was usually in a chandeliered governor's house, with many, many servants, great long tables, the finest of cutlery and glassware. It was like something out of the past. The women were some of the most exotic in the world, mixtures of French and Vietnamese. Fantastic creatures. They would all come dressed to the hilt, driving up in their Citroëns. Nobody worked very hard. All the finest imports were available: caviar, French wines and champagnes. A fantastically easy and gracious way of life, because of the tremendous number of servants and the wealth they got out of the rubber plantations and the trading of rice and the other businesses. In 1950, they still had all that.

Vietnam. They attacked Danang twice, in 1847 and 1858. After the second attack, 14 battleships from France and the Spanish Philippines rode monsoon winds south toward Saigon. Upon reaching Saigon in 1859, the French used explosives to breach the walls of Gia Dinh Citadel and captured it. Counterattacks by the Vietnamese using elephants proved futile. In 1862, the French signed a treaty with Emperor Tu Duc to take over three southern provinces, to be known as the colony of Cochinchina. Several ports were opened to French and Spanish commerce, and missionaries were promised the freedom to disseminate their faith throughout the country.

By 1867, the Mekong Delta area was added to Cochinchina. In 1873, French forces started making inroads into Tonkin with an attack on Hanoi citadel; in 1883, they attacked Hué citadel in central Vietnam. By 1887, the French controlled the entire peninsula, encompassing the colony of Cochinchina and the protectorates of Tonkin, Annam, and Cambodia. The protectorate of Laos was added in 1893.

The French governed Cochinchina directly as a colony. In Annam and Tonkin protectorates they found it expedient to allow emperors of the Nguyen dynasty to remain as puppets. Although the administrative mandarin system remained in place in Tonkin and Annam, real power was held by the French senior resident, supposedly only a technical adviser to the mandarins. The senior resident was an assistant to the governor-general in each protectorate.

Exploiting Indochina

Governor-general Paul Bert, in his short tenure in Hanoi in the mid-1880s, set about organizing France's *mission civilisatrice* (civilizing mission) in the new colonies. The French justified their rule of Indochina by claiming, as Francis Garnier phrased it, that France was bringing "into light and liberty the races and peoples still enslaved by ignorance and despotism." However, it's dubious whether the French created much more than a new version of slavery. Education of the Vietnamese was a halfhearted affair; proper education could create potential revolutionaries, and later, it did. Instituting the French penal code largely meant turning Indochina into a police state. A network of French security forces ruthlessly snuffed out any protest. Only in Cochinchina did a select few Vietnamese have the right to vote.

Paul Doumer, who became governor-general of Indochina in 1897, single-handedly put the French possessions on a profitable basis during his five years in power—building roads, bridges, lighthouses, and railways, raising revenues through a system of taxes and customs duties. His most lucrative endeavor was the creation of state monopolies on salt, alcohol, and opium. Insidiously, Doumer built an opium refinery in Saigon that concocted a new faster-burning blend to encourage consumption. Vietnamese addiction rose sharply, and opium sales accounted for one third of the colonial administration's income. Doumer assisted in the creation of powerful financial interests headed by the Banque de l'Indochine, which issued its own Indochinese currency. Such advances put the colonies on a semiautonomous basis. By the end of Doumer's term, in 1902, Hanoi was the capital of the French Indochinese Union.

The French were also keen on exploiting the mineral and lumber resources in the remote provinces of Yunnan and Guangxi in southern China, a French zone of interest after 1898. Tonkin, much closer to the rugged, mountainous southwest of China than the treaty ports of Shanghai or Canton, was the key to ferreting away this wealth. By 1900, several parts of Yunnan were opened to French trade, and by 1910 a French-engineered railroad connected Kunming with Hanoi and Haiphong.

By the 1920s, near-slave labor had transformed the jungles of Indochina with bridges, highways, harbors, and canals. Vietnam supplied raw materials to fuel French industrialization. Rice was exported despite starvation of local people. Rubber was the second biggest export of the 1920s. At one Michelin Tire Company plantation, 12,000 of 45,000 indentured workers died from malaria, dysentery, or malnutrition between 1917 and 1944. Small wonder then the Vietnamese would flee at the approach of plantation recruiters. Many Vietnamese perished working in substandard conditions on tea or coffee plantations, or in coal or tin mines. Appropriation of land for mines or other uses caused a breakdown in the land ownership system among the peasantry, and the system of taxes caused minor uprisings.

Meanwhile, the Nguyen dynasty lumbered along, with a rapid turnover of emperors as each fell out of favor with the French. The polygamous Emperor Tu Duc left behind a large imperial family, opening the way for power struggles. The dissident Emperor Ham Nghi resisted the French and was captured and exiled to Algeria. The French handpicked his successor, Dong Khanh. Another dissident, Emperor Duy Tan, staged a revolt against French rule in 1916; for his pains, he was also exiled. In 1925 his grandson Bao Dai became emperor. Schooled in France, Bao Dai retained a fondness for a decadent French lifestyle. He assumed the throne in 1932 and remained emperor during the Japanese occupation 1940–1945. Although the French attempted to revive Bao Dai's reign, he was essentially out of the picture after 1945.

The Vietminh

Communism in Vietnam is dominated by the personality of Ho Chi Minh, who left Vietnam in 1911 and spent a lengthy period in Western Europe, where he became a founding member of the French Communist Party in 1920. Ho studied revolutionary strategy in Moscow and moved on to China and Thailand before returning to Vietnam. In 1930, Ho Chi Minh and his comrades formed the Indochinese Communist Party in Hong Kong.

In 1940, Japan invaded Vietnam. At first the Japanese cooperated with the pro-German Vichy French, but they assumed direct control of Vietnam six months before World War II ended. In 1941, Ho Chi Minh slipped back into Vietnam for the first time in almost 30 years, founding the Vietminh (the League for the Independence of Vietnam) as a nationalist movement to fight the Japanese. In 1942, Ho stepped back across the Chinese border and was imprisoned by the Nationalist Chinese for a year. He was freed after making a deal to provide information on the Japanese.

When Japan surrendered in August 1945, the Allies agreed that Britain would occupy south Vietnam and the Nationalist Chinese would take over the north. The country was in complete chaos. Before the Chinese arrived, the Vietminh marched down to liberate Hanoi. On September 2, 1945, Ho Chi Minh proclaimed the Democratic Republic of Vietnam. This statement was not officially recognized internationally. Nevertheless, the last emperor of Vietnam, Bao Dai, complied with Ho Chi Minh's demands to abdicate and left for exile in France. In negotiations with the French, Ho Chi Minh agreed to accept 25,000 French colonial troops in the north for a period of five years rather than face occupation by the Nationalist Chinese. To justify his decision to angry comrades, Ho evoked ancient fears of the Chinese invader:

> *The last time the Chinese came, they stayed a thousand years. The French are foreigners. They are weak. Colonialism is dying. The white man is finished in Asia. As for me, I prefer to sniff French shit for five years than eat Chinese shit for the rest of my life.*

Meanwhile, the south quickly fell again into French hands. British troops, mainly Gurkhas, helped a small force of French paratroopers freed from prison gain control. Incredibly, the British also enlisted the help of defeated Japanese troops to fight Vietnamese insurgents. About 35,000 French reinforcements arrived in October 1945, marching off through the Mekong Delta and into the highlands to gain control of the south. They were constantly harassed by guerrillas as the retreating Vietminh burned villages and destroyed bridges. The French could take Vietnamese territory, but they could not hold it. Nevertheless, by early 1945, French General Jacques Leclerc claimed victory in the south.

In the north, the arrangement of a "free" Vietnamese state within the French Union (as the French empire was now called) was doomed to failure. In November 1946, in a dispute over the collection of customs duties, the Vietminh clashed with the French in Haiphong. The French responded by bombing Haiphong, with great loss of civilian life. By December Hanoi, too, was a battleground, with buildings aflame and tanks rumbling through the streets. The Vietminh fled to the hills of the north, and the First Indochina War was under way.

Ho Chi Minh's regime was soon recognized by the Soviet Union and the new government of Mao Zedong in China. Chinese communists began to supply arms and logistical assistance to the Vietminh across the border. In 1950, the Vietminh attacked a French force at Cao Bang near the Chinese border. The French garrison was wiped out, and the Vietminh made off with a great stock of weapons. The weary French were increasingly funded by a United States obsessed with communist expansion. By 1954, the United States was paying for 80 percent of France's Indochina military expenditure.

From an obscure, poorly armed force, the Vietminh quickly grew into a formidable military threat. Their commitment to the cause of an independent Vietnam was absolute. As Ho Chi Minh warned a French official, "You can kill 10 of my men for every one I kill of yours, but even at those odds, I will win and you will lose." This proved remarkably prophetic in the ensuing battles against the French and Americans; the North Vietnamese suffered heavy losses, but their motivation remained strong. Realizing that their losses would be catastrophic in conventional battles, the Vietminh adopted guerrilla tactics. Ho Chi Minh outlined this approach in an interview in 1946 when he compared the French to an elephant, and the Vietnamese to a tiger:

> *When the elephant is strong and rested near his base we will retreat. And if the tiger ever pauses, the elephant will impale him on his mighty tusks. But the tiger will not pause and the elephant will die of exhaustion and loss of blood.*

It remained for brilliant military strategist General Vo Nguyen Giap to implement this approach.

Dien Bien Phu

In 1954, the French sought to block Vietminh expansion into Laos by dropping six battalions of paratroopers into Dien Bien Phu, near the Laos border. The French garrison could receive supplies only by air and required 200 tons of supplies a day. Vietminh General Vo Nguyen Giap hauled heavy artillery onto the surrounding peaks, a feat the French had considered impossible. The Vietminh artillery could fire on the airfield, effectively cutting off the French garrison. After 55 days of intense bombardment, on May 7, 1954, 10,000 starving French troops surrendered to the Vietminh.

Partition

The next morning, nine delegations met in Geneva to discuss settlements in Indochina and Korea. In Vietnam, the solution presented proved little more than a cease-fire. Zhou Enlai, representing the Chinese delegation, infuriated Vietminh negotiator Pham Van Dong by proposing a partition of Vietnam. Zhou Enlai had China's interests in mind; it suited China to have a weaker, divided Vietnam at its doorstep.

The Geneva Accords of July 22, 1954, divided Vietnam in two at the 17th parallel. In the north the communists ruled under Ho Chi Minh; the south fell under the rule of Catholic leader Ngo Dinh Diem. Diem returned from self-imposed exile at Maryknoll Seminary in New Jersey in July 1954 to become prime minister of South Vietnam. Diem had previously served under Emperor Bao Dai; the United States backed his rise to power.

The Geneva Accord called for withdrawal of French troops from the north and Vietminh troops from the south. Free elections would be held in 1956 to reunify Vietnam. Civilians and soldiers had nine months to move freely between the two areas. An estimated 850,000 Vietnamese, mostly Catholic, left the north for the south, while about 80,000 people journeyed north. Ho Chi Minh and other communist leaders launched a land reform campaign in the north; thousands of real and purported landlords were tried before kangaroo courts and shot, their families left to starve. Diem staged a rigged election in 1955 to oust Bao Dai and justify his rule of the south. When Diem and the United States realized Ho Chi Minh would prevail in any honest election, the South Vietnamese announced they had no intention of honoring the Accords.

AMERICAN INTERVENTION
Trouble in the South

Vietnam became the linchpin in the United States's attempt to stop communist expansion in Southeast Asia. The late 1940s and early 1950s were the time of the Cold War, when the Soviet Union and the United States squared off across the globe. After the communist takeover of China in 1949 and the start of the Korean War in 1950, anticommunist hysteria reached fever pitch in the United States. Ho Chi Minh was identified as part of the communist conspiracy, cleverly manipulated by Moscow. In 1954, President Dwight Eisenhower expounded the "domino theory": if Vietnam succumbed to communism, other Asian nations would fall like dominoes, until even Australia was threatened. American strategy was to build up the

Know Vietnam, Cambodia & Laos

THE HO CHI MINH TRAIL

The famous Ho Chi Minh Trail was never just a single trail. It was, instead, a network of jungle paths, sometimes up to a dozen branches, running along the spine of the Truong Son Mountain Range heading through the jungles of Laos and Cambodia. The trail was the key to North Vietnam's success in the Vietnam War. It was also the major reason the war spilled over into Laos and Cambodia.

The Vietcong could survive on 15–60 tons of supplies a day coming down the trail. In 1959, when the trail was first used, the journey took up to six months. As the war progressed, the journey took six weeks; toward the end of the war, supplies could move in little more than a week on an improved surface of crushed stone. By then, the Ho Chi Minh Trail comprised some 15,000 kilometers of camouflaged roadway.

The trail was built and maintained by 300,000 full-time workers and many other part-time peasants. Perils along the trail were many. During the rainy season, streams would turn into rapids, and floods would wash away the trails. In the dense forests, marchers were so weighed down by rain-sodden packs they couldn't stand upright. Flimsy meter-wide bridges with bamboo planks and rope handrails were strung over crossings, then easily dismantled to avoid detection. Malaria and

amoebic dysentery were a constant threat. It is believed 10 percent of those who set out in the early days died from disease.

There were several modes of travel on the trail. In the beginning, most traveled on foot, wearing Ho Chi Minh sandals made from worn

© AVALON TRAVEL PUBLISHING, INC.

South Vietnamese army so it could prevent invasion from the north across the 17th parallel. To this end, from 1956 on, American advisers were sent to the south to train the Army of the Republic of Vietnam (ARVN).

Meanwhile, resistance to Diem developed under remnants of the Vietminh who had drifted south. They became known as Vietcong, short for Viet Nam Cong San (Vietnamese Communist), at first a derogatory term to describe all the South Vietnamese groups opposed to President Diem in the 1960s. The name was coined by Diem's publicists, who wished to avoid the heroic associations Vietminh conferred. In the north, the Vietcong

was christened the National Liberation Front (NLF) by Ho Chi Minh in 1960, a clear indication that the north was backing an open war in the south. The Vietminh, now fully communist-dominated, metamorphosed into the North Vietnamese Army (NVA), which operated either with Vietcong or in separate NVA units. Although the NLF (Vietcong) claimed to be independent of the NVA, the north provided direction and funding.

The Demise of Diem

In the early 1960s, President Ngo Dinh Diem's totalitarian regime was running into problems in the south. The Vietcong were making prog-

truck tires. This footwear left soldiers susceptible to snakebite and leeches, so they carried antivenin. Troops carried cooked rice rations in a linen tube hung around the body. Pack animals were sometimes used on the trail, as well as industrial-strength bicycles. The bicycles were copied or adapted from French models and were first used to ferry supplies at Dien Bien Phu. Reinforced cargo bicycles, maneuvered with extended handlebars, could carry 200 kilos of rice. In the last stages of trail use, 10,000 Chinese and Russian trucks were deployed, each carrying up to six tons of supplies.

American forces, using high-tech weaponry to destroy bridges, roads, and railways, were unable to prevent thousands of enemy soldiers from advancing on bicycles. When they encountered a downed bridge, the North Vietnamese simply formed a human chain and manhandled their bikes across the span. A modern army would have been immobilized, with its trucks and tanks unable to continue till the bridge was restored.

Attacks on the Ho Chi Minh Trail by U.S. bombers had limited success. A B-52 bomber could drop 100 350-kilogram bombs in 30 seconds, clearing a 1.5-kilometer swath through the jungle, but the effort was not worth the result. It's estimated the raids stopped only one in every 100 North Vietnamese. Trucks moved along the trail by night. In an effort to stop them, the Americans dropped hundreds of battery-powered sensors resembling plants. The Vietnamese fooled these acoustic sensors by using tape recordings of trucks; "sniffer" sensors intended to detect humans were easily deceived by leaking bags of buffalo urine hung from trees. Vietnamese engineers built submerged pontoon bridges about 30 centimeters underwater to avoid aerial detection, and the trail was well camouflaged. By 1970, the trail was defended by antiaircraft guns. In 1971, when American General Creighton Abrams tried to cut the trail west of the DMZ using ARVN troops in helicopters, half his troops were killed or wounded and Adams was forced to retreat.

Although several touring agencies claim to show travelers the trail, it's dubious whether the trail still exists. Much of its length has been reclaimed by the jungle, though a section between Khe Sanh and Aluoi via Dakrong Bridge was paved with Cuban assistance in the mid-1970s. Trekking in remote areas is dangerous because of the massive amount of unexploded ordnance. Minor trails are still maintained and active, used for smuggling goods from Laos and Cambodia into Vietnam. The bounty travels on the backs of porters, just as before. As one Hanoi official put it, "The Vietnamese have a very long tradition of guerrilla warfare. They are good at carrying things on their backs."

ress in rural villages, carrying out propaganda work and targeting village officials for selective assassination. By 1961, the Vietcong claimed to control large swaths of the countryside. Diem and his brother Nhu, head of the feared security forces, employed a Strategic Hamlets Program to try to win back control. The idea, employed by the United States in the Philippines during the Spanish-American War and by the British in Malaysia in the 1950s, was to put farmers into fortified villages surrounded by ditches, barbed wire, and spiked bamboo. This would supposedly cut them off from the Vietcong. The Vietnamese resented being uprooted and forced to move into what seemed to be concentration camps. When the Vietcong attacked, the farmers often opened the gates and let them in.

United States President John F. Kennedy came under increasing pressure to boost support for Diem. In 1961, the number of U.S. advisers in Vietnam stood at 700; within two years it was up to 16,000. Increasingly, American "advisers" went into combat and on bombing missions. Advisers of the United States believed South Vietnamese troops were not disciplined enough to defeat the Vietcong. In a 1963 engagement near Mytho, a small Vietcong force inflicted heavy casualties on a larger ARVN force.

In 1963, Diem's Catholic regime increased its vicious repression of Buddhists in the south. In May 1963, Buddhists were refused permission to display Buddhist flags or meet on the anniversary of Buddha's birthday. Nine people were killed as government troops fired on a protest march. The world was shocked by televised images of a protesting monk who set himself on fire. When Diem began exploring negotiations with Hanoi, the United States backed a coup that overthrew the government and assassinated Diem and Nhu.

The elimination of Diem did nothing to stop the political rot in South Vietnam: A series of bungling military juntas succeeded one another. Generals Ky and Thieu held the reins from 1965 on.

The American War

Although it's called the Vietnam War by the Western media, the Vietnamese have seen so many wars that they refer to this one as the American War. In June 1964, President Johnson ordered an attack on the North by U.S. bombers because of "renewed hostile actions against United States ships on the high seas in the Gulf of Tonkin." He was referring to an unsuccessful action by three North Vietnamese patrol boats that fired on the USS *Maddox,* which had been deployed "to test the effectiveness of radar installations in the north." United States bombers attacked ports and oil storage installations in North Vietnam. After the attack, the U.S. Congress approved the Gulf of Tonkin Resolution, giving the president the power to "take all necessary measures to repel any armed attacks against the forces of the United States and further aggression."

And with that, the Second Indochina War, simmering since 1954, at last erupted in earnest. American involvement escalated rapidly. Some 3,500 U.S. Marines landed in Danang in March 1965, ostensibly to protect the airfield. By the end of 1965 there were nearly 200,000 U.S. soldiers in Vietnam; by the end of 1966 there were double that number; by the beginning of 1968 about 520,000 American troops occupied the country. The Americans tried to

set up a series of firebases as a barrier along the 17th parallel, but the NVA bypassed the block, pouring troops and supplies down the Ho Chi Minh Trail through the mountains of Laos and Cambodia.

The United States invited Allied nations to rally round the flag. Australia, New Zealand, South Korea, and Thailand sent token forces; by the end of 1967, there were 8,300 Australian troops and 4,500 Korean troops in Vietnam. Meanwhile, in the North, Hanoi was receiving armaments and advice from the Russians and Chinese. Heavy arms from China were transported to North Vietnam along a railway line from Nanning built in the 1950s.

Apocalypse Now

Although they had far superior firepower, the Americans, like the French before them, were frustrated by their failure to lure the North Vietnamese into conventional battle. Guerrillas would strike and then disappear into the local community or a vast tunnel network. The Vietcong maintained political control of many villages in the south. American troops could not distinguish between guerrillas and villagers. United States soldiers on patrol often treated any Vietnamese as a threat to be liquidated. Civilian casualties were alarmingly high.

The American use of chemical warfare was condemned by the international community. Among chemical devices used were napalm, Agent Orange, and Agent Blue. The Americans also launched sustained bombing raids. During the years of the Rolling Thunder air campaign of 1965–68, well over seven million tons of bombs—twice the tonnage of bombs dropped during all of World War II—were dropped on Vietnam and Laos. Against this onslaught, the Vietcong and the NVA countered with a degree of organization and dedication unparalleled in human history. Theirs was a 50-year struggle, one that had achieved only partial success in 1954. Only their level of dedication could have withstood the exceedingly high casualty rates; few of those within the Vietcong ranks in 1964 were alive when the war ended.

Exactly who was winning the war was difficult to tell. The first significant engagement between NVA and U.S. troops occurred at Khe Sanh in late 1967. By January 1968, a force of 6,000 U.S. Marines and ARVN forces were holed up at Khe Sanh near the Lao border, surrounded by an estimated 40,000 NVA troops. The U.S. military feared another Dien Bien Phu, even though, unlike the French, the Americans had far superior air support. The battle became merely a testing ground, assuming an importance it hardly deserved. Neither side could claim victory at Khe Sanh. The Americans held their ground but abandoned the base a few months later, calling it strategically unimportant. Though NVA losses were very heavy, the North later claimed Khe Sanh a victory, as it served as a major diversion for the 1968 Tet Offensive.

The Tet Offensive

In 1968, Ho Chi Minh was ailing, and the North Vietnamese believed it would be his last Tet celebration. So instead of observing the traditional cease-fire period for the Lunar New Year, Vietcong forces unleashed more than 100 separate attacks on targets across South Vietnam on January 31st. The audacity of the Vietcong attacks astounded the Americans. In Hué, Vietcong and NVA troops held the citadel for 24 days. Groups of Vietcong attacked key targets in Saigon, including Tan Son Nhat airbase, the presidential palace, and the radio station. Commandos blasted their way into the American Embassy in an attack that lasted six hours. Later that day (February 1), the American public watched television footage of South Vietnamese Police Chief General Loan walk up to a captured Vietcong suspect and shoot him in the head. It became one of the most notorious images of the war, one that changed public opinion in the United States. Clearly, brutality was not confined to the communists.

Vietcong losses were heavy in the Tet Offensive, and NVA troops infiltrated the South in increasing numbers to replace Vietcong units. In September 1969, at the age of 79, Ho Chi Minh died.

The Secret War

There was never an official U.S. declaration of war against North Vietnam, and little information was dispensed about exactly what was going on. As early as 1964, the United States began secret bombing raids along the Ho Chi Minh Trail in Laos, using old American planes with Royal Lao markings. In March 1969, two months after he came to power, U.S. President Richard Nixon approved the first of a series of bombing raids on Cambodia. Total secrecy applied to B-52 cross-border raids directed at what was thought to be a major communist headquarters. In April 1970, American and ARVN troops pushed 30 kilometers into Cambodia. No communist headquarters were found; the raid only increased support from North Vietnam and the Vietcong for the Khmer Rouge.

American Withdrawal

Vietnam was the first fully televised war. Pictures of napalm victims and summary executions stunned the world. News of the My Lai Massacre in 1968 sent out greater shock waves. There were large demonstrations in the West, particularly in Western Europe, against American involvement.

President Richard Nixon advocated "Vietnamization," which called for South Vietnamese troops to fight the war on their own. By 1972, American troop strength was down to 95,000—the bulk of those support troops. The Americans concentrated on supplying heavy weapons to the South Vietnamese. Meanwhile, peace talks dragged on in Paris throughout 1972. In response to a North Vietnamese offensive across the 17th parallel, Nixon ordered the bombing of Haiphong and Hanoi by 200 B-52s during the 1972 Christmas season. There was great devastation on the ground, but also, because the Vietnamese wielded Russian-supplied surface-to-air missiles, heavy bomber losses. Though they weren't speaking with each other, both the Russians and the Chinese supplied North Vietnam with sophisticated weapons. The North Vietnamese also depended on shipments of Chinese rice to feed their population.

On January 27, 1973, a cease-fire was finally agreed upon in Paris. By the end of March, the last U.S. combat forces had left Vietnam, and America's messy misadventures in Indochina had come to an end. South Vietnamese President Nguyen Van Thieu retained a well-equipped army of a million men, but morale was low.

The Fall of Saigon

As with the Geneva Accord, the peace did not hold. Negotiations between North and South went nowhere. In January 1974, Thieu announced that the war had resumed, and his army attacked communist positions. On March 10, 1975, the NVA launched a major offensive, routing southern troops. Saigon fell on April 30, 1975, the last U.S. personnel fleeing by helicopter from the roof of the U.S. Embassy to ships waiting in the South China Sea. After nearly 30 years of warfare, Vietnam was unified, independent, and completely communist. The two halves of Vietnam formally unified as the Socialist Republic of Vietnam (SRV) on July 2, 1976.

AFTER UNIFICATION
Pariah State

The fruits of victory were bitter. At least three million Vietnamese were killed between 1954 and 1975. In 1995, Hanoi officials released statistics enumerating 1.1 million communist soldiers dead, and two million Vietnamese civilians killed. Vietnam was left with an appalling legacy of bomb craters and unexploded ordnance. Lives were devastated. The country's infrastructure lay in ruin, making the rebuilding of roads, railways, schools, and hospitals a high priority. The new government hoped for Western aid; Nixon had promised $3 billion in war reparations, but no money was forthcoming. Instead, the United States imposed an economic embargo on Vietnam, pressuring other Western nations to adhere to it.

The North Vietnamese rounded up south-

AN AMBASSADOR FOR PEACE

On June 8, 1972, the village of Trang Bang came under fierce aerial attack from South Vietnamese bombers. The village, about 40 kilometers west of Saigon, had been infiltrated by Viet Cong and North Vietnamese.

Nine-year-old Kim Phuc and her family had taken refuge in a Buddhist pagoda, but the pagoda suffered a direct hit, killing two of Kim's brothers and two cousins. Screaming in pain from napalm burns, Kim ran naked up the road away from the village—and was captured on film by Associated Press photographer Nick Ut (who picked her up and carried her to medical aid). One of the most widely published images of the Vietnam War, the photograph came to symbolize the madness of war and the suffering of innocent victims—it went on to win a Pulitzer Prize. Kim said, "I'm proud of the picture, because that picture stopped the war and helped people to understand and to know war is terrible."

Kim Phuc spent more than a year recuperating from her wounds in a Saigon hospital, undergoing 17 operations for her third-degree burns. She later went to Cuba and learned Spanish and English. Kim defected from Vietnam in 1992 during a stopover flight in Canada. She moved to Toronto with her husband and two children.

In 1997, at the age of 34, Kim Phuc was appointed a UNESCO goodwill ambassador. UNESCO's goodwill ambassadors (others include actress Catherine Deneuve and designer Pierre Cardin) are expected to promote the cause of peace by giving speeches wherever appropriate. The position is unpaid.

Kim said that she would "travel for peace and share with people what happened to me." Travel will be made much easier with her U.N. passport, which she obtained before her Canadian. She has established the Chicago-based Kim Foundation, a nonprofit organization accepting donations "to support programs for children throughout the world who are innocent victims of war." Kim still speaks to Nick Ut, now living in Los Angeles, once a week.

erners who had played active roles in the war and threw them into reeducation camps. Even so, they showed remarkable restraint toward their former enemies; most inmates survived their sentences. Upon release, they were given menial jobs. Austerity and repression reigned.

In December 1978, Vietnamese troops invaded Cambodia to depose the genocidal Khmer Rouge regime. The Khmer Rouge had attacked Vietnamese border towns and targeted ethnic Vietnamese for liquidation. Vietnamese troops remained in Cambodia 10 years. For putting an end to the atrocities of the Khmer Rouge, the Vietnamese received no thanks. Instead, the Chinese attacked North Vietnam in February 1979 as punishment for attacking their Cambodian ally, and both Western and Eastern nations imposed an economic embargo. Vietnam was treated as an outcast by the international community and denied bank loans that would have enabled it to rebuild its economy. The only country Vietnam could turn to for help was the Soviet Union. In the 1980s, Soviet experts arrived in force and immediately began work on Soviet naval bases. But the kind of aid coming from the Soviet bloc proved inappropriate to the country's rural needs.

Exodus of the Boat People

In 1978, the government launched an assault on capitalist activity in Saigon, particularly targeting the wealthy Chinese business community in Cholon. When China engaged Vietnam in a vicious border war in the north, a quarter of Vietnam's ethnic Chinese fled the country—the first of the "boat people." Most of the exodus left from Saigon. An estimated 675,000 people departed Vietnam by mid-1979, about 70 percent of them ethnic Chinese. Some crossed the northern border into China, but most left in boats, hoping to reach Hong Kong, Malaysia, or Thailand. An estimated 30 percent died at sea—from drowning, dehydration, or pirates. Up to a third of the boats fell victim to pirates, mostly Thai, in the South China Sea. Boats were plundered, women raped, passengers murdered.

Despite the risks of the journey, many ref-

ugees continued to leave. In early 1989, the international community slammed the door on Vietnamese refugees after an international conference on Indochinese refugees in Geneva determined that less than 10 percent fled political persecution. As refugees escaping economic hardship for a better life in the West, the later boat people were not eligible for refugee status under international law and faced repatriation. Meanwhile, they were held in grossly overcrowded camps in Southeast Asia.

In 1992, the British and Vietnamese agreed to repatriate 55,700 boat people living in camps in Hong Kong. Despite protests from the United Nations, some Vietnamese refugees were forcibly repatriated from these camps. In 1995, 22,000 boat people still lived in detention in Hong Kong. Other nations, such as Germany, have also entered into agreements with Hanoi on the repatriation of illegal immigrants.

Doi Moi

War in Cambodia and against the Chinese was a drain on the nation's already limited resources. The economic embargo took its toll. Due to failed farm-collectivization experiments, there was a drastic food shortage, and famine struck parts of the country. By 1985, inflation was running at 700 percent, and radical economic reform was required if Vietnam were to survive. In 1986, Nguyen Van Linh was appointed secretary general of the Communist Party, and the Vietnamese leadership announced a policy of *doi moi*, or "new thinking," roughly along the lines of Soviet *perestroika*. Hard-liners were replaced in 1986 and 1987 as the party embraced capitalist market principles.

Taking over as secretary general in 1991, party chief Do Muoi vowed to continue the reforms begun by Linh. After decades of international isolation, Vietnam began to establish diplomatic relations with other nations. The climate was more favorable after the withdrawal of Vietnamese troops from Cambodia in 1989 and the signing of the Cambodian Peace Agreement in late 1991. Vietnam began repairing its strained relations with China. In 1993, French President François Mitterrand visited Hanoi, the first Western head of state to visit the capital since 1954. Also in 1993 Premier Vo Van Kiet visited Japan, South Korea, Australia, and Western Europe to establish trade links, and Secretary General Do Muoi traveled to Thailand and Singapore for trade talks. In July 1995, Vietnam became the seventh member of ASEAN, another major step in ending its isolation.

Lifting the Embargo

In time for Tet 1994, U.S. President Bill Clinton finally brought hostilities to a close by announcing the lifting of the Vietnamese trade embargo. By 1995, another major legal hurdle was resolved concerning the settlement of property claims and frozen assets. Consequently, full diplomatic relations were established between Hanoi and Washington. Attending the opening of the U.S. Embassy in Hanoi in August 1995 was U.S. Secretary of State Warren Christopher. Vietnam was included in the list of the world's most promising emerging markets for U.S. business, announced by the U.S. Department of Commerce in mid-1995. And in May 1997, Pete

Peterson, the first postwar U.S. ambassador to Vietnam, took up residence in Hanoi.

America Searches Its Soul

The Vietnam War created a high level of public distrust of generals and presidents in the United States. American Presidents Lyndon Johnson and Richard Nixon, along with the top military command in Vietnam, repeatedly lied to Congress and concealed from the American people what was occurring in Indochina. For the United States, the aftermath of the war would lead to years of soul searching. Senior State Department figure George Ball called the war "the greatest single error made by America in its history." In 1995, on the 20th anniversary of the end of the war, Robert S. McNamara in his book *In Retrospect* revealed that he and the other top brass who got Americans into Vietnam "were wrong, terribly wrong." McNamara served in the Kennedy and Johnson administrations and was the architect of the U.S. buildup in Vietnam in the 1960s.

McNamara repudiated America's once-cherished "domino theory," which held that Communism had to be stopped in Vietnam

MISSING IN ACTION—ON BOTH SIDES

The first office opened by the United States in Vietnam after the war was the MIA Office in Hanoi. Clearing up the MIA issue was a U.S. precondition for lifting its economic embargo against Vietnam. The Vietnamese never really understood why the Americans were so concerned about the fate of 2,000 MIAs when there were 300,000 Vietnamese unaccounted for. It all seemed rather arrogant, but for the Americans, MIA investigation was a face-saving procedure. Some 200 "live sightings" were investigated in 1992–1993, but no Americans were ever found. From 1993 to 1994, teams of investigators were flown into Vietnam to search for remains.

The exact number of MIAs is debatable. Because of covert operations in Laos and Cambodia, some MIAs were falsely reported by the United States as missing in action in Vietnam.

The Vietnamese have a far greater MIA problem. Nguyen Manh Dau, chairman of the Policy Department of the Ministry of Defense, has appealed to the Americans for help. "Only the American side knows where many of our soldiers died," says Dau. One recent find of 85 sets of remains were unearthed thanks to documents supplied by the Vietnam Veterans of America. American veterans groups have asked members to send in photos and other material that might assist in the search for burial sites of Vietnamese soldiers. Search parties in Vietnam have been thwarted by unexploded bombs and mines and difficult terrain.

or it would spread throughout the region. McNamara writes, "We totally underestimated the nationalist aspect of Ho Chi Minh's movement. We saw him first as a Communist, and only second as a Vietnamese nationalist."

McNamara's confessions sparked angry recriminations among veterans; why had McNamara waited 25 years to reveal his opposition to the war? How could he sit back and watch 1.1 million Americans serve in Vietnam, resulting in 58,000 deaths? Vietnamese General Vo Nguyen Giap described McNamara's revelations as "honest, courageous." Vietnam vets were outraged that McNamara not only confessed to gross errors, but that he was raking in hefty royalties from a best-seller based on those errors. But then what can you expect from a man whose middle name is "Strange?" (could be an element of Doctor Strangelove in there somewhere).

Out of Sync

In November 2000, when President Clinton visited Vietnam, he was mobbed by young people wherever he went—a nightmare for security forces, but a gesture that shows the popularity of America and American values among Vietnamese youth (and more than half of Vietnam's present population was born after the war). The die-hard old guard that runs the country is out of touch with this reality: The Communist Party leadership are still preoccupied with the war, and schoolchildren are routinely shown Ho

Chi Minh museums and war museums and heroic old documentaries about the war.

But things may be changing—slowly. National elections in 1997 brought a change of government with a younger group of ministers (younger meaning in their 60s, not their 70s or 80s). Elected Prime Minister Phan Van Khai took up the fight against rampant corruption and continued with economic reforms.

Manh of the People

Every five years the Vietnamese Communist Party holds a major congress in Hanoi where factions get together to backstab. At the congress of April 2001, a major shuffle resulted in half the candidates' being sent out to pasture and fresh blood bought in. Dumped was 70-year-old Secretary General Le Kha Phieu, a conservative with a strong military background. Through secret ballot, he was replaced by someone 10 years his junior, the reform-minded Nong Duc Manh. In securing this powerful post of secretary general of the Vietnamese Communist Party, Nong Duc Manh has already achieved a number of firsts: the first secretary-general with no record of military service, the first to hold a university degree—and the first with a minority background (he's originally from the northern border area of Vietnam). And here's another first that's a hard act to follow: He may be related to Ho Chi Minh, the national icon.

Cambodia History

The forerunners of Khmer culture were the civilizations of Chenla, centered near Kompong Thom, and Funan, based in the Mekong Delta. Funan and Chenla are Chinese names for what may have originally been Khmer states. The Indianized Funan culture ruled from the 1st to 6th centuries A.D., its wealth based on maritime trade through the key port of Oc-Eo. The people of Funan were described by Chinese travelers as dark-skinned and crinkly-haired, possibly of Melanesian origin. There is scant historical knowledge about the Funan

and Chenla empires, but it appears the land-based Funan territories were absorbed by the Chenla Empire in the 7th century A.D., while coastal sections were taken over by the Srivijaya Empire of Indonesia. The Chenla Empire rose between the 3rd and 7th centuries in the hills of northern Cambodia. In the early 8th century it split into two kingdoms—one based to the north of Lake Tonle Sap, the other east of the lake. Toward the end of the 8th century, the Mekong Delta region became a vassal state of Java's powerful Sailendra dynasty, and members of Chenla's ruling family were taken to the Sailendra court.

The Rule of Angkor

The Khmers remained under Sailendra suzerainty until a Khmer prince returned to the land of his ancestors and proclaimed independence. At Phnom Kulen, 45 kilometers northeast of Angkor Wat, Jayavarman II arranged his coronation by a Brahman priest in 802 A.D. He declared himself a *devaraja,* or divine king. At this time the Hindu deities Shiva and Vishnu were worshipped as a single entity, called Harihara; early Khmer kings adopted the Hindu trinity of Shiva, Brahma, and Vishnu, each becoming the basis for cult worship. The history of this period has been reconstructed from depictions in bas-relief and more than 900 inscriptions in stone within the boundaries of the former Khmer Empire. Still, knowledge of Khmer history is vague and highly speculative.

The 200-square-kilometer plains of Angkor, situated between Phnom Kulen and Lake Tonle Sap, are comparable in size to Egypt's Nile Valley. They were inhabited first by Jayavarman II, and then by successive kings for more than 500 years. The kings established the powerful Angkorian culture, known for its brilliant achievements in architecture and sculpture. Angkor developed into one of the world's greatest urban centers and held dominion over large swaths of present-day Thailand and Vietnam.

The Khmer king's spirit was said to reside in a linga (sacred phallus, symbol of Shiva) housed in a temple-pyramid. People believed the king communicated with the gods at the summit of this structure. The all-powerful king ensured the prosperity of his kingdom. Subsequent kings transferred the *devaraja* cult to other temple-pyramids. The Khmer Empire continued to expand, vying with neighboring kingdoms—the Cham, Vietnamese, and Burmese.

Although Jayavarman II is credited with establishing the Khmer kingdom, it was 10th-century king Yasovarman I who founded the first capital city on the site now known as Angkor. Yasovarman I built a temple-pyramid at Phnom Bakheng, near the site of Angkor Wat,

ushering in a Khmer golden age. He governed an empire that stretched from the south of Laos to the Gulf of Siam. Each new king added temples, monuments, palaces, and residences to the Angkor area; surrounding these urban complexes were vast rice fields with an intricate system of canals and irrigation networks. The Angkor region borders Lake Tonle Sap, which floods annually; as the waters recede, fish are caught in abundance—this is one of the world's richest fishing grounds. An economic surplus derived from agriculture, fishing, and a royal monopoly on foreign trade enabled Angkorian kings to embark on grandiose architectural projects symbolizing their prestige and authority.

The relationship between the royal center at Angkor and the provincial frontiers was highly unstable. More or less autonomous provinces were satellites of the central court; authority extended from Angkor through an arrangement of alliances with petty rulers. The fluctuating peripheries of the empire were of secondary concern to the kings, who were preoccupied with the splendor of the royal center at Angkor.

The zenith of the Khmer Empire was achieved under Suryavarman II, who reigned roughly 1112–1152. He undertook the building of Angkor Wat and a number of other temples; under his rule, the Khmer Empire expanded into present-day Malaya, Thailand, Myanmar (Burma), and Vietnam. He deposed the King of Champa in coastal Vietnam in 1145; however, the Cham regained their independence a few years later. Toward the end of his rule, Suryavarman II mounted a disastrous foray into North Vietnam to attack the Cham again. A large number of his troops perished from fever on jungle marches.

Angkor Under Attack

Upon the death of Suryavarman II, the nation was weak and divided, prey to Cham revenge. The Cham devised a cunning method for attacking Angkor—they came across Lake Tonle Sap in war canoes from the south, guided by a Chinese pilot. They sacked Angkor in 1177 and drove out its people.

Angkor had never before been attacked. The sacking by the Cham cast a shadow over the infallibility of both Angkor's kings and the Hindu deities that were supposed to render them infallible. A new contender to the throne routed the Cham in 1181, pushing them back to Annam. Crowned Jayavarman VII, this king inaugurated Mahayana Buddhism as the nation's faith. Temples were dedicated to Lokesvara, the bodhisattva of compassion. Jayavarman VII undertook a frenzied building and social works program, constructing the city of Angkor Thom with a royal palace and temples. Angkor Thom was a thriving metropolis with a large system of reservoirs and irrigation canals. Jayavarman VII extended the boundaries of the empire from the vicinity of Pagan in Myanmar (Burma) to the Vietnam coast, and from Vientiane in Laos to the Malay Peninsula.

Fall of the Khmer Empire

After Jayavarman VII's death in 1218, the Khmer Empire declined. His sons and heirs reverted to Shivaism, and Indian Brahmans gained great influence at the court. For unknown reasons a malaise gripped the core of the Khmer Empire in the 13th and 14th centuries. Theories abound as to why Angkor declined: climate change, shift of trade from land- to sea-based empires, exhaustion of resources in warfare and on building projects, or a change of religion to Theravada Buddhism, undermining the royal and priestly hierarchy. In any case, the elaborate irrigation system, no longer properly tended, fell into disrepair and silted up. Canals became clogged, rice fields reverted to swampland, food production dwindled. Stagnant water probably led to an increase in the number of malaria-carrying mosquitoes.

To the west, Thai chieftains shook off Khmer rule and established the first Thai kingdom of Sukothai. Another Thai kingdom from the south, in Ayuthaya, expanded quickly and became a major threat to the Khmers. In the 14th century there were repeated attacks by the Siamese and counterattacks by the Khmers, with skirmishes in 1353, 1394, 1401, and 1421. When the Siamese invaded Angkor in 1431

they went on a rampage, killing, destroying, and looting. They stripped Angkor of its wealth and destroyed its infrastructure.

Khmer Dark Ages

After its magnificent beginnings, the kingdom of Cambodia fell on hard times, becoming a vassal state of the Thai kingdom of Sukothai. For the next 400 years a weak Cambodia became a political football, kicked back and forth by its powerful neighbors, Siam and Vietnam. Worse still, there were dynastic squabbles among the Khmers. In this lackluster period of Khmer history, the court—what remained of it—moved continuously. In 1434 it moved to Phnom Penh. A short-lived attempt to rekindle the capital at Angkor was stymied when the Siamese sacked it again in 1473. There were further attempts by the court to return to Angkor in the 16th and 17th centuries, but nothing came of them. In the 16th century, Khmer King Ang Chan built a fortified capital at Lovek north of Phnom Penh. Taking advantage of the Thai preoccupation with fighting the Burmese, Ang Chan started taking back lost Cambodian territory. However, after recovering from Burmese assaults, the Thais captured Angkor, Battambang, and Pursat. An attack on Lovek in 1593 caused the Khmer royal family to flee to Laos.

In 1603 the Thais released a captured prince to rule over the vassal state of Cambodia. In 1618 the Khmers tried to shake themselves loose from Siamese suzerainty, driving out the Siamese garrison. The king asked the Vietnamese for help. However, this meant the Khmer court was obliged to pay tribute to Vietnam. Successive kings would seek Siamese assistance against the domination of Vietnam.

In the early 1700s the kingdom of Cambodia was centered in Udong, to the northwest of Phnom Penh. By 1750 the Khmer royal family had split into pro-Vietnamese and pro-Siamese factions. Only the Thai wars with the Burmese and internal squabbles in Vietnam prevented these two nations from taking over Cambodia entirely. The Khmers lost control of the Mekong Delta to the Vietnamese in the late 18th century, blocking the nation's access to the sea. In 1793 the Siamese gained the western Cambodian provinces of Siem Reap and Battambang. In the 1840s Thai and Vietnamese armies fought on Cambodian territory. Cambodian King Norodom was under the control of the Siamese resident in the capital and paid tribute to the Vietnamese.

Enter the French

French designs on Cambodia were evident soon after they gained a foothold in neighboring Cochinchina (southern Vietnam). The French sought a buffer between Cochinchina and Siam, where the British had established trading interests. The French were also keen on exploring the Mekong as a trading route from China, and wanted to secure the upper reaches of the Mekong. In 1861 Admiral Charner, the French commander in Saigon, sailed up the Mekong and on to the Cambodian capital of Udong to tell King Norodom the French would help Cambodia maintain its freedom by providing military assistance.

Under French pressure, Norodom signed a treaty in 1864 whereby Cambodia became a French protectorate. This was merely a switch of masters—the French resident, Captain Doudart de Lagrée, replaced the Siamese resident. In 1867, in return for Siamese renunciation of sovereignty over Cambodia, the French ceded the provinces of Battambang and Siem Reap to the Siamese. King Norodom protested, to no effect; the two provinces were later returned to Cambodia under a 1907 treaty.

In 1884 the French tried to gain full control of Cambodia by forcing King Norodom to sign an agreement handing over all power to the French resident. This sparked an insurrection, mainly in the eastern part of the country, most likely supported by the disgruntled king. The French eventually conceded and withdrew some of their demands. However, to diminish the power of the king, they paid attention to a rival branch of the royal family, the Sisowaths, who were considered more malleable. When King Norodom died in 1904, the French discounted his heir and arranged for his half-brother, Prince Sisowath, to succeed him.

The French were not greatly interested in developing Cambodia. Tax revenues were used to build rail lines and roads; in the 1920s, private-sector investors planted rubber estates in Kompong Cham in eastern Cambodia, as well as tea, coffee, pepper, and cotton plantations.

Shaking off the French

In the late 1930s nationalism began to stir in Cambodia as intellectuals educated in France returned to their homeland. A key figure in disseminating anticolonial ideas was Son Ngoc Thanh, an ethnic Khmer from Vietnam's Mekong Delta. In 1937 he founded *Nagaravatta (Angkor Wat),* the first Cambodian-language newspaper. Son Ngoc Thanh rallied a group of Buddhist monks, rich Khmers, and Cambodian intellectuals to his cause.

To counter nationalism, in 1941 the French decided to switch royal families once again. When Sisowath's son Monivong died in 1941, they reverted to the Norodoms. Nineteen-year-old Prince Norodom Sihanouk was crowned king. The French hold on Cambodia was weakened during World War II when Indochina was occupied by the Japanese. In 1945 the Japanese took full control of Cambodia from the Vichy French and ordered Sihanouk to declare independence. Under Japanese pressure, Sihanouk appointed Son Ngoc Thanh as prime minister.

When Japan surrendered, Thanh attempted to declare a republic but was arrested by the French and sent into exile. Thanh believed only armed struggle against France and an end to the monarchy could liberate Cambodia. He conducted a guerrilla campaign from the forests of Thailand and the south of Vietnam, forming the Khmer Serei (Free Khmers). In 1946 the French secured their hold on Battambang and Siem Reap provinces. In 1949 Sihanouk negotiated partial freedom from the French; in 1953 came full independence. Sihanouk had proved himself an astute negotiator.

In 1954 the Geneva Peace Conference agreed to a temporary division of Vietnam into north and south. It also recognized Cambodia's neutrality and called on the country to hold elections based on universal suffrage. It became clear the Democratic Party, republican-minded followers of Son Ngoc Thanh, would win. There appeared to be little sympathy for the monarchy, so Sihanouk decided to wade into the elections himself. In 1955 he abdicated in favor of his father and formed a movement, the Sangkum, a loose coalition of royalist and Buddhist forces. Sihanouk was victorious at the polls and became prime minister.

Calm Before the Storm

From 1955 to 1965, Cambodia was miraculously insulated from the brutality that engulfed the rest of Indochina. Protected by the deft neutrality of Sihanouk, the country drifted along almost oblivious to the bloodshed in Vietnam and Laos. Phnom Penh offered the charm of a provincial French town. Food was stacked high in the central marketplace, and there was little evidence of the sort of slums that plagued Bangkok or Saigon. In the countryside rural folk lived around their pagodas, worked the rice fields, and fished the streams. North Vietnamese troops moved through the mountains of northeast Cambodia; deep in the forest was a ragtag band of Cambodian guerrillas. But all this seemed remote to the bulk of the population.

THE RAVAGES OF WAR
Sideshow

In 1965, suspicious of CIA involvement in plots against him, Sihanouk broke off diplomatic relations with the United States and aligned himself with China. At the same time he continued to crack down on domestic dissent. Primary targets included French-educated radicals who had returned from Paris to teach or take civil service jobs in Phnom Penh. These men and women were disillusioned by the rampant corruption in the city. Among them were Leng Sary, Son Sen, Khieu Samphan, and Saloth Sar (who later earned international infamy as Pol Pot). In 1963 a number of them headed for the jungles and mountains. In 1967 there was an anticorruption insurrection in Battam-

THE CAMBODIAN FLAG

Cambodia is the only country in the world with a building on its flag: the triple towers of Angkor Wat. That flag has been flying, in one form or another, since Cambodia gained independence from France in 1953.

The current national flag is red, white, and blue—three white towers set against a red central field bordered by two horizontal blue stripes. Vexillology, the study of flags, is particularly confusing in Cambodia because there have been more than seven versions of the Angkor temple-tower design, used by successive governments and the Khmer Rouge. If the flag features three yellow temple towers on a blood-red field, it's the flag of the Khmer Rouge. This flag flew at the United Nations during the late 1970s when the Khmer Rouge held a seat there. The flag has also, embarrassingly, popped up at functions planned for Cambodian government officials in Thailand.

From 1991 to 1993, Cambodia briefly dropped its flag—the country was under U.N. auspices and flew the U.N. flag, which featured a white outline of Cambodia on a blue field.

bang province. Sihanouk savagely put down the peasant revolt by liquidating the rioters. The uprising was blamed on leftists—remaining Phnom Penh radicals fled to join their comrades in the jungle. Sihanouk dubbed the Cambodian Communists "Khmer Rouge" (Cambodian Reds).

Meanwhile the United States sought ways of preventing the North Vietnamese Army and the Vietcong from escaping to sanctuaries in neighboring Laos and Cambodia along the Ho Chi Minh Trail. Secret raids by U.S. and South Vietnamese operatives in the late 1960s preceded the B-52 bombings of Cambodia in March 1969. These actions were referred to by the Nixon White House as "a sideshow to Vietnam." Flight crews assumed they were bombing Vietnam when in fact their targets lay inside Cambodia. President Richard Nixon and Secretary of State Henry Kissinger maintained the areas were unpopulated by all save

North Vietnamese troops, but in fact many places were populated by Cambodians. More than 3,600 B-52 sorties were flown against suspected Communist bases in Cambodia in the next 14 months. William Shawcross provided an overview in his book *Sideshow:*

By the beginning of 1969, Vietnam and Laos were torn apart by war, their people driven into camps, their societies already irrevocably destroyed. Thailand had endured no fighting, but it too had been corrupted by the commerce of war and now, under a repressive military dictatorship, served as a "land-based aircraft carrier" for the B-52 bombers that daily pounded the grounds of its Indochinese neighbors. Only Cambodia was unassailed. Her neutralism was vulnerable and abused by all parties to the conflict.

Lon Nol Regime

In March 1970 Sihanouk was deposed in a U.S.-backed coup led by General Lon Nol.

POL POT: BROTHER NUMBER ONE

Behind the Khmer Rouge bloodbath was Pol Pot, a psychopathic mass murderer. Born Saloth Sar in Kompong Thom in 1925, he was one of seven children in a rural family. The family had royal connections: His cousin had grown up a palace dancer, becoming one of King Monivong's principal wives, and his eldest sister was chosen as a royal consort. In 1928, his eldest brother, Loth Suong, began a career in palace protocol, and Saloth Sar joined him six years later. After a year in a royal monastery, he spent six years in a strict Catholic school.

In 1948, after attending technical college in Phnom Penh, Saloth Sar received a scholarship to study radio electronics in Paris. Study at a French university was the ultimate goal of ambitious Cambodians, who avidly sought scholarships. Saloth Sar failed his examinations in Paris three times—he preferred to spend his time at Marxist revolutionary meetings. He kept company with Khieu Ponnary—eight years his senior—the first Khmer woman to receive a French degree. They were married in 1956. Among their circle of student friends were Khieu Samphan, Ieng Sary, and Son Sen.

Upon returning to newly independent Cambodia in 1953, Saloth Sar taught history and geography at a private school in Phnom Penh and worked as a left-wing journalist. By 1962, he had risen to the rank of deputy general secretary in the underground Cambodian Communist Party. Members had code names such as "Free Khmer" or "Khmer Worker." Saloth Sar's *nom de guerre* was Pol Pot, meaning "Original Cambodian."

In 1963, he fled Phnom Penh in the wake of a crackdown by Sihanouk. Pol Pot was trained in guerrilla warfare and became leader of the Khmer Rouge forces, advocating armed resistance. When the Khmer Rouge took Phnom Penh in 1975, Pol Pot—who was also known as Brother Number One—ruled as virtual dictator, with Khieu Samphan as head of state. Few Cambodians had ever heard of him when he came to power. He had always kept a low profile—so low that it wasn't until 1978 that Loth Suong found out (by seeing a portrait of Pol Pot on a wall in Kompong Thom and recognizing it) that it was his own younger brother who was responsible for the genocide in Cambodia. Khieu Ponnary reputedly went mad.

Occasionally, Pol Pot was heard over the radio. His early training in radio electronics proved useful in this regard—radio was one of the few technologies retained and permitted by the Khmer Rouge. In September 1977, he gave a five-hour speech over Radio Phnom Penh, laced with Maoist rhetoric. He calmly recited the new national anthem of Democratic Kampuchea, which roughly translates as: "Bright red blood which cov-

The new regime abolished the monarchy and declared a republic; Sihanouk, in Moscow at the time, subsequently moved to Beijing, where he passed his time in exile in luxury. Lon Nol got off to a bad start. To compensate for lack of peasant support, he tried to exploit the traditional Khmer fear of the Vietnamese by launching a murderous campaign against Vietnamese civilians in the south. Lon Nol's regime soon became even more dictatorial and corrupt than Sihanouk's. In April 1970 Nixon announced that American and ARVN troops had crossed into Cambodia to attack an alleged Vietcong headquarters. The base was never found and the troops withdrew a few months later.

In early 1971, Lon Nol suffered a stroke that left him with slurred speech and a tenuous grasp on reality. Yet he remained in power for four more years, bolstered by the White House. Cambodia became heavily dependent on American aid in political, economic, and military affairs. Lon Nol's troops were poorly disciplined; the government controlled only the areas around Phnom Penh and the provincial capitals. In the

ers the towns and plains of Kampuchea, our motherland, sublime blood of workers and peasants, sublime blood of revolutionary men and women fighters!"

Under the code name "87," Pol Pot continued operations in the Cardamom Mountains. The most secretive of leaders, Pol Pot dropped out of sight—he was not seen by a Western journalist after 1979. Then, on June 25, 1997, Western reporter Nate Thayer was summoned to a Khmer Rouge stronghold in Anlong Veng—where Pol Pot was undergoing a show trial, staged by his cohorts. When Pol Pot turned on his longtime military commander Ta Mok, the strategy backfired, and Pol Pot himself was on the run. He was arrested and accused not of mass murder, but of ordering a purge of his top leaders, resulting in the deaths of Son Sen (his defense minister) and 14 of his relatives. The aging Pol Pot, a frail man with gray hair, was denounced before a crowd of 500. The tribunal sentenced Pol Pot to life imprisonment—but ruled out turning him over to a Cambodian or an international court.

Through an interpreter, reporter Nate Thayer was able to conduct the first interview with Pol Pot in 18 years. He didn't get any straight answers, however. Repeatedly pressing Pol Pot on his role in the atrocities between 1975 and 1979, Thayer was told, "My conscience is clear" or "I'm tired of talking about it," or asked, "Do I look like a savage person?" When Thayer talked about the notorious Tuol Sleng prison in Phnom Penh, where many Cambodians were murdered, the unrepentant Pol Pot said he never heard of it before 1979—and that it was a Vietnamese fabrication. He also revealed that he had a 14-year-old daughter by his second wife, Mea Som, whom he married in 1987.

Ten months after the interview, when Cambodian government troops had succeeded in flushing Khmer Rouge groups from their spheres of operation and chasing them into much less hospitable mountainous regions near the Thailand-Cambodia border, Thayer was again summoned, this time to a jungle hut in Anlong Veng. This time, he was to see for himself and to confirm for the world that the 73-year-old tyrant was dead. On April 15, 1998, Thayer identified and was allowed to photograph the body of Pol Pot, who had reportedly had a heart attack and died in his sleep. Thayer pointed out in interviews at the time that the explanation was entirely credible, given Pol Pot's longstanding infirmity, the physical stresses of his strenuous flight over challenging terrain, and the disheartening beating his soldiers had taken in combat against government forces. Others said he was poisoned. Whatever the case, Pol Pot was never brought to justice. Pol Pot—who ranks up there with Hitler, Stalin, and Mao Zedong in his ability to kill—died peacefully in his sleep.

countryside the Communists ruled, and each year they captured more territory. By 1974 only Phnom Penh remained in government hands. In April 1975, Lon Nol fled to Hawaii.

Rise of the Khmer Rouge

The obscure Khmer Rouge were thought to number only 5,000 in the 1960s. It was Prince Sihanouk who gave this insidious group its name, derisively dubbing them "Cambodian Reds." By the early 1970s the Khmer Rouge army had grown to perhaps 50,000 men and could hold its own against Lon Nol with some support from the North Vietnamese.

The dramatic change was due to several factors. When Sihanouk went into exile, he was piqued by the Lon Nol coup. He abandoned neutrality and allied himself with his former enemies, the Khmer Rouge and the North Vietnamese, against Lon Nol, South Vietnam, and the United States. The Khmer Rouge thus gained national appeal. Many Cambodians switched allegiance because the Khmer Rouge represented opposition to the corruption of the Lon Nol regime. By 1973, U.S. B-52 raids had killed at least 100,000 Cambodian civilians. Pol Pot used the bombing as both recruitment propaganda and an excuse to purge moderate socialists. Although Pol Pot was deeply resentful of foreign influence, he was forced to accept North Vietnamese help in the early 1970s. As soon as his forces were strong enough, Pol Pot appealed to Khmer nationalism—and any cadres who'd been trained by the Vietnamese were marked men.

The Year Zero

On April 17, 1975, 13 days before the fall of Saigon, the Khmer Rouge rolled into Phnom Penh. Having methodically secured the city, they ordered everyone out, including the dying in hospitals. More than two million people were sent to the countryside in the next 48 hours with neither food nor possessions. They were informed that American planes would bomb them and that there was no need to take anything because they could return in a few days. Later, they were told a different story. This was

the Year Zero in democratic Kampuchea, and Angka Loeu (the Organization on High), Pol Pot's administrative arm, would provide for a new future. Angka Loeu was run by a handful of people—all French-educated and related by revolutionary experience and/or marriage. Together they launched a bloodbath.

The Killing Fields

From 1975 to 1979 the Khmer Rouge strove to realize Pol Pot's vision of a peasant nation of self-reliant agricultural work brigades, modeled on the Khmer Empire. This was to be accomplished without machinery—everything would be done with bare hands. "We will burn the old grass and new will grow," went one slogan. A practical side of this strategy was that the Khmer Rouge could split up and isolate any possible opposition. The Khmer Rouge enforced a revolution that probably went farther and faster toward destroying a society than any other in history. They made no attempt to reeducate the urban population—they simply set about killing "traitors." Cities were emptied, imported technology (including medical equipment) was destroyed, temples were dynamited, schools and hospitals closed, and books burned—all in an attempt to turn the nation into a rural paradise. There were no medical facilities, no education, no transport. Money, telephones, and newspapers were outlawed. Books, holidays, and music were banned. Buddhism was forbidden.

Khmer Rouge methods of killing were particularly brutal. Refugees who escaped to Thailand reported that pregnant women were disemboweled, babies torn apart limb from limb, men buried up to their necks in sand and left to die, others suffocated with plastic bags over their heads. Within months of the takeover, the entire administrative order of the old regime was gone—all executed. Those evacuated from the cities were placed in rural communes and made to work as slave labor on often pointless projects. Khmer Rouge irrigation-cum-drainage systems were poorly engineered (the Khmer Rouge had killed off most of the engineers) and resulted in serious environmental damage and crop failure.

In communes the people were separated into three groups—those from the city, those from market towns, and rural people. The rural contingent was put in charge. Each citizen was required to submit a verbal autobiography to the commune and its cadres. Those who revealed they had been technicians, teachers, monks, or doctors were executed. Those who spoke French, English, or Vietnamese, or who had studied abroad, were likewise liquidated. Simply having fair skin or wearing glasses was cause for execution.

Ethnic Cleansing

Pol Pot envisioned a pure Cambodian race. National impurities were to be expunged, territory lost to Vietnam and Thailand regained. The minorities in Cambodia—Chinese, Vietnamese, Cham, and hilltribe groups—were devastated. The Muslim Cham numbered 250,000 in 1975. The Khmer Rouge emptied all 113 Cham villages in Cambodia and massacred 90,000 Cham. Islamic schools and religion and the Cham language were banned. Only half the estimated 500,000 ethnic Chinese survived the Pol Pot era, one of the worst disasters ever to befall the Chinese in Southeast Asia. China passed over the slaughter of Cambodia's Chinese because the Khmer Rouge were killing Vietnamese, and China resented Vietnam's alignment with the Soviet Union at the time. The 450,000-strong Vietnamese community had mostly been expelled under the Lon Nol regime; those who remained in 1975 were driven out by Pol Pot or murdered.

The bloodiest period of Khmer Rouge reign was in 1978, when Pol Pot's troops crushed an uprising in eastern Cambodia. Pol Pot broadcast a call not only for the extermination of the Vietnamese but also for purification in the Cambodian masses. Estimates of the number of people killed in the 1975–1979 period range from 300,000 to three million (out of a total population of around seven million in 1975). Research based on extensive interviews with survivors by two independent Western researchers puts the figure at 1.5 million dead from execution, starvation, or disease.

Barring the Chinese, communist nations refused to recognize democratic Kampuchea, but they did little else. Western nations, intent on improved relations with China, remained silent. As essayist George Steiner put it: "In previous times, we were not bombarded with the graphic demonstration of our own impotence or indifference. [In Cambodia] we knew, day by day, that 100,000 people were being buried alive, and we did nothing."

Vietnamese Occupation

In several years of border fighting with the Khmer Rouge the Vietnamese suffered the deaths of perhaps 30,000 troops and an equal number of civilians. In a move censured by the West, the Vietnamese invaded Cambodia in December 1978. Within two weeks the Vietnamese Army had pushed its former ally back to the Thai border. More than half a million people became refugees in Thailand, assisted by an international humanitarian effort. The Vietnamese installed a client regime in Phnom Penh, the People's Republic of Kampuchea (PRK), headed by Heng Samrin. Samrin had been a member of a pro-Vietnamese group within the Khmer Rouge and had defected from the Khmer Rouge in 1977, fleeing to Vietnam. Others in the PRK, such as Hun Sen, who became prime minister, were also Khmer Rouge defectors.

Vietnam's invasion was seen as part of a wider plan to combine the countries of Indochina into a single political and economic bloc—Ho Chi Minh's dream. Suddenly, the genocidal Khmer Rouge were given military support by outsiders. According to the Vietnam Veterans of America Foundation, the British and American governments provided $88 million in assistance to Pol Pot and the Khmer Rouge between 1980 and 1986. Singaporean Senior Minister Lee Kuan Yew claims in his memoirs *From Third World to First* (published in 2000) that the Chinese were the biggest backers of the Khmer Rouge—contributing much of an estimated US$1.3 billion spent to support rebel groups fighting Vietnamese and allied Cambodian forces after the Vietnamese invasion of Cambodia. Lee Kuan Yew claims the United States, China, Singapore, Malaysia, and Thailand all funneled aid to the genocidal Khmer Rouge in the form of cash, weapons, and training. The United Nations called on Vietnam to withdraw from Cambodia and seated the Khmer Rouge (as part of a coalition government) in the security council in New York. The Chinese invaded North Vietnam as a punitive measure, but this backfired and the Chinese were forced to withdraw after heavy losses.

After the Vietnamese invasion, three Cambodian factions banded together in an uneasy alliance. Apparently under pressure from the United States, the alliance was forced to include the Khmer Rouge as part of a broader plan to legitimize its operations.

The Party of Democratic Kampuchea (PDK), more commonly known as the Khmer Rouge, fielded an army of 40,000 troops. Its force was called the National Army of Democratic Kampuchea (NADK), and was mostly based in the Cardamom Mountains. The United Front for an Independent, Neutral, Peaceful, and Cooperative Cambodia (FUNCINPEC, a French acronym) was formed in 1981 by Sihanouk, then living in exile in China. This group fielded the 12,000-strong National Army of Independent Kampuchea (ANKI), otherwise known as the Armée Nationale Sihanoukiste. The Khmer People's National Liberation Front (KPNLF) was an anticommunist group headed by former Prime Minister Son Sann. It worked in cooperation with the Buddhist Liberal Democratic Party (BLDP) and commanded the 8,000-member Khmer People's National Liberation Armed Forces (KPNLAF).

These three forces made up the Coalition Government of Democratic Kampuchea (CGDK) under the nominal leadership of Sihanouk. Thailand protected Pol Pot and his followers, helping rebuild the Khmer Rouge into a potent guerrilla force.

The CGDK was arrayed against the 70,000 troops loyal to the Vietnamese-installed government of President Heng Samrin and Prime Minister Hun Sen. Its army was called the Cambodian People's Armed Forces (CPAF). In 1989 the government was renamed the Party of the State of Cambodia (SOC), with a new flag and national anthem. In a shuffle, Hun Sen rose to leadership. Under increasing economic pressure, and eager to reduce its international isolation, the Vietnamese withdrew from Cambodia in September 1989.

A FRAGILE PEACE
Paris Peace Accords
Since 1986 there had been negotiations between key players to try to resolve the crisis in Cambodia. Throughout 1991 these efforts intensified. The four warring factions—SOC, FUNCINPEC, KPNLF, and the Khmer Rouge—were repeatedly brought to the negotiating table to work out a peace deal. Argument erupted over the use of the word "genocide"—the Hun Sen government insisted any agreement should condemn the Khmer Rouge's genocidal acts, while the Khmer Rouge refused to accept any such language.

Under the auspices of the United Nations in Paris, the four factions signed a political agreement ending civil war in Cambodia on October 23, 1991. The agreement called for a 70 percent reduction of all armed forces, and for the remaining troops to be placed under the temporary jurisdiction of the United Nations Transitional Authority in Cambodia (UNTAC) pending multiparty democratic elections in 1993. Sihanouk returned to Cambodia several months later to head the Supreme National Council (SNC), a 12-member unit representing all four factions. The SOC transformed itself into the Cambodian People's Party (CPP), still headed by Hun Sen. At this point, Cambodia had three different governmental units—the Hun Sen government, the SNC, and UNTAC.

The Khmer Rouge were invited to participate in the electoral process. This anomaly was made possible by the Cambodians' hatred of the Vietnamese. In 1989 Sihanouk said,

The Khmer Rouge are tigers. But I
would rather be eaten by a Khmer Rouge

tiger than a Vietnamese crocodile, because the Khmer Rouge are true patriots. Oh, they are vicious, they are cruel; they are murderers. But they are not traitors like Hun Sen.

In the end, the Khmer Rouge did not honor the Paris treaty, claiming that Vietnamese forces still occupied Cambodia, remained in their guerrilla strongholds, refused to disarm, and declined to take part in U.N.-supervised elections.

The Blue Berets

Cambodia was placed under the jurisdiction of UNTAC in July 1992 for a period of 18 months. Monitoring elections were 22,000 U.N. personnel, including 16,000 blue beret peacekeepers from more than 30 nations, 2,500 civilian personnel, and 3,600 civilian police monitors. At the time it was the largest operation in U.N. history and cost more than $2 billion. Cambodia was awash with white U.N. vehicles—white jeeps, white tanks, white helicopters, white planes.

Apart from guiding the country through "democratic elections," the UNTAC mandate in Cambodia included demobilization of soldiers and repatriation of Cambodian refugees. Another key aspect was assistance in repairing an infrastructure severely damaged in 13 years of civil warfare—mine clearing and building of roads, transport, communications, schools, hospitals. At a cost of $800 million, United Nations High Commission for Refugees (UNHCR) resettled 350,000 Cambodian refugees from six Thai border camps. This enormous task took more than a year, with 10,000 refugees settled each week.

Other parts of the Paris Peace Accords were not implemented. Demobilization and disarmament did not occur. The Khmer Rouge refused to allow UNTAC troops to patrol areas under its control and fired at U.N. helicopters that flew over it zones. It insisted Vietnamese residents in Cambodia not be allowed to vote and attempted to disrupt the electoral process.

Not all the United Nations's work was positive: Highly paid U.N. workers contributed to massive inflation in 1992–1993. There was wide-scale prostitution in Phnom Penh and elsewhere in Cambodia catering to the highly paid foreign troops and personnel, causing a spread of AIDS. Personnel from some nations were unused to driving and caused accidents. A large amount of U.N. property disappeared—and not all of it could be attributed to theft.

The 1993 Elections

Despite setbacks in fulfilling the Paris Peace Accords, UNTAC pushed ahead with preparations for 1993 elections, launching a massive campaign to register voters. There were widespread attempts to intimidate voters; about 20 FUNCINPEC organizers and candidates were assassinated before the elections. Hun Sen's Cambodian People's Party (CPP) was implicated in these attacks, and it was also accused of restricting access of other parties to territories under government control. Both the CPP and FUNCINPEC accused each other of assassination attempts. The Khmer Rouge killed Vietnamese civilians in Siem Reap province, prompting an exodus of 30,000 Vietnamese. The Khmer Rouge threatened to resort to violence to disrupt polling, and polling stations in more remote areas were shelled.

The elections finally took place in May 1993, with a huge voter turnout. More than 20 parties were represented, but the two most popular were the CPP and FUNCINPEC. The royalist FUNCINPEC party, led by Prince Norodom Ranariddh, gained 58 seats but failed to attract sufficient support to rule outright. The CPP picked up 51 seats. CPP leader Hun Sen agreed to accept the results and persuaded members of his party to form a coalition government with FUNCINPEC. With the passage of the first constitution in September 1993, the role of UNTAC expired. Soldiers who previously served in ANKI, KPNLAF, and CPAF were issued uniforms in the newly unified Royal Cambodian Armed Forces (RCAF).

Prince Chakrapong, a son of Sihanouk and bitter rival of Ranariddh, refused to accept the election results and led an unsuccessful secession movement in the eastern provinces. In July 1994 Chakrapong and renegade General Sin

THE TROUBLE WITH CAMBODIA

Cambodia has so many problems it's hard to know where to begin. Until the problems of banditry and corrupt army soldiers are solved, travel will remain risky. If the country does settle down, there's still the reality of millions of land mines strewn throughout the nation.

Human Rights

Repression is the order of the day in Cambodia. On the heels of the U.N. peacekeeping mission, the United Nations Center for Human Rights (UNCHR) set up a base in Phnom Penh in October 1993 to assist the government in meeting its human rights obligations. This was something of a precedent in Asia. China and Indonesia swiftly announced opposition to the center, while Malaysian officials asked the United Nations to close it. In 1995 the co-premiers of Cambodia also requested the office be banished—the present government sees UNCHR activities as opposition lobbying. The UNCHR has investigated secret prisons in Battambang; the murder of newspaper editors; threats against members of parliament; ill treatment of ethnic minorities; draft, immigration, and press laws; and the corrupt conduct of military personnel.

The Cambodian judicial system is in its infancy. Many prisoners are held without trial; the majority of judges will bring a case to trial only when they receive money. Freedom of speech has come under government attack. In September 1994, a newspaper editor who had published accounts of official corruption was gunned down in Phnom Penh, the third journalist killed in Cambodia that year. In January 1995, the government filed defamation suits against two Cambodian newspapers for criticizing the co-premiers. An editor arrested for running a cartoon of the co-premiers received a one-year jail sentence and a fine of $2,000. The government also threatened to restrict circulation of some Western magazines, barred two French reporters, and launched a defamation suit against two French newspapers in Paris. The papers reported on abuses by the Cambodian military that were first reported by the UNCHR in Phnom Penh.

In mid-1995 the Cambodian parliament passed a tough new law stating, "The press shall not publish or reproduce information which affects national security and political stability." Violations are punishable by jail terms and fines of up to $6,000. Another section restricts "rude" language and pornographic pictures.

Corruption

Corruption is rampant in Cambodia. Underpaid civil servants, police, and soldiers frequently resort to other means of fund-raising, turning to extortion or bribes. Border battalions are heavily involved in smuggling. Military officials often collect pay for phantom soldiers. In 1995, the government said it had taken some steps toward cutting corruption: It reduced the number of army generals from almost 2,000 to just 200.

Banditry

Demobilized or unemployed soldiers and police have been known to turn to banditry. Bandits have staged armed robberies on the highways and byways of Cambodia, attempting to steal 4WD vehicles or motorcycles, sometimes killing the owners to do so. NGO cars are a favorite target. An hour after a car is stolen, it could be transformed and on its way to the Vietnamese border for resale. Lawlessness prevails in Phnom Penh, especially at night. Shoot-outs between security forces and bandits have revealed that some bandits are in fact local police or security forces in civilian clothing. To counter gangsterism, embassies and hotels in Phnom Penh have posted round-the-clock armed guards.

Mines

There are estimated to be three million to seven million mines in Cambodia scattered throughout rice paddies and forests. The United Nations described the carnage left by mines in Cambodia as "one of the worst modern manmade disasters of the century." Angola, Afghanistan, and Cambodia rank as the countries most afflicted by mines. Mines were the weapon of choice for former Khmer Rouge forces—they're cheap, easy to deploy, and extremely effective in immobilizing enemy forces and disrupting social and economic life. Antipersonnel mines are designed to maim, not kill, creating an economic burden for the government and terrorizing civilians.

The **Cambodian Mine Action Center** (CMAC) was set up in July 1992 under UNTAC auspices to educate people about mines, map and mark mined areas, and start mine clearing. Producing a countrywide map of mined areas is a large part of CMAC's work. About 2,000 Cambodians were trained in de-mining before UNTAC pulled out. Clearing mines is a slow and tedious process. Although the de-miners have suffered few casualties, 11 de-miners were injured by bullets during a train ambush near the Thai border. Under UNTAC's auspices fewer than 15 square kilometers were cleared of mines. De-miners pulled 40,000 mines from that bit of ground, so with possibly 300 square kilometers of mined areas remaining, there are probably three million mines left to go.

Cambodia has more amputees per capita than any other country. One in every 300 Cambodians is missing a limb. Amputees are outcasts—many rely on friends and family for care. There is an entrenched prejudice in Cambodia against physical deformity: To lose part of your physical being is to lose part of your soul. Every month, 300–600 Cambodians are killed or injured in land-mine accidents. Ironically, one of the few fields of employment open to an amputee is mine clearing.

Although mines have been laid by different factions, the main culprits were the Khmer Rouge, who were trained by British SAS troops at camps in Thailand and Malaysia in the 1980s. Mines laid include the Chinese Type 72 antitank mine and the Italian Valsella VS-50 all-plastic antipersonnel mine. Mines are cheap—under $10. Finding them is expensive. It is calculated it costs $1,000 to find a mine in Cambodia. One expert calculates that to rid itself of the mine scourge Cambodia would have to spend $7 billion—a figure equivalent to its gross domestic product for 5–7 years.

Mines are not the only obstacle laid by the former Khmer Rouge. Trip-wired booby traps are fashioned from unexploded ordnance and laid in ricefields and farms in Battambang province. There's a lot of unexploded ordnance lying around—hand grenades, 60mm and 80mm mortars, air-to-ground rockets, antipersonnel bomblets, even 250-kilogram bombs dropped from B-52s. Under UNTAC, de-mining teams destroyed 170,000 pieces of unexploded ordnance.

Song staged an unsuccessful coup. Chakrapong was allowed to fly to France in exile, and Sin Song remained under house arrest.

Kingdom of Cambodia

A surprise outcome of the U.N. elections was the reinstatement of Sihanouk as reigning monarch in August 1993. Sihanouk is a maverick with semidivine status who commands widespread respect. Though his role is largely symbolic, the king gave Phnom Penh a shot of 1960s nostalgia by returning old names to the major boulevards, reintroducing the pre-1975 flag, and issuing new currency featuring the king's portrait. A number of Cambodian ceremonies and festivals involving the king have been revived. Sihanouk eventually stepped down but kept the monarchy in place with the coronation of his son, Norodom Sihamoni.

Khmer Rouge Leadership Self-Destructs

After the election of the coalition government, war with the Khmer Rouge escalated. In November 1993 the last contingent of U.N. peacekeepers left. Long overdue but finally passed in July 1994 was a law outlawing the Khmer Rouge. Thirty-year prison terms are decreed for acts of secession and incitement to take up arms. When the Khmer Rouge office in Phnom Penh was shut down, Khmer Rouge Radio responded, "The move to close the office was a dictatorial and fascist measure by the police and troops of the communist Vietnamese puppets." The Khmer Rouge made a declaration of a new provisional government with Khieu Samphan as leader.

During a mid-1990s amnesty period for defectors, thousands left the Khmer Rouge to become government soldiers. In August 1996, the government announced a split in the Khmer Rouge: Pol Pot's brother-in-law Ieng Sary led defections that eventually totaled 10,000 guerrillas. Two months later, Ieng Sary ("Brother Number Two") was pardoned by King Sihanouk for his role in genocidal killings while serving as Khmer Rouge foreign minister (Ieng Sary claimed he had no knowledge of the killings). Ieng Sary formed a

political party, the Democratic National Union Movement (DNUM), with himself as president. He and his followers maintained rule over Pailin under nominal government control: This denied the Khmer Rouge access to important revenues from the Pailin gem and lumber production sold to the Thais.

It appears that there was infighting among remaining Khmer Rouge forces over the question of defection. In June 1997, Defense Minister Son Sen, his wife, and nine relatives were murdered, apparently on Pol Pot's orders. When Pol Pot turned on military commander Ta Mok, the strategy backfired, and Pol Pot found himself on the run. He was captured and sentenced to life imprisonment by his former cohorts in a "show trial." He was never released from the custody of his own people. In early 1998, government troops closed in pursuit of Khmer Rouge groups. Incredibly a Western reporter gained access to Pol Pot and conducted a video interview in which Pol Pot denied taking part in any massacres or ordering any mass killings. Pol Pot died in a shack near the Thai-Cambodian border in early 1998: Some say it was a heart attack, others claim it was a case of deliberate poisoning.

Political Jockeying

Meanwhile, both Prince Ranariddh and Hun Sen were involved in deals with defecting Khmer Rouge. Hun Sen feared a powerful new alignment of FUNCINPEC royalists and defecting Khmer Rouge—an alignment that once existed under Sihanouk. A new opposition party called the Khmer Nation Party (KNP) was formed by Sam Rainsy, who was ejected from FUNCINPEC for his speeches about corruption. On March 30, 1997, at a rally outside the National Assembly by the KNP protesting Cambodia's corrupt judicial system, four hand grenades ripped through the crowd—at least a dozen people were killed, and many more injured.

Hun Sen Takes Over

In a few short days in early July 1997, Hun Sen trashed the United Nations' $2 billion effort in Cambodia by setting himself up as a strongman. A military coup led to the ousting of First Prime

Minister Ranariddh, who was forced into exile. On July 5 and 6, pitched battles—with tanks, mortars, and automatic weapons—erupted in the streets of Phnom Penh between military forces loyal to Ranariddh and those loyal to Hun Sen. The fighting left at least 60 dead, and scores of Cambodians fled the city in an eerie reenactment of the civil war days of 1975. During lulls in the fighting, foreigners and wealthier Cambodians scrambled for the bullet-ridden airport to be evacuated to Bangkok. Hun Sen's RCAF commanders ruthlessly hunted down prominent FUNCINPEC supporters; the last of the FUNCINPEC forces battled with Hun Sen's RCAF troops in the northwest of Cambodia, aligning themselves with remnants of Khmer Rouge forces. In this region, an estimated 50,000 Cambodian refugees fled across the border into Thailand. Hun Sen's rule of force did not find wide acceptance. Cambodia's seat was left vacant at the United Nations after lobbying by the United States, and a number of foreign aid groups froze funding to Cambodia.

Elections of 1998

Though the 1993 U.N.-sponsored elections were a total farce in the end, there was a remarkable side-benefit: The Cambodian people developed a taste for voting. In 1998 elections, more than 90 percent of the electorate turned out to vote. After the chaos of 1997, parties had all regrouped and Ranariddh returned. Hun Sen's Cambodian People's Party (CPP) won 41 percent of the vote, with Ranariddh's FUNCINPEC capturing 31.7 percent and Sam Rainsy Party (SRP) taking 14.3 percent. A short while later, Ranariddh,

RELIVING THE HORROR

In April 1975, *New York Times* correspondent Sydney Schanberg and several other journalists were held at gunpoint on Chruoy Changvar Bridge by the Khmer Rouge. Only the pleading of Schanberg's Cambodian aide and friend Dith Pran saved them from summary execution; later they managed to gain the sanctuary of the nearby French Embassy. But Schanberg could not in turn save Dith Pran, who was forced to walk out of the embassy gates into the hands of the Khmer Rouge. Pran was one of the very few Cambodians who left the embassy and survived.

After four years of hellish experiences with the Khmer Rouge, he escaped to a refugee camp in Thailand, where eventually Schanberg found him. His haunting real-life story is portrayed in the 1984 movie *The Killing Fields,* directed by Roland Joffé and based on a series of articles by Schanberg in the *New York Times* magazine. The movie was filmed mostly in Thailand, with the Hua Hin Railway Hotel standing in for Phnom Penh's Royal Hotel.

The Killing Fields featured a stunning debut by Dr. Haing Ngor, who received an Academy Award for his portrayal of Dith Pran. Haing Ngor moved on to an acting career in which he starred in several Asian-themed movies: He reprised a similar role of a Cambodian refugee in a second movie, *Fortunes of War,* released in 1994. But for *The Killing Fields* he was not exactly acting—it was closer to reenacting. Dr. Ngor was performing an emergency operation in Phnom Penh when the Khmer Rouge broke into the hospital, demanding to know the identities of the doctors. Haing Ngor suddenly switched professions to taxicab driver. He survived Khmer Rouge atrocities and eventually reached the safety of a Thai refugee camp.

The Killing Fields is a powerful tool to keep the memory of Khmer Rouge atrocities alive. On the eve of the May 1993 elections, the film, dubbed in Khmer, was aired by state television. Haing Ngor saw the film as a way of bringing his nation's ordeal to light. "If I die now from now on, OK," Ngor said. "The film will go on for 100 years." Sadly, this turned out to be prophetic: Ngor died in Los Angeles in 1996, at the age of 55. He was gunned down by members of a Chinatown street gang who apparently tried to rob him outside his home. The three men shot Ngor when he refused to hand over a gold locket containing a picture of his wife, who died during the genocidal reign of the Khmer Rouge.

Sam Rainsy, and Hun Sun arranged for talks in Siem Reap under the auspices of King Sihanouk. Queen Monineath helpfully suggested the three leaders should play golf more often (the sport of diplomacy in Southeast Asia: Many top deals are sealed on the golf course). Golf or not, the result was that the nation got back on its feet with a FUNCINPEC-CPP coalition: Hun Sen emerged as sole prime minister while Ranariddh became chairman of the National Assembly. Sam Rainsy was left out in the cold as the opposition leader, an underdog role he has always played.

With some semblance of stability restored to the political scene, Cambodia was allowed to resume its seat at the United Nations in December 1998. And the new state of affairs won the approval of ASEAN: In April 1999, Cambodia gained its coveted admittance to the powerful economic alliance of ASEAN.

Even when things appear to be peaceful—and all the infighting and bickering appears to have died down—there's no rest for the wicked in Phnom Penh. In November 2000, a group of 70 Cambodian Freedom Fighters armed with rocket launchers and assault rifles mounted an attack on government buildings in downtown Phnom Penh. Authorities crushed the raiders within an hour. Hun Sen demanded that the United States find, detain, and extradite the Cambodian-American behind the minicoup, Chhun Yasith. But the United States and Cambodia have no extradition treaty, and this could open a whole can of worms—Chhun Yasith is from Long Beach, California. California is also home to the Government of Free Vietnam, which claims to have a secret base of active soldiers near the border of Vietnam, and also home to disgruntled Hmong exiles who support armed insurgency in Laos.

Khmer Rouge on Trial?

With mass defection of Khmer Rouge troops in the mid- to late 1990s, the death of Pol Pot in April 1998, and the capture of one-legged General Ta Mok ("the Butcher") near the Thai border early in 1999, the Khmer Rouge were snuffed out (although some soldiers retained the guns and mutated into lawless bandits).

After amnesties that went with government-sponsored Khmer Rouge defections, there came the question of whether the captured leaders should be pardoned or brought to trial for their massacres of civilians. In 1979, the leaders of the Khmer Rouge, Pol Pot and Ieng Sary, had been tried in absentia and convicted of genocide, though the verdict has not been recognized internationally. In any case, Ieng Sary was granted a royal pardon when he defected in 1996, and Pol Pot died in 1998 out of reach of the law.

There are few historic precedents for the crime of genocide beyond the Tokyo and Nuremberg war trials. There has been no attempt to prosecute those involved under the Geneva Convention's three violation headings—War Crimes, Crimes Against Humanity, and Genocide—and legal action in the World Court under the Genocide Convention has always faced Chinese and U.S. opposition. In 1994, however, the U.S. State Department established an Office of Cambodian Genocide Investigation—which is more than a little ironic in light of the fact that the United States caused the deaths of at least 50,000 Cambodians in bombing runs from 1969 to 1975 and *supported* the Khmer Rouge during the 1980s.

In January 1995, the U.S. State Department granted $700,000 to the Cambodian Genocide Project to document the Pol Pot era and drum up evidence for legal proceedings. Herein lies a problem: A number of the present leaders of Cambodia, including Second Prime Minister Hun Sen, are former members of the Khmer Rouge. And should former U.S. Secretary of State Henry Kissinger and his principal aide Winston Lord, who were primarily responsible for the secret bombing of Cambodia, be investigated also? Well, no—Kissinger ended up with a Nobel Peace Prize instead, and the Bush administration is adamant that it will not let any American stand accused of war crimes in any kind of world court (controversial British journalist Christopher Hitchens has made ongoing attempts to get Kissinger indicted for crimes against humanity). As of 2006, not a single former leader responsible for Khmer Rouge atrocities had been brought to trial.

Laos History

For much of its history, Laos has been under the thumb of its neighbors—at various times the Cambodians, Burmese, Vietnamese, Chinese, and Siamese (Thais). The result is that Laos has experienced great difficulty in establishing a national identity.

The earliest inhabitants of Laos were migrants from southern China. From the 11th century onward, parts of Laos fell under the Khmer Empire and later under Siamese influence from the Sukhothai dynasty. With the fall of Sukhothai in 1345, the first kingdom of Laos emerged under Fa Ngum, a Lao prince brought up in the court of Angkor Wat. As the Khmer Empire crumbled, Fa Ngum welded together a new empire, which he modestly christened Lan Xang (the Land of a Million Elephants). Lan Xang covered the whole of present-day Laos plus most of Issan (northeast Thailand). Fa Ngum declared himself king of the realm in 1353. Fa Ngum was unable to subdue the unruly highlanders of the northeast regions; these remained independent of Lan Xang rule.

Upon Fa Ngum's marriage to a Cambodian princess, the Khmer court gave the Lao king a sacred gold Buddha called Pra Bang. Fa Ngum made Buddhism the state religion, and Pra Bang became the protector of the Lao kingdom. Nobility pledged allegiance to the king before the statue. Named after Pra Bang was the city of Luang Prabang, the cradle of Lao culture and the center of the Lao state for the next 200 years.

Monarchs of Lan Xang

Fa Ngum's son Samsenthai, who reigned 1373–1416, consolidated the royal administration, developing Luang Prabang as a trading and religious center. His death was followed by unrest under a swift succession of lackluster monarchs. Luang Prabang came under increasing threat from incursions by the Vietnamese and later the Burmese. In 1563, King Settathirat declared Vientiane the capital of Lan Xang and built Wat Pra Keo to house the Emerald Buddha, a gift from the king of Ceylon, as a new talisman for the kingdom. Settathirat is revered as one of the great Lao kings because he protected the nation from foreign subjugation. When he disappeared in 1574 on a military campaign, the kingdom rapidly declined and was subject to Burmese invasion. There was a quick and lackluster succession of kings after Settathirat. King Souligna Vongsa, who ruled 1633–1694, returned stability and peace to the kingdom—a period regarded as Lan Xang's golden age.

Siamese Satellite

When Souligna Vongsa died in 1694 without an heir, the leadership of Lan Xang was contested, and the nation split into three kingdoms. The area around Vientiane was taken over by Souligna's nephew, supported by the Annamites from northern Vietnam; Souligna's grandson controlled the area around Luang Prabang, while another prince controlled the southern kingdom of Champassak, with Thai backing. China, Myanmar (Burma), and Vietnam briefly held sway over these kingdoms; bands of Chinese marauders terrorized the north of the country.

The power of Lan Xang waned; gradually, the Thais extended their influence over most of Laos until it became a Siamese satellite state. In the 1820s Vientiane's King Anou rebelled against Siamese interference and attacked the Thais. The Thai response was to sack Vientiane in 1827, razing most of the city.

Land of the Lotus-Eaters

In the late 19th century the king of Siam, seeking to keep Thailand free of foreign domination, ceded a large tract of territory—equivalent to what is now Laos and Cambodia combined—to the French. A series of treaties released more Lao territories to the French between 1893 and 1907. Former Lao territories were thus united again, although the three kingdoms founded in the late 17th century remained in existence, and tribal princes were able to increase their power by collaborating with the French. The French gave the new protectorate the name Laos, from *les Laos,* the plural term for the people of Laos.

Laos was a low-key French protectorate, known as the land of the lotus-eaters, where an indolent lifestyle prevailed. It was too mountainous for plantations, there was little in the way of mining, and the Mekong was not suitable for commercial navigation. The French built very few roads—the main colonial route constructed ran from Luang Prabang through Vientiane to Savannakhet and the Cambodian frontier. The French built no higher-education facilities. Some halfhearted attempts were made to cultivate rubber and coffee, but the main export under the French was opium. Only a few hundred French lived in Laos. They adopted a dissolute lifestyle with Lao or Annamite consorts and left the running of the place to Vietnamese civil servants. The king was allowed to remain in Luang Prabang, trade was left to resident Vietnamese and Chinese, and the Lao carried on farming as they had for hundreds of years.

During the colonial period, administration, health care, and education hardly made any impact or progress at all. The only significant change for ordinary folk was the presence of obnoxious tax collectors, a frequent cause of uprisings. In the lowlands, revolts were quickly put down, but in the highlands of Xieng Khuang and the Bolovens Plateau the French had trouble deploying their heavy weaponry. Sometimes a remission of taxes led to pacification.

The 50-year French sojourn in Laos came to an abrupt end in March 1945, when the Japanese took control of the government and interned the Vichy French. With the surrender of Japan in August that year, the Lao Issara (Free Laos) movement declared liberation from the French in September and set about establishing an alternative government. The Lao Issara leader was Prince Phetsarath, a nephew of the king. Other key players in the Lao Issara were his half-brothers, Prince Souvanna Phouma and Prince Souphanouvong.

King Sisavang Vong sided with the French, and the movement for Lao independence was crushed, causing Prince Phetsarath and Prince Souvanna Phouma to flee to Thailand. King Sisavang Vong was crowned constitutional monarch of all Laos in 1946. Meanwhile, the Lao Issara dissolved, and a splinter group called the Pathet Lao formed a new resistance group based in northeast Laos. The Pathet Lao were led by Prince Souphanouvong and backed by the Vietminh of North Vietnam. Prince Souvanna Phouma returned to Vientiane and joined the newly formed Royal Lao government.

The French granted full sovereignty to Laos in 1953, but the Pathet Lao regarded the royalist government as Western-dominated. When in 1954 the French made a last stand at Dien Bien Phu it ended badly, with a stunning defeat. The weary French started a withdrawal from Indochina; at this point, the United States started supplying the Royal Lao government with arms.

Civil War Skirmishes

The U.S.-backed Royal Lao Government ruled over a divided country 1951–1954. The Geneva Conference of July 1954 granted full independence to Laos but did not settle the issue of who would rule. Prince Souvanna Phouma, a neutralist, operated from Vientiane; in the south, right-wing, pro-U.S. Prince Boun Oum of Champassak dominated the Pakse area. In the far north Prince Souphanouvong led the leftist resistance movement the Pathet Lao, drawing support from North Vietnam.

In 1959 the Lao king died and was succeeded by his son, Sisavang Vatthana. Through the next few years there were a number of unsuccessful attempts to set up a coalition government to bring royalists and communists together. Souvanna Phouma became prime minister in 1956 and tried to integrate his half-brother's Pathet Lao forces into a coalition government. That government was toppled in 1958. Fighting broke out between the Royal Lao Army and the Pathet Lao in 1960; in 1961, a neutral independent government was set up under Prince Souvanna Phouma, based in Vientiane. A second attempt at a coalition government floundered in 1962 because of the widening war in Vietnam. The neutralists later joined forces with the Pathet Lao to oppose forces backed by the United States and Thailand.

The Dirty War

For the next decade, Laos was plagued by civil war, coups, countercoups, and chaos, and was dragged headlong into the Vietnam War. Laos became a pawn of the superpowers, with Hmong tribesmen trained by CIA agents, Thai mercenaries fighting for the Royal Lao government, and the Pathet Lao receiving help from the Chinese, the Russians, and the Vietminh.

During the Vietnam War, Laos was effectively partitioned into four spheres of influence: the Chinese in the north, the Vietnamese along the Ho Chi Minh Trail in the east, the Thais in western areas controlled by the U.S.-backed Royal Lao government, and the Khmer Rouge operating from parts of the south. Because of the Ho Chi Minh Trail, Laos was subjected to saturation bombing by aerial raids launched from Thailand and from within Laos. In this undeclared dirty war, the tonnage of bombs dropped by U.S. bombers on the northern Lao provinces of Xieng Khuang, Sam Neua, and Phong Saly 1964–1973 exceeded the entire tonnage dropped over Europe by all sides during World War II. It is estimated that U.S. forces flew almost 600,000 sorties—the equivalent of one bombing run every eight minutes around the clock for nine years. This air assault was shrouded in secrecy, since under the terms of the Geneva Accord of 1962 no foreign personnel were supposed to operate on Laotian territory. The Vietminh and the Chinese also violated Laos's neutrality with infantry divisions deployed in the north. In the early days of the bombing, American pilots dressed in civilian clothing flew old planes with Royal Lao markings; Thai and Hmong pilots were also trained to fly missions.

So confusing did the number of Laotian coups become that the Americans were unsure which Phoumi, Phuouma, Phoui, Souvanna, or Souvanou was in power at any given time. American journalist Malcolm Browne described this bewildering era thus:

THE RED PRINCE

Prince Souphanouvong was born in Luang Prabang, the 20th son of Prince Boun Khong, viceroy of the French protectorate, and a commoner concubine. Among his half-brothers were Prince Boun Oum and Prince Souvanna Phouma. Souphanouvong attended the exclusive Lycée Albert Serraut in Hanoi and went on to obtain a civil engineering degree from the Sorbonne in Paris in 1937. He returned to Laos and in 1945 joined the Lao Issara (Free Laos) movement against the French. In 1949 he was expelled from Laos because of his ties to Ho Chi Minh, and he helped form the Pathet Lao in 1950. Pathet Lao means "Land of the Lao." The Pathet Lao are a mysterious lot, their story cloaked in myth rather than based on hard facts.

When Laos gained independence in 1954, Souphanouvong joined the first coalition government as the Pathet Lao leader. In 1958 that government was toppled, and Souphanouvong went to prison for 15 months. Upon his release he rallied the Marxist Pathet Lao to fight U.S.-backed royalist forces. Souphanouvong was known as "the Red Prince," and the guerrilla group was known for its extreme brutality. After the Pathet Lao takeover in 1975, Souphanouvong was named to the largely ceremonial post of president, which he held until 1986. He died in January 1995 at the age of 86—the last of the communist old guard.

Laos was as improbable as the Looking Glass world ruled by the Red Queen, the White Queen and Alice. Its towns and trackless jungles swarmed with guerrillas, communist agents, Special Forces troopers, armed tribesmen, opium growers, an international corps of mercenaries and sundry camp followers. Vientiane was awash with the dollars pouring in with the foreigners. The Chinese-owned gold shops along Samsentai Street did a booming business in twenty-four-karat gold bracelets, each weighing five ounces or more. Customers included pilots of the CIA's Air America, French military advisers, Belgian mercenaries, spooks, assassins and journalists. Foreigners bought gold bracelets on the theory that if they were shot down or wounded, they could pay for help from tribesmen with gold, the only currency universally respected in Laos.

Pathet Lao Victory

In 1973, as the United States began its strategic withdrawal from Vietnam, the Pathet Lao gained the upper hand, controlling most of the country's provinces. In 1975, with the fall of Saigon and Phnom Penh, opposition to the Pathet Lao crumbled. The Pathet Lao took Pakse, Champassak, Savannakhet, and finally Vientiane without opposition, establishing the Lao People's Democratic Republic (Lao PDR).

Refugees and Reeducation

As Vientiane fell to the Pathet Lao, the country's political and professional elite fled across the Mekong into Thailand, knowing that 30 years of struggle by the Pathet Lao would not end without retribution. Tempered by 30 years of harsh existence in the remote limestone caves of the north, the new Laotian leadership brought a revolutionary puritanism that was unparalleled. Traditional religious festivals were frowned upon, Buddhist practices were discouraged, freedom of movement was curtailed, personal dress and lifestyle were monitored, and all signs of decadent bourgeois culture—rock music, dancing, Western fashion—were roundly condemned.

A combination of witch-hunts and harsh economic conditions resulted in an exodus of refugees. Getting out of Laos is simply a matter of crossing the Mekong—large numbers of Lao refugees drifted into northeast Thailand, and

more than 350,000 Laotians settled abroad. In the Lao PDR, an estimated 30,000 people were imprisoned for "political crimes," and a further 40,000 were sent to "reeducation camps," including the last king of Laos. The Lao PDR was closed to Westerners, and it established relations with Russia and Vietnam; 50,000 Vietnamese troops were stationed in the country.

With the 1988 departure of the Vietnamese, Laotian policy changed course: The Lao PDR has closed its reeducation camps, released surviving political prisoners, opened again to the West, and invited compatriots who fled across the Mekong to return. The year 1991 ushered in a period of "new thinking" *(chitanakan mai)*. Regulations eased, though state-controlled radio and television still rail against Thai rock music and decadent Western fashion.

Mending Fences

Joining ASEAN in 1997 forced Laos to open up somewhat, easing its crippling system of red tape and permits. And the crash of the kip the same year forced it to mend fences with its powerful neighbors. Laos is the only landlocked country in Southeast Asia, and its key river, the Mekong, is not navigable for the southern stretches bordering Cambodia. That means Laos has no access to large container shipping: It depends on its neighbors for road access to ports in Thailand or Vietnam. In the late 1990s, Laos made a concerted effort to patch up differences with Thailand, China, and Vietnam—with the Thais being the main beneficiaries of this policy.

Meanwhile, the Lao People's Revolutionary Party has done nothing very revolutionary about its system of government. Apart from cosmetic cabinet reshuffles, single-party life goes on in Laos unchanged and unchallenged—as it has done for 40 years.

Government

VIETNAM

There is only one political party in the Socialist Republic of Vietnam: the Vietnamese Communist Party. The VCP was founded by Ho Chi Minh in 1930 and has ruled a unified Vietnam since 1975. A new constitution approved in 1992 reinforced the party's authority by stating the VCP will continue to be the only political player in the nation. How long the VCP can maintain its Marxist-Leninist charade in the wake of economic reforms is questionable.

Although the party boasts 2.1 million members, real power is held by the 13-member Politburo. Members of the Politburo include the Communist Party general decretary (the top position), the president (second in command), and the premier. The Politburo is elected by the Central Committee, whose 100-plus members meet several times a year. The National Assembly is Vietnam's highest legislative authority, with about 500 deputies elected for five-year terms. In effect, the National Assembly rubberstamps Politburo decisions and party-initiated legislation at its twice-yearly meetings. Party Congresses, at which major policy changes are discussed and ratified, are held intermittently; recent ones were in 1986 and 1991.

Corruption is a major problem. Former party chief Nguyen Van Linh warned the party daily newspaper, *Nhan Dan*, in 1993 that

the evils of bureaucratism, corruption and bribery. . . have reached a serious level without any sign of abating. . . not a small number of people including leading cadres. . . misappropriate public funds, accept bribes and seek personal gain in an illegal manner. . . Their filthy deeds cause the people to doubt the party's leadership, breed internal disunity and erode the masses' confidence in the party.

If there is a lack of confidence, no one is allowed to show it. Dissent is simply not permitted. The government continues to prohibit an independent press and independent organizations. In 1991 three Vietnamese were arrested for advocating a multiparty system: They received sentences of 6–13 years. Others have been given harsh sentences after convictions for "activities aiming to overthrow the government." One offender was sentenced to 20 years for publishing a newsletter critical of the Vietnamese government. In 1993 a new press law went into effect prohibiting the publication of works hostile to socialism in Vietnam, or "falsifying history."

Administration

Vietnam is divided into 50 provinces. The number of provinces has fluctuated slightly, and provincial boundaries keep changing. In addition, there are three independent municipalities: Greater Hanoi, Greater Haiphong, and Greater Saigon. Everything in the SRV is controlled from Hanoi; the provinces are merely administrative cells with little independent political authority. The provincial capital is usually the largest city. Apart from widespread corruption, a great obstacle to efficient administration is an elaborate stonewalling system the Vietnamese appear to have inherited from French bureaucrats. The burgeoning bureaucracy and poorly developed legal system have stymied efforts of foreign investors; more than 100 steps are required to conclude a joint-venture contract.

CAMBODIA

On paper, Cambodia is a constitutional monarchy run by a coalition in which ministerial portfolios are divided equally between CPP and FUNCINPEC. The "coalition" controls most of the national assembly's 120 seats, which makes the idea of opposition almost irrelevant.

The behavior of those in power can hardly be called democratic. One of the assembly's few accomplishments was to vote its members a pay increase to $650 a month, in a country where

THE MERCURIAL SIHANOUK

Seven-meter-high posters of the king graced the front of the Royal Palace and other key spots around Phnom Penh for the November 1993 celebration of 40 years of independence from the French. The portraits showed the handsome Sihanouk of the 1960s, with black hair and ruby-red lips. Sihanouk, with his love of pomp and pageantry, was in his element for the celebration. Today he is in his 80s, white-haired, and in frail health. He suffers from cancer and ailments of the arteries and frequently flies to Beijing for treatment. Sihanouk bounced back into Phnom Penh in 1991 after 10 years in exile—he's good at reappearing.

Sihanouk once said it would take a Shakespeare to do literary justice to his early reign. An apt title might be: *The Man Who Would Be King—Again*. In a country buffeted by big powers, ruled by revolutionary lunatics, wracked by civil war, and bombed to bits by B-52s, Sihanouk is the ultimate survivor.

Actually, a French dramatist *did* take Sihanouk as a subject: The Shakespearean figure of the tragic king has been translated to the stage by Hélène Cixous in *The Terrible but Unfinished Story of Norodom Sihanouk, King of Cambodia*. First published in France in 1985, this satirical drama was translated into English by the University of Nebraska Press in 1994. The full-length play begins with Sihanouk's abdication in 1955 and ends with his arrest by the Khmer Rouge two decades later. The destiny of the entire country unfolds through the 50 warped characters who appear on stage—among them Pol Pot, General Giap, Henry Kissinger, and Zhou Enlai.

Considered malleable by the French, Sihanouk was installed as king in 1941, when he was 19. He managed to negotiate independence from the French with a campaign employing threats, arrogance, charm, persuasion, and ultimatums. These became his trademark tactics. He abdicated in favor of his father in 1955 to become prime minister. Head of state again in 1960, when his father died, he presided over an autocratic regime that repressed or killed opponents,

rigged elections, and pilfered funds. But he is popular among the peasants, who revere him as a god-king. During the 1950s and 1960s he promoted a national consciousness and unity of purpose that brought modest but solid prosperity to Cambodia. In 1970, while visiting Moscow, Sihanouk was deposed by the U.S.-backed General Lon Nol. Sihanouk joined the radical Khmer Rouge in a guerrilla war against Lon Nol, but after the Khmer Rouge took power in 1975 they held Sihanouk and his family virtual prisoners in the Royal Palace.

In 1979, with the approach of the Vietnamese, royal family members flew by Chinese aircraft to Beijing, where they spent the 1980s in exile. Sihanouk still occupies a large government-donated compound near Tiananmen Square in Beijing (and a 60-room lakeside palace north of Pyongyang in North Korea). He receives a hefty stipend from the Chinese government, travels in a North Korean jetliner, and is shadowed by a retinue of North Korean bodyguards. His entourage includes a bevy of chefs who specialize in different cuisines and a person who tests his food for poison. Sihanouk played a significant part in the Cambodian peace talks of 1991: Without his involvement, they would not have been successful. After the Paris Peace Accords were signed, Sihanouk returned in triumph to Phnom Penh to head the Supreme National Council, paving the way for free elections. After the 1993 U.N.-sponsored elections ushered in a coalition government, Sihanouk was once again crowned king of Cambodia.

Although he has symbolic power only, Sihanouk has dabbled—some say meddled—in policy and politics, influencing the outcome of proceedings. He is prone to ambiguous statements and rapid turnarounds of opinion. After a decree outlawed the Khmer Rouge, Sihanouk argued to include them as a political force; a few months later, he said that Pol Pot deserved to "go to the deepest hell."

Sihanouk presides over a personal household apparently riven with rivalries and intrigue. During the 1940s and 1950s Sihanouk took six wives or consorts and fathered 14 children. Two liaisons were with his aunts, both princesses; he also married a cousin. Prince Norodom Ranariddh, his eldest son, is one of two children Sihanouk fathered with a star of Cambodia's royal dance troupe. Prince Norodom Chakrapong, exiled after an attempted coup in 1994, was one of seven children born to the late Princess Pongsaomoni. Five other siblings died, some during the Khmer Rouge holocaust.

Sihanouk's current wife, Princess Monique Monineath, is the daughter of a Cambodian woman and an Italian diplomat—she caught Sihanouk's eye as a beauty queen in the early 1950s. She has become Sihanouk's principal adviser and wields considerable influence. Relations within the "family" can be a tad volatile. Princess Monique and Prince Norodom Ranariddh are known to detest one another, and before his deportation, Chakrapong swore to kill his stepbrother Ranariddh. In April 1994, Ranariddh fired the foreign minister, Prince Norodom Sirivudh, who is King Sihanouk's stepbrother.

King Sihanouk is a saxophone player and a one-man Cambodian movie industry. In 1941 the prince made his first 16mm film; in 1966 he began directing color 35mm films in Khmer with French and English subtitles. Among his works are *Apsara* (1966), *The Enchanted Forest* (1967), *The Little Prince of the People* (1967), and *Rose of Bokor* (1969). These movies recall the halcyon days of the 1960s when the king and queen rode around in an open American sports car—the plot is invariably a melodramatic love story with opulent settings and automobiles. Sihanouk claims to have spent much of his 1980s exile in Pyongyang watching countless movies with fellow film fanatic Kim Il Sung. Sihanouk's favorite filming location is the Angkor region, to which he returned to make *I Shall Never See You Again, Oh My Beloved Kampuchea* (1991), *To See Angkor Again and Die* (1994), and *Peasants in Distress* (1994).

The films are processed at a lab in Pyongyang, North Korea.

Introducing Khmer exhibits shipped for a special showing in Australia in 1992, King Norodom Sihanouk said,

> *They [the Khmer exhibits] represent the great cultural achievement of our people; they not merely celebrate the power and affluence of our great kings who built Angkor Wat in our golden age, but also the skills and artistic brilliance of the Cambodian people. As we embark on our reconstruction. . . we remain inspired by our Angkor heritage, and are confident we will once again achieve the greatness which was once ours.*

In later interviews, Sihanouk conceded that his countrymen "can't match the glory of the Angkor period," but he reckoned that they could at least rebuild the nation in the image of the socialist state he led in the 1950s and 1960s. Since then, the king has given himself to erratic emotional outbursts of dark despair over Cambodia's future. And recent events have proved him right: In 1997, Hun Sen took over the reins of government in a coup, forcing Sihanouk's son Prince Ranariddh to flee into exile. After these events, King Sihanouk threatened once again to abdicate. But Ranadriddh returned, and the monarchy stayed in place.

Finally, the aging king did get round to stepping down: His son Norodom Sihamoni was crowned monarch. Norodom Sihamoni is the son of the king and Princess Monique. For a while he lived in Paris, teaching classical Western ballet. He was also the Cambodian ambassador to UNESCO. Sihamoni shares his father's interests in film, dance, and culture—and, it seems, his penchant for indecisiveness. Sihamoni's image is displayed around the country in large posters.

the standard civil wage is around $30 a month. They're also allowed to import cars without payment of duties; some members promptly sold their duty-exempt rights to third parties. The prime ministers enjoy significant powers, approving major foreign investment deals and government contracts without parliamentary scrutiny. In 1994 they granted contracts worth $1.4 billion to five Malaysian companies, including a logging concession for 5 percent of the country's land mass, and a casino in Sihanoukville. All revenue from logging was granted to the Ministry of Defense, bypassing the central treasury. There is not much more that needs to be said about a government of this caliber.

In February 2001, the first-ever defense White Paper on Cambodia was produced. This gives some insight into Cambodia's biggest problems. At the top of the agenda is downsizing the army: With the Khmer Rouge threat neutralized, there is no need for such forces—and corruption among the military is rife. Other key concerns were the preservation of the environment and the growing problem of AIDS.

Administration

There are 20 provinces—most named after the provincial capital. Thus Battambang is the capital of Battambang province, and Siem Reap the capital of Siem Reap province.

LAOS

Since 1975, the Lao People's Revolutionary Party (LPRP) has been the sole party in power. Until his death in November 1992, the most influential party figure was President Kaysone Phomvihane, a Pathet Lao leader who held several key LPRP posts. President Kaysone Phomvihane was half-Vietnamese, and with his death, a historical link to the Vietnamese was cut. Leadership passed to Nouhak Phoumsavanh and General Khamtay Siphandone.

THE KAYSONE CULT

Since the mid-1990s, busts and statues of Kaysone Phomvihane have been popping up all over Laos—so many, in fact, that they've become navigational landmarks. The statuary is cast in North Korea and China. A beaming Kaysone also graces the 2,000-, 5,000-, 10,000-, and 20,000-kip banknotes—the iconic equivalent of Ho Chi Minh. Kaysone was a Pathet Lao leader who held several key party and government posts, including that of president of the LPRP. Being half-Vietnamese and raised on a steady diet of military warfare during the Vietnam War, the former president was Laos's last old-guard link to Hanoi: After his death, there was a slight policy shift on relations with Vietnam.

Even so, the leader is highly revered: The busts of Kaysone are sheltered by shrinelike structures. Probably the last word on the Kaysone cult is a six-meter-tall bronze statue marking a memorial outside Vientiane. The memorial is off Route 13, south near KM6, in the military compound where Kaysone Phomvihane lived until his death in November 1992. The massive bronze statue was cast by a Chinese metallurgy plant and delivered in 1996. Two other statues—more modest, at five meters—were cast in the same place and are installed in Savannakhet and Hua Phan provinces. The Chinese perfected the cottage industry of casting in the course of producing scores of waving Mao Zedong statues—many of them recalled, knocked down, or scrapped as Mao fell from grace in the Chinese Communist pantheon (and just where did all that Mao Zedong scrap metal go?).

The Kaysone statue is a marker at KM6. At the site is a memorial museum, opened in 1995. Exhibits vary from the history of the revolutionary struggle to displays of the revered leader's binoculars, radio, and revolver. There's also a model of "Kaysone Cave" in Hua Phan province, where Kaysone lived during the armed struggle to take over Laos.

Phomvihan was a comrade of Ho Chi Minh, and the LPRP government is similar in structure to that of the Socialist Republic of Vietnam, although the Marxist-Leninist base of the LPRP went through some curious revisions in the 1990s. Every 4–5 years, the LPRP convenes a congress to dictate the party's path. At the March 1991 Fifth Congress the hammer and sickle were removed from the state emblem, and the state motto was changed from "Peace, Independence, Unity and Socialism" to "Peace, Independence, Democracy, Unity and Prosperity." For "Prosperity" read "Capitalism"—free enterprise through market reforms is where the country is heading. So far "Democracy" refers only to elections within a one-party system, as when Lao citizens elect members of the Supreme People's Assembly. Advocates of multiparty democracy are dealt with harshly in Laos, drawing stiff prison sentences—the LPRP brooks no criticism.

The first official Laotian constitution was adopted in 1991, and it is only in the last few years that the government has drafted and adopted codes for common law, penal law, and foreign investment law.

Administration

Laos is divided into 16 provinces, plus the independent prefecture of Vientiane. The provinces are divided into regions *(muang)*, districts *(tasseng)*, and villages *(ban)*. Provinces, towns, and villages are administered by People's Revolutionary Committees that receive orders from the Central Committee of the LPRP.

Economy

VIETNAM

One of the world's poorest countries, Vietnam has an annual per capita income of around $300. Left with a shattered infrastructure and economy in 1975, and isolated for almost 20 years by the international community, Vietnam has lots of catching up to do to compete with Southeast Asian neighbors such as Thailand. Due to its central geographic position in Southeast Asia and its ready access to seaports, Vietnam is poised to assume an important role in the near future.

Since 1986 and the dawn of *doi moi* (new thinking), Vietnam has pursued capitalist market reforms and made remarkable economic progress. While happily patting capitalist traders on the back with one hand, the government slaps the face of those who contest Marxist doctrine with the other.

Rapprochement with the United States has meant a tremendous boost for Vietnam's economy. In July 1993, the United States stopped blocking international loans to Vietnam; within a month, the International Monetary Fund, the World Bank, and the Asian Development Bank all pledged new funds. The economic growth rate reached an all-time high of 8.8 percent in 1994, but inflation also crept up that year to 14 percent. By 2005, the inflation rate dropped to a very reasonable 3 percent. With an annual growth rate of between 7–8 percent in the period 2002–2006, Vietnam has developed into one of Asia's fastest-growing economies.

Economic facts and figures are difficult to pin down because of the "shadow economy." The per capita annual income figure of $300 does not explain how 90 percent of the families in Saigon own at least one motorbike, or how motorbikes outnumber bicycles in Hanoi. Consider the mathematics involved: A new Japanese motorbike costs around $2,500 in Vietnam, and yet a monthly state wage averages only $65. So lots of moonlighting goes on: Experts say the real income figure is more likely higher in urban areas because many people are involved in the black market or receive money from overseas relatives. Rampant smuggling, especially of Chinese goods, could mean the country's foreign purchases per annum are $500 million higher than official figures. There is heavy smuggling of Chinese goods

THE RHYTHM OF RICE

Vietnam produces about 24 million tons of rice a year. It's the world's third-largest exporter of rice after Thailand and the United States. In Vietnam, rice is the staple, eaten three times a day. The scale of production—with whole villages working together to slosh through boggy crops—gives rice growing a near-mythic quality, and there are indeed many legends associated with rice.

An estimated 8,000 strains of rice are cultivated around the world, several thousand of them in Vietnam alone. Rice planting in Vietnam gets under way twice a year, in February and July, after rains fill up the paddies. Farmers plough with the help of reluctant water buffalo, churning the mud to a gooey consistency. Rice seedlings are cultivated in patches of standing water that serve as nurseries, protected from birds by scarecrows and children. In 30–50 days the seedlings are transplanted to the fields, a task that requires hours of patient stooping in knee-deep muddy water. Within 3–4 months, the crop is ready for harvest. Farmers reap the crop by hand, cutting the stems close to the ground. The stubble is burned, and the best seeds are saved for the next cycle.

The harvested rice, still in its brown husks, is dried in the sun and threshed in pedal-driven devices. It may also be left along the shoulder of a roadway to dry, where it may be run over by cars and trucks. Only when the harvested rice is safely stored can the festivals begin.

In the north, an unusual rice festival among minority groups involves a competition between unmarried women. The task is to cook a pot of rice, suspended from a pole attached to the woman's back by a sash. Each woman must quickly chew a stick of sugarcane to produce fiber for the fire, then balance the pot of rice over the fire. To make the task more difficult, each woman is also given an infant to hold, and must contain a frog within a 1.5-meter diameter circle around the fire. The winner is the one who makes the best-tasting rice in the shortest time, keeps the frog contained, and sufficiently soothes the terrified infant.

in the north, especially electronics, compact discs, and toys. Cars and other consumer goods are smuggled into Vietnam from Thailand and Singapore by way of Cambodia and Laos to avoid 150 percent import duties.

Vietnam's main trading partners are neighboring countries: Hong Kong, Taiwan, Singapore, South Korea, and Japan. Australia, Malaysia, and France also have large investments, and U.S. investment is rising. Vietnam is a member of the Association of Southeast Asian Nations (ASEAN), comprising Brunei, Cambodia (since 1999), Indonesia, Laos (since 1997), Malaysia, Myanmar (Burma), Thailand, Singapore, and the Philippines. ASEAN membership will undoubtedly boost Vietnam's economy.

Major Economic Pursuits

Since the 1990s, foreign investment has flooded into Vietnam. Acronyms are springing up everywhere—Huda (the initial letters from Hué and Danish forming a beer brand name), Vietsovpetro (a Russian-Vietnamese petroleum venture), Artex (an arts and crafts export company). Import/export is often abbreviated to "imex," so Donimexco stands for Dong Nai Import Export Company.

Agriculture: Vietnam is mainly an agrarian nation. An estimated 70 percent of the labor force works in agriculture. The largest crops are rice, rubber, coffee, and tea. Crops can be adversely affected by recurrent flooding and typhoons: A million tons of rice were lost this way in 1994. Still, Vietnam exported 2.2 million tons of rice that year. To boost confidence, the National Assembly voted in 1993 to grant farmers long-term land-use rights.

Fishing: Vietnam's fishing fleet harvests more than one million tons of seafood annually: Exports are worth more than $500 million. After rice, fish is the most important staple in Vietnam and a major source of protein.

Industry: Major industries include chemical fertilizer, cement, textiles, steel, sawn logs, and paper. Light industry has a bright future. The combination of an educated, highly skilled workforce and low wages is attractive to foreign investors. Vietnam could become one of Asia's leading producers of computer software. Another large industry is garment-making.

Energy: Coal and oil are among Vietnam's top exports. The country may harbor large oil and gas reserves; one study estimates they may be equivalent to those of oil-rich Brunei. Vietsovpetro produced 6.7 million tons of oil from two major fields in 1994. Since Vietnam lacks pipelines and refineries, oil is shipped to other countries for refining. Foreign oil companies are actively exploring for offshore oil. Australia's Broken Hill Proprietary Company announced the discovery of commercial quantities of oil in its Dai Hung field, and Mitsubishi Oil Company also struck black gold offshore.

CAMBODIA

In the 1960s Cambodia supported itself from its own natural resources. Until 1970 it exported rice, sugarcane, coffee, cotton, rubber, spices, and fish. Civil war turned Cambodia into the beggar of Asia: In 1994 there were shortfalls of around 100,000 tons of rice that were due to drought, floods, and civil unrest. During the Pol Pot years Cambodia's economy was destroyed. The country lost its entire educated elite—engineers, architects, doctors, lawyers. The Hun Sen government that followed faced a trade and aid embargo from the West and was the only Third World country denied U.N. development aid. In the mid-1980s the State of Cambodia began a transition to a more liberal market economy, paralleling changes in Vietnam. However, the cessation of Soviet subsidies and the withdrawal of Vietnamese troops in 1989 forced the government to spend more on arms to defend itself. Cambodia's ailing economy was then given a tremendous boost in the 1992–1993 UNTAC era by the presence of highly paid U.N. personnel; simultaneously, in January 1992, the United States lifted its embargo against Cambodia to enable the U.N. project to go ahead. The arrival of U.N. personnel sparked a boom that eased the country's transition to a market-driven economy, although at first causing high inflation.

Cambodia's economy is heavily supported by foreign aid and investment.

Cambodia's government is desperate to jump-start an economy ravaged by civil war and Vietnamese occupation. The hopes of the government lie in its admittance to ASEAN, asking for the richer members of that alliance to allow Cambodia preferential trading conditions. Otherwise, Cambodia looks to foreign investors and joint ventures. The largest foreign investors are the Thais, Japanese, Malaysians, and the French. The biggest investment is concentrated in the service sector, with hotels, restaurants, and bars. The markets are flooded with goods from Thailand, Vietnam, and Singapore.

Cambodia's economy revolves around agriculture, forestry, and marine resources. About 75 percent of the workforce is employed in agriculture, producing rubber, rice, maize, cassava, fruit, and timber. Boosting agricultural production is a major government priority, a task severely hampered by the presence of land mines. Rice production shortfalls caused by drought, floods, and civil unrest were recorded in the early 1990s. Despite a ban on logging imposed in 1992, operations continue on a large scale, with most exports going to Thailand and Japan. The Khmer Rouge oversaw huge logging and gem-mining operations, selling to the Thais with the apparent involvement of the Thai military (the cut was thought to be 50 percent for Thai contractors, 5 percent for the Thai military, and 45 percent for the Khmer Rouge). There are Thai villages close to former Khmer Rouge zones where the main occupation is furniture making—all the wood used is Cambodian, as Thailand is virtually logged out.

Cambodia's tiny industrial base consists of a handful of factories making textiles and garments, furniture, farm implements, tires and rubber products, and agricultural processing. Cambodia's economy is hard to track because of the wide extent of black marketing, smuggling, corruption, and graft. The government has little central control of the economy and cannot police border zones.

LAOS

Eighty percent of Laotians are subsistence farmers, toiling away on soil that rarely produces more than one crop a year. And not always a successful crop—Laos periodically experiences rice shortages.

To its credit, Laos was the first of the three Indochinese nations to experiment with market reforms. After the complete withdrawal of Soviet aid in the 1990s, the Laotian economy has been propped up by foreign aid, particularly from Japan. The full gamut of NGOs and U.N. agencies is in evidence in Vientiane. The 1991 constitution promotes the development of a free-market economy. Laos is opening up, forging new links with its powerful neighbors. Thawed relations with Thailand and China led to a significant trade boost, and in 1997, Laos joined ASEAN. The Lao government is committed to a policy of attracting investors, even as it's adept at strangling them in red tape.

Thailand is easily the largest foreign investor in Laos, followed by France, Australia, the United States, Taiwan, Hong Kong, China, and Vietnam. Laos is especially vulnerable to its richer neighbors. Having shaken off the Vietnamese, who stationed troops in the country until 1988, Laos is not keen on becoming a Thai province either, and thus is seek-

THE FRIENDSHIP BRIDGE

The most pressing problem in Laos is weak infrastructure. Road transport in Laos is abysmal. Much of the terrain is mountainous, and the rainy season—which prevails May–September—swiftly turns the dirt roads into muck, a great hindrance to communications in a country the size of Britain. In April 1994, the Friendship Bridge, spanning the Mekong near Vientiane, linked the nation to Thailand for the first time. The $28 million bridge was funded by the Australian government, and the opening ceremony brought together the king of Thailand, Thai Prime Minister Chuan Leekpai, Australian Prime Minister Paul Keating, and Lao Prime Minister Khamtay Siphandone. Keating presented the span to Thailand and Laos, and King Bhumibol became the first Thai monarch to stroll across the Mekong.

Engineers constructing the bridge had to handle a very unusual problem: Traffic moves on the right in Laos, but on the left in Thailand. This was resolved by having bridge traffic move on the left and then spin off to the right by a fly-over exiting the bridge on the Lao side. Still, it takes drivers with a warped sense of right or left to drive the bridge, and wisely, a shuttle service has been set up. The 1.2-kilometer-long bridge will greatly affect the economy and society of Laos in trade and tourism. Laos hopes the impact will be positive, though critics say the bridge could lead to Thai exploitation of the smaller nation's natural resources, as well as increased smuggling and pollution. Says one Lao diplomat, "My gut feeling is that Laos is shaking hands with the big bad wolf." Or at least a hungry tiger. Laos finds itself caught in a buffer zone between its powerful neighbors.

The bridge provides Laos with access to the port of Bangkok, though Laos is looking toward coastal Vietnam as well. In 1994, a land crossing opened from southern Laos into Vietnam. From the border, it's a day's drive into Danang, central Vietnam's major seaport.

With the normalization of relations between Thailand, Laos, Vietnam, and China, the Friendship Bridge paves the way for a Pan-Asian highway from Singapore to Beijing. There is even a place on the Friendship Bridge for a railway, so Singapore could eventually be linked by rail through Thailand and Laos to Vietnam and China, and, ultimately, Europe. For the moment, the bridge promotes truck trade between Thailand, Laos, and China's Yunnan province. A second bridge spanning the Mekong opened in 2001 near Pakse in the deep south of Laos: This bridge lies wholly within Lao territory.

ing investment and economic help elsewhere, particularly China. Vietnam is uneasy about the prospect of Chinese trade in Laos, since these trade links also involve military agreements. The Chinese have established several signal-intelligence stations near Champassak in southern Laos capable of listening in on Vietnamese army units. And in 1993 China delivered several thousand tons of military hardware to Laos.

With a shared language and culture, the Laotians find it easy to do business with the Thais. Thailand, which logged its own teak forests out of existence, is now eyeing the tropical hardwood stands of Laos, and other hungry wolves here include neighboring Vietnam and China—also logged out. Laotian forests contain teak, mahogany, and rosewood trees. In fact, after Myanmar (Burma), Laos is the greenest country in Southeast Asia, with more than 45 percent of total land area forested. Domestic energy consumption is heavily wood-based. Concerned about overcutting, the Lao government imposed a strict quota system, but this seems to have had little effect, and forest products still form a major share of Lao exports.

Apart from logging, few Laotian resources have been tapped. Gold, bauxite, and lignite deposits lure foreign investors; geological surveys indicate reserves of lead, zinc, coal, iron ore, and precious stones. Western companies are prospecting for oil and gas.

The plunge of the Thai economy in 1997 caused the Lao kip to fall dramatically: It spiraled out of control and has been on life support ever since. The devalued currency may actually give Laos an edge, making its exports cheap enough to compete with those made with cut-rate Chinese and Vietnamese labor.

Tapping the Mekong

Laos has been called the "Battery of Thailand" because scores of dams have been planned to supply power to the Thais. One of Laos's main exports could soon be energy—generated by the mighty Mekong. So far Laos has tapped only 700 megawatts from hydroelectric projects—over 70 percent is sold to Thailand, ac-

counting for 25 percent of the country's foreign exchange earnings. Thailand plans to buy at least half the hydropower from future projects, including a large plant at Thakhek. It is estimated the Mekong and its tributaries possess a hydropower potential of 18,000 megawatts in Laos alone.

When it runs high in the monsoon season, the murky Mekong is Laos's lifeline for the transportation of goods and passengers. In the north, small cargo boats ply the Mekong between Jinghong in southern China and the Laotian town of Ban Huay Sai. Goods are then shipped to Thailand, or sent down the Mekong through Laos to Luang Prabang, Vientiane, and Savannakhet. Farther south, rapids render stretches of the Mekong unnavigable.

When French adventurers Doudart de Lagrée and Francis Garnier tried to sail upriver from Cambodia into Laos on their 1866–1868 Mekong expedition, they came up against the crashing chain of cataracts known as Khone Falls. This discovery dashed the dreams of the French to use the Mekong as a trade route from Yunnan in China down to Saigon. A century later, however, the very obstacle that stymied the French may provide Laos with its greatest trade—the power of the river itself.

Most of the Mekong's enormous hydroelectric potential, it is calculated, lies within Laos. Power exports could well be Laos's salvation, as the country has virtually nothing else to generate foreign income. Laos finds it difficult to export timber or agricultural products, but it would find it easy to export electricity to power-hungry Thailand. The Laotians could also export power to Myanmar (Burma), China, Cambodia, and Vietnam.

The source of the Mekong is the 5,000-meter Tibetan Plateau in China's Qinghai province. For half of its 4,350-kilometer length, the river runs through remote reaches of western China, and then crosses into Laos. After China, Laos is the country that sees the most of the Mekong. Nam Khong (Mother of Waters), as the Mekong is known in Laos, courses 1,800 kilometers through the country, forming most of its border with Myanmar (Burma) and

Know Vietnam, Cambodia & Laos

THE OPIUM TRADE

Laos is the world's third-largest producer of opium. The notorious "Golden Triangle," defined by Laos, Myanmar (Burma), and Thailand, provides 60 percent of the world's heroin supply. Opium growing is associated with the hilltribes that descended from southern China, particularly the Hmong and Mien. The opium poppy is grown all over northern Laos, even on steep slopes and in poor soil, and cash returns are high. Some hilltribes use opium in traditional medicine. There is significant opium addiction in Phong Saly, Hua Phan, Luang Prabang, and Xieng Khuang provinces. Most opium in Laos is smoked—nearly all refined opium is earmarked for export.

The opium poppy, *Papaver somniferum,* is one of more than 250 species of poppy. When the petals fall, the seed pod is sliced to release a milk-white juice that dries to a brown fudge that can be stored for years without losing its potency. The brown substance can be refined into heroin for easier transport—there are thought to be hidden labs in the north of Laos that handle this process. Opium is grown in 10 Laotian provinces (marijuana is planted in provinces along the Mekong River). The annual opium yield in Laos is upward of 200 tons (puny compared to Myanmar, where annual production is estimated at more than 2,200 tons). Some is used locally by hilltribe addicts; the rest is smuggled through to Thailand or China. Opium and heroin are used in bartering for Thai consumer goods. According to an official

report by the National Commission for Drug Control, Laos seized 53 kilograms of heroin, 292 kilograms of opium, and 9,402 kilograms of marijuana in 1994. Most of the heroin was intercepted at Vientiane's Wattay Airport, the cannabis in Savannakhet province.

The opium trade was once legal in Laos. The practice of growing opium was forced upon the Hmong by the French government of Indochina, which secretly sold opium to Marseilles gangsters to finance the war against the Vietminh. Later the CIA became involved in the trade, using the profits to finance U.S. operations in Indochina. Opium dens were permitted until the Pathet Lao takeover in 1975. These were small places, similar to a country pub, where patrons would drop by for a few pipes. In 1975, Vientiane featured 60 licensed dens, and a lot more unlicensed houses. There is some evidence that even after 1975, Lao army elements and provincial officials continued a clandestine role in opium and heroin production to ameliorate the disastrous financial situation of the late 1970s and 1980s.

In 1990, Laos agreed to cooperate with the United States and United Nations in narcotics control. The main thrust of the program is to substitute cash crops such as coffee or mulberry trees for opium poppies. There have been arrests of drug traffickers, but in the unruly Golden Triangle, enforcement is difficult. The Counter-Narcotics Unit, Laos's enforcement agency, was set up in 1992. It employs only 26 officials and relies heavily on foreign support.

Thailand. Leaving Laos, the Mekong moves through Cambodia before emptying into the sea in Vietnam. The Mekong is pretty much untamed: For its entire length, there is hardly any industrial buildup, and the river passes only one major city: Phnom Penh. The Mekong is at present dammed only at Manwan, north of Jinghong in China. Manwan Dam generates 1,500 megawatts of power for industry near Kunming; the Chinese plan to build eight more dams along the most turbulent sections of the river in Yunnan province. Nam Tha 3

Dam was completed in 2005 in Luang Namtha province in Laos.

The Mekong Committee, a U.N.-sponsored development agency headquartered in Bangkok, was resurrected in the 1990s to monitor the Mekong. Current committee members are Laos, Thailand, Cambodia, and Vietnam, with China and Myanmar (Burma) participating in some sessions. The committee is reviewing plans for four giant hydroelectric dams on the lower river. The first under consideration is the $2.8 billion project at Pa Mong, about 20 kilometers upstream from Vientiane. The project is controversial; critics argue that the dam would disrupt fish migration and displace 50,000 villagers as its reservoir floods 600 square kilometers of land. In the works with possible World Bank funding is the enormous Nam Theun 2 Dam, which could generate more than 1,000 megawatts of electricity. The downside of this project is that it would flood an area the size of Singapore and affect as many as 100,000 people living in and around the Nakai Plateau. Such projects are irreversible—if the environmental destruction happens, there is no going back. Half a dozen Laotian sites along the Mekong and its tributaries are being considered

for hydroelectric plants; there are also plans to dynamite rapids in the Mekong to enable year-round navigation.

Altering the course of nature comes with a price. Dams will undoubtedly disrupt fauna migration patterns, thereby threatening the livelihood of people who live by fishing. Fish catches are already down in southern Laos because of dynamite fishing on the Cambodian side of the Mekong. Very little is known about life in the Mekong; it has only recently been discovered that the Mekong contains an astonishing migratory fauna, featuring, in some places, a complete change in fish species between the dry season and the wet.

The People

VIETNAM

It is estimated that the population stands at about 83 million, which is quite dense considering the small land area.

Viet

The Viet, or Kinh, form the majority group—an estimated 85 percent of the population. The Viet are of Mongolian origin and probably migrated from southern China to settle the Red River Valley, living in limestone caves. Mixing with Malayo-Polynesian, Muong, and Tai tribes is believed to have created the Viet ethnic hybrid. The Viet are concentrated in the two great rice-producing areas—the Red River and Mekong deltas, home to more than half of the Viet population—as well as on the coastal plains and in the major cities.

There are two ongoing national demographic campaigns. The first encourages population shifts to less populated areas through the creation of new economic zones. As part of a family-planning campaign, the Viet are encouraged by the government to have no more than two children, similar to the one-child limit in China. Subtle penalties and incentives are part of the package. Minorities are not subject to these regulations.

Almost 80 percent of the Viet live outside the urban centers. Rural life is spartan in all respects: lodging, facilities, meals, transportation. Farm folk follow the simple rhythm of rice growing: sowing, harvesting, and celebrating festivals. Their diet consists of rice supplemented by fresh vegetables and fish. Men and women wear loose-fitting cotton tops and dark pants; both sexes don conical hats to ward off the sun and rain. Due to a lack of electricity, most people retire early at night. To relax, men smoke cigarettes or a pipe, while women chew betel nut, a mild stimulant that stains the mouth bright red. It also stains the teeth—first brown, then, over a long period of time, black. In former times, Vietnamese women in the north used to blacken their front teeth with a kind of lacquer, as a display of white teeth was considered shocking. The practice was discontinued under the French.

Urban Viet live in cities that are quite small by Southeast Asian standards. Space is at a premium, with families living in cramped apartments where two or three generations share a single roof—sometimes even the same room. Running water is a luxury. Most families share plumbing facilities or use communal water pumps. Shopping for fresh produce is a daily ritual, although refrigerators are finding their way into more urban homes. A private television set may turn into a local theater as neighbors crowd around to watch a popular program. The main form of private transport is the bicycle, with motorcycles making their mark in places such as Saigon and Hanoi. At night, cafés are popular hangouts for the young, the old, and the lovestruck.

The most developed urban centers are prim and proper Hanoi and her brash sister Saigon. Clothing is indicative of lifestyles here: While men in Hanoi are decked out in old army gear and baggy pants, in Saigon they wear jeans and western fashion, a legacy of American influence.

Hoa and Viet-Kieu

Although a minority, the ethnic Chinese, or Hoa, have wielded such power in the past they are now considered mainstream. More than a million Hoa inhabit Vietnam, most living in the south. They're mostly traders, merchants, and middlemen. The Hoa have successfully retained their own school system, religion, language, and customs. Traders from different parts of China—Canton, Fuzhou, Chaozhou, Hainan—form strong community centers to support their members. Before 1975, ethnic Chinese controlled most of the commerce in the south, with a large contingent in Saigon. After years of persecution following reunification, there are signs the Hoa are resuming this role in Saigon. After 1975, the boat people fleeing Vietnam were largely Hoa.

Viet-Kieu represent the estimated 2.5 million overseas Vietnamese. Roughly half that number have settled in the United States. The biggest Viet-Kieu communities live in California. Other countries containing large populations of Viet-Kieu are France (250,000), Canada (120,000), Australia (110,000), and Germany (95,000). Vietnamese communities are also scattered in eastern European countries, western Europe, China, and Thailand. Viet-Kieu are an important source of foreign exchange for the Vietnamese government. Several hundred thousand visit relatives every year; others are lured back to help finance new ventures.

BETEL NUT ADDICTS

If you see an old Vietnamese woman in the countryside with a row of black teeth, gums stained red, and lips dyed a shade of scarlet, chances are she's a devoted betel chewer. Hang around a bit longer and you'll probably see the addiction in action. After several minutes of chewing and sucking on the bitter-tasting nut, devotees spit out gobs of bright red betel juice.

Betel nut is a mild stimulant, producing a sense of euphoria similar to alcohol, and it leaves the chewer feeling slightly anesthetized. Although chewed in the belief it freshens the mouth and strengthens the teeth, betel nut chewing has been linked to oral cancer, gum disease, and the spread of tuberculosis. Many longtime enthusiasts lose teeth.

The practice of chewing betel dates to the dawn of recorded history in Asia. It was long the habit of royalty, and emperors put their finest craftsmen to work creating elaborate silver or lacquered betel boxes. These are still made as gifts.

The reddish-brown, acorn-sized betel nut is the fruit of the areca palm tree. Betel nut is served in slices rolled up in a leaf dabbed with pulverized lime to cut the acidity.

Amerasians

As living reminders of U.S. involvement in the war, Amerasians faced ostracism or discrimination by Vietnamese society and were forced onto the streets to make ends meet by begging or petty crime. For more than a decade, Amerasians fathered by U.S. soldiers were ignored by the governments of both Vietnam and the United States. Most of the estimated 40,000 Amerasians lived around Saigon. In 1989, the United States finally took responsibility for those of obvious white or black parentage, permitting them to emigrate to the United States under the U.N. Orderly Departure Program.

Montagnards

There are more than 50 minority groups in Vietnam, ranging in size from several hundred to more than a million people. Minority groups account for six million to eight million people and are mainly concentrated in the mountainous western part of the country, where they occupy two-thirds of the border areas. Most minorities are found in equal or greater numbers on either side of the border in southern China, Cambodia, Laos, northern Thailand, and Myanmar (Burma). The French collectively called them *montagnards,* or mountain people.

The Vietnamese, Chinese, French, and British designate the same group of people by different names. The Zao, for example (pronounced "zao" in the north of Vietnam and "dao" in the south), are equivalent to the Yao in Laos or Thailand, also known as the Man or Mien. The Vietnamese government defines the minority groups by linguistic families, although this division is not precise; other factors include geographical location and traditional dress.

Under French rule, most minorities were forced into unpaid labor and subjected to heavy taxes. This led to a number of minority revolts against the French. The French attempted to exploit differences between minorities and the Viet by deploying Tai and Nung as local militia and border guards. In the Central Highlands a number of ethnic groups worked with the Americans, which led to reprisals by the Viet majority after 1975.

Between 1945 and 1975 the North Vietnamese tried to gain the cooperation of ethnic groups by granting them constitutional rights similar to those of the Viet majority. In the north and northwest the government established two autonomous regions with their own administrative bodies. After 1975, however, the autonomous regions were abolished. The Vietnamese have since pursued a policy of paternalism, trying to bring the Montagnards into the fold by settling nomadic groups and foisting majority values on them.

Northern Montagnards

The largest concentration of Montagnards is in the far north of Vietnam. In some parts of the north, particularly the northwest, ethnic groups actually outnumber the Viet. Most eth-

nic clans in the north descended from China. A large number practice beliefs based on animism and ancestor worship.

Hmong-Zao Group: The Hmong (420,000) and Zao (40,000) are found in the mountains bordering China and Laos. They arrived in Vietnam from China in the 19th century.

The Hmong (also known as the Miao or Meo) are closely related to the tribes living across the border in Laos. Their preference for living at higher elevations (above 1,500 meters) allows them the isolation to pursue their ancient ways. The Hmong are found particularly in mountain areas around Dien Bien Phu, Lai Chau, and Sapa. They live in simple wooden houses and practice slash-and-burn cultivation, growing dry rice and maize. They grow hemp as their primary textile material and cultivate opium poppies. They also raise chickens, ducks, pot-bellied pigs, goats, and buffalo. The Hmong are among the poorest of the nation's minority groups, with little access to modern education or health care; they do not use written language. Hmong men often wear black pajama outfits and carry flintlock rifles. Hmong women wear elaborately embroidered dresses—black, white, red, green, or flowered, according to their clan—and large heavy earrings, bracelets, and necklaces.

The Zao (also known as Dao, Yao, Man, or Mien) share the same linguistic family and similar origins as the Hmong. They mostly inhabit Lao Cai and Ha Giang provinces near the Chinese border. Several subgroups abound, including the Red Zao. Red Zao women wear spectacular red turbans with braided or beaded sections, pompoms, or coins dangling off them, and silver neck pieces. On market day, Red Zao men wear black turbans and dark blue jackets with an embroidered patch on the back.

Tai-Kadai Group: Communities from the Tai language group arrived from China as early as the 4th century. In the northeast are the Nung, estimated at 700,000, and Tay, 1.2 million; in the northwest other Tai groups number perhaps 800,000.

The Nung live near the Chinese border in Cao Bang and Lang Son provinces. They're strongly influenced by Chinese traditions and are mostly Buddhist. The Nung share the same language, culture, and customs as the Tay and often live together in the same villages. Tay groups are more widespread in the north and northwest and are well integrated into mainstream Vietnamese culture. They've adopted Vietnamese dress and, because of intermarriage, may live in villages of mixed ethnic groups. Other Tay groups wear traditional clothes reflecting their southern Chinese origins: black pants, Chinese-style cotton tunics, and plaid woolen head-scarves. A subgroup closely related to the Tay is the Giay, numbering possibly 30,000. They live in villages built close to the Tay or Nung.

The Tai live between the Red and Black River valleys in the northwest. Tai is also spelled Thai, which invites confusion when speaking of natives of Thailand, with whom they have little in common. The Tai are valley-dwelling farmers who've mastered wet rice cultivation methods, often producing two harvests a year. The Tai compete directly with the Viet, and some cultural assimilation occurs. Tai villages are composed of 20–50 families living in raised wooden longhouses. Tai groups are identified by the colors of their dress: black, white, or red. Black Tai women, for instance, wear black sarongs and bright, tight-fitting blouses with rows of silver or metal buttons down the front. Their hair is coiled in a topknot and covered with a black turban bearing multicolored embroidery; after marriage, Black Tai women wear a silver hairpin.

Muong: The Muong live mainly around Hoa Binh and Thanh Hoa provinces to the west and south of Hanoi. This group of 900,000 are cousins of the ancient Viet and speak a similar dialect. Many Muong have been assimilated into Vietnamese society, but in remote regions they still live in longhouses on stilts and hunt with blowpipes. The Muong cultivate rice, sugarcane, tea, and coffee; silk production is also common in villages. Muong men largely wear city-bought clothing; Muong women still wear traditional garb of long black skirts, pastel blouses, and conical hats.

Tibeto-Burman Groups: Border zones in the far north contain some tiny groups from the Tibeto-Burman language family, such as Phula, Hani, Lahu, Sila, and Cong. These obscure groups are isolated and rarely encountered by visitors.

Central and Southern Montagnards
Ethnic groups in the center and south are mostly descended from people who lived in the area before the Viet pushed south from the north.

Malayo-Polynesian Group: In the Central Highlands, from the Malayo-Polynesian linguistic family, are the Jarai (or Giarai), numbering about 240,000; Ede (or Rhade), about 190,000; and Raglai, 70,000. All are of Malay and Indonesian origins. These groups are mostly matriarchal, although increasing Vietnamization since 1975 is changing this. Jarai villages comprise 50 or more longhouses with matriarchal families. The people cultivate fruit trees and rice and beans; they also hunt, fish, and raise livestock. Women take the initiative in choosing a marriage partner. The Ede build traditional longhouses and affix a pair of wooden breasts to the top, symbolizing the power of women. In Ede traditional society, the woman's family selects a husband for the daughter, and property is inherited only by daughters. Most Ede have been converted to Catholic or Protestant religions, but they retain traces of animism in the worship of spirits of the forest, stream, or hill.

The matriarchal Cham, who live in the coastal provinces south of Qui Nhon (particularly around Phan Thiet) and in the Mekong Delta province of Chau Doc, also belong to the Malayo-Polynesian group. There are an estimated 80,000 Cham, divided into two groups: the Hindu Cham, found mainly in central Vietnam, and the Muslim Cham of southern Vietnam and the Mekong Delta. Although the two groups coexist, there is no intermarriage. The Cham derive from an Indianized culture that once ruled a kingdom in coastal and South Vietnam until eclipsed by the Viet.

Mon-Khmer Group: In the Kontum and Buon Ma Thuot areas of the Central Highlands, groups from the Mon-Khmer language family include the Bahnar (150,000), Sedoun (100,000), and Mnong (65,000). The same groups also live on the Cambodian side of border. The Sedoun are a warlike people who almost annihilated the Bahnar in the 19th century. Bahnar tribespeople were sacrificed to spirits or sold into slavery in Thailand. Remaining Bahnar are concentrated in Gia Lai and Kontum provinces. They practice animism mixed with elements of Catholicism and engage in settled and shifting cultivation. The Mnong are a matriarchal group living near Buon Ma Thuot. They speak a language similar to Cambodian, have no script, and live in houses flat to the ground. The Mnong are famed as elephant hunters; elephant spirit worship is a part of their animist practices.

Other members of the Mon-Khmer language group include the Bru Van-Kieu, found in the former DMZ area and Khe Sanh, and Stieng, in Song Be province. In the Dalat area are the Lat and Koho tribespeople.

The Khmer (ethnic Cambodian) form a large contingent in the Mekong Delta, estimated at about 700,000. Some are descendants of the original Khmer Empire inhabitants displaced by the advancing Viet. Other groups are refugees from Pol Pot's reign of terror. The Khmer, practicing Theravada Buddhists, are strong in Chau Doc province, up by the Cambodian border.

CAMBODIA
The Khmers
The Khmers account for roughly 90 percent of Cambodia's 13 million people. They are a mixed race of Austro-Indonesian origin with Melanesian features, and they belong to the Mon-Khmer peoples, who most likely migrated from China 4,000 years ago. The Indianized culture of the Khmers was influenced by contact with the civilizations of Java and India; through the centuries the Khmers mixed with other groups, including the Thais, Vietnamese, and Chinese. The Khmers look physically different from Laotian, Thais, or Vietnamese. This might be the result of intermixing with Indian immigrants, who came into Cambodia from the 3rd century B.C. onward.

A common Khmer garment is the *krama,* a checkered scarf (usually blue and white or red and white). Apart from a headdress for both men and women, it can be used as a shawl, towel, belt, sunshade, or to carry goods or babies. Women like to wear brightly patterned sarongs and tops—the more eye-blinding the colors and patterns the better. This is a legacy of the Pol Pot years, when everyone was forced to wear black. The *sampot* is a Cambodian garment consisting of a rectangular piece of cloth worn around the hips and tied in front, with the gathered cloth then inserted between the legs and passed through the back of the belt.

The majority of ethnic Khmers live in small agricultural settlements. Up to three-quarters of the population occupies fertile regions between Lake Tonle Sap in the northwest and the area south of Phnom Penh. Most live in houses raised on stilts, safe from the damp, thieves, snakes, and feral animals. Structures are open on all sides to the air to allow breezes to pass through. Rural communities work on a cooperative basis, with little competition between individuals—perhaps attributable to the effect of centuries of Buddhist faith.

Minority Groups
Minority groups in Cambodia were decimated in the 1975–1979 Pol Pot era. Many were killed or starved to death; others fled across the borders into Vietnam or Thailand. The result is that less than 10 percent of the current population consists of non-Khmers.

Hilltribe Groups: A number of tribal groups inhabit the forested mountain zones of Cambodia and may number more than 200,000 people. In the Elephant Mountains to the southwest are the Saoch, in the Cardamom Mountains the Peur, in the northwest the Kuy. The largest hilltribe groups live in the northeast in Ratanakiri and Mondulkiri provinces. More than 80 percent of Ratanakiri's population of 72,000 is classified as hilltribe people, mainly Jarai, Krung, Brou, and Tampuan. The 12 ethnic minority groups of the northeast are collectively called Khmer Loeu (highlanders). Some of these groups are found across the border in Vietnam's Central Highlands or southern Laos.

Because these areas are remote and the infrastructure is weak, highlanders have little access to education or health care. Most are animist and live by hunting and slash-and-burn agriculture. They farm rice and grow vegetables and raise water buffalo and cows. Although most hilltribe people conform to Khmer dress, others retain their customs. Krung tribeswomen wear sarongs, go bare-breasted, and smoke long-stemmed pipes. Brou tribeswomen have large pierced earlobes and wear earrings sculpted from chunky ivory tusks. Their faces are tattooed, and they wear bead necklaces and brass anklets.

Cham: The historic enemy of the Angkor kings, the Cham originally came from the Vietnamese coastal kingdom of Champa. In the 15th century, the Cham were attacked by the Viet from the north and pushed south into the Mekong Delta and Cambodia, where they settled along rivers and lakes to pursue fishing. The Cham originally adhered to Hindu and Brahman beliefs, but, influenced by the Malays, they converted to Islam—most are Sunni Muslim. There are about 165,000 Cham in Cambodia. Their schools, mosques, and other buildings were all destroyed by Pol Pot's forces. About 20 mosques were rebuilt in the 1990s. The Cham live in riverside towns north of Phnom Penh, such as Kompong Chhnang and Kompong Cham, and engage in fishing, cattle trading, and silk weaving. They wear batik sarongs, similar to those found in Malaysia. Because of the laws of the Koran, intermarriage is rare with the Khmers.

Chinese: The Chinese in Cambodia number perhaps 175,000 and are found mainly in Phnom Penh and larger towns. Seafaring Chinese traders found their way to Cambodia as early as the 12th century. In the 18th and 19th centuries, large numbers of Chinese immigrated to Southeast Asia. In the French era, the Chinese were employed as middlemen and plantation workers. As in neighboring Thailand, the Chinese integrated with the community through intermarriage and controlled a significant amount of

banking, transport, and trade. After their numbers were decimated during the Khmer Rouge years, the Chinese appear to be resuming their old role, at least in Phnom Penh.

Vietnamese: The Vietnamese, numbering perhaps 150,000, usually live in separate communities in Cambodia, and are called "youn" by the Khmers—a derogatory term that means "savage from the north." The Vietnamese have always been at odds with the Khmers; the once-great Khmer Empire shrank when attacked by the Vietnamese and Thais. Khmer lands in the Mekong Delta were taken by the Vietnamese, and offshore islands are still subject to dispute. The Vietnamese settled in Cambodia as rice farmers, plantation workers, and fisherfolk. In Phnom Penh, the Vietnamese are mostly artisans or shopkeepers.

Under the Lon Nol regime, and again under Pol Pot, many Vietnamese were killed or expelled. In the 1979–1989 period the Vietnamese returned—with the Vietnamese army. After Khmer Rouge attacks in 1993, about 20,000 Vietnamese fishing people fled Lake Tonle Sap to Chrey Thom on the border of Cambodia and Vietnam. The government has drafted a new immigration law that calls into question the status of those Vietnamese who immigrated in the 1990s. The United Nations has protested the tenor of the bill.

Thai: The latest traders to arrive in significant numbers are the Thais. They were involved in border trading with the Khmer Rouge and are also numerous in Phnom Penh, where they work in joint-venture businesses.

Khmer Krom: These ethnic Cambodians live not in Cambodia, but in the south of Vietnam, mostly in the Mekong Delta. Estimates of their numbers range from one million to six million. Their ancestry dates to the 17th century, when the area was governed by Cambodia. The Cambodians call this region Kampuchea Krom: the Khmer Krom dress as Vietnamese and carry Vietnamese national identification cards but remain staunchly Khmer in their beliefs and customs. They are discriminated against by both the Cambodians and the Vietnamese.

THE HMONG

The word "Hmong" was coined in the mid-1970s by a French-educated Hmong tribesman. It means "mankind" in the Hmong language. Before this, the tribal group was known as the "Meo," which derives from Man Meo (Wild Cat), a name the French used to describe the agility of these high-mountain people. To the Hmong, however, this term has come to mean "savage" and is considered derogatory.

The Chinese developed an intense dislike for this warrior tribe and drove them out of southwest China in the 19th century, forcing them into Laos. Today, the Hmong practice slash-and-burn agriculture (growing rice and maize), raise animals, and hunt and forage to supplement their diet. Their main cash crop is opium. Refined opium is transported on horseback to markets in Thailand. Hmong embroidery is also exported to Thai markets for sale to tourists.

The French recruited the Hmong to help fight the Vietnamese communists. Under General Vang Pao, 30,000 Hmong mercenaries were recruited and paid by the CIA to fight the Pathet Lao. Nonliterate Hmong villagers were even trained to fly U.S. T-28 fighter bombers. (It is said locals in remote villages would carefully examine the undercarriages of these contraptions to determine their sex.)

Up to 100,000 Hmong perished during the Laotian civil wars, and even after 1975 the Pathet Lao government occasionally conducted mop-up operations to flush out the Hmong. The new government vigorously attempted to reduce desolating agricultural practices and resettle the unruly Hmong at lower elevations. The Hmong resented the infringement and the low esteem in which they were held (they had, and have, little access to adequate educational and medical services).

In 1975, when it became clear that the Pathet Lao would win the war, Hmong General Vang Pao and 3,000 of his closest supporters were airlifted to Thailand and eventually resettled in the United States. After two years on a ranch in Montana, Vang Pao moved to California's Central Valley, which has the largest concentration of expatriate Hmong in the world. About 200,000 Hmong now live in the United States and other

Hmong woman

Western countries. Many have not adapted well to life in the West. The Hmong seem to fare better in Thailand, although the Thais want to close the refugee camps and repatriate Hmong refugees to Laos under U.N. auspices.

Hmong refugees in camps along the Thai border have been a headache for the Lao government; the camps have been used as bases for rebel attacks on Lao territory. General Vang Pao is said to fund and direct Hmong insurgent efforts. Estimates on the size of the rebel forces on the border vary from a few hundred to several thousand troops. A variety of organizations claim to represent the resistance, including the Free Democratic Lao National Salvation Force, the Free Lao National Liberation Movement, the Chao Fa (Soldiers of the Clouds), and the Movement for Democracy in Laos.

Though resistance is thought to be weak, there are pockets where Hmong rebels are active. One such area is a mountainous zone straddling the provinces of Vientiane, Luang Prabang, and Xieng Khuang. In 1993, in a pitched battle in Xieng Khuang province, more than 100 rebels and 50 government soldiers were killed.

LAOS

Laos is largely a nation of hilltribes. The Lao—the dominant ethnic group—form only half the population; the rest is a mosaic of more than 60 hilltribe groups. Add to this ethnic stew a sprinkling of other Asians: resident Chinese, Vietnamese, Thais, and Khmers. The Chinese and Vietnamese live mainly in the towns, running restaurants or hotels, or retail and wholesale shops. The Vietnamese originally arrived with the French to serve in administrative posts. There are Indian and Khmer shopkeepers in the south of Laos.

The Lao

Also called the Lao Loum, or Low Lao, the Lao live in the Mekong River Valley and its tributaries. The Lao are racially mixed. These rice cultivators descended from southern China in the 6th and 7th centuries and are closely related to the Thais of northeastern Thailand. A large proportion—perhaps one-fifth—live in towns. Most follow Theravada Buddhism, but many also practice animism. Men wear long pants and open shirts. Women mostly wear a wraparound skirt called a *sinh,* fastened with a silver belt, and blouses of cotton or silk. The traditional hairstyle for women is a bun on top of the head, decorated with flowers and jewelry.

Hilltribe Groups

Hilltribes make up a large part of the population and in certain areas outnumber the Lao. Hilltribes in Laos are usually identified according to language, cultural practices, and favored geographic terrain. They fall into three broad groups—Lao Tai, Lao Theung, and Lao Sung—although there is overlapping.

Lao Tai: This group is closely associated with the ethnic Lao; in fact, in government statistics, the Lao Tai are included with the Lao Loum. The difference is that Lao Tai are more tribal and have retained animist beliefs. Subgroups are "color coded" and readily identifiable by their dress: White Tai, Black Tai, Red Tai.

Lao Theung: With 45 subgroups, the Lao Theung constitute the largest hilltribe contingent. They're also the poorest. The seminomadic Lao Theung are of Mon-Khmer origin and favor mountain slopes in northern and southern Laos, where they practice slash-and-burn agriculture. In the north are the Khamu; on the Bolovens Plateau dwell the Alak and Akha groups, while the Htin live in Sayaboury.

Lao Sung: The Lao Sung, or High Lao, favor the high mountains of the north. They migrated from southern China, Tibet, and Myanmar (Burma). Main groups are the animist Hmong (Meo) and Yao (Mien). They belong to the Austro-Asiatic language family, through some linguists place them in the Sino-Tibetan family. The Hmong are divided into Black, Red, White, and Striped, distinguished by their clothing. Most practice shifting cultivation, although some are settled and grow mountain rice, sugarcane, maize, tapioca, and yams. Their main cash crop is opium. The Lao Sung are animists who worship their ancestors.

Religion

In Vietnam, communism is allegedly the mass faith, and those in power closely monitor religious groups. Karl Marx believed religion to be the opium of the people, employed by repressive regimes to divert the attention of the people from their true enemies. Therefore, in a true communist society, religion does not exist. A modified version of this: Religious practices that do not harm political rule can be tolerated. This is the case in Vietnam.

During the Vietnam War, dissident Buddhists mounted a campaign against the Catholic regime of Diem, who often accused Buddhists of maintaining communist ties. But when the communists came to power they began repressing both Buddhism and Catholicism by putting them under the control of state organizations: the Buddhist Church of Vietnam, and the Council of Union of Vietnamese Catholics. Those who would not submit were placed under house arrest. Schools, hospitals, and other institutions run by religious organizations were taken over after 1975, land owned by religious groups was confiscated, many religious leaders were sent to reeducation camps, and proselytizing was severely restricted.

Since the late 1980s the official stance has softened, with more freedom allowed to Catholics, Buddhists, and other groups. There has been a resurgence of worship in pagodas and churches throughout the country. However, leaders of the Unified Buddhist Church of Vietnam have been under house arrest for decades. Religious prisoners held in jail include Evangelical Christians in the Central Highlands, Catholic priests, and a large number of Buddhist dissidents.

Early Cambodia was largely Hindu, although this was always tempered with a large measure of animism and Brahmanism. Mahayana Buddhism was favored by 12th-century King Jayavarman VII, but his successors reverted to Shivaism, with court ceremonies influenced by Indian Brahmans. Eventually it was the Theravada strain of Buddhism that took hold in Cambodia, as it did in Laos.

BUDDHISM

Buddhism focuses on suffering—its causes and eradication. It is based on the teachings of Siddhartha Gautama, born around 560 B.C. in what is now Nepal. The essence of Buddha's teachings is the Eightfold Path, also known as the Middle Path because it steers a course between materialists and ascetics. The Path consists of right understanding, right thought, right speech, right action, right livelihood, right effort, right mindfulness, and right concentration.

The ultimate goal of Buddhism is cessation of suffering, or attainment of nirvana—enlightenment, ultimate truth, gaining of wisdom. A number of Buddhist schools developed—the two largest are Theravada, which spread to southern Asia, and Mahayana, dominant in northern Asia. **Mahayana** Buddhists work toward the enlightenment (and salvation from suffering) of all beings, while **Theravada** (Hinayana) Buddhists believe in the personal quest for enlightenment. Theravadans claim to adhere to the original teachings of Buddha; Mahayana Buddhists believe in both Buddha and a vast array of bodhisattvas, or enlightened beings. Only those who dedicate themselves fully to the Path can attain enlightenment. For most adherents, the likelihood of attaining nirvana is remote because it requires such intense dedication.

A more humble pursuit involves redressing the balance of karma. Karma is cause and effect: Good deeds have good effects; bad deeds have bad effects. Many Buddhists believe they may have inherited bad karma from previous existences, a situation that must be corrected by doing good deeds in the present life.

Vietnam

Mahayana Buddhism was most likely introduced from China in the 2nd century A.D. It received royal patronage after the 9th century, and by the 12th century it was promoted to the state religion. After a lengthy period of stagnation, Mahayana Buddhism underwent a major

WAR AND THE ZEN MASTER

Zen master Thich Nhat Hanh played a major role in nonviolent opposition to the war in Vietnam. Thich Nhat Hanh was born in central Vietnam in 1926 and ordained a monk in 1942 at the age of 16. In 1964, along with a group of university professors and students, Thich Nhat Hanh founded the School of Youth for Social Service, an organization based entirely on Gandhian principles. Thousands of Buddhist monks, nuns, and laypeople were shot or imprisoned for their work, which involved the creation of projects to help war victims. Teams of young people journeyed to the countryside to build schools and health clinics or rebuild bombed villages.

In 1966, after a speaking tour of the United States, Thich Nhat Hanh was banned from returning to Vietnam by both the North and the South governments of Vietnam. Exiled in France, he traveled frequently to the United States, inspiring Martin Luther King Jr. to oppose the war. In 1969, at the request of the Unified Buddhist Church of Vietnam, Thich Nhat Hanh set up the Buddhist Peace Delegation to the Paris Peace Talks. He settled in a small community southwest of Paris. He is recognized today as one of the greatest exponents of Theravadan and Zen teachings. As a public face of Buddhism, and a crusader for world peace, Thich Nhat Hanh is perhaps second only to the Dalai Lama. He founded three monasteries in the United States and one in France and has taught tens of thousands his concepts of "engaged Buddhism," emphasizing meditation, peace, and social justice. He is a prolific speaker and writer and a tireless campaigner in a number of causes: assisting Vietnamese boat people; working with refugees in camps in Thailand, Malaysia, and Hong Kong; and applying the balm of Buddha's teachings to the psychologically damaged veterans of the Vietnam War. Handwritten copies of Thich Nhat Hanh's books continue to circulate illegally in Vietnam. Among his best-known meditation manuals are *Peace Is Every Step* and *The Miracle of Mindfulness*. *Fragrant Palm Leaves* is a lyrical collection of journal entries written in Vietnam and the United States in the 1960s, trying to make sense of the Vietnam War.

In January 2005, after more than a year of negotiations, Thich Nhat Hanh and 200 followers were allowed to return to Vietnam for four months of touring and teaching. The government even allowed four of his books to be printed. Arriving at Hanoi's Noi Bai Airport, 78-year-old Thich Nhat Hanh was greeted by more than 1,000 devotees. He had been unable to get a visa to return to his homeland for almost 30 years. He said that he hoped his visit would relax the Vietnamese government's attitude toward religion.

revival in the 1920s. Mahayana Buddhism is concentrated in the north and center of Vietnam; the most important sect is the Thien (Zen) meditation sect. Zen master Thich Nhat Hanh introduces the sect in *Vietnam, Lotus in a Sea of Fire*:

Thien (Zen) differs from orthodox religions in that it is not conditioned by any set of beliefs. In other words, Thien is an attitude or a method for arriving at knowledge and action. For Thien the techniques of right eating and drinking, of right breathing and right concentration and meditation, are far more vital than mere beliefs. A person who practices Zen meditation does not have to rely on beliefs in hell, nirvana, rebirth, or causality; he has only to rely on the reality of his body, his psychology, biology, and his own past experiences of the instructions of Zen Masters who have preceded him. His aim is to attain, to penetrate, to see; once he has attained sartori (insight) his action will conform by itself to reality.

THE GODDESS OF MERCY

A very popular deity in Vietnamese Buddhism is Quan Am, modeled on the Chinese bodhisattva Guanyin, or Goddess of Mercy. Quan Am is a female form of Avalokitesvara, the masculine Hindu bodhisattva who personifies the virtue of compassion. At some point around 1,000 years ago, Avalokitesvara underwent a transformation in China, emerging as Guanyin. The Vietnamese version of this quasifolk legend is that Avalokitesvara made the great sacrifice of renouncing his chance at nirvana, choosing instead to return to Earth as Quan Am. The Vietnamese believe this transformation took place in the grotto shrine of the Perfume Pagoda near Hanoi.

Quan Am is usually sculpted as a standing all-white female figure holding a vase of holy water, and sometimes a willow branch for sprinkling the water of compassion onto mankind. In another version she holds her adopted son in one arm and stands on a lotus blossom. Quan Am looks remarkably like the Virgin Mary, or Madonna and Child, a similarity Western missionaries probably used to their advantage.

According to Chinese legend, Quan Am was unfairly thrown out on the streets by her husband and took refuge in a monastery disguised as a monk. A woman unjustly accused Quan Am of fathering her son and then abandoning the child. Quan Am accepted the blame and took responsibility for the care of the child. She found herself once more on the streets, this time as a "father" with a "son." Only years later, when she was close to death, did she reveal her true female identity. The emperor of China, hearing her story, made Quan Am the guardian spirit of mother and child. Quan Am is believed to have the power to bestow male offspring on believers, which explains her popularity. Childless couples and those without a son make offerings to her image.

Theravada Buddhism is concentrated in the south of Vietnam, in the Mekong Delta, where adherents are found in small numbers, mostly in Khmer communities. Theravada Buddhism was most likely introduced by Indian seafarers and later reinforced by Cambodian settlers.

An estimated 60 percent of the population follows some sort of Buddhist beliefs, though considerably watered down from their original strength or mixed with other faiths. Both major schools of Buddhism are represented in Vietnam: in the north and the center, Mahayana Buddhism predominates (because of Chinese influence), while in the south, pockets of Theravada Buddhism prevail (because of Indian and Cambodian influence).

Communism and Buddhism don't see eye to eye. Communists have historically replaced Buddhist teachings with communist ideology, weakening the power of the monasteries and eliminating Buddhist privileges, isolating and discrediting the monastic leadership. Such is the case in Vietnam. The communist government declared the Buddhist Church of Vietnam, set up in 1981, as the only legal Buddhist authority. Dissident monks and émigré communities in France, Australia, and the United States support the banned Unified Buddhist Church of Vietnam (UBCV), which was the main Buddhist organization in former South Vietnam and the largest of 22 Buddhist groups in Vietnam.

The UBCV is militantly opposed to state control of Buddhism. The organization was the driving force behind a sit-down demonstration in Hué in May 1993 in support of religious freedom—the largest demonstration in Vietnam since 1975. Thich Tri Tuu, the abbot of Thien Mu Pagoda, was later sentenced to four years in prison for his part in the demonstration. In late 1994 the supreme patriarch of the UBCV, Thich Huyen Quang, who had been under house arrest since 1982, was taken into custody in Quang Ngai province. A month later, the second-highest leader of the UBCV, Thich Quang Do, was detained for committing "provocative acts." He was later sentenced to five years in jail for "undermining the policy of solidarity," a national security crime in Vietnam's criminal code.

Pagodas

Active places of Mahayana Buddhist worship in Vietnam are called pagodas, or *chua*. The Vietnamese pagoda is usually a single-storied structure with a bell tower, sacred pond, and yard at the front; a main building consisting of a front hall, central hall, and altar hall; and, at the back, living quarters for the monks or nuns, and perhaps some gardens. A multitiered Chinese-style pagoda sometimes stands on the grounds, generally housing sacred relics.

A Vietnamese pagoda is a community center of sorts. At festival time, pagodas are thronged with devotees and beggars and ablaze with incense. The grounds take on a carnival-like atmosphere. With its eclectic mix of Buddhism, Taoism, and Confucianism, the Vietnamese pagoda often functions in the area of wish-fulfillment; monks tell fortunes, sell talismans, advise on house construction location. Some pagodas are famed for statues of deities that can grant special wishes, such as pregnancy to infertile women. Another important function monks perform is to recite incantations at funerals. The pagoda becomes a repository for small funerary jars, each containing the ashes of the deceased with a photo and nameplate.

Iconography

Pagoda wall motifs often feature dragons, a divine and benevolent symbol formerly associated with the emperor. Dragons may be wrapped around columns, with forms ingeniously collaged from beer-bottle shards. Occasionally in a pagoda courtyard you'll find a dragon screen made of glazed tiles to deflect evil spirits. The dragon symbolizes power and is one of the four sacred animals of Chinese and Vietnamese mythology. The others are the phoenix, representing peace; the turtle, symbolizing long life; and the unicorn, representative of wisdom. These animals appear in paintings or statuary as temple guardians and bearers of good luck. Other common pagoda motifs include the Taoist yin-yang symbol—a circle split by an S-line—which symbolizes the fusion of opposites; and the reverse swastika, symbolizing the heart of Buddha, or long life. Actually, the

swastika is based on this symbol, not the reverse. Common statuary in pagodas includes the following.

Buddhas: Mahayana Buddhists believe in a series of Buddhas, among them Amitabha, Buddha of the Past; Sakyamuni, the historical Buddha of this age; and Maitreya, Buddha of the Future. Some Buddha sculptures are massive efforts in sandalwood or bronze, weighing up to several tons. Another figure, the Laughing Buddha, usually represents a historic wandering Chinese monk but is sometimes associated with the Maitreya Buddha.

Avalokitesvara: Mahayana adherents believe in a vast array of bodhisattvas, or enlightened beings. Avalokitesvara is the bodhisattva of compassion, usually represented with a forest of arms and multiple heads. The latter are supposed to have burst from the original head as a result of contemplating the suffering of human beings. At some point Avalokitesvara metamorphosed into a female form; in Vietnamese, this popular deity is known as Quan Am.

Chinese folk deities: Chinese-style pagodas are sometimes dedicated to Thien Hau, goddess of the sea and protector of sailors and fisherfolk. Another common figure in Chinese pagodas is Quan Cong, a deified Chinese general from the Three Kingdoms period (3rd century A.D.). Statuary depict Quan Cong as red-faced with a long beard, sometimes astride a red horse, and flanked by companions General Chau Xuong and mandarin Quan Binh. Temple guardian statuary may take the form of Chinese warriors.

Cambodia

Theravada Buddhism was imported from Sri Lanka via Myanmar (Burma) and Thailand in the late 13th century. In the 19th century, Cambodian monastic orders modeled themselves on the Thammayut (royalist) and Mahanikai sects of Theravada Buddhism in Thailand. The Thammayut sect is a stricter order than Mahanikai and operates under royal patronage. Both sects have recently been revived in Cambodia.

Before civil war erupted in Cambodia in the

late 1960s, the temple, or *wat,* was the focal point of most Cambodian communities. Monks played an active role in Cambodian nationalist movements of the 1930s and 1940s and assumed an even larger role in mass education and the elimination of illiteracy. When the Khmer Rouge came to power Theravada Buddhism was not merely prohibited—it was physically expunged. Temples were turned into storehouses, factories, slaughterhouses, and prison centers; others were closed down or demolished. The monkhood was disbanded. Monks were ordered to work in the fields or face execution. Nuns were likewise forced to abandon their faith. Buddhism was linked by the Khmer Rouge with the monarchy and thus represented an obstacle to revolutionary change. Khmer Rouge Education Minister Yun Yat observed in 1978:

> *Under the old regime peasants believed in Buddhism, which the ruling class utilized as a propaganda instrument. With the development of revolutionary consciousness, the people stopped believing and the monks left the temples. The problem gradually becomes extinguished. Hence there is no problem.*

Before 1975 Cambodia supported an estimated 64,000 monks; by the time of the Vietnamese takeover in 1979 fewer than 2,000 remained, mostly in Thai refugee camps. The rest had died from execution, starvation, or disease. Most of the country's 3,000 temples and monasteries were destroyed. Buddhism in Cambodia has not yet recovered.

In 1989 Theravada Buddhism was again sanctioned as the national religion, and novices were again accepted into monasteries. Buddhist leaders are once more highly respected leaders of the local community. Supreme Patriarch Preah Maha Ghosananda was nominated for the 1994 Nobel Peace Prize for his efforts in promoting peace and reconciliation. Ghosananda led several peace marches across Cambodia in the early 1990s and has been active in preserving the environment. Cambodian monks have set about teaching and rebuilding what the Khmer Rouge destroyed.

Buddhist practices in Cambodia hinge on accruing merit—making donations to temples or giving food to monks, for example. By becoming a monk for a short period of time, a young man can accrue merit not only for himself but also for his entire family. To release captive birds at a temple is considered meritorious, even though the birds are captured and sold for this express purpose. Common temple offerings consist of incense sticks, flowers, candles, and sometimes food.

Iconography

Buddhist statuary and art features a system derived from Pali texts of 32 special physical features of the Buddha. There are several poses, called *asanas,* and a variety of hand gestures, called *mudras,* which illustrate key events in the Enlightened One's life. Think of this as a kind of sign language—each gesture conveys a meaning to the onlooker. The seated position indicates meditation; the standing position denotes preaching; the reclining position represents Buddha's entrance into nirvana at the moment of his physical death. In Khmer art, Buddha is mostly represented in the seated meditation pose.

A popular depiction of Buddha in Khmer sculpture is the *naga*-protection pose. It shows a meditating Buddha under the shelter of a hood formed by a multiple-headed *naga.* According to Buddhist legend, on the day of Buddha's enlightenment a torrential downpour began, but Buddha was in such deep meditation he was unaware of the rain. The serpent Mucilinda coiled his body to form a throne, lifting Buddha off the ground; the serpent's cobralike multiple heads formed a large hood to shelter Buddha from the rain.

Laos

The main school of Buddhism in Laos is Theravada Buddhism. Although Theravada Buddhism was probably introduced to Laos more than 600 years ago, it wasn't until the 17th century that Buddhism was taught in Lao schools.

Before 1975, Buddhism in Laos was divided into two sects, Mahanikai and Thammayut.

The Thammayut sect, associated with Thai royalty, was banned after the 1975 Pathet Lao takeover, together with all Buddhist literature written in Thai. Buddhism was banned as a primary school subject. Since 1989 things have eased up for Buddhists in Laos, and the number of monks has increased. There is now only one official sect, the Lao Sangha (Song Lao). But the curriculum is somewhat different; Marxist doctrine is part of monastic training under the Department of Religious Affairs.

Many Buddhist practices in Laos hinge on accruing merit or doing good deeds; by following the right path in this life, it is believed a person will be able to carry over karma into the next life. Making donations to temples is a common way of accruing merit. Women accrue merit by giving food to monks who go around with alms bowls in the morning. By becoming a monk—for a week, a month, three months—young men can accrue merit for not only themselves, but also their families. Monks renounce worldly pursuits and lead simple lives devoted to study and meditation.

Iconography

Creating (or funding) artwork for temples is considered meritorious. Although Buddha declined to countenance images of himself during his lifetime, Buddha statues now abound in temples. Laypeople demanded some sort of physical presence for worship, something to focus on. In Lao sculpture and art, Buddha is usually painted or sculpted to conform with a Pali system of physical features, such as a beaklike nose, long earlobes, and tightly curled hair.

There are specific poses for Buddhas and a variety of hand gestures, known as *mudras* (see the *Iconography* section for Cambodia, above). Two distinctive Lao *mudras* are the Calling for Rain posture (a standing Buddha with long arms hanging straight down, palms inward), and the Contemplating the Bodhi Tree attitude (standing with arms crossed in front of the body), a reference to the large tree under which Buddha meditated before attaining enlightenment.

BUDDHIST HYBRIDS IN VIETNAM

In Vietnam, Confucian, Taoist, and animist beliefs are inextricably entwined with Buddhism. In fact, the Vietnamese refer to their faith as Tam Giao the Triple Religion. In the Mekong Delta are exotic homegrown hybrids such as Cao Daism and Hoa Hao Buddhism. Adherents of the sects do not believe in a superior being. Confucianism and Taoism are often referred to as Chinese folk religions.

Confucianism

Confucianism is a code of ethics derived from the teachings of Chinese philosopher Confucius (551–479 B.C.). Confucianism was introduced to Vietnam by the Chinese to bolster their rule. Confucius promoted respect for authority and family elders and enshrined the concept of imperial rule through the Mandate of Heaven. The teachings emphasize the Three Bonds: loyalty of minister to emperor, son to father, and wife to husband. When the Vietnamese established their own dynastic line, Confucianism conveniently continued under the mandarins and the royal court. Confucius himself is often worshipped as a temple deity, such as at the Temple of Literature in Hanoi.

Ancestor Worship

Ancestor worship long predates Confucianism as an animist cult, but Confucianism reinforced and enhanced the practice. Ancestor worship hinges on the belief that the soul lives on after death and protects descendants, so descendants must pay homage to the spirit of the deceased and keep them informed of important changes. Pagodas often feature a section where memorial tablets and photos of the deceased are displayed, and many Vietnamese maintain an in-house family memorial altar where incense sticks are regularly lit.

Taoism

Taoism was introduced from China around the same time as Confucianism. It derives from the works of Chinese philosopher Lao Tzu (6th–5th centuries B.C.), and is based on the *I Ching* or *The Book of Changes*. Taoism is similar to Confucianism but provides a spiritual dimension that Confucianism lacks. Taoist belief hinges on the concept of harmony, maintaining the balance between the contradictory forces of *yin* (female) and *yang* (male). The fusion of yin and yang in temporary harmony can provide people and things with a sense of direction. This fundamental law applies to just about anything: the family, the nation, or nature itself. Upsetting the yin-yang harmony leads to illness or tragedy. Taoist beliefs incorporate magic, alchemy, exorcism, faith healing, the search for immortality, and faith in spirits and ghosts. Because it functions in combination with Buddhism and Confucianism, it is not possible to give a figure for the number of adherents in Vietnam.

Cao Daism

Cao Daism is a hodgepodge of Buddhism, Confucianism, Taoism, and Catholicism, with a bit of Islam thrown in. The founder of Cao Daism was Ngo Van Chieu, a civil servant who experienced visions in the mid-1920s that led him to declare his existence as the first Cao Dai pope. The all-knowing Divine Eye, symbol of Cao Dai or Supreme Spirit, occupies the central temple altar. In 1943 Ngo Van Chieu died and was succeeded by Pham Cong Tac, who was deported to the Comoros Islands by the French. He returned to Vietnam in 1946. When Ngo Dinh Diem came to power in the south in 1954, violent resistance from the Cao Dai and Hoa Hao sects was crushed, and Pham Cong Tac fled to Cambodia. Although Cao Dai lands were confiscated and the leadership disbanded after 1975, the temples were returned in 1985. The faith is now making a comeback, with an estimated 1,000 churches in the south and two million followers. The sect is particularly strong in the Mekong Delta. Cao Dai headquarters are at Tay Ninh, 96 kilometers northwest of Saigon.

Hoa Hao Buddhism

This militant sect was founded in the village of Hoa Hao in Chau Doc province in the Mekong Delta, led by the faith healer Huynh Phu So. The breakaway Buddhist movement gained 1.5 million adherents; the faith emphasizes simplicity of worship and places little stress on ritual or temple building. Hoa Hao followers were anti-French; when the Japanese invaded Vietnam, they were supported by Hoa Hao militia. In 1947 Huynh Phu So was killed by the Vietminh for refusing to ally himself with the communists. As a result, Hoa Hao Buddhists became anticommunist. The tide turned in 1956 when a Hoa Hao leader was publicly guillotined by the Diem regime. Then elements of the Hoa Hao army sided with the Vietcong. After 1975 the Hoa Hao army was disbanded. Today the stronghold of Hoa Hao Buddhism is Chau Doc near the Cambodian border.

CATHOLICISM IN VIETNAM

Roman Catholic missionaries from France, Spain, and Portugal introduced Christianity to Vietnam in the 16th century. In the early 17th century, Portuguese Jesuits founded missions in Hanoi, Hoi An, and Danang. The mandarins perceived the Roman Catholic religion as a threat to their Confucian order of society. In the early 18th century a decree forbidding Christianity was enforced in the north; in the south, foreign missionaries were told to leave. Persecution of Catholics and Catholic missionaries led to the eventual conquest of the entire country by the French, though this seems to have been but a pretext for plundering the country's resources.

However, some resources (building materials for cathedrals) were brought in piece by piece. Gothic-style cathedral spires can be seen in Saigon, Dalat, Hué, and Hanoi. There are also Montagnard churches in places such as Dalat and Kontum; Montagnards mix Christian and animist beliefs.

Under the French, the church wielded considerable power: the Catholic Church was once the country's biggest landowner. After 1954, Catholics moved south to the protection of the Diem regime. Because of strong Catholic support for the U.S. presence in southern Vietnam, the church was the target of a backlash after 1975. Foreign nuns and priests were expelled, seminaries and schools closed, church lands confiscated, and proselytizing forbidden.

About six million people, representing about 8 percent of the population, are thought to be Catholic; Vietnam has the second-largest Catholic contingent in Southeast Asia after the Philippines. The bulk of funding for the churches comes from Catholics in the United States and France. Although communication with the Vatican is restricted, in 1994 the Archbishop of Hanoi, Pham Dinh Tung, was allowed to go to Rome to be invested by Pope John Paul II in the Vatican's 120-member college of cardinals.

The pope viewed Vietnam as a fruitful frontier, but Vietnam and the Vatican have been at loggerheads over religious freedom. The Vietnamese government insists on its right to veto all church appointments. In early 1995 Archbishop Paul Nguyen Van Binh, leader of the community in Saigon, died, and the Vatican's initial nomination was Bishop Nguyen Thuan, a nephew of former South Vietnamese President Diem. This nomination was rejected. The Vietnamese government is suspicious of the Vatican. Hanoi is concerned that elements of the Catholic community can be manipulated by external forces to act against the regime.

OTHER FAITHS

Vietnam

Minorities in Vietnam adhere to a wide variety of beliefs. In addition to those already mentioned are the following:

Protestantism: About 300,000 Protestants live in Vietnam. The largest contingent is formed of Montagnards from the Central Highlands, who were converted by French and Portuguese missionaries. The religion was introduced in 1911. Churches are called Good News Churches *(Tin Lanh).*

Hinduism: In central Vietnam, descendants of the Cham follow Hindu and Brahman beliefs, worshipping the holy trinity of Shiva, the Destroyer; Vishnu, the Preserver; and Brahma,

the Creator. A tiny Tamil community once existed in Saigon; a Hindu temple remains there, patronized by local Vietnamese and those of Indian origin.

Islam: In the 18th and 19th centuries, Cham descendants on the south coast and Mekong Delta converted to Islam. Muslim Cham, or Cham Bani, are easily distinguished by the preferred headgear of men: a crimson fez with a long golden tassel, or white Muslim prayer cap. In the Phan Rang area, men wear a white turban with red tassels. The largest Cham mosque stands in Chau Doc in the Mekong Delta.

Animism: Although superstitious practices are banned by the communist government, spirit worship is well entrenched among hilltribe groups. Animists believe powerful spirits living in forests, rocks, streams, wind, and rain must be appeased by gifts of food, flowers, and incense. Spirits can also live in animals. The Mnong tribespeople of the Central Highlands, famed as elephant catchers, practice elephant spirit worship.

Cambodia

Because the Khmers are the overwhelming majority in Cambodia, there are few religious groups other than Buddhism in evidence. The Chinese community practices Taoism and Confucianism; the Vietnamese community includes Catholics and some followers of quasi-Buddhist Mekong Delta cults; the Cham are Sunni Muslim.

To the northeast, hilltribe groups practice animism and ancestor worship. So, to some degree, do most rural Cambodians. Animism, or spirit worship, coexists with Buddhism, which has always been tolerant of it. Sacrifices are offered to the spirits of wind, water, and earth, upon which harvests depend. Spirits in all material things—trees, rivers, mountains, stones—exert a profound influence on daily life. Animist practices are evident at harvest festivals and also surface in ceremonies such as weddings and funerals. Departed ancestors become guardian spirits, who must be honored to ensure the well-being of the family.

Laos

The Lao tend to mix Buddhist, animist, and Brahman practices. Hilltribes in Laos are primarily animist. Officially, under the communist government, animism is banned, but in practice, worship of *phi*, or spirits, continues. The main image worshipped at Vientiane's Wat Simuang is the city pillar—the guardian spirit of the city. Animist worship has found its way into a number of Lao ceremonies. A common one is the *baci*, in which strings representing the guardian spirits of body organs are tied round the wrists of guests of honor.

Hilltribes believe that everything—from mountains to opium poppies—has a spirit, or *phi*. Some spirits are bad, some are good. To counter sickness and catastrophe, the *phi* must be placated. The village shaman plays an important role, capable of exorcising bad *phi* from his patients. Animal sacrifices to appease *phi* are common among hilltribe groups.

Mythology and the Arts

VIETNAM

Vietnam's artistic roots lie in Chinese culture; the Chinese dominated the area for 1,000 years. Vietnamese art forms are not as distinct as other cultures in Southeast Asia, as the Vietnamese drew heavily on Chinese prototypes. While the Vietnamese arts of poetry and water puppetry date to the 13th century, such distinct elements of Vietnamese culture as painting and the use of romanized script derive from 1920s French influence.

Language and Literature

Written Vietnamese uses a roman script with tonal markers called *quoc ngu*. The language was developed by 17th-century French Jesuit missionary Alexandre de Rhodes. The first *quoc ngu* dictionary was published in 1651, but the script was used by only the Catholic Church at first and later by the colonial administration. The study of *quoc ngu* became compulsory in secondary schools in 1906, and a new curriculum entirely in *quoc ngu* was established several years later. Not until 1920 was *quoc ngu* adopted as the national script, with the first major literary volume in *quoc ngu* published in 1925.

The Vietnamese language is variously thought to have derived from Austro-Asiatic or Sino-Tibetan languages. Because of Chinese influence, Chinese ideograms *(chu nho)* were used by scholars for formal and official documents until the 20th century. In a breakaway move, the Vietnamese devised their own characters in the 13th century. This system, called *chu nom*, used Chinese characters to render phonetic Vietnamese in popular stories, tales, and poetry. Vietnam has a well-developed heritage of poetry. Originally, folk literature (fables, legends, songs) was an oral tradition, and works were recited by itinerant storytellers. Folktales in verse glorified the deeds of Vietnamese heroes, or explained such phenomena as the origin of the watermelon, or how the water buffalo acquired wrinkled skin and horns.

A classic Vietnamese work is *Kim Van Kieu,* by poet Nguyen Du (1765–1820). The verse epic relates the bittersweet love of Thuy Kieu, princess of the Moon, for the poet Kim Trong. Thuy Kieu forsakes her lover and prostitutes herself to obtain money for her father's release from prison. The theme of the separation of the young lovers and saving the family name holds universal appeal. Carving out a special niche is 18th-century poetess Ho Xuan Huong, whose works ridicule pompous officials, praise free love, and advocate equality for women. Her trademark is poetry with both literal and pornographic levels of meaning.

Chu nom was first expressed only in verse; the French introduced the concept of prose. In the French colonial era prose came to the fore: By the 1930s, the Chinese literary tradition had been replaced by romanized Vietnamese script because of the French preference for *quoc ngu*.

POLITICALLY INCORRECT

Vietnam clamps down on writers who dare to speak out against the official state line. Some writers, however, have acquired an international reputation, which emboldens them. Since publishing is entirely a government operation in Vietnam, getting a "politically incorrect" manuscript published is quite a feat.

The Sorrow of War, by Bao Ninh, was published privately in 1991 by a group of Hanoi writers. It is the work of a North Vietnamese soldier who recalls his war experience and postwar trauma. Ninh went to war in 1965 at the age of 18. Of the 500 men who went with him, only 10 returned home after the fall of Saigon. Of those, six more committed suicide between 1976 and 1987. Bao Ninh overturns the official version of soldiers returning from the glorious front lines healthy in body and spirit. Ninh returns to a Hanoi that is a dilapidated capital, its citizens uninterested in victory parades. *The Sorrow of War* was picked up by Secker and Warburg and published in London in 1993. It has been translated into English, Swedish, and Norwegian. Bao Ninh is delighted by the international reception and by royalties that buy him more time to write.

Duong Thu Huong's 1988 novel, *Paradise of the Blind,* portrays the communist system as exploitative and corrupt. The novel is part of a trilogy—all of which are banned in Vietnam. Huong is a former anti-American resistance fighter who lives in Hanoi. In 1987, the Vietnamese Communist Party encouraged writers and artists to speak their minds, but within two years, it reversed that decision and started arresting outspoken writers. Huong was expelled from the Communist Party in 1990 for advocating democracy; in 1991, she was imprisoned for seven months on trumped-up charges. Pressure from Amnesty International and PEN helped secure her release. On a private visit to France in 1994, the dissident writer was presented the order of Chevalier des Arts et des Lettres, the country's highest literary award. The French culture minister cited her as a writer of the first order who characterized the role of Vietnamese women in the fight for liberty and independence. The award was vigorously protested by the Vietnamese government—it seems that liberty and independence are good values as long as they don't get out of hand. Huong's *Novel Without a Name,* published by William Morrow in 1995, tells the story of a 28-year-old captain in the NVA during the war.

This led to a literary renaissance in Vietnam, with the rise of novels, short stories, and essays. Although the essays and fiery anticolonial rhetoric of Ho Chi Minh propelled the communists to power, communist authorities have since clamped down on writers. A number of poets, authors, and journalists have been imprisoned by the present regime. Others have been reduced to writing "politically correct" material. A safer area than politics is the realm of love and personal relations.

Music and Dance

Traditional instruments figure prominently in festivals and as accompaniment to water puppetry and drama. Originally music played an important part in religious ceremonies, with orchestras and dance troupes sponsored by royalty.

Unique to Vietnam is the monochord *(dan bau),* which has a single brass string stretched across a trapezoidal wooden resonance chamber one meter long, 12 centimeters wide, and 15 centimeters deep. At one end is a bamboo rod with its own small sound box in the shape of a tiny gourd; at the other is a conventional peg. The instrument produces a surprising range of haunting sound and can mimic the specific tones of the Vietnamese language. Hence it's popular as accompaniment to romantic songs on film and in the theater.

Other unusual stringed instruments include the 16-string zither *(dan tranh)* and two-string vertical violin *(dan co).* Among the wind instruments, the oldest is the bamboo flute. Extremely difficult to master is the double trumpet *(ken doi),* composed of two bamboo pipes fused together, each pierced with seven holes. A popular percussion instrument is the bamboo xylophone *(to rung)*; a variation is the stone xylophone *(dan da)*.

Dance in Vietnam remains essentially a folk tradition, specific to villages and ethnic groups; performances most often take place during festivals. Occasionally, a special dance performance is staged at a tourist venue as a "cultural show." You might see the Conical Hat Dance from Hué or the Dance of the Princesses from Hanoi, a Montagnard courtship dance, or a sensuous Cham dance. In Hué, imperial song and dance routines have been resurrected for the benefit of tourists.

Drama

Today's Vietnamese theater presents three types of performances: *cheo, cai luong,* and *tuong.* All three have been employed for propaganda purposes. Cheo is the oldest form of theater—a mix of mime, dance, song, and poetry. *Cheo* became a form of peasant protest against feudal masters and later against the French—the Vietnamese version of the blues.

Cai luong, or "renovated theater," is of fairly recent origin, deriving from the days of the Nguyen dynasty and featuring spoken drama with short acts. *Cai luong* performances evolved into a nationwide protest against the French, and colonial censors banned performances of certain plays. In the 1920s, a new form of drama, *kich noi,* was introduced. After 1954, *kich noi* was used to disseminate communist doctrine to large audiences.

Tuong drama arrived from China in the 14th century. Performances follow strict rules of facial expression, stylized gestures, and accented speech; performers wear elaborate costumes and paint their faces in different colors. The story is usually an epic taken from Vietnamese legends and myths, or a historical plot portraying the lives of national heroes. The imperial Nguyen court brought *tuong* to its peak in Hué in the 19th century, making the most of the Confucian concepts embodied in *tuong*, stressing absolute authority of the monarch. In the 20th century, *tuong* moved to the stage and

became dissociated from court intrigues, centering instead on everyday life, with characters depicting people's joys and sorrows. Modern versions of *tuong* feature aspects of the life of Ho Chi Minh and other communist leaders. *Tuong* has fallen out of favor as a popular entertainment form: The last bastion of *tuong* is the city of Qui Nhon, where the Dao Tan Troupe resides.

Water Puppetry

The most original theatrical form in Vietnam is water puppetry, or *roi nuoc.* Like much original Vietnamese culture, water puppetry derives from the Red River Delta area, centered around Hanoi. This unique and exuberant form of puppetry employs the surface of the water as a stage and focuses on themes such as herding ducks, plowing with water buffalo, harvesting rice, sampan fishing, and naval battles.

Water puppetry was a folk art form long before it became a theatrical one. Performances are believed to date to the 12th century. Temporary theaters were constructed in the village pond and performances marked the beginning or end of the rice-planting cycle. Offering prayers for good crops and good rainfall was essential. The water itself became part of the festive ritual, with washing of Buddha statues, boat racing, and swimming contests. Water puppetry uses a fair dose of satire, perhaps as a way for country folk to let off steam. Traveling puppetry guilds were later able to tour with shows, and water puppetry became part of court entertainment during the Ly and Tran dynasties. Guilds exist today in a number of northern provinces; the best place to see water puppetry is in Hanoi.

In contrast to puppets controlled from above by strings, water puppets are manipulated from below, so the means of manipulation remains completely concealed. A dozen puppeteers stand waist-deep in water behind a pagoda set, meant to resemble an ancient village communal house. The puppeteers hide behind a bamboo screen in a manipulation room about 4–5 meters long and 3–4 meters wide. Invisible to the audience, the puppeteers maneuver the puppets with bamboo or wooden poles ingeniously rigged to pulleys and strings. To the audience, the lifelike puppets skipping across the water appear nothing short of magical. Sometimes a series of six or more puppets may be operated from a single base, requiring 3–4 puppeteers.

Skits presented in water puppet theater are short (sometimes only 2–3 minutes), and the entire performance lasts about an hour. Themes include satirical digs at village life, folk stories, mythology, and historical events. A light and sound show is provided by aquatic fireworks and festive, rhythmic sound effects. Sound may involve traditional instruments and snippets of *tuong* or *cheo* opera. Skits are introduced and narrated by Chu Teu, a clownish water puppet whose outward appearance is that of a strong and dignified young ploughman, albeit one wearing a loincloth and sporting pigtails. Chu Teu's role is master of ceremonies; he opens the show, introduces the program, acts as an intermediary between audience and puppet characters, and makes fun of everyone and everything. Water provides natural amplification and produces reflections that enhance the theatrical effect. Water puppets are made of lacquered wood. The hand-carved puppets are a folk art in themselves: Characters include fishermen, duck-tenders, wrestlers, emperors, and national heroes, as well as frogs, fish, turtles, phoenixes, and aquatic dragons.

Films

In 1992, former U.S. Marine Dan Thomas found himself standing in the old American Embassy compound in Saigon in full battle gear. Across the street, black smoke rose from burning tires as Vietcong troops drew nearer. Tanks flying the yellow-and-red striped flag of South Vietnam raced by. Wrong year? Bad dream? No, Dan had been sitting at Kim Café when he was recruited as an extra for a film—in effect, to play himself. The South Korean film company paid extras $30 a day, plus a $5 bonus for anyone willing to submit to a military crew cut.

These days it's easy to find American extras in Saigon. But before the days of individual travel, the Vietnamese had to settle for Russians or visiting Swedes to play the American parts. Today there's a famous bar in Saigon named after the movie *Apocalypse Now,* with a poster of the movie on the wall. Sometimes the Vietnamese confuse the movies that have been made about the war fought in their country—one T-shirt sighted in Hanoi was printed with the logo "Good Morning, Apocalypse" on the front and "Vietnam Now!" on the back.

While the Vietnamese have produced films about the war era, most of them fall into the boring propaganda documentary genre. The Vietnamese have hardly any film industry (only a few competent technicians) and no laboratory capable of processing high-quality film. However, the Vietnamese have gained experience with moviemaking during coproduction of French movies. Since deregulation in 1992, private film production companies have appeared in Vietnam, mainly producing Kung Fu flicks or melodramatic romances in imitation of those from Hong Kong.

Hollywood Combat Formulas

American television coverage and postwar movies have had an indelible effect on the way we view Vietnam—all war, all combat, faceless Vietcong. The Americans have filmed primarily in the Philippines or Thailand, and, since America didn't win the war, standard heroic combat formulas had to be tinkered with. *The Green Berets,* a John Wayne film made in 1968, is the first and only Hollywood movie about Vietnam to suggest any degree of American military success. Other movies have looked for heroism in the effort to find and rescue MIAs. Sylvester Stallone took on Vietnam singlehanded (in search of MIAs) in *Rambo: First Blood II* (1985) and won, only to find he'd been duped by Uncle Sam. Ironically, Rambo ended up a box-office hero in Asia, an icon to many Asian kids. Also in the comic-book action genre are three *Missing in Action* movies (1984–1987), starring Chuck Norris. *Hamburger Hill* (1987) is a brutal documentary-style movie about the 1969 battle in which the Americans suffered heavy losses.

Some of the combat movies tackle the moral quagmire in which the Americans found themselves in Vietnam. *Casualties of War* (1989) is based on a true story about the kidnap, rape, and murder of a Vietnamese woman by U.S. soldiers. In *Platoon* (1986), Vietnam serves largely as a backdrop for a melodramatic battle between good and evil. *Gardens of Stone* (1987) mostly derives its drama from boot camp in the States. The first half of *Full Metal Jacket* also takes place in boot camp; the second half is set in Hué during the 1968 Tet Offensive. These movies present the grunt's-eye view of combat—harrowing accounts of the war's horror told from the perspective of naive recruits who had no idea what they were getting into or why. A sequence in *Forrest Gump* is the final word on this theme of startled innocence. The lead character, though immersed in the carnage and horror of the Vietnam War, emerges completely unscathed—because he's too stupid to know what's happening.

Shaking up the formulas, other Hollywood films examine the turmoil of returning American vets and the scars and side effects of the war: *The Deer Hunter* (1978), *Coming Home* (1978), *Jacob's Ladder* (1990), and *Born on the Fourth of July* (1990), based on disabled Vietnam vet Ron Kovic's memoir. Two classics that broke out of the Hollywood mold are Francis Ford Coppola's *Apocalypse Now* (1979) and Barry Levinson's *Good Morning, Vietnam* (1987).

Most of the Hollywood films are banned in Vietnam, although some, such as *Born on the Fourth of July,* have been screened. Others find their way into video stores on the black market, either smuggled in or brought in by third parties. *Rambo* and *Good Morning, Vietnam* led the way. With the lifting of the embargo, the national cinematographic service in southern Vietnam will import and distribute films made by Paramount, MGM, and Universal Studios through an agreement with United International Pictures. It remained to be seen whether any American-made war movies about Vietnam would be allowed to play in theaters in Vietnam.

The French Are Back
The French have had enough time to come

to terms with Vietnam, and they offered a frank and perceptive view of their colonial past with a spate of movies released in 1992—*Indochine, l'Amant,* and *Dien Bien Phu.* These go for the human element; the Vietnamese are portrayed with genuine depth (and even real speaking parts). The French films also enjoy the advantage of filming on location in Vietnam. A French-Algerian coproduction called *Poussières de Vie* (Dust of Life), released in 1994, tackles the story of Son, born from a liaison between an American soldier and a Vietnamese woman, who is sent to reeducation camp in Vietnam in 1975.

French Era Classics
Indochine: Directed by Régis Wargnier, this movie is set in 1930s Vietnam. The plot involves a love triangle, with an undercurrent of Vietnamese resistance to French rule. Eliane, played by Catherine Deneuve, runs a large rubber plantation in the south. She has adopted an Annamite princess, Camille (Linh Dan Pham), after the death of the girl's parents in a plane crash. Both women fall in love with Jean-Baptiste (Vincent Pérez), a French naval officer. The movie depicts French high life contrasted with the brutal lot of Vietnamese peasants pressed into plantation service. In the middle are the elite Vietnamese ruling group, the mandarins. Times are changing for the mandarins. Tanh, Camille's intended husband, was educated in Paris, where he acquired new ideals; now he refuses to respect the shrine of his ancestors. Camille, the "Red Princess," makes a break with her adopted mother. With its glossy, Hollywood-like treatment, *Indochine* has been responsible for a boost in French tourism to Vietnam. People come looking for the exact pinnacle of limestone in Halong Bay and the exact building of Hué Citadel seen in the movie. The movie suggested to viewers that Vietnam was not, after all, all bomb-scarred landscapes—it has power and poetry, too. Halong Bay, Tam Coc Caves, the mountain landscapes of the north, the citadel and tombs of Hué, and the Hotel Continental in Saigon

all figure in the movie, which won an Academy Award for best foreign film in 1992.

L'Amant (The Lover): This 1992 release is based on the novella of the same name by Marguerite Duras. Set in the Saigon of the 1930s, it concerns a steamy affair between a French schoolgirl and the elegant son of a wealthy Chinese family. The tale of the forbidden liaison was filmed on location in Saigon and Cholon in French and English versions. It stars English actress Jane March and American actor Tony Leung and was directed by Jean-Jacques Annaud. The movie is based on a true story (and sparked controversy in France over whether the lead actor and actress actually engaged in on-screen sex).

Dien Bien Phu: Released in 1992, this film is a declaration of France's finally coming to terms with its great defeat at the hands of the Vietminh in 1954 (director Pierre Schoendoerffer was there, as a combat photographer).

Traps: The decay of French colonial rule in Vietnam is well portrayed in this Australian movie made in 1993. This movie presents a refreshingly non-Hollywood perspective. The setting is 1950s Vietnam. A journalist and his photographer wife arrive on assignment to report on colonial life. They become guests of a French rubber plantation owner and his defiant daughter. The central theme—of characters desperately trying to find themselves—echoes the attempts of a new Vietnam to find a new voice. The movie was filmed on location in Vung Tau and other parts of the south, and the Vietnamese did not attempt to modify the script. Director Pauline Chan was born and raised in Vietnam but left at the age of 15.

American Era Classics

Apocalypse Now: Francis Ford Coppola's 1979 release was very loosely based on Joseph Conrad's novel *Heart of Darkness,* set in the Belgian Congo. Coppola's crazy Colonel Kurtz is modeled on Conrad's character of the same name but also on CIA agent Anthony Posepny (Tony Poe), who operated out of northern Laos and offered tribal recruits one U.S. dollar for every set of communist ears they brought back.

In *Apocalypse Now,* rogue Green Beret Colonel Walter Kurtz (Marlon Brando) lives in an Angkor-style temple deep in Cambodia; another agent, Ben Willard (played by Martin Sheen) is dispatched from Vietnam to find him and "terminate his command." This hallucinatory movie was one of the first postwar American films on Vietnam, and one of the few to delve into America's "dirty war" in Cambodia. Coppola took a lot of risks making this movie, dodging all the Hollywood formulas in favor of a blunt and brutal approach. There is no attempt at heroic portrayal; the movie portrays the war as a kind of madness.

Apocalypse Now went way over schedule and budget. Coppola expected to finish it in a single 14-week stint on location in the jungles of the Philippines. But everything that could go wrong did—and it took three tours of duty and 238 days of shooting to complete the job (and a further 18 months to edit the 250 hours of film shot). Typhoons washed away whole sets, use of drugs was prodigious, adultery was rife, techies and crew mutinied in the rain, Sheen suffered a heart attack midway through, and Brando showed up late and totally unprepared for his role—a million-dollar joker. "Little by little we went insane," says Coppola.

Later, a movie was made about the movie, titled **Hearts of Darkness** (1991), with on-set footage shot by Coppola's wife, Eleanor, during filming in the Philippines, as well as more recent interviews with the director, cast, and crew. This is a fascinating glimpse into the madness and magic behind the scenes as the movie—like the Vietnam War—spiraled out of control and turned into a filmmaker's nightmare.

And the story is not over. In May 2001, with sanity fully restored, Francis Ford Coppola returned to Cannes to unveil a longer version of the cult classic, called *Apocalypse Now Redux.* Coppola was never happy with the final cut of the 1979 version, believing he jeopardized artistic integrity by bowing to studio pressure calling for version of just over two hours (Coppola's rough cut is known to exist in a five-hour format). To be precise, the new version is 53 minutes longer, with a mammoth running time of three hours 17 minutes. It includes a French plantation sequence in which a U.S. patrol boat lost in fog arrives at the homestead of some colonial French, who rail against their lot: Opium pipes are passed around and Willard beds the lady of the house. In another scene, Willard and his men come across a helicopter full of stranded Playboy bunnies. Coppola decided against including a 45-minute monologue from the disturbed Kurtz (Brando).

Good Morning, Vietnam: A comedy about the Vietnam War? They said it couldn't be done. In this movie, it's not only done but done brilliantly. The movie stars Robin Williams, ad-libbing his way through the script about disc jockey Adrian Cronauer, who defied both musical and military decorum on Saigon's Armed Forces Radio in 1965. The loud call "Goooooooood Morning, Vietnam!" was coined in real life by disc jockey Jean Leroy, working for the American Forces Vietnam Network. The movie also stars Tung Thanh Tran and Forest Whitaker. Directed by Barry Levinson, this 1987 movie breaks ground, showing the manipulation of truth by the American military and presenting a more sympathetic, human view of the Vietnamese. For these reasons, the movie has gained acceptance in Vietnam itself (the Vietnamese find it funny, too). The soundtrack on audiocassette turns up on cruise boats in places such as Nha Trang.

The Oliver Stone Trilogy: Epic wars demand epic movies, and director Oliver Stone set out to capture three different dimensions with three movies. Stone is himself a Vietnam vet, and *Platoon* (1986), starring Tom Berenger, Willem Dafoe, and Charlie Sheen, is easily the most gripping and realistic of the combat movies to come out of the United States. *Born on the Fourth of July* (1990) captures the anguish of a high-school football star (Tom Cruise) who is drafted, sent to Vietnam, and comes home in a wheelchair. Based on the true experience of veteran Ron Kovic, it's nevertheless liberally fictionalized. The third movie, *Heaven and Earth* (1993), captures a dimension not explored in any other American movie—the Vietnamese viewpoint. This film is based on

Le Ly Hayslip's true story, adapting events from her two books, *Child of War, Woman of Peace* and *When Heaven and Earth Changed Places.* The story is narrated by Le Ly Hayslip (played by Hiep Thi Le) with Haing S. Ngor as her father, Joan Chen as her mother, and Tommy Lee Jones as her American husband. This powerful drama unfolds in Ky La, a village close to Danang, and captures the upheavals in village life. Neither the North Vietnamese, the South Vietnamese, nor the Americans appear in a good light as they bully, abuse, and coerce the villagers. Le Ly Hayslip is caught in the middle—between North and South, Americans and Vietnamese, greed and compassion, capitalism and communism, war and peace, Father Heaven and Mother Earth. Le Ly Hayslip's faith in Buddhism—the middle way—is the key to her survival.

Ironically, Le Ly Hayslip's books have yet to be translated into Vietnamese or published in Vietnam; permission is being delayed by Culture Ministry objections to the portrayal of the North Vietnamese.

We Were Soldiers: This 2002 release, starring Mel Gibson and directed by Randall Wallace, attempts a very different docudrama approach to a major battle in Vietnam. Unusual for a Hollywood film, it puts a human face on the war, showing the courage of the soldiers. And it shows the Vietnamese soldiers in a human light. Apparently a bit too human: Vietnamese actor Don Duong, who appeared in the movie, was branded a "national traitor" by Vietnam's Ministry of Culture and Information and was placed under house arrest in Saigon. He was banned from acting for five years and forbidden to leave the country.

Operation Dumbo Drop: This 1995 Walt Disney movie provides something different: an amiable war saga for children. The Vietnam War is relatively bloodless in this adventure-comedy focusing on one good American deed. The action is inspired by a "true" story, as told to Disney by U.S. Major James Morris. In 1968, NVA troops shoot a Montagnard village's only elephant to punish villagers working with the Americans. A U.S. special forces band lands the tricky assignment of delivering a full-sized elephant to the village in time for an important ceremony. The special forces group travels to Ban Don to buy another elephant; the rest of the movie is pure Disney fantasy involving transport of the pachyderm by plane, flatbed truck, and boat, with narrow escapes, airborne antics, elephant rampages, and lots of slipping around in elephant plop. Finally, the weary elephant arrives. The movie, shot in Thailand, is directed by Simon Wincer and stars Danny Glover, Ray Liotta, and Dinh Thien Le.

The Quiet American: Based on the novel by Graham Greene, this was originally made into a movie in the 1950s. The 2002-release remake stars Michael Caine as British journalist Fowler, Brendan Fraser as CIA agent Pyle, and Vietnamese actress Do Hai Yen as Phuong (the woman in the love triangle). The movie also features another famous Vietnamese actress, Mai Hoa. It was filmed on location in Saigon, Hanoi, Ninh Binh, and Hoi An—one of the first Hollywood productions to be shot in Vietnam. Perhaps it was more acceptable to Vietnamese officials because it takes place in the pre–American-war era (although the film is prophetic about what would come to pass in Vietnam). The movie is directed by Australian filmmaker Phil Noyce, with a budget of $30 million.

Viet-Kieu Films

Cyclo: Tran Anh Hung has lived in France most of his life. On the strength of his first movie, *The Scent of Green Papaya*, a lyrical memoir of life in Saigon (filmed on a Paris soundstage and released in 1993), Tran was invited to film on location by the Vietnamese government. The result is a gritty portrait of gangsterized Saigon—a surreal, sensual, violent story focusing on the harsh life of cyclo drivers. An 18-year-old cyclo driver (unnamed, played by Le Van Loc) has his pedicab stolen by a competitor, forcing him to reimburse his boss, a ruthless woman who leads a local gang. The cyclo driver's debt precipitates his rapid descent into Saigon's underworld, with the lure of easy crime and money, and eventually entraps his

older sister (played by Tran Nu Yen Khe, the captivating star of *The Scent of Green Papaya*). Her lover (played by Tony Leung), part poet and part gangster, leads her into a prostitution ring. *Cyclo* is a visual and cerebral tour de force—and a stiff rebuke to Hung's Vietnamese government sponsors, who will probably not extend another invitation. Officials were apparently infuriated by the depiction of extreme violence.

Three Seasons: Because of the debacle over *Cyclo,* the next Viet-Kieu to come along and ask for permission (in 1997) to film on location was treated with great caution—especially since the script concerned extreme poverty and prostitution in Saigon. And this movie, *Three Seasons,* would be backed by American producers. That seemed like a tall order, but somehow director Tony Bui managed to convince the Vietnamese Ministry of Culture that even though the film showed extreme poverty, it has a theme of redemption. Tony Bui went to America when he was two years old. He returned at the age of 19 to rediscover Vietnam. Still in his mid-20s, he made *Three Seasons* on location in the Vietnamese language. With a budget of $2 million, it is the first American-backed movie to be shot on location since the 1975 fall of Saigon. The movie is about interlocking relationships, with the three seasons being dry (full of yellow and orange), wet (blues and grays)—and a third season of "growth." The movie went on to win the Grand Jury Prize at Utah's Sundance Film Festival in 1999.

Vietnamese Classics

The Girl on the River: This 1987 movie, made by Vietnam's leading director, Dang Nhat Minh, is set in the south during the Vietnam War. A flotilla of boats anchored on the banks of a river serves as a brothel for ARVN soldiers. The heroine of the movie is a prostitute who rescues an injured Vietcong leader on the run. She saves his life and they fall in love. Before he leaves, they promise to reunite after the war. However, with reunification of the country, the man becomes a high official who denies that he ever met her. His wife, a journalist, finds out about the heroine and writes an article about her, which her husband tries to have censored.

Wild Reed: This 1993 film, made with government funding accounting for half of the $60,000 budget and directed by Vuong Tuan Duc, is one of the first in Vietnam to address the tragedy of Vietnam's estimated 300,000 MIAs. It shows the anguish of a North Vietnamese officer who returns to his hometown with a Vietnamese MIA search team in 1976 to discover that his wife has remarried, believing him dead.

Other 1990s films that tackle the anguish of women in the war include *The Sound of the Violin,* about the feeling of people attending the 30th commemoration of the My Lai Massacre, and *Return to Ngu Thuy,* a story about the postwar lives of women once acknowledged as heroic soldiers.

Sand Life: While he was filming in Vietnam, Tran Anh Hung (director of *Cyclo*) presented a Vietnamese filmmaker five rolls of high-quality film. The filmmaker, Nguyen Thanh Van, used the treasured film for the beautiful night scenes in his movie *Doi Cat* (Sand Life), filmed in 1998. The film won awards in Asian festivals and picked up the Palm D'Or at Cannes. Not bad for a film made on a $65,000 budget and blocked by officials because it depicts a communist cadre with two wives. The movie tells the story of the bitter life of a middle-aged woman living alone in a southern coastal village, where she has been waiting 20 years for her husband to return. After the Geneva Agreement was signed in 1954, thousands of communist soldiers in the south regrouped in the north, believing that they could go home within a few years. But in fact 20 years passed before they were able to reunite with their families. In this movie, when the husband does eventually return in 1975, the crestfallen woman discovers he has married again and has a young daughter. The second wife follows him to the village, and the two wives face a tussle of love. The older first wife is played by actress Mai Hoa, who also appears in *The Quiet American.*

Architecture

Heavy Chinese influence is apparent in the architecture of pagodas and palaces, such as those at the imperial citadel in Hué. Very little is left of original Vietnamese architecture after years of neglect and warfare. Many older structures were made of wood, which has a limited life span. Other older structures were knocked down to make way for French buildings. Surviving examples of urban architecture with Vietnamese elements are the long narrow "tube houses" in the old quarter sectors of Hoi An and Hanoi. In Hoi An semidetached two-story mansions constructed with columns of wood sit on marble bases. Structures are held in place with large wooden nails; on the roof are "Yin and Yang" tiles, so named for the way they lock together. Merchant houses feature a shop front, family living quarters with a courtyard, and a rear storage section.

Sculpture

Sculpture lives in the past in Vietnam. Vietnamese art first flourished with the emergence of the Dongson culture in the Red River Delta near Thanh Hoa. This culture produced magnificent bronze sculptures with clear elements of Chinese style. The most renowned are huge bronze kettle drums more than a meter in height and width, with geometric and naturalist decoration on the drum head. The exact function of the drums is not known. Possibly they were used for summoning rain or buried with important deceased people. The tradition of sculpting in bronze survived, and in pagodas and temples the visitor will see elaborate sculptures in the shape of prominent deities and real and mythical animals. Sculpting of large statues in sandalwood is another medium seen in pagodas.

The former Kingdom of Champa, which flourished in coastal Vietnam in the 10th and 11th centuries, was remarkable for its sandstone sculpture. The artistic style draws on Indian influences, as the Cham culture itself existed outside the Vietnamese mainstream. The Kingdom of Champa was overrun by the Viet in the 15th century and virtually extinguished.

The finest display of Cham sculpture is in a museum in Danang; examples of Dongson and Cham art and sculpture can be seen in museums in Saigon and Hanoi.

Painting

With the exception of mural painting, folk art, and portraits on silk, painting was not a highly developed art form in Vietnam. Vietnamese painting is largely of modern origin, derived from French tutelage. In 1925 the French established the Ecole des Beaux-Arts de L'Indochine in Hanoi, training a generation of painters from across Indochina. The training was largely European; a major part of the syllabus involved the work of French Expressionists. French influence explains why Vietnamese art appeals so widely to the Western eye; it's a unique mix of European and Asian styles.

From 1945 to 1987, Vietnamese painting entered a phase of social realism. Visiting an exhibition in 1945, Ho Chi Minh was bored by the flowers and women; he said the works did not show the realities of daily life. The following year the paintings exhibited were titled *National Unity* and *General Insurrection* and featured revolutionaries and peasants. Thus a school of social realism was launched, featuring "politically correct" art that dominated the artistic arena for the next 40 years. Individual art was suppressed in favor of art that served the revolutionary cause.

In the early 1950s Bui Xuan Phai, considered the master of contemporary painting, started a campaign with other painters for more freedom of expression. The movement was severely repressed. Phai lost his teaching job at the Hanoi Fine Arts School and had trouble obtaining supplies. Often he resorted to painting on newsprint. Phai was not allowed to hold an exhibition until 1984, two years before his death. He never earned more than a few hundred dollars from his art, yet today a single Phai painting can fetch $25,000.

In modern Vietnam social realism has been completely abandoned. Movement began in 1986 with the advent of *doi moi*. Individual styles once forbidden—abstract and even surrealist art—are now common. You can find nudes, permitted since 1990; one Hanoi artist caused a sensation with a 1994 exhibition featuring male nudes. Another sensational exhibition in 1994 was called *As Seen From Both Sides,* which culled works from Vietnamese and American painters involved in the Vietnam War. The exhibition toured 14 American cities before arriving in Vietnam for shows in Hanoi and Ho Chi Minh City in 1994.

Since 1989, Vietnamese art has gained momentum on the international market. Prices for original artworks have soared, making it possible for younger artists to live off the proceeds of their work. Paintings are sold in European countries such as France and Sweden, and the Asian art centers of Hong Kong and Singapore. A Vietnamese painter's dream is an exhibition in Paris.

Folk Art

There is a vibrant tradition of village folk art in Vietnam. Villages in the Red River Delta, for example, specialize in the production of ceramics, silk weaving, woodblock printing, and the carving of furniture with mother-of-pearl inlay. These craft skills are largely of Chinese origin.

In the 15th century Emperor Le Than Ton sent an envoy to the Chinese court to investigate the art of lacquerware. Resin from the lacquer tree is milked and applied in repeated coats to wood, leather, metal, or porcelain. After lacquer application, the piece can be decorated, painted, or inlaid with mother-of-pearl. The art of mother-of-pearl inlay has been practiced for more than 1,000 years and is one of the more original folk arts in Vietnam. Pieces of mollusk shell are glued to recessed wood for trays, screens, and bowls. Pictures are also created on wood this way. Vietnamese pottery shows distinct Chinese influence in both design and execution. Among the types produced are celadon and blue and white porcelain.

Handicraft shops in Vietnam sell items with mythical animals or landscapes embroidered on silk or velvet. Another very different source of folk art comes from Montagnard groups;

these hilltribe folk excel at weaving, embroidery, and basketry.

CAMBODIA

Cambodia's cultural traditions were virtually destroyed under four years of Khmer Rouge domination and are only just beginning to recover. The return of Sihanouk has bolstered the arts—he is, for instance, a keen patron of Cambodian dance.

Most early Khmer literature has been lost or destroyed through conquest. Only stone inscriptions survive, etched in either ancient Khmer, Sanskrit, or Pali. Modern Cambodian script derives from southern India with overlays of Sanskrit: It is written from left to right with no separation between words.

Cambodian art forms derive from Hindu and Buddhist legends—the Indian epics of the *Ramayana* and the *Mahabharata*, and the *Jataka Tales*. Another Khmer epic is the poem of Angkor Wat. The *Mahabharata* is a partly narrative and partly didactic epic, describing the struggle between two family clans—the heroic Pandavas and the evil Kauravas—for possession of northern India. After 18 days of frenzied battle the Pandavas emerge victorious, and the eldest Pandava is crowned king. The *Jataka Tales*—fables detailing the previous lives of Buddha—are well known in Cambodia, in several modern adaptations. The *Jataka Tales* detail the lives of Buddha. They often take the form of parables, rather like Aesop's fables, with dramatic adventures resolved by nonviolent means. The most important lives of Buddha are the last 10, during which a particular virtue was perfected.

Modern Cambodian writing is mostly the work of exiles living abroad and is heavily influenced by French literature.

Ramayana

The *Reamker* is the Khmer adaptation of the Sanskrit epic poem the *Ramayana;* the full version of the *Reamker* takes about 50 hours to recite. The *Ramayana,* first written by Valmiki more than 2,000 years ago, is the most important myth in Southeast Asia, with varying forms extant in India, Thailand, Laos, Myanmar (Burma), and Indonesia.

The *Ramayana* tells the story of Prince Rama, an incarnation of the Hindu god Vishnu, who sets out in quest of his princess, Sita, and to destroy Ravana, a powerful demon intent on world domination. The epic portrays the struggle between good and evil with many subplots and doses of sex, drugs, violence, adventure, and magic. Subplots are embroidered with local myth and folklore. In the Cambodian version, beautiful Sita is abducted by the 10-headed, 20-armed, wicked King Tosakan, who imprisons her in his palace on the island of Lanka (Sri Lanka). Prince Rama sets off to rescue Sita; in this endeavor he is assisted by his brother Lakshman and a simian army under the mischievous monkey-god Hanuman. Overcoming impossible obstacles, the rescuers build a causeway to Lanka. After a pitched battle between the monkey army of Hanuman and the demons and giants of Tosakan, Tosakan is killed by an arrow from the magic bow of Rama, and Sita is rescued. Rama suspects her of unfaithfulness, so she throws herself on a burning pyre to prove her purity. Agni, the god of fire, takes her from the flames and reunites the couple.

The *Ramayana* is the basis for classical dance in Cambodia, which has transcended mere culture and become fused with the Cambodian national identity. Classical dancers are Cambodia's true diplomats abroad. The *Ramayana* is also the basis for folk plays and shadow plays. Shadow-play characters are cut out of leather and painted. Traveling shadow puppeteers usually perform at local festivals.

Architecture and Sculpture

From the 10th to 13th centuries, the kings of the powerful Khmer Empire erected scores of temples and military outposts. Apart from those found in present-day Cambodia, Khmer temples are also scattered across northeast Thailand, particularly at Phimai, and at Wat Phu in Laos.

Early Khmer temples were made of brick and laterite. After about A.D. 950 sandstone

KHMER DANCE

by Toni Shapiro

Dance, music, and drama have always been prominent in Cambodian life, indispensable as rites of passage and religious and national ceremonies. Traditionally, each temple in Cambodia had its own *pin peat* orchestra, an ensemble accompanying religious ceremonies, classical dance, and shadow puppet plays. It consists of xylophones, string and wind instruments, and three types of drums. Throughout the centuries, dance troupes have performed episodes from epic tales and legends for the people in temple compounds around the country.

Cambodians trace the unique stylized movements of their dances back hundreds of years to bas-relief sculptures of celestial dancers *(apsaras)* at the grand 12th-century temple of Angkor. As far back as the 7th century, inscriptions tell of dancers associated with temples. In many of the ancient Hinduized states of Southeast Asia, thousands of magnificent carvings of celestial and earthly dancers adorn temple walls. Dancers also had a place within the confines of the palace as they formed part of the king's regalia, used in the maintenance and symbolic display of royal prowess.

The Angkor Court

Along the east gallery of Angkor Wat is a panel of bas-reliefs featuring a huge stone *naga* (sacred serpent) that twists and pulls, while the mythic Sea of Milk churns in turbulence. From this movement, hundreds of flying *apsaras* are born. *Apsaras,* thought to embody purity of spirit and eternal beauty, dance to entertain the gods. They symbolize the well-being of the Cambodian people.

For centuries, royalty communicated through the medium of dance with the divine world, seeking to guarantee fertility of the land and prosperity for the people. At least once a year a sacred ceremony known as *buong suong* was installed under royal patronage. In *buong suong*

divine beings are asked for blessings in exchange for offerings of elaborately presented fruits, meats, incense, flowers, and, most important, sacred music and dance. Swathed in velvet and brocade, wearing golden tiaras or fearsome masks and delicate flowers, the dancers enact sacred stories.

New Year Ritual Dance

As part of a sequence of dances in the *buong suong* ritual, dancers would recreate the battle between the legendary figures of Moni Mekhala and Ream Eyso. The female deity Moni Mekhala is protectress of the waters, the giant Ream Eyso controller of storms. Legend has it that long ago these two were students of a wise and powerful hermit. One day the hermit offered them a challenge. Each was to collect the morning dew; the first to present a glassful of nature's gift would be the winner and would receive a magic ball. Early next morning Ream Eyso gathered as many leaves as he could, letting the droplets of dew slide from each leaf into his glass. Moni Mekhala spread a handkerchief on the grass and left it overnight; by morning, the cloth was damp. Squeezing it, she filled her glass. She arrived at the hermit's abode with a full cup of dew before the giant did.

As a reward for her ingenuity, the hermit fashioned a magic glittering ball of dew and bestowed it on her. Ream Eyso received a magic ax as a consolation prize. But the small ball of Moni Mekhala was much more powerful than Ream Eyso's ax; he *had* to have that ball. Ream Eyso stalked Moni Mekhala and threatened her; she teased and scolded him in return. In desperation and fury, Ream Eyso flung his spangled ax, barely missing the goddess. Moni Mekhala tossed her ball into the air, creating a bolt of lightning that blinded the giant. He collapsed, and Moni Mekhala glided away. But the giant did not die; seconds later, sight regained, he realized what had happened. In frustration and anger, he disappeared into the clouds.

Through this tale Cambodians trace the origin of thunder and lightning. Ream Eyso's ax crashes through the air, and Moni Mekhala's sparkling ball lights up the heavens. Together they bring rain—the symbol of renewed life, imparting fertility to Cambodia's farmlands. The confrontation between Ream Eyso and Moni Mekhala recurs every year, around the time of the Cambodian New Year in mid-April. This is the height of the hot season, just before monsoon rains wash away the dust and bring nourishment to the fields. When Cambodians see dark clouds forming in the sky, they know Ream Eyso and Moni Mekhala will soon engage in their eternal battle, flooding the rice fields. The giant will be vanquished, but only temporarily. Sooner or later he will return.

Sihanouk's Patronage

Through the centuries, Cambodian royal dancers remained, for the most part, cloistered within the palace compound. They danced for the public, as well as for deities, at the annual Water Festival in Phnom Penh, and at various sites during ritual ceremonies. Provincial troupes, some headed by retired court dancers, were found throughout the country.

After Norodom Sihanouk ascended to the throne in 1941, circumstances changed. Though they still performed at sacred and royal functions, dancers lived on their own for the first time, outside the palace walls, free to marry and raise children.

Since the middle of the 20th century, Cambodian dance has combined spirituality with a growing emphasis on secular performances held on a proscenium stage in front of an audience. Queen Kossamak, Sihanouk's mother, was particularly influential in elevating dancers to the role of international symbols of Cambodia. Besides providing domestic entertainment for foreign dignitaries in Cambodia, the Royal Dance Troupe often accompanied Sihanouk on his official visits abroad. The association

between the dancers and Cambodia grew so strong that in the 1960s a French observer noted: "Rare are the countries who by their name evoke the image of a dancer. This is the privilege of Cambodia, from where the vision of the refined dancer rises."

In the 1960s the University of Fine Arts was founded. The school offered professional training in several forms of Cambodian theater, shadow puppetry, music, and folk dance. In 1970, after a coup sent the royal family into exile, the court dancers were no longer messengers between the sovereign and the deities. Yet they continued practicing in the Royal Palace compound, performing and touring abroad.

The Khmer Rouge Years

Under the Khmer Rouge regime all dance and music, as the Cambodians knew them, were forbidden. Along with the entire urban population, dancers were sent into the countryside in 1975. Fearful the Khmer Rouge would kill them if they knew of their previous connections to the palace, many dancers tried to hide their identities, telling cadres they'd been vegetable sellers, pedicab drivers, or seamstresses.

There were some dance performances during the years of Khmer Rouge rule, but the style of dancing was unrecognizable to those who had practiced or watched this art before. One royal dancer remembers,

Sometimes they marched us and forced us to watch their dances. They wore only black and danced in place, glorifying manual labor. But I must admit part of me could sit back and recall the beautiful memories of my past, when I was practicing or performing, guided by my teachers. And I could imagine what it would be like to be dancing again.

(continued on next page)

KHMER DANCE (cont'd)

Contemporary Dance

After the Vietnamese ousted Pol Pot in 1979, surviving dancers regrouped. They discovered that close to 90 percent of their professional colleagues—dancers, musicians, actors, playwrights, poets—had perished. Almost all the delicately carved instruments and intricately embroidered costumes and accoutrements had been lost or destroyed. In one instance, artists found a priceless *roneat* (xylophone) base in use as a pig trough. The artists immediately set about reclaiming their rich cultural heritage by performing and teaching. They hoped to instill a sense of pride in their students and in their shattered communities. The school of dance, a division of the University of Fine Arts, reopened in Phnom Penh in 1980. Many of the students were children of artists who'd died. Now those children are teachers and performers, and new classes open each year.

Dance retained a high profile throughout the 1980s and continues to do so today. During the 1980s dancers toured the countryside, performed on television at New Year celebrations, and were the highlight of many national ceremonies. Dance and music were also priorities in the chaotic and dangerous refugee camps on the Thailand-Cambodia border. Since the return of royalty and renewal of open expression of religious faith, dancers have again become official messengers to the deities, asking for spiritual blessings in ceremonies staged at the Royal Palace and the temple of Angkor. Princess Bopha Devi, King Sihanouk's daughter, was a star dancer of the 1960s; she returned to Cambodia with her father and now helps oversee dance training and performances.

Dancers are invited to perform at temple festivals and for tourist groups, photojournalists, and filmmakers. The National Department of Arts sponsors performing arts festivals every year or two. Troupes and individual artists from all over the country participate. Dancers also perform at the government's request to honor visiting dignitaries and on national holidays.

Dancers from two prestigious troupes—the University of Fine Arts Troupe and the Royal Dance Troupe of the National Department of Arts—are often busy touring abroad.

Dance was previously performed for tourists in Phnom Penh's Bassac Theater, but in February 1994 this historical site was severely damaged by fire. It was going to be rebuilt. Check with a hotel receptionist or the Ministry of Culture and Fine Arts for the location of cultural performances.

Training

Annual auditions for the dance school in Phnom Penh attract more than 100 applicants. In the past, children began dancing at 5–6 years of age, when their bones and muscles were considered supple enough to be trained and molded properly. Today youngsters audition at age 8–9, after a few years of public schooling. This is necessary, school officials insist, to raise the general educational level following the devastation of the Khmer Rouge years.

Mastering Cambodian dance requires many years of discipline and dedication. Students work on technique every morning and attend academic classes in the afternoon. At the dance school, a division of the University of Fine Arts in Phnom Penh, dancers specialize in classical (court) dance, folk dance, or *lakhon khol*. Court dancers perform episodes from the *Reamker*, or Cambodian *Ramayana*.

The dancers were traditionally all female, until Sihanouk's time, when men began to dance the roles of monkeys and the hermit. *Lakhon khol* is an all-male form of masked dance-drama. This kind of troupe was attached to temples or performed at provincial governors' palaces; there is still a *lakhon khol* troupe in Kandal province. Many folk dances were created in the 1960s and '70s by teachers and students at the University of Fine Arts. They based these works on rituals, music, daily activities, movement patterns, or the dances of people in the provinces.

The first phase of dance school studies emphasizes training in rhythm and memorization of the basic positions and movements. The second phase begins after the sixth year of study and continues for another three: In this phase, students are taught to analyze the movements, emotions, and symbolism of the dance. Throughout the dancer's career, a special exercise routine is practiced; designed to encourage the hyperextension of the elbows, the deep arch of the spine, and the extreme flexibility of the fingers—all essential to the Cambodian dance aesthetic.

The first months of study are undertaken without musical accompaniment. A teacher beats out the rhythm on the floor with a wooden stick; as they move, the children sing the rhythm of the *sampho*, the drum that carries the beat in the *pin peat* ensemble. This allows the younger dancers to master both the rhythm and the basic postures and movements of Cambodian dance without being distracted by the complexity of the music. With a live orchestra, advanced students practice an expanded version of the same series of thousands of core gestures and steps. Elaborate dances and dance-dramas are constructed from combinations of these movements and postures. Individual dancers also work on perfecting movements particular to a character role in Cambodian dance or dance-drama. The role could be the graceful and gentle female (a princess or female deity), the brave and noble male (a prince or male deity), the forceful and fearsome giant, or the sprightly monkey. The monkey is a role danced only by men.

Before each performance, dancers light incense and offer prayers of thanks to their teachers and to the spirits of the dance, asking for guidance and blessings to ensure a successful performance. The dancers add an extra prayer these days—one for lasting peace in Cambodia.

Repertoire

In a stage performance, you're likely to see a combination of classical and folk dances, with perhaps a *lakhon khol* excerpt. Some of the dances are briefly described here.

Classical Dance: Apsara was choreographed in the 1950s, with costuming based on the bas-relief carvings of celestial dancers at Angkor Wat and danced by five or seven women wearing distinctive multispired crowns. The chorus sings of the delight of being surrounded by beautiful flowers in a garden. **Hanuman and Sovann Macha** is an excerpt from the *Reamker* dance-drama. Monkey-general Hanuman pursues and flirts with the golden mermaid Sovann Macha. **Moni Mekhala and Ream Eyso** is performed as part of the sacred New Year ceremony; the duet is also danced as a theatrical piece. **Tep Monorom** is a large group dance in which the women appear as celestial beings moving in and out of formation, around and across the stage, while the chorus sings of their heavenly bliss.

Folk Dances: Beh Korvanh (Cardamom Picking) is derived from the Peur people of western Cambodia, who collect spices in the Cardamom Mountains. This dance portrays aspects of Peur lifestyle and clothing. **Nesat** (Fishing) uses different kinds of real fish traps as the dancers present a comic and romantic outing in the countryside. **Tbal Kadeung** (Rice Threshing) depicts adventures in the countryside, when women become angry at the men for abandoning their tasks at the first sight of the palm juice seller. **Kangaok Pailin** (Peacock of Pailin) comes from the Pailin region and features a story of a princess who dreams of a peacock presenting a Buddhist sermon. Shortly thereafter, the princess falls ill; nobody can cure her. The king's hunter takes a female peacock into the forest and has her dance to attract a male peacock, who can speak. The hunter catches the male peacock; asked to recite sermons for the princess, the captured peacock said he'd be delighted to if only she'll set him free. She does so, and he promises to return every Buddhist holy day. Two elaborately adorned "peacocks" enact this dance of attraction, with onlookers clapping and beating drums.

was reserved for sacred temples, while brick was used for secondary structures and laterite for foundations. Wooden buildings have not survived centuries of warfare and decay.

Khmer temples were built according to symbolic criteria. The central tower, or *prasat,* was built on a pyramidal base representing sacred Mt. Meru, navel of the world in Hindu cosmology. An enclosing wall represented the earth, a moat beyond was viewed as the cosmic ocean. The spirit of the *devaraja* (divine king) was enshrined in a linga (stylized phallus, symbol of Shiva) at the center of the temple complex. People believed their king communicated directly with the gods. The central tower sanctuaries housed images of the Hindu—and later Buddhist—deities to whom the temples were dedicated. After death, the king, members of the royal family, and high priests may have been cremated, their ashes kept at the temple. A subsequent king would dedicate a new temple to shelter his special linga.

Although sandstone Khmer temples followed formulaic structural codes, there was great latitude for innovation. Most structures are oriented from east to west, with the main entrance at the east. Many structures were crudely erected, relying on gravity and a good fit between stones to hold the structure in place, although bronze clamps were sometimes employed. The arch or vault was unknown to

KHMER SCULPTURAL MOTIFS

Motifs in early Cambodian sculpture, bas-reliefs, and lintel carvings were heavily influenced by Brahmanism and Hinduism. In Hinduism are three important gods: Brahma, the Creator of the Universe; Shiva the Destroyer and Reproducer; and Vishnu the Preserver. Each inspired a cult of worship at Angkor, and each is depicted with special objects, clothing, and mount. Four-faced Brahma rides a sacred goose called Hamsa. Four-armed Vishnu rides a half-man, half-bird creature known as Garuda; Vishnu's consort is Lakshmi, goddess of beauty. Shiva carries a trident and rides Nandi, a bull; his consort is Uma. The son of Shiva and Uma is Ganesh, who has a corpulent human body and the head of an elephant. Other common figures are Indra, god of the sky, who rides a white three-headed elephant; eight-armed Yama, the judge of the dead; and two-headed Agni, god of fire, who rides a rhinoceros. Kama, the god of love, carries a bow and a case of floral arrows made of lotus, jasmine, and lily.

Linga: One of the most important motifs in Khmer sculpture is the linga, a stylized erect phallus, symbolic of Shiva and his powers of reproduction. It rests upright on a yoni base, symbolizing the female organ. The linga on a yoni base was adopted by Khmer kings as a symbol of their divine power: Each king built a new temple to shelter his special linga. Lingas were usually made of stone, but some were made of quartz and others were reputed to have been made of solid gold.

Naga: The snake or aquatic serpent figures prominently in Hindu mythology as part of fertility cults. The Khmers claim their descent from the mythical union of Indian Brahman Kaundinya and Soma, the daughter of the *naga* king. *Nagas* proliferate through Khmer temples—found in the form of stylized cobras on balustrades, finials, and bas-reliefs. The *naga* may feature five, seven, or nine fan-shaped heads. Ananta was the name of a large serpent that Vishnu reclined on during a cosmic sleep. Vasuki is a serpent that served as a rope in Churning the Sea of Milk (a Hindu creation myth) to release the essence of life. The *naga* crossed over into Buddhism, where it is considered the deity of rain and also the protector of Buddha's law.

Garuda: Half-bird, half-man, this creature is the mount of Vishnu and the enemy of the *naga.* Garuda is usually portrayed with the torso of a human and the beak, wings, legs,

Angkorian architects—they employed a false vault, known as the corbel arch.

The most distinctive feature of Khmer architecture is the sanctuary tower in the shape of a budding flower, a refinement that dominates Angkor Wat. Philip Rawson describes Angkor Wat's towers in *The Art of Southeast Asia:*

> *The tower spires have eight stories and a crown, and are square, with a series of multiple recessed profiles and center projections that makes them look octagonal. They show the full-fledged curved outline of a sprouting bud, which gives the impression that each story is rising out of the one beneath. This impression, combined with the facade motifs of all the gable-ends—which have upturned corners and rise well beyond the ridges of their roofs—is responsible for the extraordinary dynamic, rising effect of the structures.*

In the 12th century, King Jayavarman VII added a new dimension to Hindu inspiration, layering on a design that derived from Mahayana Buddhism. This led to the stunning innovation of the Buddhist temple-mountain of the Bayon and the gates of Angkor Thom.

There was no great emphasis on temple interiors in Khmer architecture—the structures were not built for the people, but for the king and high priests. Thus the interiors tend to be windowless, and many have false doors. In

and claws of an eagle. Garuda appears on lower temple walls, appearing to help support the structure, with arms stretched above his head grasping the tails of serpents.

Apsara: The celestial dancer is a Khmer innovation. Born of the action of Churning the Sea of Milk, the beautiful *apsaras* live in the heavens. These dancing angels are the epitome of female beauty at the court of Angkor, and they indulge the sexual pleasures of ultimate Khmer male incarnations. Placement of the legs in arched position with bent knees is associated with flying.

Lotus: In Buddhism, the lotus is symbolic of purity and divine birth. Like the Buddha born into an impure world, the lotus originates in impure mud and rises above the murky water to blossom high above it. The lotus may be sculpted at the base or crown of statuary. At Angkor's Neak Pean, a tower island set in an artificial lake is decorated with lotus petals at the base, and capped with lotus blossoms. *Apsara* dancers are sometimes shown in bas-reliefs dancing on a bed of lotuses.

Lokesvara: In Mahayana Buddhism, the bodhisattva of compassion is Lokesvara (Avalokitesvara in Sanskrit). It is thought the four-headed entry gates and massive stone Bayon heads at Angkor are renditions of Lokesvara, combined with features of King Jayavarman VII. The serene heads, with downcast eyes and faint smiles, are the icons of Angkor.

Guardians: Serving as guardian statues at numerous temples are Khmer-style lions, or **singhas**. These often line temple entrances and steps. Because the lion is not native to Cambodia, features are crude and stylized. A guardian appearing over temple doorways is Kala, a jawless monster with bulging eyes, grinning face, horns, claws, and pointed ears. Kala had a voracious appetite and asked Shiva for a victim to satisfy its hunger. Angered by the request, Shiva commanded Kala to devour its own body. Kala swallowed its body, but not its head. Shiva ordered the head placed over temple doors as a reminder of his powers. A similar-looking bodyless creature is the demon Rahu, with hands but no claws. Rahu may hold the moon in its mouth: According to legend, the moon is the source of the elixir of immortality. Rahu sometimes swallows the moon, causing an eclipse—the moon reappears shortly, popping out of Rahu's throat.

this sense, the buildings could be considered gigantic sculptures—ornately carved walls and lintels festoon the exterior, while the interiors are bare. The soft sandstone used at Angkor lent itself to relief sculpting: Niche and bas-relief carving in sandstone in the Angkor region is especially elaborate. In some places, such as at Banteay Srei, no exterior surface is left unadorned. Galleries at Angkor Wat and the Bayon bear huge bas-reliefs of Hindu and Khmer historical themes.

Free-standing sculpture appeared in the 9th century in the role of temple guardians. Khmer lions lined stairways, five-headed *nagas* formed balustrades, *garudas* appeared at foundation corners. Lintels bearing monsters guarded temple entrances. Temple interiors bristled with bronze and stone sculpture. Toward the end of the 12th century the development of portraiture in stone was one of the most remarkable achievements of Khmer art. A sophisticated level of bronze-casting technology was achieved at Angkor, evident in a massive bronze reclining Vishnu torso unearthed in 1936 at Angkor. A number of smaller bronze items, such as oil lamps and incense burners, survive. Wooden sculpture most likely existed at Angkor too, but none has survived. Carved wood pieces from the 18th century display the considerable skills of Khmer craftsmen.

Modern Khmer sculpture and mural painting is fostered at the School of Fine Arts in Phnom Penh, where students fashion copies of Angkor statuary in wood, marble, bronze, and concrete. The traditional Cambodian art of wood carving is particularly fine, with decorative panels, portrait heads, and other items produced at the School of Fine Arts. Other traditional crafts, such as Khmer silk weaving and silversmithing, are also being revived.

LAOS

There are two streams for the arts in Laos—classical and folk. Classical arts are strongly associated with Hindu mythology, Buddhism, and former Lao royalty, while folk arts are connected with animist Lao hilltribes. The stronger and more vibrant stream is the folk arts.

Mythology

There is very little in the way of Lao literature, ancient or modern. Older Lao manuscripts were engraved on palm leaves, bundled together, threaded, and wrapped in cloth. Many Lao sacred texts were looted by the Thais in the 19th century.

Laotian mythology is heavily dependent on the Sanskrit epic the *Ramayana,* written by the Indian poet Valmiki more than 2,000 years ago. The *Ramayana* pits lovers Rama and Sita against the wicked demon Ravana. The story parallels Western myths from the *Iliad* to *Star Wars* in focusing on the struggle between good and evil. There are good doses of sex, violence, magic, adventure, and intrigue in the *Ramayana.* The Lao version of the myth, called *Phra Lak Pralam,* parallels the original story but adds new episodes. These were later a source of inspiration for the Thai version.

The *Jataka Tales,* stories about the lives of Buddha, are also well known in Laos. The stories suggest Aesop's fables and present dramatic adventures resolved through nonviolent means. Although the *Jataka Tales* recount hundreds of Buddha's lives, the most important are the last 10, during each of which a particular virtue is perfected.

Classical Arts

As in Thailand and Cambodia, the main patron of the performing arts was royalty. When royalty and Buddhism fell out of favor under communism, the arts suffered. One casualty was classical dance based on *Ramayana* themes, once performed for the royal court. Classical Lao music is now heard only during *Ramayana* performances. A standard ensemble consists of a xylophone with bamboo crosspieces *(ranyat),* a set of bronze cymbals hung from a wooden frame *(khong wong),* bamboo flute *(khui),* and Lao-style clarinet *(pii).*

There are three main styles of temple architecture in Laos: Vientiane, Luang Prabang, and Xieng Khuang. Because Xieng Khuang province was heavily bombed during the Vietnam War, hardly any examples of this form remain. Of the other two styles, only a few significant structures have survived repeated ransacking through the centuries. None are uniquely Lao; they share features borrowed from northern Thailand. Temples in Vientiane have high-peaked roofs with three, five, or seven layers, while Luang Prabang–style temples feature dramatic, low-sweeping roofs.

Sculpture, carving, and mural design are strongly associated with temple architecture. Temple frescoes and bas-reliefs draw inspiration from the *Jataka Tales*—following the mural sequence reveals the fables. At temples in Vientiane and Luang Prabang, beautifully carved wooden doors and shutters—and entire facades—depict scenes from the *Ramayana*. Lao sculpture consists mainly of images of Buddha, the best pieces being from the 16th through 18th centuries.

Folk Arts

Hilltribe lore and customs provide Laos with its cultural identity; folk song and dance are closely related to festivals. Lao folk dances telling of the joys of life and work have survived for many centuries. The national dance is the *lam wong,* a slow revolving circle dance with men on the inside and women on the outside. Partners move their hands in graceful, expressive gestures. Music for the *lam wong* is provided by the *khen,* a handheld bamboo reed instrument related to South American pan pipes. The *khen* is difficult to play—performers must produce a continuous melody by exhaling and inhaling without catching their breath. Other instruments include the *khong wong,* hand drums, bamboo flute *(khui),* and a bowed string instrument, the *saw.*

Performed at festivals and temple fairs is *maw lam,* Lao folk theater. *Maw lam* is a combination of talking, singing, and costume drama. It's bawdy, witty, and profane, embracing topics such as sex and politics, and appears to be impervious to official censure. *Maw lam* is also heard on the radio.

Handicrafts

Weaving has a long tradition in Laos. It's mostly done by hand in villages, on simple wooden looms; skilled weavers are held in high regard. The most common type of weaving in cotton or silk is for the *sinh,* a long wraparound skirt worn by most Lao women. Exquisite pieces are also produced for ceremonial purposes, such as the shawl women wear over their shoulders at important events such as weddings or festivals. Textile-making techniques and patterns vary widely according to the hilltribe group and geographic location. Luang Prabang patterns, for example, feature gold and silver brocade, while Khmer-influenced patterns are found in the south. Motifs are often based on folktales, legendary creatures, nature, or geometric patterns. Designs from the northeast are highly prized—they have achieved "antique" status because the hilltribe weaving tradition in that zone was severely disrupted by decades of war; attempts have been made to revive lost patterns. Recipes for mixing natural textile dyes are closely guarded secrets; the dyes derive from tamarind, turmeric, and indigo, among other sources.

A quite different form of weaving involves the making of mats and baskets, which are the hilltribe method of packaging. These are woven from straw or reed. Silversmithing is important to the Hmong and Mien not only for display purposes but also as a kind of portable wealth, carried in the form of silver jewelry, ornaments, belts, and other pieces. In Luang Prabang, silversmithing was once a royal craft. Several of the smiths who made silverware for the royal palace before 1975 still work around the old capital, producing finely crafted pieces.

Customs and Conduct

TEMPLE MANNERS

Pagodas and temples are sacred places, so when visiting, dress properly (no shorts, sandals, dirty clothes, jeans, or T-shirts). Determine whether shoes must be removed. Remove your shoes and hat when approaching the central sanctuary of a temple. Ask permission if taking photos. Treat all Buddha images and statues with respect. Buddhist monks should be treated with great respect. Making a small donation to the contribution box would be appreciated. Angkor Wat, though a ruin, is also a pilgrimage site for Buddhists and Hindus.

Monks are not supposed to touch a woman; if a woman must hand something to a monk, she should place it on a table for the monk to pick up, or hand it over via a male. Women should not attempt to shake hands with a monk or sit beside him.

TERMS OF ADDRESS

Vietnam

Vietnamese names consist of three elements. The name Nguyen Van Tan breaks down as Nguyen (family name) Van (middle) and Tan (given name). The order is thus inverted from the Western, but titles are still applied to the third name. So if a title, such as General or Mr., is applied, the address becomes "Mr. Tan." In the Vietnamese White Pages for Saigon or Hanoi, residential listings are by given name followed by family name and middle name—thus, *Tan* Nguyen Van. The reason for this is that, since the Nguyen emperors allowed people to take their family name, half the population goes by the family name of Nguyen. Other common family names are Tran, Le, Phan, and Ngo. Vietnamese women do not change their names after marriage. When addressing people, you need to use the given name, and take into account age, sex, status, and other factors. It's worth taking the

time to find out how to use the system. (For more details, see the *Vietnamese Language* section later in this chapter.)

Lien Xo! means "Russian" and is chanted by children in Vietnam upon encountering any Caucasian. This becomes quite annoying if you stay in Vietnam long enough. It's a derogatory term because the Vietnamese didn't like the penny-pinching Russians. Hanoi and Moscow were closely aligned in those days, but since the collapse of the Soviet Union there are very few Russians left in Vietnam. To correct this impression, repeat your nationality in Vietnamese.

Laos

The Lao commonly use the first name, not the family name, when addressing each other.

DRESS

Caucasians in shorts remind the old folks of the colonial French, which is not a good idea. Although rural men wear shorts or rolled-up pants when slushing through rice paddies, it is not culturally acceptable for women to wear shorts. Exposure of skin by women is frowned upon, so dress modestly (covering shoulders and thighs), even in the hot and humid south.

Entry to pagodas, temples, and places such as Ho Chi Minh's mausoleum may be refused to foreigners in shorts. Travelers should be aware that Ho Chi Minh has acquired a sacred status in Vietnam; images and statues of the leader are treated with great respect.

BODY LANGUAGE

In most situations, observe how a person of your sex and age behaves, and do as he or she does. In Vietnam, a simple example of this is using a toothpick after dining. Most Vietnamese cover their mouths with the left hand, and use the toothpick with the right.

Gestures

In Vietnam, Cambodia, and Laos, the head is considered pure and sacred in Buddhism; do not touch anyone, including children, on the head. The feet, which come into contact with dust on the street, are lowly; do not point your feet at anyone, or at any Buddhist image. If sitting in a temple, either squat or sit with the legs tucked to the side so the soles of the feet point backward.

Likewise, do not point at a Buddha image with a forefinger or hand. When beckoning someone toward you, do not use a crooked single finger. Instead, gesture with palm down and four fingers cupped together.

Vietnam: Avoid touching Vietnamese people—such contact as back-slapping a guide may not be welcome. Although members of the opposite sex refrain from touching each other in public, it's common to see two young men walking hand-in-hand.

The OK symbol (thumb and forefinger pressed into a circle) is understood in Vietnam. It can also mean "zero," as in money. Crossed fingers is a bad gesture. It refers to a prostitute.

A useful gesture in Vietnam is "screwing-in-the-lightbulb," which consists of an upturned palm with fingers held as if grasping a bowl. The hand is then rotated back and forth near the ear in the rhythm used when installing a lightbulb. This can mean "I don't know," "I don't understand," or "the price is too high." The double gesture—both hands, near both ears, plus a grimace, simultaneously—really drives the point home.

Greetings

In Cambodia and Laos, as in Thailand, a commonly used greeting is the *wai* (called *sompeah* in Khmer), a prayerlike gesture with palms placed together and a slight bow of the head. There are various degrees of *wai,* and foreigners are not expected to know all the nuances; a smile and a nod are acceptable. Cambodians and Lao doing business with foreigners are also familiar with the handshake.

SAVING FACE, LOSING FACE

It is considered bad form to display anger in Vietnam, Cambodia, and Laos; instead, smile. Buddhists greatly admire the "cool heart:" restraining strong emotions and practicing moderation in all things. Stay calm, or you will lose face. In many situations, "face" is important. Do not shout when bargaining.

An important cultural note: A smile on a Vietnamese face does not necessarily indicate amusement—it can also convey anger, fear, embarrassment, disagreement. Thus, as you pick up your mangled bicycle from a head-on collision with another cyclist, the other party may smile or even manage a nervous laugh.

GIFTS

Anything foreign will do just fine, thank you—foreign cigarettes for men, foreign cosmetics for women, and so on. Items do not have to be expensive. Baseball caps with foreign logos are all the rage, as are T-shirts with foreign slogans on them (not too risqué). Foreign magazines are greatly appreciated; women prefer fashion magazines. For children, pens and balloons are ideal.

TAKING PICTURES

Vietnam

Do not photograph bridges, military installations, or strategic infrastructure. Do not photograph military parades or official functions. Photojournalists require special visas to visit Vietnam and may require special permission to photograph sensitive events or subjects.

Cambodia

You are free to photograph most things in Cambodia. Be careful, however, when dealing with armed subjects. Troops manning checkpoints are extremely touchy about photographs because the checkpoint may not be legal—set up simply for personal fund-raising. In one case, a foreigner photographed a checkpoint from a passing boat—whereupon several shots were fired across the bow. You can take pictures of soldiers—some tourists even pose with borrowed guns—but always ask first. A few cigarettes come in handy here.

Laos

Ask permission before photographing anyone within temple grounds. Avoid photographing or videotaping official functions. Some areas, such as Nam Ngum Dam, are of military importance, and no photos are permitted.

DEALING WITH POLICE

Vietnam

Most Vietnamese are terrified of the police—with good reason. If you show no fear, the police may be taken aback. In the early postwar years of travel in Vietnam, you needed permits to visit any place outside Saigon or Hanoi. The police had a field day holding passports of foreigners or asking for and receiving $100 fines for being in a place without a permit. The 1993 abolition of permits was intended to curb these corrupt practices. Now that this game is up, police are discovering other ways of extracting money. A group of foreigners in a jeep east of Pleiku was fined $7 each for touring the

"wrong village"—the total fine came to $50. Vietnamese drivers are sometimes fined $10 or so for not possessing a "license to drive foreigners around" or for carrying irregular insurance. Others have been told by a policeman on an ancient Russian motorcycle that their brand-new Toyotas are "not roadworthy."

Police often count on the fact that foreigners are pressed for time. So one tactic is to sit it out with a fat book and see what gives. Police must go to a higher authority to hold you overnight; if you're stubborn, they may give up. Keep smiling and ask, "What's the problem? I don't understand what the problem is here." Do not produce original documents, as this gives police the leverage they need for fines (e.g., if you give them $50, they return your passport). Show only photocopies and insist that the originals are elsewhere. Sometimes a five-dollar bill will expedite the case to a favorable conclusion. Packs of foreign cigarettes have a similar effect. If you must pay a fine, remember that all charges are negotiable, so bargain.

PROSTITUTION

Prostitution is a serious offense in Laos; women are usually treated with great respect.

Recreation and Shopping

VIETNAM

Adventure tourism is in its infancy in Vietnam, but things are shaping up, and there's great potential for trekking, diving, sailboarding, whitewater rafting, ocean and river kayaking, and other pursuits. Until rental equipment becomes readily available, it's a case of bring-it-yourself and do-it-yourself, or fall in with a tour.

Beaches

Resort areas are at Nha Trang Beach (with offshore islands), China Beach in Danang, and Bai Chay near Halong Bay. Along the coast are pristine beaches such as Cana, Dai Lanh, Lang Co Lagoon, and Canh Duong. Sun worshipers

should bear in mind that typhoons strike the beaches. This makes them windy—bad news for swimmers, good news for surfers. Pacific Coast beaches have quick drop-offs, which means undertow problems. On the Gulf of Thailand near Cambodia are stretches of sand near Ha Tien, and at Phu Quoc Island offshore.

Marine Sports

You can get your hands on snorkeling equipment at Nha Trang, but quality is spotty. There's limited diving equipment for rent, too. Diving is best at offshore islands. Many islands dot the coast to the north of Nha Trang. China Beach hosted an international surf meet in October 1993.

Boating

Fishing vessels can be hired for island day trips. Onboard seafood is often included with the package. Kayaking is a possibility in the Mekong Delta and at Halong Bay, but you have to bring your own equipment.

Caving

Vietnam's north is a spelunker's paradise featuring thousands of caves in limestone formations. The Halong Bay area is good for grottoes and several very deep caves. There are also huge caves at Trung Trang near Cat Ba National Park. The most spectacular caves are probably those at Phong Nha, about 45 kilometers northwest of Dong Hoi. The main cave here is eight kilometers long.

Bicycling

Vietnam moves at bicycle pace; the bicycle is as yet the main form of private transport. Bicycle hire is available in major cities. Hanoi and Hué are pleasant to cycle around. Bikes in Vietnam are used mostly for practical purposes and not for sport. During the Vietnam War cargo bicycles carted supplies. In 1994 the Back to Dien Bien Phu Bicycle Race commemorated these hardships with a race from Hanoi to Dien Bien Phu. In the rougher Central Highlands, a mountain bike is ideal. Bikes are easily ferried around on boats or other vehicles.

Hiking

In the mountains of the northwest you can hike into valleys and stay in minority villages overnight. Good areas to visit are Mai Chau, Dien Bien Phu, Lai Chau, and Sapa. You can hire a jeep to reach a trailhead, and porters can carry supplies if needed. From Sapa, you can organize a trek to the summit of Mt. Fansipan, which at 3,143 meters is Vietnam's highest peak.

Running

The Vietnam International Marathon is held alternately in Saigon and Hanoi every January. The first marathon was run in 1990. About 1,500 runners participate. The world's largest, strangest, and silliest running club—the **Hash House Harriers**—welcomes visitors to its chapters in Saigon and Hanoi. Find out when the weekly run is scheduled and show up at the trailhead in your shorts. There's a beery gathering of hares and hounds after the run.

Golf

After being banished for years under communist rule as bourgeois decadence, golf has made a comeback as "a good sport for health and the spirit." In late 1993, an 18-hole golf course was opened in Dalat, the Dalat Palace Golf Club (the site actually dates to the 1930s under the French). There are seven other golf courses in the country, and Malaysian, Singaporean, Hong Kong, and Australian interests all have joint-venture plans to develop more courses, complete with hotels, villas, swimming pools, and resort facilities. The top courses are in Dalat (Dalat Palace Golf Club), Saigon (Vietnam Golf and Country Club), and Phan Thiet (Ocean Dunes Golf Club). In the north, 18-hole courses include Daeha Golf Course and Country Club, northwest of Hanoi, and King's Island Golf and Country Club, 45 kilometers west of Hanoi.

Shopping

Shopping is low-key in Vietnam. Saigon and Hanoi are not in the same league as Bangkok or Hong Kong. But with Vietnam's long tradition of handicrafts and its ready workforce, the potential is certainly there. Vietnamese handicraft specialties include lacquerware vases, boxes, trays, and wall panels, mother-of-pearl inlay, ceramics, embroidery, and traditional clothing. Some shops in Hanoi specialize in selling items made by minority peoples—from basketry to bows and arrows. Many travelers find tailor-made clothing is a bargain in Vietnam, with top-quality family-run operations in Saigon, Hoi An, and Hanoi. You can have a custom silk *ao dai* made in Saigon—or custom silk lingerie made in Hanoi. Modern Vietnamese painting combines styles from East and West in a unique and pleasing hybrid. The widest selection of galleries and handicraft shops can be found in Hanoi, Hué, Hoi An, and Saigon.

THE ALLURING AO DAI

One of the first things the visitor notices on a trip to Vietnam is schoolgirls riding bicycles three or four abreast, the panels of their long *ao dai* dresses billowing behind them like orchid petals. Or, on a Boeing run by Vietnam Airlines, flight attendants in beautiful sky blue or pink *ao dais*. Anthony Grey described the *ao dai* in his novel *Saigon* as "demure and provocative. . . women seemed not to walk but to float gently beneath the tamarinds on the evening breeze." The *ao dai* covers everything, but its gossamer-thin fabric hides almost nothing. It's very practical, maintaining modesty but allowing ventilation and freedom of movement. It does not crush and dries quickly after washing.

Ao dai means long gown, and it is pronounced "ow yai" in the south and "ow zai" in the north. It's a close-fitting knee-length gown, split to the waist and worn over flowing white or black satin pants. The gown features a high collar and tight sleeves. The *ao dai* is adapted from a Chinese dress called the *cheong sam*, originally worn by both sexes. Pants and buttoned coats were worn by men and women during the latter years of the Nguyen dynasty. In traditional society, design and color indicated the status of the wearer: Yellow fabric was reserved for the emperor, purple for high-ranking mandarins, blue for court officials. The emperor alone could use gold brocade and the five-claw dragon design. Emperor Minh Mang imposed the wearing of pants on the entire female population of Vietnam.

The *ao dai* is of recent design. In the early 1930s Cat Tuong, a Vietnamese writer who dabbled in fashion design, modified the *cheong sam*. The new design tightened the bodice and moved the opening from the front to the shoulder and side seam. Cat Tuong also employed a greater range of colors and motifs for the *ao dai*. In the 1950s, two tailors in Saigon incorporated raglan sleeves into the design, with seams running diagonally from the collar to the underarm. As the *ao dai* evolved it became less popular as dress for men.

Between 1975 and the late 1980s, in a period of severe austerity, the *ao dai* fell from grace, and Vietnamese women switched to Western-style blouses and pants. Since 1990, however, the *ao dai* has made a bold comeback as the national dress. It is the dress seen in tourist advertising and is worn by hotel receptionists and office workers, particularly in the south. Spectacular *ao dais* with hand-painted designs on the bodice are worn for holidays—especially at Tet—and for weddings.

Although *ao dais* in standard sizes are mass-produced for work and school uniforms, Vietnamese women prefer custom-made versions. At a Saigon tailor shop, a team of specialized cutters, sewers, and fitters can mold an ensemble in several hours. The resulting *ao dai* fits the woman's figure perfectly.

Know Vietnam, Cambodia & Laos

GREAT BUYS AND TIPS

by Nancy Yildiz

The booming free-market economy in Vietnam has provided a wealth of tourist souvenirs and practical items for sale, such as cards, ceramics, T-shirts, lacquerware, paintings, stamps, and stone carvings. Many items are overpriced, so it's essential to comparison shop and bargain hard. Start by browsing through the government fixed-price stores in Saigon and Hanoi to get an idea of price range and quality. You can gain a wealth of information by chatting with the sales clerks.

One of the great buys is greeting cards with traditional Vietnamese designs hand-painted on silk, selling for $.10–.50 each. You can special-order brass or rubber stamps bearing Happy Birthday, Merry Christmas, or Thank You messages so you'll be prepared for all occasions. Cards are usually cheaper in the street stalls, but stores offer a wider selection.

Printed T-shirts are sold everywhere with various logos such as Saigon, Hanoi, or a waving Ho Chi Minh. Wearing these in Cambodia can get you in a lot of trouble; the locals detest the Vietnamese. The Vietnamese community in the United States may also take offense. Prices vary $1–3 depending on whether they're 100 percent cotton or a cotton-synthetic mix. For a wide range of hand-embroidered T-shirts with rural scenes, sailboats, and so on, try the shops in Hanoi along Hang Gai and Ly Quoc Su streets. The shirts come in all colors and sizes and make great gifts for under $3 each.

For knickknack collectors, there are handmade figurines of fishermen, cyclos, water buffalo, or silver cigarette cases and snuff boxes. Try the stores along Dong Khoi Street in Saigon and Hang Khay Street in Hanoi (south side of Hoan Kiem Lake). Be aware that the silver content varies 20–92 percent, and that prices vary accordingly. Cheaper items ($2–5) are usually made of nickel-silver alloys, not sterling silver. In the small-souvenir line, avoid buying items made of ivory or tortoiseshell; these materials derive from endangered species. For stamp collectors, stalls near the GPO in Hanoi

and Saigon sell an excellent range of modern stamps; for less than $20 you can start your own collection. Old coins and banknotes are also available but the prices are steadily climbing; unless you know what you're doing, you could get ripped off.

For Art Lovers

Galleries selling both traditional and modern paintings and woodblock prints abound in every major city. But it can be a headache determining the "right" price to pay when you're not sure whether the paintings are mass-produced or one-of-a-kind, and when little is known about the artists. Starting price is often 10–15 times higher than actual worth. Therefore, take time to shop and ask lots of questions.

For around $3–12, you can pick up mass-produced prints or silk paintings of traditional market scenes, landscapes, or portraits. Browse through the art section in government fixed-price tourist stores. Once you get a feel for the prices and what you like, try your hand at bargaining in the numerous souvenir shops or art galleries.

For more expensive paintings, $30–300 and up, including reproductions, original oils and watercolors, and woodblock prints, shop in the numerous art galleries, including the Vietnamese Art Association in Hanoi and the Ho Chi Minh Association of Fine Arts in Saigon. Ask for background information on the artist, and don't be surprised to find the same artist's work at different prices in more than one gallery. It's a time for hard bargaining; most paintings are overpriced. If you're really hooked on paintings and want to meet the artists, you'll have a better chance in Hué or Hoi An. Both have good galleries and more reasonable prices.

Hoi An, a quaint town near Danang, also offers a good selection of old and reproduction ceramics at reasonable prices. However, upon leaving Vietnam, tourists have reported that Customs may confiscate items that appear to be old. The export of Buddha images and items of "high cultural value" is forbidden.

CAMBODIA

Because of the association between crafts such as silk weaving and silversmithing with Cambodian royalty, craftsmen were targeted in the Khmer Rouge era. The skills of the few survivors are now being passed on, and Sihanouk and his entourage are again patronizing these crafts. Under the Khmer Rouge, master silk weavers were ordered to weave plain cloth or work in the fields; today Khmer silk is back in favor with the royal family, and the textile trade has resumed. The craft of silversmithing is also being revived, with small-scale handcrafting of silver boxes and jewelry. Modern Khmer sculpture and mural painting is fostered at the School of Fine Arts in Phnom Penh, where students fashion copies of Angkor statuary in wood, marble, bronze, and concrete. The traditional Cambodian art of woodcarving is particularly fine, with decorative panels, portrait heads, and other items produced at the School of Fine Arts. Handcrafted goods are on sale at a number of outlets and markets in Phnom Penh and Siem Reap.

Festivals and Holidays

VIETNAM

Public holidays and certain festivals are known as "Red Flag Days," because national flags are flown from many residences and offices.

National Holidays

January 1: New Year's Day
January/February: Tet
February 3: Anniversary of 1930 founding of Communist Party
April 30: Liberation Day, commemorating 1975 fall of Saigon
May 1: International Worker's Day (May Day)
May 19: Anniversary of the birth of Ho Chi Minh
September 2: National Day, commemorating 1945 independence proclamation by Ho Chi Minh

Lunar Calendar Festivals

On lunar festival days, many Vietnamese flock to pagodas. The lunar calendar is divided into 12 months of 29 or 30 days, making a year of about 355 days. Every four years an extra month—a leap month—is added to keep the lunar calendar in sync with the solar calendar. Due to this juggling of months, lunar calendar dates are movable. Festivals usually take place at the time of the full moon.

The Vietnamese 12-year cycle follows the Chinese zodiac, with years corresponding to rat, buffalo (or ox), tiger, cat (or rabbit), dragon, snake, horse, goat, monkey, rooster, dog, and pig. So 1998 was the Year of the Tiger, 1999 the Year of the Cat, 2000 the Year of the Dragon, and so on. (According to astrologers, a child's future can be predicted based on the hour, month, and year of birth; the shape and character of the zodiac animal in the year of birth also affects the person's fate. The animal years are further influenced by one of the five elements: metal, water, wood, fire, or earth.)

In addition to the following national festivals, there are many regional village and minority celebrations, especially in the north.

January/February: Tet, or Lunar New Year, takes place in late January or early February. In a "leap year" it can take place in early March. The country comes to a standstill at Tet for five days of holiday.

March: On the sixth day of the second lunar month is Hai Ba Trung Day, which commemorates the Trung sisters, who led a revolt against the Chinese around A.D. 40.

May: The birth, death, and enlightenment of Buddha is celebrated on the eighth day of the fourth lunar month.

August: On the 15th day of the seventh lunar month is Trung Nguyen, Wandering Souls Day. The dead, hungry and naked, re-

THE SPIRIT OF TET

Tet is Christmas, New Year, and the Fourth of July all rolled into one. It's also the day of celebration for everyone's birthday (individual birthdays are not celebrated in Vietnam; everyone is simply a year older at Tet). Tet Eve marks a special celebration that is followed by 4–5 days of festivities. Just before Tet roads are bottlenecked, but once Tet starts the roads are quiet. Most businesses close and railways shut down for four days, but a few buses operate. There's lots of activity at the pagodas and temples, and special water-puppet shows for children. Tet is best in the north, where festivities are more traditional. Other traditional sites include Hué and Hoi An.

Coming from the word *Tiet,* meaning festival, Tet marks the first days of the Lunar New Year and the start of spring. It's a time to pay debts, forgive others, correct one's faults, and start the new year with a clean slate. In common with the Western Christmas celebration, the Vietnamese buy a tree, exchange greeting cards, wish each other Happy New Year *(chuc mung nam moi!),* and eat themselves silly. Women buy peach or apricot branches and bunches of flowers several days before Tet. It's auspicious if the branches bloom on the first morning of Tet: Apricot and peach blossoms are reputed to keep demons out of the homes at this time. Some families buy an entire apricot tree and display it like a Christmas tree, decorated with greeting cards from well-wishers. Another popular choice in the south is a fruit tree with miniature oranges.

It can stand up to several meters tall, bearing more than 100 oranges.

To drive evil spirits away you have to make a lot of noise. That's where firecrackers come in. In 1995 the government placed a ban on the manufacture of fireworks because of the deaths of 71 revelers and injuries to 765 others during Tet in 1994. The ban appears to be enforced strictly, although tape-recordings of fireworks are permitted. Before the ban, massive strings of fireworks were attached to the front of a residence and ignited—and the louder the fireworks, the better.

Countdown to Tet

The countdown to Tet begins up to a month before the festival starts. Two weeks before Tet there is a noticeable increase in the number of shoppers. People buy clothes and presents for family and friends, and stock up on food for guests over the five-day holiday. Public and private buildings may get a new coat of paint. Stalls are set up to sell New Year greeting cards, candied fruit, decorations, and firecrackers. Exactly a week before Tet, in a simple household ceremony, offerings of fresh fruit, cooked food, and paper models are made to the Ong Tao, the Spirit of the Hearth. Ong Tao must leave the hearth to report household events from the old year to the Jade Emperor. The departure of the Spirit leaves the home unprotected for a week, until New Year comes.

(continued on next page)

---

turn to their relatives to eat and take a look around. If not treated with respect, ghosts can cause havoc. Offerings are made in Buddhist homes and temples, and feasts are placed on tables for the ghosts.

September: The 15th day of the eighth lunar month brings Trung Thu, the Mid-Autumn Festival. Of Chinese origin, the festival is celebrated with the baking of mooncakes and lantern parades.

November: On the 28th day of the ninth lunar month is a celebration of the birthday of Confucius.

CAMBODIA

National Holidays

January 7: National Day, celebrating the 1979 fall of the Khmer Rouge

March 8: Women's Day, with parades with floats in the main towns

April 17: Independence Day, celebrating the fall of the Lon Nol regime in 1975, with a parade in Phnom Penh. In mid-April is Cambodian New Year.

May 1: Labor Day

May 9: Genocide Day, commemorating the

THE SPIRIT OF TET (cont'd)

Houses are decorated in red and gold. Bright woodcut prints announcing the upcoming year and its featured zodiac animal adorn the walls, and people take down the print from the previous year. Everyone must wear new clothes, so clothes vendors are out in force. Families begin choosing Tet trees. Office parties are held, and Tet bonuses distributed.

Two days before Tet, people are busy cleaning their houses and decorating their Tet trees, and rushing about doing last-minute shopping. Traditionally, no cooking, cleaning, sewing, digging, or drawing of water is done during the Tet festival; everything must be arranged in advance. Some families still make traditional *banh chung*, a cake of sticky rice filled with bean paste and pork, symbolizing the earth.

On Tet Eve, everything closes early as families head home to celebrate the first dinner of Tet. Huge balloons appear on the streets, eagerly bought by homeward-bound shoppers. Elaborate offerings of chicken and glutinous rice are made to ancestors as everyone awaits the magic hour of midnight. Catholics attend pre-midnight Mass. Just before midnight, some fireworks may be set off. Families and friends meet to exchange greetings. Just after midnight, Buddhists go to their favorite pagoda to pray for a good year. Many families eat a simple meal after midnight, perhaps with some rice wine or champagne. In Hanoi, droves of young people patrol the streets on motorcycles (later there is unofficial daredevil racing).

The first person to cross the home threshold after midnight must be a person of good character, or misfortune can follow for the entire year. Not leaving anything to chance, some folks discreetly arrange their first visitor ahead of time. Elders present packets of lucky money to children.

The first day of Tet, people dress in their finest new clothes and visit relatives. Village festivities may include singing competitions, cockfighting, and Chinese chess competitions with real people as the pieces. Gambling is popular. Parks are full of holiday celebrants.

The second day of Tet involves visits to special guests and close friends. Young people looking for partners stroll to the nearest lake to make a wish that the person of their dreams will appear before them.

The third day of Tet is reserved for visits to teachers, friends, and business associates. Visitors are served candied fruit, *banh chung*, spring rolls, sausage, and drinks. Negative talk is taboo. The attitude of the first days of the New Year sets the tone for the remainder of the year. When leaving the house, elaborate wishes are exchanged, "I hope that your business may prosper and that money may flow into your house like water."

On the fourth day of Tet, people are supposed to return to work, but seldom do. In the city, people go back to their offices to wish coworkers happy New Year. It is not until the sixth day of Tet that people get serious about work again, and Vietnam returns to normal.

---

victims of Khmer Rouge rule. The main ceremony is at Choeung Ek, near Phnom Penh. June: Two parades in Phnom Penh, on June 19 a celebration of the 1951 founding of the Armed Forces, and a June 28 commemoration of the 1951 founding of the People's Revolutionary Party of Cambodia
October 31: King Sihanouk's birthday

Lunar Calendar Festivals

Festivals were banished under the Khmer Rouge because of links to Buddhism and royalty, and were downplayed by the Hun Sen government. They were revived with the return of Sihanouk, who is very fond of pomp and ceremony. Lunar festivals are movable and usually coincide with the full moon. The Royal Plowing Ceremony, held in May, was revived in 1994 after a 25-year hiatus; the Water Festival was revived in 1990.

January/February: Tet, or Chinese Lunar New Year, is celebrated by the Vietnamese and Chinese communities. Shops may be closed.

April: In mid-April is Chaul Chhnam or Cambodian New Year—three days of festive celebration, similar to Pimai in Laos and Song-

FESTIVAL OF THE REVERSING CURRENT

This Cambodian boat-race Water Festival dates to the 12th century, when Angkor King Jayavarman VII defeated the Cham in a naval battle. Linked to royalty, the three-day festival was revived in 1990 after a 20-year hiatus. In 1994 boat races were held at Siem Reap in the spectacular location of Angkor Wat moat.

A month before the festival starts, ceremonial longboats are hauled out of monastery sheds around the country, and crews begin training. The crew consists of 40 or more oarsmen. Although boat races are held in October or November in different parts of Cambodia, the biggest venue is Phnom Penh, where up to 200 longboats compete in the rowing regatta. Thousands converge on the riverbanks opposite the Royal Palace to see the arrival of the boats and oarsmen, followed by small orchestras of gongs and drums, and accompanied by monks or village dignitaries. Boat races take place in the afternoon. The oarsmen, spurred on by rhythmic singing and drumbeats, compete on a short stretch of the river. At night, dragon boats cruise up and down and fireworks soar skyward. At the climax of the festival, the king commands the Tonle Sap to reverse direction and flow to the sea, which it duly does within a few days.

kran in Thailand. It marks the beginning of the year on the traditional Khmer calendar and is celebrated with feasting, games, and offerings of food, flowers, candles, and incense to welcome the Songkran Goddess, believed to descend to Earth for three days at this time. Water-splashing, originally related to washing Buddha statues, prevails only in certain parts of the country, such as Siem Reap and Battambang. In April/May is Visak Bauchea, the commemoration of the birth and enlightenment of Buddha.

May: The Royal Plowing Ceremony is an ancient Brahman ritual, celebrating the start of the rice-planting season. In Phnom Penh the ceremony is presided over by the king. Court officials are charged with appraising the taste buds of eight royal oxen; results are used to predict the outcome of rice, corn, and bean harvests for the year that follows.

July: Start of Buddhist Lent and the rainy season proper, a time when novices join monasteries.

September: End of Buddhist Lent, sometimes celebrated with boat races. Another festival at this time is Prachum Ben, when offerings are made to ancestors.

October/November: Bon Om Tuk, the Water Festival or Festival of the Reversing Current, is held at the full moon at the end of October or beginning of November. When monsoon rains subside, the flow on the Tonle Sap River reverses, and is celebrated with three days of boat races, processions, music, and games.

LAOS

The Lao are addicted to festivals. They kick off the year with three different celebrations—Western New Year, Chinese New Year, and Lao New Year. Authorities despair that farmers would rather spend money on festivals than save funds in the bank.

Buddhist celebrations are based on the movable lunar calendar: The full moon figures prominently in these calculations. Many traditional villages still use the lunar calendar to follow the passage of the seasons. Festivities often center around local *wats,* which are transformed into country fairgrounds with games, food stalls, live music, dancing, and other entertainment.

In addition to the Gregorian calendar, the Lao follow the Buddhist-era calendar, which in Laos starts 638 years before the Christian era. Add 638 to the Western year to get the corresponding B.E. year: Thus 2005 corresponds to 2643 B.E.

Celebrating any auspicious occasion—wedding, birth, new year, recovery from illness, a welcome or a farewell—is the uniquely Lao *baci* ceremony. Of animist origins, the *baci* centers around an elaborate "tree" made from banana leaves and flowers, surrounded by rice wine, cakes, and other symbolic food. A village elder lights candles and delivers a monologue in Pali and Lao, after which villagers tie white cotton strings around participants' wrists as blessings are spoken. If you're a visitor, the blessing may be that no calamity befall you in Laos. The several dozen strings correspond to internal organs and represent good health and prosperity. After the string tying, rice wine and refreshments are served, followed by *lam wong* dancing. It is considered unlucky to take the strings off until three days pass; the strings should then be untied rather than cut.

The following list of festivals and holidays is by no means exhaustive—ethnic minorities march to a different drummer and have a great variety of festivities. *Boun* is Lao for "festival."

National Holidays

January 1: New Year's Day, celebrated with *baci* ceremonies
Mid-April: Lao New Year (Pimai), with three days of festivity
May 1: International Labor Day, with parades in Vientiane
December 2: National Day, celebrating 1975 victory by the Pathet Lao with parades and speeches

Lunar Calendar Festivals

January: The story of Prince Vessanthara's reincarnation as Buddha is celebrated with Boun Pha Vet, featuring temple recitals and theater and dance performances. This is a popular time for ordination of monks.

February: Maha Puja is an important Buddhist holy day celebrating an occasion of impromptu preaching by Buddha. Merit-making ceremonies take place during the day at temples throughout the country; at dusk there are candlelit processions around principal *wats* as the full moon rises. The festival is celebrated chiefly in the capital, Vientiane, and at Wat Phu in southern Laos. Chinese

New Year (Vietnamese Tet) in late January or early February is marked by deafening fireworks and visits to Chinese and Vietnamese temples. Many Chinese and Vietnamese businesses close for three days.

March: The Harvest Festival, or Boun Khoun Khao, is celebrated in *wats* up-country after rice has been harvested.

April: Pimai, the Lao or Buddhist New Year, occurs in the fifth lunar month, usually mid-April. There are three official days of holidays, and a few more unofficial. The entire country closes down for festivities, which are quite elaborate in Luang Prabang. People clean their houses, put on new clothes, and assemble for ceremonial washing of Buddha images in the temples. April is the hottest month, and Pimai is a good excuse to throw buckets of water over all and sundry on the streets—and that includes visitors.

May: Visakha Puja is a full-moon festival marking the birth, death, and enlightenment of Buddha. It is celebrated in local *wats,* with candlelit processions at night. The Rocket Festival, or Boun Bang Fai, takes place around the same time. This rainmaking festival is staged before the start of rice planting; rockets are burnt as a sacrifice to Phagna Thene, the god of rain. Large bamboo rockets are carried in procession by monks and then fired heavenward to loosen up the skies and bring down rain. The higher the rocket flies, the more propitious the omen. Designers of failed rockets are thrown in the mud. In some places male participants blacken their bodies with lamp soot, while women wear sunglasses and carry carved wooden phalluses. The Rocket Festival is one of the wildest festivals in the country, with plenty of music and dance—especially irreverent *maw lam* performances.

June: Khao Pansa marks the beginning of the rains retreat, when Buddhist monks are expected to stay at one monastery. This is the traditional time for young men to enter the monkhood for short periods.

August/September: Boun Kao Padabdin is the Festival of the Dead. Many cremations take place at this time, and gifts are presented to monks who chant on behalf of the deceased.

October: Boun Ok Pansa marks the end of the three-month rains retreat; monks are allowed to travel and are presented with robes, bowls, food, and other offerings. In conjunction with this is Bun Nam, the Water Festival, with longboat racing in such major towns as Vientiane, Savannakhet, Pakse, and Luang Prabang.

Longboats with crews of 50 or more, accompanied by drummers, participate in regattas.

November: In Vientiane the That Luang Festival takes place on the full moon of the 12th lunar month, usually mid-November. The festival lasts three days, with offerings to assembled monks, a weeklong fair, a parade through town, fireworks, and a candlelit procession around the sacred stupa of That Luang.

Accommodations

VIETNAM

There are more hotel rooms in the city of Bangkok than in the entire country of Vietnam. Accommodations in Vietnam are consistently higher-priced and of lower quality than their Thai counterparts. Costs for moderately priced hotels in Vietnam are roughly double the rates in Thailand. Vietnam is woefully short of hotels to meet the influx of tourists, particularly in Hanoi. Many hotels are run-down, and horror stories abound. One American tourist checked into a $175-per-night room in Saigon to discover a windowless chamber. She was informed by the management that a room with a view would cost $200. Only after she started to gather up her bags did the manager relent and give her a suite with windows.

Among the air-conditioned nightmares of Vietnam you might find some of the following: The Mosquito Pond Hotel, The Rusted French Villa, The Taxi-Girl Hotel, Khach San Boom Boom, The Rat and Roach Inn, Grand H"tel Ordinaire, The Hanoi Hilton, The Rat Bat Guesthouse, and The Boney M Karaoke Hotel. That gives you some idea of what's out there. Most towns or cities in Vietnam feature some kind of rudimentary accommodations, whether government guesthouse or Russian blockhouse. Socialist architecture has a happy knack of making things look gloomy and decrepit even before the building is completed. You might luck out and get an ancient French hotel with vintage Gallic plumbing and fixtures still in place, though not necessarily functioning properly. Some places offer cavernous bidets and bathtubs. Take care in bathrooms; the wiring in budget hotels is very dangerous, more dangerous when water is present.

Most accommodations, including guesthouses, provide mosquito nets. The net is sometimes tucked into hideaway boxes above the bed, spread with the help of wooden arms. Another type of net is hung off four poles mounted at the corners of the bed; yet another is a squarish net suspended over the bed, attached by strings to nails mounted on the walls. Check the cupboards if you don't see a net in place, or ask the staff to provide one.

Under $50

For a $5 basic fan room in the central Vietnam town of Quang Ngai you get: "1 double bed, 1 table, chairs, 1 bathroom, 1 pair of plastic slippers, sweet-scented soap for bathing, 1 neon light system and ceiling fan, and 1 thermos with enough hot water for making tea." And, you hope, 1 mosquito net and 1 roll of toilet paper. The thermos, a Chinese habit, is very useful; it provides purified water, and in a pinch can be used to soak down hot towels in lieu of a hot shower. Basic rooms go for $5–10, and may share bathrooms. "Room for Rent" is another way of saying "hotel" without attracting government taxes. Family-run places are homey—look for them. A step up are budget rooms with air-conditioning or hot water, or both. Prices are usually in the $10–20 range; government guesthouses are often in this category.

From here, prices spiral into the $20–50

NOTE ON VIETNAMESE BUSINESS NAMES

The Vietnamese government has been enforcing name changes on hotels, restaurants, and businesses. Vietnamese businesses must bear only a Vietnamese name, while joint-venture and foreign-owned businesses can retain an English name. These changes may cause some identification problems with listings in this book. A hotel featured here as Hoan Kiem Hotel may have a sign saying Khach San Hoan Kiem; a restaurant listed as Cha Ca Restaurant might appear as Nha Hang Cha Ca; other businesses may change names entirely. Enforcement of these regulations is haphazard: in Saigon, some businesses completely ignore the regulations, while others have chosen to post a large Vietnamese sign with a smaller English subtitle.

zone, depending on the number of creature comforts, gadgets, circuitry, and appliances added. With air-conditioning and phone, $20; add a color TV and fridge, $30. In this price range, you might find a renovated French hotel with lots of character—a good value. Privately run minihotels, which are now proliferating throughout Vietnam, are an excellent deal. Unlike the state-run hotels, these are proper business concerns that try hard to provide the best service and comfortable, clean and secure accommodation. What's more, these minihotels are most likely to be family owned and operated, and that's a bonus. Any chance you get, try and take a privately run minihotel over a state-run hotel.

Over $50

Business or luxury-class hotels charge $50–100 for standard rooms and $100–200 for deluxe rooms. Major hotels extract 10 percent government tax and 5–10 percent service charge on top of listed prices. Hotels accept Visa, MasterCard, Diners Club, American Express, and JCB cards, but levy a surcharge of up to 4 percent for credit cards. High-end hotels provide in-house movies, minibar, IDD, room safe, satellite TV, and individual air-conditioning control; facilities include health club, business center, and restaurants.

Hotels with international first-class standards—the Metropole and the Daewoo in Hanoi, the Dalat Sofitel Palace and the Century Hotel in Saigon—charge considerably

more. These can run $200 and up for top-end accommodations, $300–600 for a suite.

Resort Hotels

How long before Club Med makes it to Vietnam? Not long, judging by the joint-venture beach resort developments sprouting along the central coast. These luxurious places sport bungalows and villas, swimming pool, gourmet seafood, and perhaps even a nearby golf course. Resorts opened include the French joint-venture Ana Mandara Resort in Nha Trang, the Hong Kong joint-venture Furama Resort in Danang, Pansea Beach Resort and Coco Beach Resort in Phan Thiet, and Hoi An Resort and Victoria Hoi An in Cua Dai near Hoi An.

Mystery Hotels

Sometimes you run into a brick wall in Vietnam: a hotel for Vietnamese only, Asians only, even Taiwanese only. The reason for rejecting you could be one of the following: The staff have never had a foreigner stay there before and are afraid of the police; the place is deemed not comfortable for foreigners and the owner does not have a "foreigner-dealing license"; the military reserves the hotel for high-profile guests (you'll know you've found one of these if you get a gun shoved in your face). Or the hotel may be a "short-time" joint, with taxi girls lounging around the lobby; these places don't want to lose money from any of the rooms being rented out for the entire night. "Taxi girl" is a euphemism for a loose woman; the term comes from "taxi dancers," who are metered for time spent with customers on the dance floors of seedy nightclubs. Often, hotel and nightclub are under the same roof—this species is called a Karaoke TV (KTV) Hotel. Most of these are aimed at businessmen from Hong Kong, Singapore, and Taiwan, with karaoke hostesses "entertaining" in private rooms. These hotels will wave you away.

Other Options

You may arrive in a place without a hotel. Here you have to improvise. Stay in a village with a family; mime the gesture for sleeping and a kid will direct you to a possible place to sleep. Restaurants and noodlehouses are another possibility. In one case, in the Mekong Delta, we were not only welcomed through the front door—we slept on it. Two fellow travelers and I were provided with old doors as beds. Traveling in North Vietnam, we were once given impromptu beds in a village schoolhouse, under the gaze of a stucco Ho Chi Minh, at a cost of $.25 each.

Hotel Check-In

Hotels dispense forms that ask for date of arrival, visa number, visa validity, entry/exit card number, what you ate for breakfast, and other idiotic questions. The best thing to do is make photocopies of one of these completed forms and just pass them out along the way. There used to be a procedure in Vietnam in the early days of individual travel whereby all travelers carried permits listing places they wanted to visit. Hotels would demand passport and paper visa, which were then ferried off to the local police to be registered, recorded, stamped, sealed, signed, and delivered back to the hotel. You can bet a bit of money changed hands along the way. Travel permits are long gone, but for some reason the registration procedure persists; maybe money still changes hands. The policy seems to vary. Some hotels do not ask for a passport; others don't bother with "registration" if you pay up front; still others adamantly insist on retaining your passport. In one place in the Delta, the front desk even insisted on seeing the customs form.

More than one traveler has rushed out of a hotel in a bleary-eyed daze at the crack of dawn to catch an express bus, and left behind a passport at the front desk. You may well need your original passport for other transactions, such as banking or motorcycle rentals. Therefore, if the hotel insists on keeping the passport for "registration," try to retrieve it the same night or the next morning, or try to leave only a photocopy. You can argue that your passport is a valuable document that belongs to your government (which is true) and cannot be left in the care of a hotel.

CAMBODIA

Phnom Penh and Siem Reap both offer a full range of accommodations, from budget to first-class hotels. The number of hotels and guesthouses mushroomed both in Phnom Penh and up-country with the 1992–1993 UNTAC operation. Guesthouse and midrange hotels can be found in Siem Reap and Sihanoukville, the two main tourist centers up-country, with fan rooms ranging $5–25, and rooms with air-conditioning and hot water for $25–45. Facilities in hotels can be basic—the public supply of electricity and water is intermittent. Malaria is a problem up-country in Cambodia; make sure your room is equipped with a good mosquito net.

Guesthouses are a great way to mingle with a Cambodian family—in Siem Reap there are dozens of them. You get a simple fan room for perhaps $5–10: Guests lodge in a handful of rooms upstairs, and the family lives downstairs. Showering is with cold water, a bucket, and a dipper. At the other end of the scale, in Phnom Penh, the 300-room Hotel Sofitel Cambodiana offers a pool, satellite TV, business center, five restaurants; prices range $150–200, double that for suites. Luxury hotels charge an extra 10 percent government tax and 10 percent service charge. Hotels offer discounts for groups and longer stays; prices also drop in the monsoon season.

LAOS

There is a chronic lack of hotel rooms in Laos. There are very few cheap guesthouses compared to Thailand, and very little in the way of luxury-standard hotels—only a handful in Vientiane and Luang Prabang would qualify. Most rooms fall in the $15–40 range—double the cost of similar accommodation in Thailand. Hotel rooms usually feature a fan and attached bathroom; air-conditioning and hot water are available only in better hotels. Mosquito nets are generally provided in areas with malaria—Vientiane is not considered a risk. Facilities can be basic—erratic electricity and blackouts—so bring a flashlight. Up-country, hotels may be in renovated (you hope) French villas or chalets. If you really get off the track and there aren't any hotels in town, you might be allowed to stay in a government guesthouse.

Vientiane has the largest selection of hotels in the country. High-end hotels such as the Lane Xang, Royal, Riverview, and Belvedere offer a range of creature comforts, with business centers, nightclubs, restaurants, and health and sports facilities. Rooms range $40–60; suites or apartments cost $80 and up. The Singapore-managed Belvedere hotel charges $120 for a double room and more than $150 for a suite.

Food

VIETNAM

In Vietnam in the 1970s and 1980s, a thousand years of Chinese and French-influenced culinary tradition went down the drain as austerity set in and restaurants came to be regarded as bourgeois indulgences. Some of the best chefs fled the country. The Vietnamese emulated the Soviet example of giving restaurants numbers, after the street address, thus avoiding all bourgeois pretension. So you might try Restaurant 66 in Hanoi (named after its location, 66 Bat Su Street). Thang Loi Hotel in Hanoi has a Restaurant A and a Restaurant B.

Happily, in the 1990s there was a remarkable return of gourmet Vietnamese food, and now in the 21st century, the selection is greater than ever, with key ingredients in much better supply. You can eat well; a good variety of Vietnamese, French, and Chinese cuisine exists in Saigon, Hanoi, Hué, and Hoi An. Seafood is found along the coast at Nha Trang, Vung Tau, and Bai Chay. Foreigners generally find the list of exotic and endangered species on some menus to be beyond the pale—dishes here include pangolin, python, gecko, and bat. Vegetarian food is widely available—especially in marketplaces—because Mahayana Buddhist monks in Vietnam are largely vegetarian.

A peculiar phenomenon in Vietnam—and also in major tourist centers of Cambodia and Laos—is that foreigners tend to congregate in restaurants that cater only to foreigners. This happens from high-end hotel restaurants right down to traveler cafés. While this may be a function of pricing (these restaurants tend to be out of reach for locals) or location (locals are unlikely to visit the hotel venues), the main explanation appears to be that foreigners distrust the hygiene standards of local restaurants—and tour operators will actually steer them right away from these because they fear foreigners will develop stomach problems.

Use your common sense and you will not have stomach problems when eating from street stalls. Hot food, such as soups for example, should be safe. You can mix with the locals and find far cheaper food in markets or at street stalls—a hearty meal with soups and other courses for under $2. Cafés are also a source of less expensive meals; they may really be restaurants, masquerading as cafés to avoid taxes. Budget restaurants can cost up to $5 a head; moderate restaurants, with a plusher setting, perhaps $5–10 a head; classy restaurants or those in some first-class hotels in major cities may cost $10 and up per person—a lot of money in Vietnam, where the average

VIETNAMESE CUISINE

by Naomi Duguid and Jeffrey Alford

Bread, yogurt, processed cheese, coffee, beer, and fruit: If worse comes to worst in Vietnam you can survive on these familiar foods—at least in the cities. But you'll be missing out on one of the world's finest cuisines. Granted, finding what you want to eat here is not always as straightforward as it is in Thailand or Malaysia; street foods and night markets are not nearly as elaborate or abundant, and restaurants can be confusing if you aren't familiar with Vietnamese food. But with a few helpful hints, finding great food needn't be a problem.

Regional Variations

Although a wide variety of foods is found all across the country, Vietnamese cuisine can be divided into three distinctive regional cuisines: southern, central, and northern. If you've eaten at Vietnamese restaurants outside Vietnam, you'll most likely have eaten southern-style food, with its wide variety of fresh herbs and complex tropical flavors. Food from the center tends to have more chile heat than that of the other regions; shrimp paste is also used extensively. As you move north, the food has more of a Chinese feel, with greater use of preserved vegetables, tree fungus, and dried mushrooms, and fewer fresh herbs and greens. There are more stir fries, and black pepper is used instead of chiles. People from the north will tell you southern food is flamboyant and unsubtle, while those from the south say northern food lacks taste and freshness. We find it all delicious.

Flexible Flavors

The final tastes in almost any Vietnamese meal, whether a simple market soup or an elaborate feast, are determined by choices made by you—the person eating. A table salad *(xalach dia)* of assorted fresh herbs, salad greens, and sprouts, and vinegared vegetables comes as an accompaniment to almost every meal, and there are always condiments on hand. One of the most pleasurable aspects of eating Vietnamese food is the act of sampling, altering, and enhancing your food as you eat.

Vietnamese soups exemplify the freshness, complex flavors, and flexible do-it-yourself aspect of Vietnamese cuisine. Large bowls of *pho* (hot soup) are a favorite breakfast in Vietnam, and they can also be found in stalls and restaurants later in the day. The soups are hearty and delicious. The Vietnamese are famous for their soup broths—filled with noodles, bean sprouts, sprigs of fresh herbs, and lean pieces of chicken, pork, or beef. You can garnish your soup with more fresh herbs or sprouts from the table salad, or with any of the many little sauces and condiments that may be set out.

Vietnamese dipping and flavoring sauces are varied and wonderful. The most common of these is known as *nuoc mam* or *nuoc cham*. It's a pale blend of salty, pungent fish sauce diluted with fresh lime juice and sometimes vinegar, spiced with garlic and chopped chiles, and sweetened with a touch of sugar. You can drizzle it over your rice, use it as a dip for spring rolls or grilled meats, or add a spoonful to your soup. Other dipping sauces include *nuoc leo*, a peanut sauce from the Hué region now widely found throughout the country; *tuong ot*, a red hot chile sauce similar to the Thai *sriracha*; and *mam tom*, a pungent shrimp sauce also from central Vietnam. One of our favorite condiments is a simple combination often served at soup stalls and restaurants: a pile of black pepper and a pile of salt placed side-by-side on a small dish and served with a wedge of lime. You squeeze a little lime juice into the dish and blend some salt and pepper with it to make a paste into which you dip bits of meat from your soup.

Roll Your Own

The other do-it-yourself element in many Vietnamese meals comes with roll-your-own rice-paper rolls. For example, grilled chunks of lemongrass beef *(thit bo nuong)*, grilled meatballs *(nem nuong)*, or freshly steamed shrimp *(tom)* all come served with a salad plate together with a stack of moist rice papers *(banh trang)* or

(continued on next page)

VIETNAMESE CUISINE (cont'd)

fresh rice wrappers *(banh uot)*. You lay a wrapper on your open palm, put in a piece or two of meat, several strips of pickled radish, perhaps some herbs, sprouts, or rice vermicelli, and then tuck over the ends and roll it up. You now have your own unique fresh spring roll that can be dipped in *nuoc cham* or *nuoc leo,* or eaten simply on its own.

Street and Market Foods

Travelers in Vietnam sometimes complain about not getting enough to eat and of always being hungry. Vietnamese food is relatively low in fats and oils; visitors accustomed to a diet high in dairy and meat, and who may not be accustomed to eating large quantities of carbohydrates, frequently find themselves hungry simply because they're not eating enough food to maintain their normal caloric intake. One way of avoiding this "starving feeling" is to start the day with a big breakfast, and then to snack on bread and sandwiches available from street vendors frequently throughout the day. You'll also find, especially in the south, stalls selling fresh fruit—depending on the place and season, slices of fresh papaya, pineapple, or ripe jackfruit.

For breakfast, head to any neighborhood market. Generally, in the center of the market you'll find many vendors side by side, all selling hearty soups and other hot foods such as rice with curries *(cari)*. Market food is at its best, and offers the greatest selection, in the morning before the day gets hot. If you're looking for something special—say, *bun bo Hué*—simply ask someone. If it can be found nearby or in the market, people will tell you where to go. Vendors tend to specialize in one or two dishes; most street stalls and even restaurants are not set up to prepare a range of different dishes.

While breakfast in the south and north is generally soup, in rural areas it can be *xoi*—sticky rice steamed in a leaf wrapper. Often peanuts or mung beans are steamed with the rice. *Xoi* is not only healthy and delicious but also makes a great portable breakfast.

Some stalls in large markets are signposted

Com Chay, which means vegetarian. Here you can find a variety of tasty and creative dishes, centered around tofu or mushrooms.

To keep up your fluid intake—essential in the heat—you will find that bottled water is available in the cities. In hotels and guesthouses, a thermos of boiled water is usually provided. In the south, look for freshly pressed sugarcane juice available from vendors on the main streets in the afternoon and evening. Vietnamese beer is good; try Saigon Beer or 333. Vietnam grows its own tea in the region around Dalat. Tea is consumed morning to night; it's served before or after but never during a meal. For another caffeine hit, try Vietnamese coffee black and hot or iced with condensed milk, *gafe suda*—our favorite. The coffee is made in individual slow-drip filters and can be very strong.

In the late afternoon and evening, the least expensive and most entertaining food option is to go out for street food. Check out the main streets or small side streets in the center of town; there are always vendors, usually with a single specialty. You'll see a small wooden stand with a few stools and several tables set out on the sidewalk. In Hanoi and the north generally, there are fewer street stalls, but you can still find small restaurants open to the street doing a roaring trade selling soups and stir fries.

Restaurant Specialties

In addition to trying street food, you'll want to experience restaurant food. If you're in the southern part of the country and looking for a treat, head for a Bo Bay Mon or "Beef Seven Ways" restaurant. You can order just one or two dishes or go for the entire feast. Beef dishes include beef fondue *(bo nhung dam),* grilled beef-stuffed leaves *(bo la lot),* beef pâté steamed in banana leaves *(cha dum),* and beef rice soup *(chao thit bo).* Another restaurant specialty, often eaten for lunch in the south, is *banh xeo,* a kind of crepe filled with finely chopped vegetables and meat. In central Vietnam this is called *banh khoai* and looks like a cross between an omelette and a crepe. In the northern cities you'll find restaurants that have their menus posted outside, French-style, making them easy to spot for lunch or supper. Confirm prices before ordering.

We find that one of the best ways to make the most of your trip is to come with a good Vietnamese cookbook. Not only is a cookbook an excellent source of names of dishes and ingredients, it can also provide valuable insights into culture and daily life. We particularly recommend Binh Duong and Marsha Kiesel's *Simple Art of Vietnamese Cooking* and Bach Ngo and Gloria Zimmerman's *The Classic Cuisine of Vietnam*. Nicole Routhier's *The Foods of Vietnam* is also very good.

Common Street and Market Foods
Pho bo Hanoi (Hanoi soup) is a substantial beef and rice-noodle soup available in street stalls for breakfast and in some specialty restaurants all over the country.

Bun bo Hué (beef noodle soup Hué-style) is a substantial, meaty, meal-in-one noodle soup flavored with shrimp paste and a little chile heat. Found in street stalls in Hué and nearby towns in the center.

Hu tieu (Saigon soup) consists of noodles with chicken and/or pork and vegetables, either bathed in broth or served with broth on the side in a separate bowl. A satisfying meal-in-one available in some restaurants, as well as at markets and street stalls in the south.

Pho ga (Hanoi chicken soup) and **mien ga** (chicken soup with cellophane noodles) are comforting and sustaining meals-in-one. Hanoi soup is available in restaurants in Saigon and in markets and street stalls in the north, while *mien ga* is found in the south and the center.

Bo vien (beef balls) are small, slightly chewy beef meatballs served floating in a clear aromatic broth, sometimes with added rice noodles and fresh herbs. Most easily found in Saigon and Nha Trang, though available all over. Sold by street vendors, at stalls and markets, and in restaurants.

Nem nuong (grilled meatballs) are small pork meatballs, lightly spiced and grilled. Sold in street stalls, markets, and restaurants; try eating them in bread.

Cha gio (fried spring rolls) are made of rice papers wrapped around finely chopped pork, assorted vegetables, and cellophane noodles, then deep fried; served with a plate of fresh greens and dipping sauce. These snack foods are sold in markets and street stalls all over the country.

Common Vietnamese Food Words
Some food words in Vietnamese derive from French: *gato* (cake, from *gateau*), *gafe* (from *cafe*), *phomai* (cheese, from *fromage*), *biftek* (beefsteak), "*mlet* (omelette), and *xocola* (chocolate).

bun—noodles
pho—soup
cuon—salad or lettuce
goi cuon—fresh spring rolls
gao—uncooked rice
gao nep—sweet glutinous rice
com—cooked rice
ot—chiles
gung—ginger
nuoc—sauce, liquid
nuoc mam—fish sauce
thit—meat, often meaning pork
thit heo—pork
thit bo—beef
bo—beef
ga—chicken
cha—pâté
tom—shrimp
muc—squid
nuong—grilled

Jeffrey Alford and Naomi Duguid are Toronto-based travelers, writers, and photographers with a special interest in food. They are authors of two travel-story–laced cookbooks: Flatbreads and Flavors: A Baker's Atlas *(William Morrow, 1995) and* Seductions of Rice *(Artisan, 1998). They followed this up with another book,* Hot Sour Salty Sweet *(Random House, 2000), about the pleasures of eating in the Mekong region, from Yunnan to the Mekong Delta.*

daily wage is around $1. Western-style food will require Western bills. It's tastier and less expensive to keep to Vietnamese fare. So dig in—*Chuc an ngon!* (Good appetite!)

The Sandwich Bar

Banh mi (sandwiches) are made to order from delicious French-style baguettes and usually include pickled strips of white radish and carrot. You can choose a selection of pâtés and cured meats. You may want to avoid mayonnaise as a health precaution. Baguettes made from rice flour are sold in street stalls from Haiphong to the Mekong Delta from midmorning until after sunset; when there's a choice, go for the vendor who heats the bread on a grill before assembling the sandwich. You'll see a small charcoal brazier by the side of the stall or under the sandwich cart. Don't buy bread in the afternoon; by then it's really only useful as a hard-edged weapon.

To go with your bread, pâté or cheese? The pâté is homemade, the consistency of Spam, and wrapped in banana-leaf. As long as it's not too old, it's OK. Spam-pâté is usually made from pork. Cheese is usually processed in boxed segments; try either the Laughing Cow variety (La Vache Qui Rit or Vache Jolie) or the sterner nonlaughing cow (Nouvelle Vache). Palatable but poor quality. There's a cake shop in Hanoi that makes cheese similar in taste to feta. Another topping is jam—a French transplant. Varieties include papaya and pineapple.

Which came first: the duck or the egg? In Hanoi you can have both at once. The duck egg is incubated to a critical moment and then boiled, which results in a soft crunchy duck emerging from the egg. Not for the fainthearted, this dish is called *trung vit lon*, but get some coaching lessons on the correct tones as this collection of words can also refer to something quite rude.

Exotic Fruit

Vietnam offers a profusion of tropical fruit, especially in the Mekong Delta. These exotic specimens will tickle your taste buds, quench your thirst, or at the very least arouse your curiosity. Among the rarer and more exotic are dragonfruit *(thanh long)*, found in the Nha Trang area, and water coconut *(dua nuoc)* and a three-segment coconut *(thot lot)* from the Mekong Delta. Juice bars in the south turn out concoctions with crushed ice and sweetened condensed milk and other murky mixtures. Fruit is also used to make a variety of jams and jellies. You can also get exotic items such as custard apple ice cream in Saigon. Fruit is seasonal, and offerings vary from north to south.

Durian *(sau rieng)* is a round, greenish fruit studded with sharp spikes. It's the size of a football, can weigh up to 14 kilograms, and is available only in the summer in the south. Broken open with a sharp knife, it reveals white podlike sections that have the texture of a very ripe French camembert, which is why the fruit is nicknamed "the cheese that grows on trees." Despite its awful smell, durian has an exotic taste, described by 19th-century naturalist Alfred Russel Wallace thus: "A rich butter-like custard highly flavoured with almonds gives the best general idea of it, but intermingled with it come wafts of flavour that call to mind cream cheese, onion sauce, brown sherry, and other incongruities." In Asia, the smooth and highly nutritious flesh of the durian is reputed to be an aphrodisiac.

Also in the football-sized league is the jackfruit *(mit),* a cousin of the durian. Jackfruit is bright yellow and very sweet and crisp with a sweet fragrance. The large hard seeds can be steamed, shelled, and eaten. Jackfruit can grow to monstrous proportions, with some specimens weighing in at 40 kilograms. As the fruit ripens, the skin turns from green to brown, and is covered with blunt spines. The tender fruit is either eaten raw or cooked in various sweet and savory dishes.

Rambutan *(chom chom)* has hairy reddish spines surrounding a translucent fruit that tastes like lychee. Similar-tasting, but with a smooth exterior skin, is the smaller longan *(trai nhan).* Mangosteen *(mang cut)* has a leathery maroon husk with soft, delicious white flesh inside. The taste reminds Westerners alternately of cream, lemonade, and fragrant apple. When eating this fruit, avoid the large seed in the center, which can be bitter if bitten. Also watch out for mangosteen juice, which stains.

Some fruit is used in salads or for other purposes. A fresh young coconut is often cut in half and the flesh scooped out with a spoon—ice cream and candied fruit can then be served in the shell along with the coconut flesh. Star fruit *(trai khe)* is used in salads and juices; you'll know the cool, watery fruit inside is ripe when the waxy skin turns from green to deep yellow. Star fruit is also known as the star apple, or carambola.

A bit more familiar in taste for Westerners is the pomelo *(buoi)*, a relative of the grapefruit and tasting similar, though it has a huge, husky exterior. Watch out for the translucent segment skin, which can be very bitter. Uglifruit *(cam sanh)* is a grapefruit-tangerine hybrid, with dark green or mottled skin. It is often used for orange juice that is guzzled in Saigon. The persimmon *(hong)* looks like a tomato but has a stretched bright orange glossy skin. Inside, the fruit offers a smooth firm flesh.

The Java apple *(man)*, also known as rose apple, is bright red, pale pink, or greenish, and has a sweet-and-sour acquired taste. The tiny Vietnamese apple is extremely sour; a bite will bring tears to your eyes, though it doesn't appear to have much effect on the locals who happily munch away. Locals in the south also feed on tamarind, a beanlike fruit with a brittle skin, and pods that will make you pucker like you've never puckered before. The flesh is used to flavor curries and also used for cleaning brass.

Quite unlike any apple you've seen before—or are likely to see again—is the custard apple *(mang cau)*, a round fruit with a scaly, bumpy, green exterior. It looks like something from the Twilight Zone. Inside lies a white heart with black buttonlike seeds. Custard apple is excellent in fruit juices with a dash of orange juice. Pureed custard apple, watered down and pepped up with a little lime or orange juice, makes an exotic milkshake. In the same fruit family, with a similar taste but an entirely different appearance, is the spiny soursop *(mang cau xiem)*, a longish fruit with a thin skin that has rows of dark green curved spines. The white pulp offers a delicious sour-sweet flavor.

Most exotic of all is dragonfruit *(thanh long)*, so named because it grows on a creeping cactuslike plant said to resemble a green dragon. The fruit is oval-shaped, about the size of a small pineapple, magenta in color, with a smooth skin sprouting green petals. Inside, the pulpy and translucent white flesh is scattered with thousands of black crunchy seeds. The succulent flesh is an excellent thirst-quencher. The fruit is grown mostly in arid parts of Binh Dinh province around Qui Nhon, and is in great demand, with exports to Hong Kong, Taiwan, and China. Dragonfruit is in season May–September.

Café Drinks

Cafés are the ideal place to find snacks, and, with the dearth of nightlife in Vietnam, also function as gathering places. Drinks are cheap if you stick to Vietnamese fare. An imported Coke could cost $.75; a whole young coconut will cost you $.10 or $.20. Vendors cut the top off a young coconut and provide a straw. After you drink a young coconut, give it back to the waiter and he'll hack it open for you and provide a spoon to scrape out the flesh. Some vendors serve coconut milk with the fleshy bits floating in it. Coconut milk is safe to drink while still fresh in the shell; it may be a different story if transferred to a glass with ice added. Fresh fruit juice is another thirst-quencher, but untreated water may be added, or suspect ice. Bottled water is widely available and of decent quality—make sure it's sealed when you buy it.

Mainstream drinks are tea and coffee. Often, upon entering a house you may be offered green tea—a Chinese-derived habit. In cafés, you can also order black tea with lemon. Most Vietnamese prefer to drink tea, but in the cities you can easily find coffee. The coffee plant was introduced to Vietnam in the 19th century under the French. The most sought-after beans are robusta, grown in Dak Lak province, and arabica, grown in Lam Dong. Filter kits are provided to the caffeine-addicted in cafés. The

KHMER CUISINE

by Jeffrey Alford and Naomi Duguid

Khmer food is a close cousin of Thai and southern Vietnamese food but it is distinct. In Phnom Penh and Siem Reap, you will find French restaurants and a lot of Thai and Vietnamese dishes and influence—sometimes more easily than you can find Khmer food.

Traditionally, the Khmer eat two meals a day—at midmorning and in the late afternoon. As in Thailand or Vietnam, "food" is rice. Before the war and devastation of the 1970s began, Cambodia was famous throughout Southeast Asia for the quality of its rice, which resembles the aromatic jasmine rice that is the staple in much of Thailand. Depending on people's wealth and on what is available, the rice is eaten with a currylike soup-stew (called *somla*) of vegetables and fish or meat, as well as perhaps a stir-fry or a grill.

Flavorings in Khmer food begin with fish sauce (as in Thailand and Vietnam), here called *tuk trey,* though in the countryside a fermented fish paste called *prahok* may be used. Fish sauce provides flavor (a salty, slightly smoky taste) and nutrition and is the essential ingredient in most dishes. Khmer fish sauce is generally milder than Vietnamese fish sauce. Apart from its use in the kitchen it is usually served at the table, often in a small dish with several small chiles floating in it, to be used as a condiment as you are eating.

After fish sauce, the next most common flavoring is lemongrass. It is boiled to flavor soup broths or minced and used in curry pastes and marinades, giving a lemony aroma and a very agreeable tangy sharp taste. Another frequent flavoring, also on the sour side, is tamarind, extracted as a paste from the fruit of the tamarind tree.

Like central Thais, Khmer cooks have been influenced by Indian ingredients and also by the wide range of flavorings that grow in their fertile land. Curry pastes are prepared used galingasl (a rhizome that is a cousin to ginger), ginger, and chiles, though the food is less chile-hot than some Thai dishes. As in Vietnam, aromatic herbs play an important role, either as garnishes to dishes, or as cooked ingredients. Herbs used include Asian basil, holy basil, sawtooth herb, and scallions. Sauces are often topped or blended with chopped roasted peanuts.

On the street, one of the best deals in town is often the rice soup, known generically as congee in English and in Khmer as *bahbah*. Soup vendors set up from noontime on: You'll recognize them by the large pots of broth and rice they have boiling on small braziers. You can custom-order your rice soup, asking the vendor to omit extra meat or to add more herbs while assembling your bowl.

The other great street food, available especially in the cities, is a Khmer adaptation of a French legacy, the baguette. In Vietnam, the baguette has become breakfast food as well as the base for sandwiches. In Cambodia there are also baguette sandwiches, but differently presented. Instead of assembling a whole sandwich, a Khmer vendor will serve you two halves of a

waiter brings an individual filter cup containing a few teaspoonfuls of coffee grains; this sits over the regular cup and you wait about 10–15 minutes for piping-hot water to filter through. A variation of this is called French press. This method mixes coarsely ground coffee and just-off-the-boil water for a few minutes, after which the wire mesh filter is plunged through the brew to trap the grounds at the bottom of the pot. The Vietnamese add butter to their coffee to counter the bitter flavor, and some Hanoi cafés serve yolk-cream coffee—egg yolk mixed with sugar and butter. A large dollop of sweetened condensed milk is an ingredient in *caphe suda,* or iced coffee.

Imported wine is expensive in Vietnam, so try the local wines. Dalat mulberry wine looks and tastes like port; Sapa wine tastes like a plum wine. The local firewater is rice wine. You may find some imported Eastern Bloc bottles of champagne on the dusty shelves of a café—good for bathing in, but not much else. Beers are cheap and safe to drink. Brasseries et Glacières d'Indochine (BGI) is

small baguette lightly toasted and then rubbed with fresh garlic or perhaps some mayonnaise or butter or a smooth meat paste; you say what you want or don't want. Beside the bread on the plate will be slices of delicious pâté or sausage. In a small bowl there will be a little shredded pickled carrot or white radish, and on another small plate you will be given fresh herbs and perhaps some sliced cucumber, short lengths of scallion, and a wedge or two of green tomato (preferred to the red tomatoes by the Khmer). You can either assemble a sandwich, or eat the bread in one hand and spear the pieces of pâté or sausage with a small fork. Condiments on the table will almost always include Maggi sauce, *tuk trey* (Khmer fish sauce), soy sauce, and chile paste, so you can flavor your food as you wish.

In the markets you'll come on vendors selling single specialties: little grilled Vietnamese-style breads; or round rice noodles known as *khao phoun* or *banh soong*—topped with coconut milk, chopped peanuts, bits of barbecued pork, chopped herbs, and a sprinkling of sugar; or variants of the Vietnamese noodle soups *(pho)*. You can make a light and tasty meal of any of these noodle dishes and finish with some fresh fruit.

In the evening in Phnom Penh you may find small restaurants serving a form of hot pot, Khmer-style. This is a meal best eaten in company—with at least one other person and ideally in a group of four. Patrons sit at low tables and are served a steaming pot of broth placed over a small charcoal brazier. You order your remaining ingredients separately: thinly sliced beef, an

assortment of fresh herbs, a plate of mushrooms, a pile of greens, some thin pork skin, an egg or two, and some soft yellow noodles. To eat, you add the herbs and greens to the broth and then dip the beef in briefly to cook it lightly. Toss in several mushrooms at a time to cook. The eggs can be broken and then stirred into the soup too. Any ingredient that you fish out of the broth can be dipped in a flavorful sauce (fish sauce blended with chile paste) or eaten straight, as you wish. This seems to be a great meal for Khmer guys out to drink and eat and talk together, so the restaurant (or sidewalk) can get very noisy and congenial as the evening wears on.

Often in the same restaurant you can instead eat in a grill-it-yourself arrangement. A small charcoal grill is set up on your table and then you and your dining companions grill slices or skewers of meat and fish. Several dipping sauces come with, so you can check out an array of flavors. Again, this is congenial drinking food, often served to a group of men out for an evening, and usually accompanied by beer or whisky.

If you're eating in someone's home or in a good Khmer restaurant, the meal will include a *somla* (soupy stew) and maybe also *amok*, an aromatic fish curry steamed in a banana leaf, or perhaps a grilled fish. You may be also served a Khmer salad, which resembles the salads called *yam* in Thailand. In restaurants one of the most widely served (and delicious) of these is a beef and vegetable salad (often made with water buffalo), dressed with lemongrass and flavored with fish sauce, mint leaves, and coriander leaf.

a company that brewed in French colonial times, and it is back again, this time with local partner Tien Giang. BGI has breweries in Saigon, Mytho, and Danang. Huda, from Hué, is a joint-venture Danish beer; Vinagen is Canadian; Halida is a joint venture with Carlsberg; Tiger Beer comes from Singapore. Popular local brands include 333 and Saigon Export. On the streets, the locals make their own brew, called *bia hoi,* literally meaning "fresh beer." It's siphoned from a curbside keg and costs a pittance.

CAMBODIA

Cambodian staples are rice, fish, and bread. A typical Cambodian meal consists of fried or steamed rice mixed with pieces of salted, dried, or cooked fish, seasoned with chiles or garlic. Soup accompanies the meal. Popular dishes include *an sam chruk,* a roll of sticky rice filled with soybean cake and chopped pork, and *khao phoun,* a noodle dish with a coconut sauce. Freshwater fish comes from Lake Tonle Sap; seafood is also found in the Gulf of Thailand at Sihanoukville. Fish comes grilled *(trey aing)*, steamed whole *(trey chorm hoy)*, or fried with vegetables *(trey chean neung spey)*. *Somla machou banle* is sour fish soup; *somla machou bangkang* is spicy prawn soup. Special dishes include *amok*, which is fish in coconut, wrapped in a banana leaf. In former times, royal Cambodian cuisine was developed in the service of the king; there are some chefs in Cambodia who have mastered this culinary art—but restaurants serving this kind of food are rare.

Cheaper selections of food are mainly found in and around the central market in each town. Food stalls abound in these areas, selling fresh fruit and other fare. Up-country there's not much in the way of restaurants, although the selection in Siem Reap and Sihanoukville is reasonable. In Phnom Penh a large number of restaurants sprang up to cater to the U.N. trade. The restaurant variety includes French, Thai, Vietnamese, Chinese, and Western. Fresh baguettes are sold in Phnom Penh, a legacy from colonial days and a habit not even the Khmer Rouge could eradicate.

Food generally costs $2–3 for a simple meal and $5–10 per person for a restaurant meal. Larger hotels in Phnom Penh charge upscale prices. For drinks, stick to tea or coffee, beer, and imported soft drinks. Angkor Beer is the national brew. Bottled water is widely available in Phnom Penh and Siem Reap.

Restaurants and hotel bars often offer nightlife, particularly in small towns. There is a group of bars patronized by foreigners in Phnom Penh, but the city is not safe by night, and armed holdups have been reported.

LAOS

Lao food shares a lot in common with Thai (Issan) food, and selections verge on the hot and spicy (sour). Lao people also eat a lot of less-spicy Chinese food. Vietnamese food is found in Vientiane and a few other cities. In the larger towns, French cuisine is widely available, with fresh baguettes, Lao-style pâté, croissants, and Lao coffee available at street stalls and small cafés. Restaurants serve pricey dishes, includ-

ing steak and filet mignon. Cheaper selections of food are mainly found in and around the central market in each town; food stalls abound in these areas. More formal restaurants are small affairs, often a family-run shop front. In larger places such as Vientiane or Luang Prabang, hotel restaurants serve tasty fare.

For Lao cuisine, rice is the staple—either glutinous sticky rice, served in small lidded baskets and eaten with the hand, or plain white rice, eaten with a spoon (often Thai jasmine rice). Sticky rice is often rolled into a ball and dipped into various dishes. When eating Lao food it's common to share dishes—each party orders one dish, so portions are usually large. Lao dishes are cooked with fresh ingredients, using vegetables, freshwater fish, duck, beef, pork, and chicken. Spicing is tangy, using lemongrass, chiles, ginger, tamarind, coriander, lemon juice, and aromatic herbs such as marijuana. Beware of dishes with raw or undercooked freshwater fish or derivatives, as these may promote liver flukes. Particularly avoid *paddek,* made of chunks of fermented freshwater fish, and *nam paddek,* a sauce from fermented fish. The risk is higher in rural areas.

Dessert dishes include grilled bananas and sticky rice with coconut milk and black beans.

A common Lao dish is *larp,* made of minced meat, chicken, fish, or vegetables tossed with garlic, chiles, green onions, and lime juice. It's served with rice on a plate of lettuce, mint, and steamed mango leaves, and eaten by wrapping a little *larp* in the lettuce. The dish is served cold, but watch out for the hidden heat in the spicing.

Tam som is a green papaya salad made by pounding shredded green papaya and adding lime juice, chiles, garlic, and other ingredients in a mortar. At a street-side stall, the preparation involves customer participation. One of the great beauties of *tam som* is that it tastes fine without any chiles at all, so specify this as the salad is pounded in front of you at a market. *Pho* is a Lao version of Chinese noodle soup, often served with a garnish of lettuce, mint, bean sprouts, lime, and basil. Ingredients are added to the soup as desired.

Bottled water is widely available in Laos. Coffee grown on the Bolovens Plateau provides an excellent brew; it is usually served with sweetened condensed milk unless you specify otherwise. Imported soft drinks and beer are widely available. The Lao Brewery Company in Vientiane produces Beerlao (labeled Bière Larue), which is a good value; draft beer from plastic pitchers is also available in Vientiane. The local firewater is *lao lao,* a rice whiskey made from fermented sticky rice. It's usually served on ice with lime and soda or cola.

Visas and Officialdom

VIETNAM

The Vietnamese love red tape. There's so much paperwork you could wear the stuff. Make sure yours is in good shape. The more chops and seals and stamps you accumulate, the better you'll look. Carry a few extra passport photos in your wallet; you never know when you'll need them. You need documents for hotel registration, to change money, and to rent bicycles, motorcycles, or cars.

Where possible, do not hand over originals in Vietnam. Carry copies of absolutely everything, and use the copies in day-to-day transactions. Hotels will repeatedly ask for your passport, paper visa, entry card, and so on. Some even insist on seeing your customs form. Get all the material together and copy it onto double-sided pages; hand those out to hotel staff. You can also photocopy a typical hotel registration form instead of filling it in each time; just hand over a photocopy of the completed form.

In some cases you may be parted from your original documents. If, for example, you leave your passport for an extension in Hanoi, it could take three days. During this time, you may wish to travel to Halong Bay. In this case, you have to get a note from a travel agent, in English and Vietnamese, saying the agent is holding the passport for the purpose of extension. Carry photocopies of the initial pages of the passport with you. Be aware you'll have great trouble cashing traveler's checks without an original passport. Bureaucratic games in Vietnam are legendary: Hanoi stands out in this department.

Visa Types

In 1995 the Vietnamese government announced that one-month tourist visas would no longer be renewed within Vietnam. This policy has never been rigorously enforced, and it does not apply to those on business, journalist, or diplomatic visas, or to overseas Vietnamese. Even in Hanoi you can get a one-month extension for around $30. But the 1995 regulation promises hassles with visa extensions, so if you are planning to stay longer than a month in Vietnam, you might look into issue of a longer-term visa from, say, Hong Kong, or issue of a multiple-entry visa. The other alternative for staying longer in Vietnam is to exit from Saigon to Phnom Penh and pick up a new visa there for another month.

Vietnamese visas are complicated. You generally must use the visa within three months from the time of application. Unlike most visas that are stamped when you actually arrive, the Vietnamese visa specifies a fixed starting date when issued. You cannot arrive before this date; if you arrive later, you lose time on your visa. Visas are usually valid for a period of one month; extensions of 2–4 weeks are possible once in Vietnam. Individual visa applications are faxed to a "sponsoring agency" in Vietnam, which turns out to be Vietnam Tourism or some other government organ. This information is encoded at the top of your visa, next to the handwritten visa number.

The Vietnamese visa may be either stamped directly in your passport or issued on paper. If it's available, a paper visa is preferable. For a paper visa, you don't have to submit an original passport—just a photocopy of initial passport pages. On a paper visa (or in passport) request that when it says "Enter From" or "Exit From" that you are requesting an open entry at any frontier point. *Cac cua khau quoc te* (all land, sea, and air border points) is how this is written in Vietnamese on the visa. Otherwise, the issuer might try and restrict it to Hanoi (Noi Bai Airport) or Thanh Pho Ho Chi Minh (Tan Son Nhat Airport, Saigon), which is not to your advantage. Once you're in Vietnam, there's little restriction on your movements. Only a few sensitive border regions and ethnic areas require internal travel permits.

The **tourist visa** is usually single entry and valid one month. Single-entry and transit visas cost $25 (extensions $10); a multiple-entry visa costs $40–100 (extensions $16). These are basic prices; a visa costs double or triple that when obtained through a travel agent. On visa applications, be vague about things such as your profession or contacts in Vietnam. Answers such as "dedicated missionary" or "photojournalist" will cause indefinite delays.

Valid 3–6 months, the **business visa** may allow for multiple entry. Business visas cost $45–160 and up; extensions may cost more than $100. For this visa you must present an invitation letter from a Vietnamese company recognized by the Vietnamese government as a bona fide business with international trading capabilities. Some business-class hotels in Saigon can broker business visas, as can some travel agents in Hong Kong or Bangkok.

Visiting diplomats, journalists, or those visiting family in Vietnam require **special visas.** Start paperwork well in advance: The process could take several months to finalize. Journalists are expected to be escorted by an assigned Vietnamese guide—an expensive venture.

Visa Issue

Allow 2–4 weeks for processing of the visa from your home base; turnaround time is faster if a courier service is involved. The relevant embassy must fax Hanoi for approval, and this takes time. Your visa can be arranged through an agent or visa-handling service. Costs vary $25–120 for a visa via an agent; fast visas can cost up to $170; business visas or multiple entries can be more than $200. In Paris, two travelers got a visa valid for a five-month stay and a

specified entry date; visas are readily obtainable in London. In Hamburg, applications can be made through Saigon Tourist, Hamburgerstr. 132, 200 Hamburg 176; in Paris, through Vietnam Tourism, 4 Rue Cherubini, 75002 Paris. In North America numerous agents can arrange Vietnamese visas through embassies in Ottawa (Canada), Los Angeles (United States), or Mexico City. The Vietnamese Embassy in Washington, D.C., can arrange to have a 30-day visa issued within a week if you enclose a priority-mail envelope. Cost is $65. In Australia, visas are processed through the Vietnamese embassy in Canberra.

There are a number of points in Asia where you can obtain Vietnamese visas directly from the embassy in about four days: Singapore ($100) and Phnom Penh ($70). In Beijing, a one-month Vietnamese visa takes a week to get, costs $60, and is good for land crossing into Vietnam. The easiest places to obtain visas are in Bangkok or Hong Kong with only a four- to five-day turnaround time (faster if you're willing to pay through the nose). Regulations in Hong Kong and Bangkok chop and change. Sometimes paper visas are issued, sometimes the visa is stamped in the passport; sometimes it takes three days to obtain, sometimes five.

In Hong Kong, a standard visa through an agent costs $55 and takes an average of four working days to obtain. For $100 you can receive your Vietnamese visa in 24 hours; for $150 you can secure a multiple-entry three-month visa. Delays are sometimes deliberately created by the embassy maintaining that a fax has not arrived when in fact it has—in order to power trip and show the agent why it's necessary to "pay dues." (For more information on Hong Kong and Bangkok agents, see the *Getting There* section in the *Know Vietnam, Cambodia, and Laos* chapter.)

In Bangkok, a visa costs $48 (1,200 baht) and takes 4–7 working days; you can go through an agent or apply to the embassy yourself. For a visa to return in less than four working days, add $20. The embassy must fax the sponsor agency in Vietnam—your visa can be delayed if the fax is not returned or if the embassy claims it hasn't been received. One traveler preordered a visa from a Bangkok agent who forgot to get it. The agent made amends by obtaining the visa the same day.

Visa on Arrival: With prior arrangement through an agent and at least a one-week notice, a Vietnamese visa can be issued at Tan Son Nhat Airport, Saigon. You must show officials at the airport a letter of sponsorship indicating your visa is waiting. Some hardy souls have arrived at Tan Son Nhat Airport without a valid Vietnamese visa. Experiences with this vary. On a group tour, some travelers were immediately granted visas, and thus proceeded on their merry way. For individuals the story is a bit different: One lone traveler, after reciting a sob story about meeting friends, was fined $80 on arrival, placed under house arrest at expensive Tan Son Nhat Transit Hotel for several days, then bingo, received a 20-day visa. It wound up costing him a bundle, after the fine, hotel bills, and eventual visa. Moral of the story: It's better to wait four days in Bangkok or elsewhere and get your paperwork in order there.

Border Games

In the interests of fund-raising, Vietnamese border police are fond of playing mind games with travelers, gauging how much the foreigner will cough up if threatened. Borders notorious for this are Lao Bao, Lao Cai, and Moc Bai. Make sure your paperwork is border-proof. Do not reveal that you have cash U.S. dollars on your person—a payment demanded might not work with traveler's checks. Other forms of "payment," such as cigarettes (the pack or the entire carton), may expedite matters here—and won't drain your pockets.

Arrival and Departure Paperwork
Registration
When you enter the country, officials at the port of arrival will stamp your visa, then register you. In Saigon and Hanoi you must fill out laborious forms at the airport that look like a visa application all over again. You even need a passport photo for the form. At land borders, officials simply record the information in a logbook.

Entry/Exit Card
The seemingly unimportant entry/exit card you hurriedly fill out upon arrival can come back to haunt you. First, don't lose it! It can be important if you plan on leaving through land borders or obtaining a visa extension. Not having this piece of paper upon exit can create major hassles.

If you apply for a visa extension, officials often look at the box on this card listing where you plan to stay. If you put down someone's residence, chances are the visa may not be renewed. If you're applying in Danang and put down a hotel in Saigon, you're sometimes required to return to Saigon to receive the extension. Several travelers who wrote the name of an actual hotel in Saigon were told to go there and get their "license number" before applying for an extension. Solution to all this rigmarole? Write "unknown" in the appropriate box and there seems to be no problem.

Customs Declaration
The tricky box here requires specifying currencies, precious metals, and credit cards. If you put specific amounts of currency in that box, a customs officer may ask to see the color of your money; if there's a discrepancy, the officer may confiscate the difference—this has happened at land borders. A vague "traveler's checks, credit card" may suffice. Technically, you don't have to declare amounts of money under $3,000. Customs officers are touchy about the import of blank or recorded video tapes: Some foreigners have had these seized upon entry. Incoming travelers may also be required to submit any books and CDs they're carrying to review by a "cultural section"—on the lookout for content deemed to be dangerous to the nation's morality. There is no restriction on the number of rolls of film you may bring in.

Visa Extensions
Visa extensions for tourist visas—usually for 2–4 weeks—cost $15–25 and may be issued on the spot or the same day. An exception is Hanoi, where extensions could take three days or longer. Applying for visa extensions is erratic;

sometimes it works, sometimes not, depending on where you apply and also on the particular chief at the office. Most places, you can apply directly for the extension yourself. In Saigon or Hanoi, because of the volume of applications, it's best to go through an agent.

A sampling of waits and costs around the country: Saigon, two days, $20–25; Hué, five minutes, $20; Vung Tau, two hours, $20; Danang, one day, $15; Nha Trang, one day, $20–25; Hanoi, minimum three working days, sometimes five, $15–25. Travelers have reported trouble in Hanoi. After asking for a one-month extension, they were given only 10, 14, or 20 days; these extensions should have been cheaper, say $10–15 for a two-week extension. Some travelers were refused extensions altogether and told to leave the country within two days; they had to scramble for a flight to Vientiane.

The maximum number of extensions appeared to be two. Some travelers have managed to extend their initial visas for a total stay of three months. A second extension is more expensive—around $35. You are generally not permitted to apply for an extension unless you're within a week of expiration of the visa. If planning to stay longer, insist on a one-month extension the first time, or go elsewhere. Two extensions of two weeks each appear to be OK, but that might cost you $30; it's better to get one extension of one month for $20. Sometimes the visa is stamped, "No more extensions." Extension of business visas is possible and will most likely cost more than $100 through an agent.

Reentry Stamp

If you wish to return to Vietnam after crossing over to a neighboring country, you need either a new visa or a reentry stamp on your existing visa. A reentry stamp effectively turns a single-entry Vietnamese visa into a multiple-entry one. In Saigon, a reentry visa can be arranged through an agent at the same time as you apply for a Cambodian visa.

Internal Travel Permits

Before 1993, foreigners needed permits to go

anywhere. In 1993, that system was scrapped and the previously off-limits Central Highlands plus the area north of Hanoi were flung open without permit. Very few places now require permits: minority areas such as Lat village near Dalat, a few villages near the Lao border out of Buon Ma Thuot, and Kontum or Khe Sanh, and far north border areas past Hagiang. Certain water routes in the Mekong Delta may be sensitive. Permits usually cost around $5 per person.

Vietnamese Embassies
Within Asia

Some of the following embassies, such as those in Hong Kong, Cambodia, and Laos, cannot be approached directly except for diplomatic visas or business visas with invitation. Vietnamese embassies are best approached through travel agents. An exception is in Thailand, where you can apply for the visa yourself. But this will take just as long, if not longer, than having an agent procure the visa.

Cambodia: Monivong Boulevard (Achar Mean) at 436 Street, Phnom Penh, tel. 23/25481
China: 32 Guanghua Lu, Jianguomenwai, Beijing, tel. 532-1125; there is also a consulate in Kunming (2nd floor, Kai Wah International Hotel, 157 Beijing Rd., tel: 86-871/352-2669)
Hong Kong: 15F Great Smart Tower, 230 Wan Chai Rd., Wan Chai, tel. 2591-4510 (Consulate General)
Indonesia: 25 Jalan Teuku Umar, Jakarta, tel. 310-0358
Japan: 50-11 Motoyoyogi-Cho, Shibuya-ku, Tokyo 151, tel. 466-3312; there is also a consulate in Osaka
Laos: That Luang Road, Vientiane, tel. 21/413400 (also a consulate in Savannakhet)
Malaysia: 4 Pesiaran Stonor, Kuala Lumpur, tel. 484036
Myanmar (Burma): 30 Komin Kochin, Yangon, tel. 50361
North Korea: 7 Munxu St., Pyongyang
Philippines: 54 Victor Cruz, Malate, Manila, tel. 500364
Singapore: 10 Leedon Park, Singapore 267887, tel. 462-5938

South Korea: 33-1 Han Nam Dong, Yong-ku, Seoul, tel. 794-3570

Thailand: 83/1 Wireless Rd., Bangkok, tel. 251-7201

Other Embassies Abroad

Australia: 6 Timbarra Crescent, O'Malley, Canberra, ACT, tel. 866058

Belgium: Ave. de la Floride 130, 1180 Brussels, tel. 374-9370

Canada: 695 Davidson Dr., Gloucester, Ottawa, tel. 744-0698

France: 62 Rue Boileau, 75016 Paris, tel. 4524-5063

Germany: Konstantinstrasse 37, 5200 Bonn, tel. 357-0201

India: 17 Kautilya Marg Chanakyapury, Delhi, tel. 301-7714

Italy: Piazza Barberini 12, 00187 Rome, tel. 475-5286

Mexico: Calle Sierra Ventana 255, 11000 Mexico DF, tel. 540-1612

Mongolia: Enkhe-taivan, Oudamjni 47, Ulan Bator, tel. 50465

Russia: Bolshaya Pirogovskaya Ul.13, Moscow, tel. 245-0925

Sweden: Orby Slottsvag 26, 125 36 Alvsjo, Stockholm, tel. 861214

United Kingdom: 12–14 Victoria Rd., London W8 5RD, tel. 937-1912

United States: 1233 20th St. NW, Ste. 501, Washington, D.C. 20036, tel. 202/861-0737

Vietnam also maintains embassies or consulates in Eastern Europe in Bulgaria, Hungary, Romania, Czech and Slovak Republics, Poland; the Middle East in Egypt, South Yemen, and Iraq; Africa in Algeria, Angola, Libya, Madagascar, Mozambique, and Ethiopia; and Central America in Nicaragua.

Tourism Agents

Official tourism agencies in Vietnam are expensive; Vietnam Tourism and Saigon Tourist routinely charge double the price of other agencies or more. With daily tariffs of $80 and up per person, the tours cater to the well-heeled, offer the best accommodations, and feature some unimaginative itineraries. Vietnam Tourism has a monopoly on anything to do with foreigners that smells like big bucks, from cruise ships and motorcycle rallies to Central Highlands elephant safaris. Government tourist offices in the provinces are not in the least interested in individual travelers, or in shelling out free maps and travel literature. Their raison d'être is to make money, not squander it on handouts.

Far preferable to the official agencies are the services of joint-venture or private agents and transport companies, which can charge a more modest $40 a day per person. (Lists of local agents in Hanoi and Saigon are given in the respective *Services and Information* sections.) At any of these places you can hire a guide. Guides can smooth over problems with police, point you to better restaurants, and save you from being ripped off. If you want a cheaper guide, hire a moto or cyclo driver. They can usually speak a little English, and might charge a bit extra on top of the hourly vehicle rental rate. So a moto driver acting as an unofficial guide might charge $2 a day extra for guide services on top of a $5 daily moto charge. Tourism office guides want $10–20 a day and expect to travel in a hired car.

As an individual traveler you may find yourself in search of a group to cut costs. Part of the attraction here is the comfort zone; Vietnamese public transport is crowded, crammed, and excruciatingly slow. With a bit of extra effort you can launch your own expeditions by assembling a small group. This gives you a strong hand in designing and steering the tour—a lot more fun. By advertising in traveler cafés, for example, you can put together a group in your own jeep or 4WD vehicle. To visit Halong Bay, you can easily assemble a group at Bai Chay and rent a fishing boat or sailing junk for the day. Motorcycling is best done with a companion in case of an accident; team up with other riders by advertising. Bringing your own bicycle into Vietnam is easy, but finding roads that aren't heavily trafficked is difficult.

Traveler Cafés

Apart from a strong hit of coffee, traveler cafés in Vietnam are an excellent source of current information, and the owners can often fix you up with cheap guides, half- or one-day tours, motorcycle and bicycle rentals, or long-distance minibuses. You can also post notices to join up with other travelers for rented jeeps or minibuses for custom tours.

North: In Hanoi, reliable cafés include Love Planet at 25 Hang Bac, and Handspan at 80 Ma May.

Center: In Hué there are numerous small cafés along Hung Vuong Street, close to Le Loi Street. In Danang, Café Lien, opposite Danang Hotel, is the spot. In Nha Trang, Hanh Café on Tran Hung Dao Street is a good place to hang out.

South: In Saigon, Pham Ngu Lao Street has a large concentration of traveler cafés—the equivalent of Khao San Road in Bangkok. Here you'll find Sinh Café and Kim Café.

CAMBODIA

Visa on Arrival

Because there are so few Cambodian embassies and consulates, visas are issued on arrival at Pochentong Airport. You fill in a form on the spot, supply three passport photos, add a $20 bill, and the visa is stamped. It's valid for 1–4 weeks, depending on how the authorities take to you and what the prevailing policy is at the time. There has been talk of implementing a free 14-day visa on arrival, similar to Thailand's entry visa.

Paperwork Within Cambodia

Unlike Vietnam or Laos, paperwork is straightforward in Cambodia—you pay, you get what you need. The travel permit system was scrapped in 1992 under pressure from UNTAC. No permits are required for travel anywhere in Cambodia.

Cambodian Embassies and Consulates

After 1993, Cambodia designated ambassadors to Thailand, Malaysia, Singapore, Indonesia, Japan, Laos, North Korea, the European Union, France, Germany, the United States, and the U.N. relations with some of these countries had

been severed between 1973 and 1993. Cambodian embassies open at the time of writing are in Bangkok, Saigon, Hanoi, Vientiane, Delhi, Paris, Berlin, Prague, Moscow, Washington, D.C., and Havana; others were planned for Australia, New Zealand, and China. In the United States, contact the Royal Embassy of Cambodia, 4500 16th St. NW, Washington, D.C. 20022, tel. 202/726-7742. With the coup in 1997 and the loss of Cambodia's U.N. seat, it is unclear how diplomatic relations will be maintained.

Within Asia
Thailand: The Cambodian Embassy opened for business in Bangkok in 1994 after a closure of 20 years. It's at 185 Rajadamri Rd. (down an alley off Soi Sarasin just north of Lumpini Park), tel. 253-7967. A Cambodian visa can be obtained the same day or the next day for $20.

Singapore: The Cambodian Embassy is at Orchard Scotts Apartments, Block 12, Unit 03-89, Singapore, tel. 7345379.

Vietnam: In Hanoi, the Cambodian Embassy at 71A Tran Hung Dao, tel. 4/8253789 or 4/8265225, issues a visa for $20. It may only be valid for a week or two, and takes three days or longer to obtain. In Saigon, the Cambodian Consulate at 41 Phung Khac Khoan, Q1, tel. 8/8292751, issues a seven-day visa for $20, or a 14-day visa for $30. The visa is issued same day or next day.

Laos: In Vientiane, the Cambodian Embassy in the Saphathong Nua area, tel. 21/314952, issues a one-month visa for $20 in one day. You need three photos.

Touring Cambodia

Before venturing into Cambodia, always inquire about current conditions and conflicts. Because of limited access due to land mines and military activity, most travelers visit only Phnom Penh and Angkor. You could do a round-trip from Bangkok to Phnom Penh to Angkor and back to Phnom Penh for Bangkok, or fly Bangkok to Phnom Penh, take a side trip to Angkor, and exit by road or air to Saigon. Some travelers also go to Sihanoukville from Phnom Penh.

Travel agencies in Bangkok can arrange fully escorted tours to Cambodia. Escorted tours solve logistical problems and provide the security of numbers, but they often do not allow enough time to fully explore Angkor. As long as you keep to Phnom Penh, Angkor, and Sihanoukville, security should not be a problem for an individual traveler. You can usually find someone to team up with in Bangkok or in Phnom Penh to go to Angkor.

LAOS

Visas

Be careful when applying for visas; specify exactly what you want to do in Laos. Some travelers are disappointed to find themselves restricted to Vientiane Prefecture on a transit visa; businesspeople have been issued one-month visas valid only for this zone. Lao visas and other documents are issued mostly in Lao script, which means you have to double-check what you're getting. Let the travel agent know your travel plans. Any roman alphabet entries on the visa will be in French, not English.

Transit Visa: Generally valid for 5–10 days, transit visas are in theory nonextendable and supposedly valid for Vientiane Prefecture only. These visas are available in Saigon, Danang, or Hanoi and cost around $15–20. They're used by travelers seeking a cheap way back from Vietnam to Thailand, with a short stopover in Vientiane. Some travelers have been able to travel along Route 9 from Vietnam, crossing the Lao Bao border, on a transit visa. This crossing is not guaranteed, as the policy seems to change.

Tourist Visa: Valid for 30 days, a tourist visa costs $60–100 in Bangkok and takes up to five working days to obtain. If you're willing to cough up, you can get the visa back in two working days. On this visa, you can go up-country, but technically you're part of some tour. In theory, you must have a guarantee letter from a Lao tourist company under permission of the Ministry of Foreign Affairs in Laos, but a travel agency in Bangkok can act as your sponsor, in conjunction with a tour agent in Vientiane. The name of the Vientiane sponsor tour agency is

written on your visa in Lao script, and you're supposed to be its charge while in Laos. A tourist visa can be extended in Vientiane and possibly Luang Prabang for $3 a day. Otherwise, if you overstay your visa, the "fine" is $5 a day. Travelers have been able to obtain a 30-day visa direct from the Lao Embassy in Bangkok for lower rates. Lao consulates and embassies issue 30-day tourist visas. However, you must specify that you want 30 days; otherwise, they're prone to giving you only 15 days.

Visa on Arrival: The visa-on-arrival situation in Laos is not consistent. Check ahead to see if it's in operation. Or better yet, get the visa in advance. When it is available, you can get a $30 visa on arrival (valid for 15 days) in Vientiane—either at Wattay Airport or the Friendship Bridge. The visa is also available at other international air entry points—namely, Luang Prabang and Pakse. This visa is not available at other land entry points for Laos. The $30 must be paid in U.S. cash—nothing else is accepted. An extension of this visa could prove a problem.

There are some conditions stipulated for the visa on arrival, though it's doubtful that much attention is paid to these. Conditions stipulate that (a) you must have a return air ticket or a visa to enter a third country (although you could point out that Thailand doesn't require a visa on entry), (b) you must know an individual or organization to contact in the Lao PDR (make one up), (c) you are supposed to have a confirmed hotel reservation in the Lao PDR (again, make one up), and (d) you must have proof of sufficient funds for your visit.

Business Visa: Valid for 30 days, business visas are renewable in Vientiane for 30, 90, 180, or 365 days depending on circumstances. Businesspeople are the advance guard of tourism—investing in Laos and opening it up for trade—and are therefore allowed certain liberties. There are fewer up-country travel restrictions on this visa, but you're still expected to tour with an escort. You're permitted multiple entry-exit during the life of the visa.

For this visa, you need a letter of invitation stating the reason for your visit, approved by the Ministry of Foreign Affairs in Laos. However, in practice, tour agents can obtain this visa for anybody requesting it, minus the complicated paperwork. A business visa costs $12 in Bangkok for an application made directly to the embassy; through a tour agent, the cost can run 10 times that. Allow up to 10 working days to process the visa in Bangkok. Some tour agents in Vientiane and Bangkok can arrange the necessary invitation and paperwork—allow up to a month for processing if applying from abroad. No tour agency is stamped on the visa, which gives the business visa holder a choice of agents upon arrival. Business visas do not pay government tax on travel arrangements, so travel paperwork may be cheaper.

Other Visas: Letters of invitation are required for those visiting relatives or for diplomatic visas. It's very difficult for photographers and writers to obtain official permission to visit.

Visa Issue

Vientiane: A visa on arrival is issued at Wattay Airport, costing $30 and valid for 15 days. The same deal is offered for land arrivals at the Friendship Bridge near Vientiane, and at the airports in Luang Prabang and Pakse. Because Laos does not have many embassies abroad, a visa on arrival is an alternative, but not always consistent, method of processing. Other international border crossing points may issue a 15-day visa on arrival, but some border guards play games in an attempt to extract money.

Cambodia: A Lao tourist visa valid for 15–30 days is issued in Phnom Penh for around $50. It can be obtained in several working days.

Thailand: Bangkok is the most common place to obtain a Lao tourist visa, valid for 30 days. Although the visa itself costs only $12, you normally go through a travel agent who charges a service fee, making the total cost of the visa around $60 or so. Smaller Bangkok agents operate through bigger agents. The Lao Embassy deals with the following travel agents in Bangkok for tourist visas: MK Ways, tel. 254-4765; Chansiam, tel. 287-4798; Diethelm, tel. 255-9150; Exotissimo, tel. 253-5240; Tritee, tel. 233-6896; Transindo, tel. 249-1117;

JP Travel, tel. 255-2233; Precha, tel. 233-5316; Siamwing, tel. 235-4757; Prestige, tel. 314-5498; Spangle Tours, tel. 212-1583; Scenic World, tel. 513-5314; Thai-Indochina Supply Company, tel. 233-5369; and Vista Travel, tel. 281-0786 These agencies chop and change, so phone ahead to initiate contact.

You can fax ahead to Bangkok agents so the paperwork is completed by the time you arrive. Fax a photocopy of your front passport pages, and the agent will fax back a visa application. You need to transfer the fee for the visa. On arrival in Bangkok, the agent will need the actual passport for 24 hours to take it to the Lao Embassy for visa-stamping.

There are several other points in Thailand where you can arrange a Lao visa, particularly at two Mekong crossing points: Nong Khai and Chiang Khong. Some guesthouses in Nong Khai operate as travel agents and send paperwork to either Vientiane or Bangkok. One of these is the Meeting Place, at 1117 Soi Chuen Jitt, Nong Khai, tel. 42/421223, fax 42/460975. Initial charges are $12 for a Bangkok visa, or $30 for a Tha Deua border-issued visa, with additional fees charged by the agent. A tourist visa costs around $60–100 and takes 1–3 days to obtain, although it can sometimes be had in one hour also. Expect to wait longer if getting a 30-day business visa. You will most likely have the actual visa stamped in at the Friendship Bridge immigration section.

Similarly, in Chiang Khong, which lies opposite the Lao entry port of Ban Huay Sai on the Mekong, you can arrange a next-day visa for around $70. Inquire at guesthouses in Chiang Khong.

It is not exactly clear why, but in 1996, a Lao Consulate was established in up-country Thailand at Khon Kaen—which is in the middle of nowhere. Travelers can go directly to this consulate and get a one-month visa for around $30, no questions asked. The only snag is having to wait—the visa can take 2–3 working days to be issued.

Vietnam: In Hanoi, you can acquire transit visas and 15-day tourist visas. Processing requires a few days and is best done through a travel agent. You may be asked for a confirmed Hanoi–Vientiane air ticket. An extra $10 under the table will speed up proceedings. The Lao Consulate in Saigon issues transit and 15-day visas in 3–4 working days. Danang Lao Consulate General offers business visas in two days for $10; seven-day transit visas for $15, processed in two days; and tourist visas for $10. The tourist visa may require up to five days. Lao visas are also available from Rangoon but are more difficult to obtain.

Paperwork Within Laos
Arrival and Departure
You need to complete the standard arrival/departure card and customs declaration form. You can bring 500 cigarettes, two bottles of wine, and one bottle of liquor. The customs declaration form asks you to itemize cameras and valuables. Export of antiques and Buddha images from Laos is forbidden. If entering or exiting a land border in Laos, be aware that greedy border officials on both sides may cause delays by finding "irregularities" in your paperwork. A few cartons of cigarettes will work wonders here.

Extensions
Visa extensions are processed in Vientiane at the Immigration Department. The process is best handled by a travel agent, preferably the sponsoring agent indicated on your visa (if issued in Bangkok). You may have problems with extensions if no sponsor is indicated on your original visa. Visa extensions can take three days to process. Extensions cost roughly $3 for each day you intend to stay. An alternative is to simply overstay your visa—you can then negotiate a $5 per day "fine" (some have negotiated $3 a day), which you pay upon exiting. In Thailand, overstaying a Thai visa is a fixed $4 a day, so Laotian officials probably follow this parameter. It seems that visa extensions are stamped only in Vientiane, as is the case with other major paperwork. In theory you are supposed to be in a group in Laos. Your progress may be monitored at checkpoints. Some areas are off-limits because of their sensitivity—these may require special permission.

Lao Embassies and Consulates
The success rate in dealing direct with Lao embassies and consulates is low—in most places, you must go through a travel agent or passport-handling agency. However, there's no harm in trying the direct option. Travelers regularly obtain Lao visas in Bangkok, but even here an agent is preferable because the embassy is a long way out, and the agent uses a motorcycle courier both ways (the visa application process may require several visits to the embassy). Several travelers have managed to squeeze a 30-day visa out of the embassy in Paris. Staff at the Lao Embassy said they would only deal with group tours, but travelers have received visas anyway. Try a passport-handling agency on home ground. Other travelers have reported obtaining 15-day tourist visas in Beijing for $30 each, which is cheaper than in Bangkok (however, it took seven working days to be issued).

Within Asia
Cambodia: 15-17 Mao Tse Tung Blvd., Phnom Penh, tel. 23/982632

China: 2nd floor, Bldg. 3, Camellia Hotel, 154 Dong Feng East Rd., Kunming (consulate), tel. 3176623; 11 Sanlitun Dongsijie Jie, Beijing (embassy), tel. 65321224

Indonesia: Jalan Kintamani Rajac, 15 N.33 Keningantimur, Jakarta, tel. 5202673

Japan: 3-3-22 Nishi-Azabu Minato-Ku, Tokyo, tel. 541-12291

Malaysia: 1 Lorrng Damai Tiga, Kuala Lumpur, tel. 2483895

Myanmar (Burma): NA1 Diplomatic Quarters, Fraser Road, Rangoon, tel. 222482

Thailand: 520-502/1-3 Soi Ramkhamhaeng 39, Bangkapi, Bangkok, tel. 5396667. There is a visa-issuing consulate at Khonkaen, which lies between Bangkok and Nong Khai. Address is 19/1-3 Phothisarn Road, Khonkaen, tel. 43-223698

Vietnam: 22 Tran Binh Trong, Hanoi, tel. 4/8269746 (embassy); 93 Pasteur St., Saigon, tel. 8/8297667 (consulate); 12 Tran Quy Cap, Danang, tel. 51/821208 (consulate)

Outside Asia

Australia: 1 Dalman Crescent, O'Malley, Canberra, ACT

Belgium: Avenue de la Brabanconne, 19-21b 1000 Bruxelles

Cuba: Sta. Avenida No. 2808 ESQ A30 Playa, Miramar, Havana

France: 74 Ave. Raymond Poincare, 75116 Paris

Germany: Am Lessing 6, 53639 Koenigwinter, Bonn

India: E53 Panchsheel Park, New Delhi

Mongolia: 27 Stalin Ave., 2F, Apartment 10, Ulan Bator

Poland: Ul. Rejtana 15/26, 02-516, Warsaw

Russia: Ul. Katchalova 18, Moscow

Sweden: Badstrangvagen 11, 11265 Stockholm

United States 2222 S. St. NW, Washington, D.C. 20008, tel. 202/332-6416-0076; Lao PDR U.N. office, 317 E. 51 St., New York, NY 10022, tel. 212/832-2734

Tourism Agents

Agents in Vientiane can assist with visa extensions and paperwork, immigration problems, transport rentals, hotel reservations, guides, and so on. Although you can approach the Immigration Office (off Lane Xang Boulevard, near Bangkok Bank) yourself for paperwork, dealing with the staff can be tedious. Agents can speed up the process—for a price.

The large agencies have links up-country with branch offices. Larger agencies are all linked to agents in Bangkok—Raja Tours, for instance, has links with MK Ways and half a dozen other agents in Bangkok, while Lane Xang deals with Chansiam Travel, and Sodetour with Transindo. The name of the Lao agent may be stamped right on your Lao visa as your "sponsor." Although you can deal directly with Lao agents, faxes to Laos can be slow and trying. It may be easier to deal with a Bangkok agent.

Business Travel

Following are agents who deal with business trav-

elers. **Lao Investment Promotion Corporation (LIPCO)** handles business-type travelers, helping with visa issue, agents and brokers, permits and registration for companies, car rentals and guides, typing, translation, and legal work. It's in Building 1, Luang Prabang Road, P.O. Box 795, Vientiane, tel. 21/169645 or 21/169945, fax 9646. **Laovilay,** 100 Tha Deua Rd., P.O. Box 843, Vientiane, tel./fax 21/314350, handles investment documents, business license extensions, visas, car rentals, and travel arrangements.

Travel Agents

Diethelm, Namphu Square, Settathirat Boulevard, tel. 21/215920, fax 21/217151, is a Bangkok-based company that is both upscale and high-priced. It has a branch in Luang Prabang. Diethelm is the American Express agent in Vientiane.

Inter-Lao Tourisme, on the corner of Settathirat and Pangkham, tel. 21/214232, fax 21/216306, maintains links to Luang Prabang and Savannakhet. **Lane Xang Travel,** Pangkham Road, tel. 21/212469, fax 21/215777, has branches in Luang Prabang, Xieng Khuang, and Pakse; it offers lower-priced tours. **Raja Tour,** Anou Hotel, 2nd Floor, 3 Heng Boun St., tel. 21/213633, fax 21/215797, offers good links with Luang Prabang.

Sodetour (Societé de la Developpement Touristique), 16 Fa Ngum, tel. 21/216314, fax 21/216313, is run by a longtime French resident; good links to Pakse and the southeast. **Vieng Champa Tours,** Tha Deua Road, KM3, in the Vientiane Club complex, tel./fax 21/314412, handles Thai tourism. **On-Time Travel Service,** near Inter-Lao Tourisme at 35 Settathirat, books train and bus tickets in Thailand.

Other tour agents in Vientiane include: **That Luang Tours,** Fa Ngum Road, tel. 21/215809, fax 21/215346, and **Chackavane Travel and Tour,** 92 Thong Khankham, tel. 21/216444, fax 21/214743. Tour operators in Vientiane may be unreliable—go over itineraries in great detail to make sure you know what you're getting.

Health and Safety

Health care is either poor or nonexistent in most parts of Indochina. Best medical attention is to be found where embassy staff are—in capital cities such as Hanoi, Phnom Penh, or Vientiane. Western-run nongovernmental organizations (NGOs) arrange transport of medical equipment considered obsolete in the West but state-of-the-art in Vietnam. An American dentist visiting a dental school in Saigon found 1950s techniques practiced with 1940s equipment, and tattered pages of photocopied medical journals used as reference material. In southern Laos dull razor blades may be used for incisions in eye surgery if nothing else is available. In Hanoi the tendons of rat's tails may serve as sutures. Quality drugs and medical provisions are in extremely short supply.

In hospitals around Indochina injection-happy doctors tend to be aggressive in their treatment, forging ahead without proper testing data. Often they will pump foreign patients with antibiotics in search of a quick solution. Food poisoning can be a problem in hospitals. In major cities inquire through embassy staff about facilities with international standards or Western doctors in residence, as well as places for dental treatment. In 1995, Vietnam's Minister of Health signed a decree allowing for the first time foreign investors to open hospitals, clinics, medical consultancies, and medical-technical services. There is a series of efficient Western-run family medical and dental practices operating in Vietnam in Hanoi, Danang, and Saigon. For details, consult their website: www.vietnammedicalpractice.com.

Medicines and drugs are available at pharmacies in Indochina, but quality is questionable. Drugs readily deteriorate if not stored in a cool, dry place. Consult expiration dates and check for signs of tampering. Beware of drugs from eastern European nations, and be on the lookout for fake medication; the World Health Organization (WHO) reports that in some Third World countries fake drugs contain only a placebo or aspirin. Buy from air-conditioned premises if you can, as the shelf life of drugs such as antibiotics is greatly decreased in hot and humid conditions. You can easily obtain reliable medicine in Hong Kong, Singapore, and Bangkok without a prescription. Certain antimalarial drugs, however, are not sold in Bangkok.

This section is not intended to alarm travelers but to make them aware of the potential risks of traveling in Indochina. The real hazards apply to visits to remote areas, or extended stays in rural areas. You need to remain alert for symptoms of ailments, and know when it's time to get out. Advice on drugs and potions in the following sections may not apply to pregnant women, children, and those with certain medical conditions or allergies. Specialist advice should be sought from a family doctor before departure.

MEDICAL INSURANCE

Make sure you carry comprehensive medical insurance, including emergency evacuation coverage. Under some private coverage schemes you pay up front for evacuation by whatever aircraft happens to be around (if you're lucky here, it won't be a Russian one) and the insurance company reimburses you later. Helicopter charter services such as New Zealand–run Lao Westcoast Helicopter in Vientiane and VASCO, operating out of Saigon and Hanoi, can assist in emergencies. Evacuation in Indochina is largely a matter of rocketing off to Singapore, Hong Kong, or Bangkok, where there are excellent health-care facilities.

Carriers

A medical carrier such as International SOS (AEA) will cover the cost of evacuation by private jet and postevacuation expenses up to $10,000. The cost of coverage under these comprehensive schemes is around $140–180 a month. Case scenario: a motorcycle accident near Hué, with your leg fractured in three places. A private jet flies in from Singapore with a medical team on board, landing at

MEDICAL KIT

Camping and outdoor stores sell prepackaged medical kits you can customize to your needs. These come in compact versions with sterile gauze squares, adhesive tape, bandages in assorted shapes and sizes (including knuckle and fingertip bandages), antibacterial towelettes, needle, razor blade, and safety pins. Take along a small Swiss Army knife with scissors and tweezers. For travel in Indochina choose a kit that is comprehensive yet compact. A couple of people traveling together can share one kit. Following are some tips for assembling a health-care kit:

- Treating simple cuts, bites, and scratches is very important in a tropical climate as these are slow to heal and easily infected. Wounds should be kept clean; the juice of a young green coconut is quite sterile and can be used to clean wounds when purified water is not available. Bring an extra supply of bandages, antiseptic cream, and some sort of calamine lotion or antihistamine to reduce itching from bites or sunburn. To assist in cleanup take cotton swabs, dental floss, and a bar of antibacterial soap. To promote cleanliness and dryness in areas such as the feet and groin you should carry antifungal cream or talcum powder.
- Take a bottle of iodine tablets to purify water in case bottled brands are not available. Iodine tablets are cheap, require little space, and are extremely effective.
- A variety of "blockers" is essential: 15-factor sunscreen, lipscreen, mosquito repellent, earplugs (essential to reduce noise in hotels or on transport), condoms (just in case).
- Stock your own drugs: antimalarials, pain and headache medications (codeine is good), antihistamines and decongestants (cough and cold medication), medicines for stomach problems (including oral rehydration salts), and antiworm tablets. A two-week supply of antibiotics would be useful. Carry these drugs but hope you never have to use them. Don't use unless really necessary, and at all costs avoid drug "cocktails" (using several drugs at the same time). Antibiotics lose their effectiveness if used every time a minor problem occurs.
- Because of the poor health care in Indochina, it's highly recommended you carry sterile needles and syringes as anti-AIDS and anti-hepatitis protection. These needles can be used for blood samples or any injections you might require. Kits can be purchased ready-made, sealed, and labeled so you won't look like a junkie to customs officers.
- Eye irritation is a potential problem because of dust; you might want to take along eyedrop fluid. Dental care is abysmal in Indochina: Depending on the state of your dental work, consider carrying a few items to deal with problems. A tiny tube of benzocaine gel will deal with toothache. There are travel-sized dental repair kits on the market that address the calamity of lost fillings.
- If you're dependent on specific brands of medicine that may not be available in Indochina, take a supply with you. This extends to birth control pills, and to items you may well overlook. You'll make an absolute fool of yourself trying to mime contact lens solution to a shopkeeper in Hanoi who's never heard of such a thing.

Danang. You're picked up by ambulance and flown to a hospital in Singapore within 24 hours of the accident. Doctors calculate possible loss of the leg through infection if you'd arrived any later.

International SOS is a Singapore-based organization that will evacuate you to Singapore. There are branches in Hong Kong, India, Japan, Vietnam, Cambodia, and Thailand. Consult its www.internationalsos.com website for more information and all emergency locations and 24-hour alarm numbers. International SOS was taken over by AEA Group (Asian Emergency Assistance). In Singapore contact AEA at 331 N. Bridge Rd., 17F Odeon Towers, Singapore 0718, tel. 65/3382311, fax 65/3387611. In Hanoi contact International SOS at Central Building, 31 Hai Ba Trung, tel. 4/9340666, fax 4/9340556; in Saigon contact OSCAT/AEA at 65 Nguyen Du St., Q1, tel. 8/8236520, fax 8/8298551; in Vung Tau contact OSCAT/AEA at 1 Thanh Thai St., tel. 64/858776, fax 64/858779. In Phnom Penh, contact AEA at House 161, Street 51, Sang-Kat Boeung Peng, Khon Doun Penh, tel. 23/216911, fax 23/215811. In the United States, the main International SOS office is at 8 Neshaminy Complex, Ste. 207, Trevose, PA 19053, tel. 215/2441500, fax 215/442227.

INFORMATION AND INOCULATIONS

For current information on who's winning in the battle against mosquitoes, avian flu, and other viruses and bugs, contact the Centers for Disease Control and Prevention in Atlanta, Georgia, in the United States, which monitors outbreaks of disease around the globe. Check the latest information on prevention guidelines and strategies at its website, www.cdc.gov/travel/travel.com—you can refer to the travelers' health pages. The CDC's Traveler's Hotline, tel. 404/332-4565, provides information by voice recording or automated fax transmission. In England contact the Medical Advisory Service for Travellers (MASTA) at the London School of Hygiene and Tropical Medicine, tel. 071/631-4408. British Airways Travel Clinics also supply information. Highly recommended medical guides are Dirk Schroeder's *Staying Healthy in Asia, Africa, and Latin America* (Avalon Travel Publishing, 2000) and Richard Dawood's *Travellers' Health* (Oxford University Press). For pocket-sized guides, try Stephen Bezruchka's *The Pocket Doctor* (The Mountaineers) and the *Collins Gem Holiday Health* booklet (HarperCollins).

Get an armful of inoculations before you leave home; try a travel clinic, which also supplies information. Consult your family doctor about the trip. Have your teeth checked before departure. Recall all those items you're dependent on: If you wear glasses or contact lenses, take an extra set along, and carry your prescription for new lenses. You can have very nice copies of brand-name glasses made in Vietnam for really low rates. On an organized bike trip through Vietnam, one participant lost her glasses. This could have been a major problem—but it turned out to work to her advantage. She had a new set made up within a day in Nha Trang and was so pleased with the results (and the extremely reasonable price) that she went back and ordered two more sets. Meanwhile, another participant, an American—upon seeing all this in action—decided to try his luck at ordering a pair of prescription Oakley sunglasses. These too were made in short order—to the complete amazement of the American, who had been informed by the Oakley Company in the United States that such an order was not technically possible because of extreme curvature on these sports specs. Glasses are also cheap to buy in Bangkok.

Bring a good medical kit. Prepare a personal medical card to carry in your wallet. Print or type all the details on a small card, then laminate it. Include identification, with passport number, blood type, preexisting medical conditions, special medications, medical insurance details, and a name of a relative or friend to contact in an emergency.

Why go to this trouble? It's essential to have this information at your fingertips in an emergency, and it may alert others to problems. For example, some blood types, such as O-negative, are rare in Asia, which presents a potential problem for O-negative travelers with a sudden need for blood.

You don't have to show any vaccination certificates in Indochina, but it's highly recommended you get jabs or boosters against typhoid and polio/tetanus, and consider shots for hepatitis A. On the road these inoculations can be obtained at the Red Cross in Bangkok, at clinics in Hong Kong or in Singapore, and at the Swedish Clinic in Hanoi. If entering China, you'll most likely be asked to show a health certificate. Officials even scrutinize the document for a cholera vaccination, which is practically useless. To satisfy their whims, you should get that section stamped in big letters, "Cholera not medically indicated."

While all of the above are preventive measures, there are medical alternatives in Southeast Asia. A number of foreigners actually travel to Bangkok to have medical work done there because it is of international standard—and, more to the point, it is much, much cheaper (especially for cosmetic procedures). And the same goes for dental work—again a fraction of the cost of Western practices, and reliable as long as you research the dental outfits and get good recommendations from those in the know.

Coming Home

Then there's coming home. Some bugs in the system may lie dormant for six months or longer before multiplying. If you have any reason to suspect a condition or problem, get blood and/or stool tests, and inform your doctor where you've been traveling. What might be mistaken for flu could well be malaria, and a doctor in the West should be alerted to this possibility.

ACCLIMATION ILLNESSES

Sun Exposure and Prickly Heat

Adjusting to the tropics can take 2–6 weeks. Problems that can occur if you're not acclimated include heatstroke, sunburn, and prickly heat. Take it easy on arrival to allow yourself time to adapt to the new environment. Avoid strenuous activity, wear a hat, apply sunscreen, and drink plenty of fluids.

Your body deals with excess heat by turning into a kind of air-conditioning unit. Sweat glands are activated, beginning in the forehead and spreading down to the soles of the feet; skin ducts secrete fluid that is mostly water and about 1 percent salt. Cooling is accomplished by the evaporation of sweat and is quicker if helped by convection—the air movement of a breeze or fan. Sweating is the best avenue for heat loss, but sweating too much without fluid replacement is a problem. Sweating on a very hot day, you can lose a liter of water an hour, and, if working hard, you may lose up to four liters an hour. The body isn't very good at signaling when it's lost too much water; you can lose quite a lot before you begin to get thirsty. If you don't restore water and electrolytes, your blood pressure will begin to fall, and you'll feel dizzy. In a worst-case scenario, the body's heat system shuts down, leading to brain-damaging heatstroke if not countered immediately by cooling the body in water and restoring fluids and salts.

In tropical areas there's a firm correlation between clothing and health. Wear loose, light clothing; cotton is best because it breathes and will not shrink. If you wear tight synthetic clothing, particularly socks and underwear, you may fall victim to prickly heat (an itch and a heat rash) or fungal infections, particularly between the toes and in the groin. Humidity, increased perspiration, and heat favor the growth of fungi and bacteria on the skin; to counter these, stay clean, dry between the folds of the skin, and apply a light dusting of talcum powder.

If the rot persists, switch to very loose clothing. For foot problems, wear sandals for a few days. Women afflicted with groin or vaginal infections should don cotton underwear and a skirt; males with groin infections should wear loose cotton boxer-style shorts. Apply talc to affected areas to keep them dry and free of sweat. Another remedy is soap with an antibacterial agent, or antifungal cream. Infection of the urinary tract and bladder (cystitis) in women is associated with sexual activity; this infection is much more frequent in the tropics, probably because of dehydration.

If symptoms are pain and more frequent urination, drinking plenty of water should alleviate the problem. If there is no sign of improvement, antibiotics may be required.

Diarrhea

Stomach problems are common on the road. The greatest risk with diarrhea is dehydration: You have to drink plenty of clear fluids, water, unsweetened juices, or clear soups. Do not drink alcohol or milk, and avoid fruit, green vegetables, and spicy or fatty foods, as these items tend to aggravate diarrhea. Pack something for the runs; Imodium or Pepto-Bismol for minor cases, and an antibiotic for more memorable instances. Most cases of the runs resolve in a few days. If symptoms persist, with diarrhea and blood or mucus in the stool, this indicates a more serious illness, such as amoebic or bacillary dysentery. In such a case get a stool test to identify the bug.

TAINTED FOOD AND WATER

Constantly monitor the quality of your food and water in Indochina. Boil it, peel it, cook it, filter it—or forget about it. Unsanitary conditions, with cockroaches and rats running around kitchens, can be dangerous. Observe basic sanitary hygiene. Keep your hands clean when eating; watch out for restaurant face towels—if they're not clean, they can lead to eye infections.

Stick to drinking purified bottled water, even when brushing your teeth. When buying bottled water ensure the seal is intact. La Vie is a popular brand in Vietnam. Carry your own plastic water bottle when traveling. In many places in Indochina you'll be offered water with ice in it. Don't drink it! An exception might be a high-class hotel where the ice is produced in-house under sterile conditions. In Vietnam, if you buy a bottled or canned soft drink or beer, you can often ask for a small ice-bucket—keep the drink on ice near your table just like champagne. Beer is cheap and goes through a fermenting process that renders it safe to drink (don't drink too much of it, though—you can get terrific tropical hangovers). Other relatively safe drinks are tea and coffee, assuming the water used has been sufficiently boiled.

French colonial-type ceramic filters for purifying water have been spotted in first-class railway waiting rooms in Vietnam. Chinese thermoses are ubiquitous in hotel rooms in the north. This water is generally piping hot and thus a good source of drinking water. However, the problem is how to transfer it—hot water can melt plastic. One solution is to uncork the thermos and leave it to cool off overnight; your drinking water is ready the next morning. In areas where there is no bottled water you need to use iodine tablets or a personal filter.

Ensure all food is thoroughly cooked. The baguettes sold fresh daily throughout Indochina are generally safe because they're baked at extremely high temperatures—high enough to fry any bugs within. Dairy products should be avoided, although yogurt is good for your stomach as a natural antibacterial agent. Hazards to the stomach increase with salads, ice cream, unpasteurized milk, raw or undercooked eggs, and undercooked meat or seafood, particularly shellfish, crabs, and prawns if not boiled for at least 10 minutes. The latter may be infected with parasites or their larvae; in Laos, raw or undercooked fish may carry tiny worms that cause liver flukes. An American pamphlet tenders this advice for Laos: "Avoid cold buffets, custards, and any frozen desserts," which shouldn't be that difficult in Vientiane (I've never seen any custards there).

Cholera

Cholera is an acute intestinal infection caused by contaminated food or water. Symptoms include an abrupt onset of watery diarrhea, vomiting, dehydration, and muscle cramps. The available vaccine for cholera is only 50 percent effective in reducing the illness and has a brief validity period. People with severe cases respond well to simple fluid and electrolyte-replacement therapy (oral rehydration). Cholera outbreaks have been reported in Indochina, Myanmar (Burma), and China. Outbreaks occur mainly in rural areas where locals have little access to clean drinking water.

Typhoid

Typhoid fever is a bacterial infection transmitted through tainted food or water, or directly between people. Symptoms include fever, headache, loss of appetite, constipation or diarrhea, and fatigue. Typhoid fever can be treated directly with antibiotics. A vaccine is good protection against typhoid.

INFLUENZA AND RESPIRATORY PROBLEMS

Avian Flu

Sporadic lethal outbreaks of avian influenza A (H5N1) have been reported among chickens, ducks, quail, and humans in Vietnam, Cambodia, and Laos. Keep an eye on news and Internet sources to stay up-to-date on where outbreaks may have occurred: Consult www.cdc.gov/travel/. These outbreaks are not expected to diminish: It is likely that avian flu has become endemic in the region. It is now thought that ducks, not chickens, are the main reservoir of the H5N1 virus. Ducks are thought to play a silent role in transmission because unlike chickens, they spread the virus without showing any signs of illness. Avian flu is spread through saliva, nasal secretions, and feces from infected birds. Most cases of avian flu infection in humans have resulted from contact with infected birds or contaminated surfaces. It is thus important to avoid contact with live birds in markets in rural and semirural areas. If the avian flu virus strengthens its ability to transmit from human-to-human contact, an influenza pandemic could result—as humans have little or no preexisting immunity and no drugs have been devised to counter avian flu. It is uncertain whether the avian flu virus has the potential to be transmitted through food sources, as in eating chicken or eggs. If well-cooked, such food should prove no problem, but undercooked or raw poultry might be a hazard.

SARS

Severe Acute Respiratory Syndrome (SARS) was first reported in Asia in November 2002. The illness spread to more than two dozen countries worldwide before being brought under control. Symptoms include high fever, headache, and body aches. Mild respiratory problems are present at the outset, later developing into a dry cough and pneumonia. There are devices at major airports across Asia (including Hanoi and Saigon) scanning incoming passengers for high forehead temperature. There are many unknowns about SARS.

Virulent Flu Strains

Coughs, colds, and sore throats are common problems when traveling in Indochina, often related to road dust and overkill air-conditioning. Carry your own cough and cold medicines. There are virulent strains of flu running around Asia, and you may come down with a bad case. Do not treat cold symptoms lightly; you might acquire a strain of Asian flu that could lay you flat for a week, accompanied by fever and stomach problems. What at first appears to be flu may actually be more serious, perhaps the onset of typhoid or malaria. Initial symptoms can be very similar.

Tuberculosis

The "white plague" is threatening to make the comeback of the century. Vaccines, antibiotics, and improved hygiene nearly erased TB from industrialized nations; however, the disease now appears to be resistant to most of the drugs previously used to treat it. Tuberculosis thrives in crowded and dirty living conditions where both ventilation and the people are poor. The airborne bacteria are readily transmitted through coughing, sneezing, or spitting by people in an infectious stage of TB. Vietnam and Cambodia are among the hot spots for infection. TB is the number-one killer in the 15- to 45-year age group in Cambodia, according to French-based Médecins Sans Frontières (Doctors Without Borders).

MOSQUITO-BORNE DISEASES

Malaria

Malaria is prevalent in certain parts of Indochina. The major cities—Vientiane, Phnom Penh, Saigon, Danang, Hanoi—present no risk, apparently because of water pollution. Malaria-carrying mosquitoes are fussy about the water where they lay their eggs, and the water in these urban centers is too polluted for their taste. Coastal and urban areas of Vietnam are considered low-risk, as are the deltas. In remote areas of the countryside in Vietnam, Laos, and Cambodia, the risk is very real, particularly around Angkor Wat, Luang Prabang, and the jungle border zones of Vietnam.

Of the hundreds of varieties of mosquitoes in Indochina only a handful carry malaria. Of the *Anopheles* mosquitoes, males are vegetarian, feeding entirely on plant juices. The female mosquito, who bites to obtain protein sustenance for her eggs, can fly around carrying more than twice her own weight in blood. Malaria is caused by protozoa that infect red blood cells. If her human victim is infected, the mosquito ingests malarial parasites along with her quota of blood. Some of the ingested parasites are hardy enough to survive the mosquito's oral digestive juices and are passed on alive to the mosquito's next victim.

Four kinds of malaria parasite can inhabit humans. Malaria parasites can be identified by blood tests. *Falciparum,* the deadliest type, accounting for 95 percent of all malarial deaths, thrives in the hottest climates and is now resistant to chloroquine. *Vivax,* more widespread, causes fevers and anemia. The two other types of malaria—*ovale* and *malariae*—are less common. A victim can actually suffer from several malarias at once. Once the malaria parasite is in the bloodstream it's carried to the liver, where it reproduces. After an indeterminate period (anywhere from days to years later), the parasite reenters the bloodstream, producing chills and headache and diarrhea, followed by high fever and nausea. In serious cases delirium and coma follow. The malaria parasite is devious; it attacks, withdraws, and attacks again, sometimes with devastating results.

There is no guaranteed effective remedy against malaria. Every time a promising new drug appears, mosquitoes quickly mutate and develop resistance. This situation is ongoing and researchers wait for reported cases of for-

eigners with malaria from different areas before deciding how resistant the mosquitoes have become. Antimalarial drugs should be taken two weeks before entering a malarial zone, and for four weeks after leaving. Antimalarials do not prevent infection. Instead, they suppress multiplication of the parasite in the liver. If you stop taking the malarial tablets too soon, you increase the odds of developing full-blown malaria. Because of side effects, long-term use of antimalarials is not recommended.

Malarone is the magic bullet antimalarial now recommended for Indochina, but since this drug is still in the field-testing stages, it's too early to tell what side effects it may have, or how effective it is. Consult your doctor or go to a travel medical clinic—or both. Until mefloquine-resistant areas showed up in Asia, the most effective drug was Mefloquine (Lariam). This drug, however, is renowned for its host of side effects, including dizziness and gastrointestinal disturbances, which are not too bad. But others have experienced hallucinations on this drug—not what you need if you're riding a motorcycle. Infants and pregnant women should not take mefloquine. Adult dosage is 250 milligrams (one tablet) once a week.

Chloroquine is no longer effective in parts of Southeast Asia, and Fansidar is deemed too dangerous because of side effects, and has proved useless more than a third of the time in many parts of Africa under a usage survey. In mefloquine-resistant areas such as Thailand and the Philippines, the antibiotic doxycycline is recommended. This drug, however, may increase chances of sunburn. The drug proguanil (Paludrine), used simultaneously with chloroquine, is an alternative to mefloquine or doxycycline. Halofantrine (Halfan) is reserved for self-treatment of malaria after symptoms become apparent.

Keep an eye on new drugs being developed to counter malaria. One of them goes under the drug name Coartem, which combines artemether and lumefantrine. This is one of a new line of ACTs, which stands for "artemisinin-based combination therapies." Derivatives of artemisinin, a plant extract first used in China more than 2,000 years ago, combined with certain other drugs, seem to work well against *P. falciparum,* the deadliest of the malaria strains. Apart from Coartem, other artemisinin derivatives include amodiaquine and artesunate. These drugs are very expensive to buy while in experimental phases, but they do look promising.

In the 1950s, the WHO declared war on malaria with weapons varying from DDT to mosquito-killing fungi. It was believed malaria could be eradicated within a few decades, but mosquitoes have proved far more resilient than ever imagined, and the outlook for malaria control is grimmer than ever. Now the WHO's strategy is to get back to fundamentals: The best protection against malaria is to ensure you're not bitten in the first place. Especially around dusk and dawn, cover up with long-sleeved shirt, scarf, and long pants tucked into socks, and use a repellent. Mosquitoes will often swarm over one person but virtually avoid another, behavior apparently linked to scents. Biting mosquitoes seem to be turned on by sweat, lactic acid, and the scent of bananas, perfume, and cologne, among other things. If you smell "bad," mosquitoes won't want to bite you. Use some kind of mosquito repellent for exposed flesh. In Vientiane a soap called Mos-Bar is marketed for similar effects. A good natural repellent is oil of citronella. Pay special attention to areas such as the legs and ankles as mosquitoes favor ground-level meals. Tucking pants into socks is also effective.

The active ingredient in most insect repellents is DEET (diethyl meta-toluamide), which operates on the stealth principle, emitting a vapor that keeps insects from sensing your presence. DEET wards off mosquitoes, fleas, ticks, chiggers, and other insects. But it can be toxic (to you), so don't apply concentrations greater than 30 percent and avoid contact with eyes and mouth. DEET-based products can damage synthetic fibers, painted surfaces, and plastics, so avoid getting any on eyeglasses or plastic wristwatches. And, since it's highly flammable, keep it away from fire sources. An insecticide called permethrin is also highly effective, licensed for use with clothing and netting.

In air-conditioned hotels, the risk of mosquito bites is extremely low; after all, the windows are closed. Thus, in four-star hotels mosquito nets will probably not be provided. In other accommodations you may need to deploy a net around your bed at night. Check hotel room cupboards if you don't see a net installed, or ask staff to provide one. Keep the flammable nets well away from fire sources such as candles or mosquito coils. Consider carrying your own net if you're visiting rural areas or areas without hotels, or taking long train or bus trips. Mosquito netting is sold by the meter in markets in Phnom Penh and Saigon. Avoid no-see-um netting: The mesh is too fine to allow air to circulate. It's a good idea to impregnate a net with insecticide.

Dengue Fever

Dengue fever, carried by *Aedes albopictus,* or tiger mosquitoes, is a threat (a low-incidence threat) in urban areas and some larger rural towns. Dengue can take two forms: dengue hemorrhagic fever and the less severe classical dengue fever. The tiger mosquito is more active during the day, especially at dawn and dusk. Dengue fever is a bit of a mystery. If a person has symptoms, it's a matter of resting up, restoring fluids, and waiting till the fever passes. No vaccine is available. Symptoms include fever, headache, severe joint and muscle pains, and rash. Cases of dengue fever have been detected throughout Indochina, but the risk of infection is small for travelers except during periods of epidemic transmission, usually during the rainy season. In 1995 an epidemic hit the northwest of Cambodia, around Battambang, resulting in the deaths of hundreds of children. Adult fatalities from dengue fever are rare.

Japanese Encephalitis

This viral disease (JE) is spread by mosquitoes, particularly in rice-growing and pig-farming areas. It's commonly spread from pigs to humans by *Culex* mosquitoes. Risk is seasonal. In subtropical regions, JE is associated with the rainy season. Only certain mosquito species are capable of transmitting the disease, and they bite mostly at dusk and dawn. Mild symptoms are flulike at the onset, with headache and fever. More serious complications include swelling of the brain (encephalitis), which can be fatal. The chance a traveler in Asia will contract JE is very small. There's a vaccine available for JE through travelers clinics, but it's really only recommended for those who intend to make extensive visits to rural areas during transmission season. You should avoid mosquito bites at all times in these areas; use a repellent and net at night.

NOXIOUS PESTS

Worms

Intestinal worms are common in rural areas. The larvae are often present on unwashed vegetables or undercooked meat. Intestinal worms are awful to contemplate but not of great medical concern since drugs to kill them are highly effective. If you think you've picked up a worm or two, a simple stool examination on your return home will identify the culprits, and elimination is accomplished with antiworm tablets. Also be careful of infestation by the larvae of hookworms, contracted by walking barefoot on moist soil or on beaches in infected areas.

Laos presents some special worm hazards. Avoid eating raw or undercooked fish, as the fish may carry tiny worms that cause liver flukes, or opisthorchiasis. Particularly avoid eating *paddek*, chunks of fermented freshwater fish, and *nam paddek*, a sauce from fermented fish. The risk is higher in rural areas. Around Khong Island in the Mekong in southern Laos it's possible to contract liver flukes from swimming. In the same area are blood flukes, which can cause schistosomiasis (bilharzia), an infection that develops after the larvae of a flatworm have penetrated the skin. Water treated with chlorine or iodine is virtually safe, and salt water poses no risk. The medication to treat both blood and liver flukes is the praziquantel Biltricide. Schistosomiasis may also be present in parts of Vietnam.

Insects

Most are of the bothersome kind, such as bedbugs, lice, crabs, and scabies. In cheaper accommodations bedbugs can be a problem: Consider carrying antiflea powder to dust bedding. Special shampoos can counter head lice, and infected clothing should be washed in very hot water. When scratched, insect bites are easily infected in a tropical climate, and such wounds heal slowly. Avoid scratching bites, and use calamine lotion or antihistamine tablets to reduce itching. If bites become infected, treat with antibiotic cream. If heading into wet jungle areas, use sturdy footwear and tuck pants into socks to counter leeches.

Venomous Creatures

There is a low-incidence risk from venomous snakes, spiders, scorpions, centipedes, and sea creatures. Poisonous snakes such as cobras and kraits exist in Indochina, but attack only when provoked—and hardly ever if you keep still. However, the Hanuman snake, found near Siem Reap in Cambodia, is a tree snake that drops onto its victims. If bitten, clean the wound, and take yourself—and the snake, if possible—to the nearest medical facility with antivenin. Scorpions have been sighted in Cambodia in Sihanoukville; check inside your shoes in the morning and keep your bed away from the wall. Venomous species may lurk in the water: Among them are sea snakes and the stonefish, which spikes the foot that steps on it.

Plague Carriers

Vietnam is listed as a plague-infected country. Plague is spread by fleas from rats infected with the disease-causing organism. A vaccine for prevention and treatment is available but is normally only recommended for those contemplating extended stays in rural areas, or for people bent on fondling wild rodents.

Rabies

Avoid being licked, scratched, or bitten by a rabid mammal. Dogs are the greatest offenders, though monkeys also pose a risk. Rabies is a deadly disease that attacks the brain, and unless treated it can kill within two months. If bitten by a rabid animal, clean the wound thoroughly with soap and water, and then seek prompt medical attention. Vaccination against rabies is recommended only for veterinarians and animal handlers, travelers planning extended visits to areas known for rabies risk, and spelunkers risking rabies from cave bats. Preexposure vaccination (a series of shots) does not nullify the need for postexposure vaccine, though it reduces the number of injections.

OTHER HAZARDS
Hepatitis

Hepatitis is a viral infection of the liver primarily spread through contaminated food and water, dirty needles, or sexual contact via body fluids such as blood, saliva, or urine.

Hepatitis A (infectious hepatitis) is transmitted by the fecal-oral route, through direct person-to-person contact, from contaminated water or shellfish, or from fruit or uncooked vegetables contaminated through handling. Hepatitis A damages liver cells. They swell up, stop functioning, and cannot dispose of the body's toxic waste material, especially bile. When bile builds up in the blood it causes jaundice, a condition that turns the skin and eyes yellow and darkens the urine. Other symptoms include fever, fatigue, loss of appetite, nausea, aches and pains, and light stools. Havrix, a hepatitis A vaccine that provides immunity expected to last 5–10 years, is said to be extremely effective. The vaccine contains hepatitis A virus produced in cell culture and rendered harmless by treatment with formalin. Two doses at least six months apart are required. This also goes under the name Twinrix.

Hepatitis B (serum hepatitis) is transmitted through tainted blood, needles, or sexual contact. A high percentage of prostitutes carry this virus. Hepatitis B differs from hepatitis A in that it may lead to chronic liver disease or cancer. You can be immunized against hepatitis B. Other strains of hepatitis are mysterious and are still in the process of being identified by researchers. They're often lumped under the label "non-A, non-B" because they don't react in blood tests for types A or B. They appear to be more closely aligned with hepatitis B in regard to modes of transmission. There is no known vaccine or treatment for these strains.

AIDS and STDs

Acquired immunodeficiency syndrome (AIDS) is linked to human immunodeficiency virus (HIV), although researchers are hazy on how the virus operates. The HIV virus has been detected in Vietnam, Cambodia, and Laos. Cases are spreading rapidly in Vietnam because of widespread prostitution. In Cambodia prostitution was rampant during the 1992 U.N. occupation of the country and HIV has spread through the Cambodian armed forces. Laos fears its inadequate health-care system may not be able to cope with the problem.

Under U.N. auspices, a vigorous campaign is under way in all three countries to combat AIDS. The Australian government is funding 23 AIDS projects in Southeast Asia, including Vietnam and Cambodia, with the main emphasis on education.

Travelers are at risk for AIDS if they have sexual intercourse with an infected person; use contaminated, unsterilized syringes or needles for any injections or skin-piercing procedures; or encounter infected blood products. Prostitutes are a major risk: They have multiple sex partners and often associate with intravenous drug users. Condoms and spermicides decrease, but do not entirely eliminate, the risk of HIV transmission. While Western nations have virtually eliminated the risk of infection of transfusion-associated HIV, in poorer nations such as Vietnam, Cambodia, and Laos, the resources for testing blood products for HIV are limited. Western-run organizations such as the International Red Cross in Phnom Penh screen blood for the AIDS virus and hepatitis. For any medical procedures insist on the use of a sterile disposable needle, prepackaged in a sealed container. It might be worth carrying a few in your medical kit.

STDs: Since AIDS hit the scene, it seems other sexually transmitted diseases (STDs) have faded from public consciousness. Risks still exist from infected partners of genital herpes, chlamydia, gonorrhea, and syphilis. Again, the use

THE CRUSADE AGAINST AIDS

In every large city billboards carry AIDS awareness slogans hinting at the consequences of an unregulated sex industry. The SIDA posters (using the French acronym for AIDS) are displayed because the World Health Organization (WHO) will not provide funding unless public awareness posters are in place. Recently, the government has been converting slogans to read AIDS since the French acronym is identical to that of the Swedish International Development Agency (SIDA), a health-care group active in Vietnam.

Pasteur Institutes in Saigon, Nha Trang, and Dalat were set up as medical research outfits.

Among founder Alexandre Yersin's first projects was isolation of a plague bacillus; he was later involved in research on the prevention of malaria and set about planting quinine trees in Vietnam. Now the Pasteur Institutes play a role in researching a modern scourge—they've conducted research on AIDS since 1991. In 1995, 2,300 HIV-positive cases were recorded in Vietnam. The WHO estimated Vietnam may have 400,000 HIV cases at the turn of the century.

Vietnam's National Committee on AIDS prevention has initiated a program to integrate an AIDS-prevention program into the training curriculum for the national political system, medical colleges, and schools nationwide. The Australian government will pilot a project with the Vietnam Youth Project in Vietnam using *Streetwise Comics,* Australian publications that help street kids understand HIV and AIDS problems. The project will train Vietnamese staff to produce a series of bilingual minicomics on AIDS prevention.

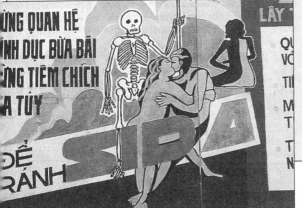

Poster warns, "To avoid AIDS, don't engage indiscriminately in sex, don't use drugs."

of condoms lessens the chances of transmission but does not provide absolute protection.

Mines and War Materiel

One of the greatest risks to life and limb in remote areas of Vietnam, Cambodia, and Laos is land mines and unexploded ordnance. In Vietnam and Laos land mines are mostly left over from the Vietnam War. There is a lot of left-over ordnance in Laos, particularly in Xieng Khuang and Savannakhet provinces. Use of a guide in such areas is recommended. In Vietnam, the risk is real only in places such

as the DMZ. If you venture into the former DMZ, follow your guide and do not stray from marked paths, do not touch or disturb any shells or mines you may come across, and do not climb inside bomb craters. Cambodia has well over three million mines, placed by both government forces and the (now-defunct) Khmer Rouge. Never approach or touch live war materiel.

Military Menaces

Insurgency exists in Laos and Cambodia. The risk in Laos is from disgruntled Hmong tribesmen, sporadic bandits, and mystery bombers. In Cambodia, banditry may be a threat, involving demobilized soldiers and police. Government

DANGER!! MINES!!

The greatest limitation to travel in the remote parts of Cambodia—surpassing even bandits and corrupt government troops—is land mines. It is unknown how many mines remain (many planted by the former Khmer Rouge), but it is certainly a huge problem. The Cambodian government is a signatory to the international land-mine treaty, drafted in Canada in 1997, banning the use, stockpiling, manufacture, and export of land mines.

The only known cases of foreigners falling victim to Cambodian mines have been UNTAC staff who ventured into known mined areas or handled unknown explosive devices. Remaining a biped is easy if you're alert to potential dangers. The following advice is adapted from a supplement published in the *Phnom Penh Post.*

Be Sensible: Bright red skull-and-crossbones signs in Khmer and English mark suspect areas. Heed the signs. Stay alert. Do not become complacent and think that because you've not seen any mines the area is safe. Realize where you are and understand the consequences of a wrong action. Don't be foolhardy and "brave" in front of your companions; you might put them into danger as well.

Use a Guide: If you must travel outside the villages, make sure you stay with a guide who knows the area and will lead the way. Do not enter any region outside a known safe area without first asking local people if there are mines about ("Mian min teh?"). Don't travel outside the towns after 1600 or before 0800: mines may be laid during the night for protection, and, in theory, retrieved in the morning.

Stay on the Path: Stick to well-trodden trails at all times. Do not go off a known safe path for any reason, and do not take a shortcut, even if it looks safe. You must do all your business (which includes the toilet) on the safe path, no matter what the circumstances. Don't go off the safe path to explore ruins or derelict military equipment. Do not walk in long grass; snakes could be a problem here as well.

Do Not Touch: Never approach or touch any mines or unexploded ordnance. The Khmer Rouge rig up live ordnance as booby traps, often with trip wires. It's not uncommon for someone to want to show you his collection of mines, or even pass one to you for inspection. If this happens, make excuses to leave.

Driving: Make sure your driver knows where he's going. Ask the locals, or take along a local guide. If you need to stop in a potentially mined area, make sure the car is away from the edge of the road so you don't have to venture off the road when you get out. Mines are commonly laid on the edges of roads and paths. If your car breaks down in a mined area, you must climb out onto the roof of the car, make your way to the back of the vehicle, and then walk in the tire tracks.

In a Mined Area: If you find yourself in a mined area, warn everyone else around you to stop walking. If you can see your footsteps, you must stand completely within them and retrace all the way back to the known safe area. If you cannot see your footsteps you must not move. Call for help and wait until someone comes to rescue you. This may take a long time, but it is better to wait one day in a minefield than to be an amputee for life. If the worst happens, and someone is injured, do not rush into the mined area to rescue him or her. Many people have been killed or injured doing this. It's better to wait and find someone who knows how to safely enter a mined area. The safest way to enter a minefield is by prodding, which is an exact technique that must be learned thoroughly before being used in the field.

soldiers may demand handouts from travelers. The police in Vietnam are after the same but are more refined in their approach, perhaps charging big-noses for "insurance" to visit a site, or fining a minibus driver for not possessing "a license to drive foreigners." Customs officials in all three countries like to supplement their meager incomes by fleecing unwary travelers.

Drugs

Marijuana is widely available in Indochina. The use of soft drugs is tolerated or ignored in Cambodia and Laos, where they're sold in the markets for less than the price of tobacco. Marijuana is sold in Vientiane, Phnom Penh, and Siem Reap as a cooking condiment. While it is not illegal in Cambodia, possession of marijuana is a serious criminal offense in neighboring Thailand. In Saigon cyclo drivers sometimes sell marijuana to travelers and then inform the police, who are always keen on extra income. Opium smoking is prevalent among the Hmong hilltribe people of Indochina, though it is officially outlawed in Vietnam. In opium-growing areas of northern Laos, especially toward the Burmese border, foreigners may be mistaken for drug traffickers or, even worse, drug enforcement agents.

On the hard-drug front Vietnam is following the lead of Thailand and Malaysia, exacting harsh penalties. In 1993, a Hong Kong–born British citizen was intercepted at Saigon Airport with five kilos of heroin; in June 1995, he was executed for drug trafficking. In April 2001, the Lao National Assembly drafted a law with severe penalties for trafficking—the death penalty for those found in possession of three kilos of opium, 500 grams of heroin, or 10 kilos of marijuana.

Reckless Driving

By far the biggest potential threat for travelers in Indochina is injury caused by vehicle collisions or road accidents. Vietnam has one of the world's highest road-fatality rates. Dr. Keystone, editor of a book on how to stay healthy in warm climates, has formulated three golden rules for staying alive abroad: Never ride a motorcycle; don't travel by road at night; and avoid overcrowded public vehicles. You can easily break those parameters in Vietnam, since Open Tour buses travel at night on the Hué to Hanoi route, and you will probably need a moto to get to the hotel when you arrive. Vietnamese drivers make a macho sport out of overtaking everything in sight—on blind corners or perilous cliff edges. Driving through the night, even Open Tour bus drivers attempt reckless overtake maneuvers. And this is doubly hazardous because drivers do not seem keen on using headlights, preferring to navigate in darkness. If you are hiring a jeep or 4WD vehicle of any sort, make it clear before you set out that the driver will not overtake in blind-corner situations, and will not attempt antics such as the double-overtake maneuver (this is where the driver attempts to overtake a truck that is already overtaking another truck on a narrow strip of road). If the trip is already under way and the driver makes a perilous move on a mountain road, signal for him to pull over and stop—and explain that there is no rush to reach the destination (you don't mind arriving half an hour later), and therefore no need to overtake all the time. Actually, you could explain that the opposite is true: You would prefer to go slower to take in the scenery and assess it for photo stops. To put that in blunter terms, you just want to live longer.

Crime

Although physical attacks are uncommon in Vietnam, theft directed at foreigners is increasing in Saigon and other big cities. Pickpockets are more common, and beggars more aggressive. Thieves will more likely be interested in your whole backpack or suitcase rather than in something inside them. Keep your bags within sight, or lock them up. Avoid black-market money changing; rates are no different from those in banks. Never change money on the street.

Petty theft is a problem in urban areas of Cambodia. Armed robberies of tourists have been reported at night in Phnom Penh; if out at night, avoid walking by yourself. Use a motorcycle-taxi or cyclo instead. Phnom Penh is prone to blackouts, making theft easier. Never travel after dark in the countryside.

There is banditry in some parts of Laos, related to opium growing and hilltribe antigovernment insurgency. Road travel may be risky, especially on the Vientiane–Luang Prabang, Vientiane–Paksane, and Luang Namtha–Ban Huay Sai roads. The alternative is to fly over all this in an aging Russian turboprop, which also has its hazardous side.

Beggars

Phnom Penh has a roving population of amputee beggars and street kids. As a wealthy foreigner, you will be an obvious target. In isolated cases it's OK to give some small riel bills to a beggar, but if there are others in sight, you risk being mobbed—which can lead to pickpocketing and other unfortunate consequences. Beggars and homeless children also abound at the major ruins of Angkor. They can be very persistent and aggressive. Kids often demand pens, sweets, or dollar bills.

For Women Travelers

In Buddhist countries harassment of Western women is usually not a problem, but it's best to be careful. However, karaoke has unfortunately altered Vietnamese males' perceptions of Western women. The only ones they've seen are the karaoke TV kind cavorting in bikinis or rolling around on beds in skimpy lingerie to the strains of Bob Marley or Boney M hits. Karaoke seems to be a synonym for sex among the Vietnamese; high-class bars offer private rooms with karaoke "hostesses." Women should be aware that certain cheap hotels, especially in the south, serve as short-time brothels patronized by Vietnamese men who drink in the lobby.

In Cambodia, there have been cases of intimidation reported by Westerners concerning Cambodian government soldiers. They will try to intimidate anyone, but they have also made approaches with sexual overtones to females in the Angkor area. A German woman was asked for a kiss—possibly a joke, but frightening when demanded by seven soldiers with guns.

Money

Credit cards are of extremely limited use in Indochina, outside of larger hotels, restaurants, and shops in major cities. Also, there may be markups of 4 percent or higher on purchases involving credit cards, and, while cash advances on credit cards are possible, commissions are high. Most visitors to Indochina carry traveler's checks and some U.S. cash. Most traveler's checks are accepted (keep to larger banks when changing; avoid hotel desks or shops). Independent money changers operating in Phnom Penh and Vientiane offer reasonable rates.

Cash U.S. dollars are the most convenient way of settling bills. However, there is no insurance against theft. What you can do is convert traveler's checks to U.S. cash at banks in major cities as needed. In Indochina commission rates vary 1–2 percent for converting traveler's checks to U.S. cash, so a $100 check nets $98–99. For easier calculations and better value, carry U.S. denomination traveler's checks. Cash U.S. dol-

lars are the coin of the realm—and practically the currency of Cambodia.

VIETNAM

An editorial in *The Asian Wall Street Journal* suggested the first thing Vietnam has to do if it's serious about joining the world economy is change the name of its currency. The word is the brunt of numerous jokes such as the businessman who wakes up in the morning and says, "I feel like a million dong!" Actually, there is such a thing as a 1,000,000-dong note. You'll occasionally see them displayed in jewelers' windows—it's much larger than regular bills, and Ho Chi Minh isn't on it. There's also a large 500,000-dong note.

At presstime for this book, the exchange rate was hovering at around 15,800 dong to the dollar. The dong comes in coins of 500, 1,000, 2,000, and 5,000 (nobody seems to like

CURRENCY CONVERSION RATES

Approximate rates for one U.S. dollar:

Vietnam	15,800 dong
Cambodia	4,000 riel
Laos	10,500 kip
Thailand	40 baht
Hong Kong	7.8 HK dollar
China	8.3 renminbi
Malaysia	3.8 ringgit
Singapore	1.65 Singapore dollar

Note: Asian currency rates are volatile. Consult an Internet currency converter to get the latest rates. Also, rates vary slightly for traveler's checks and cash. Rates may be higher for large U.S. bills. Some banks offer commission-free conversions but a slightly lower rate, while others may offer a better rate but a 1 percent or higher commission for converting traveler's checks.

using the coins); and paper bills of 200 (rare), 500, 1,000, 2,000, 5,000, 10,000, 20,000, 50,000, and 100,000. Newer incarnations of the 50,000- and 100,000-dong notes are made of a plastic-type material and have a see-through strip—apparently in an effort to stem the activities of forgers. One of the peculiar sights at a bank in Vietnam is a Mercedes unloading sacks of dong, with tellers presiding over mountains of dong that must be counted by hand (more sophisticated banks use counting machines). There must be very few bank robbers in the country—too much hard work lugging the stuff around.

ATMs usually dispense only 50,000- and 100,000-dong bills and are restricted to two million dong for each withdrawal. While the larger bills reduce your wad, the next problem is change. Nobody seems to have any. A good compromise is to change your funds into wads of 20,000-dong bills, which are less of a hassle to change. Be careful using the 20,000-dong bill—it looks very similar to the 5,000-dong bill, with the same coloration. You can tell the difference at a glance because Ho Chi Minh's

smile is more radiant on the 20,000-dong bill: It features a kind of blue halo around Uncle Ho. Bargaining in Vietnamese is quite easy because you can read off the number printed on the bill you wish to use. On the 10,000-dong bill, for example, is written *muoi nghin dong.*

Dong cannot be taken out of Vietnam—and let's face it, who would want to take it out anyway? So as you get nearer to departing Vietnamese shores, scale back your accumulation of dong. You may change dong up to the value of $500 at Vietcombank before leaving the country (produce an exchange receipt). More than $500 requires special paperwork.

U.S. Dollars

A fistful of dollars, or a fistful of dong? Because of logistical problems, larger transactions in Vietnam are usually conducted in U.S. cash dollars. You're not expected to drop 1.5 million dong on the counter for an airline ticket. The U.S. dollar is almost legal tender in Vietnam, although the government has moved to tighten the monetary system and curb everyday use of dollars and is trying to stop the unauthorized use of dollars by Vietnamese companies and shops. Airlines, telecommunications and shipping firms, and foreign companies are allowed to deal in U.S. dollars. Other cash currencies are not accepted so readily by some places, such as hotels. Euros, which are more stable than U.S. dollars, have been knocked back, and so have French francs and British pounds. This may be due to unfamiliarity, but it's also got a lot to do with the status of the U.S. dollar.

Be aware that there are fake U.S. bills circulating in Asia—black market dealers may traffic them in. Some $100-bill forgeries are state-of-the-art. Study any bills you receive (from any source) carefully. Some Vietnamese banks maintain detection equipment that will search for flaws in U.S. bills.

Banking

Vietnam's Bank of Foreign Trade (Vietcombank) will handle most transactions. Another major player is Sacombank. There is at least one Vietcombank or Sacombank in every major

Junks ply the waters of Halong Bay on the 10,000-dong note.

city. Foreign-run banks operate in Hanoi and Saigon, including Hong Kong Bank, Bangkok Bank, Banque National de Paris, Credit Lyonnais, Deutsche Bank, Britain's Standard Chartered Bank, Internationale Nederlanden Bank, and ANZ Bank. In 1995 Citibank upgraded its Hanoi office to a full branch, becoming the first American bank to operate in Vietnam since 1975. The Bank of America opened a branch in Hanoi shortly after. These banks cash traveler's checks and handle money transfers from abroad. Vietcombank and foreign banks offer cash advances on credit cards, usually with a high commission of 4 percent or more. Credit cards can be used at a number of venues in Saigon and Hanoi but less reliably elsewhere in the country. Saigon has double the number of establishments accepting credit cards than Hanoi. Accepted in Saigon are American Express, Visa, MasterCard, Diners Club, and JCB cards. Be aware that use of credit cards incurs a 3 percent charge (and 4 percent for American Express cards).

ATMs (automatic teller machines) are abundant in Hanoi and Saigon but harder to find elsewhere. You can draw on your home accounts by using your regular PIN or secret four-digit number encoded in the card's magnetic strip. If coming from the United States you may have to arrange to alter a six-digit code

to a four-digit. ATM withdrawals are restricted to two million dong each transaction. However, you can use your card to make consecutive draws of two million dong on the same day. ATMs usually dispense only 50,000- or 100,000-dong bills.

Costs

Gouging foreigners is a national sport in Vietnam. This infuriating practice is based entirely on racial and economic criteria: If you have a big nose, you pay through it. The practice will make your blood boil because it applies to just about everything. Somebody charging you triple for a coffee or a baguette can precipitate a major argument that will put you in a foul mood for the rest of the day. I was charged 50 percent above local price to send an airmail letter to Canada. One foreigner, married to a Vietnamese and living in Vietnam, is consistently charged more than his wife to place a phone call to the same place in the United States. One reason for this behavior may be that for many years under the French, the Vietnamese were treated little better than dogs. And still, today, foreigners can afford to eat in restaurants that are beyond the reach of locals and can afford privileges that the average Vietnamese cannot, such as the use of taxis or chauffeured cars.

Viet-Kieu, or overseas Vietnamese, hit middle

ground; they're charged more than locals but not as much as foreigners. If they speak fluent Vietnamese, they can probably get local prices; if not, prices are higher. The government leads the way. On Vietnam's official airline there are three prices: one for locals, another for overseas Vietnamese, a third (much higher) for foreigners. So if a foreigner and a Vietnamese friend sit down for lunch, what price is charged? Here the locals are confounded, because regardless of who pays, the Vietnamese person will scrutinize the bill. So hiring a Vietnamese guide can more than pay off by saving you from rip-offs. The same applies when shopping: The guide becomes your negotiator. A hard-nosed negotiator is a real asset on a trip through Vietnam.

To avoid misunderstandings, *always* establish the price of an item beforehand and write it down. If you're in a small restaurant or at a street stall with no menu or pricing, write up your order and have it itemized in dong, so in effect you receive the bill before you begin to eat. The same applies to a cyclo ride; some travelers even pay up front for cyclos to avoid confusion. Tipping is not expected, and bargaining the norm for services such as cyclos.

The traveler is most vulnerable to rip-offs within the first few days of arriving in Vietnam. For this purpose, hustlers will casually inquire how long you've been in the country, so don't let on. To avoid rip-offs, it's a good idea to assemble your own list of common purchases; get assistance from other travelers for the current rates. Find out the cost of a sandwich, a beer, bottled water, a cyclo ride across town, bicycle parking rates, and so on. Bear in mind that when it comes to signs in Vietnam, you're literate. You can read the bulletin boards listing prices for long-distance buses and other services. Find them. Read them. Point to them when negotiating your fare.

You won't be quoted Vietnamese prices. The magic formula for deciding foreigner prices for items such as airline tickets, train sleepers, and hotels seems to be to multiply the Vietnamese price by 2.5, so foreigners pay between two and three times more than Vietnamese. A Vietnamese price for a hotel room may be 30,000 dong ($2.80), but for a foreigner it might be $7. In some cases, the foreigner price is much more; for entry to the Perfume Pagoda near Hanoi, foreigners pay five times the local price.

CAMBODIA

The unit of currency in Cambodia is the riel, with exchange rates hovering (at press time) at 4,000 riels to the U.S. dollar. To promote use of the riel over the dollar, in 1995 the National Bank issued new notes printed by the French. The notes are in denominations of 500, 1,000, 2,000, 5,000, 10,000, 50,000, and 100,000 riel. The notes bear both a watermark and a metallic strip; all but two feature King Norodom Sihanouk. The 100,000-riel note shows both the king and queen and is worth about $25 but is not much seen in circulation.

Restaurant menus in Phnom Penh may quote three prices—dollars, riels, and Thai baht. There are no U.S. coins circulating, so if a dish is priced at $1.30 or $1.70, and you pay in dollars, you'll receive change in riels. If you pay in baht, change will come in baht or riels.

Banking

There are lots of banks in Phnom Penh and Siem Reap, but few elsewhere it seems. And even if you find a bank elsewhere, it might not want to cash your traveler's checks. Best to carry some U.S. cash up-country because you can always find locals who'll change dollars into riel. Jewelers in markets up-country will change money. Credit cards are of limited use in Cambodia, though the larger hotels in Phnom Penh will accept Visa and MasterCard. Cash advances mean high commissions.

Counterfeit Bills

Beware of fake high-denomination U.S. bills. Some are obviously of poor quality, but others are hard to distinguish from the real thing. In March 1995 two Thais and two Cambodians were arrested in Poipet for illegally importing $1.5 million in fake US$100 bills. Two months earlier Thai police in Aranyaprathet arrested two Thais with $390,000 in fake US$100 bills.

Although police confiscate the fake bills, banks in Phnom Penh may hand bad bills back, which means they remain in circulation. In early 1995 police confiscated almost 30,000 fake US$100 bills peddled by Phnom Penh money changers. A further 100,000 fake Thai baht bills were also confiscated.

LAOS

The unit of currency in Laos is the kip, with paper bill denominations: 500, and 1,000, 2,000, 5,000, 10,000, and 20,000. In 2005, the conversion rate was 10,500 kip to the dollar. The kip is useless once out of Laos, and because the biggest bill is worth less than $2, it's very impractical to carry around large amounts of kip—your pockets will overflow with the stuff. Use kip for small transactions, but pay for larger purchases in dollars or Thai baht. There

are no ATMs in Laos, but you can withdraw a load of Thai baht from an ATM across the border in Thailand and use that.

Laos has a largely cash economy. In remote areas, not even cash is used; trading is based on barter. Credit cards are rarely used in Vientiane; some hotels, restaurants, and shops in the capital accept them, and you can buy tickets on Lao Airlines with a Visa card. The agent for Visa in Vientiane is Banque pour le Commerce Extérieur. Cash advances for Visa and Master-Card are available in baht through Thai banks in Vientiane. The agent for American Express is Diethelm Travel in Vientiane.

Costs

You can keep transport expenses down by traveling overland by boat or bus. Lodging is cheap in Laos compared to neighboring nations, and food is also very reasonable.

Measurements and Communications

VIETNAM
Maps

Buy as much map material as you can outside Vietnam. The most accurate, up-to-date map of Vietnam is produced by International Travel Maps in combination with the Cartographic Mapping Institute of Hanoi (CMI). It provides topographic features, the names of provinces and provincial capitals, and realistic road and route detail; submaps offer details of central Saigon and central Hanoi. In the ITM/CMI series are also separate maps of Hanoi (single-sided), Saigon (double-sided), and the Mekong Delta. Another map on the market is Periplus Editions' *Vietnam Travel Map*, which is less detailed as a country map but carries a number of city submaps.

Within Vietnam the selection is spotty. But there are surprises. On sale is a terrific map titled *Vietnam: Ecotourism Map*, researched and published by Fauna and Flora International, a British conservation group. The double-sided map shows all national park areas in

Vietnam and has inset maps of Sapa area, Cat Tien National Park, Cat Ba National Park, and others. Invaluable are the annotations, giving hard-to-come-by snippets on wildlife, diving, trekking, kayaking, biking, and bird-watching. The map costs $6.

For about $5 you can buy an 80-page *Vietnam Atlas,* published in Hanoi, with a good selection of highway, region, and city maps (although the latter are hard to read). Useful city maps are available within Vietnam, but supply is erratic. Sometimes a good map of Hué may be on sale only in Saigon. Pick up maps where you find them, as you might not see them again. Reading Vietnamese maps presents few problems except perhaps for deciphering the keys.

Books

Because of government monitoring of printed material, it's difficult to find reading material in English or French in Vietnam. What is available may be pirated or photocopied to get around government import restrictions. A single bookstore in Bangkok will probably stock more reading material on Vietnam than you'll find in the entire city of Saigon. The material will be more intelligible, too. Government-run bookstores in Vietnam sell boring tomes of pure propaganda written in garbled English.

Media

In a halfhearted attempt to modernize Vietnam TV (VTV), the Vietnamese Ministry of Culture has replaced irrigation documentaries and folk-dance contests with spicier pirated videos from Hong Kong and the United States. Satellite TV has not made great inroads into Vietnam. Dish distribution is tightly controlled—only major hotels and embassies have been permitted to install dishes that can pick up Hong Kong–based StarTV, which includes BBC programs. Other channels pick up CNN, ABC (Australia), and VTV (Indian music station). On radio, Voice of Vietnam broadcasts in a dozen foreign languages, although broadcasts are brief. On shortwave radio you can pick up the BBC, Radio Australia, and Voice of America.

Press laws in Vietnam prohibit criticism of official government policy. Newspapers or magazines that do not comply are shut down by the Ministry of Culture for a few weeks or longer. Publishers may also be ordered to recall a particular issue. The Casting and Metallurgy Association was asked to recall a 1995 issue of *Knowledge and Technology* because only five of 24 stories concerned metals and engineering; the rest concerned crime, cannibalism, a man with 105 wives, and the secrets of embalming. Obviously, these were stories with no mettle.

Foreign magazines are often full of saucy articles and criticism of just about everything and are sold in Vietnam in upper-crust hotel lobbies. But they're priced so high that the average Vietnamese is not likely to lay hands on them. Among the foreign magazines on sale are *Newsweek, Time,* and *Paris Match.* You can also buy the *International Herald Tribune, Sydney Morning Herald, Le Monde,* and day-old copies of the *Bangkok Post.*

There are several weekly English-language newspapers produced in Vietnam, including *Saigon Times* and *Vietnam Investment Review.* *Vietnam News* is issued weekdays, as is the French *Le Courier du Vietnam.* Hotel newsstands and gift shops in Saigon and Hanoi also carry *Vietnam Today,* a business magazine published in Singapore. *Business News Indochina,* a journal published monthly in Hong Kong, is available in Vietnam.

Post Office and Courier

Post offices in Vietnam offer regular and express mail service, parcel service, telex, telegram, fax, and possibly courier services. *Poste restante* is available in major Vietnamese cities—letters all go into one big box at the main post office. Incoming mail is not guaranteed in Vietnam. Some mail arrives minus stamps; some mail arrives very late; some mail never arrives. To increase chances (from an official viewpoint), have packages addressed to "Socialist Republic of Vietnam." At one point in the 1980s, the government stopped all magazines and photos arriving by post. Outgoing mail takes about two weeks to reach the West by air. For letters and packages, it's advisable to pay a small extra fee for registration of items, and make sure stamps are cancelled in front of you. Do not fully package materials as you'll have to open up for "customs" inspection before mailing. If you're heading to Bangkok, Hong Kong, or Singapore, save your bundle and mail from there; the service is more efficient, faster, safer, and cheaper.

Vietnamese postal rates are high by Asian standards and impossibly high by local standards. An airmail postcard to Hong Kong or Sydney costs $.41; to Paris $.43; to New York, $.50. With an income of perhaps $1 a day, few Vietnamese can afford to send postcards or letters. If you want to correspond, supply your Vietnamese correspondent with stamps. Regular mail items are accepted up to two kilograms. Cheaper rates are offered for small parcels or printed matter; books can be sent as printed matter up to five kilograms. For overseas parcels, the maximum weight is five kilograms unless a postal service agreement exists with the destination country, when it can rise to 10 kilograms or more.

For greater security and speed, a courier such as DHL, UPS, or TNT is preferable, though rates are exorbitant. Courier services operate from the larger cities, including Hanoi, Haiphong, Danang, Qui Nhon, Nha Trang, and Saigon. In Hanoi and Saigon, DHL operates from the central post office, and Federal Express is not far behind.

Fax and Phone

There are bilingual phone directories for both Saigon and Hanoi: You can help yourself to detailed information on fax rates, IDD phone rates, and EMS postal rates. A bewildering number of foreign companies—French, Japanese, Australian, Malaysian, Korean, and American—supply new telecommunications equipment to Vietnam. Within Vietnam, calling can be erratic. IDD (International Direct Dialed) calls are not cheap: The first three minutes to the United States, the United Kingdom, or France direct dial cost $13.80; for a person-to-person call it's $17.62. To Australia the first three minutes cost $12 direct dial, and $15.15 person-to-person; to Hong Kong or Bangkok the rates are $11.40 direct, and $14.35 person-to-person. For operator-assisted international calls, dial 110; for direct dialing, the prefix is 00, plus country code followed by the number. For domestic calls, dial 101 to place operator-assisted calls. Dial 01 for direct domestic dialing, plus country code and number. The Vietnam country code is 84. Some area codes: Hanoi 4, Saigon 8, Haiphong 31, Danang 51, Hué 54, Qui Nhon 56, Nha Trang 58, Dalat 63, Vung Tau 64. You can buy phone cards for more convenient use of public phones. Cards may be issued in 60,000-dong, 150,000-dong, 300,000-dong, or other denominations.

Consider faxing or emailing (or using a NetPhone system) instead of telephoning. Beware of hotels that don't list fax rates. Some are prone to charging double or even triple the rate charged by the post office in the interest of fund-raising. Receiving a fax incurs charges in hotels but is usually inexpensive.

Email and Internet

One thing coming down the phone line that has the Vietnamese government very worried is the anarchic Internet. The bulletin boards of Varenet (Vietnam Academic, Research, and Education Network) have been bombarded with criticism of the Hanoi government by disgruntled expatriate Vietnamese in the United States. Varenet launched a quasicommercial Internet service in 1994 called Netnam, but the government is nervous. Cut off from events in Vietnam, exiled dissidents have tended to fade away; the Internet may allow their voices to be heard again, cheaply and instantaneously. In any event, since December 1997 there has been Internet access in Vietnam, meaning that major hotel business centers have it. Many cybercafés throng the tourist centers of Vietnam: Hanoi, Saigon, Hué, Hoi An, and Sapa. Internet access is very cheap in Vietnam but can be frustratingly slow.

Time Zone

Vietnam is all on one time zone: Greenwich mean time +7 hours; eastern standard time +12; Pacific standard time +15. Figures may vary with daylight saving time. When in Hanoi or Saigon, time in London is -7 hours; Paris -6; New York/Toronto -12; San Francisco/Vancouver -15; Sydney +3 hours.

Metric and Electric

Vietnam follows the metric system. The Vietnamese words for gram, kilogram, ton, kilometer, and liter sound almost the same as in English, though rendered with tones. Currents in Vietnam are 220V/50 cycles in urban areas and 110V/50 cycles in rural areas. There's rarely enough electricity to go around; service is erratic, with blackouts or power surges common. Wiring is often improvised, sometimes with exposed wires hanging around bathrooms. Sockets may be two-prong, with American-style flat pins (220V, mostly in the south), or Russian- and European-style round pins (mostly in the north). Don't even think about using a hair dryer.

THE LANGUAGE WAR

A battle rages in Phnom Penh over the use of French or English as the country's second language. The older generation was schooled in French; the younger generation wants to study English. Makeshift English schools proliferate in Phnom Penh temples, alleyways, and roadside shacks. While Laos and Vietnam accepted the reality of English as the language of business, pro-French King Sihanouk opted for French. First Prime Minister Ranariddh was schooled in France, as were a number of prominent members of parliament.

Cambodia is France's last bastion in Asia. France has mounted a major campaign to bring French back to Cambodia's intellectual, business, and cultural life. The French Embassy has signed exclusive deals that allow France to train and equip Cambodian government organizations—the military, legal and health professions, and the civil service. French advisers are urging that 100-year-old colonial laws continue to serve as civil and legal codes.

Cambodia's education system is mainly dependent on foreign donors; the country is the world's largest recipient of French aid on a per capita basis. France makes its multimillion-dollar contributions—programs, training, books, equipment—conditional on the use of the French language. In 1993 1,000 students at Phnom Penh's Institute of Technology staged street demonstrations against a requirement that they study French. The students wanted to study courses in English. Institute courses were taught in Russian from the mid-1980s–1992; the curriculum switched to French after France agreed to renovate laboratories—on the condition courses be taught in French. The protesting students claimed learning French as a second language would hamper Cambodia's development and international relations.

Elsewhere in Asia, Anglo-American is the language of business and law. The Cambodian Finance Ministry declared the French accounting system the only one acceptable to the new government for foreign business transactions. Critics say this will deter foreign investment. All ASEAN states use an international accounting system incompatible with the French model.

CAMBODIA

Telecommunications

Back in the 1970s Cambodia had only a few international phone lines to Moscow; today, Cambodia has the world's lowest density of telecom facilities. There are very few phone connections up-country in Cambodia. For the 1993 elections a U.N. satellite network, including a cellular phone system, was installed by Australian company OTC/Telstra at a cost of $50 million. It was handed over to Cambodia when the United Nations left and provided communication among all of Cambodia's provinces, though it quickly fell into disrepair from theft, vandalism, and lack of maintenance. The network is being refurbished by Indonesia's Indosat company; other phone systems have been installed by Thai company Shinawatra and Malaysia's Tricelcam.

Telstra brought Internet and email services to Cambodia via a satellite link to Sydney. The Thai company Samart offers a satellite phone system and handles IDD (International Direct Dialed) and mobile phone calls in Phnom Penh, Siem Reap, Sihanoukville, Battambang, and Kompong Cham. Embassies and major hotels use Samart satellite dishes for IDD and fax contact. Major hotels in Phnom Penh and elsewhere use the Samart system for IDD calling.

IDD calls from Cambodia are expensive—it's cheaper to use a NetPhone connection at an Internet café. Phnom Penh is seven hours ahead of Greenwich mean time. You can buy phone cards (embossed with Angkor Wat pictures) in denominations of $2, $5, $10, $20, $50, and $100 for use in special phone booths that can handle IDD calls. The Cambodia country code is 855; Phnom Penh IDD code is 23; Siem Reap is 63; Sihanoukville 34. Popular mobile networks are 012, 016, and 011, but calls can be very difficult at peak hours, and the networks demand loyalty, meaning that if you try to call across networks, you might well have no reception. SIM cards are difficult to buy in Cambodia unless you are a resident with papers to prove it.

Post from Cambodia is slow, expensive, and unreliable. Post offices are signposted PTT (Poste Télégraphe Téléphone). Parcel weights are accepted up to two kilograms, and everything is shipped airmail rate. One kilogram costs $26 to ship to Canada, or $10 to Bangkok. It's cheaper and more reliable to send mail from a point such as Hong Kong or Bangkok—if flying to these points, hold on to your mail. Courier offices in Phnom Penh include DHL, UPS, and TNT.

Email and Internet

Internet access is not widespread in Cambodia and remains expensive. There are many cyber-cafés in Phnom Penh and in Siem Reap, but the rest of the country has spotty cybercafé services. In Phnom Penh, some of the more expensive cybercafés have faster connections. Using a prepaid card system, PIC Online has set up WiFi hotspots in a number of cafés and hotels in Phnom Penh and Siem Reap.

Metric and Electric

Cambodia uses the metric system. Electricity, when available, is 220V/ 50 cycles. Electricity is a scarce commodity in Cambodia—even in Phnom Penh many hotels and businesses must rely on in-house generators during blackouts or when the public power is turned off.

LAOS

Until 1990 Laos maintained only a single phone line to the outside world, bar lines to the Soviet Union and Thailand. The situation has improved since then, but most of the links are to Vientiane—few other parts of the country are connected by phone. Where phones exist, IDD (International Direct Dialed) calls and faxes are expensive. A one-page fax to Europe costs $15 from Vientiane; to Bangkok a page costs $6. Vientiane is seven hours ahead of Greenwich mean time. The country code for Laos is 856.

There are post offices (PTT) in the larger towns—Vientiane, Luang Prabang, Pakse, and Savannakhet. Service may be unreliable. Courier services operating from Vientiane include DHL, TNT, and UPS.

Under the French, Laos issued beautiful postage stamps with traditional themes—temples, Buddhist art, legends, flora and fauna—all printed in Paris. Some of the modern stamps still feature these themes. Today's stamp subjects also include dinosaurs, the American Bicentennial, the 100th anniversary of Ho Chi Minh's birth, Barcelona '92 Olympics, and The War Against Drugs Campaign. The stamps may cover half a postcard—it's best to apply them first, then add the text.

Email and Internet

Cybercafés in Laos cater mainly to tourism and can be found in Vientiane, Vangvieng, Luang Prabang, Luang Namtha, and Pakse. Cost is low, but connections are slow. A cybercafé chain called Planet Online has good operations in Vientiane, Vangvieng, and Luang Prabang. It's homepage is www.laopdr.com.

Metric and Electric

Laos uses the metric system. Electricity is mostly 220 volts/ 50 cycles, using two-pin sockets, both flat and round plugs. If you're bringing 110-volt devices, you'll need a converter. A computer surge protector is a good idea.

Services and Information

VIETNAM

Tourist Information

Current information about Vietnam is difficult to find, especially outside Vietnam. Vietnam Tourism and Saigon Tourist have only a few offices abroad. You can apply through these offices for visas. Vietnam Tourism maintains offices in Indiana, at P.O. Box 53316, Indianapolis, IN 46253, USA, tel. 317/388-0788, fax 317/298-3454 (mostly deals with group tours, no individuals); in Paris at 4 rue Cherubini 75002, Paris, tel. 1/42868637, fax 1/42604332; and Singapore at 101 Upper Cross St. #02-44, People's Park Centre, Singapore 0105. Saigon Tourist staffs offices in Hamburg at Hamburger Str. 132, 200 Hamburg 76, fax 40/296705; and Tokyo at 7F Crystal Bldg. 1–2, Kanda Awajicho, Chiyoda-Ku, Tokyo 101, fax 3/3253-5757.

Traveler Network

Vietnam is changing fast, and guidebook listings often cannot keep pace. New hotels are going up, new restaurants opening, new regions opening to travelers. Keep your ears and eyes open. The best way of getting up-to-the-minute information is to frequent traveler cafés. Here you can meet travelers coming from the opposite direction, their brains bulging with fresh data. Traveler cafés serve mediocre food, but over the bowls of noodles backpackers gather to swap tales. Sauce and source: Most of the cafés maintain traveler logbooks with comments about destinations.

Business Services

Major hotels in Hanoi and Saigon offer business centers providing translation, telecommunications, and secretarial services. There are also independent operators. Software can easily handle combinations of Vietnamese and English text. Computers are slowly creeping into Vietnam, though a high percentage of software is pirated, a throwback to the days of the U.S. embargo. If bringing in electrical devices, it's best to run them off rechargeable batteries; bring a recharge unit that can be plugged into the wall. This way you don't have to worry about a sudden surge of electricity zapping a laptop computer. Power surges are common, so use a surge protector with sensitive equipment.

Business Hours

Business is most often conducted from 0700 or 0800 to 1600 or 1700, closing at midday for 1–2 hours. Market hours are 0730–1700 daily; post offices, 0730–1800 and often till 2200; embassies and consulates, 0800–1100 and 1400–1630 Monday–Friday; banks and airlines, 0800–1130 and 1300–1630, half-day Saturday, closed Sunday. Some foreign banks and airlines keep Western hours, say, 0900–1530. Museums are generally open 0800–1130 and 1300–1630 Tuesday–Sunday.

Health Care

Vietnamese health care is woefully substandard. Equipment and skills date to the 1930s, or perhaps even the Dark Ages. However, conditions are improving. Some joint-venture medical consultancies operate in Hanoi, Danang, and Saigon. However, in case of an emergency, you are best advised to evacuate to Singapore, Bangkok, or Hong Kong. Evacuation insurance is advisable. (See *Health and Safety* for a complete rundown of health hazards in Indochina.)

CAMBODIA

Traveler Network

Many travelers find the Cambodian people among the friendliest in Asia and end up staying longer than planned. Tourist information from official sources is almost nonexistent, and where it does exist, is not likely to discuss mines or bandits.

Maps and Books

An up-to-date, accurate map of Cambodia is important. For geographical detail, the finest

VIDEO STARS

In the late 1980s, expatriate Cambodian visitors left behind a few VHS camcorders for their poorer cousins. Local entrepreneurs, struck by the appeal of third-rate Indian, Vietnamese, and Soviet-bloc films, set about making two-hour dramas. In 1990, when the government organized the first Cambodian Film and Video Festival, there were more than 150 companies registered with the Ministry of Culture's Film Department. The industry has made instant celebrities of a handful of Cambodian actors and actresses. Huge, brightly painted billboards announce the current attractions.

Plots are melodramatic and little is planned. The crew of 15 shoots with just a camera, monitor, and some reflector boards. Actors mouth whatever the director tells them to say—it doesn't really matter because the scenes are dubbed with sound later anyway. The budget is $2,000–$3,000. Actors come from the University of Fine Arts Theater School, although no talented neighbor or friend is beyond consideration. Shooting takes a month, and postproduction perhaps another two weeks. Soundtracks can be pirated from any source, since there is a lack of copyright laws.

After Hollywood on the Mekong has done its job, the effort hits the big screen, where voices shake because of distortion and echo effects. Like any other moviegoers, Cambodians want escapist entertainment. This is provided with rags-to-riches stories and melodramatic and sentimental romances. Male characters drip gold jewelry, wear leather boots, drive cars, and use cellular phones; actresses wear miniskirts, use lots of makeup, and provocatively sway their hips in contrast to the modest apparel and movements of the average Cambodian woman.

Fame and fortune come to those acting in the video dramas. They can enjoy new Honda Dream motorcycles and watch their portraits sell out in local photo shops. However, there are drawbacks. Actors and actresses known for playing angry heroes or vixens are not necessarily welcomed in person by Cambodian society, with its Buddhist ethics. As one young screen idol put it, "After I graduate from university, I will stop acting, because no Cambodian family will let their daughter marry an actor."

Return of the Big Screen

The country's best-known celluloid creator is King Sihanouk, who wrote, directed, and even starred in his own movies during the 1950s and 1960s. In a country with a ruined infrastructure, it's remarkable that celluloid production has started up again. Using equipment thrown away by Vietnamese and Czech film crews, some filmmakers are now producing work in 8mm and 16mm formats. Students at Phnom Penh's National Cinema Center are instructed by Rithy Panh, who wrangled a scholarship to study film in France in the 1980s and has since been involved in Khmer-French coproductions. Panh has been hailed internationally for his feature, *The People of the Ricefields,* filmed in 1993. His 1996 feature film *A Cambodian Tragedy* was the first Khmer-language film made about the Khmer Rouge holocaust. Panh's 1998 movie *One Night After the War* was screened at Cannes. The film—set in Phnom Penh of 1992—portrays the generation that survived war and fighting. "Movies give the Cambodian people the tools to come to terms with their past," says Panh. "Once we have resolved that problem, we can move on."

Meanwhile, moving along into the 21st-century box office, 35mm film has reappeared in Cambodia. Cambodia used to have a vibrant film industry: Studios churned out 50-odd films a year for local consumption, and Phnom Penh had about

30 cinemas. Many actors were killed during the Khmer Rouge era, and Phnom Penh's cinemas were destroyed. In fact, for a long time the only places capable of screening 35mm films were minitheaters at the French Cultural Center and Russian Cultural Center in Phnom Penh. But now that is changing with the construction of Vimean Theater on Monivong Boulevard in downtown Phnom Penh. A joint Korean-Cambodian venture, this 800-seat theater uses modern American 35mm projection equipment with Dolby surround-sound.

Other parts of the country are not so lucky: The promotion crew for a movie released in 2001 had to drive around with a 35mm projector, improvising a screen. The movie is *The Snake King's Child,* directed by Fay Sam Ang, who honed his cinematic skills making MTV-type videos for TV3 in Phnom Penh. Fay Sam Ang wanted to find a copy of a 1960s classic movie about the Cambodian legend of a peasant woman seduced by the king of snakes (echoing the ancient legend of the origin of the Khmer people). But he couldn't find the print—they had all been destroyed by the fanatical Khmer Rouge. So he set out to make his own version of the mythical story. Fay Sam Ang says his movie is a kind of love story, along with liberal doses of melodrama, magic, sorcery—and snakes.

On such a low budget, there's not much money for special effects. So the director used real snakes—with seven snake handlers on the set. Borrowed from a temple, a five-meter-long python stars as the Snake King—slithering over the top of soap star Ampor Tevy and flickering its tongue at her. The actress, who was very afraid at first, came to trust the giant, but moviemaking may have proven more taxing for the python, which expired shortly after the movie shoot ended. And then there's a collection of smaller snakes that form the headdress for the female star of the movie—the daughter of the Snake King. No special effects here, either—the Medusa-like coiffure is real. The 35mm movie with Dolby sound was shot in six months on a shoestring budget of $250,000. But it raked in $100,000 in the first three days of its release in Cambodia and Thailand: That's great news for director Fay Sam Ang, because it means a privately funded Khmer-language movie can make it in the marketplace.

Meanwhile, big-budget productions have returned to Cambodia to shoot on location. A part of the action-adventure movie *Lara Croft: Tomb Raider,* starring Angelina Jolie, was filmed on location at Angkor in late 2000. The big-budget flick, made by British director Simon West, was released in 2001. This marked the first time in three decades that a big-budget movie was filmed in Cambodia (the last time was in the 1960s, when Peter O'Toole's *Lord Jim* was made then). Some of the final scenes for Hong Kong director Wong Kar-wai's *In the Mood for Love,* were filmed at Angkor—Hong Kong star Tony Leung won Best Actor Award for it at Cannes 2000. Matt Dillon's *City of Ghosts,* shot on location in Phnom Penh and nearby, was released in 2002—it has a confusing storyline about a con man who flees the United States to track down his mentor in Cambodia. French director Jean-Jacques Annaud made good use of the Angkor region as a set for the filming of *Two Brothers* (2004), a story about two tigers growing up in Cambodia. The French colonial scenes in the movie are vivid.

is *Cambodia Road Map,* published by Gecko Maps from Switzerland—the country detail is unbeatable, but the submaps of Phnom Penh and Angkor are somewhat dated. Another fine map is the Periplus *Travel Map of Cambodia,* including submaps of Phnom Penh and Angkor—all handsomely produced with annotated material. Check Canby Publications' Visitors Guide series for up-to-date maps of Phnom Penh, Siem Reap, and Sihanoukville.

You can buy some decent maps in Phnom Penh. Particularly useful are the color maps produced by Point Maps and Guides. One map offers a remarkably detailed three-dimensional overview of the city of Phnom Penh; a second map does the same for Siem Reap and the Angkor area. The maps cost a few dollars each.

Availability of books in Cambodia is limited, and much of the material is either overpriced originals or hard-to-read photocopies of books. You're better off stocking up in Bangkok or Hong Kong. It's a good idea to take along some background and cultural material on Angkor (see *Suggested Reading* in *Resources* for ideas).

Media

Cambodia has more than 30 Khmer publications, two French-language newspapers, and three English journals. The *Phnom Penh Post* is an excellent publication issued twice a month. Since its creation in 1992, it has won accolades from journalists worldwide as an essential tool for understanding events in Cambodia. The *Post* is owned by an American couple, printed in Bangkok, and maintains offices in Phnom Penh. The centerfold contains a map of Phnom Penh featuring paid advertisers; it's useful as a base map nonetheless. A second English-language newspaper is *The Cambodia Times,* published by a Malaysian public relations firm based in Kuala Lumpur. The paper is pro-government, which does not make for inspiring copy. There's also *Cambodia Daily,* in a smaller format with international news summaries. In French, *Cambodge Soir* is published three times a week, while *Le Mékong* is published monthly. The latter is available in Hong Kong, Bangkok, and Saigon.

There is one state-owned television station and one private one. Thai telecom giant Shinawatra operates a TV channel with a 100-square-kilometer radius around Phnom Penh. Satellite dishes can pick up Hong Kong's StarTV (BBC World Service Television), Australia's ATVI, and CFI, a French channel retransmitted over Phnom Penh by the French Cultural Center. On radio you can pick up Radio France Internationale (RFI), the BBC, VOA, and Radio Australia.

Services

Business centers can be found in Phnom Penh at major hotels and a few independent locations. They operate computing, translating, and secretarial services, as well as telecommunication and photocopy facilities. There are film labs in downtown Phnom Penh that sell brand-name film, but you'd be better off buying it in Bangkok or Hong Kong to ensure freshness. In Phnom Penh most offices are open 0700–1100 or 1130, followed by a lunch siesta, reopening 1400–1700 or 1730. Most are closed Sundays. Some businesses, especially joint-venture concerns, keep Western office hours of 0900–1700. Embassies are usually open mornings only.

Health Care

The standard is very poor. Most of Cambodia's doctors were killed or sent into exile during the Pol Pot era, which means a severe shortage of skilled medical staff. Foreign aid groups such as the Red Cross fill the vacuum. In serious cases, evacuation to Bangkok, Hong Kong, or Singapore is advised. A few foreign doctors and dentists operate privately in Phnom Penh—ask your embassy for recommendations. International SOS will arrange emergency evacuation from Cambodia to Singapore. It's at 161 Street 51, Sang-Kat Boeung Peng, Khon Doun Penh, tel. 23/216911, fax 23/215811.

LAOS

Tourist Information

The Lao National Tourism Authority (NTSA) was established in 1991 and as yet assists only group tours. None of the NTSA offices in Laos are useful to individuals. You're better off asking travel agents for information.

Traveler Network

Because there are so few hotels in the country, it's easy to meet other travelers. In Vientiane are a few watering holes where travelers hang out.

Maps and Books

Any kind of printed material on Laos is hard to come by—scrounge where you can. An excellent map of Laos is the GT-Rider *Guidemap,* produced in Thailand. This map carries a wealth of city and town submaps, and it is laminated so you can open it up in the rainy season. You can obtain topographical maps of most parts of Laos from the State Geographic Service in Vientiane. Good maps of Vientiane itself are available, but the rest of the place is erratic. The only bookstore of any note in the entire country is Vientiane Book Center in Vientiane.

Information Highway

The "information highway" is coming to Vientiane. Around 1992, the Lao government for the first time permitted foreign newspapers, international direct dialing, private fax machines, and satellite dishes. While these changes mean little to the average farmer, they herald a major shift in attitude. In 1994, the Lao Information and Culture Ministry started a weekly newspaper, *The Vientiane Times,* the country's first English-language newspaper since 1975. Laotians, however, worry about the spread of Thai pop culture with this new media onslaught: Most of the television, pop songs, and magazines in Laos are Thai.

Media

Lao National Radio broadcasts news in English twice a day, but most expatriates in Vientiane prefer the shortwave version on BBC, VOA, or Radio Australia. The national television station on Channel 8 broadcasts in Lao for about five hours a night. Most prefer watching Thai television, received from across the Mekong, which broadcasts a mix of Thai and English programming. Satellite dishes are starting to sprout around Vientiane; a regular dish can pick up StarTV, which includes BBC World Service, while a large dish will receive CNN. Satellite dishes are provided to the Lao market by Samart Group, the largest dish maker in Thailand. The Thai group Shinawatra signed a number of telecom and broadcasting deals with the Lao government in 1993; among them was the opportunity to set up a nongovernment television station—Vientiane's Channel 3—run by International Broadcasting Company (IBC). It will provide mostly Laotian programs.

Services

The Laotians are not big on services. The major hotels in Vientiane and Luang Prabang handle business services and recreational efforts such as the odd swimming pool. Computers are used (sparingly) in Vientiane; Lao- and Thai-style fonts can be imported into English programs through Windows. Vientiane also offers photocopy services and film labs. You're advised to bring film with you—buy it in Bangkok or Hong Kong. Outside of Vientiane and Luang Prabang, don't count on even the most basic of services. Business hours for shops and offices in Vientiane are roughly 0800–1200 and 1400–1700, Saturday 0800–1200, closed Sunday.

Health Care

By Western standards, medical care in Laos is poor to nonexistent. Carry good medical supplies with you, and if the situation warrants it, travel to Thailand for proper medical care. Equipment considered obsolete in the United States is state-of-the-art in Laos. Western doctors visiting southern Laos have witnessed the use of blunt razor blades for eye "surgery," and a hand-pumped ambu-bag fashioned from the inside of a football for resuscitation. Lao health services are severely lacking in supplies, equipment, and training.

The situation is better in Vientiane, where the Australian and Swedish embassies maintain their own clinics. In worst-case scenarios, evacuation is available by Westcoast Helicopter from Vientiane to Udon Thani in Thailand. Lao Westcoast Helicopter (tel. 21/512023) charges about $850 for the run to Udon, 50 kilometers south of Nong Khai.

Getting There

There are direct flights to Vietnam, but Bangkok, Hong Kong, Kuala Lumpur, and Singapore are the transport hubs of Asia, with frequent discount flights from Europe, North America, and Australia. For travel during the November–February peak season, book well in advance—three months or more. At Tet, the Lunar New Year, there are aerial bottlenecks all over Asia. It's best just to stay out of Asian airspace at this time.

Many travelers to Indochina stop first in Bangkok or Hong Kong because of these cities' frequent air connections, visa services, travel agents, and good information sources. You can complete all your trip preparations in either city, including last-minute purchases. For Canadian, U.S., Australian, New Zealand, and European passport holders, these cities do not require visas for stays of 14 days or less. Some are even more generous: Malaysia offers a two-month stay on arrival for U.K. or U.S. passport holders; Hong Kong and Thailand usually offer a month or longer.

The primary gateway for Vietnam, Cambodia, and Laos is Bangkok, where you'll find the most frequent air connections. An increasing number of travelers from East Asia and the United States, however, visit Indochina via Hong Kong or the Philippines. Flights from the U.S. West Coast to Hong Kong and Manila may be $100 cheaper than flights to Bangkok (though this is offset by the fact that it's cheaper to stay in Bangkok). Hong Kong handles southern China and northern Vietnam and is particularly good for connections into Hanoi.

For those keen on tracking baggage labels, some relevant air codes are: Bangkok, BKK; Hong Kong, HKG; Singapore, SIN; Kunming, KMG; Guangzhou, CAN; Hanoi, HAN; Danang, DAD; Hué, HUI; Saigon, SGN; Phnom Penh, PNH; Vientiane, VTE; Luang Prabang, LPQ.

VIETNAM

By Air

More than 25 airlines from as many countries schedule flights to Vietnam and maintain representative offices there. The national carrier, Vietnam Airlines, has offices in more than 20 countries. More connections are on the way. A number of aviation agreements have been signed to open new routes to Europe, Australia, Japan, and the United States. There will also be more frequent flights in the region from Vietnam to Bangkok, Vientiane, Phnom Penh, and Hong Kong.

There are two flight paths into Vietnam: direct, or via a staging point such as Bangkok, Hong Kong, or Singapore, with frequent connections to Saigon or Hanoi. It's generally cheaper at present to approach Vietnam from Bangkok or Hong Kong. Carriers flying into Vietnam include Cathay Pacific, Malaysia Airlines, Korean Air, Singapore Airlines, China Airlines, Air France, Thai International, Lufthansa, KLM, Philippine Airlines, and Japan Airlines. Vietnam Airlines often arranges joint service with these airlines, taking over the final leg from, say, Bangkok or Hong Kong.

The majority of flights into Vietnam are routed through Saigon. With some carriers it's possible to arrive in Hanoi and depart from Saigon, or vice versa. A third international airport is open at Danang, with possible direct flights from Singapore (other flights have been routed through Saigon or Hanoi). Another direct flight into Vietnam goes from Singapore to Vung Tau on RegionAir: This flight caters to those in the oil and gas industry, and also to businesspeople and tourists.

Customs

On entry each person is allowed 200 cigarettes or 50 cigars, one liter of spirits, and one liter of wine. On exit, your entry/exit card and customs form are collected with a cursory check only. Buddha images, antiques, or items "of high cultural value" may not be exported unless accompanied by a Customs Export permit. Dong export is not permitted, but neither is conversion back to dollars. Spend it all before you

FLYING GHOSTS

In the mid-1980s the Vietnamese government issued a series of stamps showing historic aircraft—a German Fokker Triplane from 1917, a Soviet Yakolev II from 1946. Cynics wondered if these planes weren't part of Vietnam's newest fleet. Indeed, in the embargo days, Vietnam's fleet was composed mostly of aging Russian Tupolev-134 jets and Ilyushin-18 turboprops that groaned and creaked when aloft. For hair-raising flights, nothing beat the Yakolev-40 light aircraft. In Vietnamese, Vietnam Airlines is rendered Hang Khong Vietnam, which foreigners quickly dubbed "Hang On Vietnam." Former fighter pilots specialized in vertical takeoffs and landings, learned from wartime days. Exit doors—if you could find them—were marked in Russian.

Vietnam Airlines was forced to use Russian aircraft because the embargo prevented leasing planes with American technology or parts. In 1992 Vietnam Airlines found a way around the restrictions by chartering instead of leasing planes, and by agreeing not to fly under its own name. This resulted in the acquisition of two Boeing 767s and a Boeing 737 painted completely white—somewhat disconcerting to passengers such as myself boarding in Bangkok. After our flying ghost took off, we were relieved to hear a French accent emanating from the cockpit—we hoped it was the pilot. The inflight service was uniquely Vietnamese: A hostess dressed in a dreamy ao dai trundled down the aisle to deliver a single fruit to each passenger. I gazed at the fruit in wonder: I'd never seen this species before. Here I was on an unmarked plane with an unknown fruit. A new species at 7,000 meters! Puzzled, I turned to my neighbor, a Vietnamese woman, and she instructed me in sign language how to dissect the fruit and which parts to eat. It was delicious.

In mid-1992, Vietnam Airlines bought two 80-seat ATR-72s from France. The ATR-72 is a turboprop made by Avions de Transport (ATR), a joint venture between France's Aerospatiale and Italy's Alenia Spa. With the lifting of the embargo, Vietnam Airlines is retiring its old Russian crates—the Tupolev jets—to boost the airline's safety reputation. There are maintenance concerns with the Tupolevs, which have to be flown to Moscow for checks. The airline's fleet now includes Airbus A-320s leased from Air France, an assortment of leased Boeings, and a handful of ATR-72s. Vietnam Airlines planned to more than double its fleet by the year 2000.

After getting the cold shoulder from the United States for so long, Vietnamese airline officials are suddenly being treated like royalty. Delta was the first airline to host a visit to the United States by Vietnamese executives. Nguyen Hong Nhi of Vietnam Airlines was wined and dined, given a tour of Disney World, and photographed next to a Wookie, the furry copilot in Star Wars. It was a bizarre experience for Nhi, a former air force general who shot down eight American aircraft in his MiG-21, but he said he had "a lovely time" in the States.

depart, or find an incoming traveler to change with. Departure tax for international flights is $14; departure tax for domestic flights should be included in the ticket price.

Inter-Asia Flights

Flights from Bangkok to Saigon, and Hong Kong to Hanoi take less than two hours. The airline hubs of Bangkok and Hong Kong dominate the Vietnam trade. Cheaper flights into Saigon (prices quoted are one-way) are from Bangkok, $150; Phnom Penh, $50; Kuala Lumpur, $150; Canton (Guangzhou), $140.

Cheaper flights into Hanoi (one-way) are from Vientiane, $90; Bangkok, $160; Nanning, $80; Canton, $125.

On inter-Asia flights luggage is restricted to 20 kilograms on economy class and 30 kilograms for business class. Anything above those weights may be subject to a surcharge. This means if you fly in from North America to Hong Kong with a 70-kilogram luggage allowance and you stop for several days in Hong Kong, your allowance will plummet to 20 kilograms for the Hong Kong–Hanoi leg. But if your flight is booked as one ticket with a transit in Hong Kong, the original baggage weight is allowed.

Bangkok and Hong Kong agents offer round-trip packages with visa. Bangkok agents may offer a Bangkok to Saigon entry flight and a Hanoi to Vientiane exit flight, plus Vietnamese visa, all for $240. A package from Hong Kong to Saigon and return from Hanoi to Hong Kong can be obtained for $450 including visa; the regular airfare is $540 round-trip. Flying into Hanoi from Canton rather than Hong Kong represents a big savings; the flight is only $125, but you have to add in the costs of a Chinese visa and boat to Canton, an extra $40 or so. A flight from Hong Kong to Hanoi or Saigon one-way is around $260.

Visitors from Australia often land first in Singapore (where the hotels are very expensive, as are the flights to Vietnam). Safe, sanitized Singapore is one of the few places in Asia where you won't be run over if you cross the street at random; you'll be fined for jaywalking instead. You can apply for a visa directly at the Vietnamese Embassy in Singapore (it will take 1.5 days for an express visa, three days for a normal visa, and five working days for a three-month multiple-entry visa). Singapore Airlines has flights round-trip to both Saigon and Hanoi. Shop around at travel agents for discount deals. Budget and midrange travelers in Singapore stay near Bencoolen Street. Singapore also has some excellent bookstores: the largest MPH bookstore is at 71 Stamford Rd.; a bookstore specializing in books on

EXTENDED OVERLAND ROUTES

For the ride of your life, crossing through Vietnam provides a novel if time-consuming way to get to Nepal. This is the Vietnam–Tibet–Nepal route. Start out in southern Vietnam (or Cambodia), travel north of Hanoi, and head through the Lao Cai border to Kunming. Travelers in the past have approached Kunming from Hong Kong or Beijing, but going through Vietnam puts you right in the southwest of China. From here there are several options. You could try an overland route by proceeding through Dali, Lijiang, and Zhongdian to Lhasa. This is a wild and rugged route with an ascent to the Tibetan Plateau and takes a few weeks to cover. You can shorten it by flying Zhongdian to Lhasa. And here I will pass you over to another guidebook: *Tibet—the Bradt Travel Guide* (by Michael Buckley, Bradt Publications, UK, 2003), which has all the details you'll ever need on these routes.

An alternative route involves making your way overland to Chengdu and flying to Lhasa. This generally requires booking a short tour to Tibet and staying on. Or you can head from Chengdu via the Aba Grasslands through Zoige and Songpan to Xiahe and Lanzhou. From Lanzhou you can go overland to Golmud via Lake Kokonor, then travel south over the high passes to Lhasa. Travelers on this route have been charged several hundred dollars for a truck ride from government-operated and arranged sources. From Lhasa you can overland or fly to Kathmandu, Nepal. From Kathmandu, carry on to Delhi, then cross the Amritsar border to Pakistan, and keep going to Quetta, Tehran, and Istanbul. Phew!

Karakoram Route: After visiting Vietnam, make your way to Kunming, then cut a huge arc through southwestern and western China to Kashgar before heading down the Karakoram Highway into Gilgit and Islamabad in Pakistan (you'll need a Pakistan visa before being allowed into Pakistan). From there you can overland to India via the Amritsar border into Delhi. In the reverse direction, the problem would be where to secure a Vietnamese visa.

Asia to Europe Overland: The opening of the Vietnamese-Chinese border has provided a "missing link" in Asian overland travel, and a direct Hanoi–Beijing train links

Southeast Asia is Select Books, on the third floor of Tanglin Shopping Center.

Fares from Singapore to Vietnam are pricey. On Vietnam Airlines, a one-way fare Hanoi to Singapore is $310; on Singapore Airlines, a one-way fare Saigon to Singapore is $237. It's a better value to take a Vietnam Airlines flight from Saigon to Kuala Lumpur for $150 one-way. Other flights come into Saigon from Seoul, Taipei, Manila, and Osaka; and into Hanoi from Seoul, Beijing, and Kaohsiung.

Kunming is becoming an interesting staging point. Hong Kong–Kunming is $195 one-way, and Kunming–Bangkok is $160 one-way. You can cover the Hanoi–Kunming stretch by train or bus—a very scenic ride. There's no Vietnamese consulate in Kunming.

Other International Flights

Student travel organizations (you often don't have to be a student) and bucket shops in large cities are the best sources of cheap fares. Shop around until you find the right deal. Cheaper fares may necessitate restrictions such as one-month advance purchase, nonrefundable tickets, or a three-month limit on use of return fare. Always find out how long the agency you're dealing with has been in business before buying a ticket.

From Europe: Bucket shops in London, Amsterdam, Antwerp, and Paris offer competitive flights into Hong Kong or Bangkok. From Paris, Air France operates expensive direct routes into Hanoi and Saigon; Lufthansa has direct flights from Frankfurt to Saigon. Vietnam Airlines

Hanoi all the way to Europe by rail. The major hurdle in the fine sport of border crossing is obtaining visas and paperwork. You can make the process a bit easier by carrying along some glowing recommendations on official-looking letterhead.

The world's longest railway journey just got longer. Now you can ride the rails all the way from Saigon to Moscow and beyond. From Thailand, proceed by air or boat to Cambodia, then travel overland to Saigon, and start the train journey—north to Hanoi and by rail through to Kunming and all the way to Beijing. From Beijing take the Trans-Mongolian train through Outer Mongolia and Russia to Europe. Visa issue is complicated. Mongolian visas issued on the spot in Vientiane in Laos give you three months to get there; Mongolian visa issue in Hanoi is also reportedly easy. You can pick up a two-month Chinese visa in Hanoi. You can obtain Russian and Mongolian transit visas in Beijing with a confirmed rail ticket. You can most likely extend the Mongolian visa for two weeks in Ulan Bator, and extend the Russian visa for a like period of time in Moscow.

Coming from Europe, the only visa for Russia apart from a transit visa is a business visa or personal invitation visa. These can be arranged through a contact in Russia, or through a travel agent in Scandinavia or the Baltic States. A one-month Russian business visa costs $60; a three-month multiple entry runs $90; an Uzbeki visa is $130. You can obtain a Mongolian visa in Ulan Ude.

In 1992 another Trans-Asian rail route opened, running from Beijing to Xian and then on via Urumqi to Alma Ata in Kazakhstan. From here you can travel via Tashkent to Samarkand and Bukhara in Uzbekistan, and eventually Moscow. The visa situation is tricky: Uzbekistan requires a separate visa. For more information, consult a guidebook called *The Silk Routes,* published by Trailblazer Publications, UK, 2003.

You can overland all the way from Australia to Europe via the Vietnam route. Island-hop from Australia through Indonesia to Malaysia, travel up through Thailand, cross over to Cambodia, move on to Saigon and into Hanoi and China. From Beijing take the Trans-Mongolian train all the way to Europe. Coming from the other direction, you can obtain a Vietnamese visa in Beijing or Hong Kong.

operates Boeing 767 flights on the Paris–Berlin–Dubai–Saigon–Hanoi route.

From Australia: There are flights from Sydney and Melbourne to Saigon, with onward connections to Hanoi. You can enter Hanoi and depart from Saigon. Round-trip three-month excursion fares on joint Qantas-Vietnam Airlines flights are competitive.

From Canada: Korean Airlines flies Vancouver to Seoul, where you transfer to a Saigon flight. More expensive are flights from Vancouver into Saigon via Singapore on Singapore Airlines, or into Hanoi on Cathay Pacific via Hong Kong. From Toronto or Montreal, flight paths are eastward via Bangkok.

From the United States: Since the lifting of the trade embargo, U.S. airlines are scrambling for direct routes into Vietnam. First off the mark is United Airlines, with flights into Saigon and Hanoi from San Francisco and Chicago (though these are routed through an intermediate point). Delta, Continental, and Northwest Orient are set to follow. Korean Airlines flies Los Angeles–Seoul–Saigon, and EVA Airlines offers same-day connections from San Francisco or Los Angeles via Taipei to Saigon. China Airlines also operates flights from the United States into Vietnam without overnight layovers.

By Sea

Western cruise liners and smaller vessels dock at coastal ports. A popular cruise route runs from Hong Kong with 4–5 stops along the coast of Vietnam before continuing to Bangkok, Singapore, or Manila. Commercial ports open to cruise ships include Halong Bay, Haiphong, Danang, Qui Nhon, Nha Trang, Vung Tau, and Saigon. Smaller ports open include Thanh Hoa in the north, and Mytho, Cantho, and Vinh Thai on the Mekong River. Pilotage is compulsory for all vessels entering or leaving Vietnamese ports, and paperwork must be in order for entry.

By Land

There are many land border crossings from Vietnam into neighboring nations, but only a handful at present are open to foreigners. In the north are three crossings to China, at Lao Cai, Huu Nghi (Dong Dang), and Mong Cai (Dongxing)—accomplished by train, bus, minibus, jeep, or a combination of these. In the center is the Lao Bao road crossing to Laos; you can rent vehicles along this stretch. North of this, the Cau Treo crossing leads from Vinh across to Lak Sao in Laos. In the south is the Moc Bai crossing to Cambodia—you can travel the route by taxi, minibus, bus, or moto. Long-distance cyclists have crossed all four borders. In addition there's a river crossing from Vietnam to Cambodia, from Chau Doc on the route to Phnom Penh, at the Tonle Mekong border.

You must possess relevant visas to enter or exit a land border to Vietnam. When crossing, be wary of customs and immigration officials working far from the reach of authorities in Saigon or Hanoi. They may be looking for extra income. One traveler reports a customs official counting his money to see if it matched the currency declaration. Later the traveler noticed some of the bills were missing.

CAMBODIA
By Air

Until 1998, the only international entry point was Phnom Penh, with frequent connections to Bangkok and Saigon. Phnom Penh's Pochentong Airport terminal underwent a major facelift in 1994 and was then trashed and looted during the coup in mid-1997. Cambodia must be one of the few countries in the world without a national airline. The closest Cambodia gets to a national airline is President Airlines, which is a joint-venture operation with Thailand. Siem Reap Airways is wholly owned by Bangkok Airways.

After the July 1997 coup, Hun Sen introduced an "open skies" policy, so what's running is, well, up in the air. The major connection out of Phnom Penh is to Bangkok: Thai Airways International operates daily flights for $140 one-way; others competing on this route include President Airlines and Siem Reap Airways. Other carriers flying into Phnom Penh include Malaysia Airlines, with connections to Kuala Lumpur, three flights a week, $370 round-trip, and flights to Vientiane, $170 one-way; SilkAir, frequent flights to Singapore, $300 round-trip; Dragonair, flights to Hong Kong, $366 round-trip; Vietnam Airlines, flights to Saigon daily, $50 one-way, and to Hanoi, once or twice a week, $155 one-way; Lao Airlines, to Vientiane, once a week, $150 one-way; Eva Air to Taipei, several times a week; Singapore Airlines, frequent flights between Phnom Penh and Rangoon; Shanghai Airlines, irregular flights to Shanghai; China Southern Airlines, to Guangzhou; and maybe Aeroflot (flights to Moscow).

Siem Reap is a second international air entry and exit point for Cambodia with visa-on-arrival issued for $20 in U.S. dollars only (have a passport photo handy). A direct Bangkok–Siem Reap (Angkor) route is operated by Bangkok Airways: The one-hour flight on a 70-seat ATR-72 turboprop is scheduled several times daily and costs about $240 round-trip. Since Bangkok Airways flies round-trip to Phnom Penh from Bangkok also, it might be possible to negotiate an inbound flight to Angkor and an outbound flight back via Phnom Penh if you want to see more of Cambodia. Other international direct flights into Siem Reap operate from Saigon and Hanoi (Vietnam Airlines), Luang Prabang and Pakse (Lao Airlines), Singapore (Silk Air), and there are possible connections to Taipei, Kaohsiung, Kunming and Guangzhou.

Customs

Customs on entry is simple. You declare any video, radio, TV, or audiocassette equipment, as well as amounts of money exceeding $10,000. None of this is checked on exit. You can import 200 cigarettes, one bottle of spirits, and a bottle of perfume for personal use. Export of antiques or Khmer artifacts is forbidden, a policy enforced by the National Heritage Protection Authority of Cambodia. Foreigners are liable to searches when exiting Phnom Penh or Siem Reap. International departure tax is $10.

By Sea

A popular entry point for Cambodia is the Koh Kong water crossing at the Thai border, near the town of Hat Lek. One reason for the popularity is that no visas are required in either direction—you are stamped in on the spot. Confusingly, there are half a dozen places that answer to the name of "Koah Kong"—the province of Koah Kong, Kong Island (Koh Kong), and the port town of Krong Koah Kong. Piracy is a problem on the high seas in the Gulf of Thailand—a major smuggling route.

From the Thai side take a bus to Trat and on to Ban Hat Lek. You might have to overnight at Hat Lek, because you need an early start for the daylight run to Sihanoukville. From Hat Lek, ride a long-tail through mangroves for about an hour to get to the area around Phumi Thnal Krabi, which is close to the Cambodian seaport of Koh Kong. Here you get yourself stamped into Cambodia, and take the speedboat to Sihanoukville, reaching the port same day. Sihanoukville is a relaxing place to hang around on the beach for a few days. It's only four hours by road from there to Phnom Penh.

In the reverse direction, Cambodian officials will stamp you out of Cambodia at Koh Kong, and Thai officials stamp you in for a month on the spot.

By River

A water border crossing is open between Cambodia and Vietnam, linking Phnom Penh to Chau Doc. If you're crossing from Chau Doc, a Cambodian visa can be issued at the border post; however, going in the opposite direction, you must have a Vietnamese visa in advance to enter. Some tour operators offer a combination boat and minibus service—covering the last stretch into or out of Phnom Penh by road. This defeats the purpose of the trip, which is to see river life. Stick to a boat that completes the whole run.

From the Vietnamese side, an option is to join a three-day Mekong Delta tour run by Saigon Tourist: The third day, you set off from Chau Doc and cross into Cambodia along the Mekong. The Victoria Hotel group runs its own boats along some sections of the Mekong, particularly the Chau Doc to Phnom Penh route. Boats can be chartered from the Victoria Hotel group, but this is an expensive option.

By Land

There are four land borders open into Cambodia—one from Vietnam, three from Thailand. On the Saigon to Phnom Penh route, travelers enter the country at Bavet (Cambodian side) via Moc Bai (Vietnamese side). Buses with padded seats travel this 248-kilometer route. If you are exiting Cambodia, the bus is not recommended because of hassles from soldiers and Vietnamese police along the way (it's a notorious smuggling run). A share-taxi on both sides is preferable, or at the very least for the Vietnamese part of the trip.

Another popular crossing point is in the northwest, at Poipet (Cambodian side) via Aranyaprathet (Thai side). The road route from Bangkok to Siem Reap is actually a lot faster than the road from Phnom Penh to Siem Reap, because of the superior condition of roads on the Thai side. Neither a Thai visa nor a Cambodian visa are needed for this crossing—you pick them up on the spot. Minibuses ply the route daily from Khao San Road in Bangkok to the old market area of Siem Reap for around $12 one-way.

Two other less-traveled crossing points lie at O'Smach and Pailin. Both routes pass over rough roads through former Khmer Rouge strongholds. O'Smach lies directly north of Siem Reap via the town of Anlong Veng. It takes up to eight hours to reach the border from Siem Reap on rough roads. The nearest Thai town to the border is Surin. The Pailin border crossing lies southwest of Battambang.

LAOS

By Air

The main air arrival point is Vientiane's Wattay Airport. Other international flights land in Luang Prabang (from Thailand) and Pakse (from Angkor, Cambodia). Approximate one-way fares for direct flights into Vientiane are: Bangkok, $100; Hanoi, $90; Phnom Penh, $125; Saigon, $140; Kunming, $110 (the price fluctuates to as much as $175); Guangzhou, $280; Beijing, $338. Some are stopover destinations: There's a Vientiane–Kunming–Guangzhou flight, and a Vientiane–Saigon–Phnom Penh flight. There are twice-weekly flights from Vientiane to Rangoon, but don't count on those—they could be canceled. Lao Airlines flies to Chiang Mai–Vientiane twice weekly on 70-seat ATRs; some group tours have managed to fly direct from Chiang Mai in Thailand into Luang Prabang.

Other carriers operating in Laos include Yunnan Airlines, SilkAir, Malaysia Airlines, Vietnam Airlines, Eva Air, and Air France. SilkAir (Singapore Airlines) offers twice-weekly service between Vientiane and Singapore. New routes are opening from Vientiane to Kuala Lumpur, Rangoon, and Hong Kong. Eva Air operates a Vientiane–Taipei flight via Bangkok. Lao Airlines, in a joint venture with China's Yunnan Airlines, is planning to expand services to connect Laos with Yunnan province, with more frequent connections to Kunming, and direct flights into Chengdu and Xishuangbanna (the latter started operating, but flights have been frequently canceled). Lao Airlines uses its best planes on the international routes, including Boeing 737s and French ATRs.

Most international connections to Vientiane pass through Bangkok first. Bangkok serves as the hub for international flights to Vientiane; Air France, for example, routes passengers through Bangkok, where they transfer to a Lao Airlines B-737 flight to Vientiane. Bangkok to Vientiane takes an hour; ticketing is jointly operated by Lao Airlines (mostly weekday flights) and Thai Airways International (weekends). Price is $100 one-way, but you can sometimes obtain special fares. Lao Airlines in Bangkok is at 491/17 Ground Floor, Silom Road, tel. 236-9822; Thai Airways is at 485 Silom Rd., tel. 233-3810.

If you're bumped from a Bangkok–Vientiane flight, an alternative is to fly north to Udon Thani. From Udon Thani Airport there's a Thai Airways express bus to the office in Nong

Khai, 53 kilometers north. From here, you can cross by land into Vientiane.

Customs

Airport arrival formalities are relaxed. There's no limit on the amount of foreign currency brought in—the most useful currency to carry is Thai baht. Because Thai baht is commonly accepted in Vientiane, you can eliminate the need for airport money changing by arriving with baht. You can bring in 500 cigarettes, two bottles of wine, and one bottle of liquor. The customs declaration form will ask you to itemize camera equipment and valuables. A departure tax of $10 is levied on international flights leaving Laos.

By Land and River

Laos has a number of land borders open to foreigners: two to China, one to Cambodia, five to Vietnam, and five to Thailand. More border crossings are bound to open up. At some of these international crossings, a Lao visa may be issued on arrival for $30, but this is valid for only 15 days, and the policy at land borders varies—to play it safe, have your Lao visa in hand before attempting a land crossing (and likewise for China, Vietnam, and Cambodia if entering those countries from Laos). Thailand presents no problem—a visa is always issued on the spot, free. Long-distance (overnight) express buses ply some key international routes, such as Vientiane-Bangkok, Vientiane-Jinghong, Vientiane-Vinh, Vientiane-Hanoi, and Vientiane-Siem Reap. These often charge less than $20 for the trip—which is considerably cheaper than flying, but the trade-off is the time taken to get there.

To Thailand: The Thailand-Laos border is 1,750 kilometers long, with 650 kilometers on land and the rest along the Mekong. Thai border crossings account for the majority of entries into Laos. The major crossing is at Nong Khai–Tha Deua over the Friendship Bridge. Thai transport is allowed as far as the Lao side of the bridge; then you must transfer to Lao transport. From Nong Khai to the bridge is four kilometers by minibus and costs around

$1 a person; you then take a bus across the bridge for a small fee; on the other side, a ride in a taxi or jumbo is $2–4 for the last 20 kilometers into Vientiane.

There are four other points where foreigners can cross the Mekong: at Ban Huay Sai, northwest Laos, opposite the Thai town of Chiang Khong; at Thakhek, opposite the Thai town of Nakhon Phanom; at Savannakhet, opposite the Thai town of Mukdahan; and at Chong Mek, southern Laos, about 40 kilometers west of Pakse (you cross at Chong Mek and proceed to Ubon Ratchathani in Thailand). Crossing at Thai border points without a Thai visa is not a problem—you're given a 30-day stamp that is nonextendable unless you have excellent reasons.

To Vietnam: There are five land borders open to Vietnam, and more may surface. The Taichang border crossing enters Vietnam close to Dien Bien Phu, which would place you on the northern loop to Sapa and Lao Cai in Vietnam. Reached via Sam Neua and Route 6 is the Namsoy-Nameo border crossing, opened in 2004. Namsoy is the Lao side of the border; Nameo is the first Vietnamese town past the border. Roads can be rough here, but travelers have used this route to make the run from Hanoi into Laos. Running along Route 7 in Laos is a link from Phnonsavan to the Nong Het border crossing into Vietnam, which finishes at Vinh. Once a week there is a direct bus from Phonsavan to Vinh.

Also linking close to Vinh is the Lak Sao-Cau Treo border crossing along Route 8. It is the fastest road route from Laos into the north of Vietnam and the one used by the long-distance buses from Vientiane to Hanoi. This route starts at a point between Paksane and Thakhek, and eventually leads to the Vietnamese town of Vinh. If opting for this route, don't plan to stay long in Vinh—it's a dismal place. From Vinh you have the option of heading north to Hanoi, or south to Hue.

The fourth border crossing is on Route 9: From Savannakhet you can go east and cross the border at Lao Bao, exiting to central Vietnam toward Dong Ha in the former DMZ

(Demilitarized Zone). In the reverse direction, there's a Lao Consulate in Danang to assist with paperwork.

To China: There's an exit through the border post of Ban Boten in Luang Namtha province to Mengla in China's landlocked Yunnan province. This border crossing leads to fascinating minority areas of China such as Jinghong, home to the Dai people. From Jinghong you can carry on to Kunming. Chinese visas are easy to obtain in Bangkok. Get a Lao visa in Kunming if coming from the Chinese side. Coming from China into Laos, it appears you can enter along the Mekong and be stamped into Laos at Xiengkok. From Xiengkok, there is a speedboat service to Ban Huay Sai.

To Cambodia: The Voeng Kham crossing near the lower Mekong, leading from Pakse south to Stung Treng, is open with some dickering on paperwork. Make sure you have a Cambodian or Lao visa stamped in your passport before attempting this one (no visa is issued on the spot).

VIA BANGKOK

Bangkok is like the futuristic Los Angeles in the science fiction movie *Blade Runner*—a city seemingly out of control, clogged with traffic, crawling beneath a skyline of towering apartment blocks and banks. The Big Mango is a paradox. Delve below the ugly exterior and you'll find homely neighborhoods with superb restaurants tucked down side alleys, and enough sights to keep you busy for weeks. Think of Bangkok as the Land of Plenty; it is bristling with ATMs, McDonalds, 7-Elevens, and major department stores—any last-minute supplies you need can be obtained here.

Transportwise, Bangkok is a disaster, but there are two forms of transport that move at a good pace. The Chao Phraya express boats offer comfort and speed—and lots of superb views. Also offering the views, and unprecedented speed, is the BTS (Bangkok Mass Transit System), also known as the Skytrain, which will whip you around in record time and in air-conditioned comfort—all for less than

a dollar. The Skytrain operates a north-south line that runs from Saphan Taksin on the the Chao Phraya (near Shangri-La Hotel) via Siam Square all the way up to Chatuchak Market, near the Northern Bus Terminal, and another line that runs from Siam Square all the way east along Sukhumvit past the Eastern Bus Station. One of the perhaps unintended benefits of the Skytrain is that it makes crossing deadly streets such as Silom or Sukhumvit a snap: You use the Skytrain entrances as overpasses. Get a free BTS map to figure out routes. Another rapid rail system, the MRT, runs underground and has several interchange points with the BTS, though the systems require different electronic tickets.

Airport Arrival

For a stay of up to 30 days no visa is required. You're stamped in at the airport; for overstays, there's a charge of $4 a day. Bangkok's Don Muang Airport is 25 kilometers north of the city center—a ride in can take an hour or so. Your options include taking a metered taxi, which should cost no more than 300 baht to reach town (make sure the driver turns the meter on); an airport bus service (making stops at major hotels); or a train to Hualampong Station for about 25 baht. To reach the railway station, walk over an overhead bridge through the Amari Airport Hotel and down to a platform. Air-conditioned buses also run past the airport into town, but the going is very slow.

Accommodations

Compared with other Asian capitals, Bangkok is a bargain for accommodations and food. There are several budget areas in Bangkok. The largest is the Banglamphu/Khao San Road area, a rabbit warren of guesthouses and hotels. Prices here range $10–30 for a basic room to $20–50 for one with air-conditioning. Find other guesthouses near the National Library and at Soi Kasemsan 1 near Siam Square. Midrange hotels catering to families, group tours, and business travelers are on side streets off Sukhumvit Road. Moderately priced accommodations here run $40–100 for a room; luxury hotel rooms are $100 and up. Small business hotels clustered on Sukhumvit Sois 7, 9, and 11 charge $30–60 a night. There is fierce competition among luxury hotels in Bangkok, which means walk-in customers can often negotiate 10–50 percent off list prices. Discounts are also provided in the off-season or for longer stays.

Travel Agents

There are many agencies along Khao San Road in Bangkok's premier backpacker budget zone. A more up-market strip of travel agents and airlines is along Silom Road. There are a few agents at the corner of Wireless (Wittayu) Road and Ploenchit, near the Vietnamese Embassy. A reliable general travel agent offering discount fares and unmatched ticket flexibility and refunds is **STA Travel,** part of an Australian chain with offices worldwide. STA is in Wall Street Tower, 14th floor, Room 1406, 33 Surawong Rd., tel. 236-0262, fax 237-6005, help@statravel.co.th, www.statravel.co.th. Travel agents handling the region of Indochina include:

Diethelm, 140/1 Wireless Rd., tel. 255-9150, fax 256-0248

East-West, 46/1 Sukhumvit Soi 3, tel. 253-0681

Exotissimo, 21/17 Sukhumvit Soi 4, tel. 253-5240, fax 254-7683; Silom branch at 755 Silom Rd., tel. 235-9196

Marvel Holidays, 279 Khao San Rd., tel. 282-9339, fax 281-3216

MK Ways, 57/1 Wireless Rd., tel. 254-4765, fax 254-5583; Sathorn branch at 18/4 Sathorn Tai Soi 3, tel. 212-2532

Siamwing, 173/1 Surawong Rd., tel. 253-4757, fax 236-6808

SMI Travel, 580 Ploenchit, tel. 252-5435, fax 251-1785

Thai Indochina Tour Company, 753 Silom Rd., beside Indian temple, tel. 234-1555, fax 635-0504

Thavee Travel, 65 Sukhumvit Soi 3, tel. 252-0097, fax 253-8789

Transindo, Thasos Building/10F, 1675 Chan Rd., tel. 287-3241, fax 258-3235

Vista Travel, 244 Khao San Rd., tel. 280-0348

Tickets

A number of agents offer ticket and visa package deals. A $220 package includes a Vietnamese visa and Bangkok-Saigon and Hanoi-Vientiane flights. Other flights in the region include Bangkok–Saigon $150, Bangkok–Hanoi $160, Bangkok–Kunming $160, Bangkok–Phnom Penh $125, Bangkok–Vientiane $100; all prices one-way.

Visas

Many travelers go through agents in Bangkok to arrange their visas. Agents use motorcycle couriers and know how to speed the process, so they are worth the extra fee you pay—they save you a lot of time and aggravation. You can apply directly for a one-month visa at the Vietnamese Embassy, 83/1 Wireless Rd., tel. 251-5837, a few doors down from the American Embassy. Visa cost is $48 and it takes five working days to obtain. The Lao Embassy is at 520, 502/1-3 Soi Ramkhamhaeng 39, Bangkapi, tel. 353-6667; visas can be obtained directly, though this place is so far out. The Cambodian Embassy, at 185 Rajadamri Rd. (on an alley off Soi Sarasin near Lumpini Park), tel. 253-7967, issues visas within a day (even the same day), but if arriving at a common border crossing in Cambodia you can get a visa on the spot for $20 (except for some borders, such as the Lao/Cambodian river crossing). The Chinese Embassy, at 57 Rajadapisek Rd., tel. 245-7036, issues a one-month visa within four working days for $12–100 depending on nationality. A one-day or same-day request costs more.

Supplies

It's easy to obtain U.S. cash dollars in Bangkok. Banks deduct a 1.5 percent commission when changing traveler's checks to cash. There are ATMs everywhere; use your four-digit code at machines bearing a Visa Plus or MasterCard Cirrus symbol. There's no need to convert Thai baht back to dollars on leaving Thailand if you're heading to Cambodia or Laos as you can continue to use baht there. Bangkok medical services are good. Drugstores are not as well stocked as in Hong Kong, and you should be careful with storage conditions for drugs (also check expiration dates and beware of imitations or fakes). Mefloquine (Lariam) for malaria is not available through drugstores. Mosquito nets are available; you can find the Spider, an excellent net made in Thailand for a Canadian company, at Robinsons Department Stores, in the bedding section. There are many Western-style department stores in Bangkok for last-minute supplies. Quality processing for print and E6 slide films is readily available in Bangkok, and there are CD-burning facilities offered at cybercafés.

Communications

Bangkok is well supplied with Western media tools, wired up with satellite TV, email, and Internet access; there are three English-language newspapers. Apart from hotels providing the necessary hookups, there are many independent places providing email and Internet access. Some work on a "smart card" basis—you buy a card of a fixed time limit. The Central Post Office sells a card allowing access to its terminals for three hours and a similar system is used at Bangkok International Airport.

Resources

Bangkok offers plenty of English-language material on Indochina: books, magazines, maps, phrasebooks. You can find books on the Indochina region that may be out of print in the West. Kunokuniya is a huge bookstore inside the Emporium Shopping Plaza. In the Silom area, try Asia Books on the third floor of Thaniya Plaza, and Bookazine on the ground floor of CP Tower at 131 Silom Road. At 29 Sathorn Tai Rd. is Librarie Française, with books in English, French, and Italian. In the Siam Square area is DK Book House on Soi 6, and Bangkok Books at 302 Soi 4. Along Sukhumvit is a DK Book House near the corner of Soi 8, and branches of Asia Books at 221 Sukhumvit (between Sois 15 and 17), Landmark Plaza, Times Square building, the Skydome in the World Trade Center, and Peninsula Plaza, near the Regent Hotel. There's a branch of Bookazine on the ground floor of Bangkapi Plaza at 171 Sukhumvit. Khao San Road is the big trading center for secondhand books. The biweekly *Phnom Penh Post* is available at Asia Books. Good for finding out what's happening around Bangkok is *Metro Magazine;* there is also a website (www.bkkmetro.com); or *Farang Magazine.*

VIA HONG KONG

On July 1, 1997, Hong Kong began a new life as a Special Administrative Region (SAR) of China. Supposedly, the economic, social, and legal status quo will remain for another 50 years, and it is largely business as usual. The Chinese leadership may even decide to fulfill its promise of "one country, two systems." A real test case of this is the Falun Gong sect, which is outlawed in China, but which holds demonstrations in Hong Kong. Although Hong Kong's pre-1997 democratic reforms were quickly rolled back after the handover, the press in Hong Kong is still among the freest in Asia (the local press dances around new taboos such as writing about the Falun Gong, insulting senior Communist Party leaders, advocating independence for Taiwan, Tibet, or Hong Kong, and being off the mark about the Tiananmen massacre). There have been changes in predominant language—it's shifted to Mandarin for business and commerce—and in the color of the life being lived there: The queen is gone from the postage stamps; the postboxes, once red, have been shorn of royal insignia and painted dark green (the color of post offices in China); and Hong Kong's symbol, the bauhinia flower, suddenly sprouted five red stars, one on each petal, and acquired a red background on the Hong Kong flag and other paraphernalia.

Hong Kong SAR is attached to mainland China but has more than 200 outlying islands; Hong Kong Island, Lantau, Lamma, and Cheng Chau are the largest. Ferry trips across Hong Kong Harbor to Lantau or Cheng Chau are relaxing (and cheap) escapes from the hustle and bustle of business centers such as Hong Kong Central and Kowloon.

Airport Arrival

On entry, no visa is required for most Westerners for stays of a month or longer in Hong Kong SAR (visa regulations are much the same as they were in pre-1997 days). You are in a special administrative zone, not in China Proper. The exchange rate is US$1 = HK$7.8; unless otherwise noted, prices in this section are quoted in US dollars, not HK dollars. Airport baggage is ultraexpensive, running around $10 a day per bag. Before you leave the airport, load up on free tourist maps and other literature. Next step would be to buy an Octopus card: This electronic ticket system will not only give you access to the Airport Express and MTR, it can also be used to buy goods at 711s and other merchants. From Hong Kong's Chek Lap Kok Airport on Lantau Island, there are rail, bus, and taxi connections to Hong Kong Central and Kowloon. The fastest option is to take the Airport Express train (use the Octopus card), which runs direct to HK Central. Taking the airport bus downtown requires exact change.

Accommodations

Budget accommodation is scarce in Hong Kong. You'll find budget rooms largely in Chungking and Mirador Mansions, two rather daunting tower blocks on either side of the Holiday Inn Golden Mile, at the bottom end of Nathan Road in Kowloon. The YMCA on Salisbury Road is not cheap, but it does offer some dormitory accommodations. The YHA on Mt. Davis, Hong Kong side, is for members only (you can join on the spot for a fee) and is not cheap, either. The usual YHA rules apply, including curfew. In larger hotels rates start at about $80 for a twin room in low season. Hong Kong travel agencies offer discounted rooms in the large hotels, sometimes up to 50 percent off rack rate, although rooms can be fully booked during busy months. Luxury hotel rooms start at around $200 a night.

Travel Agents

Many travel agents offer visas, ticketing, tours, and information for Vietnam and China. Laos and Cambodia are handled more from within Indochina or Bangkok. Regulations concerning overland travel into Vietnam wax and wane with the phases of the moon; always inquire about current conditions.

A highly recommended travel agency is **Phoenix Services Agency,** Room 1404, 14F, Austin Tower, 22-26 Austin Avenue, Kowloon, Hong Kong (closest MTR station is Jordan), tel. (+852) 2722-7378, fax 2369-8884, email info@phoenixtrvl.com. An experienced agent for travel in China and Vietnam with pleasant staff and friendly service, Phoenix has affiliated offices in Hanoi and Saigon, and it can arrange custom tours to Vietnam and other international travel.

Hong Kong agents dealing with Vietnam and China include **Mekong Travel,** 1210 Hollywood Plaza, 610 Nathan Rd., Kowloon, tel. 2782-1956, fax 2782-0095; and **Star Tours and Travel,** 8F Wah Ying Cheong Kin Bldg., 236 Nathan Rd., Jordan, Kowloon, tel. 2367-6663, fax 2369-6173.

Tickets

Sample ticket prices from Hong Kong include Hong Kong–Saigon–Hong Kong $480; Hong Kong–Hanoi–Hong Kong $550; Hong Kong–Hanoi/Saigon–Hong Kong $540; Hong Kong–Saigon–Bangkok–Hong Kong $590; Hong Kong–Saigon $270 one-way; Hong Kong–Hanoi $300 one-way; Hong Kong–Kunming $250 one-way. You may be able to strike better deals by packaging a round-trip flight and Vietnamese visa for $450 or less—fixed dates, may be valid for two weeks only. A cheaper way of getting in and out of Vietnam from Hong Kong is via Canton. Get a Chinese visa for $30, take a $15 boat to Guangzhou, and fly to Hanoi for $200. The total cost one-way to Hanoi is around $200. Some agents offer inexpensive Hong Kong–Guangzhou–Hanoi–Hong Kong packages. Cheaper yet, travel overland from Hong Kong to Nanning, and just keep going by land to Hanoi. There are direct flights from Hong Kong to Danang, on the Hong Kong–Danang–Saigon route, for around $350 round-trip. The Hong Kong to Danang flights are on-off: It's best to inquire if they're running or not and when.

Visas

The Chinese visa-issuing office is in the China Resources Building in Wanchai. You can approach this office yourself, but travelers often go through agents for convenience. One-month Chinese visas are easy to obtain, usually within two days. Cost depends on nationality: around $25–40 for a two- to three-month visa, $35 for double-entry, and $50–90 for a three-month multiple entry.

The Consulate General of Vietnam is on the 15th floor of Great Smart Tower, 230 Wanchai Rd., Wanchai, tel. 2591-4510, fax 2591-4524. However, you must go through a travel agent to get a visa. A one-month visa costs $45 and takes 4–7 working days to obtain. Be aware that unless you specify otherwise, the visa may start running from the date of issue (ask for leeway time to get there). You can get two- or three-month multiple-entry visas for Vietnam. A six-month multiple-entry visa is possible too.

Supplies

You can change money on just about every street corner in Hong Kong. American cash dollars are widely available from banks and money changers, and ATMs abound. Hong Kong medical facilities are very good and pharmacies are well stocked; try those attached to large department stores. Hong Kong is synonymous with shopping. Be wary of "deals" on electronic goods, as the goods may be of dubious quality and often nonreturnable. Numerous photo shops sell film. You can get slight discounts if you buy in quantity. Be aware of fakes in Hong Kong: Under Chinese control, pirate CDs, tapes, software, and all kinds of copied items have flooded in; these are brazenly manufactured in China in contravention of copyright agreements.

Resources

Hong Kong offers English-language bookstores selling books, magazines, maps, and phrasebooks, all often printed in Hong Kong. One of the biggest English-language bookstores is Page One, with several branches in Hong Kong Central, Kowloon, and Causeway Bay. In Hong Kong Central, the address is Century Square, 1-13 D'Aguilar Street. There's also Bookazine on Des Voeux Road, and Dymocks at the Star Ferry pier. In Kowloon, try Swindon's at 13 Lock Rd., or in the Ocean Centre on Canton Road in Kowloon, Times Books near Mirador Mansions, and branches of Crown's bookstores. For longer stays in Hong Kong, consult *Moon Handbooks Hong Kong* by Kerry Moran.

Getting Around

VIETNAM

By Air

Vietnam Airlines, the national carrier, operates about 15 domestic routes. Vietnam Airlines is a Third-World carrier, so expect Third-World safety standards and service. Conditions are much improved on international runs where appearances must be maintained. The smaller Pacific Airlines, a joint-stock airline with state-owned corporations as shareholders, operates on the Saigon to Hanoi route and also flies to Taiwan. It was not certain how long Pacific Airlines would remain in business. It has only a few jets at its disposal and is beset by financial problems. Vietnam Air Service Company (VASCO) operates light planes and helicopters on a charter basis. It flies helicopters from Hanoi to Haiphong, Cat Ba, and Halong Bay, and operates light planes from Saigon to Cantho, and Saigon to Con Dao Islands. There were plans to expand the helicopter service to other parts of the country.

Vietnam Airlines issues its own time-table booklet with domestic and international flights; you can track it down in Saigon or Hanoi. There are frequent flights between the cities of Hanoi, Saigon, Hué, and Nha Trang.

INDOCHINA TRAVEL TIPS

Indochina is a developing tourist region and often facilities are poor or nonexistent. So you have to be resourceful and improvise. Here are a few tips:

- Language problems? Find a local English speaker. They get to practice their English, you get a guide. It's a fair trade-off.
- Lost? It's useful to ask hotel staff for a "Card Visit," bearing the name and address of your hotel, so you can show it to a cyclo or moto driver when returning to the hotel.
- Can't find the address in a big city? You'd be surprised what's up on the Web. Head for a cybercafé and use a search engine to find it. Websites are up to date. An example: In Bangkok, I could not find a DHL courier office after looking in all kinds of (useless) phone books, but in two minutes on a computer, I came up with all the data. Use the Internet as your Yellow Pages—let the Web do the walking.
- No map of town? Check the biggest hotel in town. Sometimes there's a map painted or glued on the wall. You may not be able to get a copy, but you can probably glean enough details for orientation. If you want to photocopy a map (paper version, not concrete), and can't find a copy shop, head for the nearest film developer in town. Most have a photocopy machine tucked away somewhere. Photos and photocopies—makes sense, right?
- No regular taxis in sight? Take a cyclo for short distances, or a motorcycle-taxi for longer distances. In places such as Phnom Penh flag down the nearest motorcyclist.
- No bicycle rentals? Ask the hotel staff if you can borrow a personal bicycle. An offer of $2 will be much appreciated.
- No motorcycle rentals? Hail the nearest moto driver. Tell him to take a walk, and you'll bring the machine back in the evening. Offer $5. If you prefer to just be a passenger, hire the moto and driver by the day—the driver will act as your guide.
- Can't decide if you want to spend the day touring by bicycle or by boat? Take the bike with you on the boat. The boatman won't bat an eyelid, as bicycles go everywhere with the locals.

- No bank in sight? Find the nearest jeweler's shop. Jewelers sell gold and trade in cash U.S. dollars. Changing $200 or $300 will not faze them.
- No hotel in town? Go to a restaurant, stay late, make friends—they have a floor.... Or make the sleeping gesture (palms together under tilted head) and ask local kids where you can find a house to stay the night. They'll generally direct you to a suitable place.
- No hot shower in your hotel? Ask for a thermos of hot water (supplied in hotels in Vietnam), soak a thin towel, and apply it. This sushi-bar toweling technique will wipe off the grime and refresh you. Another technique is the bucket shower—fill up a bucket with cold water, mix part thermos-water and part cold water in a plastic ladle, pour it over yourself, and repeat procedure.
- No restaurants? Find the markets, which always have foodstalls. Market food is fresh, tasty, and cheap.
- Can't find the bus station? Go to the markets. The buses generally leave close by, and cyclos and other forms of transport are clustered around the bus station.
- Problems with police or officialdom? Try greasing palms with packs of fancy foreign cigarettes or small cash advances. If the situation is not clear, offer only cigarettes, which cannot be misconstrued as bribes. If you hand over a pack of cigarettes, the other party may just pocket it—then you press your case.
- Can't afford a long phone call back home? Use Web-based email: There are cybercafés in all major tourist locations in Indochina, catering to tourist demand. And you don't have to worry about waking people up at midnight—or getting an answering machine. Another possibility is sending a fax—post offices and hotels have fax machines around.
- The last bus already left for the place you want to go, or you missed the cursed crack-of-dawn express departure? Stand out on the main highway and flag down a long-distance bus that's passing through. Hitching is another possibility and could well be more comfortable than a bus.

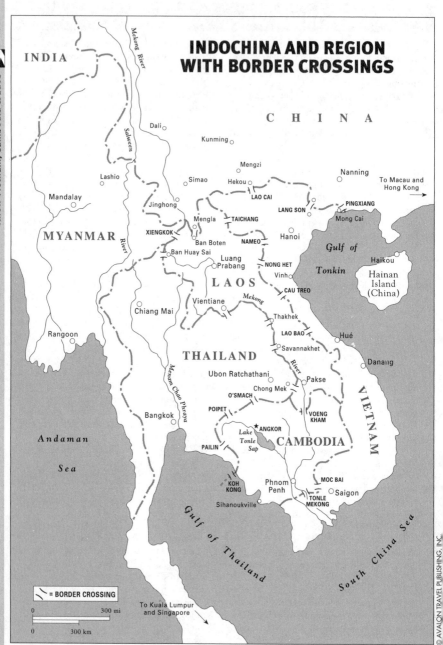

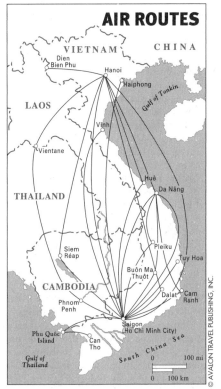

AIR ROUTES

VIETNAM   CHINA

Dien
Bien Phu   Hanoi

LAOS   Haiphong

Gulf of Tonkin

Vinh

Vientane

Huế

THAILAND   Da Nẵng

Siem   Pleiku
Réap   Tuy Hoa

Buôn Ma
Thuột

CAMBODIA   Dalat   Cam
Ranh
Phnom
Penh

Saigon
(Ho Chi Minh City)
Phu Quốc
Island   Can
Tho

Gulf of   South China Sea
Thailand   0   100 mi

0   100 km

© AVALON TRAVEL PUBLISHING, INC.

for 250,000 dong for injury, whereas a foreigner might sue for $250,000. Fares are based on distance; a two-hour flight from Hanoi to Saigon covering 1,138 kilometers costs $160 one-way, while a one-hour flight from Hanoi to Danang covering 606 kilometers costs $80 one-way. There is no discount for round-trip fares, which double the price of one-way fares. Sample fares are as follows. From Hanoi to Danang, $80; to Hué, $80; to Nha Trang, $130; to Saigon, $160. From Saigon to Dalat, $25; to Nha Trang, $45; to Danang, $85; to Hué, $85; to Haiphong, $150; to Hanoi, $160.

Domestic flights can save a long haul by bus or train. The Hué to Hanoi flight is popular here, because there's not a whole lot to miss on the road route. Saigon to Buon Ma Thuot takes only 50 minutes in a 34-seat Yakolev and costs $45; by road, the route is a much cheaper dogleg 18 hours by bus. A similar situation exists for Danang to Pleiku—a $30 flight can save a lot of time. If there's flooding in a particular region, you might consider flying over it.

Support systems for Vietnam Airlines are poor. Computer bookings are often botched; if a plane appears to be booked out, try standby. You can sometimes arrange to ride a Vietnam Airlines bus or minibus from its downtown office to the airport or vice versa. With the exception of Saigon's Tan Son Nhat Airport, airport facilities are dismal. Arrive well in advance for a domestic flight or you may find the clerks have sold your seat to another passenger. Before you board, make sure you keep your film to one side. At Saigon's Tan Son Nhat Airport are two sets of X-ray machines to pass through before you board a domestic flight.

By Train

Trains are good places to mingle. On the neutral ground of trains, people speak more freely. That's if you can hear them. Trains are noisy—engines roaring, carriages swaying around, loudspeakers screeching in the cars—so a set of earplugs is a good idea if you're trying to sleep. Trains are more expensive than buses and don't necessarily get you there any faster. However, you do have legroom, and you

The time table will inform you which Russian crates are still flying around. While Boeings and Airbuses are used on the Hanoi–Saigon route, lesser breeds such as Tupolev-134s (TU3) are used on more obscure domestic flights. The Tupolev has a tainted safety reputation, and the crew are not renowned for service, either. The Tupolev is a 70-seat Russian jet being phased out in favor of 80-seat French ATR-72s. On some trips such as the Saigon-to-Dalat run, a 34-seat Yakolev-40 (YAK40) is employed. Not recommended for those with heart problems. Baggage is limited to 20 kilograms per person on domestic flights.

Vietnam Airlines charges double to triple local price for foreigners, and you usually pay in dollars. Supposedly the increased tariff covers insurance; a Vietnamese family may settle

Know Vietnam, Cambodia & Laos

TRAIN FARES

By applying the logic absorbed from the following sample fares, you can arrive at rough calculations for the foreign price for a particular train. Some stations hand out photocopied sheets in English with price calculations and brief time tables. Odd-numbered trains are southbound; even-numbered trains are northbound.

Hanoi to Saigon, 1,726 km
S3/CM5 trains: 38/42 hours; soft seat $65; hard sleeper $91–99–108; soft sleeper $117; a/c soft sleeper $150
S7 train: 46 hours; hard seat $48; soft seat $56; hard sleeper $82–91–99; soft sleeper $108

Hué to Saigon, 1,038 km
S3/CM5 train: 24/26 hours; soft seat $40; hard sleeper $55–60–65; soft sleeper $76
S7 train: 28 hours; hard seat $29; soft seat $35; hard sleeper $50–55–60; soft sleeper $66

Hanoi to Hué, 688 km
S3/CM5 trains: 14/16 hours; soft seat $26; hard sleeper $37–40–44; soft sleeper $51
S7 train: 18 hours; hard seat $20; soft seat $23; hard sleeper $33–37–40; soft sleeper $44

can recline in soft seat class or even sleep overnight. Also, there's less chance of an accident. Comfort allows you to enjoy the scenery; the railway passes some spectacular stretches on parts of the coast, particularly between Hué and Danang.

The most common trains used by travelers are the Reunification (Thong Nhat) Expresses running between Saigon and Hanoi. Not really expresses, these rarely make it more than 40 kilometers per hour, but they sure beat local trains, which can crawl along at 15 kph. At maximum speed a train from Hanoi to Saigon takes 29 hours. Express trains are often forced to share the track with slower trains, some traveling in the opposite direction. Time tables for expresses are posted at most stations and can be viewed in hotel lobbies.

The Reunification Express runs along an old meter-gauge line begun in 1899 under the French and finished 37 years later. In 1942, when the line was used extensively by the Japanese, it was sabotaged by the Vietminh. During subsequent warfare against the French and the Americans, the line was blown to bits. In 1975 the new government started to put all the pieces back in place. To reopen the line from Hanoi to Saigon, engineers had to repair 1,334 bridges, 27 tunnels, and 1,300 switches. Vietnam now has about 3,000 kilometers of track in service. More than 100 steam engines are still running; the main power is supplied by diesel engines of old Soviet, Czech, Indian, and French stock. Several colonial-era tracks have not yet been put back into service. Dalat has a grand ghost station.

Railways are more prominent in the north. Three French-engineered rail spurs radiate from Hanoi: the Hanoi to Haiphong line, Hanoi to Lang Son line (completed 1902), and Hanoi to Lao Cai line (built 1906). In the French colonial era, the French had shares in the Yunnan Railway Company and managed the service from Haiphong through Hanoi to Lao Cai toward Kunming. Railways once drove across the Chinese border at Lao Cai and Lang Son, but service was disrupted after 1979 border clashes with the Chinese; almost two decades later, the through service was resumed. One other rail spur appearing on maps of the north is an industrial line built after 1954. This is the Dong Anh–Thai Nguyen–Kep–Bai Chay line. Thai Nguyen is an iron and steel complex, and Bai Chay is a coal-producing area.

Food

Pack food and bottled water for longer train trips. Train meals are free with your overpriced foreign ticket. They're delivered to your seat and vary from the adequate (bread and pâté) to the highly suspect (box with rice, stale vegetables, egg, and meat). Foreigners are often given a free Coke to offset the fact that they've paid more than double for their rail tickets. Attendants rove up and down the cars dispensing beer from ice buckets, tea from kettles. Newspapers and other items are also available at an extra cost. The dining car serves food to order, but the fare is not a great improvement over what you get at your seat. It's best to buy fresh food from stations along the route and hang it in plastic bags in your car. Smoking is permitted in all classes at all times, creating a stale cigarette smell. No ashtrays are provided.

Classes

In socialist Vietnam there are no classes—it's just that some seats are softer than others. Prices vary according to softness of bunk, degree of privacy, and height above the floor. If you're going to pay double or triple local price, you deserve more. Use the first-class waiting rooms at stations even if you've got a hard-seat ticket. These waiting rooms have comfortable couches to snooze on, tea service, TV, fridge, toilet, even a shower cubicle. On trains, there are two types of seats, hard *(ngoi cung)* and soft *(ngoi em)*, and usually two types of sleeper, hard sleeper *(nam cung)* and soft sleeper *(nam em)*.

Hard seats are facing high-backed benches made of wooden slats, with about 80 places in each crowded hard-seat car. On long runs, passengers sleep bolt upright, or on the floor, or string hammocks between seats. Sleep is often interrupted by screeching static on speakers placed at both ends of each car. You can stow luggage on overhead racks or under seats; it's a good idea to padlock your possessions to a piece of metal.

Soft seats resemble aircraft-style seats, but think Russian aircraft after a combat mission. Seats may be broken at the reclining angle, or have broken armrests. About 64 seats to a car, arranged in pairs on either side of the aisle. This class is less crowded, seats are numbered, and there is greater legroom. Soft seat is a good budget alternative to a hard sleeper and sometimes more comfortable because you get your own flip-down table and a reading lamp. If your train trip is daytime only, soft seat is preferable to hard sleeper, and cheaper.

A **hard sleeper** features six bunks in three tiers to each compartment. There are about seven compartments to each hard-sleeper car,

so 42 bunks to the car. This sleeper really is hard—no mattress is provided. The bunk is just hard wood with a straw mat on it, although you can try asking for a blanket. You can close the compartment door at night. Pricing varies slightly for the three levels of bunks—the top is cheapest, the middle medium-priced, the lowest the most expensive. During the day passengers may sit on the lower bunks, which have access to a window table.

A **soft sleeper** consists of four bunks in each enclosed compartment, with six compartments to a car, or 24 beds. Each bunk is supplied with a mattress and pillow; there's a mirror on the compartment door and decent lighting. This class would be the equivalent of a hard sleeper on Chinese trains. A soft sleeper is expensive, about double the price of a soft seat. To get around the expense, some travelers buy hard-class tickets, then negotiate with the conductor to upgrade to soft class once on the train (payment in cash).

A **deluxe sleeper** consists of two bunks to an enclosed compartment with thicker and softer mattresses. This class is rare. It's found only on top trains, and presumably used only by the top brass.

Pricing

A Reunification Express train is typically composed of 7–12 cars, including a dining car and a goods car for mail and heavy items such as bicycles and motorcycles. Staff may occupy half a sleeping car, sometimes shared with the goods car. The top trains are S3/S4 and CM5/CM6, offering soft seats, hard sleepers, and soft sleepers. These trains stop only at major cities and take between 38 hours (S3/S4) and 42 hours (CM5/CM6) to cover the 1,726 kilometers on the Hanoi–Saigon route. With hard seat cars are S7/S8 and S9/S10, typically composed of nine passenger cars: three hard seat, two soft seat, three hard sleeper, and one soft sleeper. These trains stop at more stations along the Hanoi to Saigon route and take 46 hours to cover the entire distance.

On Hanoi to Haiphong trains there are only hard seats or soft seats available; from Hanoi to

Lao Cai, hard seats, soft seats, and hard sleepers; from Hanoi to Dong Dang, hard seats.

Prices vary slightly for each kind of train—it depends on comfort, speed, distance, and the size of your nose. Foreigners pay 2–3 times more than Vietnamese and usually pay in dollars rounded out to the nearest figure. The markup is higher for the soft classes. Foreign prices are not usually posted at railway stations. If you're keen on calculations, you can use the posted Vietnamese prices as a rough gauge. On average, if you multiply the Vietnamese price by 2.5 you'll arrive at a dong price that roughly converts to the price a foreigner is expected to pay. Because of this pricing system, it's much cheaper to travel by bus than train—in theory there is no foreign markup on buses—but buses are nowhere near as comfortable.

Consider traveling by soft seat; it's only marginally more expensive than hard seat but a lot cheaper than a hard sleeper. For day trips, the soft seat is preferable to other classes; for overnight trips, you'll still get some sleep on a soft seat since you can recline.

As a high-paying foreigner, you'll be sold a ticket through a separate wicket dealing in U.S. dollars. You need to show your passport. To avoid disappointment, book several days in advance for sleepers—a three-day advance booking is a good idea. Travel agents can arrange your ticket for a small surcharge. Tickets can be booked by phone in major cities.

By Road
Rental Vehicles
You can assemble your own small group and hire a car and driver from numerous travel agencies and government tourism offices. Self-drive vehicle rentals are not available as yet, except for motorcycles. Vehicles ranging from a car to a minibus, or even full-sized bus, can be used for touring around a city or farther afield. Calculation of costs depends on the type of vehicle, time, distance, number of passengers, and several other variables. Russian cars are cheaper, Japanese cars more expensive. In the south you can rent museum pieces: old Peugeot 203s or Citroën Tractions. Vehicles are

mostly priced per 100 kilometers, but you can arrange hire by half or full day. Cars usually work out to $25–40 a day. An example here is driving from Hué to Danang. It's only 108 kilometers, and there's great scenery along the route. A hired car allows you to dawdle, and once you get to Danang, you could use the car to visit Hoi An, 35 kilometers farther on. Another shared route that works well by hired car is the run from Saigon to the Cambodian border. Buses along the route are often stopped by police looking for smugglers, but share-taxis or rental cars go through quickly. If you hire a vehicle for a period of 3–4 days, you pay a small surcharge to cover the driver's extra time and lodging.

4WD Vehicles
On the rugged roads of the north and Central Highlands, 4WD vehicles are the only way to go. These vehicles are higher-priced than regular cars but essential on rough roads. Modern vehicles include Toyota Land Cruisers and Japanese jeeps. A close relative of the Land Cruiser is a Mekong 4WD, assembled in Vietnam as part of a Japanese joint venture. Other joint ventures are under way with Japanese, French, American, and German companies for trucks, cars, and motorcycles to be produced in Vietnam. The incentive here is that Vietnam's import tax on new cars is 200 percent while the tax on cars assembled in Vietnam is 40 percent.

To visit the mountainous north, you can rent a Russian army jeep in Hanoi. The Gazelle is a roomy Russian model with two bucket seats in the front, room for three passengers in the back, and a luggage section with space for jerry cans right up the back. That's a total of five people. You can negotiate the number of days you need the vehicle and assemble a rough schedule, but allow flexibility for additional days and extra places to visit. Then work out a fixed price. Pay half up front, half on completion of the trip. In the south, although you don't really need a jeep to tour, reconditioned U.S. Army jeeps are a status symbol. Many are still running in pristine condition.

Traveler Bus and Minibus

Local long-distance transport can be exasperatingly slow—breakdowns due to overloading, stop and drop, moving of cargo, stampeding ducks and pigs. It can take five hours to cover a mere 100 kilometers. Thus many travelers eye the tourist buses and vans plying the coast. If you want to spend more time at the actual destination rather than getting there, consider Open Tour buses and minibuses. These are organized by traveler cafés and are popular along the Saigon to Hué section. Think of it: You can get up at 0900 instead of 0500 and still arrive at the same time, with your legs not writhing from cramps. The minibuses will actually pick you up from your hotel and may drop you at a hotel at the other end, thus avoiding transfers. The buses stop for half an hour or an hour at various scenic attractions en route, allowing you to stretch and take in the sights. On the Saigon to Hué route, for example, the bus might stop at coastal beaches, fishing villages, and the Cham Museum in Danang. You can save a lot of time by buying an "open ticket," which allows you to get on and off traveler buses at key junctions—all on the same ticket. The cost from Hanoi to Saigon works out to about $57.

The disadvantage of this method of transport is that you're insulated from the locals; you get to talk only to other travelers. When you do encounter locals, it's not under the best of circumstances. Imagine an air-conditioned tour bus descending on a small village, and 45 people streaming out, all armed to the teeth with cameras and video equipment. The way you can get round this problem is by avoiding the larger, 45-seat buses and sticking to either 24-seat buses or 12-seat minibuses.

Another disadvantage of the Open Tour is being forced to move at the same pace as the group in a regimented fashion with driver and guide barking at their charges if they're late reboarding. The Open Tour buses involve more than transport; the operator herds you into chosen restaurants along the route and also tries to book you into an affiliated hotel once you arrive at your destination. So it starts to become a real package deal. With a number of operators offering Open Tour tickets, it's best to just pick up the bus you need for the next destination—chop and change operators to make the journeys more interesting.

Public Bus and Minibus

Using regular local buses, you can travel all the way from Hanoi to Saigon for a mere $20, though you might arrive with a few loose screws and a jangled spine. Buses are dirt cheap but also uncomfortable. You're often wedged into a tiny space surrounded by curious locals, heaving children, and squawking chickens. Buy a small foam pad for bus rides, available cheaply from markets, with colorful covers. You can use the pad as a buttsaver, pillow, or backrest.

Avoid buses that stop and drop every kilometer or so. Try to track down express buses. Unfortunately, a classier bus may come equipped with a video machine; pray there's no karaoke device attached. Even these buses offer limited legroom. Space is at a premium on local buses. All buses transport goods: sacks of rice, cut wood, chicken feed, sugar, batteries strewn along the floor, bananas, bicycles, chickens stacked all over the roof. A crawler with a seat-high load may be able to do only 30 kph—if it doesn't break down. There may be other complications. On one bus, our driver noticed smoke rising, opened a hatch inside the bus to have a closer look, and a huge flame shot up. Obviously the bus had overheated a bit. Eventually the fire was doused, and after some minor surgery the bus was on its way again.

Faster but not necessarily safer are Toyota minibuses. There's a comprehensive network of these, but they're uncomfortable, with passengers stuffed in tightly. You'll also notice the distinctive red or yellow snout of the Renault van; there are many of these in central Vietnam, used for short range runs.

You can't complain about the prices on these forms of transport—about $.60 for 100 kilometers. That compares with roughly $.75/100 kilometers for a minibus, and about $4/100 kilometers for a soft seat on a train. A bus from Saigon to Dalat covers 310 kilometers in

6–7 hours for $1.80; by minibus it's marginally more, perhaps $2.20. Technically there's no foreign surcharge on buses, but you'll be charged above the Vietnamese price.

One way to gain more legroom is to buy several seats. Sometimes the driver will even size you up and *ask* you to buy several seats. This is because it's possible you'll require the space of two Vietnamese. This especially applies to minibuses, where they *really* pack them in. Sometimes in a bus or minibus, two Westerners will buy a row of three seats. Another problem is what to do with your bags. If the underseat space is filled with produce, you may end up with your luggage on your lap; it's not a good idea to put it on the rooftop. Riding local buses or minibuses for longer than 10 hours is not recommended if you value your sanity. Everybody reaches the limits of patience on bus rides. Two Western women, after enduring children vomiting on them, elbows in the ribs, and sundry other insults, drew the line at a passenger who boarded with an unidentified animal moving around inside a burlap bag. "That," shouted one of them hysterically, "is *not* sharing my seat!"

Share-Taxis

In bus depots, often situated near markets, you'll spot smaller vehicles that may be used

TOURING BY MOTORCYCLE

On your own motorcycle in Vietnam, you're free to go where you please. However, you do need good riding skills to handle the road-warrior mentality in Vietnam, and you need mechanical know-how. Your motorcycle will most certainly not be brand-new, and older models tend to break down or lose parts because of vibration on rough roads. Motorcycles can easily be transported on trains and larger boats and have also been sighted on the tops of buses.

Highway 1, the main route from Hanoi to Saigon, is not exactly the Indochina Expressway. Sometimes it's only a single lane or dirt. Motorcycles must share the road with trucks, cars, bicycles, and the occasional oxcarts, as well as large patches of rice or other crops drying in the sun. The Vietnamese must rank among Asia's most aggressive drivers. Their reckless attitude toward speed leads to many accidents, often fatal for motorcyclists because of the lack of helmets. There is nothing in the way of insurance; a common reaction at the scene of an accident is for the rider or driver to recover and take off as fast as possible. If the police arrive, damage compensation is paid on the spot.

Foreigners without Vietnamese licenses do not usually encounter problems with police, although it would be nice to at least have an International Driver's License. Police occasionally may try to make pocket money by saying your papers are not in order. If police attempt to flag you down, smile, wave back, and keep on going. If stopped, you suddenly do not understand *anything*. Just keep smiling.

Now for the good news: Gasoline is cheap in Vietnam. Unheard of for a Marxist country, Vietnam produces its own gasoline. It's a bit over $1 a U.S. gallon for unleaded gas, probably enough to carry you 100 kilometers on a motorcycle. Countdown kilometer stones (French-style, every kilometer) allow you to track your progress. There are two options for acquiring a motorcycle for touring: Rent long-term from an agency, or buy a used motorcycle and resell it after touring.

Long-Term Rental

Two Australian travelers made it all the way from Saigon to Hanoi and beyond on Honda 90cc bikes. They rented them in Saigon for $3.50 a day each, with the proviso they would send the bikes back by train at the end of the tour. It cost $30 each to ship the bikes. The owner held their paper visas as security—these were mailed on to a friend in Hanoi, who also handled putting the bikes back on a train. The leisurely tour consumed a month with many stops, perhaps 10 days of actual motorcycling. The riders traveled with shouldered backpacks, the weight resting over the rear rack. They said the best part of the ride

for short-run destinations. You can find old elongated Citroëns used as share-taxis. These classic vehicles bear record-breaking figures on the odometer (if it's not shot) and carry record-breaking numbers of passengers. Jeeps are sometimes used on dirt roads as share-taxis; there are also jeeps with elongated backs.

Motorcycle Rental

Motorcycle rental is available in Saigon, Dalat, Nha Trang, Hué, Danang, Hoi An, and Hanoi. Greater numbers of travelers frequent these cities— thus the cottage industry of motorcycle rental. The owner will want to keep your passport, paper visa, credit card, or plane ticket

as security for a newer Japanese bike. Before renting consider what may happen if there's an accident or the bike is stolen. Also consider your riding skills. Reckless drivers abound in Vietnam, and if you have an accident, medical facilities are very poor.

The most common motorcycle in Vietnam is a Honda. A rental will likely be a scooter such as the Honda 50cc, 70cc, or 90cc. Top of the line for rentals is a Honda Dream 100cc, a nightmare if it gets stolen, because it will set you back a few thousand dollars. The renter is generally responsible for theft or damage to the bike. Apparently the legal limit for riding a bike without a Vietnamese license is 70cc,

was the coastal strip from Saigon to Hué. The biggest problems along the route were 1) trucks; 2) more trucks; 3) holes in the road, big ones in the south, fewer but deeper ones in the north; 4) riders making sudden U-turns (they collected three bicycles this way); and 5) rain.

From Hanoi, a number of Westerners have rented 125cc and 175cc Russian motorcycles to head northwest to Sapa via Dien Bien Phu. From Sapa, you can aim for the railway at Lao Cai and then load yourself and your bike onto a train bound for Hanoi. Some ride the full loop, though this is exhausting because of bad road conditions. On a larger bike you can stow one small bag over the gas tank at the front and place another small bag sideways at the back.

Buying a Motorcycle

Japanese imports are very expensive. In Saigon, Honda 50cc, 90cc, and 125cc motorcycles sell in the $1,300–1,600 range. Honda Cubs are imported from Japan; the Honda Dream 100 is imported from Thailand and Indonesia. Top of the line is a gleaming Honda Dream II, which can cost $2,500 new. Apart from Hondas, Suzuki, Yamaha, and Kawasaki hold a small share of the market. Big-engined bikes are forbidden for import to Vietnam; the ones around before the rules came down are sold for high profits. Travelers often settle for Russian motorcycles, which are

fairly hardy beasts and have a good spare-parts pool. You can buy a used Minsk 175cc in Hanoi or Saigon for $250–350, or new for $500–600. You can probably sell the bike for $100 less than you paid for it. Bikes such as the Minsk 125cc and 175cc are easily sold, but others, such as a Czech-made Jawa 350cc, present problems because spare parts are hard to find.

You need papers of some nature to resell the bike. Foreigners are not supposed to possess ownership papers, but this is bypassed by registering under a Vietnamese friend's name. You can have your plates made up in Saigon at Ben Thanh market. Regular plates are white with black lettering; police and government plates are green with white lettering; army plates are red with white lettering. The NN prefix indicates a plate for a foreign businessperson; NG on a white plate with red lettering indicates a diplomat. Green (government) plates would be nice, because police are less likely to bother you.

Three on one bike? An enterprising Englishman bought a 750cc Ural with a sidecar in Saigon for $800. He was on his way to Hanoi, where he was counting on selling the Russian bike for $700. The Ural was hard to maneuver on rough roads, so he took it easy. To cut costs, he picked up travelers en route for a small charge—one passenger in the sidecar, a second sitting behind the driver.

but nobody takes much notice, and licenseless foreigners rent higher-powered Russian and Czech bikes. Helmets are not mandatory in Vietnam. You can buy one for $10–35; they are more commonly worn in the north than in the south.

A place such as Saigon requires skilled riding. There are estimated to be more than a million motorcycles in the city, vastly outnumbering cars. Accidents between motorcycles are common.

Motos

Motorcycle-taxis are known in Vietnamese as *xe moto om* or *honda om* (Honda cuddle), "Honda" being generic for any kind of motorcycle. They're excellent for touring around a town or covering short-haul destinations. As a backpacker you develop a kind of symbiotic relationship with motos, as they fill in those crucial 10-kilometer gaps between highway and hotel, or airport and town. An express bus, for example, may drop you 10 kilometers outside Nha Trang. A moto can take you and your pack straight to a hotel. You can hire a moto like a taxi for a one-way trip, or by the hour, or by the half or full day. As a touring vehicle, motos are great. The driver takes care of all the traffic and mechanical problems, leaving you to focus on the scenery. In effect, the moto driver is your guide. The charge should be around $5–7 for a full day of touring.

The most important part of a moto is the driver. Before you board, take quick stock of his apparent sanity and physical condition. Any tell-tale scars? Skid marks on the elbows? Does he shake a lot (indicating either amphetamine use or bad suspension on the bike)? No helmet is supplied when riding a moto, so tell your driver to go slowly. Moto drivers in Vietnam have an alarming habit of using hand gestures when showing you around, leaving only one hand to control the handlebars.

Motos can also be used for touring up to 40 or 50 kilometers out of town. If carrying luggage, two bags are better; you can strap a small backpack sideways on a motorcycle. Moto operators deal a lot with market freight.

They often have rear side racks to carry loads and rubber straps to hold them in place. Once you get over the sight of a huge pig slung across the back of a motorcycle, you realize a backpack is not a problem. Balance is. So it's wise to adapt your luggage to suit. A big backpack will make for an unstable load on a moto, especially if you're still wearing it. Better to have two smaller packs—you can throw one up front on the gas tank, or strap it to sidesaddle racks at the back, or wear a day pack. On a Honda 70cc scooter, a smaller pack will fit nicely wedged down vertically between handlebars and seat. The driver's knees hold it in place.

Cyclos

Cyclos, or bicycle trishaws, were introduced in Hanoi in the early 1930s, replacing rickshaws. Cyclos are a leisurely way to take in the sights and you can turn them into touring vehicles by hiring one by the hour or the half day. Cyclo drivers often make good guides, charging around $3 for the day. Cyclos are great for short hauls.

Fares are negotiable, usually 2,000 dong a kilometer, or $.80 an hour. Negotiate for cyclo prices by holding up the relevant number of digits on your hand; make sure it's dong, not dollars, you're talking about. Foreigners can get into nasty arguments with cyclo drivers over disputed fares. To save argument, some travelers prefer to pay up front.

When you first arrive in Vietnam cyclos seem quaint; by the time you leave you may never want to ride in one again. Unfortunately, cyclo drivers can be very aggressive, and they think that foreigners cannot walk from point A to point B unassisted. If the foreigner has luggage and is still walking, she or he must be absolutely crazy. Cyclo drivers will relentlessly pursue you along the streets of Saigon, Nha Trang, or Danang. Even if you're sitting in a cyclo, another driver will pull up and ask you if you want a cyclo! If you're riding a rented bicycle, a cyclo driver will sidle up and ask if you're tired, demanding to transport you *and* the bicycle back to your hotel.

In cities such as Saigon, Hanoi, and Haiphong,

major hotels maintain a small fleet of luxury cyclos with padded seats, plush armrests, front suspension, sunroof, even headlights. The suspension-model cyclos are used for VIPs or by family members for marriage negotiation visits; fares on these models don't run much higher than for regular ratty cyclos. You can squeeze two passengers into one cyclo, or take one cyclo for each passenger and travel in a convoy.

In the Mekong Delta there are variants on bicycle-taxis. You can find a bicycle-buggy, consisting of a detachable bicycle and a driver up front hauling a two-wheel wooden chariot behind. On a flat road, this contraption can haul four passengers. A bare bicycle is often used to ferry chickens and ducks around markets; passengers sit on a wooden and metal rack over the back wheel, and an extra child can be carried up front on the top frame. These are called *xedap om* (bicycle cuddle). Foreigners rarely use them.

Bicycles

The bicycle is the prime mode of personal transport in Vietnam, though mopeds and motorbikes are taking over in Saigon and Hanoi. There are an estimated 20 million bicycles in Vietnam, roughly one bike for every three people— a per-head ratio similar to China's. Sturdy Chinese-made bicycles are flooding the market in Vietnam, with lesser breeds arriving from Thailand. Vietnam also makes its own bicycles in French-built factories. More than 100,000 bikes are produced annually. The Huu Nghi (Friendship) model costs $20, and the Doan (Corporate) model costs up to $35. You get what you pay for; the bikes have a habit of falling apart quickly. A smuggled Chinese bicycle sells for $60 and up.

Bicycles in Vietnam are used not only as the "family car" but also as freight vehicles. In rural areas you'll see bike riders performing impossible balancing acts: transporting a score of live geese or a load of fish traps that totally obscures the bike. Heavy loads are transported on industrial bicycles that are not ridden but pushed. These are ingeniously decked out with heavy-duty panniers; when the full load of pottery or whatever is in place, the bike can be steered by means of a handlebar extension. When the industrial bike has no load, it can be ridden.

Bike Rental: You can rent a bike in places where travelers gather—Saigon, Nha Trang, Hué, Hanoi—for about a dollar a day. Bike-repair stands abound on street corners and repairs are very cheap. Before cycling off on a rental, check the tires, make sure the wheels spin freely, and determine that at least one brake works. Also check the saddle height; your leg should be almost fully extended from the saddle position to the pedal at its lowest point to maximize leg power. Pay attention to one-way streets downtown: Be especially careful when cycling near schools in the morning, or in market areas.

In busy areas such as markets, always park in designated bike parking areas, which have attendants who require a token fee. This is to prevent your rental bike's being either towed officially or stolen unofficially. Bike parking spots may have thousands of bikes that all look like yours. Mark your vehicle! Put a brightly colored wrapper on the back rack or wherever, or tie some cloth onto the handlebars. If you're in a busy area and there's no bike parking in sight, try to find a bicycle-repair place and lock your bike close to the owner. When you return, pay the bike repairman a small fee for watching the bike.

Because they lack gears, rented bikes are not suitable for long-distance forays, although you can easily cover 10 kilometers in an hour by bike, making a destination within 20 kilometers feasible as long as the going is flat. Bike-repair stands are easy to find and very cheap.

Buying a Bike: In Saigon, a Phoenix 10-speed from Shanghai costs $100 with rack, water-bottle cage, and fenders (mudguards). For $130 you can buy a Taiwan-made 10-speed or even an 18-gear pseudo-mountain bike. About $190 will secure a Federal 12-speed with real Shimano shifters and a tube made in Indonesia. Sometimes you can get your hands on used Western bikes sold by ship hands visiting Saigon. A Japanese bike with Shimano equipment costs around $260.

BIKING VIETNAM

by Patrick Morris

Cycling is often the best way to explore and experience a place, removing the barriers between you and native people that are common with other means of transportation. Nowhere is this truer than in Vietnam—a place dominated by two-wheeled vehicles and foot traffic. To make your journey more enjoyable, here is some practical information culled through several seasons of leading cycling tours throughout the country.

Packing

Thorough preparation can save headaches later on. First and foremost—don't overpack! Besides quality bicycle parts and certain other essentials, almost anything forgotten can be bought cheaply in Bangkok, Saigon, or Hanoi. I've even had good cycling shorts made in a few days in Saigon for $10. Bring a tough bicycle. A mountain bike with multiuse tires for the pavement and dirt is the best all-around choice. Pack spare parts and critical gear such as spokes, tubes, a sturdy pump, cables, extra chain, and a spare water bottle or two. Bring along tools such as a spoke wrench, tire irons, and chain tool or one of the new all-in-one, multifunction tools.

For easy access to such things as maps and a camera, a handlebar bag or rear-mounted rack with bag is indispensable. A handlebar bell is required equipment—the louder the better. Many cyclists find a rear-view mirror attached to a helmet or glasses useful. Padded gloves ease the shock from rough roads. Carry a photocopy of your passport and use it instead of the original when possible. I've even had success flashing my California driver's license. Bring a couple of good maps and a guide-book, neither of which should be assumed entirely accurate—some roads are just not there anymore. A phrasebook is also handy for at least pointing to unpronounceable words. For gifts, children like pens, and sharing pictures from home is always great at breaking the ice.

The box your bike flies over in is an excellent place to stuff your helmet and other supplies for the trip over as the weight limit is frequently very high. Deflate your tires and avoid packing bottled items as your bike may fly into Vietnam in an unpressurized cabin, which can lead to exploded tubes and shampoo containers.

On the Road

On the bike, wear a hat, long-sleeved cotton shirt, and plenty of sunscreen on exposed skin. A wide-brimmed hat helps protect your face and neck (the ubiquitous Vietnamese green pith helmets are excellent for this and cost only a few dollars). Flying insects, trucks kicking up debris, and children occasionally throwing things make sunglasses a good idea. Don't overdo the first few days of riding as your body adjusts to the climate, jet lag, and food. Fatigue can quickly compromise your health. Everything, including cycling, is much more difficult in the tropics. That, combined with poor road conditions, makes it wise to scale back distance projections made at home.

Drink fluids constantly—heat stroke is a real possibility. Bottled water is scarce in rural areas but there is always plenty of boiled tea, bottled sodas, and beer. Always check bottle seals for tampering—sometimes bottled water is merely refilled. *Nuoc mia* is sugarcane juice made at roadside stalls and is very refreshing. Coconut juice is also common. Carry lots of small bills and ask the price before drinking anything or your bill may double or triple. Because the Vietnamese seldom drink water, asking or gesturing for it may get you a glass of rice wine instead! Intense heat combined with vigorous cycling may make ice unavoidable, but in my experience it is usually safe—except for in Hoi An, where stomach flu has cropped up several times. Raw vegetables can be a problem: Try to always eat cooked foods or fruits you can peel. Speaking of stomach problems, carry toilet paper, as there is none outside the hotels. Rural toilets can be shockers—a bush may actually be preferable. Cookies and other sweets are well stocked in numerous cafés and shops that line the roads. These cafés are the best spots to find shade, cool down, and perhaps nod off for a while. Also, don't be afraid to step into peoples' homes. In Vietnam you are always a welcome guest.

Infections can happen very rapidly—treat cuts and abrasions quickly and thoroughly. Second-skin bandages are handy for covering areas exposed to the rigors of cycling. Pharmacies are well stocked and present in even small towns.

Bicycle theft is typically not a worry, as everyone will seem to be watching you or your bike. However, curious tinkering is common—gears are changed, and cyclometers, water bottles, and pouches can disappear. Keeping an eye on your things when suddenly surrounded by 100 children can be difficult—keep important stuff tucked away. Solo travelers are always at a disadvantage. This is especially true for women. At midday, amused harassment by beer-guzzling karaoke lounge lizards is not uncommon. Don't be afraid to yell or hit back, but stopping and calling the attention of the locals may be best. Two men were arrested for harassing one woman on our tour after locals called the police. Hotel laundry is rough—you may prefer to wash your own delicates, such as cycling shorts. Also make sure to double-check all your clothes have been returned. The Vietnamese day starts at sunup—every day. At the hotel, ask for a room off the street. Earplugs may help even if you don't sleep in, as some cities, such as Saigon, have constant noise.

Rideable Routes

Don't feel driven to cycle the entire length of Vietnam. Some areas are definitely worth skipping—if only to conserve energy for the better routes in the mountains. The Mekong Delta has an enormous amount of traffic and narrow roads and rather plain scenery. Highway 1 can be a nightmare to cycle. However, the Central Highlands are sparsely trafficked with the bonus of cooler weather and excellent landscape. The roads around the border areas of northern Vietnam are also sparsely trafficked, and Cat Ba Island in the Halong Bay area is great for cycling.

On Highway 1, skipping the ride from Hué to Hanoi may conserve your good impression of Vietnam. The area has notoriously bad roads and some areas curiously lacking the usual Vietnamese graciousness. Rocks are thrown and last time we rode through Quang Tri province, the friendly police in Dong Ha invited us out for beer but left us with the $50 tab. Our $7-a-night hotel also added $20 onto our bill for good measure. The train is a much better way to cover this area. Make sure the train you are on has a cargo car for your bicycle or it will arrive later than you do. Hué train station is notorious for overcharging on bike fees. From Yen Bai (a train stop approximately

(continued on next page)

BIKING VIETNAM (cont'd)

100 kilometers north of Hanoi) to the Chinese border is very scenic, especially to Lao Cai on a sparsely driven road. The area around Sapa is very mountainous and challenging—but incredibly beautiful.

Riding on Highway 1 can be unnerving. Cyclists are at the bottom of the food chain: There are no traffic lines on the road and there are no traffic laws. You are supposed to get out of the way and drivers will expect you to in confrontations. Luckily the Vietnamese drivers honk constantly. Always ride far to the right and be prepared to bail out to the side of the road. Likewise, you should use your bell frequently. People do not look when crossing or turning unless they hear an engine or horn. An easy way to get killed cycling in Vietnam, or in much of the world, is to wear earphones or ride at night. Rocks, holes, drying rice and coffee, darting children, chickens, dogs, and water buffaloes mean you must give adequate attention to the road ahead. Tired? Wave down a truck. Anyone with room will stop. This road service is usually at no charge, but a dollar or two goes a long way.

Unlike Bangkok, Saigon and Hanoi are still rideable cities, where bicycle and scooter traffic still dominate the wide, tree-lined streets. Although swarms of two-wheeled traffic crossing each other like schools of fish can be intimidating at first, it can soon become exhilarating. Sunday night "cruising" in Saigon is not to be missed. After nightfall, the city center becomes packed with two-wheeling Vietnamese of all ages, dressed up and going *di troi*—around.

Local Encounters

Vietnamese police pretty much leave travelers alone. Rural areas north of Hanoi, border regions, Quang Tri province, and occasionally Danang can be hazardous to your wallet. Arrest or physical force is unheard of, but an English lesson on demand—or in one case, a bucket shower given to me by frontier police—may be required. Smiling and playing stupid—but unintimidated—may get you going again quickly. If the police do stop you, show only a copy of your passport (if you hand over your original passport, they may hold it for money).

Fun diversions? Pulling off the highway into a schoolyard is an experience not to miss. A couple of hundred screaming children swarming around you is quite a charge. In fact, heading just off the main road anywhere in rural areas will put you in places many foreigners have never been. Expect Vietnamese on bicycles and motor scooters to ride with you to practice English. You may also be invited to their homes—these invitations provide the finest travel experiences in Vietnam, so try not pass too many of them up. Finding a box to repack your bike in after your trip is next to impossible, but Vietnam Airlines will let you fly your bike out without a bike-box and usually will care for it well.

Patrick Morris leads tours through Vietnam, Cambodia, Sumatra, and Turkey for VeloAsia, a Northern California–based adventure cycling company, website: www.veloasia.com.

Bicycle Touring: Foreigners have explored large swaths of Vietnam by bicycle. Some have even traversed the length of China before taking on Vietnam as an afterthought, and then carried on through Laos into Thailand. You can cycle through land borders in Vietnam. A mountain bike or hybrid is preferable for touring.

The best bike routes are those away from heavy traffic. Unfortunately, Highway 1 is becoming very busy with truck traffic. It's therefore unpleasant for cycling, although bicyclists have found parts of the coast agreeable. Between Buon Ma Thuot and Pleiku in the Central Highlands is a great road for cycling. However, there are no places to stay. The Mekong Delta has good routes. There are small towns with hotels, and you can transport the bike on local ferries for the best of both worlds. Cycling can be sweaty work in the delta. Another route involving ferry hops is Hanoi to Halong Bay and beyond on the coast road. Cat Ba Island has little traffic. It's a bit hilly, but a great place to ride.

Cyclists should note that prevailing winds blow northeast in summer and southwest in winter. To avoid head winds, you should head north in summer (July), but south in winter (January). Typhoon season is October–December for the central and north coast. Cycling in the north is more difficult because accommodations, bottled water, and food variety are not as common as in the south. It's unpleasant to be reduced to drinking jugs of bitter tea or consuming bowls of *pho*.

Bicycles can easily be transported on trains and boats or on the tops of buses. Domestic flights are trickier because of a 20-kilogram weight restriction. A bicycle counts as a 50-kilogram weight on trains—say, $1.50 from Hué to Hanoi. However, foreigners are often charged $5 for "foreign bikes," even though they're lighter than local bikes. An English couple figured that since they were paying so much extra for their rail ticket they didn't have to follow regulations, so they just wheeled their bikes straight onto hard-seat class. On buses or boats, the cost should be about no more than a third of a regular passenger fare.

Around Town

The public bus system in Vietnamese cities is useless: slow, crowded, and cumbersome. And you have to figure out where the bus lines travel. Foreigners can easily afford better transport. Options include rented bicycle or motorcycle, cyclo (bicycle trishaw) or moto (motorcycle-taxi), or rented car. Do not underestimate the power of walking; Vietnamese towns such as Hoi An are easily covered on foot. A number of walking, bicycle, and boat tour suggestions have been included in this book because these are ideal ways of taking in the surroundings. Bicycle rentals are cheap—perhaps $1–2 a day. Chinese models are better. Use designated bicycle parking spots for security. If you don't want to ride yourself, you can hire a cyclo.

In a place such as Saigon, a rented motorcycle requires skilled riding and can be a liability because you're not supplied with a helmet. If nervous about riding, the solution is simple: Hire a moto driver, so you become a passenger. In Danang a rented motorcycle is great, allowing you to get out of town to nearby sights. Motorcycles are rented for $5–10 a day depending on quality.

Cyclos and motos can be hired by the hour or day; always negotiate rates before setting out. A cyclo ride is a relaxing way of getting around; you can hire one for as little as $2 a day. More luxurious and expensive models with sunroofs and other gadgets are available outside ritzy hotels. Motos, good for longer-distance touring or anything involving hills, charge roughly $7 a day. Occasionally, you might hop on a lambro (short for Lambretta, or small three-wheel vehicle), which shuttles along fixed routes.

Travel agencies in most towns can arrange car hire by the half or full day, or travel by minibus or larger vehicle. Taxis do not cruise the streets, but they may be available from ranks near the train station or local market. In Saigon and Hanoi are metered taxis, though these are expensive, charging $2 on boarding and $.70 a kilometer.

In Hué and Hoi An, you can rent a local boat to tour the area. You pay by the hour or arrange a half-day rate. Prices range from $3 for a few

HEROES OF THE BOULEVARDS

You'll find the streets in cities throughout Vietnam invariably emblazoned with the same 20 or so names—a miniglossary of Vietnamese revolutionary heroes and heroines. This system gets confusing; you become hazy about whether the Army Hotel was on Pham Ngu Lao Street in Hanoi or Saigon. And that place called Number 3 Hotel—was that on Le Loi Boulevard in Hanoi or Hué? Hotels are often named after the street or town. You'll see a Dien Bien Hotel in Dien Bien Phu town and on Dien Bien Phu Street in Haiphong.

Streets in Vietnam once bore French names: governors-general, administrators, admirals, literary figures, and so forth. In Saigon there was Rue Paul Bert, Rue Admiral Courbat, Rue d'Espagne, Quai de Belgique, Place Pigneau de Béhaine, Boulevard Bonnard, and streets named after Kipling and Rousseau. After the French left in 1954, naturally all the names in North and South Vietnam were changed. After reunification in 1975, there were further name changes, especially in the south. A few French names remain in the medical hero line: Pasteur, Curie, Calmette, and Yersin. Hotels previously known by French names—the Hotel Majestic and Hotel Continental in Saigon—underwent name changes after 1975 but are now reverting to the original names because it's easier on tourists. This process of name-changing is ongoing. You may find that different maps do not agree on street or hotel names.

Even the name of Vietnam's greatest revolutionary hero hasn't stuck. After 1975, Saigon was changed to Ho Chi Minh City. The tongue-twister never caught on, and most still call it Saigon. In any case, Ho Chi Minh City refers to Greater Saigon, which is the size of a province. The inner city is known all around as Saigon.

In historical order, here are some sources of names for the byways and boulevards of Vietnamese cities:

Hai Ba Trung: named after the famous Trung sisters, who temporarily ousted the Chinese around A.D. 40.

Ly Thuong Kiet: military commander who led campaigns against the Chinese and Cham in the 12th century.

Tran Hung Dao: Vietnamese general who defeated a Mongol fleet dispatched by Kublai Khan in the 13th century.

Le Loi: Vietnamese leader who ended several decades of Chinese Ming rule in 1427.

Trung Trac: Nguyen Trung Trac was executed by the French in 1868. The resistance leader turned himself in to protect his relatives, held hostage by the French in Rach Gia.

Le Qui Don: 18th-century encyclopedist and historian.

Nguyen Hue: named after one of the brothers of the 18th-century Tay Son rebellion, who later became Emperor Quang Trung.

Duy Tan: emperor who lent support to an armed uprising against the French in 1916.

Phan Boi Chau: nationalist in the early 1900s, imprisoned by the French.

Nguyen Thai Hoc: communist leader guillotined by the French in 1930.

Tran Phu: first secretary general of the Communist Party of Indochina, killed by the French in 1931.

Nguyen Thi Minh Khai: the first Communist Party secretary for Saigon, she was executed by the French in 1941.

Hoang Van Thu: leader of the Vietnamese Communist Party, executed by the French in 1944.

Dien Bien Phu: famous battle site where the Vietminh defeated the French in 1954.

30 Thang 4 Street: commemorates the fall of Saigon on April 30, 1975. Individual towns often have a "fall" date posted on a major artery—in Dalat, for example, there's a boulevard called Duong 3 Thang 4, which refers to the April 3, 1975, liberation of the town.

hours up to $15 for a half day for the entire boat, holding six passengers and up.

Other Modes of Travel
Hitching

Some travelers have had great success hitchhiking. The concept is alien to most Vietnamese, but the idea of chatting in English or French must be appealing to bored drivers. Getting around by hitching can be much faster than by bus, and a good deal more comfortable. Minor payment is expected.

Hiking

The best way to see rural villages and minority areas in Vietnam is to start walking, preferably with a guide. Your guide can arrange for overnight stays in villages, which means you can keep on walking. A fit hiker could cover 20 kilometers a day in this fashion. Longer hikes can also be undertaken in national parks. The best places for this kind of walking are in the north.

Boat Transport

Around Hué or Hoi An you can rent a sampan to cruise along the town's river; at the Perfume Pagoda or Tam Coc Caves a small boat is the only way to get around. In Halong Bay and at Nha Trang you can club together with others to rent a fishing vessel to tour offshore islands. At Halong you can also sleep overnight on vessels fitted with bunks. Some refitted junks are also available for hire—essentially yachts with maroon cotton panels for sails.

Because of a lack of bridges, you'll often use ferry crossings in Vietnam. Waterways are a lifeline for goods and passenger transport in some areas. The waterways of the Mekong Delta are best toured by large wooden craft leaving from points such as Cantho or Chau Doc. Ferries run to the delta from Saigon. You can sleep overnight using a hammock on one of these vessels. They're usually overloaded with goods and have no safety equipment. Out of Haiphong, much larger rusting hulks are used as ferries to ports along the northern coast.

Kayaking has been tried with success in the Mekong Delta. An Australian couple brought in fold-up kayaks by plane and paddled up to the Cambodian border. Their tour lasted a couple of weeks; they had a few brushes with police, but nothing serious. The kayakers stayed with families and on sampans, sometimes mooring alongside, sometimes lifting the kayaks aboard a boat. They packed the kayaks onto a regular ferry to return to Saigon. The Halong Bay area north of Hanoi holds great potential for kayaking, with many islands scattered through the region. SeaCanoe Thailand, a sea kayak operator from Phuket, Thailand, has been permitted to conduct short trips in this area, as well as Mountain Travel Sobek, an American tour operator.

Tours

International adventure travel operators stage trips some individuals may find difficult because of logistics, equipment, or permission requirements. Weighed against this are the cost ($100–150 and up per person per day) and the slow group pace. You might find yourself chafing at the restrictions. Regardless of whether or not you join a tour, you can garner plenty of ideas from the following short sampling of adventure travel operators.

Tours for Veterans

Going back to Vietnam can be a healing experience for a person who fought there—possibly even alleviating what psychotherapists have identified as post-traumatic stress disorder (loosely characterized by a set of symptoms including depression and withdrawal, drug and alcohol dependence, and inability to hold a job). Certainly the ability to walk around rural Vietnam without worrying about snipers or booby traps must offer a new perspective.

An early returnee, Patrick Campbell, summed up the experience this way: "Before I came over here, I thought of Vietnam the way I left it: helicopters and shooting and ducking and dodging. I thought that way until three or four days after I got back [to Vietnam]. By then I could see that it wasn't like that anymore." Patrick was involved in building a

Know Vietnam, Cambodia & Laos

VIETNAM ROUTE STRATEGIES

Most travelers start or end trips to Vietnam from Hanoi or Saigon. Because of weak infrastructure and horribly overcrowded buses and minibuses, many opt for rented vehicles, throwing together their own small groups, or joining traveler minibuses. For adequate leg space, travel by train is a viable option.

Vietnam is a skinny country—a glance at the map will show the main route runs from Saigon to Hanoi or the reverse. Many fly into Hanoi, work their way toward Saigon, and fly out of Saigon (or the reverse). A good route taking in the Central Highlands is Hanoi to Hué to Danang to Quang Ngai to Pleiku to Buon Ma Thuot to Nha Trang to Dalat to Saigon or the reverse. Or you could spend all your time looping around the north, or around the south. Some travelers start in the south, explore the Mekong Delta, proceed up to Nha Trang, and turn back to Saigon. Others arrive in Hanoi from Hong Kong, loop around the northwest and north, and fly from Hanoi on to Bangkok.

The opening of land border crossings to Cambodia, Laos, and China has created new overland routes through Vietnam. The land routes are: into Cambodia, Saigon–Moc Bai–Phnom Penh; into Laos, Dong Ha–Lao Bao–Savannakhet and Vinh–Cau Treo–Lak Sao–Paksane; and into China, Hanoi–Lao Cai–Kunming, Hanoi–Lang Son–Nanning or Hanoi–Mong Cai–Zhanjiang. You can travel from Bangkok through Laos to the Lao Bao border, proceed into Vietnam near Khe Sanh, continue from here to Hanoi, cross to Nanning, and carry on overland to Hong Kong. Another viable route is to enter Vietnam from China, proceed south to Saigon, take the road to Phnom Penh, and then, after a side trip to Angkor, plane-hop from Phnom Penh to Bangkok. In the other direction, starting in Saigon, you could go overland to Lao Cai, head for Kunming, and fly from Kunming to either Bangkok or Hong Kong.

In Vietnam you have to base your trip on the weather. A monsoon will not only make it difficult for you to see the sights, it will also render certain areas completely inaccessible because of roads of mud. Visiting in the dry season, I had to completely change plans when typhoons and flooding hit central Vietnam. With several different climate zones, there is no best time to visit. Keep in mind that certain parts of Vietnam—especially in the north—can dip to freezing at night around December.

The onset of Tet, the Lunar New Year, creates special traffic hazards—commuters wheeling around on motorcycles or bicycles with entire peach trees or miniature orange trees strapped to the sides. Airline seats are booked solid and roads are jammed as every Tan Thanh and his dog try to get home for the sacred family dinner. But once those dinners get under way, consider this: The highways are empty for five days. Everybody stays home at Tet. The hitch is that the railways, bus companies, and other transport companies shut down or scale back operations. Attractions are open for the holidays—if you've arranged your own transport, you'll have the place to yourself. Lunar New Year is celebrated over much of Southeast Asia in different guises; air transport in the entire region is chockablock.

---

medical clinic in Vung Tau in 1988. The project was under the auspices of Vietnam Veterans Restoration Project (VVRP), which has since completed six additional projects in Vietnam—building clinics and supplying medical and alternative energy technology. In 1994 VVRP worked to set up a facility near Saigon to house Vietnamese amputees being fitted for artificial limbs. The limbs are provided free by another American NGO, Vietnam Assistance for the Handicapped. For more information on the work of VVRP, contact Steve Stratford, P.O. Box 369, Garberville, CA 95542, tel. 707/923-3357. The founder of VVRP, Fredy Champagne, organizes tours to Vietnam for vets and is involved with bicycle and motorcycle tours. Contact him at Vietnam Friends, P.O. Box 69, Garberville, CA 95542, tel./fax 707/923-3658.

Agencies in Vietnam have been set up by Vietnamese veterans to assist tours to former battlefields, as well as arrange meetings with former field commanders and officers from

ARVN, Vietcong, and NVA units. One problem disabled veterans face in Vietnam is a complete lack of wheelchair access in the country. Tour companies don't have any wheelchair-lift equipped vans, and visitors in wheelchairss must be carried up and down stairs by a porter. There has been little attempt to make restaurants or hotels accessible.

Ecotouring and Hiking

A few outfits are delving into the rainforests. Top Guides organizes tours in north Vietnam led by wildlife biologists from Vietnam and Malaysia. The route goes through Tai villages and into thick jungle; you stay in longhouses or camp out. The group studies the habitat of local species, including the endangered langur monkey. Contact Top Guides, 1825 San Lorenzo Ave., Berkeley, CA 94707, tel. 800/867-6777.

Many tour organizers and traveler cafés operate hiking tours to visit mountain areas and minority groups in the north. Overnight tours stay in villages or camp out. The café also offers four-day hikes around Mai Chau. If you're joining a tour like this, a sleeping bag is an asset; it gets cold in the mountains. Some U.S. operators are offering short hiking tours in the northwest to visit minority groups. Contact: The Global Spectrum, 1901 Pennsylvania Ave. NW, Washington, D.C. 20006, tel. 800/419-4446; All Adventure Travel, 5589 Rapahoe #208, Boulder, CO 80303, tel. 800/537-4025; Asian Pacific Adventures, 826 S. Sierra Bonita Ave., Los Angeles, CA 90036, tel. 213/935-3156; Geographic Expeditions, 2627 Lombard St., San Francisco, CA 94123, tel. 800/777-8183; and Overseas Adventure Travel, 349 Broadway, Cambridge, MA 02139, tel. 800/221-0814.

In the future, specialized tours—such as those for bird-watchers—will no doubt be offered. Birdlife abounds in Vietnam's handful of national parks and reserves in both North Vietnam and the Mekong Delta region. Some have been established with the help of the World Wildlife Fund (WWF). Wildlife enthusiasts should keep an eye on research projects run by nonprofit research organizations such as Earthwatch in the United States. Projects are classed as study tours; you pay your own way to assist a research project, but the tours are tax-deductible in the United States.

Bicycling

In the spirit of cultural exchange and exploration, San Francisco–based VeloAsia Cycling Adventures offers innovative small-group trips at reasonable prices. Director of this nonprofit project, Patrick Morris, supports environmentally friendly, nonimpact tourism. These fun tours aim for a complete experience, focusing on sightseeing and fine dining at destinations along the route, alternate activities such as swimming and hiking, and cultural spiels from local guides. The trip focuses on the Hanoi–Saigon route, with add-ons possible (such as a Halong Bay kayaking trip). Customized itineraries can be arranged. Contact VeloAsia, 1283 12th Ave., San Francisco, CA 94122, tel. 415/731-4311 or 888/833-4533, fax 415/651-8869, info@veloasia. com, www.veloasia.com.

Several other outfits offer bicycle touring, including Exotissimo and Back Roads. Cycle Vietnam organizes trips from Hanoi to Saigon, featuring 1,000 kilometers of cycling, the remainder by tour bus. Its annual biking adventure may attract up to 50 bicyclists, though not all riding in one pack. Contact Cycle Vietnam, P.O. Box 4481, Portland, OR 97208, tel. 800/661-1458, fax 503/331-1458.

Motorcycling

In Hanoi, a handful of agencies can arrange adventurous tours of the mountainous north by Minsk—the legendary Russian motorcycle. Or you can hire your own Minsks and head off with friends in your own small group. The Minsk is a hardy beast—used extensively by moto drivers around Sapa and other parts of the north.

Touring by motorcycle is bound to be exciting, but even the most skilled riders have had trouble with unpredictable driving maneuvers of the Vietnamese. Make sure you have good evacuation insurance. Here's why: Read over the following cautionary tale. In October 1992 a group of French riders took on La Route Mandarine between Saigon and Hanoi. The group of

17 participants rode big-engined bikes—some flown in—accompanied by a press entourage. Eleven bikes were 1957 Harley-Davidson Sportsters, once used as the police escort for South Vietnamese President Nguyen Van Thieu, rebuilt and restored for the trip. The group rode as a convoy with biking police at the front and rear; the pack was followed by mechanics, interpreters, organizers, and security police in vans, as well as an ambulance. Along the route, the group donated books, medical supplies, and equipment to local schools and hospitals. After leaving Saigon, they headed up to Nha Trang. South of Danang, there was an accident with a truck, and four bikes went down. The leader, Daniel Roussel, suffered serious injury and was airlifted to Singapore. Farther north the group encountered an early monsoon; about 160 kilometers short of Hanoi, the riders had to cancel the last leg because of washed-out roads and ferry crossings.

Luxury Train Trips

Several operators run luxury train trips in Vietnam. This mostly consists of adding luxury cars (with dining car and sleepers) to existing trains. A good ride is the overnight train from Hanoi to Sapa, with accommodation described as "extremely soft." It's not the Orient Express, but it sure is a step up from the wooden bunks that go with the regular cars. The luxury carriages make the journey several times a week and are run by Victoria Sapa Hotel, with an office in Hanoi and deluxe hotel in Sapa. A precondition of using the Victoria's rail cars is that you have to stay at its hotel in Sapa. Other luxury trips may operate in central Vietnam, out of Danang.

Kayaking

Quite a few Hanoi-based companies offer kayaking at Halong Bay and Cat Ba Island in the north. The kayaks are loaded onto the mothership, usually a modified junk. Quality and condition of the kayaks can be dodgy—there is little maintenance going on. Some outfits use inflatable kayaks; others use plastic sit-on-tops (not the best as you get wet). A select few use enclosed fiberglass kayaks. Trails of Indochina has some kayaks in very good condition, catering to upscale clients. Catering more to backpackers is Handspan, with its own stable of kayaks. Also look at Seacanoe, http://seacanoe. com. Kayaking allows you to get much closer to the karst formations of Halong Bay and to reach nooks and crannies that other craft cannot enter. Easily the best area for exploring by kayak is off the east coast of Cat Ba—you need a good guide to find the best coves and caves.

Sailing on a Junk

An armada of modified junks plies the waters of Halong Bay in the north. The term "junk" is a misnomer since the red sails on these boats are mostly decorative. On day trips, these junks can take up to 40 passengers. Better to stick with a smaller vessel that takes fewer than 10 passengers if you want to appreciate the views. The Huong Hai Company, based in Halong Bay, has a fleet of more than 30 deluxe junks (all named *Huong Hai*), but perhaps only a third of these are live-aboards with cabins. These superjunks have two-berth cabins with hot shower, and they serve gourmet seafood—and the price tag is around $170 a day.

In the south, French joint-venture organization Voiles Vietnam offers cruising on the *Song Saigon,* billed as the largest traditionally built junk in Asia. The luxury 26-meter vessel features five cabins and carries 10 passengers; for day trips, the vessel can carry larger groups. Best season is November–April with a Mekong Delta itinerary, with some trips up to Phnom Penh from Mytho on the Mekong. Trips can be customized; regular itineraries range 2–6 days at $200 per person per day. Contact Voiles Vietnam, 17 Pham Ngoc Thach, Q3, Saigon, tel. 8/8231589, fax 8/8231591.

Cruising

Western cruise liners have been docking at Halong Bay, Haiphong, Hué, Danang, Qui Nhon, Nha Trang, Vung Tau, and Saigon since 1992. Among the available boats are the *Caledonian Star* via Lindblad Tours; the *Europa,* Hapag Lloyd; *Ocean Pearl,* Pearl Cruises and Croisières Paquet; *Song of Flower,* Seven

Seas Cruise Line; *Golden Odyssey,* Royal Cruise Line; and *Sea Goddess,* Cunard Line. These vessels hold 100–800 passengers each. Smaller vessels allow for greater maneuverability and the freedom to explore areas and call on ports not accessible to larger ships. A popular cruise route travels from Hong Kong, stopping 4–5 times along the coast of Vietnam before continuing to Bangkok, Singapore, or Manila. Onshore and inshore touring falls under the auspices of Vietnam Tourism. At Halong Bay, for example, passengers must transfer to motorboats or junks to tour the karst islets.

Seven Seas Cruise Line started itineraries to Vietnam in 1993, offering 10-night cruises from Hong Kong to Singapore on the 125-meter *Song of Flower.* The 170-passenger vessel passes through the Gulf of Tonkin and Halong Bay and docks in Hong Gai, Danang, Nha Trang, and Saigon. A second itinerary runs from Hong Kong to Saigon, with stops at Hainan Island, Hong Gai, Haiphong, Qui Nhon, and Nha Trang. The tariff for a 10-day cruise ranges $6,000–9,000 per person, based on double occupancy, and including airfare, pre- and postcruise hotel nights, and shore excursions. The *Song of Flower* offers a full range of onboard facilities, including casino, video and book library, health club, hot tub, and sauna—in effect a five-star floating hotel. Onboard lectures were delivered by none other than Bob Haldeman, former White House chief of staff under President Richard Nixon. For more details, contact Radisson Seven Seas Cruise Line, 600 Corporate Dr., Ste. 410, Fort Lauderdale, FL 33334, tel. 800/333-3333, fax 305/772-3763.

Some other addresses for Vietnam cruises: Cunard Line, 555 5th Ave., New York, NY 10017, tel. 800/221-4770; and Pearl Cruises, 6301 N.W. 5th Way #4000, Fort Lauderdale, FL 33309, tel. 305/772-8600.

CAMBODIA
By Air
While travel by air is the safest way to go, a second option is fast boats upriver to Siem Reap or Kratie. Domestic flights operate several times daily to Siem Reap, and several times weekly to Battambang, Koh Kong, and Sihanoukville. Less frequent flights head for Stung Treng, Ratanakiri, and Mondulkiri. Domestic service is on old Russian crates—Tupolevs (Tu-134) and Antonovs (An-24). RAC flies a few French ATR turboprops on the Siem Reap run. Other domestic carriers are starting up since deregulation. These include Siem Reap Airways and Kampuchea Air. Schedules are prone to rapid change and planes may be cancelled. One-way flights from Phnom Penh include Siem Reap, $55, up to three flights a day; Battambang, $45, three times a week; Sihanoukville, $40, several flights a week; Koh Kong, $50, four flights weekly; Stung Treng, $45, twice weekly. Round-trip tickets are usually double. Domestic departure tax is $4.

By Boat
With such dismal roads in Cambodia, travel by fast boat is preferable. There is a fast boat service to Siem Reap, Kompong Cham, and Kratie for around $25 one-way. It's better to take a fast boat because the slow cargo boats may be stopped at marine checkpoints. Soldiers have, on occasion, fired a few shots across the bow of a boat to indicate it should come ashore to pay "taxes." Stung Treng is only accessible by slow boat when the waters run high, in the postmonsoon season, around September–January. In seasons when the waters are low, boat trips take longer because the captain has to navigate the shoals, exposed rock, and other obstacles. On overnight boat trips you need to bring a hammock and mosquito net, and your own food and water. A small library of books would be a good idea in case you run aground upriver.

By Train
Cambodia has two French-built rail lines: south from Phnom Penh to Kampot and Sihanoukville; and north from Phnom Penh to Pursat, Battambang, and Sisophon. Service depends on whether the track or engines have been blown up.

There are 600 kilometers of track. Service is a far cry from the heyday of the 1960s, when 30 trains carried a total of two million passengers a year. The railway company has 10 French locomotives dating from the 1960s, four Czech engines purchased a few years ago, and five shunting locomotives. All but two are marred by war damage. The French are funding a project to restore old trains and tracks in Cambodia, but the task is daunting. The rail system was a favorite target of the former Khmer Rouge, who vowed to "cut the railway into pieces." In the first half of 1995, for example, a total of 327 stretches of railway track were blown up, along with 12 bridges.

Trains remain the most dangerous form of transport in Cambodia and are used only by the poor. The worst route is the Phnom Penh to Battambang line. Trains are supposed to run daily here, but in the course of six months only 2–3 trains typically complete the journey. The line may run only as far as Pursat if the track on the Pursat-Battambang section has been blown up or bridges are down. RCAF soldiers assigned to guard the line sometimes stand on the tracks with rifles and grenade launchers to stop trains and ask for money, batteries, shoes, radios, or just a free ride. A dozen illegal checkpoints operate along the route.

In better times, the Battambang line actually ran all the way to Bangkok. The section from Battambang to Sisophon was used to repatriate refugees from Thailand.

Rail is essentially for moving freight in Cambodia—passengers are an afterthought. Trains move at crawl speed, around 15 kilometers per hour on the Battambang run, taking 16 hours to cover the distance. Phnom Penh to Kampot requires seven hours. Cars are often old Indian stock, with wooden seats and metal shutters—most are crammed with goods, with a few cars up front reserved for female passengers. Men sit on the roofs of the cars, which can get very hot in the midday sun.

An unusual modification to the 1960s French locomotive on the Kampot run is a steel plate across the cabin with two visors cut for visibility—this to reduce the chance of the engineer's being taken out by a bullet during the Khmer Rouge era. There used to be two flatbed cars out front on a Cambodian train—if the train hit a mine, the flatbeds would be blown up, not the precious engine (passengers would ride the flatbeds for a reduced fare, but the ultimate cost might have been their lives). In the 1980s and early 1990s, there were numerous train ambushes by the Khmer Rouge. Although trains carried their own militia, armed with AK-47s, they were unsuccessful in fending off attacks. The Sihanoukville–Phnom Penh train, loaded with port goods, was attacked by Khmer Rouge forces four times in 1993 and at least that many times again in 1994. Some trains were assaulted with rockets. In early 1995, a force of 20 Khmer Rouge stopped a train by exploding mines on the track 50 kilometers north of Phnom Penh. After the train came to a halt, the Khmer Rouge ran toward the cars, firing AK-47s and grenade launchers. Eight passengers were killed and another 30 injured. The guerrillas robbed the passengers of valuables and looted sacks of rice from the train. Government soldiers arrived about six hours later. The Khmer Rouge have melted away; as of early 1999, the group became defunct. But remnants of those forces remain, and sporadic banditry still occurs—even targeting trains.

By Bus

Malaysian-run air-conditioned coaches ply the route from Phnom Penh to Sihanoukville on Route 3. These buses have tinted windows, a hostess aboard serving drinks, and the best highway in Cambodia to ride—a very smooth trip, costing around $4. The only other viable road route at present is along Route 1, connecting Phnom Penh to Saigon—there are some a/c buses on this route, too. Elsewhere in Cambodia you will not be so lucky—either with road conditions or with the vehicles. Very few foreigners use the vintage Dodge buses with wooden seats that provide bone-jarring rides over Cambodia's rough roads. These are packed to the gills with produce, and progress is painfully slow.

By Share-Taxi

A packed—but smoother and faster ride than local Dodge buses—is provided by share-taxis, sometimes referred to as "death-taxis." These collective taxis operate on set routes. They usually depart from the town marketplace; in Phnom Penh they leave from half a dozen market depots partway up the line. Share-taxis keep piling people in, leaving when critical mass is achieved. They may drop off and pick up passengers along the fixed route. A ride is $5 a head, or you can commandeer the whole taxi for $20 a day.

Start early in the day—off by 0730—and try and complete the journey by 1400 hours. By late afternoon checkpoint soldiers are drunker and more aggressive. Travel toward nightfall is dangerous. Main routes have tollbooths with soldiers—and they're hungry. Like waiters, the soldiers depend on "tips" and "taxes" for their real income. Donations are expected in the form of foreign-brand cigarettes or small riel bills tossed from the taxi. In the early days of Cambodia travel, a Western photographer's driver used to throw out entire packs as he approached checkpoints—the soldiers would be so busy scrambling for them, they wouldn't think to stop the car. Avoid stopping at any checkpoints or at bridges guarded by soldiers—it's best to simply reduce speed and toss money out of the car.

Around Town

You can flag down a moto driver just about anywhere for a pillion ride. In Siem Reap, a popular way of getting around is by *remork,* which is a motorcycle-pulled chariot that seats two. You can use *remork* or moto drivers as tour guides. In Phnom Penh, cyclos are more common. You can also rent your own motorcycle in some places such as Sihanoukville. Motorcycling is not recommended in Phnom Penh because of erratic traffic maneuvers: A better choice would be a bicycle rental (though these are hard to find in the capital). Taxis are operated by major hotels and can be hired by the day.

LAOS

By Air

The pride of the Lao domestic air fleet are French-Italian 70-seat ATR-72 turboprops, used on high-profile routes such as Vientiane to Luang Prabang; on more obscure runs, the plane could be a 50-seater Russian Antonov-24—a turbo that drones on, with dry-ice effects in the cabin. With a reduction in trade with Moscow, Laos has found it difficult to stock parts for its aging Russian crates. Smaller planes include Chinese-made Yun-7s and Yun-12s—these are very scary. As for in-flight service: There isn't any. Lao Airlines has been known to send the occasional trolley down the aisle on a domestic flight—a flat soda is about all you can expect. Stewardesses are clad in the *sinh,* the national dress. Buy domestic tickets at Lao Airlines in Vientiane, or obtain them through a tour agent.

Domestic route airfares will continue to increase. One-way fares (foreigner price) from Vientiane: Muang Sai (Udomxay), $49; Luang Namtha, $57, with four flights a week; Phonsavan (Xieng Khuang, Plain of Jars), $32, daily; Luang Prabang, $40, daily; Ban Huay Sai, $64, three times a week; Thakhek, $49; Savannakhet, $54, four flights a week; Saravan, $86, once a week; Pakse, $95, four flights a week. Return fares are double the one-way price. There are some interprovincial flights, such as Luang Prabang to Phonsavan (Xieng Khuang, Plain of Jars).

Flights to other locations, such as Viengxay, Sayaboury, Sam Neua, and Lak Sao may be available—inquire. In the north, Luang Prabang is emerging as an air hub, with connections on Yun-12 aircraft to Ban Huay Sai, Xieng Khuang, Phong Saly, and direct flights to Chiang Mai in Thailand and to Bangkok. In the south, there are connections on light aircraft from Pakse to Saravan, Savannakhet, Attapeu, and Moung Khong. Several times a week there is a direct flight from Pakse to Siem Reap (Angkor, Cambodia).

Be aware that flights can be heavily booked, particularly if the plane is the only way in, as is the case with Luang Namtha, poorly served by road—and reached by light plane with only 17 seats. Weight limit for domestic flights is 20 kilograms; domestic departure tax is $.50. Flights leave in the morning and usually return the same day.

Helicopter: For those with money to burn, Lao Westcoast Helicopter, tel. 21/512023, offers charter operations throughout Laos on AS350B Squirrel helicopters. The New Zealand-backed company operates from a hangar near Wattay Airport and is involved in seismic and aerial surveys, resource exploration, and medical evacuation.

By Boat

Stretches of the Mekong are navigable in high water. Decrepit wooden cargo boats ply these routes: Fares are dirt cheap and the boats are basic. For travelers, the main stretch of the Mekong undertaken is from Ban Huay Sai to Pakbeng and Luang Prabang. This is a trip of several days, although a long-tail speedboat can cut the time to a mere six hours. Speedboat travel can be highly hazardous to yourself (if the boat hits rocks) and to your hearing (they make an incredible racket). If you want to see the scenery, long-tail speedboat is not the way to go. In some places, however, you may have no choice as long-tail speedboat is the only option: as, for instance, on the journey from Ban Huai Say to Xiengkok (a jumping-off point to Muang Sai). From Vientiane to Luang Prabang, boat service is spotty: You can take a ferry from Vientiane to a point midway along the route; from there you would have to hire a speedboat. The section of the Mekong from Vientiane to Pakse is rarely used by passenger boats now—travel by road is far faster and cheaper. Cargo boats may ply the route from Vientiane to Savannakhet in the rainy season. Because the Mekong runs wide on these routes, the scenery is a fair way off: For closer viewing, going up tributaries such as the Nam Ou out of Luang Prabang) is preferable. You can do a combination of tributaries and main Mekong via a loop from Luang Prabang.

By Road

The main highway is Route 13, which on paper snakes from Luang Prabang through Vientiane and south past Muang Paksane to Savannakhet, Pakse, and the Cambodian border. The route is mostly paved, and long-distance overnight buses ply the entire Vientiane-Pakse section. Long-distance express buses run from Vientiane via Luang Prabang to Luang Namtha, which means you can cover the entire country from far north to deep south this way. Certain roads are considered unsafe because of bandits and opium warlords—there have been attacks on buses on the Kasi–Phonsavan and Luang Namtha–Ban Huay Sai roads, with deaths resulting from shoot-outs. Laos is not the easiest place to get around by land. Infrastructure is weak—there is no railroad, and the roads are often dirt. Roughly half the road bridges in Laos need to be replaced. Cratered and potholed roads are dust bowls in the dry season and rivers of muck in the wet season—bridges may be down during this time, and rivers too deep to drive through. In the rainy season, the water level is sufficient that the Mekong is navigable for much of its length. Boats and buses work in tandem: in the dry season, river water is low, so passengers take buses; in the wet season, roads may be washed out and rivers run high, so people take boats.

Jeep Rentals

Up-country, you can rent minibuses and cars (with Lao driver), but because of the nature of the terrain, your best bet is a 4WD vehicle such as a jeep. A jeep runs $20–50 a day up-country, and 3–4 travelers can defray expenses; a guide costs $5 a day and up for one group. Vehicles for rent are mostly of the rugged 4WD type—jeeps, Land Rovers, or converted pickup trucks. The price includes cost of gasoline.

Rental agencies are usually open 0800–1700. Pay by time rather than distance—some drivers want to restrict driving distances to save on gasoline and may exaggerate the time needed to reach a destination. It's best to retain control over the itinerary; also, indicate

LAOS ROUTE STRATEGIES

Nothing is certain in Laos. You can chart a route through the country, but you may be stymied by red tape, transport mode restrictions, poor transport, or bad weather. Coming up with an ideal route is a matter of juggling the variables of land border crossings, transport restrictions, and the complications of obtaining appropriate visas. You can base yourself in Thailand and make a loop through Laos, or attempt overland routes such as Thailand–Laos–Vietnam–China. A simple south/north route is to enter Laos from Thailand near Pakse (or enter from Cambodia south of Pakse), and then exit north into China at the Ban Boten border and continue overland to Kunming. The following route ideas are Bangkok-based; a number of variations of these routes are possible.

Bangkok Loop: Start in Bangkok, take a train to Nong Khai, and cross to Vientiane. Make a round-trip to Luang Prabang. From Vientiane travel by land or air to Pakse, exit to Thailand at Chong Mek, and take a train back to Bangkok from Ubon Ratchathani. Obtain a Thai multiple-entry visa if planning long stays in Thailand. Because flights to the southern tip of Laos are expensive, a one-way flight to Pakse and traveling overland from Pakse back to Thailand makes sense. Another viable route, involving more plane hops, is to start in Bang-

kok, travel to Vientiane and Luang Prabang, fly from Vientiane to Phnom Penh, explore Cambodia, and then fly from Phnom Penh back to Bangkok.

Bangkok–Hanoi–Kunming: Start in Bangkok, head north, enter Laos through Ban Huay Sai, take a boat along the Mekong to Luang Prabang, and then continue by road to Vientiane. Travel south by road and exit the Cau Treo border to Vinh in Vietnam, or continue farther south to Savannakhet and exit Lao Bao into Vietnam, arriving at Dong Ha. From Dong Ha either go north to Hanoi or south to Saigon. There are several variations on this route. You could proceed from Luang Prabang overland to Phonsavan and cross the border at either Nong Het or Nameo into northern Vietnam, and head for Hanoi.

From Hanoi you can proceed north to Sapa and cross the Lao Cai border to Kunming in China. From Kunming you can fly to Bangkok for little more than the cost of the Hanoi–Bangkok flight. Or you can carry on through China to the end of the Eurasian continent.

Transiting Vientiane: Fly from Hanoi into Vientiane. Make your way from there to Luang Prabang, and then take a boat upstream on the Mekong to Ban Huay Sai, exiting into Thailand.

clearly if you wish to stop frequently to take photos or visit villages. Misunderstandings can arise—halfway through a tour, the guide will suddenly bring up a new fee. Get your agreement written down at the outset with cost breakdown as a guarantee against such abrupt changes of mind.

Local Transport
The locals get around by small bus, *songtao* (a converted pickup truck with two rows of seats in the back), or truck. Trucks feature two rows of seats in the back to carry passengers over longer distances, such as sections of the Vientiane–Luang Prabang route. They are not known for their suspension.

Around Town
In Vientiane and the smaller towns, you can use cyclos (also called *samlors*) for shorter distances; you should also be able to rent a bicycle. Motorized transport consists of three-wheelers carrying up to four passengers, similar to *tuk-tuks;* or jumbos, a larger version seating up to eight passengers. You can hire motorcycle sidecar-taxis in places such as Luang Prabang or Pakse. These vehicles seat two and are a blast for open-air touring. In Vientiane, Luang Prabang, and Savannakhet are a few rental cars of Russian ancestry for hire by visiting businesspeople or tourists—these are often attached to hotels. Metered taxis from Thailand made their debut in Vientiane with the opening of the Friendship Bridge.

Tours
Group Tours
Tours can be booked through a Bangkok travel agency. You can customize a group tour—Bangkok agencies will assist a group of four, three, two, or even one. A typical package running five days, four nights from Bangkok to Vientiane to Luang Prabang runs about $900 per person including flights and hotels. Another possibility is to link up with a travel agent in Vientiane and make arrangements on the spot. (A list of agents is provided in the *Vientiane* section.) Here you can oscillate between group tour and individual travel, and control your schedule better. It's a good idea to build in free time to wander around on your own.

Individual Travel
Solo travel in Laos is in constant flux. Sometimes the doors are flung wide open, and travelers pour in. Then a tourist is caught stealing a Buddha image from a temple, and the doors are slammed shut again. Or a big party conference is happening in Vientiane, and all visa-on-arrival procedures are shut down.

Authorities may frown on the use of certain modes of transport by individuals. While you can rent a motorcycle in Vientiane, authorities will not be too thrilled if you use that motorcycle to go far afield, although individuals have taken overnight trips. For some reason, renting a motorcycle in Luang Prabang is not allowed, although it is in Vangvieng. At the Plain of Jars, travelers have been instructed not to use local buses or *tuk-tuks*. Long-distance cycling is not approved of, though foreigners have mountain-biked in many regions (some have bought their bikes in Vientiane).

Laos is more geared toward group visits. If you don't start off in a group, you may well join an impromptu one at various points along the way for economic reasons—getting together with fellow travelers, for example, if going up-country to defray the costs of hired jeeps or chartered boats. With 3–4 travelers in a jeep safari pool, the cost of a guide remains the same, and you can share a hotel room and transport costs. In Phonsavan, for instance, travelers band together to hire a van for a day trip to the jar sites, which are widely scattered.

What to Pack

Packs and Carry Bags
If you're traveling independently, avoid a suitcase or a large backpack with a frame. It's better to divide your load into two smaller soft packs: an oversize day pack for camera gear and valuables (this bag never leaves your sight), and a medium duffel bag or travel bag for the main load of clothing and other items. Ideally, these bags should be airline carry-on size, measuring about 50 by 40 by 25 centimeters, or 52 liters in volume. In theory, carry-on weight is five kilos, but airlines rarely check. If the check-in clerk is fussy, you can compress a soft duffel bag to a smaller size with webbing straps. Some travel bags can be used as foam-padded backpacks or carried suitcase-style with a handle. The carrying capacity can also expand. Most likely, with two smaller bags, you could take the lot onto an aircraft as carry-on—depending on freight weight for that flight, and the mood of the check-in clerk.

In Indochina the two-bag system enables easy maneuvering on buses, trains, and planes. You can fit gear into overhead racks on buses or trains, and store it under the seat in minibuses. On motorcycle-taxis, place the main load over the gas tank or on the rear rack, or wedge it between handlebars and seat. The system also works well for leaving one bag behind in a hotel when you head off on two- or three-day trips. Lockable zips keep out prying fingers. Inside, nylon stuff sacks separate and serve as waterproofing; resealable food bags are excellent for this function too. A garbage bag is good for protecting the entire pack from rain or dust.

Clothing
For hot climates cotton clothing or a cotton/

LIGHTEN YOUR LOAD

There are many reasons why you should cut baggage weight and bulk. The most obvious is that if you have less to carry, you enjoy greater mobility: You can walk straight onto a plane with hand luggage, and you don't have to stash gear on the roof of a bus. Bags out of sight are prone to petty pilfering or outright loss. Carrying only hand luggage is very liberating. And if the worst should happen—if it should all disappear—you have less to lose. The biggest decision you'll have to make is what size bags to take. Packs themselves can be quite heavy, especially those with elaborate internal frame systems, padded hip belts, and webbing.

Before leaving home assemble all your baggage on the floor, and separate items into essential, optional, and dubious categories. Discard the dubious, reconsider the optional, and cut the essential in half. Then double the amount of money you'll take. You need to leave some space in your bags for purchases along the way. (Also leave space for the money you'll need to make those purchases. Remember, if you change $200 in Vietnam, you may have a stack of dong the size of a shoebox. You have to carry that somewhere.)

Well before you set off, pack all your gear exactly as you would on the road. Wear the same shoes you'll use on the road and walk a dozen blocks with your gear—or, better yet, hike up the nearest mountain. See how you feel. If you stagger around like a drunk, cut the gear down until manageable. Remember that in a tropical climate you'll develop big sweat patches wherever a heavy bag presses on your clothing. If you want to find out where the real weight lies, use a postal scale to weigh your gear.

There are several ways to cut corners on baggage weight and bulk. Clothing is one of the biggest offenders. Bring only items with multiple uses. A sarong, or two-meter length of dress material, easily purchased in Asia, can be used as scarf, sheet, dress, or beach towel. Avoid heavy items such as towels, which will just turn to soggy mildew in your pack. Instead take a sport towel, a thin synthetic sponge strip the size of a scarf that will dry quickly and can be put to many uses. Cut clothing to a bare minimum and prepare to wash what you do bring frequently, using hotel laundry services. That's preferable to carrying it around all the time. You can always buy extra clothing or have it tailor-made along the way if need be.

Miniaturizing toiletry supplies is an excellent way of saving weight and bulk. Secure tiny plastic bottles from a camping store and decant shampoo, powders, and potions into them. Eliminate heavy glass bottles and repackage their contents in smaller plastic containers. If carrying drugs, be sure to transfer the identifying labels. Saw the end of your toothbrush—you don't need the full length, and the smaller brush will fit more easily into a toiletry bag. You don't really need a hefty bar of soap; pick up a few miniature airline washroom soap packets to fill in for the times when your hotel doesn't supply soap. Males should consider whether they really need to shave—not shaving will cut down on gear. Women travelers should consider leaving perfume and cosmetics at home.

When traveling, use the post office to mail souvenirs, purchases, and excess gear back home. It's expensive to post gear out, but think about the advantages: You won't have to carry the stuff, and the chances of its getting stolen are greatly reduced.

polyester mix is best. Dress loosely—tight-fitting nylon or polyester clothing will play havoc with your body's ventilation system. Choose clothing that is lightweight, washes quickly, and dries fast. Jeans are heavy, bulky, hot, and take a long time to dry. You really need only two sets of clothing—one to wear, and one to wash. Darker clothing doesn't show dirt, but lighter colors deflect heat and are less likely to attract mosquitoes. Long-sleeved shirts protect against mosquito bites. Also take modesty into account, especially with women's clothing. You can buy clothing en route in Indochina, but ready-made sizes often do not fit larger-framed Westerners. This problem is solved by custom-ordering clothes in a place such as Saigon or Phnom Penh. All you have to do is hand over a shirt or skirt, and the tailor will copy it. Shoes, however, are more difficult to find—make sure yours will last the distance.

Be prepared for adverse weather conditions. Carry a hat and sunglasses with UV block to counter harmful rays. You need a pair of sturdy, lightweight walking shoes; make sure they're not too tight, as your feet can swell in a hot climate. Although you can wear sandals in southern Vietnam, shoes are advisable to protect against cuts and scrapes when riding a bicycle or walking over sharp limestone rocks. The Vietnamese coast is prone to lashing winds and rain; waterproof yourself with a light jacket and hood. If your trip coincides with the monsoon season, take more substantial gear for wet weather.

If you start out in tropical Thailand, you tend to overlook the fact you can freeze your ass off in the highlands of Laos, or in Vietnam's Central Highlands and the far north. If you're planning to visit highland areas, pack a pile sweater. Layering of T-shirt, shirt, pile sweater, and rain jacket should ward off the cold. In Hanoi you can buy a Chinese parka for the north and then resell it to another traveler.

Mosquito Net

The mosquito net presents a dilemma: Should you rely on the quality of mosquito nets in hotels in Indochina? Generally they're OK. But for the odd time when you're without a net, is it worth carrying one? Depends where you go. If you're planning any remote-area travel, you should definitely carry a net to avoid malaria. This includes visits to hilltribe villages where you may stay overnight, or roughing it on overnight boat trips. You can buy mosquito netting and army surplus nets quite cheaply in markets in Saigon or Phnom Penh.

There are several kinds of mesh used in mosquito nets. At all costs avoid no-see-um netting: The mesh is so fine that air doesn't circulate, and you'll boil in a humid tropical climate. There are a number of compact, lightweight mosquito nets on the market. In England you can buy the Micronet, made by Lifesystems; another quality net is produced by Safariquip.

The best netting on the market is white nylon fire-retardant mesh made in Thailand. This knitted mesh will keep mosquitoes out but is large enough to allow good air circulation. This mesh is used in some nets made by Coghlan's and Thai Occidental (both Canadian companies). The trend is now toward the use of finer mesh, which unfortunately does not suit humid climates. Coghlan's manufactures a variety of lightweight nets that are reasonably priced (look for the larger-size mesh). The simplest Coghlan's net weighs 200 grams, packs small, and costs $15—it has grommet holes for suspension from walls. Contact Coghlan's at 121 Irene St., Winnipeg, Manitoba, tel. 204/284-9550, fax 204/475-4127. Thai Occidental makes a well-designed net called the Spider that sells for around $50. This net is ideal if you're going to be spending a lengthy period in malaria-exposed areas. The half-kilogram net can be deployed indoors over a twin bed, or outdoors suspended from a line stretched between two trees. You can order a Spider from Thai Occidental, 5334 Yonge St., Toronto, Canada, fax/phone 416/496-2490; orders can be shipped within three days anywhere in the world.

Other Sleeping Gear

A sleeping bag may be useful in northern Vietnam or Laos for trekking or roughing it in villages, but it is otherwise unnecessary in Indochina. Hot climates require breezy beds; a sheet sleeping bag or sarong will do fine, or take a whole bed along in the form of a hammock, available for a few dollars in Vietnam or Cambodia. Locals string up hammocks on overnight boat trips in Indochina; hammocks are even deployed on trains in Vietnam. You can buy silk sleeping sheets at silk shops along Hang Gai street in Hanoi.

Useful Gadgets

A flashlight is essential because blackouts are common and because of lack of lighting in rural areas. Actually, two flashlights would be a good idea. Carry a miniature pocket flashlight for finding your way down unlit alleys, or for finding your hotel room or the washroom in a blackout. Maglites are good. For exploring caves or dark pagodas you need a larger model with a strong beam; some are waterproof and can be attached to your head for hands-free operation. Flashlight battery life is short, so bring plenty of backup batteries. Remove or invert batteries when the unit is not in use to avoid burnout. Avoid lithium batteries as they cannot be replaced in Indochina.

You will constantly need purified drinking water in Indochina. Locally produced mineral water is sold in cheap plastic bottles that break easily, so take along a tough plastic water bottle with a leak-proof seal for carrying water on day trips or train trips. For remote areas where you must rely on river water, consider taking a small filter, particularly an inexpensive compact model with an iodine filter. Otherwise, use iodine tablets. These are sold under the label Potable Aqua in Europe and the United States, or Coghlan's in Canada. The maker produces another bottle called Neutralizer, with tablets to remove the unpleasant iodine taste in the water. You can use Gatorade crystals to achieve the same effect; these also supply potassium and sodium.

Take a Swiss Army pocketknife with blade, scissors, tweezers, and can opener, or buy a cheap Chinese copy in Vietnam. Heavy-duty duct tape is invaluable for emergency repairs to equipment—you can carry a smaller amount by rerolling the tape. A pocket compass is very useful for city orientation and map use. A wristwatch with built-in alarm is good for those bus departures at the break of dawn. A small solar-powered calculator is useful for dealing with confusing currency exchange rates. Newshounds might consider a palm-sized shortwave radio to pick up the BBC, VOA, Radio France International (RFI), and Radio Australia.

If you are conducting any kind of business, a GSM mobile phone is very handy. You can pick up a SIM card in Vietnam (Vinaphone), Laos (Tango), or Thailand (DTAC), buy a top-up card, and you're in business. Cambodia sells SIM cards only to foreigners resident in the country—this policy could change.

Electrical Devices

The best advice on electrical devices is not to rely on them totally. Be sure to have backup power in the form of rechargeable nickel-cadmium or nickel metal-hydride battery packs. For sensitive equipment use a voltage regulator or surge protector; blackouts are common. Be sure to bring along an adapter with a variety of plugs on it—buy one with a built-in surge protector. You will be faced with a confusing array of plug types: Wiring in most Indochina hotels dates to the French era and would never pass Western safety inspections. Plugs vary from dual European round prongs to American flat parallel pins—there's no standardization. Power circuits are often overloaded. Power runs the gamut from 220 volts in urban areas to 110 volts in towns and the countryside; it's best to bring switchable 220/110-volt devices. Standard alkaline batteries are usually available in the cities of Indochina, including AAAs, but lithium varieties may be more difficult to find.

Toiletries

Items such as soap, toothpaste, shampoo, deodorant, and cosmetics are available in the major cities of Indochina, although local brands are of poor quality and Western brands are expensive. Carry a minimal amount to save on weight. Carry back-up supplies of toilet paper (flat packs). Speaking of backups, many sewage systems in Vietnam cannot cope with toilet paper; if there's a bin provided, place used paper in that, not the toilet. Tampons and sanitary pads are unavailable in rural areas. Pack items such as nail clippers and a nailbrush, which serves double duty for quick cleaning of clothing.

Medical Kit

Don't skimp here: Take time to carefully read over the *Health and Safety* section of this book for details on packing your medical kit, medical insurance, emergency evacuation, inoculations, and health hazards.

Photography

Take along a supply of batteries for your camera; you may find them on the road, or you may not. You can buy film in Hong Kong or Bangkok, strip off the cardboard packaging to reduce bulk, and put the film canisters into Ziploc bags. Do your best to keep film cool and dry; the greatest damage is done by humidity. Do not mail film from Indochina; you may never see it again. A bonded courier service is more reliable, though not cheap.

Shooting with a digital camera means never having to worry about airport X-ray scanners again. However, it means having to worry about batteries (digital devices are notorious battery hogs) and it means having to worry about running out of memory. Internet cafés in cities and major tourist centers of Indochina can assist with burning your pictures to CD to solve the latter problem, and in some places you can even burn to DVD. Back to the battery problem: Be sure that you have a converter so your battery charger can communicate with the local electric circuits. A good converter will have a surge protector feature so it serves a dual function.

Documents and Printed Matter

Your most valuable documents are your passport and stamped or paper visas. Take along a dozen photocopies of initial passport pages for visa applications and other uses. Bring a stack of passport photos—20 is about right. Be fussy about your passport photo and dress formally: Remember that the person issuing the visa will most likely never see you, just the photo. Keep some passport photos in your wallet. An International Health Certificate is required only in China. An International Driver's License is good identification. An important personal document is medical insurance and a card showing your blood type and any other important medical information. Assemble all document numbers, addresses, and phone and fax numbers on single pages and then use reduction double-sided photocopies to compress the material. Pack documents in a thin resealable bag to protect them from rain.

Baggage Security

The three things I'd really hate to go missing are documents, money, and camera gear, especially shot pictures. The rest is dispensable—inconvenient if lost, but replaceable. Travelers tend to carry a lot of cash in Vietnam, Cambodia, and Laos because banking is inefficient. It's impossible to insure cash, so wear a money belt or neck pouch, and sew inner pockets on pants or vest. Make it hard for a would-be thief to figure out where you keep your stash of cash. Keep large denomination U.S. bills in a spot you must practically disrobe to reach; stick smaller U.S. bills in a more accessible spot, such as a button-down shirt pocket; and carry local currency in yet a third location. Some hotels have safes: You can place your valuables in an envelope, signing along the sealed part of the envelope; hotel staff will then tape it and put it in the safe. This is OK for a night out in a larger city, but don't leave a credit card in a hotel safe; somebody might decide to use it while you're out. Keep your passport tucked away on your person; show photocopies on demand rather than the original document.

Budget hotels in Vietnam often offer rooms with two metal rings on the door, through which you loop the hotel padlock. Bring a small brass padlock or combination lock with a long reach on it, because some rings are wide on door closures. It's better to use your own padlock than one supplied by the hotel; the hotel key can be picked up by anyone, and sometimes the keys fit other locks as well. It depends how you feel about the hotel. Definition of a secure hotel: one where you have no second thoughts about leaving your camera behind in the room. If the hotel is family-run, grandma will make sure no one gets to your stuff.

When on the move keep your luggage in sight—on trains, on buses, on minibuses. Do not store anything on the roof if at all possible. If on a train, padlock luggage to the overhead rack. There are some compact retractable cable locks that can be purchased for this purpose. You will most likely want to leave your main luggage behind at a hotel when heading off for a three-day trip to the Mekong Delta or Halong

Bay. For this reason it's good to have zippered luggage: A small padlock secures two zips together and prevents petty theft. But beware: If you padlock through the *top* rings of the zippers, they can still be easily separated and the contents rifled. What you want to do is padlock through the *bottom* rings of joining zippers. Some pack makers now use zips that fold over one another, with brackets for padlocks.

When storing luggage, add a few labels, both inside and out, with your passport number on them. Tell the hotel staff person you'd like him or her to check the passport number before returning the gear. Another reason for using passport ID is that if the hotel gives you a receipt for the luggage and you lose it, you have a backup method of retrieving the gear.

Glossary

VIETNAM

Annam—former French protectorate of central Vietnam

ao dai—Vietnamese traditional dress, originally worn by both sexes, but now worn by women

ben xe—bus station

bonze—monk

Cao Daism—a mix of Catholic, Buddhist, Confucian, and Taoist beliefs, originating in the Mekong Delta in the 1920s

Cham—people who inhabited the central coast of Vietnam. They rose to prominence in the 10th and 11th centuries A.D. and were eclipsed by the Viet in the late 15th century.

Champa—the former coastal kingdom of the Cham people, with its capital at Vijaya, near present-day Qui Nhon

chua—active temple or pagoda

Cochinchina—former French colony of southern Vietnam

Confucianism—Chinese code of ethics based on the teachings of the philosopher Confucius (from the 5th century B.C.)

doi moi—"renovation" or new political thinking, a policy announced in 1986

Hoa Hao—breakaway Buddhist faith from the Mekong Delta, emphasizing simplicity of worship and abandonment of ritual

Ho Chi Minh Trail—a network of jungle trails that served as a conduit for supplies and soldiers from North Vietnam through border areas of Laos and Cambodia into South Vietnam during the 1959–1975 period

Huey—American helicopter, derived from model names UH-1A, UH-1B, and UH-1D

khach san—hotel

lien xo—Russian, also applied to all foreigners who look like Russians. The term is derogatory since Vietnamese have a poor opinion of Russians.

Maitreya—the Buddha of the Future

Montagnards—minorities of Vietnam, from the French word for mountain people

nha khach—hotel or guesthouse

nuoc mam—fish sauce, flavoring many Vietnamese dishes

overseas Vietnamese—see Viet-Kieu

pagoda—eight-sided tower; also commonly denotes a temple

Quan Am—bodhisattva of compassion, a female deity usually sculpted as a standing all-white figure holding a vase of holy water, sometimes with a willow branch to sprinkle the water

Quan Cong—a deified Chinese general from the Three Kingdoms period (3rd century A.D.); a guardian depicted in statuary as red-faced with a long beard, sometimes on a red horse

quoc ngu—romanized Vietnamese script

R&R—Rest and Recreation, or vacation leave for American soldiers during the Vietnam War days

song—river

Taoism—belief system based on the teachings of Chinese philosopher Lao Tzu from the 6th century B.C. Taoism emphasizes the pursuit of harmony.

Tet—Vietnamese Lunar New Year

Thien Hau—goddess of the sea, and patroness of sailors and fisherfolk; a figure seen in some pagodas of Chinese origin

Tonkin—former French protectorate of northern Vietnam

Vietcong—short for Vietnamese communist; at first a derogatory name coined to describe all the South Vietnamese groups opposed to President Diem in the 1960s. Other terms used for the Vietcong were VC and Charlie (short for Victor Charlie). These terms no longer carry a derogatory meaning.

Viet-Kieu—overseas Vietnamese, who are often resented by locals when they return because of their wealth and arrogance

Vietminh—nationalist and communist group led by Ho Chi Minh in the fight against the Japanese and the French in the 1940s and 1950s

CAMBODIA

anastylosis—taking apart the main sanctuary of a crumbling site, numbering the pieces, building a new concrete base, and reassembling the structure piece by piece

apsara—celestial dancer or angelic nymph. The seductive *apsaras* promise a joyful existence for those who attain the ultimate incarnation.

asura—mythical demon

Avalokitesvara—see Lokesvara

banteay—Khmer citadel

baray—artificial lake or spillway reservoir

bas-relief—sculptural relief in which the projection from the surrounding surface is slight

bodhisattva—an enlightened being who delays achieving nirvana to help others attain this ultimate goal on the Buddhist path

Brahma—four-headed Hindu deity of Creation

deva—male god or celestial power

devaraja—divine king. As part of a cult instituted by Jayavarman II, the Khmer king was an emanation of a deity and would be reunited with that deity upon death.

devata—goddess

Ganesh—elephant-headed Hindu deity worshipped as the remover of obstacles

Garuda—mythical figure having the beak and talons of an eagle and the torso of a man; the mount of Vishnu

Hanuman—mischievous white monkey of the Ramayana; chief of the monkey army

Indra—Vedic god of war and thunder

Kala—mythical monster sculpted in stone with wide face, bulging eyes, claws, and pointed ears

Khmer Krom—ethnic Cambodians living in the south of Vietnam, mainly in the Mekong Delta region

Khmer Rouge—quasi-Marxist military group that rose to power in Cambodia in 1975 and launched a bloodbath until ousted in 1979. Khmer Rouge leadership self-destructed in 1998 and its guerrilla warfare came to an end.

koh—island

kompong—port or river town

krama—checkered Khmer all-purpose scarf

linga—phallic sculpture, symbolic of Shiva

lintel—stone or wood crossbeam resting on two upright posts. On a Khmer temple, it is above a door or window opening and supports the pediment.

Lokesvara—bodhisattva of compassion

Meru—mythical golden mountain at the center of the Hindu universe

naga—snake or serpent deity, usually a cobra with multiple heads

Mahabharata—Hindu epic narrating the

struggle between two warring families for control of northern India

pediment—triangular upper section above a temple doorway

phnom—mountain or hill; can also refer to temple or sacred site

pilaster—column used on the side of an open doorway

prasat—main tower of a temple

preah—holy, sacred; used as honorific title for important Buddhist images or abbots

Ramayana—Indian cycle of legends, known all over Asia, portraying the trials of lovers Rama and Sita

Ravana—demon king who abducts Sita in the *Ramayana* legend

Reamker—Cambodian name for the *Ramayana*

Shiva—Hindu deity, the Destroyer and Reproducer

singha—mythical lion

stela—stone panel inscribed with historical data

stung—river

Tonle Sap—"sweet water"; name of the inland sea in northwest Cambodia, and of the river linking it to the Mekong

varman—suffix denoting "protected by," often incorporated into the title of Khmer kings

Vishnu—Hindu deity, the Preserver

wat—Thai word for temple with monks in residence, also spelled vat

LAOS

asana—hand gesture of the Buddha in statuary

baci—traditional Lao welcoming ceremony

ban—village

boun—Lao festival

Hmong—ethnic group whose people favor mountainous terrain

Jataka Tales—series of mythological life stories of the Buddha

jumbo—three- or four-wheeled vehicle that can take 6–8 passengers

kuti—monks' residence

lam wong—traditional slow-moving circle dance

mudra—pose of the Buddha in statuary

naga—snake or serpent deity, usually a cobra with multiple heads

Pathet Lao—military arm of the communist party, based in northeast Laos until it came to power in 1975

phi—spirits believed by animists to live in trees, forests, and mountains

Phra Lak Pralam—Lao version of the *Ramayana*

Pimai—Lao Lunar New Year, taking place in mid-April

pra—holy, sacred; used as honorific title for important Buddhist images or abbots

Ramayana—Indian cycle of legends, known all over Asia, portraying the trials of lovers Rama and Sita

sangha—the Buddhist brotherhood or community

sim—main temple

sinh—sarong or strip of woven cloth worn by Lao women

songtao—pickup truck converted to carry passengers

talad—market

tham—cave

thanon—street or road

that—(pronounced "tat") bell-shaped monument similar to a stupa, and containing sacred relics or ashes of important person

Trimurti—Hindu trinity, comprised of Brahma, Vishnu, and Shiva

viharn—secondary prayer hall or sermon hall

yaksha—fierce temple guardian; may be good or evil

ABBREVIATIONS

ARVN—Army of the Republic of Vietnam, until 1975

ASEAN—Association of Southeast Asian Nations

B.E.—Buddhist Era

BLDP—Buddhist Liberal Democratic Party

CPP—Cambodian People's Party

cyclo—from French cyclo-pousse, or bicycle-powered trishaw

DMZ—demilitarized zone

EFEO—Ecole Française d'Extrême Orient (French School of the Far East)

FCCC—Foreign Correspondents Club of Cambodia

FUNCINPEC—United Front for an Independent, Neutral, Peaceful, and Cooperative Cambodia, from a French acronym

GH—guesthouse

GPO—general post office

IDD—international direct dialing

kph—kilometers per hour

KS—Khach San (Vietnamese for hotel)

lambro—a three-wheel van, after the brand-name Lambro 550cc

Lao PDR—Lao People's Democratic Republic

LPRP—Lao People's Revolutionary Party

moto—motorcycle-taxi

MP—Member of Parliament

NBCA—National Biodiversity Conservation Area—multi-use zones in Laos

NGO—nongovernmental organization

NLF—National Liberation Front

NVA—North Vietnamese Army, until 1975

RAC—Royal Air Cambodge

RCAF—Royal Cambodian Armed Forces

SRV—Socialist Republic of Vietnam

UBND—Uy Ban Nhan Dan, or People's Committee

UNCHR—United Nations Center for Human Rights

UNDF—United Nations Development Programme

UNESCO—United Nations Educational, Scientific, and Cultural Organization

UNHCR—United Nations High Commissioner for Refugees

UNTAC—United Nations Transitional Authority of Cambodia, 1992–93

VASCO—Vietnam Air Service Company

WAF—Vietnam Veterans of America Foundation

WHO—World Health Organization

Communicating

The more you can communicate and interact with locals while on the road, the more you'll get out of your trip. The language sections that follow are starter kits for Vietnamese, Khmer, and Lao. You're advised to brush up on any French you know, as it's useful in all three countries. If you speak some Thai, you can take advantage of the fact that Laotian and Cambodian vocabularies draw from the same word base as Thai. English is a kind of lingua franca in Asia, and many Asians are keen to practice. You can conduct a lot of transactions, particularly in large cities, in English.

Attempt to get at the basics of the native language, even if it is only simple vocabulary. Languages may appear daunting to tackle, but the actual number of words you need to handle basic situations is minimal.

Vietnamese and Lao are tonal languages. Basic phrases in tonal languages are some-

times identical to insults, give or take a tone. In Lao, the word for "friend" (moo, spoken with a midtone) is a few tones away from the word for "pig." Cambodian is nontonal. You can't learn exact tones from phrasebooks; you can really only grasp them from imitating a native speaker or repeatedly listening to a tape. Before you travel, it's worth getting your hands on an audiotape. Hearing the foreign phrase spoken twice, followed by the phrase in English, will attune your ear to the nuances of pronunciation. Think of it this way: Can you really get an idea of what a symphony sounds like from just looking at sheet music? Some travelers carry a minicassette recorder to record locals.

Strategies

Carry a pocket-sized phrasebook; they're inexpensive and light. If you're interested in attaining the pidgin plateau of communication, concentrate on verbs, nouns, pronouns, and adjectives. Once you've mastered a few of those, skip any pretense at making whole sentences or observing grammar rules; just combine gestures with basic vocabulary to get your message across. Take along small blank cards that can fit in your wallet. Write down frequently used constructions in local script and transliteration. Or add them directly to your phrasebook.

Flattery: A positive attitude will take you a long way. Go at it with gusto: Enthusiasm works wonders for improving communication, and flattery will get you everywhere. The most important words to grasp in the new language are "good," "very good," "delicious," and "beautiful." These can be accompanied by a thumbs-up gesture. Once you've learned the right words, try these on your host or hostess (point at things or areas if you don't know the word): "Your house is beautiful!" "The wine is terrific!" "I love this country!" Enjoy the language of food: Sit back and allow your host to force-feed you, uttering grunts of appreciation. Avoid negatives, but learn the word for "OK." This can have a negative connotation by inference; for example, "OK" meaning "that's enough food, thank you" with an accompanying hand gesture.

Pictures and Numbers: Pictures communicate quickly. Take along photos of your family, your dog, your city. Examination of pictorial subjects—theirs and yours—can lead to long dialogue. Written Arabic numerals are universal, so use them to exchange statistical information such as: How many years married? How many children do you have? How many ducks? How many water buffalo? Prices can be negotiated by holding up fingers for digits. In Vietnam each finger represents 1,000 dong, so three fingers means 3,000 dong. Beware, however: Some foreigners have been unpleasantly surprised when the bill comes to $3!

Gestures: Use mime, facial expressions, and hand gestures to ham it up and cut through the language barrier. However, some Western gestures are considered rude, such as beckoning using the forefinger. This is used for animals in Asia. To beckon people, use the full hand, palm down, and motion with all fingers wriggling together. In a restaurant, to ask the waiter for the bill, write up an imaginary bill in the air. To indicate to a taxi driver you want the airport, slap the right hand off a horizontal, stationary left palm in imitation of a plane taking off.

Brain Teasers: In Vietnam, thanks to Jesuit missionaries, you're semiliterate. In Laos and Cambodia, you may well consider yourself a total illiterate. But are you really? If you're any good at puzzle patterns, you can start decoding those script squiggles. Try it with destinations by matching symbols on a road sign to those on a bilingual map, for example. Phrasebooks can aid your use of script and attempts to decode it. Phrasebooks also make excellent gifts upon departure—your hosts may use them for figuring out English.

Vietnamese Phrasebook

Vietnamese is a tonal language, possibly derived from Austro-Asiatic or Sino-Tibetan languages; Chinese has been a major influence on Vietnamese literature. There are three main dialects in Vietnam—northern, central, and southern—although the language is mutually intelligible.

Good Morning, Vietnam: The minute you open your mouth in Vietnam you put your foot in it because the first thing you need to say is "hello." Unfortunately, "hello" is quite complicated in Vietnamese. There is no way round "hello," as the Vietnamese rarely use "good morning" or "good evening." A straight "hello" is rude—you need to address the person as well. You can wing it, and get away with chào, bạn, (hello, my friend) if talking to a younger person or chào, các bạn (hello, my friends). But this won't work with older folk. If you're looking for a catch-all "friends, Romans, countrymen," there isn't one. You have to take into account the person's sex, age, and level of familiarity (formal or informal). Vastly underestimating or overestimating a woman's age can be a big faux pas!

The correct forms of address are as follows: chào ông—when addressing an old man; chào anh—to a young man; chào bà—to an old woman; chào cô—to a young woman; chào chị—to an older woman; chào em—to younger people; chào cháu—to a young child; chào các bạn—hello friends, if addressing a younger audience. If you know the given name, add that. So now it's chào cô Lan—hello young woman Lan. The conversation may then lead to "How old are you?" or "Where are you going?" or "What are you doing?" Some Vietnamese like this gambit with foreigners: "How much money do you make?" With some perseverance, you can build up a stock of simple phrases such as đẹp lắm or rât đẹp, both mean beautiful or very pretty. These will get you through a variety of situations.

Tones: The sound of Vietnamese has been likened to the twittering of birds. Mastering the sing-song warblelike tones is essential to conveying correct meaning. The same word can mean six different things, depending on the tone— "ma" for instance, can mean ghost, mother, but, tomb, horse, or rice seedling.

As satirist P.J. O'Rourke puts it: "Cơm (cooked rice), không (no), cam (orange), câm (not allowed) and kem (ice cream) are all pronounced, to the American ear, "kum." Thus you can ask someone for an ice cream and wind up in the market with a forbidden orange dog."

The six tones are rendered (with "o" as an example only): midtone, no marker; ó high rising, starts high and rises sharply; ò low falling, starts low and falls to lowest level of voice range; ỏ low rising, starts low, dips, and rises to high point; õ high broken, starts above midtone, dips slightly, rises abruptly; and ọ low broken, starts below normal range, falls abruptly and immediately to a lower level and gets cut off. In addition to these markers the vowels a, e, i, o, and u carry special marks such as a hat or a little hook for sounds that have no approximations to English sounds. Go over the Vietnamese phrases that follow with a Vietnamese speaker to get the sounds correct. Or record the speaker on a cassette, listen repeatedly, and mimic.

Negatives and Questions: Vietnamese sentences follow the word order: subject, verb, object. To make a negative, simply add the word không between subject and verb. Question words are usually placed at the end of the sentence. Take the affirmative statement without the answer and add the question word. For example, "This book is how much?" For yes/no questions, the word có (yes) is added before the verb, and the word không (no) is added at the end of the sentence to make the question. The word order is thus: subject, có, verb, object, không? The trickiest question in Vietnamese is a negative one. "You haven't gone to the market yet, have you?" is answered in the positive "Yes," meaning "Yes, I haven't."

Reading: After being completely illiterate in Thailand, China, Laos, and Cambodia, it comes as quite a shock to suddenly find that in Vietnam you can actually recognize the letters on signs, street names, museum labels, and even the odd newspaper headline. For this you can thank Alexandre de Rhodes, the 17th-century French Jesuit who devised quốc ngữ script—basically to convert the Bible into Vietnamese, and the people into Catholics. Alexandre de Rhodes also came up with the system of tone markers above and below the letters. This replaced a system with Chinese–based ideographs. Quốc ngữ set Vietnam apart from the rest of continental Asia.

If you have trouble getting your message across with tonal pronunciation, try writing it down, adding the tone markers if you can. Without the appropriate tone markers, the roman alphabet can still be understood, although the Vietnamese person would have to guess at the meaning. Expect the odd transliteration methods, which derived from French. Gion–Xồn is Johnson; xàlách is salad. Signs like Cồm Chay (vegetarian) or Cảnh Sát (police) are handy to recognize.

Phrasebooks and Tapes: Many dirt-cheap phrasebooks and dictionaries are sold in Saigon and Hanoi for English-Vietnamese or French-Vietnamese. If your pronunciation doesn't work, you can at least count on pointing to phrasebook or dictionary entries. Vietnam boasts an exceptional 92 percent literacy rate. Ho Chi Minh personally promoted this cause, proclaiming, "an ignorant nation is a weak nation." Because of the unusual sounds in Vietnamese, you can go only so far in learning the language from a phrasebook. It is preferable to listen to a tape to attune your ear at least to recognizing the sounds.

Language learning can be monotonous, so to add spice, try the multimedia approach—photographs, sound effects, maybe even some video. Virginia–based company The Rosetta Stone sells CD-ROMs that are used by the Peace Corps, among other clients. You can find out more about them at their www.rosettastone.com website. They have a complete 250-hour 92-lesson Vietnamese language course on CD-ROM retailing for a whopping $195 (or the same thing online for the same price); considerably more affordable is a CD-ROM called "Vietnamese Explorer," which contains the first 22 lessons of the longer version for just $25.

The more conventional approach to language learning is the text-and-tape approach. **The Language 30** series, produced by Educational Services Corporation for U.S. government personnel, consists of a booklet and two cassettes, with 100 minutes of recording. Phrasebooks are also issued by Lonely Planet, Rough Guides, and Editions Duang Kamol (Bangkok). **Colloquial Vietnamese,** a package with book and two 60-minute cassettes, by Tuan Duc Vuong and John Moore, costs about $50 (published by Routledge, London). A Viet-Anh and Anh-Viet dictionary makes sense, but unfortunately those on the market abroad are hefty and expensive tomes—impractical to lug around.

PRONUNCIATION

Vietnamese transliteration varies from English pronunciation, and sounds vary slightly from north (N) to south (S). Some variants include:

c—"k"

ch—at the beginning of a word is pronounced "ch" as in "cheek"; at the end of a word it's "ck" as in "lick"

đ—"z" (N) and "y" (S); for example, the national dress áo dài is pronounced áo zài (N) or áo yài (S)

Đ—"d" as in "dog"

gì—"z" (N) and "y" (S)

kh—"ch" as in the German "Bach"

nh—in the beginning or middle of a word, pronounced ñ as in the Spanish "mañana"; at the end of a word it's "ng" as in "running away"

ph—"f"

r—"z" (N) and "r" (S)

th—"t" as in "tea," but strongly aspirated

tr—"ch"(N) and "tr" (S)

s—"s" (N) and "sh" (S)

x—"s"

OPENERS

Hello (my friend)	Chào bạn (bạn tôi)
Goodbye	Tạm biệt nhé
Pleased to meet you	Hân hạnh được gặp bạn
How are you?	Bạn có khỏe không?
Very well, thank you	Cám ơn bạn, tôi khỏe
Where are you going?	Bạn đi đâu đấy?
What's your name?	Tên bạn là gì?
My name is …	Tên tôi là…
I only speak a little Vietnamese	Tôi chỉ nói một ít setiếng Việt
I don't understand	Tôi không hiểu
Do you understand?	Bạn có hiểu không?

GETTING PERSONAL

Where are you from?	Bạn từ đâu đến?
Canadian/	Canada/Úc/Anh

Australian/British American/ French/Russian	Mỹ/Pháp/Nga
Vietnamese/Lao/Thai	Việt Nam/Lào/Thái
Cambodian/Chinese	Cam-pu-chia/ Trung Hoa
My job is …	Việc làm của tôi là…
How old are you?	Bạn bao nhiêu tuổi?
married/single	có gia đình/độc thân
husband/wife	chồng/vợ
mother/father	mẹ/cha
children/son/daughter	con cái/con trai/ con gái
older brother/sister	anh/chị
younger brother/sister	em trai/em gái

FLATTERY

good/very good	tốt/tốt lắm
The food is great!	Món ăn ngon lắm!
Terrific food!	Ngon tuyệt!
Cheers!	Chúc mừng!
To your health!	Chúc sức khỏe!
I love this town!	Tôi thích thành phố này!
very beautiful	rất đẹp
very interesting	rất thích
I had a great time!	Tôi có một thời gian tuyệt vời
Good luck!	Chúc bạn may mắn!

NEGATIVES, QUESTIONS, AND REQUESTS

yes/no	vâng (N), có (S)/ không
okay/no problem	được/không sao
not okay/no good	không được/không tốt
please/thank you	làm ơn/cám ơn bạn
enough, thank you	đủ rồi, cám ơn
I want/need	Tôi muốn/cần
don't want/don't like	tôi không muốn/ không thích
sorry, excuse me	xin lỗi
don't know	không biết

Can I take a photo? — Tôi có thể chụp hình nhé?

What's this called in Vietnamese? — Cái này tiếng Việt gọi là gì?

What does that mean? — Cái nghĩa đó là gì?

Can you write it down for me? — Bạn có thể viết ra đây không?

where/where is? — đâu?/ở đâu?

when?/who?/ why?/how? — khi nào?/ai?/ tại sao?/thế nào?

how much/many? — bao nhiêu?

how long?/how far? — bao lâu?/bao xa?

RED TAPE

passport — giấy thông hành

tourist/ business person — du khách/ thươnggia

visa/Thai visa — chiếu khán/chiếu khán của Thái

I want to extend my visa — Tôi muốn gia hạn chiếu khán

travel permit — giấy phép du lịch

I need a translator — Tôi cần thông dịch viên

What is the problem? — Có vấn đề gì đấy?

MEDICAL

sick — ốm đau (N)/bệnh (S)

diarrhea/ headache/fever — tiêu chảy/ nhức đầu/sốt

cold/sore throat — cảm/đau họng

Please help! — giúp tôi với!

need a doctor/dentist — cần một bác sĩ/ nha sĩ

emergency — khẩn cấp

hospital — bệnh viện

drugstore — nhà thuốc tây

ASKING/GIVING DIRECTIONS

I want to go to … — tôi muốn đi đến…

I want to see … — tôi muốn gặp…

how many kilometers to…? — bao nhiêu ki lô mét đến…?

how long will it take to get to…? — Đi bao lâu thì tới…?

turn right/turn left — queo phải/queo trái

straight ahead — đi thẳng

fast/slow — nhanh/chậm

slow down/ take it easy! — chậm lại/ cútừ từ!

Stop here! — Dừng lại!

Wait here — Đợi ở đây

Let's go! — Chúng ta hãy đi!

north/south — bắc/nam

east/west — đông/tây

map — bản đồ

Where can I get a map? — Tôi có thể mua bản đồ ở đâu?

TRANSPORT

timetable — lịch trình

Please write down the timetable. — Xin viết lịch trình ra.

ticket — vé

Can you buy a ticket for me? — Bạn có thể mua hộ tôi cái vé?

Where can I leave my luggage? — Tôi có thể để hành lý ở đâu?

plane/helicoptor — máy bay/máy bay lên thẳng (N), trực thăng (S)

bus/minibus — xe buýt/xe ô-tô con

express bus — xe buýt tốc hành

bus station/ minibus station — bến xe buýt/ bến xe con

Where is the bus station? — Bến xe buýt ở đâu?

How many buses a day are there? — Một ngày có bao nhiêu chuyến xe buýt?

What time is the first bus? — Mấy giờ bắt đầu có chuyến xe thứ nhất?

What time is the last bus? — Mấy giờ bắt đầu có chuyến xe cuối?

When does the next bus leave? — Chuyến xe tới xuất hành vào giờ nào?

When does the bus arrive? — Khi nào xe buýt tới?

railway station	ga xe lửa
express train	tàu tốc hành
hard seat/soft seat	ghế ngồi cứng
	(ghế gỗ)/ghế ngồi
	mêm (ghế mềm)
hard sleeper/	giường nằm cứng
soft sleeper	(giường gỗ)/
	giường nằm mềm
	(giường nệm)
What time is	Chuyến tàu tới
the next train?	chạy vào lúc mấy
	giờ?
taxi/taxi station	tắc xi/bến xe tắc xi
motorcycle-taxi	xe mô–tô ôm
cyclo (trishaw)	xe xích lô
truck/4WD vehicle	xe vận tải/xe díp
boat/boat dock	tàu thủy/bến tàu
ferry/ferry dock	phà/bến phà

RENTALS

motorcycle	xe mô–tô
bicycle	xe đạp
Where can I	Tôi có thể thuê
rent a bicycle?	xe đạp ở đâu?
How much per hour?	Bao nhiêu tiên
	một giờ?
How much for	Bao ýnhiêu tiền
one day?/half a day?	một ngày?/nửa
	ngày?
Where can I	Tôi có thể
rent a motorcycle?	thuê mô–tô ở đâu?
driver/guide	tài xế/người
	hướng dẫn
Where can I hire	Tôi có thể thuê
a car and driver?	ô–tô con và tài
	xế ở đâu?
Where can I hire	Tôi có thể thuê
a minibus?	xe buýt nhỏ ở đâu?
Where can I hire	Tôi có thể thuê
a boat?	tàu thủy ở đâu?

PLACES

airport	phi trường
airline office	phòng bán vé
	máy bay
embassy	tòa đại sứ

post office	bưu điện
bank	ngân hàng
(foreign exchange)	(đổi tiền ngoại)
tourism bureau	văn phòng du lịch
bookshop	cửa hàng sách
gas station	trạm xăng
police station	đồn công an
market	chợ
temple/pagoda/church	đền/chùa/nhà thờ
museum/theatre	bảo tàng/rạp hát

DINING OUT

restaurant/café	nhà hàng ăn
	uống/quán nước
Let's eat!	chúng ta hãy
	ăn/mời bạn!
Please bring	Làm ơn cho
the menu	xem thực đơn
not hot (spicy) please	xin đừng làm cay
May I have…	Tôi có thể có…
fried rice/	cơm rang/
steamed rice	cơm nóng
sticky rice	xôi
croissant/	bánh sừng bò/
French bread	bánh mì Pháp
sandwich/	bánh mì kẹp/
noodle soup	tô mì sợi
chicken/	thịt gà/
pork/beef	thịt lợn/thịt bò
fish/shrimp	cá/tôm
vegetables/fruit	rau/quả
vegetarian food	món ăn chay
hot/cold	nóng/lạnh
salad	sà lách
I'll have the	Cho tôi cùng
same thing	món đó
water/cold water	nước/nước lạnh
boiled mineral water	nước suối
	đóng chai
boiled water	nước sôi
no ice, thanks	không đá, cám ơn
hot tea/hot coffee	trà nóng/
	cà phê nóng
lemon/sugar	chanh/đường
beer/soft drink	bia/nước ngọt
fruit juice	nước quả (N)/nước
	trái cây (S)

young coconut — nước dừa tươi
two beers please — xin cho hai chai bia
the bill please — làm ơn tính tiền

HOTEL

a good hotel — một khách sạn tốt
budget hotel — khách sạn bình dân
(family-run) guesthouse — nhà khách(gia đình làm)
air-conditioned — có điều hòa không khí
fan — quạt
telephone — điện thoại
room with bath — phòng có buồng tắm
single room (one bed) — phòng một giường
double room (two beds) — phòng hai giường
triple room — phòng ba
dormitory — nhà ngủ
toilet — nhà vệ sinh
toilet paper — giấy đi cầu
men's toilet/ women's toilet — nhà vệ sinh nam/ nhà vệ sinh nữ
shower/hot shower — vòi tắm hương sen/vòi tắm hương sen có nước nóng
sheets/towel — khăn trải giường/ khăn tắm
blanket — chăn đắp (N)/mền đắp (S)
thermos of hot water — bình thủy nước nóng
mosquito net — màn ngủ (N)/ mùng (S)
May I see the room, please? — Tôi có thể xem Phòng được không?
Can you give me a discount? — Bạn có thể bớt cho tôi được không?

BARGAINING

How much is this? — Cái này bao nhiêu?
Do you have … ? — Bạn có…?
big/small — lớn/nhỏ
old/new — củ/mới
expensive — đắt (N)/mắc (S)

Do you have anything cheaper? — Bạn có cái nào rẻ hơn không?
Can you give me a better price? — Bạn có thể cho tôi một giá thấp hơn không?
I will come back. — Tôi sẽ trở lại

TIME AND NUMBERS

today/now — hôm nay/bây giờ
tonight — đêm nay
yesterday/tomorrow — hôm qua/ngày mai
morning/ afternoon/evening — sáng/ chiều/tối
year/month/ day/hour — năm/tháng/ ngày/giờ
Monday — Thứ Hai
Tuesday — Thứ Ba
Wednesday — Thứ Tư
Thursday — Thứ Năm
Friday — Thứ Sáu
Saturday — Thứ Bảy
Sunday — Chủ Nhật
zero — không
one — một
two — hai
three — ba
four — bốn
five — năm
six — sáu
seven — bảy
eight — tám
nine — chín
ten — mười
twenty — hai mươi
thirty — ba mươi
fourty — bốn mươi
fifty — năm mươi
sixty — sáu mươi
seventy — bảy mươi
eighty — tám mươi
ninety — chín mươi
one hundred — một trăm
five hundred — năm trăm
one thousand — một nghìn
two thousand — hai nghìn
five thousand — năm nghìn

ten thousand	mười nghìn	cave	hang động
twenty thousand	hai mươi nghìn	valley	thung lũng
fifty thousand	năm mươi nghìn	highway	xa lộ
one hundred thousand	một trăm nghìn	bridge	cầu
		city	thành phố
one million	một triệu	boulevard	đại lộ
		street	phố (N)/đường (S)
		town square	bùng binh
		gardens/	vườn/
		park	vườn hoa (công viên)

GEOGRAPHICAL TERMS

district	quận
forest	rừng
jungle	rừng nhiệt đới
mountain	núi
river	sông
beach	bãi tắm
bay	vịnh
island	đảo
lake	hồ
waterfall	thác

Khmer Phrasebook

The Cambodian language belongs to the Mon-Khmer family. Khmer is spoken throughout the Kingdom of Cambodia and by several million people in southwest Vietnam and northeast Thailand. Due to the influence of Buddhism and Brahmanism in Cambodia, many Sanskrit and Pali words entered the Khmer language. A large proportion of words in Cambodian share the same base as the Thai language, though the linguistic association is not immediately recognizable in the spoken language because Thai is tonal, and Khmer is nontonal.

Although Khmer is nontonal, pronunciation can be difficult. There are consonants that sound between d and t, between ch and j, or between b and p. There is no standard system of transcribing Cambodian script into roman letters to suit an English speaker. Many sounds in Cambodian do not have precise English equivalents. The following phrase list attempts only an approximation of the correct sounds. You should go over the phrases with a native speaker to attune your ear.

Polite forms: When addressing someone, it's polite to take into account the person's sex, age, and social standing. There are a variety of polite forms of "you," depending on whether you're addressing a man, a woman, a boy, a girl, or a person older than 60. In general, address a man of high standing *lohk* (mister) and a woman of high standing *lohk srei* (madam); for addressing someone the same age or of equal standing, use *neak* (my friend) or use the person's name. Certain Khmer forms are spoken only by women (*jah,* meaning "yes," for example) or by men (*baat,* meaning "yes").

Useful Phrases: Opening conversation gambits in the UNTAC era: "Thank you for showing me your wonderful gun;" "I am delighted to accept your invitation to lie down on the ground;" "Please accept my watch and this quantity of U.S. dollars as a small sign of the high regard in which I hold you." Jokes aside, one of the most useful phrases to know in Cambodian is: *mian min teh?* (any mines around here?). The word for mine is easy—it's *min.*

Negatives and Questions: Questions are indicated by adding the question-words *reu teh* or just *teh* to the end of a sentence, spoken with an upward inflexion. Since Cambodian is nontonal, you can make a question by using an upward inflexion to a statement alone, as in English. Question words such as where, what, when, and why are placed at the end of a sentence, as in, *this coconut is how much?* Negatives are formed by inserting *meun*, (meaning "no") before the verb.

Reading: Khmer has a mammoth 74-letter alphabet with 33 consonants and a remarkable number of vowels and diphthongs. Some letters have no current usage. The alphabet derives from southern India. Examination of early Cambodian stele inscriptions reveals that two different kinds of writing were in use simultaneously: one was based directly on Hindu; the other developed and adapted to Cambodian. The latter became the established medium, and has changed only slightly over the centuries. The writing system is extremely complicated to the Western eye. Vowels and dipthongs may be above, below, before, and after consonants. Consonants may be written below text as subscript.

Phrasebooks and Tapes: Crude photocopied language materials can be bought cheaply at the central market in Phnom Penh. These are more often intended for Cambodians learning English, so they might have important omissions, such as transliteration of Cambodian sounds. It's helpful to have the transliteration and the Cambodian script side-by-side. Useful is a palm-size version of Seam and Blake's *English-Khmer Dictionary,* originally printed in Bangkok, which uses its own phonetic system with exclamation marks. For serious attempts at the language, try *Colloquial Cambodian* by David Smyth, with a book and two tapes for $50.

The following phrases are transcribed as if addressing a man—the particle is *lohk;* to address a woman, substitute *lohk srei;* to address someone of equal standing, substitute *neak.* The word *sohm* (as rhyming with "home") denotes politeness.

Know Vietnam, Cambodia & Laos

OPENERS

hello	joom reap soo-uh (suisdei)
goodbye	leah sun hi
Pleased to meet you …	Knyom reek reuh na toybon chewuhk lohk …
How are you?	Sohm lohk sok sabei chea teh?
Very well, thank you.	Baat sok sabei, awkun. (spoken by men)/Jah sok sabei, awkun. (spoken by women)
Where are you going?	Sohm lohk, dtiw nah?
What's your name?	Sohm lohk, chmou ei?
My name is …	Knyom chmou …
I only speak a little Khmer.	Knyom ne-yeay pee-uh-saw Kmei bantec, bantuec.
I don't understand.	Knyom meun yul teh.
Do you understand?	Sohm lohk, yul reu teh?

GETTING PERSONAL

Where are you from?	Lohk mohk pee srok nah?
Canadian/ Australian/British	Kanada/ Ostralee/Anglae
American/ French/Russian	Amerikang/ Barang/Rossey
Vietnamese/Lao/ Thai	Vietnam/Layo/Tai
Cambodian/Chinese	Kmei/Jhen
My job is …	Knyom tve kah …
How old are you?	Sohm lohk, ayut bpon mahn?
married/single	riapkah/kom law
husband/wife	pdei/prawpun
mother/father	madei/owpuhk
children/son/daughter	kon/kon bproh/ kon srey
older brother/sister	bong bproh/bong srey

younger brother/sister   puh-own bproh/puh-
own srei

FLATTERY

good/very good	lu-awh/lu-awh nah
The food is great!	Mahop chngainh!
terrific food	mahop nee ochar nah
I love this town!	Knyom sraalanh khoom nee!
very beautiful	suh-awt nah
very interesting	coor chat aram nah
I had a great time!	Pbehl vilea nee lu-awh nah!
good luck	somnang lu-awh

NEGATIVES, QUESTIONS, AND REQUESTS

yes/no	baat (spoken by men) jah (by women)/baat teh (men) jah teh (women)
okay/no problem	ban/meun ei teh
not okay/no good	meun ban/meun lu-awh
please/thank you	sohm/awkun
enough, thank you	krup kroen hai, awkun
I want/need	knyom jong/knyom treu kah
don't want/don't like	knyom meun jong bahn/meun jol jet
sorry, excuse me	sohm toe/ot-toe
don't know	meun dong
Can I take a photo?	Dta knyom at tot rub bahn teh?
What's this called in Khmer?	Nee kay how tah avei?
What does that mean?	Dta peak nee mienei jong meitch?
Can you write it down for me?	Dta lohk at sohsei, bahn teh?
where?/where is?	ai nah?/ti nah?
when?/who?	ongkal?/neak-na?
why?/how?	hat-ei?/jong meitch?

how much/many?	tlai bpon mahn?
how far?	chngei bpon mahn?

RED TAPE

passport	lee keut chlong-daehn
tourist/businessperson	taih suhcha/neak choom new-one
visa	visa
extend a visa	visa bpun-jia bpehl
I need a translator.	Knyom treu kah neak bop bpraeh.
What is the problem?	Mien panyaha ei?

MEDICAL

sick/very sick	chue/chue klong
diarrhea/ headache/ fever/stomach ache	riak/chue kbal/ krun kdow/chue phuah
cold/sore throat	padasay/johk bom-bpoung ko
please help	sohm jewy bong
need a doctor/ dentist	treu kah krew bpet/ bpet tahmenh
emergency	bon toen
hospital	moonty bpet
drugstore	hong luek tnam

ASKING/GIVING DIRECTIONS

I want to go to …	Knyom jong dtiw …
I want to see …	Knyom jong kheun …
How many kilometers to …?	Bpon mahn kilo dtiw …?
turn right/turn left	bot dtiw sdam/bot dtiw chwaingh
straight ahead	dtiw dtrong
fast/slow	loeun or chop chop/ djuet or muey muey
slow down/ take it easy	sohm dtiw muey muey
Stop here	chop tee nee
Wait here.	Jaam tee nee.
Let's go!	Dtiw kah dtiw!
north/south	jeung/tbohng

east/west	kaet/lehj
map	paehn-tee

TRANSPORT

timetable	dah rahng bpehl
ticket	somboht
Can you buy a ticket for me?	Sohm lohk, atting somboht owee knyom baan teh?
Where can I leave luggage?	Dta kon lai na my bao knyom at took vallee robah knyom?
plane/ helicopter	joo-uhn haw/ helikopter
bus/minibus	lawn kroang
bus station	chamnot lawn kroang
Where is the bus station?	Chamnot lawn kroang niw kon lei na?
What time is the first bus?	Lawn kroang tee muey chain maowng bpon mahn?
When does the bus arrive?	Dta lawn kroang mohk dal niw maowng bpon mahn?
railway station	sattani rot pleung
train	rot pleung
taxi/taxi station	tak-si/sattani tak-si
motorcycle-taxi	moto dop
cyclo (trishaw)	cyclo
three-wheeler	lambretta
truck	lahn truck tome
small boat	dtuk
medium-size boat	kanoht
big boat	kobpal
ferry	salang
boat dock	kompong tei

RENTALS

motorcycle	moto
bicycle	kong
Where can I	Kon lei na
rent a bicycle?	knyom joul kong chee?
How much per hour?	Muey maowng tlei bpon manh?
half a day	kanlah tngei
Where can I rent a motorcycle?	Kon lei na knyom al joul moto?
driver	neak bowk lawn (car)
	neak bowk moto (moto)
	neak bowk taksi (taxi)
	neak bowk cyclo (cyclo)
guide	neak nai noum

PLACES

I want to go to …	Knyom jong dtiw tee …
airport	jomnot joo-uhn haw
airline office	krohmhun ahkasjo
embassy	stahn-doot
post office	praisinee
bank	tanee-akeea
tourism bureau	kariyalei samrap puok taih suhcha
bookshop	hong luek see-uh-piw
gas station	satani preng
police station	bot polis
market	psah
temple	wat
museum/theatre	sahrah-munti/ rohng kohn

DINING OUT

restaurant/café	poachania tahn/ hong cafe
Let's eat!	Dta, onjeunh tiw nyam!
Please bring the menu.	Sohm owee see-uh-piw menu.
not hot (spicy) please	ot heul teh
May I have…	Knyom jong…
fried rice/steamed rice	mae cha/mae saw
sticky rice	mae donap

French bread	Nom pong
sandwich/	noum sandwit/
noodle soup	guay tiao
chicken/pork/	sik moan/sik chrouk/
beef	sik ko
fish/shrimp	sik trey/sik mongeya
vegetables/fruit	bunlae/plei cheu
hot/cold	kdow/trocheat
salad	salat
I'll have the	knyom jong man
same thing	doich knia
water/cold water	teuk/teuk trocheat
bottled water	teuk suh-awt
boiled water	teuk bpu
no ice, thanks	min dak teuk-awh
	teh, awkun
tea/coffee	teuk tai/kahfay
lemon/sugar	kroj mah/skaw saw
young coconut	dong kchei
two beers, please	sohm owee knyom
	beer pi
the bill, please	sohm owee kut loy

HOTEL

a good hotel	sonta kia lu-awh
(family-run)	pteah pneu
guesthouse	
air-conditioned	machine trocheat
fan	kong ha
telephone	tourosap
room with bath	bantuop mien bon
	dtoop teuk
single room	bantuop mien tei
(one bed)	krey muey
double room	bantuop mien tei
(two beds)	krey pee
triple room	bantuop tom mein
	krey buey
toilet/paper	bong kuen barah/
	bong kuen setrei
men's toilet/	mun koun bproh/
women's toilet	mun koun setrey
shower/	nguet teuk/
hot shower	nguet teuk kadow
sheets/towel	kome raht took/
	kone saeng choot
	kluen

thermos of hot water	boam toam teuk
	kadow
blanket	pouy
mosquito net	mung
Can I see the room?	Jong dtiw meul
	bantuop sen,
	bahn teh?

BARGAINING

How much is this?	Nee talei bpon
	manh?
Do you have …?	Sohm lohk,
	mien …?
big/small	tom/toic
old/new	ja/tmei
expensive	tlei
Do you have	Sohm lohk,
anything cheaper?	mien evei towk
	cheang nee?
Can you give me	Sohm lohk,
a better price?	choe talei bantec?
discount	bahn-choe domlay
I will come back.	Knyom bon troe lop
	mohk vanh.

TIME AND NUMBERS

today	tngay nee
now	aylao nee
tonight	yoop nee
yesterday/tomorrow	msel minh/suh-eik
morning/afternoon/	preuk/ reuseal/
evening	langeat
year/month/	chnam/kei/
day/hour	tngei/mowng
Monday	Tngay chan
Tuesday	Tngay awng keah
Wednesday	Tngay bput
Thursday	Tngay prohoea
Friday	Tngay sok
Saturday	Tngay saow
Sunday	Tngay atut
zero	sohn
one	muoy
two	pi
three	buey
four	buon

five	pram	50,000	pram meun
six	pram muoy	100,000	muoy saen
seven	pram pi	one million	muoy lee-uhn
eight	pram buey		
nine	pram buon		
10	dop		

GEOGRAPHICAL TERMS

11	dop muoy		
12	dop pi	district	songkhat
13	dop buey	forest	prey cheu
14	dop buon	jungle	prey
15	dop pram	mountain/hill	phnom
20	mapuey	river	tonle (stung)
30	sam sup	beach	chne samot
40	sae sup	bay	choe samot
50	ha sup	island	koh
60	hok sup	lake	boeng
70	jet sup	waterfall	teuk tliak
80	bpad sup	cave	rung phnom
90	kaow sup	highway	ploechit
100	muoy roy	bridge	spean
500	pram roy	city	krong
1,000	muoy poan	river town	kompong
2,000	pi poan	boulevard	moha vithei
5,000	pram poan	street	pleu
10,000	muoy meun	market	psah
20,000	pi meun	gardens/park	soun chbah
		temple	wat

Lao Phrasebook

by Alison Norman

The Lao spoken and written in Vientiane sets the standard for language in Laos. The Vientiane version of Lao is one of the many dialects of the Thai language family, which also encompasses Thailand and Laos, extends to northern Vietnam, northern Myanmar (Burma), southern China, and even parts of Bangladesh. Within Laos there are different dialects as you move from north to south, and even 60 kilometers from Vientiane, at Phon Hong, the tones of standard Lao begin to change.

Any effort the foreign traveler makes to learn and use standard Lao will be greeted with delight by the locals. If you have spent any time in Thailand prior to visiting Laos, you can use any Thai that you have acquired, as most Laotians understand Thai. Laotians are bombarded by Thai media-radio, TV, newspapers, magazines, textbooks. Therefore, they have picked up both spoken and written Thai. The reverse, however, does not apply—very few Thais can understand Lao. With the exception of Issan people in the northeast, Thais usually cannot understand spoken Lao, and only a few elderly Issan folk can read Lao script.

Tones: Lao is a tonal language with six distinct tones, which are placed on syllables. Hence a monosyllabic word only carries one tone, but a polysyllabic word may have several. Tones affect meaning, and therefore cannot be left out of speech. Tones are somewhat easier to produce than to hear. To help convey your meaning, you can mimic the tone patterns by tilting your head up or down to match the particular tone by nodding, or by moving your chin from side to side as you speak. You may look a bit odd but if the words you produce are understood, it's worth it! In Lao dictionaries, the six tones in Lao are: (with "o" as an example only) low tone, no marker; ō midtone, normal voice pitch; ò high falling; ǒ low rising; ó high pitch; and ô low falling. An example of the variation in tones follows: the Lao word for

"almost rotten" is mòo; the word for "pig" is mòo; while the word for "friend" is mo-o. Just think what you could accidentally say: "You're a real pig!"

Lao has 20 consonant sounds and 28 vowel/diphthong sounds. Most of the consonants are similar to English with the exception of the initial "ng," and the hard "p," "t," and "g," which are not aspirated. The vowels are more difficult, as quite a few are not found in English. The best way to learn them is to listen to a Lao speaker on tape or in person.

Negatives and Questions: While pronunciation is complex, Lao grammar is simple. To make a negative, just put the word "bor" in front of an adjective or verb—for example, "bor dii" (not good); "bor mak" (don't like). To make a question, put the word "bor" at the end—for example, "dii bor (is it good?); "mak bor" (do you like it?). Be careful to keep the tone on "bor" low in a question; don't make it a rising intonation as in English. Verb tenses are easy to deal with in Lao. To render a past tense, you simply add "layo" after the verb—for example "gin layo" (ate, or have eaten), "maa layo" (came, or has come). To form a future tense, you just put "si" in front of the verb—for example, "si gin" (will eat). It doesn't matter who the subject of the verb is—I, you, she, he, they—the subject has no effect on the verb at all, and is not usually stated if it is obvious to whom the speaker is referring.

Script: Lao script is modeled on early Thai script, written from left to right with no spacing between words. Reading and writing this script presents a real challenge. Unless you are planning a long stay in Laos, or have an intense academic interest, it is unlikely you will want to tackle the written word. However, if you have already mastered Thai script, you will find Lao easy to read, and much easier to spell than Thai. Lao script has 32 consonant symbols, 28 vowel/diphthong symbols, three classes of consonants, and tone markers. The

Lao disagree on the spelling of many words, especially those derived from Sanskrit. The traveler will not fare much better with transliteration of Lao into the roman alphabet. Transliteration of Lao is extremely confusing because standardization does not exist, and while the French provided spelling for Lao words, the British transliterated Thai. Hence the Thai name "Sunthorn" is spelled "Sounthone" in Laos, even though the pronunciation and derivation is identical. The French often use "x" for an "s" sound (as in the province of Xieng Khuang), and rarely have a "w" sound; the French wrote "v" in transliteration even though this sound does not exist in Lao. Vientiane is actually pronounced "Wiang Jun."

Phrasebooks: A handy pocket-sized phrasebook is *Lao Phrasebook,* by Joe Cummings (Lonely Planet, 1995) with Lao script for all vocabulary included. For Lao language materials, your best bet is to scour bookstores in Bangkok. Check places like Asia Books. The Lao, Cambodian, and Vietnamese material is usually grouped together and is easy to find. In Vientiane you can try Raintree Books, the sole bookstore that caters to foreigners. The bookstore stocks Russell Marcus's *English-Lao Dictionary; Lao for Beginners,* by Russell Marcus and Tatsuo Hoshino, as well as Klaus Werner's *Learning Lao.* Using your own cassette player to record Lao sounds would be extremely useful.

TONES

The following tones appear on the phrases below. The letter "o" is used as an example.

low tone	(o) no marker
midtone	(ō) normal voice pitch
high falling	(ò)
low rising	(ǒ)
high pitch	(ó)
low falling	(ô)

OPENERS

hello	sábai dee
goodbye	laá gōn der

Pleased to meet you.	Nyiňdee teá hòo júk jaò.
How are you?	Sábai dee bōr?
Very well, thank you	Sábai dee, kop jai.
Where are you going?	Jaò jà pai sǎi?
What's your name?	Jào sēr nyǎng?
My name is ...	Kôy sēr ...
I only speak a little Lao.	Kôy wòw láo dài nòy nȳng.
I don't understand.	Kôy bōr kao jai.
Do you understand?	Jaò kâo jai bōr?

GETTING PERSONAL

Where are you from?	Jào maa tēh sǎi?
Canadian/	kanada/
Australian/British	australie/angkǐt
American/	amerika/
French/Russian	farangsêt/sowiet
Vietnamese/Lao/Thai	vietnam/laó/tai
Cambodian/Chinese	káměn/jeen
My job is ...	Kôy hed wiǎk...
How old are you?	Jào anȳu taōdai?
married/single	tāng ngárn/sôat
husband/wife	pǔa/mǐa
mother/father	mē h/pōr
children/son/daughter	lùke/lùke sái/ lùke sǎo
older brother/ older sister	ài/èay
younger brother/ younger sister	noǹg sái/ noǹg sǎo

FLATTERY

good/very good	dee/dee lǎi
The food is great!	Ahařn sàp lǎi!
terrific food	sàp ēe lěe
Cheers! To your health!	Nyōke nyōke! Peāy soukhaphap!
I love this town!	Kôy hūk meuǎng nèe!
very beautiful	ngárm laǎy
very interesting	son jaī laǎy
I had a great time.	Mūan lǎi.
Good luck!	Sowk dee!

NEGATIVES, QUESTIONS, AND REQUESTS

yes/no	mēn/bōr–mēn
okay/no problem!	tóke lóng/ bōr meě punhǎa!
not okay/no good	bōr toké lońg/ bōr dee
please/thank you	kalouna/kop jai
enough, thank you	pór làyo, kop jai
I want/need	koỷ yârk dai/ toǹg garn
don't want/don't like	bōr yǎrk dai/ bōr mūk
sorry/excuse me	kǒr toàt/kǒr ápái
don't know	bōr hoò
Can I take a photo?	Kôy kǒr tāi hòop dài bōr?
What's this called?	An neè ern wāa nyǎng?
What does that mean?	An neè mǎi kwárm wāa nyǎngdai?
Can you write it down for me?	Jaò kiǎn bòk hâi kôy dài bōr?
where?/where is?	yoū sǎi?/theè neè yoū sǎi?
when?/who? why?/how?	meūadai?/mēn pāi? pen yāng?/ yāngdai?
how much/how many?	taōdai?/laǎy tāodai?
how long? (time)	doan parndai?
how far?(distance)	kài parndai?

RED TAPE

passport	but pārn dan
tourist/businessperson	nuk tōng tiāo/ pōr káa
visa/Thai visa	wisa/ wisa meǔang tai
I want to extend my visa.	Kôy toǹgkarn kǒr tōr wisa.
travel permit	but ánōonỳart tōng tiāo
I need a translator.	Kôy toǹggarn koń pleh pasāa.
What is the problem?	Meě punhǎǎ yāng?

MEDICAL

sick	bōr sábai
diarrhea/ headache/fever	pānyàrt lóng toǹg/jép húa/kai
cold/sore throat	pen wát/jép kór
Please help.	Suǎy nēh.
need a doctor/dentist	toǹggarn haǎ mŏr/mŏr kâyo
emergency	gá tún hǔn
hospital/clinic	hóng pān ýabarn/ hóng mŏr
drugstore	bōn kǎi yaa

ASKING/GIVING DIRECTIONS

I want to go to …	Kôy tonggarn pai …
I want to see …	Kôy yârk bӯng …
How many kilometers to …?	Júk ǵilómēt pai …?
How long will it take to get to …?	pai thӯng … sài weláa tāodai?
turn right/turn left	loūay kwǎa/ loūay sàai
straight ahead	pai sēr sēr
fast/slow	wái/sàa
slow down/take it easy	saà lóng/jai yen yen
Stop here!	Yóot tēe nèe!
Wait here.	Tâa yōu nèe.
Let's go!	Pai gun tōr!
north/south	taŕng nêua/taŕng tài
east/west	tawún ôk/tawán tóke
Where can I get a map?	Kôy já aw phan tee yōu sǎi?

TRANSPORT

timetable	táláng weláá
Please write down the time table.	Garuna kiǎn táláng weláá sai but.
ticket	but
Can you buy a ticket for me?	Garuna sèr but hâi kôy dài bōr?
Where can I leave my luggage?	Kôy já páa hêp wài sǎi?
plane/helicopter	hӯa bin/helikopter
bus/minibus	rōte may pájum

bus station	tańg/rōte may sŏng tăyo
Where is the	sátařnee rōte may
bus station?	Sátařnee rōte may yōu săi?
How many buses	Rōte may měe júk
a day are there?	tiāo tōr mèr?
What time is	Wéláa júk móng rō
the first bus?	te may tiāo tée nӯng?
What time is	Wéláa júk móng rō
the last bus?	te may tiāo soótài?
When does the	Rōte may tiāo tōr
next bus leave?	pai já ôk júk móng?
When does	Wéláá tōrdai rōte
the bus arrive?	may já maa hot?
taxi/taxi station	taxi/sátărnee taxi
motorcycle sidecar-taxi	saăm lòr rōte júk
cyclo (trishaw)	saăm lòr
truck/4WD vehicle	rōte bantūk/ rōte gabah
boat/boat dock	hӯa/tār hӯa
ferry/ferry dock	hӯa bák/tār hӯa bák

RENTALS

motorcycle	rōte júk
bicycle	rōte teěp
Where can I	Kôy já sāo rōte
rent a bicycle?	teěp yōu săi?
How much per hour?	Sūamóng nӯng lákáa tāodai?
How much for	Mèr nӯng tāodai?
one day? Half a day?	Kӯng mèr tāodai?
Where can I	Kôy já sāo rōtejúk
rent a motorcycle?	yōu săi?
driver/guide	kón kup rōte/ pôu nē núm
Where can I hire	Kôy já sāo rōte léh
a car and driver?	cháng kón kuprōt yōu săi?
Where can I	Kôy já sāo rōte soňg
rent a minibus?	tăyo yōu săi?
Where can I	Kôy já sāo hӯa
rent a boat?	jarňg yōu săi?

PLACES

airport	sanaăm bin
airline office	hónggarn kǎi peè yón
embassy	sátărn toòt
post office	hónggarn pai sáneě
bank	tā ná kárn
(foreign exchange)	
tourism bureau	gom tōng tiāo
bookshop	harn kǎi pěrm
gas station	bōn kǎi naàm mán
police station	hông garn tumruat
market	tálârt
temple	wāt
church	bôat
museum	hǒr pēe pit tá pun
movie theater	hông sinay

DINING OUT

restaurant/café	harn ahǎrn/gafe
Let's eat!	Serń gin!
Please bring the menu	Garuna ao láigarn ahǎrn hâi nēh.
not hot (spicy) please	garuna yāa hēt pét laǎy
May I have…	Kǒr… dài bōr
fried rice/steamed rice	kûa kâo/kâo là là
sticky rice	kâo niǎo
French bread/sandwich	kâo jē e/kâo jē e patay
Chinese noodle soup/	phō chin/
Vietnamese soup	phō viet
chicken/pork/beef	gāi/mǒo/sèen
fish/shrimp	paa/guňg
vegetables/fruit	púck/mârk mài
vegetarian food	ahǎrn púck
hot/cold	hòn/yen
water/cold water	naàm/naàm yen
mineral water/	naàm gan/
boiled water	naàm tom
no ice, thanks	bōr ao naàm gòn
hot tea/coffee	sa hòn/gáfé
lemon/sugar	mârknao/numtarn
beer	bia
fruit juice	naàm mârk mài
the bill, please	kǒr bai gép ngerń

HOTEL

a good hotel	hónghém sān dee
budget hotel	hónghém tŷk tŷk
air-conditioned	hông ai yen
room with bath	hông thée měe
	hông naàm
single room (one bed)	hông poû diao
	(tiang diao)
double room (two beds)	hông sŏng kón
	(sŏng tiang)
triple room	hông saăm kón
dormitory	hŏr pūck
toilet	hông naàm (in rural
	areas: wēet)
men's toilet/	hông naàm pôu
women's toilet	sái/hông naàm
	pôu nyĭng
shower	bōn arp naàm
sheets/towel	pâ pu tiang/
	pâ sēt tua
mosquito net	mùng
May I see	Kôy kŏr bȳng hông
the room, please?	dài bōr?
Can you give	Jào lot lá káa
me a discount?	dài bōr?

BARGAINING

How much is this?	Nèe rákáa tōrdai?
Do you have … ?	Měe … bōr?
big/small	nyai/nòy
old/new	gāo/mài
expensive	páng
Do you have	Mēe naýo tŷk gwāa
anything cheaper?	nèe bōr?
Can you give	Lot lákáa dài bōr?
me a better price?	
I will come back.	Kôy já maa eêk.

TIME AND NUMBERS

today/now	mèr nèe/diao nèe
tonight	mèr láng
yesterday/tomorrow	mèr wárn nèe/
	mèr ern
morning/	ton sào/
afternoon/evening	bai/láng

year/month/day	pee/deuan/mèr
Monday	wań jun
Tuesday	wań angkárn
Wednesday	wań pōot
Thursday	wań pāhárt
Friday	wań sōok
Saturday	wań saŏ
Sunday	wa áatīt
one	nȳng
two	sŏng
three	sǎrm
four	sēe
five	haâ
six	hóke
seven	jét
eight	bât
nine	gao
ten	síp
twenty	sáo
thirty	sǎrm síp
forty	sēe síp
fifty	haâ síp
sixty	hóke síp
seventy	jét síp
eighty	bât síp
ninety	gao síp
one hundred	hòy
five hundred	haâ hòy
one thousand	pún
two thousand	sŏng pún
five thousand	haâ pún
ten thousand	síp pún
twenty thousand	sáo pún
fifty thousand	haâ síp pún
one hundred thousand	hòy pún
one million	larn nȳng

GEOGRAPHICAL TERMS

district	kâte
forest	paā
jungle	paā dong
mountain	poú
river	hûay–nām
beach	hârt–sai
island	don
lake	thapay
waterfall	naàm tóke

cave	tûm	city	meuăng
valley	hôm poú	boulevard	tánŏn nyai
highway	tārng luăng	street	tanŏn
bridge	kŏōah	gardens/park	suăn/suăn sătárānā

Suggested Reading

Books on Vietnam, Cambodia, and Laos fall into the feast-or-famine category. There are probably more books written about the Vietnam War than any other conflict in modern history, yet when it comes to the extension of the same conflict in Laos, only a handful of books can be found. Even more gaping holes exist in coverage of contemporary Indochina. Among the following books, some are either hard to find or out of print. These are marked with an asterisk (*). Your best chances of finding these books are in Hong Kong, Bangkok, or Singapore, although you might also find them in a library collection. The Bangkok-based publisher White Lotus (http://thailine.com/lotus) specializes in reprints of older material, with a good list for Indochina titles. The Gioi Publishers in Hanoi prints glossy booklets on such subjects as ethnic groups, water puppetry, traditional painting, folk sculpture, and traditional medicine—these are available in Vietnam.

INDOCHINA

Evans, Grant, and Kelvin Rowley. *Red Brotherhood at War.* New York: Routledge, Chapman & Hall, 1990. Good coverage of politics and history in Vietnam, Cambodia, and Laos since 1975.

Lewis, Norman. *A Dragon Apparent.* London: Eland Books, 1991. Well-written and lucid account of travels in 1949, right before the fall of the French empire in Indochina. This classic by Englishman Norman Lewis was first published in 1951.

The Mekong

The Mekong courses through Laos, Cambodia, and Vietnam. A broad overview of the people and places on the river is provided by the following coffee-table books.

Alford, Jeffrey, and Naomi Duguid. *Hot Sour Salty Sweet.* New York: Random House, 2000. A culinary and cultural journey along the Mekong, with recipes from Yunnan, Laos, Cambodia, and Vietnam.

Hoskin, John, and Allen Hopkins. *The Mekong: A River and Its People.* Bangkok: Post Publishing, 1991. Takes in life along the murky river from its source in China to the South China Sea. A CD-ROM title, *Beyond the Nine Dragons* produced by Black Box, Inc., of Hong Kong, is based on this book. The CD-ROM offers the added dimension of sound and video.

Sesser, Stan. *Life Along the Mekong.* New York: RDR Books, 2002. Subtitled: Asia's river people from China to Vietnam. By a journalist affiliated with *The New Yorker.*

Yamashita, Michael. *Mekong: A Journey on the Mother of Waters.* New York: Takarajima Books, 1995. Grand voyage along the Mekong by a *National Geographic* photographer.

VIETNAM
History

Duiker, William. *Ho Chi Minh.* New York: Hyperion, 2000. Running to a whopping 700 pages, this is the definitive biography of the enigmatic leader.

Taylor, Keith. *The Birth of Vietnam.* Berkeley: University of California Press, 1991. Covers early history.

Wintle, Justin. *The Vietnam Wars—Wars of the Modern Era*. London: Weidenfeld and Nicholson, 1991. Good summary not only of the Vietnam-American War but of all the conflicts in Vietnamese history.

The French in Vietnam

Fall, Bernard. *Street Without Joy*. Pennsylvania: Stackpole Books, 1994. Covers the 1946–1954 period. Another tome by French scholar Fall is *Hell Is a Very Small Place* (New York: Da Capo Press, 1985), about the siege of Dien Bien Phu.

The Americans in Vietnam

Requiem: By the Photographers Who Died in Vietnam and Indochina. New York: Random House, 1997. Coordinated by editors Tim Page and Horst Faas, this project brings together astounding images from the war—from the likes of Larry Burrows and Sean Flynn to little-known Vietnamese photographers. With some, it shows pictures from the combat photographer's last roll of film—or the last shot. A photo exhibition based on the book toured the United States and also appeared in Vietnam at places such as the War Crimes Museum in Saigon. The website www.wardogs.com/requiem.html showcases some of the pictures.

Fitzgerald, Frances. *Fire in the Lake*. New York: Random House, 1989. First published at the height of the conflict in 1972, this Pulitzer-prize winner presents some interesting Vietnamese perspectives on the war.

Halberstam, David. *The Making of a Quagmire*. 1965. Excellent account of America's early involvement in the war.

Herr, Michael. *Dispatches*. New York: Avon Books, 1978. This work offers a firsthand account of events in Vietnam told by a war correspondent for *Esquire*. Herr also collaborated on screenplays for *Apocalypse Now* and *Full Metal Jacket*.

Karnow, Stanley. *Vietnam: A History*. New York: Viking Penguin, 1983. Authoritative and detailed history of Vietnam, concentrating on the American War era—well researched and easy to follow. This classic was written to accompany the PBS documentary series *Vietnam: A Television History*.

MacPherson, Myra. *Long Time Passing: Vietnam and the Haunted Generation*. New York: Doubleday, 1993. Includes more than 500 interviews with men and women involved in the war.

Mangold, Tom, and John Penycate. *The Tunnels of Cu Chi*. London: Pan Books, 1986. Intriguing reconstruction of tunnel warfare at Cu Chi by two BBC journalists, based on interviews with Vietnamese and American survivors.

McNamara, Robert S. *In Retrospect: The Tragedy and Lessons of Vietnam*. New York: Random House, 1995. The former U.S. Secretary of Defense delivers his confessional—25 years after the fact. This bestselling account outraged American vets; it delighted the Vietnamese government. McNamara followed up with another corker, *Argument Without End* (self-explanatory title, published 1999).

Prochnau, William. *Once upon a Distant War*. New York: Times Books, 1995. Relates the adventures of five war correspondents covering the conflict.

Sheehan, Neil. *A Bright Shining Lie*. New York: Vintage Books, 1989. Vietnam War history woven around a biography of American commander John Paul Vann. Sheehan followed this Pulitzer-Prize winner with a slim volume, *After the War Was Over* (New York: Vintage, 1991), about a postwar visit to Hanoi and Saigon. A two-hour made-for-TV movie of *A Bright Shining Lie* was released in 1998.

Vietnamese Writers on the War

Hayslip, Le Ly. *When Heaven and Earth*

Changed Places. London and New York: Penguin, 1989. This autobiographical account formed the basis for the Oliver Stone movie *Between Heaven and Earth.* Hayslip's books have yet to be published in Vietnam because of the Culture Ministry's objections to the way the North Vietnamese are portrayed.

Huong, Duong Thu. *Novel Without a Name.* New York: William Morrow, 1993. Tells the story of a 28-year-old captain in the NVA during the war. Huong is one of Vietnam's very few outspoken dissidents. Her 1988 novel *Paradise of the Blind* (New York: Viking Penguin, reprinted 1994) portrays the communist system as exploitative and corrupt.

Ninh, Bao. *The Sorrow of War.* London: Secker and Warburg, 1993, and Pantheon Books in the United States. The voice of a Vietnamese soldier who recalls his war experience and postwar trauma. Bao Ninh overturns the official version of soldiers returning from the glorious front lines healthy in body and spirit.

*Tang, Truong Nhu. *A Vietcong Memoir.* New York: Random House, 1986. This memoir covers the 1961–1975 period; written by a young revolutionary who became disillusioned after 1975 and left Vietnam.

Modern Vietnam
Kamm, Henry. *Dragon Ascending.* New York: Arcade Publishing, 1996. By senior foreign correspondent and bureau chief of the *New York Times,* this book goes behind the scenes to interview Vietnamese military, writers, and dissidents, as well as ordinary people.

Illustrated Accounts
Bakaert, Jacques, and Tim Hall. *Vietnam: A Portrait.* Hong Kong: Elsworth Books, 1993. A pictorial guide to the country.

Népote, Jacques, and Xavier Guillaume. *Illustrated Guide to Vietnam.* Hong Kong: Odyssey Guides, 1992. Strong cultural background material.

Smolan, Rick, and Jennifer Erwitt. *Passage to Vietnam.* Against All Odds Productions, 1994. For this book, 70 photojournalists were allowed a seven-day period to photograph Vietnam. They shot more than 200,000 photos and 100 hours of video. The best 200 photo frames are featured in this book, which was assembled, start to finish, in 12 weeks in 1994. A separate *Passage to Vietnam* CD-ROM includes the book's text and photos, plus video interviews and six interactive "passages" covering such subjects as river life, street life, history and the war, and a host of "side trips" exploring aspects of Vietnamese culture and commerce.

West, Helen, ed. *Vietnam.* Singapore: Insight Guides, 1994. This officially sanctioned guide is good for reading before you go, but not something you'd want to pack in a suitcase or backpack.

Culture and Customs
Ellis, Claire. *Culture Shock! Vietnam.* Singapore: Times Editions, 1995. A guide to the customs of Vietnam—from how to eat with gusto to taboos when making business deals. Particularly useful for the resident foreigner. In the same series is *Culture Shock! Succeed in Business: Vietnam,* by Kevin Chambers, (Times Editions, 1997) which is targeted for business travelers. This book describes the investment climate in Vietnam and covers such topics as protocol for meetings and labor management; it also briefly details forays into Cambodia and Laos.

Travel Narratives
Quite a lot in the travelogue department. Easily the best is Andrew Pham's book.

Fenton, James. *All the Wrong Places.* New York: Atlantic Monthly Press, 1988. Covers a handful of destinations in Asia, with a longish section on southern Vietnam. British poet Fenton finds poetry in the sacking of the American embassy as Saigon falls.

Hunt, Christopher. *Sparring with Charlie.* New York: Doubleday, 1996. American writer Hunt tackles Highway One on a Minsk motorcycle: He has a perfectly awful time when he goes in search of the Ho Chi Minh Trail and an even harder time explaining why he's doing this in the first place.

Muller, Karen. *Hitchhiking Vietnam.* Boston: Globe Pequot, 1998. Contrary to the title, very few of the miles in this book were covered by hitchhiking. Muller later refers to "hitching a ride" with Western touring motorcyclists. A stunt from start to finish.

Page, Tim. *Derailed in Uncle Ho's Victory Garden.* London: Simon & Schuster, 1995. One of the most celebrated photographers of the Vietnam War returns 20 years later to visit old haunts. The prose is uneven and jarring: Page did not make his name through writing.

Pham, Andrew. *Catfish and Mandala.* New York: Picador, 1999. This superbly crafted book is far and away the best travelogue on modern Vietnam. Pham, who escaped Vietnam by boat in 1975 (at the age of eight), settled with his family in California. At the age of 27, to the horror of his parents, he decides to quit his engineering job and return to Vietnam to discover his roots. He sets off on a rickety 18-speed bicycle to tackle the road from Saigon to Hanoi—and all that lies between. This is much more than a travelogue—it's about Pham's whole life, revealing family secrets and intrigue and offering uncanny insight into Vietnam. One of the most unlikely seriocomic travel adventures on record. A terrific read.

Visser, Carolijn. *Voices and Visions: A Journey Through Vietnam Today.* London: Paladin, 1994. Translated from the Dutch original, this book includes travels from Saigon to Hanoi and encounters with dissident writers and a surviving princess.

Wintle, Justin. *Romancing Vietnam.* London:

Penguin, 1991. Goes beyond the Rambo curtain and the Hanoi gloss on this extensive 1989 trip—at times self-centered and trivial, but other times bang on.

Fiction

Balaban, John, and Nguyen Qui Duc (editors). *Vietnam: A Traveler's Literary Companion.* San Francisco: Whereabouts Press, 1996. An excellent array of contemporary Vietnamese fiction. In choosing the 17 stories here, the editors have avoided both the Vietnam War and politics, concentrating instead on the roots of Vietnamese culture and a sense of place. Stories vary from factual to surreal.

Butler, Robert Olen. *A Good Scent from a Strange Mountain.* New York: Viking Penguin, 1993. A selection of superbly crafted stories that offer uncanny insight into the Vietnamese mindset.

Butler, Robert Olen. *The Deep Green Sea.* New York: Henry Holt and Company, 1997. Love and war—a story about a Vietnam vet who returns to modern Saigon and falls for a mixed-race Vietnamese woman, orphaned during the war. The voices of both alternate in narrating the story. Butler's female persona is astounding.

Duras, Marguerite. *The Lover.* London: Flamingo, 1986. A lyrical novella set in Saigon and southern Vietnam in the 1930s; it portrays a love affair between a French schoolgirl and a man from a wealthy Chinese family.

Greene, Graham. *The Quiet American.* London: Penguin, 1973. This novella, first published in 1955, relates a love triangle between a British correspondent, his Vietnamese mistress, and a young American obsessed with channeling economic aid. Uncannily prophetic on what was about to pass in Indochina.

Grey, Anthony. *Saigon.* London: Pan Books, 1983. This blockbuster adventure novel deftly brings to life the French colonial era and American occupation, spanning the years 1925–1975. Packed with sex, violence, colonialism, and revolutionary action, this book is a terrific read.

Koch, Christopher. *Highways to a War*. New York: Viking Penguin, 1995. Set in South Vietnam and Cambodia, this novel relates the story of an Australian combat photographer who travels a long road through the Vietnam War, then strays into Khmer Rouge territory and disappears. The characters are fictional; the background events portrayed are very real.

O'Brien, Tim. *Going After Cacciato*. New York: Doubleday, 1978. Award-winning novel about a soldier's decision to walk away from the war—an intense mix of horror, fantasy, comedy, and reality.

CAMBODIA

Current print material on Cambodia is hard to track down, with many books now out of print.

History and Politics

Chanda, Nayan. *Brother Enemy*. New York: Collier Books, 1988. Covers Cambodia in the context of Indochina 1975–1985.

Chandler, David. *A History of Cambodia*. Colorado: Westview Press, 1992. Revised second edition of this well-written history.

Chandler, David. *Brother Number One: A Political Biography of Pol Pot*. Colorado: Westview Press, 1992.

Kiernan, Ben. *How Pol Pot Came to Power*. New York: Routledge, Chapman & Hall, 1985. A history of communism in Cambodia 1930–1975 by one of the world's leading Khmer-speaking scholars.

Osborne, Milton. *Sihanouk: Prince of Light, Prince of Darkness*. Sydney: Allen & Unwin,

1994. By an Australian specialist on Cambodia, who, however, made no attempt to interview the king.

Ponchaud, François. *Cambodia: Year Zero*. London: Penguin, 1977. An account of Cambodia under the Khmer Rouge.

Shawcross, William. *Cambodia's New Deal: A Report*. New York: Carnegie Endowment for International Peace, 1994. This 110-page book analyzes the impact of the United Nations in Cambodia, 1991–1993, from a reporter who has closely followed the situation in Cambodia. His earlier books are now out of print. *Sideshow: Kissinger, Nixon and the Destruction of Cambodia* (New York: Simon & Schuster, 1979) covers the events of 1969–1978. *Quality of Mercy: Cambodia, Holocaust and Modern Conscience* (New York: Simon & Schuster, 1984) covers the 1978–1983 period.

Personal Accounts

Bizot, Francois. *The Gate*. New York: Knopf, 2003. The incredible true story of Francois Bizot, a young French ethnologist captured by the Khmer Rouge in 1971 in the Cambodian countryside. After three months of intense interrogation, he managed to talk his way out—an incredible feat—and was released. Because of his Khmer language skills, Bizot became the intermediary between the French Embassy and the Khmer Rouge leadership after the fall of Phnom Penh in 1975. John Le Carre called this book "a contemporary classic."

Gray, Spalding. *Swimming to Cambodia*. New York: Theatre Communications Group, 1985. Spalding Gray's irreverent account of his role as an extra in the movie *The Killing Fields*. Gray turned his thoughts into a performance theater monologue. Available in book format or on video.

Gilboa, Amit. *Off the Rails in Phnom Penh*. Bangkok: Asia Books, 1998. This lively book chronicles the decadence of Western expats in more detail than you'd really want to contemplate. The usual chaos and mayhem in the capital are deftly encapsulated in this tome.

Hall, Kari, and Dith Pran. *Beyond the Killing Fields.* New York: Aperture Foundation, 1992. Documentary photography, with an introduction by Dith Pran, who survived the Khmer Rouge years.

Ngor, Haing. *Surviving the Killing Fields.* London: Chatto & Windus, 1985. Haing Ngor was the principal actor in the movie *The Killing Fields.* The book relives his own experience as a survivor of the Khmer Rouge pogrom. Haing Ngor did not survive America itself—he was gunned down in Los Angeles in 1996.

Swain, Jon. *River of Time.* London: Minerva, 1996. Recounts tumultuous times in Cambodia and Vietnam—a love and war account. Swain, a war reporter, was captured by the Khmer Rouge during the fall of Phnom Penh, and he would have been executed if not for the intervention of Dith Pran, a story recounted in the movie *The Killing Fields.*

*Szymusiak, Molyda. *The Stones Cry Out.* London: Sphere Books, 1988. Subtitled: a Cambodian childhood 1975–1980. Szymusiak was a teenager at the time of the Khmer Rouge takeover; she escaped to Thailand and migrated to France.

Ancient Khmer Empire

Ishizawa, Yoshiaki, and Hitoshi Tamura. *Along the Royal Roads to Angkor.* New York: Weatherhill Inc, 1999. A photobook covering the network of former royal roads of the Angkorian empire, extending from Cambodia into present-day Thailand and Vietnam.

Angkor

Angkor has an entire genre to itself, with many books varying from scholarly works to cof-

fee-table photobooks. The most impressive all-round effort is *Ancient Angkor* by Michael Freeman and Claude Jacques (see below).

Angkor: The Serenity of Buddhism. London: Thames & Hudson, 1993. Large-format book featuring moody black-and-white photos by French master lensman Marc Riboud, with text by Jean Lacouture and Jean Boisselier.

*Brand, Michael. *The Age of Angkor: Treasures from the National Museum.* Canberra: The Australian National Gallery, 1992. A glossy catalog, in book form, of Khmer artworks that toured Australia in 1992.

*Coedes, George. *Angkor: An Introduction.* London: Oxford University Press, 1986. A lucid account from prominent Angkorologist George Coedes, but no new material has been added since 1961 when the book was first published in French.

Dagens, Bruno. *Angkor: Heart of an Asian Empire.* New York: Harry Abrams, 1995. Excellent background material on restoration at Angkor by former member of the EFEO, with numerous illustrations.

Freeman, Michael, and Roger Warner. *Angkor: The Hidden Glories.* Boston: Houghton Mifflin, 1990. Coffee-table photobook.

Giteau, Madeleine. *Khmer Sculpture and the Angkor Civilization.* New York: Harry Abrams, 1965.

Jacques, Claude, and Michael Freeman, *Ancient Angkor.* New York: Weatherhill, 1999 (originally published by River Books, Bangkok). An excellent tome on all counts: lucid text, great photos by Michael Freeman, and wonderful maps. Use this one as your guide to Angkor.

McDonald, Malcolm. *Angkor and the Khmer.* Singapore: Oxford University Press, 1987. Reprint of original from 1958.

Rooney, Dawn. *Angkor: Introduction to the Temples.* Hong Kong: Odyssey Illustrated Guides, 2001 (4th ed.). Detailed guide to Angkor with good illustrations.

Roveda, Vittorio. *Khmer Mythology: Secrets of Angkor.* Bangkok: River Books, 1997. Delves into the mythological database of ancient Angkor.

Standen, Mark, and John Hoskin. *Passage Through Angkor.* Bangkok: Asia Books, 1995. Moody pictures by English photographer Mark Standen form the basis for this hardback, issued in English and French versions. Among the stunning images is one of lightning striking Angkor's central tower (which is a bad omen!).

*Ta-kuan, Chou (Zhou Daguan). *The Customs of Cambodia.* Bangkok: The Siam Society, 1992. The original manuscript is around 700 years old—the only eyewitness account, albeit a brief one, of the glories of the Angkor court.

LAOS

Current print material on Laos is extemely difficult to come by—the best source is Bangkok, where you might find books on Lao textiles and handicrafts. You're more likely to stray across material on Laos tucked into books on the Indochina region.

The Secret War

*Castle, Timothy. *At War in the Shadow of Vietnam.* New York: Columbia University Press, 1993. Details covert U.S. activity and military aid to the royal Lao government 1955–1975. The book is based on declassified materials as well as on interviews with dozens of American and Laotian participants.

Hamilton-Merritt, Jane. *Tragic Mountains: The Hmong, the Americans, and the Secret Wars for Laos, 1942–92.* Bloomington: University of Indiana Press, 1993.

Robbins, Christopher. *The Ravens.* New York: Bantam Press, 1988. Ravens was the code name for the U.S. pilots who fought in the secret war on Laos. This book, by a British journalist, was the first to reveal many details hidden from the U.S. public. Robbins' earlier book *The Invisible Air Force* (published 1979) was the basis for the 1990 comedy film, *Air America,* starring Mel Gibson.

Warner, Roger. *Back Fire: The CIA's Secret War in Laos and Its Link to War in Vietnam.* New York: Simon & Schuster, 1995.

Modern Laos

Sesser, Stan. *The Lands of Charm and Cruelty.* New York: Knopf, 1993. The 50-page essay, "Laos—The Forgotten Land," included in this book, is one of five essays on Asia published in *The New Yorker* in the early 1990s.

*Stieglitz, Perry. *In a Little Kingdom: The Tragedy of Laos, 1960–1980.* New York: Sharpe, 1990.

Stuart-Fox, Martin. *A History of Laos.* Cambridge: Cambridge University Press, 1997. Wide-ranging history that provides essential background on modern Laos and the challenges it now faces. Stuart-Fox is the author of two other titles on Lao history and politics.

Stuart-Fox, Martin. *Buddhist Kingdom, Marxist State: The Making of Modern Laos.* Bangkok: White Lotus Books, 1996. Coverage of Laos up until 1994. An earlier book by Stuart-Fox, *Laos: Politics, Economics and Society,* (New York: Pinter Publishers, 1983) contains some detail on post-1979 reform.

Culture and Customs

Connors, Mary. *Lao Textiles and Traditions.* Singapore: Oxford University Press, 1996. This booklet focuses on the historical and cultural background of the Lao-Tai, whose lives are intimately linked to their traditions and textiles.

Gosling, Betty. *Old Luang Prabang*. Singapore: Oxford University Press, 1996. The old royal capital of Luang Prabang is probably the best-preserved traditional town in Asia—this short book delves into the cultural treasure trove.

Mansfield, Stephen. *Culture Shock! Laos*. Singapore: Times Editions, 1997. Tells you how to reset your body language to ingratiate yourself with Laotians and divulges snippets such as exactly how much money to leave in an envelope at a wedding if you're invited. Designed for the resident foreigner but equally useful for travelers.

Travel Narratives

Du Pont De Bie, Natacha. *Ant Egg Soup*. UK: Sceptre, 2004. Subtitled "The Adventures of a Food Tourist in Laos"—which sums it up. Natacha samples fried cricket and other exotica, and comes back with the recipes too.

Internet Resources

It's just a click away, so click away. Getting connected will make a big difference to your journey to Indochina. All kinds of travel information can be brought up on the Web by using search engines—things such as airline schedules, tour operators, currency conversion rates, and weather forecasts for Hanoi, Saigon, Phnom Penh, and other cities. The Internet is an invaluable resource for trip preparation: You can even take an intensive online Vietnamese language course (see the *Vietnam Online* section).

Even once your trip is under way, Web crawling is an extremely useful method for obtaining information quickly because of the dearth of good bookstores and libraries in all three countries (mostly a matter of censorship and import restrictions).

Internet access of course relies on the presence of cybercafés. These are found in any site with a significant tourist presence in Vietnam, Cambodia, or Laos. You should be aware that if you leave out a single speck of a Web address—including misplaced hyphens, dots, or slashes—the browser may not find it. If an address doesn't appear to work, play around with those dots and slashes, or try shortening it and try again. Should you not be able to access a site, it has either folded, mutated to another address, or you've hit a firewall. Because of political sensitivity, certain sites are blocked by firewalls set up by officialdom in Vietnam and Laos (less likely in

Cambodia). There are ways of getting around a firewall—you have to enter the address on a different system.

Staying ahead of the game is very important in Indochina. With the Internet you can find out which new borders may be open and which areas may not be safe to visit at the moment. The guide you now hold is not a phone book, nor a Web directory; although there may well be an email address and a website for the Scandinavian Bakery in Vientiane, you won't find them listed here, because sites such as that have narrow interest. But you could find that information on the Web by accessing the online Yellow Pages (Golden Pages in Laos) and searching the restaurant category. Help yourself to all that on the Internet. Here are some starting points.

Cybercafés
www.cybercafes.com
www.netcafeguide.com

These sites have listings of thousands of cafés around the world. The Norway-based Internet café site is just the tip of the iceberg, of course, as many more cafés are not listed.

Searching for It
www.google.com
www.metacrawler.com

If you can't find it, the Internet can find it for you—but the trick is to narrow down the search so you don't get zillions of sites. Both Google and Metacrawler group together other search engines so you get the best of the Web. On Metacrawler, click on "phrase" to narrow the search. Example: You need to find the DHL office in Bangkok, and fast. Type "DHL" into the box for Metacrawler, hit the Search button, and the home site should come up. Of course, no big surprise here—it's www.dhl.com—but other sites are not so easy to find.

amazon.com
Although Amazon is a vast catalog of millions of books, it has an excellent search function that can be done by subject area. And if you're looking for ideas, you can check the "Browse Subjects" section of the mighty Amazon website—click on "Travel," and you can search listings by country. There's more than just books, too; you can search this site for music and videos, among other things.

Weather
But first, the weather report. Plan your trip around the weather as much as possible; monsoons and typhoons are no fun.

www.accuweather.com
Here you can find five-day forecasts for more than 800 cities around the globe, with some coverage of Vietnamese cities.

asia.weather.yahoo.com/asia
This site features city reports and forecasts. You can customize it for Laos, Cambodia, or Vietnam.

www.cnn.com/weather
Through this CNN site you can access reports and forecasts for cities in Vietnam, Cambodia, and Laos—complete with satellite map overviews.

Travel Warnings
www.fco.gov.uk/travel
The British Foreign Office warnings are

much more readable and down-to-earth than those of the U.S. State Department.

travel.state.gov/travel/warnings.html
The U.S. State Department warnings are often exaggerated. If you read this stuff you would never set foot in Asia. Things are not as bad as it makes out: The State Department is overly cautious.

www.dfait-maeci.gc.ca
Here are the Canadian Department of Foreign Affairs warnings; click on Travel for advice.

www.dfat.gov.au
The Australian government warning site.

Current Travel Information
Staying right up to date is critical in Indochina. Keep an ear to the ground for changing politics and heed current safety warnings. The following sites contain updates and news relevant to the entire region.

www.canbypublications.com
This is excellent for recent border-crossing information and anything to do with Cambodia travel.

www.pmgeiser.com
Run by Peter Geiser, this Swiss site is good not just for Vietnam, Cambodia, and Laos, but also for neighboring China and Myanmar (Burma). Click on the relevant flag.

www.visit-Mekong.com
This site covers Mekong region countries—China (Yunnan), Myanmar (Burma), Thailand, Laos, Cambodia, and Vietnam. It is done with official input, but it offers links to travelers' tales.

www.mekongexpress.com
James Michener runs this online travel agency, but it also functions as a good resource for the traveler contemplating the Mekong region countries.

www.thingsasian.com

This site is run by California-based Global Directions, which used to publish a magazine devoted to Vietnam. All that information has been transferred to cyberspace and expanded to include Asia and beyond.

Touring Ideas

Outfitters specializing in the Indochina trade have excellent websites that offer current news about not only their own trips, but also about the region in general. They often include photo galleries and good links. You can lift lots of ideas for routes and touring from these sites, which target adventurous travel in Indochina.

www.exotissimo.com

This place runs some very innovative tours, such as bicycling in Cambodia and longer trekking forays in Vietnam's far north. The site also has a newsletter update section.

www.vietnamadventures.com

Hosted largely by Buffalo Tours in Vietnam.

www.veloasia.com

San Francisco–based Veloasia, a small bicycle touring company with a big heart, operates this site.

seacanoe.com

This site is run by a pioneer kayak operator at Halong Bay.

www.transmekong.com

This company runs short and longer-distance boat tours in the Mekong Delta region.

www.wildside-asia.com

This company mounts exploratory kayak trips in the region.

Asia News

www.timeasia.com/travel

The Travel Watch section tackles some highly controversial topics. You can search the Travel Watch archives for ideas. This site is also based in Hong Kong.

www.channelnewsasia.com

This site is from Singapore's Mediacorp. The section on "Do's and Taboos" is good.

www.asiaobserver.com

Journalist John Sandvand runs this website. From here you can access a dozen more Asian news sources, including the *Tribbie (International Herald Tribune)*.

www.scmp.com

This is the website for the *South China Morning Post,* the leading newspaper in Hong Kong.

www.bangkokpost.com

Find the best daily English newspaper in Bangkok online here.

www.phnompenhpost.com

This site offers fine journalism from the foreign-run, biweekly paper.

www.bbc.co.uk/worldservice/eastasiatoday

The BBC site is a mixed-media website with some audio and video clips.

www.dfn.org

The Digital Freedom Network, operating from New Jersey, gives lesser-known voices a chance to be heard.

www.rfa.org

Washington, D.C.–based Radio Free Asia hosts broadcasts in Vietnamese language, Khmer, and Lao. This site may be blocked.

www.voa.gov

The online version of the Voice of America is also based in Washington, D.C.—and may also be blocked.

www.asiasource.org

Run by the Asia Society from New York, this site has a culture/art bias but also carries other news.

Banking
www.visa.com
www.mastercard.com
The latest additions to the expanding network of cash-dispensing machines can be found by using the ATM locators on these sites. Search by country and by city.

Health
A very mixed bag here. What you are looking for is current information on the latest drugs. Often the site talks about a drug but fails to discuss side effects of that drug (an example is medication for malaria, which is notorious for side effects).

www.drwisetravel.com
This Canadian website, run by Dr. Mark Wise, steals the show from other contenders by offering lucid, user-friendly advice on preparing for your trip.

www.cdc.gov/travel
The Centers for Disease Control and Prevention (CDC) in Atlanta, Georgia, maintains a website with the latest information on prevention guidelines and strategies, as well as news about outbreaks. You can refer to the travelers' health pages.

www.who.int/en
World Health Organization website where you can check for disease outbreaks.

www.tripprep.com
Shoreland's Travel Health Online is a Wisconsin-based site that offers excellent individual country profiles for health matters; it relies heavily on CDC information.

travelhealth.co.uk
This is a simple, well-organized website with recommendations largely taken from the World Health Organization—a bit dry at times.

www.internationalsos.com
Website of medical insurance and emergency evacuation group with facilities in Vietnam, Cambodia, and other parts of Southeast Asia—best in the business.

Backchat
For discussion and posting of questions, try these newsgroups. If you have no method of accessing them, go in via this site: groups.google.com.

news:soc.culture.vietnamese
news:soc.culture.cambodia
news:soc.culture.laos
news:soc.culture.hmong
www.vietline.com
This site for the Vietnamese community contains lots of discussion groups and questions posed. It is U.S.–based, so you might meet a firewall.

VIETNAM ONLINE
Surfing Vietnam is difficult at times because of tighter control of the Net; there may be firewalls blocking off sensitive sites—such as ones that show the old striped South Vietnamese flag!

Vietnamese Language
www.travlang.com/languages
No time to take language lessons? Here's a thought: You can study Vietnamese language online—at your own pace, when you want. San Jose–based Travlang allows you to click on sound files for pronunciation of phrases. For Vietnamese, you can sample The Rosetta Stone (Vietnamese CD-ROM) with a choice of buying the CD-ROM or engaging in online lessons. Not available for Khmer or Lao yet.

Gateway Sites
www.vietgate.net
A variety of Vietnamese community links in the United States, Canada, and Australia are provided here, but you might hit a firewall.

www.vietnamonline.com
This is a Bangkok-based site with no connections with the Vietnamese government. It has a Yellow Pages section and business-oriented material.

www.vietnamonline.net

This Hanoi-based business portal and official site contains some travel and cultural information, and embassy and airline listings. It has a Travel section and some archives for *Vietnam Investment Review* (newspaper).

Embassy Site

www.vietnamembassy-usa.org

This Washington site has a list of Vietnamese embassies and consulates, and some business information and links.

City Homepage

www.hanoitourism.gov.vn

A window on Hanoi, from the folks who run the town.

Town Homepage

www.hoianworldheritage.org

With a little help from the United Nations, this ancient town has set up its own Web presence—and even fills you in on Hué, Danang, and the surrounding region.

CAMBODIA ONLINE

Cambodia has the most liberal Web access of the three countries in this book, and it also has the greatest variety of sites (independent ones, too). But connections may be slow and have bad lines (these may be mobile phone connections, not landlines).

Gateway Sites

www.gocambodia.com

This ace site from Phnom Penh offers an online Yellow Pages (but listings seem to be paid for) and lots of links.

www.canbypublications.com

A great effort by Kenneth Cramer, publisher of quarterly miniguides to Phnom Penh, Siem Reap, and Sihanoukville, this site contains a wealth of usable information for the traveler, with good material on border crossings in Cambodia.

www.cambodia.org

The Cambodian Information Center is a nonprofit site operated by volunteers. It includes news archives, photos, academic and cultural essays, and other resources.

www.cambodia-web.net

This slick-looking site is authorized by the government and set up in association with the Ministry of Tourism. It has some hotel listings and online Yellow Pages referrals.

Embassy Site

www.embassy.org/cambodia

This easy-to-navigate site set up by the Royal Cambodian Embassy in Washington, D.C., offers good links and broad range of information.

City Homepage

www.phnompenh.gov.kh

Every city should have one: This is the Phnom Penh Municipality site—set up to reassure you that all is well in Phnom Penh (which it isn't) and encourage you to venture out and see the sights and delights of this fair city (daylight hours only recommended).

Angkor Homepage

www.angkor.com

Every ruin should have one: This portal to Angkor, set up by Ron Morris, features excellent links for travel-related matters, plus snippets of history. A comprehensive site for Angkor aficionados.

Airlines

www.bangkokair.com
www.siemreapairways.com

Huge tropical fish and palm trees—or Angkorian artwork—are painted on the planes for Bangkok Airways, which also owns the carrier Siem Reap Airways.

News

www.phnompenhpost.com

This is an excellent biweekly newspaper printed in Bangkok.

www.cambodiadaily.com
The daily broadsheet from Phnom Penh has uneven quality: sometimes fine reporting, other times a washout.

LAOS ONLINE

You're scraping the barrel when it comes to Laos—not a lot of sites up, and what exists on the Internet is thin. But let's hope the offerings will improve, so keep trolling.

Gateway Sites

www.global.lao.net
An Internet community of Lao students, professionals, and friends around the world hosts this site. It is not affiliated with the Lao PDR government.

www.visit-laos.com
The official site of Lao Tourism has a good layout, with lots of good links. The attached travelers' tales are freelance.

www.laopdr.com
This site is from the homepage of Planet On-line, which is a partly Western-run network of cybercafés in Laos, and has links to the Lao Golden Pages.

Golden Pages

gp.laopdr.com
There are no Yellow Pages in Laos: They're called the Golden Pages. There's a longish listing obtained from this site: You could click on "travel agents," for example, and that would bring up quite a slew.

Embassy Site

www.laoembassy.com
This Washington, D.C.–based site has some useful information.

News

vientianetimes.com
"The Gateway to Democracy!" proclaims the top header for this website. Fat chance. Read: Lao government mouthpiece. It is the only English-language newspaper in Laos, produced biweekly in Vientiane.

Index

Acknowledgments

This is a lengthy book, and with it goes a long list of thank-yous to those who have contributed directly or indirectly. A guidebook depends on the network that supports it.

Special thanks to Bill Newlin for getting this project underway over a beer in Hong Kong, and for smoothing the path. Patrick Morris, cyclist extraordinaire, provided gritty details on road conditions in Vietnam, minutiae along the way, and a host of missing links—the kind of information that comes from long hours in the saddle. Patrick contributed an article on the Central Highlands by motorcycle, and another piece on Cycling Vietnam. Scott Harrison and D'Arcy Richardson wrote pages of detailed notes on everything from what kind of spice was being used in Hoi An to exactly how many people you can fit in a bus loaded with logs to window height. Scott provided some excellent photographs.

My gratitude to culinary anthropologists Jeff Alford and Naomi Duguid for their articles on Vietnamese, Khmer, and Luang Prabang cuisine. Thanks to Nancy Yildiz for tips on shopping in Vietnam and weaving in Laos, to Toni Shapiro for her article on Khmer dance, to Hans Kemp for his piece on classic Saigon cars, and to Gary McFarlane for his tale on strolling through minefields in Cambodia, and his bicycle touring odyssey through Central Asia and Indochina. Special thanks to the Caveman, John Gray of SeaCanoe, for input on kayaking the nooks and crannies of Halong Bay.

Guides, experts, and those whose brains I've picked include the following. In Hanoi and Saigon, Rocky Dang showed me the snake village and organized great trips to Cuc Phuong and Mai Chau, and later up the coast to Mong Cai. In the quest for the best artworks, eclairs, and croissants in Hanoi, there is no finer guide. In Hanoi, thanks also to Justine Cole, Michael Sharp, Digby, Laura, Rita Leroux, Tran Bang Tam, Hoang Van Cuong, Nguyen The Vy, and Mr. Liem. Fredy Champagne provided a host of details on touring in Vietnam and special information on touring for veterans. In Phnom Penh, staff at Phnom Penh Post were most helpful: Kathleen Hayes, Alan Pierce, Richard McDonough, and Bill Irwin. In Siem Reap, Ian Kerr and Rudolf Knuchel were extra-helpful and hospitable. In Vientiane, my thanks to Elsie Webber; for supplementary material on Laos, thanks to Noah Shepherd, Phil Schlesinger, Mike McBeth, and Mick O'Shea of Wildside.

In Bangkok, Kevin Miller coordinated logistics and assisted with research material—and helped sort out the fish at Lake Tonle Sap and the rivers of northern Laos. Jock Montgomery and Annie Miniscloux got some projects moving that have fed back into this book in a number of productive ways. Thanks to the Artasia crew, too. In Hong Kong, Daryl Bending, Lisa Humphries, and Barbara Bale provided valuable information on the China connection and all sorts of other peculiarities.

Fellow travelers make a big difference: popping up everywhere was the much-traveled Martin Saunders, who hails from the U.K., but whose real home is Southeast Asia, from where he contributed valuable material on Laos and Chinese border areas. Stuart Washington provided doses of black humor, and Ken Hadzima, motorcycle outrider in Laos. Others along the trail: Thysje Strypens, Brendan Baker, Philippe Hamal, Herman Hilbers, Carola Bisschop, Alice Daunt, Micaela Small, Ilya Gutlin, Stefan Samuelsson, Jonathan Vandevoorde, Simone Ros, John Connell, Dennis Griffin, and John Porter and Gabriella Toth.

In Vancouver, I'd like to thank Jack and Lan Joyce of ITM for assistance with maps and expert advice, Peter Sevcik and Irene Holman and the clan, Tony McCurdy of Wanderlust Books, Dwight Elliott of the Travel Bug, Anne Smith for industrious clipping, and Carolyn Carvajal for help with video, maps, and fine art touches. Tom Quinn assisted in fine-tuning background material on belief systems. For assistance with language sections: Patsie Lamarre (for French and Captain Haddock suggestions), Alison Norman (Lao language), My Van Truong and Ngo Van Nham (Vietnamese), and Sokhanar Oun (Cambodian).

And finally, special thanks to much-traveled Le Van Sinh, the man who started Saigon's original Sinh Cafe and who has explored every back road in the country.

U.S.~Metric Conversion

1 inch	=	2.54 centimeters (cm)
1 foot	=	.304 meters (m)
1 yard	=	0.914 meters
1 mile	=	1.6093 kilometers (km)
1 km	=	.6214 miles
1 fathom	=	1.8288 m
1 chain	=	20.1168 m
1 furlong	=	201.168 m
1 acre	=	.4047 hectares
1 sq km	=	100 hectares
1 sq mile	=	2.59 square km
1 ounce	=	28.35 grams
1 pound	=	.4536 kilograms
1 short ton	=	.90718 metric ton
1 short ton	=	2000 pounds
1 long ton	=	1.016 metric tons
1 long ton	=	2240 pounds
1 metric ton	=	1000 kilograms
1 quart	=	.94635 liters
1 US gallon	=	3.7854 liters
1 Imperial gallon	=	4.5459 liters
1 nautical mile	=	1.852 km

To compute Celsius temperatures, subtract 32 from Fahrenheit and divide by 1.8. To go the other way, multiply Celsius by 1.8 and add 32.

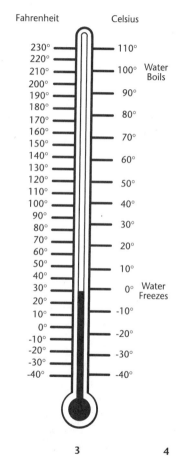